FOOTBALL OUTSIDERS™
ALMANAC 2020

THE ESSENTIAL GUIDE TO THE 2020 NFL AND COLLEGE FOOTBALL SEASONS

Edited by Aaron Schatz

With

Thomas Bassinger • Ian Boyd • Bill Connelly • Parker Fleming • Brian Fremeau
Derrik Klassen • Bryan Knowles • Rivers McCown • Dan Pizzuta • Andrew Potter
Scott Spratt • Mike Tanier • Vincent Verhei • Robert Weintraub • Carl Yedor

Copyright 2020 EdjSports, LLC

ISBN: 979-8666296882

Table of Contents

PLAYERS

COLLEGE FOOTBALL

FURTHER RESEARCH

Introduction

This is the 16th straight year that the Football Outsiders staff has written an annual previewing the upcoming football season, but this one feels a little different than the others. This time, it's possible there's no football season to preview.

You don't need us to tell you about how the COVID-19 pandemic has changed life in America over the past few months. Sports, like everything else in American society, was shut down and then forced to do things differently. But so far the NFL, unlike other leagues, hasn't been forced to do things *too* differently.

The combine, held right before the country shut down in March, was no different from any other year. Even after the shutdown, we had free agency just like we always have free agency. The April draft was a little different because the league didn't all come together in one location to usher the top draft picks from a green room onto a stage where they could shake Roger Goodell's hand. This year, every team handled its draft remotely, and the broadcast took us into the living rooms of both incoming rookies and NFL executives. But 255 players still got drafted to specific NFL teams, and then a bunch of other players signed as undrafted free agents like any other year.

Things got a little bit different after that. There were no rookie minicamps this year. There were no OTAs. Teams had their offseason meetings over Zoom instead of in person. But we've all been preparing to have a 2020 season. The schedule for this season was announced like usual. Rumors that the schedule was built to allow for certain weeks to be cancelled or postponed weren't completely false, but they were certainly overstated.[1] Training camps are set to open on July 28. The Houston Texans are planning to go to Kansas City to start the season against the defending champion Chiefs on the night of September 10.

At Football Outsiders, it was business as usual this offseason. We ran our usual content over the offseason months. We worked on an upgraded KUBIAK fantasy football projection system. We've done all our usual work in preparing the book you currently hold in your hand (or see on your computer screen). *Football Outsiders Almanac 2020* contains everything you're used to from our preseason annuals. We've got in-depth statistics on every NFL team, fantasy football projections, skill player writeups, and previews of the top 50 college squads.

And here's the sad truth: it all might mean nothing.

So far, this offseason hasn't been too different for the NFL. But depending on the spread of the COVID-19 epidemic between now and the planned start of the season, plans for the NFL could change dramatically. The league already made the decision to cut the preseason in half. The entire preseason could yet be cancelled. Regular-season games could be delayed or cancelled. Even if all the games are played, they will likely be played without fans in attendance. And we don't know what the effect of COVID-19 will be on rosters. What will happen when players inevitably test positive? Will entire position groups have to quarantine?

The situation is even worse for college football. College teams already had to give up their spring games and practices. Can you have college football if students aren't back at school taking classes in the fall? How do you manage the sport nationally when each conference and even each individual university are making their own decisions about the pandemic? So far, the Big Ten and Pac-12 announced a decision to cancel all non-conference games between the date we finished the college football section of this book and the date we are releasing it.

We're acknowledging these questions here because for the rest of this book, we mostly ignore them. Although there are a few mentions of this abnormal offseason, particularly for teams trying to install new playbooks and systems, *Football Outsiders Almanac 2020* is mostly written as if the 2020 season will go off as planned, without a hitch.

With that in mind, let's talk about what's in this book for those of you who may be reading *Football Outsiders Almanac* for the first time. Football analytics has come a very long away since Football Outsiders first pioneered analytical writing about the NFL back in 2003. This summer, ESPN sports analytics writer Seth Walder compiled a list of analytics staffers for each NFL team. Only two teams, Tampa Bay and Tennessee, had nobody on the list.

More NFL teams are following more of the precepts of football analytics. Teams are more aggressive on fourth downs than ever before. Teams are passing more than ever before. Teams are using play-action more than ever before. And teams are spreading out defenses more than ever before.

Off the field, analysts working for the NFL have developed new metrics (a.k.a. "Next Gen Stats") using the tracking systems that are now installed in every player's pads and in every football used on the field. The NFL now provides some of that data to the public to create new analytics in their annual Big Data Bowl. Those who don't have access to this tracking data have created their own new metrics using game charting data, such as the data collected by our partners at Sports Info Solutions. And a whole community of analysts has sprouted up on Twitter, developing new ways to look at the game and debating the great questions of current NFL fandom.

At its heart, the football analytics revolution is about learning more about the intricacies of the game instead of just accepting the boilerplate storylines produced by insipid pregame shows and crotchety old players from the past. It's about not accepting the idea that some guy "just wins." It's about understanding that the "skill players" aren't the only guys on the team with skills. It's about gaining insight into the complexity behind the modern offense, and why just shoving the ball into the line hoping to gain yardage is usually a bad idea. It's about understanding the dramatic way that strength of schedule affects the way

---

1 Week 2 can be rescheduled if necessary, because every team shares its bye week with its Week 2 opponent; Weeks 3 and 4 have no division games in case they need to be cancelled.

we see a team's performance, especially at the college level. It's about figuring out which player skills translate from college to the pros, and which skills just produce meaningless scoutspeak. And it's about accepting that the pass dominates the run in the National Football League, and that it's been that way for at least 30 years.

As the original football analytics website, Football Outsiders is still doing our part to challenge conventional wisdom and look deeper inside the numbers. Yes, there are a lot of tables of numbers in this book, but words are the meat of our analysis; numbers are just the spice. There's a rumor that stat analysts don't watch game tape. In reality, stat analysts watch more tape than most beat writers or national Internet columnists, and *a lot* more tape than the average fan. We take everything we learn off the tape, synthesize it with the statistics, and deliver it to you.

Everybody who writes about football uses both statistics (whether they be basic yardage totals or more advanced stats like ours) and scouting (whether scouting reports by professionals or just their own eyes). The same goes for us, except that the statistics portion of our analysis is far more accurate than what you normally see from football coverage. Those numbers are based on two ideas:

1) **Conventional football statistics are heavily dependent on context.** If you want to see which teams are good and which are bad, which strategies work and which do not, you first need to filter out that context. Down and distance, field position, the current score, time left on the clock, the quality of the opponent—all of these elements influence the objective of the play and/or its outcome. Yet, the official NFL stats add together all yardage gained by a specific team or player without considering the impact of that particular yardage on wins and losses.

A close football game can turn on a single bounce of the ball. In a season of only 16 games, those effects can have a huge impact on a team's win-loss record, thus obscuring the team's true talent level. If we can filter out these bits of luck and random chance, we can figure out which teams are really more likely to play better for the rest of the season, or even in the following season.

2) **On any one play, the majority of the important action is not tracked by the conventional NFL play-by-play.** That's why we started the Football Outsiders game charting project in 2005. We now partner with both ESPN Stats & Info and Sports Info Solutions to collect data on every single NFL regular-season and postseason play. We know how many pass-rushers teams send on each pass, how often teams go three-wide or use two tight ends, how often teams use a play-action fake, and which defensive backs are in coverage, even when they don't get a tackle in the standard play-by-play.

There's also a third important precept that governs the work we do at Football Outsiders, although it's more about how to interpret numbers and not the numbers themselves. **A player's production in one year does not necessarily equal his production the next year.** This also applies to teams, of course. Even when stats are accurate, they're often extremely variable from year to year and subject to heavy forces of regression to the mean. Field goal percentage, red zone performance, third-down performance on defense, interceptions and fumble recoveries—these are but a few examples. In addition, the age curves for football players are much steeper than in other sports. Old players break down faster, and young players often improve faster. Many football analysts concentrate on looking at what players did last year. We'll talk about that as well, but we're more interested in what players are going to do *this* year. Which performances from a year ago are flukes, and which ones represent long-term improvement or decline? What will one more year of experience do to this player's production? And how will a player's role change this year, and what does it mean for the team?

As with past books, *Football Outsiders Almanac 2020* starts off with "Pregame Show" (reviewing the most important research we've done in past books) and "Statistical Toolbox" (explaining all our stats). Once again, we preserve the ridiculousness of the football season for posterity with another version of "The Year in Quotes" and we introduce you to some of the more promising (and lesser-known) young bench players with our 14th annual list of Top 25 Prospects chosen in the third round or later.

Each NFL team gets a full chapter covering what happened in 2019 and our projections for the upcoming season. Are there reasons to believe that the team was inherently better or worse than its record last year? What did the team do in the offseason, and what does that mean for the team's chances to win in 2020? Each chapter also includes all kinds of advanced statistics covering 2019 performance and strategic tendencies, plus detailed commentary on the major units of the team: offensive line, defensive front seven, defensive secondary, and special teams.

"Skill players" (by which we mean "players who get counted in fantasy football") get their own section in the back of the book. We list the major players at each position alphabetically, along with commentary and a 2020 KUBIAK projection that will help you win your fantasy football league.

Next comes our preview of the college football season. We go in-depth with the top 50 projected teams in the nation. Just like with our NFL coverage, the goal of our college previews is to focus as much as possible on "why" and how," not just "which team is better." We're not just here to rank the Football Bowl Subdivision teams from 1 to 130. We break things down to look at offense and defense, pass and run, and clear passing situations compared to all plays.

As noted earlier, all of these predictions for the upcoming season are predicated on the idea that there will be an upcoming season and that it will look something like what we're used to. Things are going to be different, but we don't know how different. Hopefully, you can enjoy *Football Outsiders Almanac 2020* as a season preview and not as an alternate history novel.

Aaron Schatz
Auburn, MA
July 15, 2020

P.S. Don't forget to visit FootballOutsiders.com every day for fresh coverage of the NFL and college football, plus the most intelligent football discussion threads on the Internet. That coverage and intelligent discussion will continue this year whether the football continues or not.

Pregame Show

It has now been 17 years since we launched Football Outsiders. In that time, we've done a lot of primary research on the National Football League, and we reference that research in many of the articles and comments in *Football Outsiders Almanac 2020*. New readers may come across an offhand comment in a team chapter about, for example, the idea that fumble recovery is not a skill, and wonder what in the heck we are talking about. We can't repeat all our research in every new edition of *Football Outsiders Almanac*, so we start each year with a basic look at some of the most important precepts that have emerged from Football Outsiders research. You will see these issues come up again and again throughout the book.

You can also find this introduction online at http://www.footballoutsiders.com/info/FO-basics, along with links to the original research in the cases in which that research appeared online instead of (or as well as) in print.

Our various methods for projecting NFL success for college prospects are not listed below but are referenced at times during the book. Those methods are detailed in an essay on page 450.

You run when you win, not win when you run.

If we could only share one piece of anti-conventional wisdom with you before you read the rest of our book, this would be it. The first article ever written for Football Outsiders was devoted to debunking the myth of "establishing the run." There is no correlation whatsoever between giving your running backs a lot of carries early in the game and winning the game. Just running the ball is not going to help a team score; it has to run successfully.

There is also no evidence that running the ball more early in the game creates the opportunity for longer gains late in the game, i.e. the so-called "body blows" thesis. And there is no evidence that passing the ball too frequently puts the defense on the field too much and tires it out.

Why does nearly every beat writer and television analyst still repeat the tired old school mantra that "establishing the run" is the secret to winning football games? The biggest issue is confusing cause and effect. There are exceptions, but for the most part, winning teams have a lot of carries because their running backs are running out the clock at the end of wins, not because they are running wild early in games.

A sister statement to "you have to establish the run" is "team X is 8-1 when running back John Doe runs for at least 100 yards." Unless John Doe is possessed by otherworldly spirits the way Adrian Peterson was a couple years ago, the team isn't winning because of his 100-yard games. He's putting up 100-yard games because his team is winning.

At this point, it's hard to figure out why so many commentators and fans still overrate the importance of the running game. One problem has always been history. Older NFL analysts and fans came of age during the 1970s, when the rules favored the running game much more than those in the modern NFL. We used to have to explain that optimal strategies from 1974 are not optimal strategies for today. But this would seem to be a smaller problem now than it was ten years ago; most current NFL analysts played the game in the '90s or beyond, when the game was heavily pass-centric.

Another issue may be a confusion of professional football with other levels. As you go down the football pyramid, from NFL teams to FBS to FCS to Division II and so on down to high school, at every level further down the running game becomes more important. To give an example, the Carolina Panthers led the NFL in 2018 with 5.1 yards per carry—but that average was lower than five different teams in the SEC. Strategies that win on Saturday do not necessarily win on Sunday.

A great defense against the run is nothing without a good pass defense.

This is a corollary to the absurdity of "establish the run." With rare exceptions, teams win or lose with the passing game more than the running game—and by stopping the passing game more than the running game. Ron Jaworski puts it best: "The pass gives you the lead, and the run solidifies it." The reason why teams need a strong run defense in the playoffs is not to shut the run down early; it's to keep the other team from icing the clock if they get a lead. You can't mount a comeback if you can't stop the run.

Running on third-and-short is more likely to convert than passing on third-and-short.

On average, passing will always gain more yardage than running, with one very important exception: when a team is just 1 or 2 yards away from a new set of downs or the goal line. On third-and-1, a run will convert for a new set of downs 36% more often than a pass. Expand that to all third or fourth downs with 1 or 2 yards to go, and the run is successful 40% more often. With these percentages, the possibility of a long gain with a pass is not worth the tradeoff of an incomplete that kills a drive.

This is one reason why teams have to be able to both run and pass. The offense also has to keep some semblance of balance so they can use their play-action fakes—you can't run a play-fake from an empty set—and so the defense doesn't just run their nickel and dime packages all game. Balance also means that teams do need to pass occasionally in short-yardage situations; they just need to do it less than they do now. Teams pass roughly 60% of the time on third-and-2 even though runs in that situation convert 20% more often than passes. They pass 68% of the time on fourth-and-2 even though runs in that situation convert twice as often as passes.

You don't need to run a lot to set up play-action.

Of course, the idea that you have to run a little bit so play-action will work doesn't mean you have to run as often as NFL teams currently do. There's no correlation between a team's rushing frequency or success rate rushing and its play-action effectiveness over the course of either a single game or an entire season. That doesn't mean there wouldn't be a correlation at an extreme run/pass ratio, but we have yet to see an NFL team that even comes close to what that extreme might be.

Standard team rankings based on total yardage are inherently flawed.

Check out the schedule page on NFL.com, and you will find that each game is listed with league rankings based on total yardage. That is still how the NFL "officially" ranks teams, but these rankings rarely match up with common sense. That is because total team yardage may be the most context-dependent number in football.

It starts with the basic concept that rate stats are generally more valuable than cumulative stats. Yards per carry says more about a running back's quality than total yardage, completion percentage says more than just a quarterback's total number of completions. The same thing is true for teams; in fact, it is even more important because of the way football strategy influences the number of runs and passes in the game plan. Poor teams will give up fewer passing yards and more rushing yards because opponents will stop passing once they have a late-game lead and will run out the clock instead. For winning teams, the opposite is true. For example, which team had a better pass defense last year: Cincinnati or Tennessee? According to the official NFL rankings, Cincinnati (3,917 yards allowed on 530 passes and sacks, 7.4 net yards per pass) was a better pass defense than Tennessee (4,080 net yards allowed on 641 passes and sacks, 6.4 net yards per pass).

Total yardage rankings are also skewed because some teams play at a faster pace than other teams. For example, last year Tampa Bay (6,366) had more yardage than Kansas City (6,067). However, the Chiefs were the superior offense and much more efficient; they gained those yards on only 156 drives while the Buccaneers needed a league-high 194 drives.

A team will score more when playing a bad defense and will give up more points when playing a good offense.

This sounds absurdly basic, but when people consider team and player stats without looking at strength of schedule, they are ignoring this. In 2012, for example, rookie Russell Wilson had a higher DVOA rating than fellow rookie Robert Griffin III because he faced a more difficult schedule, even though Griffin had slightly better standard stats. A more recent example: in 2019, Seattle and Houston both had 5.7 yards per play on offense. Seattle was the better offense by DVOA in part because Seattle played the third-hardest schedule of opposing defenses in the league while Houston played an average schedule of opposing defenses.

If their overall yards per carry are equal, a running back who consistently gains yardage on every play is more valuable than a boom-and-bust running back who is frequently stuffed at the line but occasionally breaks a long highlight-worthy run.

Our brethren in the baseball analytics world believe that the most precious commodity in baseball is outs. Teams only get 27 of them per game, and you can't afford to give one up for very little return. So imagine if there was a new rule in baseball that gave a team a way to earn another three outs in the middle of the inning. That would be pretty useful, right?

That's the way football works. You may start a drive 80 yards away from scoring, but as long as you can earn 10 yards in four chances, you get another four chances. Long gains have plenty of value, but if those long gains are mixed with a lot of short gains, you are going to put the quarterback in a lot of difficult third-and-long situations. That means more punts and more giving the ball back to the other team rather than moving the chains and giving the offense four more plays to work with.

The running back who gains consistent yardage is also going to do a lot more for you late in the game, when the goal of running the ball is not just to gain yardage but to eat clock time. If you are a Giants fan watching your team with a late lead, you don't want to see three straight Saquon Barkley stuffs at the line followed by a punt. You want to see a game-icing first down.

A common historical misconception is that our preference for consistent running backs means that "Football Outsiders believes that Barry Sanders was overrated." Sanders wasn't just any boom-and-bust running back, though; he was the greatest boom-and-bust runner of all time, with bigger booms and fewer busts. Sanders ranked in the top five in DYAR five times (third in 1989, first in 1990, and second in 1994, 1996, and 1997).

Rushing is more dependent on the offensive line than people realize, but pass protection is more dependent on the quarterback himself than people realize.

Some readers complain that this idea contradicts the previous one. Aren't those consistent running backs just the product of good offensive lines? The truth is somewhere in between. There are certainly good running backs who suffer because their offensive lines cannot create consistent holes, but most boom-and-bust running backs contribute to their own problems by hesitating behind the line whenever the hole is unclear, looking for the home run instead of charging forward for the 4-yard gain that keeps the offense moving.

Further research has shown that rushing success is also heavily dependent on scheme as well as how the defense sets up against the play, in particular how many men the defense puts in the box (i.e., in between the offensive tackles). Research from this year's NFL Big Data Bowl suggests that the results of a running play can be almost entirely predicted using the movement of the blockers and defenders, without needing to consider the identity of the running back at all. It's research like this that's given birth to the popular Twitter saying that "running backs don't matter." That's a bit of an extreme; it's more likely that running backs matter a little bit, but much less than NFL wisdom has historically believed, and most of the differentiation between different backs comes from their skills in the passing game.

In addition, "running backs don't matter" is sometimes mistaken for the idea that the running game doesn't matter. The latter is a bit of an analytical strawman, even if analytics has shown that the running game is less important than the passing game.

As for pass protection, some quarterbacks have better instincts for the rush than others and are thus better at getting out of trouble by moving around in the pocket or throwing the ball away. Others will hesitate, hold onto the ball too long, and lose yardage over and over.

Note that "moving around in the pocket" does not necessarily mean "scrambling." In fact, a scrambling quarterback will often take more sacks than a pocket quarterback, because while he's running around trying to make something happen, a defensive lineman will catch up with him.

Shotgun formations are generally more efficient than formations with the quarterback under center.

From 2013 to 2017, offenses averaged roughly 5.9 yards per play from Shotgun (or Pistol), but just 5.1 yards per play with the quarterback under center. In 2018 and 2019 that gap has closed a bit, but offenses still averaged 5.8 yards per play from Shotgun or Pistol compared to 5.4 yards per play with the quarterback under center. This wide split exists even if you analyze the data to try to weed out biases like teams using Shotgun more often on third-and-long, or against prevent defenses in the fourth quarter. Shotgun offense is more efficient if you only look at the first half, on every down, and even if you only look at running back carries rather than passes and scrambles.

It's hard to think of a Football Outsiders axiom that has been better assimilated by the people running NFL teams since we started doing this a decade ago. In 2001, NFL teams only used Shotgun on 14% of plays. Five years later, in 2006, that had increased slightly, to 20% of plays. By 2012, Shotgun was used on a 47.5% of plays (including the Pistol, but not counting the Wildcat or other direct snaps to non-quarterbacks). In 2016, the league as a whole was up to an average of 64.4% of plays from Shotgun or Pistol. Last year, that average was at 64.9% .

There's an interesting corollary here which we are just starting to study, because there does seem to be one split where offenses are *less* efficient from shotgun: play-action. In 2019, offenses averaged 8.1 yards per play when using play-action from an under-center formation, compared to 7.0 yards per play when using play-action from a Shotgun formation. A number of teams that are near the top of the league in play-action usage, such as the Rams and Patriots, are also near the bottom of the league in using Shotgun.

Wide receivers must be judged on both complete and incomplete passes.

Here's an example from last season: Stefon Diggs had 1,130 receiving yards while Robby Anderson had 779 receiving yards, even though the two receivers were just one target apart. Each receiver ran his average route roughly 15 yards downfield. But there was a big reason why Diggs had a much better season than Anderson: Diggs caught 67% of intended passes and Anderson caught just 54%.

Some work has been done on splitting responsibility for incomplete passes between quarterbacks and receivers, but not enough that we can incorporate this into our advanced stats at this time. We know that wide receiver catch rates are almost as consistent from year to year as quarterback completion percentages, but it is also important to look at catch rate in the context of the types of routes each receiver runs. A few years ago, we expanded on this idea with a new plus-minus metric, which is explained in the introduction to the chapter on wide receivers and tight ends.

The total quality of an NFL team is four parts offense, three parts defense, and one part special teams.

There are three units on a football team, but they are not of equal importance. Work by Chase Stuart, Neil Paine, and Brian Burke suggests a split between offense and defense of roughly 58-42, without considering special teams. Our research suggests that special teams contributes about 13% to total performance; if you measure the remaining 87% with a 58-42 ratio, you get roughly 4:3:1. When we compare the range of offense, defense, and special teams DVOA ratings, we get the same results, with the best and worst offenses roughly 130% stronger than the best and worst defenses, and roughly four times stronger than the best and worst special teams.

Offense is more consistent from year to year than defense, and offensive performance is easier to project than defensive performance. Special teams are less consistent than either.

Nobody in the NFL understood this concept better than former Indianapolis Colts general manager Bill Polian. Both the Super Bowl champion Colts and the four-time AFC champion Buffalo Bills of the early 1990s were built around the idea that if you put together an offense that can dominate the league year after year, eventually you will luck into a year where good health and a few smart decisions will give you a defense good enough to win a championship. (As the Colts learned in 2006, you don't even need a year, just four weeks.) Even the New England Patriots, who are led by a defense-first head coach in Bill Belichick, have been more consistent on offense than on defense since they began their run of success in 2001.

Teams with more offensive penalties generally lose more games, but there is no correlation between defensive penalties and losses.

Specific defensive penalties of course lose games; we've all sworn at the television when the cornerback on our favorite team gets flagged for a 50-yard pass interference penalty. Yet overall, there is no correlation between losses and the total of defensive penalties or even the total yardage on defensive penalties. One reason is that defensive penalties often represent *good* play, not bad. Cornerbacks who play tight coverage may be just on the edge of a penalty on most plays, only occasionally earning a flag. Defensive ends who get a good jump on rushing the passer will gladly trade an encroachment penalty or two for ten snaps where they get off the blocks a split-second before the linemen trying to block them.

In addition, offensive penalties have a higher correlation from year to year than defensive penalties. The penalty that correlates highest with losses is the false start, and the penalty that teams will have called most consistently from year to year is also the false start.

Recovery of a fumble, despite being the product of hard work, is almost entirely random.

Stripping the ball is a skill. Holding onto the ball is a skill. Pouncing on the ball as it is bouncing all over the place is not a skill. There is no correlation whatsoever between the percentage of fumbles recovered by a team in one year and the percentage they recover in the next year. The odds of recovery are based solely on the type of play involved, not the teams or any of their players.

The Cleveland Browns are a good example. In 2018, the Browns recovered 14 of 23 fumbles by opponents (61%). The next year, the same defense recovered just six of 17 fumbles by opponents (35%).

Fumble recovery is equally erratic on offense. In 2018, the Miami Dolphins recovered a league-low three of 13 fumbles on offense (23%). In 2019, the Dolphins recovered 13 of 20 fumbles on offense (65%).

Fumble recovery is a major reason why the general public overestimates or underestimates certain teams. Fumbles are huge, turning-point plays that dramatically impact wins and losses in the past, while fumble recovery percentage says absolutely nothing about a team's chances of winning games in the future. With this in mind, Football Outsiders stats treat all fumbles as equal, penalizing them based on the likelihood of each type of fumble (run, pass, sack, etc.) being recovered by the defense.

Other plays that qualify as "non-predictive events" include two-point conversions, blocked kicks, and touchdowns during turnover returns. These plays are not "lucky," per se, but they have no value whatsoever for predicting future performance.

Field position is fluid.

As discussed in the Statistical Toolbox, every yard line on the field has a value based on how likely a team is to score from that location on the field as opposed to from a yard further back. The change in value from one yard to the next is the same whether the team has the ball or not. The goal of a defense is not just to prevent scoring, but to hold the opposition so that the offense can get the ball back in the best possible field position. A bad offense will score as many points as a good offense if it starts each drive 5 yards closer to the goal line.

A corollary to this precept: The most underrated aspect of an NFL team's performance is the field position gained or lost on kickoffs and punts. This is part of why players such as Cordarrelle Patterson can have such an impact on the game, even when they aren't taking a kickoff or punt all the way back for a touchdown.

The red zone is the most important place on the field to play well, but performance in the red zone from year to year is much less consistent than overall performance.

Although play in the red zone has a disproportionately high importance to the outcome of games relative to plays on the rest of the field, NFL teams do not exhibit a level of performance in the red zone that is consistently better or worse than their performance elsewhere, year after year. The simplest explanation why is a small(er) sample size and the inherent variance of football, with contributing factors such as injuries and changes in personnel.

Injuries regress to the mean on the seasonal level, and teams that avoid injuries in a given season tend to win more games.

There are no doubt teams with streaks of good or bad health over multiple years. However, teams who were especially healthy or especially unhealthy, as measured by our adjusted games lost (AGL) metric, almost always head towards league average in the subsequent season. Furthermore, injury—or the absence thereof—has a huge correlation with wins and a significant impact on a team's success. There's no doubt that a few high-profile teams have resisted this trend in recent years. The Patriots often deal with a high number of injuries, and the 2017 Eagles obviously overcame a number of important injuries to win the championship. Last year, the team with the lowest AGL on offense, Baltimore, finished with the best offensive DVOA. The team with the lowest AGL on defense, New England, finished with the best defensive DVOA. Meanwhile, out of the ten teams with the highest overall AGL, only San Francisco made the playoffs.

By and large, a team built on depth is better than a team built on stars and scrubs.

Connected to the previous statement, because teams need to go into the season expecting that they will suffer an average number of injuries no matter how healthy they were the previous year. You cannot concentrate your salaries on a handful of star players because there is no such thing as avoiding injuries in the NFL. The game is too fast and the players too strong to build a team based around the idea that "if we can avoid all injuries this year, we'll win."

Running backs usually decline after age 28, tight ends after age 29, wide receivers after age 30, and quarterbacks after age 32.

This research was originally done by Doug Drinen (former editor of Pro Football Reference) in 2000. A few players have had huge seasons above these general age limits, particularly at the quarterback position, but the peak ages Drinen found still apply to the majority of players.

As for "non-skill players," research we did in 2007 for *ESPN The Magazine* suggested that defensive ends and defensive backs generally begin to decline after age 29, linebackers and offensive linemen after age 30, and defensive tackles after age 31. However, because we still have so few statistics to use to study linemen and defensive players, this research should not be considered definitive.

The strongest indicator of how a college football team will perform in the upcoming season is their performance in recent seasons.

It may seem strange because graduation enforces constant player turnover, but college football teams are actually much more consistent from year to year than NFL teams. Thanks in large part to consistency in recruiting, teams can be expected to play within a reasonable range of their baseline program expectations each season. Our Program F/+ ratings, which represent a rolling five-year period of play-by-play and drive efficiency data, have an extremely strong (.76) correlation with the next year's F/+ rating.

Championship teams are generally defined by their ability to dominate inferior opponents, not their ability to win close games.

Football games are often decided by just one or two plays: a missed field goal, a bouncing fumble, the subjective spot of an official on fourth-and-1. One missed assignment by a cornerback or one slightly askew pass that bounces off a receiver's hands and into those of a defensive back 5 yards away and the game could be over. In a blowout, however, one lucky bounce isn't going to change things. Championship teams—in both professional and college football—typically beat their good opponents convincingly and destroy the cupcakes on the schedule.

Aaron Schatz

Statistical Toolbox

After 17 years of Football Outsiders, some of our readers are as comfortable with DVOA and ALY as they are with touchdowns and tackles. Yet to most fans, including our newer readers, it still looks like a lot of alphabet soup. That's what this chapter is for. The next few pages define and explain all of all the unique NFL statistics you'll find in this book: how we calculate them, what the numbers mean, and what they tell us about why teams win or lose football games. We'll go through the information in each of the tables that appear in each team chapter, pointing out whether those stats come from advanced mathematical manipulation of the standard play-by-play or tracking what we see on television with Sports Info Solutions game charting. This chapter covers NFL statistics only. College metrics such as FEI and SP+ are explained in the introduction to the college football section on page 391.

We've done our best to present these numbers in a way that makes them easy to understand. This explanation is long, so feel free to read some of it, flip around the rest of the book, and then come back. It will still be here.

Defense-Adjusted Value Over Average (DVOA)

One running back runs for three yards. Another running back runs for three yards. Which is the better run?

This sounds like a stupid question, but it isn't. In fact, this question is at the heart of nearly all of the analysis in this book.

Several factors can differentiate one three-yard run from another. What is the down and distance? Is it third-and-2, or second-and-15? Where on the field is the ball? Does the player get only three yards because he hits the goal line and scores? Is the player's team up by two touchdowns in the fourth quarter and thus running out the clock, or down by two touchdowns and thus facing a defense that is playing purely against the pass? Is the running back playing against the porous defense of the Panthers, or the stalwart defense of the Vikings?

Conventional NFL statistics value plays based solely on their net yardage. The NFL determines the best players by adding up all their yards no matter what situations they came in or how many plays it took to get them. Now, why would they do that? Football has one objective—to get to the end zone—and two ways to achieve that, by gaining yards and achieving first downs. These two goals need to be balanced to determine a player's value or a team's performance. All the yards in the world won't help a team win if they all come in six-yard chunks on third-and-10.

The popularity of fantasy football only exacerbates the problem. Fans have gotten used to judging players based on how much they help fantasy teams win and lose, not how much they help *real* teams win and lose. Typical fantasy scoring further skews things by counting the yard between the

one and the goal line as 61 times more important than all the other yards on the field (each yard worth 0.1 points, a touchdown worth 6.0). Let's say DeAndre Hopkins catches a pass on third-and-15 and goes 50 yards but gets tackled two yards from the goal line, and then Kenyan Drake takes the ball on first-and-goal from the two-yard line and plunges in for the score. Has Drake done something special? Not really. When an offense gets the ball on first-and-goal at the two-yard line, they are going to score a touchdown five out of six times. Drake is getting credit for the work done by the passing game.

Doing a better job of distributing credit for scoring points and winning games is the goal of **DVOA**, or Defense-adjusted Value Over Average. DVOA breaks down every single play of the NFL season, assigning each play a value based on both total yards and yards towards a first down, based on work done by Pete Palmer, Bob Carroll, and John Thorn in their seminal book, *The Hidden Game of Football*. On first down, a play is considered a success if it gains 45% of needed yards; on second down, a play needs to gain 60% of needed yards; on third or fourth down, only gaining a new first down is considered success.

We then expand upon that basic idea with a more complicated system of "success points," improved over the past four years with a lot of mathematics and a bit of trial and error. A successful play is worth one point, an unsuccessful play zero points with fractional points in between (for example, eight yards on third-and-10 is worth 0.54 "success points"). Extra points are awarded for big plays, gradually increasing to three points for 10 yards (assuming those yards result in a first down), four points for 20 yards, and five points for 40 yards or more. Losing three or more yards is -1 point. Interceptions average -6 points, with an adjustment for the length of the pass and the location of the interception (since an interception tipped at the line is more likely to produce a long return than an interception on a 40-yard pass). A fumble is worth anywhere from -1.7 to -4.0 points depending on how often a fumble in that situation is lost to the defense—no matter who actually recovers the fumble. Red zone plays get a bonus: 20% for team offense, 5% for team defense, and 10% for individual players. There is a bonus given for a touchdown that acknowledges that the goal line is significantly more difficult to cross than the previous 99 yards (although this bonus is nowhere near as large as the one used in fantasy football).

(Our system is a bit more complex than the one in *Hidden Game* thanks to our subsequent research, which added larger penalty for turnovers, the fractional points, and a slightly higher baseline for success on first down. The reason why all fumbles are counted, no matter whether they are recovered by the offense or defense, is explained in the essay "Pregame Show.")

Every single play run in the NFL gets a "success value" based on this system, and then that number gets compared to the average success values of plays in similar situations for all players, adjusted for a number of variables. These include down and distance, field location, time remaining in game, and the team's lead or deficit in the game score. Teams are always compared to the overall offensive average, as the team made its own choice whether to pass or rush. When it comes to individual players, however, rushing plays are compared to other rushing plays, passing plays to other passing plays, tight ends to tight ends, wideouts to wideouts, and so on.

Going back to our example of the three-yard rush, if Player A gains three yards under a set of circumstances in which the average NFL running back gains only one yard, then Player A has a certain amount of value above others at his position. Likewise, if Player B gains three yards on a play on which, under similar circumstances, an average NFL back gains four yards, that Player B has negative value relative to others at his position. Once we make all our adjustments, we can evaluate the difference between this player's rate of success and the expected success rate of an average running back in the same situation (or between the opposing defense and the average defense in the same situation, etc.). Add up every play by a certain team or player, divide by the total of the various baselines for success in all those situations, and you get VOA, or Value Over Average.

Of course, the biggest variable in football is the fact that each team plays a different schedule against teams of disparate quality. By adjusting each play based on the opposing defense's average success in stopping that type of play over the course of a season, we get DVOA, or Defense-adjusted Value Over Average. Rushing and passing plays are adjusted based on down and location on the field; passing plays are also adjusted based on how the defense performs against passes to running backs, tight ends, or wide receivers. Defenses are adjusted based on the average success of the *offenses* they are facing. (Yes, technically the defensive stats are "offense-adjusted." If it seems weird, think of the "D" in "DVOA" as standing for "opponent-Dependent" or something.)

The biggest advantage of DVOA is the ability to break teams and players down to find strengths and weaknesses in a variety of situations. In the aggregate, DVOA may not be quite as accurate as some of the other, similar "power ratings" formulas based on comparing drives rather than individual plays, but, unlike those other ratings, DVOA can be separated not only by player, but also by down, or by week, or by distance needed for a first down. This can give us a better idea of not just which team is better, but why, and what a team has to do in order to improve itself in the future. You will find DVOA used in this book in a lot of different ways—because it takes every single play into account, it can be used to measure a player or a team's performance in any situation. All Pittsburgh third downs can be compared to how an average team does on third down. Derek Carr and Marcus Mariota can each be compared to how an average quarterback performs in the red zone, or with a lead, or in the second half of the game.

Since it compares each play only to plays with similar circumstances, it gives a more accurate picture of how much better a team really is compared to the league as a whole. The list of top DVOA offenses on third down, for example, is more accurate than the conventional NFL conversion statistic because

it takes into account that converting third-and-long is more difficult than converting third-and-short, and that a turnover is worse than an incomplete pass because it eliminates the opportunity to move the other team back with a punt on fourth down.

One of the hardest parts of understanding a new statistic is interpreting its scale, or what numbers represent good performance or bad performance. We've made that easy with DVOA. For each season, ratings are normalized so that 0% represents league average. A positive DVOA represents a situation that favors the offense, while a negative DVOA represents a situation that favors the defense. This is why the best offenses have positive DVOA ratings (last year, Baltimore led the NFL at 27.7%) and the best defenses have negative DVOA ratings (with New England on top at -25.5%).

The scale of offensive ratings is wider than the scale of defensive ratings. In most years, the best and worst offenses tend to rate around +/- 30%, while the best and worst defenses tend to rate around +/- 20%. For starting players, the scale tends to reach roughly +/- 40% for passing and receiving, and +/- 30% for rushing. As you might imagine, some players with fewer attempts will surpass both extremes.

Team DVOA totals combine offense and defense by subtracting the latter from the former because the better defenses will have negative DVOA ratings. (Special teams performance is also added, as described later in this essay.) Certain plays are counted in DVOA for offense and not for defense, leading to separate baselines on each side of the ball. In addition, although the league ratings for offense and defense are always 0%, the league averages for passing and rushing separately are *not* 0%. Because passing is more efficient than rushing, the average for team passing is always positive and the average for team rushing is always negative. However, ratings for individual players only compare passes to other passes and runs to other runs, so the league average for individual passing is 0%, as are the league averages for rushing and the three separate league averages for receiving by wide receivers, tight ends, and running backs.

Some other important notes about DVOA:

- Only four penalties are included in DVOA. Two penalties count as pass plays on both sides of the ball: intentional grounding and defensive pass interference. The other two penalties are included for offense only: false starts and delay of game. Because the inclusion of these penalties means a group of negative plays that don't count as either passes or runs, the league averages for pass offense and run offense are higher than the league averages for pass defense and run defense.

- Aborted snaps and incomplete backwards lateral passes are only penalized on offense, not rewarded on defense.

- Adjustments for playing from behind or with a lead in the fourth quarter are different for offense and defense, as are adjustments for the final two minutes of the first half when the offense is not near field goal range.

- Offense gets a slight penalty and defense gets a slight bonus for games indoors.

How well does DVOA work? Using correlation coefficients, we can show that only actual points scored are better than DVOA at indicating how many games a team has won (Table 1) and DVOA more stable from year to year than either wins or points scored (Table 2).

(Correlation coefficient is a statistical tool that measures how two variables are related by using a number between 1 and minus-1. The closer to minus-1 or 1, the stronger the relationship, but the closer to 0, the weaker the relationship.)

Table 1. Correlation of Various Stats to Wins, 2006-2019

Stat	Offense	Defense	Total
Points Scored/Allowed	.755	-.686	.916
VOA (no opponent adjustment)	.730	-.552	.883
DVOA	.708	-.491	.866
Yards Gained/Allowed per Play	.531	-.348	.698
Yards Gained/Allowed	.537	-.380	.670

Table 2. Correlation of Various Stats from Year to Year, 2006-2019

Stat	Correlation
DVOA	.470
Yardage Differential	.468
Point Differential	.426
Pythagorean Wins	.415
Yards per Play Differential	.396
Wins	.335

Special Teams

The problem with a system based on measuring both yardage and yardage towards a first down is what to do with plays that don't have the possibility of a first down. Special teams are an important part of football and we needed a way to add that performance to the team DVOA rankings. Our special teams metric includes five separate measurements: field goals and extra points, net punting, punt returns, net kickoffs, and kick returns.

The foundation of most of these special teams ratings is the concept that each yard line has a different expected points value based on the likelihood of scoring from that position on the field. In *Hidden Game*, the authors suggested that the each additional yard for the offense had equal value, with a team's own goal line being worth -2 points, the 50-yard line 2 points, and the opposing goal line 6 points. (-2 points is not only the value of a safety, but also reflects the fact that when a team is backed up in its own territory, it is likely that its drive will stall, forcing a punt that will give the ball to the other team in good field position. Thus, the negative point value reflects the fact that the defense is more likely to score next.) Our studies have updated this concept to reflect the actual likelihood that the offense or defense will have the next score from a given position on the field based on actual results from the past few seasons. The line that represents the value of field position is

not straight, but curved, with the value of each yard increasing as teams approach either goal line.

Our special teams ratings compare each kick or punt to league average based on the point value of the position of the kick, catch, and return. We've determined a league average for how far a kick goes based on the line of scrimmage for each kick (almost always the 35-yard line for kickoffs, variable for punts) and a league average for how far a return goes based on both the yard line where the ball is caught and the distance that it traveled in the air.

The kicking or punting team is rated based on net points compared to average, taking into account both the kick and the return if there is one. Because the average return is always positive, punts that are not returnable (touchbacks, out of bounds, fair catches, and punts downed by the coverage unit) will rate higher than punts of the same distance which are returnable. (This is also true of touchbacks on kickoffs.) There are also separate individual ratings for kickers and punters that are based on distance and whether the kick is returnable, assuming an average return in order to judge the kicker separate from the coverage.

For the return team, the rating is based on how many points the return is worth compared to average, based on the location of the catch and the distance the ball traveled in the air. Return teams are not judged on the distance of kicks, nor are they judged on kicks that cannot be returned. As explained below, blocked kicks are so rare as to be statistically insignificant as predictors for future performance and are thus ignored. For the kicking team they simply count as missed field goals, for the defense they are gathered with their opponents' other missed field goals in Hidden value (also explained below).

Field goal kicking is measured differently. Measuring kickers by field goal percentage is a bit absurd, as it assumes that all field goals are of equal difficulty. In our metric, each field goal is compared to the average number of points scored on all field goal attempts from that distance over the past 15 years. The value of a field goal increases as distance from the goal line increases. Kickoffs, punts, and field goals are then adjusted based on weather and altitude. It will surprise no one to learn that it is easier to kick the ball in Denver or a dome than it is to kick the ball in Buffalo in December. Because we do not yet have enough data to tailor our adjustments specifically to each stadium, each one is assigned to one of four categories: Cold, Warm, Dome, and Denver. There is also an additional adjustment dropping the value of field goals in Florida (because the warm temperatures allow the ball to carry better).

The baselines for special teams are adjusted in each year for rule changes such as the introduction of the special teams-only "k-ball" in 1999, movement of the kickoff line, and the 2016 change in kickoff touchbacks. Baselines have also been adjusted each year to make up for the gradual improvement of kickers over the last two decades.

Once we've totaled how many points above or below average can be attributed to special teams, we translate those points into DVOA so the ratings can be added to offense and defense to get total team DVOA.

There are three aspects of special teams that have an impact on wins and losses, but don't show up in the standard special teams rating because a team has little or no influence on them. The first is the length of kickoffs by the opposing team, with an asterisk. Obviously, there are no defenders standing on the 35-yard line, ready to block a kickoff after the whistle blows. However, over the past few years, some teams have deliberately kicked short in order to avoid certain top return men, such as Devin Hester and Cordarrelle Patterson. The special teams formula now includes adjustments to give teams extra credit for field position on kick returns if kickers are deliberately trying to avoid a return.

The other two items that special teams have little control over are field goals against your team, and punt distance against your team. Research shows no indication that teams can influence the accuracy or strength of field goal kickers and punters, except for blocks. As mentioned above, although blocked field goals and punts are definitely skillful plays, they are so rare that they have no correlation to how well teams have played in the past or will play in the future, thus they are included here as if they were any other missed field goal or botched punt, giving the defense no additional credit for their efforts. The value of these three elements is listed separately as "Hidden" value.

Special teams ratings also do not include two-point conversions or onside kick attempts, both of which, like blocks, are so infrequent as to be statistically insignificant in judging future performance.

Defense-Adjusted Yards Above Replacement (DYAR)

DVOA is a good stat, but of course it is not a perfect one. One problem is that DVOA, by virtue of being a percentage or rate statistic, doesn't take into account the cumulative value of having a player producing at a league-average level over the course of an above-average number of plays. By definition, an average level of performance is better than that provided by half of the league and the ability to maintain that level of performance while carrying a heavy work load is very valuable indeed. In addition, a player who is involved in a high number of plays can draw the defense's attention away from other parts of the offense, and, if that player is a running back, he can take time off the clock with repeated runs.

Let's say you have a running back who carries the ball 250 times in a season. What would happen if you were to remove this player from his team's offense? What would happen to those 250 plays? Those plays don't disappear with the player, though some might be lost to the defense because of the associated loss of first downs. Rather those plays would have to be distributed among the remaining players in the offense, with the bulk of them being given to a replacement running back. This is where we arrive at the concept of replacement level, borrowed from our friends at Baseball Prospectus. When a player is removed from an offense, he is usually not replaced by a player of similar ability. Nearly every starting player

in the NFL is a starter because he is better than the alternative. Those 250 plays will typically be given to a significantly worse player, someone who is the backup because he doesn't have as much experience and/or talent. A player's true value can then be measured by the level of performance he provides above that replacement level baseline, totaled over all of his run or pass attempts.

Of course, the *real* replacement player is different for each team in the NFL. Last year, the player who was originally the third-string running back in San Francisco (Raheem Mostert) ended up as the starter with a higher DVOA than original starter Tevin Coleman. Sometimes a player such as Mostert will be cut by one team and turn into a star for another. On other teams, the drop from the starter to the backup can be even greater than the general drop to replacement level. (The 2011 Indianapolis Colts will be the hallmark example of this until the end of time.) The choice to start an inferior player or to employ a sub-replacement level backup, however, falls to the team, not the starter being evaluated. Thus we generalize replacement level for the league as a whole as the ultimate goal is to evaluate players independent of the quality of their teammates.

Our estimates of replacement level are computed differently for each position. For quarterbacks, we analyzed situations where two or more quarterbacks had played meaningful snaps for a team in the same season, then compared the overall DVOA of the original starters to the overall DVOA of the replacements. We did not include situations where the backup was actually a top prospect waiting his turn on the bench, since a first-round pick is by no means a "replacement-level" player.

At other positions, there is no easy way to separate players into "starters" and "replacements," since unlike at quarterback, being the starter doesn't make you the only guy who gets in the game. Instead, we used a simpler method, ranking players at each position in each season by attempts. The players who made up the final 10% of passes or runs were split out as "replacement players" and then compared to the players making up the other 90% of plays at that position. This took care of the fact that not every non-starter is a freely available talent.

As noted earlier, the challenge of any new stat is to present it on a scale that's meaningful to those attempting to use it. Saying that Aaron Rodgers' passes were worth 193 success value points over replacement in 2019 has very little value without a context to tell us if 193 is good total or a bad one. Therefore, we translate these success values into a number called "Defense-adjusted Yards Above Replacement, or DYAR. Thus, Dalton was eighth among quarterbacks with 794 passing DYAR. It is our estimate that a generic replacement-level quarterback, throwing in the same situations as Dalton, would have been worth 794 fewer yards. Note that this doesn't mean the replacement level quarterback would have gained exactly 794 fewer yards. First downs, touchdowns, and turnovers all have an estimated yardage value in this system, so what we are saying is that a generic replacement-level quarterback would have fewer yards and touchdowns (and more turnovers) that would total up to be equivalent to the value of 794 yards.

Problems with DVOA and DYAR

Football is a game in which nearly every action requires the work of two or more teammates—in fact, usually 11 teammates all working in unison. Unfortunately, when it comes to individual player ratings, we are still far from the point at which we can determine the value of a player independent from the performance of his teammates. That means that when we say, "In 2019, Aaron Jones had rushing DVOA of 12.0%," what we really are saying is, "In 2019, Aaron Jones, playing in Matt LaFleur's offensive system with the Green Bay offensive line blocking for him and Aaron Rodgers selling the fake when necessary, had a DVOA of 12.0%."

DVOA is limited by what's included in the official NFL play-by-play or tracked by our game charting partners (explained below). Because we need to have the entire play-by-play of a season in order to compute DVOA and DYAR, these metrics are not yet ready to compare players of today to players throughout the league's history. As of this writing, we have processed 35 seasons, 1985 through 2019, and we add seasons at a rate of roughly two per year (the most recent season, plus one season back into history.)

In addition, because we need to turn around DVOA and DYAR quickly during the season before charting can be completed, we do not have charting data such as dropped passes incorporated into these advanced metrics.

Pythagorean Projection

The Pythagorean projection is an approximation of each team's wins based solely on their points scored and allowed. This basic concept was introduced by baseball analyst Bill James, who discovered that the record of a baseball team could be very closely approximated by taking the square of team runs scored and dividing it by the sum of the squares of team runs scored and allowed. Statistician Daryl Morey, now general manager of the Houston Rockets, later extended this theorem to professional football, refining the exponent to 2.37 rather than 2.

The problem with that exponent is the same problem we've had with DVOA in recent years: the changing offensive levels in the NFL. 2.37 worked great based on the league 20 years ago, but in the current NFL it ends up slightly underprojecting teams that play high-scoring games. The most accurate method is actually to adjust the exponent based on the scoring environment of each individual team. Kansas City games have a lot of points. Buffalo games feature fewer points.

This became known as Pythagenport when Clay Davenport of Baseball Prospectus started doing it with baseball teams. In the middle of the 2011 season, we switched our measurement of Pythagorean wins to a Pythagenport-style equation, modified for the NFL.[1] The improvement is slight, but noticeable due to the high-scoring teams that have dominated the last few years.

Pythagorean wins are useful as a predictor of year-to-year improvement. Teams that win a minimum of one full game more than their Pythagorean projection tend to regress the following year; teams that win a minimum of one full game less than their Pythagorean projection tend to improve the following year, particularly if they were at or above .500 despite their underachieving. The Dallas Cowboys had the worst Pythagorean luck in 2019, going 8-8 despite 10.7 Pythagorean wins. On the other side, there are teams that seem set for a reversion of luck. The Green Bay Packers went 13-3 despite having only 9.7 Pythagorean wins. Houston, New Orleans, and Seattle also had over two more wins compared to their Pythagorean projections.

Adjusted Line Yards

One of the most difficult goals of statistical analysis in football is isolating the degree to which each of the 22 men on the field is responsible for the result of a given play. Nowhere is this as significant as the running game, in which one player runs while up to nine other players—including not just linemen but also wideouts and tight ends—block in different directions. None of the statistics we use for measuring rushing—yards, touchdowns, yards per carry—differentiate between the contribution of the running back and the contribution of the offensive line. Neither do our advanced metrics DVOA and DYAR.

We do, however, have enough play-by-play data amassed that we can try to separate the effect that the running back has on a particular play from the effects of the offensive line (and other offensive blockers) and the opposing defense. A team might have two running backs in its stable: RB A, who averages 3.0 yards per carry, and RB B, who averages 3.5 yards per carry. Who is the better back? Imagine that RB A doesn't just average 3.0 yards per carry, but gets exactly 3 yards on every single carry, while RB B has a highly variable yardage output: sometimes 5 yards, sometimes -2 yards, sometimes 20 yards. The difference in variability between the runners can be exploited not only to determine the difference between the runners, but the effect the offensive line has on every running play.

At some point in every long running play, the running back passes all of his offensive line blocks as well as additional blocking backs or receivers. From there on, the rest of the play is dependent on the runner's own speed and elusiveness and the speed and tackling ability of the opposing defense. If Nick Chubb breaks through the line for 50 yards, avoiding tacklers all the way to the goal line, his offensive line has done a great job—but they aren't responsible for the majority of the yards gained. The trick is figuring out exactly how much they *are* responsible for.

For each running back carry, we calculated the probability that the back involved would run for the specific yardage on that play based on that back's average yardage per carry and

---

1 The equation, for those curious, is 1.5 x log ((PF+PA)/G).

the variability of their yardage from play to play. We also calculated the probability that the offense would get the yardage based on the team's rushing average and variability using all backs *other* than the one involved in the given play, and the probability that the defense would give up the specific amount of yardage based on its average rushing yards allowed per carry and variability.

A regression analysis breaks the value for rushing yardage into the following categories: losses, 0-4 yards, 5-10 yards, and 11+ yards. In general, the offensive line is 20% more responsible for lost yardage than it is for positive gains up to four yards, but 50% less responsible for additional yardage gained between five and ten yards, and not at all responsible for additional yardage past ten yards.

By applying those percentages to every running back carry, we were able to create **adjusted line yards (ALY)**, a statistic that measured offensive line performance. (We don't include carries by receivers, which are usually based on deception rather than straight blocking, or carries by quarterbacks, although we may need to reconsider that given the recent use of the read option in the NFL.) Those numbers are then adjusted based on down, distance, situation, opponent and whether or not a team is in the shotgun. (Because defenses are generally playing pass when the quarterback is in shotgun, the average running back carry from shotgun last year gained 4.51 yards, compared to just 4.11 yards on other carries.) The adjusted numbers are then normalized so that the league average for adjusted line yards per carry is the same as the league average for RB yards per carry. Adjusted line yards numbers are normalized differently in each season, so that normalization is based on that year's average for RB yards per carry rather than a historical average.

The NFL distinguishes between runs made to seven different locations on the line: left/right end, left/right tackle, left/right guard, and middle. Further research showed no statistically significant difference between how well a team performed on runs listed as having gone up the middle or past a guard, so we separated runs into just five different directions (left/right end, left/right tackle, and middle). Note that there may not be a statistically significant difference between right tackle and middle/guard either, but pending further research (and for the sake of symmetry) we still list runs behind the right tackle separately. These splits allow us to evaluate subsections of a team's offensive line, but not necessarily individual linesmen, as we can't account for blocking assignments or guards who pull towards the opposite side of the line after the snap.

Success Rate

Success rate is a statistic for running backs that measures how consistently they achieve the yardage necessary for a play to be deemed successful. Some running backs will mix a few long runs with a lot of failed runs of one or two yards, while others with similar yards-per-carry averages will consistently gain five yards on first down, or as many yards as necessary on third down. This statistic helps us differentiate

between the two.

Since success rate compares rush attempts to other rush attempts, without consideration of passing, the standard for success on first down is slightly lower than those described above for DVOA. In addition, the standard for success changes slightly in the fourth quarter when running backs are used to run out the clock. A team with the lead is satisfied with a shorter run as long as it stays in bounds. Conversely, for a team down by a couple of touchdowns in the fourth quarter, four yards on first down isn't going to be a big help.

The formula for running back success rate is as follows:
- A successful play must gain 40% of needed yards on first down, 60% of needed yards on second down, and 100% of needed yards on third or fourth down.
- If the offense is behind by more than a touchdown in the fourth quarter, the benchmarks switch to 50%, 65%, and 100%.
- If the offense is ahead by any amount in the fourth quarter, the benchmarks switch to 30%, 50%, and 100%.

The league-average success rate in 2019 was 47.8%. Success Rate is not adjusted based on defenses faced and is not calculated for quarterbacks and wide receivers who occasionally carry the ball. Note gain that our calculation of success rate for running back is different from the success rate we use as a basis for DVOA, and other success rate calculations you may find across the Internet.

Approximate Value

Approximate Value is a system created by Doug Drinen of Pro Football Reference. The goal is to put a single number on every season of every NFL player since 1950, using a very broad set of guidelines. The goal is not to make judgments on individual seasons, but rather to have a format for studying groups of seasons that is more accurate than measuring players with a very broad brush such as "games started" or "number of Pro Bowls." Skill players are rated primarily using basic stats, while offensive linemen and defensive players are rated in large part based on team performance as well as individual accolades and games started. Advanced stats from Football Outsiders play-by-play breakdown are not part of this system. It is obviously imperfect—"approximate" is right there in the name—but it's valuable for studying groups of draft picks, groups of players by age, and so on. The system is introduced and explained at https://www.pro-football-reference.com/blog/index37a8.html

Expected Points Added

Expected Points Added (EPA) seeks to measure the value of individual plays in terms of points. This is done by calculating the expected average next score before and after each play based on a number of variables including down, distance, field position, and remaining timeouts. This is similar to the system of expected points that underlies our special teams methodology. A freely available model for EPA has become popular in football analysis on the Internet over the last couple seasons, and that model is used a few places in this book.

KUBIAK Projection System

"Skill position" players whom we expect to play a role this season receive a projection of their standard 2020 NFL statistics using the KUBIAK projection system. The KUBIAK system has been overhauled and is newly upgraded for 2020 with work done by Scott Spratt.

The new KUBIAK combines two things:

- Projected player efficiencies based on their regressed per-play production from recent seasons and that of players with similar roles and combine measurements
- Workload projections based on team and player tendencies and the anticipated effect of projected team qualities on their teams' run-pass ratios.

It then adjusts those projections for expected team context each week, capturing the typical changes players in similar roles see because of factors including the venue, weather, and opponent. These preseason projections are an extension of the weekly fantasy projections available as part of our premium FO Plus package on FootballOutsiders.com. Please note that the new KUBIAK system does a better job of accounting for the possibility of injuries, and therefore overall projections will come out a little lower than in previous years. The exception comes in the Quarterbacks chapter, where each quarterback is still given a 16-game projection to help readers understand the expectations if circumstances force a backup quarterback to start for an extended period.

Each player with a KUBIAK projection also comes with a Risk variable for fantasy football, which measures the likelihood of the player hitting his projection. The default rating for each player is Green. As the risk of a player failing to hit his projection rises, he's given a rating of Yellow or, in the worst cases, Red. The Risk variable is based not only on age and injury probability, but also how a player's projection compares to his recent performance as well as our confidence (or lack thereof) in his offensive teammates. A few players with the strongest chances of surpassing their projections are given a Blue rating. Most players marked Blue will be backups with low projections, but a handful are starters or situational players who can be considered slightly better breakout candidates.

When we named our system KUBIAK, it was a play on the PECOTA system used by our partners at Baseball Prospectus—if they were going to name their system after a long-time eighties backup, we would name our system after a long-time eighties backup. Little did we know that Gary Kubiak would finally get a head coaching job the very next season. After some debate, we decided to keep the name, although discussing projections for Denver players was a bit awkward for a while.

To clear up a common misconception among our readers, KUBIAK projects individual player performances only, not teams.

2020 Win Projection System

In this book, each of the 32 NFL teams receives a **2020 Mean Projection** at the beginning of its chapter. These projections stem from three equations that forecast 2020 DVOA for offense, defense, and special teams based on a number of different factors. The system starts by considering the team's DVOA over the past three seasons and, on offense, a separate projection for the starting quarterback. We also incorporate a measure that's based on the net personnel change in DYAR among non-quarterbacks (for offense) and the net change in Approximate Value above replacement level (for defense). Other factors include coaching experience, recent draft history, certain players returning from injury, and combined tenure on the offensive line.

These three equations produce precise numbers representing the most likely outcome, but also produce a range of possibilities, used to determine the probability of each possible offensive, defensive, and special teams DVOA for each team. This is particularly important when projecting football teams, because with only 16 games in a season, a team's performance may vary wildly from its actual talent level due to a couple of random bounces of the ball or badly timed injuries. In addition, the economic structure of the NFL allows teams to make sudden jumps or drops in overall ability more often than in other sports.

This projection system was built using the years 2003-2014. For the five years since, 2015-2019, the mean DVOA forecast by this new projection system had a correlation coefficient with actual wins of .503. By comparison, previous year's point differential had a correlation of .416, and previous year's wins had a correlation of just .331.

The next step in our forecast involves simulating the season one million times. We use the projected range of DVOA possibilities to produce 1,000 different simulated seasons with 32 sets of DVOA ratings. We then plug those season-long DVOA ratings into the same equation we use during the season to determine each team's likely remaining wins for our Playoff Odds Report. The simulation takes each season game-by-game, determining the home or road team's chance of winning each game based on the DVOA ratings of each team as well as home-field advantage. A random number between 0 and 100 determines whether the home or road team has won that game. We ran 1,000 simulations with each of the 1,000 sets of DVOA ratings, creating a million different simulations. The simulation was programmed by Mike Harris.

We use a system we call a "dynamic simulation" to better approximate the true distribution of wins in the NFL. When simulating the season, each team had 2.0% DVOA added or subtracted after a win or loss, reflecting the fact that a win or loss tends to tell us whether a team is truly better or worse than whatever their mean projection had been before the season. Using this method, a team projected with 20.0% DVOA which goes 13-3 will have a 40.0% DVOA entering the playoffs, which is much more realistic. This change gave us more projected seasons at the margins, with fewer seasons at 8-8 and more seasons at 14-2 or 2-14. The dynamic simulation also meant a slight increase in projected wins for the best teams, and a slight decrease for the worst teams. However, the conservative nature of our projection system still means the distribution of mean projected wins has a much smaller spread than the actual win-loss records we will see by the end of December. We will continue to experiment with changes to the simulation in order to produce the most accurate possible forecast of the NFL season in future years.

Game Charting Data

Each of the formulas listed above relies primarily on the play-by-play data published by the NFL. When we began to analyze the NFL, this was all that we had to work with. Just as a television broadcast has a color commentator who gives more detail to the facts related by the play-by-play announcer, so too do we need some color commentary to provide contextual information that breathes life into these plain lines of numbers and text. We added this color commentary with game charting.

Beginning in 2005, Football Outsiders began using a number of volunteers to chart every single play of every regular-season and postseason NFL game. To put it into perspective, there were over 54,000 lines of play-by-play information in each NFL season and our goal is to add several layers of detail to nearly all of them.

It gradually became clear that attempting to chart so much football with a crew of volunteers was simply not feasible, especially given our financial resources compared to those of our competitors. Over the past few years, we have partnered with larger companies to take on the responsibilities of game charting so that we can devote more time to analysis.

In 2015, Football Outsiders reached an agreement with Sports Info Solutions to begin a large charting project that would replace our use of volunteers. We also have a partnership with ESPN Stats & Info and use their data to check against the data collected by Sports Info Solutions. All charting data for the 2019 season is provided by one of these two companies.

Game charting is significantly easier now that the NFL makes coaches' film available through NFL Game Rewind. This tape, which was not publicly available when we began charting with volunteers in 2005, includes sideline and end zone perspectives for each play, and shows all 22 players at all times, making it easier to see the cause-and-effect of certain actions taken on the field. Nonetheless, all game charting is still imperfect. You often cannot tell which players did their jobs particularly well or made mistakes without knowing the play call and each player's assignment, particularly when it comes to zone coverage or pass-rushers who reach the quarterback without being blocked. Therefore, the goal of game charting from both ESPN Stats & Info and Sports Info Solutions is *not* to "grade" players, but rather to attempt to mark specific events: a pass pressure, a blown block, a dropped interception, and so on.

We emphasize that all data from game charting is unofficial.

Other sources for football statistics may keep their own measurements of yards after catch or how teams perform against the blitz. Our data will not necessarily match theirs. Even ESPN Stats & Info and Sports Info Solutions have a number of disagreements, marking different events on the same play because it can be difficult to determine the definition of a "pressure" or a "dropped pass." However, any other group that is publicly tracking this data is also working off the same footage, and thus will run into the same issues of difficulty and subjectivity.

There are lots of things we would like to do with all-22 film that we simply haven't been able to do yet, such as charting coverage by cornerbacks when they aren't the target of a given pass, or even when pass pressure prevents the pass from getting into the air. Unfortunately, we are limited by what our partners are able to chart given time constraints.

In the description of data below, we have tried to designate which data from 2019 comes from ESPN Stats & Info group (ESPN S&I), which data comes from Sports Info Solutions (SIS), and where we have combined data from both companies with our own analysis.

Formation/Personnel

For each play, we have the number of running backs, wide receivers, and tight ends on the field courtesy of ESPN S&I. Players were marked based on their designation on the roster, not based on where they lined up on the field. Obviously, this could be difficult with some hybrid players or players changing positions in 2019, but we did our best to keep things as consistent as possible.

SIS also tracked this data and added the names of players who were lined up in unexpected positions. This included marking tight ends or wide receivers in the backfield, and running backs or tight ends who were lined up either wide or in the slot (often referred to as "flexing" a tight end). SIS also marked when a fullback or tight end was actually a sixth (or sometimes even seventh) offensive lineman, and they marked the backfield formation as empty back, single back, I formation, offset I, split backs, full house, or "other." These notations of backfield formation were recorded directly before the snap and do not account for positions before pre-snap motion.

SIS then marked defensive formations by listing the number of linemen, linebackers, and defensive backs. There will be mistakes—a box safety may occasionally be confused for a linebacker, for example—but for the most part the data for defensive backs will be accurate. Figuring out how to mark whether a player is a defensive end or a linebacker is a different story. The rise of hybrid defenses has led to a lot of confusion. Edge rushers in a 4-3 defense may play standing up because they used to play for a 3-4 defense and that's what they are used to. A player who is usually considered an outside linebacker for a 3-4 defense may put his hand on the ground on third down (thus looking like a 4-3 defensive end), but the tackle next to him is still two-gapping (which is generally a 3-4 principle). SIS marked personnel in a simplified fashion by designating any front seven player in a standing position as a linebacker and designating any front seven player in a crouching position as a defensive lineman.

For the last three years, we also have data from SIS on where receivers lined up before each of their pass targets (wide, slot, tight, or backfield) and what routes they ran.

Rushers and Blockers

ESPN Stats & Info provided us with two data points regarding the pass rush: the number of pass-rushers on a given play, and the number defensive backs blitzing on a given play. SIS also tracked this data for comparison purposes and then added a count of blockers. Counting blockers is an art as much as a science. Offenses base their blocking schemes on how many rushers they expect. A running back or tight end's assignment may depend on how many pass-rushers cross the line at the snap. Therefore, an offensive player was deemed to be a blocker if he engaged in an actual block, or there was some hesitation before running a route. A running back that immediately heads out into the flat is not a blocker, but one that waits to verify that the blocking scheme is working and then goes out to the flat would, in fact, be considered a blocker.

Pass Play Details

Both companies recorded the following data for all pass plays:

- Did the play begin with a play-action fake, including read-option fakes that developed into pass plays instead of being handed to a running back?
- Was the quarterback in or out of the pocket?
- Was the quarterback under pressure in making his pass?
- Was this a screen pass?

SIS game charting also marks the name of the defender who caused the pass pressure. Charters were allowed to list two names if necessary, and could also attribute a hurry to "overall pressure." No defender was given a hurry and a sack on the same play, but defenders were given hurries if they helped force a quarterback into a sack that was finished by another player. SIS also identified which defender(s) caused the pass pressure which forced a quarterback to scramble for yardage. If the quarterback wasn't under pressure but ran anyway, the play could be marked either as "coverage scramble" (if the quarterback ran because there were no open receivers) or "hole opens up" (if the quarterback ran because he knew he could gain significant yardage). All pressure data in this book is based on SIS data.

Some places in this book, we divide pass yardage into two numbers: distance in the air and yards after catch. This information is tracked by the NFL, but the official scorers often make errors, so we corrected the original data based on input from both ESPN S&I and SIS. Distance in the air is based on the distance from the line of scrimmage to the place where the receiver either caught or was supposed to catch the pass. We do not count how far the quarterback was behind the line or horizontal yardage if the quarterback threw across the field. All touchdowns are counted to the goal line, so that distance in the air added to yards after catch always equals the official yardage total kept by the league.

Incomplete Passes

Quarterbacks are evaluated based on their ability to complete passes. However, not all incompletes should have the same weight. Throwing a ball away to avoid a sack is actually a valuable incomplete, and a receiver dropping an otherwise quality pass is hardly a reflection on the quarterback.

This year, our evaluation of incomplete passes began with ESPN Stats & Info, which marked passes as Overthrown, Underthrown, Thrown Away, Batted Down at the Line, Defensed, or Dropped. We then compared this data to similar data from SIS and made some changes. We also changed some plays to reflect a couple of additional categories we have kept in past years for Football Outsiders: Hit in Motion (indicating the quarterback was hit as his arm was coming forward to make a pass), Caught Out of Bounds, and Hail Mary.

ESPN S&I and SIS also marked when a defender dropped an interception; Football Outsiders volunteers then analyzed plays where the two companies disagreed to come up with a final total. When a play is close, we tend to err on the side of not marking a dropped interception, as we don't want to blame a defender who, for example, jumps high for a ball and has it tip off his fingers. We also counted a few "defensed" interceptions, when a quarterback threw a pass that would have been picked off if not for the receiver playing defense on the ball. These passes counted as dropped interceptions for quarterbacks but not for the defensive players.

Defenders

The NFL play-by-play lists tackles and, occasionally, tipped balls, but it does not definitively list the defender on the play. SIS charters attempted to determine which defender was primarily responsible for covering either the receiver at the time of the throw or the location to which the pass was thrown, regardless of whether the pass was complete or not.

Every defense in the league plays zone coverage at times, some more than others, which leaves us with the question of how to handle plays without a clear man assigned to that receiver. Charters (SIS employees in 2015-2019, and FO volunteers in previous seasons) had three alternatives:

- We asked charters to mark passes that found the holes in zone coverage as Hole in Zone, rather than straining to assign that pass to an individual defender. We asked the charter to also note the player who appeared to be responsible for that zone, and these defenders are assigned half credit for those passes. Some holes were so large that no defender could be listed along with the Hole in Zone designation.
- Charters were free to list two defenders instead of one. This could be used for actual double coverage, or for zone coverage in which the receiver was right between two close defenders rather than sitting in a gaping hole. When two defenders are listed, ratings assign each with half credit.
- Screen passes and dumpoffs are marked as Uncovered unless a defender (normally a linebacker) is obviously shadowing that specific receiver on the other side of the line of scrimmage.

Since we began the charting project in 2005, nothing has changed our analysis more than this information on pass coverage. However, even now with the ability to view all-22 film, it can be difficult to identify the responsible defender except when there is strict man-to-man coverage.

Additional Details

All draw plays were marked, whether by halfbacks or quarterbacks. Option runs and zone reads were also marked.

Both SIS and ESPN S&I when the formation was pistol as opposed to shotgun; the official play-by-play simply marks these plays all as shotgun.

Both SIS and ESPN S&I track yards after contact for each play.

SIS charters marked each quarterback sack with one of the following terms: Blown Block, Coverage Sack, QB Fault, Failed Scramble, or Blitz/Overall Pressure. Blown Blocks were listed with the name of a specific offensive player who allowed the defender to come through. (Some blown block sacks are listed with two blockers, who each get a half-sack.) Coverage Sack denotes when the quarterback has plenty of time to throw but cannot find an open receiver. QB Fault represents "self sacks" listed without a defender, such as when the quarterback drops back, only to find the ball slip out of his hands with no pass-rusher touching him. Failed Scramble represents plays where a quarterback began to run without major pass pressure because he thought he could get a positive gain, only to be tackled before he passed the line of scrimmage.

SIS tracked "broken tackles" on all runs or pass plays. We define a "broken tackle" as one of two events: Either the ball-carrier escapes from the grasp of the defender, or the defender is in good position for a tackle but the ballcarrier jukes him out of his shoes. If the ballcarrier sped by a slow defender who dived and missed, that did not count as a broken tackle. If the defender couldn't bring the ballcarrier down because he is being blocked out of the play by another offensive player, this did not count as a broken tackle. It was possible to mark multiple broken tackles on the same play. Broken tackles are not marked for special teams.

How to Read the Team Summary Box

Here is a rundown of all the tables and stats that appear in the 32 team chapters. Each team chapter begins with a box in the upper-right hand corner that gives a summary of our statistics for that team, as follows:

2019 Record gives each team's actual win-loss record. **Pythagorean Wins** gives the approximate number of wins expected last year based on this team's raw totals of points scored and allowed, along with their NFL rank. **Snap-Weighted Age** gives the average age of the team in 2019, weighted based on how many snaps each player was on the field and ranked from oldest (New England, first at 28.6) to youngest (Jack-

sonville, 32nd at 25.5). **Average Opponent** gives a ranking of last year's schedule strength based on the average DVOA of all 16 opponents faced during the regular season. Teams are ranked from the hardest schedule of 2019 (Los Angeles Rams) to the easiest (New England).

Total DVOA gives the team's total DVOA rating, with rank. **Offense, Defense**, and **Special Teams** list the team's DVOA rating in each category, along with NFL rank. Remember that good offenses and special teams have positive DVOA numbers, while a negative DVOA means better defense, so the lowest defensive DVOA is ranked No. 1 (last year, New England).

2020 Mean Projection gives the average number of wins for this team based on the 2020 Win Projection System described earlier in this chapter. Please note that we do not expect any teams to win the exact number of games in their mean projection. First of all, no team can win 0.8 of a game. Second, because these projections represent a whole range of possible values, the averages naturally tend to drift towards 8-8. Obviously, we're not expecting a season where no team goes 4-12 or 12-4. For a better way to look at the projections, we offer **Postseason Odds**, which give each team's chance of making the postseason based on our simulation, and **Super Bowl Appearance** odds, which give each team's chance of representing its conference in Super Bowl LV. The average team will make the playoffs in 43.8% of simulations (now a higher number due to the expansion to seven playoff teams per conference), and the Super Bowl in 6.3% of simulations.

Projected Average Opponent gives the team's strength of schedule for 2020; like the listing for last year's schedule strength in the first column of the box, this number is based not on last year's record but on the mean projected DVOA for each opponent. A positive schedule is harder, a negative schedule easier. Teams are ranked from the hardest projected schedule (Carolina, first) to the easiest (Indianapolis, 32nd). This strength of schedule projection does not take into account which games are home or away, or the timing of the bye week.

The final column of the box gives the team's chances of finishing in four different basic categories of success:

- On the Clock (0-4 wins; NFL average 12%)
- Mediocrity (5-7 wins; NFL average 32%)
- Playoff Contender (8-10 wins; NFL average 36%)
- Super Bowl Contender (11+ wins; NFL average 20%)

The percentage given for each category is dependent not only on how good we project the team to be in 2020, but the level of variation possible in that projection, and the expected performance of the teams on the schedule.

You'll also find a table with the team's 2020 schedule placed within each chapter, along with a graph showing each team's 2019 week-to-week performance by single-game DVOA. The second, dotted line on the graph represents a five-week moving average of each team's performance, in order to show a longer-term view of when they were improving and declining. After the essays come statistical tables and comments related to that team and its specific units.

Weekly Performance

The first table gives a quick look at the team's week-to-week performance in 2019. (Table 3) This includes the play-offs for those teams that made the postseason, with the four weeks of playoffs numbered 18 (wild card) through 21 (Super Bowl). All other tables in the team chapters represent regular-season performance only unless otherwise noted.

Table 3. 2019 Patriots Stats by Week

Wk	vs.	W-L	PF	PA	YDF	YDA	TO	Total	Off	Def	ST
1	PIT	W	33	3	465	308	+1	75%	69%	0%	6%
2	at MIA	W	43	0	379	184	+3	86%	8%	-91%	-14%
3	NYJ	W	30	14	381	105	-1	68%	18%	-51%	-2%
4	at BUF	W	16	10	224	375	+3	-3%	-39%	-44%	-8%
5	at WAS	W	33	7	442	223	+1	66%	11%	-46%	9%
6	NYG	W	35	14	427	213	+2	46%	-8%	-58%	-5%
7	at NYJ	W	33	0	323	154	+5	74%	-2%	-68%	8%
8	CLE	W	27	13	318	310	+3	-6%	-11%	-20%	-16%
9	at BAL	L	20	37	342	372	0	35%	27%	5%	14%
10	BYE										
11	at PHI	W	17	10	298	255	+1	21%	-6%	-12%	15%
12	DAL	W	13	9	282	321	+1	32%	-13%	-51%	-6%
13	at HOU	L	22	28	448	276	-1	-29%	-2%	24%	-3%
14	KC	L	16	23	278	346	+1	25%	-5%	-39%	-9%
15	at CIN	W	34	13	291	315	+5	16%	-14%	-18%	11%
16	BUF	W	24	17	414	268	-1	44%	37%	0%	7%
17	MIA	L	24	27	352	389	-2	-29%	-9%	32%	12%
18	TEN	L	13	20	307	272	-1	-5%	-14%	-3%	6%

Looking at the first week for the New England Patriots in 2019, the first five columns are fairly obvious: New England opened the season with a 33-3 win at home against Pittsburgh. **YDF** and **YDA** are net yards on offense and net yards against the defense. These numbers do not include penalty yardage or special teams yardage. **TO** represents the turnover margin. Unlike other parts of the book in which we consider all fumbles as equal, this only represents actual turnovers: fumbles lost and interceptions. So, for example, the Patriots forced one more turnover than the Steelers in Week 1 but committed one more turnover than the Jets in Week 3.

Finally, you'll see DVOA ratings for this game: Total **DVOA** first, then offense (**Off**), defense (**Def**), and special teams (**ST**). Note that these are DVOA ratings, adjusted for opponent, so a loss to a good team will often be listed with a higher rating than a close win over a bad team. For example, the Patriots have a positive DVOA for their Week 9 loss to Baltimore, but a negative DVOA for their Week 8 win over Cleveland.

Trends and Splits

Next to the week-to-week performance is a table giving DVOA for different portions of a team's performance, on both offense and defense. Each split is listed with the team's rank among the 32 NFL teams. These numbers represent regular season performance only.

Total DVOA gives total offensive, and defensive DVOA in all situations. **Unadjusted VOA** represents the breakdown of play-by-play considering situation but not opponent. A team whose offensive DVOA is higher than its offensive VOA played a harder-than-average schedule of opposing defenses; a team with a lower defensive DVOA than defensive VOA player a harder-than-average schedule of opposing offenses.

Weighted Trend lowers the importance of earlier games to give a better idea of how the team was playing at the end of the regular season. The final four weeks of the season are full strength; moving backwards through the season, each week is given less and less weight until the first three weeks of the season, which are not included at all. **Variance** is the same as noted above, with a higher percentage representing less consistency. This is true for both offense and defense: Tennessee, for example, was very consistent on defense (1.7%, first) but inconsistent on offense (14.1%, 31st). **Average Opponent** is that the same thing that appears in the box to open each chapter, except split in half: the average DVOA of all opposing defenses (for offense) or the average DVOA of all opposing offenses (for defense).

Passing and **Rushing** are fairly self-explanatory. Note that rushing DVOA includes all rushes, not just those by running backs, including quarterback scrambles that may have begun as pass plays.

The next three lines split out DVOA on **First Down**, **Second Down**, and **Third Down**. Third Down here includes fourth downs on which a team runs a regular offensive play instead of punting or attempting a field goal. **First Half** and **Second Half** represent the first two quarters and last two quarters (plus overtime), not the first eight and last eight games of the regular season. Next comes DVOA in the **Red Zone**, which is any offensive play starting from the defense's 20-yard line through the goal line. The final split is **Late and Close**, which includes any play in the second half or overtime when the teams are within eight points of each other in either direction. (Eight points, of course, is the biggest deficit that can be made up with a single score, a touchdown and two-point conversion.)

Five-Year Performance

This table gives each team's performance over the past five seasons. (Table 4) It includes win-loss record, Pythagorean Wins, **Estimated Wins**, points scored and allowed, and turnover margin. Estimated wins are based on a formula that estimates how many games a team would have been expected to win based on 2019 performance in specific situations, normalized to eliminate luck (fumble recoveries, opponents' missed field goals, etc.) and assuming average schedule strength. The formula emphasizes consistency and overall DVOA as well as DVOA in a few specifically important situations. The next columns of this table give total DVOA along with DVOA for offense, defense, and special teams, and the rank for each

Table 4. Eagles Five-Year Performance

Year	W-L	Pyth W	Est W	PF	PA	TO	Total	Rk	Off	Rk	Def	Rk	ST	Rk	Off AGL	Rk	Def AGL	Rk	Off Age	Rk	Def Age	Rk	ST Age	Rk
2015	7-9	6.7	6.8	377	430	-5	-11.2%	22	-10.1%	26	3.0%	17	1.9%	10	22.7	5	27.3	12	27.2	11	26.7	15	26.9	2
2016	7-9	9.0	9.9	367	331	+6	14.4%	5	-5.5%	20	-12.4%	4	7.5%	2	20.4	3	17.7	4	27.0	11	26.9	9	27.0	3
2017	13-3	12.0	11.1	457	295	+11	23.4%	5	10.1%	8	-12.3%	5	0.9%	16	29.0	13	24.4	9	27.1	12	26.9	9	26.4	7
2018	9-7	8.5	8.0	367	348	-9	-0.1%	16	-0.3%	16	0.0%	15	0.2%	15	46.0	22	71.0	31	27.9	5	27.6	3	25.5	26
2019	9-7	8.8	9.2	385	354	-3	6.6%	11	2.6%	14	-4.0%	12	0.0%	19	30.3	10	54.1	29	27.8	3	27.2	4	25.6	21

among that season's 32 NFL teams.

The next four columns give the adjusted games lost (AGL) for starters on both offense and defense, along with rank. (Our total for starters here includes players who take over as starters due to another injury and then get injured themselves, such as Trevor Siemian or Vernon Davis last year. It also includes important situational players who may not necessarily start, such as pass-rush specialists and slot receivers.) Adjusted games lost was introduced in *Pro Football Prospectus 2008*; it gives a weighted estimate of the probability that players would miss games based on how they are listed on the injury report. Unlike a count of "starter games missed," this accounts for the fact that a player listed as questionable who does in fact play is not playing at 100% capability. Teams are ranked from the fewest injuries (2019: Baltimore on offense, New England on defense) to the most (2019: Washington on offense, New York Jets on defense).

Individual Offensive Statistics

Each team chapter contains a table giving passing and receiving numbers for any player who either threw five passes or was thrown five passes, along with rushing numbers for any players who carried the ball at least five times. These numbers also appear in the player comments at the end of the book (except for runs by wide receivers). By putting them together in the team chapters we hope we make it easier to compare the performances of different players on the same team.

Players who are no longer on the team are marked with an asterisk. New players who were on a different team in 2019 are in italics. Changes should be accurate as of July 1. Rookies are not included.

All players are listed with DYAR and DVOA. Passing statistics then list total pass plays (**Plays**), net yardage (**NtYds**), and net yards per pass (**Avg**). These numbers include not just passes (and the positive yardage from them) but aborted snaps and sacks (and the negative yardage from them). Then comes average yards after catch (**YAC**), as determined by the game charting project. This average is based on charted receptions, not total pass attempts. The final three numbers are completion percentage (**C%**), passing touchdowns (**TD**), and interceptions (**Int**).

It is important to note that the tables in the team chapters contain Football Outsiders stats, while the tables in the player comments later in the book contain official NFL totals, at least when it comes to standard numbers like receptions and yard-

age. This results in a number of differences between the two:

- Team chapter tables list aborted snaps as passes, not runs, although aborted handoffs are still listed as runs. Net yardage for quarterbacks in the team chapter tables includes the lost yardage from aborted snaps, sacks, and intentional grounding penalties. For official NFL stats, all aborted snaps are listed as runs.
- Football Outsiders stats omit kneeldowns from run totals and clock-stopping spikes from pass totals.
- "Skill players" who played for multiple teams in 2019 are only listed in team chapters with stats from that specific team; combined stats are listed in the player comments section.

Table 5. Jaguars Passing

Player	DYAR	DVOA	Plays	NtYds	Avg	YAC	C%	TD	Int
G.Minshew	193	-5.0%	503	3086	6.1	5.4	60.8%	21	6
N.Foles*	-77	-21.3%	125	669	5.4	4.6	66.4%	3	2
M.Glennon	-6	-20.2%	11	53	4.8	3.0	60.0%	1	0

Rushing statistics start with DYAR and DVOA, then list rushing plays and net yards along with average yards per carry and rushing touchdowns. The final two columns are fumbles (**Fum**)—both those lost to the defense and those recovered by the offense—and Success Rate (**Suc**), explained earlier in this chapter. Fumbles listed in the rushing table include all quarterback fumbles on sacks and aborted snaps, as well as running back fumbles on receptions, but not wide receiver fumbles.

Table 6. Falcons Rushing

Player	DYAR	DVOA	Plays	Yds	Avg	TD	Fum	Suc
D.Freeman*	-19	-11.1%	184	661	3.6	2	2	41%
B.Hill	14	-4.1%	78	323	4.1	2	0	44%
M.Ryan	38	18.1%	25	156	6.2	1	1	-
I.Smith	27	13.7%	22	106	4.8	1	0	55%
Q.Ollison	-3	-11.1%	22	50	2.3	4	1	55%
K.Smith	5	4.6%	5	8	1.6	0	0	80%
K.Barner*	9	58.5%	4	28	7.0	0	0	75%
T.Gurley	58	-2.4%	223	858	3.8	12	3	48%

Receiving statistics start with DYAR and DVOA and then list the number of passes thrown to this receiver (**Plays**), the number of passes caught (**Catch**) and the total receiving yards (**Yds**). Yards per catch (**Y/C**) includes total yardage per reception, based on standard play-by-play, while yards after catch

(YAC) is based on information from our game charting project. Finally we list total receiving touchdowns, and catch percentage (C%), which is the percentage of passes intended for this receiver which were caught. Wide receivers, tight ends, and running backs are separated on the table by horizontal lines.

Table 7. Browns Receiving

Player	DYAR	DVOA	Plays	Ctch	Yds	Y/C	YAC	TD	C%
J.Landry	182	4.1%	138	83	1174	14.1	5.3	6	60%
O.Beckham	79	-5.4%	133	74	1035	14.0	4.4	4	56%
D.Ratley	21	-1.9%	24	12	200	16.7	3.9	1	50%
A.Callaway*	-3	-15.0%	15	8	89	11.1	5.5	0	53%
R.Higgins*	-11	-27.0%	11	4	55	13.8	2.3	1	36%
K.Hodge	-7	-21.3%	10	4	76	19.0	2.3	0	40%
D.Harris*	-17	-16.0%	27	15	149	9.9	4.5	3	56%
R.Seals-Jones*	28	10.2%	22	14	229	16.4	6.8	4	64%
D.Njoku	-10	-23.7%	10	5	41	8.2	3.2	1	50%
S.Carlson	12	17.5%	7	5	51	10.2	4.2	1	71%
A.Hooper	130	12.5%	97	75	787	10.5	4.4	6	77%
N.Chubb	-4	-15.3%	49	36	278	7.7	8.8	0	73%
K.Hunt	71	14.2%	44	37	285	7.7	7.5	1	84%
D.Hilliard	24	16.5%	15	12	92	7.7	8.6	0	80%
D.Johnson	14	35.0%	7	6	71	11.8	7.2	0	86%

Performance Based on Personnel

These tables provide a look at performance in 2019 based on personnel packages, as defined above in the section on marking formation/personnel as part of Sports Info Solutions charting. There are four different tables, representing:

- Offense based on personnel
- Offense based on opponent's defensive personnel
- Defense based on personnel
- Defense based on opponent's offensive personnel

Most of these tables feature the top five personnel groupings for each team. Occasionally, we will list the personnel group which ranks sixth if the sixth group is either particularly interesting or nearly as common as the fifth group. Each personnel group is listed with its frequency among 2019 plays, yards per play, and DVOA. Offensive personnel are also listed with how often the team in question called a running play instead of a pass play from given personnel. (Quarterback scrambles are included as pass plays, not runs.)

Offensive personnel are given in the standard two-digit format where the first digit is running backs and the second digit is tight ends. You can figure out wide receivers by subtracting that total from five, with a couple of exceptions. Plays with six or seven offensive linemen will have a three-digit listing such as "611" or "622." Any play with a non-quarterback taking a direct snap from the quarterback position was counted as "Wildcat." This personnel group only appears on the table for Pittsburgh, listed as "WC."

When defensive players come in to play offense, defensive backs are counted as wide receivers and linebackers as tight ends. Defensive linemen who come in as offensive linemen are counted as offensive linemen; if they come in as blocking fullbacks, we count them as running backs. Taysom Hill (and any other quarterback who lines up at another position) is counted based on where he lines up in the formation.

We no longer give giving personnel data based on the number of defensive linemen and linebackers. This is because of the difficulty in separating between the two, especially with our simplified designation of players as defensive linemen or linebackers based simply on who has a hand on the ground. There are just too many hybrid defensive schemes in today's game: 4-3 schemes where one or both ends rush the passer from a standing position, or hybrid schemes that one-gap on one side of the nose tackle and two-gap on the other. Therefore, defensive personnel is listed in only five categories:

- Base (four defensive backs)
- Nickel (five defensive backs)
- Dime+ (six or more defensive backs)
- Big (either 4-4-3 or 3-5-3)
- Goal Line (all other personnel groups with fewer than four defensive backs)

11, or three-wide personnel, was by far the most common grouping in the NFL last year, used on 59% of plays. However, this was a drop of 5% from the year before. After 11 personnel came the standard two-tight end set 12 personnel (19% of plays) and the more traditional 21 personnel (7.8%). Defenses lined up in Base on 27% of plays, Nickel on 56% of plays, Dime+ on 16% of plays, and either Big or Goal Line on 1.4% of plays. Table 8 lists the average performance from the ten most common personnel groups in 2019. Note that be-

Table 8. NFL Offensive Performance by Personnel Group, 2019

Pers.	Plays	Pct	Yds	DVOA
11	18,904	58.6%	5.8	6.0%
12	6,201	19.2%	5.6	1.8%
21	2,507	7.8%	5.7	4.3%
22	906	2.8%	5.2	6.3%
13	886	2.7%	5.2	-1.4%
10	780	2.4%	5.8	9.0%
611	505	1.6%	5.4	-2.9%
612	438	1.4%	4.5	-4.2%
20	340	1.1%	4.9	-10.2%
621	143	0.4%	4.3	-10.2%

cause we don't track personnel grouping on penalties, those negative plays are all missing from this analysis, so the average offensive DVOA for this table is 4.2% rather than 0.0%.

On Table 9, which shows the same numbers from the defensive perspective, the average DVOA is still 0.0%.

Table 9. NFL Defensive Performance by Personnel Group, 2019

Pers.	Plays	Pct	Yds	DVOA
Nickel	18,045	55.9%	5.7	1.5%
Base	8,610	26.7%	5.4	-3.9%
Dime+	5,172	16.0%	6.0	3.0%
Goal Line	244	0.8%	1.0	-1.9%
Big	181	0.6%	3.6	-19.5%
10 Men	27	0.1%	6.2	62.9%

Strategic Tendencies

The Strategic Tendencies table presents a mix of information garnered from the standard play-by-play a well as charting from both Sports Info Solutions and ESPN Stats & Information. It gives you an idea of what kind of plays teams run in what situations and with what personnel. Each category is given a league-wide **Rank** from most often (1) to least often (32) except as noted below. The sample table shown here (Table 10) lists the NFL average in each category for 2019.

The first column of strategic tendencies lists how often teams ran in different situations. These ratios are based on the type of play, not the actual result, so quarterback scrambles count as "passes" while quarterback sneaks, draws and option plays count as "runs."

Runs, first half and **Runs, first down** should be self-evident. **Runs, second-and-long** is the percentage of runs on second down with seven or more yards to go, giving you an idea of how teams follow up a failed first down. **Runs, power situations** is the percentage of runs on third or fourth down with 1-2 yards to go, or at the goal line with 1-2 yards to go. **Runs, behind 2H** tells you how often teams ran when they were behind in the second half, generally a passing situation. **Pass, ahead 2H** tells you how often teams passed when they had the lead in the second half, generally a running situation.

In each case, you can determine the percentage of plays that were passes by subtracting the run percentage from 100 (the reverse being true for "Pass, ahead 2H," of course).

The final entry in the first column gives the percentage of each offense's plays that were coded as **Run-Pass Options** by SIS charters.

The second column gives information about offensive formations and personnel, as tracked by Sports Info Solutions.

The first three entries detail formation, i.e. where players were lined up on the field. **Form: Single Back** lists how often the team lined up with only one player in the backfield, **Form: Empty Back** lists how often the team lined up with no players in the backfield, and **Form: Multi Back** lists how often the team lined up with two or three players in the backfield.

The next three entries are based on personnel, no matter where players were lined up in the formation. **Pers: 3+ WR** marks how often the team plays with three or more wide receivers. **Pers: 2+ TE/6+ OL** marks how often the team plays with either more than one tight end or more than five offensive linemen. **Pers: 6+ OL** marks just plays with more than five offensive linemen. Finally, we give the percentage of plays where a team used **Shotgun or Pistol** in 2019. This does not count "Wildcat" or direct snap plays involving a non-quarterback.

The third column shows how the defensive **Pass Rush** worked in 2019.

Rush 3/Rush 4/Rush 5/Rush 6+: The percentage of pass plays (including quarterback scrambles) on which Sports Info Solutions recorded this team rushing the passer with three or fewer defenders, four defenders, five defenders, and six or more defenders.

Edge Rusher Sacks/Interior DL Sacks/Second Level Sacks: These numbers list how often sacks came from each level of the defense. Second-level sacks are those that come from linebackers who are not edge rushers, plus sacks from defensive backs.

The fourth column has more data on the use of defensive backs.

4 DB/5DB/6+ DB: The percentage of plays where this defense lined up with four, five, and six or more defensive backs, according to Sports Info Solutions.

Man Coverage: The percentage of passes where this defense was in some sort of man coverage, according to Sports Info Solutions.

CB by Sides: One of the most important lessons from game charting is that each team's best cornerback does not necessarily match up against the opponent's best receiver. Most cornerbacks play a particular side of the field and in fact cover a wider range of receivers than we assumed before we saw the charting data. This metric looks at which teams prefer to leave their starting cornerbacks on specific sides of the field.

To figure CB by Sides, we took the top two cornerbacks from each team and looked at the percentage of passes where that cornerback was in coverage on the left or right side of the field, ignoring passes marked as "middle." For each of the two cornerbacks, we took the higher number, right or left, and

Table 10. Average Strategic Tendencies, 2019

Run/Pass		Rk	Formation		Rk	Pass Rush		Rk	Secondary		Rk	Strategy		Rk
Runs, first half	37%	--	Form: Single Back	80%	--	Rush 3	9.0%	--	4 DB	27%	--	Play Action	25%	--
Runs, first down	49%	--	Form: Empty Back	8%	--	Rush 4	65.0%	--	5 DB	56%	--	Offensive Motion	40%	--
Runs, second-long	27%	--	Form: Multi Back	12%	--	Rush 5	20.3%	--	6+ DB	16%	--	Avg Box (Off)	6.56	--
Runs, power sit.	57%	--	Pers: 3+ WR	63%	--	Rush 6+	5.7%	--	Man Coverage	33%	--	Avg Box (Def)	6.56	--
Runs, behind 2H	28%	--	Pers: 2+ TE/6+ OL	30%	--	Edge Rusher Sacks	56.6%	--	CB by Sides	76%	--	Offensive Pace	30.67	--
Pass, ahead 2H	48%	--	Pers: 6+ OL	4%	--	Interior DL Sacks	24.4%	--	S/CB Cover Ratio	26%	--	Defensive Pace	30.64	--
Run-Pass Options	6%	--	Shotgun/Pistol	65%	--	Second Level Sacks	19.0%	--	DB Blitz	11%	--	Go for it on 4th	1.52	--

then we averaged the two cornerbacks to get the final CB by Sides rating. Teams which preferred to leave their cornerbacks in the same place last season, such as Chicago and Seattle, will have high ratings. Teams that did more to move their best cornerback around to cover the opponent's top targets, such as New England and Arizona, will have low ratings.

S/CB Cover Ratio: This is our attempt to track which teams like to use their safeties as hybrid safety/corners and put them in man coverage on wide receivers. This ratio takes all pass targets with a defensive back in coverage, and then gives what percentage of those targets belonged to a player who is rostered as a safety, ranging from Kansas City, which used safety Tyrann Mathieu as a nickelback (39%) to the New York Jets, who had very defined roles for their two starting safeties (14%).

DB Blitz: We have data on how often the defense used at least one defensive back in the pass rush courtesy of ESPN Stats & Info.

Finally, in the final column, we have some elements of game strategy.

Play action: The percentage of pass plays (including quarterback scrambles) which began with a play-action fake to the running back. This percentage does not include fake end-arounds unless there was also a fake handoff. It does include flea flickers.

Offensive motion: The percentage of offensive plays which began with a man in motion before the snap.

Average Box: These items list the average number of men in the box faced by each team's offense and the average number of men in the box used by this team's defense. Note that for 2020, we have switched from using ESPN Stats & Info box counts to Sports Info Solutions box counts. Because of differences in the way each organization defines the box, this year's box counts are roughly 0.35 higher than in past years.

Offensive Pace: Situation-neutral pace represents the seconds of game clock per offensive play, with the following restrictions: no drives are included if they start in the fourth quarter or final five minutes of the first half, and drives are only included if the score is within six points or less. Teams are ranked from quickest pace (New England, 27.7 seconds) to slowest pace (Los Angeles Chargers, 33.1 seconds).

Defensive Pace: Situation-neutral pace based on seconds of game clock per defensive play. This is a representation of how a defense was approached by its opponents, not the strategy of the defense itself. Teams are ranked from quickest pace (Tampa Bay, 27.9 seconds) to slowest pace (New England, 32.7).

Go for it on fourth: This is the aggressiveness index (AI) introduced by Jim Armstrong in *Pro Football Prospectus 2006*, which measures how often a team goes for a first down in various fourth down situations compared to the league average. A coach over 1.00 is more aggressive, and one below 1.00 is less aggressive. Coaches are ranked from most aggressive to least aggressive.

You may notice on the Strategic Tendencies sample table that the average Aggressiveness Index for 2019 was 1.52, far above the multi-year average of 1.00. There is no question that NFL coaches, some following the example of the Super Bowl LII Champion Philadelphia Eagles, have been more aggressive on fourth downs in the past two seasons than in the 30 years that came before. Twenty-nine out of 34 head coaches (including those who coached partial seasons) had an Aggressiveness Index above 1.00, and John Harbaugh of Baltimore set the all-time AI record at 3.95.

Following each strategic tendencies table, you'll find a series of comments highlighting interesting data from that team's charting numbers. This includes DVOA ratings split for things like different formations, draw plays, or play-action passing. Please note that all DVOA ratings given in these comments are standard DVOA with no adjustments for the specific situation being analyzed. The average DVOA for a specific situation will not necessarily be 0%, and it won't necessarily be the same for offense and defense. For example, the average offensive DVOA on play-action passes in 2019 was 25.3%, while the average defensive DVOA was 18.6%. The average offensive DVOA when the quarterback was hurried was -62.8%; even if we remove sacks, scrambles, and intentional grounding and only look at actual passes, the average offensive DVOA was -5.4%. Across the league last year, there was pressure marked on 30.3% of pass plays.

How to Read the Offensive Line Tables

SIS charters mark blown blocks not just on sacks but also on hurries, hits, and runs stuffed at the line. However, while we have blown blocks to mark bad plays, we still don't have

Table 11. Packers Offensive Line

Player	Pos	Age	GS	Snaps	Pen	Sk	Pass	Run	Player	Pos	Age	GS	Snaps	Pen	Sk	Pass	Run
Billy Turner	RG	29	16/16	1101	2	6.0	21	12	Corey Linsley	C	29	16/16	974	2	1.8	8	7
David Bakhtiari	LT	29	16/16	1100	12	2.8	12	5	Bryan Bulaga*	RT	31	16/16	922	6	3.0	17	3
Elgton Jenkins	LG	25	16/14	986	7	0.5	12	3	Rick Wagner	RT	31	12/12	772	3	3.5	17	11

Year	Yards	ALY	Rank	Power	Rank	Stuff	Rank	2nd Lev	Rank	Open Field	Rank	Sacks	ASR	Rank	Press	Rank	F-Start	Cont.
2017	4.13	4.60	5	66%	11	16%	2	1.10	19	0.51	24	51	8.6%	28	35.1%	28	11	21
2018	4.70	4.71	7	65%	21	18%	12	1.49	2	0.80	20	53	7.9%	21	29.0%	16	16	33
2019	4.47	4.63	5	54%	27	17%	6	1.28	9	0.69	20	36	6.4%	10	29.2%	12	20	44

2019 ALY by direction:	Left End 4.55 (8)	Left Tackle: 3.10 (29)	Mid/Guard: 5.02 (3)	Right Tackle: 4.86 (6)	Right End 4.36 (15)

a metric that consistently marks good plays, so blown blocks should not be taken as the end all and be all of judging individual linemen. It's simply one measurement that goes into the conversation.

All offensive linemen who had at least 160 snaps in 2019 (not including special teams) are listed in the offensive line tables along with the position they played most often and their **Age** as of the 2020 season, listed simply as the difference between birth year and 2020. Players born in January and December of the same year will have the same listed age.

Then we list games, games started, snaps, and offensive penalties (**Pen**) for each lineman. The penalty total includes declined and offsetting penalties. Finally, there are three numbers for blown blocks in 2019.

- Blown blocks leading directly to sacks
- All blown blocks on pass plays, not only including those that lead to sacks but also those that lead to hurries, hits, or offensive holding penalties
- All blown blocks on run plays; generally, this means plays where the running back is tackled for a loss or no gain, but it also includes a handful of plays where the running back would have been tackled for a loss if not for a broken tackle, as well as offensive holding penalties on running plays

As with all player tables in the team chapters, players who are no longer on the team have an asterisk and those new to the team in 2020 are in italics.

The second offensive line table lists the last three years of our various line stats.

The first column gives standard yards per carry by each team's running backs (**Yds**). The next two columns give adjusted line yards (**ALY**) followed by rank among the 32 teams.

Power gives the percentage of runs in short-yardage "power situations" that achieved a first down or touchdown. Those situations include any third or fourth down with one or two yards to go, and any runs in goal-to-go situations from the two-yard line or closer. Unlike the other rushing numbers on the Offensive Line table, Power includes quarterbacks.

Stuff gives the percentage of runs that are stuffed for zero or negative gain. Since being stuffed is bad, teams are ranked from stuffed least often (1) to most often (32).

Second-Level (**2nd Lev**) Yards and **Open-Field** Yards represent yardage where the running back has the most power over the amount of the gain. Second-level yards represent the number of yards per carry that come five to ten yards past the line of scrimmage. Open-field yards represent the number of yards per carry that come 11 or more yards past the line of scrimmage. A team with a low ranking in adjusted line yards but a high ranking in open-field yards is heavily dependent on its running back breaking long runs to make the running game work, and therefore tends to have a less consistent running attack. Second-level yards fall somewhere in between.

The next five columns give information about pass protection. That starts with total sacks, followed by adjusted sack rate (**ASR**) and its rank among the 32 teams. Some teams allow a lot of sacks because they throw a lot of passes; adjusted sack rate accounts for this by dividing sacks and intentional grounding by total pass plays. It is also adjusted for situation (sacks are much more common on third down, particularly third-and-long) and opponent, all of which makes it a better measurement than raw sacks totals. Remember that quarterbacks share responsibility for sacks, and two different quarterbacks behind the same line can have very different adjusted sack rates. We've also listed **Pressure Rate**: this is the percentage of pass plays where we have marked pass pressure, based on Sports Info Solutions charting. Sacks or scrambles due to coverage are not counted as passes with pressure.

F-Start gives the number of false starts, which is the offensive penalty which best correlates to both wins and wins the following season. This total includes false starts by players other than offensive linemen, but it does not include false starts on special teams. Houston led the league with 30, Dallas was last with 6, and the NFL average was 15.4. Finally, Continuity score (**Cont.**) tells you how much continuity each offensive line had from game-to-game in that season. It was introduced in the Cleveland chapter of *Pro Football Prospectus 2007*. Continuity score starts with 48 and then subtracts:

- The number of players over five who started at least one game on the offensive line;
- The number of times the team started at least one different lineman compared to the game before; and
- The difference between 16 and that team's longest streak where the same line started consecutive games.

Indianapolis led the NFL with a perfect continuity score of 48. The lowest score last season was 20 for Miami.

Finally, underneath the table in italics we give 2019 adjusted line yards in each of the five directions with rank among the 32 teams. The league average was 4.07 on left end runs (**LE**), 4.25 on left tackle runs (**LT**), 4.37 on runs up the middle (**MID**), 4.20 on right tackle runs (**RT**), and 4.23 on right end runs (**RE**).

How to Read the Defensive Front Tables

Defensive players make plays. Plays aren't just tackles—interceptions and pass deflections change the course of the game, and so does the act of forcing a fumble or beating the offensive players to a fumbled ball. While some plays stop a team on third down and force a punt, others merely stop a receiver after he's caught a 30-yard pass. We can measure opportunities in pass coverage thanks to our charting partners at Sports Info Solutions.

Defensive players are listed in these tables if they made at least 20 plays during the 2019 season, or if they played at least eight games and played 25% of defensive snaps in those games. Defensive players who were with two teams last year are only listed with the final team they played with.

Defensive Linemen/Edge Rushers

As we've noted earlier in this toolbox: as hybrid defenses become more popular, it becomes more and more difficult to

Table 12. 49ers Defensive Line and Edge Rushers

Defensive Line	Age	Pos	G	Snaps	Plays	TmPct	Rk	Stop	Dfts	BTkl	Runs	St%	Rk	RuYd	Rk	Sack	Hit	Hur	Dsrpt
						Overall						vs. Run					Pass Rush		
DeForest Buckner*	26	DT	16	824	62	7.8%	8	51	17	2	47	77%	44	3.0	84	7.5	6	25	4
Sheldon Day*	26	DT	16	330	14	1.8%	--	10	2	2	10	80%	--	2.5	--	1.0	1	7	0
D.J. Jones	25	DT	11	307	23	4.2%	81	18	9	1	21	76%	45	2.4	56	2.0	0	4	0

Edge Rushers	Age	Pos	G	Snaps	Plays	TmPct	Rk	Stop	Dfts	BTkl	Runs	St%	Rk	RuYd	Rk	Sack	Hit	Hur	Dsrpt
						Overall						vs. Run					Pass Rush		
Nick Bosa	23	DE	16	789	48	6.0%	27	35	20	4	32	72%	54	2.0	25	9.0	16	62	2
Arik Armstead	27	DE	16	788	55	6.9%	15	46	22	5	35	74%	45	2.1	32	10.0	7	28	2
Solomon Thomas	25	DE/DT	16	428	21	2.6%	83	16	4	4	15	73%	49	1.7	18	2.0	5	9	1
Dee Ford	29	DE	11	232	14	2.6%	--	14	10	2	4	100%	--	2.3	--	6.5	1	7	1
Ronald Blair	27	DE	9	201	21	4.7%	--	16	11	3	18	72%	--	2.2	--	3.0	0	5	0
Kerry Hyder	29	DE	16	447	17	2.1%	90	12	3	3	15	73%	49	2.5	46	1.0	3	28	0

tell the difference between a defensive end and an outside linebacker. What we do know is that there are certain players whose job is to rush the passer, even if they occasionally drop into coverage. We also know that the defensive ends in a two-gapping 3-4 system have a lot more in common with run-stuffing 4-3 tackles than with smaller 4-3 defensive ends.

Therefore, we have separated defensive front players into three tables rather than two. All defensive tackles and defensive ends from 3-4 teams are listed as **Defensive Linemen**, and all ranked together. Defensive ends from 4-3 teams and outside linebackers from 3-4 teams are listed as **Edge Rushers**, and all ranked together. Most 4-3 linebackers are ranked along with 3-4 inside linebackers and listed simply as **Linebackers**. For the most part this categorization puts players with similar roles together. Some players who have hybrid roles are ranked at the position more appropriate to their role, such as J.J. Watt as an edge rusher despite playing defensive end in a nominally 3-4 scheme.

The tables for defensive linemen and edge rushers are the same, although the players are ranked in two separate categories. Players are listed with the following numbers:

Age in 2020, determined by 2020 minus birth year, plus position (**Pos**) and the number of defensive **Snaps** played in 2019.

Plays (**Plays**): The total defensive plays including tackles, assists, pass deflections, interceptions, fumbles forced, and fumble recoveries. This number comes from the official NFL gamebooks and therefore does not include plays on which the player is listed by the Football Outsiders game charting project as in coverage but does not appear in the standard play-by-play. Special teams tackles are also not included.

Percentage of team plays (**TmPct**): The percentage of total team plays involving this defender. The sum of the percentages of team plays for all defenders on a given team will exceed 100%, primarily due to shared tackles. This number is adjusted based on games played, so an injured player may be fifth on his team in plays but third in **TmPct**.

Stops (**Stop**): The total number of plays which prevent a "success" by the offense (45% of needed yards on first down, 60% on second down, 100% on third or fourth down).

Defeats (**Dfts**): The total number of plays which stop the offense from gaining first down yardage on third or fourth down, stop the offense behind the line of scrimmage, or result in a fumble (regardless of which team recovers) or interception.

Broken tackles (**BTkl**): The number of broken tackles recorded by SIS game charters.

The next five columns represent runs only, starting with the number of plays each player made on **Runs**. Stop rate (**St%**) gives the percentage of these run plays which were stops. Average yards (**AvYd**) gives the average number of yards gained by the runner when this player is credited with making the play.

Finally, we have pass rush numbers, starting with standard NFL **Sack** totals.

Hit: To qualify as a quarterback hit, the defender must knock the quarterback to the ground in the act of throwing or after the pass is thrown. We have listed hits on all plays, including those cancelled by penalties. (After all, many of the hardest hits come on plays cancelled because the hit itself draws a roughing the passer penalty.) Our count of hits does not add in sacks; that count is referred to elsewhere as "knockdowns."

Hurries (**Hur**): The number of quarterback hurries recorded by Sports Info Solutions game charters. This includes both hurries on standard plays and hurries that force an offensive holding penalty that cancels the play and costs the offense yardage.

Disruptions (**Dsprt**): This stat combines two different but similar types of plays. First, plays where a pass-rusher forced an incomplete pass or interception by hitting the quarterback as he was throwing the ball. These plays are generally not counted as passes defensed, so we wanted a way to count them. Second, plays where the pass-rusher batted the ball down at the line of scrimmage or tipped it in the air. These plays are usually incomplete, but occasionally they lead to interceptions, and even more rarely they fall into the hands of offensive receivers. As with the "hit in motion" disruptions, some plays counted as tips by Football Outsiders were not counted as passes defensed by the NFL.

Defensive linemen and edge rushers are both ranked by percentage of team plays, run stop rate, and average yards per run

Table 13. Seahawks Linebackers

Linebackers	Age	Pos	G	Snaps	Plays	TmPct	Rk	Stop	Dfts	BTkl	Runs	St%	Rk	RuYd	Rk	Sack	Hit	Hur	Tgts	Suc%	Rk	AdjYd	Rk	PD	Int
						Overall						vs. Run				Pass Rush				vs. Pass					
Bobby Wagner	30	MLB	16	1080	165	20.4%	1	76	21	10	88	57%	51	4.6	71	3.0	3	7	49	35%	63	8.1	57	6	1
K.J. Wright	31	OLB	16	1021	143	17.7%	5	72	24	10	69	57%	54	4.4	66	0.0	1	3	56	52%	32	6.5	36	11	3
Mychal Kendricks*	30	OLB	14	664	75	10.6%	49	42	10	16	40	53%	69	4.8	74	3.0	0	7	20	55%	23	10.4	65	4	1

tackle. The lowest number of average yards earns the top rank (negative numbers indicate the average play ending behind the line of scrimmage). Defensive linemen and edge rushers are ranked if they played at least 40% of defensive snaps in the games they were active. There are 97 defensive linemen and 91 edge rushers ranked.

Linebackers

Most of the stats for linebackers are the same as those for defensive linemen. Linebackers are ranked in percentage of team plays, and also in stop rate and average yards for running plays specifically. Linebackers are ranked in these stats if they played at least five games and at least 35% of defensive snaps in the games they were active, with 84 linebackers ranked.

The final six columns in the linebacker stats come from Sports Info Solutions game charting.

Targets (**Tgts**): The number of pass players on which game charters listed this player in coverage.

Success rate (**Suc%**): The percentage plays of targeting this player on which the offense did not have a successful play. This means not only incomplete passes and interceptions, but also short completions which do not meet our baselines for success (45% of needed yards on first down, 60% on second down, 100% on third or fourth down).

Yards per pass (**Yd/P**): The average number of yards gained on plays on which this defender was the listed target.

Passes defensed (**PD**): Beginning with this book, we are using the NFL's count of passes defensed rather than computing our own separate total.

These stats are explained in more detail in the section on secondary tables. There are 68 linebackers are ranked in the charting stats, based on hitting one of two minimums: 16 charted passes with fewer than eight games started, or 12 charted passes with eight or more games started. As a result of the different thresholds, some linebackers are ranked in standard stats but not charting stats.

Further Details

Just as in the offensive tables, players who are no longer on the team are marked with asterisks, and players who were on other teams last year are in italics. Defensive front player statistics are not adjusted for opponent.

Numbers for defensive linemen and linebackers unfortunately do not reflect all of the opportunities a player had to make a play, but they do show us which players were most active on the field. A large number of plays could mean a strong defensive performance, or it could mean that the linebacker in question plays behind a poor part of the line. In general, defensive numbers should be taken as information that tells us what happened on the field in 2019, but not as a strict, unassailable judgment of which players are better than others—particularly when the difference between two players is small (for example, players ranked 20th and 30th) instead of large (players ranked 20th and 70th).

After the individual statistics for linemen and linebackers, the Defensive Front section contains a table that looks exactly like the table in the Offensive Line section. The difference is that the numbers here are for all opposing running backs against this team's defensive front. As we're on the opposite side of the ball, teams are now ranked in the opposite order, so the No. 1 defensive front is the one that allows the fewest adjusted line yards, the lowest percentage in Power situations, and has the highest adjusted sack rate. Directions for adjusted line yards are given from the offense's perspective, so runs left end and left tackle are aimed at the right defensive end and (assuming the tight end is on the other side) weakside linebacker.

How to Read the Defensive Secondary Tables

The first few columns in the secondary tables are based on standard play-by-play, not game charting, with the exception of broken tackles. Age, total plays, percentage of team plays, stops, and defeats are computed the same way they are for other defensive players, so that the secondary can be compared to the defensive line and linebackers. That means that total plays here includes passes defensed, sacks, tackles after receptions, tipped passes, and interceptions, but not pass plays on which this player was in coverage but was not given a tackle or passed defense by the NFL's official scorer.

The middle five columns address each defensive back's role in stopping the run. Average yardage and stop rate for running plays is computed in the same manner as for defensive linemen and linebackers.

The third section of statistics represents data from Sports Info Solutions game charting. We do not count pass plays on which this player was in coverage, but the incomplete was listed as Thrown Away, Batted Down, or Hit in Motion. Hail Mary passes are also not included.

Targets (**Tgts**): The number of pass plays on which game charters listed this player in coverage.

Target percentage (**Tgt%**): The number of plays on which this player was targeted divided by the total number of charted passes against his defense, not including plays listed as Uncovered. Like percentage of team plays, this metric is adjusted

Table 14. Chiefs Defensive Secondary

Secondary	Age	Pos	G	Snaps	Plays	TmPct	Rk	Stop	Dfts	BTkl	Runs	St%	Rk	RuYd	Rk	Tgts	Tgt%	Rk	Dist	Suc%	Rk	AdjYd	Rk	PD	Int
							Overall						vs. Run						vs. Pass						
Tyrann Mathieu	28	SS	16	1095	87	10.6%	20	34	14	15	22	27%	60	5.8	26	53	13.1%	7	10.7	55%	27	5.4	13	12	4
Charvarius Ward	24	CB	16	1062	84	10.2%	8	27	11	9	32	28%	70	10.4	79	80	20.4%	37	13.0	65%	6	6.9	25	10	2
Juan Thornhill	25	FS	16	1011	62	7.5%	48	15	10	15	28	29%	57	9.6	58	25	6.7%	49	15.2	56%	24	5.7	18	5	3
Bashaud Breeland	28	CB	16	927	55	6.7%	54	19	8	10	14	36%	63	7.1	58	53	15.5%	75	15.7	57%	25	7.1	31	8	2
Daniel Sorensen	30	SS	16	574	56	6.8%	56	28	13	9	22	50%	15	7.1	41	37	17.4%	1	8.5	62%	13	6.1	21	4	2
Kendall Fuller*	25	CB	11	507	51	9.0%	--	19	6	5	21	38%	--	7.3	--	23	12.3%	--	10.5	35%	--	9.0	--	2	0
Morris Claiborne*	30	CB	8	198	14	3.4%	--	4	1	2	6	33%	--	6.2	--	5	6.8%	--	20.4	40%	--	8.8	--	0	0

Year	Pass D Rank	vs. #1 WR	Rk	vs. #2 WR	Rk	vs. Other WR	Rk	WR Wide	Rk	WR Slot	Rk	vs. TE	Rk	vs. RB	Rk
2017	23	29.5%	31	-6.0%	14	0.8%	18	2.3%	20	19.6%	26	-5.9%	12	-23.1%	3
2018	12	-9.2%	9	-23.8%	5	21.6%	29	-9.8%	13	-0.1%	16	19.1%	25	7.3%	21
2019	6	-32.3%	3	-10.4%	7	5.1%	20	-48.4%	1	4.3%	12	-19.5%	4	-2.0%	18

based on number of games played.

Average depth of target (**aDOT**): The average distance in the air beyond the line of scrimmage of all passes targeted at this defender. It does not include yards after catch and is useful for seeing which defenders were covering receivers deeper or shorter. This is also often referred to as "Air Yards."

Success rate (**Suc%**): The percentage plays of targeting this player on which the offense did not have a successful play. This means not only incomplete passes and interceptions, but also short completions which do not meet our baselines for success (45% of needed yards on first down, 60% on second down, 100% on third or fourth down). Defensive pass interference is counted as a failure for the defensive player similar to a completion of equal yardage (and a new first down).

Yards per pass (**Yd/P**): The average number of yards gained on plays on which this defender was the listed target.

Passes defensed (**PD**) and Interceptions (**Int**) represent the standard NFL count for both stats.

Cornerbacks need 50 charted passes or eight games started to be ranked in the defensive stats, with 85 cornerbacks ranked in total. Safeties require 20 charted passes or eight games started, with 74 safeties ranked in total. Strong and free safeties are ranked together.

Just like the defensive front, the defensive secondary has a table of team statistics following the individual numbers. This table gives DVOA figured against different types of receivers. Each offense's wide receivers have had one receiver designated as No. 1, and another as No. 2. (Occasionally this is difficult, due to injury or a situation with "co-No. 1 receivers," but it's usually pretty obvious.) The other receivers form a third category, with tight ends and running backs as fourth and fifth categories. The defense is then judged on the performance of each receiver based on the standard DVOA method, with each rating adjusted based on strength of schedule. (Obviously, it's a lot harder to cover the No. 1 receiver of the Atlanta Falcons than to cover the No.1 receiver of the Washington Redskins.) **Pass D Rank** is the total ranking of the pass defense, as seen before in the Trends and Splits table, and combines all five categories plus sacks and passes with no intended target.

The "defense vs. types of receivers" table should be used to analyze the defense as a whole rather than individual players. The ratings against types of receivers are generally based on defensive schemes, not specific cornerbacks, except for certain defenses that really do move one cornerback around to cover the opponent's top weapon (i.e., Arizona). The ratings against tight ends and running backs are in large part due to the performance of linebackers.

In addition, we list each team's numbers covering receivers based on where they lined up before the snap, either wide or in the slot. The "vs. Other WR" number has sometimes been misrepresented as measuring coverage of slot receivers, but in the modern NFL, the team's No. 1 or No. 2 receiver will often be working predominantly out of the slot, while other receivers will switch back and forth between the two positions. The listing of coverage of wide receivers in the slot also includes wide receivers lined up tight in a tight end position.

How to Read the Special Teams Tables

The special teams tables list the last three years of kick, punt, and return numbers for each team.

The first two columns list total special teams DVOA and rank among the 32 teams. The next two columns list the value in actual points of field goals and extra points (**FG/XP**) when compared to how a league average kicker would do from the same distances, adjusted for weather and altitude, and rank among the 32 teams. Next, we list the estimated value in actual points of field position over or under the league average based on net kickoffs (**Net Kick**) and rank that value among the 32 teams. That is followed by the estimated point values of field position for kick returns (**Kick Ret**), net punting (**Net Punt**), and punt returns (**Punt Ret**) and their respective ranks.

The final two columns represent the value of "**Hidden**" special teams, plays which throughout the past decade have usually been based on the performance of opponents without this team being able to control the outcome. We combine the opposing team's value on field goals, kickoff distance, and punt distance,

Table 15. Bengals Special Teams

Year	DVOA	Rank	FG/XP	Rank	Net Kick	Rank	Kick Ret	Rank	Net Punt	Rank	Punt Ret	Rank	Hidden	Rank
2017	-2.4%	21	2.7	14	-2.9	24	-5.3	31	-6.0	22	-0.2	17	4.8	11
2018	2.6%	7	1.0	14	2.9	8	8.6	3	-1.2	18	1.6	13	-10.8	27
2019	4.6%	1	8.1	6	5.1	6	8.7	1	4.2	12	-3.2	25	-10.3	29

adjusted for weather and altitude, and then switch the sign to represent that good special teams by the opponent will cost the listed team points, and bad special teams will effectively hand them points. We have to give the qualifier of "usually" because, as explained above, certain returners such as Cordarrelle Patterson will affect opposing special teams strategy, and a handful of the missed field goals are blocked. Nonetheless, the "hidden" value is still "hidden" for most teams, and they are ranked from the most hidden value gained (Buffalo, 15.5 points) to the most value lost (Philadelphia, -13.5 points).

We also have methods for measuring the gross value of kickoffs and punts. These measures assume that all kickoffs or punts will have average returns unless they are touchbacks or kicked out of bounds, then judge the kicker or punter on the value with those assumed returns. We also count special teams tackles; these include both tackles and assists, but do not include tackles on two-point conversions, tackles after onside kicks, or tackles of the player who recovers a fumble after the punt or kick returner loses the ball. The best and worst individual values for kickers, punters, returners, and kick gunners (i.e. tackle totals) are listed in the statistical appendix at the end of the book.

Administrative Minutia

Receiving statistics include all passes intended for the receiver in question, including those that are incomplete or intercepted. The word passes refers to both complete and incomplete pass attempts. When rating receivers, interceptions are treated as incomplete passes with no penalty.

For the computation of DVOA and DYAR, passing statistics include sacks as well as fumbles on aborted snaps. We do not include kneeldown plays or spikes for the purpose of stopping the clock. Some interceptions which we have determined to be "Hail Mary" plays that end the first half or game are counted as regular incomplete passes, not turnovers.

All statistics generated by ESPN Stats & Info or Sports Info Solutions game charting, or our combination of the two sources, may be different from totals compiled by other sources.

Unless we say otherwise, when we refer to third-down performance in this book we are referring to a combination of third down and the handful of rushing and passing plays that take place on fourth down (primarily fourth-and-1).

Aaron Schatz

The Year In Quotes

THERE IS NO HUNTING LIKE THE HUNTING OF CHILDREN

"If they all flipped and attacked you how many could you take?"

—Twitter user @44DesignCo to Baker Mayfield, asking what would happen if the squads of children at the Cleveland Browns quarterback's summer camp suddenly turned violent.

"Which age group? As a general thought, I say at least 50+"

—Mayfield, in response.

"You're selling yourself short. Gotta escape the pocket, reset, and take out 8-10 at a time."

—New England Patriots quarterback Tom Brady, interjecting with the wisdom of a seasoned veteran. (Tom Brady via Twitter)

'THE INNER MACHINATIONS OF MY MIND ARE AN ENIGMA'

"Which part of the pig's skin is actually a football?"

"At which point does it change from going up the street to down the street?"

"Why do we use toothbrushes more than once, if they dirty after first use?"

"What shape is the sky?"

"So ummm...what's on the other side of a black hole?"

"If the sun is hot why is it cold in outer space?"

—Indianapolis Colts quarterback Jacoby Brissett has turned his Twitter page into a sea of life's greatest mysteries and unanswered questions. Unrelated: is weed legal in Indiana yet? (Jacoby Brissett via Twitter)

SPEED KILLS, BUT TWITTER BURNS HURT FOREVER

"Tom Brady can't run 2 yards how the hell is he a 96? If those ratings were based on the entire Super Bowl winning team, sure. As an individual, he's not a 96."

"I 100% could run faster and further than Tom. So could 50% of high schoolers, 80% of college players, and 99% of pros. Learn how to unbiasedly access the totality of a player, then adjust these numbers and I could possibly take you seriously."

—A fan by the name of Matt got #madonline and took to Twitter when Yahoo Sports revealed the list of top *Madden* rankings, highlighting New England Patriots quarterback Tom Brady's rank of 96 overall.

"I'm so much faster than you Matt."

—Brady's as quick to a comeback as he is on the field. (Yahoo!)

KEEP BOTH HANDS ON YOUR CONTROLLER, PLEASE

"My rating? I've got an 80 on [Madden] Ultimate Team, so I'ma go play with myself today, see how it feel ... that came out weird."

—New York Jets rookie defensive tackle Quinnen Williams may be in his first year playing professional football, but he can already crack jokes at the podium like a savvy veteran. Either that, or he needs to work on word choice with Jets PR. (SNY Jets via Twitter)

THE YEAR IN GRUDEN

"Everybody has dreams right now, don't they guys? Alright, everybody in the NFL, 'I have a dream of making it in the NFL,' 'I got a dream of winning a Super Bowl,' 'I got a dream of being in the Pro Bowl.' I'm really not into dreams anymore, OK? I'm into f*cking nightmares. ... You've got to end somebody's dream. You've got to take their job, you've got to take their heart."

—The Oakland Raiders had the "honor" of hosting HBO's *Hard Knocks* before the 2019 season, and head coach Jon Gruden took center stage. Combine this quote with the show's orchestral score and you'll be hard pressed to find a brick wall you can't run through. (Viral Sports via Twitter)

"Every win I'm going down there. I've got facepaint all over me, I got to see some costumes I have not seen before at any football games. Awesome."

—Gruden delivered this quote about his trips to the Black Hole after every win with a permanent smile plastered on his face. (NFL on ESPN via Twitter)

"I think I smoked my first cigarette thinking I was Fred Biletnikoff."

—Gruden was asked who his favorite Raider was growing up, and he threw out an all-time answer. (John Shipley, Jaguars Maven via Twitter)

KNOWING YOUR OPPONENT GOES BEYOND THE SCOUTING REPORT

"Say I was playing a big receiver at whatever school. I would look up his Instagram and slide in his girlfriend's DMs before the game."

—Jacksonville Jaguars cornerback Jalen Ramsey sought out every competitive advantage he could against his opponents in college. If that meant stealing their girl in the process, so be it. (Barstool Sports via Instagram)

GETTING IN PLAYERS' HEADS, EVEN IN RETIREMENT

Steve Smith Sr.: *"Cam, can you come here real quick? So I've got him on my [fantasy football] bench, D.J. Moore. I ain't benching DeAndre Hopkins, should I let John Brown [inaudible]?"*

Cam Newton: *"That's kinda disrespectful. John Brown, he ain't no asset. He got a lot of choice selections. I'm giving you insider trading so don't report me."*

Smith: *"No I'm just saying. So, should I take [Moore] off the bench? Because currently he's on the bench."*

Newton: *"Yeah, yeah, yeah, you gotta start him."*

Smith: *"What if I just flex? What if I put him at flex?"*

Newton: *"I don't understand that."*

Smith: *"That just mean an extra guy, right?"*

Newton: *"Yeah, yeah, yeah."*

Smith: *"So put him at flex? Because he's not a real wide receiver yet. He's just kinda developing."*

Newton: *"I wouldn't say all that now!"*

Smith, to Moore: *"Should I start you or John Brown? It's a legit question, is it not?"*

Moore, who stood directly next to Smith during this entire exchange: *"Start me."*

Smith: *"Start you? You give me two points, I'll slap the sh*t out of you."*

—Retired wide receiver and Hall of Fame trash talker Steve Smith Sr. may have left the league several years ago, but he still knows how to get under people's skin. Just ask Carolina Panthers wide receiver D.J. Moore, who stood next to Smith while he contemplated fantasy moves with quarterback Cam Newton. (Coach Coleman via Twitter)

HEMORRHAGING CAP SPACE

"Picture you were a driver of a car and you had a wreck and your hand was almost severed off, but you don't understand your anatomy. You look down, you're spurting blood, you open the door, and run to the woods, and either die bleeding to death or shock. The educated man looks down, knows his anatomy, squeezes and knows his best chance is to wait for help. That's because he's been there a lot and done that. So I'm squeezing and waiting for help."

—Dallas Cowboys owner Jerry Jones gives an oddly specific and very graphic analogy to illustrate his team's current contract negotiations with quarterback Dak Prescott, running back Ezekiel Elliott, and wide receiver Amari Cooper. (Jon Machota, The Athletic via Twitter)

HOT MIC!

"I've never had my butt fingered."

—A microphone on the Packers bench picked up whispers of some strange happenings during a punt by the Chicago Bears. (Barstool Sports)

FULLBACKS CRAVE CONTACT

*"The biggest collision I ever had was like two years ago I think. Me and Myles Jack, we were running like an iso play, and we just f*cking collided. And you kinda get your head bounced back, seeing stars. ... First of all I felt like my head was just like totally a different shape. And I looked at him and we were like 'F*****************ck!' Both of us dapped each other up, and I end up running off the field, and I take off my helmet and checking that my head isn't a different shape. Turn my facemask around and it was just f*cking caved in. Like my whole facemask, so I got to keep that."*

—Green Bay Packers fullback Danny Vitale talks about the hardest hit he's ever laid as a lead blocker on the play. When asked what even happened on the play, Vitale responded, "Hell if I know!". (Pardon My Take via Twitter)

WORSE PLUMBING THAN THE MUSHROOM KINGDOM

"The bathrooms flooded last year, won't miss that."

—Kansas City Chiefs head coach Andy Reid was asked about the nostalgia heading back to the Oakland Coliseum for possibly the last time, so he gave an answer only Andy could. (Matt Derrick, ChiefsDigest.com via Twitter)

"Not gonna tell you I'm gonna miss it. ... This year we didn't have to dodge sewage."

—The following week, Reid doubled down, now regaling the media with stories of literally evading human waste. (Phil Barber, Press Democrat via Twitter)

EXCESSIVE CELEBRATION

"Must have been some post-Super Bowl celebrations ... we're really pumping 'em out."

—New England Patriots head coach Bill Belichick had a string of players miss games early in the season for the births of children, about nine months after New England's Super Bowl LIII run. (OMF on WEEI via Twitter)

FLY LOVEBIRDS FLY

"Please win if you do I will ask out this girl in my class"

—Deep in the mentions of an Eagles pregame tweet was this singular cry for help from an Eagles fan named JV. If the Eagles would beat the Green Bay Packers, he'd ask a girl out from his class.

"Go get her, JV"

—After a last-second pick in the end zone to seal victory, the Eagles gave JV their blessing. (Eagles via Twitter)

THE YEAR IN LAMAR

"Not bad for a running back."

—Baltimore Ravens quarterback Lamar Jackson silenced some of his critics after the Ravens walloped the Dolphins by a score of 59-10. Many speculated the Ravens were implementing an extremely run-heavy offense for their quarterback after watching him throw for 1,200 yards and six touchdowns all of his rookie season. In this game alone, Jackson threw for 324 yards and five scores. (Jonas Shaffer, Baltimore Sun via Twitter)

"So I'm calling my buddy who was director of player personnel with the Ravens who I worked with back in the day, and he's got his son with him going to Little League practice. So he's calling me, it's like the week of the draft, I'm like, 'What's going on, you doing well?' 'Yeah, I'm doing well, what's going on? We're just taking our son to practice.' So I start asking him about players, he's being vague and everything. So I ask his son in the backseat. I go, 'Hey, what's going on?' 'Hi, Mr. Jeremiah, how's it going?' And I go 'Who's your favorite player in the draft?' And he goes, 'Oh, Lamar Jackson.' I'm like, frick, I should've known, man. He already let his son known that he's gonna be a Raven, I should've seen the signs."

—NFL Network's Daniel Jeremiah recalls a story from the 2018 draft, where he unknowingly got the son of the Baltimore Ravens' director of player personnel to reveal their eventual selection of Jackson. (Pardon My Take)

"We're feeling more confident of being able to contain him—not shut him down—but slow him down and contain him. We had film on him. We felt better. Then, we do a very good job of slowing him down running, and he starts using the arm. He beats us in the air. I'm saying, 'I can't believe this.' I started to question, 'What are we doing as coaches?' I looked in the mirror. 'Is there something I am not doing to put my kids in position to be successful?'

"Fast-forward two years later and I'm watching Florida State and Louisville. I can't believe what he's doing against one of the top teams in college football. I feel a lot better. Fast-forward another two years, he's in the NFL, and no one can tackle him, and I said, 'I can't believe this.' Fast-forward to this year, and I feel like, 'Hey, maybe I should go coach in the NFL.' I did just as good of a job stopping him."

—Village Academy head coach Don Hanna coached against Jackson in high school and was sent into a spiral after Jackson decimated his team. Hanna slowly gained his coaching confidence back as Lamar continued to dominate at every level. (The Ringer)

"Yeah I saw that. ... It still is low."

—Jackson still felt slighted after EA Sports raised his speed rating in Madden 20 to a 96. This was the highest speed rating ever given to a quarterback in Madden history. (SportsCenter via Twitter)

"Soo uhh @michaelvick how would you stop someone like...well kinda like yourself but the 2019 version?? I need tips for the game"

—Los Angeles Rams cornerback Jalen Ramsey seeks advice on stopping Jackson … from one of the few quarterbacks who have ever played like Lamar Jackson. (SportsCenter via Twitter)

"Come. See. Me. LJ. MVP. If you got a problem, come see me. ... That's all I'll say. Man, people have been trying me, but they can't validate their opinions. So, LJ for MVP."

—Ravens running back Mark Ingram led the charge on Jackson's MVP campaign. (Baltimore Ravens via Twitter)

THE YEAR IN MINSHEW

"I grabbed a bottle of Jack Daniel's and a hammer. I go into my room, take a pull of Jack Daniel's, put my hand down on the table and boom-boom-boom, 1, 2, 3, and hit the hell out of my hand."

—When asked what he would do to be able to play more football, Jacksonville Jaguars quarterback Gardner Minshew told the story of how he tried to get a medical redshirt in college by mashing his hand with a hammer. (Pardon My Take via Twitter)

"Probably saw more middle fingers today than I have in my whole life. They have a good time man, it was fun to ruin that for them."

"It's a piece of football history. Something special to be a part of. It'll be like an Aflac trivia question in like 20 years, so it's definitely gonna be cool to be a part of that."

—Minshew had some all-time trash talk after scoring 17 unanswered points and beating the Oakland Raiders 20-16 in Week 15. What a perfect send-off for the Oakland Coliseum. (Ben Murphy, First Coast News via Twitter)

WHO HAS TIME FOR THE ARTS WHEN YOU HAVE FOOTBALL TO COACH?

"Hey, not all of Mozart's paintings were perfect, huh? And hey, that end result, though. That sucker's gonna sell for a million dollars."

—Kansas City Chiefs head coach Andy Reid was charged up as he delivered this line to his team following a tight 34-30 victory over the Detroit Lions. Who cares that he thought classical composer Wolfgang Amadeus Mozart was a painter? It's not the wildly inaccurate historical claim that matters, it's the energy with which you make that wildly inaccurate claim. (Mike Kreiger via Twitter)

A WISE MAN ONCE SAID...

"A dog that poop fast don't poop for long, man. It's a good division, man. There's gonna be a lot of games we've got to win down the stretch, you know what I mean? But the most important is the next one, you know we can't really watch what's going on too much."

—Chicago Bears linebacker Khalil Mack had a colorful idiom to describe his team's "one game at a time" mindset. (SportsCenter via Twitter)

DISS IS THE KIND OF TWITTER CONTENT I'M LOOKING FOR

"If you think about it... unicorns make way more sense than giraffes. A horse with a horn vs a long necked horse with cheetah spots tf?"

—Seattle Seahawks tight end Will Dissly has a point. (Will Dissly via Twitter)

A FANCY BEVERAGE FOR A BIG PAYDAY

Reporter: *"What's the celebration or what's the first big purchase?"*

Darren Waller: *"Uhh ... I'm not really spending away on a lot of things. I went to Walgreen's last night and bought some Perrier. That's my favorite."*

—Oakland Raiders tight end Darren Waller popped some bubbly (not that kind) after signing an extension with the Silver & Black through 2023. (Oakland Raiders via Twitter)

THE BOOGEYMEN ARE REAL

"I'm seeing ghosts."

—New York Jets quarterback Sam Darnold got caught on mic admitting to feeling pressured by the New England Patriots defense during a 33-0 loss on Monday Night Football. Darnold coughed up four interceptions and a fumble during that stretch. (Dan Roche, WBZ via Twitter)

NOT TECHNICALLY INDESTRUCTABLE, BUT CLOSE ENOUGH

Reporter: *"Not a lot of people have come back from broken necks."*

Jason Pierre-Paul: *"Not a lot of people have come back from blowing off their hand, too."*

—Tampa Bay Buccaneers defensive end Jason Pierre-Paul is no stranger to devastating injuries. When a reporter informed Pierre-Paul, who was out with a cervical fracture in his neck, that players don't often return from broken necks, JPP had to remind her who she was dealing with. (Surf And Turf Pod via Twitter)

GET YOU A HYPE MAN LIKE GEORGE KITTLE

"I'm so happy he's on my team!"
"Sign him to a 20-year deal now!"
"BOOOOOOOOOSA!"

—A mic'd up San Francisco tight end George Kittle is by far the world's biggest fan of 49ers defensive end Nick Bosa. (San Francisco 49ers via Twitter)

IT'S FOOTBALL, NOT BLOODSPORT

"The Russians were so unknowledgeable about football, they asked Mackovic how many ambulances he would need for the game. He told them Illinois always had one on hand as a precaution.

"They said, 'Well, you'll need to take away the dead.' I said, 'Well, we're not counting on anyone dying.' They thought the game was vicious like that, that we killed off players. They assured us a hospital was close by."

—In an excerpt from the *Chicago Tribune*'s piece on a failed college football game in Russia between Illinois and USC, former Illinois coach John Mackovic revealed that the Russians definitely overestimated how violent the game of football really was. (Chicago Tribune)

WINSTON'S WISDOM

"The glass is always full. It might be half-full with water, it's still full with air."

—No, we can't really make sense out of Tampa Bay Buccaneers quarterback Jameis Winston's podium musings, either. (B/R Gridiron via Twitter)

NATIONAL FOOD-BALL LEAGUE

"Matthew Judon: Body built by Taco Bell."

—Baltimore Ravens linebacker Matthew Judon made a splash during Sunday Night Football after dropping this tagline during defensive intros. (Baltimore Ravens via Twitter)

"I'll tell you what the key was, the Popeye's chicken sandwiches I ate this week."

—Houston Texans quarterback Deshaun Watson is fueled by a different fast food joint. (Bloomberg Tic Toc via Twitter)

HOLD THAT TIGER

"We're gon' beat their ass in recruiting, we're gon' beat their ass every time they see us. 'Roll Tide,' what? F*ck you!"

—LSU head coach Ed Orgeron's postgame speech to his team got caught on a player's Instagram Live feed, and it would have any Alabama hater ready to charge into battle. (Barstool Sports via Twitter)

SOMEONE GET TARIK A STEPLADDER

"Who keeps putting the towels on the top shelf? Damn!"

—Vertically challenged Chicago Bears running back Tarik Cohen could be heard in the background of a postgame interview looking to find the culprit keeping his towels out of reach. (NFL on ESPN via Twitter)

JINX!

"Somebody's gonna get their ass whooped today. And it ain't gonna be us."

—Jacksonville Jaguars cornerback D.J. Hayden gave this inspiring quote in the tunnel before his team promptly got their asses whooped by the Tennessee Titans 42-20. (Ben Murphy, AP via Twitter)

THIS IS WHY THEY WENT TO SCHOOL FOR JOURNALISM

"I asked James Washington if a stadium full of duck calls could actually summon a giant flock of ducks to Heinz Field. He thought about it for a second and said the crowd noise would probably drown the calls out, but it's possible."

—ESPN's Brooke Pryor asks the hard-hitting questions to Pittsburgh Steelers wide receiver James Washington after Heinz Field banned duck calls from the stadium. (Brooke Pryor, ESPN via Twitter)

EVERYBODY'S WONDERING

"I've got the guy at Rouses, or at freaking Whole Foods, asking me about the freaking two-point play. I looked at him, the guy from the meat section. I said. 'Hey, your steaks don't look too good right now, worry about your freaking meat.' Driving me crazy."

—Fans were happy to remind New Orleans Saints head coach Sean Payton about a decision to go for two that played a key role in a 48-46 loss to San Francisco in Week 14. (The Athletic)

'TIS BUT A FLESH WOUND

"As long as my leg is not halfway off."

—Tennessee Titans running back Derrick Henry wasn't going to let a hamstring injury keep him out of a game during Tennessee's playoff run. (B/R Gridiron via Twitter)

A HIT HE'LL NEVER (BE ALLOWED TO) FORGET

"Now I tell my child to take the trash out, he tell me, 'Shut up before I go get Bosher.'"

—As a member of the Carolina Panthers, Atlanta Falcons running back Kenjon Barner took a devastating hit from Falcons punter Matt Bosher on a return. A year later, Barner and Bosher became teammates, but Barner's kid wouldn't let him forget that one highlight takedown. (The Checkdown via Instagram)

WHAT'S UNDER THE TREE?

"Getting socks on Christmas is the equivalent of drafting an offensive lineman in the first round. Not flashy or exciting, but you know if they do their job, you'll appreciate them at some point later on."

—NFL analyst Jordan Reid dropped this comparison on Christmas morning.

"Nah, lineman aren't socks. We are underwear. We are the layer that protects the most near and dear object to all."

—Former NFL guard Geoff Schwartz amends this comparison, conjuring up some unholy imagery on such a wholesome day. (Geoff Schwartz via Twitter)

'WAIT, THIS IS SUPPOSED TO BE HARD?'

"In my fourth year in college we played in the Citrus Bowl; we came back and we threw a touchdown pass to win the game. My fifth year we played Alabama in the Orange Bowl and we won in overtime. So I actually felt like 'Oh, here's another bowl game that I get a chance to play in.' I'm glad I didn't have the perspective of how hard it actually was to win the Super Bowl. ... I really realized how hard it was in 2010, [2011] after we hadn't won in a lot of years, and I was like 'God, I never realized how hard it is to win the Super Bowl.'"

—New England Patriots quarterback Tom Brady joined NFL Network as one of the quarterbacks on the NFL 100 list, and Cris Collinsworth asked Brady about the pressure he overcame to win his first Super Bowl. (NFL Network)

DR. JAMEIS & MR. WINSTON

"There's so much good and so much outright terrible."

"With another quarterback? Oh yeah. If we can win with this one, we can definitely win with another one, too."

—Tampa Bay Buccaneers head coach Bruce Arians had a mixed final assessment of quarterback Jameis Winston, who finished the season with 5,000 yards, 30 touchdowns, and 30 interceptions. (B/R Gridiron via Instagram and Rick Stroud, Tampa Bay Times via Twitter)

CELEBRATORY CHAMPIONSHIP CAPICOLA

"We've got a nice week ahead of us. I've got [my wife] Kelly and my three boys with me. We'll probably go get a ham sandwich, got to bed, and wake up tomorrow and do it again."

—After capping a 15-0 season off with a Heisman Trophy winner and a National Championship over undefeated Clemson—in the city of New Orleans, no less—most coaches would have a long night of celebration ahead. LSU head coach Ed Orgeron was just excited about spending time with his family. (SportsCenter via Twitter)

WHO'S LAUGHING NOW?

"At the end of the day, we're in a blessed situation. We're in the playoffs. We're one of 12 teams in the playoffs. We have a chance to go on a revenge tour. What better way to start off than with Tennessee, who we lost to last year. Got big motivation."

—New England Patriots linebacker Kyle Van Noy dropped this quote early in the leadup to the Patriots' wild-card matchup against the Titans, claiming that losing the bye and having media members doubt the team allowed the Patriots to enact their revenge tour. (WEEI Radio)

"That organization has so much class. So like, my guy Kyle Van Noy calling it a revenge tour. ... Just play ball, Kyle. Like, you know, I'm sure you're gonna see this. But he's one of the hyenas. He's on a revenge tour. 'Why not start with the Titans?' Honestly, he's gonna ride the wave of the Patriots, but Tom Brady doesn't do that. Julian Edelman doesn't do that. Devin McCourty, Gilly Lock [Stephon Gilmore] don't do that. And Kyle Van Noy's running his mouth, giving us bulletin board material about his revenge tour. His revenge tour ended early."

—Tennessee Titans cornerback and former New England Patriot Logan Ryan responded to Kyle Van Noy's "revenge tour" comments after ending said tour with a win in Foxborough. Ryan also referenced "the hyenas," which came from a hype video Patriots quarterback Tom Brady posted to social media earlier that day. (CBS Boston)

"They want hyenas? They got the f*cking hyenas!"

—Tennessee Titans head coach Mike Vrabel, another ex-Patriots player, piles onto the Brady hype video, embracing the hyena identity. (Sports Illustrated)

THE AUDACITY!

"10.5. We already got fitted for [our Championship rings]."

—LSU quarterback Joe Burrow pointed to his ring finger as celebration during the National Championship Game in a 42-25 win over Clemson. When prompted about what size ring he wears in a postgame interview, Burrow revealed the team was already fitted for rings BEFORE the National Championship Game. (ESPN via Twitter)

STILL WISH YOU WERE IN THE NFL?

"Nothing new. My fingernails continue to get ripped off."

—Philadelphia Eagles center Jason Kelce reveals what it's like to play every snap of a 17-game NFL season. Hint: it's painful. (Bo Wulf, The Athletic via Twitter)

THE MUSINGS OF MARSHAWN

"This is a vulnerable time for a lot of the young dudes, you feel me? They don't be taking care of their chicken right, you feel me? So if it was me, and if I had an opportunity to let these young sahabs know something, I'd say take care of y'all money, 'cause that sh*t don't last forever.

"I've been on the other side of retirement. And it's good when you can do what the f*ck you want to. So I'll tell y'all right now while y'all in it, take care of y'all bread, so when y'all done, you can go ahead and take care of yourself.

"So while y'all at it right now take care of y'all bodies, you know what I mean? Take care of y'all chicken, you feel me? Take care of y'all mentals, 'cause look, we ain't lasting that long. You know, I had a couple players who I played with that they're no longer here no more, they're no longer. You feel me? So start taking care of y'all mentals, y'all bodies, and y'all chicken for when y'all ready to walk away. You'll walk away and you'll be able to do what you want to do."

—Seattle Seahawks running back Marshawn Lynch is notorious for his press conferences, but he took the time after being eliminated by the Green Bay Packers to send a message to his young sahabs (friends) in the NFL to take care of their chicken (money) and bread (also money). (New York Daily News)

KEEP THAT SHOULDER WARM

"It's funny that you say that, because someone said that we hadn't thrown a pass for 96 minutes in the championship game of real time. I do know that when Kyle [Shanahan] called the pass, I could hear him tell Jimmy [Garoppolo] the play. I did think, 'Man, we haven't passed that in a long time.' But it turned out fine. But it was funny, I always get nervous."

—49ers offensive line coach John Benton sounds prepared for the big game, but did admit he got a little nervous when his team had to pass for the first time in over 90 minutes during the NFC Championship Game. Quarterback Jimmy Garoppolo passed only eight times during against Green Bay, completing six for 77 yards. (The Athletic)

THE THINGS WE DO FOR FASHION

Frank Clark: *"New Louis Vuitton season, so I had to bring 'em out."*

Cooper Manning: *"They prescription?"*

FC: *"No, not at all. Actually I can't see anything."*

—Kansas City Chiefs defensive end Frank Clark broke out some new Louis Vuitton glasses to add a little flair to his look, but at what cost? (FOX Sports NFL)

BLAST FROM THE PAST

Question: *"What are you looking forward to most about your class reunion?"*

Spencer Shaw: *"Seeing Patrick Mahomes' Super Bowl ring."*

—A high school classmate of Kansas City Chiefs quarterback Patrick Mahomes predicted his massive early success and immortalized it by getting it into the yearbook.

"He was just one of those special athletes. You knew he was going to succeed in whatever he did because he had that 'it' factor and a drive to work hard. If he was leaning more toward playing baseball after high school, I might've said that I was looking forward to seeing his World Series ring. He was that kind of special talent."

—Shaw, who played basketball with Mahomes in high school, pontificates on the Super Bowl MVP's all-around athleticism. (Washington Post)

ELITE COMPANY

"It's like watching Denzel [Washington] in a movie or LeBron James in the playoffs."

—When asked what it was like to see Patrick Mahomes in the fourth quarter of the Super Bowl, cornerback Tyrann Mathieu likened the quarterback to some of the best in their fields. (The Checkdown via Twitter)

BREAKFAST OF CHAMPIONS

- *"7 eggs*
- *Cottage cheese*
- *Grits*
- *Peanut butter*
- *Banana*
- *Gatorade"*

—Minnesota Vikings team reporter Eric Smith broke down the shake that helped Ben Bartch of the Saint John's Johnnies put on over 70 pounds, transforming from a tight end into a tackle.

"I'd gag sometimes, but that's what you have to do."

—Bartch on the "magic shake." (Eric Smith, Minnesota Vikings via Twitter)

THIS IS WHY CALLER ID IS SO IMPORTANT

"I declined a call from Green Bay, Wisconsin. I tried to call back and my call didn't go through and I had no idea what I just did."

—Newest Green Bay Packers offensive lineman Jon Runyan Jr. almost couldn't call himself that after rejecting the team's first call to announce his selection. (The Checkdown via Instagram)

JUST GET OUT OF THIS MAN'S WAY

"What I love most about the game is that I can literally go out there and hit a man consistently, and pound him, and the police won't come. That is the most enjoyable moment about ball. Just to go out there and just really abuse somebody. They won't say nothing about it in the press, anything. I ain't in no headlines in handcuffs. No mugshots, no nothing. I'm out here just physically abusing a man."

—Auburn Tigers defensive lineman Marlon Davidson gave one of the most poetically violent answers ever heard at the combine when asked what he loves most about football. (Trevor Sikkema, The Draft Network via Twitter)

HEY, CAN I GRAB AN EIGHTH OF SOME 'BAKED-ER MAYFIELD?'

"According to the State Medical Board of Ohio, someone submitted a petition to add 'Bengals/Browns Fans' as a qualifying condition under the Ohio Medical Marijuana Control Program."

—Amidst the medicinal legalization of marijuana in the state of Ohio, one informed citizen decided to incite real and lasting change in his community. Unfortunately, the State Medical Board of Ohio did not recognize the suffering that Browns and Bengals fans go through year after year as a legitimate ailment. What a shame. (Danny Eldredge, Hannah News via Twitter)

WE SHOULD ALL BE SO SLOPPY

Jeff Okudah: *"Sloppy in what way?"*

Reporter: *"Sloppy like ... *inaudible* penalties and stuff like that."*

JO: *"I had zero pass interferences, zero holdings, so put the tape on again. I think you might see something else."*

—Ohio State cornerback Jeffrey Okudah took a reporter to task over some inaccurate critiques of his game. (PFF via Twitter)

A SHORT LIST TO REMEMBER

"I remember everybody drafted in front of me…"

—New York Jets safety Jamal Adams posted this self-motivating quote to Twitter.

"Brah it was only 5 people lol"

—New Orleans Saints cornerback Marshon Lattimore poked a little hole in Adams' previous sentiment. Adams was drafted sixth overall in 2017. (Marshon Lattimore via Twitter)

COULDN'T HAVE FOUND A BETTER OPPORTUNITY

"I wanna play in the snow so bad."

—Buffalo Bills running back Zack Moss sent this wish out into the Twittersphere back in 2015…

"We have the perfect place in mind."

… and in classic draft day fashion, the Bills decided to dig up some old tweets. (Buffalo Bills via Twitter)

THE 'BEST' QUOTE FROM DRAFT WEEK?

"I was always trying to be the best, because I hold myself to the standard that I am the best. So if I feel like I'm the best, and I'm not playing like I'm the best, then you're not the best. As soon as the doctors pulled me [out of the womb] and they had me, and they handed me like 'Here, you've got a baby boy,' I was the best.' I had 'The Best' written across my forehead."

—Atlanta Falcons defensive tackle Marlon Davidson may have slid to Day 2 of the draft, but don't tell him he's anything but the best. (Trevor Sikkema, The Draft Network via Twitter)

IF AN ATHLETE WORKED OUT BUT DIDN'T POST IT, DID IT EVEN HAPPEN?

"Someone's coming for that starting RB job"

—Detroit Lions fan account @LionsFanReport posted this to Twitter attached to two images: one showing workouts from running back D'Andre Swift, and one of running back Kerryon Johnson.

"I assure you it's scientifically possible to workout and NOT post about it…I'm with the ignorance tho if you wanna get started"

—Johnson assured people that not every single workout has to be posted to social media for it to count. (Going Deep via Twitter)

CHARGED-UP COMMENTS

"Bro, we didn't have fans anyway."

—Denver Broncos running back Melvin Gordon is ready to potentially play in empty football stadiums this year after playing in a near-empty soccer stadium for the L.A. Chargers. (B/R Gridiron via Instagram)

PIRATES DRINK RUM, BUCCANEERS DRINK HENNESSEY

"It's surreal. He's about to be my quarterback bro. I've been on that Hennessey, man. Oh, I'm drinking. I got Tom Brady."

—Buccaneers wide receiver Mike Evans has every reason to celebrate his new quarterback. (David Jacoby, ESPN via Twitter)

QUOTE OF THE YEAR

Taylor Lewan: *"Matt Neely (an assistant for the show) said he would cut off his dick for a, uno, Super Bowl, and I said no I would not do that. Would you cut your dick off for a super bowl?"*

Mike Vrabel: *"Been married 20 years. Yeah, probably."*

Lewan: *"You've got three?!"*

Vrabel: *"As a player … You guys will be married for 20 years one day. You won't need it."*

Lewan: *"If you come home with a bag of ice, and [your wife] is like 'Oh honey what did you do.' 'I cut … my dick off, we're gonna win a Super Bowl,' she'd be like 'eh,' or would she be upset?"*

Vrabel: *"She'd be like do you want me to do it? Do you want to do it now?"*

—Tennessee Titans head coach and father of three Mike Vrabel is looking to get a lot lighter downstairs if it means his ring hand can get a little heavier. (Bussin' With the Boys Podcast)

compiled by Cale Clinton

Full 2020 Projections

The following table lists the mean DVOA projections for all 32 NFL teams. We also list the average number of wins for each team in our one million simulations, along with how often each team made the playoffs, reached the Super Bowl, and won the NFL Championship.

Full 2020 Projections

| Team | Avg Wins | Postseason Odds | | | Mean DVOA Projections | | | | | | | | | Schedule | |
		Make Playoffs	Reach Super Bowl	Win Super Bowl	Total DVOA	Rk	Off DVOA	Rk	Def DVOA	Rk	ST DVOA	Rk		Average Opponent	Rk
KC	10.6	81.5%	26.8%	15.9%	22.5%	2	20.4%	1	-0.2%	14	1.9%	2		1.0%	6
NO	10.5	80.0%	26.6%	15.5%	23.2%	1	17.0%	2	-5.2%	2	1.0%	8		0.2%	12
BAL	10.0	73.7%	18.2%	10.1%	16.4%	3	10.5%	3	-2.9%	11	3.0%	1		-1.1%	25
PIT	9.0	58.6%	9.0%	4.6%	7.0%	5	4.2%	11	-3.9%	9	-1.1%	27		-2.1%	31
IND	8.9	58.3%	8.4%	4.1%	6.0%	6	4.4%	10	-1.0%	13	0.6%	11		-2.2%	32
TB	8.9	55.7%	9.1%	4.5%	8.6%	4	6.0%	6	-3.9%	8	-1.3%	29		1.2%	5
DAL	8.8	57.4%	8.3%	3.9%	5.9%	7	8.9%	4	1.4%	22	-1.6%	31		-1.6%	29
SEA	8.7	52.9%	7.3%	3.4%	5.3%	8	8.4%	5	2.3%	25	-0.8%	24		-1.2%	27
NE	8.5	54.8%	7.5%	3.7%	4.7%	9	5.4%	7	2.4%	26	1.8%	3		-0.5%	21
PHI	8.5	51.9%	7.0%	3.2%	4.1%	10	0.3%	15	-4.2%	6	-0.5%	18		-0.1%	15
LAR	8.4	48.2%	6.1%	2.8%	3.2%	13	2.0%	12	-1.7%	12	-0.5%	21		-0.7%	23
SF	8.4	48.2%	6.3%	2.9%	4.0%	11	-0.2%	17	-4.0%	7	0.2%	14		0.3%	11
ATL	8.1	43.4%	5.4%	2.5%	3.9%	12	4.5%	9	0.1%	15	-0.5%	19		2.8%	2
TEN	8.1	45.6%	4.7%	2.1%	-0.5%	14	1.0%	14	1.1%	21	-0.3%	15		-1.3%	28
ARI	8.1	42.7%	4.4%	2.1%	-0.5%	15	1.5%	13	0.8%	18	-1.2%	28		-1.7%	30
DET	8.0	43.2%	4.5%	1.9%	-1.3%	17	-1.7%	21	0.2%	16	0.5%	12		-1.1%	26
Team	Avg Wins	Postseason Odds			Mean DVOA Projections									Schedule	
		Make Playoffs	Reach Super Bowl	Win Super Bowl	Total DVOA	Rk	Off DVOA	Rk	Def DVOA	Rk	ST DVOA	Rk		Average Opponent	Rk
BUF	7.9	43.4%	4.2%	1.8%	-1.6%	18	-8.8%	28	-7.6%	1	-0.4%	16		-0.1%	16
GB	7.8	40.5%	4.2%	1.8%	-1.0%	16	5.1%	8	5.5%	30	-0.7%	22		0.5%	10
CHI	7.8	39.8%	3.9%	1.6%	-2.5%	21	-7.6%	25	-4.7%	3	0.4%	13		-0.2%	17
LV	7.7	38.1%	3.6%	1.5%	-1.8%	19	0.3%	16	1.1%	20	-1.0%	26		1.8%	4
MIN	7.6	37.6%	3.7%	1.6%	-2.3%	20	-0.4%	18	1.4%	23	-0.5%	20		0.8%	7
HOU	7.5	36.7%	3.3%	1.4%	-3.3%	23	-0.6%	20	4.0%	27	1.3%	5		-0.3%	19
LAC	7.5	35.4%	2.9%	1.3%	-3.2%	22	-5.0%	23	-3.1%	10	-1.3%	30		0.6%	8
CLE	7.5	34.4%	2.5%	1.0%	-5.1%	24	-0.5%	19	4.1%	28	-0.5%	17		-0.6%	22
NYJ	7.4	35.9%	2.7%	1.1%	-5.7%	25	-11.4%	31	-4.6%	4	1.1%	7		0.0%	14
JAX	7.1	29.9%	1.9%	0.8%	-8.9%	28	-9.1%	29	1.0%	19	1.2%	6		-1.0%	24
DEN	7.0	28.5%	2.0%	0.8%	-5.9%	26	-9.3%	30	-4.3%	5	-0.9%	25		2.7%	3
NYG	7.0	28.8%	2.0%	0.8%	-8.8%	27	-8.1%	26	2.0%	24	1.3%	4		0.5%	9
CIN	6.7	23.3%	1.2%	0.5%	-12.8%	29	-6.9%	24	6.7%	31	0.9%	9		-0.3%	20
MIA	6.4	21.9%	1.0%	0.3%	-15.0%	30	-8.7%	27	5.5%	29	-0.7%	23		-0.2%	18
WAS	6.0	17.2%	0.7%	0.2%	-17.7%	32	-17.8%	32	0.7%	17	0.9%	10		0.1%	13
CAR	5.7	12.7%	0.6%	0.2%	-16.9%	31	-3.7%	22	11.0%	32	-2.2%	32		3.6%	1

Arizona Cardinals

2019 Record: 5-10-1	**Total DVOA:** -5.8% (20th)	**2020 Mean Projection:** 8.1 wins	**On the Clock (0-4):** 9%
Pythagorean Wins: 6.0 (23rd)	**Offense:** 3.8% (13rd)	**Postseason Odds:** 42.7%	**Mediocrity (5-7):** 32%
Snap-Weighted Age: 26.8 (4th)	**Defense:** 7.2% (23rd)	**Super Bowl Odds:** 4.4%	**Playoff Contender (8-10):** 40%
Average Opponent: 4.0% (3rd)	**Special Teams:** -2.4% (26th)	**Proj. Avg. Opponent:** -1.7% (30th)	**Super Bowl Contender (11+):** 18%

2019: A second hit of the reset button shows much more success.

2020: Can the young QB rise up to the challenge? We'll see.

It's not very often that you see a team draft a quarterback in the first round one year only to follow that up with another first-round quarterback pick immediately afterward. However, Arizona's 2018 season was such a disaster that Arizona fired head coach Steve Wilks and traded Josh Rosen after one season in the desert. Enter Kliff Kingsbury and Kyler Murray. The first-year coach-quarterback combo brought life to an abysmal Arizona offense and led to some massive improvement. The defense was not great, but the team took a major step forward even if they only ended up with two more wins than in 2018 by season's end.

In 2019, Arizona went from being the worst offense in the league by a comfortable margin to being slightly above average, no easy feat for a first-year quarterback-coach combination. Even without an ideal health situation on the offensive line, the Cardinals managed to finish second in the league in rushing DVOA. Murray's rushing ability had a lot do with that, as he finished third in quarterback rushing DYAR behind two players (Lamar Jackson and Josh Allen) who each had more rushing opportunities. Dating back to 1986, Arizona had the third-largest year-over-year improvement in offensive DVOA that we have ever measured (Table 1). Normally it would be hard to continue to improve on a more than 40% increase in offensive DVOA, but Arizona may be able to do just that thanks to the acquisition of DeAndre Hopkins via trade in the offseason.

There is also some room for positive regression from the offensive line simply because of better luck on the injury front. While Arizona suffered fewer adjusted games lost from the offensive line in 2019 than in 2018, they still had the most in the league for the second straight year. Breaking in a young quarterback behind a patchwork offensive line does not exactly seem like an ideal situation, but Murray and Kingsbury found a way to make it work.

The heights that Arizona's offense can reach will ultimately revolve around the 2019 first overall pick's ability to be productive through the air. Murray finished his rookie season with 305 passing DYAR, 21st in the league and the ninth-most from a rookie quarterback since the 2011 CBA. He will need to take the next step for the Arizona offense to truly soar, and some improvement in avoiding sacks would likely help his cause. The diminutive 2018 Heisman Trophy winner entered the league having only spent one full season as a college start-

er, and Oklahoma's offensive line that year featured four 2019 draftees and another potential 2021 first-rounder. It's possible that Murray was simply accustomed to having a dominant line in front of him, leading to a tendency to hold onto the ball waiting for a juicy opportunity down the field. Whether it was a product of his past experience or simply an adjustment period that comes from facing NFL defenses, Murray was among the league leaders in sacks taken. Murray's scrambling ability does help him avoid some sacks, so this could also be a stylistic aspect of his game that Arizona will just have to accept (à la Russell Wilson or Deshaun Watson). But for that tradeoff to be worth it, he will need to continue to develop.

Murray certainly showed flashes of that sort of development on the way to his Offensive Rookie of the Year honors. His Week 9 outing against a dominant 49ers defense was the best performance against Robert Saleh's group all season, as Murray finished with 10.0 yards per attempt for the game and Arizona as a whole finished with a 51.0% offensive DVOA. However, against a similarly tough Steelers group a few weeks later, Arizona struggled to get anything going on offense while Murray threw three interceptions. If Murray and the Cardinals can improve their consistency week to week, they could easily become an offensive force to be reckoned with in the NFC West.

Table 1: Biggest Year-to-Year Improvements in Offensive DVOA, 1986-2019

Year	Team	Year N-1	Rank	Year N	Rank	Change	Year N+1	Rank
2011	CAR	-35.8%	32	18.2%	4	54.0%	7.2%	10
2017	LAR	-37.8%	32	11.1%	6	48.9%	24.6%	2
2019	**ARI**	**-41.1%**	**32**	**3.8%**	**13**	**44.9%**	**--**	**--**
1999	OAK	-24.2%	29	20.5%	2	44.7%	17.3%	6
1991	DAL	-23.6%	28	17.6%	4	41.3%	23.6%	2
1998	BUF	-18.0%	28	19.4%	4	37.4%	12.7%	7
2016	DAL	-15.6%	31	19.9%	3	35.5%	6.7%	10
1992	PHI	-24.6%	26	10.5%	5	35.1%	6.3%	8
2013	PHI	-10.8%	25	22.9%	3	33.7%	1.1%	13
1993	SEA	-41.3%	28	-7.8%	20	33.5%	-11.8%	25

2020 Cardinals Schedule

Week	Opp.	Week	Opp.	Week	Opp.
1	at SF	7	SEA	13	LAR
2	WAS	8	MIA	14	at NYG
3	DET	9	BUF	15	PHI
4	at CAR	10	at SEA (Thu.)	16	SF (Sat.)
5	at NYJ	11	BYE	17	at LAR
6	at DAL (Mon.)	12	at NE		

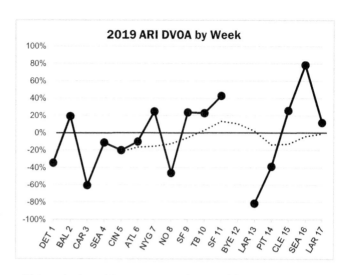

Arizona's young quarterback was not the only key figure for the Cardinals new to the NFL in 2019; head coach Kliff Kingsbury entered the league after being fired as the head coach of Texas Tech. Kingsbury had spent six seasons in Lubbock blending impressive offensive numbers with a general lack of success in terms of wins and losses in the Big 12. Texas Tech is by no means a traditional collegiate powerhouse, so it was not particularly surprising that Kingsbury was unable to break through to the upper echelon of the league. Still, this meant that Kingsbury's 2019 hiring was met with some consternation from Cardinals fans.

Fortunately for Kingsbury, he does not have to worry about recruiting disadvantages anymore and was able to focus on just coaching up the offense and strategic decision-making in his first season in the NFL. He initially struggled with fourth-down decisions over the first few weeks of the season, repeatedly settling for field goals on short fourth downs in the red zone instead of going for it, but over time, he developed a more aggressive approach and finished in the middle of the pack in EdjSports' Head Coaching Rankings.

Even without an ideal level of aggressiveness, Kingsbury helped make some major improvements to Arizona's offense. In spite of not having the best possible personnel available, Kingsbury's version of the Air Raid offense looked promising in Year 1. The Cardinals led the league in the percentage of snaps where they used 10 personnel (one running back, no tight ends), but Kingsbury was not wedded to just that one formation, as it was not even their most-used personnel grouping. The Cardinals may have leaned more toward their four-receiver sets had their depth at the position been better, but outside of Christian Kirk and Larry Fitzgerald, Arizona's receiving corps left much to be desired. The addition of Hopkins may lead to a shift toward more four-receiver sets, which in turn will spread defenses out even wider to create more running lanes for Murray and running back Kenyan Drake.

In addition to leading the league in 10 personnel usage, Arizona employed an empty backfield 15% of the time, more frequently than any other team in 2019. Combined with their most common personnel groupings (Arizona lined up in 10, 11, and 12 personnel 92% of the time), this suggests that Kingsbury wants to make use of his running backs in the passing game. Before injuries derailed his season, David Johnson was one of Arizona's primary targets, and the aforementioned Drake was involved as a receiver as well after taking over for Johnson.

With Johnson and his large contract off to Houston, Drake will be playing this season on the transition tag, and if his late-season usage is any indication, Kingsbury seems likely to feature Drake in 2020. Arizona is reportedly considering a long-term extension for Drake, but they would be wise to learn from their experience with Johnson and proceed with caution. Drake does not represent the same level of injury risk that Johnson did, but the replaceable nature of the running back position should at least give Arizona some pause. They don't have to look beyond their division for examples. Raheem Mostert began 2019 buried on the San Francisco depth chart and eventually starred in a run to the Super Bowl. Chris Carson of Seattle was originally a seventh-round pick and has started for multiple seasons. Drake himself was available for just a sixth-round pick at the trade deadline. Meanwhile, the Rams are regretting the huge contract extension they handed Todd Gurley; he's not even on their team anymore.

The biggest strategic question for Kingsbury is likely how much emphasis he shifts toward the highly talented and productive Hopkins after acquiring him in the trade that sent Johnson to the Texans. Kirk and Fitzgerald were essentially a two-man show at receiver with most of the remaining targets heading to the running backs, but trading for Hopkins has the knock-on effect of sliding each receiver one peg down the totem pole in terms of defensive attention. Despite missing three games, Kirk still finished with 108 targets, which is a 16-game pace of 133, and Fitzgerald eclipsed the century mark as well in spite of a slight decline in his share of snaps. Over in Houston, Hopkins vacuumed up 10 targets per game on his way to another All-Pro season, and he will certainly deserve another heavy workload this fall.

Even though the Cardinals frequently trailed in 2019, they only finished in the middle of the pack in terms of total pass attempts. So there should be room for Arizona to get Hopkins his looks without sacrificing all the opportunities for the incumbent duo, though it might make sense to reduce Fitzgerald's workload a bit more considering his advancing age. Kirk and Fitzgerald's receiving volume will likely take a bit of a dip with Hopkins in the fold, but the two of them should have the opportunity to be more efficient with the looks they do get.

Fitzgerald could essentially become an overqualified third option behind Hopkins and Kirk, taking some of the pressure off of 2019 second-round pick Andy Isabella. Isabella struggled to earn much playing time as a rookie. He failed to exceed 40% of the team's offensive snaps in any game despite Arizona's wide receiver-heavy personnel groups, though he began to take on a bit more of a role as the season progressed. While Isabella did not have a particularly productive rookie season, if he is able to replicate even a fraction of how productive he was at the University of Massachusetts, he could make for a scary third or fourth option. In that case, Kingsbury and Murray would have no shortage of receiving choices at their disposal for 2020.

The plethora of receiving options available seems to have Murray in position to make a leap in 2020, but it's hard to imagine Arizona making a playoff run without some improvement on the defensive side of the ball as well. In Vance Joseph's first season as defensive coordinator, the Cardinals took a bit of a step back while transitioning back to a 3-4 and particularly struggled against the pass. While the unit as a whole was comfortably below average, there were absolutely some bright spots that should continue to make a positive impact in the immediate future.

Since coming over from New England, edge rusher Chandler Jones has done nothing but produce, and 2019 was no exception. In addition to having another excellent season rushing the passer, Jones tied for the league lead in forced fumbles. In the secondary, Budda Baker filled a do-everything role at strong safety, sticking his nose in against the run and leading all safeties in solo tackles while simultaneously posting the best coverage success rate of any of Arizona's defensive backs. Cornerback Patrick Peterson did not have the best year after getting a late start because of a performance-enhancing drug suspension, but he appeared to return to form over the last three weeks of the season, starting with his effective shadowing of Odell Beckham Jr., and should be highly motivated entering a contract year.

Even with those three players in the fold, the Cardinals will need more juice against the pass if they are going to have success in 2020, and the biggest move they made to address their deficiencies there was drafting Clemson do-it-all defender Isaiah Simmons in the first round. While Simmons is technically listed on Arizona's roster as a linebacker, he offers the ability to fill a variety of roles and assignments. Clemson defensive coordinator Brent Venables used Simmons as a pass-rusher (he finished with seven sacks), a middle-of-the-field safety, and both an inside and outside linebacker, often varying his assignments from snap to snap depending on matchups. At the NFL level, he is a little on the lighter side among linebackers, but his explosive athletic ability should serve him well in coverage.

Simmons' versatility would be wasted if he were pigeonholed into just one position, though it may be smart to limit his responsibilities a bit as he is entering the league amidst a highly unusual offseason. The Cardinals' plan is to start him off at inside linebacker, but he should take on a more expansive role as he shows he can handle it. They view him as a mistake-eraser that will eventually be able to make the rest of the Arizona defenders' lives easier, though that may not happen immediately in his rookie year.

Arizona could have really used another defender like Simmons to help with defending tight ends last season, as they finished dead last in DVOA when opposing tight ends were targeted. In a division with George Kittle of the 49ers, having an answer in coverage for that kind of a matchup problem is critical. The Cardinals struggled as well with the likes of T.J. Hockenson and an aging Greg Olsen; they clearly needed to make some personnel changes if Joseph's scheme is going to work.

Some growing pains were to be expected after changing schemes in back-to-back seasons, and Arizona was definitely low on bodies in the secondary prior to Peterson's return from suspension. However, if the defense is going to take a step forward, they can't really afford to have such a glaring weakness in coverage. The Broncos finished in the top 10 in defensive DVOA in both of Joseph's seasons as Denver's head coach, so it seems reasonable that a bit of a defensive talent infusion could really make his scheme hum.

With another year in Joseph's system and some additional investment on defense, we expect Arizona to take a step towards being around average on defense, which should absolutely help their cause as they try to return to the postseason for the first time since 2015. An expanded playoff field makes that task a bit easier than it was in the past, and Arizona should also benefit from what we expect to be one of the league's softest schedules. Their divisional schedule in the NFC West will be tough, but the AFC East looks weak, as does the bottom of the NFC East and early-October opponent Carolina. We do not expect the Cardinals to jump to the league's upper echelon, but their schedule could potentially help them sneak into the playoffs.

The addition of Hopkins has Arizona pegged by many as a team on the rise, and Kyler Murray showed flashes of excellent play during his rookie season. If Murray can make a real leap, which seems very possible given the improved weapons around him, the Cardinals could definitely outperform their projections and become a real threat to make a playoff run on their own merit instead of just being propped up by a weak schedule. Murray may not be ready to make the transition from promising youngster to comfortably above average, and if that's the case, it will be tough for Arizona to make some serious noise. Even if it doesn't all come together this season, the future is bright in the desert, and the offensive improvement Murray and Kingsbury catalyzed in their first season together while adapting to the NFL game bodes well for what they could eventually become.

Carl Yedor

2019 Cardinals Stats by Week

Wk	vs.	W-L	PF	PA	YDF	YDA	TO	Total	Off	Def	ST
1	DET	T	27	27	387	477	+1	-34%	-32%	13%	10%
2	at BAL	L	17	23	349	440	0	19%	18%	-11%	-9%
3	CAR	L	20	38	248	413	-1	-60%	-33%	30%	3%
4	SEA	L	10	27	321	340	-1	-11%	-9%	-7%	-10%
5	at CIN	W	26	23	514	370	0	-20%	20%	30%	-9%
6	ATL	W	34	33	442	444	0	-10%	39%	45%	-3%
7	at NYG	W	27	21	245	263	+3	25%	12%	-28%	-15%
8	at NO	L	9	31	237	510	+1	-46%	-28%	22%	4%
9	SF	L	25	28	357	411	0	24%	51%	19%	-8%
10	at TB	L	27	30	417	457	+1	23%	7%	-12%	4%
11	at SF	L	26	36	266	442	0	43%	46%	0%	-3%
12	BYE										
13	LAR	L	7	34	198	549	-1	-82%	-65%	26%	9%
14	PIT	L	17	23	236	275	-1	-39%	-20%	6%	-13%
15	CLE	W	38	24	445	393	+1	26%	39%	9%	-4%
16	at SEA	W	27	13	412	224	+1	79%	19%	-55%	4%
17	at LAR	L	24	31	393	424	-5	12%	18%	7%	2%

Trends and Splits

	Offense	Rank	Defense	Rank
Total DVOA	3.8%	13	7.2%	23
Unadjusted VOA	1.8%	14	10.8%	26
Weighted Trend	9.8%	7	4.3%	22
Variance	10.9%	28	6.2%	19
Average Opponent	-2.5%	5	1.4%	10
Passing	1.8%	20	20.7%	27
Rushing	14.7%	2	-11.3%	12
First Down	4.3%	11	1.3%	18
Second Down	4.4%	12	17.4%	29
Third Down	1.6%	16	3.2%	18
First Half	4.5%	8	5.6%	24
Second Half	3.0%	15	8.7%	22
Red Zone	6.2%	10	5.2%	19
Late and Close	3.6%	14	13.9%	29

Five-Year Performance

Year	W-L	Pyth W	Est W	PF	PA	TO	Total	Rk	Off	Rk	Def	Rk	ST	Rk	Off AGL	Rk	Def AGL	Rk	Off Age	Rk	Def Age	Rk	ST Age	Rk
2015	13-3	12.1	11.6	489	313	+9	27.4%	3	15.7%	4	-15.6%	3	-4.0%	29	22.8	6	42.8	24	28.2	3	26.0	26	25.8	21
2016	7-8-1	9.4	7.7	418	362	0	1.3%	16	-6.0%	21	-13.6%	3	-6.3%	30	45.5	22	49.8	21	28.3	1	25.9	29	25.5	27
2017	8-8	6.1	5.6	295	361	-4	-10.8%	22	-18.0%	30	-12.7%	4	-5.5%	28	73.6	32	34.5	15	28.6	1	28.1	2	26.5	6
2018	3-13	2.8	2.5	225	425	-12	-40.7%	32	-41.1%	32	0.5%	18	1.0%	11	59.8	29	32.5	15	26.1	25	27.2	4	26.2	9
2019	5-10-1	6.0	7.1	361	442	-1	-5.8%	20	3.8%	13	7.2%	23	-2.4%	26	45.6	19	39.4	20	27.3	6	26.7	9	26.0	10

2019 Performance Based on Most Common Personnel Groups

ARI Offense					ARI Offense vs. Opponents					ARI Defense					ARI Defense vs. Opponents			
Pers	Freq	Yds	DVOA	Run%	Pers	Freq	Yds	DVOA	Run%	Pers	Freq	Yds	DVOA	Pers	Freq	Yds	DVOA
11	35%	5.7	12.0%	33%	Base	21%	5.4	0.3%	55%	Base	38%	6.0	10.7%	11	55%	6.3	3.6%
10	33%	5.5	3.7%	19%	Nickel	63%	5.8	9.7%	32%	Nickel	57%	6.4	7.5%	12	19%	5.9	20.3%
12	24%	5.8	8.2%	59%	Dime+	16%	5.4	6.2%	23%	Dime+	2%	4.7	-27.4%	21	9%	7.5	28.3%
20	2%	10.7	73.1%	36%	Goal Line	0%	-1.0	-136.1%	0%	Goal Line	1%	1.0	21.0%	22	4%	6.2	3.5%
13	2%	2.5	-14.1%	79%						Big	1%	2.2	-48.9%	611	4%	3.0	-43.3%
21	2%	5.6	-45.5%	56%													

Strategic Tendencies

Run/Pass		Rk	Formation		Rk	Pass Rush		Rk	Secondary		Rk	Strategy		Rk
Runs, first half	36%	18	Form: Single Back	75%	26	Rush 3	5.8%	21	4 DB	38%	2	Play Action	28%	11
Runs, first down	45%	26	Form: Empty Back	15%	1	Rush 4	54.4%	29	5 DB	57%	17	Offensive Motion	31%	27
Runs, second-long	31%	7	Form: Multi Back	10%	18	Rush 5	29.0%	4	6+ DB	2%	26	Avg Box (Off)	6.23	32
Runs, power sit.	50%	26	Pers: 3+ WR	71%	11	Rush 6+	10.9%	1	Man Coverage	35%	11	Avg Box (Def)	6.59	15
Runs, behind 2H	28%	17	Pers: 2+ TE/6+ OL	27%	16	Edge Rusher Sacks	70.0%	5	CB by Sides	58%	30	Offensive Pace	28.35	4
Pass, ahead 2H	49%	15	Pers: 6+ OL	1%	25	Interior DL Sacks	17.5%	23	S/CB Cover Ratio	25%	21	Defensive Pace	31.12	24
Run-Pass Options	12%	4	Shotgun/Pistol	88%	2	Second Level Sacks	12.5%	24	DB Blitz	16%	4	Go for it on 4th	1.82	8

The Cardinals ran 35.3% of plays without a tight end or sixth offensive lineman in the personnel. That's the highest rate since the 2015 Jets were at 43.1%. The Cardinals averaged 5.7 yards and 5.0% DVOA on these plays, slightly above NFL averages of 5.5 yards and 1.9% DVOA. ◐ Another way to put that: Arizona led the league with four or more wide receivers on 33.4% of plays; second-place Jacksonville was way down at 8.4%. ◐ All those four-wide sets are really good at clearing out room for the running backs, and the Cardinals had 47% of their running back carries against a small box of six men or fewer. Only Kansas City faced small boxes more often. Yet the Cardinals had a better DVOA running the rest of the time (12.7%) than they did against a six-man box (-1.9%). ◐ Although Arizona led the NFL in empty backfields, they were below average with 5.4 yards and 1.0% DVOA on these plays. NFL average was 6.1 yards and 13.3% DVOA. ◐ The Cardinals were out ahead of the rest of the league with 69 wide receiver or tight end screens last season; no other offense was above 53. The Cardinals had a very good 22.6% DVOA on these plays. ◐ Arizona used pistol on 6.1% of plays, which was second in the league behind Baltimore. The Cardinals had 21.2% DVOA and 7.1 yards per play from the pistol. ◐ Arizona receivers dropped a league-low 3.3% of passes in 2019. ◐ Arizona's offense was once again poor when it came to breaking tackles, ranking just 25th in total broken tackles and the percentage of plays with at least one broken tackle. The defense was also poor in this area: 153 broken tackles was more than any other defense except for Cleveland (tied) and Jacksonville. ◐ Two years ago, the Cardinals used nickel personnel more than any other defense; last year, they used base personnel more than any defense other than Seattle. ◐ The Arizona defense ranked sixth in the league in pressure on first and second downs but fell to 29th on third and fourth downs. ◐ The Cardinals had the league's biggest gap in defensive DVOA between plays with pressure (-71.1% DVOA, 12th in the NFL) and plays without pressure (63.3% DVOA, 29th).

Passing

Player	DYAR	DVOA	Plays	NtYds	Avg	YAC	C%	TD	Int
K.Murray	305	-3.1%	588	3410	5.8	5.3	65.0%	20	12
B.Hundley	-43	-62.3%	13	38	2.9	6.8	45.5%	0	0

Rushing

Player	DYAR	DVOA	Plays	Yds	Avg	TD	Fum	Suc
K.Drake	236	35.5%	123	643	5.2	8	0	54%
D.Johnson*	-9	-10.8%	94	345	3.7	2	0	43%
K.Murray	87	8.5%	82	550	6.7	4	1	-
C.Edmonds	84	31.7%	60	303	5.1	4	0	40%
C.Kirk	55	55.6%	10	93	9.3	0	0	-
B.Hundley	17	44.7%	5	44	8.8	0	0	-

Receiving

Player	DYAR	DVOA	Plays	Ctch	Yds	Y/C	YAC	TD	C%
L.Fitzgerald	90	-2.0%	109	75	804	10.7	4.6	4	69%
C.Kirk	67	-5.1%	108	68	709	10.4	4.2	3	63%
D.Byrd*	30	-4.6%	46	32	359	11.2	4.7	1	70%
K.Johnson	-105	-45.6%	42	21	187	8.9	2.0	1	50%
P.Cooper*	33	0.4%	33	25	243	9.7	2.8	1	76%
A.Isabella	44	33.4%	13	9	189	21.0	15.6	1	69%
T.Sherfield	-11	-22.6%	13	4	80	20.0	2.5	0	31%
D.Hopkins	224	6.2%	150	104	1165	11.2	3.7	7	69%
C.Clay*	75	45.3%	24	18	237	13.2	5.3	1	75%
M.Williams	51	30.0%	19	15	202	13.5	6.9	1	79%
D.Arnold	35	49.0%	10	6	102	17.0	4.5	2	60%
D.Johnson*	114	29.2%	47	36	370	10.3	6.3	4	77%
K.Drake	24	-2.3%	35	28	171	6.1	9.3	0	80%
C.Edmonds	-2	-15.3%	21	12	105	8.8	8.8	1	57%

Offensive Line

Player	Pos	Age	GS	Snaps	Pen	Sk	Pass	Run	Player	Pos	Age	GS	Snaps	Pen	Sk	Pass	Run
D.J. Humphries	LT	27	16/16	1063	14	3.0	23	5	J.R. Sweezy	RG	31	16/16	1018	7	1.0	16	7
A.Q. Shipley*	C	34	16/16	1058	3	3.5	11	13	Justin Murray	RT	27	14/12	857	4	5.0	22	2
Justin Pugh	LG	30	16/16	1039	3	5.0	18	3	Mason Cole	LG	24	16/2	215	1	1.0	4	1

Year	Yards	ALY	Rank	Power	Rank	Stuff	Rank	2nd Lev	Rank	Open Field	Rank	Sacks	ASR	Rank	Press	Rank	F-Start	Cont.
2017	3.38	4.02	17	68%	9	20%	13	0.90	32	0.30	32	52	8.1%	26	29.7%	11	17	26
2018	3.58	4.00	25	69%	10	16%	6	0.98	30	0.36	31	52	9.2%	26	35.4%	29	19	17
2019	4.61	4.12	22	74%	4	18%	8	1.30	8	0.97	9	50	8.4%	26	27.7%	6	13	31
2019 ALY by direction:			Left End 4.23 (13)			Left Tackle: 4.61 (8)			Mid/Guard: 4.23 (20)			Right Tackle: 4.10 (17)			Right End: 3.27 (25)			

They weren't quite decimated by injuries as much as they were in 2018, but for the second straight year, the Cardinals led the league in adjusted games lost by offensive linemen. ◐ Free-agent right tackle signing Marcus Gilbert missed the entire season because of a torn ACL, and his backup Jordan Mills went on IR in Week 5. These injuries opened the door for former undrafted free agent Justin Murray to take over at right tackle for the remainder of the season, though Murray may struggle to hold onto the gig with rookie third-round pick Josh Jones in the fold and Gilbert returning from injury with designs on reclaiming his spot. Some observers had Jones going as early as the first round, so it appears Arizona got good value when they selected the University of Houston product. ✎ J.R. Sweezy came over from Seattle for the 2019 campaign and started every game at right guard. While he was not particularly impressive in pass protection, he is by no means on an expensive deal. ✎ Veteran center A.Q. Shipley managed to hold off former Michigan lineman Mason Cole for the starting role in 2019, but Cole will take over for 2020 and beyond. Cole started all 16 games as a rookie during Arizona's nightmare 2018, then filled in at left guard last year amidst some injury-induced reshuffling midseason. Armed with more experience, he should be better positioned for success entering his third year. ✎ Justin Pugh was the primary starter at left guard for Arizona, though he did moonlight at right tackle for a few games because of the injuries. Pugh came into the league as a tackle, but guard is a better fit for him given his struggles in pass protection. ✎ Rounding out the Cardinals offensive line was left tackle D.J. Humphries, who started every game for the first time in his career and earned a three-year deal to be Kyler Murray's blindside protector for the foreseeable future. Humphries ranked fifth in the league in penalties in 2019, but when playing with a scrambling savant like Murray at quarterback, some holding penalties are unavoidable. ✎ Speaking of which: 40% of Arizona's sacks were what we might call "non-pressure sacks," those marked "coverage sack," "failed scramble" or "self sack." In particular, the Cardinals had 15 failed scramble sacks, when no other offense had more than 10.

Defensive Front

Defensive Line	Age	Pos	G	Snaps	Plays	TmPct	Rk	Stop	Dfts	BTkl	Runs	St%	Rk	RuYd	Rk	Sack	Hit	Hur	Dsrpt
						Overall							vs. Run				Pass Rush		
Corey Peters	32	DT	16	827	37	4.2%	51	28	10	3	31	74%	52	2.1	38	2.5	3	20	#N/A
Rodney Gunter*	28	DE	13	622	29	4.1%	76	25	10	3	23	83%	22	2.0	28	3.0	8	18	0
Zach Kerr*	30	DE	12	332	20	3.0%	--	18	4	4	19	89%	--	1.3	--	0.0	2	13	1
Jonathan Bullard	27	DE	9	315	22	4.4%	87	16	7	3	18	72%	63	1.8	22	1.5	5	7	1
Jordan Phillips	*28*	*DT*	*16*	*548*	*31*	*3.9%*	*64*	*21*	*16*	*4*	*18*	*44%*	*97*	*2.6*	*62*	*9.5*	*6*	*14*	*0*

Edge Rushers	Age	Pos	G	Snaps	Plays	TmPct	Rk	Stop	Dfts	BTkl	Runs	St%	Rk	RuYd	Rk	Sack	Hit	Hur	Dsrpt
						Overall							vs. Run				Pass Rush		
Chandler Jones	30	OLB	16	1095	58	6.6%	21	47	24	8	27	74%	47	2.0	26	19.0	11	43	7
Terrell Suggs*	38	OLB	15	710	39	4.7%	48	31	15	7	31	74%	46	2.1	27	6.5	5	23	4
Cassius Marsh*	28	OLB	16	436	35	4.0%	--	30	9	5	22	95%	--	1.1	--	2.5	3	14	5
Devon Kennard	*29*	*OLB*	*16*	*946*	*58*	*6.8%*	*17*	*39*	*12*	*8*	*44*	*61%*	*78*	*3.2*	*73*	*7.0*	*14*	*33*	*6*

Linebackers	Age	Pos	G	Snaps	Plays	TmPct	Rk	Stop	Dfts	BTkl	Runs	St%	Rk	RuYd	Rk	Sack	Hit	Hur	Tgts	Suc%	Rk	AdjYd	Rk	PD	Int
						Overall							vs. Run				Pass Rush				vs. Pass				
Jordan Hicks	28	ILB	16	1160	156	17.7%	6	80	31	21	87	62%	35	4.4	63	1.5	5	11	47	36%	60	9.9	63	6	3
Haason Reddick	26	ILB	16	710	81	9.2%	51	51	24	12	45	67%	19	3.7	32	1.0	3	20	42	50%	36	7.1	43	6	0
Joe Walker*	28	ILB	16	543	58	6.6%	69	28	11	10	39	56%	56	3.3	20	0.0	1	2	21	57%	15	7.0	42	0	0
De'Vondre Campbell	*27*	*OLB*	*16*	*937*	*133*	*16.8%*	*9*	*64*	*22*	*8*	*70*	*60%*	*42*	*4.2*	*59*	*2.0*	*1*	*7*	*39*	*33%*	*65*	*7.9*	*54*	*5*	*2*

Year	Yards	ALY	Rank	Power	Rank	Stuff	Rank	2nd Level	Rank	Open Field	Rank	Sacks	ASR	Rank	Press	Rank
2017	3.36	3.34	3	62%	12	23%	6	0.96	6	0.56	6	37	5.9%	24	30.2%	17
2018	4.92	4.32	14	80%	32	20%	12	1.46	30	1.28	30	49	8.8%	3	28.8%	22
2019	4.22	4.17	14	57%	4	22%	5	1.29	24	0.74	16	40	7.0%	16	30.5%	15
2019 ALY by direction:		*Left End: 4.31 (19)*			*Left Tackle: 3.84 (9)*			*Mid/Guard: 4.43 (18)*			*Right Tackle: 2.16 (1)*			*Right End: 5.29 (24)*		

Arizona's pass defense was a mess in 2019 but that was through no fault of Chandler Jones. Jones finished just a half-sack off the league lead and also had more hurries than any other season since arriving in Arizona in 2016. ✎ After being cut by Detroit, Devon Kennard joins the Cardinals to serve as Jones' pass-rush partner. ✎ De'Vondre Campbell should be the new starting inside linebacker at first after spending four years with the Falcons. He will pair with Jordan Hicks, who was an iron man in his first year with the Cardinals, to make up the inside linebacker duo in Arizona's 3-4. However, rookie Isaiah Simmons may push one of the inside linebackers to the bench in some passing situations if he is anywhere near as impactful as he was in college. Simmons seems likely to fit in as a coverage linebacker early on, but his exact responsibilities may vary from week to week given his effectiveness as a pass-rusher in college. In all likelihood, we are going to see all of these linebackers on the field a lot in 2020. ✎ Haason Reddick has bounced around in the linebacker group since being drafted in 2017 without really being able to lock down a position. The 2020 season will be make-or-break for him moving forward as he slides to inside linebacker without much of a projected role. ✎ Corey Peters brought a veteran presence to Arizona's defensive line rotation at nose tackle and played a major role in the team's improvement against the run from 2018 to 2019. The Cardinals hope to get more out of 2019 third-round pick Zach Allen, and he appears to have a path to a starting spot at defensive end that would help Arizona's interior group get a little younger. ✎ Counteracting that youth infusion will be veteran Jordan Phillips, who slots in at the other defensive end position across from Allen coming off a career high in sacks in 2019, though his 9.5 sacks paired with 14 hurries is almost certain to regress in a role likely to involve more two-gapping responsibilities. ✎ Arizona also added a pair of defensive tackles—Utah's Leki Fotu and LSU's Rashard Lawrence—in the fourth round of the draft to bring in some younger depth for its defensive front.

Defensive Secondary

Secondary	Age	Pos	G	Snaps	Plays	TmPct	Rk	Stop	Dfts	BTkl	Runs	St%	Rk	RuYd	Rk	Tgts	Tgt%	Rk	Dist	Suc%	Rk	AdjYd	Rk	PD	Int
Budda Baker	24	SS	16	1146	152	17.3%	1	64	25	15	75	52%	12	6.0	29	39	8.7%	27	10.0	54%	32	9.0	56	6	0
Byron Murphy	22	CB	16	1132	87	9.9%	10	30	16	13	14	29%	68	7.4	61	92	20.8%	33	11.0	42%	78	6.9	27	10	1
Patrick Peterson	30	CB	10	710	59	10.7%	53	20	8	5	16	25%	72	6.9	52	58	20.9%	32	11.3	50%	53	7.9	49	7	2
Jalen Thompson	22	FS	15	618	59	7.1%	60	19	6	8	16	25%	63	11.6	70	19	7.9%	38	6.9	47%	49	7.3	34	3	1
Chris Jones	25	CB	11	279	25	4.1%	--	7	3	7	5	0%	--	8.0	--	24	22.0%	--	18.5	54%	--	8.2	--	6	0
Kevin Peterson	26	CB	14	261	18	2.3%	--	6	2	5	0	0%	--	0.0	--	21	20.6%	--	9.9	33%	--	8.7	--	2	0
Deionte Thompson	23	SS	11	259	18	3.0%	--	4	1	3	7	29%	--	9.1	--	4	3.9%	--	8.3	25%	--	14.5	--	0	0

Year	Pass D Rank	vs. #1 WR	Rk	vs. #2 WR	Rk	vs. Other WR	Rk	WR Wide	Rk	WR Slot	Rk	vs. TE	Rk	vs. RB	Rk
2017	10	11.4%	23	-19.8%	6	-9.9%	9	-4.7%	15	-8.4%	9	-14.6%	7	-0.5%	17
2018	8	-0.7%	14	13.6%	23	-6.7%	12	-9.8%	12	11.0%	24	3.0%	17	-3.1%	14
2019	27	15.3%	27	-3.3%	12	30.2%	31	7.7%	23	19.2%	27	28.2%	32	31.7%	29

Patrick Peterson missed the first six games of the 2019 season because of a performance-enhancing drug suspension, and when he returned he did not perform up to his previous standards, finishing 53rd in success rate and 49th in yards per pass allowed. The two prior years, Peterson ranked seventh and fourth in success rate in coverage. ✎ Peterson's suspension and the broken leg Robert Alford suffered during training camp led to rookie cornerback Byron Murphy taking on a larger role than was originally intended right away. Arizona sees Murphy as a great fit for slot corner, but with the absences of Arizona's projected starters on the outside, he had to bounce around to plug gaps. Alford should return to start on the outside in 2020; hopefully he's better than he was for Atlanta in 2018, when he ranked 79th in both of our cornerback charting stats. ✎ More time for Murphy was better than the alternatives of Chris Jones and Kevin Peterson, a pair of former undrafted free agents who both had to fill in at times in 2019 and did not particularly impress. ✎ Safety Budda Baker earned his first Pro Bowl nod for his defensive play in 2019 after making the roster for special teams in 2017. One of the few Cardinals defenders to start every game, the third-year pro led all NFL safeties with 152 plays made and 25 defeats. ✎ Rookie Jalen Thompson, a fifth-round pick in the 2019 supplemental draft, took over the free safety position a month into the season and made an early impact.

Special Teams

Year	DVOA	Rank	FG/XP	Rank	Net Kick	Rank	Kick Ret	Rank	Net Punt	Rank	Punt Ret	Rank	Hidden	Rank
2017	-5.5%	28	-8.9	28	-5.5	27	-2.1	20	-10.0	27	-0.9	20	-7.5	27
2018	1.0%	11	-5.1	25	2.6	11	-1.5	19	6.5	5	2.3	12	9.5	7
2019	-2.4%	26	0.4	17	0.6	14	-4.5	30	-9.8	30	1.4	10	1.9	15

Zane Gonzalez earned a second-round restricted free agent tender despite not being very good in 2019. He had a very average year in field goals and extra points, with 89% field goal accuracy that was inflated a bit by a large number of chip shots. Still, that's better than what the Cardinals had gotten in previous years. Gonzalez also was near the bottom of the league in gross kickoff value, with the Cardinals finishing in the middle of the pack in net kickoffs thanks to a good coverage unit. ✎ Arizona's punt coverage, on the other hand, was pretty brutal, but the ageless Andy Lee was about average in terms of gross points of field position value from punts only. Lee dealt with some injuries in 2019, so undrafted rookie Ryan Winslow filled in for two games. Winslow signed a reserve/future contract with Arizona at the end of the season, so the two former Pittsburgh Panthers may end up with more time to bond. ✎ Arizona got next to nothing from its kickoff return unit between rookie wide receiver Andy Isabella and return specialist Pharoh Cooper, who rejoined the team in October after being cut at the end of training camp. Fellow wide receiver Christian Kirk was a talented punt returner in college, but given that he was one of Arizona's primary targets in 2019, he did not get a chance to contribute much in the return game. Cooper signed with the Panthers, so there should be some competition for the returner roles, though Isabella seems to have the inside track on kick returns while Kirk is the likely favorite for punt return duties.

Atlanta Falcons

2019 Record: 7-9	Total DVOA: -5.3% (17th)	2020 Mean Projection: 8.1 wins	On the Clock (0-4): 9%
Pythagorean Wins: 7.5 (19th)	Offense: 2.0% (15th)	Postseason Odds: 43.4%	Mediocrity (5-7): 32%
Snap-Weighted Age: 27.0 (3rd)	Defense: 4.5% (20th)	Super Bowl Odds: 5.4%	Playoff Contender (8-10): 41%
Average Opponent: 3.1% (5th)	Special Teams: -2.9% (28th)	Proj. Avg. Opponent: 2.8% (2nd)	Super Bowl Contender (11+): 18%

2019: This is your last chance, Dan Quinn.

2020: Seriously, *this* is your last chance, Dan Quinn.

As Jameis Winston took a shotgun snap and threw a pass at the start of overtime of the Buccaneers' Week 17 game against the Falcons, the football world was captivated. That isn't something one would expect about a play in a game between two below-.500 teams whose playoff hopes had already been dashed. But Winston had thrown his 29th interception of the season in the second quarter on a route miscommunication with Justin Watson—playing because of injuries to normal starters Mike Evans and Chris Godwin and likely light on practice reps. This was Winston's last chance to make history.

Defensive end John Cominsky got his fingertips on the pass and slowed its flight, but the play still needed just seven seconds. Falcons linebacker Deion Jones jumped tight end Cameron Brate's curl route, secured the interception, and jogged the 27 yards needed to score the game-winning touchdown with his ball arm stretched out in celebration. The fans of chaos delighted in Winston's 30th interception, a total no quarterback had reached in a season since Vinny Testaverde did it—also for the Bucs—in 1988. That Winston reached the benchmark with his seventh pick-six of the season—an outright NFL record—made it even more comical.

The Falcons probably pulled some humor from their victory over a divisional rival and their punctuating of the end of the Winston era in Tampa Bay. But if they were as interested in the results of an otherwise meaningless game as the masses, it was for a different reason. That overtime victory closed out a streak of four consecutive Falcons wins to end the season, a perfect December that included a 29-22 upset win over the eventual NFC champion 49ers in San Francisco. Last February's Super Bowl was the third since the Falcons' most recent berth and the subsequent and infamous collapse from a 28-3 third-quarter lead. But the team's rally in the fourth quarter of the 2019 season gave them hope that a return trip to the Super Bowl could still happen before Matt Ryan retires and while 77-year-old team owner Arthur Blank can still appreciate it, and it informed their approach to the offseason.

But that hope doesn't survive closer scrutiny.

The Falcons enjoy a high baseline of success because their greatest team strength is in the passing game. Passing is the most consistent aspect of team offense, which itself is more consistent than either defense or special teams from one year to the next. The team may not have come close to repeating their 540 points scored from their standout 2016 season, but they have remained in the top 12 of passing offense DVOA in the three years since. Even in a down year relative to his exceptional standards, Matt Ryan finished 14th out of 34 qualified quarterbacks in 2019 in both DYAR and DVOA. Receivers Julio Jones and Calvin Ridley each finished in the top seven in DYAR at their position, and after extending Jones last September, the Falcons have all three cornerstone players under team control until at least 2023.

To return to the (near) top of the mountain, the Falcons need their defense to elevate closer to their offense. That seemed destined to happen in 2017. In 2016, the breakouts of four young defenders motivated the unit's improvement from a 10.3% DVOA—where higher rates are worse—and 28.8 points allowed per game in the first half of the year to a 3.0% DVOA and 21.0 points allowed per game in the second half, propelling them to the Super Bowl. And Grady Jarrett, Vic Beasley, Deion Jones, and Keanu Neal all started that next season between 22 and 25 years old with just one or two years accrued on their inexpensive rookie contracts.

But the defense's on-paper promise didn't translate. Beasley's best season in the last three years produced just 26.5 pass pressures, 8.0 fewer than in his All-Pro 2016 season. He needed all three of those years to better his sack total from that one amazing season. Jones and Neal haven't suffered the same steep decline in on-field productivity, but they've spent 38 of a possible 64 games on the sidelines the last two years with respective foot and knee and Achilles injuries. All told, the Falcons have finished 20th or worse in defensive DVOA each of the last three seasons.

To their credit, the Falcons quickly identified their deficiencies and tried to correct them. They drafted defensive end Takk McKinkley, defensive tackle Deadrin Senat, linebacker Duke Riley, and cornerback Isaiah Oliver with four of their five Day 1 and Day 2 draft picks in 2017 and 2018. But so far in their careers, those players have not fulfilled their potential either. That's especially true for the first-rounder McKinley, who has averaged just 24 pass pressures and 5.5 sacks per year in his three seasons.

The Falcons have paid some members of their defensive core—Jarrett and Jones landed four-year extensions for $68 million and $57 million, respectively. They've let or likely will soon let other members go—Beasley left as a free agent this offseason, and the team declined McKinley's fifth-year

2020 Falcons Schedule					
Week	Opp.	Week	Opp.	Week	Opp.
1	SEA	7	DET	13	NO
2	at DAL	8	at CAR (Thu.)	14	at LAC
3	CHI	9	DEN	15	TB
4	at GB (Mon.)	10	BYE	16	at KC
5	CAR	11	at NO	17	at TB
6	at MIN	12	LV		

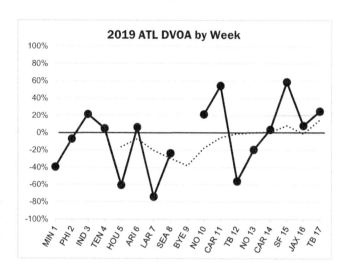

option. But regardless of approach, the Falcons have lost the value they used to have in underpaid young players, and they haven't replaced them with a new set of blue-chip draftees on inexpensive rookie contracts.

That has put the team on a downward trajectory from 11 wins in 2016 to 10 the next year to just seven in each of the last two seasons, and without the cap flexibility to reverse course.

Many teams would interpret those trends as signals to rebuild, in particular because their previous year's firings of all three of their coordinators carried an unwritten expectation that head coach Dan Quinn—who reclaimed the team's defensive play calling, and with it the full extent of credit or blame for the unit's success or lack of it—would return to the playoffs in 2019 or follow his former assistants out the door. But the Falcons' December sweep and the lasting image of Jones' outstretched arm on a season-ending pick-six provide the perfect narrative for the team to roll it back one more time.

The Quinn-as-defensive-coordinator experiment got off to a rocky start and hit a quick nadir in Week 5 when Deshaun Watson's Texans scored 53 points against the Falcons. That outburst exposed weaknesses beyond Beasley and McKinley's inability to generate pressure. Oliver struggled to stay with speedy and savvy receiver Will Fuller, who used quick cuts and picks near the line to find space en route to a 217-yard, three-touchdown day. And Oliver's plight didn't relent. He faced tough assignments in receivers including DK Metcalf and Brandin Cooks in subsequent weeks after presumed No. 1 cornerback Desmond Trufant suffered a turf toe injury. With no available help from the injured free safety Neal, Oliver managed just a 46% coverage success rate in 2019, 10th lowest of the 66 cornerbacks who saw 50 or more passes thrown their way. Ryan's passing offense was in its usual position in the top half of the league, but that was not enough to counterbalance a defense that allowed 20 or more points to the team's first eight opponents of the season. The Falcons entered their bye week at 1-7, effectively eliminated from playoff contention before the start of November.

Quinn avoided the firing that many thought would come in the team's week off, and he responded with what at the time seemed like a desperate decision to hand some of his defensive play-calling duties to Raheem Morris. Morris began his Falcons tenure as a secondary coach, but at the time of his advancement, he was coaching receivers on the opposite side of the ball. Desperate or not, Morris' promotion paid immediate dividends. The Falcons defense held the Saints and Panthers

to nine and three respective points in a pair of road wins coming out of the team's bye week. Morris rode that momentum and that of the team's undefeated December to an official title of defensive coordinator.

The Falcons had experienced a similar statistical renaissance before. You'll notice that Table 1 looks very similar to a table from the Atlanta chapter of last year's *Almanac*. Including in their Super Bowl season, the team had shown marked improvements in defensive DVOA and points allowed from the first half to the second half in the three previous seasons. And trusting DVOA as the truer indicator of team quality, none of those improvements carried over to the next season. But Morris provides a *reason* that the defense improved in 2019, and so he is a reason the team can be optimistic that 2020 will be different.

Table 1. Falcons' Second-Half Defensive Improvements

Season	Weeks 1-9				Week 10-17			
	DVOA	Rk	Pts Allowed	Rk	DVOA	Rk	Pts Allowed	Rk
2016	10.3%	26	28.8	28	3.0%	23	21.0	13
2017	13.0%	28	21.5	14	-2.1%	11	17.9	5
2018	22.3%	31	28.3	29	4.0%	22	24.6	22
2019	15.7%	29	31.3	30	-7.8%	10	18.6	8

Quinn and team president Rich McKay have raved over Morris' leadership and communication skills, and perhaps he will be able to draw better play out of a group whose greater sample of ineffectiveness suggests they may be undertalented. That said, the narrative that Morris authored the team's second-half defensive turnaround last season is flawed. At the very least, he had some co-writing assistance from the team's strength of schedule split (Table 2).

The 2016 Falcons defense improved despite facing better offenses in the second half of that season. The team was justified in its belief that they could maintain that progress into the next season. However, the Falcons' defensive improvements in 2017, 2018, and, yes, 2019 all followed second-half

Table 2. Falcons' Strength of Opposing Offense

Season	Weeks 1-9		Week 10-17	
	DVOA	Rk	DVOA	Rk
2016	-2.8%	32	-1.4%	21
2017	3.1%	4	-1.6%	20
2018	4.1%	1	1.1%	11
2019	0.2%	18	-3.0%	24

schedules against significantly worse offenses. And while the schedule may not fully explain the team's jumps from four forced turnovers and a 22.9% defensive DVOA in the red zone (fourth-worst in football) in the first half of 2019 to 16 forced turnovers and a -27.7% defensive DVOA in the red zone (seventh-best) in the second half, it does hint at the important truth that full-season defensive DVOA rates better predict future efficiency (0.38 correlation from 2002 to 2019) than second-half defensive DVOA rates (0.32 correlation).

The Falcons have been in and remain in a difficult position. No team has ever come closer to the ultimate prize of a championship and yet come up short. That bitter ending demanded the efforts they have made to take more bites at the apple. The trajectory of their ultimately disappointing seasons since and the fact that a bad defense is more likely than a bad offense to improve from one year to the next provided them with reasonable assurances that they could avenge their Super Bowl loss.

And maybe they still can. The division-rival Saints have demonstrated how one stellar draft class can propel a good team to several years of Super Bowl contention. Maybe cornerback A.J. Terrell, defensive tackle Marlon Davidson, center Matt Hennessy, and linebacker Mykal Walker can do for the Falcons what Marshon Lattimore, Ryan Ramczyk, Marcus Williams, and Alvin Kamara did for the Saints. Those draft picks play the positions where the Falcons could most use some upgrades, and the same can be said for defensive end free agent and tight end trade additions Dante Fowler and Hayden Hurst. But that 2017 Saints draft class is lauded as much because of the rarity of its success as its success itself. Teams seldom hit on every pick in the first four rounds. The Falcons know that from the first-hand experience of their recent draft classes.

If the Falcons fall short of an historically successful draft, it won't be a disaster in 2020. Even with an average draft impact, we project the team to finish with an above-average overall DVOA. That stems from a typically above-average offensive DVOA and a modest improvement in defensive DVOA that captures the belabored point of defensive regression and the very real upgrades they made at defensive end in Fowler, cornerback in Terrell, and hopefully safety in a healthy Neal, whom the team kept on his fifth-year option when they could have released him to save $6.5 million in cap space. Those decisions, plus the trade of a second-round pick for Hurst, are good ones for a team in a championship window.

The problem comes if, as the defensive research suggests, the Falcons are misreading their chances to be competitive this season. With the expanded playoffs, the 12th-best team has a better chance of a postseason berth than it did in prior years. But the Falcons aren't a typical 12th-best team. They are the peak Tampa Bay Rays from the 2000s American League East when they spent less than half as much money as the division-rival Yankees and Red Sox. In a salary-capped NFL, the Saints and Buccaneers don't have that same financial advantage, but they have realized one in the value over cost of star players on rookie contracts such as the Saints' 2017 draft class and the Bucs' trio of Chris Godwin, Vita Vea, and Devin White. Those savings allowed the Saints and Bucs the luxury of signing free agents such as Malcolm Jenkins, Emmanuel Sanders, and Tom Brady, which in turn propelled them to first and fifth in projected DVOA this season. The Falcons were forced to backload Fowler's contract to fit him on their books and couldn't sign any other player to a multi-year deal or even a one-year deal worth more than Todd Gurley's $5.5 million this offseason. It's not a fair fight, and that—plus the NFC South's misfortune of non-divisional matchups with the NFC North and AFC West—is why our mean projection for Atlanta includes the league's second-hardest schedule and results in an under-.500 record.

If the Falcons fall short again in 2020, then it likely will cost Quinn his job and kick off a rebuild. But that may be a year too late. The team's decision to cling to their current core this offseason likely extended the valley of their eventual rebuild. Fowler's back-loaded contract spikes to $18.6-million and $19.6-million cap hits the next two years, and as it stands today, the Falcons have the third-lowest available cap space in 2021 followed by the lowest available cap space in 2022. Fans will happily take that future losing if it comes on the heels of a Super Bowl victory. It just doesn't seem likely that the current Falcons have that high of a ceiling.

Scott Spratt

2019 Falcons Stats by Week

Wk	vs.	W-L	PF	PA	YDF	YDA	TO	Total	Off	Def	ST
1	at MIN	L	12	28	345	269	-3	-39%	-16%	17%	-6%
2	PHI	W	24	20	367	286	0	-7%	-19%	-21%	-9%
3	at IND	L	24	27	397	379	-1	22%	49%	28%	0%
4	TEN	L	10	24	422	365	-1	5%	1%	-13%	-9%
5	at HOU	L	32	53	373	592	0	-61%	-9%	47%	-4%
6	at ARI	L	33	34	444	442	0	6%	39%	29%	-3%
7	LAR	L	10	37	224	381	-3	-74%	-51%	9%	-14%
8	SEA	L	20	27	510	322	-3	-23%	18%	29%	-12%
9	BYE										
10	at NO	W	26	9	317	310	-1	21%	-12%	-30%	3%
11	at CAR	W	29	3	349	347	+4	55%	6%	-40%	8%
12	TB	L	22	35	337	446	0	-56%	-28%	31%	3%
13	NO	L	18	26	348	279	-3	-20%	-18%	-9%	-10%
14	CAR	W	40	20	461	345	+4	4%	15%	21%	10%
15	at SF	W	29	22	290	313	+1	59%	37%	-22%	1%
16	JAX	W	24	12	518	288	-1	8%	23%	2%	-12%
17	at TB	W	28	22	373	329	+2	25%	3%	-13%	10%

Trends and Splits

	Offense	Rank	Defense	Rank
Total DVOA	2.0%	15	4.5%	20
Unadjusted VOA	0.5%	16	8.7%	24
Weighted Trend	2.8%	12	-0.2%	15
Variance	7.2%	16	6.7%	21
Average Opponent	-1.4%	8	2.2%	7
Passing	16.3%	12	17.0%	25
Rushing	-10.4%	22	-10.7%	14
First Down	-3.6%	19	3.7%	20
Second Down	-2.8%	15	8.3%	24
Third Down	21.8%	6	0.0%	16
First Half	-8.0%	16	8.6%	25
Second Half	6.8%	12	-0.4%	12
Red Zone	0.1%	17	3.0%	18
Late and Close	9.7%	8	-4.4%	15

Five-Year Performance

Year	W-L	Pyth W	Est W	PF	PA	TO	Total	Rk	Off	Rk	Def	Rk	ST	Rk	Off AGL	Rk	Def AGL	Rk	Off Age	Rk	Def Age	Rk	ST Age	Rk
2015	8-8	7.8	5.8	339	345	-7	-16.3%	26	-7.3%	23	6.9%	22	-2.1%	22	10.0	2	18.4	4	27.5	8	26.9	14	26.7	5
2016	11-5	10.9	11.8	540	406	+11	19.8%	3	24.6%	1	7.3%	26	2.5%	7	18.5	2	32.3	12	27.8	5	26.0	25	27.3	2
2017	10-6	9.1	8.5	353	315	-2	1.4%	15	8.1%	9	5.6%	22	-1.2%	19	10.4	4	4.5	2	27.4	8	25.7	25	26.5	5
2018	7-9	7.8	7.5	414	423	+1	-3.0%	18	8.8%	8	13.3%	31	1.4%	10	32.2	13	43.7	26	28.1	4	26.4	13	26.7	3
2019	7-9	7.5	7.6	381	399	-5	-5.3%	17	2.0%	15	4.5%	20	-2.9%	28	15.5	5	37.7	19	27.7	4	26.4	13	26.3	8

2019 Performance Based on Most Common Personnel Groups

ATL Offense					ATL Offense vs. Opponents					ATL Defense					ATL Defense vs. Opponents			
Pers	Freq	Yds	DVOA	Run%	Pers	Freq	Yds	DVOA	Run%	Pers	Freq	Yds	DVOA	Pers	Freq	Yds	DVOA
11	60%	5.9	10.2%	17%	Base	34%	5.6	0.8%	53%	Base	24%	6.6	15.1%		11	61%	5.8	3.5%
12	15%	6.0	4.4%	46%	Nickel	49%	5.7	15.3%	23%	Nickel	71%	5.9	0.4%		12	17%	5.6	-7.2%
21	12%	5.3	1.3%	54%	Dime+	17%	6.4	0.9%	5%	Dime+	2%	6.8	83.0%		21	6%	6.3	3.8%
10	3%	5.9	-0.9%	8%	Goal Line	0%	0.3	-128.9%	50%	Goal Line	1%	0.9	-4.4%		13	5%	5.6	10.3%
22	3%	5.6	13.1%	74%						Big	3%	2.8	-46.5%		611	3%	8.7	43.2%
13	2%	4.5	-12.0%	73%											10	2%	8.2	26.4%

Strategic Tendencies

Run/Pass		Rk	Formation		Rk	Pass Rush		Rk	Secondary		Rk	Strategy		Rk
Runs, first half	33%	29	Form: Single Back	75%	25	Rush 3	11.1%	12	4 DB	24%	20	Play Action	22%	25
Runs, first down	40%	31	Form: Empty Back	7%	19	Rush 4	65.0%	15	5 DB	71%	6	Offensive Motion	36%	18
Runs, second-long	19%	31	Form: Multi Back	17%	9	Rush 5	20.7%	16	6+ DB	2%	28	Avg Box (Off)	6.45	26
Runs, power sit.	52%	21	Pers: 3+ WR	65%	18	Rush 6+	3.2%	24	Man Coverage	39%	5	Avg Box (Def)	6.80	3
Runs, behind 2H	21%	32	Pers: 2+ TE/6+ OL	23%	22	Edge Rusher Sacks	60.7%	12	CB by Sides	87%	8	Offensive Pace	29.92	9
Pass, ahead 2H	51%	9	Pers: 6+ OL	2%	16	Interior DL Sacks	32.1%	8	S/CB Cover Ratio	31%	6	Defensive Pace	29.75	5
Run-Pass Options	6%	13	Shotgun/Pistol	58%	23	Second Level Sacks	7.1%	31	DB Blitz	5%	31	Go for it on 4th	1.25	21

Atlanta ran only 17% of the time when they had three or more wide receivers in the game, the lowest rate in the league. They ranked 29th in DVOA on these runs. ●, Atlanta receivers were second in the league in both fewest drops and lowest rate of drops. ●, The Falcons had the worst DVOA in the league on passes at or behind the line of scrimmage. ●, For the fourth straight year, the Falcons were particularly strong with an empty backfield. Last year, this meant 6.8 yards per pass and 25.3% DVOA. ●, Atlanta recovered just three of 16 fumbles on defense. ●, Falcons opponents threw just 15% of their passes to the middle of the field, dead last in the league (compared to a league average of 24%). ●, One reason the Falcons didn't send a lot of defensive back blitzes may have been that they were terrible on these plays: league-worst 9.1 net yards allowed per pass with 56.0% DVOA. ●, Atlanta tied for the smallest gap between where their two safeties made their average play, suggesting interchangeable safeties instead of more-defined roles as free and strong safety. ●, The Atlanta defense increased from 29th in average box count in 2018 to third in 2019.

Passing

Player	DYAR	DVOA	Plays	NtYds	Avg	YAC	C%	TD	Int
M.Ryan	732	6.5%	663	4152	6.3	4.0	66.3%	26	14
M.Schaub	217	37.6%	67	561	8.4	5.3	76.9%	3	1

Rushing

Player	DYAR	DVOA	Plays	Yds	Avg	TD	Fum	Suc
D.Freeman*	-19	-11.1%	184	661	3.6	2	2	41%
B.Hill	14	-4.1%	78	323	4.1	2	0	44%
M.Ryan	38	18.1%	25	156	6.2	1	1	-
I.Smith	27	13.7%	22	106	4.8	1	0	55%
Q.Ollison	-3	-11.1%	22	50	2.3	4	1	55%
K.Smith	5	4.6%	5	8	1.6	0	0	80%
K.Barner*	9	58.5%	4	28	7.0	0	0	75%
T.Gurley	58	-2.4%	223	858	3.8	12	3	48%

Receiving

Player	DYAR	DVOA	Plays	Ctch	Yds	Y/C	YAC	TD	C%
J.Jones	299	11.6%	157	99	1394	14.1	3.5	6	63%
C.Ridley	310	30.6%	93	63	866	13.7	2.2	7	68%
R.Gage	-8	-14.1%	74	49	446	9.1	3.1	1	66%
M.Sanu*	45	1.2%	42	33	313	9.5	3.7	1	79%
J.Hardy*	8	-8.5%	26	19	195	10.3	4.3	0	73%
C.Blake	-41	-34.3%	24	11	91	8.3	2.2	0	46%
L.Treadwell	53	31.7%	16	9	184	20.4	6.3	1	56%
A.Hooper*	130	12.5%	97	75	787	10.5	4.4	6	77%
L.Stocker*	-61	-75.5%	14	8	53	6.6	4.5	0	57%
J.Graham	55	74.0%	10	9	149	16.6	8.1	1	90%
H.Hurst	89	28.1%	39	30	349	11.6	4.9	2	77%
D.Freeman*	51	-0.9%	70	59	410	6.9	5.8	4	84%
B.Hill	23	16.5%	14	10	69	6.9	5.4	1	71%
I.Smith	-1	-14.7%	14	11	87	7.9	6.5	0	79%
K.Barner*	-6	-30.6%	8	6	22	3.7	4.5	0	75%
T.Gurley	0	-13.8%	49	31	207	6.7	6.3	2	63%

Offensive Line

Player	Pos	Age	GS	Snaps	Pen	Sk	Pass	Run	Player	Pos	Age	GS	Snaps	Pen	Sk	Pass	Run
Jake Matthews	LT	28	16/16	1189	7	5.0	21	2	James Carpenter	LG	31	11/11	692	7	5.0	16	3
Alex Mack	C	35	16/16	1182	7	2.5	11	5	Jamon Brown	RG	27	10/9	602	6	0.0	7	6
Kaleb McGary	RT	25	16/16	1128	6	13.5	37	9	Chris Lindstrom	RG	23	5/5	315	1	0.5	7	5
Wes Schweitzer*	LG/RG	27	15/7	711	5	2.0	12	6	Justin McCray	LT/RT	28	15/4	332	4	2.5	11	2

Year	Yards	ALY	Rank	Power	Rank	Stuff	Rank	2nd Lev	Rank	Open Field	Rank	Sacks	ASR	Rank	Press	Rank	F-Start	Cont.
2017	4.25	4.35	8	64%	17	21%	20	1.25	6	0.85	10	24	4.8%	8	31.5%	19	17	34
2018	4.59	4.08	24	60%	27	25%	31	1.29	13	1.30	2	42	6.6%	14	28.2%	12	15	28
2019	3.73	3.98	24	65%	16	21%	27	1.08	25	0.52	27	50	6.6%	13	32.1%	24	19	27
2019 ALY by direction:			Left End 3.21 (27)			Left Tackle: 4.56 (11)			Mid/Guard: 3.79 (31)				Right Tackle: 4.08 (18)			Right End: 4.74 (12)		

The Falcons' offensive line ended the season on their own high note with Ty Sambrailo catching a 35-yard touchdown pass, the longest in NFL history for a lineman. Little else went right for a unit that has gotten worse in run-blocking in three consecutive seasons. ●, The Falcons tried to stem the tide of that decline by drafting right guard Chris Lindstrom and right tackle Kaleb McGary in the first round in 2019—the latter by virtue of a trade that cost the team its second- and third-round picks that season. That investment didn't pay immediate dividends as Lindstrom broke his foot in Week 1 and missed the bulk of the season while McGary floundered as a rookie, leading the league with 46 blown blocks and 13.5 sacks allowed. He also failed to improve from the first half (21 blown blocks) to the second half (25) of the season, but both he and Lindstrom almost certainly will do more for the team in 2020 than they did in their rookie years. ●, The Falcons signed James Carpenter and Jamon Brown to compete for the left guard position last offseason, but they both ended up as starters for much of the season following Lindstrom's injury. Neither player excelled in his role, and both players ranked in the bottom half of snaps per blown block.

Still, they'll have chances to rebound in 2020 thanks to $5.4-million and $8.4-million respective dead cap figures that prevent them from being released before 2021. ❧ Lindstrom, McGary, Carpenter, and Brown are big linemen and perhaps curious fits for a zone-blocking run scheme that tends to favor speed over size. Based on appearance, they fit better with offensive coordinator Dirk Koetter's traditional commitment to power-blocking and could suggest a transition away from the Kyle Shanahan offensive philosophy, even if that transition didn't show up in a decline in outside zone carries in 2019. ❧ Left tackle Jake Matthews and center Alex Mack are the holdover stars from the Super Bowl team. But after blowing just 13 combined blocks in 2018, Matthews and Mack combined for 39 blown blocks last season. At 28 years old, Matthews is the better bet to rebound in 2020. And the Falcons seem to agree. They selected Temple center Matt Hennessy in the third round to eventually take over for the 34-year-old Mack and to round out a bench that includes the loser of the Carpenter-Brown left guard starting battle, free-agent addition Justin McCray, swing tackle John Wetzel, and undrafted sophomore Matt Gono.

Defensive Front

Defensive Line	Age	Pos	G	Snaps	Plays	Overall TmPct	Rk	Stop	Dfts	BTkl	Runs	vs. Run St%	Rk	RuYd	Rk	Pass Rush Sack	Hit	Hur	Dsrpt
Grady Jarrett	27	DT	16	821	69	8.7%	3	52	25	7	61	72%	64	1.9	25	7.5	9	31	2
Tyeler Davison	28	DT	16	568	55	7.0%	13	32	7	1	52	56%	95	2.7	70	1.0	1	5	0
Jack Crawford*	32	DT	16	436	27	3.4%	74	20	7	2	18	83%	19	2.2	40	0.5	5	9	1
Jacob Tuioti-Mariner	24	DT	8	188	14	3.5%	--	10	4	0	12	75%	--	1.5	--	0.0	1	5	0

Edge Rushers	Age	Pos	G	Snaps	Plays	Overall TmPct	Rk	Stop	Dfts	BTkl	Runs	vs. Run St%	Rk	RuYd	Rk	Pass Rush Sack	Hit	Hur	Dsrpt
Vic Beasley*	28	DE	16	774	44	5.6%	37	35	18	7	27	78%	28	2.9	59	8.0	4	25	1
Takkarist McKinley	25	DE	14	557	29	4.2%	62	20	10	2	23	70%	62	2.9	64	3.5	11	23	3
Allen Bailey	31	DE	15	521	24	3.2%	74	19	6	5	23	78%	27	2.4	44	1.0	2	7	0
Adrian Clayborn*	32	DE	15	446	16	2.2%	91	13	9	2	9	78%	28	1.8	19	4.0	4	24	0
Dante Fowler	26	OLB	16	890	61	7.2%	13	51	25	8	40	80%	21	2.9	58	11.5	4	39	8
Charles Harris	25	DE	14	436	22	3.0%	84	11	3	1	19	42%	89	3.8	85	0.5	6	7	1

Linebackers	Age	Pos	G	Snaps	Plays	Overall TmPct	Rk	Stop	Dfts	BTkl	Runs	vs. Run St%	Rk	RuYd	Rk	Pass Rush Sack	Hit	Hur	Tgts	vs. Pass Suc%	Rk	AdjYd	Rk	PD	Int
Deion Jones	26	MLB	16	965	115	14.6%	20	45	22	19	61	41%	79	5.3	79	0.0	4	7	41	59%	13	5.2	14	5	1
De'Vondre Campbell*	27	OLB	16	937	133	16.8%	9	64	22	8	70	60%	42	4.2	59	2.0	1	7	39	33%	65	7.9	54	5	2
Foyesade Oluokun	25	MLB	16	312	56	7.1%	--	29	7	3	32	59%	--	3.7	--	0.0	1	0	11	91%	--	3.5	--	0	0
Deone Bucannon	28	ILB	14	247	26	3.5%	--	10	2	2	13	46%	--	3.8	--	0.0	1	3	6	33%	--	8.7	--	0	0

Year	Yards	ALY	Rank	Power	Rank	Stuff	Rank	2nd Level	Rank	Open Field	Rank	Sacks	ASR	Rank	Press	Rank
2017	3.84	4.15	19	76%	29	20%	17	1.09	13	0.51	4	39	6.6%	16	29.5%	22
2018	4.66	5.07	31	74%	27	14%	32	1.25	18	0.80	15	37	6.6%	25	25.7%	30
2019	4.25	4.29	19	64%	15	22%	6	1.24	22	0.77	18	28	5.8%	28	27.0%	27
2019 ALY by direction:			Left End: 4.47 (24)			Left Tackle: 3.11 (3)			Mid/Guard: 4.4 (15)			Right Tackle: 4.59 (21)			Right End: 5.34 (25)	

The Falcons have no buyer's remorse for Grady Jarrett. After signing a four-year, $68-million extension prior to the 2019 season, Jarrett responded with career highs of 25 defeats, 31 hurries, and 7.5 sacks and made his first Pro Bowl. ❧ Free-agent addition Tyeler Davison was supposed to be Jarrett's complementary run-stuffer, but despite reaching a career high of 55 combined tackles, Davison declined from an 80% run stop rate in three seasons as a starter for the Saints to 56% in 2019 for the Falcons. The Falcons still extended Davison for three years and $12 million this offseason, but a team option to release him after 2020 for just a $2.4-million cap hit makes his long-term marriage with the team tenuous. ❧ Part of Davison's uncertainty stems from the Falcons selection of defensive tackle Marlon Davidson in the second round of the 2020 draft. At just 303 pounds, Davidson comes from Jarrett's undersized mold. As a frequent pass-rusher, he even led his 2019 Auburn team with 6.5 sacks. The Falcons will hope that he can become Jarrett's running mate, something that undersized 2018 third-rounder Deadrin Senat never managed. Senat spent the majority of 2019 as a healthy inactive. ❧ The Falcons have made even greater efforts to increase their pass rush in recent seasons, but first-rounders Vic Beasley and Takk McKinley famously failed to deliver on their promise. Their combined total of 48 hurries trailed nine individual defenders from 2019. ❧ With Beasley gone in free agency, the Falcons will try again to boost their pass rush with free-agent additions Dante Fowler and Charles Harris. Fowler's 39 hurries and 11.5 sacks for the Rams in 2019 were career highs, but 2019 was also his only full season alongside two-time defensive player of the year Aaron Donald. Harris may be a first-round bust like McKinley, but he did showcase some positional versatility as the Dolphins switched to a 3-4 under Brian Flores in 2019, a welcome trait for a team that lost veteran outside linebacker De'Vondre Campbell in free agency. ◈ Deion Jones will have even more responsibility in 2020 with linebacker conversions like Harris and Deone Bucannon alongside him. Unfortunately for the team, Jones has slipped from a 14.5% broken tackle rate before his broken foot in 2018 to a 20.0% rate since. It would help the team tremendously if Fresno State fourth-rounder Mykal Walker could contribute as a rookie this season. Walker's strong statistical production in college clashes with some of the scouting reports that criticize his physicality and ability to stack and shed offensive linemen.

Defensive Secondary

Secondary	Age	Pos	G	Snaps	Plays	Overall TmPct	Rk	Stop	Dfts	BTkl	vs. Run Runs	St%	Rk	RuYd	Rk	vs. Pass Tgts	Tgt%	Rk	Dist	Suc%	Rk	AdjYd	Rk	PD	Int
Ricardo Allen	29	FS	16	969	92	11.6%	13	35	16	11	40	43%	36	8.7	50	37	10.0%	17	11.4	59%	18	7.7	41	8	2
Isaiah Oliver	24	CB	16	944	72	9.1%	21	26	8	9	15	53%	29	5.3	30	81	22.4%	22	12.3	46%	69	9.5	72	11	0
Damontae Kazee	27	SS	16	817	72	9.1%	36	18	10	14	27	22%	67	9.8	59	26	8.3%	33	12.1	50%	43	9.7	62	3	3
Kendall Sheffield	24	CB	16	708	46	5.8%	73	8	3	6	10	20%	77	8.3	65	40	14.7%	82	8.9	38%	83	8.3	60	3	0
Desmond Trufant*	30	CB	9	535	24	5.4%	85	12	8	7	4	75%	8	4.5	22	31	15.1%	78	13.2	39%	82	10.3	79	7	4
Blidi Wreh-Wilson	31	CB	14	339	31	4.5%	--	13	5	4	6	33%	--	6.0	--	32	24.6%	--	12.4	56%	--	7.4	--	7	0
Kemal Ishmael*	29	SS	14	288	41	5.9%	--	17	5	6	24	58%	--	3.4	--	15	13.6%	--	9.5	27%	--	10.1	--	0	0

Year	Pass D Rank	vs. #1 WR	Rk	vs. #2 WR	Rk	vs. Other WR	Rk	WR Wide	Rk	WR Slot	Rk	vs. TE	Rk	vs. RB	Rk
2017	20	14.6%	25	19.3%	25	-7.9%	12	-2.3%	16	17.8%	23	-2.3%	14	8.4%	21
2018	29	15.8%	27	-6.3%	11	16.7%	27	14.7%	28	5.6%	21	0.9%	15	13.5%	28
2019	25	4.0%	18	29.4%	30	20.7%	27	15.2%	27	16.4%	25	-11.0%	6	-7.9%	13

It's difficult to disentangle the Falcons' secondary troubles from their lack of a pass rush, but it remains clear that the team's cornerbacks underwhelmed in 2019. Earlier in the chapter, we highlighted Isaiah Oliver's struggles as he filled in as the team's No. 1 corner for an injured Desmond Trufant, but Kendall Sheffield (38%), Trufant (39%), and Jamar Taylor (40%) all had even worse coverage success rates than Oliver (46%). Among corners who saw 30 or more targets, they were all in the bottom 20. It's little wonder the team was below average in DVOA against every wide receiver grouping. ◈ The Falcons used their 16th overall pick on Clemson cornerback A.J. Terrell, who should replace the departing Trufant as the team's top corner and ease Oliver's, Sheffield's, and Blidi Wreh-Wilson's assignments if he can transition comfortably to the NFL in his rookie season. If Terrell has a difficult transition, then the Falcons will likely draw heavy criticism for selecting him ahead of corners including Jeff Gladney, Trevon Diggs, Jaylon Johnson, and Kristian Fulton, whom many scouts ranked ahead of Terrell. ◈ Safety Ricardo Allen returned from his 2018 Achilles tear to play the full 2019 season, but fellow safety Keanu Neal compounded his 2018 ACL tear with an Achilles tear in Week 3. Neal has now missed 28 of a possible 32 games for the Falcons the last two seasons. The team could have cut the former Pro Bowler to save $6.4 million in cap space, but they opted to retain him in the final year of his rookie deal. Atlanta could really use the 48 stops and 18 defeats from his Pro Bowl 2017 season given the team's undermanned linebacker corps.

Special Teams

Year	DVOA	Rank	FG/XP	Rank	Net Kick	Rank	Kick Ret	Rank	Net Punt	Rank	Punt Ret	Rank	Hidden	Rank
2017	-1.2%	19	6.4	9	-4.5	25	-3.6	25	-1.0	19	-3.1	25	-3.0	16
2018	1.4%	10	12.0	1	-0.7	18	-2.4	22	1.0	16	-2.7	21	-11.3	28
2019	-2.9%	28	-4.8	25	1.6	13	-1.1	16	-5.6	24	-4.3	27	5.9	8

Two of the team's three long-time Matts had likely their last seasons with the Falcons in 2019, concluding a combined 20 years with the team. Punter Matt Bosher suffered and later re-aggravated a groin injury that limited him to three games. Short-term replacement Matt Wile fared better than Kasey Redfern but suffered his own groin injury, paving the way for long-time Patriots punter Ryan Allen to close out the second half of the season and potentially win the job for 2020. Allen's 41.9 yards per punt average—more than 4.0 yards below his career average—won't help. ◈ The 44-year-old Matt Bryant wasn't the team's first plan for 2019, but poor preseason performances by Giorgio Tavecchio and Blair Walsh had them re-signing Bryant on the eve of the regular season. He promptly missed five of 14 attempts and an extra point before being released at the end of October. ◈ Desperation likely led the Falcons to audition Younghoe Koo after Bryant's release. Koo infamously missed three of his first six career attempts for the Chargers in 2017 and hadn't kicked in the league since. But Koo took advantage of his second chance, converting 23 of 26 attempts and authoring what may have been the most improbable result of the 2019 season when he initiated three successful onside kicks (including one called back due to a penalty) against the Saints on Thanksgiving. That was more successes than the entire league had managed to that point of the season. Of course, the Falcons still lost the game.

❧ The Falcons escaped their two-year stint in the bottom three teams in average starting field position with a 29.2-yard-line average in 2019 (seventh), but they can't thank their return game for the boost. Even with a kickoff return touchdown, Kenjon Barner finished in the bottom half of both kickoff and punt returners in yards per return. Undrafted receiver Chris Rowland could earn those returner jobs in 2020—he had both kickoff and punt returns for touchdowns at Tennessee State. Brandon Powell and Olamide Zaccheaus are candidates as well.

Baltimore Ravens

2019 Record: 14-2	**Total DVOA:** 41.8% (1st)	**2020 Mean Projection:** 10.0 wins	**On the Clock (0-4):** 2%
Pythagorean Wins: 13.4 (1st)	**Offense:** 27.7% (1st)	**Postseason Odds:** 73.7%	**Mediocrity (5-7):** 14%
Snap-Weighted Age: 26.5 (13rd)	**Defense:** -12.7% (4th)	**Super Bowl Odds:** 18.2%	**Playoff Contender (8-10):** 39%
Average Opponent: -2.2% (23rd)	**Special Teams:** 1.5% (9th)	**Proj. Avg. Opponent:** -1.1% (25th)	**Super Bowl Contender (11+):** 45%

2019: Regular-season domination, playoff faceplant.

2020: Super Bowl or Bust.

The Baltimore Ravens' championship window is wide-open, thanks to the brilliant play of their MVP quarterback Lamar Jackson—who is also quite conveniently entering only the third year of his rookie contract, giving the front office the financial flexibility to go all in on a Super Bowl run. Few teams can match Baltimore's balance of an explosive (if unconventional) offense and a lockdown defense. The coaching staff under John Harbaugh returns mostly whole. When offensive coordinator Greg Roman, the architect of the historically effective running game, did not get a head coaching gig, it was an important if unheralded early victory for the 2020 Ravens. By most accounts the draft was an unmitigated success, loading the team with still more young talent. The Ravens are also right at the top of the league in applying analytics, particularly when it comes to in-game decisions. From top to bottom, it is hard to find many flaws in the organization.

Of course, this was the case last year, too, and (mostly) the season before as well, and it didn't stop the Ravens from flaming out of the playoffs on both occasions. The team leapt through the aforementioned championship window but missed grabbing the fire escape and plummeted to the street below.

So will the 2020 Ravens joyously bound through the open window and land on a parade float, or will they once again be defenestrated like a Russian whistleblower?

2019 was shaping up to be a dream season in the Inner Harbor. Baltimore won 14 games, including its last 12 straight, cruising to the top seed in the AFC. They led the league in points scored and point differential by a wide margin. But for the second straight season with Jackson under center, Harbaugh's group came up limp in its first playoff game, once again losing dismally at home, this time to Tennessee. Baltimore dominated the box score, rolling up 530 yards and 29 first downs, but Jackson threw a pair of interceptions and Derrick Henry ran roughshod through the Ravens all night. It was a sudden and ignominious end to what had been four months of nearly uninterrupted success.

The 2019 Ravens ran away with the DVOA title, beating the second-place Patriots by a full 11.0% and ending the season as one of the top 10 regular-season teams in DVOA history (Table 1). They were tops in both rushing and passing offense and fourth in passing defense. The Ravens also led the league in all our crucial offensive drive metrics, including points, yards, plays, and time of possession per drive, along with success rate. Unlike previous powerhouse teams from the Charm City, these Ravens shot to the top in style, as Jackson proved an unstoppable, untackleable, unmissable force, a whirling dervish while carrying the ball and a hugely efficient passer when throwing it. Lamar was NFL RedZone Must-See TV, a weekly highlight package that began in Week 1 with a 17-of-20, 324-yard, five-touchdown passing masterpiece in Miami. He rushed for 120 yards the following Sunday against the Cardinals, and each weekend thereafter added a new plank to his MVP candidacy, which eventually ended with Jackson winning the award unanimously.

Table 1. Top Regular-Season Teams by Total DVOA, 1985-2019

Year	Team	W-L	Total DVOA
1991	WAS	14-2	56.9%
2007	NE	16-0	52.9%
1985	CHI	15-1	52.5%
1987	SF	10-2*	47.0%
2010	NE	14-2	44.6%
1996	GB	13-3	42.0%
2019	**BAL**	**14-2**	**41.8%**
2013	SEA	13-3	40.0%
1995	SF	11-5	40.0%
2012	SEA	11-5	38.7%
2015	SEA	10-6	38.1%
2004	PIT	15-1	37.6%

Strikebreaker games not included.

Jackson topped the NFL in QBR, ranked second in passing DVOA, and finished sixth in passing DYAR, all while working without an established threat at wide receiver. He also notably improved his passing precision, upping his completion percentage from 58.2% to 66.1%, yet somehow he was still dogged by the "inaccurate" and "just a runner" stigmas that accompanied him out of Louisville. But wow, could he run—with 1,206 yards Jackson shattered Michael Vick's single-season record for quarterbacks, while piling up an astounding 273 rushing DYAR, nearly triple that of the next highest quarterback, Josh Allen.

The Ravens were dominant on the ground beyond Jackson,

2020 Ravens Schedule

Week	Opp.	Week	Opp.	Week	Opp.
1	CLE	7	PIT	13	DAL (Thu.)
2	at HOU	8	BYE	14	at CLE (Mon.)
3	KC (Mon.)	9	at IND	15	JAX
4	at WAS	10	at NE	16	NYG
5	CIN	11	TEN	17	at CIN
6	at PHI	12	at PIT (Thu.)		

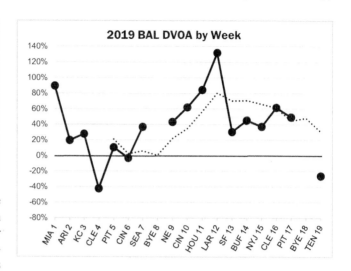

2019 BAL DVOA by Week

thanks to a powerhouse line that paved the way for two of the top 11 running backs by DYAR in the league, Mark Ingram and Gus Edwards. (The running back room got even deeper on draft day, when Baltimore added the sensational J.K. Dobbins from Ohio State in Round 2.) Defenses were powerless to slow down the ground-based attack—Baltimore rushed it nearly 100 more times, and for nearly 1,000 more yards, than the second-place running team (San Francisco), and at 5.5 yards per attempt averaged a full half-yard more than the Cardinals and Titans, who were a distant second in that stat. Baltimore was the only team in the league with more runs than pass plays (including sacks). Even if we count Jackson's scrambles as pass plays, the Ravens still ran the ball 51% of the time, the highest rate since the 2011 Tim Tebow Broncos at 53%. While the rest of the NFL was obsessed with finding new ways to wing it, Baltimore zagged into throwback football and was incredibly successful.

The threat of Jackson's incredible efficiency by air or by land emboldened Harbaugh to be almost comically aggressive on fourth down, going for it on an unheard-of 23% of qualifying all-or-nothing downs while shattering the Aggressiveness Index record at 3.95. In other words, Harbaugh went for it roughly four times as often as the average coach, by far the most often of any coach since we've tracked the data. The Ravens were successful, too, going 17-for-24 on fourth downs, a 70.8% clip. Unfortunately, in the playoff loss to Tennessee the Ravens went 0-for-4 on fourth down, a major factor in the upset loss. After swinging his *huevos* around all season, Harbaugh got kicked in the onions at the worst possible time.

There were a few other reasons that Baltimore's high efficiency attack was unusual for the modern NFL. Far more than any other team, the Ravens utilized the pistol formation made popular by the college game, with Jackson a few steps behind the center (similar to shotgun) but with a running back further behind him and ready to take a handoff. Baltimore used the pistol on 53.3% of offensive plays. No other offense in the league used the pistol on more than 6.1% of offensive plays. The Ravens had almost 500 more pistol plays than the next-highest offense (Arizona). The Ravens had 26.1% DVOA on pistol plays, and 28% of pistol plays were passes or scrambles while 72% were planned runs.

Baltimore also featured more tight ends than a 1970s roller disco movie. The Ravens set a modern NFL record by targeting the troika of Mark Andrews, Nick Boyle, and Hayden Hurst on an amazing 42% of the team's passes (Table 2).

Table 2. Highest Rate of Targeting Tight Ends, 1985-2019

Year	Team	TE Pct	Main Tight Ends
2019	**BAL**	**42%**	**M.Andrews, N.Boyle, H.Hurst**
1985	TB	40%	J.Bell, J.Giles, C.Magee
2011	NE	39%	R.Gronkowski, A.Hernandez
2019	**PHI**	**39%**	**Z.Ertz, D.Goedert**
2015	TEN	37%	D.Walker, A.Fasano, C.Stevens
2005	TEN	36%	E.Kinney, B.Sciafe, B.Troupe
2018	PHI	36%	Z.Ertz, D.Goedert
2012	HOU	34%	O.Daniels, J.Casey, G.Graham
2005	WAS	34%	C.Cooley, R.Royal
2006	CLE	33%	K.Winslow, S.Heiden

Note: Rate does not include passes with no intended receiver.

Realizing that enemy defenses will adjust, and so heavy a burden on an offense that ignores wide receivers is probably unsustainable, Baltimore took steps in the offseason to get some passing game diversity. Only a single wideout, rookie burner Marquise "Hollywood" Brown, cracked 50 targets (he was 42nd in the league in DYAR), and Willie Snead and Miles Boykin are limited and inexperienced, respectively. So the Ravens dealt Hurst to Atlanta for a second-round pick and added to the wide receiver room, drafting Texas slot powerhouse Devin Duvernay in the third round and draftnik-crush James Proche from SMU in the sixth. In a sign of the team's desperation for downfield explosiveness, rumors flew during the spring that the Ravens would try to bring in Antonio Brown, if only because Josh Gordon remains unavailable.

Even with depth questions at the wide receiver position, the Ravens still used 11 personnel as their main grouping. And being the Ravens, Baltimore ran it on almost half the snaps they lined up in three-wide formations (48%), and did so with great effectiveness, to the tune of 20.0% DVOA, both league-high totals. They also topped the NFL with an unholy 82.9% DVOA when they lined up with an empty backfield, gaining 8.2 yards per play.

The common denominator to all of these numbers is Jackson's ability to create big plays given any sort of space. His versatility and terrifying speed and quickness allowed Roman to answer any adjustment made by enemy defenses with even more deadly counterattacks. Sit back in zone? OK, we will run it down your throat. Load the box to stop Lamar? OK, we will line up in 11 personnel to force you to defend the perimeter, or we'll throw it over the top. Key on our pistol formation zone-read plays? OK, we will empty the backfield and zip it to a tight end past your onrushing ends. And if you get us into third down and launch a blitz, our pass protection is best in the league at pressure rate on the money down, so watch helplessly as Jackson runs or throws past the sticks.

With Jackson in command all things are possible, and our projection naturally has the Ravens as strong favorites to win the AFC North and compete with Kansas City for the AFC title. Yet there are still pitfalls that can entrap Baltimore.

First and foremost, the team will be without perhaps its second-best and second-most irreplaceable player, right guard Marshal Yanda, who retired after 13 seasons, two first-team All-Pro honors, and a trip to the Pro Bowl every year since 2011 (except 2017, when he was injured). Yanda, a man so ornery he once tasered himself just to see what it felt like, goes out on top—he was typically awesome in 2019, committing zero penalties in 987 snaps and anchoring one of the league's best front fives. Only Zack Martin had a better ratio of snaps per blown block than Yanda. It is highly unlikely the running game suddenly will cease to function without him in there, but it is also hard to believe there won't be any falloff due to his absence.

Meanwhile, the run defense didn't just have a bad game against Tennessee—it was the weak link of the team, coming in at 20th in DVOA. Sure, it is much better to be stout against the pass than the run, but Baltimore remains vulnerable to teams like the Titans that are well-suited to ram it down the Ravens' throats and keep the ball from Jackson as much as possible. The team spent three premium draft picks on helping this part of the defense: two inside linebackers, including first-rounder Patrick Queen of LSU and third-rounder Malik Harrison of Ohio State, along with another third-round pick, nose tackle Justin Madubuike of Texas A&M. Expecting instant impact from these guys is a lot to ask, however, so look for opponents to try and make hay on the ground in 2020. If nothing else, Ravens games should be over much more quickly than the average NFL contest.

The Ravens' pass rush didn't get home enough in 2019, ranking just 15th in adjusted sack rate. However, the Ravens ranked third in defensive pressure rate, which suggests improvement in sacks next season. Defensive coordinator Wink Martindale dialed up the pressure with scheme—no team rushed five more than Baltimore, and only Arizona sent six pass-rushers more often. The Ravens also attacked this area in the offseason with two major personnel moves. First, they placed the franchise tag on leading pass-rusher Matt Judon to make sure they didn't open up a hole at outside linebacker. Then they traded a mere fifth-round pick to Arizona for the venerable Calais Campbell, who has the same number of sacks over the last two seasons as Judon (16.5) and remains a force despite his advancing years. The Ravens have historically made very good use of players nearing their last rodeo, and the 34-year-old Campbell would seem to fill the veteran leadership role quite nicely.

There may be a few nits to pick, and of course, an injury to Jackson would cripple Baltimore's hopes (not to mention depress the league's overall entertainment value considerably), but it is hard to conjure any other scenario where the Ravens aren't a contender in 2020. However, thus far in Jackson's brief foray into pro football, his sh-t hasn't worked in the playoffs, to borrow a line from Billy Beane.

The Ravens are among this century's most successful teams one-fifth of the way in, appearing in 25 playoff games since 2000—tied for fifth-best in the NFL (with arch-rival Pittsburgh, coincidentally)—and winning a pair of Super Bowls. Surprisingly, only seven of those games have been played at home, with the team just 3-4 in Baltimore, while going 12-6 on the road or in neutral sites (by contrast, Pittsburgh has played 13 postseason games at home, going 8-5). Pick any memorable Ravens postseason game—Flacco-to-Jacoby Jones, the Ray Lewis pick-six, the Lee Evans drop—and it invariably happened somewhere other than on a Maryland gridiron. The team had a golden opportunity last season to reverse that trend but flopped.

Maybe it behooves Baltimore to be good—but not too good—in 2020. Save some of that greatness for when the calendar turns to 2021.

Robert Weintraub

2019 Ravens Stats by Week

Wk	vs.	W-L	PF	PA	YDF	YDA	TO	Total	Off	Def	ST
1	at MIA	W	59	10	643	200	+3	90%	46%	-36%	8%
2	ARI	W	23	17	440	349	0	20%	14%	9%	15%
3	at KC	L	28	33	452	503	0	28%	43%	18%	3%
4	CLE	L	25	40	395	530	-2	-42%	-11%	38%	7%
5	at PIT	W	26	23	277	269	-1	11%	-12%	-8%	15%
6	CIN	W	23	17	497	250	0	-3%	12%	-1%	-17%
7	at SEA	W	30	16	340	347	+2	37%	5%	-31%	1%
8	BYE										
9	NE	W	37	20	372	342	0	43%	50%	2%	-5%
10	at CIN	W	49	13	379	307	+2	62%	50%	-14%	-3%
11	HOU	W	41	7	491	232	+2	85%	39%	-52%	-6%
12	at LAR	W	45	6	480	221	+2	132%	64%	-60%	8%
13	SF	W	20	17	283	331	0	30%	23%	1%	9%
14	at BUF	W	24	17	257	209	0	45%	-3%	-48%	0%
15	NYJ	W	42	21	430	310	+2	37%	75%	4%	-34%
16	at CLE	W	31	15	481	241	0	62%	44%	-14%	4%
17	PIT	W	28	10	304	168	0	49%	5%	-26%	18%
18	BYE										
19	TEN	L	12	28	530	300	-3	-26%	-22%	11%	8%

Trends and Splits

	Offense	Rank	Defense	Rank
Total DVOA	27.7%	1	-12.7%	4
Unadjusted VOA	27.7%	1	-16.8%	4
Weighted Trend	32.0%	1	-20.4%	2
Variance	7.3%	17	7.2%	24
Average Opponent	-1.8%	7	-5.2%	30
Passing	47.2%	1	-16.5%	4
Rushing	21.5%	1	-7.0%	20
First Down	17.6%	4	-8.5%	8
Second Down	32.8%	1	-15.3%	6
Third Down	40.8%	2	-16.5%	5
First Half	37.7%	1	-12.4%	7
Second Half	18.0%	5	-13.0%	4
Red Zone	45.1%	1	-12.0%	8
Late and Close	8.5%	11	-4.3%	16

Five-Year Performance

Year	W-L	Pyth W	Est W	PF	PA	TO	Total	Rk	Off	Rk	Def	Rk	ST	Rk	Off AGL	Rk	Def AGL	Rk	Off Age	Rk	Def Age	Rk	ST Age	Rk
2015	5-11	6.0	7.5	328	401	-14	-3.0%	17	-5.2%	20	5.1%	20	7.3%	1	70.0	32	26.8	11	26.5	18	27.1	10	25.6	27
2016	8-8	8.6	9.1	343	321	+5	7.4%	12	-7.5%	24	-9.9%	6	4.9%	4	29.5	12	31.2	11	28.0	3	27.2	5	26.1	18
2017	9-7	10.5	10.4	395	303	+17	18.6%	7	-4.5%	21	-13.9%	3	9.2%	1	62.1	28	42.9	22	27.3	10	27.0	6	25.7	22
2018	10-6	10.8	11.0	389	287	-5	17.0%	6	0.9%	15	-13.1%	3	2.9%	6	17.1	5	11.5	2	26.3	20	27.6	2	25.7	21
2019	14-2	13.4	13.0	531	282	+10	41.8%	1	27.7%	1	-12.7%	4	1.5%	9	9.7	1	59.1	31	25.7	31	27.3	3	26.7	4

2019 Performance Based on Most Common Personnel Groups

BAL Offense					BAL Offense vs. Opponents					BAL Defense				BAL Defense vs. Opponents			
Pers	Freq	Yds	DVOA	Run%	Pers	Freq	Yds	DVOA	Run%	Pers	Freq	Yds	DVOA	Pers	Freq	Yds	DVOA
11	46%	6.3	27.9%	49%	Base	40%	6.3	28.7%	61%	Base	9%	5.0	-19.4%	11	70%	5.4	-10.2%
12	18%	7.1	38.0%	28%	Nickel	49%	6.5	29.1%	47%	Nickel	46%	5.4	-9.4%	12	14%	5.1	-25.9%
22	15%	5.0	12.5%	75%	Dime+	7%	7.8	102.7%	15%	Dime+	44%	5.3	-14.8%	10	4%	5.6	11.8%
21	11%	6.9	23.8%	72%	Goal Line	2%	0.6	21.5%	79%	Goal Line	1%	-0.9	-15.9%	21	4%	5.8	-3.8%
13	6%	8.6	91.4%	34%	Big	2%	4.3	10.7%	64%					611	2%	3.7	12.4%
23	2%	0.8	37.7%	81%													

Strategic Tendencies

Run/Pass		Rk	Formation		Rk	Pass Rush		Rk	Secondary		Rk	Strategy		Rk
Runs, first half	50%	1	Form: Single Back	65%	31	Rush 3	7.4%	16	4 DB	9%	32	Play Action	33%	1
Runs, first down	61%	1	Form: Empty Back	12%	4	Rush 4	47.4%	32	5 DB	46%	25	Offensive Motion	62%	3
Runs, second-long	35%	4	Form: Multi Back	24%	5	Rush 5	34.3%	1	6+ DB	44%	2	Avg Box (Off)	6.83	3
Runs, power sit.	79%	2	Pers: 3+ WR	47%	29	Rush 6+	10.9%	2	Man Coverage	43%	4	Avg Box (Def)	6.47	21
Runs, behind 2H	34%	3	Pers: 2+ TE/6+ OL	43%	4	Edge Rusher Sacks	54.1%	19	CB by Sides	80%	15	Offensive Pace	32.22	27
Pass, ahead 2H	44%	27	Pers: 6+ OL	2%	22	Interior DL Sacks	13.5%	28	S/CB Cover Ratio	16%	30	Defensive Pace	30.00	7
Run-Pass Options	3%	26	Shotgun/Pistol	95%	1	Second Level Sacks	32.4%	1	DB Blitz	28%	1	Go for it on 4th	3.95	1

Baltimore led the league with 168 broken tackles. 🏈 The Ravens had a league low of 27 runs from under-center formations and had just 1.9 yards per carry on those runs. But their DVOA was just slightly below average because 20 of those 27 runs came with just 1 or 2 yards to go. 🏈 Baltimore receivers were tied for the league low with just 16 drops. 🏈 Despite using play-action on a league-high 33% of pass plays, Baltimore was better without play-action (7.4 yards, 58.7% DVOA) than with play-action (7.0, 43.7%). 🏈 The Ravens threw a league-high 36% of passes in the middle of the field. They ranked seventh in DVOA on passes up the middle. 🏈 Baltimore opponents targeted running backs on a league-low 15% of passes. 🏈 The Baltimore defense didn't just send more defensive back blitzes than any other defense; they were also more successful than almost any other defense. Only San Francisco had a better DVOA than Baltimore's -41.3%, and only San Francisco and Buffalo allowed fewer average yards on these plays than Baltimore's 4.6. 🏈 On both sides of the ball, Baltimore was roughly league average in pressure on first and second downs. But on third downs, the Ravens offense allowed the least amount of pressure and the Ravens defense caused the most.

Passing

Player	DYAR	DVOA	Plays	NtYds	Avg	YAC	C%	TD	Int
L.Jackson	1261	34.9%	422	3021	7.2	5.1	66.4%	36	6
R.Griffin	14	-5.9%	43	206	4.8	3.7	60.5%	1	2

Rushing

Player	DYAR	DVOA	Plays	Yds	Avg	TD	Fum	Suc
M.Ingram	257	19.8%	202	1018	5.0	10	2	60%
L.Jackson	273	20.5%	156	1229	7.9	7	7	-
G.Edwards	126	11.8%	133	710	5.3	2	2	56%
J.Hill	13	-2.6%	58	225	3.9	2	0	36%
R.Griffin	5	-6.6%	15	70	4.7	0	0	-

Receiving

Player	DYAR	DVOA	Plays	Ctch	Yds	Y/C	YAC	TD	C%
M.Brown	98	4.2%	71	46	584	12.7	4.9	7	65%
W.Snead	88	12.4%	46	31	339	10.9	4.1	5	67%
S.Roberts*	62	10.4%	35	21	271	12.9	3.3	2	60%
M.Boykin	50	16.2%	22	13	198	15.2	0.9	3	59%
M.Andrews	123	12.1%	98	64	852	13.3	4.5	10	65%
N.Boyle	18	-0.8%	43	31	321	10.4	5.2	2	72%
H.Hurst*	89	28.1%	39	30	349	11.6	4.9	2	77%
M.Ingram	145	74.6%	29	26	247	9.5	8.5	5	90%
J.Hill	9	-3.4%	15	8	70	8.8	10.1	0	53%
P.Ricard	12	4.0%	11	8	47	5.9	6.5	1	73%
G.Edwards	15	24.7%	7	7	45	6.4	6.4	0	100%

Offensive Line

Player	Pos	Age	GS	Snaps	Pen	Sk	Pass	Run	Player	Pos	Age	GS	Snaps	Pen	Sk	Pass	Run
Bradley Bozeman	LG	26	16/16	1125	6	3.0	9	5	Matt Skura	C	27	11/11	734	2	1.0	4	5
Orlando Brown	RT	24	16/16	1125	5	2.5	7	7	Patrick Mekari	C	23	12/5	436	4	0.0	4	2
Marshal Yanda*	RG	36	15/15	987	0	0.0	4	4	James Hurst*	LT	29	16/2	196	0	1.0	2	5
Ronnie Stanley	LT	26	14/14	955	5	0.0	7	2	D.J. Fluker	RG	29	14/14	876	7	3.3	17	6

Year	Yards	ALY	Rank	Power	Rank	Stuff	Rank	2nd Lev	Rank	Open Field	Rank	Sacks	ASR	Rank	Press	Rank	F-Start	Cont.
2017	4.22	4.36	6	69%	7	20%	14	1.27	5	0.70	17	27	4.3%	4	26.1%	6	11	30
2018	4.53	4.59	9	78%	1	15%	3	1.33	7	0.67	24	32	6.1%	8	28.5%	14	23	29
2019	4.97	4.73	3	61%	23	13%	2	1.37	2	0.95	11	28	6.0%	8	28.2%	8	12	36
2019 ALY by direction:			Left End 5.78 (1)			Left Tackle: 3.94 (22)			Mid/Guard: 4.68 (8)			Right Tackle: 5.00 (4)			Right End: 4.73 (13)			

Left tackle Ronnie Stanley had a rock solid season, leading all NFL tackles in snaps per blown block with no sacks allowed while being named first team All-Pro. 🏈 The massive Orlando Brown Jr., may not be as dominant as his father was, or as Stanley is, but he gets the job done just fine on the right side. Stanley is 26 and Brown 24, meaning the team appears set on the edge for the foreseeable future. 🏈 All eyes will be on the battle to fill Marshal Yanda's spot at right guard. (He can never actually be replaced.) Four different players could be vying for the job: rookies Tyre Phillips (third round, Mississippi State) and Ben Bredeson (fourth round, Michigan); Ben Powers, a 2019 fourth-round pick out of Oklahoma; and D.J. Fluker, who started at right guard for Seattle a year ago but ranked 26th at the position in snaps per blown block. 🏈 The monstrous Phillips (6-foot-5, 345 pounds) played left tackle in Starkville, but a lack of agility likely will make him a guard in pro ball. He may stay on the left side, however. Powers is considered a tough blocker with good footwork. The strong, squat Bredeson has the most upside. If no clear choice emerges in training camp, the Ravens may start off the season by rotating guards. 🏈 Bradley Bozeman is secure for now at left guard, and Matt Skura holds down the center spot.

Defensive Front

Defensive Line	Age	Pos	G	Snaps	Plays	Overall TmPct	Rk	Stop	Dfts	BTkl	Runs	vs. Run St%	Rk	RuYd	Rk	Pass Rush Sack	Hit	Hur	Dsrpt
Brandon Williams	31	DE	14	536	33	5.3%	45	22	4	3	32	66%	78	3.4	95	1.0	7	6	0
Michael Pierce*	28	DT	14	489	35	5.6%	38	26	7	2	31	71%	69	2.0	29	0.5	2	12	1
Chris Wormley*	27	DE	16	457	35	4.9%	38	26	6	2	29	72%	61	2.3	49	1.5	4	5	3
Jihad Ward	26	DT	14	404	8	1.3%	97	7	1	2	5	80%	27	2.8	76	1.0	5	17	2
Derek Wolfe	30	DE	12	535	35	5.6%	54	24	12	2	27	59%	89	3.0	85	7.0	7	14	1

Edge Rushers	Age	Pos	G	Snaps	Plays	Overall TmPct	Rk	Stop	Dfts	BTkl	Runs	vs. Run St%	Rk	RuYd	Rk	Pass Rush Sack	Hit	Hur	Dsrpt
Matt Judon	28	OLB	16	807	53	7.4%	9	40	22	7	34	76%	31	2.2	35	9.5	27	44	2
Jaylon Ferguson	25	OLB	14	507	32	5.1%	47	24	9	3	24	75%	39	3.1	72	2.5	6	15	0
Tyus Bowser	25	OLB	16	399	22	3.1%	--	15	8	1	10	50%	--	3.9	--	5.0	6	22	0
Calais Campbell	34	DE	16	833	57	7.2%	12	44	21	11	47	74%	44	1.6	16	6.5	19	44	3

Linebackers	Age	Pos	G	Snaps	Plays	Overall TmPct	Rk	Stop	Dfts	BTkl	Runs	vs. Run St%	Rk	RuYd	Rk	Pass Rush Sack	Hit	Hur	Tgts	vs. Pass Suc%	Rk	AdjYd	Rk	PD	Int
Patrick Onwuasor*	28	ILB	14	484	62	9.9%	56	32	9	11	29	55%	63	3.7	31	3.0	3	6	14	36%	--	12.2	--	1	0
Josh Bynes*	31	ILB	12	401	49	9.1%	68	32	11	7	36	67%	19	2.3	4	1.0	2	3	8	38%	--	8.1	--	4	2
L.J. Fort	30	ILB	16	258	27	3.8%	--	14	6	6	13	46%	--	4.2	--	2.0	3	7	8	50%	--	3.5	--	1	0

Year	Yards	ALY	Rank	Power	Rank	Stuff	Rank	2nd Level	Rank	Open Field	Rank	Sacks	ASR	Rank	Press	Rank
2017	4.12	3.85	7	62%	14	21%	15	1.10	14	0.87	26	41	6.8%	13	29.6%	20
2018	3.52	3.90	5	72%	25	19%	16	1.07	5	0.29	2	43	8.1%	6	32.8%	7
2019	4.41	4.11	10	68%	24	19%	16	1.16	16	1.01	29	37	7.1%	15	35.0%	3

2019 ALY by direction:	Left End: 1.98 (2)	Left Tackle: 3.3 (5)	Mid/Guard: 4.35 (13)	Right Tackle: 4.62 (22)	Right End: 3.59 (11)

Baltimore thought they had signed defensive lineman Michael Brockers to team with Brandon Williams and Calais Campbell, but issues with his ankle voided the deal. The team made a nice ad lib, picking up Derek Wolfe on a one-year contract. Wolfe had 7.0 sacks in 12 games with the Broncos on only 21 hits and hurries, suggesting the sacks may fall in 2020. Wolfe replaces Michael Pierce, who left in free agency. Third-round rookie Justin Madubuike (Texas A&M) is a penetrator who can play the nose or bounce to 3-technique. Edge rusher Pernell McPhee returns after missing most of 2019 with a torn triceps. He had 3.0 sacks and nine hurries in seven games. McPhee's usage in 2020 depends on the development of a pair of recent high draft picks, second-year man Jaylon Ferguson and third-year reserve Tyus Bowser. Both have flashed on occasion but require more consistency. The Ravens put the franchise tag on leading sacker Matt Judon, then worked out a deal where he signed a one-year contract for $16.8 million, the midpoint between the franchise-tag numbers for defensive ends and linebackers. He is critical for Baltimore's championship hopes but also a near-certainty to leave in free agency next offseason. It's possible, even likely, that the Ravens will start a pair of rookies at inside linebacker. Patrick Queen was a first-round pick out of LSU, an extremely fast and rangy player with work to do to develop at the next level, especially as he displayed first-round talent only in the latter half of 2019. If there was a veteran lining up next to him who allowed Queen to merely pursue and wreck plays, that would be ideal, but the other inside linebacker could well be third-rounder Malik Harrison from Ohio State. Harrison is a thumper with good hands but has only average quickness and figures to be a matchup target in the short passing game. How quickly the rookies develop will be a key element to the success of the Ravens defense in 2020.

Defensive Secondary

Secondary	Age	Pos	G	Snaps	Plays	TmPct	Rk	Stop	Dfts	BTkl	Runs	St%	Rk	RuYd	Rk	Tgts	Tgt%	Rk	Dist	Suc%	Rk	AdjYd	Rk	PD	Int
						Overall						vs. Run						vs. Pass							
Marcus Peters	27	CB	16	998	67	9.4%	15	27	15	8	12	50%	34	4.3	20	79	19.9%	44	11.8	52%	49	7.2	33	14	5
Marlon Humphrey	24	CB	16	979	79	11.0%	4	42	15	18	17	53%	31	5.9	37	78	19.1%	54	10.9	67%	5	5.0	4	14	3
Earl Thomas	31	FS	15	911	53	7.9%	50	20	13	8	26	27%	61	8.9	55	13	3.4%	73	16.9	85%	1	5.2	12	4	2
Brandon Carr*	34	CB	16	763	55	7.7%	42	23	10	12	17	41%	48	9.2	72	50	15.7%	73	11.7	58%	19	6.5	18	6	0
Chuck Clark	25	SS	16	757	77	10.8%	19	36	9	10	39	46%	27	4.6	11	28	8.9%	26	7.0	46%	53	6.6	25	9	1
Jimmy Smith	32	CB	9	410	36	9.0%	--	15	9	2	6	17%	--	8.7	--	44	25.8%	--	11.7	59%	--	5.8	--	6	1
Tony Jefferson*	28	SS	5	289	25	11.2%	--	11	0	8	13	62%	--	4.6	--	7	5.8%	--	11.1	57%	--	3.3	--	3	0
Anthony Averett	26	CB	9	225	16	4.0%	--	3	1	3	2	50%	--	0.5	--	33	35.2%	--	14.2	55%	--	6.7	--	2	0

Year	Pass D Rank	vs. #1 WR	Rk	vs. #2 WR	Rk	vs. Other WR	Rk	WR Wide	Rk	WR Slot	Rk	vs. TE	Rk	vs. RB	Rk
2017	2	-24.7%	4	-39.7%	2	-1.0%	16	-26.7%	4	-17.4%	5	19.6%	29	-16.8%	6
2018	3	-9.7%	8	-26.2%	2	-11.6%	8	-32.5%	2	-4.4%	12	16.1%	22	-44.7%	1
2019	4	-16.1%	6	3.1%	19	-31.6%	2	-15.8%	9	-13.9%	5	-5.6%	10	-10.8%	8

Baltimore clearly believes in its defensive backs, using at least five of them at a time more than any other defense. ✒ The strength of Baltimore's secondary is shown by their performance when there's no quarterback pressure. Baltimore ranked fifth in defensive DVOA without pressure after ranking first in that metric in 2018. ✒ Marcus Peters hasn't exactly been a model citizen since turning pro, as the fan who caught the penalty flag he heaved into the stands in disgust back in his Kansas City days could attest. And in six games with the Rams in 2019 he was awful, allowing 10.9 yards per pass with a 45% success rate. But once he donned the purple, he was a corner transformed, shaving his yards per pass to 5.9 and upping his success rate to 54%. Now that he has been given a rich new deal the only question is whether he can keep his head on straight. ✒ Marlon Humphrey was one of the best corners of the league (fourth in yards per pass, fifth in success rate), though he garnered a fraction of the public attention Peters did. ✒ The Ravens declined an option on Brandon Carr, which leaves Tavon Young as the slot corner. Young lost last year to a neck injury and has only been healthy in one of the last three seasons. He had a 51% success rate and allowed 7.6 yards per pass in 2018. ✒ Oft-injured Jimmy Smith returns as a depth corner and could play some safety. ✒ Earl Thomas may have enjoyed some questionable quarantine activities, but he's aces on the field, leading all safeties in success rate in coverage and providing the Ravens with the Gold Glove centerfielder they always seem to have. ✒ Chuck Clark emerged as a fearsome hitter and run-stopper at strong safety. He and Thomas form a top-of-the-league combo.

Special Teams

Year	DVOA	Rank	FG/XP	Rank	Net Kick	Rank	Kick Ret	Rank	Net Punt	Rank	Punt Ret	Rank	Hidden	Rank
2017	9.2%	1	19.0	1	6.6	4	12.3	1	4.1	12	3.9	5	-7.0	24
2018	2.9%	6	11.0	3	0.9	15	-1.3	18	-3.4	25	7.5	2	8.3	9
2019	1.5%	9	14.1	1	0.5	17	-1.4	21	-6.4	25	0.5	14	-3.7	23

Another great year by über-kicker Justin Tucker pushed the Ravens to a top-ten ranking, though they weren't as strong in other spots. ✒ Punter Sam Koch's performance continues to erode, though not dramatically, and his coverage teams were poor. ✒ The return game was particularly ordinary, leading the team to bring in De'Anthony Thomas midway through the season, an addition that failed to provide a jolt. At the moment Thomas is in line to handle return duties in 2020 as well, which means the Ravens are comfortable with mediocre returns so long as Lamar Jackson gets to do his thing, regardless of starting field position (and the team was sixth in average starting line of scrimmage anyway).

Buffalo Bills

2019 Record: 10-6	Total DVOA: 3.0% (13rd)	2020 Mean Projection: 7.9 wins	On the Clock (0-4): 11%
Pythagorean Wins: 9.8 (10th)	Offense: -7.2% (21st)	Postseason Odds: 43.4%	Mediocrity (5-7): 34%
Snap-Weighted Age: 26.7 (7th)	Defense: -11.5% (6th)	Super Bowl Odds: 4.2%	Playoff Contender (8-10): 39%
Average Opponent: -3.9% (30th)	Special Teams: -1.2% (21st)	Proj. Avg. Opponent: -0.1% (16th)	Super Bowl Contender (11+): 16%

2019: If only we could play "all-time quarterback" like when we were kids.

2020: It's time for Josh Allen to prove us wrong.

For a moment, let us pretend there are only 21 starting football players on a team. Let us excuse the quarterback from the conversation. With that out of the way, the coast is clear to declare the Buffalo Bills one of the best, most complete rosters in the NFL. They serve as a model for all struggling franchises to claw themselves back into relevance.

Something about writing that does not sit right with my soul. It defies all I know as a young football observer, but it is the truth. Through quality drafting, an excellent eye for undrafted free agents, and a free-agency strategy geared toward throwing many cheap darts at a board and hoping they hit (and many of them have), general manager Brandon Beane and head coach Sean McDermott rescued Buffalo from perennial losing. Even if imperfect, the Bills are now poised to be regular contenders in the AFC and on the cusp of winning their first playoff game in what feels like an eternity (since 1995).

And while both sides of the roster have been constructed well over the past couple of years, one side of the ball carries more of the team's success than the other. McDermott has built a defensive powerhouse in Buffalo. After finishing as a middle-of-the-pack defense in McDermott's rookie head coaching season of 2017, the Bills produced a top-six finish in defensive DVOA in both 2018 and 2019. Moreover, Buffalo finished top-five in pass defense DVOA in each of those two seasons. Only the Baltimore Ravens share that achievement over that span.

Mind you, McDermott put together this secondary after cornerback Stephon Gilmore, arguably the best defensive back in the league over the past two seasons, was allowed to walk in free agency to join Buffalo's AFC East rival New England Patriots during the 2017 offseason. That was, of course, an early error in the Beane/McDermott era, but they have recovered from it in a way nobody could have expected them to. Even with an All-Pro in the rearview mirror, McDermott's Bills are one of the league's true No Fly Zones.

2020 is shaping up to be more of the same for the Buffalo defense. The Bills go into the season with our best mean defensive projection. With only a few pieces shuffling around in the front seven and no loss of starting players in their elite secondary, it is no wonder the Bills are poised to dominate on defense once again. There's less predicted statistical regression because, unlike most stellar defenses, the 2019 Bills depended on a very ordinary rate of takeaways. Our numbers account

for schedule strength but given how shaky the offenses around the AFC East look right now, the Bills are likely to look even more dominant on the field than they do in the stats. How the Bills arrive at that point of dominance may look different this year than in years past, though—at least up front.

Since McDermott arrived in Buffalo, edge/linebacker hybrid Lorenzo Alexander had been an integral part of the defense's schematic identity. Alexander often played an off-ball linebacker position in base sets and on run downs, while transitioning to a pass-rushing edge role in sub packages or clear passing situations. His playing time at either spot varied week-to-week depending on opponent and necessity, but his flexibility moving all around the field allowed McDermott to put together one of the best front sevens in the league despite not having a true ace pass-rusher along the lines of a Von Miller or T.J. Watt. Even their four-man rush packages had some variety with Alexander in the mix. As such, Buffalo used three pass-rushers on just 1.8% of their snaps, lowest in the league, in part because they could craft their blitz and pressure packages around the uncertainty Alexander presented to offenses.

Unfortunately for the Bills, Alexander stepped away from the game this offseason after 15 years in the NFL, the last four of which he spent in Buffalo. With Alexander out of the fold early in the offseason, Buffalo had the opportunity to replace him with a similar player (including former Patriots defender Kyle Van Noy), but instead opted to go in the other direction. Rather than try to replace a unique player, the Bills are turning to a more "standard" approach. The Bills added former New Orleans Saints linebacker A.J. Klein, who previously played under McDermott in Carolina, as well as defensive end Mario Addison, also a former McDermott-era Panther. In essence, Buffalo replaced one player's responsibility with two separate players, which is bound to cut out some of Buffalo's flexibility among their edge defenders and linebackers.

In exchange for versatility at edge and linebacker, the Bills are leaning into depth and flexibility along the defensive line. Not only did the Bills sign Addison, who may be the team's least flexible acquisition up front this offseason, but they also signed hybrid end/tackle Quinton Jefferson from the Seahawks and defensive tackle Vernon Butler from the Panthers. Iowa's 6-foot-5, 275-pound "big" end A.J. Epenesa also landed in Buffalo as the team's second-round pick. With Jefferson and Epenesa each able to flex around from 3-technique

2020 Bills Schedule

Week	Opp.	Week	Opp.	Week	Opp.
1	NYJ	7	at NYJ	13	at SF (Mon.)
2	at MIA	8	NE	14	PIT
3	LAR	9	SEA	15	at DEN (Sat.)
4	at LV	10	at ARI	16	at NE (Mon.)
5	at TEN	11	BYE	17	MIA
6	KC (Thu.)	12	LAC		

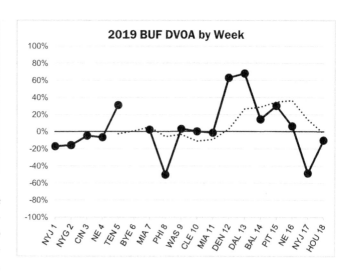

to 5-technique, as well as a standard 6-technique defensive end position in Epenesa's case, Buffalo has the tools to constantly keep a fresh lineup in the game while also being able to put together crafty sub packages for third-down passing situations. As Alexander departs and all of these new pieces arrive, expect McDermott and defensive coordinator Leslie Frazier to show off more of their creativity with the big men up front rather than with hybrid linebackers.

As different as Buffalo's front may look in 2020, adaptation along the front seven does not take away from the core of their defensive identity: the secondary. As far as change in the defensive backfield goes, there is hardly anything of note. Buffalo's top five defensive backs in snap count last year (Tre White, Levi Wallace, Taron Johnson, Jordan Poyer, and Micah Hyde) all return for 2020 and are likely to assume their starting roles again. The only potential tweak in Buffalo's starting lineup would be Josh Norman, who signed a one-year "prove it" deal with the Bills this offseason, though there is no guarantee he plays over Wallace on the outside. Norman is a quality role player and insurance policy at worst, a marginal upgrade over Wallace at best. As evidenced by two years of elite pass defense, though, Buffalo's secondary ain't broke, so there is no need to fix it by forcing Norman into the lineup.

By all accounts, Buffalo's pride and strength as a team will continue to be rooted in a shutdown pass defense. It's an important strength, because if you're a regular Football Outsiders reader, you know that teams in the modern NFL primarily win by passing the ball and stopping the pass. That being said, it is time to return one particular player to the discussion. The Bills still have to address the elephant in the room—the quarterback room, to be specific. McDermott and Frazier will have no problem leading their Pro Bowl-laden defense to the league's upper echelon once again, but the question remains as to whether third-year quarterback Josh Allen can allow the *team* to climb to the league's upper echelon for the first time in the modern era. If Buffalo wants to seize the AFC East for the first time since 1995, the offense needs to catch up to the defense.

The first two seasons of Allen's career have provided few encouraging signs, but McDermott's six years of toiling away as the defensive coordinator for the Carolina Panthers during the Cam Newton era prepared the fourth-year head coach for this season, a pivotal moment in the Bills' franchise history. Hopefully.

After seeing firsthand how Carolina failed to keep a respectable offense around Newton, McDermott came to Buffalo in 2017 with the perfect "what not to do" experience for building around a potential franchise quarterback. The Bills selected Allen in the first round of the 2018 NFL draft, the dawn of McDermott's second year in town, and have spent each following offseason injecting the offense with enough talent for Allen to prove himself the savior that upstate New York has been waiting for since Jim Kelly. Despite the efforts to build around the young quarterback, last year's offense was seemingly not enough to propel Allen to stardom.

Save for left tackle Dion Dawkins, the Bills bought and/or drafted Allen an entirely new offensive line heading into the 2019 season. Rookie third-round pick Cody Ford manned the right tackle position, while veteran free-agent signings Quinton Spain, Mitch Morse, and Jon Feliciano commanded the middle of the unit. Though not quite the 2016 Dallas Cowboys, the Bills finished 15th in adjusted line yards (4.32) and 22nd in pressure rate allowed (31.2%) in 2019, both of which were sizable improvements over their 2018 rankings of 30th (3.89) and 28th (35.3%), respectively.

New weapons were added all around Allen too. Speedster John Brown and slot savant Cole Beasley were both signed in free agency to save a desolate wide receiver corps previously led by Zay Jones and Kelvin Benjamin, neither of whom are on the roster anymore. (Benjamin was not on *any* roster last year.) Buffalo also added the ever-steady Frank Gore in the backfield, as well as rookie running back Devin Singletary. Mid-round tight end draft pick Dawson Knox finished off the key additions from Buffalo's 2019 offseason that allowed Allen to improve from "bad" to "mediocre" in his second season.

If that were not investment enough, Beane took another huge swing at adding offensive talent this offseason by trading a first-round pick for Minnesota Vikings wide receiver Stefon Diggs. Shocking as it is, Diggs has never even made the Pro Bowl during his impressive career, but that is not to say he hasn't been productive. In two of the past three seasons (2017 and 2019), Diggs finished top-10 in DYAR among wide receivers, with a publicly turbulent first season with Vikings quarterback Kirk Cousins in 2018 serving as the receiver's only recent low point. As Brown stretches the field and Beasley hammers out tough yardage underneath, Diggs is the do-everything-else component that may fully unlock the Bills passing game. And yet, all of these offensive renovations will be for naught if Allen does not become a new player. Though his growth from Year 1 to Year 2 was encouraging, the bar set by his rookie season was terribly low. Allen's production as a second-year player was still lackluster both by league-average standards and by recent two-year quarterback standards (Table 1).

Table 1. Josh Allen vs. 2019 League Median

Metric	Allen (rk)	Median
ESPN's Total QBR	47.3 (26)	53.7 (Tom Brady, Daniel Jones)
Passing DYAR	-21 (28)	454 (Carson Wentz, Ryan Fitzpatrick)
Passing + Rushing DYAR	79 (25)	496 (Jared Goff, Jacoby Brissett)
Adjusted Net Yards Per Attempt (ANY/A)	5.71 (24)	6.25 (Carson Wentz, Tom Brady)

Minimum 200 passes, 34 qualifiers.

By any reasonable measure, Allen was a below-average quarterback in 2019. A common defense for Allen's poor production last season is that his year-long numbers are bogged down by a significantly worse first half of the season compared to the second half of the season, which is true. In fact, DYAR supports this claim. Over the first eight games of the year, Allen produced a passing DYAR of -182—about -23 DYAR per game. Conversely, over the final eight games of the year, Allen pumped out 161 DYAR—good for just a hair over 20 DYAR per game. In turn, Buffalo went from the 29th offense in passing DVOA from Weeks 1 to 9 to 10th in passing DVOA through Weeks 10 to 17, sandwiching them between the Chargers and Raiders over the back half of the season. A significant portion of that split in production boils down to nothing more than Allen having thrown seven interceptions through the first eight games as opposed to just two over the final eight games, but the young passer was still "better" nonetheless.

As evidenced by research regarding Baker Mayfield and the Cleveland Browns from last year's *Almanac,* however, improvement by a quarterback through the back half of one season does not necessarily roll over into improvement for the next season. There is little to no correlation between success in the second half of one season and success the following season, from both young quarterbacks and veterans alike. While one could make the claim that a player showed progress on film—and Allen did to some degree in regards to choosing his battles more carefully—that progress is not certain to bear fruit the following season, even if it may in the long term.

Allen's profile compared to other young quarterbacks in the modern era is not up to snuff, either. Among 43 quarterbacks drafted since 2004 who started at least 17 games in their first two seasons, Allen's adjusted net yards per attempt over his first two years ranks just 29th. His performance falls just behind Trent Edwards, Jacoby Brissett, and Mike Glennon (Ta-

ble 2). Allen's 5.16 adjusted net yards per attempt also falls about one-third of a yard short of 5.50 adjusted net yards per attempt, which appears to be a reasonable threshold for production through a player's first two seasons. Not every player who cleared the threshold maintained success in the NFL (Derek Anderson and Josh Freeman, especially), but a majority of those who fell below the threshold either faded out of the league or only stuck around as backups. Ryan Tannehill, Eli Manning, and Alex Smith serve as a small handful of exceptions whom Allen may be able to follow, but he is fighting against the odds.

Table 2. Similar Career Starts to Josh Allen by ANY/A, 2004-2019

Rk	Player	Team	Years	ANY/A
24	Jason Campbell	WAS	2005-06	5.38
25	Sam Darnold	NYJ	2018-19	5.37
26	Trent Edwards	BUF	2007-08	5.36
27	Jacoby Brissett	NE/IND	2016-17	5.31
28	Mike Glennon	TB	2013-14	5.22
29	**Josh Allen**	**BUF**	**2018-19**	**5.16**
30	Ryan Tannehill	MIA	2012-13	5.10
31	Blake Bortles	JAX	2014-15	5.07
32	Eli Manning	NYG	2004-05	4.99
33	Mark Sanchez	NYJ	2009-10	4.83
34	Brandon Weeden	CLE	2012-13	4.82
35	Colt McCoy	CLE	2010-11	4.74

Rank out of 43 qualifying quarterbacks with 17 or more starts in Years 1-2

Likewise, passing DYAR presents a poor outlook based on Allen's young career, perhaps even more damning than ANY/A. Since 2004, 13 quarterbacks other than Allen produced negative DYAR scores in each of their first two seasons (min. 100 passes in each season): Alex Smith, Charlie Frye, Vince Young, Sam Bradford, John Skelton, Blaine Gabbert, Brandon Weeden, Geno Smith, EJ Manuel, Zach Mettenberger, C.J. Beathard, Josh Rosen, and Sam Darnold. Of that group, Smith is the only one to go on to a "good" career, while Bradford resides by himself in a well-paid purgatory. If we extended this list prior to 2004, it would also be largely unspectacular outside of an anomalous success case in Troy Aikman, who was a turnover machine in 1989 and 1990 before attending six consecutive Pro Bowls, winning three Lombardis, and eventually landing in the Hall of Fame.

If history is any indication, Allen is also unlikely to take a massive leap from Year 2 to Year 3, as is the case with most young quarterbacks. Per a Football Outsiders study back in 2012, quarterbacks with at least 100 pass attempts tend to improve by an average of 12.8% DVOA from their first to second season, marking the largest jump in production between any two seasons of a player's career. Naturally, it makes sense that a player's best point of progress would be following their rookie season. Allen very much lived up to that expectation, going from -35.9% DVOA as a rookie to -11.8% in 2019, nearly doubling the averaging jump a young quarterback experiences.

The leap many are expecting Allen to take this season occurs much less frequently, however. Throughout the rest of a quarterback's career, the average change in DVOA from year-to-year is between 3.5% and -5.5%, which can more or less be chalked up to variance and variable changes around the quarterback rather than change in the quarterback themselves. Even doubling the upper limit of average change from year to year, which would come to about 7%, Allen would still only finish next season around -4% DVOA, which would have ranked outside the top 20 for 2019.

We can stop the barrage of statistics against Allen here. Not only will most other numbers bear out similar results, but Allen is a player whose identity and fan support is rooted at least somewhat in the belief that his value will never show itself in the numbers properly. While there are arguments to be made for Allen through that scope, as there have been for Cam Newton for years, that is a generally flimsy case to be made, even more so given Allen has nowhere near the same pedigree as someone such as Newton. Despite how turbulent the middle portion of his career became, Newton was a Heisman- and National Championship-winner in college, earned Rookie of the Year in 2011, and broke a number of rookie quarterback records, including passing yards, rushing yards, rushing touchdowns, and total touchdowns. The latter two records still stand today. While Allen has flashed potential, his list of accomplishments pales in comparison to Newton's college and early NFL career. (How ironic that these two players often compared to one another will now battle for AFC East supremacy.)

The point of putting a microscope to Allen's production is not to doom him to a failed career. Rather, it is to show just how much Allen would need to improve to be an "average" NFL quarterback, let alone a good one. Allen may very well take another step forward in 2020, and the addition of Diggs alone is almost a guarantee that he will see a boost in production to some degree, but it would be a much more reasonable assumption of growth to say Allen will be an average quarterback instead of a potential top-10 passer who will carry the Bills to the promised land.

Buffalo's story as it relates to Allen is a story all too common in recent years. As seen with the Chicago Bears with Mitchell Trubisky and the Jacksonville Jaguars with Blake Bortles, the NFL now seems to always have a defensive powerhouse whose quarterback teeters right on the edge of competence— a quarterback whose selection was widely criticized on his draft night, more specifically. The Bears and Jaguars each found different levels of success in maintaining their defensive prowess, but both teams quickly got firm answers on their quarterbacks being bad following their lone season of hope.

Reducing the Bills' season down to nothing more than Allen's development (or lack thereof) may feel like too narrow a lens, but there is little else to point to that could signal a bad year in Buffalo. The roster has been built up about as successfully as any coach and general manager duo could ask for over the past three years, and the defensive coaching staff is as proven as any in the league. Now is the time to see whether the Bills can take over the AFC East or find themselves once again searching for a new quarterback.

Derrik Klassen

2019 Bills Stats by Week

Wk	vs.	W-L	PF	PA	YDF	YDA	TO	Total	Off	Def	ST
1	at NYJ	W	17	16	370	223	-3	-17%	-12%	7%	1%
2	at NYG	W	28	14	388	370	+2	-16%	3%	10%	-9%
3	CIN	W	21	17	416	306	+2	-5%	-19%	-21%	-7%
4	NE	L	10	16	375	224	-3	-6%	-29%	-45%	-23%
5	at TEN	W	14	7	313	252	-1	31%	2%	-27%	2%
6	BYE										
7	MIA	W	31	21	305	381	+2	2%	9%	17%	10%
8	PHI	L	13	31	253	371	0	-50%	-34%	12%	-5%
9	WAS	W	24	9	268	243	0	3%	-15%	-8%	10%
10	at CLE	L	16	19	344	368	0	0%	-2%	-5%	-2%
11	at MIA	W	37	20	424	303	+1	-1%	2%	-9%	-13%
12	DEN	W	20	3	424	134	0	63%	18%	-46%	-1%
13	at DAL	W	26	15	356	426	+2	68%	35%	-35%	-1%
14	BAL	L	17	24	209	257	0	15%	-41%	-42%	13%
15	at PIT	W	17	10	261	229	+3	30%	-5%	-34%	1%
16	at NE	L	17	24	268	414	+1	7%	18%	19%	7%
17	NYJ	L	6	13	309	271	-2	-49%	-46%	-1%	-4%
18	at HOU	L	19	22	425	360	0	-10%	-15%	-3%	3%

Trends and Splits

	Offense	Rank	Defense	Rank
Total DVOA	-7.2%	21	-11.5%	6
Unadjusted VOA	-4.5%	19	-13.6%	5
Weighted Trend	-5.1%	19	-12.7%	6
Variance	5.1%	7	5.2%	12
Average Opponent	-1.0%	12	-5.4%	31
Passing	-0.6%	23	-13.4%	5
Rushing	-3.1%	17	-8.9%	18
First Down	-0.2%	15	-13.7%	7
Second Down	-11.1%	24	-9.5%	9
Third Down	-15.1%	25	-9.9%	12
First Half	-8.7%	25	-17.8%	4
Second Half	-5.5%	19	-5.3%	9
Red Zone	-13.9%	22	-8.5%	11
Late and Close	-10.1%	21	-7.2%	13

Five-Year Performance

Year	W-L	Pyth W	Est W	PF	PA	TO	Total	Rk	Off	Rk	Def	Rk	ST	Rk	Off AGL	Rk	Def AGL	Rk	Off Age	Rk	Def Age	Rk	ST Age	Rk
2015	8-8	8.5	8.8	379	359	+6	2.7%	12	9.8%	9	8.6%	24	1.5%	12	35.9	18	47.8	28	26.2	21	26.4	21	26.5	9
2016	7-9	8.5	7.4	399	378	+6	1.0%	17	10.7%	10	7.8%	27	-1.9%	22	37.6	18	60.8	28	26.6	19	27.2	6	27.3	1
2017	9-7	6.3	6.8	302	359	+9	-9.8%	21	-11.1%	26	1.6%	15	2.9%	10	28.9	12	18.0	8	27.8	2	26.8	11	27.5	1
2018	6-10	5.0	6.5	269	374	-5	-18.2%	28	-27.5%	31	-14.5%	2	-5.1%	32	15.3	4	15.7	6	26.2	24	26.6	10	27.1	2
2019	10-6	9.8	7.8	314	259	+4	3.0%	13	-7.2%	21	-11.5%	6	-1.2%	21	46.5	20	18.1	3	26.7	16	26.4	14	27.2	2

2019 Performance Based on Most Common Personnel Groups

BUF Offense					BUF Offense vs. Opponents					BUF Defense				BUF Defense vs. Opponents			
Pers	Freq	Yds	DVOA	Run%	Pers	Freq	Yds	DVOA	Run%	Pers	Freq	Yds	DVOA	Pers	Freq	Yds	DVOA
11	71%	5.5	-1.1%	34%	Base	23%	4.6	-14.4%	60%	Base	22%	4.7	-13.7%	11	59%	5.3	-9.8%
12	10%	5.6	0.3%	47%	Nickel	53%	5.6	6.0%	38%	Nickel	77%	5.1	-9.3%	12	15%	4.7	-16.4%
21	9%	5.2	-4.5%	45%	Dime+	22%	5.9	-0.7%	21%	Goal Line	1%	-1.0	-59.6%	21	10%	5.5	0.7%
13	4%	5.1	15.0%	78%	Goal Line	2%	-0.1	-18.3%	75%					20	6%	4.2	-21.2%
22	4%	2.4	-42.9%	89%	Big	1%	3.3	-67.2%	50%					612	3%	3.5	27.1%

Strategic Tendencies

Run/Pass		Rk	Formation		Rk	Pass Rush		Rk	Secondary		Rk	Strategy		Rk
Runs, first half	37%	15	Form: Single Back	77%	22	Rush 3	1.8%	32	4 DB	22%	21	Play Action	24%	19
Runs, first down	47%	20	Form: Empty Back	12%	3	Rush 4	72.4%	8	5 DB	77%	3	Offensive Motion	27%	31
Runs, second-long	31%	8	Form: Multi Back	11%	14	Rush 5	19.3%	17	6+ DB	0%	32	Avg Box (Off)	6.66	6
Runs, power sit.	80%	1	Pers: 3+ WR	72%	9	Rush 6+	6.6%	12	Man Coverage	30%	23	Avg Box (Def)	6.83	2
Runs, behind 2H	31%	12	Pers: 2+ TE/6+ OL	19%	29	Edge Rusher Sacks	38.6%	31	CB by Sides	82%	12	Offensive Pace	30.11	11
Pass, ahead 2H	41%	29	Pers: 6+ OL	0%	29	Interior DL Sacks	40.9%	3	S/CB Cover Ratio	22%	26	Defensive Pace	32.52	31
Run-Pass Options	9%	8	Shotgun/Pistol	62%	21	Second Level Sacks	20.5%	16	DB Blitz	14%	9	Go for it on 4th	1.40	15

Josh Allen threw in the short middle of the field much more often than in his rookie year (from 13% to 21% of passes) and was much more successful (from dead last to 10th in DVOA). 🏈 For the second straight year, Allen was close to the top of the league in frequency facing defensive back blitzes. In fact, he faced them even more often in his second season, 16.0% of passes. He struggled on these plays with just 3.3 yards per play and -67.0% DVOA. 🏈 The Bills ranked second in the league with 7.1% of passes dropped by receivers. 🏈 Buffalo had a wacky and extreme home-field *dis* advantage on offense, with -19.0% DVOA in home games but 4.6% DVOA in road games. (We mention this strictly for curiosity's sake, as it's not the kind of thing that carries over from year to year.) 🏈 Sean McDermott defenses have always shown very strong personnel tendencies: near the top of the league in nickel with no dime. 🏈 Buffalo opponents threw only 14% of passes deep (16 or more air yards), the lowest figure in the league. The Bills ranked second in defensive DVOA on these passes, trailing only the Patriots. 🏈 Although they weren't as strong as they had been in 2018, the Bills were once again above average against both running back (-24.9% DVOA) and wide receiver (-17.6% DVOA) screens.

Passing

Player	DYAR	DVOA	Plays	NtYds	Avg	YAC	C%	TD	Int
J.Allen	-21	-11.8%	497	2827	5.7	5.0	59.4%	20	9
M.Barkley	-122	-52.0%	53	344	6.5	5.8	54.0%	0	3

Rushing

Player	DYAR	DVOA	Plays	Yds	Avg	TD	Fum	Suc
F.Gore*	-50	-15.2%	166	599	3.6	3	0	45%
D.Singletary	75	3.7%	151	775	5.1	2	4	50%
J.Allen	100	6.5%	95	523	5.5	9	6	-
T.Yeldon	-2	-11.4%	17	63	3.7	0	1	53%
I.McKenzie	21	4.5%	8	49	6.1	0	0	-
T.Jones	14	21.9%	9	40	4.4	0	0	67%
S.Diggs	44	103.1%	5	61	12.2	0	0	-

Receiving

Player	DYAR	DVOA	Plays	Ctch	Yds	Y/C	YAC	TD	C%
J.Brown	205	11.0%	115	72	1060	14.7	3.0	6	63%
C.Beasley	112	1.3%	106	67	778	11.6	5.0	6	63%
I.McKenzie	-24	-21.0%	39	27	254	9.4	7.6	1	69%
D.Williams	23	2.9%	19	12	166	13.8	4.2	1	63%
Z.Jones*	-60	-52.0%	18	7	69	9.9	2.7	0	39%
R.Foster	-44	-42.1%	18	3	64	21.3	10.7	0	17%
A.Roberts	-27	-61.7%	7	3	20	6.7	1.7	0	43%
S.Diggs	272	24.0%	95	63	1130	17.7	4.7	6	67%
D.Knox	-23	-14.0%	50	28	388	13.9	5.1	2	56%
T.Kroft	-11	-20.2%	14	6	71	11.8	4.5	1	43%
T.Sweeney	7	1.7%	13	8	114	14.3	4.8	0	62%
D.Singletary	-47	-35.2%	41	29	194	6.7	6.7	2	71%
F.Gore*	4	-9.6%	16	13	100	7.7	6.8	0	81%
T.Yeldon	18	8.8%	15	13	124	9.5	9.2	0	87%
P.DiMarco	-7	-31.3%	7	5	41	8.2	6.2	0	71%

Offensive Line

Player	Pos	Age	GS	Snaps	Pen	Sk	Pass	Run	Player	Pos	Age	GS	Snaps	Pen	Sk	Pass	Run
Quinton Spain	LG	29	16/16	1086	4	0.5	11	6	Ty Nsekhe	RT	35	10/1	368	5	0.5	5	1
Dion Dawkins	LT	26	16/16	1039	11	3.0	16	4	Spencer Long	C	30	14/0	175	0	1.0	2	4
Jon Feliciano	RG	28	16/16	970	5	2.5	11	5	Daryl Williams	LG/LT	28	16/12	851	2	9.0	17	6
Mitch Morse	C	28	16/16	932	9	1.0	7	9	Evan Boehm	RG	27	13/8	601	4	0.5	5	7
Cody Ford	RT	24	16/15	755	8	7.5	16	4									

Year	Yards	ALY	Rank	Power	Rank	Stuff	Rank	2nd Lev	Rank	Open Field	Rank	Sacks	ASR	Rank	Press	Rank	F-Start	Cont.
2017	3.96	3.67	27	61%	22	26%	27	1.17	15	0.90	8	47	9.3%	31	32.7%	23	10	34
2018	3.53	3.89	30	68%	14	21%	23	0.92	32	0.43	30	41	8.0%	23	35.3%	28	20	32
2019	4.26	4.32	15	58%	24	22%	28	1.27	10	0.78	17	40	7.8%	23	31.6%	23	22	37
2019 ALY by direction:			Left End 3.67 (21)			Left Tackle: 4.59 (10)			Mid/Guard: 4.54 (12)				Right Tackle: 2.95 (29)			Right End: 6.15 (1)		

Guards Quinton Spain and Jon Feliciano ranked 35th and 43rd, respectively, in snaps per blown block among 106 qualifying interior offensive linemen. In neither of the previous two seasons did Buffalo have both of their top guards finish in the top half in snaps per blown block. ❧ In the last three years, the Bills' rank in adjusted line yards on runs around right end has gone from first to 27th and then back to first. Some of last year's improvement can be credited to rookie Cody Ford as a road-grader, but of course Ford wasn't around when the Bills ranked No. 1 in 2017. That kind of variance is pretty rare and inconsistent with the rest of the line's year-to-year figures, so the performance on runs around right end figures to come back to earth next season. ❧ Only five teams had at least four offensive linemen start all 16 games last season, one of which was the Bills. The only starting lineman to not start all 16 games was Ford, who missed just one start. ❧ Despite being sixth in snaps for the Bills, backup tackle Ty Nsekhe led the team's offensive linemen with four false starts. ❧ Left tackle Dion Dawkins' seven holding penalties tied for the fifth-most in the league. Additionally, Dawkins committed over 10 total penalties for the second year in a row. Dawkins' 15 penalties in 2018 were the second-most in the league, while his 12 penalties in 2019 tied for 11th. ❧ The Bills finished sixth in pass plays per blown block, meaning they did not often blow blocks in pass protection, yet only finished 23rd in adjusted sack rate. Quarterback Josh Allen has a tendency to hold onto the ball, so it is possible Allen's play style is not getting the most of Buffalo's pass-blocking efficiency. ❧ Though unlikely to unseat Nsekhe as the primary backup tackle, former Carolina Panthers guard/tackle Daryl Williams adds much-needed depth to the Bills' offensive line. Considering how important guards are in Buffalo's run scheme, which is laden with pulling concepts, it is a savvy move for them to target depth at that position, especially given their injury fortune last year. That said, Williams ranked just 90th out of 106 interior offensive linemen in snaps per blown block, most of which he surrendered in the pass game. Hopefully another year removed from his 2018 injury can shore up some of those issues.

Defensive Front

Defensive Line	Age	Pos	G	Snaps	Plays	TmPct	Rk	Stop	Dfts	BTkl	Runs	St%	Rk	RuYd	Rk	Sack	Hit	Hur	Dsrpt
						Overall						vs. Run				Pass Rush			
Ed Oliver	23	DT	16	567	45	5.6%	28	34	12	2	31	77%	38	2.8	74	5.0	4	18	2
Jordan Phillips*	28	DT	16	548	31	3.9%	64	21	16	4	18	44%	97	2.6	62	9.5	6	14	0
Star Lotulelei	31	DT	16	488	20	2.5%	88	16	5	7	16	75%	48	2.1	37	2.0	1	4	0
Corey Liuget*	30	DT	10	180	13	2.7%	--	13	7	0	11	100%	--	-0.4	--	1.0	2	2	0
Vernon Butler	26	DT	14	449	31	4.3%	67	27	11	1	24	83%	19	2.3	45	6.0	4	7	0

Edge Rushers	Age	Pos	G	Snaps	Plays	TmPct	Rk	Stop	Dfts	BTkl	Runs	St%	Rk	RuYd	Rk	Sack	Hit	Hur	Dsrpt
						Overall						vs. Run				Pass Rush			
Trent Murphy	30	DE	16	685	35	4.3%	50	26	13	5	23	70%	62	2.2	36	5.0	6	25	2
Jerry Hughes	32	DE	16	676	26	3.2%	73	20	11	9	15	80%	21	2.1	31	4.5	6	32	4
Shaq Lawson*	26	DE	15	486	34	4.5%	53	32	21	5	23	91%	4	0.4	2	6.5	12	30	2
Mario Addison	33	OLB	15	746	33	4.3%	57	20	13	2	20	40%	90	5.5	91	9.5	5	25	1
Quinton Jefferson	27	DE	14	602	28	4.0%	64	23	8	5	21	76%	34	1.9	24	3.5	8	21	6

Linebackers	Age	Pos	G	Snaps	Plays	TmPct	Rk	Stop	Dfts	BTkl	Runs	St%	Rk	RuYd	Rk	Sack	Hit	Hur	Tgts	Suc%	Rk	AdjYd	Rk	PD	Int
						Overall						vs. Run				Pass Rush				vs. Pass					
Tremaine Edmunds	22	MLB	16	995	125	15.5%	15	74	24	12	73	64%	24	2.8	10	1.5	2	5	32	63%	8	4.7	8	9	1
Matt Milano	26	OLB	15	905	109	14.4%	25	67	23	13	55	64%	29	3.3	18	1.5	5	10	32	78%	2	4.0	5	9	0
Lorenzo Alexander*	37	OLB	16	501	58	7.2%	66	33	13	6	31	45%	78	4.3	62	2.0	8	20	10	30%	--	6.7	--	9	0
A.J. Klein	29	OLB	15	766	69	9.4%	54	41	12	12	36	69%	14	3.9	39	2.5	2	4	36	53%	31	8.1	56	2	1

Year	Yards	ALY	Rank	Power	Rank	Stuff	Rank	2nd Level	Rank	Open Field	Rank	Sacks	ASR	Rank	Press	Rank
2017	4.48	4.18	21	76%	28	22%	10	1.36	32	1.00	29	27	5.4%	28	27.0%	31
2018	4.14	4.15	10	62%	9	26%	1	1.33	24	0.76	13	36	6.9%	19	33.3%	4
2019	4.37	4.15	12	59%	8	25%	4	1.32	26	0.90	26	44	7.2%	13	31.1%	12
2019 ALY by direction:		Left End: 2.43 (3)			Left Tackle: 4.35 (18)			Mid/Guard: 4.17 (8)			Right Tackle: 4.57 (19)			Right End: 4.78 (20)		

Tremaine Edmunds and Matt Milano were the only linebacker pair to each rank in the top 10 for coverage success rate. Likewise, Milano and Edmunds were the only linebacker pair to each rank in the top 10 for yards allowed per pass. ● Edmunds and Milano also both cut down on their missed tackles in 2019. After each of them missed 18 tackles in 2018, Edmunds only missed 12 tackles and Milano missed 13, while both played more snaps than they did in 2018. Milano, specifically, played 164 more snaps in 2019. ● First-round pick Ed Oliver's five sacks were the most among rookie interior defensive linemen and double that of the next-best mark (Dexter Lawrence and Quinnen Williams, 2.5 sacks). ● Jordan Phillips recorded just one sack with nine hurries in 2018 before racking up 9.5 sacks with only 14 hurries in 2019—a stark difference in the success of his rushes. Between Oliver and Phillips, the Bills went from getting 14% of sacks from interior linemen (30th in 2018) to 41% of sacks (third in 2019). Phillips is now in Arizona, but his sack rate was already in line to regress. ● Free-agent signee Vernon Butler played his first season of more than 350 snaps in 2019. After recording just two sacks in the previous three seasons, Butler recorded six sacks with just seven hurries last season. Do not expect Butler to counteract the likely interior sack rate regression. ● The Bills are one of just two teams to rank top-five in stuff rate in each of the past two seasons, the other being the Philadelphia Eagles. ● Second-round pick A.J. Epenesa out of Iowa has the length, strength, and rock-solid technique to slot into Shaq Lawson's old role as the strongside end and run-defense specialist. Epenesa does not have particularly impressive bend or speed, but he can still be a valuable pocket-pusher and can even flex to a defensive tackle role in clear passing situations.

Defensive Secondary

Secondary	Age	Pos	G	Snaps	Plays	TmPct	Rk	Stop	Dfts	BTkl	Runs	St%	Rk	RuYd	Rk	Tgts	Tgt%	Rk	Dist	Suc%	Rk	AdjYd	Rk	PD	Int
												vs. Run					vs. Pass								
Jordan Poyer	29	SS	16	991	107	13.3%	6	46	18	13	66	48%	21	6.4	34	21	5.6%	59	15.0	43%	64	8.3	48	3	2
Micah Hyde	30	FS	16	983	73	9.1%	37	27	13	9	37	49%	20	8.7	51	21	5.7%	58	11.8	48%	48	8.1	46	2	1
Tre'Davious White	25	CB	15	965	75	9.9%	18	40	22	11	17	47%	38	4.6	25	78	21.4%	29	11.2	60%	14	5.9	9	17	6
Levi Wallace	25	CB	16	799	84	10.4%	7	27	12	12	20	35%	64	7.8	63	80	26.5%	3	10.1	44%	71	7.0	28	9	2
Taron Johnson	24	CB	12	498	54	8.9%	--	26	12	16	20	40%	--	8.1	--	31	16.5%	--	11.0	58%	--	6.0	--	5	0
Kevin Johnson*	28	CB	16	341	37	4.6%	--	19	10	5	11	45%	--	6.3	--	30	23.3%	--	11.2	70%	--	4.4	--	5	0
Siran Neal	26	SS	15	177	27	3.6%	--	11	6	3	10	60%	--	4.4	--	9	13.5%	--	6.3	67%	--	4.9	--	0	0
Josh Norman	33	CB	12	612	46	6.9%	79	14	3	6	11	36%	61	11.9	81	40	18.6%	58	16.9	38%	84	11.1	84	6	1

Year	Pass D Rank	vs. #1 WR	Rk	vs. #2 WR	Rk	vs. Other WR	Rk	WR Wide	Rk	WR Slot	Rk	vs. TE	Rk	vs. RB	Rk
2017	12	-0.1%	14	-29.7%	3	-28.0%	1	-10.0%	11	-22.7%	3	-3.9%	13	5.9%	20
2018	2	-11.2%	7	14.9%	24	-33.0%	2	-15.1%	6	-7.4%	8	-40.0%	2	-10.2%	9
2019	5	-32.8%	2	-20.7%	4	-8.1%	12	-24.4%	6	-16.7%	3	-0.3%	14	-5.8%	14

Buffalo's two primary linebackers cut down on missed tackles, yet the team still finished with the seventh-highest rate of missed tackles in the league. What gives? Four of Buffalo's defensive backs missed at least 10 tackles, with nickelback Taron Johnson leading the group by missing 31.6% of tackle opportunities. ◥ In a league rife with year-to-year inconsistency in coverage, star cornerback Tre'Davious White has established himself as consistently elite. In each of the past two seasons, White landed himself top-15 in success rate and top-10 in yards per target allowed. Even as a rookie in 2017, White posted a 54% success rate, which landed him in the top 25. White's All-Pro campaign last season was no fluke. ◥ Levi Wallace's increased playing time as the team's No.2 cornerback was a trial by fire. Wallace's 26.5% target rate was double that of what he faced the year before. The divide between Wallace's poor success rate and solid yards per pass allowed suggests he did well to defend passes down the field but gave up too many short-to-intermediate receptions. ◥ Free-agent signing Josh Norman is no guarantee to be an upgrade over Wallace, either. Norman's 2019 success rate of 38% was nearly 10% worse than his previous low since 2014 (47% in 2017). Likewise, Norman's 11.1 yards per pass allowed in 2019 was the only time in his career in which he allowed more than 10 yards per pass. ◥ The Bills' S/CB cover ratio dropped by 10% in 2019. While that may be partly due to variance, it may also have to do with an influx of slot cornerback talent. Not only did Taron Johnson post a second-straight season of 55%-plus success rate, but Kevin Johnson and Siran Neal, who filled in for Taron Johnson in the slot at various points, posted a combined 69% success rate on 39 total targets between them. ◥ Seventh-round pick Dane Jackson out of Pittsburgh fits Sean McDermott's profile as a press-man cornerback. Though not the best athlete down the field, Jackson has the snappy footwork and tough demeanor at the line of scrimmage to be molded into a contributor.

Special Teams

Year	DVOA	Rank	FG/XP	Rank	Net Kick	Rank	Kick Ret	Rank	Net Punt	Rank	Punt Ret	Rank	Hidden	Rank
2017	2.9%	10	11.5	4	2.0	15	-4.9	29	4.3	11	1.8	11	-9.0	29
2018	-5.1%	32	-5.4	26	-1.6	25	-2.3	21	-9.1	27	-7.3	31	-5.2	22
2019	-1.2%	21	3.2	12	-5.1	29	4.1	6	-9.4	29	1.2	12	15.5	1

Buffalo special teams finished below average in large part because of their kickoff and punting woes. Buffalo was one of just four teams to finish outside the top 25 in both net kickoffs and net punting. ◥ Corey Bojorquez just might be the worst punter in the league—he was third-worst in gross punt value in 2018, and dead last in 2019. Buffalo brought in Kaare Vedvik, who has not recorded a single regular-season punt since entering the league in 2018, though he was a punter/kicker combination in college at Marshall. ◥ On kickoffs, the problem was more about coverage than Stephen Hauschka, who had above-average gross kickoff value. ◥ Andre Roberts finished seventh in kickoff return value (4.4 points) in 2019 after finishing first (14.3) in 2018. The only other two players to rank in the top-10 in each of the past two seasons are Cordarelle Patterson and Jakeem Grant. ◥ New addition Tyler Matakevich tied for the league lead with 16 special teams tackles in Pittsburgh last season. ◥ Buffalo was dead last in the league with only 10 penalties on special teams. ◥ The Bills benefited from particularly poor opponent performance on field goals, worth -14.8 weather-adjusted points below average. Opponents missed four extra points and were just 16-of-26 on field goals. They missed four field goals within 40 yards, although to give the Bills credit, two of those were Buffalo blocks. (Much of this, but far from all of it, was due to Cairo Santos of the Titans going 0-for-4 in Week 5.) Further contributing to Buffalo's high "hidden" special teams, opponents were also poor on punt distance against the Bills.

Carolina Panthers

2019 Record: 5-11	**Total DVOA:** -26.7% (31st)	**2020 Mean Projection:** 5.7 wins	**On the Clock (0-4):** 33%
Pythagorean Wins: 4.9 (29th)	**Offense:** -14.3% (28th)	**Postseason Odds:** 12.7%	**Mediocrity (5-7):** 45%
Snap-Weighted Age: 26.6 (9th)	**Defense:** 8.2% (25th)	**Super Bowl Odds:** 0.6%	**Playoff Contender (8-10):** 18%
Average Opponent: 3.3% (4th)	**Special Teams:** -4.1% (31st)	**Proj. Avg. Opponent:** 3.6% (1st)	**Super Bowl Contender (11+):** 4%

2019: A team built around Cam Newton fails without him.

2020: A team built around Teddy Bridgewater is what, exactly?

On the spectrum of acceptance of losing, *Football Outsiders Almanac* writers and readers are likely on the comfortable end while new NFL team owners are likely on the uncomfortable end. For me, it has been a thrill to see the Browns and Dolphins inherit the 76ers' tanking mantle, making moves such as trading for Brock Osweiler's regrettable $72-million contract and trading away myriad productive veterans in order to stockpile draft picks and raise the ceiling of future editions of their teams. But whatever their original intentions, respective Browns and Dolphins owners Jimmy Haslam and Stephen Ross—who both purchased their teams in the last 15 years and have yet to enjoy a playoff win—seemed unwilling to see that tanking through to its natural conclusion. Haslam gave general managers Sashi Brown and John Dorsey just two seasons apiece to architect their attempted Browns rebuilds. Ross has been more patient with his GM Chris Grier, but he also enabled Grier's chosen head coach Brian Flores to right a ship that was better off sinking, pivoting in-season to veteran quarterback Ryan Fitzpatrick, whose subsequent five wins as a starter robbed the team of the agency it could have had in selecting a franchise quarterback in the 2020 draft.

David Tepper is probably uncomfortable. With a background in hedge fund management, he is the wealthiest of an extremely wealthy set of NFL owners. But it took Tepper a decade to transition from minority stakeholder in the Steelers to owner of the Panthers, and his first two seasons at the helm of his own team ended sourly with Carolina collapsing after promising 6-2 and 5-3 starts to finish 1-7 and 0-8 in the second halves of 2018 and 2019.

Tepper was ready to move on from long-time head coach Ron Rivera and star quarterback Cam Newton, and it is hard to blame him. Tepper has only ever seen Rivera and Newton at their worst. The defensive-minded Rivera had led the Panthers to above-average defensive DVOA finishes in six straight seasons before the unit fell to 22nd and 25th the last two years. Newton, meanwhile, played with an injured shoulder for much of 2018 and missed most of 2019 with a foot injury. And even longtime followers of the Panthers struggled to find the vocabulary to explain Newton's success when he had it. His traditional statistics like his career 59.6% completion rate and touchdown:interception ratio of less than 2:1 paint a picture of a below-average passer, an opinion his -3.0% career passing DVOA seems to confirm.

One needs similar creativity to see Newton's brilliance as his coaches needed to build an offense around him that could benefit from it. Since 2011, the Panthers have converted 61.6% of their short-yardage plays—defined here as third or fourth downs with 3 or fewer yards to gain or plays within 3 yards of the end zone—in Newton's starts. That puts Newton's Panthers in the company of the teams with the best pocket passers of the last decade (Table 1). But unlike for those traditionally quarterbacked teams that often convert these plays with quick and accurate throws, the Panthers' successes there rarely showed up in Newton's passing stats.

Table 1. Best Short-Yardage Conversion Rates, 2011-2019

Team	Starting Quarterback	Conv%
DAL	Dak Prescott	67.2%
NO	Drew Brees	62.3%
PIT	Ben Roethlisberger	62.1%
CAR	**Cam Newton**	**61.6%**
DEN	Peyton Manning	60.0%
ARI	Carson Palmer	59.8%
PHI	Carson Wentz	59.0%
KC	Alex Smith	58.9%
LAC	Philip Rivers	58.9%

Min. 50 Games Started
Only includes starts with listed team.

That short-yardage metric is particularly compelling for Newton's Panthers because it highlights their differences from the other teams of the 2010s with prolific running quarterbacks such as Russell Wilson's Seahawks (57.2%, 17th), Marcus Mariota's Titans (55.1%, 24th), and Colin Kaepernick's 49ers (53.8%, 28th). Newton isn't like other running quarterbacks. He doesn't scramble for new first downs, something that pocket passers can frequently do just as well as dual-threat quarterbacks because of how defenses scheme to stop them. Newton typically does his damage on designed runs where defenders fail to stop him or by making zone reads to hand off to players left open because defenders try too hard to stop the quarterback.

Newton may be the most powerful quarterback in league

2020 Panthers Schedule

Week	Opp.	Week	Opp.	Week	Opp.
1	LV	7	at NO	13	BYE
2	at TB	8	ATL (Thu.)	14	DEN
3	at LAC	9	at KC	15	at GB
4	ARI	10	TB	16	at WAS
5	at ATL	11	DET	17	NO
6	CHI	12	at MIN		

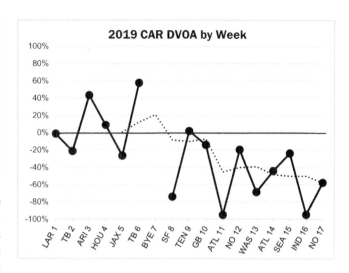

2019 CAR DVOA by Week

history, but his best offenses were ballets that required the synchronized efforts of the players around him and uninterrupted strings of small successes. They only worked with a player of Newton's skill set in the starring role, and that is something that became a huge problem for the team when he suffered injuries the last two seasons. The shoulder injury took away Newton's deep ball—a relative strength compared to his shorter passing—and allowed defenses to pack in and overwhelm an offense whose run reliance worked best against a team compelled to respect the possibility of a big passing play. The foot injury forced the team to play backups Kyle Allen and Will Grier, neither of whom share Newton's singular combination of size, strength, and athleticism. They fell prey to a bottom-five pass-protecting offensive line (8.6% adjusted sack rate) whose relative strengths in run-blocking (4.30 adjusted line yards, 17th) made more sense for an offense with Newton under center and whose weaknesses Newton may have papered over had he been healthy.

Newton may be healthy now. His incentive-laden, one-year deal with the Patriots is not much of an indicator either way, and the pandemic has disrupted the offseason practices that could have showcased his health. But even when he has been healthy, Newton has never been consistent. Perhaps because of the many hits he takes with his playing style or perhaps because of the inconsistency of his footwork and passing mechanics, Newton took the Panthers on a rollercoaster ride even before 2018. Between 2011 and 2017, the Panthers had the highest mean absolute deviation of year-to-year DVOA, score differential, and winning percentage in football.

Again, it makes sense that Tepper would want to move on. But the execution of his transition to a new chapter in Carolina carries the hallmarks of a new owner who wants to win immediately, an impulse that sometimes sabotages a team's chances to reach the heights needed to compete for a Super Bowl in the long run.

That is not meant to be a criticism of Tepper's new coaching staff. Head coach Matt Rhule inherited struggling—and in the latter case sanctioned—programs at Temple and Baylor that went 4-7 and 7-6, respectively, the year before he arrived; he turned them into 10- and 11-game winners in just three seasons. He has a similar challenge in front of him in Carolina.

Rhule outed himself as a non-regular reader of Football Outsiders when, reflecting upon a team research project that showed his Temple Owls were undefeated in his games with a 150-yard rusher, he told Football Scoop reporters that "I figured it out, let's run for 150 yards, we'll win and I can get my

wife a new kitchen and pay for my daughter to go to private school." One hopes that some insincere bravado was lost in translation when Rhule mused "Run the football and stop the run—you can win games by not doing that, but you'll never control them."

Fortunately, Rhule doesn't need to motivate me. He needs to motivate likeminded men. And regardless of Rhule's own analytical leanings, his college successes suggest an agnosticism to specific schemes. At Temple, he relied on frequent 22 personnel to run his preferred brand of smashmouth football—with a dual-threat passer at the helm in P.J. Walker, who after standing out in the latest iteration of the XFL has rejoined his former head coach as a quarterback prospect for the Panthers. But at Baylor, Rhule won with an antithetical offensive approach, a spread offense with modern RPO concepts. He may be more of a CEO than an X's-and-O's coach, and that style absolutely can work in the NFL with the right assistant coaches around him.

As such, the fate of this version of the Panthers may rest on the shoulders of offensive coordinator Joe Brady and defensive coordinator Phil Snow. Brady is the next in line of the Sean McVay brand of young quarterback whisperers. While still in his 20s, Brady designed and even called some plays for a Saints offense that finished sixth and second in DVOA in his two seasons with the team. At 30, he architected LSU's transition to a modern spread offense that resulted in an undefeated championship season, an FBS-record 726 points, and an FBS-record 60 passing touchdowns from Heisman winner and middling-prospect-turned-No.-1-pick Joe Burrow. Brady's resume is short but unimpeachable.

The Panthers' decision to pair Brady with free-agent quarterback Teddy Bridgewater makes a lot of sense. Bridgewater worked with Brady when he was Drew Brees' backup in New Orleans. The Panthers' hot start to the 2019 season took them out of the race for Burrow, and so Bridgewater was the only starting-caliber quarterback the Panthers could have signed who was familiar with Brady's offense, likely a requisite for short-term success given the practice challenges teams face with the pandemic this offseason.

Still, Bridgewater strikes me as a floor-raising but ceiling-lowering choice at quarterback. He is Alex Smith with better press. He, Smith, and Sam Bradford are the only three of 39 qualified quarterbacks with negative air yards less expectations (ALEX) on third and fourth downs over 1,000 or more overall pass attempts since 2014 (Table 2). Across all downs, Bridgewater is tied for the third-lowest average depth of target (aDOT).

Table 2. Lowest ALEX, 2014-2019

Player	aDOT	ALEX
Alex Smith	6.9	-0.7
Teddy Bridgewater	**7.2**	**-0.7**
Sam Bradford	6.7	-0.4
Case Keenum	7.4	0.0
Jared Goff	7.9	0.3
Dak Prescott	8.2	0.7
Mitchell Trubisky	8.2	0.7
Brock Osweiler	8.4	0.7
Blake Bortles	7.9	0.8
Derek Carr	7.5	0.9
Joe Flacco	7.5	0.9
Andy Dalton	8.0	0.9

Min. 1,000 Pass Attempts
ALEX limited to third and fourth downs; aDOT represents all downs.

That hyper-conservative nature can win games for teams like Bridgewater's Saints and Smith's Chiefs that enjoy a talent advantage over their opponents at other positions. But the Panthers don't appear to have that. Their poor pass-blocking line may have gotten worse following a cost-saving offseason trade of their lone Pro Bowl lineman Trai Turner for older veteran Russell Okung. Receivers Curtis Samuel and newcomer—and another Rhule Temple alum—Robby Anderson have deep speed, but that trait may be wasted with the least aggressive quarterback in football. Christian McCaffrey and D.J. Moore are strong performers with the quickness and after-the-catch ability (they have exceptional-for-their-positions 8.3 and 5.8 average yards after the catch since 2018) to complement Bridgewater, but even their standout 2019 campaigns couldn't stem the tide of a winless second half of the season.

Rhule and Brady most likely will not face the quick hook that pulled recent Browns coaches if the Bridgewater-McCaffrey-Moore triumvirate fails to have immediate success. But if the team stumbles in 2020, it's unclear whether Rhule and Brady can even have a Plan B. The team committed $33.0 and $38.2 million guaranteed dollars to Bridgewater and McCaffrey this offseason that effectively binds them to the team for at least the next two and three seasons, respectively. Bridgewater may have made the most sense for Brady, but his base contract will pay more than four times the amount that any of the more accomplished Andy Dalton, Jameis Winston, and Newton could earn even if they fully realize the incentives of their new deals. And while McCaffrey's position-leading 386 receiving DYAR and marketability provide the narratives to support his record-setting running back contract, the same could be said for the megadeals recent receiving-capable backs such as Todd Gurley, David Johnson, and Le'Veon Bell

signed … and that their teams almost immediately regretted.

The irony of all of this is that the Panthers' short-term prospects are likely disproportionately tied to relatively unheralded defensive coordinator Phil Snow's ability to turn around a defense that devolved to become truly dreadful in Rivera's last year with the team. Carolina's 18.6% run defense DVOA was the fifth worst in history (1985-present), which made it impossible for the team to rally when they fell behind in games.

To complicate matters, the Panthers lost their only blue-chip defender from that 2019 team and likely the best overall player in the team's history, Luke Kuechly. Kuechly was decidedly not the problem with the team's run defense last season. His 10.6% blown tackle rate landed him in his usual company of the best linebackers in football. Based on his wistful retirement announcement, his decision to walk away at 29 years old reflected a concern for his long-term health rather than any belief in a decline in the quality of his performance or his desire to play.

Kuechly is far from the only loss the Panthers defense suffered this offseason. The greater part of their defensive line rotation left in free agency, including defensive ends Mario Addison and Bruce Irvin and defensive tackles Gerald McCoy, Dontari Poe, and Vernon Butler. Top cornerbacks James Bradberry and Ross Cockrell departed as well, and the team released starting safety Eric Reid. In all, the team will turn over the primary starters at eight of 11 defensive positions in 2020.

In the long term, we're optimistic for the team's potential turnaround on defense. They used their top pick in 2019 on pass-rusher Brian Burns, who threatened the team lead with 7.5 sacks as a part-time player in his rookie season. His class-leading 96.1% SackSEER rating offers him the potential to be a better pass-rusher at his peak than the Panthers had in any veteran last season. In addition, the Panthers made an unprecedented investment of all seven of their 2020 draft picks in defensive players, including a trio of first- and second-round picks in tackle Derrick Brown, end Yetur Gross-Matos, and safety Jeremy Chinn. Brown was scouts' unanimous choice for the top defensive tackle in the class and should directly address the unit's biggest deficiency in run defense. Gross-Matos and Chinn are possible Day 1 starters as well. It turns out it is easy to draft for team needs when your team has holes at practically every position.

The Panthers' youth-driven defensive makeover follows the script of previous successful rebuilds like those of the 49ers and Buccaneers defenses in recent seasons, but it stands out next to offensive roster moves that seem to target a quick fix. Brown's strength and Chinn's athleticism will allow them to make plays that many veteran tackles and safeties couldn't, but the broader trends show that older defenses—as measured by snap-weighted age—perform better in defensive DVOA, and with similar correlation strength since 2006 (-0.160) to how older offenses perform in offensive DVOA (0.168).

Had they retained Newton, the Panthers could have hoped that their bipolar tendencies returned them to another peak season. Had they fully embraced a youth movement on both sides of the ball, they could have been bad but exciting, earned a top 2021 draft pick with little stress, and perhaps discovered some prospects for future team contributors in unheralded players who would likely only play for a team with no urgency to win games. With the in-between approach that I assume is motivated by Tepper's desire to fast-track a successful team, they could be stuck in the middle.

That isn't where we project the team. Carolina has the second-worst mean DVOA projection and the lowest mean win forecast for 2020. (The hardest projected schedule in the league, bolstered by three strong division rivals, certainly doesn't help.) But their proximity to other bottom-third teams in our projections makes it unlikely the Panthers will land the top overall pick if they hit or exceed their expected wins total. Some poor teams will almost certainly fall short of their projections as injuries and bad luck hit. The Panthers could have been bad enough to stay worse than those teams with even luck. But with their win-now offensive additions, they

may end up a respectable loser and win just enough games to miss out on the 2021 quarterback prospects such as Trevor Lawrence and Trey Lance that could actually raise the team's long-term ceiling.

Even though they abruptly abandoned their apparent plan to lose midway through the 2019 season, the Dolphins still landed the original apple of their tanking eye, Tua Tagovailoa. One could read that result as a karmic reward for reembracing the integrity of the sport—bad teams don't necessarily have to tank in the short term to become competitive in the long term. Still, with the worst mean win forecast in football, it's not clear what the Panthers have gained by committing themselves to Bridgewater on offense, while it's clear what they have risked. In trying to win the battle of 2020 respectability, the Panthers may well have lost the war.

Scott Spratt

2019 Panthers Stats by Week

Wk	vs.	W-L	PF	PA	YDF	YDA	TO	Total	Off	Def	ST
1	LAR	L	27	30	343	349	-2	-1%	9%	9%	-1%
2	TB	L	14	20	352	289	-1	-21%	-17%	17%	12%
3	at ARI	W	38	20	413	248	+1	43%	12%	-32%	-1%
4	at HOU	W	16	10	297	264	-1	9%	-28%	-35%	2%
5	JAX	W	34	27	445	507	+3	-27%	16%	29%	-14%
6	at TB	W	37	26	268	407	+6	58%	13%	-34%	10%
7	BYE										
8	at SF	L	13	51	230	388	-2	-74%	-47%	21%	-7%
9	TEN	W	30	20	370	431	+2	2%	16%	7%	-7%
10	at GB	L	16	24	401	388	-2	-14%	4%	21%	2%
11	ATL	L	3	29	347	349	-4	-95%	-70%	9%	-16%
12	at NO	L	31	34	351	418	0	-20%	5%	11%	-14%
13	WAS	L	21	29	278	362	-2	-68%	-42%	29%	2%
14	at ATL	L	20	40	345	461	-4	-44%	-16%	28%	0%
15	SEA	L	24	30	414	428	-2	-24%	-12%	21%	9%
16	at IND	L	6	38	286	324	-3	-95%	-34%	16%	-45%
17	NO	L	10	42	329	379	-3	-58%	-37%	20%	0%

Trends and Splits

	Offense	Rank	Defense	Rank
Total DVOA	-14.3%	28	8.2%	25
Unadjusted VOA	-17.0%	28	10.1%	25
Weighted Trend	-20.0%	30	14.2%	28
Variance	7.1%	14	4.8%	7
Average Opponent	-0.5%	15	2.9%	5
Passing	-19.8%	31	-0.7%	11
Rushing	0.7%	9	18.6%	32
First Down	-0.5%	16	5.9%	22
Second Down	-17.4%	28	8.8%	26
Third Down	-38.5%	30	12.7%	23
First Half	-16.5%	28	4.6%	23
Second Half	-12.3%	26	12.2%	28
Red Zone	-15.3%	24	26.9%	30
Late and Close	-23.0%	29	17.6%	30

Five-Year Performance

Year	W-L	Pyth W	Est W	PF	PA	TO	Total	Rk	Off	Rk	Def	Rk	ST	Rk	Off AGL	Rk	Def AGL	Rk	Off Age	Rk	Def Age	Rk	ST Age	Rk
2015	15-1	12.4	11.1	500	308	+20	26.0%	4	10.1%	8	-18.4%	2	-2.4%	23	28.0	13	44.3	27	27.0	14	28.1	3	26.8	3
2016	6-10	7.1	6.7	369	402	-2	-5.5%	24	-8.4%	25	-5.3%	10	-2.5%	25	36.8	17	37.2	15	27.0	12	26.2	23	26.6	6
2017	11-5	9.0	10.3	363	327	-1	13.0%	9	-0.5%	17	-8.8%	7	4.7%	6	30.1	14	10.3	5	26.3	25	28.4	1	26.6	4
2018	7-9	7.8	7.8	376	382	+1	0.5%	14	6.0%	11	5.4%	22	-0.2%	18	51.1	25	51.5	27	26.7	16	28.9	1	26.6	5
2019	5-11	4.9	3.9	340	470	-14	-26.7%	31	-14.3%	28	8.2%	25	-4.1%	31	36.5	14	29.7	14	26.1	27	27.4	2	26.0	12

2019 Performance Based on Most Common Personnel Groups

CAR Offense					CAR Offense vs. Opponents					CAR Defense				CAR Defense vs. Opponents			
Pers	Freq	Yds	DVOA	Run%	Pers	Freq	Yds	DVOA	Run%	Pers	Freq	Yds	DVOA	Pers	Freq	Yds	DVOA
11	68%	5.2	-14.7%	23%	Base	28%	5.3	-11.7%	52%	Base	32%	6.7	15.4%	11	56%	6.0	6.3%
12	18%	5.5	1.3%	49%	Nickel	57%	5.1	-13.9%	27%	Nickel	66%	5.7	2.6%	12	20%	6.5	21.0%
21	6%	6.2	-9.4%	34%	Dime+	14%	5.9	-2.4%	12%	Dime+	1%	6.2	38.8%	10	7%	4.1	-31.3%
22	5%	4.9	-16.2%	83%	Goal Line	1%	0.6	-53.4%	80%	Goal Line	1%	0.7	25.5%	21	5%	6.8	-1.7%
13	2%	2.9	-29.6%	56%	Big	1%	2.0	20.4%	75%					612	3%	7.5	57.3%
622	1%	0.1	-28.4%	64%										611	3%	9.1	27.8%

Strategic Tendencies

Run/Pass		Rk	Formation		Rk	Pass Rush		Rk	Secondary		Rk	Strategy		Rk
Runs, first half	33%	28	Form: Single Back	80%	18	Rush 3	1.9%	31	4 DB	32%	6	Play Action	31%	6
Runs, first down	44%	27	Form: Empty Back	7%	20	Rush 4	71.8%	11	5 DB	66%	9	Offensive Motion	51%	6
Runs, second-long	24%	22	Form: Multi Back	13%	11	Rush 5	23.9%	7	6+ DB	1%	30	Avg Box (Off)	6.56	17
Runs, power sit.	52%	24	Pers: 3+ WR	68%	14	Rush 6+	2.4%	28	Man Coverage	19%	31	Avg Box (Def)	6.73	6
Runs, behind 2H	25%	25	Pers: 2+ TE/6+ OL	26%	17	Edge Rusher Sacks	53.8%	20	CB by Sides	67%	23	Offensive Pace	28.56	5
Pass, ahead 2H	45%	23	Pers: 6+ OL	1%	23	Interior DL Sacks	29.2%	10	S/CB Cover Ratio	25%	17	Defensive Pace	30.80	20
Run-Pass Options	9%	9	Shotgun/Pistol	72%	9	Second Level Sacks	17.0%	17	DB Blitz	8%	19	Go for it on 4th	1.70	10

Despite the troubles at quarterback and Christian McCaffrey's awesome season, the Panthers' run/pass ratio in the first half of games went down from 2018 when they ranked fourth in the league. ✎ At the same time, the Panthers' pace picked up significantly, at least when games were close, as they went from 26th to fifth in situation-neutral pace. ✎ The Panthers ranked No. 2 in DVOA running on first downs. On every other down/play combination, they ranked 25th or worse. ✎ The Panthers had the league's biggest yardage discrepancy between runs from shotgun (3.8 yards, -5.4% DVOA) and runs from under-center formations (5.8 yards, 9.5% DVOA). ✎ Carolina had 4.0% of plays from pistol formations, fourth in the league, but had a -37.5% DVOA and averaged 3.8 yards on these plays. ✎ Carolina threw a league-low 16% of passes in the middle of the field and had the worst DVOA in the league on passes up the middle. ✎ Carolina committed a league-low 37 penalties on offense, including declined and offsetting. ✎ The listed Aggressiveness Index number is for Ron Rivera; Perry Fewell had an AI of 3.70 in his four games, but that's a very small sample with only two qualifying fourth-down attempts.

Passing

Player	DYAR	DVOA	Plays	NtYds	Avg	YAC	C%	TD	Int
K.Allen*	-395	-22.4%	536	2916	5.4	5.4	62.2%	17	16
C.Newton*	19	-8.0%	94	529	5.6	4.1	56.8%	0	1
W.Grier	-180	-60.6%	58	184	3.2	6.4	53.8%	0	3
T.Bridgewater	340	15.3%	208	1283	6.2	5.6	68.2%	9	2

Rushing

Player	DYAR	DVOA	Plays	Yds	Avg	TD	Fum	Suc
C.McCaffrey	278	14.9%	287	1387	4.8	15	1	47%
K.Allen*	4	-9.0%	25	108	4.3	2	1	-
C.Samuel	97	54.2%	19	130	6.8	1	0	-
R.Bonnafon	14	15.2%	16	116	7.3	1	0	38%
W.Grier	-23	-71.8%	7	20	2.9	0	1	-
A.Armah	-3	-18.4%	6	11	1.8	1	0	17%
D.Moore	32	59.8%	6	40	6.7	0	0	-
C.Newton*	-48	-230.2%	5	-2	-0.4	0	2	-
J.Scarlett	-4	-27.3%	4	9	2.3	0	0	50%
T.Bridgewater	-19	-32.7%	15	44	2.9	0	0	-
M.Davis	-28	-65.9%	11	25	2.3	0	0	18%

Receiving

Player	DYAR	DVOA	Plays	Ctch	Yds	Y/C	YAC	TD	C%
D.Moore	167	3.2%	135	87	1175	13.5	4.5	4	64%
C.Samuel	-21	-15.1%	105	54	627	11.6	2.8	6	51%
J.Wright*	-124	-39.6%	58	28	296	10.6	3.2	0	48%
C.Hogan*	-33	-42.0%	15	8	67	8.4	3.6	0	53%
B.Zylstra	20	8.4%	12	8	106	13.3	1.3	0	67%
D.White	-14	-32.1%	9	4	51	12.8	7.0	0	44%
Ro.Anderson	66	-4.2%	96	52	779	15.0	3.7	5	54%
S.Roberts	62	10.4%	35	21	271	12.9	3.3	2	60%
P.Cooper	33	0.4%	33	25	243	9.7	2.8	1	76%
G.Olsen*	4	-6.5%	82	52	597	11.5	3.9	2	63%
I.Thomas	-41	-27.1%	30	16	136	8.5	4.8	1	53%
C.McCaffrey	386	34.8%	142	116	1005	8.7	8.5	4	82%
R.Bonnafon	13	14.9%	9	6	57	9.5	8.7	0	67%
M.Davis	-9	-33.4%	8	7	22	3.1	3.9	0	88%

Offensive Line

Player	Pos	Age	GS	Snaps	Pen	Sk	Pass	Run	Player	Pos	Age	GS	Snaps	Pen	Sk	Pass	Run
Taylor Moton	RT	26	16/16	1123	6	4.0	16	9	Dennis Daley	LT/RG	24	14/9	691	4	9.0	21	5
Matt Paradis	C	31	16/16	1111	3	1.0	14	5	Greg Little	LT	23	4/3	230	3	4.0	10	3
Trai Turner*	RG	27	13/13	900	3	4.0	14	2	John Miller	RG	27	13/13	797	3	1.5	10	7
Daryl Williams*	LG/LT	28	16/12	851	2	9.0	17	6	*Russell Okung*	*LT*	*32*	*6/6*	*262*	*6*	*0.0*	*3*	*1*
Greg Van Roten*	LG	30	11/11	719	2	0.0	6	5									

Year	Yards	ALY	Rank	Power	Rank	Stuff	Rank	2nd Lev	Rank	Open Field	Rank	Sacks	ASR	Rank	Press	Rank	F-Start	Cont.
2017	3.61	3.78	25	72%	5	19%	12	0.94	30	0.53	22	35	7.1%	19	29.3%	9	9	30
2018	4.62	4.55	11	67%	18	17%	7	1.27	17	0.97	12	32	6.1%	10	28.9%	15	16	34
2019	4.84	4.30	17	43%	32	18%	10	1.20	15	1.26	1	58	8.6%	29	30.4%	20	9	28
2019 ALY by direction:			Left End 3.32 (25)			Left Tackle: 4.16 (19)			Mid/Guard: 4.41 (18)			Right Tackle: 4.41 (13)			Right End: 4.44 (14)			

The Panthers' decision to trade 27-year-old, five-time Pro Bowl right guard Trai Turner for 32-year-old, two-time (but two years removed from his last) Pro Bowl left tackle Russell Okung was one of the most interesting of the offseason. The easy explanation is that Turner carries an extra year on his contract for an extra $7.5 million in total cap hit, but that explanation doesn't fully satisfy. The team's other offseason moves refute a presumed plan to rebuild, and Turner is the kind of player that a competitive team would presumably want to have locked into a long-term contract. Instead, that trade seems to suggest that the Panthers believe a good left tackle is more valuable than a really good right guard. 🏈 Whatever his recent accolades, Okung will address a glaring team weakness if he can continue the excellent 1.3% blown block rate he provided the Chargers the last two seasons. Since Michael Oher's stellar 2015 season, the Panthers have cycled through turnstiles at left tackle including Mike Remmers, Matt Kalil, Chris Clark, and Dennis Daley. The team's second-round pick last year, Greg Little, was supposed to stabilize the left side of the team's offensive line, but an ankle injury limited him to just four games in his rookie season. Now healthy, Little and Okung—who had his own health scare in 2019 when a pulmonary embolism kept him out of the first two months of the season—offer the Panthers more optimism at left tackle than they've had in years. Little may even provide both short- and long-term insurance at right tackle for Taylor Moton, who like Okung is entering the final year of his current contract. 🏈 Daley wasn't solely responsible for the 2019 team's 8.6% adjusted sack rate, fourth-worst in football, and the Turner-for-Okung trade likely won't make the Panthers' offensive line one of the game's best in pass protection. Free-agent addition Matt Paradis blew a career-high 14 pass blocks in his first year with the team in 2019. Daryl Williams blew 17. And both Williams and Greg Van Roten—the team's only starter who did not allow a sack—left the team in free agency this offseason.

Defensive Front

Defensive Line	Age	Pos	G	Snaps	Plays	TmPct	Overall Rk	Stop	Dfts	BTkl	Runs	St%	vs. Run Rk	RuYd	Rk	Sack	Hit	Pass Rush Hur	Dsrpt
Gerald McCoy*	32	DE	16	711	39	4.7%	43	37	10	5	31	94%	3	1.5	13	5.0	9	27	2
Vernon Butler*	26	DE	14	449	31	4.3%	67	27	11	1	24	83%	19	2.3	45	6.0	4	7	0
Kyle Love*	34	DT	15	422	9	1.2%	--	8	2	2	8	88%	--	2.0	--	0.0	2	10	2
Dontari Poe*	30	DT	11	416	21	3.7%	86	15	6	2	13	69%	71	3.2	92	4.0	2	9	0

Edge Rushers	Age	Pos	G	Snaps	Plays	TmPct	Overall Rk	Stop	Dfts	BTkl	Runs	St%	vs. Run Rk	RuYd	Rk	Sack	Hit	Pass Rush Hur	Dsrpt
Mario Addison*	33	OLB	15	746	33	4.3%	57	20	13	2	20	40%	90	5.5	91	9.5	5	25	1
Bruce Irvin*	33	OLB	13	623	37	5.5%	46	29	17	4	26	69%	64	2.7	49	8.5	9	23	0
Brian Burns	22	OLB	16	483	23	2.8%	78	19	10	4	12	75%	39	2.3	37	7.5	9	19	0
Efe Obada	28	DE	16	311	24	2.9%	--	15	1	1	21	62%	--	3.4	--	0.0	3	8	1
Marquis Haynes	27	OLB	11	214	10	1.8%	--	5	2	0	7	43%	--	3.1	--	1.0	1	5	0
Stephen Weatherly	*26*	*DE*	*16*	*424*	*24*	*2.7%*	*--*	*17*	*8*	*2*	*21*	*67%*	*--*	*2.4*	*--*	*3.0*	*7*	*19*	*0*

Linebackers	Age	Pos	G	Snaps	Plays	TmPct	Rk	Stop	Dfts	BTkl	Runs	St%	Rk	RuYd	Rk	Sack	Hit	Hur	Tgts	Suc%	Rk	AdjYd	Rk	PD	Int
						Overall						vs. Run				Pass Rush					vs. Pass				
Luke Kuechly*	29	ILB	16	1086	156	19.0%	3	88	20	9	89	65%	22	3.4	23	0.0	5	6	53	55%	24	6.0	30	12	2
Shaq Thompson	26	ILB	14	984	112	15.6%	24	54	18	15	48	60%	41	4.3	60	3.0	2	7	51	53%	27	4.8	10	3	0
Jermaine Carter	25	ILB	16	263	25	3.0%	--	14	3	4	18	67%	--	3.1	--	0.5	1	2	11	45%	--	5.6	--	0	0
Tahir Whitehead	30	OLB	16	961	108	14.0%	22	42	13	9	64	50%	73	4.4	65	0.0	2	4	38	37%	59	11.1	66	1	0

Year	Yards	ALY	Rank	Power	Rank	Stuff	Rank	2nd Level	Rank	Open Field	Rank	Sacks	ASR	Rank	Press	Rank
2017	3.89	3.51	5	47%	2	26%	4	1.12	18	0.94	27	50	9.1%	3	32.9%	6
2018	4.71	3.97	8	78%	31	24%	7	1.40	27	1.32	31	35	6.8%	20	31.6%	10
2019	5.32	4.89	30	74%	29	17%	22	1.49	32	1.41	31	53	8.8%	3	28.6%	22
2019 ALY by direction:		Left End: 3.41 (7)			Left Tackle: 5.13 (29)			Mid/Guard: 5.16 (31)			Right Tackle: 4.57 (20)			Right End: 4.62 (17)	

The Panthers had the third-best defensive front in adjusted sack rate (8.8%) but the third-worst defensive front in adjusted line yards (4.89). That's a split that can work for a team with an explosive offense such as the Chiefs but proved devastating for the Panthers with their bad offense in 2019. ◗ The team's defensive front will look very different in 2020 than it did in 2019, but it's unclear how much if any that should improve things. The team subtracted Dontari Poe and his poor 69% run stop rate in free agency, but they also lost Gerald McCoy and Vernon Butler, whose 94% and 83% run stop rates were quite good. ◗ The team's top draft pick, Derrick Brown out of Auburn (No. 7 overall), was the consensus top defensive tackle in the class and should anchor the team's new-look defensive line. At 6-foot-5 and 326 pounds, Brown has the size one would expect of a run-stopping anchor, but he may do his best work as an interior pass-rusher. Returning lineman Kawann Short had similar versatility against both the run and the pass before a shoulder injury limited him to two games in 2019. From 2015 to 2018, Short led Carolina linemen in stops every season, and he led them in defeats three times in four years. His return to form would be the most likely path for an immediate, dramatic improvement of the team's run defense. ◗ With Mario Addison and Bruce Irvin also on new teams, 2019 first-rounder Brian Burns and 2020 second-round Penn State product Yetur Gross-Matos will be charged with maintaining the team's strong outside pass rush. And despite their lack of experience, their 96.1% and 61.6% respective SackSEER ratings suggest they can do so. ◗ Even with experience from Shaq Thompson and Tahir Whitehead, off-ball linebacker could be Carolina's biggest weakness in the front seven. Thompson did not buckle under the responsibility of his first year as a three-down player in 2019, but he and Whitehead combined for only 96 stops, barely beating Kuechly's total of 88 despite collectively playing almost twice as many defensive snaps. Meanwhile, the team lacks quality depth throughout the defensive front and could endure a similar fall from grace if they suffer as many injuries in 2020 as they did in 2019.

Defensive Secondary

Secondary	Age	Pos	G	Snaps	Plays	TmPct	Rk	Stop	Dfts	BTkl	Runs	St%	Rk	RuYd	Rk	Tgts	Tgt%	Rk	Dist	Suc%	Rk	AdjYd	Rk	PD	Int
						Overall						vs. Run							vs. Pass						
Tre Boston	28	FS	16	1127	79	9.6%	32	20	10	15	32	19%	70	12.8	73	22	5.3%	64	17.8	50%	41	7.5	37	11	3
Eric Reid*	29	SS	16	1115	135	16.4%	2	52	12	16	77	43%	35	6.3	33	46	11.1%	15	11.5	33%	68	10.8	69	6	0
James Bradberry*	27	CB	15	1038	77	10.0%	16	22	9	8	20	20%	77	10.5	80	75	19.5%	49	14.9	52%	48	6.9	26	12	3
Donte Jackson	25	CB	13	745	48	7.2%	72	23	9	12	18	39%	53	6.6	46	53	19.2%	52	17.4	53%	41	10.5	80	8	3
Ross Cockrell*	29	CB	14	743	69	9.6%	28	30	10	12	23	52%	33	6.2	41	57	20.7%	35	13.3	61%	10	6.3	13	8	2
Javien Elliott*	27	CB	16	444	39	4.7%	--	17	7	7	14	57%	--	6.8	--	22	13.4%	--	9.8	36%	--	8.6	--	2	1
Eli Apple	25	CB	15	954	62	8.4%	35	16	4	4	12	25%	72	8.3	66	64	15.2%	77	12.1	53%	38	8.6	61	4	0
Juston Burris	27	FS	14	419	37	5.3%	69	19	8	6	18	44%	30	6.0	30	12	7.9%	39	10.2	67%	7	4.8	7	7	2

Year	Pass D Rank	vs. #1 WR	Rk	vs. #2 WR	Rk	vs. Other WR	Rk	WR Wide	Rk	WR Slot	Rk	vs. TE	Rk	vs. RB	Rk
2017	11	9.5%	19	5.4%	20	3.4%	19	1.6%	19	11.7%	20	-22.2%	4	-3.0%	14
2018	24	-15.0%	5	29.5%	32	-2.9%	15	-4.2%	20	5.4%	19	17.2%	24	-15.1%	5
2019	11	-10.7%	8	8.0%	23	-22.6%	4	-28.0%	4	7.7%	19	7.4%	22	-3.0%	17

Starting cornerbacks James Bradberry and Ross Cockrell turned in bounce-back and career years in coverage, respectively, each limiting opposing receivers to less than 7.0 yards per target. But as has become a running theme in this chapter, both players departed as free agents. A 53% coverage success rate may suggest that third-year corner Donte Jackson could handle the responsibility of being the team's top corner, but he was also routinely beaten over the top on a 17.4-yard average depth of target, easily the deepest of any Panthers cornerback. An already uncomfortable 10.5 yards per target could get even worse if the 5-foot-10 Jackson has to match up with the No. 1 receivers in his division such as Julio Jones, Michael Thomas, and Mike

Evans in 2020. And he'll have little help from a cornerback group that otherwise includes journeyman Eli Apple, fourth-round rookie Troy Pride from Notre Dame, and no one else with NFL experience to speak of. ◗ At least Jackson will have help from a trio of talented safeties. Veteran Tre Boston reverted to his poor 2017 form in run defense in his return to the Panthers in 2019, but he continued to play well in pass defense. He limited receivers to 7.5 yards per target despite a team-leading 17.8-yard aDOT and finished second on the Panthers with 11 passes defensed. He'll have fifth-round rookie Kenny Robinson behind him. Robinson was a more productive college safety than his Day 3 status would indicate, but he was expelled from West Virginia for academic fraud. Robinson was frank in an admission of his cheating in a letter he wrote for *The Players Tribune*, the same letter where he named himself the most NFL-ready safety prospect in the 2020 draft. Robinson does not seem to lack for confidence, but he also may be right on that latter point. He played and was productive in the short-lived XFL in 2019 prior to being drafted. ◗ Finally, second-round draft pick Jeremy Chinn from Southern Illinois should start for the Panthers immediately at strong safety. His exceptional 4.45s 40 time, 41-inch vertical jump, and 138-inch broad jump each placed him in the top three safeties as this year's combine and suggest an athleticism that the Panthers hope will help him make plays in both run and pass defense.

Special Teams

Year	DVOA	Rank	FG/XP	Rank	Net Kick	Rank	Kick Ret	Rank	Net Punt	Rank	Punt Ret	Rank	Hidden	Rank
2017	4.7%	6	6.3	10	2.2	14	5.3	6	7.8	5	1.9	10	-0.2	13
2018	-0.2%	18	3.4	10	-1.2	20	-3.6	27	3.6	12	-3.1	24	-11.6	30
2019	-4.1%	31	1.9	13	3.0	10	-2.9	26	-17.3	32	-5.4	30	6.1	7

The Panthers have been oddly obsessed with kicker Graham Gano since they first signed him in 2012 following his release by Washington. Since then, the team has extended Gano on a pair of long-term contracts. The first of those contracts induced them to cut seventh-round gem Harrison Butker in the 2017 preseason; the second paid him $9 million in practical guarantees—still in the top five of kickers two years after he signed it—and would have stuck the team with close to a $6-million dead cap hit had they cut him after he hurt his leg last year and went on injured reserve. ◗ Fortunately for the team's finances, they found a replacement for Gano in 2019 in undrafted second-year kicker Joey Slye. Somehow, Slye is an even more extreme version of the already extreme Gano. With maybe the strongest leg in football, Slye allowed just three returns on 70 kickoffs, good for a rate of 4.3% that was easily the lowest among regular kickers. He also converted eight of 11 field goal attempts from both 40 to 49 yards and from 50 or more yards, the latter total being a franchise record for a season. Slye's problem was consistency. He missed three kicks in two different games, including a three-point loss to the division-rival Saints in November. And on just 35 extra points plus five field goal attempts under 30 yards, Slye missed eight easy kicks on the season. That more than anything else is why the inexpensive Slye will have to win a camp battle with a now-healthy Gano to keep his job in 2020. ◗ The Panthers' last-place performance on punts was almost entirely due to Carolina native Nyheim Hines' two-touchdown game in Indianapolis in Week 16. Punter Michael Palardy was average in gross punt value, and the Panthers punt coverage team allowed only 1.3 estimated points worth of returns in the other 15 games of the season. ◗ Six different Panthers returned at least one kick and six different Panthers returned at least one punt in 2019. Unsurprisingly then, the team finished in the bottom seven of both kick and punt return value and second-to-last in special teams DVOA. As the saying goes, if you have six returners, do you have one? ◗ The team retained just four of those eight total returners for 2020—Reggie Bonnafon, DeAndrew White, Brandon Zylstra, and D.J. Moore—and free-agent addition Pharoh Cooper may consolidate that work in any case. He was the primary kick and punt returner for the Cardinals last season, although in the past two years he has not come close to matching his 2017 All-Pro season with the Rams.

Chicago Bears

2019 Record: 8-8	Total DVOA: -2.1% (15th)	2020 Mean Projection: 7.8 wins	On the Clock (0-4): 11%
Pythagorean Wins: 7.4 (20th)	Offense: -10.1% (25th)	Postseason Odds: 39.8%	Mediocrity (5-7): 35%
Snap-Weighted Age: 26.4 (14th)	Defense: -7.2% (8th)	Super Bowl Odds: 3.9%	Playoff Contender (8-10): 38%
Average Opponent: 2.5% (9th)	Special Teams: 0.9% (13rd)	Proj. Avg. Opponent: -0.2% (17th)	Super Bowl Contender (11+): 16%

2019: The Bears continue to fall further and further off the Pace.

2020: Don't go chasing water-Foles.

It is a truth universally acknowledged that the Chicago Bears, in possession of a good defense, must be in want of a quarterback.

"Quarterback issues in Chicago" could have been the headline for Bears season previews dating back to the 1960s. Or better yet, a David Mamet play: *Quarterback Perversity in Chicago*. The Bears have been in an endless loop, flipping between not having a quarterback, worrying about the development of a young quarterback, and complaining about the inconsistences of their quarterback. With Chicago opting to not pick up Mitchell Trubisky's fifth-year option, we're back to Stage 1 on the endless Bears quarterback carousel. At least they're staying very much on brand.

Trubisky became the ninth first-round quarterback under the current CBA to not have his fifth-year option picked up, joining luminaries such as Paxton Lynch, Johnny Manziel, and EJ Manuel. Despite his postseason statements that Trubisky would remain the starting quarterback and that the team believed in the progress he was making, general manager Ryan Pace really had little option other than to pass on the fifth-year option. It's a bit reductive to say that the 2019 Bears failed just because of poor quarterback play, but when you have a good defense and solid skill position players, it's hard to not keep coming back to the man under center when diagnosing the team's problems.

Remember, Pace and the Bears valued Trubisky so much that they gave up three mid-round picks to go and get him, rather than risk even the possibility of being stuck with Deshaun Watson or Patrick Mahomes. It was a classic case of being overly confident in your ability to evaluate talent.

First-round quarterbacks are a coin toss, even for the best minds in the league. Those nine quarterbacks who haven't had their fifth-year options picked up since 2011 represent nearly half of the 20 quarterbacks drafted in the first round over that time period. It was certainly not unreasonable to have had Trubisky over Watson and Mahomes in 2017. Our own QBASE quarterback projection system had Trubisky in the middle of that pack, with one great season at North Carolina balanced out by being unable to win the starting job before that. The problem was less that the Bears drafted Trubisky first and more that they traded up one spot to get him when there were other quality quarterback prospects on the board. Those mid-round picks ended up becoming Alvin Kamara and Fred

Warner, making the decision to trade up sting all the more. Even if Trubisky had turned out to be a great player or the mid-round picks they used to seal the deal turned into below-average players, the trade would have been ill-advised. The fact that Trubisky has flopped just puts it into sharper contrast.

This has been the legacy of the Ryan Pace era to date. Through six offseasons, no one gives up draft picks quite like Pace's Chicago Bears. Based on their draft position over the last six years, the Bears should have made picks worth 281.8 Approximate Value points, per Chase Stuart's draft model. Instead, their picks have been worth 246.0 points, the biggest drop-off in the league. Pace has traded up to make his first pick in three of his six drafts in Chicago, each time paying a value premium to make the move, and he also gave up two first-rounders for Khalil Mack. Some of these moves have worked out better than others, but if you're constantly giving draft capital away, you're going to have to draft better than league average to make up for the missed opportunities. When you put all your eggs in one basket, they'd better be from a golden goose.

The trouble is, there's precious little evidence that general managers can routinely draft above league average over a reasonable sample size. That isn't to say there's no skill involved whatsoever, but the level of luck and variance involved vastly outweighs individual scouting and evaluation. And, even if you try to parse the noise, Pace's early results haven't exactly set the world on fire. Pace has had three first-rounders eligible for fifth-year options, and the team has declined to pick up two of them. That's not gold in that basket; Pace's selections tend to lay entirely different sorts of eggs. Which brings us back, as all things Chicago do eventually, to the man throwing ducks under center.

You can't argue that the Bears didn't give Trubisky a chance to succeed in 2019. The Bears spent $41.1 million on wide receivers last season, third-most in the league, and used their top two draft picks on skill position players. Theoretically, Trubisky should have had no end to his weapons, with the salary-cap savings from having a quarterback on a rookie deal being funneled to provide him aid. After all, Trubisky had seen his numbers jump from 2017 to 2018 with Matt Nagy bringing in a quick-hitting offense that maximized Trubisky's athletic prowess while deemphasizing some of his mental struggles. In his second year in the system, it looked like 2019

2020 Bears Schedule

Week	Opp.	Week	Opp.	Week	Opp.
1	at DET	7	at LAR (Mon.)	13	DET
2	NYG	8	NO	14	HOU
3	at ATL	9	at TEN	15	at MIN
4	IND	10	MIN (Mon.)	16	at JAX
5	TB (Thu.)	11	BYE	17	GB
6	at CAR	12	at GB		

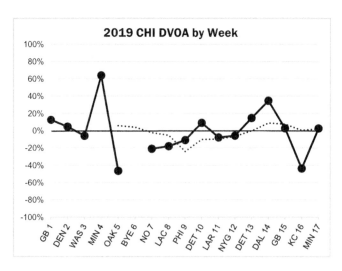

was going to be a chance for Trubisky to show what kind of quarterback he really was.

Going back to 1985, there have been 47 quarterbacks to qualify for our leaderboards with at least 200 pass plays in each of their first three seasons. Trubisky's third-year DVOA of -11.8% ranks 35th in that group. His highest DVOA, 3.6% in 2018, ranks 30th. His average DVOA of -8.3% ranks 29th. He is one of 15 players on that list to have multiple seasons with DVOA below -10.0%. No matter how you slice it, Trubisky has been a massive disappointment to this point.

One way to put Trubisky's start into context is to compare him to players with similar career arcs through their first three seasons—players who struggled as rookies, showed signs of life in Year 2, and then collapsed back in upon themselves in Year 3. To find a list of similar quarterbacks in the DVOA era, we compared Trubisky's DVOA through his first three seasons to each of those 47 three-year qualifiers. To put more emphasis on Trubisky's most recent season, we weighted each player's performance so that Year 1 counted once, Year 2 counted twice, and Year 3 counted three times. That produces a list of comparable rough starts to careers—and it's not the world's most inspiring list (Table 1).

Table 1. Similar Quarterbacks to Mitchell Trubisky, 2017-2019

Rk	Player	Team	Years	Year 1 DVOA	Year 2 DVOA	Year 3 DVOA	Year 4 DVOA
--	Mitchell Trubisky	CHI	2017-2019	-16.8%	3.6%	-11.8%	---
1	Drew Bledsoe	NE	1993-1995	-8.7%	1.5%	-11.0%	7.5%
2	Mark Sanchez	NYJ	2009-2011	-26.5%	-4.3%	-12.5%	-29.4%
3	Tony Banks	STL	1996-1998	-31.2%	-2.1%	-13.1%	-18.0%
4	Charlie Batch	DET	1998-2000	4.9%	6.5%	-14.8%	-3.6%
5	Christian Ponder	MIN	2011-2013	-31.5%	-6.1%	-13.5%	3rd-stringer
6	Josh Freeman	TB	2009-2011	-31.1%	13.9%	-13.7%	-8.0%
7	Marcus Mariota	TEN	2015-2017	-13.2%	11.1%	-3.3%	-8.5%
8	Kyle Boller	BAL	2003-2005	-26.0%	-14.6%	-9.3%	Backup
9	Joey Harrington	DET	2002-2004	-20.9%	-18.2%	-9.9%	-15.2%
10	Blake Bortles	JAX	2014-2016	-40.7%	-9.9%	-10.0%	0.3%

There is one name in that ragged flock that should give Trubisky fans some hope. Drew Bledsoe has the closest career arc to Trubisky through three years. After making the Pro Bowl in Year 2, he struggled significantly in 1995, dropping even below his rookie season with an -11.0% DVOA, in part

because of a lingering shoulder injury that affected his timing and mechanics. Healthier and working with a new quarterback coach in 1996, Bledsoe's accuracy and ability to read defenses took a significant step up, and the Patriots made the Super Bowl. While Bledsoe's and Trubisky's quarterbacking styles couldn't be much more different, the basic path of improvement could still be there. Perhaps new quarterbacks coach John DeFilippo can have the same impact on Trubisky, helping him to streamline his decision-making progress and do a better job of identifying trouble spots on the defense before he throws the ball at them. Couple that with a shift in offensive philosophy to give Trubisky more schemed throws and easier reads, and it's possible, albeit unlikely, Trubisky could still be a viable option under center. Then again, you look at the other nine closest comparisons, and they make one long for the glory days of Jay Cutler.

Many of the concerns we had about Trubisky in last year's *Almanac* repeated themselves or got worse in 2019. Trubisky was the sixth-worst quarterback out of a clean pocket, with a 31.5% DVOA—he simply does not process the game quickly enough to take advantage of positive situations. Two years ago, Trubisky was one of the best quarterbacks when under pressure, but that's a volatile stat, inconsistent from year to year. His DVOA under pressure fell from -14.1% in 2018 to -74.8% in 2019—he wasn't as lucky last year as he had been in 2018.

While the days of being unable to throw to his left are a thing of the past, Trubisky's mechanics are still shaky, and his execution leaves a lot to be desired. He's unwilling or unable to get the ball into tight windows or push it downfield; he saw both his average depth of target and ALEX drop from 2018 to 2019. Even his legs failed him. Trubisky produced the second-most rushing DYAR in the league in 2018, but he dropped from 114 rushing DYAR in 2018 to -12 a year ago. Some of that was due to nagging injuries; the Bears didn't want to risk aggravating the shoulder injury that cost him a start, and he did suffer a hip pointer later in the season. But Trubisky was running less even in September, before the injuries occurred, and that's due to a change in offensive philosophy. Both coach and quarterback made a point on several occasions that their goal was for Trubisky to keep working through his progressions rather than take off and scramble for extra yardage. Nagy still called more than his fair share of quarterback runs—22 of them, sixth-most in the league. But scrambles fell from sixth to 16th, and Chicago's DVOA on scrambles fell from 103.0% to 10.6%, 27th in the league. Essentially, Trubisky's scrambles went from a part of his game where he could take advantage of defensive weaknesses to a last-resort option, and the effectiveness dropped off accordingly.

Truth be told, there's not a lot of difference, for good or for ill, between 2018 and 2019 Trubisky in his actual passing. He can still produce solid numbers when his pre-snap reads are well-defined and he can deliver the ball quickly; it's when you start forcing him to make decisions on his own that things start going south. Trubisky's receivers dropped more passes in 2019 than 2018. He was put in worse positions thanks to a less-dominant defense. Opposing defenses had an extra year of footage of Nagy's offense to work with after entering 2018 working off just a handful of Nagy-called games from Kansas City. Those three facts alone basically sum up the difference between 2018 Trubisky and 2019 Trubisky. The improvement between 2017 and 2018 Trubisky can, in retrospect, mostly be attributed to an improved situation around him and unsustainably strong play under pressure more than an actual step forward from Trubisky himself. And so the Bears found themselves in a position where they absolutely could not enter the 2020 season with Trubisky as the only quarterback on the roster.

Enter Nick Foles, Super Bowl LII MVP. With Foles rendered expendable in Jacksonville by the emergence of Gardner Minshew, the Bears saw their opportunity to get an established starter, a playoff-tested veteran who will help Chicago earn their first postseason victory since the 2010 season. Problem solved!

Well, about that…

First of all, the acquisition of Foles represents a massive misread of the 2020 quarterback market. Established starters Jameis Winston and Andy Dalton were available on one-year deals for $3 million or less, essentially nothing in the world of quarterbacks. Cam Newton's one-year contract with New England is almost entirely based on incentives. Foles' contract was a nightmare for Jacksonville, and the Jags were operating from a very weak negotiating position with $57 million remaining on his deal over three years. It seemed likely that the Jaguars would have to bundle Foles with a pick in order to free up some salary-cap space, as in the Brock Osweiler trade back in 2017. Instead, the Bears sent a fourth-round pick to the Jaguars for Foles' services, eating most of the guaranteed money that essentially ensures Foles will be on the roster through 2021. From a financial perspective, it's at least as confusing as when Pace brought in Mike Glennon on a three-year, $45-million deal in 2017—financial evaluation of quarterbacks is clearly not one of Pace's strengths.

All that being said, there's every reason to believe that Foles is a better fit in Chicago than Winston or Dalton would have been. Foles worked with Nagy in Kansas City and both offensive coordinator Bill Lazor and quarterbacks coach John DeFilippo in Philadelphia, so he should be familiar with the system—a major selling-point in an offseason shortened by COVID-19. So what if the Bears ended up overpaying for Foles; it's more important to find the *right* guy than the *most cost-effective* guy. And as Foles is going to be a massive improvement over Trubisky, whatever the Bears had to do to bring him into the fold was worth it, right?

Well, about *that*…

Mitch Trubisky has had a better regular-season DVOA than Nick Foles in each of his three seasons in the league—in fact, Foles hasn't topped Trubisky's high-water mark of 3.6% since 2013, and has been below Trubisky's -11.0% DVOA from 2019 in half of his eight career seasons.

This is not entirely a fair comparison, of course. Foles didn't qualify for the main quarterback leaderboards in either 2017 or 2019. In 2019, he missed a large chunk of the season with a broken clavicle, and his 2017 numbers do not include the postseason run, where Foles' 69.4% DVOA and 586 DYAR dazzled and amazed. Trubisky's three-game high-water mark is a relatively paltry 31.0% in 2018, in Weeks 4-7. Still, it shows that the argument for Foles being better than Trubisky isn't entirely cut-and-dried, especially when you take into account the fact that Foles is six years older than Trubisky, has a lengthy injury history, and has never started all 16 games in a season.

The argument for Foles is all upside—that 2017 playoff run, the magical 2013 season. We're talking a dozen games, about a quarter of his track record as a starting quarterback. Foles has shown, in streaks, an ability to be one of the top quarterbacks in the league, but the majority of his career has been as a replacement-level player. If you distributed out Foles' best games around his career, rather than having them all piled up next to one another, you'd consider him a frustratingly erratic bundle of potential, rather than someone capable of leading a team anywhere.

Then again, doesn't "frustratingly erratic bundle of potential" describe Trubisky pretty well, too? There were portions of last season where Good Trubisky seemed to rear his head once again. He played very well in Weeks 13 and 14 against the Lions and Cowboys, going 52-for-69 for six touchdowns and two interceptions, 155 DYAR, and a DVOA of 22.7%. That's a very positive line for a young quarterback, one you can build on going forward. Healed up from his early-season shoulder injury, it looked briefly like Trubisky was going to finish the year on a high note … before putting up progressively worse numbers in each of his last three games. Frustratingly erratic.

To put Foles' and Trubisky's erratic performances into context, we can look at how frequently their starts hit certain DVOA thresholds. Looking back at all games in which either passer had at least ten attempts, including the playoffs, how often do we get Good Foles or Good Trubisky? How often do they torpedo their teams' chances with horrible play?

Figure 1 shows why a team looking to contend in 2020 would prefer Foles to Trubisky. Terrible Foles does tend to show up a bit more frequently than terrible Trubisky—not by a ton, but by enough that it shouldn't be too surprising that his overall DVOA is lower. But Foles has put up a positive-

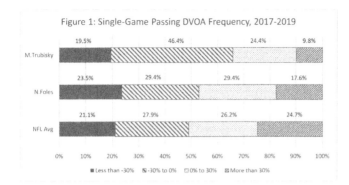

Figure 1: Single-Game Passing DVOA Frequency, 2017-2019

DVOA game a little under half the time in the last three years, while Trubisky's hanging down around a third. Foles' three 30%-plus games are all that 2017 playoff run, but three great games in 17 tries is a much better rate than Trubisky's four in 41. If the Bears are going to contend in 2020, it's going to be thanks to a great defense, with the offense doing all it can to not serve as a massive anchor. Foles seems more likely to produce that than Trubisky.

Of course, Foles has been more likely than not to put up a negative DVOA game over the past three seasons, meaning he's not really a solution at the position, just a less-bad option for now. He's almost certainly not going to become the first Bears quarterback to make repeated Pro Bowl berths since Ed Brown. If we were to look at Foles' entire career, more than half of his games (54.4%) do clock in with a positive DVOA, but that's almost entirely because of his amazing 2013 season. Perhaps Foles and Trubisky can bond over that—both of them had their one Pro Bowl year come in their second season, aided by a new head coach making their debuts as full-time NFL playcallers, and then came back to earth the next year when opposing defenses had an extra year of film to work with. The parallels don't work entirely—Chip Kelly's first year in Philadelphia produced a 22.9% offensive DVOA compared to Nagy's -3.4% in 2018, and Foles was leaps and bounds better than Trubisky in their respective Pro Bowl seasons—but it's interesting to note that the Bears now employ two quarterbacks who arguably had their best seasons more from the element of surprise than their own innate strengths.

Who should Bears fans hope is behind center? Foles probably gives the better median result. He's a known quantity at this point, and while he's not a long-term solution at the position, he's an above-average stopgap. But the odds of Foles improving on his recent performances is relatively slim; in fact, the odds of Foles even matching his performance from the 2017 postseason run are relatively slim. He's a low-ceiling, higher-floor sort of player. If he wins the starting job, Bears fans should spend their Saturdays this season scouting Trevor Lawrence, Justin Fields and the rest of next year's quarterback class.

On the other hand, the best-case scenario for the Bears probably involves Trubisky winning the starting job and bouncing back significantly in Year 4. It's rare, but not unheard of, for a quarterback to finally find their footing later in their career. A player's strengths and weaknesses are more or less set in stone after three full seasons as a starter, but that doesn't mean a new scheme or better play calling can't help emphasize the

former and minimize the latter. Foles likely gives the Bears offense the best chance of avoiding embarrassment in 2020. But the odds of Trubisky bouncing back to above-2018 levels of performance are better than the odds of Super Bowl Foles lasting an entire season. Bears fans should be rooting for Trubisky to win his starting job back, if only because that is the most likely path to a successful season in Chicago.

Whichever quarterback ends up under center, he's going to have to get more help from his supporting cast on offense than Trubisky had in 2019, where the Bears featured Allen Robinson and a whole passel of question marks.

The fact that Chicago's offensive line ranked 21st in adjusted sack rate can, in part, be explained away by Trubisky's lack of pocket awareness; the Bears actually only allowed a better-than-average 17.5 sacks on blown blocks. The same excuse does *not* apply to their poor performance in run-blocking, where they ranked 29th in adjusted line yards and 31st in power situations. And yet, Pace didn't do much to bolster the line, only adding penalty-magnet Germain Ifedi and ex-Packer Jason Spriggs to the fold. Ifedi may end up replacing the retired Kyle Long, and run-blocking *is* his forte, but the Bears are counting on a lot of improvement from the pieces already in place. The poor blocking up front goes a long way to explaining why David Montgomery ranked 40th out of 45 qualified running backs with a -13.0% DVOA, and why he averaged a terrible 3.67 yards per carry, the worst total for a Bears primary running back since Matt Forte in 2009. A competent rushing attack would go a long way to helping take some of the load off of the passing game, but the Bears haven't managed an above-average attack since Forte left town in 2015. Opposing defenses know Chicago can't run and can spend all day teeing off on the quarterback. That's not ideal.

Pace also made some interesting choices when trying to add playmakers to take some of the load off of Robinson in the passing game. Bears quarterbacks had 439 DYAR when targeting Robinson in 2019 and 326 DYAR targeting everyone else. (These totals do not include all the DYAR those quarterbacks lost on sacks.) Nagy's offense in Kansas City had success with Travis Kelce as a big-bodied target, and Trey Burton had some prosperity in that role in 2018 before struggling with injuries in 2019. To bolster the tight end position, Pace signed Jimmy Graham to a two-year, $16-million contract, which does include a no-trade clause but does not include a time machine to 2016, the last time Graham had more than 40 DYAR in a season or a DVOA higher than 5.0%. The decision to sign Graham is the single most baffling move of the offseason, made all the more baffling when the Bears used their top draft pick on Cole Kmet out of Notre Dame—that gave the Bears 10 tight ends on the roster, an odd position to prioritize over the offensive line or secondary. Assuming the Bears do not decide to pull out a five-tight end offense, we're projecting Graham to replace Burton as the primary move tight end and Kmet to eventually supplant Demetrius Harris as the in-line tight end, but Graham's best days were already in his rearview mirror a contract ago, while rookie tight ends notoriously are slow starters. The Bears are unlikely to get a very solid performance out of their many, many tight ends this season.

That leaves the Bears' wideouts to pick up the slack, but shuffling ineffective speed receivers with Ted Ginn replacing Taylor Gabriel doesn't inspire much confidence there either. The Bears' receivers remain the strongest point of their offense. Robinson returned to health and had his best season since 2015, while slot receiver Anthony Miller put up a respectable -1.0% DVOA over the last seven weeks of the year as he moved ahead of Gabriel on the depth chart; he actually had more DYAR than Robinson over that final stretch. We're not exactly showering that unit with high praise; the fact that it is the best position group on offense is more of a condemnation of the rest of the team.

Everything lines up for yet another year where the offense derails a solid defensive performance. We expect the Bears defense to be very good once again in 2020, albeit more like it was last season as opposed to 2018's great numbers. Holes in the secondary likely mean second-round pick Jaylon Johnson will have to be a Day 1 contributor, and we're not entirely sure Pace made the right decision to keep Danny Trevathan over Nick Kwiatkoski at linebacker, but this is still a very solid group of players. For all the criticism Pace has gotten for his offseason, adding Robert Quinn and his 37 pass pressures a year ago is a significant (albeit expensive) upgrade over Leonard Floyd; pairing him with Khalil Mack should give the Bears the best pass rush in the division and possibly the conference. As we always write, defense is less consistent than offense from year to year, but if this unit can take a step back

to where it was when the Bears made the playoffs just two years ago, that would take a massive load off of the offense's shoulders. In 2018, the Bears' offense started with the sixth-best field position in the league, compared to 16th a year ago.

Still. The Bears haven't had a positive offensive DVOA since 2015, and they haven't had a multiple-year stretch of above-average offensive play since Jim Harbaugh was under center. At some point, this just gets ridiculous. Nagy and Pace aren't on the hot seat just yet. They were Coach and Executive of the Year in 2018; the business is harsh but not *that* harsh. But if the Bears can't find their way to something approaching offensive competence soon, there will be questions as to Nagy's ability to run an offense. And if they can't get out of the eternal rebuild into a sustained period of contention, there will be questions about Pace's ability to produce results. Those questions are bouncing around as whispers now, and they will only increase in volume if the season goes according to our projections, with the Bears finishing in last place in a weak division. We are not won over by the Bears' offseason moves. The old adage that "when you have two quarterbacks, you have none" may not always be true, but it certainly feels like the case in Chicago. It's hard to imagine 2021's starter currently wearing the navy blue and burnt orange—and until Chicago gets that sorted out, it's hard to see the Bears going anywhere significant.

Bryan Knowles

2019 Bears Stats by Week

Wk	vs.	W-L	PF	PA	YDF	YDA	TO	Total	Off	Def	ST
1	GB	L	3	10	254	213	-1	13%	-26%	-34%	4%
2	at DEN	W	16	14	273	372	+1	5%	6%	7%	6%
3	at WAS	W	31	15	298	356	+4	-6%	-4%	-13%	-15%
4	MIN	W	16	6	269	222	+2	64%	6%	-50%	8%
5	at OAK	L	21	24	236	398	0	-46%	-36%	23%	13%
6	BYE										
7	NO	L	25	36	252	424	-2	-21%	-20%	12%	11%
8	LAC	L	16	17	388	231	-1	-18%	-24%	-19%	-13%
9	at PHI	L	14	22	164	373	-1	-11%	-20%	3%	13%
10	DET	W	20	13	226	357	+1	9%	-5%	-18%	-4%
11	at LAR	L	7	17	267	283	+1	-8%	-18%	-21%	-10%
12	NYG	W	19	14	335	243	-1	-6%	-18%	-23%	-10%
13	at DET	W	24	20	419	364	0	15%	14%	4%	5%
14	DAL	W	31	24	382	408	-2	35%	19%	-11%	5%
15	at GB	L	13	21	415	292	-3	3%	-10%	-16%	-3%
16	KC	L	3	26	234	350	0	-44%	-29%	20%	5%
17	at MIN	W	21	19	337	300	+2	3%	-6%	-10%	-1%

Trends and Splits

	Offense	Rank	Defense	Rank
Total DVOA	-10.1%	25	-7.2%	8
Unadjusted VOA	-11.5%	26	-3.9%	11
Weighted Trend	-9.4%	25	-6.8%	10
Variance	2.6%	1	3.8%	4
Average Opponent	1.2%	22	3.7%	1
Passing	2.8%	19	-4.1%	8
Rushing	-17.6%	29	-11.0%	13
First Down	-3.9%	21	0.5%	16
Second Down	-19.6%	30	-10.1%	8
Third Down	-5.8%	20	-16.5%	4
First Half	-20.6%	30	-12.9%	6
Second Half	0.1%	16	-1.9%	11
Red Zone	-18.1%	25	9.5%	22
Late and Close	-4.0%	18	-15.3%	6

Five-Year Performance

Year	W-L	Pyth W	Est W	PF	PA	TO	Total	Rk	Off	Rk	Def	Rk	ST	Rk	Off AGL	Rk	Def AGL	Rk	Off Age	Rk	Def Age	Rk	ST Age	Rk
2015	6-10	6.3	6.8	335	397	-4	-5.7%	19	6.9%	10	11.3%	31	-1.2%	21	63.6	30	40.3	23	27.4	10	25.8	31	26.2	13
2016	3-13	4.7	6.2	279	399	-20	-8.3%	25	-2.6%	17	5.0%	23	-0.6%	18	84.0	31	87.5	32	26.7	16	26.0	24	26.2	11
2017	5-11	6.2	5.9	264	320	0	-16.0%	25	-15.1%	28	-1.5%	14	-2.4%	23	56.4	25	68.1	30	26.6	20	26.1	17	26.0	10
2018	12-4	11.6	10.7	421	283	+14	19.4%	5	-3.4%	20	-26.0%	1	-3.2%	26	20.3	6	14.2	4	26.1	26	26.0	22	26.1	11
2019	8-8	7.4	7.7	280	298	0	-2.1%	15	-10.1%	25	-7.2%	8	0.9%	13	36.9	15	28.5	13	26.0	29	26.9	6	26.4	7

2019 Performance Based on Most Common Personnel Groups

CHI Offense				CHI Offense vs. Opponents					CHI Defense				CHI Defense vs. Opponents			
Pers	Freq	Yds	DVOA	Pers	Freq	Yds	DVOA	Run%	Pers	Freq	Yds	DVOA	Pers	Freq	Yds	DVOA
11	60%	4.9	1.0%	Base	15%	3.9	-37.8%	74%	Base	31%	4.8	-18.7%	11	61%	5.5	-1.7%
21	11%	4.2	-10.6%	Nickel	52%	4.9	1.1%	36%	Nickel	62%	5.1	-4.4%	12	24%	4.5	-25.1%
12	9%	5.0	-15.4%	Dime+	33%	5.0	-1.6%	17%	Dime+	6%	7.8	22.7%	21	8%	3.9	-21.1%
10	6%	7.0	32.6%	Goal Line	0%	1.0	127.1%	100%	Goal Line	0%	7.0	98.2%	22	2%	6.1	5.0%
20	4%	3.3	-55.6%										611	1%	6.7	12.2%
611	3%	3.3	-46.3%										13	1%	2.9	-35.2%
612	3%	2.8	-26.4%										621	1%	5.2	30.7%

Run% column for CHI Offense: 11→30%, 21→32%, 12→66%, 10→15%, 20→9%, 611→80%, 612→96%

Strategic Tendencies

Run/Pass		Rk	Formation		Rk	Pass Rush		Rk	Secondary		Rk	Strategy		Rk
Runs, first half	33%	27	Form: Single Back	83%	13	Rush 3	11.9%	9	4 DB	31%	9	Play Action	21%	27
Runs, first down	47%	22	Form: Empty Back	8%	17	Rush 4	64.1%	18	5 DB	62%	14	Offensive Motion	29%	30
Runs, second-long	28%	14	Form: Multi Back	9%	22	Rush 5	20.8%	15	6+ DB	6%	20	Avg Box (Off)	6.31	30
Runs, power sit.	52%	25	Pers: 3+ WR	72%	8	Rush 6+	3.2%	23	Man Coverage	30%	22	Avg Box (Def)	6.46	24
Runs, behind 2H	26%	22	Pers: 2+ TE/6+ OL	17%	31	Edge Rusher Sacks	42.2%	28	CB by Sides	98%	1	Offensive Pace	31.51	22
Pass, ahead 2H	45%	25	Pers: 6+ OL	7%	6	Interior DL Sacks	35.9%	5	S/CB Cover Ratio	25%	18	Defensive Pace	30.61	15
Run-Pass Options	15%	2	Shotgun/Pistol	77%	5	Second Level Sacks	21.9%	14	DB Blitz	6%	28	Go for it on 4th	2.26	2

You can see Nagy's connection to Andy Reid in some of the stats: box counts, among other things. Chicago had 45% of its running back carries against small boxes (six or fewer), which was third in the league. Reid's Chiefs ranked first at 53%. ● However, the Bears continued to struggle on short passes, contrary to Nagy's history with Reid. Chicago ranked 26th in DVOA on passes at or behind the line of scrimmage after ranking 31st in Nagy's first season. The Bears had another poor year on running back screens, gaining just 4.2 yards per pass with -26.6% DVOA. ● Chicago was better on wide receiver screens. They used 53 of them, second behind Arizona, and were around league average with 5.5 yards per pass and slightly above average with 14.7% DVOA. ● Chicago gained just 4.1 yards on RPOs, the lowest figure among the six teams that used them on at least 10% of plays. ● Chicago opponents dropped 38 passes, or 7.3%. Both figures ranked second in the NFL. ● This was the second straight year Chicago's defense was No. 1 in "CB by Sides."

Passing

Player	DYAR	DVOA	Plays	NtYds	Avg	YAC	C%	TD	Int
M.Trubisky	5	-11.0%	551	2909	5.3	4.3	63.5%	17	9
C.Daniel*	-9	-13.2%	71	387	5.5	3.0	70.3%	3	2
N.Foles	-77	-21.3%	125	669	5.4	4.6	66.4%	3	2

Receiving

Player	DYAR	DVOA	Plays	Ctch	Yds	Y/C	YAC	TD	C%
A.Robinson	165	0.4%	154	98	1147	11.7	2.6	7	64%
A.Miller	34	-7.6%	85	52	656	12.6	4.2	2	61%
T.Gabriel*	24	-5.8%	48	29	353	12.2	2.7	4	60%
J.Wims	-83	-39.8%	39	18	186	10.3	2.5	1	46%
C.Patterson	-32	-35.1%	17	11	83	7.5	6.5	0	65%
R.Ridley	19	25.0%	7	6	69	11.5	2.5	0	86%
T.Ginn	22	-7.7%	56	30	421	14.0	1.6	2	54%
T.Davis	-2	-14.6%	11	8	111	13.9	8.1	0	73%
T.Burton*	-65	-49.1%	24	14	84	6.0	2.6	0	58%
A.Shaheen	-9	-17.1%	13	9	74	8.2	4.2	0	69%
B.Braunecker	5	0.0%	11	6	59	9.8	4.2	1	55%
J.Horsted	28	43.0%	10	8	87	10.9	3.8	1	80%
J.Holtz	22	34.6%	8	7	91	13.0	11.3	0	88%
J.Graham	38	2.1%	60	38	447	11.8	6.5	3	63%
D.Harris	-17	-16.0%	27	15	149	9.9	4.5	3	56%
T.Cohen	-36	-20.1%	104	79	456	5.8	5.4	3	76%
D.Montgomery	15	-5.5%	35	25	185	7.4	6.2	1	71%
M.Davis*	-9	-33.4%	8	7	22	3.1	3.9	0	88%

Rushing

Player	DYAR	DVOA	Plays	Yds	Avg	TD	Fum	Suc
D.Montgomery	-46	-13.0%	242	889	3.7	6	2	46%
T.Cohen	-23	-17.2%	64	215	3.4	0	0	42%
M.Trubisky	-12	-17.6%	42	189	4.5	2	2	-
C.Patterson	32	-7.5%	17	103	6.1	0	0	-
M.Davis*	-28	-65.9%	11	25	2.3	0	0	18%
C.Daniel*	-10	-38.3%	6	6	1.0	0	0	-

Offensive Line

Player	Pos	Age	GS	Snaps	Pen	Sk	Pass	Run	Player	Pos	Age	GS	Snaps	Pen	Sk	Pass	Run
James Daniels	C/LG	23	16/16	1091	4	2.0	14	13	Cornelius Lucas*	RT	29	16/8	516	0	1.5	6	2
Cody Whitehair	C/LG	28	16/16	1091	4	1.5	5	5	Kyle Long	RG	32	4/4	258	2	1.0	3	3
Charles Leno	LT	29	16/16	1088	13	5.0	20	5	Ted Larsen*	LG/RG	33	12/2	169	0	1.5	5	1
Rashaad Coward	RG	26	13/10	673	4	1.0	15	5	Germain Ifedi	RT	26	16/16	1124	13	3.5	18	8
Bobby Massie	RT	31	10/10	626	3	4.5	16	5									

Year	Yards	ALY	Rank	Power	Rank	Stuff	Rank	2nd Lev	Rank	Open Field	Rank	Sacks	ASR	Rank	Press	Rank	F-Start	Cont.
2017	4.08	3.65	28	58%	26	26%	28	1.20	11	0.97	6	39	7.7%	23	30.3%	13	18	27
2018	3.83	3.92	28	67%	18	21%	22	0.96	31	0.63	26	33	6.0%	7	26.4%	8	16	33
2019	3.56	3.86	29	50%	31	18%	16	0.89	31	0.39	30	45	7.3%	21	29.5%	14	15	26

2019 ALY by direction:	Left End 3.19 (28)	Left Tackle: 4.84 (6)	Mid/Guard: 4.03 (25)	Right Tackle: 2.72 (32)	Right End: 3.30 (24)

Over the last two seasons, the Bears' offensive line has been ranked 28th and 29th in adjusted line yards. With Germain Ifedi as the only significant free-agent signing and no draft picks used on the line until the seventh round, it'll be up to Juan Castillo—previously an offensive line coach in Philadelphia, Baltimore, and Buffalo—to whip the line into shape. ● Ifedi will battle for the right guard spot that opened when Kyle Long retired. Ifedi struggled as a tackle for the Seahawks, especially in pass protection; it's hoped that kicking inside will help accentuate his run-blocking prowess. He'll fight with incumbent Rashaad Coward for the open spot. ● The Bears flipped Pro Bowl center Cody Whitehair and left guard James Daniels to begin the 2019 season in a move that helped no one. The idea was that Daniels was a natural center and was most comfortable there, while Whitehair was forced into center because of lack of options as a rookie. That's all fair and good, but both players were just fine in their 2018 positions, and miscommunications and misidentified pass protections early on in 2019 meant that the switch was a net negative for both players. Daniels went back to guard and Whitehair back to center in Week 10. For the season, Whitehair ranked second out of 35 centers in snaps per blown block, while Daniels ranked 34th. ● For what it's worth, Whitehair has struggled with shotgun snaps, which is an issue when the Bears run shotgun 77% of the time. ● 2019 was the worst season of Charles Leno's career. While Leno's rank in blown blocks improved, he was flagged 13 times and struggled against power rushes; according to NFL Next Gen Stats, the Bears ended up having to give him help in pass protection more than a third of the time. ● The Bears ranked dead last in adjusted line yards at right tackle at 2.72. Bobby Massie missed six games, which hurt their overall totals there, but he wasn't exactly a world-changer when he was in the lineup; ex Packers-disappointment Jason Spriggs and 2019 UDFA Alex Bars might have a chance at cracking the starting lineup here.

Defensive Front

Defensive Line	Age	Pos	G	Snaps	Plays	TmPct	Rk	Stop	Dfts	BTkl	Runs	St%	Rk	RuYd	Rk	Sack	Hit	Hur	Dsrpt
					Overall							vs. Run				Pass Rush			
Roy Robertson-Harris	27	DE	15	552	32	4.1%	62	22	5	5	23	65%	79	2.8	78	2.5	9	12	2
Nicholas Williams*	30	DT	16	540	44	5.3%	31	37	7	2	33	85%	14	2.5	58	6.0	4	9	2
Eddie Goldman	26	DT	15	472	29	3.7%	71	22	2	2	27	78%	34	2.2	44	1.0	2	7	0
Bilal Nichols	24	DE	13	453	28	4.2%	75	20	4	2	25	72%	65	2.4	53	0.0	2	5	1
Brent Urban	29	DE	13	248	18	2.7%	--	13	1	2	15	73%	--	2.9	--	0.0	1	5	3
John Jenkins	*31*	*DT*	*16*	*486*	*35*	*4.2%*	*50*	*26*	*3*	*3*	*33*	*73%*	*58*	*2.8*	*71*	*1.0*	*0*	*9*	*1*

Edge Rushers	Age	Pos	G	Snaps	Plays	TmPct	Rk	Stop	Dfts	BTkl	Runs	St%	Rk	RuYd	Rk	Sack	Hit	Hur	Dsrpt
					Overall							vs. Run				Pass Rush			
Khalil Mack	29	OLB	16	943	51	6.2%	25	42	17	6	34	76%	31	3.9	86	8.5	7	53	5
Leonard Floyd*	28	OLB	16	916	41	5.0%	40	28	10	9	27	70%	57	2.9	59	3.0	11	33	5
Robert Quinn	*30*	*DE*	*14*	*658*	*36*	*5.0%*	*49*	*26*	*16*	*7*	*21*	*52%*	*84*	*2.3*	*42*	*11.5*	*15*	*37*	*4*

Linebackers	Age	Pos	G	Snaps	Plays	TmPct	Rk	Stop	Dfts	BTkl	Runs	St%	Rk	RuYd	Rk	Sack	Hit	Hur	Tgts	Suc%	Rk	AdjYd	Rk	PD	Int
					Overall							vs. Run				Pass Rush				vs. Pass				
Roquan Smith	23	ILB	12	734	102	16.5%	30	54	17	6	61	64%	26	4.1	48	2.0	0	2	39	54%	25	5.5	20	2	1
Danny Trevathan	30	ILB	9	572	71	15.3%	58	43	8	7	46	70%	12	3.2	17	1.0	3	6	20	35%	62	8.6	61	1	0
Nick Kwiatkoski*	27	ILB	16	518	71	8.6%	58	36	14	7	39	56%	56	4.0	42	3.0	0	9	20	55%	22	3.4	1	4	1
Kevin Pierre-Louis*	29	ILB	14	215	35	4.8%	--	24	8	2	18	72%	--	2.8	--	0.0	2	10	12	83%	--	3.0	--	3	1

Year	Yards	ALY	Rank	Power	Rank	Stuff	Rank	2nd Level	Rank	Open Field	Rank	Sacks	ASR	Rank	Press	Rank
2017	4.16	4.50	30	79%	30	14%	32	1.06	9	0.62	11	42	7.6%	8	29.9%	19
2018	3.63	3.97	9	58%	4	20%	14	0.98	4	0.45	4	50	7.5%	12	33.4%	3
2019	3.89	4.26	17	66%	19	14%	29	0.93	2	0.54	6	32	6.6%	22	29.6%	20
2019 ALY by direction:	*Left End: 4.48 (26)*		*Left Tackle: 3.98 (12)*			*Mid/Guard: 4.58 (23)*			*Right Tackle: 4.69 (25)*			*Right End: 2.06 (2)*				

Chicago's defensive stats (pressures, adjusted line yards, adjusted sack rate, etc.) all fell from 2018 to 2019—a function both of the year-to-year variance defensive stats have and the worse situations they were put into by a struggling offense. ❧ 5-tech end Akiem Hicks only suited up for five games in 2019 due to an elbow injury, and his presence was sorely missed. When healthy, Hicks is one of the top run defenders in football, and his presence in the pass rush helps take attention away from the edge rushers; he had six hurries in the Bears' first four games before getting hurt. ❧ Roy Robertson-Harris has been a heck of a find as a UDFA, graduating to play more than half of Chicago's defensive snaps for the first time in 2019. Even if he is still primarily a passing-down player, don't be surprised if the Bears give him more general work, biting into Bilal Nichols' play time. ❧ Add in Eddie Goldman at nose tackle—his 78% run stop success rate just missed the top 20 at his position—and the Bears' interior line may be the best in football. ❧ Fifth-round pick Trevis Gipson (Tulsa) is a project who will get to sit and learn for most of 2020. Lance Zierlein compared him to Robertson-Harris—he's long, athletic, and agile; he just needs to learn to convert those traits into polished technique. He's in the right place to learn. ❧ Robert Quinn set a career high for pass pressures in 2019 with 37 and had the highest pass rush win rate among edge rushers for the second year in a row, per ESPN Analytics. His 33% pass rush win rate was just a *touch* higher than Leonard Floyd's 11% a year ago. ❧ The addition of Quinn and the return of Hicks should help Khalil Mack see a few fewer double-teams—as if he needed it, ranking sixth with 53 pass pressures a year ago. And that was in a self-described off season, as Mack's worst years would be career highlights for most mere mortals. ❧ The Bears can thank their inside linebacker corps for their high ranking in second-level and open-field yards; both Roquan Smith and Danny Trevathan ranked in the top 20 in run stop rate among inside linebackers. ❧ Said linebacker corps took a hit, however, as the top three non-Smith linebackers from 2019 all needed new deals. The Bears opted for Trevathan over Nick Kwiatkoski, valuing experience and run defense (70% stop rate versus 56%) over youth and pass coverage (35% success rate versus 55%).

Defensive Secondary

Secondary	Age	Pos	G	Snaps	Plays	Overall TmPct	Rk	Stop	Dfts	BTkl	Runs	vs. Run St%	Rk	RuYd	Rk	Tgts	vs. Pass Tgt%	Rk	Dist	Suc%	Rk	AdjYd	Rk	PD	Int
Kyle Fuller	28	CB	16	1089	94	11.4%	2	39	10	6	17	41%	48	6.6	47	83	19.5%	50	12.3	46%	68	8.8	68	12	3
Ha Ha Clinton-Dix*	28	SS	16	1086	83	10.1%	24	21	9	11	33	36%	48	7.3	42	31	7.3%	43	8.1	52%	36	5.5	14	5	2
Eddie Jackson	27	FS	16	1079	65	7.9%	47	26	14	13	28	46%	26	6.9	39	33	7.8%	40	10.1	67%	6	3.8	5	5	2
Prince Amukamara*	31	CB	15	910	63	8.1%	44	24	12	6	13	38%	55	5.1	27	55	15.4%	76	14.2	55%	33	8.1	54	10	0
Buster Skrine	31	CB	16	742	52	6.3%	60	20	8	13	9	78%	5	4.6	24	58	20.0%	43	9.5	55%	29	6.2	12	5	0
Tashaun Gipson	30	FS	14	882	60	8.4%	51	19	8	12	24	29%	56	8.8	53	26	7.1%	44	11.8	46%	54	9.8	63	8	3

Year	Pass D Rank	vs. #1 WR	Rk	vs. #2 WR	Rk	vs. Other WR	Rk	WR Wide	Rk	WR Slot	Rk	vs. TE	Rk	vs. RB	Rk
2017	14	10.4%	20	-16.5%	7	19.4%	26	4.2%	23	5.6%	15	-6.2%	11	-3.4%	13
2018	1	-30.4%	1	-24.2%	3	-20.3%	4	-19.6%	3	-31.2%	1	-33.6%	3	-9.5%	10
2019	8	-17.3%	5	2.1%	17	-29.4%	3	2.1%	21	-27.1%	2	2.9%	16	-9.1%	12

The Bears ranked fifth against short passes with a -17.8% DVOA but just 22nd against the deep ball with a 38.8% DVOA. They were third-worst on passes marked deep right. ✎ Since the Bears played the most cornerbacks by side, you can blame at least some of that poor performance on the left cornerback. Kyle Fuller made the Pro Bowl again in 2019, but the stats show he had a poor year in coverage. He gave up 8.8 yards per target, 68th out of 85 qualifiers. Thirty-three players had double-digit targets in the deep right zone; Fuller had the worst success rate of any of them and gave up 20.5 average yards on these passes. He has been better than that historically, but Chuck Pagano's system appears not to agree with him so much. ✎ Chicago cut Prince Amukamara before free agency for cap reasons. Second-round pick Jaylon Johnson (Utah) may need to start from Day 1 to replace him; he's a very physical press corner, so he makes sense as a direct one-to-one replacement. There's no doubting Johnson's ball skills or his instincts, but there are some concerns over his lack of top-line athletic numbers and his history of shoulder injuries, which dropped him into the second round. ✎ The Bears also picked up Artie Burns, who never really panned out as a first-round pick for the Steelers. Burns' success rate peaked at 58% in 2017, but he struggled and was phased out of the lineup the last two seasons. A change of scenery might help. ✎ Buster Skrine bounced back from a poor 2018 with the Jets to rank 12th in yards per target last season. Ideally, either Johnson or Burns will succeed on the outside, letting Skrine continue to work in the slot. ✎ Tashaun Gipson was signed to try to fill the strong safety hole Chicago has had since Adrian Amos walked. Gipson's 27% broken tackle rate in Houston a year ago would have been the worst on Chicago's defense. ✎ Eddie Jackson's new deal makes him the highest-paid safety in football. He wasn't as impactful as he was in his breakout 2018 season when he intercepted six passes, but he still ranked in the top 10 among safeties in success rate and yards per target; some added pressure up front might give him more opportunities to make those splash plays.

Special Teams

Year	DVOA	Rank	FG/XP	Rank	Net Kick	Rank	Kick Ret	Rank	Net Punt	Rank	Punt Ret	Rank	Hidden	Rank
2017	-2.4%	23	-6.0	25	-2.2	23	-1.2	17	-12.3	30	9.7	2	-12.3	31
2018	-3.2%	26	-10.2	29	-1.5	22	-6.2	31	-2.5	22	4.4	9	-17.1	32
2019	0.9%	13	-4.6	23	-3.5	24	7.5	2	2.0	16	3.3	6	2.2	13

The Bears spent all of 2019's offseason worrying about their kicking game. While they saw some slight improvement there last season, they were still significantly below average. ✎ Eddy Pineiro started the season fairly adequately, worth 4.0 FG/XP points above average through Week 7, fifth in the league. After that, everything fell apart, highlighted by a six-game stretch in which he failed to make a field goal from longer than 30 yards out. ✎ 2019 was the first time Pat O'Donnell and the Bears punt unit had positive value since 2015. ✎ The Bears had their best kickoff return season since 2010, as Cordarelle Patterson's arrival gave Chicago a legit weapon. His 7.8 points of return value were second in the league, behind only Brandon Wilson in Cincinnati. ✎ Patterson wasn't on the fans' Pro Bowl ballot, because the Bears instead had punt returner Tarik Cohen as their one eligible name. Cohen was fine in 2019, but Patterson was special, and the coaches and players ballots rightfully put the correct Bear on the team.

Cincinnati Bengals

2019 Record: 2-14	Total DVOA: -25.3% (29th)	2020 Mean Projection: 6.7 wins	On the Clock (0-4): 21%
Pythagorean Wins: 4.3 (30th)	Offense: -16.5% (29th)	Postseason Odds: 23.3%	Mediocrity (5-7): 43%
Snap-Weighted Age: 26.2 (24th)	Defense: 13.4% (30th)	Super Bowl Odds: 1.2%	Playoff Contender (8-10): 28%
Average Opponent: 2.9% (6th)	Special Teams: 4.6% (1st)	Proj. Avg. Opponent: -0.3% (20th)	Super Bowl Contender (11+): 7%

2019: Toothless Tigers.

2020: In Joe We Trust.

At long last, Marvin Lewis was gone, and the Cincinnati Bengals were on to a fresh start. The new coach, Zac Taylor, had youth and vision and a shiny Sean McCoy imprimatur. This would be a "New Dey," a riff on the Bengals motto "Who Dey?" trotted out by the marketing department when Taylor was hired.

Then the season began. And Lewis was kicking back in his easy chair, cackling, pulling the cork on another big bottle of *schadenfreude*.

Cincinnati won only twice all season, earning the ignominious "honor" of the top choice in the draft. The offense was brutal, the defense worse. It all came to a head in a 49-13 destruction by the Ravens when Lamar Jackson, a player the Bengals coulda/shoulda drafted in 2018, spin-cycled his way through the defense for a meme-memorable touchdown run. The distance between the two division rivals was never more stark.

In Taylor's defense, he was hamstrung by horrendous misfortune long before the season even began. Jonah Williams, the team's first-round draft pick and heir apparent at left tackle, tore his labrum in minicamp and was done for the season before folks in Cincy started wearing shorts. Shortly afterwards, left guard Clint Boling unexpectedly retired due to injury concerns of his own. And on the first day of training camp, star wideout A.J. Green went down with a torn ankle tendon, never to return in 2019. The team had scarcely begun to dig into Taylor's new system and already the left side of the line and the main downfield weapon were gone.

Unsurprisingly, perhaps, the Bengals set new standards for anemia before finally getting it together a bit late in the season. The team was 30th in points per game, 29th in points per drive, 31st in touchdowns. They broke the plane just 20 times in the first 14 games until exploding for eight in the final two contests (against the Dolphins and Browns).

Prior to that wild Miami game, Cincinnati somehow managed to go 42 second-half drives without a touchdown. 42! It was a display of post-halftime ineptitude so remarkable the NFL should join Major League Baseball and retire that number league-wide. The Streak of Shame started in Week 8, which is precisely when Taylor, offensive coordinator Brian Callahan, and offensive line coach Jim Turner ripped up the run scheme that was on a pace for historic futility and found some success with the changes they made (Table 1). Yet it still didn't translate into touchdowns in the third and fourth quarters, proving that slinging it remains far more important than hauling it when it comes to offensive production. For the season, only a dozen of their 85 drives after halftime resulted in touchdowns.

Table 1. Cincinnati Offense Pass vs. Run, 2019

Weeks	Pass Yd/At	DVOA	Rk	Run Yd/At	DVOA	Rk
Weeks 1-8	5.80	-5.2%	26	3.17	-31.4%	32
Weeks 10-17	5.53	-20.6%	28	4.63	3.5%	8

The failure to draft a replacement for Andy Dalton at quarterback over the past several years cast the Bengals into a period of wandering in the wilderness. Dalton was bad enough in 2019 to be benched for fourth-round pick Ryan Finley, who was even more terrible, leading to the Red Rifle's triumphant "comeback." Dalton was more celebrated in Cincinnati for being better than an overmatched rookie on an awful team than for any of his actual good stretches of play over the years.

One can make a case for those three games Dalton spent on the bench being the most crucial of the season: the losses that resulted, the first two directly attributable to Finley's awful play, helped to cement Cincinnati's spot at the top of the 2020 draft and allowed them a chance to at last move on from Dalton's eternal mediocrity.

Move on and move up—to the quarterback who just finished the greatest single collegiate season anyone ever saw.

Joe Burrow, of course, won the Heisman Trophy and led LSU to a 15-0 national championship season, besting an unprecedented schedule of top opponents along the way. He broke the single-season record with 60 touchdown passes (he also ran for five more), against just six interceptions. He led the nation in completions, yards, yards per attempt, and passer rating. Only Colt McCoy of the 2008 Texas Longhorns had a better completion percentage (76.7% to 76.3%), and LSU wasn't running a dink-and-dunk offense—only 11.3% of Burrow's passes were at or behind the line of scrimmage, by far the lowest of any quarterback last season. Burrow's adjusted yards per attempt is fourth all-time (the prior two top overall

2020 Bengals Schedule					
Week	Opp.	Week	Opp.	Week	Opp.
1	LAC	7	CLE	13	at MIA
2	at CLE (Thu.)	8	TEN	14	DAL
3	at PHI	9	BYE	15	PIT (Mon.)
4	JAX	10	at PIT	16	at HOU
5	at BAL	11	at WAS	17	BAL
6	at IND	12	NYG		

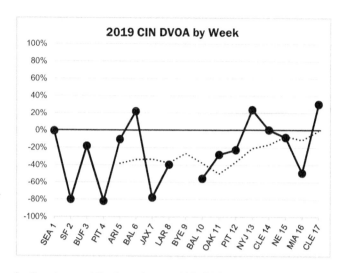

2019 CIN DVOA by Week

picks, Kyler Murray and Baker Mayfield, are slightly ahead of Burrow, as is Tua Tagavailoa's 2018).

Burrow's intangibles got even raver reviews than his pin-point passes. If you listen to LSU people and the defeated opposition left strewn in his wake, Burrow is some combination of Joe Montana, Tom Brady, and Sully Sullenberger, a peerless leader with nerves of steel and a work ethic that made him the most popular cat in the Tigers' locker room. Burrow also possesses a confidence bordering on cockiness that, fairly or not, stands in stark contrast to the blandness offered to the public by one Andrew G. Dalton. To cite just one example, not since Michael Jordan has any athlete made smoking a stogie, as Burrow did after winning the national title, look so damn cool. Video of him puffing away became an Internet meme and a T-shirt showing it has been a hot seller in the southern Ohio region.

Those inclined to search for flaws generally center on Burrow's quasi-suspect arm strength. Josh Allen or Jeff George he is not, but Burrow is hardly bringing a popgun to a shootout, and a slight mechanical flaw in his delivery—the premature lifting of his back foot—is a correction that should keep the odd throw from hanging in the air. His hands also measured slightly less than ideal, causing Burrow to sarcastically contemplate retirement on his Twitter feed. His advanced age (he will turn 24 before the 2020 season is over) is a legitimate knock, though the resulting maturity and steeliness he displayed at LSU surely is connected to that.

The more worrying factor for Bengals fans is that No. 1 overall picks, quarterbacks or otherwise, don't exactly have a great track record of turning into dominant players, especially in recent years. Can Burrow escape that trend? QBASE, our quarterback projection system, docks Joey B. for his lack of starting experience—he played only two years on the Bayou after famously transferring from Ohio State, and his junior season scarcely resembled his historic senior campaign. He is still easily the highest-ranked prospect in this class by our metrics, and if we filter for quarterbacks who started fewer than three seasons, Burrow is the second-best projection we've ever calculated, trailing only Alex Smith (Table 2).

Burrow isn't a prospect on the John Elway/Andrew Luck level, and no rookie should have to be burdened with the expectations of turning a franchise around immediately, especially such a nondescript squad as Cincinnati. Making things worse were the pigskin chattering classes (made up in fair measure by former Bengals) attempting to speak into existence a "Burrow won't play for that losing Bengals organization" campaign. On

its face it was ridiculous that an Ohio kid as classy and humble as Burrow would think that way, and Cincy can hardly be described as a destination quarterbacks go to die. Recent seasons were bleak, but the Bengals did make the playoffs five straight years to begin the decade, a fact that seemed to disappear down the memory hole in certain precincts.

Coincidentally or otherwise, there seemed to be a cause and effect when it came to free agency. The Stripes have long eschewed buying players, preferring to draft and develop, a wise course up until new rules limiting practice time re-framed the value of established veterans. Whether it was to prove to Burrow that his new team was indeed worthy, or just an overdue and necessary revamping of a two-win roster, the Bengals cannonballed into the free agency pool, got out, and jack-knifed back in again.

The porous defense—30th in DVOA—was the main area of focus. Cincinnati brought in a top-rated tackle (D.J. Reader), a pair of corners from old pal Mike Zimmer's defense in Minnesota (Trae Waynes and Mackenzie Alexander), a punishing safety (Vonn Bell), and a wise hand at linebacker (Josh Bynes). They signed depth corners LaShaun Sims from the Titans and Winston Rose, who led the CFL in interceptions

Table 2. Top QBASE Projections for 1-Year and 2-Year Starters, 1997-2020

Player	School	Year	QBASE
Alex Smith	Utah	2005	798
Joe Burrow	**LSU**	**2020**	**759**
Cam Newton	Auburn	2011	698
Tua Tagovailoa	**Alabama**	**2020**	**653**
Kyler Murray	Oklahoma	2019	595
JaMarcus Russell	LSU	2007	570
Sam Bradford	Oklahoma	2010	545
Vince Young	Texas	2006	536
Dwayne Haskins	Ohio State	2019	527
Tim Couch	Kentucky	1999	474

while with the Winnipeg Blue Bombers. The team also drafted three linebackers to try to improve the worst unit on the team.

The roster turnover will hopefully mesh with defensive coordinator Lou Anarumo's scheme better than the replaced group. Much as the offense was ruined by injuries over the summer, the defense got such a late start it never really began to jell until the season was lost. Anarumo wasn't hired until late February, and it took a while for his methods to sink in with the players. The weighted DVOA (25th) indicates some improvement later in the season, and players such as safety Jessie Bates and corner William Jackson talked openly about how their initial confusion subsided by December. Of course, Cincy's main issues were porous tackling, bad angles, and a lack of speed, which shouldn't be scheme-dependent. The Bengals were tied for 24th in the NFL in missed tackles, and the three players who missed the most tackles in the league were all Bengals—Bates (24), the now-departed Nick Vigil (23), and Shawn Williams (22). To cite just one example in a season full of them, the Bengals conjured a way to lose to Devlin "Duck" Hodges and Pittsburgh when Jackson took a strange angle and completely whiffed on James Washington, who subsequently scored when (since released) corner B.W. Webb tripped over his own feet while trying to prevent the touchdown.

The good news is that Burrow will be surrounded by weaponry in the offensive huddle superior to that of the usual 2-14 team—or the 2019 Patriots. Green has missed the last year and a half due to leg injuries, throwing his long-term viability into doubt, but he is in Cincinnati's plans for 2020 at the least, and if healthy he remains a force who opens up everything else. Tyler Boyd topped 1,000 yards for the second straight season despite the slop around him. John Ross has been injury-plagued through two seasons, but when upright has scored 10 touchdowns on 116 targets.

The Bengals also drafted a receiver they hope will grow along with Burrow into the next Dalton-Green combo. Clemson wideout Tee Higgins, picked at the top of the second round, was a Cincinnati fan, one of the few and proud, growing up. He now gets to learn the trade from Green, his boyhood idol. Higgins is a tremendous leaper with an immense catch radius and a knack for big plays (25 touchdowns in his two years as a regular), though his 40-yard dash time left something to be desired and almost certainly knocked him out of the first round.

The offensive line still profiles to be a problem, though the coaching staff clearly thinks more of the big uglies than anyone else, having mostly let it be during the offseason. A lot will be placed upon the shoulders of Turner, the line coach; his main achievement in 2019 seemed to be infuriating tackle Cordy Glenn, whose concussion in the preseason turned into a months-long war of words and wills inside the O-line room. At least getting Williams back, akin to adding another first-round pick, should up the talent level of what is otherwise a pretty banal group.

Aside from the new faces, there are other reasons to believe in a turnaround, however moderate it may be. The schedule, which replaces the NFC West with the East and includes the AFC South, profiles to be somewhat easier. Cincinnati was winless in seven one-score games last year. Only three other teams since 1989 lost six or more one-score games without winning any of them. Cincy suffered an excruciating loss by a single point in Seattle on opening day, a defeat that set the tone for the heartbreak to come. Even when the Bengals scored a shocking 16 points in the final seconds to force overtime at Miami, they managed to lose. In the big picture, of course, this was highly beneficial—it prevented the team and its fans from having to talk themselves into Justin Herbert or Jordan Love—and the strong likelihood is that the team finds a way to win at least a couple of those close calls this year.

Then there are the positive signs of growth shown by Taylor in his first season, which seems hard to believe during a two-win nightmare. He showed a willingness to adjust, as shown by the junking of his preferred zone-based running offense halfway through the schedule, and to use his best players, regardless of draft or contractual status, exemplified by the decision to bench former first-round center Billy Price. And the team certainly didn't quit down the stretch, if any coach can really have a quantifiable effect on that.

In terms of strategy, Taylor's scheme tendencies reflected his time spent alongside Sean McVay with the Rams, especially in using 11 formations. Only one other team used multiple running backs less often, and no team used three wide receivers more often. The team re-signed C.J. Uzomah and drafted Drew Sample, but only the highly breakable Tyler Eifert made much of a dent at the tight end spot (and he left for Jacksonville in the offseason). How Taylor deploys his tight ends will be an interesting subplot to the new Burrow-led offense. At LSU, Burrow threw nearly half his passes to slot receivers, which in that system often included tight end Thaddeus Moss. Uzomah and Sample have the ability to replicate the Gerald Everett/Tyler Higbee combo that was effective in Los Angeles, and perhaps exceed it with Burrow throwing them the ball.

Of course, Burrow is the key to everything, not just the tight ends. A big-time quarterback is the tide that lifts the entire franchise fleet, from the on-field product to merchandise sales to season tickets to, in this particular case, an overdue boost to the morale of the city vis-a-vis its pro football team. Optimism is running high in the Queen City for the first time in years, thanks to the Tiger King. It can be argued that Burrow is the most important player to don the black and orange in team history, as many locals believe another period of blah play, coinciding with the end of the current stadium lease (set to expire in 2026), could push the Brown/Blackburn family to move the team in the not-so-distant future. That won't happen if Burrow leads a renaissance, which, god willing, would include a long-awaited postseason win, a civic event the fan base hasn't had to enjoy since 1991.

This is all assuming we have a season, and what could be more Bengals than at last landing a franchise quarterback, only to not even play ball?

Robert Weintraub

2019 Bengals Stats by Week

Wk	vs.	W-L	PF	PA	YDF	YDA	TO	Total	Off	Def	ST
1	at SEA	L	20	21	429	232	-2	0%	-16%	-23%	-8%
2	SF	L	17	41	316	571	0	-80%	-20%	58%	-2%
3	at BUF	L	17	21	306	416	-2	-18%	-21%	-2%	1%
4	at PIT	L	3	27	175	326	-1	-82%	-41%	37%	-4%
5	ARI	L	23	26	370	514	0	-10%	11%	25%	3%
6	at BAL	L	17	23	250	497	0	22%	2%	0%	21%
7	JAX	L	17	27	291	460	-4	-78%	-74%	15%	12%
8	at LAR	L	10	24	401	470	0	-39%	-1%	46%	7%
9	BYE										
10	BAL	L	13	49	307	379	-2	-56%	-27%	38%	10%
11	at OAK	L	10	17	246	386	0	-28%	-50%	-17%	5%
12	PIT	L	10	16	244	338	-1	-22%	-21%	3%	2%
13	NYJ	W	22	6	277	271	0	24%	25%	0%	-1%
14	at CLE	L	19	27	451	333	+1	1%	1%	11%	11%
15	NE	L	13	34	315	291	-5	-8%	-10%	1%	2%
16	at MIA	L	35	38	430	502	0	-49%	-35%	28%	14%
17	CLE	W	33	23	361	313	+2	30%	16%	-14%	1%

Trends and Splits

	Offense	Rank	Defense	Rank
Total DVOA	-16.5%	29	13.4%	30
Unadjusted VOA	-19.3%	30	12.9%	30
Weighted Trend	-15.5%	27	10.1%	25
Variance	6.7%	11	5.6%	15
Average Opponent	-3.8%	4	-1.3%	23
Passing	-12.2%	28	25.0%	28
Rushing	-10.6%	23	2.4%	28
First Down	-19.9%	29	10.3%	27
Second Down	-13.4%	26	16.9%	28
Third Down	-14.6%	24	13.6%	25
First Half	-5.7%	21	16.1%	31
Second Half	-25.5%	31	9.9%	24
Red Zone	-35.7%	31	-8.4%	12
Late and Close	-27.3%	30	7.2%	24

Five-Year Performance

Year	W-L	Pyth W	Est W	PF	PA	TO	Total	Rk	Off	Rk	Def	Rk	ST	Rk	Off AGL	Rk	Def AGL	Rk	Off Age	Rk	Def Age	Rk	ST Age	Rk
2015	12-4	11.7	12.3	419	279	+11	27.9%	2	18.6%	2	-7.1%	10	2.2%	8	9.4	1	23.4	8	26.2	23	28.1	2	26.5	10
2016	6-9-1	8.3	8.0	325	315	+3	4.0%	13	7.5%	11	0.8%	17	-2.7%	28	23.8	7	26.1	8	26.7	17	28.2	1	26.4	7
2017	7-9	6.2	6.7	290	349	-9	-12.6%	24	-6.5%	22	3.7%	17	-2.4%	21	42.0	21	37.0	18	26.6	19	26.4	14	25.1	29
2018	6-10	5.9	7.2	368	455	+1	-9.7%	23	-3.3%	19	9.0%	27	2.6%	7	55.3	27	42.6	23	25.6	29	25.8	25	25.6	23
2019	2-14	4.3	4.3	279	420	-14	-25.3%	29	-16.5%	29	13.4%	30	4.6%	1	55.9	28	27.3	11	26.1	26	26.3	15	25.9	15

2019 Performance Based on Most Common Personnel Groups

CIN Offense					CIN Offense vs. Opponents					CIN Defense					CIN Defense vs. Opponents			
Pers	Freq	Yds	DVOA	Run%	Pers	Freq	Yds	DVOA	Run%	Pers	Freq	Yds	DVOA		Pers	Freq	Yds	DVOA
11	76%	5.3	-9.1%	29%	Base	19%	4.5	-26.7%	54%	Base	29%	5.9	10.4%		11	53%	6.8	20.5%
12	17%	4.6	-6.8%	57%	Nickel	62%	5.3	-6.0%	35%	Nickel	49%	6.6	19.8%		12	17%	5.7	-0.8%
611	2%	7.2	47.5%	76%	Dime+	19%	5.2	-14.3%	13%	Dime+	20%	6.5	6.4%		21	6%	5.6	-6.3%
13	1%	3.9	7.2%	33%	Goal Line	0%	0.0	-131.2%	100%	Goal Line	1%	0.8	-12.5%		13	6%	7.0	38.2%
21	1%	3.8	-76.9%	43%						Big	1%	2.7	-21.7%		22	5%	6.2	16.4%
															10	3%	8.3	53.3%

Strategic Tendencies

Run/Pass		Rk	Formation		Rk	Pass Rush		Rk	Secondary		Rk	Strategy		Rk
Runs, first half	38%	13	Form: Single Back	90%	4	Rush 3	6.2%	18	4 DB	29%	14	Play Action	22%	21
Runs, first down	45%	24	Form: Empty Back	9%	13	Rush 4	62.2%	20	5 DB	49%	22	Offensive Motion	35%	19
Runs, second-long	27%	18	Form: Multi Back	2%	31	Rush 5	23.4%	8	6+ DB	20%	10	Avg Box (Off)	6.41	28
Runs, power sit.	57%	15	Pers: 3+ WR	78%	1	Rush 6+	8.2%	8	Man Coverage	34%	12	Avg Box (Def)	6.64	12
Runs, behind 2H	28%	18	Pers: 2+ TE/6+ OL	22%	26	Edge Rusher Sacks	72.6%	4	CB by Sides	71%	20	Offensive Pace	29.25	7
Pass, ahead 2H	53%	7	Pers: 6+ OL	3%	13	Interior DL Sacks	17.7%	22	S/CB Cover Ratio	28%	10	Defensive Pace	31.30	27
Run-Pass Options	4%	19	Shotgun/Pistol	70%	12	Second Level Sacks	9.7%	29	DB Blitz	12%	14	Go for it on 4th	1.57	13

You can see some of the similarities between the Sean McVay offense and the Zac Taylor offense in the table above, including lots of three-wide sets and single-back formations. But why aren't the Bengals using more play-action? ◥ Another Bengals-Rams similarity: the Bengals were third with 11.8% of passes qualifying as max protect (seven or more blockers, at least two more blockers than pass-rushers). The Rams were second in the same metric. ◥ Cincinnati was a shocking sixth in DVOA on passes to the middle of the field, but 30th to the left side and dead last to the right side. ◥ The Bengals offense improved from 31st to 13th in broken tackles. ◥ Cincinnati's defense had a big gap between man coverage (6.9 yards per pass, 20.9% DVOA) and zone coverage (9.0 yards per pass, 54.2% DVOA). ◥ Cincinnati sent over twice as many defensive back blitzes as the year before but still didn't have many sacks from second-level defenders.

Passing

Player	DYAR	DVOA	Plays	NtYds	Avg	YAC	C%	TD	Int
A.Dalton	19	-10.6%	558	3230	5.8	4.9	60.4%	16	14
R.Finley	-290	-59.8%	98	388	4.0	5.0	47.1%	2	2

Rushing

Player	DYAR	DVOA	Plays	Yds	Avg	TD	Fum	Suc
J.Mixon	90	-0.9%	278	1137	4.1	5	0	46%
G.Bernard	-52	-33.5%	53	170	3.2	0	0	32%
A.Dalton	7	-7.7%	24	77	3.2	4	3	-
R.Finley	22	35.4%	9	77	8.6	0	0	-
A.Erickson	12	8.2%	5	33	6.6	0	0	-

Receiving

Player	DYAR	DVOA	Plays	Ctch	Yds	Y/C	YAC	TD	C%
T.Boyd	3	-12.4%	148	90	1046	11.6	3.9	5	61%
A.Tate	-5	-13.4%	80	40	575	14.4	3.4	1	50%
A.Erickson	-55	-22.0%	78	43	529	12.3	5.3	0	55%
J.Ross	36	-4.5%	56	28	506	18.1	7.1	3	50%
D.Willis	-8	-19.0%	16	9	82	9.1	1.8	0	56%
S.Morgan	-53	-82.5%	10	3	18	6.0	3.3	0	30%
T.Eifert*	22	-1.8%	63	43	436	10.1	2.6	3	68%
C.Uzomah	-34	-19.6%	40	27	242	9.0	5.0	2	68%
D.Sample	2	-0.8%	6	5	30	6.0	2.6	0	83%
J.Mixon	86	19.3%	45	35	287	8.2	9.5	3	78%
G.Bernard	-55	-38.5%	43	30	234	7.8	7.3	0	70%

Offensive Line

Player	Pos	Age	GS	Snaps	Pen	Sk	Pass	Run	Player	Pos	Age	GS	Snaps	Pen	Sk	Pass	Run
Trey Hopkins	C	28	16/16	1122	1	5.5	18	10	John Jerry*	LT	34	11/5	460	3	6.3	20	4
Bobby Hart	RT	26	16/16	1111	8	5.0	12	11	Cordy Glenn*	LT	31	6/5	295	0	1.5	5	2
John Miller*	RG	27	13/13	797	3	1.5	10	7	Andre Smith	LT	33	6/5	260	4	2.5	13	2
Michael Jordan	LG	22	14/9	658	5	3.5	10	10	Alex Redmond	RG	25	3/2	195	1	2.8	4	2
Billy Price	LG	26	16/8	604	3	2.3	15	9	Xavier Su'a-Filo	LG	29	11/4	309	1	1.0	3	7

Year	Yards	ALY	Rank	Power	Rank	Stuff	Rank	2nd Lev	Rank	Open Field	Rank	Sacks	ASR	Rank	Press	Rank	F-Start	Cont.
2017	3.70	3.79	24	59%	24	18%	9	1.17	12	0.41	31	40	7.2%	20	28.9%	8	10	28
2018	4.61	4.10	22	71%	7	20%	20	1.30	11	1.19	3	37	7.0%	19	27.6%	10	27	30
2019	3.95	3.90	26	67%	13	22%	29	1.10	23	0.70	19	48	7.3%	20	24.8%	3	19	21

2019 ALY by direction: Left End 4.90 (6)   Left Tackle: 2.90 (30)   Mid/Guard: 3.81 (30)   Right Tackle: 3.38 (25)   Right End: 5.55 (4)

Cincinnati's offensive line finished with a combined 164 blown blocks, second in the league to Miami. Yet the Bengals ranked third in the NFL in pressure rate, mainly due to abandonment of the deep passing game. ◥ As for the run game, going between the tackles was a non-starter, with the Bengals near the bottom on any rushes not charted as end runs. In those, however, Cincy was top six on both sides. ◥ With Jonah Williams lost early on and Cordy Glenn in a Trent Williams-like dispute with the team over his concussion, the Bengals were helpless for most of the season at left tackle, reduced to giving John Jerry and Andre Smith 720 combined snaps. The exception came in the last two games, when Fred Johnson, a guard claimed off waivers from Pittsburgh, played the spot with surprising verve. The expectation is for Johnson to battle Bobby Hart to start at right tackle. Hart has been so maligned he may have reached the point of being a bit underrated. ◥ Trey Hopkins is hardly among the top centers in the NFL—he had 28 blown blocks and allowed 5.5 sacks—but by recent Bengals standards he's Jim Otto. As such, he was extended in the offseason, and is what passes for a mainstay in the lineup. ◥ Guard was a nightmare in 2019 and doesn't figure to be a strong suit in 2020. Xavier Su'a-Filo has been mediocre since being taken with the 33rd pick in 2014 and came off the bench in Dallas last season, but the Bengals signed him to play on the right side to replace John Miller, who was hardly the weak link in 2019. ◥ The inside track for left guard belongs to Michael Jordan, who will most decidedly not have a ten-hour documentary produced about his play. A mid-round pick from Ohio State last year, Jordan struggled as a rookie and was benched, but began to come around in the final furlong. If Fair Jordan stumbles, that might open the door for another Buckeye, former first-round pick Billy Price, who is otherwise headed for Bustville. ◥ Nimble-footed sixth-round pick Hakeem Adeniji out of Kansas has a lot of fans among draftniks and provides depth at both tackle and guard.

Defensive Front

Defensive Line	Age	Pos	G	Snaps	Plays	Overall TmPct	Rk	Stop	Dfts	BTkl	Runs	vs. Run St%	Rk	RuYd	Rk	Sack	Pass Rush Hit	Hur	Dsrpt
Geno Atkins	32	DT	16	836	47	5.7%	27	34	13	2	39	69%	71	2.7	67	4.5	6	26	0
Andrew Billings*	25	DT	16	670	35	4.2%	49	22	6	4	33	61%	86	2.5	61	1.0	3	8	1
Josh Tupou	26	DT	16	475	27	3.3%	77	23	6	1	27	85%	13	1.7	20	0.0	0	3	0
D.J. Reader	26	DT	15	629	51	6.7%	19	40	7	2	46	78%	33	2.6	63	2.5	11	14	2

Edge Rushers	Age	Pos	G	Snaps	Plays	Overall TmPct	Rk	Stop	Dfts	BTkl	Runs	vs. Run St%	Rk	RuYd	Rk	Sack	Pass Rush Hit	Hur	Dsrpt
Sam Hubbard	25	DE	15	871	78	10.1%	1	56	18	10	57	75%	38	2.8	53	8.5	5	37	3
Carlos Dunlap	31	DE	14	755	70	9.7%	3	54	25	3	47	70%	59	2.9	65	9.0	13	36	8
Carl Lawson	25	DE	12	467	23	3.7%	80	13	7	4	15	53%	82	2.7	52	5.0	19	20	0
Andrew Brown	25	DE	14	250	14	1.9%	--	8	1	3	13	62%	--	2.9	--	0.0	2	7	0

Linebackers	Age	Pos	G	Snaps	Plays	Overall TmPct	Rk	Stop	Dfts	BTkl	Runs	vs. Run St%	Rk	RuYd	Rk	Sack	Pass Rush Hit	Hur	Tgts	vs. Pass Suc%	Rk	AdjYd	Rk	PD	Int
Nick Vigil*	27	OLB	16	1009	116	14.0%	21	67	16	23	74	62%	34	3.9	40	1.0	4	9	33	64%	7	5.6	23	5	1
Germaine Pratt	24	MLB	16	443	71	8.6%	61	34	4	10	54	57%	48	4.1	53	0.0	0	4	14	36%	61	11.9	68	0	0
Preston Brown*	28	MLB	10	440	53	10.3%	71	25	4	3	32	56%	60	4.0	43	0.0	0	4	9	33%	--	8.7	--	0	0
Josh Bynes	31	ILB	12	401	49	9.1%	68	32	11	7	36	67%	19	2.3	4	1.0	2	3	8	38%	--	8.1	--	4	2
Austin Calitro	26	OLB	13	236	40	6.2%	--	19	4	8	21	57%	--	4.8	--	1.0	1	2	12	67%	--	4.0	--	1	0

Year	Yards	ALY	Rank	Power	Rank	Stuff	Rank	2nd Level	Rank	Open Field	Rank	Sacks	ASR	Rank	Press	Rank
2017	4.06	4.38	29	70%	25	19%	25	1.26	26	0.49	3	41	6.3%	19	33.8%	5
2018	4.94	4.99	30	77%	29	14%	30	1.41	28	1.01	21	34	7.1%	16	26.5%	28
2019	4.58	4.55	24	66%	20	21%	9	1.36	28	0.88	24	31	6.3%	24	31.4%	11
2019 ALY by direction:		Left End: 5.34 (31)			Left Tackle: 4.67 (23)			Mid/Guard: 4.45 (19)			Right Tackle: 4.27 (15)			Right End: 4.37 (15)		

The Bengals' sack rate was mediocre, and when the sacks came, they came in waves—20 of the team's 31 sacks came in just five games. The pressure rate was much stronger, 12th in the league, which bodes well for an increase in sacks. ◥ One key will be if edge rusher Carl Lawson can play an entire campaign, which he hasn't done since his rookie year in 2017. When he is healthy, Lawson regularly caves in the left side of enemy pockets. ◥ Sam Hubbard isn't a dominant rusher, but he is relentless and versatile, allowing him to get 8.5 sacks and 37 hurries. ◥ Atkins and end Carlos Dunlap remain effective, if on the back end of their productive careers. Dunlap in particular had a quietly strong 2019, second in the league with eight pass disruptions after leading the league with 10 in 2018. ◥ The undeniable weak spot on the defense, and the team, was line-backer, as evidenced by the team's 28th rank in second-level yards and in covering tight ends, while ranking 31st in covering opposing running backs. The Bengals were also dead last in DVOA against passes thrown at or behind the line of scrimmage. After watching the unit get embarrassed week after week, the team jettisoned almost everyone, save Germaine Pratt, a rookie who emerged as a solid player. ◥ Josh Bynes was brought in from the Ravens to provide some veteran leadership, but Cincy mainly attacked its wanting linebacker corps in the draft, taking three players. Third-rounder Logan Wilson of Wyoming and fourth-rounder Akeem Davis-Gaither of Appalachian State both played under the watchful eyes of Bengals coaches at the Senior Bowl. Both are much more athletic than the guys trotted out last year, save Pratt. ◥ The wild card is seventh-round pick Markus Bailey, a borderline first-round talent who was severely injured twice at Purdue. If he can buck the Bengals trend and actually stay healthy, he would help immensely.

Defensive Secondary

Secondary	Age	Pos	G	Snaps	Plays	TmPct	Rk	Stop	Dfts	BTkl	Runs	St%	Rk	RuYd	Rk	Tgts	Tgt%	Rk	Dist	Suc%	Rk	AdjYd	Rk	PD	Int
Jessie Bates	23	FS	16	1083	109	13.2%	8	26	10	23	55	16%	73	9.8	60	20	5.4%	62	13.8	55%	26	8.8	53	9	3
Shawn Williams	29	SS	16	1024	115	13.9%	3	45	16	22	58	47%	25	5.5	20	39	11.2%	14	11.0	49%	44	9.2	59	3	1
B.W. Webb*	30	CB	15	851	44	5.7%	77	12	7	5	8	13%	83	9.0	69	55	19.0%	57	14.8	44%	73	12.9	85	7	1
William Jackson	28	CB	14	849	40	5.5%	83	12	7	4	6	0%	85	19.5	85	51	17.6%	62	11.9	61%	13	6.6	21	3	1
Darqueze Dennard*	29	CB	9	502	42	9.0%	--	22	8	3	20	65%	--	5.1	--	29	16.9%	--	8.0	69%	--	4.3	--	5	0
Dre Kirkpatrick*	31	CB	6	345	37	11.9%	--	14	6	6	16	25%	--	8.3	--	25	21.3%	--	10.2	52%	--	8.0	--	4	0
Vonn Bell	26	SS	13	893	91	14.2%	14	38	17	11	37	59%	4	4.9	13	31	7.9%	37	11.9	45%	58	9.0	55	5	1
Trae Waynes	28	CB	14	782	66	8.6%	48	33	10	8	12	75%	8	1.3	1	78	23.6%	13	11.4	47%	63	7.6	43	8	1
Mackensie Alexander	27	CB	13	541	41	5.7%	--	19	8	1	9	44%	--	5.7	--	42	18.4%	--	10.5	52%	--	6.0	--	5	1
LeShaun Sims	27	CB	14	336	31	4.2%	--	11	0	7	12	33%	--	5.3	--	26	19.9%	--	14.2	54%	--	7.0	--	2	0

Year	Pass D Rank	vs. #1 WR	Rk	vs. #2 WR	Rk	vs. Other WR	Rk	WR Wide	Rk	WR Slot	Rk	vs. TE	Rk	vs. RB	Rk
2017	17	-14.4%	8	-4.4%	15	22.2%	28	-10.5%	9	11.9%	21	19.6%	30	-5.6%	11
2018	25	-2.6%	13	21.7%	28	-14.5%	7	7.9%	24	-3.8%	13	2.7%	16	22.0%	31
2019	28	22.3%	30	-2.5%	14	21.5%	28	30.1%	32	4.6%	14	10.9%	28	34.3%	31

Like the linebacker corps, the defensive backfield desperately needed an overhaul, and it sure received one in the offseason. ● William Jackson appeared to be an emerging lockdown corner two years ago, but hasn't taken the next step, though he had good numbers in 2019. One thing holding him back: he revealed in a June interview that he played the entire 2019 season with a torn labrum. ● Dre Kirkpatrick was swapped out for expensive free-agent signing Trae Waynes. Both irritated their fans with coverage gaffes, but the difference point is in the run game—Waynes is a superb tackler, Kirkpatrick an indifferent one. ● Likewise, the Bengals brought in sure-tackling Mackenzie Alexander to replace Darqueze Dennard at slot corner, although DD was actually superior in our numbers, except in one critical area—games played. Dennard's contract with Jacksonville fell through after the Alexander signing; perhaps his future is as a Chris Crocker-type annual mid-season signing after injuries hit. ● Free safety Jessie Bates struggled to find his way in coordinator Lou Anarumo's scheme, but in the back half of the season, he figured it out, and showed the skill he had as a stalwart rookie in 2018. ● Vonn Bell was another free agent seemingly signed with Lamar Jackson in mind. Bell was one of the best run-stopping safeties in the league in 2019. His addition may lead to Shawn Williams assuming more of a linebacker-hybrid role. Williams missed a raft of tackles in 2019 but in fairness played most of the way with a severe thigh injury.

Special Teams

Year	DVOA	Rank	FG/XP	Rank	Net Kick	Rank	Kick Ret	Rank	Net Punt	Rank	Punt Ret	Rank	Hidden	Rank
2017	-2.4%	21	2.7	14	-2.9	24	-5.3	31	-6.0	22	-0.2	17	4.8	11
2018	2.6%	7	1.0	14	2.9	8	8.6	3	-1.2	18	1.6	13	-10.8	27
2019	4.6%	1	8.1	6	5.1	6	8.7	1	4.2	12	-3.2	25	-10.3	29

If you thought 2019 was a full-on disaster for the Bengals, think again! The special teams unit coached by Darrin Simmons was best in the NFL in overall DVOA, mainly on the strength of excellent kick returns by Brandon Wilson, who led the league in return value by a wide margin despite missing the final month of the season to injury. ● Number one here does not mean greatness, however. The Bengals had the lowest special teams DVOA of any team to finish first in the league since the 1992 Detroit Lions. ● Cincy's luckless season extended to the consistency of enemy kickers, which is why the Bengals ranked 29th in Hidden Points. ● Punter Kevin Huber and kicker Randy Bullock were very solid, although neither wows anyone with powerful legs. ● Alex Erickson has stayed in the league mainly on the strength of his special teams play, but his punt returns were the weak link in 2019.

Cleveland Browns

2019 Record: 6-10		Total DVOA: -9.7% (23rd)		2020 Mean Projection: 7.5 wins	On the Clock (0-4): 13%
Pythagorean Wins: 6.4 (22nd)		Offense: -4.5% (20th)		Postseason Odds: 34.4%	Mediocrity (5-7): 38%
Snap-Weighted Age: 25.7 (31st)		Defense: 6.0% (22nd)		Super Bowl Odds: 2.5%	Playoff Contender (8-10): 37%
Average Opponent: 2.7% (8th)		Special Teams: 0.8% (15th)		Proj. Avg. Opponent: -0.6% (22nd)	Super Bowl Contender (11+): 13%

2019: Kitchen's Nightmares.

2020: The Mystery Ingredient is … (chairman voice) PLAY-ACTION.

Last year's forecast for the Cleveland Browns largely came true. The empirical one, we mean. The final projections we listed on our website, FootballOutsiders.com, had the Browns finishing below average with 4.8% offensive DVOA, 4.8% defensive DVOA, and -0.7% special teams DVOA. We thought they would win eight games; they won six. Their offense wound up slightly overprojected, as they finished with -4.5% offensive DVOA. The special teams and defensive DVOA both wound up within two percentage points of expectations.

We lead with this because it is a departure from the conventional wisdom of last preseason, which built the pressure and anticipation for a super-sleeper, playoff-caliber Browns team. There was a lot of wish-casting on Baker Mayfield's last eight games of 2018, Odell Beckham's talent, and the idea that Freddie Kitchens could galvanize the team together, and this brewed optimism that just wasn't borne out by the numbers. The tea has been bubbling on that ever since the franchise re-incorporated in 1999, with just one playoff appearance and one 10-win season to show for the last 21 years. The Browns have been criticized for everything under the sun and in every possible way you can criticize a franchise: that is what happens when this level of losing takes hold.

We are most intimately familiar with criticisms that the Browns have turned over coaching staffs too quickly and that analytics have ruined them, because that is the main tenor of what has come of late. Yet earlier iterations of this franchise did things exactly the opposite way and still lost. Butch Davis and Romeo Crennel each got fourth years despite showing little in the way of growth. Initial general manager Dwight Clark came from the Bill Walsh/Carmen Policy football school. Davis had full personnel control. Phil Savage came in as former Ravens director of college scouting and player personnel, where he had helped create a defense so good it made future Browns quarterback Trent Dilfer a Super Bowl winner. Tom Heckert was a football lifer who had a phenomenal run as Andy Reid's general manager and came to Cleveland for three years and flopped.

If you count Crennel as a Patriots hire, the Browns hired from one of the great '90s dynasties and three of the six teams with the highest winning percentages of the 2000s. It got them to the exact same nowhere that analytics and quick firings did. Moreover, it's not like this version of the Browns has fired

a Belichick-level head coach. For all the fuss about coaches who didn't get enough of a chance, it's not like Rob Chudzinski suddenly became a superstar when the Browns let him go. It's not like Pat Shurmur changed the Giants into an offensive juggernaut. The best head coach the Browns let go of was Kyle Shanahan, and Shanahan wasn't even part of a deposed regime: he straight-up left the organization in 2015 for opposing Johnny Manziel's ascent to starter.

Continuing in that vein of bad coaching and quick resets, we have to stand on the mountaintop and say that Kitchens proved a lot about how unprepared he was for the job in 2019, way more than enough to make a convincing case to fire him. Offensive coordinator Todd Monken had no control of the play calling and referred to his Thursday media sessions as a "dentist appointment" because he didn't have final say. This is despite Monken running an offense in Tampa Bay that finished with a 24.0% pass offense DVOA in 2018 with the notable handicap of starting Ryan Fitzpatrick, something that garnered Monken actual head-coaching interviews. Beckham reportedly asked a different team to "come get him" every week. Jarvis Landry and Kitchens openly feuded on the sidelines. Kitchens didn't do anything to head off the ugly brawl between the Steelers and Browns that left star defensive end Myles Garrett suspended for swinging his helmet at Pittsburgh backup Mason Rudolph—in fact, he would wear a shirt that said "Pittsburgh started it." We could reel off paragraphs about the pure leadership dysfunction before we even bring up things like "calling a draw on fourth-and-9 against the Rams," or how the multiple-tight end sets the Browns ran in 2018 became a thing of the past.

Cleveland's recent issues are largely a byproduct of a lack of a cohesive vision. Owner Jimmy Haslam had the organization on two different tracks—analytics (Sashi Brown, Paul DePodesta) and traditional football men (Hue Jackson, John Dorsey)—without ever getting the two sides on the same page. As Football Outsiders is one of the birthplaces of public football analytics, the Browns chapter of *Football Outsiders Almanac* has essentially become a proxy debate for their effectiveness. The problem with this is that analytics can only make you more likely to succeed, not guarantee it. The analytical mindset in and of itself is helpful, but marrying it to football is a lot more complex than we give it credit for, in particular when it comes to interpersonal and identity conflicts. There's a reason

2020 Browns Schedule

Week	Opp.	Week	Opp.	Week	Opp.
1	at BAL	7	at CIN	13	at TEN
2	CIN (Thu.)	8	LV	14	BAL (Mon.)
3	WAS	9	BYE	15	at NYG
4	at DAL	10	HOU	16	at NYJ (Sat.)
5	IND	11	PHI	17	PIT
6	at PIT	12	at JAX		

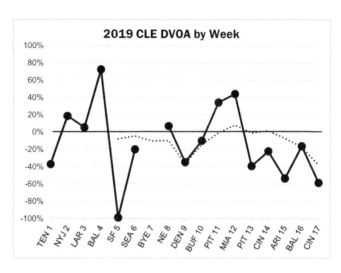

2019 CLE DVOA by Week

that Football Outsiders writers aren't a head-coaching market inefficiency waiting to be exploited.

The analytics unit would routinely do a great job of providing the Browns with draft capital and cap space, two tools for building a football team that are very important provided that they are given to someone who wields them well. The Browns too often would not wield them well, as evidenced by Manziel, Corey Coleman, and Justin Gilbert, among others. Football Outsiders ran a study by Benjamin Ellinger this summer that concluded the Browns accumulated more draft capital than any team over the past five years and had more draft return than any team over that same timespan. But in measuring the return against the capital, the Browns finished fourth-to-last in the NFL, ahead of only the Raiders, Bengals, and Jets (Table 1).

Table 1: Cleveland Browns Drafts, 2015-2019

Team	Capital	Rank	Team	Return	Rank	Team	Return vs. Capital	Rank
CLE	**5.02%**	**1**	**CLE**	**4.06%**	**1**	ARI	84%	28
SF	3.93%	2	BAL	4.06%	1	**CLE**	**81%**	**29**
TB	3.73%	3	IND	4.05%	3	OAK	79%	30
OAK	3.72%	4	SF	3.92%	4	CIN	78%	31
NYG	3.66%	5	NYG	3.55%	5	NYJ	71%	32

Numbers represent percentage of all draft capital or return among all 32 teams in a given draft. Capital measured with Chase Stuart's draft value chart. Return measured by Approximate Value.

What happened this offseason in Cleveland was something of a consolidation of power for the analytics section of the front office. DePodesta took over as the senior personnel man in the building after a mutual parting of ways with Dorsey, and the analytics department wooed a sympathetic set of ears in new head coach and former Vikings offensive coordinator Kevin Stefanski. Stefanski's one season coordinating the Vikings offense established a run-centric focus with a minor in play-action passing and ended with Minnesota rebounding from a down first year with Kirk Cousins to become a top-10 passing DVOA offense.

If 2019's offseason was about the flashy moves, 2020's was about adding the meat and potatoes to sustain the team. One of the major problems that Cleveland faced last year was a lack of talent at tackle. Greg Robinson was named the starter

on the left side after some good play down the stretch in 2018, and that faith went about as well as it ever has in Robinson's career. Steelers import Chris Hubbard was at right tackle. The two of them helped contribute to Mayfield's year of taking the snap, dropping back, and immediately tiptoeing to his right out of the pocket like a cat that saw something it wanted to sniff. Neither was a tackle you should leave on an island. The Browns signed ex-Titans tackle Jack Conklin to a huge deal, then buffered that by selecting Alabama tackle Jedrick Willis in the first round. By signing Austin Hooper to a huge contract and drafting Harrison Bryant when he surprisingly was on the board in the fourth round, the Browns also protected themselves against future David Njoku injuries and have set themselves up well to run Stefanski's primary formation curveball last year in Minnesota. Only the Eagles (54%) ran two tight ends more often than the Vikings (35%) on first and second downs last season.

The changes effectively remove most of the excuses for Mayfield's 2019 season. The narrative of Mayfield's 2018 was one that was hard to ignore because when you see good things happen as a player gets more starts, it's easy to believe that the player is growing. What 2019 showed us was that Mayfield at this point in his career is heavily influenced by his situation.

Oklahoma schemed up Mayfield in an RPO-based, play-action-heavy game plan to get him into his comfort zone and disguise the fact that he still had some flaws as a dropback passer. He's small for a starting quarterback and deals with it by taking extra steps to better see the field on his straight dropbacks, which puts his tackles at a major disadvantage in handling wide rushers. As mentioned earlier, when Mayfield has to put even more space between himself and the pass-rushers, he has a tendency to drift to his right. As much as we generally poke fun at the height-obsessed nature of NFL scouting—the same complex that has missed the Russell Wilsons and Drew Breeses for the trees—Mayfield is an example of where that stereotype comes from in the first place. The footwork he demonstrated last year to create space for his vision helped get him sacked. Everything out of that same basic "five steps and a cloud of dust" concept became a little too slow, and Kitchens leaned into it extremely hard for the first eight weeks as the Browns waddled around as an offense like their pants were around their legs. Through the first eight weeks of the year, Mayfield had -23.9% passing DVOA, a number that put him ahead of only Luke Falk, Josh Allen, Josh Rosen, and Sam Darnold. That is not the murderer's row in which you want to see your former No. 1 pick. From Week 9 on, Mayfield's passing DVOA was -0.2%, which doesn't sound great but ranked him 15th among quarterbacks during that stretch.

The 2019 Browns averaged 8.4 yards per attempt out of play-action. They averaged just 5.8 yards out of non-play-action passes, a 2.6-yard difference that put them in the top five in the NFL. The 2018 Browns as a whole barely improved while using play-action, but that changed drastically after Kitchens was installed. From Week 9 on, the 2018 Browns averaged 10.0 yards per attempt using play-action passes. Mayfield's splits in 2018 with two or more tight ends on the field are also stark in a good way: 63 dropbacks and an average of 10.3 yards per play, as compared to 7.6 without. In 2019, Mayfield averaged 7.5 yards per play with two or more tight ends on the field and 5.8 without.

More RPOs will also help Mayfield and the whole Browns offense. Cleveland gained 5.7 yards per play on RPOs in 2019, the highest average among the six teams that used them at least 10% of the time.

Your belief in the Browns this year is likely to bank heavily on how you feel about the concept of the post-hype sleeper and, specifically, how you feel about Stefanski's ability to pull off a major offensive coup for this team. It has not been uncommon over the last five seasons for new coaching to drag a team's offense up heavily. Sean McVay's takeover with the Rams is perhaps the most instructive example of a team that improved heavily specifically because of a coaching staff, and there's also the obvious similarity between Goff and Mayfield as first overall picks. Even beyond that, Kellen Moore, Kliff Kingsbury, and the Pat Shurmur/Stefanski 2017 Vikings each had major offensive DVOA turnarounds in the last three seasons. And, in theory, Stefanski's Minnesota offense, heavy on play-action and two-tight end sets, seems to avoid the schematic failings of Mayfield's 2019 season.

What 2018 taught us is that an efficient, well-managed Browns offense should be considered within the scope of out-comes for this team. And given the fact that there are now seven playoff teams in each conference, and the AFC has been fairly top-heavy for years, any kind of good offense would be enough to carry the Browns to playoff contention even if nothing else improved. But that's not the only reason to believe that they'll improve: they're presumably getting 16 games of Myles Garrett this year, they're likely to get more Olivier Vernon than they got in 2019, and they should be better against the run as a wave of new linebackers and safeties have been signed or drafted over the past two years.

As we dig deep on these teams and write these chapters, a lot of what we present as an optimistic outcome feels silly sometimes. "If Nick Foles can be healthy and be a major upgrade, the Jaguars can compete this year!" "If Andy Dalton can be managed à la Jared Goff, this Bengals team under new head coach Zac Taylor has some sneaky upside!" and so on. But with the Browns, there is a very realistic path to contention this year if you believe that Kitchens was a bungler. The talent has been massively upgraded over the past two offseasons. They have someone in charge who looks to be a good fit for Mayfield's talents—someone who has overseen a couple of different offensive resurgences in Minnesota and who just last year rebounded around a talented run game and scheme protecting a quarterback in Kirk Cousins who, if we're being honest with ourselves, has always been a few throws short of elite. Even if Mayfield doesn't improve on a talent level, there's reason to believe a more careful management of his game will change a lot about this offense. Nick Chubb is every bit capable of going Dalvin Cook on the league, and no NFL team has a better backup running back than Kareem Hunt.

The numbers? They don't see it. The offensive projection gets a little boost from Austin Hooper, but that just brings the Browns to the level of average. The defensive projection sees no reason why the Browns should be significantly better than they were a year ago. The numbers believe it will be another Browns winter of third at best in the AFC North. And, certainly, after this many years of the usual, you can't blame the numbers.

Rivers McCown

2019 Browns Stats by Week

Wk	vs.	W-L	PF	PA	YDF	YDA	TO	Total	Off	Def	ST
1	TEN	L	13	43	346	339	-3	-37%	-32%	10%	5%
2	at NYJ	W	23	3	375	262	0	19%	-5%	-13%	10%
3	LAR	L	13	20	270	344	+2	5%	-16%	-21%	0%
4	at BAL	W	40	25	530	395	+2	72%	50%	-22%	0%
5	at SF	L	3	31	180	446	-4	-99%	-83%	19%	3%
6	SEA	L	28	32	406	454	-3	-20%	-12%	11%	4%
7	BYE										
8	at NE	L	13	27	310	318	-3	7%	-7%	-12%	2%
9	at DEN	L	19	24	351	302	+1	-35%	1%	32%	-4%
10	BUF	W	19	16	368	344	0	-10%	2%	6%	-6%
11	PIT	W	21	7	293	236	+4	34%	16%	-30%	-12%
12	MIA	W	41	24	467	284	+1	44%	38%	-11%	-5%
13	at PIT	L	13	20	279	323	-1	-39%	-5%	27%	-7%
14	CIN	W	27	19	333	451	-1	-22%	-13%	17%	8%
15	at ARI	L	24	38	393	445	-1	-53%	-10%	39%	-5%
16	BAL	L	15	31	241	481	0	-16%	-1%	21%	6%
17	at CIN	L	23	33	313	361	-2	-58%	-38%	33%	13%

Trends and Splits

	Offense	Rank	Defense	Rank
Total DVOA	-4.5%	20	6.0%	22
Unadjusted VOA	-7.6%	22	6.7%	21
Weighted Trend	-1.2%	16	11.6%	26
Variance	9.0%	25	4.8%	6
Average Opponent	-4.7%	1	-2.5%	26
Passing	1.3%	21	6.4%	17
Rushing	1.4%	8	5.6%	30
First Down	2.4%	13	20.7%	31
Second Down	-4.2%	19	-1.0%	14
Third Down	-19.3%	26	-14.2%	10
First Half	-2.6%	17	2.6%	20
Second Half	-6.6%	20	9.4%	23
Red Zone	-25.5%	28	16.1%	27
Late and Close	-15.3%	24	8.0%	25

Five-Year Performance

Year	W-L	Pyth W	Est W	PF	PA	TO	Total	Rk	Off	Rk	Def	Rk	ST	Rk	Off AGL	Rk	Def AGL	Rk	Off Age	Rk	Def Age	Rk	ST Age	Rk
2015	3-13	4.0	4.5	278	432	-9	-23.0%	30	-13.2%	27	10.5%	29	0.7%	15	36.0	19	33.2	16	27.4	9	27.1	8	25.6	25
2016	1-15	3.3	1.5	264	452	-12	-30.4%	31	-13.4%	29	14.5%	30	-2.5%	26	45.2	21	50.0	22	26.7	15	25.1	32	24.5	32
2017	0-16	3.3	3.3	234	410	-28	-27.2%	32	-20.1%	32	2.0%	16	-5.1%	27	19.9	7	35.9	16	24.9	32	24.5	32	24.1	32
2018	7-8-1	7.1	7.5	359	392	+7	-2.8%	17	-1.1%	17	-2.5%	12	-4.2%	30	9.1	1	38.8	22	25.6	30	24.9	31	25.4	27
2019	6-10	6.4	6.2	335	393	-8	-9.7%	23	-4.5%	20	6.0%	22	0.8%	15	15.4	4	41.4	23	26.3	22	25.4	30	25.0	32

2019 Performance Based on Most Common Personnel Groups

CLE Offense					CLE Offense vs. Opponents						CLE Defense					CLE Defense vs. Opponents			
Pers	Freq	Yds	DVOA	Run%	Pers	Freq	Yds	DVOA	Run%		Pers	Freq	Yds	DVOA		Pers	Freq	Yds	DVOA
11	56%	5.6	-3.0%	26%	Base	27%	5.7	-3.6%	54%		Base	12%	6.1	13.9%		11	56%	5.9	2.1%
12	23%	6.2	7.8%	61%	Nickel	48%	6.0	6.3%	39%		Nickel	85%	5.8	1.6%		12	21%	5.9	10.8%
20	8%	6.9	44.2%	39%	Dime+	24%	5.5	0.4%	15%		Dime+	2%	13.4	145.7%		21	7%	8.2	7.8%
21	6%	5.8	-1.9%	43%	Goal Line	1%	-0.1	-10.9%	54%		Goal Line	1%	0.3	0.6%		22	4%	6.0	28.3%
13	2%	4.4	31.4%	33%												13	4%	4.8	2.4%
																10	3%	5.1	10.1%

Strategic Tendencies

Run/Pass		Rk	Formation		Rk	Pass Rush		Rk	Secondary		Rk	Strategy		Rk
Runs, first half	36%	22	Form: Single Back	80%	17	Rush 3	4.6%	23	4 DB	12%	31	Play Action	28%	12
Runs, first down	51%	12	Form: Empty Back	8%	14	Rush 4	59.6%	23	5 DB	85%	1	Offensive Motion	31%	28
Runs, second-long	29%	12	Form: Multi Back	12%	13	Rush 5	26.5%	5	6+ DB	2%	25	Avg Box (Off)	6.52	21
Runs, power sit.	50%	26	Pers: 3+ WR	65%	17	Rush 6+	9.2%	6	Man Coverage	28%	26	Avg Box (Def)	6.65	11
Runs, behind 2H	33%	5	Pers: 2+ TE/6+ OL	28%	15	Edge Rusher Sacks	50.0%	24	CB by Sides	86%	9	Offensive Pace	32.23	28
Pass, ahead 2H	46%	19	Pers: 6+ OL	3%	12	Interior DL Sacks	22.4%	16	S/CB Cover Ratio	30%	7	Defensive Pace	30.28	11
Run-Pass Options	11%	5	Shotgun/Pistol	67%	16	Second Level Sacks	27.6%	8	DB Blitz	19%	2	Go for it on 4th	1.84	7

Cleveland was third in the NFL with 159 broken tackles, led by Nick Chubb's 74 which was second in the league. But while Chubb breaks a ton of tackles, the guy does have his limits. Overall, Cleveland had just 2.4 yards per carry and -37.2% DVOA when facing a heavy box of eight or more defenders, compared to a 5.6-yard average and 8.8% DVOA on other running back carries. ◥ Cleveland led the league with 43 running back screens. They had 15.6% DVOA on these plays with 6.2 average yards, both close to the NFL averages of 12.0% DVOA and 6.7 yards. ◥ The Browns brought a lot of defensive back blitzes and got good results. The Browns had -15.4% DVOA and allowed 5.8 net yards per pass on these plays. On other blitzes, they had 34.9% DVOA and allowed 7.6 net yards per pass. ◥ Cleveland's defense led the NFL with 10 sacks attributed to an untouched pass-rusher by SIS charters. ◥ If the Browns want to be one of the league's better defenses, they have to improve their tackling. Only Jacksonville was charted with more broken tackles on defense. At least that's a step better than the year before, when the Browns missed the most tackles in the league. ◥ Cleveland tied for the smallest gap between where their two safeties made their average play, suggesting interchangeable safeties instead of more-defined roles as free and strong safety.

Passing

Player	DYAR	DVOA	Plays	NtYds	Avg	YAC	C%	TD	Int
B.Mayfield	48	-9.8%	573	3516	6.1	5.7	59.7%	22	21
C.Keenum	51	-8.1%	260	1565	6.0	5.0	65.3%	11	5

Receiving

Player	DYAR	DVOA	Plays	Ctch	Yds	Y/C	YAC	TD	C%
J.Landry	182	4.1%	138	83	1174	14.1	5.3	6	60%
O.Beckham	79	-5.4%	133	74	1035	14.0	4.4	4	56%
D.Ratley	21	-1.9%	24	12	200	16.7	3.9	1	50%
A.Callaway*	-3	-15.0%	15	8	89	11.1	5.5	0	53%
R.Higgins*	-11	-27.0%	11	4	55	13.8	2.3	1	36%
K.Hodge	-7	-21.3%	10	4	76	19.0	2.3	0	40%
D.Harris*	-17	-16.0%	27	15	149	9.9	4.5	3	56%
R.Seals-Jones*	28	10.2%	22	14	229	16.4	6.8	4	64%
D.Njoku	-10	-23.7%	10	5	41	8.2	3.2	1	50%
S.Carlson	12	17.5%	7	5	51	10.2	4.2	1	71%
A.Hooper	130	12.5%	97	75	787	10.5	4.4	6	77%
N.Chubb	-4	-15.3%	49	36	278	7.7	8.8	0	73%
K.Hunt	71	14.2%	44	37	285	7.7	7.5	1	84%
D.Hilliard	24	16.5%	15	12	92	7.7	8.6	0	80%
D.Johnson	14	35.0%	7	6	71	11.8	7.2	0	86%

Rushing

Player	DYAR	DVOA	Plays	Yds	Avg	TD	Fum	Suc
N.Chubb	162	4.5%	298	1493	5.0	8	2	45%
K.Hunt	26	7.9%	43	173	4.0	2	1	53%
B.Mayfield	48	21.9%	24	144	6.0	3	1	-
D.Hilliard	15	17.3%	13	49	3.8	2	0	46%
D.Johnson	0	-10.2%	4	21	5.3	0	0	0%
C.Keenum	-12	-36.8%	6	16	2.7	1	2	-

Offensive Line

Player	Pos	Age	GS	Snaps	Pen	Sk	Pass	Run	Player	Pos	Age	GS	Snaps	Pen	Sk	Pass	Run
Joel Bitonio	LG	29	16/16	1066	3	2.5	6	5	Wyatt Teller	RG	26	15/9	569	2	2.5	6	5
J.C. Tretter	C	29	16/16	1066	4	2.0	4	7	Eric Kush*	RG	31	16/7	453	4	1.5	7	2
Christopher Hubbard	RT	29	14/13	916	8	5.5	21	10	Justin McCray*	LT/RT	28	15/4	332	4	2.5	11	2
Greg Robinson*	LT	28	15/14	876	12	4.5	15	2	Jack Conklin	RT	26	16/16	957	7	2.8	18	5

Year	Yards	ALY	Rank	Power	Rank	Stuff	Rank	2nd Lev	Rank	Open Field	Rank	Sacks	ASR	Rank	Press	Rank	F-Start	Cont.
2017	4.15	4.09	14	74%	4	19%	11	1.23	8	0.75	15	50	7.6%	22	32.9%	24	11	39
2018	4.61	4.24	18	50%	32	23%	29	1.27	16	1.16	4	38	6.7%	16	27.7%	11	11	38
2019	4.85	4.46	10	53%	29	18%	14	1.34	5	1.17	2	41	7.2%	18	28.1%	7	23	26
2019 ALY by direction:		Left End 2.13 (32)			Left Tackle: 4.84 (5)			Mid/Guard: 4.73 (5)			Right Tackle: 4.54 (10)			Right End: 3.22 (27)				

Jack Conklin's career year could not have come at a better time. The Titans were so down on his play in 2018 that they declined his fifth-year option. He has been roundly inconsistent in pass protection, but stellar as a run blocker. It's hard to square the money he's making against a career that has pointed more towards above-average than special play, but he's an upgrade. ◥ Right guard has been an open question since the Browns traded Kevin Zeitler last offseason. It was supposed to be Austin Corbett's job, but he got traded to the Rams for a fifth-round pick at midseason. Wyatt Teller, who was acquired from the Bills at last cuts, split time with now-departed Eric Kush. 2019 sixth-rounder Drew Forbes (Southeast Missouri) is the only other non-UDFA vying for the spot. ◥ Jedrick Willis will likely be moving from right tackle at Alabama to left with the Browns, which inspires some "could Alabama beat an NFL team?" chuckles but shouldn't actually be a big deal. Tyron Smith was also a college right tackle. "Jed going over to the left side, I think the sky is the limit for him," offensive coordinator Alex Van Pelt told

Browns reporters over a Zoom call. 🏈 Hard to do much but give plaudits to both Joel Bitonio and J.C. Tretter, who have been consistently above average for the Browns the last three seasons. Last year, each one ranked in the top five at his position for snaps per blown block. Tretter was an extremely successful free-agency strike by Cleveland from Green Bay, and the Browns re-upped him to a three-year, $32.5-million extension last November. 🏈 The nominal backup tackle is ex-Texan Kendall Lamm, who is more of a right tackle than a swing tackle. He played fairly well in his small starting sample last year, inspiring the typical "Kendall Lamm should start for the rest of the season" articles by MavenBarker aggregation types.

Defensive Front

Defensive Line	Age	Pos	G	Snaps	Plays	TmPct	Rk	Stop	Dfts	BTkl	Runs	St%	Rk	RuYd	Rk	Sack	Hit	Hur	Dsrpt
						Overall							vs. Run				Pass Rush		
Larry Ogunjobi	26	DT	15	797	50	6.7%	18	44	12	5	40	88%	10	1.7	17	5.5	7	19	1
Sheldon Richardson	30	DT	16	791	66	8.3%	4	48	12	7	53	72%	66	3.4	94	3.0	6	26	3
Devaroe Lawrence*	28	DT	11	226	9	1.6%	--	4	3	1	8	38%	--	2.5	--	0.0	2	1	0
Eli Ankou	26	DT	9	183	6	1.3%	--	4	0	1	6	67%	--	3.8	--	0.0	0	2	0
Andrew Billings	25	DT	16	670	35	4.2%	49	22	6	4	33	61%	86	2.5	61	1.0	3	8	1

Edge Rushers	Age	Pos	G	Snaps	Plays	TmPct	Rk	Stop	Dfts	BTkl	Runs	St%	Rk	RuYd	Rk	Sack	Hit	Hur	Dsrpt
						Overall							vs. Run				Pass Rush		
Myles Garrett	25	DE	10	556	29	5.8%	63	22	16	2	19	63%	75	3.5	83	10.0	10	22	2
Olivier Vernon	30	DE	10	519	26	5.2%	70	20	6	6	20	70%	61	3.4	80	3.5	7	23	0
Chad Thomas	25	DE	16	472	26	3.3%	70	15	7	4	15	53%	82	2.9	62	4.0	2	12	1
Adrian Clayborn	32	DE	15	446	16	2.2%	91	13	9	2	9	78%	28	1.8	19	4.0	4	24	0

Linebackers	Age	Pos	G	Snaps	Plays	TmPct	Rk	Stop	Dfts	BTkl	Runs	St%	Rk	RuYd	Rk	Sack	Hit	Hur	Tgts	Suc%	Rk	AdjYd	Rk	PD	Int
						Overall							vs. Run				Pass Rush				vs. Pass				
Joe Schobert*	27	MLB	16	1079	141	17.7%	7	77	24	18	87	56%	59	4.3	61	2.0	2	9	36	53%	30	6.0	31	9	4
Mack Wilson	22	OLB	16	958	88	11.0%	37	49	14	14	41	63%	30	4.4	64	1.0	1	13	37	59%	11	5.4	18	7	1
B.J. Goodson	27	ILB	15	256	35	4.7%	--	17	1	3	28	50%	--	4.8	--	0.0	0	1	6	50%	--	5.0	--	0	0

Year	Yards	ALY	Rank	Power	Rank	Stuff	Rank	2nd Level	Rank	Open Field	Rank	Sacks	ASR	Rank	Press	Rank
2017	3.35	3.27	2	56%	8	30%	1	1.08	12	0.60	8	34	6.5%	17	29.6%	21
2018	4.75	4.21	11	63%	10	23%	9	1.51	31	1.16	28	37	6.7%	23	27.1%	27
2019	4.96	4.62	26	76%	30	18%	19	1.38	30	1.13	30	38	7.0%	18	32.2%	9
2019 ALY by direction:		Left End: 4.37 (22)			Left Tackle: 3.16 (4)			Mid/Guard: 4.56 (22)			Right Tackle: 5.56 (31)			Right End: 5.98 (31)	

Over the last two years, Myles Garrett has 23.5 sacks and 55 hurries in a little under 1,600 snaps. Obviously, what happened on Thursday Night Football against the Steelers will mar his reputation for a bit, but he's one of the brightest young pass-rushers in the NFL and an overwhelming physical specimen. Six extra games of him will definitely make a difference if it happens. 🏈 In his first year with the Browns, Olivier Vernon—and let's be honest, mostly his sprained knee—underwhelmed to the point where the possibility of the Browns releasing him and signing Jadeveon Clowney was a talking point long into June. Vernon has a great track record but is quickly approaching the 30/10/16 zone: He'll turn 30 in October, has a cap number of over $10 million ($15.5 million in this case), and hasn't started 16 games since 2016. He's also on the last year of his deal. The only real depth on the edge is the crafty veteran Adrian Clayborn, so the Browns are hoping for a healthy Vernon year. 🏈 Larry Ogunjobi has honestly been a bit of a disappointment the last few seasons, at least compared to how stellar he was in 2017. He's a solid interior player, but if he doesn't win instantly, he often is putting himself out of position as a run defender. Nose tackle Andrew Billings will help provide some early-down stability, and maybe free up Ogunjobi on early downs to save more energy for third-and-long. 🏈 Sheldon Richardson is the same stellar 3-technique he has been since he was drafted in 2013, but is coming up on the last year of guaranteed money in his deal. Cleveland spent a third-rounder on Missouri's Jordan Elliott, a player very much in that Richardson mold, to grow for a year behind Richardson. Elliott had 5.5 sacks and 16.5 tackles for loss over his last two years with the Tigers. 🏈 With Joe Schobert off to Jacksonville, Browns linebackers coach Jason Tarver described the position as an open competition. "We have a mix of body types and athletes. We're going to see who works best together and who takes advantage of their reps when we do get to practice. We do think we have the pieces to run coach [Joe] Woods' schemes," Tarver told reporters in a Zoom call. 🏈 2019 fifth-rounder Mack Wilson ran with the ones last season after Christian Kirksey was lost to a chest injury but showed too much of the run-game indecision he showed at Alabama in 2018. Sione Takitaki, the 2019 third-rounder who was behind Wilson most of the season, has more of a classic run defense profile without quite as much speed. ❧ This year's third-rounder, LSU's Jacob Phillips, was the run-stuffing complement to Patrick Queen's three-down linebacker skill set. Phillips defensed just five passes in 34 games with the Tigers and might be purely a two-down stuffer, making him a curious Day 2 pick. ❧ The only veteran in the room at this point is ex-Giants and Packers linebacker B.J. Goodson, who didn't have much of a role last season in Green Bay and is around to eat snaps in case some of the youth doesn't come through.

Defensive Secondary

Secondary	Age	Pos	G	Snaps	Plays	Overall TmPct	Rk	Stop	Dfts	BTkl	vs. Run Runs	St%	Rk	RuYd	Rk	vs. Pass Tgts	Tgt%	Rk	Dist	Suc%	Rk	AdjYd	Rk	PD	Int
Denzel Ward	23	CB	12	767	55	9.2%	51	21	11	11	16	13%	83	13.4	84	70	25.0%	6	12.6	63%	7	6.6	19	11	2
Damarious Randall*	28	FS	11	731	67	12.2%	43	18	9	8	35	17%	72	10.7	67	21	7.9%	36	10.8	52%	35	7.6	39	6	0
Greedy Williams	23	CB	12	696	49	8.2%	63	18	7	11	18	61%	22	7.0	54	50	19.7%	48	12.6	46%	67	9.3	71	2	0
T.J. Carrie*	30	CB	16	691	54	6.8%	--	26	12	7	21	76%	--	4.5	--	47	18.7%	--	9.1	38%	--	8.2	--	4	1
Jermaine Whitehead*	27	FS	8	509	43	10.8%	67	16	6	15	19	53%	10	6.5	35	13	7.0%	45	8.8	31%	69	7.9	44	2	1
Juston Burris*	27	FS	14	419	37	5.3%	69	19	8	6	18	44%	30	6.0	30	12	7.9%	39	10.2	67%	7	4.8	7	7	2
Sheldrick Redwine	24	SS	12	383	37	6.2%	--	12	1	11	18	50%	--	5.2	--	7	5.0%	--	14.0	43%	--	9.6	--	2	0
Morgan Burnett*	31	SS	8	377	43	10.8%	67	18	7	3	23	52%	11	4.0	6	15	10.9%	16	14.2	47%	51	8.0	45	2	1
Eric Murray*	26	FS	9	364	24	5.4%	--	17	5	5	13	92%	--	3.0	--	13	9.8%	--	11.6	62%	--	5.2	--	1	0
Terrance Mitchell	28	CB	15	332	23	3.1%	--	9	4	1	6	50%	--	8.7	--	24	19.8%	--	9.8	46%	--	8.1	--	3	1
Karl Joseph	27	SS	9	590	51	11.8%	61	17	8	8	26	42%	37	4.5	9	11	4.7%	67	10.3	27%	72	11.7	71	3	1
Andrew Sendejo	33	SS	15	395	43	6.1%	--	17	9	7	15	40%	--	5.8	--	13	7.5%	--	9.5	46%	--	9.3	--	4	3
Kevin Johnson	28	CB	16	341	37	4.6%	--	19	10	5	11	45%	--	6.3	--	30	23.3%	--	11.2	70%	--	4.4	--	5	0

Year	Pass D Rank	vs. #1 WR	Rk	vs. #2 WR	Rk	vs. Other WR	Rk	WR Wide	Rk	WR Slot	Rk	vs. TE	Rk	vs. RB	Rk
2017	26	22.0%	29	-7.5%	12	-6.4%	13	10.8%	27	1.4%	14	27.8%	32	24.9%	30
2018	7	-3.6%	12	-15.8%	8	-25.4%	3	-7.9%	15	-21.3%	2	-12.5%	9	4.4%	17
2019	17	10.2%	25	14.7%	25	-5.0%	13	10.4%	25	1.0%	10	-6.4%	9	13.4%	25

Denzel Ward has played two seasons and has two top-10 finishes in success rate. That'll do nicely. This year he drew more targets than he did under Gregg Williams in 2018, with a 22.3% figure in 2018 against 25.0% in 2019. ❧ Greedy Williams has all the physical tools to be a good press-man corner but had the typical rookie growing pains in his first season. Williams held Courtland Sutton to 6 yards on four targets in Week 9 but allowed 80 yards on four targets to Damiere Byrd in Week 15. Don't be too hasty to judge his first season. ❧ The No. 1 option at slot corner is likely former Texans first-rounder Kevin Johnson, coming off a small rebound season in Buffalo. Johnson has been pretty solid when he has been healthy but has just two 16-game seasons and zero seasons with more than 10 starts so far in the NFL. He also has a history of concussions. ❧ The Browns rebuilt their safety corps with veteran Andrew Sendejo and former Raiders first-round pick Karl Joseph. Joseph has shown flashes of great play but was never really able to earn Jon Gruden's trust. He has done some nice work as a box safety, but the Raiders used him most often as a deep safety last year. Sendejo strung together a nice little career as a Mike Zimmer sub-package player before the Eagles signed him in 2019, only to waive him in November and send him right back to the Vikings. On a one-year deal, turning 33 in September, Sendejo is more of a bandage than a long-term solution. ❧ Grant Delpit was one of the great enigmas of #draftszn—preseason college mocks had him as a clear top-15 pick and he was awesome as a true freshman, but his tackling was dinged heavily by LSU watchers and draftniks this year and whispers that the Tigers didn't exactly trust him in coverage were loud. It's clear Delpit has the talent to be something, but whether he gets there or not was such an open question that he slid all the way to the second round.

Special Teams

Year	DVOA	Rank	FG/XP	Rank	Net Kick	Rank	Kick Ret	Rank	Net Punt	Rank	Punt Ret	Rank	Hidden	Rank
2017	-5.1%	27	-3.5	21	-6.0	28	2.1	9	-11.5	29	-6.8	30	-4.8	21
2018	-4.2%	30	-9.8	28	0.8	16	-5.3	30	-10.8	30	4.2	10	0.4	15
2019	0.8%	15	0.7	16	6.2	2	-1.4	20	1.4	17	-3.0	23	3.5	11

Listen, we're biased, but Jamie Gillan's nickname (Scottish Hammer) and aesthetic (Thor-esque long hair) are exactly what punting should be all about. Well, that and caber tossing. Gillian's first season was solid but not exemplary. ● Austin Seibert's rookie season also fell into that same kind of memory hole: he was solid on kickoffs, solid on field goals and extra points, but there wasn't any grand hidden value. In fact… ● The biggest improvement on Browns special teams last year was their kick-off coverage team, and the two players that did the best job there were 2019 last-cuts waiver claim KhaDarel Hodge and backup running back Dontrell Hilliard, who combined for 18 return stops on 22 tackles. ● Hilliard was also the main punt and kick returner last year, with positive value on kickoffs and negative value on punts. The Browns added former Rams returner JoJo Natson to the mix this offseason. Jarvis Landry still gets broken out as a punt returner in big situations as well.

Dallas Cowboys

2019 Record: 8-8	Total DVOA: 17.2% (6th)	2020 Mean Projection: 8.8 wins	On the Clock (0-4): 5%
Pythagorean Wins: 10.9 (5th)	Offense: 24.2% (2nd)	Postseason Odds: 57.4%	Mediocrity (5-7): 25%
Snap-Weighted Age: 26.7 (6th)	Defense: 3.0% (19th)	Super Bowl Odds: 8.3%	Playoff Contender (8-10): 43%
Average Opponent: -3.0% (26th)	Special Teams: -3.9% (30th)	Proj. Avg. Opponent: -1.6% (29th)	Super Bowl Contender (11+): 27%

2019: The definition of insanity is doing the same thing over and over but expecting different results.

2020: Please welcome the Cowboys to a brave new world of sanity.

The 10-year hamster wheel of the Jason Garrett era in Dallas finally came to a stop after the 2019 season. Each year, the wheel touched all the same points: have impressive talent, underperform, run it back again the following year. The players and coordinators changed, but the general path remained the same.

Throughout Garrett's time at the helm, he excelled at being exactly Jason Garrett. He wasn't a big enough personality to ever ruffle any of the Joneses' feathers, but that bland personality carried over to game plans and preparation. His status as head coach was seemingly in question at the end of every season, but there was just enough support around the building for him to stay in charge.

Jerry Jones wasn't oblivious to the situation. He had a sense something needed to change, but he switched all the pieces around Garrett and left the head coach in place. It was the staffing equivalent of wiping down a countertop without moving anything that had been sitting on the counter.

By nearly all accounts the Cowboys were a good team in 2019 and one that should have contended at the top of the conference. They finished sixth in overall DVOA with 11.2 estimated wins but still limped to an 8-8 record and missed the playoffs completely in a weak division. It was another disappointing finish for the Cowboys and one that eventually sealed Garrett's fate as head coach.

While Jones allowed Garrett to wander around the Cowboys facility as his contract was about to expire, the owner was searching for his replacement. Garrett wasn't officially let go until a replacement was found about a week after Black Monday. Former Green Bay Packers coach Mike McCarthy will be the new head coach in Dallas after a year out of the league. Reports say that during that year away, McCarthy spent time self-scouting, watching film, and studying analytics to improve his process. He even told NBC's Peter King his plan was to build a 10-person analytics team as part of his next coaching gig. All of that played into McCarthy's pitch to Jones, made during a Saturday night sleepover at Jones' mansion. At his introductory press conference, McCarthy admitted that some of the claims like "watching every play of the 2019 season" were exaggerated in an attempt to get hired.

McCarthy may have discovered data-driven enlightenment during his year wandering in the NFL wilderness, but he regularly followed two analytics-friendly strategies even during his time with the Packers: heavy passing rates on early downs and aggressive fourth-down decision-making.

McCarthy had some high-profile blunders with short field goals in the playoffs, but over his final five years with the Packers, he ranked no worse than 10th in any season by Aggressiveness Index. He was in the top five each year from 2015 to 2018 and ranked first twice, including his final season of just 12 games in 2018. Meanwhile, Garrett found himself in the top 10 just once since 2014 (eighth in 2017) and was 22nd or worse three times, including 25th in 2019.

The pass-heavy shift for McCarthy came on later in his tenure with the Packers. Green Bay was around the middle of the league in early-down pass rate in 2014 (18th) and 2015 (11th) but ranked no lower than fifth in each season from 2016 to 2018. Over that five-year span, the Cowboys ranked no higher than 26th in early-down pass rate and finished 32nd twice.

One of McCarthy's main responsibilities now will be to mix in his new ideas with the changes that had already worked for the Cowboys in 2019. One of the keys there, and potentially the most positive development of McCarthy's tenure so far, was the decision to keep Kellen Moore as both offensive coordinator and playcaller.

Moore helped bring the Dallas offense into the 21st century last season with wild modern techniques like pre-snap motion and route concepts that properly spaced out receivers on the field. Both of these were revolutionary ideas compared to the stagnant design of the 2018 offense which still might have looked outdated had the '90s-era Cowboys been the ones executing it. Early on, the Moore offense was even more forward-thinking. The Cowboys used play-action on 40% of pass plays in their season-opening three-game win streak but dropped to just 23% of pass plays for the rest of the season. There was some speculation that Garrett inserted himself more in the offense after a flat 12-10 loss to the New Orleans Saints in Week 4.

The turnaround wasn't only about play-action and pre-snap motion. Dallas was just 14th in rate of pre-snap motion usage. The final numbers for both rate and performance with play-action stayed essentially identical from 2018 to 2019 (25% of pass plays both years with 8.3 yards per attempt in 2018 and 8.4 in 2019). The biggest difference was how well the Cowboys did on *non*-play-action passes, where they ranked second in yards per attempt last season after finishing 23rd the year prior.

2020 Cowboys Schedule

Week	Opp.	Week	Opp.	Week	Opp.
1	at LAR	7	at WAS	13	at BAL (Thu.)
2	ATL	8	at PHI	14	at CIN
3	at SEA	9	PIT	15	SF
4	CLE	10	BYE	16	PHI
5	NYG	11	at MIN	17	at NYG
6	ARI (Mon.)	12	WAS (Thu.)		

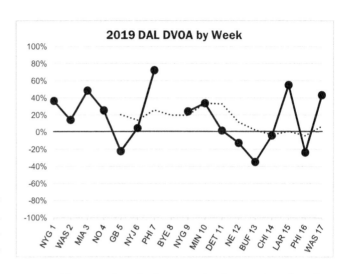

2019 DAL DVOA by Week

Moore's offense, especially early on, was a sign of how change and new ideas from the previous norms could positively impact the franchise. Now, the future success of the offense could hinge on how much change there will be from the 2019 offense and how well Moore and McCarthy can mesh.

Keeping Moore as the playcaller could help aid the offense in a few areas. First, it allows McCarthy to focus more on big-picture coaching details and limits the probability of 14 slant-flat calls per game, a predictable pattern that helped tank McCarthy as a playcaller in Green Bay. Moore's presence can also help fight off some regression that could be coming for the offense.

As impressive as the improvement on offense was for the Cowboys in 2019, there's some concern of the Plexiglass Principle heading into 2020. Dallas went from 24th in offensive DVOA in 2018 to second last season, a jump that is typically followed by a dip the following year. However, it wouldn't be hard to talk oneself into the legitimate reasons for the 2019 turnaround sticking through 2020—a more modern passing game, another full season of Amari Cooper, the plusses of the other skill position talent, and a quarterback who has been able to take advantage of his ideal surroundings. Dallas still has a top-five offensive projection, but there's a strong chance their DVOA rating will be lower than it was a year ago.

On top of the natural expectation of regression, the Cowboys will be dealing with some personnel losses on the offense. Clearly, the biggest of those is five-time Pro Bowler Travis Frederick at center. Frederick retired in March at age 29 due in part to his battle with Guillain-Barré Syndrome, an autoimmune disease that attacks the nervous system. It had already forced him to miss the 2018 season.

Dallas still finished eighth in adjusted line yards in 2018 without Frederick, but the line had ranked fourth the previous season and jumped back up to second last year. So much of the Cowboys' foundation over the past few seasons has relied on the offensive line being great, not just good. There are a number of center options on the roster including veteran Joe Looney (who replaced Frederick in 2018), 2019 third-rounder Connor McGovern, and fourth-round rookie Tyler Biadasz. Regardless of who wins the starting job for 2020, he's likely to be a steep drop-off in quality from Frederick in the middle of that line.

Some losses, though, might show up more in our projections than in the results on the field, such as the impact of Randall Cobb. Whenever a team loses DYAR on offense, the projection will take a hit for the upcoming year. Historically

teams suffer more from losing a productive receiver than they gain by adding one, but it's worth asking how much the Dallas passing game may have helped Cobb's numbers rather than the other way around. The Cowboys were one of just two teams, along with the Tampa Bay Buccaneers, to have three receivers finish with over 100 DYAR in 2019. But Cobb was still a distant third behind Cooper and Michael Gallup.

It's not as if Cobb's replacement will be some afterthought at wide receiver. His spot in the lineup will be taken by the 17th overall pick in the 2020 NFL draft, CeeDee Lamb. Lamb had a Playmaker Score projection similar to Cooper or Odell Beckham Jr., and his fall to the Cowboys at 17 was quite a surprise. He has the ability to be the top receiver on an offense but won't have to take on that responsibility immediately, unlike some other rookie wide receivers over the past few seasons.

Lamb can work his way into the rotation starting as the No. 3, and last year's offense already showed the potential to support three productive wide receivers. McCarthy also isn't a stranger to offenses with deep receiver groups. The 2010 Packers offense that won the Super Bowl and finished fifth in pass offense DVOA featured Donald Driver, Greg Jennings, James Jones, and Jordy Nelson. The following year, Cobb was added to the mix.

There should also be plenty of opportunities to get Lamb involved in the passing game with 166 vacated targets from Cobb and Jason Witten. Dallas was 12th in its usage of 11 personnel last season, and with little valuable depth behind Blake Jarwin at tight end, we could see an increase in three-receiver sets for the coming year.

The selection of Lamb was the first in a widely lauded draft class for the Cowboys. Objectively, it's already the best class ever drafted from a yacht. Of course, collective praise doesn't guarantee success on the field, given that past studies have shown no correlation between draft grades and career Approximate Value over expectation.

This draft class might have no choice but to be good because, while there's a lot of new elements surrounding the 2020 Dallas Cowboys, some of the old Cowboys habits hit them hard this offseason. After years of shelling out big contract extensions and following those up with restructures to work around the cap, Dallas entered the offseason with Dak

Prescott, Amari Cooper, and Byron Jones slated to become free agents and enough cap space to sign two of the three at most. Jones ended up as the odd man out and left for the Miami Dolphins.

Even with Cooper and Prescott under contract for 2020, the degree of difficulty in keeping this core together has risen exponentially. With neither of those two on their rookie contracts and top-of-the-market prices for the likes of Demarcus Lawrence, Zack Martin, Tyron Smith, and Ezekiel Elliott on the books, there are few bargains on the Dallas roster with the potential for surplus value. That window was wasted, and another era of extensions and restructures could be on the horizon. In a worst-case scenario, there could be more decisions to face like the one with Jones where there is little choice but to move on from a talented young player. The Cowboys have now reached the stage where they need to restock the roster with those talented youngsters.

Part of the well-received draft class was the act of doubling up at corner in an effort to replace Jones with Alabama's Trevon Diggs in the second round and Tulsa's Reggie Robinson II in the fourth. Per Sports Info Solutions charting, both were among the best corners in the draft class by yards allowed per man coverage snap. However, there's a difference between good process in drafting and immediately forcing those rookies into big roles, and that's where the Cowboys might find themselves at corner.

As a whole, the defense isn't expected to be much worse without Jones on the outside, but that has more to do with the lack of overall success on that side of the ball last season than it does with Jones. Individually, Jones was one of the better outside corners in the league and ranked 11th in yards allowed per play.

The entire structure of the Dallas defense was troubling last year. Former Seattle Seahawks defensive coordinator Kris Richard took over more responsibility after helping the Dallas defense to a No. 9 ranking in DVOA in 2018 as defensive backs coach/passing game coordinator/de facto defensive coordinator. Richard expanded on his attempt to replicate the Seahawks' Legion of Boom defense without any legion or boom.

Richard stuck to the old script with a Cover-3-heavy approach as Dallas used the seventh-highest rate of zone defense in the league last season and ranked just 28th in the rate of straight man-to-man coverage. Richard wasn't interested in the illusion of the Cowboys doing anything other than expected on defense. On an offseason podcast, veteran safety George Iloka, who spent the 2019 training camp with the team, said Richard told him to go back to his spot on the field after he tried to creep into the box to disguise coverage before the snap. Showing the offense what's coming and daring them to beat it works with Richard Sherman and Earl Thomas, less so with Jeff Heath and Anthony Brown.

There's no guarantee the scheme is going to improve in 2020, though it will at least give some different looks. At defensive coordinator, McCarthy brought in Mike Nolan, whom McCarthy served under as offensive coordinator when Nolan was the head coach of the San Francisco 49ers. Nolan spent the past three seasons as the linebackers coach for the New

Orleans Saints and hasn't been a defensive coordinator since the 2014 season. His three-year stint as the coordinator for the Atlanta Falcons saw a No. 8 defense by DVOA in 2011 drop to 12th in 2012, 28th in 2013, and 32nd in 2014.

New Orleans' linebackers have been productive over the past few seasons, especially on the blitz. The Saints were one of the most blitz-heavy teams in the league last year (they sent five or more on 30% of plays, which ranked eighth) and that could give more value to where the most talent lies on the defense (Jaylon Smith and Leighton Vander Esch) and feed some life to a pass rush that might need the extra boost. There's now a lack of depth on the edge for a team with the fourth-highest rate of rushing four last season.

In free agency, the defense lost Lawrence's pass-rush partner Robert Quinn. Quinn was a rare bargain free agent and Pass Rush Win Rate superstar per ESPN, but he turned his 2019 season into a massive deal with the Chicago Bears. Also gone is Michael Bennett, who worked in four sacks in half a season as a rotational edge rusher. There's not a lot left on the roster to fill those spots. Whether pass rush or coverage is more important to a defense, the Cowboys don't look like they have the talent at either to lift up the other.

Blitzing more could be a useful strategy for the Cowboys, who were quite good at it last season even with such a low frequency. Dallas registered pressure 55% of the time when rushing five or more, tied for the league lead with New Orleans. They allowed 6.5 yards per play (16.3% DVOA) with four pass-rushers but only 4.3 yards per play (-10.2% DVOA) with five or more.

With the talent discrepancy on offense and defense, the Cowboys are likely to find themselves in a number of shootouts this season. While we expect the offense to be able to win a majority of those, that brings us to the biggest looming question over the season: what is Dak Prescott's contract situation?

Prescott is currently in line to play on the franchise tag, which will cost $31.5 million, a hefty raise from his $2.1-million cap hit in 2019. At this point, the leverage is in Prescott's hands. He could play on the tag this year and anticipate a tag again in 2021, which would be closer to $40 million. A third tag would push Prescott over $50 million for the 2022 season.

Even if Prescott was only a quarterback who needed an ideal situation around him to succeed (a weak argument used against paying Prescott), the current Cowboys offense looks to be pretty ideal for the upcoming season. That might not be the case in a few years after the offensive line slowly gets picked away, but that side of the ball is set up to win now.

Should the offense take off again in 2020, the Cowboys could be in for a more expensive extension with Prescott. But if they don't agree on a deal, Dallas could be in for an even bigger gamble with an attempt to find another quarterback who could replicate Prescott's production. Teams typically don't voluntarily go that route for a reason—it's quite hard to do.

Viewing Prescott as that type of replaceable player also undercuts what he's been able to do at the position. Quarterbacks don't really fluke themselves into leading the league in DYAR, which Prescott did in 2019. They especially don't fluke themselves into finishing in the top five twice, which Prescott has done after finishing fourth in his rookie season of 2016. Despite down years in 2017 and 2018, Prescott has more passing DYAR over the past four seasons than Aaron Rodgers, Kirk Cousins, or Russell Wilson (Table 1).

Table 1. Cumulative Passing DYAR, 2016-2019

Player	Team	2016	2017	2018	2019	Total
Drew Brees	NO	1,599	1,390	1,631	1,316	5,936
Matt Ryan	ATL	1,885	1,084	1,232	712	4,913
Tom Brady	NE	1,286	1,595	1,034	550	4,465
Philip Rivers	LAC	498	1,412	1,316	714	3,940
Patrick Mahomes	KC	—	54	2,031	1,320	3,405
Ben Roethlisberger	PIT	807	1,270	1,204	69	3,350
Dak Prescott	**DAL**	**1,302**	**375**	**112**	**1,541**	**3,330**
Derek Carr	OAK	1,164	709	392	1,064	3,329
Aaron Rodgers	GB	1,279	334	817	794	3,224
Kirk Cousins	WAS/MIN	1,317	395	595	795	3,102
Russell Wilson	SEA	569	530	673	1,265	3,037
Matthew Stafford	DET	761	1,004	396	776	2,937

Sure, there's a big difference between building around a quarterback making $2 million and one making over $30 million, but Dallas already missed out on the chance to take advantage of that window by sticking with the status quo for too long. And unlike the other top-of-the-market deals Jerry Jones has given out in the past, there is still room for surplus value with a big quarterback contract.

The 2020 season is a fresh start for the Cowboys, the biggest change for the franchise in quite some time. Even when Jason Garrett was hired as head coach, it wasn't a significant organizational shift since he had already been the offensive coordinator for three and a half seasons before he initially took over in an interim role in 2010.

This isn't just about a move at head coach. For the Cowboys, this feels like a potential overhaul in philosophy for team building, game management, and strategy on both sides of the ball. There's finally something different going on in Dallas, and how much the Cowboys embrace the change will shape the franchise for 2020 and beyond. It will go a lot better if they embrace their star quarterback for 2020 and beyond as well.

Dan Pizzuta

2019 Cowboys Stats by Week

Wk	vs.	W-L	PF	PA	YDF	YDA	TO	Total	Off	Def	ST
1	NYG	W	35	17	494	470	+2	37%	55%	20%	1%
2	at WAS	W	31	21	474	255	-1	14%	40%	27%	1%
3	MIA	W	31	6	476	283	0	49%	36%	-14%	-1%
4	at NO	L	10	12	257	266	-2	26%	-5%	-35%	-5%
5	GB	L	24	34	563	335	-3	-22%	13%	16%	-19%
6	at NYJ	L	22	24	399	382	+1	5%	35%	32%	2%
7	PHI	W	37	10	402	283	+3	72%	19%	-41%	12%
8	BYE										
9	at NYG	W	37	18	429	271	+1	24%	25%	-13%	-14%
10	MIN	L	24	28	443	364	-1	34%	45%	10%	-2%
11	at DET	W	35	27	509	312	-1	2%	30%	22%	-7%
12	at NE	L	9	13	321	282	-1	-13%	-4%	-17%	-26%
13	BUF	L	15	26	426	356	-2	-35%	10%	29%	-15%
14	at CHI	L	24	31	408	382	+2	-4%	29%	28%	-6%
15	LAR	W	44	21	475	289	+1	55%	41%	-7%	7%
16	at PHI	L	9	17	311	431	-1	-24%	-12%	17%	5%
17	WAS	W	47	16	517	271	+1	44%	17%	-26%	1%

Trends and Splits

	Offense	Rank	Defense	Rank
Total DVOA	24.2%	2	3.0%	19
Unadjusted VOA	24.2%	2	-1.8%	14
Weighted Trend	21.5%	4	3.6%	21
Variance	3.8%	2	6.0%	18
Average Opponent	-0.6%	13	-4.5%	28
Passing	39.4%	5	13.2%	23
Rushing	8.9%	3	-10.4%	15
First Down	13.8%	6	19.2%	30
Second Down	29.0%	2	-2.9%	12
Third Down	37.6%	3	-19.8%	3
First Half	12.7%	6	2.4%	19
Second Half	37.1%	1	3.6%	19
Red Zone	34.7%	2	-7.4%	13
Late and Close	44.6%	1	-11.4%	8

Five-Year Performance

Year	W-L	Pyth W	Est W	PF	PA	TO	Total	Rk	Off	Rk	Def	Rk	ST	Rk	Off AGL	Rk	Def AGL	Rk	Off Age	Rk	Def Age	Rk	ST Age	Rk
2015	4-12	5.2	4.4	275	374	-22	-18.0%	27	-15.6%	31	4.1%	19	1.8%	11	34.7	16	30.5	15	26.9	15	25.9	29	25.7	23
2016	13-3	11	11.8	421	306	+5	20.3%	2	19.9%	3	1.1%	18	1.6%	9	37.9	19	39.2	16	26.6	20	26.3	20	26.1	16
2017	9-7	8.6	8.9	354	332	-1	5.3%	13	6.5%	10	5.8%	25	4.6%	7	8.0	2	26.4	10	26.8	18	25.1	30	25.9	15
2018	10-6	8.4	7.0	339	324	+2	-5.2%	21	-6.6%	24	-3.5%	9	-2.1%	23	42.0	20	33.2	16	25.5	31	24.7	32	25.8	14
2019	8-8	10.9	11.2	434	321	-1	17.2%	6	24.2%	2	3.0%	19	-3.9%	30	11.3	2	24.5	7	27.0	13	26.2	18	26.9	3

2019 Performance Based on Most Common Personnel Groups

DAL Offense					DAL Offense vs. Opponents					DAL Defense				DAL Defense vs. Opponents			
Pers	Freq	Yds	DVOA	Run%	Pers	Freq	Yds	DVOA	Run%	Pers	Freq	Yds	DVOA	Pers	Freq	Yds	DVOA
11	67%	7.2	39.0%	30%	Base	22%	5.7	4.5%	61%	Base	32%	5.0	-8.0%	11	64%	5.4	5.7%
12	19%	5.9	0.6%	60%	Nickel	62%	6.4	22.0%	38%	Nickel	63%	5.7	10.8%	12	17%	5.9	8.1%
21	9%	5.0	8.1%	55%	Dime+	14%	9.2	86.7%	11%	Dime+	4%	4.1	-11.8%	21	6%	5.9	9.3%
13	2%	3.3	-51.7%	67%	Goal Line	1%	1.0	102.8%	83%	Goal Line	1%	0.1	-24.1%	13	3%	2.4	-52.6%
20	1%	1.0	-86.1%	33%	Big	1%	3.2	-54.3%	56%					22	2%	3.7	-12.2%
22	1%	3.1	-51.8%	44%										612	2%	6.0	-2.1%

Strategic Tendencies

Run/Pass		Rk	Formation		Rk	Pass Rush		Rk	Secondary		Rk	Strategy		Rk
Runs, first half	41%	5	Form: Single Back	86%	8	Rush 3	3.3%	27	4 DB	32%	7	Play Action	25%	14
Runs, first down	52%	11	Form: Empty Back	5%	28	Rush 4	76.3%	4	5 DB	63%	12	Offensive Motion	40%	14
Runs, second-long	21%	27	Form: Multi Back	9%	20	Rush 5	17.8%	20	6+ DB	4%	22	Avg Box (Off)	6.55	19
Runs, power sit.	58%	13	Pers: 3+ WR	69%	12	Rush 6+	2.6%	26	Man Coverage	27%	27	Avg Box (Def)	6.56	16
Runs, behind 2H	23%	28	Pers: 2+ TE/6+ OL	23%	25	Edge Rusher Sacks	62.8%	10	CB by Sides	90%	5	Offensive Pace	28.26	2
Pass, ahead 2H	45%	21	Pers: 6+ OL	1%	27	Interior DL Sacks	12.8%	30	S/CB Cover Ratio	27%	14	Defensive Pace	30.66	18
Run-Pass Options	7%	12	Shotgun/Pistol	64%	18	Second Level Sacks	24.4%	10	DB Blitz	7%	25	Go for it on 4th	1.16	25

Dak Prescott had a league-high 41 of his passes (7.2%) dropped by receivers. On the other side of the ball, the Cowboys had just 19 passes dropped by opponents, a league-low 3.6%. 🖐 Dallas threw just 11.8% of passes at or behind the line of scrimmage, the lowest rate in the league. 🖐 Connected: Dallas was dead last with only nine wide receiver or tight end screens. They ran 20 running back screens, which was also below average. 🖐 For the second straight year, Dallas was dead last with only 3.7% of pass plays going max protect (seven or more blockers with at least two more blockers than pass-rushers). 🖐 Dallas used pistol on 4.3% of plays, third in the league, but had just -24.4% DVOA and 4.0 yards per play from pistol. 🖐 The Cowboys offense was 15th in the league in the first quarter of games, then had the best DVOA in the league from the second quarter on. 🖐 Not included in the pass-rush defense numbers earlier in the chapter: the Cowboys were absolutely destroyed by screens last season. Wide receiver screens got them for 7.6 yards per play and 56.6% DVOA, while running back screens gained 8.5 yards per play with 54.8% DVOA. Dallas was below average against screens in 2018 as well but not to anywhere near the same extent.

Passing

Player	DYAR	DVOA	Plays	NtYds	Avg	YAC	C%	TD	Int
D.Prescott	1541	27.1%	619	4734	7.6	4.8	65.3%	30	9

Rushing

Player	DYAR	DVOA	Plays	Yds	Avg	TD	Fum	Suc
E.Elliott	324	16.5%	301	1358	4.5	12	3	56%
T.Pollard	71	11.6%	86	455	5.3	2	1	52%
D.Prescott	71	15.6%	41	287	7.0	3	1	-
T.Austin*	20	22.6%	6	47	7.8	1	1	-

Receiving

Player	DYAR	DVOA	Plays	Ctch	Yds	Y/C	YAC	TD	C%
A.Cooper	324	22.3%	119	79	1189	15.1	3.0	8	66%
M.Gallup	233	13.5%	113	66	1107	16.8	5.0	6	58%
R.Cobb*	119	5.4%	83	55	828	15.1	6.0	3	66%
T.Austin*	1	-12.1%	24	13	177	13.6	6.5	1	54%
D.Smith	24	20.5%	9	5	113	22.6	6.4	1	56%
C.Wilson	-9	-28.2%	8	5	46	9.2	2.2	0	63%
T.Jones	-12	-29.9%	10	4	61	15.3	2.8	0	40%
J.Witten*	38	-0.5%	83	63	529	8.4	2.6	4	76%
B.Jarwin	52	12.1%	41	31	365	11.8	5.1	3	76%
B.Bell	-40	-50.1%	15	8	67	8.4	1.1	0	53%
E.Elliott	99	12.6%	71	54	420	7.8	7.3	2	76%
T.Pollard	12	-2.7%	20	15	107	7.1	9.0	1	75%

Offensive Line

Player	Pos	Age	GS	Snaps	Pen	Sk	Pass	Run	Player	Pos	Age	GS	Snaps	Pen	Sk	Pass	Run
Travis Frederick	C	29	16/16	1124	1	2.0	12	10	Connor Williams	LG	23	11/11	733	6	0.0	8	2
Zack Martin	RG	30	16/16	1122	2	0.5	3	5	Xavier Su'a-Filo*	LG	29	11/4	309	1	1.0	3	7
La'el Collins	RT	27	15/15	1007	5	1.5	12	3	Cameron Fleming*	LT	28	14/3	259	4	1.5	8	0
Tyron Smith	LT	30	13/13	889	8	2.0	12	4	Cameron Erving	LT	28	13/8	594	7	4.5	30	4

Year	Yards	ALY	Rank	Power	Rank	Stuff	Rank	2nd Lev	Rank	Open Field	Rank	Sacks	ASR	Rank	Press	Rank	F-Start	Cont.
2017	4.26	4.66	4	77%	3	17%	4	1.16	16	0.67	19	32	6.4%	15	31.9%	21	10	30
2018	4.46	4.61	8	75%	3	18%	11	1.31	9	0.87	14	56	9.7%	28	34.1%	26	11	32
2019	4.68	4.91	2	76%	2	13%	1	1.42	1	0.72	18	23	4.3%	2	29.6%	15	6	25

2019 ALY by direction:	Left End 4.08 (14)	Left Tackle: 5.73 (1)	Mid/Guard: 4.74 (4)	Right Tackle: 4.90 (5)	Right End: 4.96 (9)

The biggest change on this line isn't in the personnel, but at the coaching spot. Joe Philbin will replace Mark Colombo, who is now in New York with the Giants. The line as a whole gelled better in 2019 than when Paul Alexander came in and tried to tinker too much with players' techniques in 2018. Philbin has plenty of experience coaching offensive line and has been adaptable to players and schemes. ● Only the Ravens (9.0) allowed fewer sacks than the Cowboys (9.5) on plays labeled as blown blocks. ● Filling the hole at center left by the retired Travis Frederick will not be easy. Joe Looney played that part in 2018, but 2019 third-round pick Conner McGovern and 2020 fourth-round pick Tyler Biadasz will be in competition. Biadasz had the lowest blown run block rate and third-lowest blown pass block rate among draft-eligible centers. ● Left guard was the question heading into 2019, but Connor Williams had an impressive second-year turnaround before a torn ACL ended his season in Week 13. His blown block rate went down and he did not allow a sack, but most importantly he did not look overmatched as often as he did in 2018. He's expected to be ready to return by Week 1. ● Even down seasons for Tyron Smith are among the best at the position. Smith improved in both penalties and sacks allowed from 2018 but blown blocks went up in both run- and pass-blocking. The concern for the soon-to-be 30-year-old tackle remains his injury history. He has played exactly 13 games in each of the past four seasons. ● There might not be a better right side of an offensive line, where right guard Zack Martin remained dominant and right tackle La'el Collins turned into one of the better right tackles in football by cutting down his penalties, blown blocks, and sacks allowed from 2018.

Defensive Front

Defensive Line	Age	Pos	G	Snaps	Plays	TmPct	Rk	Stop	Dfts	BTkl	Runs	St%	Rk	RuYd	Rk	Sack	Hit	Hur	Dsrpt
						Overall						vs. Run				Pass Rush			
Maliek Collins*	25	DT	16	782	20	2.4%	89	14	9	3	16	63%	83	1.5	12	4.0	6	34	0
Christian Covington*	27	DT	16	487	29	3.5%	69	24	6	5	25	84%	18	1.9	26	1.0	2	10	1
Antwaun Woods	27	DT	10	322	22	4.3%	83	18	3	3	20	90%	6	2.2	41	0.0	1	3	0
Gerald McCoy	32	DE	16	711	39	4.7%	43	37	10	5	31	94%	3	1.5	13	5.0	9	27	2
Dontari Poe	30	DT	11	416	21	3.7%	86	15	6	2	13	69%	71	3.2	92	4.0	2	9	0

Edge Rushers	Age	Pos	G	Snaps	Plays	TmPct	Rk	Stop	Dfts	BTkl	Runs	St%	Rk	RuYd	Rk	Sack	Hit	Hur	Dsrpt
						Overall						vs. Run				Pass Rush			
Demarcus Lawrence	28	DE	16	687	46	5.6%	35	37	17	4	33	82%	16	1.4	14	5.0	11	50	7
Robert Quinn*	30	DE	14	658	36	5.0%	49	26	16	7	21	52%	84	2.3	42	11.5	15	37	4
Michael Bennett*	35	DE	15	564	31	4.0%	60	27	17	4	22	82%	16	1.2	9	6.5	10	24	3
Kerry Hyder*	29	DE	16	447	17	2.1%	90	12	3	3	15	73%	49	2.5	46	1.0	3	28	0
Dorance Armstrong	23	DE	15	269	14	1.8%	--	11	3	1	10	90%	--	1.9	--	2.0	3	7	0

Linebackers	Age	Pos	G	Snaps	Plays	TmPct	Rk	Stop	Dfts	BTkl	Runs	St%	Rk	RuYd	Rk	Sack	Hit	Hur	Tgts	Suc%	Rk	AdjYd	Rk	PD	Int
						Overall						vs. Run				Pass Rush				vs. Pass					
Jaylon Smith	25	MLB	16	1013	151	18.4%	4	75	27	13	81	57%	52	4.1	54	2.5	1	12	45	47%	45	5.4	19	9	1
Sean Lee	34	OLB	16	649	90	10.9%	38	45	9	15	48	50%	73	4.2	58	1.0	0	3	31	48%	39	3.7	4	4	1
Leighton Vander Esch	24	OLB	9	528	75	16.2%	52	42	13	15	39	69%	15	3.4	22	0.5	2	3	22	41%	55	6.8	40	3	0
Joe Thomas	29	MLB	15	252	30	3.9%	--	14	6	6	11	55%	--	3.8	--	0.0	0	1	6	33%	--	9.3	--	1	0

Year	Yards	ALY	Rank	Power	Rank	Stuff	Rank	2nd Level	Rank	Open Field	Rank	Sacks	ASR	Rank	Press	Rank
2017	4.12	3.95	11	83%	32	22%	11	1.25	25	0.76	20	38	6.7%	14	35.5%	2
2018	3.88	3.87	3	67%	20	25%	5	1.16	10	0.76	14	39	6.5%	27	32.2%	8
2019	4.05	4.05	8	66%	20	21%	10	1.16	15	0.78	19	39	6.8%	19	33.9%	6

2019 ALY by direction:	Left End: 4.36 (21)	Left Tackle: 3.91 (11)	Mid/Guard: 4.41 (17)	Right Tackle: 2.78 (3)	Right End: 3.43 (10)

Dallas finished in the top eight of pressure rate over the past three seasons, but that will be hard to replicate in 2020 with the current depth on the roster. Demarcus Lawrence was one of the league's most disruptive pass-rushers (eighth in QB hurries), but his help on the edge has vanished from the roster. Robert Quinn and Michael Bennett, who combined for 18.0 sacks and 61 hurries, are both gone. ● The responsibility for helping Lawrence on the edge now falls to Tyrone Crawford, a veteran coming off a hip injury who has bounced around from the edge to interior in his seven seasons, along with a reinstated-from-suspension Aldon Smith (who hasn't played in the NFL since 2015) and 2020 fifth-round pick Bradlee Anae from Utah. Anae doesn't have the long speed of a top pass-rusher, but he lived off his quick-twitch explosion on the way to 13.0 sacks and 54 pressures in 2019. ● The interior of the line is significantly stronger with the veteran free-agent signings of Gerald McCoy and Dontari Poe added to second-year tackle Trysten Hill. Hill's rookie season was wasted for multiple reasons: he lost playing time to off-field issues like falling asleep in meetings, then looked overmatched when he did get on the field. Still, there's talent there for this 2019 second-rounder to become an above-average interior disruptor if everything can come together. 2020 third-round pick Neville Gallimore was also added to the mix. The Oklahoma product can flash pass-rush upside as a rotational tackle in his rookie season. ● Leighton Vander Esch only played nine games due to a neck injury, but that allowed Jaylon Smith to flourish with more responsibilities. Smith finished ninth among defenders in total defeats with a nearly even split against the run and pass. Over the past two seasons, Smith has rushed the passer on 11.6% and 9.7% of his pass snaps, per SIS, and he has been an effective blitzer. Those rates could increase under Mike Nolan. ● Veteran Sean Lee was brought back as the third linebacker. While his instincts have remained top-notch for the position, his first step has not.

Defensive Secondary

Secondary	Age	Pos	G	Snaps	Plays	Overall TmPct	Rk	Stop	Dfts	BTkl	vs. Run Runs	St%	Rk	RuYd	Rk	vs. Pass Tgts	Tgt%	Rk	Dist	Suc%	Rk	AdjYd	Rk	PD	Int
Chidobe Awuzie	25	CB	16	1040	93	11.3%	3	34	7	12	23	39%	52	8.3	64	86	21.3%	30	13.2	53%	37	8.1	53	14	1
Xavier Woods	25	FS	15	997	80	10.4%	29	23	10	11	39	28%	58	10.3	65	23	6.0%	55	6.3	43%	62	7.6	38	5	2
Byron Jones*	28	CB	15	938	50	6.5%	65	17	5	3	13	23%	76	6.8	51	54	14.9%	81	12.1	54%	36	6.1	11	6	0
Jeff Heath*	29	SS	13	732	66	9.9%	46	28	12	4	24	58%	6	4.9	14	37	13.0%	9	9.0	51%	37	6.2	23	7	0
Jourdan Lewis	25	CB	16	596	55	6.7%	--	27	15	5	7	43%	--	5.6	--	41	17.7%	--	9.4	54%	--	9.2	--	6	2
Darian Thompson	27	FS	15	435	41	5.3%	--	20	8	5	26	50%	--	4.1	--	14	8.3%	--	15.5	43%	--	10.9	--	3	0
Anthony Brown	27	CB	9	289	22	4.8%	--	12	4	5	6	83%	--	1.5	--	21	18.7%	--	12.1	48%	--	7.0	--	5	0
Ha Ha Clinton-Dix	28	SS	16	1086	83	10.1%	24	21	9	11	33	36%	48	7.3	42	31	7.3%	43	8.1	52%	36	5.5	14	5	2
Daryl Worley	25	CB	15	962	66	9.1%	25	24	5	11	19	47%	37	5.6	34	73	19.0%	55	13.7	56%	26	8.7	66	8	1
Maurice Canady	26	CB	13	403	47	8.1%	--	16	6	3	11	36%	--	7.1	--	43	25.7%	--	11.2	51%	--	6.7	--	5	1

Year	Pass D Rank	vs. #1 WR	Rk	vs. #2 WR	Rk	vs. Other WR	Rk	WR Wide	Rk	WR Slot	Rk	vs. TE	Rk	vs. RB	Rk
2017	18	10.7%	21	13.5%	23	-14.9%	8	-15.2%	6	18.8%	25	12.5%	25	14.5%	28
2018	16	-11.7%	6	-24.1%	4	6.9%	22	-4.6%	19	-8.1%	7	4.7%	19	12.5%	26
2019	23	4.8%	20	16.0%	26	5.7%	21	-10.1%	13	22.7%	30	8.3%	23	-1.5%	20

Without Byron Jones, the Cowboys will have to figure out how they want to assemble their secondary pieces to fill the hole left on the outside. ● Chidobe Awuzie was the No. 2 for most of last season and had a similar coverage success rate to Jones, though he allowed 2 more yards per play. Some of that came from getting torched on double-moves during the regular season. Per SIS charting, Awuzie allowed 141 yards off double-moves in 2019, the third-highest total in the league, which included a 92-yard touchdown against Robby Anderson in Week 6. There has been talk about a move to safety for Awuzie, but that won't be determined until camp. If a few big plays can be erased by an improvement in discipline, Awuzie could still be salvaged as a quality outside corner. ● With a need at the position, the Cowboys doubled up at corner in the draft with second-round pick Trevon Diggs of Alabama and fourth-round pick Reggie Robinson II from Tulsa. Both tied for third in this draft class by yards allowed per man coverage snap according to SIS. Either could easily push Anthony Brown from a starting role, at least one on the outside, early in the season. Neither rookie has much experience in the slot. ● Xavier Woods has turned into an above-average free safety after coming into the league as a fifth-round pick in 2017. Woods was often asked to play the single-high safety role in the Cover-3 alignment, but it could be a new day for him in the back end of the secondary with a new scheme and more help beside him.   Ha Ha Clinton-Dix was brought in as a free agent after a year in Chicago and offers a significant improvement over Jeff Heath. Clinton-Dix has played both deep and in the box, which could allow the Cowboys to move pieces around and also play more 2-high coverages than they have over the past few seasons to help out the corners.

Special Teams

Year	DVOA	Rank	FG/XP	Rank	Net Kick	Rank	Kick Ret	Rank	Net Punt	Rank	Punt Ret	Rank	Hidden	Rank
2017	4.6%	7	-7.0	26	4.5	8	2.3	8	16.9	2	6.2	3	14.8	2
2018	-2.1%	23	-2.6	23	-3.4	26	-0.8	15	-2.5	21	-1.1	18	-4.1	21
2019	-3.9%	30	1.7	14	-4.9	28	-7.1	32	-7.6	26	-1.8	21	2.6	12

John Fassel will take over as special teams coordinator with the goal of orchestrating a much-needed improvement in all facets of a special teams unit that has been among the league's worst for the past two seasons. Fassel led the Rams' special teams to five straight top-10 finishes in DVOA from 2013 to 2017, though the Rams ranked 17th and 23rd over the past two seasons.   Brett Maher was one of four kickers to convert every extra point attempt, but he was one of the most inconsistent field goal kickers in the league. His 66.7% conversion rate, which included a 1-for-5 clip between 40 and 49 yards, was second-worst. He was cut after Week 14 and replaced by Kai Forbath, whose strong performance in the final three games lifted Dallas above zero in placekicking value. The Cowboys will have a training-camp battle between Forbath and free-agent signing Greg Zuerlein, coming off an inconsistent season of his own with the Rams.   Chris Jones has been the Cowboys' full-time punter since 2013 but is now coming off back-to-back seasons with negative punt value; he finished second-worst in gross punt value in 2019. While he has two rushing attempts over the past two seasons, he has no NFL pass attempts, which is something to keep in mind with Fassel, king of the fake punt.   Tony Pollard took over as the lead kick returner but finished dead last in return value among all players with at least five returns.   The Cowboys will have to replace Tavon Austin on punt returns, but that shouldn't be too difficult, as he was also among the league's worst in punt return value. Cedrick Wilson is the only returning player who returned a punt in 2019, and he only returned two. This is a role that could potentially go to CeeDee Lamb, who returned punts for Oklahoma.

Denver Broncos

2019 Record: 7-9	Total DVOA: -9.0% (22nd)	2020 Mean Projection: 7.0 wins	On the Clock (0-4): 17%
Pythagorean Wins: 6.9 (21st)	Offense: -10.8% (26th)	Postseason Odds: 28.5%	Mediocrity (5-7): 42%
Snap-Weighted Age: 26.1 (25th)	Defense: -3.7% (13th)	Super Bowl Odds: 2.0%	Playoff Contender (8-10): 32%
Average Opponent: 0.4% (15th)	Special Teams: -1.9% (24th)	Proj. Avg. Opponent: 2.7% (3rd)	Super Bowl Contender (11+): 9%

2019: John Elway finally tries modern offense for the first time. And he likes it!

2020: Don't waste another minute of your crying. We're nowhere near the end. But the best is ready to begin.

From Peyton Manning's retirement after the triumphant 2015 season until very recently, the Broncos were among the worst-run organizations in the NFL. With John Elway acting as executive vice president, general manager, and semi-legendary emperor-deity, they drafted abysmally, juggled coaches haphazardly, played the free-agent market poorly, and adhered stubbornly to outdated offensive strategies. In four short years, the Broncos slid from the Super Bowl into mediocrity and irrelevance.

Football Outsiders Almanac is proud to announce that there is light at the end of the tunnel. Productive drafts and a new willingness to build a modern offense should soon get the Broncos back on track.

That said, they're still in the tunnel.

The Broncos' futility over the last three seasons largely stems from their epic mid-decade draft drought. From 2013 through 2017, the Broncos drafted just five players whose career Approximate Value (from Pro Football Reference) exceeded 20 by the end of last season: Sylvester Williams, Matt Paradis, Mike Schofield, Justin Simmons, and Garrett Bolles. An Approximate Value of 20 isn't a very high threshold—Bolles reached it simply by racking up starts at an important position—and none of those players have reached 30 yet. For comparison's sake, the Lions selected 13 players whose Approximate Value has passed 20 in that span, five of whom (Darius Slay, Ziggy Ansah, Larry Warford, Kyle Van Noy, and Laken Tomlinson) have passed 30. And Williams, Paradis, and Schofield were no longer even on the Broncos roster when they achieved their very minor milestone. The Broncos went five full years without drafting a star and barely even mustered some adequate starters during that span.

It's difficult to pinpoint the cause of the Great Draft Famine of 2013 to 2017. Research tells us that draft success and failure are far more random than anyone involved in the NFL would like to admit, so probability dictates even a well-run organization is susceptible to an occasional wicked slump of critical-failure dice rolls. Throw in one high-profile blunder (Paxton Lynch) and the fact that the Broncos were contenders in the first seasons of famine (so they picked late in the draft and had a veteran roster with limited opportunities for youngsters), and perhaps the drought was more about perceptions and circumstances than managerial errors.

But there was another layer to the Broncos' late-decade failures. Much of what we perceive as drafting (good or bad) is really the result of coaching and player development (good or bad). The Broncos of the post-Super Bowl years were almost certainly not making the most of the players they did select. This was an era in which Gary Kubiak retired from coaching and took on a vague consigliere role within the organization, Vance Joseph cycled through offensive coordinators, and Elway meddled in position coaching decisions. Elway's preference for a vintage 1990s-style offense became an organizational mandate, then self-parody. And by 2017 and 2018, a shadow cabinet of Super Bowl holdovers in the locker room held a great deal of sway over the Mighty Mountain King. If you want to make sure third- through seventh-round picks never develop, swap out their position coaches every few months, yoke them to outdated schemes, and take advice from the players they were selected to replace.

The weak drafts, staff politicking, and Elway's peculiar taste in mid-century offensive furnishings trapped the Broncos in a feedback loop. Elway, with the support of the Super Bowl-era veterans, fooled himself into believing that the Broncos were just one veteran pocket passer away from a return to the playoffs, even as the depth chart crumbled. So Elway overpaid Case Keenum, then traded for Joe Flacco. He undermined Vance Joseph by keeping Kubiak at his right hand and firing assistants; Joseph was never much more than a glorified defensive coordinator, and he made in-game decisions like one. Elway then replaced Joseph with Vic Fangio, who promised to be even more conservative and inattentive to the offense than Joseph, albeit with a touch of gruff trucker-grandpa charm.

But even as Elway noodled with his staff and made the worst possible quarterback decisions, signs of hope began to spring from the ground in Denver. Bradley Chubb, Courtland Sutton, and Phillip Lindsay headlined an impressive rookie crop in 2018. Another productive draft class followed in 2019. Fangio mixed his grouchy drill sergeant routine with attention to detail and an ability to relate to players, earning the trust of both Elway and the outspoken defensive veterans, even though the Broncos started the 2019 season with four straight losses.

Midway through last season, the Broncos traded Emmanuel Sanders (plus a fifth-round pick) to the 49ers for third- and fourth-round draft picks, then transitioned from injured/disenchanted Flacco to veteran third-stringer Brandon Allen and

2020 Broncos Schedule

Week	Opp.	Week	Opp.	Week	Opp.
1	TEN (Mon.)	7	KC	13	at KC
2	at PIT	8	BYE	14	at CAR
3	TB	9	at ATL	15	BUF (Sat.)
4	at NYJ (Thu)	10	at LV	16	at LAC (Sat.)
5	at NE	11	LAC	17	LV
6	MIA	12	NO		

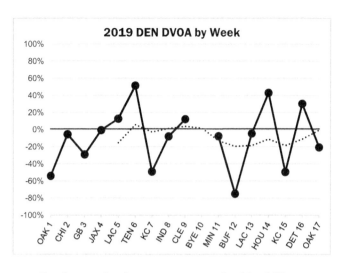

finally to Drew Lock. The moves signaled that Elway finally realized after four years that the Broncos were a rebuilding team. The Sanders trade also further weakened the Peyton-era ruling council in the locker room, while Flacco's mediocrity and mutterings about the play calling may finally have shaken Elway's faith in the church of tall pocket-passer fundamentalism. The Broncos went 4-1 down the stretch, and the team appeared energized, both by a quarterback who didn't need a forklift to move around the pocket and a roster-wide sense that they were no longer living in the shadow of the 2011-2015 teams.

This offseason brought an impressive influx of talent, both through the draft—Jerry Jeudy, KJ Hamler, Lloyd Cushenberry, and others—and through free-agent acquisitions Jurrell Casey, A.J. Bouye, and Melvin Gordon. Offensive coordinator Pat Shurmur also arrived to liberate the Broncos from a dreary dynasty of Kubiak lieutenants. The offense of Lock, Sutton, Noah Fant, Jeudy, Hamler, Gordon, and Lindsay, with an improving offensive line in front of them, has the potential to be very good someday. The defense led by Von Miller, Chubb, Simmons, Casey, Bouye, Kareem Jackson, and others has the potential to be very good right now.

So why are we projecting the Broncos for six or seven wins instead of 10 or 11?

First of all, a late-season hot streak is a poor predictor of future performance. Even if a 4-1 finish had predictive value, there was less to the Broncos' late surge than meets the eye. Their win over the Texans was impressive, though it helped that they used a few big plays to take an early 21-0 lead over an erratic team having one of its regularly scheduled self-destructive fits. The Broncos posted a negative total DVOA in the narrow Chargers and Raiders wins; they beat the Chargers 23-20 with the help of a pair of 50-plus-yard Brandon McManus field goals and beat the Raiders 16-15 in a game when they netted just 238 yards of total offense (and benefited from two more long McManus field goals).

So the Broncos' late hot streak looked like a case of a 7-9 team finding its true level after underperforming early in the year, not a sign that they solved all (or even very many) of their problems. Their 2020 schedule is the third-toughest in the league, per DVOA. The AFC West has no particularly weak teams and the NFC South makes for particularly difficult opponents (the AFC East, less so). Denver's second-place finish last year means the Broncos start the season with the Titans and Steelers. The Broncos could improve while treading water in the standings due to their strength of schedule.

It's also dangerous to project a young quarterback based

on a few impressive late-season starts. Lock's ability to run a little, throw from a variety of platforms, and improvise are all traits that could help him develop into a front-line starter, and he showed remarkable improvement from last year's Hall of Fame game (when he looked like a teenaged fan who had run onto the field on a dare) to a guy who truly belonged in the huddle by December. But some of Lock's top highlights were 50/50-type plays which could easily have been interceptions if, for example, Noah Fant didn't wrestle the ball away from a Texans defender in the end zone. Lock remains a boom-or-bust prospect, despite some encouraging evidence of boom.

Shurmur also shouldn't be mistaken for Kyle Shanahan. He has been a head coach or offensive coordinator for 11 years, and while his teams finished in the top five in DVOA twice, they finished 23rd or lower seven times. His two best seasons came with the Keenum-led Vikings in 2017 and Chip Kelly's 2013 Eagles: one of those successes appears far more repeatable than the other.

At least Shurmur's offense is more modern and multiple than the Ask Madden scheme Bill Musgrave and Rick Scangarello trotted out for the last two years; the Scangarello/Flacco offense, with its dump-offs to the flat and play-action bombs that even a drunk in the bleachers could see coming, was practically a nighttime cold remedy. Shurmur could recreate the 2017 Vikings with the Broncos' current personnel. But he could also recreate last year's Giants, who finished 23rd in DVOA as their inexperienced quarterback mixed highlights with strip-sacks in critical situations.

The final reason to be skeptical of a quick turnaround is the fact that the Broncos are missing an entire generation of talent because of the draft famine. There's Miller, and there are lots of up-and-comers, but there are only a handful of significant players on the Broncos roster who are truly in their prime, and most of them (all but Simmons, essentially) are recent imports. Sweeping out aging, increasingly disgruntled defensive veterans should help the Lock generation establish its own identity, but the roster remains lean due to years of neglect.

Expectations among Broncos fans may be a little too high right now. Lock drew some Patrick Mahomes comparisons leaving Mizzou, and there will always be a vocal contingent of over-enthusiastic fans who project a rookie quarterback with some 16-15 victories straight to MVP status. Fangio's lovably irascible goombah personality plays well with fans and the media. The Sutton-Jeudy-Fant-Lindsay offense is talented enough to inspire some Chiefs daydreams. And while the Bouye and Casey additions do little more than offset the Chris Harris-Derek Wolfe subtractions, they give the impression that the still-formidable defense got better in the offseason.

In reality, the Broncos have merely stabilized after years of slow defensive and rapid offensive deterioration. Just as the draft famine which started in 2013 didn't fully cripple the team until 2016, the relief which started coming in 2018 won't reach the win-loss column for at least another year.

The good news is that we are talking about a talented young quarterback and his growing supporting cast instead of laughing at some overpaid journeyman and musing over what percentage of snaps should be taken under center in a mid-21st century offense. Elway is no longer making things worse by swilling quack medicine to cure his offense.

The Broncos may be trending in the positive direction. They should be fun to watch and competitive. They're still going to lose a lot of football games. But after years of famine, there's at least hope that there will soon be another feast.

Mike Tanier

2019 Broncos Stats by Week

Wk	vs.	W-L	PF	PA	YDF	YDA	TO	Total	Off	Def	ST
1	at OAK	L	16	24	344	357	0	-54%	-8%	38%	-8%
2	CHI	L	14	16	372	273	-1	-6%	7%	8%	-4%
3	at GB	L	16	27	310	312	-3	-29%	-16%	16%	4%
4	JAX	L	24	26	371	455	-1	-1%	23%	16%	-8%
5	at LAC	W	20	13	350	246	+1	13%	-11%	-47%	-23%
6	TEN	W	16	0	270	204	+2	52%	-29%	-74%	7%
7	KC	L	6	30	205	271	-1	-49%	-50%	-21%	-19%
8	at IND	L	13	15	279	318	+1	-8%	-7%	-2%	-2%
9	CLE	W	24	19	302	351	-1	12%	10%	-2%	1%
10	BYE										
11	at MIN	L	23	27	394	321	+1	-8%	-12%	5%	9%
12	at BUF	L	3	20	134	424	0	-75%	-52%	21%	-2%
13	LAC	W	23	20	218	359	+1	-5%	-26%	-7%	14%
14	at HOU	W	38	24	391	414	+2	43%	41%	0%	2%
15	at KC	L	3	23	251	419	0	-49%	-39%	15%	5%
16	DET	W	27	17	348	191	0	30%	31%	-15%	-16%
17	OAK	W	16	15	238	477	0	-21%	-44%	-14%	10%

Trends and Splits

	Offense	Rank	Defense	Rank
Total DVOA	-10.8%	26	-3.7%	13
Unadjusted VOA	-8.9%	25	-2.0%	13
Weighted Trend	-13.5%	26	-5.8%	12
Variance	8.1%	20	7.4%	25
Average Opponent	2.8%	29	3.2%	4
Passing	-8.2%	27	1.9%	14
Rushing	-6.4%	19	-10.0%	16
First Down	1.7%	14	-5.2%	11
Second Down	-17.4%	29	3.7%	17
Third Down	-23.6%	28	-11.7%	11
First Half	-2.9%	19	-12.3%	8
Second Half	-19.1%	28	4.8%	20
Red Zone	-21.2%	27	-35.4%	2
Late and Close	-6.7%	19	9.4%	26

Five-Year Performance

Year	W-L	Pyth W	Est W	PF	PA	TO	Total	Rk	Off	Rk	Def	Rk	ST	Rk	Off AGL	Rk	Def AGL	Rk	Off Age	Rk	Def Age	Rk	ST Age	Rk
2015	12-4	9.7	10.7	355	296	-4	17.7%	8	-8.7%	25	-25.8%	1	0.7%	14	40.9	21	18.0	3	28.3	2	26.5	19	25.6	26
2016	9-7	9.1	8.5	333	297	+2	3.7%	14	-12.3%	28	-18.3%	1	-2.3%	24	25.2	8	34.0	13	26.6	18	26.7	12	25.1	30
2017	5-11	5.4	5.6	289	382	-17	-21.1%	29	-19.0%	31	-5.3%	10	-7.4%	30	26.4	10	38.1	19	27.1	14	26.7	12	25.0	30
2018	6-10	7.4	8.7	329	349	+7	6.6%	13	1.1%	14	-9.7%	5	-4.2%	31	47.5	24	26.0	11	26.6	18	26.9	7	25.4	28
2019	7-9	6.9	6.6	282	316	+1	-9.0%	22	-10.8%	26	-3.7%	13	-1.9%	24	52.0	25	48.3	27	25.8	30	26.9	7	25.1	31

2019 Performance Based on Most Common Personnel Groups

DEN Offense					DEN Offense vs. Opponents					DEN Defense				DEN Defense vs. Opponents			
Pers	Freq	Yds	DVOA	Run%	Pers	Freq	Yds	DVOA	Run%	Pers	Freq	Yds	DVOA	Pers	Freq	Yds	DVOA
11	51%	4.8	-18.0%	31%	Base	37%	6.1	0.7%	53%	Base	27%	4.9	-7.3%	11	59%	5.7	-3.9%
21	21%	6.0	-0.3%	43%	Nickel	44%	5.0	-6.5%	37%	Nickel	65%	5.5	-6.4%	12	25%	5.7	-0.5%
12	13%	5.1	7.8%	43%	Dime+	19%	4.1	-31.4%	17%	Dime+	8%	7.0	43.8%	21	8%	4.6	-21.0%
22	6%	4.9	-12.8%	61%	Goal Line	1%	0.6	31.7%	57%	Goal Line	0%	0.0	-103.4%	22	2%	5.5	24.7%
31	3%	8.3	27.1%	73%										13	2%	2.8	-28.7%
														611	2%	3.5	-14.7%

Strategic Tendencies

Run/Pass		Rk	Formation		Rk	Pass Rush		Rk	Secondary		Rk	Strategy		Rk
Runs, first half	40%	8	Form: Single Back	67%	29	Rush 3	12.5%	7	4 DB	27%	18	Play Action	23%	20
Runs, first down	57%	4	Form: Empty Back	9%	12	Rush 4	64.6%	16	5 DB	65%	10	Offensive Motion	47%	8
Runs, second-long	28%	14	Form: Multi Back	24%	3	Rush 5	21.1%	14	6+ DB	8%	18	Avg Box (Off)	6.60	13
Runs, power sit.	52%	21	Pers: 3+ WR	52%	28	Rush 6+	1.8%	30	Man Coverage	32%	18	Avg Box (Def)	6.32	31
Runs, behind 2H	33%	4	Pers: 2+ TE/6+ OL	23%	24	Edge Rusher Sacks	38.8%	30	CB by Sides	61%	29	Offensive Pace	31.45	21
Pass, ahead 2H	54%	5	Pers: 6+ OL	0%	30	Interior DL Sacks	51.3%	1	S/CB Cover Ratio	35%	4	Defensive Pace	31.40	28
Run-Pass Options	2%	27	Shotgun/Pistol	55%	24	Second Level Sacks	10.0%	28	DB Blitz	4%	32	Go for it on 4th	0.68	32

The arrival of Vic Fangio meant some big changes for the Broncos' defensive tendencies. Denver went from first to 18th in frequency of using base defense, while going from 31st to 10th in frequency of nickel. They went from fourth to 31st in average men in the box on defense. They went from 25th to third in how often they sent the standard four pass-rushers. And they went from leading the league in sacks by edge rushers (72% in 2018) to being near the bottom of the league (39% in 2019). They had more sacks by interior linemen, similar to Fangio defenses of the past. ✎ The Broncos were the NFL's No. 2 defense against passes behind the line of scrimmage, trailing only Tampa Bay, but they were average against passes beyond the line of scrimmage. ✎ Denver ranked seventh in offensive DVOA in the first quarter of games, but 29th in offensive DVOA for the rest of the game. ✎ The Broncos ranked 10th running the ball on third downs but 29th passing the ball. ✎ Denver was one of three teams that never used six offensive linemen. ✎ It's a very small sample, but Drew Lock had an impressive 41.9% DVOA against the blitz.

Passing

Player	DYAR	DVOA	Plays	NtYds	Avg	YAC	C%	TD	Int
J.Flacco*	-144	-18.8%	287	1635	5.7	5.3	65.8%	6	5
D.Lock	138	2.2%	162	994	6.1	5.5	64.1%	7	3
B.Allen*	-115	-30.5%	93	456	4.9	6.0	46.4%	3	2
J.Driskel	-91	-24.2%	114	639	5.6	4.7	60.2%	4	4

Rushing

Player	DYAR	DVOA	Plays	Yds	Avg	TD	Fum	Suc
P.Lindsay	94	1.9%	224	1011	4.5	7	0	50%
R.Freeman	-12	-11.0%	132	500	3.8	3	0	41%
D.Lock	1	-10.9%	13	73	5.6	0	1	-
B.Allen*	21	41.2%	7	42	6.0	0	0	-
J.Flacco*	1	-9.3%	7	24	3.4	0	0	-
M.Gordon	8	-7.5%	162	615	3.8	8	3	51%
J.Driskel	52	37.0%	21	152	7.2	1	0	-

Receiving

Player	DYAR	DVOA	Plays	Ctch	Yds	Y/C	YAC	TD	C%
C.Sutton	189	5.7%	124	72	1112	15.4	4.9	6	58%
D.Hamilton	-21	-18.0%	52	28	297	10.6	4.6	1	54%
E.Sanders*	71	6.9%	44	30	367	12.2	3.9	2	68%
T.Patrick	11	-7.8%	31	16	218	13.6	2.4	0	52%
D.Spencer	-46	-89.6%	8	6	31	5.2	5.5	0	75%
N.Fant	6	-5.9%	66	40	562	14.1	8.3	3	61%
J.Heuerman	-4	-9.7%	20	14	114	8.1	3.0	1	70%
A.Beck	13	9.1%	12	9	90	10.0	7.4	1	75%
T.Fumagalli	-7	-19.4%	9	6	38	6.3	2.3	1	67%
N.Vannett	10	0.9%	22	17	166	9.8	3.9	0	77%
R.Freeman	10	-10.1%	50	43	256	6.0	6.0	1	86%
P.Lindsay	-69	-39.7%	48	35	196	5.6	6.9	0	73%
D.Booker*	-9	-33.6%	9	6	57	9.5	7.3	0	67%
M.Gordon	19	-7.3%	55	42	296	7.0	7.6	1	76%

Offensive Line

Player	Pos	Age	GS	Snaps	Pen	Sk	Pass	Run	Player	Pos	Age	GS	Snaps	Pen	Sk	Pass	Run
Garett Bolles	LT	28	16/16	1024	17	5.5	19	4	Ronald Leary*	RG	31	12/12	765	8	0.0	5	9
Connor McGovern*	C	27	16/16	1024	0	1.5	5	7	Austin Schlottmann	RG	25	16/4	260	1	0.5	5	1
Dalton Risner	LG	25	16/16	986	3	3.0	12	6	Graham Glasgow	RG	28	15/15	886	3	0.0	11	5
Elijah Wilkinson	RT	25	15/12	844	9	9.5	21	4									

Year	Yards	ALY	Rank	Power	Rank	Stuff	Rank	2nd Lev	Rank	Open Field	Rank	Sacks	ASR	Rank	Press	Rank	F-Start	Cont.
2017	4.03	4.31	9	65%	15	18%	7	1.11	18	0.51	26	52	9.1%	29	31.1%	16	17	28
2018	4.88	4.75	6	71%	7	18%	14	1.42	5	1.01	10	34	6.3%	11	32.1%	20	9	31
2019	4.24	4.45	11	69%	8	15%	3	1.17	17	0.61	23	41	8.1%	25	32.2%	25	11	29

2019 ALY by direction: Left End 3.95 (16)   Left Tackle: 5.20 (3)   Mid/Guard: 4.49 (13)   Right Tackle: 4.79 (9)   Right End: 3.48 (21)

Left tackle has become the weak link on an otherwise-respectable offensive line. Garrett Bolles committed 13 holding penalties last season (seven of them declined), two false starts, one block below the waist, and one unnecessary roughness foul. That gives him 34 holding penalties (14 declined) and 46 total penalties in his three-year career, not to mention some of the ugliest blown blocks ever to go viral on Twitter. 🏈 The Broncos declined the fifth-year option on Bolles' rookie contract and are expected to give Elijah Wilkinson the chance to compete with Bolles for the starting job. But don't expect an easy victory for Wilkinson. Bolles improved substantially when Drew Lock took over at quarterback (it helps to not be blocking for an elm tree), and Wilkinson is making an unusual right guard-to-right tackle-to-left tackle career transition. 🏈 Second-year Colorado native Dalton Risner is the rising star of the Broncos offensive line. He made several All-Rookie teams, but he told Troy Renck of Denver's KMGH-TV that the recognition brought him no satisfaction. "I am not proud of that honor. People bring it up, and I try not to be rude. That's not what I am after. I want to just dominate. I thought I had a good year, but (bleep) Troy, I wasn't All-Pro. I wasn't in the Pro Bowl. That's not cool with me." Risner is locked in at left guard now, but he could move outside to challenge or replace Ja'Wuan James (who missed most of last season with a lingering knee injury) at right tackle if Wilkinson slides across the formation. 🏈 New right guard Graham Glasgow had similar blown-block numbers to Risner. He flew under the radar in terms of free-agent name recognition but not in terms of dollar value, signing a four-year, $44-million contract. 🏈 The new center will be LSU product Lloyd Cushenberry III, a third-round rookie from the all-intangibles team. Cushenberry had an exceptional Senior Bowl week, knocking Javon Kinlaw to the turf and out of action for the week with a minor injury on one memorable rep.

Defensive Front

Defensive Line	Age	Pos	G	Snaps	Plays	TmPct	Rk	Stop	Dfts	BTkl	Runs	St%	Rk	RuYd	Rk	Sack	Hit	Hur	Dsrpt
						Overall						vs. Run					Pass Rush		
Shelby Harris	29	DE	16	649	58	6.9%	14	45	12	1	40	73%	59	2.5	57	6.0	0	17	9
Derek Wolfe*	30	DE	12	535	35	5.6%	54	24	12	2	27	59%	89	3.0	85	7.0	7	14	1
Mike Purcell	29	DT	13	417	48	7.1%	24	34	9	7	47	72%	62	1.3	7	0.0	3	8	1
Dre'Mont Jones	23	DE	14	290	16	2.2%	--	12	8	1	8	50%	--	4.6	--	3.5	3	9	1
Adam Gotsis*	28	DE	9	282	18	3.8%	92	14	5	4	15	80%	27	1.8	21	0.0	0	2	2
DeMarcus Walker	26	DE	10	225	23	4.4%	--	17	6	3	14	64%	--	2.4	--	4.0	1	6	0
Jurrell Casey	*31*	*DE*	*14*	*722*	*44*	*5.9%*	*34*	*38*	*11*	*5*	*36*	*86%*	*12*	*1.8*	*22*	*5.0*	*5*	*20*	*0*
Christian Covington	*27*	*DT*	*16*	*487*	*29*	*3.5%*	*69*	*24*	*6*	*5*	*25*	*84%*	*18*	*1.9*	*26*	*1.0*	*2*	*10*	*1*

Edge Rushers	Age	Pos	G	Snaps	Plays	TmPct	Rk	Stop	Dfts	BTkl	Runs	St%	Rk	RuYd	Rk	Sack	Hit	Hur	Dsrpt
						Overall						vs. Run					Pass Rush		
Von Miller	31	OLB	15	853	48	6.1%	33	36	19	5	34	68%	66	3.0	67	8.0	11	52	3
Malik Reed	24	OLB	15	475	25	3.2%	76	18	9	4	17	82%	14	1.6	17	2.0	4	14	0
Jeremiah Attaochu	27	OLB	12	325	17	2.7%	--	17	7	4	11	100%	--	0.8	--	3.5	2	10	1
Justin Hollins	24	OLB	15	272	23	2.9%	--	14	3	2	14	57%	--	3.7	--	1.0	1	9	2
Bradley Chubb	24	OLB	4	243	21	10.0%	86	16	5	4	17	76%	31	3.2	77	1.0	5	9	1

Linebackers	Age	Pos	G	Snaps	Plays	TmPct	Rk	Stop	Dfts	BTkl	Runs	St%	Rk	RuYd	Rk	Sack	Hit	Hur	Tgts	Suc%	Rk	AdjYd	Rk	PD	Int
						Overall						vs. Run					Pass Rush				vs. Pass				
Todd Davis	28	ILB	14	915	134	18.3%	11	53	18	7	72	40%	81	5.6	82	0.0	1	6	48	48%	42	6.1	33	1	0
A.J. Johnson	29	ILB	15	743	96	12.2%	32	54	22	7	62	58%	45	4.5	69	1.5	3	9	17	53%	29	6.8	39	3	1
Josey Jewell	26	ILB	15	221	34	4.3%	--	19	8	2	20	65%	--	4.0	--	1.5	0	2	7	57%	--	7.1	--	0	0

Year	Yards	ALY	Rank	Power	Rank	Stuff	Rank	2nd Level	Rank	Open Field	Rank	Sacks	ASR	Rank	Press	Rank
2017	3.44	3.37	4	45%	1	26%	3	0.91	3	0.60	9	33	6.9%	11	32.7%	7
2018	4.78	4.58	23	73%	26	14%	30	1.14	8	1.16	29	44	8.0%	9	30.2%	17
2019	4.00	4.28	18	58%	6	18%	21	1.08	10	0.56	8	40	7.6%	11	28.3%	24
2019 ALY by direction:		Left End: 2.68 (4)			Left Tackle: 4.86 (26)			Mid/Guard: 4.46 (20)			Right Tackle: 4.92 (28)			Right End: 2.65 (6)	

Jurrell Casey is the new arrival. Bradley Chubb is returning from an ACL injury. And Von Miller is a COVID-19 survivor. 🏈 Casey, who has been named to five straight Pro Bowls, became expendable in Tennessee when the Titans decided to re-sign Ryan Tannehill and franchise-tag Derrick Henry, maxing out their short-term cap space; the Broncos acquired Casey and his salary for a mere seventh-round pick. The wisdom of these decisions is a topic for another chapter. Casey is a modest upgrade over Derek Wolfe (now in Baltimore) but an upgrade nonetheless. Casey told reporters after the trade that he was looking forward to playing with Miller and Chubb. "What else can a guy like me—who loves the pass rush and getting after the quarterback—ask for but to have two great edge rushers who can collapse the pocket and make the job a lot easier for me, where I don't have to push a hundred guys backward and push them too far?" Bradley Chubb told Troy Renck of KMGH-TV that his knee was "doing great" in late March, before the strictest of the social distancing rules took effect. "I am in rehab every day. Me and one of the trainers are working out. It's just the two of us." Malik Reed, Jeremiah Attaochu, and Justin Hollins took turns on the right edge in Chubb's absence (with Miller also moving across the formation more frequently), but none was an adequate replacement. Chubb's return essentially adds a Pro Bowler to the Broncos roster. Miller, who suffers from asthma, was tested for COVID-19 in early spring after developing a cough that his inhaler could not suppress. He announced a positive result on April 16, then Tweeted in May that he had recovered and was COVID-19-negative. There were some reports that Miller had been working out with teammates before the positive result, but he announced that he was self-isolating immediately after the diagnosis, and fortunately there are no signs that the virus spread beyond him. Miller reported some lingering symptoms later in the spring, but in June he held an online version of his annual pass-rusher summit. There are no indications that his performance will suffer due to long-term effects of the illness, and he's expected to join Chubb and Casey in making the Broncos' front seven one of the most formidable units in the NFL. Vic Fangio is under the impression that Todd Davis is a crackerjack coverage linebacker capable of neutralizing Austin Ekeler types and holding his own against Travis Kelce if called upon. Davis even lined up as a slot defender frequently last season. But Davis was among the least effective coverage linebackers in the NFL, and he was even worse in 2018, when he ranked 60th in coverage success rate and 65th in yards allowed per pass. While Davis struggled, undrafted first-year starter A.J. Johnson was a revelation as an in-the-box enforcer and situational blitzer at age 28. Unfortunately, the 255-pound Johnson is ill-suited for Ekeler-chasing duties, so Davis will keep drawing the tough coverage assignments.

Defensive Secondary

Secondary	Age	Pos	G	Snaps	Plays	Overall TmPct	Rk	Stop	Dfts	BTkl	vs. Run Runs	St%	Rk	RuYd	Rk	vs. Pass Tgts	Tgt%	Rk	Dist	Suc%	Rk	AdjYd	Rk	PD	Int
Justin Simmons	27	FS	16	1075	108	12.9%	9	44	21	6	45	33%	53	8.0	48	34	8.7%	28	9.9	74%	3	3.6	3	15	4
Chris Harris*	31	CB	16	1067	62	7.4%	49	18	6	4	14	29%	68	6.4	43	58	14.9%	80	13.4	45%	70	10.9	83	6	1
Kareem Jackson	32	SS	13	862	81	11.9%	30	39	15	13	34	59%	5	3.8	4	29	9.2%	21	9.4	59%	19	5.1	10	10	2
Will Parks*	26	FS/CB	14	555	33	4.5%	71	15	4	8	16	50%	15	3.7	3	30	14.8%	4	11.8	63%	9	5.8	19	2	1
Isaac Yiadom	24	CB	16	517	42	5.0%	81	16	3	11	8	75%	8	2.6	3	46	24.4%	9	12.9	43%	74	8.2	56	4	0
Davontae Harris	25	CB	16	434	35	4.2%	--	11	5	7	6	33%	--	10.2	--	46	29.1%	--	10.7	43%	--	6.3	--	3	0
Duke Dawson	25	CB	14	346	21	2.9%	--	9	3	4	6	50%	--	19.7	--	14	11.1%	--	7.1	43%	--	9.5	--	2	0
A.J. Bouye	29	CB	14	946	73	10.5%	20	19	8	10	18	39%	53	7.5	62	83	23.6%	14	12.1	42%	79	9.7	74	8	1

Year	Pass D Rank	vs. #1 WR	Rk	vs. #2 WR	Rk	vs. Other WR	Rk	WR Wide	Rk	WR Slot	Rk	vs. TE	Rk	vs. RB	Rk
2017	15	-33.6%	2	-13.3%	9	28.5%	30	-28.6%	3	-2.1%	12	19.8%	31	5.6%	19
2018	4	-5.8%	11	0.1%	17	-36.4%	1	-7.7%	16	-14.2%	3	-9.3%	12	5.4%	18
2019	14	11.2%	26	-9.0%	8	-20.7%	5	13.3%	26	-14.5%	4	-11.9%	5	-11.5%	6

Last year, the Broncos secondary consisted of the typically exceptional Chris Harris, one of the best safety tandems in the NFL in Justin Simmons and Kareem Jackson, and a rotating cast of second and nickel cornerbacks, including (but not limited to) Isaac Yiadom, Davontae Harris, Duke Dawson, and Will Parks. Harris, who did his best work in years past as a slot defender, often found himself matched up against Tyreek Hill, DeAndre Hopkins, or Odell Beckham while the safeties provided support for the cornerback randos. Many of the assignments were just too much for Harris, who allowed 12.4 yards per pass when covering opponent's top wideouts. As a result, the Broncos ranked 26th in DVOA against top receivers but did a fine job shutting down just about everyone else. Harris is gone, but newcomer A.J. Bouye, rookie Michael Ojemudia, and returnee Bryce Callahan should fill the void and relegate Yiadom, Dawson, and others to dime/reserve roles or the waiver wire. Callahan missed all of last season with complications from foot surgery, but he was an effective nickelback for the Bears who should fill Harris' traditional slot role. Bouye's play in Jacksonville slipped from its 2016-2017 peak, but like many former Jaguars, he may benefit from a move to an organization which does not actively antagonize its best players. He may be better suited for No. 1 receiver duties at this point in his career than Harris was. Ojemudia was the standout of a weak cornerback crop at the Senior Bowl: a big, physical corner/safety tweener from Iowa who will give the Broncos better matchup options. Like other Broncos units, the secondary has many questions but high upside, whereas in past seasons it only had the former.

Special Teams

Year	DVOA	Rank	FG/XP	Rank	Net Kick	Rank	Kick Ret	Rank	Net Punt	Rank	Punt Ret	Rank	Hidden	Rank
2017	-7.4%	30	-10.3	29	-9.8	31	-3.6	24	-8.8	26	-4.5	27	-2.6	15
2018	-4.2%	31	0.3	15	-1.4	21	-6.4	32	-9.3	28	-4.3	27	11.4	4
2019	-1.9%	24	4.5	8	-4.0	26	3.3	8	-11.9	31	-1.4	17	-0.5	18

Rookie KJ Hamler will compete with journeyman Dionte Spencer for the return chores. Hamler's return stats at Penn State are nothing special—he averaged 6.0 yards per return on 37 punts and 23.5 yards per return on 44 kickoffs across two seasons—but he has lots of college experience as a return man, plus the jitterbug traits teams look for in a punt returner. The 28-year-old, 170-ish pound Spencer was a star return man and productive receiver in the CFL for several years before winning the Broncos return chores last year and performing fairly well. Hamler has youth and more offensive utility on his side, so barring a case of fumblitis, he should win the job. ◥ Kicker Brandon McManus' touchback rate increased from 57.5% in 2018 to 76.4% last year, the sixth-best rate in the NFL and the highest of McManus' career. McManus was also perfect inside 40 yards (15-of-15, though with one missed extra point) for the second straight season. Long kickoffs and reliable short field goals will keep a kicker in the league a long time, no matter how his numbers on longer field goal attempts fluctuate. ◥ Punter Colby Wadman was just 27th in average gross punt distance, an unacceptable performance at altitude. He has been replaced by free-agent signing Sam Martin, formerly of Detroit, who our metrics scored as average in gross punt value last season and a few points above average the season before.

Detroit Lions

2019 Record: 3-12-1	**Total DVOA:** -12.0% (25th)	**2020 Mean Projection:** 8.0 wins	**On the Clock (0-4):** 9%
Pythagorean Wins: 5.9 (24th)	**Offense:** -2.8% (18th)	**Postseason Odds:** 43.2%	**Mediocrity (5-7):** 33%
Snap-Weighted Age: 26.3 (20th)	**Defense:** 10.7% (28th)	**Super Bowl Odds:** 4.5%	**Playoff Contender (8-10):** 40%
Average Opponent: 1.3% (11st)	**Special Teams:** 1.4% (10th)	**Proj. Avg. Opponent:** -1.1% (26th)	**Super Bowl Contender (11+):** 18%

2019: Preseason FO favorite Detroit stumbles to its worst season in a decade.

2020: This time we mean it. The Lions will contend, if Matt Patricia can get out of their way.

Rejoice, Detroit Lions fans!

It has been over a generation since the boys in Honolulu Blue have hoisted a divisional title, back in the days of Barry Sanders and Pat Swilling. Well, bust out your flannel shirts and crank Nirvana's *Unplugged*, because the glory days of the '90s are here once again. The always infallible and never incorrect Football Outsiders predictions have the Lions ending up with the most projected wins in the division, and will be rolling into the playoffs…

… Wait, why are you looking at us like that?

Oh, right. Last season's final projections *also* had the Lions with the most projected wins in the division. They missed it by *just* that much, finishing with their worst record since 2009 and only 9.5 games out of first place. That would be a promising season for the Detroit Tigers, perhaps, but it's the furthest the Lions have been from a division title since Jim Schwartz's 2009 squad finished a full 10 games behind Brett Favre and the Vikings. It's fair to be at least a little skeptical of any projection which says that no, this time, it will be different!

So this is where the caveats come in. Most importantly, last year's mean projection was just 8.3 wins, and this year's is even lower than that. We are not projecting the Lions to suddenly become world-beaters, storming their way through the season as a dominant team. Instead, our mean projections have the Lions as a below-average offense and an average defense; a world of mediocrity. Just like last season, the Lions have the most projected wins in the NFC North more because of a lack of faith in the other teams in the division, rather than a sudden love of Honolulu Blue. While the Lions have been busy adding talent this offseason, their three divisional rivals have been stuck in neutral, or worse. To butcher a phrase, the Lions don't have to outrun the rest of the NFC to win their division; they just need to outrun the Bears (and the Vikings, and the Packers).

Then again, all that held true last year as well. Every year, when we publish our final projections, we make sure to note that a few of them will look strange to you. A few of them look strange to *us*. The Lions were Exhibit A last season, and we were down on them in our subjective staff predictions compared to the division-leading statistical forecast. That being said, Vegas had their over/under at 6.5 wins, but we thought that their improvement would get them comfortably past that mark, with an efficient offense and a "semi-competent" defense in the second year of the Matt Patricia era. A 7-9, possibly even 8-8 record

seemed like obtainable goals, even if "divisional favorites" seemed like an overreach. In the end, of course, they couldn't even reach *those* heights, and as such, Patricia and general manager Bob Quinn are justly on the hot seat entering 2020. So we can understand why going back to the well a second time would bring with it well-deserved skepticism from Detroiters.

However, it's important to remember that while the Lions were undeniably bad last season, they were also unlucky. They had six estimated wins in 2019, which is our metric of the number of games a team should have won if it had faced an average schedule of opponents and had average luck, emphasizing DVOA in the most important specific situations (i.e., red zone defense, first-quarter offense, performance in the second half of close games). While Detroit still had the lowest estimated win total in the division last season, that two-and-a-half-game difference plays a huge role in how you perceive the Lions' 2019 season; 6-10 is still disappointing, but a lot more promising than 3-12-1. It's not just estimated wins, either—the Lions had 5.9 Pythagorean wins, which is based solely on points scored and allowed. They finished a dreadful 3-8-1 in one-score games, a statistic that tends to revert to the mean over time. The Lions ranked 24th in adjusted games lost. They had poor fumble luck, recovering just four of 11 fumbles on offense. This is not to try to say that we were right, somehow, and that the Lions were an average team in disguise; you don't go 3-12-1 without being bad. But they weren't *quite* as bad as their record would suggest, and they're operating off of a higher floor than a cursory glance would indicate.

And then you have the splits. While Detroit's overall DVOA was very similar in 2018 and 2019, just rising from -13.8% to -12.0%, it was not evenly spaced throughout the year. Through the first nine weeks of the season, Detroit had a 5.1% offensive DVOA and a 38.7% passing DVOA, fourth-best in the league. That collapsed to -11.0% and -12.0%, respectively, over the last half of the season. That's the effect of Matthew Stafford fracturing his back and missing the last eight games of the season. You can see a similar split defensively. From Weeks 1 to 7, the Lions had a 1.9% defensive DVOA and a 6.8% pass defense DVOA—below average, but something you could live with behind a decent offense. After the Quandre Diggs trade, however, the Lions fell to a 16.3% defensive DVOA and a league-worst 39.0% pass defense DVOA. The Stafford/Diggs Lions were a bit unlucky to be sitting at 2-3-

2020 Lions Schedule

Week	Opp.	Week	Opp.	Week	Opp.
1	CHI	7	at ATL	13	at CHI
2	at GB	8	IND	14	GB
3	at ARI	9	at MIN	15	at TEN (Sat.)
4	NO	10	WAS	16	TB (Sat.)
5	BYE	11	at CAR	17	MIN
6	at JAX	12	HOU (Thu.)		

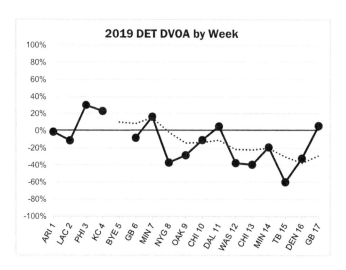

2019 DET DVOA by Week

1, but they were an average team very much in the wild-card race, at the very least. Losing your star quarterback and blowing up your defensive chemistry are not, it turns out, particularly positive events for your team.

So, there's your entry point into an optimistic view for 2020. Stafford will be back, better than ever. The defense has been retooled to best fit what the Lions want to do. They are unlikely to be as unlucky as they were a season ago. The rest of the division has stagnated or taken a step back. There is a path to a division title for Detroit, and our projections respond accordingly.

Now, let's dive into that and see where the logic holds up, and where it begins to break down.

Matt Patricia was hired for his defensive chops, but they've yet to actually show up on the field. Detroit has ranked 28th in defensive DVOA in each of the past two seasons, with a DVOA of 9.0% or worse in each of his two years. The last time the Lions had a defensive DVOA that bad in consecutive seasons was 2008 and 2009 as Jim Schwartz's team imploded—we keep coming back to say that Patricia's team is the worst the Lions have been in a decade, don't we? We were supposed to see Patricia's defensive vision come to fruition in 2019. His first season was a write-off, as the Lions didn't have nearly the talent needed to make Patricia's unique, multiple-front defense really go. In came three ex-Patriots in Trey Flowers, Justin Coleman, and Rashaan Melvin, as well as two defensive draft picks in the first three rounds. With that not quite paying dividends last year, Patricia has adjusted his strategy to … bring in three ex-Patriots in Jamie Collins, Duron Harmon, and Danny Shelton, as well as two defensive draft picks in the first three rounds. Well, at least there's consistency in the plan.

This did not work last season, not even in the early part of the year when the defense was merely below average. The Lions' pressure rate ranked 28th in the league and improved from the previous year by a grand total of 0.5%. While Flowers himself had a very good season, the idea was that he would unlock the rest of the front. Instead, the pass rush at the other end stayed more or less constant—Devon Kennard and Romeo Okwara went from a combined 50.5 pressures in 2018 to 57.0 in 2019—while the interior of the line collapsed. Snacks Harrison had given the line a boost at the end of 2018, but he was ineffective all throughout last season, out of shape and physically under par. Mike Daniels and A'Shawn Robinson massively underperformed as well. Patricia's defenses really are built from the middle out—they don't blitz much and rely on the line to be self-sufficient. The more the defensive line can handle its assignments without needing extra

help, the more creative Patricia can be with formations and packages and fronts; when they're regularly losing battles, that limits what he can do. The hope is by bringing in Shelton (who knows how to play this defense from his time in New England) and adding new fresh blood in Julian Okwara, the defensive front will have the talent needed to actually achieve Patricia's vision. Second time's the charm?

Self-sufficiency is the watchword in the secondary as well. The Lions copied the Patriots model in coverage. Both teams finished first or second in man coverage and last or second-to-last in keeping cornerbacks on specific sides. Both teams finished in the top five in plays with six or more defensive backs on the field. The idea is to flood the field with a stable of defensive backs who can win in man coverage. The key difference between the Patriots and Lions, of course, is that the Patriots were good at this and the Lions were not. The Lions had a DVOA of 46.7% when defending passes in man coverage, 26th in the league, and significantly worse than the league average of 27.9%. They were actually better when dropping into a zone (31.5% DVOA). And yes, it should be noted once again that the Lions were specifically better in man when Diggs was still on the roster, at 23.2% DVOA, 13th in the league.

We keep saying "Quandre Diggs was traded" like it was just one of those things that happens—it snowed today, Matthew Stafford hurt his back, Quandre Diggs was traded. But no, this was an active decision made by Patricia and Quinn that has never fully been explained. Diggs has said that the trade was a move to control the locker room, and that does fit the pattern. Patricia is leaving a string of disgruntled defenders in his wake, with a veritable smorgasbord of *Survivor* elimination-esque confessionals trashing him. From Diggs ("I think it was more of just a control thing") to Robert Ayers ("Let's just say me and the head coach didn't agree") to Darius Slay ("I felt there was no mutual respect as a man"), you can create quite a greatest hits collection from these post-release interviews. That's not to say that every ex-Lion has something to say, but there's a growing track record there. The culture Patricia is trying to create in his locker room has not gone over well with some of his key players, and where talent has clashed with culture, culture has won out.

It's superficial to say that trading Diggs away is the sole reason for the Lions' defensive collapse, though it should be noted that the Seahawks' defense saw a corresponding upgrade once Diggs arrived. No one safety is responsible for a drop-off as large as we saw from Detroit last season, especially one that has a history of missed tackles. But it's worth noting that Lions players were *not* happy with the move—Diggs was a team captain, voted by the players. Slay notably avoided the locker room when reporters were allowed in after the trade and refused to talk to ex-defensive coordinator Paul Pasqualoni for two weeks after the move. He wasn't the only one disgruntled, either; the locker room was very public on Twitter trying to understand and deal with the ramifications of the trade. If your veterans are upset and checking out of the season in mid-October, it has to be hard to get the motivation up to play week in and week out.

And remember, the Lions had just signed Diggs to a contract extension; he ended up playing six games on that extension before the trade. There is a perfectly logical argument that Diggs was eventually expendable; that the presence of Tracy Walker and Will Harris meant that the future of the position was with players Patricia had acquired and not with a holdover from the old regime. That doesn't explain the timing of the trade, or making the trade so soon after giving him a contract extension, or using the fifth-round pick from the trade to bring in a different veteran safety in Duron Harmon. Nor does it explain why the Lions' defensive philosophy remained the same throughout the season, even as the results started taking an abrupt turn for the worse.

Whether you blame it on Diggs; or a sour locker room; or opponents figuring out Patricia's schemes; or second-half injuries to players such as Tracy Walker, A'Shawn Robinson, and Rashaan Melvin; or just the random variation that happens in a 16-game season, the Lions defense was significantly worse down the stretch. And yet, watching the Lions defensive philosophy remained the same, whether you were watching them in Week 2 or Week 16. It didn't matter whether Pasqualoni or Patricia was making play calls—and there is intentional confusion on the part of the Lions as to just how much Patricia was doing and when—the Lions defense stubbornly stuck to its base ideas, with unimaginative and predictable play calling. Forget in-game adjustments, it seemed like the Lions struggled to make in-season adjustments. The much-hyped defensive line was not getting it done at the point of attack, but Patricia did not deviate and call more blitzes, bringing no help to his overmatched front unit. The Lions sent just three pass-rushers more often than any other team in the league, and only rushed five or more 11% of the time, dead last. The scheme wasn't fit to the players: Damon Harrison was playing out of position, the non-Slay cornerbacks were unable to successfully cover receivers one-on-one, and the linebackers simply looked overwhelmed trying to handle the myriad of different roles Patricia's defense requires out of them.

Is that the fault of a lack of players fit for the system? Or is it a fault of the coaching staff trying to fit square pegs into round holes? The honest answer is a little from Column A and a little from Column B. Patricia's defense would look better if he had New England's talent to run it with, but you would think a purported defensive guru and student of Bill Belichick would be a little more apt at getting the very best out of his players. Fair or not, Patricia's also fighting against the less-than-stellar reputation ex-Belichick assistants have had in the NFL. Ex-Patriots assistants have now coached 22 seasons and put up just four years of positive DVOA; Belichick's former defensive assistants are just two for 14 in above-average defenses as head coaches. Right or wrong, there's a sense that the Patriot way does not work without Belichick at the helm, and the assistants who go out there and live off that success are quickly revealed to be less than ready to do the job.

All that being said, there is no quicker cure for a defense than adding boatloads of players. The old maxim is that while you can hide weaknesses on offense with scheme, you need raw talent on defense to be competitive. There's some evidence supporting that—early-round draft picks tend to have a more predictable immediate impact on defense, and there's a stronger correlation between blue-chip recruits and college success on defense rather than offense. Our projection system is neutral on whether talent helps more on defense than on offense, but it certainly gives the Lions credit for bringing in so many new players with strong track records. Just because this strategy didn't work last season doesn't mean that it won't work in 2020.

Duron Harmon is an upgrade over Quandre Diggs, at least in Patricia's system. While both players are roughly equally skilled in coverage, Harmon is both more willing and more adept in the run game; he has higher run stop rates and fewer missed tackles than Diggs. He's more of a jack-of-all-trades than Diggs was, a key point in the big nickel system Patricia loves using. There would be a lot less concern in Detroit had the Lions just done a one-for-one trade there rather than holding on to an extra fifth-round draft pick for four months. Jamie Collins had a career renaissance in his return to New England and a return to his old responsibilities after being lost in Cleveland. His experience should be a big boost for the middle of the defense; couple him with second-year improvement from Jahlani Tavai and you have the makings of a solid linebacker corps. Desmond Trufant's days as a shutdown corner are behind him, but he is a veteran of the sort of man-to-man schemes Patricia wants to run. While Snacks Harrison is a better player than Danny Shelton, he's a nose tackle, not a 3-tech. Shelton is a more natural fit at the role Harrison was asked to play in Detroit. Jeff Okudah is the best cornerback prospect in years; it's almost impossible to find a significant flaw in his game. Julian Okwara had the sixth-highest SackSEER rating in this year's draft class. There's a lot to like here.

There's plenty of room for optimism, as long as you keep your expectations somewhat realistic. Some people point to Trey Flowers' 7.0 sacks and call him a bust, but Flowers actually set a career high in quarterback pressures; he just didn't have help from the rest of his line to mop up his pressures. Flowers is joined by the returning Walker and Coleman, and when you add in all that new talent, you get what looks like, on paper, a very solid unit. The Lions could feature as many as six new starters, and at least four of them are direct upgrades from last year's opening day starter at the position. Yes, there might be extended growing pains thanks to the shortened offseason, but that's where bringing in veterans of the scheme comes in handy; the learning curve is shortened. Yes, there are still question marks in the secondary, as Okudah might be a year away from being a tippy-top guy and Trufant might be a year or two past his best buy date, but they'll be helped out significantly by that improved defensive front. Whether the improvement will come from the addition of players who know and can execute Patricia's scheme, or it's because there's just so much talent there that they can succeed despite their coach is, at some level, immaterial—this should be a much-improved unit. There are no excuses for the Lions not to have their best defense since the early Teryl Austin days—which admittedly would sound more impressive if Austin hadn't been fired to make way for Patricia, but hey, you have to crawl before you can walk.

As for the offense, it's a shame Matthew Stafford ended up missing half the season. His 28.8% DVOA was the highwater mark of his career, and very nearly beat out his career-best eight-game streak (31.9% in Weeks 8 to 15 of 2017). While we're not projecting Stafford to hit quite those highs again in 2020, it's pretty clear that Stafford took very well to Darrell Bevell's offense right off the bat. Stafford's average depth of target skyrocketed, going from 7.2 in 2018 to 11.1 last season, highest in the NFL. The book on Stafford has always been that while he excels as a deep-ball thrower, his processing in the short game isn't always up to par. While previous coordinators have tried to give Stafford more options underneath to work with, Bevell more or less decided to build the plane out of the black box.

While Stafford was healthy, the Lions dialed up 79 deep shots, 33 on first down—both the most in the league over that time span. It's not that they were all successful; Detroit actually ranked higher on short passes (fourth with a 45.0% DVOA) than on deep passes (13th at 110.6%). Note that, yes, the Lions' DVOA was higher on deep passes than short passes even though the rank was lower. That's partially selection bias (if the deep route isn't open, you generally check down rather than throwing into coverage), but it also goes to show you the benefit of the overall philosophy of letting Stafford and his big arm rip; even his short passes travelled an average of 5.1 yards in the air, and Next Gen Stats had him leading the league in aggressiveness (the percentage of throws into tight windows, where a defender is within 1 yard or fewer of the intended receiver), rising from 16.0% in 2018 to 23.4% last season. It was exciting and it was dynamic and it produced tons of big plays—and it was effective, too. That 38.7% team passing DVOA during Stafford's starts would have been the best passing DVOA ever recorded for Detroit. Stafford was clicking on the deep ball with the old guard in Kenny Golladay and Marvin Jones; he was finding a rapport in the shorter passing game with newcomers Danny Amendola and T.J. Hockenson. And then he got hurt, because of course he did, because the Lions can't have nice things.

That's not to say that a healthy Stafford would have necessarily maintained that pace throughout the season; while Bevell's passing attack played to his strengths, he has never really been a top-five quarterback like he was in 2019 and some regression to the mean was likely inevitable. Nor was the offense perfect.

Bevell does love his running attack to extremes, even when it's less effective than passing. The Lions ranked 29th with a -25.5% rushing DVOA in the weeks Stafford was healthy, and yet they still rushed the ball 54% of the time on situation-neutral first downs, ninth-most in the league. The fear would be that taking D'Andre Swift in the second round—not to mention a second running back later, and two guards—leads to a significant increase in run usage and only a moderate increase in rushing DVOA, playing into Bevell's worst traits.

Still, even if the healthy offense is less efficient in 2020, and Stafford is closer to his career averages than 2020's peak, that's bound to be better than the offense that cratered under Jeff Driskel and David Blough. Take an already very bad rushing game, take away the quarterback and replace him with sub-replacement level players, and you get poor results. Projecting the 2020 offense has to be more about what Detroit did in September and October and not about how they stumbled to close out the year.

There are concerns, for sure. Back injuries can linger, so it's unclear how Stafford will be able to come back. Graham Glasgow and Rick Wagner are gone, so the Lions will need two new starters on the right side of an already questionable offensive line—and note that Stafford and the Lions' offense dropped 5.6 yards per play when under pressure in the first half of 2019, significantly more than league average. The Lions have a running back committee to work out between Swift, Kerryon Johnson, and Bo Scarbrough, and it may take some time to figure out where each back is best used. The Lions have roughly zero depth at wideout, so if Golladay, Jones, or Amendola goes down, there are big question marks as to who would replace them. There are enough concerns to keep our model from projecting the Lions to be one of the better offenses in the league, but there's enough potential there to make dreams of a top-half, or even top-10 offense, not entirely out of the question.

And that's the thing—the Lions' don't *need* to have a league-best offense or a league-best defense in order to return to the postseason. If we're right that their divisional rivals are in one state of floundering or another, sheer competence on both sides of the ball might be all Detroit needs to reach the postseason for the first time since 2016. Then again, we said this last year, almost verbatim. Our closing paragraph in *Football Outsiders Almanac 2018* claimed that "a solid, efficient offense and a semi-competent defense could make Detroit a more complete team than their peers. Coming off a down season in a chaotic division, a dose of stability is just what the Lions need now and moving forward." We repeat that sentiment once again here, noting that yet another influx of defensive talent and the return of a healthy Stafford should give the Lions their best chance yet of recapturing a division title. The Lions have an argument for the best roster, top-to-bottom, in the division, so it's fair for our projections to put them atop the flawed NFC North. The $64,000 question is whether this coaching staff can turn that on-paper talent into on-field results. If they can't, rest assured that a different administration will get a crack at it in 2021.

Bryan Knowles

2019 Lions Stats by Week

Wk	vs.	W-L	PF	PA	YDF	YDA	TO	Total	Off	Def	ST
1	at ARI	T	27	27	477	387	-1	-1%	-4%	-20%	-17%
2	LAC	W	13	10	339	424	0	-11%	5%	5%	-11%
3	at PHI	W	27	24	287	373	+2	30%	3%	-7%	20%
4	KC	L	30	34	447	438	+1	23%	9%	-3%	12%
5	BYE										
6	at GB	L	22	23	299	447	+3	-8%	-29%	-1%	20%
7	MIN	L	30	42	433	504	-1	17%	54%	38%	0%
8	NYG	W	31	26	375	370	-1	-37%	-11%	25%	-1%
9	at OAK	L	24	31	473	450	-2	-28%	6%	25%	-9%
10	at CHI	L	13	20	357	226	-1	-11%	-6%	15%	11%
11	DAL	L	27	35	312	509	+1	5%	18%	18%	5%
12	at WAS	L	16	19	364	230	-2	-37%	-39%	-25%	-23%
13	CHI	L	20	24	364	419	0	-39%	3%	38%	-4%
14	at MIN	L	7	20	231	354	-2	-19%	-14%	-5%	-10%
15	TB	L	17	38	295	495	-2	-60%	-30%	36%	6%
16	at DEN	L	17	27	191	348	0	-32%	-11%	39%	18%
17	GB	L	20	23	305	432	0	6%	-4%	-4%	5%

Trends and Splits

	Offense	Rank	Defense	Rank
Total DVOA	-2.8%	18	10.7%	28
Unadjusted VOA	-5.0%	20	11.2%	28
Weighted Trend	-6.0%	21	15.8%	30
Variance	4.7%	6	4.5%	5
Average Opponent	-0.6%	14	1.2%	11
Passing	13.9%	15	26.1%	29
Rushing	-13.6%	27	-9.3%	17
First Down	-14.0%	27	9.9%	25
Second Down	4.3%	13	4.2%	19
Third Down	7.2%	11	23.6%	28
First Half	2.0%	13	9.5%	26
Second Half	-7.6%	21	11.9%	27
Red Zone	-13.8%	21	-1.5%	16
Late and Close	-11.8%	23	12.4%	28

Five-Year Performance

Year	W-L	Pyth W	Est W	PF	PA	TO	Total	Rk	Off	Rk	Def	Rk	ST	Rk	Off AGL	Rk	Def AGL	Rk	Off Age	Rk	Def Age	Rk	ST Age	Rk
2015	7-9	6.9	7.4	358	400	-6	1.2%	13	1.8%	13	1.6%	16	1.0%	13	22.8	7	59.4	30	26.2	24	27.3	6	26.2	15
2016	9-7	7.7	5.3	346	358	-1	-15.6%	27	-0.6%	15	18.5%	32	3.5%	6	54.5	27	35.6	14	26.2	25	26.4	18	25.9	21
2017	9-7	8.9	8.4	410	376	+10	5.5%	12	4.4%	12	4.0%	19	5.1%	5	27.0	11	44.3	23	26.6	21	26.0	21	26.0	9
2018	6-10	7.0	6.1	324	360	-5	-15.2%	26	-5.2%	23	9.0%	28	-0.9%	20	40.9	19	33.9	17	26.8	15	26.2	17	26.5	8
2019	3-12-1	5.9	6.0	341	423	-5	-12.0%	25	-2.8%	18	10.7%	28	1.4%	10	56.5	29	31.3	17	26.6	20	26.3	16	25.9	14

2019 Performance Based on Most Common Personnel Groups

DET Offense					DET Offense vs. Opponents					DET Defense					DET Defense vs. Opponents			
Pers	Freq	Yds	DVOA	Run%	Pers	Freq	Yds	DVOA	Run%	Pers	Freq	Yds	DVOA		Pers	Freq	Yds	DVOA
11	61%	5.7	2.0%	26%	Base	28%	5.3	-3.4%	58%	Base	19%	5.7	15.1%		11	50%	6.3	10.2%
12	16%	5.8	18.5%	50%	Nickel	61%	5.4	-0.2%	30%	Nickel	46%	5.9	6.4%		12	17%	5.7	-1.8%
21	10%	5.7	-5.5%	61%	Dime+	10%	7.7	27.7%	12%	Dime+	34%	6.3	11.0%		21	12%	5.3	14.5%
22	3%	6.2	-21.9%	72%	Goal Line	1%	0.6	28.8%	75%	Goal Line	1%	6.8	42.7%		10	9%	6.4	22.3%
13	3%	4.5	1.3%	50%											22	3%	5.3	1.3%
612	2%	5.4	-10.2%	81%											13	3%	7.3	18.1%
															611	3%	4.7	-9.9%

Strategic Tendencies

Run/Pass		Rk	Formation		Rk	Pass Rush		Rk	Secondary		Rk	Strategy		Rk
Runs, first half	40%	7	Form: Single Back	76%	24	Rush 3	27.0%	1	4 DB	19%	27	Play Action	24%	17
Runs, first down	49%	14	Form: Empty Back	11%	6	Rush 4	60.9%	21	5 DB	46%	26	Offensive Motion	38%	15
Runs, second-long	34%	6	Form: Multi Back	14%	10	Rush 5	9.0%	32	6+ DB	34%	5	Avg Box (Off)	6.47	25
Runs, power sit.	44%	29	Pers: 3+ WR	64%	19	Rush 6+	3.1%	25	Man Coverage	55%	1	Avg Box (Def)	6.20	32
Runs, behind 2H	28%	16	Pers: 2+ TE/6+ OL	26%	18	Edge Rusher Sacks	55.4%	16	CB by Sides	52%	32	Offensive Pace	30.12	12
Pass, ahead 2H	58%	1	Pers: 6+ OL	2%	18	Interior DL Sacks	16.1%	25	S/CB Cover Ratio	25%	20	Defensive Pace	29.32	2
Run-Pass Options	5%	16	Shotgun/Pistol	61%	22	Second Level Sacks	28.6%	7	DB Blitz	6%	30	Go for it on 4th	0.93	29

The Lions passed more than any other offense when they were ahead in the second half, a dramatic change from 2018 when they ranked 24th at just 22% passes when ahead in the second half. ❧ Detroit was fourth with 11.7% of pass plays going max protect (seven or more blockers with at least two more blockers than pass-rushers). ❧ The Lions offense was dead last with just 91 broken tackles and broken tackles on only 8.1% of plays. ❧ Detroit ranked eighth in DVOA against passes to the offensive left but 31st against passes to the offensive right, a weird split considering that the Lions played their cornerbacks on specific sides less than any other defense. ❧ Man coverage means opponents throw deep more often. The three teams that played the most man coverage—Detroit, Miami, and New England—were also the three defenses that faced the highest rate of deep passes (16 or more yards through the air). ❧ Not only did the Lions send only three pass-rushers more often than any other defense, they also were at their best when sending only three pass-rushers: 9.1% DVOA with three, 37.8% DVOA with four, and 34.7% DVOA when blitzing. This doesn't seem to be a permanent tendency, however, as in 2018 the Lions were much worse when sending only three pass-rushers.

Passing

Player	DYAR	DVOA	Plays	NtYds	Avg	YAC	C%	TD	Int
M.Stafford	776	28.8%	307	2360	7.7	4.8	64.7%	19	5
D.Blough	-101	-19.5%	188	880	4.7	3.5	54.0%	4	5
J.Driskel*	-91	-24.2%	114	639	5.6	4.7	60.2%	4	4
C.Daniel	-9	-13.2%	71	387	5.5	3.0	70.3%	3	2

Rushing

Player	DYAR	DVOA	Plays	Yds	Avg	TD	Fum	Suc
K.Johnson	-26	-13.7%	113	403	3.6	3	1	52%
B.Scarbrough	10	-5.7%	89	377	4.2	1	1	56%
T.Johnson	28	3.5%	63	273	4.3	0	0	44%
J.McKissic*	23	6.5%	38	205	5.4	0	0	47%
J.Driskel*	52	37.0%	21	152	7.2	1	0	-
C.Anderson*	-23	-42.6%	16	43	2.7	0	0	38%
M.Stafford	-19	-40.1%	14	63	4.5	0	2	-
T.Carson*	-4	-18.0%	12	34	2.8	0	0	25%
P.Perkins*	-6	-21.3%	12	29	2.4	0	0	25%
W.Hills	26	37.4%	10	21	2.1	2	0	50%
D.Blough	2	-7.7%	7	32	4.6	0	1	-
C.Daniel	-10	-38.3%	6	6	1.0	0	0	-

Receiving

Player	DYAR	DVOA	Plays	Ctch	Yds	Y/C	YAC	TD	C%
K.Golladay	279	18.0%	116	65	1190	18.3	4.7	11	56%
D.Amendola	18	-10.2%	97	62	678	10.9	3.3	1	64%
M.Jones	180	11.8%	91	62	779	12.6	1.7	9	68%
M.Hall	98	108.2%	11	7	261	37.3	5.1	1	64%
C.Lacy	-3	-16.5%	10	3	60	20.0	3.0	0	30%
G.Allison	-98	-35.8%	55	34	287	8.4	3.2	2	62%
T.Hockenson	-41	-18.1%	59	32	367	11.5	6.3	2	54%
L.Thomas*	-21	-18.9%	28	16	173	10.8	4.8	1	57%
J.James	-28	-23.9%	27	16	142	8.9	4.1	0	59%
J.McKissic*	12	-8.2%	42	34	233	6.9	7.0	1	81%
T.Johnson	-45	-40.2%	31	24	109	4.5	3.9	0	77%
K.Johnson	39	29.3%	15	10	127	12.7	11.6	1	67%
N.Bawden	-20	-63.1%	6	4	17	4.3	5.0	0	67%

Offensive Line

Player	Pos	Age	GS	Snaps	Pen	Sk	Pass	Run	Player	Pos	Age	GS	Snaps	Pen	Sk	Pass	Run
Taylor Decker	LT	27	15/15	1039	10	5.3	24	8	Rick Wagner*	RT	31	12/12	772	3	3.5	17	11
Frank Ragnow	C	24	15/15	1018	5	1.0	9	10	Kenny Wiggins	LG/RG	32	14/3	449	2	1.5	6	3
Graham Glasgow*	RG	28	15/15	886	3	0.0	11	5	Tyrell Crosby	RT	25	16/5	403	7	1.3	18	2
Joe Dahl	LG	27	13/13	820	2	2.3	8	5	Halapoulivaati Vaitai	RT	27	16/3	481	5	3.0	15	5

Year	Yards	ALY	Rank	Power	Rank	Stuff	Rank	2nd Lev	Rank	Open Field	Rank	Sacks	ASR	Rank	Press	Rank	F-Start	Cont.
2017	3.31	3.16	32	45%	32	27%	31	0.94	29	0.52	23	47	7.5%	21	30.6%	15	10	16
2018	4.10	4.14	20	68%	14	22%	27	1.18	22	0.74	23	41	6.3%	12	27.0%	9	10	28
2019	3.94	4.21	20	64%	19	18%	12	1.12	22	0.54	25	43	7.2%	19	30.2%	18	16	25
2019 ALY by direction:		Left End 3.89 (18)			Left Tackle: 5.57 (2)			Mid/Guard: 4.43 (16)			Right Tackle: 3.16 (27)			Right End: 3.23 (26)				

While the offensive line has improved since Patricia took over, the Lions haven't ranked above average in adjusted line yards since 2013, and they have been above average in adjusted sack rate just once in the past six years. With a blown block every 7.2 snaps, you can see why the Lions used so much max protect. ❧ The weak part of the line in 2019 was right tackle, where Rick Wagner and Tyrell Crosby combined for 49 blown blocks. Wagner was cut and the Lions brought ex-Eagle Halapoulivaati Vaitai in to fill the void. Vaitai has only started 20 games in four seasons in the league, but still received a massive five-year deal to nail down the right side. When he has played, he has looked worth the money, especially carving out paths in the running game—but *caveat emptor* on small sample sizes. ● It's slightly more surprising that Detroit let Graham Glasgow walk in free agency, but the Lions chose to spend their big bucks on the outside rather than the interior. That makes both guard spots question marks entering 2020. ● There are questions about Joe Dahl's long-term health after injuring his back in December, but he was clearly the better part of the guard rotation last season. Assuming Dahl is healthy, Kenny Wiggins will be involved in a battle royal for the right guard position. Anything but another rotation, please. ● Third-round pick Jonah Jackson (Ohio State) will also be part of that battle for a starting role. Jackson's missing the sort of power you would love in an interior lineman, but he makes up for it with smooth footwork and impeccable technique, especially in pass protection. The more the Lions pass, the better a fit Jackson will be. ● Frank Ragnow still struggled a bit with consistency in Year 2, ranking 25th among centers in blown blocks after ranking 29th at left guard as a rookie. That being said, he's terrific when he's on, as he has quickly become one of the top run-blocking interior linemen in the league. If he can get rid of the one or two plays a game where he whiffs, you can remove "one of" from that description. ● Thirty-two blown blocks for Taylor Decker is not what you want to see out of someone coming up for a big contract extension, but it's worth noting that most of Decker's poor games were right at the beginning of the season, possibly due to a nagging back injury. A fully healthy and clean season would make Detroit a lot more comfortable finding room to re-sign Decker, who is playing on his fifth-year option in 2020. ● Fourth-round pick Logan Stenberg (Kentucky) might be too tall for his own good—at 6-foot-6, he struggles to get and stay low for leverage. That didn't hurt him in college, where he didn't allow a sack in his final two seasons, and he's got power to spare. He was nicknamed "Mr. Nasty" as a Wildcat due to a penchant for playing through (and occasionally after) the whistle. As long as that doesn't make him "Mr. Penalty Flag," he has some potential, depending on where the Lions want to go with their interior line rebuild.

Defensive Front

Defensive Line	Age	Pos	G	Snaps	Plays	TmPct	Rk	Stop	Dfts	BTkl	Runs	St%	Rk	RuYd	Rk	Sack	Hit	Hur	Dsrpt
					Overall							vs. Run					Pass Rush		
Damon Harrison*	32	DT	15	534	52	6.5%	21	40	7	8	45	76%	47	2.1	36	2.0	0	5	3
A'Shawn Robinson*	25	DT	13	532	43	6.2%	35	26	8	3	36	58%	92	3.1	88	1.5	0	11	2
John Atkins	28	DT	12	411	20	3.1%	90	10	1	5	20	50%	96	2.7	69	0.0	0	5	0
Mike Daniels*	31	DT	9	207	10	2.1%	--	9	3	1	7	86%	--	1.9	--	1.0	1	8	1
Kevin Strong	24	DT	8	174	6	1.4%	--	5	0	0	5	80%	--	2.4	--	0.0	0	3	1
Nicholas Williams	30	DT	16	540	44	5.3%	31	37	7	2	33	85%	14	2.5	58	6.0	4	9	2
Danny Shelton	27	DT	16	508	61	8.1%	5	43	6	3	56	68%	75	2.8	75	3.0	4	11	0

Edge Rushers	Age	Pos	G	Snaps	Plays	TmPct	Rk	Stop	Dfts	BTkl	Runs	St%	Rk	RuYd	Rk	Sack	Hit	Hur	Dsrpt
					Overall							vs. Run					Pass Rush		
Devon Kennard*	29	OLB	16	946	58	6.8%	17	39	12	8	44	61%	78	3.2	73	7.0	14	33	0
Trey Flowers	27	DE	15	716	51	6.4%	29	37	12	6	40	73%	52	2.8	55	7.0	15	47	2
Romeo Okwara	25	DE	14	611	28	3.8%	69	16	4	3	21	57%	79	3.3	78	1.5	9	24	0

Linebackers	Age	Pos	G	Snaps	Plays	TmPct	Rk	Stop	Dfts	BTkl	Runs	St%	Rk	RuYd	Rk	Sack	Hit	Hur	Tgts	Suc%	Rk	AdjYd	Rk	PD	Int
					Overall							vs. Run				Pass Rush				vs. Pass					
Jarrad Davis	26	MLB	11	661	63	10.8%	65	36	9	14	44	61%	38	3.7	34	2.0	4	14	21	33%	66	11.9	67	1	0
Christian Jones	29	OLB	13	617	53	7.7%	72	31	5	7	30	60%	42	4.1	51	2.0	2	7	20	50%	37	8.3	59	4	0
Jahlani Tavai	24	MLB	15	604	59	7.4%	67	33	9	8	42	62%	36	3.6	30	2.0	1	8	17	59%	12	6.5	38	2	1
Jalen Reeves-Maybin	25	OLB	16	300	24	2.8%	--	11	2	3	16	63%	--	3.1	--	0.0	1	3	13	46%	--	7.2	--	0	0
Jamie Collins	31	OLB	16	833	86	11.4%	34	60	29	16	47	77%	6	3.1	12	7.0	2	19	17	53%	28	5.5	21	7	3
Reggie Ragland	27	OLB	14	237	28	3.9%	--	17	5	4	15	73%	--	2.1	--	2.0	1	3	10	60%	--	3.9	--	0	0

Year	Yards	ALY	Rank	Power	Rank	Stuff	Rank	2nd Level	Rank	Open Field	Rank	Sacks	ASR	Rank	Press	Rank
2017	4.18	4.32	25	61%	11	17%	29	1.23	24	0.66	13	35	6.1%	22	28.1%	27
2018	4.68	4.47	20	52%	1	15%	28	1.20	14	1.10	26	43	8.1%	5	26.3%	29
2019	4.09	4.55	23	74%	28	12%	32	1.07	9	0.48	3	28	5.0%	31	26.8%	28
2019 ALY by direction:		Left End: 3.64 (9)			Left Tackle: 5.05 (28)			Mid/Guard: 4.71 (25)			Right Tackle: 4.32 (16)				Right End: 4.65 (19)	

The Lions haven't ranked above 27th in pressure rate since 2015, despite the head coaching switch from the offensive-minded Jim Caldwell to Patricia. ● One ex-Pat move that *did* pay off was importing Trey Flowers. Flowers was the first Lion to top 30 hurries, much less 40, since we moved to SIS charting in 2015. ● *Two brothers, both alike in pedigree / In fair Detroit, where we lay our scene / From off the edge provide new weaponry / As simple moves make passers' shirts unclean.* Romeo Okwara is joined by his brother, third-round pick Julian from Notre Dame. Julian projects as a better version of his brother—he has superior top-end speed and a powerful bull rush. Those traits didn't always show up on the field on Saturdays, he doesn't play the run, and a broken leg ended his 2019 season, so he dropped to third round. He'll be a situational pass-rusher this season, but it may take some time before he's ready for every-down action; remember, Romeo needed a couple seasons to become a regular contributor in the NFL. With that in mind, it's best to be patient and hold your horses on Julian's immediate development. *For never was a story with more woah / Then this of Julian and his Romeo.* ✎ It's notable that Danny Shelton set career highs in most counting stats last season, thriving as a starter in Bill Belichick's defense. That's not to say that 2019 was necessarily his best year. Some of those raw tackle and pressure numbers come from playing on an uber-talented Patriots unit; he was arguably a better player as a bright spot on some terrible Browns teams in his first couple seasons. His best-case scenario doesn't match the potential of a motivated Damon Harrison, who left the team in free agency. Then again, the Lions didn't see much of motivated Damon Harrison a year ago, so a more engaged Shelton might end up being an upgrade. ✎ A'Shawn Robinson's departure opens up a hole at 3-tech; between him and Harrison leaving, the Lions need to replace over 1,000 snaps on the interior of their line. The returning Da'Shawn Hand, ex-Bear Nick Williams, and John Atkins will all need to play more significant roles in 2020. ✎ Jamie Collins is all over the field, for good or ill. In New England last season, Collins' 29 defeats ranked third in the league behind only T.J. Watt (36) and Lavonte David (30). However, 20 of those defeats came in the first eight games of the regular season, with only nine in the final eight games. Collins is also one of only three linebackers to be charted with at least 15 broken tackles in both 2018 and 2019; Alec Ogletree and Joe Schobert are the other two. ✎ Stats can be misleading! Christian Jones' run stop rate improved from 44% to 60% last season. This is not because he suddenly became better at playing the run; quite the opposite. You only show up on the play-by-play sheet if you actually get into position to make a play. Those failed run tackles from 2018 ended up being plays where Jones wasn't anywhere near the ballcarrier in 2019. ✎ Jarrad Davis allowed 11.9 yards per pass attempt in coverage. That wasn't just worst among qualified linebackers in 2019; that's the worst mark recorded since Anthony Hitchens in 2015.

Defensive Secondary

| Secondary | Age | Pos | G | Snaps | Overall | | | | | | vs. Run | | | | | vs. Pass | | | | | | | | | |
					Plays	TmPct	Rk	Stop	Dfts	BTkl	Runs	St%	Rk	RuYd	Rk	Tgts	Tgt%	Rk	Dist	Suc%	Rk	AdjYd	Rk	PD	Int
Justin Coleman	27	CB	16	975	66	7.8%	40	27	13	5	6	67%	11	6.7	48	86	20.5%	36	11.8	50%	56	8.1	55	13	1
Rashaan Melvin*	31	CB	13	879	79	11.5%	19	27	9	4	18	56%	27	6.2	40	81	21.4%	28	13.7	47%	65	8.7	63	11	0
Darius Slay*	29	CB	14	871	59	7.9%	50	20	6	5	8	25%	72	12.6	83	76	20.3%	40	15.2	53%	42	7.8	47	13	2
Tracy Walker	25	FS	13	850	108	15.7%	10	40	14	13	50	48%	23	5.3	16	44	12.0%	12	12.9	43%	63	9.9	64	8	1
Tavon Wilson*	30	SS	16	848	97	11.4%	15	43	11	14	47	57%	7	4.3	7	30	8.2%	34	7.1	50%	38	6.9	27	5	0
Will Harris	25	SS	16	674	39	4.6%	--	16	6	8	14	43%	--	11.4	--	15	5.2%	--	13.0	53%	--	9.8	--	3	0
Amani Oruwariye	24	CB	9	217	21	4.4%	--	8	3	2	2	0%	--	12.5	--	18	19.3%	--	11.9	39%	--	9.7	--	3	2
Darryl Roberts	30	CB	13	727	67	10.2%	29	15	5	6	12	17%	80	10.0	76	64	22.2%	25	10.0	44%	72	7.2	35	6	1
Duron Harmon	29	SS	16	669	27	3.6%	73	10	6	4	9	44%	30	6.0	30	10	3.6%	72	14.8	60%	17	9.2	58	5	2
Desmond Trufant	30	CB	9	535	24	5.4%	85	12	8	7	4	75%	8	4.5	22	31	15.1%	78	13.2	39%	82	10.3	79	7	4
Jayron Kearse	26	FS	15	275	33	4.0%	--	18	6	2	14	57%	--	4.0	--	19	16.4%	--	11.9	74%	--	4.0	--	6	1

Year	Pass D Rank	vs. #1 WR	Rk	vs. #2 WR	Rk	vs. Other WR	Rk	WR Wide	Rk	WR Slot	Rk	vs. TE	Rk	vs. RB	Rk
2017	16	-25.6%	3	11.3%	22	5.8%	20	-5.0%	12	-2.5%	11	12.9%	26	-12.7%	8
2018	31	21.5%	32	19.4%	27	39.5%	32	19.3%	31	34.0%	31	19.4%	26	-6.6%	11
2019	29	-2.3%	13	22.0%	29	3.3%	19	-6.0%	17	13.2%	22	8.7%	24	24.6%	27

The Lions basically stapled Darius Slay to their opponent's top receiver in 2019. No team ran more man coverage than Detroit, and no team moved their corners around more than Detroit, as they ranked 32nd in keeping their corners to one side or the other. Losing Slay is a *wee* bit of a problem then, considering that Detroit ranked 13th against No. 1 wide receivers, and nearly at the bottom of the league against every other type. ✎ Who will take over Slay's role as top corner? To start the year, it might be Desmond Trufant. Trufant's days as a top cover corner are behind him; ranking 82nd out of 85 qualified corners in success rate is very concerning, and he hasn't had a success rate of over 50% since 2015. Trufant's seven years of experience and the loss of rookie minicamp might give Trufant the edge, at least at first, but Jeff Okudah should take the job by the end of the year, and possibly by the end of September. ✎ Okudah was nearly always the top athlete on the field in college and won't be too far behind the curve against NFL receivers. Finding flaws in Okudah's film is a game of picking nits; there's not a single area of his game that causes meaningful concern. You could argue that he could be a little quicker on route recognition, but that will come with experience. He should be one of the top corners in the game within a couple of years. ✎ Justin Coleman responded to being made the highest-paid slot corner in football with his worst performance in years. Context matters, though. Detroit's defense had a -0.3% DVOA when Coleman was targeted in Weeks 1 to 7. After Quandre Diggs left, that soared to 83.1%, indicating that at least part of Coleman's struggles came from the overall collapse of the Lions secondary last year. ◥ In New England, Duron Harmon came on the field as the third safety in their big nickel set, playing about 60% of their defensive snaps. In Detroit, he'll be expected to be an every-down player, going from pseudo-starter to full-fledged starter. He has certainly played well enough to earn the extra responsibilities and has been solid against the run when asked, so there shouldn't be too much concern about him having to handle a larger chunk of the work. ◥ Harmon's the single-high free safety in the Lions' big nickel scheme. Tracy Walker will be the Joker safety; playing closer to the line fits his skill set better than playing deep does, though Walker and Harmon can occasionally flop responsibilities to disguise coverages. That leaves Will Harris to fill the third safety role vacated by Tavon Wilson, which was the original idea for him before Diggs was traded. Adding Harmon should improve all three safety slots.

Special Teams

Year	DVOA	Rank	FG/XP	Rank	Net Kick	Rank	Kick Ret	Rank	Net Punt	Rank	Punt Ret	Rank	Hidden	Rank
2017	5.1%	5	7.3	8	5.8	5	-4.0	27	-1.5	20	17.9	1	6.4	6
2018	-0.9%	20	0.2	16	2.6	10	-0.7	14	-3.1	24	-3.5	25	20.0	2
2019	1.4%	10	4.5	9	-14.0	32	4.5	4	8.3	5	4.0	5	9.2	3

Ban the kickoff! No team was above average in all aspects of special teams in 2019, but the Lions would have pulled that feat off if the NFL had used the old AAF rules. Detroit's explicit strategy was to try to land kickoffs right around the goal line. As a result, they finished dead last in touchback percentage and allowed more kickoff return yards than any team in football. The strategy didn't work; their -14.0 kickoff points below average was by far the worst in the league. ◥ Most of the damage there was done by Matt Prater (-9.2 net kickoff points) instead of Sam Martin (-4.9); Martin had the worst *gross* kickoff value in the league but better results avoiding the long return. ◥ With Martin gone, expect second-year UDFA Jack Fox out of Rice to win the battle for the open punting job. Arryn Siposs is a five-year Aussie Rules veteran and has a fun rollout kick but has never handled kickoffs before. Fox's kickoff expertise gives him the upper hand. ◥ Primary returner Jamal Agnew is switching positions from cornerback to wide receiver. With only 21 defensive snaps last season, the writing was on the wall there. Agnew was fourth in kickoff return value and sixth in punt return value, so no matter which position meetings he's going to, he has a solid NFL role.

Green Bay Packers

2019 Record: 13-3	Total DVOA: 7.7% (10th)	2020 Mean Projection: 7.8 wins	On the Clock (0-4): 10%
Pythagorean Wins: 9.8 (9th)	Offense: 6.5% (8th)	Postseason Odds: 40.5%	Mediocrity (5-7): 35%
Snap-Weighted Age: 26.6 (12nd)	Defense: -1.1% (15th)	Super Bowl Odds: 4.2%	Playoff Contender (8-10): 39%
Average Opponent: -0.8% (17th)	Special Teams: 0.1% (18th)	Proj. Avg. Opponent: 0.5% (10th)	Super Bowl Contender (11+): 16%

2019: With the addition of a pair of Smiths, Green Bay started something they couldn't finish.

2020: Nothing's changed, I still Love you (only slightly less than I used to).

There are two different ways to view the Green Bay Packers' 2019 season.

With the glass half-full, it was a fantastic year—the most successful campaign since the Super Bowl XLV win back in 2010. It came as a huge relief after an offseason filed with nail-biting and concerns. Would Aaron Rodgers and Matt LaFleur be able to coexist, or would the frosty relationship between franchise quarterback and head coach continue under a new regime? Would LaFleur's faster and more versatile offense succeed where Mike McCarthy's couldn't? And was it really so strange to think a pair of Smiths could kickstart a defense that had fluctuated between bad and dreadful over the previous three seasons? What difference would Za'Darius and Preston make to a unit that hadn't ranked in the top 10 in pressure rate since 2015?

All these concerns were waylaid, the optimist will say, by the results on the field. The Packers hadn't won more than a dozen games since 2011 and hadn't earned a first-round bye since 2014. Sure, the season ended with a familiar refrain—the third loss in a conference championship game this decade. And sure, there were still some question marks and holes on the roster. But this was Year 1 of the LaFleur regime; he hadn't had enough time to fully turn the roster over from the McCarthy era or fully install his system. A 13-3 conference championship game loss as a preview for what the LaFleur Packers will look like when everything spins up to full speed sounds enticing. With plenty of draft capital and a decent amount of cap space at their disposal, LaFleur and Brian Gutekunst could make a few big splashes—a top receiving prospect here, a stud run defender there—and position the Packers as favorites in the NFC in 2020.

With the glass half-empty, calling the Packers a 13-3 team is significantly misrepresenting their actual performance a year ago. Teams with a 7.7% DVOA historically can be expected to go 9-7, maybe 10-6 if things bounce their way—good, but not first-round-bye good. In fact, the Packers ended up with the second-worst DVOA ever for a 13-3 team, just pipped to the line by Peyton Manning and the 1999 Colts (Table 1).

One common counterargument to a team overperforming its DVOA is that while a team may play at one level for the majority of a game, they can kick it into a higher gear in key moments. We can account for that in some ways with our estimated wins stat. We take into account not only offense,

defense, and special teams, but also consistency, red zone production, and performance in the second-half when the score is close—the most key moments of a game—and from there, estimate how many games a team "should" have won had they played an average schedule with average luck. The problem is, the Packers weren't breaking any records there, either. Both their offensive and defensive DVOA in the red zone were in the top 10, but only the bottom of the top 10. They ranked just 15th in late and close situations with a 3.3% DVOA and were 21st in variance.

As a result, they come out with 9.9 estimated wins. Again, that's better than what you would expect a team with their DVOA to do, but also a full 3.1 games below their actual production. That was the worst in the league in 2019, 23rd-worst in the DVOA era, and the worst since the 2016 Texans somehow turned a 29th-place DVOA finish into a 9-7 record.

Again, we need to stress that even if our advanced stats do not view the Packers to be as good as their record indicated, they were still a good team in 2019. After several years of irrelevancy, the Packers were a top-10 squad in LaFleur's first season. A good first season, showing significant steps forward, with obvious areas in which the team could improve? That's a solid foundation to build upon. With plenty of draft capital and a decent amount of cap space at their disposal, LaFleur and Gutekunst could shore up their roster with young, inexpensive players that LaFleur could mold into short-term rota-

Table 1. Worst 13-3 Teams of the DVOA Era, 1985-2019

Year	Team	DVOA	W-L Year N+1	DVOA Year N+1
1999	IND	4.0%	10-6	19.9%
2019	**GB**	**7.7%**	—	—
2012	ATL	9.1%	4-12	-10.4%
2009	SD	13.5%	9-7	15.4%
2001	CHI	15.8%	4-12	-12.5%
1999	TEN	15.9%	13-3	33.3%
2010	ATL	16.3%	10-6	13.9%
2001	PIT	17.3%	10-5-1	6.8%
2011	SF	18.6%	11-4-1	29.5%
1991	BUF	19.1%	11-5	16.0%

2020 Packers Schedule

Week	Opp.	Week	Opp.	Week	Opp.
1	at MIN	7	at HOU	13	PHI
2	DET	8	MIN	14	at DET
3	at NO	9	at SF (Thu.)	15	CAR (Sat.)
4	ATL (Mon.)	10	JAX	16	TEN
5	BYE	11	at IND	17	at CHI
6	at TB	12	CHI		

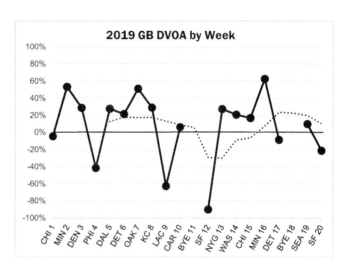

2019 GB DVOA by Week

tional pieces and long-term cornerstones, setting the Packers up to stay atop the NFC North through the early 2020s.

Two ways to look at the 2019 season. Two logical paths forward for the front office. Would Green Bay splurge and try to add the one or two difference-makers to get them over the top? Or would they concentrate on depth and building a long-term contender?

The Packers did not choose to do either of those things.

It is not overly surprising that the Packers didn't go on a free-agent shopping spree, with Rick Wagner, Christian Kirskey, and Devin Funchess the only notable names coming in. Green Bay splurged on their defense last season to good results, but you can't build a team solely on pricy free-agent deals. Breaking the bank for an Emmanuel Sanders or D.J. Reader wouldn't have really been feasible without leaving the team severely hamstrung in years to come. No, the baffling part of the Green Bay offseason came in a 48-hour period starting on April 23, when the Packers turned their top three draft picks into tight end Josiah Deguara, running back A.J. Dillon, and most shockingly, quarterback Jordan Love.

Let's try to understand what the Packers were doing here and see how that will affect their 2020 season.

Taking Jordan Love signals an impending end to the Aaron Rodgers era. From 1990 to 2019, there were 76 quarterbacks taken in the first round. Sixty-nine of them ended up starting at least one season, and that should tick up to 70 with Dwayne Haskins this year. The only exceptions in the 21st century are Johnny Manziel and Paxton Lynch. It's about as safe a bet as you can possibly make that Love will, sooner or later, get his chance under center at Lambeau.

Drafting a replacement for the quarterback who was just named to the All-Decade team is a hard sell, especially when Rodgers has made no indication that he plans to start winding his career down anytime soon. The Packers just gave Rodgers a four-year extension in 2018! Yes, he's turning 37 this season, but we have seen more and more quarterbacks play into the late 30s and even early 40s in recent years, in part because of some of the rule emphases that were put into place after Rodgers broke his collarbone in 2017. We've seen players such as Tom Brady, Drew Brees, and Philip Rivers play well into what would typically be considered their dotage in recent seasons; 37 is the new 32.

But here's the thing—Aaron Rodgers isn't AARON RODGERS anymore, and he hasn't been for some time.

The Rodgers that was named to the All-Decade team, the one who won the Super Bowl and multiple MVPs, was one of

the greatest passers the league has ever seen; a sure-fire first-ballot Hall of Famer. But that's in the past. Rodgers hasn't been a top-10 quarterback by DVOA or passed 1,000 DYAR since 2016. It's not just the lingering aftereffects of a broken collarbone, either. He hasn't put together back-to-back seasons with 10.0% DVOA or more since the 2013-2014 campaigns. Rodgers still carries with him the reputation and cache of being one of the league's best quarterbacks, but his play hasn't lived up to his reputation in some time. There are certainly some extenuating circumstances—a crumbling relationship with Mike McCarthy and the junior varsity squad of receivers Rodgers had to deal with last season are the two most commonly cited—but that does not explain the extent of Rodgers' drop-off, nor can it be used as an excuse going forward.

The problem isn't with Rodgers' ability to deliver big plays. Rodgers had the fourth-most DYAR in the league on deep shots last season, with an above-average 71.5% DVOA despite not having a reliable deep option apart from Davante Adams. Nor is it his decision making. Even in these past three seasons of middling results, Rodgers has been the best quarterback at avoiding negative plays. Since 2017, Rodgers is tops in the league with just a 0.85% interception rate. That last stat does come with a couple caveats, mind you. Rodgers takes a sack on 7.1% of his dropbacks, seventh-most in the league since 2017, and led the league in throwaways last season with 36. Some plays where other quarterbacks would take a risk, Rodgers ends up swallowing the ball or giving up on the play. Still, as long as you can hit big plays on a regular basis and you're not turning the ball over, you've got a role in any offense.

No, Rodgers' problem in recent years has been the every-down, routine throws. There's no denying that Rodgers has been plagued by drops and inconsistencies in his receiving corps in recent years, but some of those issues come from Rodgers all of a sudden having trouble putting the ball on the numbers. According to SIS charting, Rodgers was on target on just 68.2% of his throws in 2019, 18th out of 33 qualified passers and the worst in the division, even falling behind Mitchell Trubisky. Rodgers drops to 20th in catchable passes at just 74.3%.

This isn't just a one-year blip, either. Using our model, Rodgers was averaging a completion percentage above expectation (CPOE) of 3.9% through the first decade of his career; it fell to 2.8% in 2017 and then to -0.1% and 0.1% in the past two seasons. Rodgers has built his career on accuracy and catchability of his passes, especially deep downfield. He led the league in CPOE in 2013 and finished in the top 10 in all but one year from 2008 to 2017. Now, he fails to crack the top 20. And in other CPOE models, Rodgers does even worse. In the NFL Next Gen Stats model, which accounts for elements such as pass pressure and receiver separation thanks to tracking chip data, Rodgers has come out with a negative CPOE in each of the past three seasons. The only other three quarterbacks to do that were Andy Dalton, Eli Manning, and Joe Flacco. Yikes.

Again, to be clear, Rodgers has still been an above-average quarterback, even through this decline. He produces more good plays than any of the other names in that previous paragraph, he remains one of the top quarterbacks when under pressure, and there's reason to hope that some of these numbers can go up with another year in LaFleur's system. But this isn't just a statistical artifact or numbers-on-a-page scouting; it's not a joke cooked up by Athletic columnist and chaotic-neutral analytics imp Ben Baldwin. This is showing up on film and is the primary reason the Packers haven't had a top-10 passing offense since 2016. Add in the fact that Rodgers is on the back end of his career, and you can understand why the franchise needed to find a successor for Rodgers sooner or later.

But was it too soon? Calculating aging curves for quarterbacks in their late 30s is very tough, as there just has not been a significant number of players good enough to last that long. Rodgers is only the 21st quarterback in the DVOA era to qualify for our passing leaderboards in each of his age 34, 35, and 36 seasons. For what it's worth, the other 20 averaged two more seasons as a starter, and 1.25 seasons as an above-average starter, after their age-36 seasons. The three quarterbacks Rodgers' last three seasons resemble most are Mark Brunell, who ended up throwing just 46 more passes as a backup after age 36; John Elway, who won two Super Bowls when he was 37 and 38; and … Brett Favre, including his first season with a first-round quarterback named Aaron Rodgers sitting on the bench behind him. That's quite a range of possible outcomes.

There's enough evidence and reason for concern to make the Jordan Love pick a surprising one as opposed to a strictly bad one. If Love ends up being a great quarterback, it will go down as a fantastic pick! Regardless of the eventual outcome, it was a heck of a bold statement to make. By picking Love this year, the Packers are essentially saying that Love (plus a year or two in the system) is better than any passer they would have the chance to draft in 2021 or 2022. They're willing to give up years of the benefits of having a quarterback on a rookie pay scale in order to have their guy now. Love won't help the 2020 Packers, barring an absolute disaster. Rodgers' contract extension is large enough that it's unlikely Love will start for the *2021* Packers, barring an utter collapse and rebuild. For a team that both hopes to contend this season and had some significant holes on the roster, it certainly wasn't the obvious choice.

No, the major problem with the draft wasn't grabbing Love, but rather the missed opportunity to help the offense in 2020. This year's receiver class was touted as the best in recent memory, talented at the top and deep, to boot. The Packers had arguably the worst receiving corps of any contending team in 2019. They were charted with 35 dropped passes, fourth-most in the league. Rodgers seemed to have almost no chemistry with any of his non-Davante Adams targets, with his DVOA dropping from 9.0% to -2.8% when you remove Adams from the equation. Adams ranked 13th in the league with 22.6% of Green Bay's targets, but that's including the four games he missed with a toe injury; remove those, and his 29.7% target rate would have been second behind only Michael Thomas, as would his 11 targets per game. And the Saints went out and added Emmanuel Sanders to take some of the load off of Thomas, while the Packers spent most of the offseason twiddling their thumbs. If you can get odds on Adams leading the league in targets in 2020, snap it up.

After Adams, the rest of the Packers' depth chart is a collection of possibilities and could-bes with nary a solid, established option in the lot. Allen Lazard finished with a very respectable 14.6% DVOA, but that's almost solely due to his three-catch, 103-yard game against the Giants. Take that out and not only does his DVOA drop to 2.1%, but he also falls off the table of qualified receivers, dropping underneath the 50-target threshold. Lazard is pretty clearly the second-best receiver the Packers have but asking him to be more than a third or fourth option as a rotational guy at this point requires a lot of projection. But he's a better choice as your second guy than big free-agent acquisition Devin Funchess. Funchess has one career season with a positive DVOA, and one season inside the top 60 in DYAR. The concern isn't that he's coming off of a broken collarbone which cost him 2019; the concern is that even in the one year where Funchess rode a zillion dig routes to above-average production, he still was a drop machine—not something the Packers need more of in 2020.

After those three, the Packers have a motley crew of players who have never turned potential into production (Marquez Valdes-Scantling, Jake Kumerow, Equanimeous St. Brown) and lottery tickets (CFL vet Reggie Begelton; UDFAs Darrell Stewart and Malik Taylor). Starting tight end Jace Sternberger flashed in college, but no tight end has ever exceeded 500 yards in a LaFleur offense, while only one season of Jermichael Finley has topped 700 yards for Rodgers. It is certainly possible that enough of these players will take the steps forward needed to produce a quality corps this season; that small-sample-size Lazard and 2017 Funchess will both show up throughout 2020. It's more likely, however, that a lack of a proven, dynamic playmaker behind Adams will force Green Bay to funnel their passing game through one man yet again.

Another way that LaFleur and company have indicated they'll handle the receiver issue is by reducing the amount of three-receiver sets they use in favor of two-tight end or two-back sets—in a sense, switching allegiances to more of the Kyle Shanahan branch of the Shanahan/McVay offensive philosophy. You would think, with the issues the Packers had with the receiving depth chart, that going away from three-wide sets would make sense, but Green Bay was actually significantly better in 11 personnel than they were in general, with a DVOA of 21.5% compared to just 2.1% with two tight ends on the field. The difference, however, is highly impacted by play selection, rather than play quality. The Packers passed 75% of the time in 11 personnel and just 42% if the time in 12 personnel, and while the Packers were higher *ranked* as a rushing offense, they were still more efficient as a passing offense. And, as the Packers did not have two receiving threats at tight end last year, thanks to Sternberger's injury, the Packers were better throwing out of 11 personnel, 22.6% DVOA to 12.2%. Covering for a weakness by using more of a formation you were less successful at is an interesting choice, to say the least, though Sternberger replacing Jimmy Graham will likely be a significant benefit in and of itself.

There's no guarantee that a first- or second-round receiver would have solved the Packers' receiving woes, of course, but it remains baffling that with a draft class this touted, the best addition to the wideout room was Funchess. Nor did Green Bay use their draft picks to shore up their other notable points of weakness. The loss in the NFC Championship Game was due, in large part, to an inability to even slow down San Francisco's running game; finding an interior lineman to boost the team's 31st-ranked defensive adjusted line yards would have made a lot of sense. If the Packers are really committed to focusing on the run more in 2020, taking another swing at a guard to replicate Elgton Jenkins' success and replace Billy Turner would have made plenty of sense as well. You could make an argument for an inside linebacker or some depth at cornerback to help shore up the defense There were plenty of ways that it would have been logical for Green Bay to go.

Instead, they used a second-round pick on running back AJ Dillon, despite Aaron Jones having a top-10 season in both DYAR and DVOA and Jamaal Williams being a perfectly cromulent change-of-pace option. Yes, both Jones and Williams are free agents after 2020, but a) that's a problem for next year's Packers to solve, and b) you can get quality performances out of running backs from non-premium draft positions—as indicated by, for example, Jones' success as a fifth-round pick. Dillon had the second-highest BackCAST projection in this year's draft class, making him a logical choice for a team looking for a running back, with an emphasis on running. However, Dillon has roughly zero value in the passing game, which is a significant issue in a league where more and more backs have to produce as receivers to justify their place on the roster and in the starting lineup. This was a luxury pick at a less important position that wasn't a need going into the draft. Then they took Josiah Deguara in the third round, a tight end who was invited to the Senior Bowl as a fullback; he's more a replacement for Dan Vitale than Jimmy Graham. There is an argument to be made for drafting talent rather than for need, but Green Bay seemed to go out of its way to avoid addressing any of the issues they had on either side of the ball in 2019.

As a result, any significant improvement on offense in 2020 is going to have to come from players becoming more familiar with LaFleur's scheme, rather than an increase in overall talent. Drafting replacements for two of your three best players on offense, rather than addressing holes elsewhere, is not the sort of move a team expecting to contend this season does. There's either more faith in internal improvement than we have, or *less* faith in the team's ability to build on last season's successes in Green Bay's front office. It is hard to see, on paper, anywhere that the Packers are better off offensively now than they were 12 months ago.

And they will need to be better, not just because of the likely regression to the mean in terms of luck, but also because our projections have the defense sliding backwards, too.

The Packers' jump from 10.1% to -1.1% in defensive DVOA last season was the fifth-largest jump in the league. Part of that was due to the arrival of the pair of Smiths, with Za'Darius and Preston becoming the first Green Bay duo to rack up double-digit sacks since Reggie White and Bryce Paup in 1993. But it wasn't just the Smiths who played well—the Packers' secondary, with the addition of Darnell Savage and Adrian Amos, helped produce the Packers' best pass DVOA since 2015. Yes, their run defense was quite poor, but NFC Championship Game aside, it's much more important to be able to stop the pass than it is to stop the run. A defense that produced 17 interceptions and a 3.1% interception rate, both third in the league, did just fine, right?

Our model is very down on the Packers' defense repeating what they were able to do in 2019. First and foremost, there's less year-to-year correlation in defensive performance than there is on offense. This is especially true when you're seeing a big jump from one year to the next—a jump of that size is generally caused by both an increase in skill (which is replicable) and an increase in luck (which is not). The Plexiglass Principle states that teams which significantly improve or decline in one season have a tendency to relapse or bounce back in the next, and the Packers' pass defense is a definite candidate for plexiglass regression in 2020.

Secondly, the Packers' pass defense was highly dependent on the interception, which is a problem, as interceptions are very inconsistent from year to year. The Packers pass defense DVOA drops from -1.3% to 20.5% if you remove interceptions from the equation, the third-biggest decline in the league last season. Green Bay's rank in pass defense was more a product of big plays than steady, down-to-down success, and that is not sustainable. In addition, their DVOA was padded a bit due to fortunate injury luck. DVOA knows Green Bay performed well against Kansas City and Detroit's passing offenses. It does *not* know that they faced Matt Moore and David Blough instead of Patrick Mahomes and Matthew Stafford; Green Bay's pass defense falls to positive numbers if you only include games played against starting quarterbacks. The Packers face a tough slate of opposing quarterbacks this season; any slip in their big-play percentage in the secondary could see a disproportional slide in their performance.

And then there's the lack of defensive reinforcements. The Packers really missed a Mike Daniels type at defensive tackle to clog up running lanes, and no such player has been added. With Blake Martinez gone, the Packers needed two new quality starting linebackers; they added the oft-injured Christian Kirksey and fifth-round pick Kamal Martin, which is uninspiring. Cornerback depth is questionable, especially with Tramon Williams apparently done. The only added cornerback was seventh-round pick Vernon Scott, who is most likely destined for the practice squad. There are a lot of negative indicators and trends the defense is going to have to overcome to approach even last year's average performance.

And that's kind of the running theme—the Packers will have to do a lot of work just to be as good as they were last season, even before taking into account how fortunate they were to be 13-3 rather than 10-6. You can't really point to anywhere on the roster and go yes, this team is better in 2020 at this position. There's potential because every NFL team has potential, but the biggest, most significant moves the Packers made this offseason were designed to help the team two or three years from now, not in 2020.

That's not to say the Packers will be a bad team or anything, barring a significant decline from their superstars. Their average projected win total is below .500, but not by a ton. There are plenty of simulations where they return to double-digit wins and the NFC North crown, and we would not at all be surprised at that outcome. The Packers still have the highest mean projected DVOA in the division, with the only real difference between them and the Lions coming down to strength of schedule. It's just that, even if you accept that the Packers were fortunate to be as successful as they were last season, it felt like they were in a position to become clear and decisive favorites in the division. Instead, a baffling offseason has Green Bay firmly in the middle of the Pack.

Bryan Knowles

2019 Packers Stats by Week

Wk	vs.	W-L	PF	PA	YDF	YDA	TO	Total	Off	Def	ST
1	at CHI	W	10	3	213	254	+1	-5%	-26%	-18%	4%
2	MIN	W	21	16	335	421	+2	53%	16%	-32%	5%
3	DEN	W	27	16	312	310	+3	29%	22%	-12%	-5%
4	PHI	L	27	34	491	336	-2	-42%	6%	36%	-12%
5	at DAL	W	34	24	335	563	+3	28%	18%	-6%	4%
6	DET	W	23	22	447	299	-3	21%	4%	-17%	1%
7	OAK	W	42	24	481	484	+2	51%	74%	17%	-6%
8	at KC	W	31	24	374	337	+1	29%	37%	3%	-5%
9	at LAC	L	11	26	184	442	0	-63%	-30%	36%	4%
10	CAR	W	24	16	388	401	+2	6%	14%	15%	7%
11	BYE										
12	at SF	L	8	37	198	339	-1	-90%	-31%	50%	-8%
13	at NYG	W	31	13	322	335	+3	27%	12%	-10%	6%
14	WAS	W	20	15	341	262	0	21%	3%	-7%	11%
15	CHI	W	21	13	292	415	+3	17%	6%	-8%	3%
16	at MIN	W	23	10	383	139	-2	62%	-1%	-67%	-3%
17	at DET	W	23	20	432	305	0	-9%	-13%	-5%	-1%
18	BYE										
19	SEA	W	28	23	344	375	0	10%	22%	11%	-1%
20	at SF	L	20	37	358	354	-3	-21%	25%	40%	-7%

Trends and Splits

	Offense	Rank	Defense	Rank
Total DVOA	6.5%	8	-1.1%	15
Unadjusted VOA	5.6%	11	-1.1%	16
Weighted Trend	4.2%	9	0.0%	16
Variance	6.9%	13	8.1%	27
Average Opponent	0.4%	20	-0.2%	17
Passing	17.3%	11	-1.3%	9
Rushing	8.2%	4	-0.8%	23
First Down	-1.6%	17	1.9%	19
Second Down	15.8%	6	3.9%	18
Third Down	5.8%	14	-14.7%	8
First Half	3.2%	10	-3.2%	13
Second Half	10.0%	10	1.1%	17
Red Zone	16.1%	8	-16.0%	7
Late and Close	3.3%	15	-22.5%	3

Five-Year Performance

Year	W-L	Pyth W	Est W	PF	PA	TO	Total	Rk	Off	Rk	Def	Rk	ST	Rk	Off AGL	Rk	Def AGL	Rk	Off Age	Rk	Def Age	Rk	ST Age	Rk
2015	10-6	9.3	9.9	368	323	+5	9.9%	10	2.2%	11	-7.3%	9	0.4%	17	27.8	12	28.2	13	26.7	16	26.3	23	25.5	28
2016	10-6	9.1	9.8	432	388	+8	12.3%	7	16.6%	4	2.5%	20	-1.9%	21	34.8	16	42.5	17	26.8	14	25.8	30	25.4	28
2017	7-9	6.2	7.7	320	384	-3	-3.3%	17	0.3%	15	4.9%	20	1.3%	14	45.1	23	39.4	21	27.0	16	25.5	28	25.2	28
2018	6-9-1	7.4	8.0	376	400	0	-3.1%	19	11.1%	7	10.1%	29	-4.1%	29	26.2	8	63.5	30	27.6	8	25.8	24	25.2	31
2019	13-3	9.8	9.9	376	313	+12	7.7%	10	6.5%	8	-1.1%	15	0.1%	18	39.5	17	26.2	9	28.1	2	25.5	29	25.5	24

2019 Performance Based on Most Common Personnel Groups

GB Offense					GB Offense vs. Opponents					GB Defense					GB Defense vs. Opponents			
Pers	Freq	Yds	DVOA	Run%	Pers	Freq	Yds	DVOA	Run%	Pers	Freq	Yds	DVOA	Pers	Freq	Yds	DVOA
11	62%	5.9	21.5%	25%	Base	29%	5.9	10.4%	55%	Base	19%	5.9	-11.6%	11	59%	6.1	1.1%
12	20%	5.3	2.1%	58%	Nickel	56%	5.6	18.0%	29%	Nickel	28%	5.2	-4.9%	12	15%	5.4	0.5%
21	13%	5.7	2.7%	44%	Dime+	13%	6.3	12.4%	21%	Dime+	51%	6.1	5.0%	21	12%	5.5	-5.7%
13	3%	6.1	14.6%	61%	Goal Line	1%	0.8	-66.3%	50%	Goal Line	0%	1.0	82.2%	22	5%	5.1	-11.8%
22	1%	5.8	5.1%	50%						Big	1%	2.2	-31.2%	13	3%	7.2	20.3%
														20	3%	2.7	-39.2%

Strategic Tendencies

Run/Pass		Rk	Formation		Rk	Pass Rush		Rk	Secondary		Rk	Strategy		Rk
Runs, first half	34%	23	Form: Single Back	81%	16	Rush 3	11.3%	11	4 DB	19%	25	Play Action	27%	13
Runs, first down	48%	16	Form: Empty Back	9%	10	Rush 4	71.0%	12	5 DB	28%	30	Offensive Motion	44%	10
Runs, second-long	30%	10	Form: Multi Back	10%	17	Rush 5	15.8%	26	6+ DB	51%	1	Avg Box (Off)	6.49	24
Runs, power sit.	52%	21	Pers: 3+ WR	62%	20	Rush 6+	2.0%	29	Man Coverage	32%	17	Avg Box (Def)	6.40	28
Runs, behind 2H	27%	19	Pers: 2+ TE/6+ OL	24%	21	Edge Rusher Sacks	69.5%	6	CB by Sides	70%	21	Offensive Pace	31.06	18
Pass, ahead 2H	54%	3	Pers: 6+ OL	1%	26	Interior DL Sacks	18.3%	20	S/CB Cover Ratio	26%	16	Defensive Pace	31.06	22
Run-Pass Options	10%	6	Shotgun/Pistol	62%	19	Second Level Sacks	12.2%	25	DB Blitz	10%	17	Go for it on 4th	1.29	19

Green Bay had the league's biggest gap between success running against light boxes (six or fewer: 5.5 yards, 31.5% DVOA) and other boxes (seven or more: 3.9 yards, -11.3% DVOA). ◖ The Packers had the league's biggest gap between runs from shotgun (37.7% DVOA, 5.5 yards per carry) and runs from under center (-14.9%, 3.9). ◖ Green Bay ranked second in the NFL by throwing 24.9% of passes at or behind the line of scrimmage. ◖ Green Bay's offense finished fifth in pressure allowed on first and second downs but 26th on third and fourth downs. ◖ The Packers defense struggled when blitzing last season, allowing 7.8 net yards per pass with 30.2% DVOA. ◖ Possibly connected: The Packers had the NFL's biggest gap between defense in man coverage (8.9 yards per pass, 40.1% DVOA) and zone coverage (6.8 yards per pass, 6.2% DVOA). ◖ The Packers spent less time in tied games than any other team last season, just 7:39 per game.

Passing

Player	DYAR	DVOA	Plays	NtYds	Avg	YAC	C%	TD	Int
A.Rodgers	794	9.0%	605	3707	6.1	5.7	62.3%	26	4

Rushing

Player	DYAR	DVOA	Plays	Yds	Avg	TD	Fum	Suc
A.Jones	207	12.0%	236	1091	4.6	16	2	56%
J.Williams	31	-1.5%	107	460	4.3	1	0	53%
A.Rodgers	61	35.9%	27	202	7.5	1	0	-
T.Carson*	-11	-49.1%	6	15	2.5	0	0	33%
D.Williams	-6	-46.0%	5	11	2.2	0	0	20%

Receiving

Player	DYAR	DVOA	Plays	Ctch	Yds	Y/C	YAC	TD	C%
D.Adams	139	0.6%	127	83	997	12.0	4.7	5	65%
M.Valdes-Scantling	-13	-15.5%	56	26	452	17.4	5.8	2	46%
G.Allison*	-98	-35.8%	55	34	287	8.4	3.2	2	62%
A.Lazard	118	14.6%	52	35	477	13.6	3.7	3	67%
J.Kumerow	48	20.1%	21	12	219	18.3	7.4	1	57%
J.Graham*	38	2.1%	60	38	447	11.8	6.5	3	63%
M.Lewis	13	2.5%	19	15	156	10.4	5.5	1	79%
R.Tonyan	10	4.5%	15	10	100	10.0	2.6	1	67%
A.Jones	35	-5.1%	68	49	474	9.7	8.9	3	72%
J.Williams	103	27.4%	45	39	253	6.5	7.2	5	87%
D.Vitale*	13	3.3%	12	7	97	13.9	8.0	0	58%

Offensive Line

Player	Pos	Age	GS	Snaps	Pen	Sk	Pass	Run	Player	Pos	Age	GS	Snaps	Pen	Sk	Pass	Run
Billy Turner	RG	29	16/16	1101	2	6.0	21	12	Corey Linsley	C	29	16/16	974	2	1.8	8	7
David Bakhtiari	LT	29	16/16	1100	12	2.8	12	5	Bryan Bulaga*	RT	31	16/16	922	6	3.0	17	3
Elgton Jenkins	LG	25	16/14	986	7	0.5	12	3	Rick Wagner	RT	31	12/12	772	3	3.5	17	11

Year	Yards	ALY	Rank	Power	Rank	Stuff	Rank	2nd Lev	Rank	Open Field	Rank	Sacks	ASR	Rank	Press	Rank	F-Start	Cont.
2017	4.13	4.60	5	66%	11	16%	2	1.10	19	0.51	24	51	8.6%	28	35.1%	28	11	21
2018	4.70	4.71	7	65%	21	18%	12	1.49	2	0.80	20	53	7.9%	21	29.0%	16	16	33
2019	4.47	4.63	5	54%	27	17%	6	1.28	9	0.69	20	36	6.4%	10	29.2%	12	20	44
2019 ALY by direction:			Left End 4.55 (8)			Left Tackle: 3.10 (29)			Mid/Guard: 5.02 (3)			Right Tackle: 4.86 (6)			Right End: 4.36 (15)		

The Packers ranked in the top 10 in both adjusted line yards and adjusted sack rate. While they've been near the top of the league in run blocking for years, it was their first top-10 appearance in sack rate since 2007, and the first time they've pulled off the double since 2003. ❧ Elgton Jenkins was very sharp as a rookie, doubly so when you consider he hadn't played guard in two years. He gave up only a half-sack and had just three blown blocks in the running game. On the docket for 2020: fewer penalties, as his 10 accepted flags tied the league lead at his position. ❧ ESPN's Pass Block Win Rate loves the Packers' offensive line. Jenkins ranked eighth with a 95% success rate, which makes him the weak link on the left side between league leaders David Bakhtiari (96%) and Corey Linsley (98%). ❧ Despite having all those league leaders, the Packers offensive line was just good, and not great. Jenkins, Bakhtiari, and Linsley averaged one blown block every 63.8 snaps, which is great. The right side of the line averaged a blown block every 37.5 snaps, which is somewhat less ideal. ❧ Bryan Bulaga was the better player on the right, but he's gone. Ex-Lion Rick Wagner is his replacement; Wagner has generally been serviceable to good, but is coming off of his career-worst season; perhaps blocking for Aaron Rodgers and not David Blough will help. ❧ Right guard Billy Turner ranked 32nd out of 35 right guards in snaps per blown block; he's a good versatile backup being used as an every-down starter. ❧ Lane Taylor, the starter at left guard before Jenkins, is still around to provide depth. ❧ The Packers drafted three different interior linemen in the sixth round: Jake Hanson (Oregon), Jon Runyan (Michigan), and Simon Stepaniak (Indiana).

Defensive Front

Defensive Line	Age	Pos	G	Snaps	Plays	TmPct	Rk	Stop	Dfts	BTkl	Runs	St%	Rk	RuYd	Rk	Sack	Hit	Hur	Dsrpt
						Overall						vs. Run				Pass Rush			
Kenny Clark	25	DT	16	879	63	7.9%	7	52	15	5	52	81%	26	2.2	43	6.0	2	32	1
Dean Lowry	26	DE	16	642	49	6.1%	20	37	4	3	46	74%	54	2.6	65	0.0	2	12	2
Tyler Lancaster	26	DE	16	381	30	3.8%	--	24	5	0	27	78%	--	2.3	--	1.5	0	2	0

Edge Rushers	Age	Pos	G	Snaps	Plays	TmPct	Rk	Stop	Dfts	BTkl	Runs	St%	Rk	RuYd	Rk	Sack	Hit	Hur	Dsrpt
						Overall						vs. Run				Pass Rush			
Za'Darius Smith	28	OLB	16	883	53	6.6%	20	40	25	7	36	64%	73	2.3	41	13.5	23	66	0
Preston Smith	28	OLB	16	880	59	7.4%	10	40	19	7	32	63%	77	3.3	79	12.0	9	35	3
Kyler Fackrell*	29	OLB	16	422	19	2.4%	87	11	6	4	8	38%	91	4.6	90	1.0	8	27	1
Rashan Gary	23	OLB	16	245	20	2.5%	--	10	2	3	17	47%	--	4.3	--	2.0	1	10	0

Linebackers	Age	Pos	G	Snaps	Plays	TmPct	Rk	Stop	Dfts	BTkl	Runs	St%	Rk	RuYd	Rk	Sack	Hit	Hur	Tgts	Suc%	Rk	AdjYd	Rk	PD	Int
						Overall						vs. Run				Pass Rush				vs. Pass					
Blake Martinez*	26	ILB	16	1035	157	19.7%	2	73	20	17	98	53%	68	4.4	67	3.0	0	6	40	38%	57	7.1	45	2	1
B.J. Goodson*	27	ILB	15	256	35	4.7%	--	17	1	3	28	50%	--	4.8	--	0.0	0	1	6	50%	--	5.0	--	0	0

Year	Yards	ALY	Rank	Power	Rank	Stuff	Rank	2nd Level	Rank	Open Field	Rank	Sacks	ASR	Rank	Press	Rank
2017	3.81	3.93	9	56%	7	20%	21	1.08	10	0.57	7	37	7.3%	9	29.0%	26
2018	4.32	4.78	27	63%	10	15%	29	1.15	9	0.62	7	44	7.7%	10	30.8%	14
2019	4.87	4.96	31	71%	27	13%	31	1.32	27	0.84	22	41	7.5%	12	34.8%	4
2019 ALY by direction:			Left End: 4.41 (23)			Left Tackle: 4.66 (22)			Mid/Guard: 5.38 (32)			Right Tackle: 4.65 (23)			Right End: 4.17 (14)

The Packers jumped from 14th to fourth in pressure rate, the first time they've hit the top ten there since 2015. ❧ Za'Darius Smith and Preston Smith became just the second set of Packers to record double-digit sacks since the NFL started recording individual sacks in 1982. The Packers haven't had anyone record double-digit sacks in back-to-back seasons since Clay Matthews in 2009 and 2010; it has been a long time since the Packers could boast an elite pass-rusher. ❧ Preston Smith is basically a one-speed player; point him at the quarterback and let him go. Za'Darius Smith, on the other hand, contributes to run defense as well; he was second on the team with nine rush defeats. That'd make him a decent enough player even if he wasn't second in the league in quarterback hurries. ❧ Add in Kenny Clark, and the Packers were one of only two teams with three players with 30 or more hurries. ❧ After signing a big extension last season, Dean Lowry took a significant step back in run defense in 2019. His stop rate was about the same as it was a year ago, but the misses became worse, with significant cold stretches where he wasn't involved in the play at all. ❧ With Blake Martinez and B.J. Goodson walking in free agency, the inside linebacker position is a ghost town. The Packers *did* add Christian Kirksey, reuniting him with Mike Pettine. He hasn't been healthy since 2017, but he was third in the league that season with 31 defeats, a rare bright spot on some terrible Browns teams. ❧ If Kirksey can't stay healthy, or the Packers ever want to have two linebackers on the field, they'll have to turn to Oren Burks or Ty Summers, who had a combined 57 defensive snaps last season. ❧ The Packers added Minnesota's Kamal Martin in the fifth round, but he lacks the flow-to-the-ball or play recognition skills needed to be a solid defensive contributor, at least as an inside linebacker. He's a solid and willing tackler, so he'll be able to carve out a role on special teams, but he's not an ideal fit for Pettine's system.

Defensive Secondary

Secondary	Age	Pos	G	Snaps	Plays	TmPct	Rk	Stop	Dfts	BTkl	Runs	St%	Rk	RuYd	Rk	Tgts	Tgt%	Rk	Dist	Suc%	Rk	AdjYd	Rk	PD	Int
						Overall						**vs. Run**					**vs. Pass**								
Adrian Amos	27	FS	16	1047	89	11.2%	17	33	13	6	40	38%	43	7.9	47	40	9.5%	18	10.1	45%	59	8.6	52	8	2
Jaire Alexander	23	CB	16	1038	75	9.4%	14	35	14	14	8	38%	57	5.8	36	97	23.3%	16	12.2	61%	12	7.2	36	17	2
Darnell Savage	23	SS	14	871	60	8.6%	49	19	9	13	28	32%	55	7.9	45	26	7.5%	41	13.6	62%	14	4.7	6	5	2
Kevin King	25	CB	15	812	81	10.8%	9	32	15	13	15	53%	29	5.3	30	73	22.4%	21	13.9	52%	47	9.8	77	15	5
Tramon Williams*	37	CB	16	772	47	5.9%	--	20	10	6	12	33%	--	7.9	--	41	13.3%	--	10.4	54%	--	8.4	--	8	2
Chandon Sullivan	24	CB	16	356	34	4.3%	--	17	9	3	8	75%	--	5.0	--	21	14.7%	--	12.3	76%	--	3.5	--	6	1
Will Redmond	27	SS	13	276	29	4.5%	--	6	2	7	16	31%	--	8.0	--	7	6.3%	--	11.3	29%	--	8.3	--	1	0

Year	Pass D Rank	vs. #1 WR	Rk	vs. #2 WR	Rk	vs. Other WR	Rk	WR Wide	Rk	WR Slot	Rk	vs. TE	Rk	vs. RB	Rk
2017	27	31.9%	32	22.1%	26	-9.4%	10	8.3%	26	28.1%	31	4.1%	21	17.3%	29
2018	28	9.0%	22	14.9%	25	-4.1%	13	4.1%	22	13.6%	25	20.8%	27	25.1%	32
2019	9	1.4%	15	-29.7%	3	-12.8%	9	-12.6%	12	-13.0%	6	9.8%	26	-17.0%	4

Green Bay used their defensive backs in a more conventional way in 2019. While they still led the league in dime usage, with at least six defensive backs on the field 51% of the time, they no longer ranked near the top of the league in CB/S cover ratio or defensive back blitzes. At this point, their high dime usage is as much a factor of lack of depth at linebacker as anything else, and the Packers' lack of urgency to add linebackers to the roster indicate they're more than fine with the status quo. ❧ Jaire Alexander's breakout season, where he hit a 61% success rate, is all the more impressive considering he was playing parts of 2019 with injuries to his knee and groin. ❧ Kevin King finally remained healthy for the lion's share of a season. His success rate was decent enough for a second cornerback, though it should be noted that his 4.9 YAC allowed was 12th-worst in the league; when he slipped up in coverage, it often resulted a big play. ❧ With it looking more and more like Tramon Williams' career has finally come to an end, the Packers will likely turn to Josh Jackson to fill the third cornerback role. The 2018 second-round pick played just over 100 snaps last season and wasn't particularly impressive doing so; Green Bay may be better off calling up the 37-year-old Williams and seeing if he has one more go in the tank. ❧ Adrian Amos replacing Ha Ha Clinton-Dix at free safety was a much-ballyhooed talking point a year ago, especially when Clinton-Dix joined the Bears. For the Packers, it ended up being something of a wash—Amos' 45% success rate wasn't significantly different from Clinton-Dix's 48% success rate the year before, and his run defense was a bit sharper, but not by much. If we had to pick a winner, we'd side with Amos, but it was close. ❧ The top of All-Rookie Darnell Savage's to-do list for his sophomore season? Clean up his tackling. Savage's 25% broken tackle rate was the worst on the team for anyone with at least 20 tackles.

Special Teams

Year	DVOA	Rank	FG/XP	Rank	Net Kick	Rank	Kick Ret	Rank	Net Punt	Rank	Punt Ret	Rank	Hidden	Rank
2017	1.3%	14	-2.8	19	0.1	17	0.2	13	5.1	9	4.0	4	-12.0	30
2018	-4.1%	29	-0.1	18	-4.5	28	-4.5	29	-2.1	19	-9.2	32	1.1	13
2019	0.1%	18	6.9	7	-0.4	19	-1.2	17	0.2	18	-4.8	28	-6.1	26

Tyler Ervin saved the Packers from a disastrous special teams year. Before Ervin arrived, Green Bay had -8 yards total on punt returns, a near-impossible feat; the NFL record low is 27. Ervin dragged the Packers back into positive numbers on his very first return, and while the punt return unit was still the weak link on special teams, it at least wasn't historically bad. Ervin also ended the season as the best kickoff returner the Packers had, producing more value on six returns than Tremon Smith did on 13. ❧ Mason Crosby produced his first positive FG/XP season since 2016, making more than 90% of his field goals for the first time in his career. You don't see many kickers setting career highs at age 35. Crosby's 6.9 points above expectation was the best mark for a Packers kicker since Ryan Longwell in 2003. ❧ JK Scott didn't wow in Year 2, finishing 24th in yards per punt and just barely scraping above average for the punt unit as a whole. Still, with no competition on the roster, at least the Packers have stopped swapping their punter out every season.

Houston Texans

Sunday, October 29, 2017. The Texans are slated to play the Seattle Seahawks after a bye week. Since his first full week as the starter in Week 3, Deshaun Watson's Texans have scored at least 33 points in four straight games, including a 57-point pasting of the Tennessee Titans. Watson drops 38 on the Legion of Boom, in Seattle, and even though the Texans lose a heartbreaker to Russell Wilson, it is hard to deny that the Texans have every reason to be optimistic. They have one of the best talent cores in the NFL, with J.J. Watt waiting to rejoin the fold in 2018, and they have a burgeoning star quarterback on a rookie deal.

In the week of practice after that game, Watson would tear his ACL and miss the rest of the season. Duane Brown would be shipped to Seattle for two draft picks. It is hard to understate the impact these two events have had on the franchise.

With Watson sitting out the rest of the season, we had only a small sample size of him dominating. That meant that instead of running what had taken the league by storm—the college concepts from Clemson that led him to easy reads, emphasized the middle of the field, and used play-action often—Houston's coaching staff was able to instead weld him on to an offensive structure that scored more than 17 points just once in the final nine games of the season. It is purely conjecture that the Texans would have kept Watson in the offense that he ran as a rookie—in fact, it may be somewhat inevitable that head coach (and, now, general manager) Bill O'Brien would have forced his predictable and drab offense on Watson. But with a larger sample size of dominance, even someone as stubborn as O'Brien may have been forced to concede that there was nothing worth fixing. Instead, the good play with Watson merited a contract extension for O'Brien.

General manager Rick Smith, in his last major move before he went "on leave" to help his wife deal with cancer—he wasn't asked back—sent Brown to the Seahawks for second- and third-round picks. Brown had feuded with management about a new contract in an extended holdout and was upset at owner Bob McNair for his infamous "inmates running the prison" comment. He was getting up there in age, but graceful tackles tend to hold up pretty well as they get older and this is something that could have been covered over with money. The Texans never truly replaced Brown in the 2018 offseason, which contributed to Watson getting sacked a league-high 62 times. The Texans tried to replace him with Matt Kalil in the

2019 offseason, which helped contribute to the desperation that fueled the Laremy Tunsil trade. The Texans dealt two first-round picks (2020 and 2021) and a second-round pick (2021) for one of the best young tackles in the NFL.

The impact of the Tunsil trade still hasn't even begun to be fully felt. In the short term, it worked: Tunsil was a part of the reason the Texans were able to win the AFC South last year despite not being appreciably good. Houston is now locked into two straight draft classes without a first-round pick; had to surrender a market-setting three-year, $66-million extension to Tunsil; and had to trade another star player just to get a top-40 pick in this year's draft. This despite the fact that Tunsil's first year in Houston could charitably be called rocky: he led the league in false starts, missed two games, and was good rather than dominant.

Including the draft picks they made prior to the Tunsil trade, the Texans have essentially put three first-round picks and two second-round picks into their offensive line. Table 1 shows just how much impact the trade had on the overall offensive profile of the team, including Watson's sack and pressure rates, in 2019.

Table 1. Houston DVOA and Pressure with Deshaun Watson, 2017-2019

Year	Off DVOA	Rk	Adjusted Sack Rate	Rk	Pressure Rate	Rk
2017*	8.0%	11	10.4%	31	40.9%	32
2018	-3.5%	21	11.6%	32	38.5%	32
2019	0.4%	16	8.4%	27	34.1%	29

*Includes Watson starts only.

It is not groundbreaking to point out that sacks are a quarterback stat. But we lead with this because even with all that has happened in the year and change since O'Brien fired his general manager, the stunning amount of waste and churn invested in changing absolutely nothing about his offense is mind-blowing.

When it comes to keeping the quarterback clean, the offensive design may be more important than the players themselves.

2020 Texans Schedule

Week	Opp.	Week	Opp.	Week	Opp.
1	at KC (Thu.)	7	GB	13	IND
2	BAL	8	BYE	14	at CHI
3	at PIT	9	at JAX	15	at IND (Sat.)
4	MIN	10	at CLE	16	CIN
5	JAX	11	NE	17	TEN
6	at TEN	12	at DET (Thu.)		

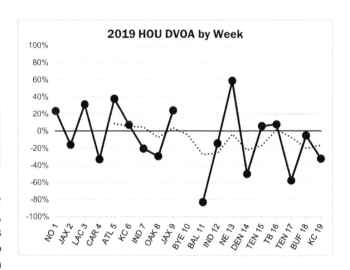

There were several games last season where Watson was rarely sacked or hurried—including one of the games Tunsil missed, in London against the Jaguars. There were also several games where O'Brien left the offense adrift and made Watson get into third or fourth reads to complete passes, games where Watson took a ton of sacks against aggressive coverage.

It is hard to say how different this team would look if they had just paid Brown. They might have spent those picks on offensive linemen anyway, and it's not like the Texans have been blowing teams away with their draft picks when they made them. But with four extra stabs at the good cost-controlled player pool, the future would look a lot less bleak than it does today.

This is our 16th preseason annual and 12th edition of *Football Outsiders Almanac*. There have been plenty of times we've had to write a chapter about the Andy Dalton Cincinnati Bengals or the Philip Rivers Chargers. We've had to stretch to find enough interesting things to get a good word count. Bill O'Brien's tenure as general manager is … not that.

Bill O'Brien's general manager tenure, to riff on a good stand-up set about someone who is definitely not Bill O'Brien, is a bit like John Mulaney's take that there is a horse loose in the hospital. "I have no idea what's going to happen next, and neither do any of you, and neither do your parents, because there's a horse loose in the hospital," Mulaney says. "No one knows what the horse is going to do next, least of all the horse. He's never been in a hospital before! He's as confused as you are." Sometimes the updates are just odd. "Bill O'Brien has decided that he needs tough, smart, and dependable players." Huh, that's weird, I thought most NFL players were like that. Then sometimes out of nowhere, O'Brien will trade DeAndre Hopkins, a universally beloved All-Pro receiver, for a running back who hasn't had a good season since 2016 and a second-round pick. And we'll all be like "aw, that's what I thought you'd do, you dumb (expletive) horse."

In last year's Texans chapter, we talked about how this was essentially a team operating without an ethos, a franchise that appeared to be in limbo. Well, that take aged pretty poorly. It is hard to distill exactly what O'Brien's ethos is at this moment, but if we had to sum it up in a word, it would be "reactionary." Hopkins openly admitted in an interview with *Sports Illustrated* this offseason that he knew that if he asked for an extension, he would be traded. Jadeveon Clowney, dealt for Jacob Martin and some change under the futon, was told he should just sign his franchise tender rather than report because he was already getting traded. The black hole at left tackle that

general manager Brian Gaine tried to solve with Kalil—who had a player profile that never should have been trusted in the first place—led to the panicked Tunsil trade. O'Brien felt the left tackle position was set up to fail, reacted strongly, and in doing so got his pocket picked by Chris Grier. This was hardly the only position where panic moves took place.

After a huge mistake in Week 1 allowed the Saints to beat the Texans on a last-minute field goal, slot corner Aaron Colvin was released. After Week 1! They spent heavily to get Colvin in 2018, talked up his comeback from injuries all offseason, then just let him go to play second-round rookie Lonnie Johnson right away. Then, they decided that Johnson was wanting and the cornerback injuries were mounting, so they would be the team that would fix Gareon Conley at the cost of a third-round pick. But after just six starts, the Texans decided not to pick up Conley's fifth-year option, although he'll still be on the roster for 2020. Running back has a similar story: O'Brien decided he was done with D'Onta Foreman in the preseason, so he had to trade a third-round pick to get Duke Johnson. Then, at final cuts, he found Carlos Hyde, who had a pretty solid season as an early-down back for the Texans. But after Hyde dragged his feet on a two-year, $10-million offer from O'Brien, he traded for David Johnson. Piss O'Brien off and the names will change, the situation will generally stay the same, and the Texans will have fewer draft picks or stars when it's all said and done.

How did O'Brien become the only person with any power in Houston? He happened to be in the right place at the right time. McNair passed during the 2018 season, meaning that the only person who had the sway to reel in O'Brien's baser instincts was gone. Gaine, who was fired as we were going to press last year, was just another guy reporting to O'Brien. The ownership transition has settled with McNair's son Cal being the face of ownership over his mother Janice. If it was possible to be even more hands-off than the man who gave Gary Kubiak *eight* seasons, Cal has somehow done it. O'Brien and McNair didn't speak for weeks after the Hopkins trade, and when they broke the silence, McNair gave only a carefully choreographed interview with team website reporters in which he said he thought fans "would be real excited that your leadership of the team can make bold moves." The scary thing is, if O'Brien were somehow deposed—he is under contract through 2022—there is literally nobody in this building who knows anything about football and has power. Assistant GM Jack Easterby, empowered through friendship with O'Brien, is a former pastor who came up with the Patriots as a character coach. He's more likely to share a quote about working through adversity on Twitter than he is to successfully diagnose football strategy off the all-22. Everyone in the building with a coaching background is a long-time O'Brien employee at this point. This would almost undoubtedly be a "head coach hired by search firm" situation.

It is this situation in which Watson finds himself shackled. His rookie contract has been wasted on O'Brien. He has no power to get out of Houston without making himself a pariah. Our No. 1 projected defense last year—we would not have made this projection had Clowney's departure been a part of the simulation, we promise—cratered to 26th in DVOA. Six of the top 11 players by snap counts are gone from the 2018 defense that finished seventh in DVOA; only Watt, Benardrick McKinney, Justin Reid, Whitney Mercilus, and Zach Cunningham remain. Watt has played 32 games in four seasons and is 31, and his future in the NFL is tenuous. The Texans have also demoted Romeo Crennel out of the coordinator position to be an upstairs supervisor for Anthony Weaver, who has never been a coordinator anywhere before and has only promised to add a heavy dash of Rex Ryan to the Crennel base.

Instead of Hopkins, Watson will be throwing passes to Randall Cobb and Brandin Cooks. Cooks has already suffered five concussions, has always had issues with press coverage, and had one 100-yard game all season last year in the broken Jared Goff Rams offense. Cobb turns 30 in August and had a lower receiving DVOA than Blake Jarwin last year in one of the league's best offenses. Will Fuller is phenomenal and never healthy.

Since taking over as general manager, O'Brien has downgraded the talent on this roster swiftly at the cost of several draft picks. There remain flashes of genius in his play calling in games such as the Week 6 win in Arrowhead, and those flashes will keep optimistic fans teased just enough to continue believing. However, all too often the narrative that starts "O'Brien is a good playcaller" ends with O'Brien having assumed too much of a role in every other bit of the operation to do a good job. There were reports that O'Brien was coming in late to the offensive install and changing things to his liking each week. Maybe offensive coordinator Tim Kelly, another O'Brien lifer who will apparently call plays next year, will make a change in the offense that will be beneficial. It may depend on whether he can go a full offseason without angering O'Brien.

Watson will be enough for this team to be competitive in the AFC South—he's simply that good—but the anchor around his neck that is O'Brien's ego will keep the Texans from ever being a real contender. When it comes down to brass tacks, you can spot this team a 24-0 lead in Arrowhead and the score still won't be close. In the self-preservation that it took to save his job in a lame-duck 2017 season, O'Brien's ego manifested in a way that makes spite the only real motivator for him.

The defining moment of the 2019 Texans season happened in a game where Houston choked away a chance at home-field advantage by losing to the Broncos, at home, in a game they trailed at halftime 31-3. TMZ would eventually unearth footage of a fan shouting "you suck" at O'Brien, and a feisty O'Brien relating to that fan repeatedly that "you suck, too, motherf*cker!" while Hopkins restrained and pulled O'Brien away.

Nowhere in his defense of himself did O'Brien ever admit that he didn't suck, you see.

Rivers McCown

2019 Texans Stats by Week

Wk	vs.	W-L	PF	PA	YDF	YDA	TO	Total	Off	Def	ST
1	at NO	L	28	30	414	510	0	23%	35%	9%	-2%
2	JAX	W	13	12	263	281	+1	-16%	-37%	-19%	2%
3	at LAC	W	27	20	376	366	0	31%	37%	2%	-3%
4	CAR	L	10	16	264	297	+1	-33%	-44%	-7%	5%
5	ATL	W	53	32	592	373	0	38%	40%	-4%	-6%
6	at KC	W	31	24	472	309	-1	7%	19%	6%	-5%
7	at IND	L	23	30	391	383	-1	-20%	-1%	28%	8%
8	OAK	W	27	24	388	378	0	-29%	-11%	23%	5%
9	at JAX	W	26	3	410	356	+3	24%	12%	-8%	5%
10	BYE										
11	at BAL	L	7	41	232	491	-2	-83%	-46%	36%	-1%
12	IND	W	20	17	396	296	-1	-14%	-1%	12%	-1%
13	NE	W	28	22	276	448	+1	59%	49%	0%	10%
14	DEN	L	24	38	414	391	-2	-50%	-4%	50%	3%
15	at TEN	W	24	21	374	432	-1	6%	0%	1%	6%
16	at TB	W	23	20	229	435	+3	8%	-34%	-25%	16%
17	TEN	L	14	35	301	467	-1	-57%	-8%	54%	5%
18	BUF	W	22	19	360	425	0	-5%	-4%	6%	6%
19	at KC	L	31	51	442	434	0	-32%	21%	54%	1%

Trends and Splits

	Offense	Rank	Defense	Rank
Total DVOA	0.4%	16	9.0%	26
Unadjusted VOA	1.5%	15	10.8%	27
Weighted Trend	-2.7%	18	14.0%	27
Variance	9.2%	26	5.2%	13
Average Opponent	0.0%	17	3.4%	2
Passing	13.7%	16	19.4%	26
Rushing	-0.1%	11	-5.0%	22
First Down	-5.7%	23	-20.5%	3
Second Down	-1.8%	14	24.1%	32
Third Down	15.9%	8	45.5%	32
First Half	-6.9%	23	4.0%	22
Second Half	8.1%	11	14.2%	30
Red Zone	6.0%	11	27.7%	31
Late and Close	6.2%	12	4.3%	22

Five-Year Performance

Year	W-L	Pyth W	Est W	PF	PA	TO	Total	Rk	Off	Rk	Def	Rk	ST	Rk	Off AGL	Rk	Def AGL	Rk	Off Age	Rk	Def Age	Rk	ST Age	Rk
2015	9-7	8.8	7.8	339	313	+5	-4.8%	18	-8.5%	24	-9.3%	8	-5.7%	32	48.6	25	13.4	2	26.5	17	26.2	24	25.8	20
2016	9-7	6.5	4.6	279	328	-7	-21.9%	29	-21.2%	30	-5.8%	9	-6.5%	31	50.7	24	51.4	23	25.7	30	26.5	17	26.2	12
2017	4-12	5.5	5.1	338	436	-12	-20.0%	28	-9.9%	24	5.6%	23	-4.5%	26	60.7	27	45.6	25	26.1	30	26.0	18	26.1	8
2018	11-5	10.3	9.1	402	316	+13	7.1%	11	-3.5%	21	-7.1%	7	3.5%	5	42.5	21	42.8	24	25.5	32	26.7	9	25.7	20
2019	10-6	7.8	7.3	378	385	0	-5.8%	19	0.4%	16	9.0%	26	2.9%	5	50.5	23	27.7	12	26.3	21	26.6	11	26.0	11

2019 Performance Based on Most Common Personnel Groups

\	HOU Offense				\	HOU Offense vs. Opponents				\	HOU Defense				\	HOU Defense vs. Opponents		
Pers	Freq	Yds	DVOA	Run%	Pers	Freq	Yds	DVOA	Run%	Pers	Freq	Yds	DVOA	Pers	Freq	Yds	DVOA
11	60%	6.1	15.4%	32%	Base	20%	5.4	8.5%	47%	Base	29%	6.1	-0.1%	11	64%	6.5	15.3%
12	35%	5.3	-2.4%	44%	Nickel	66%	5.8	5.8%	40%	Nickel	51%	5.8	2.6%	12	16%	4.7	-27.9%
21	2%	3.5	-50.3%	59%	Dime+	14%	6.7	17.0%	7%	Dime+	19%	8.2	48.4%	21	7%	8.3	48.2%
611	1%	10.5	34.6%	36%						Goal Line	0%	0.5	-13.3%	13	6%	6.6	4.3%
13	1%	3.0	1.0%	64%						Big	0%	1.0	-20.0%	22	4%	5.5	0.0%
20	1%	6.8	23.9%	50%													

Strategic Tendencies

Run/Pass		Rk	Formation		Rk	Pass Rush		Rk	Secondary		Rk	Strategy		Rk
Runs, first half	36%	21	Form: Single Back	76%	23	Rush 3	12.2%	8	4 DB	29%	15	Play Action	24%	18
Runs, first down	53%	8	Form: Empty Back	15%	2	Rush 4	60.0%	22	5 DB	51%	19	Offensive Motion	37%	16
Runs, second-long	21%	26	Form: Multi Back	9%	19	Rush 5	23.3%	9	6+ DB	19%	13	Avg Box (Off)	6.43	27
Runs, power sit.	41%	31	Pers: 3+ WR	61%	22	Rush 6+	4.5%	19	Man Coverage	39%	6	Avg Box (Def)	6.47	23
Runs, behind 2H	32%	10	Pers: 2+ TE/6+ OL	37%	6	Edge Rusher Sacks	61.7%	11	CB by Sides	77%	17	Offensive Pace	30.49	14
Pass, ahead 2H	50%	14	Pers: 6+ OL	2%	21	Interior DL Sacks	25.0%	14	S/CB Cover Ratio	19%	29	Defensive Pace	30.14	10
Run-Pass Options	9%	7	Shotgun/Pistol	81%	3	Second Level Sacks	13.3%	23	DB Blitz	9%	18	Go for it on 4th	1.62	12

It appears the Texans accounted for opposing personnel less than other offenses. The Texans ran a league-low 47% of the time when opponents were in base defense but ranked fourth running 40% of the time when opponents were in nickel defense. (League averages were 58% and 34%, respectively.) ⬥ The Texans finally figured out how to break some tackles on offense, tied for 15th with 118 broken tackles after ranking 31st for three straight years. ⬥ The Texans offense used a league-low five running back screens for the second straight season. ⬥ Houston recovered 10 of 14 fumbles on defense. ⬥ Houston's defense ranked third in the league against deep passes (16 or more yards through the air) but 29th against short passes. In particular, Houston was destroyed by short middle passes, with the worst DVOA in the league on these passes. ⬥ The Texans defense had only one sack charted as a coverage sack. ⬥ The Texans were once again excellent when they blitzed a defensive back, ranking third in the league with -22.2% DVOA on these plays. ⬥ Houston ranked seventh in defensive DVOA in the first quarter of games, but 30th for the rest of the game.

Passing

Player	DYAR	DVOA	Plays	NtYds	Avg	YAC	C%	TD	Int
D.Watson	722	9.5%	538	3580	6.7	5.0	67.7%	26	12
A.McCarron	-96	-43.6%	42	182	4.3	6.2	56.8%	0	1

Rushing

Player	DYAR	DVOA	Plays	Yds	Avg	TD	Fum	Suc
C.Hyde*	54	-3.3%	245	1086	4.4	6	4	52%
Du.Johnson	21	-2.0%	83	410	4.9	2	1	48%
D.Watson	77	9.9%	69	435	6.3	7	4	-
T.Jones*	14	21.9%	9	40	4.4	0	0	67%
G.Howell	-4	-24.5%	5	10	2.0	0	0	20%
A.McCarron	19	48.3%	5	39	7.8	1	0	-
Da.Johnson	-9	-10.8%	94	345	3.7	2	0	43%
B.Cooks	32	48.1%	6	52	8.7	0	0	-

Receiving

Player	DYAR	DVOA	Plays	Ctch	Yds	Y/C	YAC	TD	C%
D.Hopkins*	224	6.2%	150	104	1165	11.2	3.7	7	69%
W.Fuller	82	1.8%	71	49	670	13.7	4.5	3	69%
K.Stills	162	24.7%	55	40	561	14.0	3.6	4	73%
K.Coutee	-37	-25.5%	36	22	254	11.5	6.4	0	61%
D.Carter	39	21.8%	14	11	162	14.7	5.2	0	79%
S.Mitchell	-15	-45.1%	6	2	37	18.5	7.0	0	33%
R.Cobb	119	5.4%	83	55	828	15.1	6.0	3	66%
B.Cooks	71	0.0%	72	42	583	13.9	4.0	2	58%
J.Akins	6	-5.6%	55	36	418	11.6	6.8	2	65%
D.Fells	75	15.6%	48	34	341	10.0	4.9	7	71%
Du.Johnson	125	24.6%	62	44	410	9.3	8.2	3	71%
C.Hyde*	-36	-50.3%	16	10	42	4.2	5.1	0	63%
Da.Johnson	114	29.2%	47	36	370	10.3	6.3	4	77%

Offensive Line

Player	Pos	Age	GS	Snaps	Pen	Sk	Pass	Run	Player	Pos	Age	GS	Snaps	Pen	Sk	Pass	Run
Nick Martin	C	27	16/16	1049	4	0.0	5	11	Tytus Howard	RT	24	8/8	502	5	1.0	12	5
Zach Fulton	RG	29	15/15	980	8	1.5	12	14	Roderick Johnson	RT	25	16/3	374	1	4.0	14	4
Max Scharping	LG	24	16/14	962	6	0.0	11	6	Chris Clark*	RT	35	8/7	349	4	2.5	9	3
Laremy Tunsil	LT	26	14/14	942	18	1.0	13	4	Greg Mancz	C/G	28	9/1	161	0	1.0	2	2

Year	Yards	ALY	Rank	Power	Rank	Stuff	Rank	2nd Lev	Rank	Open Field	Rank	Sacks	ASR	Rank	Press	Rank	F-Start	Cont.
2017	3.78	3.89	20	63%	18	21%	18	0.99	26	0.51	25	54	9.2%	30	36.9%	31	20	23
2018	4.01	3.93	27	63%	23	20%	21	1.09	26	0.83	17	62	11.6%	32	38.5%	32	24	23
2019	4.52	4.13	21	81%	1	18%	11	1.26	12	0.93	12	49	8.4%	27	34.2%	28	30	21
2019 ALY by direction:			Left End 4.41 (10)			Left Tackle: 3.19 (27)			Mid/Guard: 4.45 (15)			Right Tackle: 2.84 (30)			Right End: 4.01 (18)			

2019 first-round pick Tytus Howard had an up-and-down rookie year after being shuffled between left guard and right tackle by the Texans during training camp. The power and agility project to make a good right tackle out of him, but he landed on IR with a torn MCL after trying to rehab and play through it. 🏈 2019 second-round pick Max Scharping was parked at left guard from Week 3 on and had a solid season as a pass-blocker that showed some real upper-level flashes. He was a bit slow on pulls though, and that's a big part of what Bill O'Brien likes to emphasize. 🏈 Nick Martin had his best season by far in 2019, leading Texans linemen in snaps per blown block. He's still not playing up to the huge extension he signed before the season, which averages $11 million per year, but he wasn't the liability that he had been in 2018 or 2017. 🏈 At right guard, Zach Fulton remains the starter despite being rumored to be on the chopping block at just about every phase of the offseason. On the eve of June, he agreed to a restructured contract that saves the Texans $2 million in cap space this year in exchange for guaranteeing his $5 million base salary. In-house competition from Senio Kelemete and Greg Mancz, who both played some each of the last two years, should push Fulton. But the guaranteed salary will win out despite some pedestrian phone booth play over the last few years. 🏈 The swing tackle role is up for grabs! Roderick Johnson, the incumbent, played fairly well but never appeared to have the confidence of the staff, who rotated him with 35-year-old Chris Clark after Howard was done for the season. They non-tendered Johnson as a restricted free agent and signed him to a cheaper deal, then drafted North Carolina legacy lineman Charlie Heck in the fourth round. Yes, that's Kansas City offensive line coach Andy Heck's son. Yes, he's 6-foot-8 and 311 pounds. Yes, those two things have overshadowed a fairly pedestrian college profile. How did you guess?

Defensive Front

Defensive Line	Age	Pos	G	Snaps	Plays	Overall TmPct	Rk	Stop	Dfts	BTkl	Runs	vs. Run St%	Rk	RuYd	Rk	Pass Rush Sack	Hit	Hur	Dsrpt
D.J. Reader*	26	DT	15	629	51	6.7%	19	40	7	2	46	78%	33	2.6	63	2.5	11	14	2
Charles Omenihu	23	DE	14	448	15	2.1%	94	11	5	3	7	57%	93	3.6	96	3.0	3	20	2
Angelo Blackson	28	DE	15	432	19	2.5%	91	16	3	1	17	88%	9	1.3	9	0.0	1	5	1
Brandon Dunn	28	DT	16	401	25	3.1%	--	22	1	4	24	88%	--	2.8	--	1.0	3	5	0
Carlos Watkins	27	DE	10	268	24	4.7%	80	19	3	2	19	79%	31	2.9	80	1.0	1	7	1

Edge Rushers	Age	Pos	G	Snaps	Plays	Overall TmPct	Rk	Stop	Dfts	BTkl	Runs	vs. Run St%	Rk	RuYd	Rk	Pass Rush Sack	Hit	Hur	Dsrpt
Whitney Mercilus	30	OLB	16	968	50	6.1%	26	41	23	6	36	75%	39	2.3	37	7.5	8	28	1
Brennan Scarlett	27	OLB	15	494	49	6.4%	28	25	7	4	35	51%	86	4.3	88	3.5	4	10	2
J.J. Watt	31	DE	8	482	27	6.6%	68	22	10	2	18	72%	53	2.4	43	4.0	18	38	4

Linebackers	Age	Pos	G	Snaps	Plays	Overall TmPct	Rk	Stop	Dfts	BTkl	Runs	vs. Run St%	Rk	RuYd	Rk	Pass Rush Sack	Hit	Hur	vs. Pass Tgts	Suc%	Rk	AdjYd	Rk	PD	Int
Zach Cunningham	26	ILB	16	955	138	16.9%	8	87	14	17	96	71%	11	2.7	9	2.0	0	9	35	51%	33	8.0	55	2	0
Benardrick McKinney	28	ILB	14	863	104	14.6%	29	60	11	7	62	68%	16	3.8	37	1.0	4	9	20	25%	68	10.2	64	3	0

Year	Yards	ALY	Rank	Power	Rank	Stuff	Rank	2nd Level	Rank	Open Field	Rank	Sacks	ASR	Rank	Press	Rank
2017	3.93	3.86	8	70%	25	22%	7	1.11	17	0.75	17	32	6.2%	21	29.0%	24
2018	3.11	3.56	1	67%	18	25%	3	0.88	2	0.21	1	43	7.4%	13	29.0%	20
2019	4.62	4.50	22	59%	7	14%	27	1.14	13	1.00	28	30	5.2%	29	28.3%	25
2019 ALY by direction:		Left End: 3.71 (10)			Left Tackle: 4.17 (13)			Mid/Guard: 4.76 (26)			Right Tackle: 3.86 (10)			Right End: 5.17 (23)		

There's probably not a non-quarterback in football that matters as much to his team's fate this season as J.J. Watt. He came back from the torn pectoral he suffered in late October and was a factor against the Bills in the playoffs, which is wild to even type out. He's still incredibly effective when he actually plays. 14 games of him would be a huge boost. Four games of him and the rest of this unit might collapse. ● D.J. Reader's departure should leave early-down roles for both Brandon Dunn and Angelo Blackson, neither of whom has really demonstrated all that much in terms of splash plays. Second-round pick Ross Blacklock (TCU) could push them for a spot in the base defense if he can be more stout than he was in college, but the former Horned Frog will likely play inside on passing downs right away due to his slippery nature. ● Whitney Mercilus got a huge contract extension after Week 17, but he was objectively a bit of a flop in a season-long role outside after the Texans ditched Jadeveon Clowney. 7.5 sacks are nice, but only two of them happened without Watt in the lineup, both against Tampa Bay in Week 16. ● Jonathan Greenard (Florida) led the SEC in sacks last year and is an extremely smart rusher who was sub-standard athletically. A 4.87s 40-yard dash and weak jump drills that led to a negative explosion score in SackSEER is a recipe for making it to the third round. However, Greenard is such a strong run defender that he might push incumbent Jack linebacker Brennan Scarlett for early-down snaps right away. ● Zach Cunningham had a breakout year in 2019, leading the NFL in successful run stops. Benardrick McKinney played well against the run as well but missed some time with a concussion suffered in Week 15 and may be getting close to his expiration date. Neither middle linebacker is great against the pass, and Dylan Cole got some dime snaps on account of that up until tearing his ACL in late November.

Defensive Secondary

Secondary	Age	Pos	G	Snaps	Plays	TmPct	Rk	Stop	Dfts	BTkl	Runs	St%	Rk	RuYd	Rk	Tgts	Tgt%	Rk	Dist	Suc%	Rk	AdjYd	Rk	PD	Int
						Overall					vs. Run					vs. Pass									
Justin Reid	23	SS	15	932	83	10.9%	23	28	10	14	35	37%	45	10.5	66	36	9.3%	20	12.0	58%	20	7.4	35	5	2
Tashaun Gipson*	30	FS	14	882	60	8.4%	51	19	8	12	24	29%	56	8.8	53	26	7.1%	44	11.8	46%	54	9.8	63	8	3
Vernon Hargreaves	25	CB	15	870	67	8.5%	32	20	8	16	11	64%	18	4.2	19	80	23.2%	18	13.3	39%	80	9.5	73	6	1
Gareon Conley	25	CB	14	784	63	8.8%	41	27	8	8	12	42%	46	7.3	59	65	19.7%	46	15.2	54%	35	9.1	69	13	1
Bradley Roby	28	CB	10	662	46	9.0%	76	20	10	11	10	60%	23	6.1	39	58	21.1%	31	11.6	52%	50	7.6	42	8	2
Johnathan Joseph*	36	CB	14	632	64	9.0%	36	28	11	10	5	40%	50	10.0	76	70	26.7%	2	13.5	50%	57	8.6	62	13	1
Lonnie Johnson	25	CB	14	543	45	6.3%	--	15	4	10	10	30%	--	7.2	--	46	20.4%	--	11.9	48%	--	8.7	--	7	0
Jahleel Addae*	30	FS	16	534	45	5.5%	--	16	9	5	16	25%	--	9.7	--	18	8.1%	--	7.4	56%	--	7.5	--	3	2
Eric Murray	26	FS	9	364	24	5.4%	--	17	5	5	13	92%	--	3.0	--	13	9.8%	--	11.6	62%	--	5.2	--	1	0
Jaylen Watkins	29	SS	14	305	27	4.0%	--	11	7	8	10	40%	--	6.2	--	16	16.2%	--	11.3	38%	--	9.4	--	1	0

Year	Pass D Rank	vs. #1 WR	Rk	vs. #2 WR	Rk	vs. Other WR	Rk	WR Wide	Rk	WR Slot	Rk	vs. TE	Rk	vs. RB	Rk
2017	25	12.4%	24	37.8%	30	16.6%	24	6.3%	24	33.6%	32	15.2%	27	-16.7%	7
2018	18	19.6%	31	0.9%	18	3.8%	20	-6.3%	18	25.9%	28	16.3%	23	-21.3%	3
2019	26	-1.1%	14	11.4%	24	-10.0%	10	-2.6%	20	6.4%	18	0.0%	15	21.7%	26

Cornerback was the No. 1 revolving door for the Texans last year, a position where there are no less than seven players that saw time and are in play for spots this year. 🏈 So naturally, let's start at safety: one of O'Brien's sneaky dumb moves was letting safety Tashaun Gipson aggravate his back injury in a meaningless Week 17 game, so he followed that up with a dumb offseason move of releasing Gipson to pay Eric Murray. Murray is kind of a corner/safety tweener without much real success at either spot. You may remember his safety work from his role with the Chiefs in the Monday Night game against the Rams that feels like it happened in 2015, the one where the Rams scored 54 points. 🏈 Justin Reid played through a torn labrum for the entirety of the 2019 season, which explains why he wasn't quite as good as he had been as a rookie. He'll continue to be the safety the Texans creep into the box. His average yardage on run tackles last year was a bit artificially high because of a couple of specific tackles after very long gains, in particular taking down Jonnu Smith after a 57-yard backfield toss play.

Bradley Roby got paid bank,
Gareon Conley make-or-break,
Lonnie Johnson's second year,
Phillip Gaines is somehow here,
Vernon Hargreaves complicates,
John Reid, rookie, Penn State,
Johnathan Joseph's Houston career ends
Cornell Armstrong breaks instead of bends
Crossen, Thomas, Jaylen Watkins,
Give some special teams vets a spin
At least DeMarcus Faggins is gone,
We're looking for a denouement!

Don't give up every third-and-loooooong/Roby's a solid starter when he is healthy/maybe two of the rest of you can be too, if you aren't this unit is in troub-bllllllle/until O'Brien trades his 2022 first for Jalen Ramsey.

Special Teams

Year	DVOA	Rank	FG/XP	Rank	Net Kick	Rank	Kick Ret	Rank	Net Punt	Rank	Punt Ret	Rank	Hidden	Rank
2017	-4.5%	26	-5.8	24	0.1	18	-5.3	30	-10.7	28	-1.1	21	-16.9	32
2018	3.5%	5	4.4	8	7.8	1	0.5	11	4.5	11	0.5	14	-2.5	19
2019	2.9%	5	-1.9	20	4.7	8	0.1	14	10.5	2	1.0	13	-7.6	28

John Christian Ka'iminoeauloameka'ikeokekumupa'a (Ka'imi) Fairbairn wrangled himself a four-year contract this off-season that placed him squarely among the NFL's elite kickers as far as total compensation. It was not Fairbairn's best year, though some of his misses were notably pointed out to be the result of poor holding. Still, five missed extra points is a lot for an elite kicker. The Texans have been excellent at kickoffs over the past two seasons, but Fairbairn's kicks have generated less value than the coverage. ✎ Bryan Anger punted well for the Texans after taking Trevor Daniel's job in Week 3. The result: a three-year extension that grants Anger a total value just inside of the top 10 among punters, which feels a bit aggressive for a player who has mostly been below average throughout his career. But if he repeats last season's performance, the Texans will be happy. ✎ Main returner DeAndre Carter is agile, spry, and fumbles often on contact. ✎ Backup safety A.J. Moore, a 2018 UDFA, has led the Texans in return stops each of the last two years. Eleven of his 12 special teams tackles last season were stops, meaning they ended a return before it reached average value. He also played a small part in some blitz packages near the end of the season.

Indianapolis Colts

2019 Record: 7-9	Total DVOA: -5.0% (16th)	2020 Mean Projection: 8.9 wins	On the Clock (0-4): 5%
Pythagorean Wins: 7.7 (17th)	Offense: -3.1% (19th)	Postseason Odds: 58.3%	Mediocrity (5-7): 24%
Snap-Weighted Age: 25.7 (30th)	Defense: 2.3% (17th)	Super Bowl Odds: 8.4%	Playoff Contender (8-10): 42%
Average Opponent: -4.5% (31st)	Special Teams: 0.4% (16th)	Proj. Avg. Opponent: -2.2% (32nd)	Super Bowl Contender (11+): 28%

2019: The franchise quarterback has retired, long live the franchise quarterback!

2020: ... short live the franchise quarterback!

Over the past two decades, no franchise has exemplified the importance of the quarterback position quite like the Indianapolis Colts. Since the turn of the century, in 16 seasons in which either of their former No. 1 overall draft pick franchise quarterbacks started more than half of their games, they only had a single losing record—which came all the way back in 2001—and made the playoffs 14 times. The only franchise with more playoff appearances over that span was the New England Patriots.

In the other four seasons, without those franchise quarterbacks, the Colts did not have a single winning record and finished 4-12 or worse twice.

Following Andrew Luck's shock retirement, last season's roster might have been good enough to buck that trend. However, an injury to Jacoby Brissett forced backup's backup Bryan Hoyer onto the field, and Hoyer's mistakes cost the team winnable games against Pittsburgh and Miami. The Steelers defeat was particularly demoralizing: the backup quarterback threw a pick-six, then the legendary clutch kicker missed a 43-yard game-winner in the last two minutes. But the horrible home loss to Miami is when the wheels really came off a wagon that seemed playoff-bound through the first half of the season. The defense played well, but the offense's -75.3% DVOA was one of the ten worst single-game ratings for any offense in 2019.

Those morale-sapping losses against the easiest portion of their schedule dropped the Colts to 5-4, and even after Brissett's return the Colts only had one more game with a positive overall DVOA the rest of their season. That second-half collapse led ultimately to another losing record. Had the Colts instead been 7-2 after Week 10, this offseason might have looked vastly different.

Following Brissett's return to the lineup in the Week 11 victory over the Jaguars, the team's offensive DVOA dropped over 10%, from 8.2% in Weeks 1 to 9 to -5.1% from Weeks 11 to 17. Brissett's passing DVOA took an even deeper plunge, from 13.0% in Weeks 1 to 9 to -8.9% in Weeks 11 to 17. Meanwhile, the team's defensive DVOA barely budged and the special teams unit, while still bad, was not quite as terrible in the second half as the first. By season's end the offense, defense, and special teams all ranked between No. 16 and No. 19 in the DVOA tables.

It is possible that Brissett's injury—a sprained MCL in the knee of his plant leg—was still causing him trouble early in the second-half skid, but he should have been long recovered by the time he played the worst three games of his campaign in Weeks 15 to 17. Two seasons as a starter have demonstrated that Brissett is a capable quarterback, but one who straddles the line between a top backup and a below-average starter. Conservatism may be his biggest flaw: his average completion was caught 5.1 yards beyond the line of scrimmage, the second-lowest of any passer with at least 300 attempts per NFL Next Gen Stats, and he had the second-longest average time to throw. His performance in the second half of the season demonstrated that even if the Colts had averted catastrophe against Pittsburgh and Miami to all but secure a winning season, that would not have reduced the need for an upgrade. Luck's abrupt retirement put the Colts in arguably the worst "good" situation possible for an NFL team. Their well-crafted roster was far too good for the Colts to bottom out like they did in 2012—when their 2-14 record dropped Luck into their collective laps—or even 2017, but they were not quite good enough to contend. They needed what they always need: a franchise quarterback.

Which is where Philip Rivers comes in. Rivers, as readers will surely know, is the most prolific passer in Chargers history. Fewer people realize that he is the sixth-most prolific passer by both yardage and touchdowns in league history, or that assuming he plays the full 2020 season at his usual level, he will almost certainly surpass Dan Marino for fifth in both categories—he needs barely 2,000 yards and 23 touchdowns to catch Marino. Even as he approaches 39 years old, that should be a reasonable expectation; Rivers has famously never missed a start since taking over in 2006, not even when he tore his ACL ahead of the 2007 AFC Championship Game. Including playoffs, Rivers has started 235 consecutive games, the second-longest streak in history behind Brett Favre's 321.

Yet despite his all-time great production, including two No. 1 finishes in DVOA in 2008 and 2009 and a league-leading 4,710 passing yards in 2010, Rivers has never really been regarded as the best quarterback in the league—usually not even one of the top two or three. A large part of the reason for that is a lack of playoff success: Rivers' Chargers teams only won five playoff games in his 14 seasons as the starter, and only made the playoffs six times. They only made a single AFC Championship Game, which they lost limply to

2020 Colts Schedule

Week	Opp.	Week	Opp.	Week	Opp.
1	at JAX	7	BYE	13	at HOU
2	MIN	8	at DET	14	at LV
3	NYJ	9	BAL	15	HOU (Sat.)
4	at CHI	10	at TEN (Thu.)	16	at PIT
5	at CLE	11	GB	17	JAX
6	CIN	12	TEN		

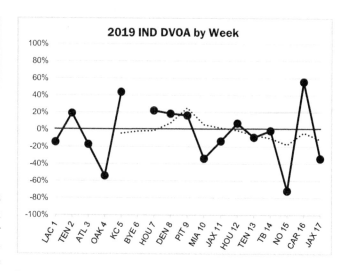

2019 IND DVOA by Week

the Patriots without scoring a single touchdown. (That was the game where Rivers played with a torn ACL.) Even when they made the postseason, his teams were better known for the nature of their defeats—the Marlon McCree interception-fumble against the Patriots in 2006, getting run all over by the Patriots in 2018—than their victories. Their most memorable playoff win of that era brought acclaim for punter Mike Scifres, not Rivers. Five of their playoff exits came at the hands of the AFC's Big Three quarterbacks—Peyton Manning, Tom Brady, and Ben Roethlisberger. In another era or the opposite conference, Rivers might be a certainty for the Hall of Fame. It is a darkly humorous twist of fate that even the one time in his career that Rivers was a free agent, Tom Brady eclipsed him as the most famous free-agent quarterback in history.

Still, like Brady, Rivers landed in his preferred location. In Indianapolis, he reunites with Frank Reich, who coached him from 2013 through 2015 in San Diego. The first of those years, when Reich was his quarterbacks coach, Rivers' 34.8% DVOA was the second-best of his career. The following two years, with Reich promoted to offensive coordinator, were roughly as prolific though not quite so efficient. Rivers is already familiar with Reich's playbook, which should help ease the transition amid historically challenging circumstances. He gets to play home games indoors for the first time in his career, in a stadium that might actually sound like a home stadium (pandemic permitting), on a team that has a very strong chance of making the postseason. Though his targets are inferior in Indianapolis—no Hunter Henry, no Keenan Allen, no Mike Williams, and no back nearly as prolific a receiver as Austin Ekeler—the offensive line is better, T.Y. Hilton is no slouch, and if the supporting cast was good enough to be a wild-card contender with Brissett at quarterback, it should be good enough to be a division contender with Rivers.

There are reasons to be wary of the current version of Rivers, however. Last year he passed for just 23 touchdowns, his lowest tally since 2008, and he threw 20 interceptions, one short of his career high. Scouts pointed to a significant decline in Rivers' arm strength, never his defining trait in the first place, which became more evident as the season progressed. By DVOA, three of Rivers' best six passing performances of the season came in the last four weeks. However, he achieved that by drastically dropping his average depth of target—from 9.5 yards in the first 12 games to 7.9 yards in the final four. There is more to arm strength than just throwing deep, and this does demonstrate that Rivers has the awareness to compensate for his fading arm, but there were definitely reasons to

be concerned despite the strong efficiency numbers.

Reich certainly understands concerns about Rivers' difficult 2019 season. When addressing them, he pointed to circumstances such as the Chargers' record causing Rivers to force throws he would not normally attempt, and there may be something to that: Rivers threw nine of his 20 interceptions while trailing in the fourth quarter, six of those within the last two minutes. (Whether Rivers would normally attempt such throws is debatable. Since 2006, Rivers has attempted more passes while trailing by at least four points in the last two minutes than anybody else; among the 28 players with at least 100 qualifying attempts, only Ryan Fitzpatrick, Blake Bortles, and Chad Henne have worse interception rates.)

Even with that unusually poor touchdown-to-interception ratio, however, Rivers was an above-average passer by DVOA, and the Chargers had a top-ten pass offense DVOA for the 11th time in Rivers' 14 years as their starting quarterback. The Colts, meanwhile, have only achieved a rank that high once since Peyton Manning's final season as their starter: they ranked exactly tenth in 2018, Luck's healthiest season. Reich points to 2018, when Rivers finished third in DVOA, as evidence that the quarterback still has plenty left. Even accounting for the decline in 2019, our numbers agree: we do not expect the Colts to have an elite offense with Rivers at quarterback, but we do expect them to be above average. That should be enough to realize Reich's twin hopes: that the Colts will make the postseason, and Rivers will be in Indianapolis for several seasons beyond the single year for which he is currently contracted. Rivers already has a high school coaching job lined up for the conclusion of his playing career, but the school is in no hurry and he has stated that he intends to take it one year at a time. A successful season that expands his undersized playoff resumé on a contending Colts team may make next season's decision easier even than this season's. (The reverse, of course, is true: a year of struggle may be enough to persuade Rivers that it's time to change careers.)

On defense, the biggest criticism of the recent Colts teams is a lack of impact defenders. Darius Leonard and Anthony Walker are IDP fantasy stars, and Bobby Okereke had a strong rookie year, but the impact of a great linebacker corps is simply not as great as that of an elite pass-rusher or a shutdown corner. That appears to have informed the team's headline off-season moves on defense: a trade for 49ers defensive lineman DeForest Buckner, and the free-agent signing of 2017 All-Pro cornerback Xavier Rhodes. The prospects for each player diverge widely: Buckner is a 26-year-old defensive tackle with 19.5 sacks in his past two seasons who should be approaching the prime of his career, whereas Rhodes is a 30-year-old cornerback coming off a terrible season. Buckner should become the key player on the defensive line; Rhodes' position is more precarious, though he will likely be given first shot at earning a starting job at outside corner. The rest of the defense is more or less as you were: free-agent signing T.J. Carrie will compete with the young trio of Kenny Moore, Rock Ya-Sin, and Marvell Tell for the other two cornerback spots, and third-round pick Julian Blackmon should enter the safety rotation in place of Clayton Geathers, but the Colts return 11 of the 13 defenders who started at least eight games for Matt Eberflus in 2019.

The defining trait of that defense was its averageness. It ranked No. 17 in DVOA overall, No. 19 against both pass and run. No. 15 in adjusted line yards, No. 18 in second-level yards, No. 11 in open-field yards. No. 21 in adjusted sack rate, No. 18 in pressure rate. No. 19 in both yards per drive and points per drive. The Colts did have a top-six finish in interceptions per drive, which is likely to regress, but they were also the worst defense against short-yardage runs, which is also likely to regress. This defense has neither great strengths nor great weaknesses. Even the signing of Buckner is no reason to expect a major leap forward, and though they did enjoy above-average health last year, it was not so far above average

that they should fear the impact of regression. Neither good enough to win games on its own nor bad enough to cost them, an adequate defense projects to remain just that.

That defense fits the story of our 2020 Colts projection: a team that has made enough improvements, and should benefit from enough positive regression, to leap all the way from average across the board to ... well, slightly above average across the board. The offensive projection lands amid a cluster of teams on the fringes of the top ten after ranking 19th in 2019, whereas we are forecasting milder improvements for the defense and special teams. We also project the Colts with the easiest schedule in the NFL, which should help propel them from visitor to host in the NFL's first six-game wild-card weekend. They are still well short of the top teams in the conference, however, and hardly prohibitive favorites even in their own division.

It is probably an overstatement to suggest that the Colts are "all-in" on 2020, but the 38-year-old quarterback does limit their current window. They have addressed their biggest weaknesses with their biggest signings, and they appear to have used their remaining draft picks well for depth and future potential. Rivers may prove to be a coup, and Buckner was an aggressive move, but otherwise the offseason has been appropriately safe for a team that had no reason to rip up the roster. The Colts are no closer to a long-term solution at their most critical position, but the stopgap solution should bring enough to return them to the postseason in what should be one of 2020's safest bets.

Andrew Potter

2019 Colts Stats by Week

Wk	vs.	W-L	PF	PA	YDF	YDA	TO	Total	Off	Def	ST
1	at LAC	L	24	30	376	435	+2	-14%	31%	25%	-21%
2	at TEN	W	19	17	288	243	-2	19%	6%	-23%	-9%
3	ATL	W	27	24	379	397	+1	-17%	22%	43%	4%
4	OAK	L	24	31	346	377	-1	-54%	-37%	14%	-3%
5	at KC	W	19	13	331	324	0	44%	7%	-30%	7%
6	BYE										
7	HOU	W	30	23	383	391	+1	22%	17%	-3%	3%
8	DEN	W	15	13	318	279	-1	19%	8%	-1%	10%
9	at PIT	L	24	26	328	273	-1	16%	15%	-16%	-15%
10	MIA	L	12	16	300	229	-1	-34%	-75%	-41%	0%
11	JAX	W	33	13	389	308	-1	-13%	1%	10%	-4%
12	at HOU	L	17	20	296	396	+1	8%	4%	-1%	3%
13	TEN	L	17	31	391	292	-1	-9%	-13%	-18%	-14%
14	at TB	L	35	38	309	542	+3	-1%	22%	25%	2%
15	at NO	L	7	34	205	424	0	-72%	-24%	40%	-8%
16	CAR	W	38	6	324	286	+3	56%	-5%	-10%	51%
17	at JAX	L	20	38	275	353	-1	-34%	-21%	15%	2%

Trends and Splits

	Offense	Rank	Defense	Rank
Total DVOA	-3.1%	19	2.3%	17
Unadjusted VOA	-0.4%	18	2.0%	18
Weighted Trend	-9.2%	24	1.1%	18
Variance	7.2%	15	5.9%	17
Average Opponent	3.5%	32	-0.6%	19
Passing	-2.3%	24	8.8%	19
Rushing	1.5%	7	-7.2%	19
First Down	-7.1%	24	-2.3%	13
Second Down	-5.2%	21	4.3%	20
Third Down	7.1%	12	8.6%	22
First Half	2.7%	12	-3.3%	12
Second Half	-9.0%	23	8.5%	21
Red Zone	2.6%	14	-2.8%	14
Late and Close	-11.0%	22	-7.3%	12

Five-Year Performance

Year	W-L	Pyth W	Est W	PF	PA	TO	Total	Rk	Off	Rk	Def	Rk	ST	Rk	Off AGL	Rk	Def AGL	Rk	Off Age	Rk	Def Age	Rk	ST Age	Rk
2015	8-8	6.0	5.5	333	408	-5	-12.9%	23	-15.6%	30	-2.2%	13	0.5%	16	26.2	11	44.1	26	27.1	13	28.6	1	26.3	11
2016	8-8	8.5	7.0	411	392	-5	-4.6%	23	3.7%	12	12.5%	29	4.1%	5	26.8	9	60.4	26	25.8	27	28.0	2	25.9	20
2017	4-12	4.2	4.3	263	404	+5	-22.8%	31	-17.8%	29	8.7%	27	3.7%	8	65.7	30	45.2	24	26.4	24	25.7	24	25.3	27
2018	10-6	10.3	10.0	433	344	+2	12.6%	8	8.2%	10	-3.4%	10	0.9%	12	57.0	28	51.6	28	25.8	28	25.3	28	25.7	19
2019	7-9	7.7	7.4	361	373	+2	-5.0%	16	-3.1%	19	2.3%	17	0.4%	16	38.6	16	26.7	10	26.0	28	25.6	25	25.1	29

2019 Performance Based on Most Common Personnel Groups

IND Offense					IND Offense vs. Opponents					IND Defense				IND Defense vs. Opponents			
Pers	Freq	Yds	DVOA	Run%	Pers	Freq	Yds	DVOA	Run%	Pers	Freq	Yds	DVOA	Pers	Freq	Yds	DVOA
11	61%	5.4	4.5%	37%	Base	21%	5.4	2.3%	58%	Base	33%	5.1	-7.2%	11	57%	6.4	8.4%
12	24%	5.7	-5.4%	43%	Nickel	67%	5.4	-3.2%	41%	Nickel	47%	6.3	12.6%	12	20%	5.7	-8.9%
13	6%	5.6	-24.4%	58%	Dime+	11%	6.1	19.2%	9%	Dime+	20%	6.2	-4.0%	21	6%	6.3	6.4%
21	4%	6.1	18.8%	50%	Goal Line	0%	1.4	-86.1%	60%	Goal Line	0%	-0.5	-20.4%	22	4%	4.1	-4.9%
612	3%	4.5	-13.0%	93%										13	3%	2.6	-32.9%
														621	3%	4.2	-12.0%

Strategic Tendencies

Run/Pass		Rk	Formation		Rk	Pass Rush		Rk	Secondary		Rk	Strategy		Rk
Runs, first half	40%	10	Form: Single Back	92%	2	Rush 3	7.8%	15	4 DB	33%	5	Play Action	30%	8
Runs, first down	49%	15	Form: Empty Back	6%	23	Rush 4	73.2%	6	5 DB	47%	24	Offensive Motion	37%	17
Runs, second-long	39%	2	Form: Multi Back	2%	32	Rush 5	14.3%	27	6+ DB	20%	11	Avg Box (Off)	6.56	16
Runs, power sit.	62%	7	Pers: 3+ WR	62%	20	Rush 6+	4.6%	18	Man Coverage	29%	25	Avg Box (Def)	6.49	19
Runs, behind 2H	39%	2	Pers: 2+ TE/6+ OL	34%	9	Edge Rusher Sacks	54.9%	17	CB by Sides	66%	26	Offensive Pace	31.79	25
Pass, ahead 2H	52%	8	Pers: 6+ OL	4%	10	Interior DL Sacks	15.9%	26	S/CB Cover Ratio	28%	9	Defensive Pace	31.77	29
Run-Pass Options	7%	11	Shotgun/Pistol	68%	15	Second Level Sacks	29.3%	6	DB Blitz	10%	16	Go for it on 4th	1.65	11

Indianapolis increased its run/pass ratio from the year before in each category listed above. ◗ The Colts' offensive pace slowed down substantially, as they dropped from second (28.5 seconds) to 25th (31.8 seconds) in situation-neutral pace. Philip Rivers' Chargers were dead last at 33.1 seconds. ◗ Indianapolis ranked 14th with 124 broken tackles after ranking in the bottom six in broken tackles for the previous four seasons. Marlon Mack had 39 broken tackles and three other backs each had at least a dozen. ◗ The Colts were one of three teams that used play-action on over 10% of third-down passes. (New England and Philadelphia were the others.) ◗ Once again, as in 2018, the Colts defense was much better against passes to the offensive left (-3.7% DVOA, 15th) than the offensive right (15.0% DVOA, 30th) even though they don't tend to play cornerbacks on specific sides. ◗ The gap was bigger in DVOA than in yardage, but the Colts were significantly better in zone coverage (20.8% DVOA, 7.5 yards per pass) than in man coverage (49.7% DVOA, 8.2 yards per pass). ◗ The Indianapolis defense ranked just 25th in pressure on first and second downs but improved to sixth on third and fourth downs. ◗ Indianapolis dropped from third in the league with 141 penalties in 2018 to dead last with only 101 penalties in 2019, including declined and offsetting.

Passing

Player	DYAR	DVOA	Plays	NtYds	Avg	YAC	C%	TD	Int
J.Brissett	414	2.6%	473	2786	5.9	5.6	61.5%	18	6
B.Hoyer*	-175	-53.1%	70	332	4.7	4.5	53.8%	4	4
P.Rivers	714	6.6%	625	4332	6.9	5.5	66.7%	23	20

Rushing

Player	DYAR	DVOA	Plays	Yds	Avg	TD	Fum	Suc
M.Mack	102	1.0%	247	1091	4.4	8	0	52%
N.Hines	38	8.4%	52	199	3.8	2	0	52%
J.Wilkins	64	20.9%	51	307	6.0	2	0	57%
J.Williams*	21	2.0%	49	235	4.8	1	0	53%
J.Brissett	57	10.1%	45	237	5.3	4	1	-
P.Rivers	-10	-41.9%	7	30	4.3	0	0	-

Receiving

Player	DYAR	DVOA	Plays	Ctch	Yds	Y/C	YAC	TD	C%
Z.Pascal	121	8.4%	72	41	607	14.8	5.8	5	57%
T.Hilton	76	1.6%	68	45	501	11.1	4.7	5	66%
M.Johnson	42	3.7%	33	17	277	16.3	2.5	2	52%
C.Rogers*	-11	-17.9%	28	16	179	11.2	4.3	2	57%
P.Campbell	-104	-73.4%	24	18	127	7.1	5.9	1	75%
D.Cain*	-2	-14.3%	14	4	52	13.0	2.8	0	29%
D.Inman*	-15	-39.0%	8	4	49	12.3	2.8	0	50%
J.Doyle	3	-6.7%	72	43	448	10.4	5.0	4	60%
E.Ebron*	21	-1.1%	52	31	375	12.1	5.0	3	60%
M.Alie-Cox	14	13.6%	11	8	93	11.6	7.5	0	73%
R.Travis*	-29	-70.7%	6	4	51	12.8	7.8	0	67%
T.Burton	-65	-49.1%	24	14	84	6.0	2.6	0	58%
N.Hines	-24	-21.5%	58	44	320	7.3	7.2	0	76%
M.Mack	-4	-18.5%	17	14	82	5.9	5.7	0	82%
J.Wilkins	-9	-31.5%	11	7	43	6.1	4.6	0	64%

Offensive Line

Player	Pos	Age	GS	Snaps	Pen	Sk	Pass	Run	Player	Pos	Age	GS	Snaps	Pen	Sk	Pass	Run
Mark Glowinski	LT	32	16/16	1092	2	3.5	15	6	Quenton Nelson	LG	24	16/16	1060	3	0.0	8	8
Anthony Castonzo	RG	28	16/16	1092	9	2.3	28	7	Ryan Kelly	C	27	16/16	1033	7	0.0	12	8
Braden Smith	RT	24	16/16	1091	5	7.3	34	9									

Year	Yards	ALY	Rank	Power	Rank	Stuff	Rank	2nd Lev	Rank	Open Field	Rank	Sacks	ASR	Rank	Press	Rank	F-Start	Cont.
2017	3.63	3.98	18	81%	2	20%	16	1.00	25	0.44	29	56	10.0%	32	37.0%	32	20	20
2018	4.55	4.83	4	59%	28	18%	9	1.34	6	0.74	22	18	4.1%	2	25.9%	6	15	24
2019	4.58	4.41	12	69%	7	20%	22	1.35	4	0.97	10	32	6.0%	7	34.8%	29	11	48
2019 ALY by direction:			Left End 2.99 (30)			Left Tackle: 4.98 (4)			Mid/Guard: 4.54 (11)			Right Tackle: 4.47 (12)			Right End: 5.84 (2)			

No other team can surpass the recent offensive line continuity of the Colts: they return all five starters for the second straight offseason. All five started every game in 2019, after only Quenton Nelson achieved that feat the previous year. ◐ The Colts allowed the fifth-worst pressure rate on offense in 2019, but the fault for this most likely lies with quarterback Jacoby Brissett rather than the offensive line: Brissett took an average of 2.93 seconds to release the ball, second-longest of any quarterback, per NFL Next Gen Stats. Incoming quarterback Philip Rivers' Chargers were exactly league median in pressure rate, and Rivers had the fifth-shortest average time to throw. ◐ Brissett was not the only reason, however: the Colts took a dramatic negative swing in blown blocks. They blew a block every 5.9 pass plays, after only blowing one every 15.1 pass plays in 2018. Pass-blocking on the right side of the line was the biggest issue: both Mark Glowinski and Braden Smith ranked in the bottom six at their position in this statistic, mainly due to 62 combined blown pass blocks. Both players were above average in 2018. ◐ Fifth-round pick Danny Pinter (Ball State) converted to offensive tackle from tight end midway through his college career. He is technically sound but lacks the physical profile to be an effective NFL tackle. His most likely destination is the practice squad as a developmental interior lineman.

Defensive Front

Defensive Line	Age	Pos			Overall						vs. Run					Pass Rush			
			G	Snaps	Plays	TmPct	Rk	Stop	Dfts	BTkl	Runs	St%	Rk	RuYd	Rk	Sack	Hit	Hur	Dsrpt
Grover Stewart	27	DT	16	632	31	3.9%	63	25	5	1	27	78%	34	2.4	51	3.0	3	15	1
Denico Autry	30	DT	14	631	35	5.0%	47	29	11	2	26	77%	39	2.0	31	3.5	6	20	5
Margus Hunt*	33	DT	16	456	17	2.1%	93	10	1	5	15	60%	87	3.2	91	0.0	0	6	0
Tyquan Lewis	25	DT	9	228	5	1.1%	--	4	1	2	4	75%	--	2.3	--	0.0	1	10	0
DeForest Buckner	26	DT	16	824	62	7.8%	8	51	17	2	47	77%	44	3.0	84	7.5	6	25	4
Sheldon Day	26	DT	16	330	14	1.8%	--	10	2	2	10	80%	--	2.5	--	1.0	1	7	0

Edge Rushers	Age	Pos	G	Snaps	Plays	TmPct	Rk	Stop	Dfts	BTkl	Runs	St%	Rk	RuYd	Rk	Sack	Hit	Hur	Dsrpt
					Overall							vs. Run				Pass Rush			
Justin Houston	31	DE	16	685	43	5.3%	38	37	20	3	28	82%	15	2.1	28	11.0	8	28	2
Jabaal Sheard*	31	DE	13	579	27	4.1%	67	23	11	7	15	93%	3	1.4	13	4.5	4	26	3
Al-Quadin Muhammad	25	DE	16	489	26	3.2%	72	21	8	6	19	84%	12	2.1	29	3.0	6	21	1
Ben Banogu	24	DE	16	273	12	1.5%	--	9	5	1	7	57%	--	3.0	--	2.5	3	16	1

Linebackers	Age	Pos	G	Snaps	Plays	TmPct	Rk	Stop	Dfts	BTkl	Runs	St%	Rk	RuYd	Rk	Sack	Hit	Hur	Tgts	Suc%	Rk	AdjYd	Rk	PD	Int
					Overall							vs. Run				Pass Rush				vs. Pass				
Darius Leonard	25	OLB	13	837	128	19.6%	12	69	28	9	65	55%	62	4.6	72	5.0	2	10	31	48%	40	5.0	11	7	5
Anthony Walker	25	MLB	16	820	125	15.5%	14	76	15	18	65	68%	17	3.2	15	2.5	1	6	40	63%	9	5.3	16	2	1
Bobby Okereke	24	OLB	16	478	60	7.5%	64	32	5	7	35	51%	71	3.5	26	1.0	0	0	17	47%	44	7.9	53	2	0

Year	Yards	ALY	Rank	Power	Rank	Stuff	Rank	2nd Level	Rank	Open Field	Rank	Sacks	ASR	Rank	Press	Rank
2017	3.96	4.09	16	64%	18	20%	20	1.11	16	0.69	15	25	4.5%	31	31.7%	10
2018	3.84	3.96	7	65%	14	25%	4	1.10	7	0.69	10	38	5.3%	29	28.0%	25
2019	4.11	4.24	15	83%	32	20%	13	1.18	18	0.65	11	41	6.6%	21	30.1%	18
2019 ALY by direction:			Left End: 3.77 (11)			Left Tackle: 4.62 (21)			Mid/Guard: 4.16 (7)			Right Tackle: 4.41 (17)			Right End: 4.61 (16)	

The Colts pass rush is another clear example of a unit where the team has no major weak spots but also no standout performers. Justin Houston's 28 charted hurries were the fifth-lowest tally for a team-leading player, but seven of the eight defensive linemen with at least 100 defensive snaps had 10 or more hurries. The only exception was veteran Margus Hunt, who is now in New Orleans. ◆ Incoming defensive tackle DeForest Buckner should help with that: Buckner had 25 hurries in San Francisco. Buckner is not just a pass disruptor though: his 17 defeats were the third-most of any defensive tackle, and they were split almost equally between run and pass. Buckner also injects some needed youth into a line for which three of last season's four primary starters will be over 30 on opening day. ◆ We would like to see more playing time for last year's second-round pick Ben Banogu, a SackSEER favorite due to his explosion off the line. ◆ Despite missing three games to injury, Darius Leonard had the most pass defeats of any off-ball linebacker and the second-most of any player behind only sack leader Shaq Barrett. ◆ 2019 third-round pick Bobby Okereke stood out during his rookie season, especially in pass coverage. He played mainly as a strongside/third linebacker in base defense, but also started at middle linebacker during Leonard's injury absence. ◆ Sixth-round draft pick Rob Windsor was a productive player at Penn State, but he lacks the size and strength to play defensive tackle in the NFL. He may find a depth role at defensive end after some time on the practice squad. ◆ Fellow sixth-rounder Jordan Glasgow (Michigan) projects as a safety/linebacker tweener in the NFL, but he was probably drafted more for his special teams prowess. He was an excellent tackler and special teams standout in college.

Defensive Secondary

Secondary	Age	Pos	G	Snaps	Plays	TmPct	Rk	Stop	Dfts	BTkl	Runs	St%	Rk	RuYd	Rk	Tgts	Tgt%	Rk	Dist	Suc%	Rk	AdjYd	Rk	PD	Int
					Overall							vs. Run					vs. Pass							
Rock Ya-Sin	24	CB	15	864	66	8.8%	30	28	10	4	17	53%	31	3.9	16	50	15.5%	74	14.4	48%	60	10.6	81	5	1
Malik Hooker	24	FS	13	796	54	8.3%	59	18	9	11	24	38%	43	11.0	68	17	5.7%	57	15.6	29%	71	13.5	72	3	2
Pierre Desir*	30	CB	12	694	61	10.1%	45	21	8	8	9	44%	44	7.0	54	60	23.2%	17	14.4	43%	76	9.8	75	11	3
Kenny Moore	25	CB	11	641	64	11.6%	34	38	15	7	25	76%	7	2.8	5	42	17.6%	63	10.3	43%	77	7.5	41	3	2
Khari Willis	24	SS	14	631	72	10.2%	39	28	6	11	40	40%	39	5.8	25	19	8.1%	35	6.6	58%	21	5.6	16	1	0
Clayton Geathers*	28	SS	15	535	49	6.5%	63	15	4	8	30	40%	39	6.3	32	18	9.0%	23	9.6	22%	74	9.9	65	1	1
George Odum	27	FS	16	288	30	3.7%	--	11	10	3	6	50%	--	6.0	--	12	11.2%	--	8.7	58%	--	7.8	--	0	0
Marvell Tell	24	CB	13	255	27	4.1%	--	12	5	0	5	60%	--	4.6	--	30	31.5%	--	11.7	60%	--	8.5	--	5	0
Xavier Rhodes	30	CB	15	807	69	8.4%	37	25	12	7	12	67%	11	3.2	9	62	18.2%	59	11.4	32%	85	9.8	76	6	0
T.J. Carrie	30	CB	16	691	54	6.8%	--	26	12	7	21	76%	--	4.5	--	47	18.7%	--	9.1	38%	--	8.2	--	4	1
Michael Thomas	30	SS	16	306	43	5.0%	--	19	14	4	13	62%	--	4.8	--	18	16.1%	--	10.1	33%	--	10.6	--	3	0

Year	Pass D Rank	vs. #1 WR	Rk	vs. #2 WR	Rk	vs. Other WR	Rk	WR Wide	Rk	WR Slot	Rk	vs. TE	Rk	vs. RB	Rk
2017	32	7.6%	18	22.7%	27	28.5%	31	22.3%	32	18.4%	24	9.9%	23	27.9%	31
2018	20	1.8%	17	-27.9%	1	-3.8%	14	-12.1%	8	-8.4%	6	21.2%	29	12.3%	25
2019	19	7.7%	22	7.2%	22	24.9%	29	7.4%	22	19.3%	28	4.1%	18	-11.1%	7

Incoming former All-Pro cornerback Xavier Rhodes led the NFL with 139 penalty yards in 2019. Ninety-nine of those yards came on just four pass interference fouls. Rhodes also had the worst coverage success rate of any player with at least four starts or 25 pass targets. ❧ Fellow newcomer T.J. Carrie played all 64 games over the past four seasons for Oakland and Cleveland, with 33 starts. In that time, he has never stood out in our charting numbers, for better or worse. He is roughly the definition of a slightly below average starter. ❧ An in-house name to watch at cornerback is converted former USC safety Marvell Tell. Tell started two games in place of Pierre Desir in his rookie season, when he showed off his size, athleticism, and tackling ability. Another year of development may see him ascend to a starting role. ❧ At midseason, rookie slot cornerback Rock Ya-Sin was something of a punchline for his penalties. However, those issues were basically confined to Week 8: five of his nine total penalty flags were earned in that one game. Ya-Sin was a very assured tackler: his 7.5% broken tackle rate was the best on the team and the fifth-best among all defensive backs with at least 30 solo tackles. ❧ In contract to Ya-Sin's individual success, the Colts defense allowed a broken tackle on 11.8% of plays, the seventh-worst rate in the league. Seven different defenders failed to secure at least 20% of their tackles (minimum 10 solo tackles), including both starting safeties. Tackling was particularly important for the Colts because they allowed the fourth-most pass completions of any team. Only the Chargers allowed their opponents to complete a higher percentage of their passes. ❧ Third-round pick Julian Blackmon (Utah) is a coverage safety with experience at cornerback who fits the versatile profile NFL teams covet. He could quickly find a home at free safety or as a third safety/big nickelback.

Special Teams

Year	DVOA	Rank	FG/XP	Rank	Net Kick	Rank	Kick Ret	Rank	Net Punt	Rank	Punt Ret	Rank	Hidden	Rank
2017	3.7%	8	0.4	16	1.6	16	-1.2	18	20.2	1	-2.6	23	5.0	9
2018	0.9%	12	-1.9	22	-1.5	24	-1.1	17	9.1	3	0.1	15	-8.6	26
2019	0.4%	16	-13.3	31	-1.3	21	-2.8	25	2.4	14	17.0	1	-11.7	31

Field-goal kicking was a major issue for the Colts all year. They converted only 84.6% of extra points, the worst rate of any team in the league, and had the fourth-worst rate of successful field goals. Adam Vinatieri's 78.6% conversion rate on extra points was the second-worst ever for a kicker with at least 20 attempts, better than only Steve Little of the 1979 St. Louis Cardinals. Vinatieri's 68% field-goal rate was terrible, but not historically so: two other kickers have had lower rates in just the past two years while attempting at least 20 field goals. ❧ Vinatieri hopes to kick again this season after finishing 2019 on injured reserve, but it is unlikely to be in Indianapolis. The Colts kept 2019 rookie Chase McLaughlin and signed Georgia's iconic kicker Rodrigo Blankenship as an undrafted free agent. Those two will compete directly to be Vinatieri's long-term replacement. ❧ Rigoberto Sanchez has been a very average punter over the past three seasons. ❧ Though listed as a cornerback, sixth-round pick Isaiah Rodgers (UMass) is more likely to make the roster as a kick returner. Rodgers has sub-4.3s speed, and he holds the school record for kick return yards. ❧ The Colts averaged 17.4 yards per punt return, by far the best figure in the league. The next-best figure was the Jets, at 11.4 yards per return. Nyheim Hines scored two touchdowns on just nine punt returns, averaging 31.2 yards per return. That is the highest average in history for a player with multiple punt return touchdowns. ❧ Only the Eagles lost more than the Colts' -11.7 points of hidden value on special teams. No opposing placekicker missed an extra point against the Colts all year, and opponents missed only two field goals, both from 45 yards or more.

Jacksonville Jaguars

2019 Record: 6-10	**Total DVOA:** -17.8% (28th)	**2020 Mean Projection:** 7.1 wins	**On the Clock (0-4):** 17%
Pythagorean Wins: 5.3 (26th)	**Offense:** -9.5% (24th)	**Postseason Odds:** 29.9%	**Mediocrity (5-7):** 41%
Snap-Weighted Age: 25.5 (32nd)	**Defense:** 11.0% (29th)	**Super Bowl Odds:** 1.9%	**Playoff Contender (8-10):** 33%
Average Opponent: -2.8% (25th)	**Special Teams:** 2.7% (6th)	**Proj. Avg. Opponent:** -1.0% (24th)	**Super Bowl Contender (11+):** 10%

2019: It wasn't a failed season. It was pre-successful.

2020: All we need is a defense and an offense and some rule changes.

One of the many long-running gags in the recently-ended NBC series *The Good Place* is the unrelenting optimism of fictional Jacksonville resident and Jaguars fan Jason Mendoza. The first series introduces him, eventually, as a seemingly diehard fan of Blake Bortles. Later, one piece of evidence that our heroes have messed up the mortal timeline is Bortles' Jaguars reaching the AFC Championship Game. When Bortles is cut during the fourth season, Jason's not-a-robot wife hesitates to tell him the news for fear of crushing his spirits; instead, his reaction is euphoria that they have now signed Super Bowl champ Nick Foles. No matter what, Jason's reaction to any news is consistently the most blindly optimistic of any character.

Jason is probably meant to represent the irrationality of all sports fans, but it was no accident that the writers chose the Jaguars as the prop. As the franchise appears headed for yet another multi-year rebuild—beginning at least their fifth such rebuild in the past 20 years—the gags remain more accurate than the changing cast of quarterbacks. To be a Jaguars fan in the 2010s was to hunt for optimism anywhere you could find it: it was the decade of Blaine Gabbert and Blake Bortles, of Gus Bradley and the return of Tom Coughlin. In just the past season, the franchise traded away All-Pro cornerback Jalen Ramsey, was called out publicly by the NFLPA for their handling of player discipline under aforementioned former general manager Coughlin, and earned their 10th top-10 draft pick in the past 11 seasons.

2020 has not started off any better. The offseason so far includes a very public Twitter spat between star pass-rusher Yannick Ngakoue and Executive VP Tony Khan, reported failed attempts to trade starting running back Leonard Fournette, and a salary-dump trade of the team's most effective front seven defender, Calais Campbell. The core of the roster from the franchise's most successful season this century has been completely gutted. That quarterback is now a free-agent backup, and both starting receivers are now backups on other teams. None of the players from that vaunted 2017 secondary are still on the roster. Of the #SACKSONVILLE pass rush, only Ngakoue remains—and only grudgingly at the time of writing. Ngakoue's expected departure would leave only six players, total, who started at least 10 games just three years ago. This is part of the problem with always rebuilding in discrete cycles: even if everything comes together as it did in 2017, everybody gets expensive at the same time and the roster is dismantled more quickly than it was assembled.

The quickest way to break that cycle is to draft a franchise quarterback, a task at which the Jaguars have failed time and time again. While there would be a certain enjoyable irony in a team that threw so many first-round picks at the problem finding their answer in the sixth round, such an outcome for Gardner Minshew is far from assured. Minshew can argue that he had the best rookie quarterback season in Jaguars franchise history: Byron Leftwich had a superior 5.5% DVOA in 2003, but Minshew had a higher completion percentage, fewer interceptions, and more attempts, yards, and touchdowns. Despite this unusual rookie success, the coaching staff saw enough limitations to bench him as soon as Nick Foles was healthy. Though they subsequently relented, Minshew's passing DVOA after returning to the lineup in Week 13 was -21.4%, versus -0.4% in his surprise stint from Weeks 2 to 9. Four of his best five games came in that initial stretch, and the fifth was the meaningless season finale against Indianapolis. While Minshew showed enough promise to let Jaguars fans believe that he *could be* the answer, he will have to take a significant step forward in his second year. Otherwise, particularly given his undoubted charisma on and off the field, he appears destined for a career as the clichéd "most popular guy in town" backup quarterback.

If Minshew is to take that step forward, he will likely need assistance from a supporting cast which appears marginally stronger than last season. The offensive line is unchanged from 2019: three of the previously mentioned six remaining starters from 2017 have been joined by left guard Andrew Norwell, a big-money signing from Carolina in 2018, and by 2019 second-round pick Jawaan Taylor at right tackle. The line is not excellent, but it is far from the liability faced by many other passers. Despite the trade rumors swirling around him this offseason, Fournette is likely to be the starting running back throughout the final season of his rookie contract. (That is, admittedly, tepid news: Fournette has not reached positive rushing DYAR since his rookie season, and he has been an off-field headache more than once.) A team with a strong track record for developing young second-round wide receivers added Laviska Shenault to a corps that already includes DJ Chark, Chris Conley, and Dede Westbrook, all of whom had productive seasons in 2019. Receiving back Chris

2020 Jaguars Schedule

Week	Opp.	Week	Opp.	Week	Opp.
1	IND	7	BYE	13	at MIN
2	at TEN	8	at LAC	14	TEN
3	MIA (Thu.)	9	HOU	15	at BAL
4	at CIN	10	at GB	16	CHI
5	at HOU	11	PIT	17	at IND
6	DET	12	CLE		

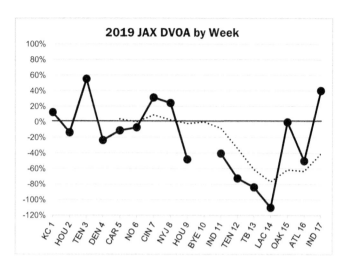

2019 JAX DVOA by Week

Thompson joins from Washington to provide a route-running option out of the backfield. Tight end Tyler Eifert also joins from Cincinnati where, when healthy—which is admittedly seldom for long—he was once one of the better receiving tight ends in the league. If the young quarterback can improve on his weaknesses from last season, the pieces are in place for this to be a more effective offense.

The man now tasked with ensuring that happens is Thompson's former Washington head coach and Eifert's former Bengals offensive coordinator, Jay Gruden. Gruden's favored offense is a West Coast system that relies heavily on a mobile quarterback for rollouts and bootlegs, a featured running back, and the ability for any eligible player to become a pass target. Gruden's arrival should be good news for Fournette, assuming Fournette can stay healthy and happy: Gruden's featured backs tend to be near the league lead in carries and yards, and he has drawn 1,000-yard seasons out of Cedric Benson, BenJarvus Green-Ellis, and Alfred Morris, all of whom were less talented than Fournette. Thompson should reprise his Washington role as the traditional receiving-down back, from which he led all backs in receiving DYAR in 2017. Minshew should contribute as a runner too, a role in which he added over 350 yards mainly as a scrambler in 2019.

Gruden is also accustomed to working with limited young passers. He coached Andy Dalton and the Bengals to the playoffs three years running as Marvin Lewis' offensive coordinator before being lured to Landover, where he helped mold Kirk Cousins into a $20-million-a-year player. He also drew occasional production in Washington from the likes of Colt McCoy and Josh Johnson, players who are usually closer to the roster bubble than the starting lineup. Minshew's mobility and improvisational skills should suit an offense that typically incorporates a lot of bootlegs and rollouts, with the caveat that no offense at this level can be built around the off-script plays that provided so many of Minshew's highlights. Minshew needs to get more effective at running plays as they are drawn up, a task which Gruden's offense should make easier for him. Gruden's scheme should also suit the skill sets of Westbrook and Shenault at wide receiver. On the surface, this looks like an uncharacteristically astute hire by the Jaguars front office.

If there is an obvious criticism, it is that Gruden's offense seldom enjoys much objective success: only one finish above No. 12 in DVOA in either Cincinnati or Washington, versus three finishes No. 28 or lower. His more successful Bengals and Washington offenses had better No. 1 receivers than the Jaguars do (A.J. Green, DeSean Jackson), better quarterbacks

(Andy Dalton, Kirk Cousins), and far superior offensive lines. However, Gruden's offenses have averaged -4.4% DVOA since 2011, which depressingly would be Jacksonville's second-best offensive DVOA over that span. The Jaguars have not had an above-average offense since 2010, whereas even Washington achieved that a couple of times with Gruden at the helm. This may be a match mired in mediocrity rather than one made in heaven, but even mediocrity has been beyond the Jaguars offense for most of the past 10 years.

The other huge concern facing the Jaguars offense is its fragility. We have already mentioned Eifert's injury history: despite his talent, he only started three games for the Bengals last season and was used sparingly throughout the campaign. That enabled him to play all 16 games for the first time in his career; he has missed at least half the season four times in his seven seasons as a professional. Shenault was widely considered a first-round talent who dropped to the second round because of his injury record. Fournette has battled persistent ankle problems since his college days. Thompson has played 16 games only once in seven years. The Jaguars have already been over 100 adjusted games lost on offense in each of the past two seasons, yet they added at least two notoriously fragile players (Eifert, Shenault) to that mix.

On a team-wide level we would usually expect some positive regression from a high tally of adjusted games lost, but individual players who tend to get injured do not typically get injured less as they get older. A full season from the team's best offensive players would give the Jaguars a chance of posting their best offense since the days of David Garrard and Maurice Jones-Drew, but the history of these players is against them. The backup pool at every position is mostly young Day 3 picks, waiver claims, and undrafted free agents, so the team can ill-afford any loss of playing time from its starters. That is, and will likely always be, a precarious position for a team playing this sport.

Those concerns are reflected in our offensive projection, which has the Jaguars amid a cluster of teams in similar situations near the bottom end of the rankings. The Bears, Giants, Bills, Jaguars, and Broncos are projected within a couple of percentage points of one another, and are all in much the same boat: young, mobile quarterbacks who have a bunch of highlight plays, but who need to become more accurate and consistent from one down to the next. (Miami almost matches that description too, but rookie Tua Tagovailoa is a slightly different case.) There is a decent chance that one or two of those players will make the leap next season, and every one of those fanbases believes it will be their guy; that's part of the optimism of sports. Unfortunately, the only guaranteed outcome is that somebody is going to be disappointed.

Our defensive projection is more favorable, mainly based on the same regression toward the mean that caused us to be wary of the team heading into the 2018 season. Then, the team had posted an exceptionally high DVOA after several below-average years. Now, the team has posted an uncharacteristically low DVOA after two straight years near the top. Even without that track record, our system would expect them to improve through natural regression, but we generally expect units that make an unusually large improvement or decline to fall somewhere between the two extremes the following season.

However, the player turnover on defense is much more pronounced than on offense, and that turnover may be underrepresented in our projection. In the small three-game sample Ramsey played last season before his hamstring injury and subsequent trade, the Jaguars pass defense posted a DVOA of -8.7%, which would have been good for seventh in the season-long table. That would also have been roughly in line with their 2018 rating of -5.2% (sixth). In the 13 games without Ramsey, their 21.3% DVOA would have ranked No. 28, which is more in keeping with the Gus Bradley era than the Ramsey-era defenses. Ramsey's departure came early last season, so he is not considered a loss in this offseason's projection. In Ramsey's absence, A.J. Bouye had his worst season in Jacksonville, also reducing the importance of Bouye in our accounting for starters lost. Free-agent signing Rashaan Melvin is a solid veteran, and top draft pick CJ Henderson has all the attributes required to be the franchise's next star cornerback, but the lack of depth and experience is again a worry. Henderson will probably have to perform as a shutdown player immediately if the Jaguars defense is to rebound anywhere close to their 2018 performance.

We also need to consider that last season the team still had the services of Calais Campbell and Yannick Ngakoue, one of whom has already moved on while the other seeks a tag-and-trade or similar agreement. Campbell will be 34 on opening day and had his lowest sack and defeats totals since 2015, so we might have expected a performance decline from him anyway. Ngakoue's expected departure is not a factor in the projection, because he technically remains on the roster and might yet play the season under the franchise tag. Those have been the team's top two pass-rushers since 2017, and despite an excellent rookie season from Josh Allen, he, Duwuane

Smoot, and first-round rookie K'Lavon Chaisson are not (yet) nearly so imposing a combination. Joe Schobert's arrival in free agency filled the biggest hole in the front seven, so even without Ngakoue this is probably the strongest unit on the team. If the front office could somehow bring Ngakoue back into the fold, the pass rush would again be the clear strength of the defense, although Campbell's presence on and off the field will be difficult to replace. Our projection envisages a degree of upward regression toward the team's previous performance mean, but that strong performance was driven more by talent than scheme and most of that top-level talent has now been replaced in a very short period of time. There is still a lot of talent on this defense, headlined by Allen's 10.5-sack rookie season and augmented by the arrival of Schobert and Henderson, but there are reasons to be skeptical of how quickly that will translate to improvement.

In one sense, given the exodus of established talent and the impression that the team is preparing for another rebuild, outside expectations are so low that the Jaguars can hardly lose this season. If they are better than expected, it probably means Gardner Minshew has established himself as a viable starting quarterback and the coaching staff has done enough to earn an extension. If they are as bad as (or worse than) expectations, they have a possible interim/successor with head coaching experience, they will be in a strong position to select the top prospect in April's draft, and they can choose to pair him with whichever head coach they deem appropriate.

In the other, less abstract sense, we expect the Jaguars to lose *plenty* this season. Though reaching the median projection of seven wins would hardly be considered disastrous, it would probably mean a change of coaching staff and quarterback unless Minshew excels and is let down by other units. Our model again expects the Jaguars to finish last in the AFC South and to make yet another pick somewhere around the top 10 of the draft. This was a 6-10 squad last season that appears to have weakened rather than strengthened during the offseason, and our projection still includes a contribution from Ngakoue that looks unlikely to materialize. That puts the team firmly in rebuild mode unless they get the sort of surprise even Jason Mendoza might struggle to believe.

In Jason's fictional universe, even the vaunted Good Place turned out neither to be as good as advertised, nor to stay good for long. It took four long, challenging seasons to get there, only for it to end in disappointment and for all the key contributors to the success to ultimately move on. The future, for those who remained, was left vague and uncertain.

Any ongoing similarities to the Jacksonville Jaguars are surely coincidental.

Andrew Potter

2019 Jaguars Stats by Week

Wk	vs.	W-L	PF	PA	YDF	YDA	TO	Total	Off	Def	ST
1	KC	L	26	40	428	491	-2	13%	46%	35%	2%
2	at HOU	L	12	13	281	263	-1	-13%	-38%	-22%	3%
3	TEN	W	20	7	292	340	+1	55%	21%	-28%	6%
4	at DEN	W	26	24	455	371	+1	-23%	10%	31%	-2%
5	at CAR	L	27	34	507	445	-3	-11%	21%	38%	6%
6	NO	L	6	13	226	326	-1	-7%	-26%	-18%	1%
7	at CIN	W	27	17	460	291	+4	31%	-13%	-47%	-3%
8	NYJ	W	29	15	389	213	+2	25%	2%	-31%	-8%
9	HOU	L	3	26	356	410	-3	-48%	-27%	17%	-4%
10	BYE										
11	at IND	L	13	33	308	389	+1	-41%	-21%	22%	2%
12	at TEN	L	20	42	369	471	+1	-72%	-10%	62%	0%
13	TB	L	11	28	242	315	-3	-84%	-84%	5%	6%
14	LAC	L	10	45	252	525	0	-110%	-24%	93%	7%
15	at OAK	W	20	16	262	364	0	0%	-6%	6%	12%
16	at ATL	L	12	24	288	518	+1	-50%	-13%	40%	3%
17	IND	W	38	20	353	275	+1	41%	16%	-11%	13%

Trends and Splits

	Offense	Rank	Defense	Rank
Total DVOA	-9.5%	24	11.0%	29
Unadjusted VOA	-8.7%	23	11.6%	29
Weighted Trend	-16.1%	28	16.0%	31
Variance	9.0%	24	14.0%	32
Average Opponent	2.6%	27	0.1%	15
Passing	0.1%	22	12.2%	22
Rushing	-14.5%	28	9.7%	31
First Down	-8.0%	25	4.1%	21
Second Down	-9.7%	23	17.6%	30
Third Down	-12.0%	23	15.4%	27
First Half	-14.5%	27	11.2%	30
Second Half	-5.3%	18	10.8%	26
Red Zone	-27.0%	29	7.3%	20
Late and Close	2.4%	17	-0.6%	19

Five-Year Performance

Year	W-L	Pyth W	Est W	PF	PA	TO	Total	Rk	Off	Rk	Def	Rk	ST	Rk	Off AGL	Rk	Def AGL	Rk	Off Age	Rk	Def Age	Rk	ST Age	Rk
2015	5-11	6.2	5.8	376	448	-10	-16.0%	25	-5.4%	21	9.7%	26	-0.9%	20	24.7	10	43.4	25	25.6	30	26.4	22	25.4	29
2016	3-13	5.8	5.4	318	400	-16	-10.4%	26	-11.3%	27	-3.1%	12	-2.3%	23	52.0	26	24.3	6	25.6	31	25.9	28	25.5	26
2017	10-6	11.9	9.0	417	268	+10	13.2%	8	-0.3%	16	-16.2%	1	-2.7%	24	31.5	15	4.1	1	26.1	28	25.9	22	26.0	11
2018	5-11	5.7	6.1	245	316	-12	-8.1%	22	-22.0%	30	-9.4%	6	4.4%	4	87.1	32	15.4	5	26.3	21	26.2	16	25.6	24
2019	6-10	5.3	6.6	300	397	-1	-17.8%	28	-9.5%	24	11.0%	29	2.7%	6	55.4	27	44.8	25	25.3	32	25.6	26	25.8	17

2019 Performance Based on Most Common Personnel Groups

JAX Offense					JAX Offense vs. Opponents					JAX Defense					JAX Defense vs. Opponents			
Pers	Freq	Yds	DVOA	Run%	Pers	Freq	Yds	DVOA	Run%	Pers	Freq	Yds	DVOA		Pers	Freq	Yds	DVOA
11	66%	5.8	-0.5%	20%	Base	23%	5.3	-4.5%	70%	Base	30%	6.3	11.0%		11	57%	6.3	10.5%
12	16%	5.3	-5.6%	63%	Nickel	59%	5.6	-2.2%	22%	Nickel	60%	6.2	11.2%		12	22%	6.4	9.7%
10	8%	4.9	-30.8%	4%	Dime+	16%	6.1	-14.4%	6%	Dime+	9%	6.0	5.3%		21	9%	7.0	33.2%
13	5%	4.5	-13.5%	83%	Goal Line	1%	1.5	-83.3%	88%	Goal Line	1%	0.3	29.7%		22	4%	7.0	22.5%
611	4%	7.3	11.0%	86%	Big	1%	3.0	-14.0%	93%						611	3%	7.0	51.8%

Strategic Tendencies

Run/Pass		Rk	Formation		Rk	Pass Rush		Rk	Secondary		Rk	Strategy		Rk
Runs, first half	34%	25	Form: Single Back	84%	12	Rush 3	3.5%	26	4 DB	30%	10	Play Action	14%	31
Runs, first down	41%	30	Form: Empty Back	4%	32	Rush 4	72.0%	10	5 DB	60%	15	Offensive Motion	21%	32
Runs, second-long	28%	17	Form: Multi Back	12%	12	Rush 5	16.9%	24	6+ DB	9%	17	Avg Box (Off)	6.56	18
Runs, power sit.	59%	9	Pers: 3+ WR	74%	5	Rush 6+	7.6%	9	Man Coverage	33%	14	Avg Box (Def)	6.75	5
Runs, behind 2H	26%	23	Pers: 2+ TE/6+ OL	26%	19	Edge Rusher Sacks	67.4%	8	CB by Sides	62%	28	Offensive Pace	32.72	30
Pass, ahead 2H	48%	17	Pers: 6+ OL	6%	8	Interior DL Sacks	9.8%	32	S/CB Cover Ratio	27%	13	Defensive Pace	30.67	19
Run-Pass Options	6%	14	Shotgun/Pistol	68%	14	Second Level Sacks	22.8%	12	DB Blitz	12%	13	Go for it on 4th	1.84	6

Jacksonville led the NFL with 159 penalties in total, including declined and offsetting. That included being No. 1 in offensive penalties (75) and special teams penalties (27). ✎ Many teams try to protect their rookie quarterbacks with higher run/pass ratios, but not the Jaguars, whose run/pass ratios fell compared to 2018. ✎ The Jaguars offense allowed only one "non-pressure sack," a single coverage sack. ✎ Jacksonville used play-action less than any offense except Pittsburgh's even though the Jaguars were very good at it. They had the league's second-largest gap in DVOA between play-action passes (8.8 yards, 55.7% DVOA) and other pass plays (5.7 yards, -7.5% DVOA). That's a big change from 2018, when Jacksonville had a reverse split and a higher DVOA rating without play-action. ✎ Jaguars opponents threw a league-high 28% of passes to their No. 1 receivers. ✎ The Jacksonville defense allowed a league-worst 6.4 average yards after the catch, highlighted by an average of 11.4 yards after the catch on passes behind or at the line of scrimmage. Maybe this is partly due to the Jaguars being the worst tackling defense in the league, with 158 broken tackles and a broken tackle on 14.2% of all plays. ✎ Jacksonville was the worst defense in the league against wide receiver screens, allowing 10.1 yards per pass and 64.9% DVOA.

Passing

Player	DYAR	DVOA	Plays	NtYds	Avg	YAC	C%	TD	Int
G.Minshew	193	-5.0%	503	3086	6.1	5.4	60.8%	21	6
N.Foles*	-77	-21.3%	125	669	5.4	4.6	66.4%	3	2
M.Glennon	-6	-20.2%	11	53	4.8	3.0	60.0%	1	0

Rushing

Player	DYAR	DVOA	Plays	Yds	Avg	TD	Fum	Suc
L.Fournette	0	-8.6%	265	1152	4.3	3	0	42%
G.Minshew	48	8.1%	54	353	6.5	0	2	-
R.Armstead	-23	-26.0%	35	108	3.1	0	0	29%
D.Ozigbo	0	-9.4%	9	27	3.0	0	0	44%
D.Westbrook	13	17.2%	5	27	5.4	0	0	-

Receiving

Player	DYAR	DVOA	Plays	Ctch	Yds	Y/C	YAC	TD	C%
D.Chark	134	1.9%	118	73	1008	13.8	4.3	8	62%
D.Westbrook	-73	-21.8%	101	66	660	10.0	4.7	3	65%
C.Conley	68	-2.7%	90	47	775	16.5	5.1	5	52%
K.Cole	105	24.8%	35	24	361	15.0	4.1	3	69%
J.O'Shaughnessy	34	19.3%	20	14	153	10.9	5.8	2	70%
S.DeValve*	12	3.3%	18	12	140	11.7	5.1	0	67%
G.Swaim*	-42	-52.7%	17	13	65	5.0	3.2	0	76%
N.O'Leary*	-9	-18.5%	13	9	72	8.0	2.3	1	69%
J.Oliver	-15	-44.1%	6	3	15	5.0	1.7	0	50%
T.Eifert	22	-1.8%	63	43	436	10.1	2.6	3	68%
L.Fournette	-17	-17.0%	101	76	524	6.8	7.2	0	76%
R.Armstead	48	19.3%	24	14	144	10.3	8.0	2	58%

Offensive Line

Player	Pos	Age	GS	Snaps	Pen	Sk	Pass	Run	Player	Pos	Age	GS	Snaps	Pen	Sk	Pass	Run
Andrew Norwell	LG	29	16/16	1108	7	3.5	10	6	Cam Robinson	LT	25	14/14	885	11	8.5	24	8
Jawaan Taylor	RT	23	16/16	1108	14	9.5	19	11	A.J. Cann	RG	29	16/16	791	3	2.5	12	3
Brandon Linder	C	28	16/16	1104	12	0.0	5	4	Will Richardson	LT	24	15/2	442	5	2.0	13	2

Year	Yards	ALY	Rank	Power	Rank	Stuff	Rank	2nd Lev	Rank	Open Field	Rank	Sacks	ASR	Rank	Press	Rank	F-Start	Cont.
2017	4.16	4.12	13	62%	19	19%	10	0.98	27	0.96	7	24	4.4%	5	33.2%	25	17	26
2018	3.47	4.12	21	69%	12	19%	19	0.98	29	0.29	32	53	9.3%	27	33.6%	25	14	22
2019	4.17	3.88	27	63%	20	20%	23	1.02	27	1.09	4	41	7.0%	16	29.4%	13	16	44
2019 ALY by direction:			Left End 3.88 (19)			Left Tackle: 4.49 (13)			Mid/Guard: 4.06 (22)			Right Tackle: 3.61 (24)			Right End: 1.15 (32)		

Among offensive linemen, only Rams veteran Andrew Whitworth was penalized for more yards than Jaguars rookie Jawaan Taylor. Taylor's 15 called penalties included eight offensive holding calls and five false starts. Other than that, his play was strong, and he is the unquestioned starter after playing every snap of his rookie season. ✎ The remainder of the line is also expected to look much the same this year as last. The same starting five played the last 14 games after Cam Robinson returned from his ACL rehab in Week 3. ✎ If there is to be a change, the most likely spot is right guard. Third-year backup Will Richardson opened the season filling for Robinson at left tackle, but occasionally replaced A.J. Cann at guard during the remainder of the season. If he cannot crack the starting lineup, Robinson will at least be the first option off the bench. ✎ Center Brandon Linder had his best season, leading all centers in snaps per blown block with no sacks allowed. ✎ Fourth-round pick Ben Bartch (St. John's University of Minnesota) is a highly regarded former tight end who converted to tackle in college and made a positive impression at the Senior Bowl. He lacks experience and finesse, but his technique and athleticism are already good, and his strength should improve with professional conditioning. He will likely begin as a gameday inactive, but he is widely expected to earn his way into the starting lineup eventually, whether at tackle or guard.

Defensive Front

Defensive Line	Age	Pos	G	Snaps	Plays	TmPct	Rk	Stop	Dfts	BTkl	Runs	St%	Rk	RuYd	Rk	Sack	Hit	Hur	Dsrpt
						Overall							vs. Run				Pass Rush		
Abry Jones	29	DT	16	565	31	3.9%	60	19	6	2	25	60%	87	3.0	87	2.0	0	7	0
Taven Bryan	24	DT	16	487	33	4.2%	56	24	8	6	28	71%	68	2.1	39	2.0	7	17	0
Akeem Spence*	29	DT	15	375	18	2.4%	--	13	1	1	17	71%	--	2.5	--	0.0	1	5	0
Al Woods	33	DT	14	459	32	4.5%	59	23	7	2	29	76%	46	1.7	18	1.0	1	10	1

Edge Rushers	Age	Pos	G	Snaps	Plays	TmPct	Rk	Stop	Dfts	BTkl	Runs	St%	Rk	RuYd	Rk	Sack	Hit	Hur	Dsrpt
						Overall							vs. Run				Pass Rush		
Calais Campbell*	34	DE	16	833	57	7.2%	12	44	21	11	47	74%	44	1.6	16	6.5	19	44	3
Yannick Ngakoue	25	DE	15	803	46	6.2%	32	40	19	7	27	85%	9	1.4	12	8.0	10	30	6
Josh Allen	23	DE	16	646	42	5.3%	39	32	17	8	27	67%	69	3.4	82	10.5	13	29	0
Dawuane Smoot	25	DE	16	412	17	2.1%	--	15	7	2	9	89%	--	1.6	--	6.0	2	8	0

Linebackers	Age	Pos	G	Snaps	Plays	TmPct	Rk	Stop	Dfts	BTkl	Runs	St%	Rk	RuYd	Rk	Sack	Hit	Hur	Tgts	Suc%	Rk	AdjYd	Rk	PD	Int
						Overall							vs. Run				Pass Rush				vs. Pass				
Myles Jack	25	MLB	11	627	69	12.7%	55	36	12	12	41	61%	39	4.1	50	0.5	1	5	28	46%	47	7.4	51	4	1
Quincy Williams	24	OLB	11	504	48	8.8%	74	21	5	19	31	55%	65	3.4	25	0.0	0	4	14	43%	54	7.1	44	0	0
Donald Payne*	26	MLB	9	351	61	13.7%	63	21	5	6	32	50%	73	4.8	75	1.0	0	0	12	33%	--	8.1	--	1	0
Leon Jacobs	25	OLB	14	329	36	5.2%	80	21	6	4	23	61%	40	3.3	19	2.0	0	5	4	25%	--	4.8	--	1	0
Najee Goode*	31	OLB	10	299	26	5.3%	82	9	1	9	13	31%	83	7.8	84	1.0	0	4	13	54%	--	7.1	--	2	0
Austin Calitro*	26	OLB	13	236	40	6.2%	--	19	4	8	21	57%	--	4.8	--	1.0	1	2	12	67%	--	4.0	--	1	0
Joe Schobert	27	MLB	16	1079	141	17.7%	7	77	24	18	87	56%	59	4.3	61	2.0	2	9	36	53%	30	6.0	31	9	4

Year	Yards	ALY	Rank	Power	Rank	Stuff	Rank	2nd Level	Rank	Open Field	Rank	Sacks	ASR	Rank	Press	Rank
2017	4.27	4.37	28	59%	9	20%	19	1.16	20	0.76	19	55	9.1%	2	34.3%	3
2018	4.07	3.87	4	61%	7	21%	11	0.90	3	1.03	22	37	7.1%	15	33.2%	5
2019	5.31	4.62	27	64%	17	18%	17	1.38	29	1.60	32	47	8.1%	6	31.8%	10
2019 ALY by direction:			Left End: 3.86 (14)			Left Tackle: 4.7 (24)			Mid/Guard: 4.52 (21)			Right Tackle: 5.05 (30)			Right End: 5.97 (30)	

Calais Campbell played three seasons in Jacksonville and led the team in defeats every one of those seasons. 2019 was his first season below 30 defeats for the Jaguars. He also led the team with 44 hurries in 2019, 14 ahead of Yannick Ngakoue and 15 ahead of rookie Josh Allen. By almost every meaningful measure you can find, Campbell was the team's best front seven defender throughout his three-year stay. ✎ The team's second first-round pick, edge defender K'Lavon Chaisson, was a two-year starter at LSU, mainly as a stand-up speed rusher. Chaisson is a strong tackler with good run discipline, and he should go straight into the team's pass-rusher rotation regardless of who else is on the roster. ✎ The third-round pick of defensive tackle DaVon Hamilton (Ohio State) is primarily aimed at the team's weakness against the run. Hamilton is a powerful nose tackle accustomed to plugging gaps and taking on double-teams. He should quickly find a role on rushing downs. ✎ Fourth-round pick Shaquille Quarterman (Miami) is also primarily a run defender who is not considered to have the athletic range required of a starter in the NFL. He should make the team as a backup for rushing downs and special teams. ✎ With the signing of Joe Schobert comes a sizeable reshuffle of the linebacker group. Schobert is expected to supplant Myles Jack at inside linebacker, with Jack moving to the weakside spot and Leon Jacobs being the primary strongside/third linebacker ahead of Quincy Williams. That would relegate Williams to a backup role: Williams' 40.4% broken tackle rate in 2019 was the worst of any defender with at least 16 solo tackles. ✎ Nose tackle Abry Jones is a good example of how small sample sizes make football stats so inconsistent. Last year, he was near the bottom of the league with a 60% stop rate on run tackles. One year earlier, he was near the top of the league at 92%.

Defensive Secondary

Secondary	Age	Pos	G	Snaps	Plays	Overall TmPct	Rk	Stop	Dfts	BTkl	vs. Run Runs	St%	Rk	RuYd	Rk	vs. Pass Tgts	Tgt%	Rk	Dist	Suc%	Rk	AdjYd	Rk	PD	Int
Jarrod Wilson	26	FS	16	1069	76	9.6%	31	28	11	9	32	44%	32	10.0	63	34	8.6%	30	11.1	44%	60	9.1	57	4	2
A.J. Bouye*	29	CB	14	946	73	10.5%	20	19	8	10	18	39%	53	7.5	62	83	23.6%	14	12.1	42%	79	9.7	74	8	1
Tre Herndon	24	CB	16	918	67	8.5%	27	22	7	14	20	35%	64	6.5	44	69	20.2%	41	15.8	52%	44	8.2	57	13	3
Ronnie Harrison	23	SS	14	846	79	11.4%	26	34	13	10	35	37%	45	7.3	43	27	8.6%	29	11.2	63%	11	8.4	50	9	2
D.J. Hayden	30	CB	15	656	47	6.3%	70	25	10	6	15	60%	23	6.9	53	29	11.9%	85	8.2	69%	3	4.4	2	6	0
Rashaan Melvin	*31*	*CB*	*13*	*879*	*79*	*11.5%*	*19*	*27*	*9*	*4*	*18*	*56%*	*27*	*6.2*	*40*	*81*	*21.4%*	*28*	*13.7*	*47%*	*65*	*8.7*	*63*	*11*	*0*

Year	Pass D Rank	vs. #1 WR	Rk	vs. #2 WR	Rk	vs. Other WR	Rk	WR Wide	Rk	WR Slot	Rk	vs. TE	Rk	vs. RB	Rk
2017	1	-58.4%	1	-14.1%	8	-8.5%	11	-36.4%	1	-23.9%	2	2.3%	20	-1.6%	16
2018	6	-15.9%	4	-1.6%	16	-8.3%	11	-8.0%	14	-9.1%	5	-5.9%	13	-12.9%	8
2019	22	-11.4%	7	6.2%	20	18.2%	25	-3.1%	19	5.6%	15	23.0%	30	25.8%	28

First-round cornerback CJ Henderson was first-team All-SEC twice and second-team once during his three-year career as a starter for the Florida Gators. He has a reputation for physical man coverage, but most reports suggest that he needs to improve his tackling and ball skills. He is expected to start immediately. ● The other incoming expected starter, Rashaan Melvin, was a very assured tackler in 2019: his 6.9% broken tackle rate was the third-best of any defensive back with at least 30 solo tackles. The man Melvin will probably replace, 2018 undrafted free agent Tre Herndon, was not: his 26.9% rate was fourth worst by the same criteria. ● Nickelback D.J. Hayden allowed only 4.4 yards per pass target, the sixth-best figure among cornerbacks with at least 20 pass targets. This marked his second successive year-on-year improvement in that figure since joining the Jaguars. ● The safety position is unlikely to change much. Both Ronnie Harrison and Jarrod Wilson started every game until Harrison's late-season injury, and the team appears content to return the same starters this year. The one addition they did make in the draft, fifth-round safety Daniel Thomas (Auburn), can play either box or deep safety to an adequate backup standard, but he may be best suited to a role on kick coverage. ● In addition to their first-round pick, the team added two late-round rookies to pad out cornerback depth. Fourth-round pick Josiah Scott (Michigan State) is probably too small to play outside corner but appears well suited to a nickel role. Seventh-round cornerback Chris Claybrooks (Memphis) is most likely to earn a spot playing special teams, where he has experience as a return specialist and the elite speed to play on coverage units.

Special Teams

Year	DVOA	Rank	FG/XP	Rank	Net Kick	Rank	Kick Ret	Rank	Net Punt	Rank	Punt Ret	Rank	Hidden	Rank
2017	-2.7%	24	-3.6	22	-8.8	30	-0.5	15	-4.4	21	3.8	6	-7.0	23
2018	4.4%	4	3.7	9	4.0	5	-0.9	16	10.7	1	4.5	8	0.2	16
2019	2.7%	6	8.5	3	0.5	15	-2.4	24	12.2	1	-5.1	29	2.1	14

The Jaguars were at or above average in all kicking phases of special teams, but below average in both return phases. ● Kicker Josh Lambo handled all but two of the team's kickoffs through Week 6, but punter Logan Cooke handled almost all of them from Weeks 7 to 15 while Lambo played through a groin injury. Cooke's kickoffs produced a lower touchback rate and allowed a longer average return than Lambo's. ● Lambo was the most accurate field goal kicker in the league in 2019, making 33 of his 34 field goal attempts. Lambo has made more than 90% of his field goal attempts every year since joining the Jaguars from the Chargers. He made only 81.3% during his two years in San Diego. ● Cooke's 44.5-yard net punting average tied for second-best in the league, behind only Dolphins punter Matt Wile. Cooke's punt unit has added more than 10 points of net expected value during both of his seasons. His two years as the Jaguars punter have been the second-best and third-best in team history by our numbers. ● 43 of the team's 154 punt return yards came on one single return by Dede Westbrook. Westbrook's other 22 punt returns averaged 4.0 yards, which would have been the second-lowest figure in the league for any player with at least 10 punt returns. Even including Westbrook's long return, the team average of 5.0 yards per return was the third-worst mark behind Washington and Green Bay. ● Michael Walker's two lost fumbles on kickoffs were a big part of what cost the Jaguars kick return team in our metrics; the team's official average of 24.2 yards per kick return ranked eighth in the league.

Kansas City Chiefs

2019 Record: 12-4	Total DVOA: 30.2% (3rd)	2020 Mean Projection: 10.6 wins	On the Clock (0-4): 1%
Pythagorean Wins: 11.6 (4th)	Offense: 22.8% (3rd)	Postseason Odds: 81.5%	Mediocrity (5-7): 10%
Snap-Weighted Age: 26.2 (21st)	Defense: -3.4% (14th)	Super Bowl Odds: 26.8%	Playoff Contender (8-10): 35%
Average Opponent: 0.4% (14th)	Special Teams: 4.1% (2nd)	Proj. Avg. Opponent: 1.0% (6th)	Super Bowl Contender (11+): 54%

2019: A new blockbuster franchise arrives for a new generation of fans.

2020: The sequel runs dangerously over budget.

The ingredients of the Chiefs' success are mostly easy to acquire. Yet the recipe may be impossible to replicate.

The quarterback was a 10th overall pick with an erratic streak from a program, system, and conference known for producing statistical mirages. Metrics such as QBASE liked him but didn't adore him. Quarterback-needy teams including the Browns, Jets, Jaguars, and 49ers all passed on him. There's a quarterback or two who looks indistinguishable from the 2017 version of Patrick Mahomes in almost every draft class. Those quarterbacks are rarely the first ones off the board, meaning they're available to any team willing to do something bold.

The coach was a retread who was run out of town after overstaying his welcome at his last stop. His defining characteristic among casual fans prior to this season was his inability to manage the clock or win "the big game." There's a veteran coach or two like the 2014 version of Andy Reid hanging around the unemployment line almost every January.

The top offensive weapon was a major-program washout turned small-school speedster with serious character questions and a 40 time whispered down the lane from a pro day at West Alabama. The No. 2 receiver was a former top-five draft pick on his third team in three years, with a checkered career and a cosmology H.P. Lovecraft would consider "a little out there." The All-Pro tight end was a third-round pick who spent his rookie season on the injured reserve. The running backs didn't really matter. There are Tyreek Hill and Travis Kelce lookalikes lurking in every draft class, some Sammy Watkins types in the diva-receiver discount rack each year, and bushels of Damien Williams and Shady McCoy at every roadside running back stand.

The left tackle, the first overall pick seven years ago, looked like a bust in his first three seasons and was injured for half of last year. His replacement, as well as the starting center and right tackle, were all cast off by the Browns at various times. The right guard is from Canada. It doesn't take a Cowboys-level investment to build a Chiefs-level offensive line.

The defense? What defense? The only big name was yet another veteran cast off by two teams the two previous years. The top pass-rusher was a second-round pick who took two full seasons to develop. Half of the starters were anonymous and replaceable. The Chiefs ranked 29th in the NFL in positional spending on defense in 2019. Sometimes it showed. It's a snap to build a Chiefs-caliber defense, if that's your goal for some reason.

The Chiefs didn't need a Herschel Walker or Khalil Mack blockbuster trade to get where they are. They didn't "tank" for two to seven years. They didn't find Tom Brady hiding in the sixth round of the draft like a magic lamp in a cavern. They didn't identify and pluck the latest fair-haired coaching wunderkind from the bottom of some other team's staff or the top of the Big 12 statistical rankings. They just found the right coach, the right quarterback, the right scheme, and the right supporting cast from among all the choices hiding in plain sight over the last seven years.

Yet copycats around the NFL will soon learn that copying the Chiefs is a great way to get coaches and executives fired. That's because truly emulating the Chiefs, rather than just re-skinning your current organization to look like them, requires the right balance of patience and risk: two resources NFL teams are terrible at managing.

We're focusing on the Chiefs' impact on the NFL moving forward instead of the 2020 team itself because there is no suspense in our 2020 projection. The Chiefs offense will be about as good this year as last year, with any expected regression from their peak performance offset by the fact that the Chiefs were hardly at their peak when Matt Moore was their starter for two-and-a-half games. The Chiefs defense also projects to be no better or worse than last season. The Chiefs' out-of-division schedule is rough, but their AFC West foes are in various stages of rebuilding, so they should coast to the playoffs and battle the Ravens for conference supremacy.

It will be a blast to watch, but it's not very interesting to talk about. We all know that Mahomes and the Chiefs have replaced the Tom Brady-less Patriots as the NFL's royalty. What we don't know is how the rest of the league will change as a result. The one thing that's certain is that we will see some Chiefs impersonators over the next few years, and many of those imitations won't be very flattering.

Finding the Next Mahomes is easier said than done. Baker Mayfield and Jared Goff produced better QBASE projections; neither is on track to be Mahomes. Drew Lock and Jordan Love had similar-looking college highlights, but that's the rub: Mahomes mixed transcendent moments with a little bit of slapstick comedy at Texas Tech. "Finding" another Mahomes really means meshing a quarterback of Mahomes' talent and potential with a head coach like Reid.

2020 Chiefs Schedule

Week	Opp.	Week	Opp.	Week	Opp.
1	HOU (Thu.)	7	at DEN	13	DEN
2	at LAC	8	NYJ	14	at MIA
3	at BAL (Mon.)	9	CAR	15	at NO
4	NE	10	BYE	16	ATL
5	LV	11	at LV	17	LAC
6	at BUF (Thu.)	12	at TB		

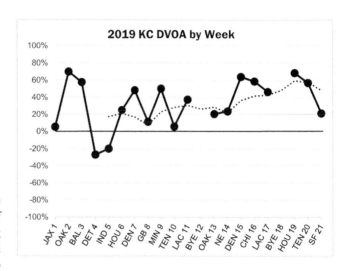

And just who is the next Reid? Is he someone who rose and fell at another organization and now needs a change of scenery, like Mike McCarthy or Ron Rivera? Is he a young quarterback whisperer, like Reid was when the Eagles hired him in 1998 and a half-dozen Mini McVays now claim to be? Is he one of the many Reid disciples now coaching in the NFL? And what happens if the next Reid arrives and spends three years earning wild-card berths and losing playoff games behind a journeyman quarterback? Does he get fired and replaced with the latest Belichick Buddy?

Scouring the waiver wire, Last Chance Universities, and occult bookshops for offensive playmakers can bring all sorts of problems down on a team. If drafting speed, speed, and more speed was the answer, the Raiders would have won five Super Bowls in the 2000s. Waiting six years for a left tackle to learn on the job can get your quarterbacks crunched. Building a defense on the cheap is obviously dangerous.

And suppose a team finds everything it needs and recreates what the Chiefs did last year, except that they face a properly coached opponent instead of the Texans in the first round of the playoffs and cannot come back from a 24-0 deficit? The Chiefs were a Mahomes miracle and a few Bill O'Brien brain brownouts away from entering this offseason as playoff also-rans with 177 bucks in cap space (precisely and literally, at one memorable point) and a quarterback with only one post-season victory on his resume seeking a record-setting contract. That's a formula no organization wants to duplicate. But it's a possible fate for any Chiefs imitator that only gets things 95% right, or simply gets unlucky at the wrong time.

The Chiefs' success will be difficult to copy because its two key components, risk and patience, are opposing forces. An organization that takes too many risks ends up like Reid's Dream Team 2011 Eagles, last year's Browns, or any other of the less-dramatic teams that went "all in" and then went bust as a result. An organization that's too patient saddles up Andy Dalton or sticks with Jason Garrett three years too long. Balancing the push and pull of patient roster development and risk management requires subtlety, and most NFL decision-makers don't handle subtleties very well. The Patriots have balanced patience (lots of slow-cooked talent on the lines, low urgency in any particular draft class or free agent crop) with risk (from Randy Moss to Antonio Brown) for decades, but it helped to have Brady around to gloss over the occasional mistake. Reid has been fiddling with the dials since the days of Terrell Owens, then Michael Vick. Last year was the first time he finally got things right.

Reid's willingness to take chances for elite talent is a defining feature of his career and a hallmark of the Chiefs' 2019 success. Let's be blunt here: we're not advocating for an organization to hold its nose and turn a blind eye to crimes like domestic violence, and the Chiefs have been lucky to thread a very fine needle with Hill. It's both prudent *and* commendable, however, to have a proper support network and culture in place for any player who fits into the NFL's very broad square-peg category, from those striving to put criminal behavior behind them to guys with really weird subreddits to the politically outspoken to players like Tyrann Mathieu guilty only of being independent-minded (and also enjoying lots of weed).

Reid may take chances on individuals like Vick or Hill more than some of us are comfortable with, but he does what he can to bring out the best in those individuals on and off the field, even though the success rate will never be 100%. Shrewd Chiefs imitators will seek ways to work with troubled talent or brash personalities. But for some, like Reid's former thought partner John Dorsey when he left to run the Browns, the focus will be on merely finding the talent and leaving the rest to others.

Schematic adaptability is another nearly inimitable hallmark of Reid's success. Last year's Chiefs ran an offense based on the old Mike Holmgren West Coast Offense engine but fuel-injected with spread-option and Air Raid components. Again, it looks easy to copy, and every Norv Turner and Brian Schottenheimer in the league has duct-taped a read-option package onto the back of their 20-year-old playbooks in recent years. Reid moved past that type of jerry rig with Vick in 2010; he now runs a fully integrated hybrid system which not only looks like a greatest hits package of every successful offensive concept of the 21st century but is designed with both the talents and needs of young quarterbacks like Mahomes in mind.

Copying Reid's playbook isn't enough, as Matt Nagy and the Bears are rapidly learning. It's the adaptability and open-minded approach that matter. The Ravens (coached by an early Reid disciple) captured that spirit of innovation with their Lamar Jackson offense last year while embracing a completely different set of concepts. The Eagles (coached by a lifelong Reid disciple) added RPOs to the mix on the fly three years ago to win a Super Bowl. The Patriots, of course, spent 20 years morphing and adjusting their offense, and the transitions had as much to do with Brady's success as the other way around, so there's plenty of evidence of the value of offensive innovation.

Reid's flexibility, both with game-planning and personnel management, provides a clearer blueprint for copycats of what NOT to do than what to do. Rigid, conservative offensive systems are bad news, but we've already name-dropped Schottenheimer, so let's not belabor the point. Playing it safe with a mid-tier quarterback is also a great way to get stuck in endless divisional-round limbo. Reid may have lingered too long with Alex Smith and late-era Donovan McNabb, but he also sought outside-the-box exit strategies (Vick, Kevin Kolb) long before the day he traded up for Mahomes. The Packers may well have taken a cue from the Chiefs by trading up for a Mahomes Extra Lite in Love to eventually replace Aaron Rodgers, though: a) the Packers have their own fascinating history of quarterback succession plans; and b) the likely real issue in Green Bay is that Rodgers is an absolutely awful person to work with.

To appreciate the uniqueness of how the Chiefs built their Super Bowl team, contrast them with the Minnesota Vikings, who built a talent-laden roster and stable infrastructure over the last few years but overcommitted to safe schemes, above-average-by-design quarterback play and the old-school running-and-defense philosophy. The Vikings made lots of great decisions during the Mike Zimmer/Rick Spielman era. Position-by-position, last year's Vikings may have been more talented than last year's Chiefs. But the Vikings slammed their head into the ceiling of their own risk aversion for years and are now in the process of being torn to shreds by the salary cap.

The Chiefs also face a looming cap emergency, which makes the Vikings case study so interesting. As mentioned earlier, the Chiefs were flirting with cap space equal to the amount in a recent college graduate's checking account early in the spring. It blossomed to nearly $5 million thanks to some restructurings by early June, just enough to sign their draft picks. Nearly $180 million is already earmarked for 2021, and that doesn't include Mahomes' next contract, which is likely to reset the entire NFL salary structure. Defensive tackle Chris Jones, one of two irreplaceable defenders (along with Mathieu), was franchise-tagged at press time: if he signs a long-term deal, it may free up a little operating capital for 2020, but it will just complicate the Mahomes extension and every other financial decision for the next few years.

The Chiefs are winning now, of course, so it makes sense to overclock the salary cap for another two years to stay in win-now mode. It's another example of shrewd risk management at work: the Chiefs are spending all the money and resources they can to remain great, in contrast with a team like the Vikings, whose adherence to the (normally sound) strategy of keeping their veteran core intact maxed them out at being very good. At some point soon, however, the Chiefs will be forced to shed the kind of talent that cannot be replaced while picking at the end of each round of the draft. Reid's adaptability and Mahomes' excellence will be tested as the Chiefs organizational strategy slowly boils down to Reid + Mahomes + Whatevs = Contention. It's yet another Patriots-tested model for success, but it comes with no guarantees.

The cap is the most likely force standing between the Chiefs and a decade-long dynasty. Defensive innovation is less likely to play a role. The Chiefs offense has helped spur the rise of "positionless" defenders and six-defensive back base packages, and we're likely to see more Derwin James-, Isaiah Simmons-, Minkah Fitzpatrick-, and, um, Tyrann Mathieu-like defenders roaming all over the field as countermeasures for Chiefs-flavored offenses in the future. But there will be no "figuring out" Mahomes, just as there was no figuring out Brady or Peyton Manning. Also, all the divergent offensive innovations taking place at the same time will make it impossible for teams to build their defenses simply to stop the Chiefs: a focus on playing on their heels to stop Mahomes and Hill will get them walloped by the Titans, Ravens, or 49ers. And if some defensive coordinator finds some silver bullet of an adjustment, Reid will simply counter-adjust.

It's tempting to look past 2020—lord, it's soooo tempting to look past 2020 in every conceivable way—and see an NFL that has changed for the better as a result of the Chiefs success: better opportunities for a diverse (including ethnically) group of quarterbacks, a continuation of the explosion of offensive innovation we've seen in the last few seasons; defenses which are less rigid and more dynamic, a more welcoming and development-oriented environment (while still maintaining high standards and consequences) for individuals who don't fit the cookie cutter, and a genuine desire to both make daring decisions and give them the time and resources they need to bear fruit. But this is the NFL, so we're more likely to see lots of lip service to all of those virtues from teams flailing around in search of Mahomes and Hill clones while firing coaches who try anything different and replacing them with their friends' sons.

Either way, we get to watch Mahomes for many, many years to come. And that's a good thing.

Mike Tanier

2019 Chiefs Stats by Week

Wk	vs.	W-L	PF	PA	YDF	YDA	TO	Total	Off	Def	ST
1	at JAX	W	40	26	491	428	+2	5%	49%	46%	2%
2	at OAK	W	28	10	467	307	+1	70%	25%	-46%	-1%
3	BAL	W	33	28	503	452	0	58%	59%	-1%	-2%
4	at DET	W	34	30	438	447	-1	-27%	0%	13%	-14%
5	IND	L	13	19	324	331	0	-20%	-15%	5%	0%
6	HOU	L	24	31	309	472	+1	25%	31%	8%	2%
7	at DEN	W	30	6	271	205	+1	48%	2%	-43%	3%
8	GB	L	24	31	337	374	-1	11%	31%	23%	3%
9	MIN	W	26	23	377	308	-1	50%	23%	-14%	14%
10	at TEN	L	32	35	530	371	0	6%	40%	23%	-11%
11	at LAC	W	24	17	310	438	+3	37%	7%	-21%	9%
12	BYE										
13	OAK	W	40	9	259	332	+3	21%	0%	-7%	14%
14	at NE	W	23	16	346	278	-1	24%	1%	-17%	6%
15	DEN	W	23	3	419	251	0	64%	41%	-21%	2%
16	at CHI	W	26	3	350	234	0	59%	47%	-2%	9%
17	LAC	W	31	21	336	366	+1	46%	20%	5%	31%
18	BYE										
19	HOU	W	51	31	434	442	0	68%	83%	-1%	-15%
20	TEN	W	35	24	404	295	0	57%	66%	8%	-1%
21	SF	W	31	20	397	351	0	21%	16%	2%	7%

Trends and Splits

	Offense	Rank	Defense	Rank
Total DVOA	22.8%	3	-3.4%	14
Unadjusted VOA	22.8%	3	-1.2%	15
Weighted Trend	20.9%	5	-5.3%	13
Variance	4.7%	5	5.8%	16
Average Opponent	0.7%	21	1.7%	8
Passing	44.1%	2	-9.3%	6
Rushing	-1.7%	14	4.2%	29
First Down	23.9%	2	-2.0%	14
Second Down	7.9%	9	1.7%	16
Third Down	46.1%	1	-14.3%	9
First Half	32.6%	2	-6.9%	11
Second Half	11.2%	8	-0.2%	14
Red Zone	-3.4%	19	-23.8%	5
Late and Close	11.7%	6	5.1%	23

Five-Year Performance

Year	W-L	Pyth W	Est W	PF	PA	TO	Total	Rk	Off	Rk	Def	Rk	ST	Rk	Off AGL	Rk	Def AGL	Rk	Off Age	Rk	Def Age	Rk	ST Age	Rk
2015	11-5	11.2	11.4	405	287	+14	25.2%	5	11.7%	6	-11.6%	6	2.0%	9	30.2	14	35.4	18	25.8	28	27.4	5	25.8	19
2016	12-4	10.1	9.7	389	311	+16	13.5%	6	2.9%	13	-2.8%	14	7.8%	1	32.9	13	66.9	30	25.9	26	26.5	16	25.1	31
2017	10-6	10.0	10.0	415	339	+15	10.6%	10	15.9%	4	10.7%	30	5.3%	4	42.1	22	38.7	20	26.3	26	27.1	5	25.9	16
2018	12-4	11.0	13.1	565	421	+11	32.9%	1	34.2%	1	6.9%	26	5.6%	2	35.3	16	24.8	10	26.0	27	26.2	15	25.7	18
2019	12-4	11.6	12.1	451	308	+8	30.2%	3	22.8%	3	-3.4%	14	4.1%	2	32.2	13	43.6	24	27.0	12	25.6	27	26.2	9

2019 Performance Based on Most Common Personnel Groups

KC Offense					KC Offense vs. Opponents					KC Defense					KC Defense vs. Opponents			
Pers	Freq	Yds	DVOA	Run%	Pers	Freq	Yds	DVOA	Run%	Pers	Freq	Yds	DVOA	Pers	Freq	Yds	DVOA
11	59%	6.9	31.9%	26%	Base	11%	4.0	-7.6%	69%	Base	27%	5.9	-1.6%	11	59%	5.8	-2.6%
12	31%	6.0	13.1%	40%	Nickel	66%	6.6	27.1%	34%	Nickel	38%	5.8	0.7%	12	21%	5.9	2.9%
21	4%	6.2	26.7%	65%	Dime+	22%	7.1	36.7%	19%	Dime+	34%	5.2	-13.2%	21	10%	4.1	-21.1%
22	4%	3.9	20.1%	74%						Goal Line	0%	1.0	41.9%	22	3%	6.3	-15.9%
621	1%	2.8	14.5%	100%										13	3%	6.0	2.0%

Strategic Tendencies

Run/Pass		Rk	Formation		Rk	Pass Rush		Rk	Secondary		Rk	Strategy		Rk
Runs, first half	28%	32	Form: Single Back	89%	5	Rush 3	9.4%	13	4 DB	27%	17	Play Action	32%	3
Runs, first down	43%	28	Form: Empty Back	5%	30	Rush 4	64.2%	17	5 DB	39%	28	Offensive Motion	56%	5
Runs, second-long	23%	23	Form: Multi Back	6%	25	Rush 5	17.3%	23	6+ DB	34%	6	Avg Box (Off)	6.24	31
Runs, power sit.	59%	11	Pers: 3+ WR	60%	23	Rush 6+	9.1%	7	Man Coverage	36%	10	Avg Box (Def)	6.41	26
Runs, behind 2H	29%	15	Pers: 2+ TE/6+ OL	36%	7	Edge Rusher Sacks	52.2%	22	CB by Sides	88%	6	Offensive Pace	29.10	6
Pass, ahead 2H	53%	6	Pers: 6+ OL	1%	24	Interior DL Sacks	26.7%	11	S/CB Cover Ratio	39%	1	Defensive Pace	31.10	23
Run-Pass Options	20%	1	Shotgun/Pistol	78%	4	Second Level Sacks	21.1%	15	DB Blitz	14%	5	Go for it on 4th	1.09	27

The Chiefs were good at manipulating opposing box counts … and then not taking real advantage of it. 53% of Kansas City's runs came against a box of six or less. Yet the Chiefs had basically the same DVOA running against those small boxes (-9.3%) as they did the rest of the time (-6.1%). ◐ Kansas City was the worst offense in the league running on second-and-long, with just 2.3 yards per carry and -70.7% DVOA. Just one year earlier, they were the best offense in the league on second-and-long, with 6.8 yards per carry and 39.4% DVOA. ◐ Andy Reid is renowned for being a strong designer of screen passes, so it is worth noting that the Chiefs were below average on screens in 2019: -0.6% DVOA on wide receiver screens and -15.0% DVOA on running back screens. ◐ Kansas City led the league in RPOs but gained a below-average 4.6 yards per carry on these plays. ◐ For two years, Patrick Mahomes has been even better against a blitz than against the standard four pass-rushers. Last year he had 73.0% DVOA against blitzes compared to 58.2% against four pass-rushers and "only" 26.8% against three. ◐ The Chiefs were fourth in the NFL in broken tackles for the second straight season. ◐ Kansas City was the strongest defense in the league against passes in the short middle of the field. ◐ Adding Tyrann Mathieu took the Chiefs from 28th to first in safety/cornerback cover ratio. The Chiefs also nearly tripled their rate of defensive back blitzes compared to 2018. ◐ Penalties are still a problem for the Chiefs. They didn't lead the league as they did in 2018, but they still finished tied for sixth with 140 total penalties, including declined and offsetting. The Chiefs were in the top dozen for both offensive and defensive penalties. The Chiefs also benefited from penalties on opponents, especially on offense, where opposing defenses committed a league-high 74 penalties.

Passing

Player	DYAR	DVOA	Plays	NtYds	Avg	YAC	C%	TD	Int
P.Mahomes	1320	30.0%	501	3901	7.8	6.1	66.0%	26	5
M.Moore	172	15.5%	98	594	6.1	4.9	65.6%	4	0

Rushing

Player	DYAR	DVOA	Plays	Yds	Avg	TD	Fum	Suc
Dam.Williams	8	-6.8%	111	500	4.5	5	1	50%
L.McCoy*	20	-4.1%	101	465	4.6	4	2	49%
Dar.Williams	-15	-15.7%	41	141	3.4	3	1	56%
D.Thompson	16	1.6%	38	128	3.4	1	0	58%
P.Mahomes	66	28.1%	31	230	7.4	2	1	-
S.Ware*	2	-5.6%	17	51	3.0	0	0	65%
T.Hill	4	-30.2%	8	23	2.9	0	0	-
A.Sherman	7	18.0%	4	9	2.3	0	0	75%
D.Washington	7	-7.0%	108	387	3.6	3	0	50%

Receiving

Player	DYAR	DVOA	Plays	Ctch	Yds	Y/C	YAC	TD	C%
S.Watkins	3	-12.3%	90	52	673	12.9	5.7	3	58%
T.Hill	237	22.4%	89	58	860	14.8	4.8	7	65%
D.Robinson	61	1.0%	55	32	449	14.0	3.2	4	58%
M.Hardman	181	44.1%	41	26	538	20.7	11.2	6	63%
B.Pringle	40	22.9%	16	12	170	14.2	5.3	1	75%
T.Kelce	203	14.8%	136	97	1229	12.7	4.2	5	71%
B.Bell*	-40	-50.1%	15	8	67	8.4	1.1	0	53%
R.Seals-Jones	28	10.2%	22	14	229	16.4	6.8	4	64%
Dam.Williams	24	-3.7%	37	30	213	7.1	7.7	2	81%
L.McCoy*	-34	-32.2%	35	28	181	6.3	8.1	1	82%
Dar.Williams	57	38.9%	19	15	167	11.1	11.9	1	79%
D.Thompson	-12	-34.8%	10	9	43	4.8	6.9	0	90%
S.Ware*	-30	-85.8%	7	5	22	4.4	3.0	0	71%
D.Washington	74	21.1%	41	36	292	8.1	6.8	0	88%

Offensive Line

Player	Pos	Age	GS	Snaps	Pen	Sk	Pass	Run	Player	Pos	Age	GS	Snaps	Pen	Sk	Pass	Run
Mitchell Schwartz	RT	31	16/16	1054	5	1.5	31	4	Eric Fisher	LT	29	8/8	469	3	1.0	13	4
Austin Reiter	C	29	16/16	1053	8	1.0	6	6	Martinas Rankin	LG	26	6/5	277	0	0.5	4	2
Laurent Duvernay-Tardif	RG	29	14/14	907	3	3.5	11	8	Stefen Wisniewski*	LG	31	11/2	208	0	0.0	1	1
Andrew Wylie	LG	26	11/11	723	3	2.0	10	5	Mike Remmers	RT	31	14/14	881	5	3.5	13	7
Cameron Erving*	LT	28	13/8	594	7	4.5	30	4									

Year	Yards	ALY	Rank	Power	Rank	Stuff	Rank	2nd Lev	Rank	Open Field	Rank	Sacks	ASR	Rank	Press	Rank	F-Start	Cont.
2017	4.66	4.14	12	82%	1	18%	8	1.23	9	1.17	2	37	6.7%	17	31.4%	18	18	24
2018	4.66	4.37	16	72%	4	18%	13	1.27	18	1.01	11	26	5.4%	5	33.2%	24	24	28
2019	4.15	3.88	28	63%	21	19%	18	0.92	29	1.02	7	25	4.9%	4	32.5%	26	8	28
2019 ALY by direction:			Left End 4.02 (15)			Left Tackle: 2.35 (32)			Mid/Guard: 3.87 (28)			Right Tackle: 5.93 (1)			Right End: 3.34 (23)			

When Patrick Mahomes was injured against the Broncos and Matt Moore was forced to start against the Packers and Vikings, Cam Erving and Martinas Rankin were starting at left tackle and left guard in place of injured Erik Fisher and Andrew Wylie. It's a testament to Andy Reid's game-planning that the Chiefs won two of those games, and that Moore survived to enjoy all the delights and wonders of 2020. Rankin, a third-round reach the Texans gave up on after one season, was replaced by Stefen Wisniewski, who came out of semi-retirement to play well down the Super Bowl stretch. Erving, a former first-round bust for the Browns, played poorly but did just enough to hold down the fort until Fisher returned in Week 11. ➤ Erving is now in Dallas and Wisniewski in Pittsburgh, but the Chiefs found enough cap space to sign Mike Remmers as their new first lineman off the bench. Remmers is a modest upgrade over Erving: a replacement-level spot starter at every line position except center during his career with the Giants, Vikings, Panthers, and Chargers. Rankin also remains on hand, as Reid loves to tinker with O-line projects (and also cannot afford to spend for a replacement). ➤ Overall, the Chiefs offensive line is set. Mitchell Schwartz is an All-Pro caliber lineman and perhaps the league's most mobile and versatile right tackle. Fisher is who he is. Wylie may get a push from third-round pick Lucas Niang (TCU), a massive Marcus Cannon type with surprising quickness but a worrisome 2019 hip injury. Austin Reiter is a Reid system-fit at center who ranked sixth at his position in snaps per blown block last season. However, he could get a push from undrafted rookie Darryl Williams, who is even more of a Reid system-fit at center (three-year starter at Mississippi State, team captain, academic standout, dad bod). ➤ And then there's right guard Laurent Duvernay-Tardif, who has a medical degree and spent the early weeks of the pandemic volunteering in a long-term care facility in his hometown outside Montreal. Per articles about Duvernay-Tardiff's laudable service, he's dating a woman named Florence Dubé-Moreau. We've now exceeded our quota of really, really French names for one team chapter.

Defensive Front

Defensive Line	Age	Pos	G	Snaps	Plays	TmPct	Rk	Stop	Dfts	BTkl	Runs	St%	Rk	RuYd	Rk	Sack	Hit	Hur	Dsrpt
						Overall						**vs. Run**					**Pass Rush**		
Chris Jones	26	DT	13	655	40	6.0%	40	33	16	7	26	77%	39	2.7	66	9.0	13	35	4
Derrick Nnadi	24	DT	16	603	49	6.0%	22	33	8	3	46	65%	79	2.3	47	1.0	1	12	0
Khalen Saunders	24	DT	12	305	23	3.7%	--	17	0	0	19	74%	--	2.6	--	1.0	1	2	1
Mike Pennel	29	DT	8	156	24	5.8%	--	16	6	1	22	68%	--	2.3	--	1.0	1	3	0
Devaroe Lawrence	28	DT	11	226	9	1.6%	--	4	3	1	8	38%	--	2.5	--	0.0	2	1	0

Edge Rushers	Age	Pos	G	Snaps	Plays	TmPct	Rk	Stop	Dfts	BTkl	Runs	St%	Rk	RuYd	Rk	Sack	Hit	Hur	Dsrpt
						Overall						**vs. Run**					**Pass Rush**		
Frank Clark	27	DE	14	735	40	5.6%	41	31	19	9	25	68%	65	1.6	15	8.0	10	24	6
Tanoh Kpassagnon	26	DE	16	702	31	3.8%	60	19	10	5	21	52%	84	3.9	87	4.0	7	23	2
Alex Okafor	29	DE	10	431	22	4.3%	82	14	7	3	15	47%	88	4.3	89	5.0	4	13	1
Emmanuel Ogbah*	27	DE	10	416	35	6.8%	52	29	13	3	25	76%	35	2.7	50	5.5	6	16	3
Taco Charlton	26	DE	10	403	21	4.0%	85	15	6	1	14	64%	72	3.2	76	5.0	2	15	0

Linebackers	Age	Pos	G	Snaps	Plays	TmPct	Rk	Stop	Dfts	BTkl	Runs	St%	Rk	RuYd	Rk	Sack	Hit	Hur	Tgts	Suc%	Rk	AdjYd	Rk	PD	Int
						Overall						**vs. Run**					**Pass Rush**				**vs. Pass**				
Damien Wilson	27	OLB	16	714	82	10.0%	43	41	6	5	47	64%	28	4.0	41	1.5	2	8	27	48%	41	5.6	22	1	0
Anthony Hitchens	28	MLB	15	705	88	11.4%	39	32	8	11	52	46%	77	5.5	81	2.0	2	3	29	45%	50	7.2	46	1	0
Ben Niemann	25	MLB	16	409	50	6.1%	73	14	8	4	17	24%	84	5.8	83	0.0	1	4	23	43%	52	6.0	29	1	0
Reggie Ragland*	27	OLB	14	237	28	3.9%	--	17	5	4	15	73%	--	2.1	--	2.0	1	3	10	60%	--	3.9	--	0	0
Darron Lee*	26	MLB	16	160	23	2.8%	--	8	1	5	11	36%	--	4.8	--	0.0	0	2	7	14%	--	12.7	--	0	0

Year	Yards	ALY	Rank	Power	Rank	Stuff	Rank	2nd Level	Rank	Open Field	Rank	Sacks	ASR	Rank	Press	Rank
2017	4.23	4.35	26	60%	10	20%	23	1.35	31	0.55	5	31	5.8%	26	30.3%	16
2018	4.97	5.28	32	78%	30	15%	27	1.57	32	0.72	12	52	8.0%	7	31.5%	11
2019	4.89	4.81	28	71%	26	14%	30	1.45	31	0.89	25	45	7.7%	10	30.0%	19
2019 ALY by direction:			Left End: 3.79 (12)			Left Tackle: 5.22 (30)			Mid/Guard: 4.67 (24)			Right Tackle: 5.66 (32)			Right End: 5.35 (26)

Chris Jones is great at generating pressure in the middle of the line and swatting down passes in the Super Bowl. But he's apparently terrible at video games. He shared his PSN and Twitch IDs on social media in May, announcing that "there's about to be a lot of 'Call of Duty,' a lot of 'Madden NFL 20,' a lot of 2K, a lot of action and adventure games." Tyreek Hill quickly responded "But your [sic] trash," with Anthony Hitchens and Patrick Mahomes also piling on and roasting Jones' shortcomings as a gamer. Jones is the best player in the Chiefs' defensive front by a wide margin—Frank Clark is a fine edge rusher, but the rest of the starters are interchangeable/replaceable—and he remained franchise-tagged at press time. The Chiefs need to lock him into a long-term deal both to retain his services and create cap flexibility; it will be hard to budget for Mahomes without knowing how much Jones will cost them. The team must do everything it can to keep Jones happy while he's tagged. Perhaps they should consider letting him win at 2K once in a while. ◥ Linebacker William Gay, a second-round pick, is the only significant newcomer on the front seven. Gay was suspended for eight games at the start of the 2019 season as part of a major academic fraud scandal that involved several Mississippi State athletes. He then missed the Music City Bowl, reportedly for getting into a practice altercation with freshman quarterback Garrett Shrader. In between the incidents, Gay was a high-energy defender with a great size-speed combination and the explosiveness to blast through traffic and deliver big hits, but his play recognition and angles to the ball were very hit-or-miss. Gay will be mentored by Hitchens, who is great at calling out pre-snap adjustments but bad at nearly everything else, and he should be able to quickly overtake the veteran on the depth chart.

Defensive Secondary

Secondary	Age	Pos	G	Snaps	Plays	TmPct	Rk	Stop	Dfts	BTkl	Runs	St%	Rk	RuYd	Rk	Tgts	Tgt%	Rk	Dist	Suc%	Rk	AdjYd	Rk	PD	Int
						Overall						vs. Run						vs. Pass							
Tyrann Mathieu	28	SS	16	1095	87	10.6%	20	34	14	15	22	27%	60	5.8	26	53	13.1%	7	10.7	55%	27	5.4	13	12	4
Charvarius Ward	24	CB	16	1062	84	10.2%	8	27	11	9	32	28%	70	10.4	79	80	20.4%	37	13.0	65%	6	6.9	25	10	2
Juan Thornhill	25	FS	16	1011	62	7.5%	48	15	10	15	28	29%	57	9.6	58	25	6.7%	49	15.2	56%	24	5.7	18	5	3
Bashaud Breeland	28	CB	16	927	55	6.7%	54	19	8	10	14	36%	63	7.1	58	53	15.5%	75	15.7	57%	25	7.1	31	8	2
Daniel Sorensen	30	SS	16	574	56	6.8%	56	28	13	9	22	50%	15	7.1	41	37	17.4%	1	8.5	62%	13	6.1	21	4	2
Kendall Fuller*	25	CB	11	507	51	9.0%	--	19	6	5	21	38%	--	7.3	--	23	12.3%	--	10.5	35%	--	9.0	--	2	0
Morris Claiborne*	30	CB	8	198	14	3.4%	--	4	1	2	6	33%	--	6.2	--	5	6.8%	--	20.4	40%	--	8.8	--	0	0

Year	Pass D Rank	vs. #1 WR	Rk	vs. #2 WR	Rk	vs. Other WR	Rk	WR Wide	Rk	WR Slot	Rk	vs. TE	Rk	vs. RB	Rk
2017	23	29.5%	31	-6.0%	14	0.8%	18	2.3%	20	19.6%	26	-5.9%	12	-23.1%	3
2018	12	-9.2%	9	-23.8%	5	21.6%	29	-9.8%	13	-0.1%	16	19.1%	25	7.3%	21
2019	6	-32.3%	3	-10.4%	7	5.1%	20	-48.4%	1	4.3%	12	-19.5%	4	-2.0%	18

Tyrann Mathieu had a Defensive Player of the Year-caliber season. He served as both the Chiefs' strong safety and their starting slot corner, mixing in some snaps at deep safety and four or five blitzes per game. He held his own in man coverage against some of the league's best slot receivers and tight ends, played the run well, and used his instincts and preparation in coverage to make plays on the ball against other defenders' receivers. What was remarkable about Mathieu's season was that it was not that much better than his 2017 season with the Cardinals or his 2018 season with the Texans. There has been a "one-year wonder" or "has-been" narrative around Mathieu for a while, and it was never true. Matthieu freelances, whiffs on some tackles, gets mismatched when forced to cover DeAndre Hopkins types and will let his coaches know when he doesn't agree with something, making him an easy player to criticize after a mistake or move on from if you are Bill O'Brien. He appears to have found a home with Andy Reid's Chiefs. ◥ Oh yeah, the rest of the secondary. Juan Thornhill was an active, aggressive playmaker as a rookie, but a Week 17 ACL injury could slow him this season; special-teams ace Daniel Sorenson played poorly in Thornhill's absence (though he sniffed out the Texans fake punt in the playoffs) and remains the likely starter next to Mathieu if Thornhill isn't ready. Charvarius Ward, who played exceptionally in the first half of last season but faded a bit down the stretch, is locked in at right cornerback. Bashaud Breeland, who played poorly in the first half of the season but rebounded late in the year and delivered a key Super Bowl interception, is back at left cornerback on a one-year contract. Breeland was arrested during an offseason traffic stop but participated in the team's virtual OTAs. Fourth-round pick L'Jarius Sneed is listed as a cornerback, though he was more of a ball-hawking free safety at Louisiana Tech. Sneed is a toolsy prospect with a 4.37s combine 40 but a tendency to grab in man coverage against mid-major receivers. ◥ There's little other depth worth mentioning; when the cash-strapped Chiefs need extra manpower in the secondary, they just ask Mathieu to do more or hope Patrick Mahomes throws another touchdown to put the game out of reach.

Special Teams

Year	DVOA	Rank	FG/XP	Rank	Net Kick	Rank	Kick Ret	Rank	Net Punt	Rank	Punt Ret	Rank	Hidden	Rank
2017	5.3%	4	11.8	3	7.1	2	0.0	14	6.2	8	1.7	12	5.0	8
2018	5.6%	2	3.1	11	5.3	3	6.8	4	7.0	4	6.0	3	10.9	5
2019	4.1%	2	8.1	5	6.1	3	4.2	5	-0.6	19	2.6	7	5.5	9

Special teams coordinator Dave Toub is among the best in the business, and his coverage units are usually sound. ● Mecole Hardman returned a kickoff for a touchdown last season and helped spark the playoff comeback against the Texans with a 58-yard punt return. Tyreek Hill is always waiting in the wings if the Chiefs really want to frighten the opposing punting unit. ● Harrison Butker is 87-of-92 on field goal attempts of less than 50 yards in his first three seasons. ● And then there's the punting situation. The Chiefs let Dustin Colquitt leave after 14 seasons. Tyler Newsome and Tommy Townsend are expected to compete for the job. Newsome was Notre Dame's punter for four years but was unimpressive for the Chargers last preseason (42.1 gross yards per punt, with zero punts inside the 20 on seven tries). Townsend received an $82,500 contract and $7,500 signing bonus as an undrafted rookie out of Florida, making him the favorite to win the job. He's a former high school safety who ran a 4.73s combine 40, making him a potential fake punt threat. And with a name like Tommy Townsend, you can also bet that he sure plays a mean pinball.

Las Vegas Raiders

2019 Record: 7-9	Total DVOA: -11.6% (24th)	2020 Mean Projection: 7.7 wins	On the Clock (0-4): 12%
Pythagorean Wins: 5.2 (28th)	Offense: 5.6% (9th)	Postseason Odds: 38.1%	Mediocrity (5-7): 36%
Snap-Weighted Age: 26.2 (22nd)	Defense: 14.8% (31st)	Super Bowl Odds: 3.6%	Playoff Contender (8-10): 37%
Average Opponent: -1.5% (21st)	Special Teams: -2.3% (25th)	Proj. Avg. Opponent: 1.8% (4th)	Super Bowl Contender (11+): 14%

2019: *Child's Play XIX: Chucky vs. Antonio Brownzilla*

2020: *Child's Play XX: Viva Las Vegas!*

It's now Year 3 of the Jon Gruden Era, Year 2 of the Mike Mayock Era, and Year 5 since their lone winning season of the last 17 years, and the Raiders are quite literally wandering in the desert.

There is no clarity or forward momentum at quarterback. Despite five first-round picks in the last two drafts, there's no substantial young nucleus. The closest thing the team has to an established star on its roster is Darren Waller, a 27-year-old reclamation-project tight end coming off what looked like a fluke season. Any sense we have of what the Raiders offense and defense are supposed to look like if the team ever becomes a true contender comes from tea-leaf readings of Gruden's early 21st Century successes and Mayock's draft predilections, not from anything the team has done in the last three offseasons. The Raiders appear further away from the Super Bowl now than they did on the day that Gruden was hired.

Back then, you may recall, the Raiders were led by what appeared to be a trio of rising superstars (Derek Carr, Amari Cooper, and Khalil Mack) who had just followed up a 12-4 2016 season with a 6-10 pratfall. But neither Gruden nor owner Mark Davis was interested in building around that promising infrastructure. Instead, the Raiders began lurching from business model to business model like would-be entrepreneurs with a cool idea for a new combination gastropub/laundromat/dating app/blood-thinning medication:

First came the great veteran pension program of 2018, when Gruden stuffed the roster with Jordy Nelson, Brandon LaFell, Dominique Rodgers-Cromartie, Leon Hall, Frostee Rucker, and other fading stars, aging journeymen, and holdovers from coordinator Paul Guenther's early 2010s Bengals defenses. Most of the veterans did little more than bloat the Raiders payroll (eating up money which could have been used to extend Mack or lure a blue-chip newcomer) while providing replacement-level production.

Next, Davis had a falling out with some agents and ordered outgoing general manager Reggie McKenzie to trade away Mack and Cooper. McKenzie acquired a haul of draft picks in return, so the Raiders lit an analytics-scented candle to cover the odor of the remaining roster.

Gruden then hired Mayock to replace McKenzie and complete a made-for-TV front office structure. Given three first-rounders to work with, Mayock indulged his obsessions for Clemson players and guys with "high football character." He began by using the fourth overall pick on Clemson's Clelin Ferrell, an edge rusher that SackSEER ranked (in Nathan Forster's 2019 words) as a "thoroughly average draft prospect who does not belong in the first two rounds." He then proved that the whole analytics thing was just a ruse by adding a running back (Josh Jacobs) and box safety (Jonathan Abram) later in the first round.

Meanwhile, the Raiders engaged in some stealth marketing for *Joker* by trading for Antonio Brown and letting him destroy Gruden and Mayock's credibility for a few months.

Finally, this offseason finds the Raiders launching their Vegas residency with a Greatest Hits tour: some clunky veteran arrivals (Nelson Agholor, Prince Amukamara, etc.) to fill roles that should have been filled through the draft the last few years; an Al Davis tribute (Henry Ruggs, The Fastest Man in the Draft Class); more draft reaches (Damon Arnette, the third- to sixth-best player on Ohio State's defense, drafted 20th overall); yet another former television broadcaster to add to the rat pack (Jason Witten); and a little bit of new material which may be inconsequential, but could mark the beginning of Gruden's Spinal Tap Jazz Odyssey (Marcus Mariota).

Mariota arrives at a strange time. Carr posted the highest DYAR and second-highest DVOA of his career, finishing sixth and eighth in the NFL respectively while throwing to Darren Waller and a bunch of guys such as Hunter Renfrow and Zay Jones. He did this even though he was still very much Derek Carr, finishing 32nd among qualifying quarterbacks in average depth of target. Carr and the Raiders offense outperformed their (post-AB meltdown) expectations last season, particularly during the six-game stretch between Week 4 and Week 10 when their offensive DVOA exceeded 10% in every game, helping lift the Raiders' record to 6-4 and making them look briefly like wild-card contenders. Adding a veteran potential challenger would have made sense when Carr's future was uncertain in 2018 or 2019. He's now starting to look like the type of heady system fit that Gruden adores. He's far superior to the jittery, perpetually banged-up Mariota, though Mariota is also a Gruden type: gutsy, mobile, and popgun-armed, like Rich Gannon or Rodney Peete.

Carr and Gruden have made strange bedfellows since Day 1. Jordy Nelson shed light on their dynamic on Pat McAfee's podcast in May, saying that Carr and Gruden sometimes "clash" and "get a little fiery at each other" but ultimately "get

2020 Raiders Schedule

Week	Opp.	Week	Opp.	Week	Opp.
1	at CAR	7	TB	13	at NYJ
2	NO (Mon.)	8	at CLE	14	IND
3	at NE	9	at LAC	15	LAC (Thu.)
4	BUF	10	DEN	16	MIA (Sat.)
5	at KC	11	KC	17	at DEN
6	BYE	12	at ATL		

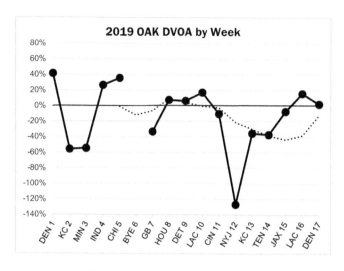

2019 OAK DVOA by Week

along great," in part because Carr is so smart and dedicated in the film room.

Nelson's remarks reveal a lot about how Gruden makes decisions. He's well known to be a management-through-conflict type who thinks of the occasional cussing match as a bonding activity. Carr won Gruden's respect by proving that he could give as well as he could get (and master all that Spider 2 Y Banana verbiage), but adding Mariota is a way to escalate the tension at a point when both sides risk growing complacent. And Carr should be challenged. Heck, he should have been challenged two years ago. The problem with any Carr-Mariota competition is that the winner will be Carr or Mariota. Gruden's preference for fiery/brainy quarterbacks prevents the Raiders from acquiring better quarterbacks.

And then there's Mayock, who has now also put his stamp on the roster, for better and for worse. Mayock looks at Clemson prospects the way Quentin Tarantino looks at Margot Robbie's feet, loves major-program talents who have Howlin' Commando personalities, and doesn't care at all about relative positional values and how they relate to draft capital and scarcity. Mayock is astute enough to hit some mid-round home runs like Maxx Crosby or Maurice Hurst. But his top picks suggest something that was whispered among NFL circles when he was hired: he can spot the talent, but he spent his TV years asking general managers around the league where prospects would actually be drafted, allowing him to cross-check and modulate his opinions. He therefore lacks the ability to gauge for himself whether Ferrell and Arnette are first-round picks or guys he can pick up later, after selecting some higher-upside talent.

As for free agents and trade acquisitions, it's not clear whether Gruden or Mayock has the stronger voice. Many of the moves have Gruden's fingerprints (who else would relish the chance to mix it up with the likes of AB, Marshawn Lynch, and Richie Incognito?), and Mayock was always more of a draftnik than a pro personnel expert. Davis forced the Mack and Cooper trades and almost certainly has input on AB-level decisions, and Guenther can probably make requests for the bargain-bin defensive veterans. The salary cap, meanwhile, appears to be managing itself, largely because the Raiders don't have very many good players to pay.

So after three offseasons of rebuilding, the Raiders roster looks like it was put together by a bunch of guys who only bother doing the fun parts of their jobs. Gruden draws up plays and fumes charmingly when things go wrong; Mayock gabs on the phone into the night with Dabo Sweeney's assistants; Davis issues decrees and beefs with agents the way he thinks

his father did. Together they transform tons of draft picks and money into an almost-.500 roster.

If the Raiders have any identity after this offseason, it's as Kansas City Chiefs cosplayers. Like their rivals in Denver, the Raiders loaded up on offensive firepower in free agency and thoroughly rebuilt the receiving corps. Gruden and Carr/Mariota will now have a variety of speed demons (Ruggs, Tyrell Williams), possession threats (Waller, Agholor), slot specialists (Renfrow, converted Wildcat quarterback Lynn Bowden), broken-down Hall of Famers (Witten), and others to choose from in the passing game. Jacobs is a sturdy, young running back, and the offensive line, while expensive, is structurally sound. Gruden, for all his big-picture faults, still has almost as many game-planning tricks up his sleeve as Andy Reid.

Unfortunately (and unlike their Denver archenemies), whatever gains the Raiders are making on offense will likely be offset by their shortcomings on defense. Guenther is part of the problem. He enters his third season as coordinator after leading the Raiders from 30th to 31st in defensive DVOA last season. Missed assignments and miscommunication plagued the Raiders, particularly at the end of last season, when they should have been showing progress. Guenther, it must be noted, is a true Gruden guy: they quarrel on the sideline, then carpool to team headquarters together (or at least they did in Oakland). Like Carr, Guenther benefits from Gruden's personality-based management system. But Carr has at least gotten some results.

Guenther has a little more to work with this season, but not much. The defensive line has the potential to be solid. Ferrell was mediocre as a rookie and could stay that way, but Crosby and Hurst were bargains, and P.J. Hill should grow into a quality run-stuffer. But there are no late-round steals like Crosby or Hurst reinforcing the back seven of the defense, so the Raiders are hoping to get production and improvement from Mayock's overdrafted top picks (Arnette, Abram, Trayvon Mullen), a whole battalion of veteran free-agent defensive backs (Amukamara, Lamarcus Joyner, Damarious Randall, Jeff Heath, Nevin Lawson), and yet another sampler platter of journeyman linebackers (with Cory Littleton and Nick Kwiatkoski replacing Vontaze Burfict, Tahir Whitehead, and others). The Raiders should get a boost from Littleton's ability in coverage, Abram's high-energy play in the box, and the overall increase in defensive depth. They should also enjoy some regression in the turnover area, where they tied for the league low with takeaways on just 8.9% of drives. Even so, this defense looks destined for another bottom-third-of-the-league finish.

The Raiders will never get past the almost-a-wild-card team stage until they acquire some superstars besides their head coach and GM. Perhaps Ruggs and/or Crosby can develop into players of that caliber, with Jacobs, Abram, Ferrell, Kolton Miller, and others justifying Gruden and Mayock's faith in max-effort overachievers. A young playoff-caliber nucleus could coalesce in Las Vegas. But there should be much, much

more in the cupboard after three years and all those extra draft picks. And the Raiders are going to need a lot more than some speedsters, small-school wonders, and tough guys if they hope to be led to the Super Bowl someday by Carr or Mariota.

For all their blockbuster trades, sideline tiffs, catchy quotes, AB-produced Arkham City cutscenes, and simmering quarterback controversies, the Raiders are rather dull on the field. That's unlikely to change unless their decision-makers stop vamping and start planning, communicating, and acting like a real front office instead of guys who play an NFL owner, coach, and a general manager on TV.

Mike Tanier

2019 Raiders Stats by Week

Wk	vs.	W-L	PF	PA	YDF	YDA	TO	Total	Off	Def	ST
1	DEN	W	24	16	357	344	0	42%	46%	14%	10%
2	KC	L	10	28	307	467	-1	-56%	-37%	16%	-2%
3	at MIN	L	14	34	302	385	-1	-55%	-11%	35%	-9%
4	at IND	W	31	24	377	346	+1	27%	12%	-15%	0%
5	CHI	W	24	21	398	236	0	36%	33%	-8%	-6%
6	BYE										
7	at GB	L	24	42	484	481	-2	-33%	26%	76%	16%
8	at HOU	L	24	27	378	388	0	7%	21%	9%	-5%
9	DET	W	31	24	450	473	+2	6%	35%	29%	0%
10	LAC	W	26	24	278	315	+3	17%	16%	-10%	-9%
11	CIN	W	17	10	386	246	0	-11%	-26%	-23%	-8%
12	at NYJ	L	3	34	208	401	-1	-127%	-61%	58%	-7%
13	at KC	L	9	40	332	259	-3	-35%	-16%	3%	-17%
14	TEN	L	21	42	355	552	0	-37%	6%	46%	4%
15	JAX	L	16	20	364	262	0	-7%	7%	8%	-7%
16	at LAC	W	24	17	366	284	0	16%	27%	20%	8%
17	at DEN	L	15	16	477	238	0	2%	-4%	-13%	-7%

Trends and Splits

	Offense	Rank	Defense	Rank
Total DVOA	5.6%	9	14.8%	31
Unadjusted VOA	6.1%	9	14.6%	31
Weighted Trend	3.0%	11	15.1%	29
Variance	8.4%	23	7.7%	26
Average Opponent	1.3%	23	-0.7%	20
Passing	25.4%	7	30.2%	30
Rushing	-7.9%	21	-5.1%	21
First Down	3.2%	12	23.2%	32
Second Down	-5.0%	20	4.5%	21
Third Down	25.9%	5	13.7%	26
First Half	18.4%	3	10.5%	27
Second Half	-8.2%	22	18.9%	31
Red Zone	-7.7%	20	11.4%	24
Late and Close	10.3%	7	2.1%	20

Five-Year Performance

Year	W-L	Pyth W	Est W	PF	PA	TO	Total	Rk	Off	Rk	Def	Rk	ST	Rk	Off AGL	Rk	Def AGL	Rk	Off Age	Rk	Def Age	Rk	ST Age	Rk
2015	7-9	6.9	7.4	359	399	+1	0.1%	14	-1.3%	18	-1.5%	15	-0.1%	19	23.6	9	33.4	17	26.2	20	26.6	17	27.2	1
2016	12-4	8.8	8.9	416	385	+16	8.2%	10	12.2%	8	4.3%	22	0.3%	14	32.9	14	48.5	19	26.5	21	26.6	13	26.9	5
2017	6-10	6.0	7.7	301	373	-14	-6.6%	19	4.0%	13	10.3%	29	-0.2%	17	10.1	3	33.4	14	27.6	4	26.6	13	25.8	17
2018	4-12	3.7	4.7	290	467	-7	-21.0%	31	-7.1%	25	12.3%	30	-1.6%	22	39.3	17	38.0	21	27.6	9	27.1	6	26.7	4
2019	7-9	5.2	7.3	313	419	-2	-11.6%	24	5.6%	9	14.8%	31	-2.3%	25	52.4	26	41.1	22	26.8	15	25.8	22	25.8	18

2019 Performance Based on Most Common Personnel Groups

OAK Offense					OAK Offense vs. Opponents						OAK Defense					OAK Defense vs. Opponents			
Pers	Freq	Yds	DVOA	Run%	Pers	Freq	Yds	DVOA	Run%		Pers	Freq	Yds	DVOA		Pers	Freq	Yds	DVOA
11	53%	6.5	14.6%	33%	Base	37%	5.4	3.9%	60%		Base	19%	6.5	8.3%		11	61%	6.2	17.3%
12	16%	5.8	3.9%	38%	Nickel	51%	6.2	8.0%	36%		Nickel	74%	6.2	18.2%		12	18%	6.1	8.9%
22	11%	4.8	-1.4%	71%	Dime+	11%	7.3	30.7%	6%		Dime+	6%	5.9	-21.0%		21	10%	7.0	16.0%
13	9%	5.4	-4.2%	40%	Goal Line	1%	3.0	22.1%	58%		Goal Line	1%	0.7	3.6%		13	4%	6.1	11.6%
21	7%	5.8	25.1%	66%												22	3%	4.0	-2.0%

Strategic Tendencies

Run/Pass		Rk	Formation		Rk	Pass Rush		Rk	Secondary		Rk	Strategy		Rk
Runs, first half	41%	4	Form: Single Back	77%	20	Rush 3	4.0%	24	4 DB	19%	26	Play Action	22%	24
Runs, first down	59%	2	Form: Empty Back	5%	29	Rush 4	80.4%	2	5 DB	74%	4	Offensive Motion	31%	26
Runs, second-long	22%	25	Form: Multi Back	18%	6	Rush 5	10.0%	31	6+ DB	6%	21	Avg Box (Off)	6.66	7
Runs, power sit.	56%	18	Pers: 3+ WR	53%	26	Rush 6+	5.6%	15	Man Coverage	37%	8	Avg Box (Def)	6.41	27
Runs, behind 2H	32%	8	Pers: 2+ TE/6+ OL	40%	5	Edge Rusher Sacks	79.7%	1	CB by Sides	73%	19	Offensive Pace	31.80	26
Pass, ahead 2H	45%	26	Pers: 6+ OL	3%	15	Interior DL Sacks	20.3%	18	S/CB Cover Ratio	36%	3	Defensive Pace	30.34	13
Run-Pass Options	4%	23	Shotgun/Pistol	52%	28	Second Level Sacks	0.0%	32	DB Blitz	8%	22	Go for it on 4th	0.90	30

No matter where they move, the Raiders will always be the Raiders. Of course they were near the top of the league in penalties last year: fourth in total flags, second in yardage, and first in both for defense specifically. ❧ The Raiders offense ranked third in DVOA in the first half of games but fell to 22nd after halftime. ❧ The Raiders ranked second in DVOA passing the ball on third downs but 22nd rushing the ball on third downs. ❧ Only New Orleans and San Francisco threw deep (16 or more air yards) less often than the Raiders. ❧ Philip Rivers was the only quarterback blitzed less often than Derek Carr, but Carr shredded blitzes when he saw them. He went from 6.7 yards per play and 19.0% DVOA with four pass-rushers to 9.7 yards and 66.4% DVOA with five or more. However, this doesn't match Carr's splits in 2017 or 2018 so it may have been a fluky one-year trend. ❧ The Raiders' share of sacks from interior linemen fell by more than half, from 46% to 20%. Their share of sacks from edge rushers more than doubled, from 31% to 80%. And yes, they had no sacks whatsoever from either linebackers or defensive backs.

Passing

Player	DYAR	DVOA	Plays	NtYds	Avg	YAC	C%	TD	Int
D.Carr	1064	18.7%	540	3858	7.1	5.9	70.9%	21	8
M.Glennon*	-6	-20.2%	11	53	4.8	3.0	60.0%	1	0
M.Mariota	-62	-17.0%	183	1031	5.6	6.4	60.5%	7	2

Rushing

Player	DYAR	DVOA	Plays	Yds	Avg	TD	Fum	Suc
J.Jacobs	126	3.5%	242	1152	4.8	7	1	51%
D.Washington*	7	-7.0%	108	387	3.6	3	0	50%
J.Richard	8	-3.6%	39	145	3.7	0	0	46%
D.Carr	-49	-60.6%	19	84	4.4	2	5	-
A.Ingold	-10	-21.1%	10	17	1.7	0	0	70%
M.Mariota	-2	-13.7%	23	130	5.7	0	1	-

Receiving

Player	DYAR	DVOA	Plays	Ctch	Yds	Y/C	YAC	TD	C%
H.Renfrow	112	7.9%	71	49	605	12.3	6.1	4	69%
T.Williams	204	27.2%	64	42	651	15.5	4.5	6	66%
Z.Jones	-31	-28.4%	27	20	147	7.4	2.9	0	74%
K.Doss	26	11.6%	14	11	133	12.1	5.2	0	79%
M.Ateman	-2	-15.2%	10	5	116	21.1	3.2	0	50%
T.Davis*	-15	-35.0%	10	7	83	11.9	7.9	0	70%
R.Grant*	-21	-37.7%	9	4	14	3.5	1.3	0	44%
N.Agholor	-123	-35.0%	69	39	363	9.3	3.4	3	57%
D.Waller	234	22.0%	117	90	1145	12.7	6.4	3	77%
F.Moreau	72	29.6%	25	21	174	8.3	4.6	5	84%
D.Carrier	-19	-21.8%	19	13	108	8.3	3.9	1	68%
J.Witten	38	-0.5%	83	63	529	8.4	2.6	4	76%
J.Richard	39	2.7%	43	36	323	9.0	6.6	0	84%
D.Washington*	74	21.1%	41	36	292	8.1	6.8	0	88%
J.Jacobs	28	4.6%	27	20	166	8.3	9.2	0	74%
A.Ingold	19	25.8%	6	6	44	7.3	6.3	1	100%
D.Booker	-9	-33.6%	9	6	57	9.5	7.3	0	67%

Offensive Line

Player	Pos	Age	GS	Snaps	Pen	Sk	Pass	Run	Player	Pos	Age	GS	Snaps	Pen	Sk	Pass	Run
Kolton Miller	LT	25	16/16	1037	4	7.0	22	9	David Sharpe	RT	25	9/2	270	3	1.5	14	2
Rodney Hudson	C	31	15/15	919	3	0.3	4	8	Jordan Devey	LG/RG	32	4/4	234	2	0.0	2	0
Richie Incognito	LG	37	12/12	778	8	0.0	4	3	Brandon Parker	RT	25	11/3	195	2	2.0	9	2
Gabe Jackson	RG	29	11/11	715	4	4.8	11	10	Greg Van Roten	LG	30	11/11	719	2	0.0	6	5
Trenton Brown	RT	27	11/11	595	5	0.3	3	7	Eric Kush	RG	31	16/7	453	4	1.5	7	2
Denzelle Good	RG/LG	29	16/5	348	2	1.0	4	2									

Year	Yards	ALY	Rank	Power	Rank	Stuff	Rank	2nd Lev	Rank	Open Field	Rank	Sacks	ASR	Rank	Press	Rank	F-Start	Cont.
2017	4.14	4.17	11	62%	21	22%	22	1.17	14	0.73	16	24	4.6%	7	23.1%	3	18	26
2018	4.24	4.49	13	53%	31	18%	10	1.31	8	0.60	28	52	8.7%	25	28.3%	13	22	28
2019	4.26	4.63	6	58%	24	17%	7	1.14	21	0.67	22	29	5.9%	6	25.7%	4	14	22
2019 ALY by direction:			Left End 3.34 (24)			Left Tackle: 4.55 (12)			Mid/Guard: 4.71 (7)			Right Tackle: 5.73 (2)			Right End: 4.00 (19)			

As of late May, the Raiders were poised to spend $57.7 million in cap space on their offensive line in 2020, per OverTheCap.com. That's the highest figure in the league and nearly $4 million more than the second-place Cowboys. The offensive line is one of the team's strengths, but they are not quite getting what they are paying for, and some of their money would be better spent at other positions or saved for when the team is truly ready to contend. 🏈 Trent Brown will earn $21.3 million to provide solid-when-healthy service at right tackle; as usual, doing business with the Patriots came with a very steep price and mildly disappointing results. 🏈 Pro Bowl center Rodney Hudson restructured his contract to save cap space this season. That will only make him more expensive in future years, but Hudson is worth paying a premium. 🏈 Gabe Jackson and Richie Incognito will eat over $15 million at guard; the Raiders signed the 37-year-old Incognito to a two-year extension in December, because he's such a reliable individual in the best of circumstances and there's no way that will backfire on them. (We're all fortunate we didn't see a maskless Incognito going HAM in a Costco in April.) Jackson had a bit of an off year, dropping from third to 31st at his position in snaps per blown block. 🏈 Fourth-round pick John Simpson, a fine prospect and mounting evidence of Mike Mayock's Clemson fetish, is an eventual replacement at one of the guard spots. 🏈 If you don't think the depth chart is littered with 30-something journeymen, then you don't know Mayock and Gruden and have never heard of Eric Kush or Jordan Devey. 🏈 The most affordable member of the offensive line is 2018 first-round pick Kolton Miller, who made huge strides as a pass protector in his sophomore season. Miller still has blooper-reel games against some elite pass-rushers, but most left tackles outside the All-Pro tier do; in typical weeks, and when given some schematic help, he's smooth and reliable. The Raiders have one more affordable Miller year before they must start planning for fifth-year options or extensions; hopefully, they'll have a plan for getting younger and cheaper at other positions.

Defensive Front

Defensive Line	Age	Pos	G	Snaps	Plays	TmPct	Rk	Stop	Dfts	BTkl	Runs	St%	Rk	RuYd	Rk	Sack	Hit	Hur	Dsrpt
						Overall						vs. Run				Pass Rush			
Johnathan Hankins	28	DT	16	682	51	6.6%	16	41	14	9	47	79%	32	1.6	16	1.5	4	12	1
P.J. Hall	25	DT	16	557	25	3.2%	78	21	6	4	23	83%	22	2.0	31	1.5	2	17	0
Maurice Hurst	25	DT	16	537	21	2.7%	82	15	8	2	14	57%	93	2.6	64	3.5	4	21	2
Maliek Collins	25	DT	16	782	20	2.4%	89	14	9	3	16	63%	83	1.5	12	4.0	6	34	0

Edge Rushers	Age	Pos	G	Snaps	Plays	TmPct	Rk	Stop	Dfts	BTkl	Runs	St%	Rk	RuYd	Rk	Sack	Hit	Hur	Dsrpt
						Overall						vs. Run				Pass Rush			
Maxx Crosby	23	DE	16	768	50	6.5%	22	43	23	13	32	84%	11	0.3	1	10.0	7	35	5
Clelin Ferrell	23	DE	15	659	43	6.0%	36	34	15	5	31	71%	56	2.7	48	4.5	4	17	4
Benson Mayowa*	29	DE	15	316	14	1.9%	--	11	10	0	3	33%	--	5.3	--	7.0	5	18	0
Josh Mauro*	29	DE	13	285	20	3.2%	--	16	4	2	19	79%	--	1.7	--	0.0	0	3	1
Carl Nassib	27	OLB	14	656	34	4.6%	56	27	15	6	24	83%	13	0.9	4	6.0	6	24	0

Linebackers	Age	Pos	G	Snaps	Plays	TmPct	Rk	Stop	Dfts	BTkl	Runs	St%	Rk	RuYd	Rk	Sack	Hit	Hur	Tgts	Suc%	Rk	AdjYd	Rk	PD	Int
						Overall						vs. Run				Pass Rush				vs. Pass					
Tahir Whitehead*	30	OLB	16	961	108	14.0%	22	42	13	9	64	50%	73	4.4	65	0.0	2	4	38	37%	59	11.1	66	1	0
Nicholas Morrow	25	OLB	16	748	71	9.2%	50	37	10	10	39	54%	66	4.1	47	0.0	4	9	41	51%	34	7.3	48	4	1
Will Compton*	31	ILB	9	245	39	9.0%	77	21	6	5	23	70%	12	3.5	27	0.0	0	1	7	29%	--	12.0	--	0	0
Cory Littleton	27	ILB	16	1051	141	16.6%	10	75	19	4	69	57%	54	4.7	73	3.5	2	7	49	49%	38	6.4	35	9	2
Nick Kwiatkoski	27	ILB	16	518	71	8.6%	58	36	14	7	39	56%	56	4.0	42	3.0	0	9	20	55%	22	3.4	1	4	1

Year	Yards	ALY	Rank	Power	Rank	Stuff	Rank	2nd Level	Rank	Open Field	Rank	Sacks	ASR	Rank	Press	Rank
2017	4.10	4.26	22	67%	22	19%	24	1.11	15	0.68	14	31	6.1%	23	27.8%	28
2018	4.76	4.63	25	65%	16	17%	20	1.29	22	1.05	25	13	3.5%	32	22.0%	32
2019	3.82	3.89	4	70%	25	22%	7	1.12	11	0.56	9	32	6.1%	27	29.6%	21
2019 ALY by direction:			Left End: 4.18 (17)			Left Tackle: 4.25 (16)			Mid/Guard: 3.45 (4)			Right Tackle: 4.19 (13)			Right End: 4.97 (21)

Four of Maxx Crosby's 10 sacks came in Week 11 against the Bengals, when Ryan Finley was at quarterback and backup journeyman John Jerry was the left tackle. Another 1.5 sacks came against the Broncos in the season finale, with Crosby lining up against Jake Rodgers (a seventh-round pick in 2015 making the first start of his career) at right tackle for most of that game. Crosby is an exciting prospect with arms that reach all the way to Reno and some slick moves, but his production should be taken with a grain of salt until he proves that he can generate sacks against starting-caliber offensive linemen and non-rookie quarterbacks. 🏈 Jon Gruden defended Clelin Ferrell's tepid 2019 production when speaking to reporters in late December. "He's not a specialized pass-rusher that comes in 30 snaps a game and cuts it loose. A lot of the production that we've got from Ferrell is production that no one really knows about." Luke Straub of Raiders Wire noted after Gruden's quote that Ferrell played just 29 snaps in the previous week's game against the Titans, but let's set that aside for now. Ferrell did indeed come around a bit as a run defender in the second half of the year. He's also a fourth overall pick, so he's expected to do the things that folks know about in addition to the things they don't. 🏈 The Raiders have not selected a linebacker in the first three rounds of the draft since Sio Moore in 2013, unless you consider Khalil Mack a "linebacker" instead of an edge rusher. Free agent Cory Littleton, one of the best coverage linebackers in the business, will upgrade a unit otherwise made up of veteran castoffs and late-round projects. The Raiders also list third-round hybrid safety Tanner Muse as a linebacker. If you can guess Muse's alma mater, Mike Mayock will reward you with a bright orange stuffed tiger.

Defensive Secondary

Secondary	Age	Pos	G	Snaps	Plays	Overall TmPct	Rk	Stop	Dfts	BTkl	vs. Run Runs	St%	Rk	RuYd	Rk	vs. Pass Tgts	Tgt%	Rk	Dist	Suc%	Rk	AdjYd	Rk	PD	Int
Daryl Worley*	25	CB	15	962	66	9.1%	25	24	5	11	19	47%	37	5.6	34	73	19.0%	55	13.7	56%	26	8.7	66	8	1
Erik Harris	30	SS	16	919	76	9.9%	28	24	6	12	37	35%	51	7.9	46	24	6.6%	52	13.4	50%	39	7.2	32	8	3
Lamarcus Joyner	30	FS/CB	14	724	52	7.7%	57	20	8	8	13	38%	42	5.3	17	46	15.9%	3	8.7	43%	61	6.7	26	3	0
Trayvon Mullen	23	CB	16	689	58	7.5%	47	25	9	7	15	47%	40	5.7	35	57	20.8%	34	11.2	56%	27	7.1	30	10	1
Karl Joseph*	27	SS	9	590	51	11.8%	61	17	8	8	26	42%	37	4.5	9	11	4.7%	67	10.3	27%	72	11.7	71	3	1
D.J. Swearinger*	29	SS	9	497	52	12.0%	57	17	4	11	30	43%	33	6.0	28	20	9.4%	19	11.3	30%	70	10.1	66	3	0
Maurice Canady*	26	CB	13	403	47	8.1%	--	16	6	3	11	36%	--	7.1	--	43	25.7%	--	11.2	51%	--	6.7	--	5	1
Nevin Lawson	29	CB	11	307	28	5.3%	--	17	3	1	9	67%	--	3.9	--	21	17.2%	--	12.7	57%	--	7.3	--	5	0
Curtis Riley*	28	FS	16	283	32	4.2%	--	7	4	5	15	27%	--	5.3	--	8	7.1%	--	15.6	50%	--	14.0	--	1	0
Prince Amukamara	31	CB	15	910	63	8.1%	44	24	12	6	13	38%	55	5.1	27	55	15.4%	76	14.2	55%	33	8.1	54	10	0
Jeff Heath	29	SS	13	732	66	9.9%	46	28	12	4	24	58%	6	4.9	14	37	13.0%	9	9.0	51%	37	6.2	23	7	0
Damarious Randall	28	FS	11	731	67	12.2%	43	18	9	8	35	17%	72	10.7	67	21	7.9%	36	10.8	52%	35	7.6	39	6	0

Year	Pass D Rank	vs. #1 WR	Rk	vs. #2 WR	Rk	vs. Other WR	Rk	WR Wide	Rk	WR Slot	Rk	vs. TE	Rk	vs. RB	Rk
2017	30	22.3%	30	14.9%	24	25.8%	29	15.2%	29	28.0%	30	0.1%	16	13.9%	27
2018	32	-27.0%	2	-5.3%	13	27.8%	30	-16.0%	5	0.1%	17	39.7%	32	7.2%	20
2019	30	18.4%	28	32.0%	31	-4.7%	14	16.9%	29	15.4%	24	9.3%	25	34.0%	30

Love the Player/Question the Pick: A Raiders Short Story

Johnathan Abram was one of the hardest hitters in the nation when he left Mississippi State. Frankly, he was too hard a hitter: he once got ejected from an intrasquad spring game for almost decapitating a teammate, and his college career was dotted with targeting ejections. But Abram sounds like a cross between a young coach and an aspiring broadcaster during interviews, and he explained (to the media, and presumably to teams) at the 2019 Senior Bowl how he planned to work on lowering his strike point and taking other technical steps to avoid becoming Vontaze Burfict 2.0. Many of us walked away impressed with the smart, instinctive, aggressive box safety, penciling him in as a second- or third-round pick. Mike Mayock walked away impressed and penciled him in as the 27th overall pick.

Abram tore his rotator cuff in the season opener last year, playing through the injury (and making some one-armed tackles) in that game before landing on IR. He returns this season to a secondary of tough, thirsty, young try-hards, including rookies Damon Arnette and Amik Robertson and promising second-year cornerback Clemson McTiger (Trayvon Mullen, as if Mayock needs to know a Clemson player's name before drafting him), plus Jon Gruden and Paul Guenther's usual assortment of journeyman veterans. Abram's return is a plus for the secondary, but how much of a plus can an inexperienced box safety who could still be a source of unnecessary roughness penalties really be? Abrams just doesn't fit the athletic profile to have Jamal Adams or Harrison Smith-like impact.

As at many other positions, the problem isn't that the Raiders are acquiring bad players, but that they burn so much draft capital, money, and time in pursuit of pretty good ones instead of outstanding ones.

Special Teams

Year	DVOA	Rank	FG/XP	Rank	Net Kick	Rank	Kick Ret	Rank	Net Punt	Rank	Punt Ret	Rank	Hidden	Rank
2017	-0.2%	17	-4.3	23	2.2	13	4.7	7	4.8	10	-8.6	31	-3.8	18
2018	-1.6%	22	2.8	12	-4.4	27	0.1	12	-12.0	32	5.3	6	2.2	11
2019	-2.3%	25	-7.8	28	2.5	12	0.7	11	-5.5	23	-1.6	18	-6.0	25

Daniel Carlson remains the Raiders kicker, with no challenger on the roster at press time. Carlson, you may recall, was the Vikings fifth-round pick in 2018 whom the team cut after just two games and three missed field goals in four attempts; he went 16-of-17 on field goals for the Raiders over the final 10 games of 2018. But the Raiders ranked 23rd in the NFL in touchback percentage with Carlson kicking off last year, and he went 6-of-12 beyond 40 yards and missed two extra points. Carlson is a major reason why the Raiders special teams were below average last season and are projected to be below average this season. ❧ Jalen Richard is listed as the primary return man, having taken the chores back after Trevor Davis (now with the Bears) fumbled the job away at the end of last season. With the arrival of Henry Ruggs, Lynn Bowden, and others, the Raiders have no shortage of return options. ❧ A.J. Cole was average in gross punt value, but the Raiders had trouble the last couple of years with punt coverage.

Los Angeles Chargers

2019 Record: 5-11	Total DVOA: -6.8% (21st)	2020 Mean Projection: 7.5 wins	On the Clock (0-4): 13%
Pythagorean Wins: 7.8 (16th)	Offense: 3.8% (12nd)	Postseason Odds: 35.4%	Mediocrity (5-7): 38%
Snap-Weighted Age: 26.7 (5th)	Defense: 5.4% (21st)	Super Bowl Odds: 2.9%	Playoff Contender (8-10): 37%
Average Opponent: -2.2% (24th)	Special Teams: -5.1% (32nd)	Proj. Avg. Opponent: 0.6% (8th)	Super Bowl Contender (11+): 13%

2019: Ol' man Rivers stops rolling along.

2020: "Does this new quarterback make us look younger and hipper?"

A bold new era of Chargers football is upon us. For the first time since 2005, the Chargers starting quarterback will not be named Philip Rivers. For the first time since 2001, he will not be named Rivers or Drew Brees. The future belongs to Justin Herbert, even if the immediate present nominally belongs to Tyrod Taylor.

Otherwise, not much has changed.

Anthony Lynn is still the head coach, Gus Bradley the defensive coordinator, Tom Telesco the general manager. The Chargers will still be couch-surfing in Los Angeles, now as the Todd in the Rams' Bojack mansion of a new stadium. They remain a team with a penny-pinching reputation and an almost nonexistent regional fan base. While their quarterback got nearly a generation younger in the offseason, the rest of the roster got older, thanks to the signings of over-30 free agents Chris Harris, Bryan Bulaga, and Linval Joseph. Look past the quarterback, the new address, and the spiffy retro-chic uniforms and the Chargers reboot was remarkably soft. But that's understandable, since they lack practice when it comes to paradigm shifts.

The quarterback change came at just the right time. Rivers' long career in Southern California, like an archaeological age, can be broken into three distinct eras. In the early Norv Turner Era (2007-12), the Chargers emerged from the Late Schottenheimer Period as Super Bowl contenders anchored by stars like Rivers, LaDainian Tomlinson, Antonio Gates, Shawne Merriman, and others. Those teams fell short of expectations due to Turner's limitations as a head coach, the front office's tightfisted habits, and just generally never being as good as the Patriots.

Then came the Mike McCoy era (2013-16). Rivers appeared to be fading, though McCoy's subsequent flops as the offensive coordinator of the Broncos and Cardinals suggest that he might have been the actual culprit for the slump. The Chargers fell from playoff contention to 4-12 and 5-11 seasons in 2015 and 2016. Telesco then replaced contentious A.J. Smith as general manager and steadily added talent such as Keenan Allen, Melvin Ingram, Joey Bosa, and others. That set the stage for the ongoing Anthony Lynn Era (2017-present), during which Rivers and the Chargers rebounded with the help of their new stars and Bradley's next-gen defense, only to discover once again in 2018 that they were not quite as good as the Patriots.

The Chargers fell from contention last year for a variety of reasons: abysmal first-quarter play calling, which led to coordinator Ken Whisenhunt's dismissal; a strange need to "feature" Melvin Gordon when he returned from his holdout (this second point was closely related to the first); the usual Chargers injury rash on defense, which prevented them from running Bradley's trendy full-time dime packages; typically inexplicable Chargers kicker catastrophes. But by the end of the year, Rivers was clearly one of the problems. He threw seven fourth-quarter interceptions, six of them in the final two minutes of games in which the Chargers were trailing. The Chargers ranked 28th in the NFL in late-and-close DVOA as a result, and Rivers' comeback efforts in late-season games against the Raiders and Chiefs were excruciating to watch.

Even in his prime, Rivers was an awkward-looking athlete, but in the second half of last season it looked like he needed all the muscle he could muster to push the ball downfield, and even his ball placement on routine crossing routes to Allen became spotty. Rivers was already performing his first encore after his McCoy Era slump. It made no sense for the Chargers to recommit to him after a 5-11 season, so they let Rivers walk and selected Herbert with the sixth overall pick.

Our QBASE projection method likes Herbert a lot. His projected bust-success rates and expected DYAR in years 3 through 5 are on par with those of Joe Burrow and Tua Tagovailoa, well above Jordan Love or the many Jake Fromm types among this year's second-tier quarterback prospects. Herbert was a two-year starter who also started several games as a freshman and sophomore for a major program, producing impressive (though not overwhelming) rate stats throughout his career, two strong indicators of future NFL success.

On the down side, game-by-game breakdowns of Herbert's production reveal a lot of fluff, including 626 passing yards, 10 touchdowns, and 70-plus completion percentage in two games against Nevada and Montana last season. Scouting of some of his Pac-12 games reveals some mid-game slumps and other issues that didn't always appear in the stat sheet. Herbert's decision-making and accuracy on throws more than 10 yards downfield were highly suspect in midseason, at about the same time Burrow overtook him as the top quarterback prospect in the nation and Tua's injury turned him into Schrodinger's Quarterback.

There were also deafening whispers about Herbert's mental

2020 Chargers Schedule

Week	Opp.	Week	Opp.	Week	Opp.
1	at CIN	7	at MIA	13	NE
2	KC	8	JAX	14	ATL
3	CAR	9	LV	15	at LV (Thu.)
4	at TB	10	BYE	16	DEN (Sat.)
5	at NO (Mon.)	11	at DEN	17	at KC
6	NYJ	12	at BUF		

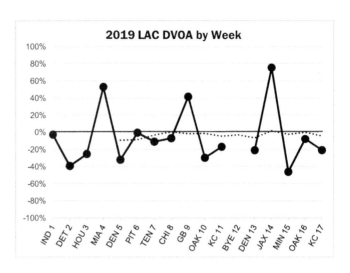

2019 LAC DVOA by Week

makeup down the "insider" lane. What I personally was told (by a source who is not typically full of beans) was that Herbert was sensitive and lacked the self-confidence needed to be the face of an NFL franchise. Whereas Baker Mayfield might hear midday talk-show criticism and start a Twitter beef with the host, Herbert (per the whispers) would hear it and curl into a little ball. Franchise quarterbacks, of course, are supposed to tune the chatter out

The perception-versus-reality element of the Herbert criticism is tough to parse out, particularly in our little analytical publication. Herbert is a soft-spoken Pacific Northwest guy who wears his hair shaggy; quarterback prospects have been castigated by the rumormongers for far less. He was easy to brand as a free-falling prospect when Burrow zoomed past him and he laid an egg in a loss against Arizona State, and that may have magnified some of his minor flaws.

Herbert began to turn the narrative around in December, not by producing gaudy stats, but by demonstrating his skills as a gutsy, hard-scrambling game manager in the Pac-12 Championship Game win over Utah and in the Rose Bowl over Wisconsin. Herbert then performed well and competed hard in both Senior Bowl activities and the combine, answering forthright questions from reporters (and, behind closed doors, decision-makers) about his demeanor and perceived lack of confidence.

In some NFL circles, a headfirst dive for a first down and a firm handshake mean more than four-touchdown games in the Pac-12. By March, Herbert could do all three. As a result, he may have landed in a better situation than Burrow with the drifting Bengals and Tua with the long-range rebuilding Dolphins.

Herbert has plenty of weapons. Allen is among the league's most gifted and reliable receivers, as well as perhaps the most unappreciated. He became an almost full-time short safety valve last year as the Chargers offense struggled and Rivers lost faith in everything except the shallow crossing route, and he should reprise that role to become Herbert's favorite security blanket. Hunter Henry and Mike Williams are finally emerging from the myriad of injuries and setbacks which befall most Chargers top draft picks. Williams is now a formidable deep threat, while Henry can put up Travis Kelce numbers if he can further limit his injuries and mistakes. Austin Ekeler is an Alvin Kamara/Christian McCaffery type, but at a wholesale price (even after a contract extension). Gordon's departure is a case of addition by subtraction, not because Gordon was terrible but because Lynn and Whisenhunt insisted on force-feeding him early-game carries to prove some point.

Herbert also has a rebuilt veteran offensive line, with newcomers Bryan Bulaga and Trai Turner anchoring the right side and holdover Mike Pouncey in the middle. There are question marks on the left side, but rookie quarterbacks rarely get to play behind lines with as many established starters as the Chargers have on the payroll.

Defensively, the Chargers hope to bounce back to 2018 form with the return of Derwin James. Bradley coached as if he didn't have a Plan B when James (as well as second-round pick Nasir Adderley) got hurt last season, leaving the Chargers without the manpower to deploy six defensive backs in their base defensive package. With his secondary depleted, Bradley blitzed even less than the year before. Los Angeles rushed more than four defenders on just 12.1% of opposing pass attempts, tied with Detroit for the lowest rate in the league. As a result, the Chargers recorded just 30 sacks and finished 25th in the NFL in both adjusted sack rate and pressure rate. Bosa and Ingram combined for 18.5 sacks, but no one else recorded more than 2.5.

The low sack rate would be tolerable if the lack of blitzes made the Chargers less vulnerable to the deep ball. But the Chargers ranked 24th in the NFL in DVOA in both passes over the middle and deep passes. James' absence hurt here, as did the fact that 36-year-old Thomas Davis was still being used as a coverage linebacker, and it didn't help that just-another-guy defenders like Michael Davis and Roderic Teamer were thrust into important roles.

Former All-Pro cornerback Chris Harris, coming off a disappointing year in which the Broncos moved him from the slot to the outside, was signed to upgrade the Chargers cornerback corps. Rookie Kenneth Murray, who is blessedly gifted but sometimes bites on head-fakes like a tabby cat leaping on a squeaky toy, is expected to replace Davis in the middle of the field. But James, who played exceptionally after returning from injury late in the season, is the crucial cog to the Chargers defense. With James, they have the personnel to prevent teams like the Chiefs from dictating the rules of engagement. Without him, the Chargers defense is two edge rushers, some slot defenders, and a lot of hustle.

With James back and the Harris-Bulaga-Joseph acquisitions, it would be tempting to ignore Rivers' 2019 struggles and predict a typical 9-7-ish Chargers season if he were still on the team. The veterans the Chargers signed even came with such low price tags that they could have added them and given Rivers an extension while barely scraping the salary-cap ceiling. Telesco and the organization deserve credit for not saddling up one last time with Rivers in an attempt to sell season tickets and relive past semi-glories.

Still, it's hard to visualize the Chargers' long game. Yes, the veteran supporting cast should aid Herbert's development and keep the Chargers out of the cellar. But Harris, Bulaga, Pouncey, Ingram, Joseph, Casey Heyward, and perhaps even Allen will be on the decline by the time Herbert enters his early peak. The Chargers run the risk of returning to the rut which defined the late Rivers era when Herbert comes of age: good enough to be in the playoff conversation in most seasons, but usually in the category labeled "wild-card hunt."

In the AFC West Young Nucleus arms race, the Chargers appear to be ahead of the Raiders (who don't have all that much to show for lots of extra picks over the last two seasons} but slightly behind the Broncos (who have learned how to recognize talent in the draft and are a step ahead at quarterback). Herbert, James, Murray, Adderley, Jerry Tillery, and some still-young veterans such as Mike Williams and Desmond King could form the core of future playoff teams if everyone develops and the top draft picks finally stop suffering Spinal Tap drummer fates. But the Chargers spent so many years trying to build a young nucleus to support Rivers that the first wave of young guys are now in their prime (Bosa, Henry) or already gone (Gordon). If the Chargers were truly hoping to gain traction on a youth movement, they should have committed to it: no Harris, Joseph, or Bulaga, no trading picks to move up for Murray.

The Chargers may also be hoping for a Chiefs/Ravens-style sudden lurch to contention while Herbert is young and affordable. Even Herbert's fiercest supporters, however, would be reluctant to compare him to Patrick Mahomes or Lamar Jackson. There's also nothing in Lynn's or Telesco's background to suggest that they are capable of building an outside-the-box powerhouse (Bradley at least has Seahawks cred and his dime defense). So the Chargers' rebuilding strategy, such as it is, appears to be to start developing Herbert now and figure out the rest later.

The Chargers left home without a stadium two years ago and shacked up with a Major League Soccer team, of course, so coherent planning may not be the organization's strong suit. They've also had great quarterbacks around to cover their missteps and keep the team competitive since the turn of the millennium. For a long time, running the Chargers has meant surrounding Rivers (or Brees) with a handful of stars, rolling the dice, and getting pretty good results. Telesco, Lynn, and the organization obviously know that there's more to it than that, but so far, they have not demonstrated much of a grasp of the particulars.

The Chargers won't be very good this year, but they will be competitive. And at least they won't be wheeling Rivers out to play out the string in front of hostile crowds at their Airbnb of a temporary stadium. Herbert is someone new to root for, the skill position stars and quirky defense will be fun to watch, the new retro uniforms are cherry, the new digs palatial. The Chargers may not be thinking too far down the road, but at least they are no longer living in limbo. That's a step in the right direction.

Mike Tanier

2019 Chargers Stats by Week

Wk	vs.	W-L	PF	PA	YDF	YDA	TO	Total	Off	Def	ST
1	IND	W	30	24	435	376	-2	-3%	29%	34%	2%
2	at DET	L	10	13	424	339	0	-39%	-10%	13%	-15%
3	HOU	L	20	27	366	376	0	-25%	11%	34%	-3%
4	at MIA	W	30	10	390	233	+1	53%	22%	-23%	7%
5	DEN	L	13	20	246	350	-1	-32%	-43%	4%	15%
6	PIT	L	17	24	348	256	-2	-1%	22%	15%	-7%
7	at TEN	L	20	23	365	403	0	-11%	-4%	10%	3%
8	at CHI	W	17	16	231	388	+1	-7%	-2%	-4%	-10%
9	GB	W	26	11	442	184	0	42%	43%	-8%	-10%
10	at OAK	L	24	26	315	278	-3	-30%	-23%	3%	-4%
11	KC	L	17	24	438	310	-3	-17%	-7%	-11%	-21%
12	BYE										
13	at DEN	L	20	23	359	218	-1	-21%	-17%	-8%	-12%
14	at JAX	W	45	10	525	252	0	75%	68%	-7%	0%
15	MIN	L	10	39	345	344	-6	-46%	-33%	11%	-2%
16	OAK	L	17	24	284	366	0	-8%	10%	16%	-1%
17	at KC	L	21	31	366	336	-1	-21%	11%	7%	-25%

Trends and Splits

	Offense	Rank	Defense	Rank
Total DVOA	3.8%	12	5.4%	21
Unadjusted VOA	4.7%	13	5.9%	20
Weighted Trend	3.7%	10	1.5%	19
Variance	8.2%	22	2.5%	2
Average Opponent	2.2%	26	-0.3%	18
Passing	22.0%	9	10.5%	20
Rushing	-11.0%	24	0.0%	25
First Down	12.8%	8	0.9%	17
Second Down	-7.8%	22	-5.0%	11
Third Down	3.9%	15	28.2%	29
First Half	3.5%	9	10.8%	28
Second Half	4.1%	13	0.2%	15
Red Zone	-15.2%	23	28.2%	32
Late and Close	-21.1%	28	2.4%	21

Five-Year Performance

Year	W-L	Pyth W	Est W	PF	PA	TO	Total	Rk	Off	Rk	Def	Rk	ST	Rk	Off AGL	Rk	Def AGL	Rk	Off Age	Rk	Def Age	Rk	ST Age	Rk
2015	4-12	5.9	6.0	320	398	-4	-14.8%	24	0.9%	15	10.4%	28	-5.3%	31	55.0	26	29.6	14	27.6	7	25.9	30	26.5	7
2016	5-11	7.7	6.9	410	423	-7	-1.1%	19	-3.2%	18	-6.8%	7	-4.8%	29	61.7	28	65.7	29	27.9	4	25.7	31	25.7	24
2017	9-7	10.5	8.4	355	272	+12	7.9%	11	10.6%	7	-4.7%	12	-7.5%	31	35.4	17	31.9	13	27.6	5	25.7	26	25.4	25
2018	12-4	10.6	11.0	428	329	+1	22.6%	3	20.7%	3	-4.7%	8	-2.8%	25	30.7	11	52.2	29	27.8	7	25.7	26	25.4	29
2019	5-11	7.8	5.8	337	345	-17	-6.8%	21	3.8%	12	5.4%	21	-5.1%	32	51.7	24	40.3	21	27.3	7	26.7	10	25.5	23

2019 Performance Based on Most Common Personnel Groups

LAC Offense					LAC Offense vs. Opponents						LAC Defense					LAC Defense vs. Opponents			
Pers	Freq	Yds	DVOA	Run%	Pers	Freq	Yds	DVOA	Run%		Pers	Freq	Yds	DVOA		Pers	Freq	Yds	DVOA
11	71%	6.4	9.8%	28%	Base	16%	4.7	0.1%	55%		Base	29%	4.3	-16.2%		11	56%	6.2	14.0%
21	14%	5.4	9.5%	48%	Nickel	57%	6.1	-5.8%	38%		Nickel	51%	5.9	7.9%		12	17%	5.1	-0.2%
12	7%	5.0	-33.3%	39%	Dime+	26%	7.0	47.3%	14%		Dime+	19%	6.8	31.2%		22	7%	5.3	38.2%
22	3%	4.8	-2.7%	73%	Goal Line	1%	0.8	68.0%	67%		Goal Line	0%	2.0	141.8%		21	6%	4.1	-42.5%
611	1%	5.9	-6.4%	73%												13	5%	4.6	-26.3%

Strategic Tendencies

Run/Pass		Rk	Formation		Rk	Pass Rush		Rk	Secondary		Rk	Strategy		Rk
Runs, first half	36%	19	Form: Single Back	81%	15	Rush 3	6.3%	17	4 DB	29%	11	Play Action	21%	26
Runs, first down	46%	23	Form: Empty Back	10%	7	Rush 4	81.5%	1	5 DB	51%	20	Offensive Motion	49%	7
Runs, second-long	20%	29	Form: Multi Back	8%	23	Rush 5	11.4%	29	6+ DB	19%	12	Avg Box (Off)	6.32	29
Runs, power sit.	59%	10	Pers: 3+ WR	72%	10	Rush 6+	0.7%	32	Man Coverage	12%	32	Avg Box (Def)	6.42	25
Runs, behind 2H	24%	26	Pers: 2+ TE/6+ OL	14%	32	Edge Rusher Sacks	74.1%	3	CB by Sides	67%	25	Offensive Pace	33.14	32
Pass, ahead 2H	45%	24	Pers: 6+ OL	3%	11	Interior DL Sacks	10.3%	31	S/CB Cover Ratio	29%	8	Defensive Pace	32.32	30
Run-Pass Options	2%	31	Shotgun/Pistol	71%	11	Second Level Sacks	15.5%	19	DB Blitz	6%	27	Go for it on 4th	1.40	16

The Chargers recovered a league-low 32% of fumbles, including just three out of 15 fumbles on defense. ✎ Los Angeles targeted running backs on a league-high 31% of passes, and their opponents targeted running backs on a league-high 25% of passes. ✎ The Chargers ranked 30th in offensive DVOA in the first quarter of games, then improved to seventh the rest of the game. ✎ This was the second straight year the Chargers defense ranked No. 1 in frequency of sending the standard four pass-rushers. ✎ The Chargers had a league-low 18 passes dropped by opponents. ✎ The Chargers had the league's smallest gap in DVOA between defense with pressure (-36.8%, 30th in the NFL) and defense without pressure (31.3% DVOA, 14th).

Passing

Player	DYAR	DVOA	Plays	NtYds	Avg	YAC	C%	TD	Int
P.Rivers*	714	6.6%	625	4332	6.9	5.5	66.7%	23	20
T.Taylor	23	59.3%	6	33	5.5	4.8	66.7%	1	0

Rushing

Player	DYAR	DVOA	Plays	Yds	Avg	TD	Fum	Suc
M.Gordon*	8	-7.5%	162	615	3.8	8	3	51%
A.Ekeler	-8	-10.0%	132	559	4.2	3	1	45%
J.Jackson	50	34.9%	29	200	6.9	0	0	62%
T.Pope*	-22	-76.1%	10	20	2.0	0	0	30%
D.Watt*	10	9.2%	7	10	1.4	1	0	86%
P.Rivers*	-10	-41.9%	7	30	4.3	0	0	-

Receiving

Player	DYAR	DVOA	Plays	Ctch	Yds	Y/C	YAC	TD	C%
K.Allen	232	7.3%	149	104	1199	11.5	3.5	6	70%
M.Williams	235	20.6%	90	49	1001	20.4	3.8	2	54%
A.Patton	-4	-15.3%	17	6	56	9.3	4.7	0	35%
T.Benjamin*	-84	-78.9%	16	6	30	5.0	3.2	0	38%
D.Inman*	19	7.0%	13	8	132	16.5	2.4	0	62%
D.Jennings	-19	-52.5%	6	2	17	8.5	7.0	0	33%
H.Henry	136	19.0%	76	55	652	11.9	2.9	5	72%
V.Green	18	12.4%	13	9	78	8.7	4.3	1	69%
L.Kendricks*	-7	-22.4%	7	3	50	16.7	2.3	0	43%
A.Ekeler	320	38.8%	108	92	993	10.8	10.2	8	85%
M.Gordon*	19	-7.3%	55	42	296	7.0	7.6	1	76%
J.Jackson	-33	-74.9%	11	9	22	2.4	4.2	0	82%

Offensive Line

Player	Pos	Age	GS	Snaps	Pen	Sk	Pass	Run	Player	Pos	Age	GS	Snaps	Pen	Sk	Pass	Run
Michael Schofield*	RG	30	16/16	1071	1	1.5	12	6	Mike Pouncey	C	31	5/5	309	0	0.5	3	2
Dan Feeney	LG	26	16/16	1046	8	3.5	14	9	Russell Okung*	LT	32	6/6	262	6	0.0	3	1
Trenton Scott	LT	26	16/9	836	9	7.0	28	8	Trey Pipkins	LT	24	13/3	254	3	3.0	8	4
Sam Tevi	RT	26	14/14	794	4	7.0	19	7	Bryan Bulaga	RT	31	16/16	922	6	3.0	17	3
Scott Quessenberry	C	25	16/9	634	2	1.0	3	7	Trai Turner	RG	27	13/13	900	3	4.0	14	2

Year	Yards	ALY	Rank	Power	Rank	Stuff	Rank	2nd Lev	Rank	Open Field	Rank	Sacks	ASR	Rank	Press	Rank	F-Start	Cont.
2017	3.93	3.71	26	58%	25	24%	26	1.17	13	0.78	12	18	4.2%	3	31.8%	20	17	26
2018	4.91	4.80	5	67%	18	18%	16	1.46	4	1.05	7	34	6.4%	13	32.4%	22	10	38
2019	4.13	4.37	13	68%	12	20%	21	1.16	19	0.68	21	34	6.2%	9	30.3%	19	16	27
2019 ALY by direction:			Left End 3.92 (17)			Left Tackle: 4.35 (15)			Mid/Guard: 4.22 (21)			Right Tackle: 4.37 (15)			Right End: 5.34 (5)			

Philip Rivers' sack rate (and, by extension, the Chargers' sack rate) hovered between 5.2% and 5.9% in every season from 2013 through last year except for 2017, when it dipped to a league-best 3.0%. The Chargers' adjusted sack rate ranged from 5.4% to 6.6% in that span, reaching 4.2% (third overall) in 2017. Rivers was the one constant throughout that era, which started with the Nick Hardwick/King Dunlap offensive lines and ended with the Mike Pouncey/Russell Okung group. Quarterbacks have more influence over their sack totals and rates than their offensive lines do, so when Okung's groin injury left Trey Pipkins and Trent Scott as the starting left tackles, it didn't make a noticeable difference in the sack totals, though it surely contributed to Rivers' woes elsewhere. 🏈 Needless to say, things will be different with Justin Herbert and/or Tyrod Taylor at quarterback. Taylor's career sack rate is 9.4%, and while Herbert wasn't too sack-prone at Oregon (his career rate was 5.4%), rookies tend to be easy prey. So expect the Chargers' sack rate to rise in 2020. 🏈 The Chargers line itself is also in transition. The arrivals of newcomers Bryan Bulaga and Trai Turner make the right side formidable on paper, Pouncey anchors things in the middle, and Dan Feeney will get pushed by perma-project Forrest Lamp at left guard. That leaves Scott, Pipkins, and question marks at left tackle. Lamp or Sam Tevi (last year's starting right tackle) could move to the left side, or Bulaga could slide across the formation after a decade on the right, but none of these sound like ideal solutions at a critical position. 🏈 Look, if I were a team whose first-round picks always suffer *Final Destination*-like fates, and I just drafted a quarterback sixth overall, I would probably spend a bazillion dollars on a left tackle. But you do you, Chargers.

Defensive Front

Defensive Line	Age	Pos	G	Snaps	Plays	TmPct	Rk	Stop	Dfts	BTkl	Runs	St%	Rk	RuYd	Rk	Sack	Hit	Hur	Dsrpt
Justin Jones	24	DT	12	507	31	5.4%	58	25	4	4	26	77%	39	2.3	50	0.0	3	13	1
Brandon Mebane*	35	DT	13	411	27	4.3%	70	17	2	5	23	61%	85	3.3	93	1.0	1	5	0
Damion Square	31	DT	16	411	29	3.8%	66	17	2	1	22	59%	90	2.4	55	0.0	1	6	1
Jerry Tillery	24	DT	15	360	16	2.2%	--	11	5	2	10	70%	--	3.4	--	2.0	0	6	0
Linval Joseph	32	DT	13	559	44	6.2%	36	28	10	2	37	62%	84	2.9	83	3.0	3	6	0

Edge Rushers	Age	Pos	G	Snaps	Plays	TmPct	Rk	Stop	Dfts	BTkl	Runs	St%	Rk	RuYd	Rk	Sack	Hit	Hur	Dsrpt
Joey Bosa	25	DE	16	846	66	8.6%	2	52	28	8	47	77%	30	1.9	23	11.5	19	49	1
Melvin Ingram	31	DE	13	677	53	8.5%	16	43	19	7	36	81%	20	2.8	56	7.0	4	38	4
Uchenna Nwosu	24	OLB	16	365	26	3.4%	--	17	9	4	18	61%	--	3.8	--	2.0	6	12	0
Isaac Rochell	25	DE	16	278	11	1.4%	--	6	3	1	9	44%	--	2.9	--	1.0	0	7	1

Linebackers	Age	Pos	G	Snaps	Plays	TmPct	Rk	Stop	Dfts	BTkl	Runs	St%	Rk	RuYd	Rk	Sack	Hit	Hur	Tgts	Suc%	Rk	AdjYd	Rk	PD	Int
Thomas Davis*	37	OLB	16	816	114	14.8%	19	59	11	19	69	58%	47	3.9	38	1.0	0	2	32	56%	18	6.0	32	2	0
Drue Tranquill	25	ILB	15	382	65	9.0%	62	31	12	3	31	52%	70	4.5	68	0.0	0	1	15	67%	--	7.8	--	1	0
Kyzir White	24	OLB	16	376	41	5.3%	75	23	2	1	31	58%	45	4.1	49	0.0	0	0	8	50%	--	5.5	--	2	1
Denzel Perryman	28	ILB	14	367	68	10.1%	53	41	6	20	47	72%	9	3.1	13	0.0	0	0	15	53%	26	5.8	27	1	1
Nick Vigil	27	OLB	16	1009	116	14.0%	21	67	16	23	74	62%	34	3.9	40	1.0	4	9	33	64%	7	5.6	23	5	1

Year	Yards	ALY	Rank	Power	Rank	Stuff	Rank	2nd Level	Rank	Open Field	Rank	Sacks	ASR	Rank	Press	Rank
2017	4.82	4.31	24	64%	18	20%	16	1.27	28	1.26	32	43	7.8%	7	30.6%	15
2018	4.38	4.37	17	71%	23	19%	18	1.21	15	0.83	16	38	6.7%	24	30.8%	15
2019	4.29	4.35	20	63%	14	17%	23	1.06	8	0.78	20	30	6.2%	25	28.2%	26

2019 ALY by direction:	Left End: 3.14 (5)	Left Tackle: 4.36 (19)	Mid/Guard: 4.89 (29)	Right Tackle: 4.46 (18)	Right End: 2.48 (5)

Joey Bosa and Melvin Ingram are awesome. Let's check in on some of the other guys. ❧ Linval Joseph replaces (finally) Brandon Mebane, who spent his last four seasons with the Chargers as an expensive big-name blocking sled. Joseph, now 31, is still the player Mebane claimed to be: a 328-pound double-team-muncher in the middle who clogs running lanes and will create opportunities for Bosa and Ingram. ❧ Jerry Tillery avoided the Chargers' top draft-pick injury curse. Instead, he was just mostly terrible. The Chargers tried to use him as a rotational tackle, but double-teams knocked Tillery back into the stadium tunnel, and his playing time dipped late in the season. Tillery is a high-effort/character guy, and the team asked him to get bigger and stronger in the offseason. Joseph's presence may allow Tillery to take more snaps out at 5-tech, where double-teams are less common. ❧ Kenneth Murray recorded 257 total tackles (29.5 tackles for a loss) in his final two seasons at Oklahoma, performed well at the combine, and has an exemplary off-field reputation. (He's the guy who administered roadside CPR and saved a motorist's life in 2018.) Murray's tape is also full of little mistakes, which were magnified by draft hipsters because a) when a defender is in position to make 20 plays per game, it's easy to spot the two he misses; and b) draft hipsters love to tweet "Aha! I spotted a mistake in coverage. So this guy secretly stinks. Bask in my extreme scouting knowledge!" Murray's college tape is reminiscent of Luke Keuchly's, and his mistakes (biting too hard on fakes, mostly) are easily ironed out. That said, Murray's ironing probably won't be finished by the time the season starts, so for 2020 the Chargers may have traded Thomas Davis getting outrun by backs and tight ends 10 years younger than him for Murray getting juked by backs and tight ends three years older than him. ❧ Speaking of broken tackles, free-agent signing Nick Vigil tied for the league lead with Cincinnati last year. Without the benefit of OTAs, it's hard to tell if the Chargers will be depending on Vigil to start on the strong side or if he's just depth material. There's a lot of personnel here to shape into a unit around Murray in the middle.

Defensive Secondary

Secondary	Age	Pos	G	Snaps	Plays	Overall TmPct	Rk	Stop	Dfts	BTkl	vs. Run Runs	St%	Rk	RuYd	Rk	vs. Pass Tgts	Tgt%	Rk	Dist	Suc%	Rk	AdjYd	Rk	PD	Int
Rayshawn Jenkins	26	FS	16	977	56	7.3%	53	10	7	9	28	18%	71	11.1	69	13	4.1%	71	23.9	46%	55	18.2	74	4	3
Casey Hayward	31	CB	16	956	40	5.2%	78	16	7	5	6	17%	80	7.0	54	44	14.2%	83	13.1	55%	32	6.8	23	8	2
Michael Davis	25	CB	12	669	48	8.3%	61	25	5	8	10	90%	1	2.1	2	42	19.4%	51	12.8	55%	31	7.2	34	9	2
Desmond King	26	CB	15	591	52	7.2%	52	25	10	2	10	60%	23	4.1	17	31	16.2%	70	8.1	39%	81	10.1	78	2	0
Roderic Teamer	23	FS	7	384	41	12.2%	--	17	5	3	17	65%	--	6.4	--	14	11.2%	--	9.0	29%	--	12.4	--	2	1
Brandon Facyson	26	CB	16	331	36	4.7%	--	13	4	5	17	53%	--	3.4	--	23	21.4%	--	13.5	35%	--	8.0	--	1	0
Jaylen Watkins*	29	SS	14	305	27	4.0%	--	11	7	8	10	40%	--	6.2	--	16	16.2%	--	11.3	38%	--	9.4	--	1	0
Derwin James	24	FS	5	299	35	14.6%	--	23	6	3	21	62%	--	4.3	--	5	5.2%	--	2.8	80%	--	1.0	--	1	0
Adrian Phillips*	28	SS	7	282	32	9.5%	--	9	3	5	14	29%	--	4.9	--	9	9.8%	--	4.2	56%	--	5.1	--	0	0
Chris Harris	31	CB	16	1067	62	7.4%	49	18	6	4	14	29%	68	6.4	43	58	14.9%	80	13.4	45%	70	10.9	83	6	1

Year	Pass D Rank	vs. #1 WR	Rk	vs. #2 WR	Rk	vs. Other WR	Rk	WR Wide	Rk	WR Slot	Rk	vs. TE	Rk	vs. RB	Rk
2017	9	-11.8%	10	0.5%	17	-25.2%	3	-17.3%	5	-6.1%	10	0.9%	18	-21.3%	5
2018	10	10.3%	23	-2.6%	15	3.1%	19	7.2%	23	4.6%	18	-52.4%	1	9.7%	23
2019	20	7.7%	23	0.1%	16	-13.3%	8	-14.5%	10	11.9%	21	-1.7%	13	-1.9%	19

With Derwin James injured for most of the year (see: Chargers Top Draft Picks, Curse of, cited elsewhere in this chapter), the Chargers were unable to deploy the every-down dime personnel groups that they used so successfully in 2018. The Chargers used six defensive backs on just 14% of snaps last season, as opposed to 64% in 2018. They used more dime packages when James returned late in the season (31%), and on paper, the Chargers have one of the league's most versatile secondaries if Gus Bradley wants to experiment with more full-time dime:

Casey Hayward: One of the NFL's most consistent outside cornerbacks. Heyward prefers the left side but will move across the formation and shadow receivers if called upon.

Derwin James: Box safety/Will linebacker/slot corner/devastating blitzer. The straw that stirs this drink.

Chris Harris: Best known as one of the league's premier slot corners, Harris was asked to line up outside more often for the Broncos last year and struggled with the new assignment. He allowed 7.1 yards per pass with a 48% success rate against opponents lined up in the slot, compared to 13.1 yards per pass with a 39% success rate against opponents lined up wide. Harris is now 31 years old but should be able to return to his previous high level of performance if his usage matches his talents.

Desmond King: Extra-thirsty coach's-dream type with a skill set halfway between Harris and James.

Rayshawn Jenkins: Big eyeball test-winning free safety, started 16 games last year but was one of the weak links in the Chargers defense. He'll face competition from…

Nasir Adderley: Last year's second-round pick; cousin (twice removed) of the Packers and Cowboys Hall of Famer. Adderley suffered a hamstring injury last summer that lasted until he landed on IR in October. Adderley has the skills of a free safety who doubles as a matchup corner against bigger receivers, meaning he could push Jenkins down the depth chart.

Others: Brandon Facyson, Michael Davis, and Roderic Teamer all started games and played a few hundred snaps last season. Davis in particular had good charting numbers.

It may be impossible to build a secondary that can cover the Chiefs receivers one week and then stop the Ravens or Titans from hammering them the next. But Bradley and the Chargers deserve credit for trying.

Special Teams

Year	DVOA	Rank	FG/XP	Rank	Net Kick	Rank	Kick Ret	Rank	Net Punt	Rank	Punt Ret	Rank	Hidden	Rank
2017	-7.5%	31	-22.2	32	-7.4	29	-3.9	26	-6.1	24	2.3	9	-4.7	20
2018	-2.8%	25	-5.9	27	1.5	13	-3.2	26	-11.3	31	4.8	7	-3.4	20
2019	-5.1%	32	-5.6	26	-6.7	30	-3.3	28	-7.6	27	-2.5	22	13.3	2

Last season was a typical one for Chargers kickers, which means this will take a while. Mike "Money Badger" Badgley, having won the job the previous season, suffered a groin injury the Friday before the season opener. Rookie punter Ty Long took over double duties and actually performed well, but Badgley's injury lingered and lingered, so the Chargers signed Chase McLaughlin. He went 1-of-4 from 40-to-49 yards (Long had been 5-of-5) and was released the moment Badgley was healthy so he could go on to sign with the 49ers and then the Colts later in the season. Badgley was reliable down the stretch, but Long took over kickoff duties because Badgley doesn't have the leg for them. The Chargers will take a limited kicker (and a versatile punter) over their usual two to seven ineffective and hazard-prone kickers. ✎ Despite an off year in 2019, Desmond King is one of the league's better punt returners, in addition to being a quality multi-purpose defensive back and the kind of guy who makes color commentators shout things like "See that Desmond King guy? You know what he is? He's a FOOTBALL PLAYER." ✎ Chargers opponents were particularly bad on field goals, which is likely to regress in 2020. They were worth an estimated -14.2 points below field position after adjusting for weather and altitude. Opponents missed six extra points and were just 23-of-33 on field goals with two misses within 35 yards.

Los Angeles Rams

2019 Record: 9-7	Total DVOA: 5.2% (12nd)	2020 Mean Projection: 8.4 wins	On the Clock (0-4): 7%
Pythagorean Wins: 8.8 (12th)	Offense: 0.3% (17th)	Postseason Odds: 48.2%	Mediocrity (5-7): 29%
Snap-Weighted Age: 26.4 (19th)	Defense: -6.4% (9th)	Super Bowl Odds: 6.1%	Playoff Contender (8-10): 42%
Average Opponent: 5.4% (1st)	Special Teams: -1.5% (23rd)	Proj. Avg. Opponent: -0.7% (23rd)	Super Bowl Contender (11+): 22%

2019: The Rams reach for the brass ring but miss and fall off the merry-go-round instead.

2020: Another ride 'round the carousel, but did they miss their best chance?

The Los Angeles Rams find themselves in a bit of a tough spot because they have gambled and lost. Two years ago, they realized that they had the NFL's most prized commodity—a starting quarterback on a rookie contract—and went all in, doing everything they could to add talent for those two seasons, knowing it would leave them deep in debt in 2020 and beyond. And it very nearly won them a Super Bowl, but now they are left struggling to pay off those old bills. As noted wagering enthusiast Hunter S. Thompson once wrote: "Gambling can turn into a dangerous two-way street when you least expect it. Weird things happen suddenly, and your life can go all to pieces."

L.A. general manager Les Snead had acquired quarterback Jared Goff with a bold trade in the 2016 draft; a year later he hired Sean McVay, then and still the youngest head coach in the NFL. In their first season together, the Rams won their division for the first time since 2003. A home loss to Atlanta quickly knocked the Rams out of the playoffs, however, leaving them craving more success.

And so the Rams went on a wild spending spree, doing all they could to supplement their quarterback with as much veteran talent as possible on both sides of the ball. Over the next two years, the Rams added Clay Matthews, Ndamukong Suh, and Eric Weddle in free agency, while trades were made for Brandin Cooks, Dante Fowler, Marcus Peters, and Aqib Talib. They were still dealing into last season, shipping Peters to Baltimore in October for peanuts, then sending three draft picks to Jacksonville to get Jalen Ramsey the next day. Along the way, the Rams also managed to dole out big money to their young offensive stars—Todd Gurley became the league's highest-paid running back in 2018, while Goff reset the market for quarterbacks a year later with an extension that kicks in this season.

Two years later, what do they have to show for it? One Super Bowl loss, in which they scored a record-low three points, and a follow-up campaign in which they were eliminated from the playoffs before Week 17. Their 2019 season was one of frustrating inconsistency—they beat the Saints and the Seahawks but fell to the Buccaneers and Steelers, and they finished 30th in DVOA variance. Most of that fluctuation was due to the rollercoaster performance of Wade Phillips' defense, but on the whole L.A. played better on that side of the ball than they had in their Super Bowl season—it's their offense that really

collapsed (Table 1). And those veteran acquisitions? Gone. Of the ten players named in the last paragraph, only Goff and Ramsey remain. Even Gurley is out the door, released in March with four years left on his deal. So turbulent has been the Rams' roster churn that half of their 22 starters in the Super Bowl against New England have left town, including seven on defense.

Table 1. Teams That Dropped from Offensive DVOA Over 20% to Offensive DVOA Below 5%, 1986-2019

Year	Team	Year N-1	Rk	Year N	Rk	Year N+1	Rk
1988	CLE1	22.7%	3	-2.7%	19	5.2%	8
1997	BAL	22.8%	1	1.8%	15	-7.3%	21
1999	DEN	34.5%	1	3.4%	14	19.6%	3
1999	SF	28.8%	2	-1.7%	16	18.8%	4
2000	WAS	22.4%	1	3.8%	12	-11.5%	26
2002	STL	20.5%	2	-10.2%	26	-7.5%	22
2003	OAK	22.0%	2	-9.1%	24	-0.5%	14
2005	NYJ	20.8%	4	-19.8%	31	5.6%	12
2006	DEN	26.9%	2	-4.8%	18	9.5%	8
2006	SEA	28.5%	1	-11.2%	27	6.6%	11
2007	SD	25.7%	2	4.6%	14	18.8%	3
2010	DAL	21.7%	3	-4.7%	21	5.9%	12
2014	PHI	22.9%	3	1.1%	13	-10.1%	26
2015	DEN	20.0%	3	-8.7%	25	-12.3%	28
2015	GB	24.7%	1	2.2%	11	16.6%	4
2019	**LAC**	**20.7%**	**3**	**3.8%**	**12**	--	--
2019	**LAR**	**24.6%**	**2**	**0.3%**	**17**	--	--
AVERAGE (THRU 2018)		*24.3%*	*2.1*	*-3.7%*	*19.1*	*3.8%*	*13.5*

The Rams have suddenly found their cupboards bare, with no cash left in the envelope for groceries. L.A. had the least cap space in the league this offseason, in part because they had the fourth-most dead money. Notable veteran acquisitions were limited to Leonard Floyd and A'Shawn Robinson, a pair of highly drafted disappointments in Chicago and Detroit. And there was little help to be found in the draft because,

2020 Rams Schedule

Week	Opp.	Week	Opp.	Week	Opp.
1	DAL	7	CHI (Mon.)	13	at ARI
2	at PHI	8	at MIA	14	NE (Thu.)
3	at BUF	9	BYE	15	NYJ (Sat.)
4	NYG	10	SEA	16	at SEA
5	at WAS	11	at TB (Mon.)	17	ARI
6	at SF	12	SF		

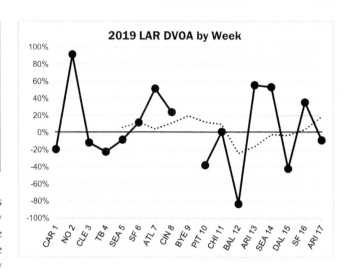

2019 LAR DVOA by Week

as usual, the Rams didn't have a first-round pick. L.A. has not made a selection in the first round of the draft since they took Goff first overall in 2016. Their other first-rounders were given up in trades for veterans (Cooks, Ramsey) or for more picks, replacing the mid-round selections they had given away for players who have since departed.

As a result of all those deals, the Rams have been left starved for young talent. According to Chase Stuart's draft value chart at Football Perspective, only the Kansas City Chiefs have had less draft capital than the Rams over the last five years. The Chiefs at least came out of that half-decade with a Super Bowl win, Patrick Mahomes, and Frank Clark signed to a long-term deal. The Rams have a Super Bowl loss, Jared Goff, and Jalen Ramsey ready to hit free agency in 2021.

It's hard to look at the Rams' roster and find any position where they are likely to be better in 2020 than they were in 2019. So you might be surprised to see that we have the Rams as playoff contenders, with a higher projection than you might be seeing elsewhere this preseason. The computer sees a team that ranked second in DVOA two years in a row before falling to 12th last season and assumes that last year was the anomaly. Our projection system balances that three-year trend with the loss of talent such as Cooks and Fowler this offseason and ends up with a mean forecast that would put the Rams right about where they were last year: just outside the DVOA top ten, on the cusp of making it to the postseason.

Now, it's certainly possible that our projection system is overestimating the chances of a rebound when a lot of players responsible for that past performance are no longer here. Most teams with similar three-year runs have been able to make the needed acquisitions to plug whatever holes have opened up on the roster. It looks like the Rams have barely managed to tread water, failing to address the myriad issues on their offensive line or on defense. And it's hard to imagine that the defense is helped by the loss of Wade Phillips, one of the best coordinators in NFL history.

But despite missing the postseason, this was still a good team in 2019, and the strongest parts of that team have survived. That starts with one the NFL's deepest wide receiver groups, with second-round rookie Van Jefferson joining holdovers Robert Woods, Cooper Kupp, and Josh Reynolds. That is crucial, because no coach leans more heavily on his wide receivers than McVay. Rams wide receivers are asked to catch a lot of passes (249 last season, second only to Atlanta), and they are asked to make plays with the ball in their hands (a league-high 5.8 yards after catch per reception). They are

asked to run the ball (32 carries for 200 yards, both the highest totals in the league). They are asked to block on runs outside the tackles (41% of L.A.'s runs went up the middle; only Minnesota had a lower rate). They are even asked to block on pass plays—McVay's affection for max-protect bootlegs out of bunch formations means that Woods and Kupp were left protecting Goff rather than trying to get open more often than you would expect.

On the rare occasions when those wide receivers can't get open, the Rams have a pair of reliable tight ends in Tyler Higbee and Gerald Everett. It has been a while since L.A. had more than one usable tight end—they were last in the league in two-tight end sets in both 2017 and 2018 but climbed out of the bottom ten in 2019, using multiple tight ends on nearly one-quarter of their offensive snaps. At running back, you can expect L.A. to replace Gurley by grouping veterans Malcolm Brown and Darrell Henderson into a committee with second-round rookie Cam Akers.

On the other side of the ball, the Rams still have Aaron Donald, the league's best defensive player, coming off his fifth consecutive appearance on the NFL's All-Pro team. Any defensive front with Donald on the field is likely to have the edge over the opposition, and he's not alone on the interior—Michael Brockers will return for his ninth season in a horned helmet, and the Rams also added veteran free agent Robinson.

There's not a lot to like behind that line, however. The L.A. defense improved somewhat following the Ramsey trade, but the corner's individual coverage statistics were unimpressive. The Rams lost Weddle to retirement and slot corner Nickell Robey-Coleman in free agency, with no incoming veterans to replace them. With Ramsey and Troy Hill starting at corner, Taylor Rapp and John Johnson at safety, and Darious Williams presumably stepping in at nickelback, the other defensive backs on the Rams roster played a combined 191 defensive snaps in 2019. Rookie safeties Terrell Burgess (third round, Utah) and Jordan Fuller (sixth round, Ohio State) are likely to see plenty of action.

That's still more than the Rams have at linebacker, where their top three players—Cory Littleton, Fowler, and Matthews—all left in free agency. Samson Ebukam's struggles as a starter early in his career inspired the Rams to go get Fowler and Matthews, but now those two are gone and Ebukam's a starter again. His bookend will be Leonard Floyd, who made waves as a rookie in Chicago but has been quiet since. At least Ebukam and Floyd have started in the NFL. With Littleton out the door, the only inside linebacker in town who can say the same is Troy Reeder, who started eight games as an undrafted rookie last year. With options here so sparse, look for first-year defensive coordinator Brandon Staley to play a lot of nickel and dime sets by default.

And this is the problem with the Rams roster: it is impossibly top-heavy. Goff and Donald each have a cap hit of $25 million or more, making the Rams the only team with two players taking up such a big chunk of cap space. Indianapolis is the only other team with two players with cap hits of even $20 million or more. (The Colts actually have three players over the $20-million mark: quarterbacks Philip Rivers and Jacoby Brissett and defensive lineman DeForest Buckner.) With so little money spent anywhere else, the Rams absolutely need Goff and Donald to deliver if they are going to advance far into the playoffs. We know Donald is up to the task, but can the same be said for Goff?

The Rams' investment in Goff goes beyond the $110 million in guaranteed money they have given him, which remains an NFL record. There's also the matter of the trade the Rams made to get him, giving up two picks in the first round, two in the second, one in the third, and one in the fourth. Referring back to the Stuart draft value chart and accounting for the two late-round picks L.A. got back from Tennessee in the deal, we find that the Rams gave the Titans an equal value for the first overall draft pick—plus the *second* overall draft pick, and a fourth-rounder for good measure. Between draft capital and big fat checks, the Rams have devoted more of their resources to Goff than any other team has in their passer, and they need him to perform at nothing less than an MVP level to justify that cost.

It looked like Goff was heading that way in L.A.'s two playoff seasons of 2017 and 2018, as he ranked fifth in passing DVOA and sixth in DYAR in both years, but then he fell to 18th and 15th in those categories last season. Despite L.A.'s bevy of receivers, only four teams had a worse DVOA on deep passes: the Jets, Pittsburgh, Carolina, and Washington. And Goff was at his worst when the Rams needed him most— he had a negative DVOA when his team was losing. That includes a DVOA of -40.4% when L.A. was down by one score in the fourth quarter, with only one touchdown and four turnovers (one of which was returned for a score by Tampa Bay).

It's important that Goff and the Rams play better in 2020 because this roster isn't likely to change much in the years to come. For better or worse, they're married to Goff and his contract for several seasons. His deal and Donald's are likely to have major cap implications through 2023. And they've already given up next year's first-round draft pick in the Ramsey trade.

It really is hard to overstate what a mess Snead has made of the Rams' salary cap. Even though Gurley was cut, he'll eat up $17.3 million of the Rams' cap space this year, then $8.4 million in 2021. When Brandin Cooks was traded to Houston in April, the Rams took on a record $21.8 million in dead money, which means their cap space in 2020 actually went *down*. They're on the hook for $2 million more in dead money after releasing Clay Matthews. They've still got to find a way to sign Ramsey because they can't afford to lose a corner after trading away two first-round picks for him last October.

In defense of Snead, the Rams' financial woes run beyond any decisions made in his office. According to an article by the *Los Angeles Times'* Sam Farmer in May, construction costs of SoFi Stadium have doubled to $5 billion, and NFL owners voted unanimously to provide Rams owner Sam Kroenke with $500 million in financing to ensure the stadium is completed. Per *Forbes*, Kroenke is still worth $10 billion, so it's not as if the team will be filing for bankruptcy or anything. But there are other signs that the Rams are having trouble paying bills— both Gurley and Matthews said publicly that the team owed them money after they were released. Matthews went so far as to file a grievance with the players' association in an attempt to collect his payday. Snead insisted that the payments were not late and that Gurley and Matthews would get their money on time, but it's certainly a bad look for one team to have so many economic question marks.

We turn once more to our gaming savant, Hunter S. Thompson: "There are many harsh lessons to be learned from the gambling experience, but the harshest one of all is the difference between having Fun and being Smart." The Rams have certainly had their Fun. But if they're going to return to the Super Bowl any time soon, they're going to have work harder on being Smart.

Vincent Verhei

2019 Rams Stats by Week

Wk	vs.	W-L	PF	PA	YDF	YDA	TO	Total	Off	Def	ST
1	at CAR	W	30	27	349	343	+2	-19%	6%	5%	-21%
2	NO	W	27	9	380	244	0	91%	27%	-60%	4%
3	at CLE	W	20	13	344	270	-2	-12%	-28%	-16%	1%
4	TB	L	40	55	518	464	-3	-22%	7%	38%	8%
5	at SEA	L	29	30	477	429	-1	-8%	16%	25%	0%
6	SF	L	7	20	157	331	+1	12%	-19%	-31%	-1%
7	at ATL	W	37	10	381	224	+3	52%	-2%	-54%	0%
8	CIN	W	24	10	470	401	0	24%	32%	12%	4%
9	BYE										
10	at PIT	L	12	17	306	273	-2	-38%	-49%	-10%	2%
11	CHI	W	17	7	283	267	-1	1%	-16%	-17%	0%
12	BAL	L	6	45	221	480	-2	-83%	-60%	23%	0%
13	at ARI	W	34	7	549	198	+1	56%	18%	-49%	-12%
14	SEA	W	28	12	455	308	-1	54%	35%	-23%	-4%
15	at DAL	L	21	44	289	475	-1	-42%	-24%	23%	5%
16	at SF	L	31	34	395	334	+1	36%	23%	-22%	-9%
17	ARI	W	31	24	424	393	+5	-9%	9%	15%	-2%

Trends and Splits

	Offense	Rank	Defense	Rank
Total DVOA	0.3%	17	-6.4%	9
Unadjusted VOA	-0.4%	17	-3.2%	12
Weighted Trend	-1.7%	17	-7.5%	8
Variance	8.2%	21	9.2%	29
Average Opponent	-2.4%	6	3.3%	3
Passing	15.0%	13	-1.3%	10
Rushing	-7.3%	20	-12.5%	10
First Down	-3.7%	20	-15.8%	5
Second Down	5.3%	11	0.9%	15
Third Down	0.3%	17	0.0%	17
First Half	3.0%	11	-2.1%	14
Second Half	-2.6%	17	-10.7%	7
Red Zone	22.2%	7	11.7%	25
Late and Close	3.0%	16	-20.7%	4

Five-Year Performance

Year	W-L	Pyth W	Est W	PF	PA	TO	Total	Rk	Off	Rk	Def	Rk	ST	Rk	Off AGL	Rk	Def AGL	Rk	Off Age	Rk	Def Age	Rk	ST Age	Rk
2015	7-9	6.5	7.9	280	330	+5	-2.2%	16	-15.0%	29	-10.5%	7	2.4%	7	31.9	15	48.6	29	25.2	32	26.1	25	24.9	32
2016	4-12	3.3	4.6	224	394	-11	-28.6%	30	-37.8%	32	-2.0%	15	7.1%	3	7.6	1	21.9	5	25.5	32	26.0	26	25.4	29
2017	11-5	11.6	11.3	478	329	+7	27.7%	2	11.1%	6	-9.8%	6	6.8%	2	3.3	1	27.4	12	26.0	31	26.0	19	25.0	31
2018	13-3	11.2	12.5	527	384	+11	24.0%	2	24.6%	2	0.5%	17	-0.2%	17	11.0	2	27.0	13	27.1	12	26.5	11	25.8	15
2019	9-7	8.8	9.1	394	364	0	5.2%	12	0.3%	17	-6.4%	9	-1.5%	23	29.8	9	30.8	16	26.3	24	26.8	8	25.4	25

2019 Performance Based on Most Common Personnel Groups

LAR Offense					LAR Offense vs. Opponents					LAR Defense				LAR Defense vs. Opponents			
Pers	Freq	Yds	DVOA	Run%	Pers	Freq	Yds	DVOA	Run%	Pers	Freq	Yds	DVOA	Pers	Freq	Yds	DVOA
11	73%	5.9	4.4%	29%	Base	27%	6.0	11.2%	51%	Base	34%	5.4	-7.0%	11	53%	5.2	-8.5%
12	21%	5.2	2.9%	60%	Nickel	61%	5.6	10.4%	34%	Nickel	23%	5.4	0.0%	12	22%	5.7	1.7%
10	3%	5.4	45.4%	22%	Dime+	11%	5.8	-40.6%	12%	Dime+	42%	5.1	-11.5%	21	8%	5.6	-13.2%
13	2%	6.2	23.0%	75%	Goal Line	0%	1.5	31.9%	0%	Big	1%	3.0	26.9%	10	5%	4.8	0.0%
														612	3%	1.6	-48.0%

Strategic Tendencies

Run/Pass		Rk	Formation		Rk	Pass Rush		Rk	Secondary		Rk	Strategy		Rk
Runs, first half	34%	24	Form: Single Back	87%	7	Rush 3	6.0%	19	4 DB	34%	3	Play Action	32%	2
Runs, first down	45%	25	Form: Empty Back	11%	5	Rush 4	66.4%	14	5 DB	23%	32	Offensive Motion	41%	13
Runs, second-long	27%	19	Form: Multi Back	2%	30	Rush 5	23.3%	10	6+ DB	42%	3	Avg Box (Off)	6.61	11
Runs, power sit.	57%	16	Pers: 3+ WR	77%	2	Rush 6+	4.4%	20	Man Coverage	29%	24	Avg Box (Def)	6.49	18
Runs, behind 2H	21%	30	Pers: 2+ TE/6+ OL	23%	23	Edge Rusher Sacks	51.0%	23	CB by Sides	76%	18	Offensive Pace	28.30	3
Pass, ahead 2H	48%	18	Pers: 6+ OL	0%	30	Interior DL Sacks	40.0%	4	S/CB Cover Ratio	36%	2	Defensive Pace	31.19	26
Run-Pass Options	0%	32	Shotgun/Pistol	44%	31	Second Level Sacks	9.0%	30	DB Blitz	6%	29	Go for it on 4th	1.15	26

The Rams' move towards using more 12 personnel really came in the second half of the season. In the first eight games of the season, the Rams used 12 or 13 personnel on 14.3% of plays. From Week 10 onwards, that more than doubled to 31.6% of plays. ✇ The Rams led the league with 27% of passes targeting "other wide receivers" not classified as the top two (Brandin Cooks and Robert Woods). Los Angeles targeted running backs on a league-low 10% of passes; no other offense was below 15%. ✇ The Rams never run out of shotgun, or almost never. Only 4.2% of shotgun plays were runs out of the backfield, compared to a league average of 20.5%. ✇ Once again, the Rams were excellent on wide receiver screens: sixth with 6.8 yards per pass and fourth with 37.3% DVOA. Those ranks were fourth and second, respectively, in 2018. ✇ This was the third straight year the Rams didn't run a single play with six offensive linemen. However, the Rams found plenty of other players to block. They were second in the league with 11.8% of plays charted as max protect (seven or more blockers with at least two more blockers than pass-rushers). ✇ The Rams' total rate of blitzing increased from 20.5% in 2018 to 27.7% last season. ✇ The Rams' defense had a much bigger problem with broken tackles than the year before, going from 86 broken tackles (second) to 130 (tied for 19th). ✇ The "CB by Sides" number is really two numbers. It was 95% in the first part of the season with Aqib Talib and Marcus Peters as the starting cornerbacks but only 63% in the second half of the season once Jalen Ramsey arrived and played across from Troy Hill. The first number would have ranked second for the season, the latter number 26th.

Passing

Player	DYAR	DVOA	Plays	NtYds	Avg	YAC	C%	TD	Int
J.Goff	552	2.0%	649	4422	6.8	5.7	63.2%	22	16

Rushing

Player	DYAR	DVOA	Plays	Yds	Avg	TD	Fum	Suc
T.Gurley*	58	-2.4%	223	858	3.8	12	3	48%
M.Brown	25	-0.1%	69	255	3.7	5	0	46%
D.Henderson	-5	-11.6%	39	147	3.8	0	0	46%
J.Goff	-32	-36.7%	19	46	2.4	2	1	-
R.Woods	59	24.9%	17	115	6.8	1	0	-
B.Cooks*	32	48.1%	6	52	8.7	0	0	-
J.Reynolds	8	-5.9%	5	23	4.6	0	0	-

Receiving

Player	DYAR	DVOA	Plays	Ctch	Yds	Y/C	YAC	TD	C%
R.Woods	94	-4.0%	139	90	1134	12.6	6.4	2	65%
C.Kupp	205	7.1%	134	94	1161	12.4	5.7	10	70%
B.Cooks*	71	0.0%	72	42	583	13.9	4.0	2	58%
J.Reynolds	-11	-16.1%	43	21	326	15.5	6.6	1	49%
T.Higbee	79	5.5%	89	69	734	10.6	5.6	3	78%
G.Everett	-13	-10.4%	60	37	408	11.0	4.8	2	62%
J.Mundt	-26	-58.3%	7	4	26	6.5	2.5	0	57%
T.Gurley*	0	-13.8%	49	31	207	6.7	6.3	2	63%
D.Henderson	2	-8.1%	6	4	37	9.3	9.3	0	67%
M.Brown	-19	-71.9%	6	2	16	8.0	3.5	0	33%

Offensive Line

Player	Pos	Age	GS	Snaps	Pen	Sk	Pass	Run	Player	Pos	Age	GS	Snaps	Pen	Sk	Pass	Run
Andrew Whitworth	LT	39	16/16	1121	14	0.5	7	5	Brian Allen	C	25	9/9	581	4	1.5	9	4
Austin Blythe	RG/C	28	15/15	1019	3	1.0	16	15	Austin Corbett	LG	25	11/7	548	4	0.0	7	4
David Edwards	RG	23	16/10	698	7	2.0	12	9	Bobby Evans	RT	23	9/7	477	0	1.0	15	7
Rob Havenstein	RT	28	9/9	636	8	5.0	15	5	Joseph Noteboom	LG	25	6/6	391	1	0.0	2	3

Year	Yards	ALY	Rank	Power	Rank	Stuff	Rank	2nd Lev	Rank	Open Field	Rank	Sacks	ASR	Rank	Press	Rank	F-Start	Cont.
2017	4.53	4.70	3	50%	29	22%	23	1.42	1	0.82	11	28	5.6%	9	29.8%	12	20	42
2018	5.00	5.49	1	68%	13	15%	2	1.58	1	0.84	16	33	5.4%	6	25.2%	4	11	48
2019	3.80	4.27	19	65%	18	21%	26	1.23	14	0.44	29	22	3.7%	1	31.5%	22	21	30
2019 ALY by direction:			Left End 3.75 (20)			Left Tackle: 4.04 (20)			Mid/Guard: 4.64 (10)				Right Tackle: 3.94 (21)			Right End: 4.12 (17)		

In 36 regular-season and playoff games in 2017 and 2018, not a single Rams lineman missed a start due to injury. That all changed in 2019, when only left tackle Andrew Whitworth made it through the season unscathed. None of the other starters in Week 1—left guard Joseph Noteboom, center Brian Allen, right guard Austin Blythe, or right tackle Rob Havenstein—were starting at the same position after Week 10. Noteboom and Allen were both shelved with torn knee ligaments, and Blythe was moved to left guard and then to center to fill in for them. Havenstein had his own knee injury, a bad meniscus, but he was healthy enough to return—or at least, he would have been, if he hadn't been Wally Pipped by third-round rookie Bobby Evans. ✇ Does this mean the Rams are likely to have a healthier line in 2020? Not necessarily. L.A. ranked eighth in most adjusted games lost by offensive linemen and 12th in continuity score. These results, not the perfect marks of the prior two seasons, are the norm in the modern NFL. ✇ Whitworth is the only sure thing going into this fall; he signed a new three-year, $30-million contract to stay with the team. Among qualifying tackles, only Baltimore's Ronnie Stanley had a better rate of snaps per blown block. He's 39 years old, however, and had talked about retirement in years past, so it's doubtful he'll see the end of that deal. ❧ Everything else is still as messy now as it was at the end of 2019. The Rams re-signed Whitworth and Blythe but failed to add any linemen in free agency, and they ignored the position in the draft until taking Clemson's Tremayne Anchrum in the seventh round. Your guess is as good as ours about who ends up where. Will Noteboom and Allen recover from their knee injuries? Will Les Snead find a trade partner for Havenstein, who has three years left on his contract and is due $8.1 million in salary this season? What will they do with Austin Corbett, who started the last seven games at left guard after a midseason trade, or with David Edwards, a fifth-round rookie last year who started two games at left guard and eight games at right? ❧ Allen, by the way, is best known as the first NFL player to test positive for COVID-19, though he only reported mild symptoms in April and is expected to suffer no lasting effects. ❧ The Rams had the lowest adjusted sack rate in the league last year, but that's a deceiving measure of the offensive line. They suffered only one "non-pressure" sack (those marked as coverage sacks, failed scrambles, or "QB fault/self sack") all year, tied with Jacksonville for the fewest in the league. Their 22nd-place ranking in pressure rate allowed is a more accurate indicator of their pass protection last season.

Defensive Front

Defensive Line	Age	Pos	G	Overall Snaps	Plays	TmPct	Rk	Stop	Dfts	BTkl	vs. Run Runs	St%	Rk	RuYd	Rk	Pass Rush Sack	Hit	Hur	Dsrpt
Aaron Donald	29	DT	16	937	50	5.9%	23	44	26	8	32	84%	16	0.7	4	12.5	11	48	3
Michael Brockers	30	DE	16	777	64	7.6%	10	46	12	6	53	72%	66	2.7	68	3.0	4	21	3
Sebastian Joseph-Day	25	DT	16	487	45	5.3%	33	33	9	1	40	73%	59	2.0	30	2.0	3	11	1
Morgan Fox	26	DE	16	355	18	2.1%	--	13	3	0	15	67%	--	3.4	--	2.0	1	11	0
Greg Gaines	24	DT	10	184	13	2.5%	--	10	2	2	11	82%	--	1.8	--	0.5	1	2	1
A'Shawn Robinson	25	DT	13	532	43	6.2%	35	26	8	3	36	58%	92	3.1	88	1.5	0	11	2

Edge Rushers	Age	Pos	G	Overall Snaps	Plays	TmPct	Rk	Stop	Dfts	BTkl	vs. Run Runs	St%	Rk	RuYd	Rk	Pass Rush Sack	Hit	Hur	Dsrpt
Dante Fowler*	26	OLB	16	890	61	7.2%	13	51	25	8	40	80%	21	2.9	58	11.5	4	39	8
Clay Matthews*	34	OLB	13	620	39	5.7%	44	23	13	12	24	50%	87	3.0	66	8.0	7	25	4
Samson Ebukam	25	OLB	16	571	50	5.9%	30	40	14	8	38	82%	18	1.8	20	4.5	7	24	2
Leonard Floyd	28	OLB	16	916	41	5.0%	40	28	10	9	27	70%	57	2.9	59	3.0	11	33	5

Linebackers	Age	Pos	G	Overall Snaps	Plays	TmPct	Rk	Stop	Dfts	BTkl	vs. Run Runs	St%	Rk	RuYd	Rk	Pass Rush Sack	Hit	Hur	vs. Pass Tgts	Suc%	Rk	AdjYd	Rk	PD	Int
Cory Littleton*	27	ILB	16	1051	141	16.6%	10	75	19	4	69	57%	54	4.7	73	3.5	2	7	49	49%	38	6.4	35	9	2
Troy Reeder	26	ILB	16	300	53	6.3%	--	25	2	13	36	61%	--	3.7	--	0.0	0	0	12	33%	64	7.4	50	0	0

Year	Yards	ALY	Rank	Power	Rank	Stuff	Rank	2nd Level	Rank	Open Field	Rank	Sacks	ASR	Rank	Press	Rank
2017	4.65	4.36	27	63%	16	18%	28	1.14	19	1.19	31	48	7.9%	5	31.5%	11
2018	4.91	4.49	21	68%	21	16%	22	1.36	25	1.12	27	41	7.0%	17	36.0%	1
2019	4.16	4.26	16	62%	12	16%	24	1.18	18	0.61	10	50	8.1%	7	32.7%	8
2019 ALY by direction:		Left End: 4.28 (18)			Left Tackle: 4.28 (17)			Mid/Guard: 4.04 (6)			Right Tackle: 4.68 (24)			Right End: 5.09 (22)		

Aaron Donald remains the best penetrating defensive tackle the world has seen since John Randle was in his prime in the 1990s. He led the NFL in tackles for loss in each of the last two seasons. He also led all interior linemen in sacks and defeats (tied in the latter category with Pittsburgh's Cameron Heyward); he has finished in the top three at the position in those categories every year since 2015. ❧ Michael Brockers, a rock for the Rams defensive line since they drafted him 14th overall in 2012, reached a deal with Baltimore in free agency. L.A. looked to replace him by signing A'Shawn Robinson, formerly of the Detroit Lions. Then Brockers failed his physical with Baltimore, rendering his Ravens contract null and void, and the Rams were only too happy to welcome him back into their flock. The doctors in Baltimore weren't happy with the state of Brockers' ankle, but if he's healthy— and the Rams are as qualified as anyone to make informed decisions on his health, having worked with him for eight years—then this could turn into a dominant defensive front. Robinson never developed into more than a rotational piece in the Motor City, but then he never got to play alongside linemen as talented as Donald and Brockers, either. ❧ Dante Fowler was overshadowed by Donald's dominance, but he quietly had the best year of his career, ranking seventh among edge rushers in defeats. Now he's gone, along with Clay Matthews. That's 19.5 sacks that just walked out the door. Replacing them will be Samson Ebukam (9.5 sacks in three seasons with the Rams) and Leonard Floyd, late of the Chicago Bears. The ninth overall draft pick in 2016, Floyd made the All-Rookie team that year, collecting 7.0 sacks in only 12 games. However, he has just 11.5 sacks in 42 games since. He did not collect a sack in the second half of last season despite starting every game. Floyd did have 33 hurries, however; the other 14 players with 30 to 35 hurries last season averaged 7.4 sacks apiece. ◥ The Rams also used a third-round pick on Alabama's Terrell Lewis. Lewis only played two seasons for the Crimson Tide, missing all of 2018 with a torn ACL and then skipping his senior season to enter the draft. He left Tuscaloosa with only 7.0 career sacks. SackSEER is cautiously optimistic about him, impressed with his combine jumps (37-inch vertical, 124-inch broad). ◥ Cory Littleton's departure leaves Troy Reeder the only available inside linebacker with any experience of note. An undrafted rookie last season, Reeder was a starter for one season at Penn State who later transferred to Delaware. He made his first NFL start in Week 5 against Seattle and promptly made a team-high 13 tackles, then had 10 the next week against San Francisco. He never made more than six after that and finished the season without making a single sack, tackle for loss, or pass breakup. ◥ The other options at the position are, in alphabetical order:

- Travin Howard, a seventh-round pick in 2018 who spent his rookie year on the practice squad and played barely 100 defensive snaps last season;
- Micah Kiser, a fifth-round pick in 2018 who spent all of his rookie year on special teams and missed all of 2019 with a torn pec;
- Clay Johnston, a seventh-round rookie out of Baylor; and
- Kenny Young, a fourth-round pick of the Ravens in 2018 who came to the Rams in the Marcus Peters trade and proceeded to play zero snaps on defense.

Analytics have suggested that off-ball linebacker is one of the less important positions on the defense, but even with that caveat, this depth chart is extremely skimpy.

Defensive Secondary

Secondary	Age	Pos	G	Snaps	Plays	TmPct	Rk	Stop	Dfts	BTkl	Runs	St%	Rk	RuYd	Rk	Tgts	Tgt%	Rk	Dist	Suc%	Rk	AdjYd	Rk	PD	Int
							Overall						**vs. Run**						**vs. Pass**						
Eric Weddle*	35	FS	16	1043	112	13.2%	7	32	16	10	49	35%	52	6.8	38	21	5.5%	61	15.6	43%	65	8.3	49	4	0
Taylor Rapp	23	SS	15	831	107	13.5%	11	52	23	9	53	49%	19	5.5	19	45	14.7%	5	7.0	47%	50	7.8	43	8	2
Jalen Ramsey	26	CB	12	791	55	8.7%	56	18	7	4	11	36%	61	10.2	78	58	19.7%	47	12.6	48%	59	8.3	58	5	1
Nickell Robey-Coleman*	28	CB	16	714	42	5.0%	--	22	16	12	9	67%	--	3.3	--	42	16.0%	--	10.0	55%	--	6.5	--	7	0
Troy Hill	29	CB	14	546	49	6.6%	74	17	5	4	16	38%	57	6.8	49	50	24.9%	7	13.1	62%	8	5.3	6	8	2
John Johnson	25	SS	6	399	53	16.7%	--	17	5	10	26	42%	--	5.3	--	11	7.5%	--	10.5	55%	--	6.4	--	2	2
Marqui Christian*	26	FS	16	375	33	3.9%	72	13	4	8	10	50%	15	5.1	15	24	17.4%	2	10.4	54%	30	6.1	22	2	0
Darious Williams	27	CB	12	221	16	2.5%	--	8	4	2	2	0%	--	19.0	--	17	20.9%	--	12.8	53%	--	9.6	--	4	2

Year	Pass D Rank	vs. #1 WR	Rk	vs. #2 WR	Rk	vs. Other WR	Rk	WR Wide	Rk	WR Slot	Rk	vs. TE	Rk	vs. RB	Rk
2017	3	-5.4%	12	-24.8%	4	-16.8%	7	-10.4%	10	-16.0%	6	1.2%	19	-9.8%	9
2018	9	15.9%	28	-12.2%	9	9.9%	24	3.0%	21	10.2%	23	-22.1%	5	-18.1%	4
2019	10	-18.0%	4	-5.9%	9	-2.6%	16	-22.3%	7	6.4%	17	6.6%	21	9.3%	22

Jalen Ramsey's coverage stats were underwhelming, to say the least. However, after a rough start with the team, his numbers drastically improved. Between completions and pass interference fouls, he gave up at least 69 yards in each of his first three appearances and an average of 75.3 yards per game. He didn't allow more than 56 yards in any of his six games after that, and his average fell to 22.8. That includes two games where he wasn't thrown at even once, against Arizona in Week 13 and Dallas in Week 15 (not coincidentally, Amari Cooper only had one catch in two targets in that game). And though Ramsey gave up some big plays early in drives, he was dominant once opponents crossed the 50—his 13 targets in Rams territory resulted in five completions for 35 yards without a first down (let alone a touchdown), plus a 19-yard DPI. Most importantly, L.A.'s pass defense DVOA plummeted to -13.0% in his nine starts, down from 14.6% in their other seven games. Unfortunately, their run defense collapsed in those nine games, limiting L.A.'s overall defensive improvement in the second half of the year. ◥ Troy Hill allowed 5.3 yards per pass, exactly half of the 10.6 he allowed on 39 targets the year before. He has played at least a dozen games for L.A. in each of the past four seasons, but last year's nine starts were a career high; it remains to be seen if he can survive a whole season. ◥ New nickelback Darious Williams played nearly 80% of his 221 defensive snaps in the last three weeks of the year, starting the last two games. He played only four snaps on defense as an undrafted rookie out of Alabama-Birmingham in 2018. He's an unknown commodity, is what we're getting at. ◥ John Johnson only missed 11 defensive snaps in the first five games, but then a shoulder injury in Week 6 knocked him out for the rest of the season. Taylor Rapp, a second-round rookie out of Washington, moved from a rotational role into the starting lineup and turned into a big-play machine, finishing as one of seven safeties to rack up more than 20 defeats. Eric Weddle's retirement leaves Johnson and Rapp as the starting duo now, with a pair of rookies (Terrell Burgess, third round, Utah and Jordan Fuller, sixth round, Ohio State) for depth. Burgess is a high-motor flexible chess piece who can play strong safety or nickel corner; Fuller is more of a centerfielder.

Special Teams

Year	DVOA	Rank	FG/XP	Rank	Net Kick	Rank	Kick Ret	Rank	Net Punt	Rank	Punt Ret	Rank	Hidden	Rank
2017	6.8%	2	11.3	5	-0.3	19	9.2	2	10.3	3	3.7	7	40.6	1
2018	-0.2%	17	-4.9	24	1.1	14	-3.0	25	3.4	13	2.6	11	10.4	6
2019	-1.5%	23	-2.9	21	-4.3	27	-1.3	18	2.2	15	-1.0	16	-6.4	27

Oh, how the mighty have fallen. After five straight seasons in the top eight in special teams DVOA, the Rams slipped to 17th in 2018 and dropped all the way to 23rd last year, their worst ranking since 2012. Only one unit had a strong season: Johnny Hekker and his coverage squad. And even there, while Hekker's leg was as strong as ever, he struggled to pin opponents deep. He only had 22 punts downed inside the 20 with five touchbacks. That's a ratio of 4.4-to-1, the worst of his career and barely half his career ratio of 8.3-to-1 coming into the season. He remains a deadly weapon on fakes; he threw for a pair of first downs last season, bringing his career total to 13 in eight NFL seasons. ● Greg Zuerlein, L.A.'s other stalwart in the kicking game, also had the worst year of his career in terms of field goal percentage (72.7%) and kickoff average (63.6 yards). He signed with Dallas in free agency. The Rams scoured the earth in search of his replacement, finding candidates in the draft (Sam Sloman, a seventh-rounder out of Miami-Ohio), American minor leagues (AAF/XFL refugee Austin MacGinnis), and the Canadian game (Yugoslavian-born Lirim Hajrullahu, who played six years in the CFL, winning the Grey Cup with the Toronto Argonauts in 2017). ● Free agency also cost the Rams JoJo Natson, who handled punt and kickoff return duties for L.A. for two years but now resides in Cleveland. His spot will be taken by either Nsimba Webster or Greg Dortch, who were both undrafted rookies last season. Dortch averaged just 7.0 yards on four punt returns for the Panthers, but Webster's 2.6-yard average on seven returns (one of them fumbled!) was even worse for the Rams.

Miami Dolphins

2019 Record: 5-11	Total DVOA: -37.4% (32nd)	2020 Mean Projection: 6.4 wins	On the Clock (0-4): 24%
Pythagorean Wins: 3.6 (32nd)	Offense: -13.9% (27th)	Postseason Odds: 21.9%	Mediocrity (5-7): 44%
Snap-Weighted Age: 25.7 (29th)	Defense: 22.1% (32nd)	Super Bowl Odds: 1.0%	Playoff Contender (8-10): 25%
Average Opponent: 0.4% (13rd)	Special Teams: -1.3% (22nd)	Proj. Avg. Opponent: -0.2% (18th)	Super Bowl Contender (11+): 6%

2019: Tua Tagovailoa, no matter what.

2020: Well, they got him. Now what?

The Fish Tank is over. Last offseason's premier talking point of organizational disaster and an opportunity for an analytically inclined rebuild through "purposeful" losing, the Fish Tank came as quickly as it went, needing just one 5-11 season to complete its life cycle. Miami never fell to the embarrassing lows of the 2016-2017 Cleveland Browns, who won a single game in two seasons, as many of us expected them to. The Dolphins did not even earn the first overall pick, as is the plan for any tanking organization. It was clear from the beginning of last season, though, that the Dolphins were not going to be competing for a playoff spot, and it was not until they stumbled into a stretch of Fitzmagic during the second half of the year that they looked like a semi-competent football team.

That stretch of Fitzmagic nearly squandered the efforts of the tank job. Heading into last year, the obvious "Tank For ___" candidate was Alabama's Tua Tagovailoa, who was fresh off one of the most efficient passing seasons ever in his first year as the Crimson Tide's starting quarterback. A heaven-sent Trevor Lawrence ultimately led the Clemson Tigers over Alabama in the National Championship Game, but that loss alone was not enough to knock Tagovailoa off his pedestal as the presumptive first overall pick. With the Dolphins being the only team with a clear M.O. to tank for the top pick—or at least it seemed like it at the time—Tagovailoa was already being locked into Miami a year out.

Of course, arriving at first overall is not how things worked out for either party. The Dolphins ripped off five wins after an 0-7 start to the year, while Tagovailoa suffered (another) injury that ended his season prematurely—a hip dislocation that some are concerned may bring long-term issues. Injury be damned, Tagovailoa may have still gone first overall if not for Joe Burrow's Cinderella season at LSU. Burrow went from Day 3 afterthought to a clearly superior prospect to Tagovailoa in an instant, pushing Tagovailoa down to the next quarterback slot in the draft. Call it luck if you please, but Tagovailoa's minor fall in favor coincided perfectly with Miami's surprising act of competence on the field over the back half of 2019. Miami ended up with their guy even after botching their draft capital by being a better team than they perhaps thought they were; truly the "best of both worlds" scenario for a team in the Dolphins' position.

Although Tagovailoa appeared to be Miami's target all along, it is still worth examining how they decided on selecting him over the likes of Oregon's Justin Herbert and Utah State's Jordan Love with the fifth overall pick. At the surface level, who can blame the Dolphins for being enamored with one of the most efficient passers in the history of college football? Burrow went ahead of Tagovailoa in large part because he managed to somehow one-up Tagovailoa's record-breaking numbers from 2018—the season that cemented Tagovailoa's spot as a future top pick in the draft.

QBASE projections paint Tagovailoa as an exceptionally productive passer as well. As always, our projection system sees a prospect with only one or two years of starting experience as a significant gamble. There are also penalties levied unto his profile for having the most stacked supporting cast in QBASE's history; he may have thrown to as many as four first-round wide receivers by the time all of them leave college. Nonetheless, Tagovailoa finished with the fourth-best all-time (since 1997) QBASE projection among one- and two-year starters. (A full table can be found in the Cincinnati chapter, page 48.) Tagovailoa's 653 mean DYAR projection for Years 3 through 5 ranks only behind Alex Smith, Joe Burrow, and Cam Newton, as well as just above Kyler Murray in fifth place. The jury is still out on fellow 2020 draftee Burrow, but Smith and Newton each have had successful careers while Murray looked exceptionally capable as a rookie despite a disastrous supporting cast dragging down his numbers.

Tagovailoa looked the part of a starting NFL quarterback on film, too. Though Alabama's offense did provide plenty of easy production via heavy doses of run/pass options and play-action as well as exceptional wide receiver talent, Tagovailoa showed off the sharp decision-making, touch accuracy, and ample (even if unspectacular) physical tools necessary to be a cornerstone NFL passer. There was room to nitpick Tagovailoa's game in relation to him being crowned as a clear No. 1 pick, as he was before the 2019 season, but there is no denying that Tagovailoa was up to snuff for a first-round quarterback.

What is most impressive (or perhaps fortunate) about Miami's tank strategy is not that they stuck to their guns at fifth overall and ended up with Tagovailoa despite all the change the 2019 season brought to his draft stock but how carefully and effectively they have tried to build the roster around him in the right way. In particular, Tagovailoa's injury history and

2020 Dolphins Schedule

Week	Opp.	Week	Opp.	Week	Opp.
1	at NE	7	LAC	13	CIN
2	BUF	8	LAR	14	KC
3	at JAX (Thu.)	9	at ARI	15	NE
4	SEA	10	NYJ	16	at LV (Sat.)
5	at SF	11	BYE	17	at BUF
6	at DEN	12	at NYJ		

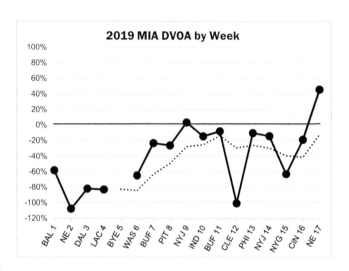

potentially long-term hip issue sets him up as a quarterback who will always need pass protection that is better than league average. The Dolphins have made sure to meet that condition so far. Trading away stud left tackle Laremy Tunsil early last year seems counterintuitive to that end, but Miami made up for his absence by filling out the entire offensive line this offseason.

While starting lineups are far from locked in, the Dolphins are bound to see at least two new starters in Week 1 with potential for a couple more as the season rolls on. Guard Ereck Flowers and center Ted Karras were both signed in free agency this offseason to bolster an atrocious offensive line that finished dead last in adjusted line yards and third-worst in pressure rate last season. Neither Flowers nor Karras are world-beaters by any means, but even upgrading to "competent" is a major improvement. The Dolphins also drafted three offensive linemen, one on each day of the draft: USC tackle Austin Jackson in the first round, Louisiana guard Robert Hunt in the second, and Georgia guard Solomon Kindley early in the fourth. Given Miami's two left tackles (Julie'n Davenport and J'Marcus Webb) combined for a stunning 63 blown blocks and guard Michael Dieter finished with 37 more (seventh-most in the league), *any* improvement along Miami's offensive line, even if marginal, would be welcomed.

Tagovailoa does not need to be rushed into action behind a gelling offensive line, either. Whether he needs extra time to heal from his hip injury or to digest the playbook in an unprecedented style of offseason, Tagovailoa will have the comfort of sitting for as long as he needs to in 2020 behind everyone's favorite scraggly veteran, Ryan Fitzpatrick. Fitzmagic quietly posted the eighth-best QBR in the league last year and had the Dolphins offense humming down the stretch. Of course, the Dolphins staff will not hesitate to bench Fitzpatrick whenever Tagovailoa is ready, but the 15-year vet can keep the team competitive while the rookie tries to find his sea legs.

Regardless of how many games each quarterback starts, however, readers should temper their expectations for an immediate turnaround by the offense. The Dolphins offense has finished outside the top 25 in DVOA for three seasons in a row. Sure, two of those years were under the perpetually underwhelming and conservative Adam Gase while part of last year's rating can be attributed to quarterback Josh Rosen's putrid performance, but it is not as though the Dolphins made enough clear upgrades this offseason to suggest they will immediately right the ship—barring an all-time great rookie year from Tagovailoa, which nobody should be expecting. Massive

jumps in offensive DVOA are not as common as they are for defensive DVOA, either. That is not to say they are impossible—just look at the San Francisco 49ers and Dallas Cowboys last year compared to 2018—but they are, in general, not as likely to happen. There is plenty of reason to believe in the Dolphins' rebuild on offense, but it is more than likely they are still a year or two away, even if some of their new cornerstone pieces are now in place.

Volatility instead favors a defensive turnaround. Last year's Miami defense ended up as one of the ten worst we've ever tracked since 1985. Yet defenses in the NFL fluctuate between excellent and awful all the time. No team in recent memory encapsulates that volatility like the 2015-2017 New York Giants, who took a ride on the DVOA roller coaster from 30th to second to 24th. Now, that amount of volatility is a bit extreme and quite rare. All-time bad defenses do not tend to figure things out in one offseason, hence Miami's low projection for 2020. Of the previous 20 worst defenses in DVOA, only the 2008-2009 Denver Broncos and 1985-1986 Houston Oilers turned around to field an above-average defense the following year. However, the Dolphins are taking the right steps in re-tooling the roster after stripping it down last year. Climbing out of the depths of DVOA hell into the top half of the league is unlikely, but there is plenty of reason to believe the Dolphins can be respectably mediocre rather than outright atrocious.

Flores and the Miami front office have subscribed to a growing school of thought regarding defensive construction in the modern era: building from the back forward, rather than from the lines out. Like trading away Tunsil while needing desperately to fix the offensive line, sending away versatile safety Minkah Fitzpatrick early last year was counterintuitive to the philosophy of building the defense through the secondary, but the Dolphins have since allocated a lot of resources toward fixing their defensive backfield, particularly the cornerback spot.

With NFL offenses operating primarily out of 11 personnel, the value in having three or four quality cornerbacks has never been higher. The Dolphins came out of last offseason securing at least one good cornerback, Xavien Howard, for the foreseeable future. Howard ended up missing a majority of the 2019 season, but signing him to a long-term deal without hesitation looked to be a signal for where Flores' head was at with regards to the defense—and it was. It seems finishing last season 29th in snaps with five defensive backs on the field (36%) was more a product of injuries and circumstance than it was Flores' ideal game plan.

To kick things off this offseason, Miami landed the best defensive back on the market in former Dallas Cowboys cornerback Byron Jones. A former safety, Jones allowed just 6.8 yards per target with a 61% coverage success rate in 2018 before crushing the competition again in 2019 by allowing 6.1 yards per target with a 54% coverage success rate. Consistent production at cornerback is tough to come by, but between his record-breaking athleticism recorded at the NFL combine, vine-like arms, and exceptional comfort in pressing at the line of scrimmage, few cornerbacks in the league are as equipped as Jones to handle the league's best wideouts week-in, week-out.

However, it is worth noting that Jones will be playing in a very different defense from the one he played in with the Cowboys. Dallas played man coverage on 27% of snaps last season, just 27th in the league, while locking their cornerbacks to a particular side of the field (i.e., Jones almost always played to the offense's left). Dallas ranked fifth in our "CB by Sides" metric. Miami, on the other hand, had the league's third-highest man coverage rate at 46% while moving cornerbacks around and ranking just 27th in "CB by Sides." Jones is more than talented enough to make the transition, but do not be startled if it takes him some time to adjust.

Miami's first-round cornerback, conversely, will not have any trouble transitioning to Flores' defense. Auburn's Noah Igbinoghene was the last of Miami's three first-round picks this offseason, marking their second notable investment at the position. Just two years removed from playing wide receiver under Auburn head coach Gus Malzahn, Igbinoghene has made a fantastic early transition to cornerback, oddly enough as a hyper-aggressive press corner and eager run defender. Wide receiver-to-cornerback converts tend to be ballhawk types or have excellent vision in reading route combinations as well as the quarterback in zone coverage, but Igbinoghene is as natural and willing a press cornerback as anyone who has been playing the position for a decade, while some of his ball skills and eyes in zone coverage need some ironing out.

Sorting out what Flores is going to do in the secondary is the easy part, though. With as many investments as the team has made at the position, it is clear Flores wants as many cornerbacks who can handle man coverage as often as possible—a page straight out of the Bill Belichick book of defense. What Belichick—and now his many disciples, including Flores—does up front, however, is much trickier to set in stone from where we sit and much tougher to put into practice from where the coaches sit.

Across the board, Miami had the worst defensive front in football last year. The Dolphins finished dead last in both pressure rate (23.8%) and adjusted line yards (5.00). Miami's average of 4.46 yards allowed on running back carries was significantly better than their putrid adjusted line yards, which

suggests their linebackers fulfilled their duties in run defense, but that alone is hardly enough to redeem last year's front seven. Flores is trying to follow the Belichick blueprint as closely as possible, but in order to do so, many renovations were needed this offseason to turn the Dolphins' front into a respectable unit, let alone a good one. Last year's collection of UDFAs, practice squad players, and future backups simply was not cutting it.

At defensive end, the Dolphins signed Shaq Lawson and Emmanuel Ogbah, both of whom weigh around 270 pounds and have credentials as stout run defenders. Neither are ace pass-rushers, but in Flores' scheme, that is fine considering much of their pressure is expected to be created through deception and overwhelming blitzes, not one-on-one matchups on the edge. These two will take a lot of their snaps at 5-technique, with stints at 3-technique and a "standard" defensive end spot weaved in throughout. Trey Flowers and Deatrich Wise are the most recent Patriots to fill this role. The other, bigger defensive end position will be reserved for Christian Wilkins, last year's first-round pick. Wilkins' role is not so much a traditional defensive end as it is a hybrid 3- and 5-technique, similar to Lawrence Guy in New England.

Outside of Lawson/Ogbah and Wilkins will be a more hybrid outside-the-tackle position for players such as Vince Biegel, who surprised with quality play last year after being cast away from multiple teams, and the newly acquired Kyle Van Noy, a former Flores-era Patriot. Generally one of their two outside players is closer to a pass-rushing type (Biegel and rookie Curtis Weaver fill this role), whereas the other is more of a linebacker playing on the edge, which should be a role filled exclusively by Van Noy. The Dolphins' attempt at this last year with the likes of Sam Eguavoen, Trent Harris, and Andrew Van Ginkel was putrid, especially considering the "Van Noy role" is central to how the front can function because of how valuable it is to have a stand-up edge player who can defend the run and the pass.

The concern with Flores' defense is that he will suffer the same fate as the disciple before him, in this case Matt Patricia. Heading into Year 2 with the Lions last offseason, Patricia set out to build a defense that looks awfully like the one Flores is building now. The Lions shelled out a ton of cash for Trey Flowers (Lawson) and Justin Coleman (Jones), while also spending a Day 2 pick on a run-stopping linebacker Jahlani Tavai (similar to the Dolphins signing Elandon Roberts). Patricia already had Devon Kennard as his "Van Noy" and Darius Slay to match what the Dolphins now have with Howard, too. The defense had been built in Patricia's image, even if not with elite talent across the board, and was supposed to perform as a much-improved unit. They did not. In fact, the Lions finished 28th in defensive DVOA in 2019, the same as they did in 2018.

So, what gives? Why was Patricia's defense still a bust despite him having many of "his" guys, and how can Flores avoid the same fate? The short answer is Flores is a better, more creative tactician than Patricia. Of course, Miami's atrocious defense last year may not reflect that sentiment, but that unit was so deprived of talent that Belichick himself would not have even made them an average unit. Detroit's downfall last year, on the other hand, was Patricia's unwillingness to adapt and find new ways to win, both over the course of a game and over the course of the season. Flores has already proven he is not so stubborn.

For example, it is no surprise that coaches from the Belichick tree love rushing three defenders. The Lions and Dolphins finished first and second, respectively, in that measure last season (the Patriots finished fifth), and playing that style of defense is not a crime in and of itself. What separates the two coaches is that many of Flores' non-three-man rush combinations were five- and six-man pressure packages rather than standard four-man rushes. The same cannot be said of Patricia. In all, the Lions rushed five or more defenders on just 12.1% of snaps last year, while Flores' Dolphins rushed five or more defenders on 27.9% of snaps, putting them a bit above league average. Flores forced a number of conflicts by showing enough variety in his calls that offenses had to worry about everything, whereas Patricia was content with playing some variation of Cover-1 all game from conservative three- and four-man rush packages, regardless of how well it was working.

Granted, Patricia was supposed to be all of the things Flores looked to be last year, so it is entirely possible Flores falls back into a conservative pattern the same way Patricia did. But, perhaps subjectively, Flores appears better equipped and a more forward-thinker than his former defensive coaching mate in New England.

Therein lies the conundrum with Miami's current state. Our own projections still see the Dolphins as a bottom-feeder team despite all their improvements. Some of this is the assumed quality of a rookie quarterback, the uncertainty of the offense, and a sweeping overhaul of the defense that leaves room only for speculation as to how the unit will function together. It's probably reasonable to assume the Dolphins will not go from having a top-five pick to reaching for the playoffs.

And yet, the culture and foundation Flores and Co. have laid appears galvanizing even from the outside, and the manner in which Miami's front office approached the rebuild suggests they have the modern game in mind. Legitimate success is likely another year out for the Dolphins, but the ingredients are there for them to surprise in some capacity this year.

Derrik Klassen

2019 Dolphins Stats by Week

Wk	vs.	W-L	PF	PA	YDF	YDA	TO	Total	Off	Def	ST
1	BAL	L	10	59	200	643	-3	-58%	-21%	40%	3%
2	NE	L	0	43	184	379	-3	-108%	-80%	25%	-2%
3	at DAL	L	6	31	283	476	0	-82%	-38%	31%	-13%
4	LAC	L	10	30	233	390	-1	-83%	-34%	40%	-9%
5	BYE										
6	WAS	L	16	17	271	311	-2	-65%	-52%	18%	5%
7	at BUF	L	21	31	381	305	-2	-23%	8%	32%	1%
8	at PIT	L	14	27	230	394	-3	-26%	-6%	26%	6%
9	NYJ	W	26	18	316	321	+1	3%	34%	14%	-17%
10	at IND	W	16	12	229	300	+1	-14%	-58%	-42%	2%
11	BUF	L	20	37	303	424	-1	-8%	2%	28%	18%
12	at CLE	L	24	41	284	467	-1	-100%	-35%	68%	2%
13	PHI	W	37	31	409	386	0	-10%	19%	23%	-6%
14	at NYJ	L	21	22	362	374	0	-14%	-7%	10%	3%
15	at NYG	L	20	36	384	412	+2	-63%	-33%	26%	-5%
16	CIN	W	38	35	502	430	0	-19%	6%	15%	-9%
17	at NE	W	27	24	389	352	+2	46%	52%	5%	0%

Trends and Splits

	Offense	Rank	Defense	Rank
Total DVOA	-13.9%	27	22.1%	32
Unadjusted VOA	-15.0%	27	20.1%	32
Weighted Trend	-5.5%	20	17.8%	32
Variance	12.3%	29	5.0%	10
Average Opponent	-4.5%	2	-4.7%	29
Passing	-2.5%	25	41.3%	32
Rushing	-26.8%	32	1.9%	27
First Down	-24.2%	31	17.8%	28
Second Down	-3.0%	16	23.3%	31
Third Down	-10.5%	22	29.2%	30
First Half	-8.0%	24	16.9%	32
Second Half	-19.8%	29	27.4%	32
Red Zone	3.0%	13	16.6%	28
Late and Close	-8.4%	20	25.7%	32

Five-Year Performance

Year	W-L	Pyth W	Est W	PF	PA	TO	Total	Rk	Off	Rk	Def	Rk	ST	Rk	Off AGL	Rk	Def AGL	Rk	Off Age	Rk	Def Age	Rk	ST Age	Rk
2015	6-10	5.8	5.8	310	389	-3	-19.0%	29	-7.3%	22	9.0%	25	-2.7%	24	22.3	4	40.0	22	25.5	31	26.6	16	25.3	30
2016	10-6	7.5	8.9	363	380	+2	1.0%	18	1.8%	14	1.6%	19	0.8%	12	46.9	23	60.6	27	26.3	23	26.9	10	25.6	25
2017	6-10	4.9	5.6	281	393	-14	-19.8%	27	-13.1%	27	9.4%	28	2.6%	12	65.3	29	60.8	28	27.3	11	27.1	4	25.8	19
2018	7-9	5.1	5.0	319	433	+5	-16.5%	27	-8.9%	26	6.5%	25	-1.1%	21	66.3	30	26.8	12	27.3	10	26.1	20	25.8	17
2019	5-11	3.6	3.1	306	494	-10	-37.4%	32	-13.9%	27	22.1%	32	-1.3%	22	43.0	18	57.0	30	26.6	19	25.1	32	25.3	27

2019 Performance Based on Most Common Personnel Groups

MIA Offense					MIA Offense vs. Opponents					MIA Defense					MIA Defense vs. Opponents			
11	58%	5.5	3.9%	19%	Base	20%	3.5	-30.5%	56%	Base	32%	5.4	6.6%		11	59%	6.3	27.7%
12	24%	4.9	-28.4%	34%	Nickel	64%	5.6	0.6%	25%	Nickel	36%	6.8	27.4%		12	20%	6.4	9.0%
21	8%	3.9	-29.6%	43%	Dime+	15%	5.0	-23.9%	8%	Dime+	31%	6.4	31.5%		21	8%	6.6	31.5%
13	3%	4.0	-23.2%	74%	Goal Line	0%	-2.2	-145.1%	60%	Goal Line	1%	0.5	42.8%		13	3%	5.3	-7.1%
611	2%	3.3	-28.5%	55%											22	3%	3.1	2.3%

Strategic Tendencies

Run/Pass		Rk	Formation		Rk	Pass Rush		Rk	Secondary		Rk	Strategy		Rk
Runs, first half	32%	30	Form: Single Back	80%	19	Rush 3	21.1%	2	4 DB	32%	8	Play Action	18%	29
Runs, first down	40%	32	Form: Empty Back	9%	11	Rush 4	51.0%	31	5 DB	36%	29	Offensive Motion	32%	24
Runs, second-long	19%	30	Form: Multi Back	10%	15	Rush 5	21.6%	13	6+ DB	31%	7	Avg Box (Off)	6.52	20
Runs, power sit.	50%	26	Pers: 3+ WR	60%	24	Rush 6+	6.3%	13	Man Coverage	46%	3	Avg Box (Def)	6.71	7
Runs, behind 2H	21%	31	Pers: 2+ TE/6+ OL	33%	11	Edge Rusher Sacks	43.5%	27	CB by Sides	64%	27	Offensive Pace	30.24	13
Pass, ahead 2H	55%	2	Pers: 6+ OL	4%	9	Interior DL Sacks	26.1%	12	S/CB Cover Ratio	9%	32	Defensive Pace	30.31	12
Run-Pass Options	4%	24	Shotgun/Pistol	69%	13	Second Level Sacks	30.4%	3	DB Blitz	8%	20	Go for it on 4th	1.74	9

The Dolphins had 39 dropped passes, second in the league behind Dallas. ❧ The Dolphins were 31st among offenses with only 93 broken tackles. ❧ This is not a misprint: Miami led the NFL with 8.6 yards per play from empty-backfield formations and ranked second with 50.8% DVOA. Limit that to Ryan Fitzpatrick at quarterback, and the numbers go up to 9.2 yards and 74.7% DVOA. ❧ The Dolphins led the NFL with the biggest DVOA gap between shotgun performance (0.3% DVOA, 21st) and performance with the quarterback under center (-41.0% DVOA, 32nd). ❧ The Dolphins were one of the most frequent teams to use dime personnel last year after never using it in 2018. ❧ Miami's pass defense was consistently bad no matter how many pass-rushers they used. The Dolphins were 27th in DVOA with three rushers, 32nd with four rushers, and 31st with five or more rushers. ❧ Man coverage means opponents throw deep more often. The three teams that played the most man coverage—Miami, Detroit, and New England—were also the three defenses that faced the highest rate of deep passes (16 or more yards through the air). ❧ Miami's rate in S/CB Cover Ratio would nearly double from 9% to 17% if we counted Eric Rowe as a safety in the games where the starting lineup listed him as a safety, roughly half the season. However, the Dolphins would still rank 30th in the league. ❧ Miami recovered 13 of 20 fumbles on offense but only four of 15 fumbles on defense.

Passing

Player	DYAR	DVOA	Plays	NtYds	Avg	YAC	C%	TD	Int
R.Fitzpatrick	432	1.3%	541	3314	6.1	4.0	62.3%	20	13
J.Rosen	-409	-63.0%	125	476	3.8	5.5	53.2%	1	5

Rushing

Player	DYAR	DVOA	Plays	Yds	Avg	TD	Fum	Suc
K.Ballage	-75	-33.9%	74	135	1.8	3	0	32%
P.Laird	-34	-23.0%	62	168	2.7	2	0	29%
M.Walton*	33	6.7%	53	201	3.8	0	0	45%
K.Drake*	-34	-27.7%	47	174	3.7	0	2	40%
R.Fitzpatrick	33	2.2%	42	259	6.2	5	3	-
M.Gaskin	-3	-10.3%	36	133	3.7	1	0	42%
S.Perine*	0	-9.2%	5	16	3.2	0	0	40%
A.Wilson	21	32.4%	5	45	9.0	0	0	-
D.Turner	-13	-93.6%	4	6	1.5	0	0	25%
M.Breida	33	-1.8%	123	623	5.1	1	2	46%
J.Howard	113	14.2%	119	525	4.4	6	0	53%

Receiving

Player	DYAR	DVOA	Plays	Ctch	Yds	Y/C	YAC	TD	C%
D.Parker	283	14.9%	128	72	1202	16.7	3.7	9	56%
A.Wilson	-53	-23.7%	62	43	351	8.2	4.2	1	69%
P.Williams	32	-5.9%	60	32	428	13.4	1.9	3	53%
A.Hurns	64	5.2%	47	32	416	13.0	3.0	2	68%
I.Ford	3	-11.7%	35	23	244	10.6	3.7	0	66%
J.Grant	-52	-33.1%	33	19	164	8.6	4.6	0	58%
M.Hollins	-41	-37.1%	22	10	125	12.5	3.3	0	45%
M.Gesicki	-51	-16.3%	89	51	570	11.2	3.4	5	57%
D.Smythe	-20	-31.0%	14	7	65	9.3	1.4	0	50%
C.Walford*	-7	-20.8%	8	4	57	14.3	6.8	0	50%
K.Drake*	-1	-14.1%	33	22	174	7.9	7.4	0	67%
P.Laird	39	8.6%	30	23	204	8.9	7.7	0	77%
K.Ballage	-65	-66.6%	24	14	63	4.5	6.2	0	58%
M.Walton*	-28	-39.1%	21	15	89	5.9	7.1	0	71%
M.Gaskin	-14	-32.9%	12	7	51	7.3	6.6	0	58%
M.Breida	39	19.5%	22	19	120	6.3	6.7	1	86%
J.Howard	17	6.7%	14	10	69	6.9	6.9	1	71%

Offensive Line

Player	Pos	Age	GS	Snaps	Pen	Sk	Pass	Run	Player	Pos	Age	GS	Snaps	Pen	Sk	Pass	Run
Michael Deiter	LG	24	16/15	1004	4	4.8	29	6	Julie'n Davenport	LT	25	8/8	535	1	3.5	18	6
Jesse Davis	RT	29	15/15	981	4	6.0	35	10	Deion Calhoun	RG	24	11/7	476	2	0.5	12	3
Daniel Kilgore*	C	33	13/13	882	4	1.5	11	6	Ted Karras	C	27	15/15	1046	3	1.0	13	8
Evan Boehm	RG	27	13/8	601	4	0.5	5	7	Ereck Flowers	LG	26	16/16	960	5	1.5	13	2
J'Marcus Webb*	LT	32	14/8	549	8	4.5	30	5									

Year	Yards	ALY	Rank	Power	Rank	Stuff	Rank	2nd Lev	Rank	Open Field	Rank	Sacks	ASR	Rank	Press	Rank	F-Start	Cont.
2017	4.09	3.26	30	71%	6	27%	30	1.09	20	1.07	4	33	5.8%	11	29.6%	10	21	30
2018	4.79	4.47	14	62%	24	18%	15	1.29	12	1.02	8	52	10.5%	31	36.3%	31	16	26
2019	2.96	3.17	32	70%	6	26%	32	0.86	32	0.25	31	58	8.6%	28	36.7%	31	10	20

2019 ALY by direction:	Left End 2.86 (31)	Left Tackle: 3.13 (28)	Mid/Guard: 3.41 (32)	Right Tackle: 2.73 (31)	Right End: 2.48 (31)

Not only did Miami's adjusted line yards plummet from the year before, but they were one of only two offensive lines to drop from 2018 in all five directions that we track. (The Rams were the other.) ✎ Miami allowed a league-high 161 quarterback knockdowns, including both passes and sacks cancelled by penalty. Ryan Fitzpatrick's knockdown rate on 22.6% of passes was the highest in the league for a quarterback with at least 200 passes, and Josh Rosen was even higher at 23.1%. ✎ For as bad as Miami's offensive line was, they seldom committed penalties. Only four teams in the league are not returning a single offensive lineman with more than five penalties last season, one of which is the Dolphins. Perhaps they were losing their reps so quickly they didn't even have time to hold their opponents. ✎ Free-agent signing Ereck Flowers, who converted to full-time guard just last season, is a major upgrade for the Dolphins interior. At offensive tackle, Flowers' heavy feet and tendency to overreach when engaging made him a liability in the pass game. These traits were less of a detriment when asked to play in a phone booth as a guard. The tutelage of Bill Callahan, one of the better offensive line coaches around, also likely played a hand; Flowers won't get to bring Callahan with him to Miami. Flowers ranked 34th of 106 interior offensive linemen in snaps per blown block (64.0), while none of Miami's three qualifying guards finished higher than 74th. Deion Calhoun and rookie Michael Deiter each finished in the bottom five. ✎ By most analysts' big boards, the Dolphins got the "best of the rest" first-round tackle in USC's Austin Jackson. A two-year college starter who will not turn 21 years old until early August, Jackson is a terribly raw technician who will struggle if forced to play right away, but he has all the physical tools to be a worthwhile project on a rebuilding team, as the Dolphins are. Jackson cleared the 80th percentile in the 40-yard dash, vertical jump, and broad jump at the NFL combine. ✎ Both of Miami's offensive guard draft picks—Louisiana's Robert Hunt in the second round and Georgia's Solomon Kindley in the fourth round—are mountainous men who play with a bulldozing mentality. Putting a premium on that style of interior offensive linemen signals what the Dolphins want to be up front.

Defensive Front

Defensive Line	Age	Pos	G	Snaps	Plays	Overall TmPct	Rk	Stop	Dfts	BTkl	Runs	vs. Run St%	Rk	RuYd	Rk	Pass Rush Sack	Hit	Hur	Dsrpt
Christian Wilkins	25	DT	16	741	58	7.0%	12	44	6	2	52	77%	39	2.5	59	2.0	2	20	1
Davon Godchaux	26	DT	16	729	76	9.1%	2	49	6	7	70	64%	82	3.0	86	2.0	6	9	1
John Jenkins*	31	DT	16	486	35	4.2%	50	26	3	3	33	73%	58	2.8	71	1.0	0	9	1

Edge Rushers	Age	Pos	G	Snaps	Plays	Overall TmPct	Rk	Stop	Dfts	BTkl	Runs	vs. Run St%	Rk	RuYd	Rk	Pass Rush Sack	Hit	Hur	Dsrpt
Vince Biegel	27	OLB	15	636	56	7.2%	19	42	12	6	45	76%	37	3.1	71	2.5	12	23	0
Charles Harris*	25	DE	14	436	22	3.0%	84	11	3	1	19	42%	89	3.8	85	0.5	6	7	1
Taco Charlton*	26	DE	10	403	21	4.0%	85	15	6	1	14	64%	72	3.2	76	5.0	2	15	0
Avery Moss	26	DE	11	353	25	4.4%	75	19	0	3	24	75%	39	3.2	74	0.0	0	3	0
Trent Harris	25	OLB	11	254	22	3.8%	--	12	3	3	18	56%	--	5.0	--	1.5	1	7	0
Kyle Van Noy	29	OLB	15	832	59	8.3%	8	39	16	5	43	63%	76	3.2	75	6.5	11	46	3
Shaq Lawson	26	DE	15	486	34	4.5%	53	32	21	5	23	91%	4	0.4	2	6.5	12	30	2
Emmanuel Ogbah	27	DE	10	416	35	6.8%	52	29	13	3	25	76%	35	2.7	50	5.5	6	16	3

Linebackers	Age	Pos	G	Snaps	Plays	TmPct	Rk	Stop	Dfts	BTkl	Runs	St%	Rk	RuYd	Rk	Sack	Hit	Hur	Tgts	Suc%	Rk	AdjYd	Rk	PD	Int
																Pass Rush									
					Overall							vs. Run								vs. Pass					
Jerome Baker	24	ILB	16	1093	128	15.4%	18	66	21	8	72	67%	19	4.0	46	1.5	3	11	36	47%	43	6.5	37	4	1
Sam Eguavoen	27	ILB	16	630	40	4.8%	78	25	10	8	30	57%	53	4.0	43	3.5	5	11	8	63%	--	5.9	--	1	0
Raekwon McMillan	25	ILB	13	524	72	10.7%	57	41	3	11	61	62%	33	3.8	36	0.0	3	5	8	25%	--	10.8	--	1	0
Kamu Grugier-Hill	26	OLB	10	304	22	4.7%	83	11	6	6	14	57%	50	3.7	33	0.0	1	2	9	56%	--	6.9	--	0	0
Elandon Roberts	26	ILB	16	210	29	3.8%	--	17	2	1	20	70%	--	3.4	--	1.0	2	4	7	57%	--	7.0	--	1	0

Year	Yards	ALY	Rank	Power	Rank	Stuff	Rank	2nd Level	Rank	Open Field	Rank	Sacks	ASR	Rank	Press	Rank
2017	4.13	3.94	10	50%	3	24%	5	1.26	27	0.85	25	30	5.7%	27	27.7%	29
2018	4.53	4.36	16	65%	15	20%	15	1.29	21	1.04	23	31	6.3%	28	28.5%	23
2019	4.46	5.00	32	65%	18	14%	28	1.32	25	0.53	5	23	4.4%	32	24.1%	31
2019 ALY by direction:		Left End: 6.55 (32)			Left Tackle: 4.61 (20)			Mid/Guard: 4.87 (28)			Right Tackle: 4.77 (26)			Right End: 6.67 (32)		

Like the offensive line, the Miami front seven plunged to the bottom of the league in adjusted line yards. Like the offense, the Miami defense dropped in rank in all five directions; this time, the Jaguars were the only other defense that had this issue. ❧ Miami was the only team in the league where no defender managed 25 hurries last season; Vince Biegel led the team with 23. ❧ Interior run defense was a nightmare for the Dolphins last year, but the selection of Alabama's Raekwon Davis in the second round looks to quell that. What Davis lacks in pass-rush skills, he makes up for in stout run defense and positional flexibility anywhere between the tackles, which is an advantage Flores' creativity should be able to make use of. ❧ Whatever your image of a traditional pass-rusher looks like, fifth-round pick Curtis Weaver does not fit it. Weaver has a short, pudgy build at 6-foot-2 and 265 pounds, as well as a short wingspan, which suggests he should be more of a pocket-pusher, but he plays like a true arc-bending edge threat. Weaver's 34 career sacks at Boise State are a Mountain West record, and he's SackSEER's favorite late-round prospect. ❧ Sorting out potential playing time for free-agent linebacker Elandon Roberts is tricky. While he notched slightly higher marks in run stop rate and yards allowed than any of Miami's linebackers, he also played behind a significantly better defensive line which gave him cleaner looks. Roberts is not a major upgrade for passing downs either, so it seems like more of the same for Miami's linebackers.

Defensive Secondary

Secondary	Age	Pos	G	Snaps	Plays	TmPct	Rk	Stop	Dfts	BTkl	Runs	St%	Rk	RuYd	Rk	Tgts	Tgt%	Rk	Dist	Suc%	Rk	AdjYd	Rk	PD	Int
					Overall							vs. Run							vs. Pass						
Eric Rowe	28	CB/SS	16	1086	89	10.7%	6	37	11	6	47	45%	43	5.2	29	54	12.1%	84	12.4	61%	11	6.4	17	8	1
Nik Needham	24	CB	12	752	65	10.4%	38	31	14	10	17	47%	38	6.8	50	74	24.0%	11	12.0	58%	18	7.7	44	11	2
Jamal Perry	26	CB	14	609	57	7.8%	--	19	11	10	19	26%	--	8.7	--	48	19.2%	--	10.5	52%	--	7.8	--	6	1
Bobby McCain	27	FS	9	548	27	5.8%	74	7	5	13	10	20%	69	12.4	72	10	4.4%	68	11.8	50%	40	7.3	33	3	2
Adrian Colbert	27	FS	6	363	22	7.1%	--	5	1	9	8	25%	--	9.1	--	4	2.7%	--	18.0	75%	--	2.8	--	2	0
Steven Parker	25	FS	14	340	22	3.0%	--	4	3	3	9	11%	--	7.9	--	9	6.5%	--	14.4	33%	--	14.0	--	3	2
Xavien Howard	27	CB	5	325	21	8.1%	--	8	2	3	5	40%	--	13.4	--	23	17.3%	--	11.7	43%	--	7.0	--	4	1
Ryan Lewis	26	CB	13	294	29	4.3%	--	8	4	1	5	60%	--	3.8	--	29	24.1%	--	17.1	52%	--	7.9	--	5	1
Ken Webster	24	CB	8	231	20	4.8%	--	7	1	1	8	75%	--	6.4	--	24	25.3%	--	17.2	46%	--	8.4	--	1	0
Reshad Jones*	32	FS	4	190	28	13.5%	--	14	6	3	18	61%	--	6.9	--	10	12.8%	--	5.9	30%	--	10.2	--	1	0
Byron Jones	28	CB	15	938	50	6.5%	65	17	5	3	13	23%	76	6.8	51	54	14.9%	81	12.1	54%	36	6.1	11	6	0

Year	Pass D Rank	vs. #1 WR	Rk	vs. #2 WR	Rk	vs. Other WR	Rk	WR Wide	Rk	WR Slot	Rk	vs. TE	Rk	vs. RB	Rk
2017	29	11.2%	22	-8.2%	11	15.4%	23	0.0%	17	9.7%	19	17.1%	28	1.8%	18
2018	23	7.0%	21	5.5%	21	-2.2%	17	26.0%	32	-5.7%	10	-0.3%	14	20.2%	30
2019	32	26.0%	31	21.9%	28	-3.3%	15	17.9%	30	17.1%	26	11.3%	29	55.4%	32

A slew of injuries and a lean towards dime coverage put the Dolphins in a rare category for defensive back deployment last season. Only one other team, the Cleveland Browns, joined the Dolphins in having 10 defensive backs record over 175 snaps. A handful of other players earned between 100 and 175 snaps, as well. ❧ Only three of those 10 defensive backs were on the Dolphins' roster before the 2019 season—Bobby McCain, Xavien Howard, and Reshad Jones. Neither of the latter two players appeared in more than five games or made it past Week 11 due to injury, and Jones is no longer with the team. ❧ Returning a healthy Howard to the lineup will be a boon for the Dolphins secondary. In both 2017 and 2018, Howard ranked in the top 20 in coverage success rate among cornerbacks, highlighted by a stellar 60% success rate in 2018. Howard's 11 interceptions also tied Darius Slay for the most among cornerbacks over that span. 🏈 Not including his rookie season in 2015, new cornerback Byron Jones has never allowed more than 6.8 yards per target or held a success rate lower than 54%. Jones' long, tall frame can make it relatively troubling for him to defend quicker routes within 10 yards because it is not as easy for him to sink his hips and drive down, but his open-field speed, physicality, and length are such that he rarely gives up receptions elsewhere. 🏈 Among all rookie defenders last season, UDFA cornerback Nik Needham earned the second-most passes defended (11), trailing only Tampa Bay's Jamel Dean (17). In tandem with his solid-to-good success rate and yards allowed figures, as well as considering how much tougher it is to play man coverage than zone coverage, it seems as though Flores has already found a diamond in the rough. 🏈 Eric Rowe and McCain should give Miami a pair of former cornerbacks as starting safeties. 🏈 Third-round pick Brandon Jones (Texas) does not fit the profile of a smooth, versatile safety, but considering Miami had the lowest S/CB cover ratio in the league, that should be a less pronounced issue on this particular team. Expect Jones to be more of a box safety with underneath coverage responsibilities, as well as a potential pseudo-linebacker.

Special Teams

Year	DVOA	Rank	FG/XP	Rank	Net Kick	Rank	Kick Ret	Rank	Net Punt	Rank	Punt Ret	Rank	Hidden	Rank
2017	2.6%	12	3.4	12	5.3	6	-1.5	19	6.6	6	-0.6	19	6.4	5
2018	-1.1%	21	1.9	13	-5.8	29	2.9	6	-10.5	29	6.0	4	11.8	3
2019	-1.3%	22	-1.3	19	-1.6	22	3.4	7	-2.8	21	-4.3	26	-3.5	21

After a middling rookie year on kickoffs in 2018, Jason Sanders ranked second in the league in gross kickoff value last season. Sanders did his job, even if the coverage unit did not reciprocate. 🏈 Matt Haack had a fairly average year as a punter and won't have any competition in camp. The highlight of his season was throwing a touchdown to Sanders off a gimmick fake field goal against Philadelphia in Week 13. 🏈 Wide receiver Jakeem Grant is one of just two kick returners worth at least 5.0 points of field position over average in each of the last two seasons, with the other being Cordarrelle Patterson. Grant shares punt return duties with Preston Williams. 🏈 Marcus Sherels, previously one of the best punt returners in the league in Minnesota, returned six punts in five games with the Dolphins last year, worth -2.0 points of estimated field position.

Minnesota Vikings

2019 Record: 10-6	**Total DVOA:** 15.3% (7th)	**2020 Mean Projection:** 7.6 wins	**On the Clock (0-4):** 12%
Pythagorean Wins: 10.8 (7th)	**Offense:** 4.6% (10th)	**Postseason Odds:** 37.6%	**Mediocrity (5-7):** 37%
Snap-Weighted Age: 26.6 (11st)	**Defense:** -9.9% (7th)	**Super Bowl Odds:** 3.7%	**Playoff Contender (8-10):** 37%
Average Opponent: -1.3% (20th)	**Special Teams:** 0.8% (14th)	**Proj. Avg. Opponent:** 0.8% (7th)	**Super Bowl Contender (11+):** 14%

2019: A return to 2017's form produces a return to 2017's postseason disappointments.

2020: Sensible financial planning sometimes means sucking it up and paying your bills.

The Minnesota Vikings knew what they were getting into.

In an attempt to recapture the magic that brought them to the NFC Championship Game in 2017, the Vikings were willing to pay tomorrow for continuity today. They extended Kyle Rudolph, re-signed Anthony Barr, and restructured Everson Griffen, squeezing every drop out of a tight salary-cap window, knowing they would have to pay for it in 2020. Rick Spielman, Rob Brzezinski, and the rest of the Vikings did a remarkable job keeping the core of the Vikings together for years and years, but eventually, the piper does come calling.

In some ways, this worked—the Vikings rebounded from a disappointing 2018 as they made their return to the post-season. Kirk Cousins played more like the $84-million man Minnesota hoped he would be, ranking in the top 10 in both DVOA and DYAR. A top-10 offense, led by a huge bounce-back season from Stefon Diggs and the rare sight of a healthy Dalvin Cook, was paired with a top-10 defense for only the fourth time in Vikings DVOA history (going back to 1985). All that salary-cap manipulation kept together a defensive core that had been intact since 2016, starting a streak of four straight top-10 DVOA seasons. The painful taste of missing the playoffs by half a game in 2018 was washed out of Vikings' fans heads, and a thrilling upset over the Saints in the wild-card round had Minnesota fans thinking something special might be in the cards.

That all came crashing down in the divisional round as the offensive line folded like a pack of cards, and the euphoria of the Saints upset was replaced with the cold, hard reality of salary-cap hell. The Vikings entered the 2020 offseason more than $11 million over the projected cap, the third-biggest deficit in NFL history. There's only so much salary-cap wizardry a team can pull off—the Vikings set themselves up to have a window of contention, hit their ceiling, and now have to deal with the aftermath.

And so, what shall be known as the great bloodletting of the 2020 offseason began. Out went Xavier Rhodes, Everson Griffen, Mackensie Alexander, Trae Waynes, Linval Joseph, Stephen Weatherly, and Jayron Kearse. That's a combined 348 defensive starts over the past few seasons, all out the door in one fell swoop. The offense didn't lose as much raw talent, but the trade of Diggs to Buffalo hurts, a lot. As strained as the relationship between Diggs, Cousins, and the Vikings organization as a whole was at times, he was a No. 1-caliber

receiver, second in yards per target in 2019. That's a lot of starters to lose at one time, and it seems a near certainty that the Vikings will be a less talented team in 2020. Our projections have them as basically a bog-standard, average team—one that will win its fair share of games, and could possibly contend for a division title in what we see as a very, very weak NFC North, but not one that should be hoping for a massive success right away. How could they, after seeing such a tumultuous offseason?

Well, what if we were to tell you that the Vikings had the best offseason in the division, and are set up the best for future contention? The team might not start reaping the rewards for the 2020 offseason for a year or two, but the Vikings' front office did a strong job with the situation they found themselves in.

First of all, let's admit that "best offseason in the division" is somewhat damning with faint praise. The Bears misjudged the quarterback market, the Lions spent all spring overpaying free agents, and the Packers forgot the wide receiver position existed. Losing a top-10 receiver does limit how successful an offseason could be, though at least the Vikings didn't pull a Bill O'Brien; they actually received fair compensation for giving up a star player.

The Vikings honestly cleared their salary-cap problems fairly effectively. $20 million in dead cap space isn't ideal, but only Diggs, Rhodes, Joseph, and Josh Kline actually count against the Vikings' cap this season. That could have been significantly worse; it ends up not even being the most dead money in the division. Extensions for Cousins and Danielle Hunter helped carve out extra room, and they were even able to re-sign Anthony Harris and add Michael Pierce to the defense. It's almost as if the front office knew what it was doing when it signed players in the first place and had a plan for bloodletting their contracts when the bill came due. And going into an offseason in the red isn't a death sentence. There were 14 teams between 2015 and 2018 which started the offseason above the salary cap; they actually *improved* by an average of 3.6% DVOA in the following season, and only three saw their DVOA fall by more than 10% (Table 1).

In part, that's because the contracts you dump end up being the bloated ones for veterans who aren't living up to their price tag—and that's true for the Vikings, as well. One of the metrics we use to help project teams is "net Approximate Value over replacement." This takes the value of all the veteran

2020 Vikings Schedule

Week	Opp.	Week	Opp.	Week	Opp.
1	GB	7	BYE	13	JAX
2	at IND	8	at GB	14	at TB
3	TEN	9	DET	15	CHI
4	at HOU	10	at CHI (Mon.)	16	at NO (Fri./Xmas)
5	at SEA	11	DAL	17	at DET
6	ATL	12	CAR		

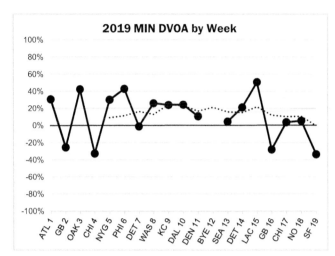

2019 MIN DVOA by Week

talent a team adds in an offseason and subtracts the value of all the players they lost. The Vikings did end up in a net negative here, with those 336 starts headed out the window, but not by as much as you might think. Their defensive net AV over replacement was only -11 AV—not great, but not anywhere close to the worst of 2019, much less an all-time bad number. Losing Griffen hurts, and Joseph and Alexander have been useful cogs at various points, but most of the players the Vikings lost defensively had name recognition above and beyond their actual on-field performance. Heck, we should probably give the Vikings positive credit for moving on from Rhodes, who was the worst qualifying cornerback in football by our charting, with a paltry 32% success rate and 9.8 yards allowed per pass. It's a net talent loss, for sure, but not a terrible one.

But the most important thing the Vikings did in the offseason was rack up roughly 10 zillion draft picks. The Vikings made 15 selections in the 2020 draft, which is a record since the NFL reduced the draft down to seven rounds in 1994. They've also set themselves up nicely for 2021, with as many as 12 picks already on the books thanks to projected compensatory selections. It wasn't the most draft *value* a team managed to gather—12 of Minnesota's 15 picks came on Day 3, so the total overall value was relatively limited—but that's a lot of bites at the apple to find cost-effective replacements for the players who left. The Vikings have had some success finding late-round contributors in Spielman's tenure as well. Diggs is the obvious one, but players such as Shamar Stephen, Ben Gideon, and Stephen Weatherley all have been useful contributors over the past few seasons. The majority of these late-round picks won't work out, of course, but the Vikings did exactly what they needed to do, casting a net far and wide to fill in the void caused by all those departures. Some of them are bound to hit.

Missing Stefon Diggs? Justin Jefferson had the third-highest Playmaker Score projection in a loaded draft class. Offensive line causing issues? Ezra Cleveland's athleticism makes him a perfect fit for Gary Kubiak's zone-blocking scheme. Missing three cornerbacks from a year ago? Welcome Jeff Gladney in the slot, Cameron Dantzler out wide, and Harrison Hand on the bench. Lost a bunch of defensive contributors? Have nine rookies ready to fill out the back end of the roster. With the undrafted free-agent pool disrupted by the ongoing pandemic, locking up key developmental prospects with a passel of sixth- and seventh-round picks is a great strategy. And if this draft class doesn't work out, the Vikings still have all those

picks waiting next year. For a team in somewhat of a reboot, that much draft flexibility is a wonderful asset.

Of course, that's all wonderful for the future Vikings, but that doesn't really help that much with 2020, which is going to be a pretty significant transitional year.

Our projections have Mike Zimmer's defense falling out of the top 10 for the first time since 2015. Some of that is the exodus of established starters. Zimmer's scheme is one of the most complex in the league, and it would be a tall ask for a bunch of new players to get up to speed in a normal offseason, much less one where rookie camps and minicamps are going to be massively disrupted. Zimmer will have his hands full getting everyone on the same page early on in the season.

Some more of that is standard regression, especially when it comes to the run defense. The Vikings led the league with a 49% power success rate, and that's generally not sustainable; teams that allow a short-yardage conversion rate of 50% or

Table 1. Teams Starting Offseason Above Salary Cap, 2015-2019

Year	Team	Cap Deficit (millions)	Year N-1 DVOA	Year N DVOA	Change
2015	NO	-$23.2	-0.9%	-18.7%	-17.8%
2019	PHI	-$16.0	-0.1%	6.6%	+6.7%
2020	**MIN**	**-$11.4**	**15.3%**	--	--
2017	DAL	-$11.3	20.3%	5.3%	-15.0%
2015	ARI	-$10.1	-6.4%	27.4%	+33.8%
2016	NO	-$9.8	-18.7%	-1.9%	+16.8%
2018	PHI	-$9.4	23.4%	-0.1%	-23.5%
2017	NYJ	-$7.4	-32.4%	-17.2%	+15.2%
2015	NE	-$4.9	22.1%	22.6%	+0.5%
2019	JAX	-$4.3	-8.1%	-17.8%	-9.7%
2016	MIA	-$3.7	-19.0%	1.0%	+20.0%
2016	BUF	-$3.5	2.7%	1.0%	-1.7%
2020	JAX	-$3.4	-17.8%	--	--
2015	PIT	-$1.7	12.1%	21.3%	+9.2%
2015	KC	-$1.6	10.4%	25.2%	14.8%
2015	STL	-$1.1	-3.8%	-2.2%	1.6%

Based on salary cap situation immediately following previous year's Super Bowl.

lower see their defensive DVOA get worse by an average of 4.0% the next season. With no players in the top 60 in success rate last season, concerns about Xavier Rhodes falling off a cliff, and the continued inconsistency of Trae Waynes, we would have been concerned about the performance of the secondary even if the Vikings hadn't lost their top three cornerbacks. As it is, Mike Hughes (with a 47% success rate) is the only cornerback the Vikings have who qualified for our leaderboards last season.

The biggest problem the Vikings' defense will have to solve, however, is the loss of Griffen, who had 40 pass pressures in 2019. Every other hole the Vikings had on defense was filled, at least in theory: rookies in the secondary, Michael Pierce up front. But there is no replacing Griffen, and the Vikings didn't particularly try. That will put a lot more pressure on Danielle Hunter to continue to shoulder the load of the Vikings' pass rush. Hunter had 59 pass pressures a year ago, fourth in the league, and became the youngest player to ever record 50 career sacks; he is a superstar in every sense of the word. But he's going from having Griffen as a wingman to … Ifeadi Odenigbo? Anthony Zettel? Eddie Yarbrough? Stephen Weatherly was third on the Vikings last season with 19 pass pressures, but he's gone as well. Those are some big, big shoes for Odenigbo to fill; he had only 15 pass pressures last season. Odgenigbo is a great example of one of those late-round picks whom the Vikings have been able to develop, and he flashed as a second-year player last season, but he's going to have to take a significant step forward if he's going to fill the shoes of the Vikings' No. 2 guy.

The Vikings basically had to choose between keeping Griffen or Anthony Harris; by using the franchise tag on the latter, they kept together Harris and Harrison Smith as the best safety duo in the league. A defense with Harris, Smith, Hunter, and Eric Kendricks can only be so bad, but it does look like the Minnesota offense will have to carry more of the load if the Vikings hope to be competitive next year.

Gary Kubiak was brought in last season to help Kevin Stefanski run the offense, and he's going to take full charge of the offense now that Stefanski has gone to Cleveland. You can credit the changes Kubiak and company made last season for the rebound season from Kirk Cousins, but further changes are needed to last year's scheme in order to really get Minnesota firing on all cylinders.

In last year's *Almanac*, we bemoaned the fact that the Vikings forgot the play-action pass existed in 2018. Case Keenum's league-leading 30% play-action pass rate in 2017 fell to just 21% with Cousins under center in 2018. Well, Stefanski and Kubiak brought it back with a vengeance, returning the play-action rate to that 30% mark and making it the foundational part of their offense. Feeding off of their strong zone-running attack, the Vikings' play-action offense was a fantastic explosive-play machine. Minnesota's passing DVOA rose from 10.3% without play action to 34.8% with it, gaining an average of 2.2 extra yards per play. For a team that wants its identity to be run-first, -second, and -third—only Baltimore ran more on first down than the Vikings did last season—the ability to draw defenders into the box and deliver over the top

with big chunk plays is critical. It's something the Vikings should lean on even more heavily in 2020, because it plays directly into Cousins' strengths as a passer. Cousins is at his best when he's using bootlegs and play-action to get into set looks and patterns against a defense, rather than just dropping back and scanning the whole field. Cousins was a square peg in a round hole in 2018, but 2019 is much more the level of quarterbacking Minnesota fans can expect from him. There's a reason his DVOA jumped from 2.7% to 14.3%.

The problem with Minnesota's offense is the outdated, old-school philosophy that Zimmer still embraces. Zimmer wants his offense to control the ball with a ground-based, low-risk attack that avoids making big mistakes, allowing his defense to take charge. That's not going to work so well with a defense in transition. In addition, last year's play calling was basically the epitome of the "establish the run" mentality and, well, the Vikings were bad at it. In situation-neutral game states (i.e., early and close, before the score or clock starts dictating strategy), the Vikings ran the ball 61% of the time on first downs, seventh-most in the league. And yet they had a -17.6% DVOA when running on first downs, and just a 35% success rate. Their average run DVOA last season was buoyed by a 13.4% DVOA on second down, where they ran more on second-and-long than any other offense. It turns out that, like essentially every other team in the league, the Vikings are good at running the ball when opponents expect them to pass, and struggle when opponents expect them to carry it.

While 2019 was a high-water mark in first-down runs for Zimmer, it's entirely within his standard parameters. Since he took over the head coaching job in 2014, the Vikings have run on 54.4% of their first-half first downs, seventh-most in the league. In that time, Minnesota has averaged a -12.6% rushing DVOA on first downs in a league which tends to average closer to -8.0 or -9.0%. Zimmer's ideal offense, as he reiterated last October, involves staying ahead of the chains, turning first-and-10s into second-and-3s instead of second-and-10s with an effective, consistent, early-down rushing attack, which in turns forces stacked boxes and opens up the pass.

The problem is, that doesn't actually *work*. The preponderance of evidence, time and time again, shows that play-action works whether or not you've "established the run." Twenty-eight teams, including Minnesota, had significantly higher DVOAs passing on first down than running last season. When the Vikings ran on first-and-10, they averaged 4.2 yards and picked up a first down 10.6% of the time. When they passed on first-and-10, they averaged 7.7 yards and picked up a first down 25.6% of the time. If Zimmer wants to set up those second-and-3s where the playbook is wide-open, he should really let Cousins throw the ball more—it's a credit to Minnesota's offensive stars that they managed a top-10 DVOA in the face of questionable play calling.

And here's where Kubiak might end up significantly boosting the Vikings offense as he takes over play-calling duties. Like Zimmer, Kubiak has a run-first mindset, using that patented Shanahan outside zone blocking to set up the pass, so it's not surprising that the two are thick as thieves. But despite Kubiak's reputation, he has been much more judicious in how he mixes the run and the pass. While there has been some variation in the 22 years he has served as a head coach or offensive coordinator—passing more when you have Peyton Manning and running more when you have Joe Flacco isn't an inconsistent offensive philosophy—Kubiak's teams generally run on first down less frequently than the average team (Table 2). Hopefully, Kubiak can convince Zimmer that you can be a tough-nosed, grind-it-out football team without sacrificing first downs to Dalvin Cook slamming into an eight-man box over and over again.

Table 2. Kubiak's Run/Pass Ratio: First Downs, First Half

Years	Team	Run%	Rank	Run DVOA
2015-2016	DEN	46.7%	29	-10.1%
2014	BAL	52.5%	14	-6.2%
2006-2013	HOU	49.0%	25	-8.3%
1995-2005	DEN	51.2%	24	12.6%
2014-2019	Zimmer	54.4%	7	-12.6%

Otherwise, the Vikings offense should look very similar to last season, as much of Kubiak's influence was already felt in last year's offensive shift. The Vikings were the first team since the 2015 Titans to use 11 personnel on fewer than one-third of their offensive plays, which is perhaps fitting for a team that hasn't found a successful third wide receiver in years. This is going to be a bit of a learning curve for first-round pick Justin Jefferson, who lined up almost exclusively in the slot a year ago at LSU. He's a versatile player with decent size, so there's no reason to believe he can't be successful on the outside, but the Vikings used a slot receiver less than any other team in football last season; there's a slight mismatch between Jefferson's past production and the Vikings' offensive philosophy.

The Vikings also have an issue with Dalvin Cook who, as of press time, is threatening a holdout over his contract. Cook, when he has been in the lineup, has been a boon to the Vikings offense. It's not just his top-10 rushing DVOA or his top-five receiving DVOA, though the fact that he joined only Mark Ingram and Christian McCaffrey in hitting both of those benchmarks in 2019 says a lot about the type of player Cook is. The Vikings' offense just also runs smoother with Cook in the lineup, a fact that Cook's agents attempted to reiterate by pointing out the Expected Points Added differences with and without Cook on the field, an advanced stats position we have to admire. Kirk Cousins' EPA per dropback with Cook on the field was +0.25; without Cook, it dropped to +0.03. There is little doubt the Vikings are significantly better with Cook in the backfield than with Alexander Mattison or Michael Boone.

The issue is that Cook allegedly wants to approach or top Christian McCaffrey's $64 million a year deal, when a) Mc-Caffrey has been better than Cook, b) Cook has missed 19 games due to injury in the last three years, and c) $16 million a year for any running back is highly questionable, considering the level of performance teams can squeeze out of backs on minimum deals. The wise move in the long term would be to not give in to those demands, but if Cook does hold out, or is disgruntled and isn't the same player in 2020, that's a significant blow to an offense that needs him to carry more of the load in 2020. It's an offense that is already hurting from the loss of Stefon Diggs, and still has problems with the interior offensive line that got exposed against San Francisco in the playoffs. The Vikings are stuck between a rock and a hard place with Cook, much like any other team trying to figure out how to properly reward successful running backs looking to cash in on their first non-rookie contract. In the end, we suspect that Cook will report to training camp, if for no other reason than an extended holdout would cost him his unrestricted free agency status for 2021. It's a tricky issue for the Vikings to solve, but it may be an issue that will affect the 2021 team more than the 2020 squad.

Despite the question marks, the offensive improvements the Vikings made last season feel more real and sustainable than the fluke Case Keenum year in 2017. They have a real chance to put up a positive offensive DVOA for the second straight year, something they haven't managed to do since the 2003-04 seasons. For all the criticism that the Vikings' front office has received about some of their decisions, Minnesota does appear to have a solid plan in place to sustain offensive growth.

Ultimately, though our projections don't believe it will be enough to overcome the probable growing pains of the young defense. You can piece together an optimistic scenario where the Vikings' young players immediately make an impact, the offense takes another step forward, and the defense remains adequate. Couple that with a weak division and it's not at all impossible that the Vikings could return to the playoffs in 2020. Anything more than that seems overly optimistic, however. This is a substantial reset moment for the franchise, and while they do seem to be in good hands with a workable plan, the most likely outcome this year is a step back to regroup before their next contending window opens up.

Bryan Knowles

2019 Vikings Stats by Week

Wk	vs.	W-L	PF	PA	YDF	YDA	TO	Total	Off	Def	ST
1	ATL	W	28	12	269	345	+3	31%	19%	-17%	-5%
2	at GB	L	16	21	421	335	-2	-25%	-15%	-3%	-13%
3	OAK	W	34	14	385	302	+1	43%	27%	-11%	4%
4	at CHI	L	6	16	222	269	-2	-33%	-32%	1%	0%
5	at NYG	W	28	10	490	211	0	30%	5%	-19%	6%
6	PHI	W	38	20	447	400	+1	43%	35%	-5%	3%
7	at DET	W	42	30	504	433	+1	-1%	39%	36%	-5%
8	WAS	W	19	9	434	216	+1	26%	3%	-21%	3%
9	at KC	L	23	26	308	377	+1	24%	8%	-16%	0%
10	at DAL	W	28	24	364	443	+1	24%	17%	-5%	2%
11	DEN	W	27	23	321	394	-1	11%	14%	-6%	-9%
12	BYE										
13	at SEA	L	30	37	354	444	-1	5%	1%	-1%	2%
14	DET	W	20	7	354	231	+2	21%	-7%	-30%	-1%
15	at LAC	W	39	10	344	345	+6	51%	-4%	-44%	10%
16	GB	L	10	23	139	383	+2	-28%	-56%	-21%	7%
17	CHI	L	19	21	300	337	-2	4%	-9%	-5%	8%
18	at NO	W	26	20	362	324	+1	6%	4%	-9%	-7%
19	at SF	L	10	27	147	308	0	-33%	-42%	-5%	3%

Trends and Splits

	Offense	Rank	Defense	Rank
Total DVOA	4.6%	10	-9.9%	7
Unadjusted VOA	7.6%	7	-9.8%	7
Weighted Trend	2.7%	13	-11.2%	7
Variance	5.9%	8	2.9%	3
Average Opponent	2.6%	27	1.7%	9
Passing	19.3%	10	-7.6%	7
Rushing	-3.1%	16	-13.1%	8
First Down	-10.9%	26	-0.8%	15
Second Down	9.9%	7	-22.0%	3
Third Down	26.6%	4	-6.9%	13
First Half	-0.9%	14	-8.8%	10
Second Half	10.7%	9	-11.1%	6
Red Zone	9.9%	9	-30.0%	3
Late and Close	9.3%	10	-9.0%	10

Five-Year Performance

Year	W-L	Pyth W	Est W	PF	PA	TO	Total	Rk	Off	Rk	Def	Rk	ST	Rk	Off AGL	Rk	Def AGL	Rk	Off Age	Rk	Def Age	Rk	ST Age	Rk
2015	11-5	9.8	9.5	365	302	+5	5.7%	11	0.0%	16	-1.8%	14	3.9%	4	35.8	17	21.7	5	26.4	19	27.5	4	25.7	22
2016	8-8	8.6	8.6	327	307	+11	-1.7%	20	-9.8%	26	-6.6%	8	1.5%	10	92.4	32	28.2	10	27.1	10	27.8	3	26.3	10
2017	13-3	11.7	12.0	382	252	+5	25.0%	4	12.0%	5	-13.9%	2	-0.9%	18	41.9	20	7.1	3	26.9	17	27.9	3	25.7	23
2018	8-7-1	8.5	8.9	360	341	0	8.1%	10	-1.3%	18	-10.3%	4	-0.9%	19	35.0	15	35.2	19	26.9	13	26.7	8	25.5	25
2019	10-6	10.8	10.4	407	303	+11	15.3%	7	4.6%	10	-9.9%	7	0.8%	14	11.7	3	13.9	2	26.3	23	27.2	5	25.7	20

2019 Performance Based on Most Common Personnel Groups

MIN Offense					MIN Offense vs. Opponents					MIN Defense					MIN Defense vs. Opponents			
Pers	Freq	Yds	DVOA	Run%	Pers	Freq	Yds	DVOA	Run%	Pers	Freq	Yds	DVOA	Pers	Freq	Yds	DVOA
12	36%	5.6	-3.1%	30%	Base	51%	6.2	5.2%	57%	Base	26%	4.7	-21.8%	11	59%	5.2	-7.0%
21	22%	6.2	3.6%	57%	Nickel	33%	5.2	4.3%	40%	Nickel	72%	5.5	-3.4%	12	19%	6.5	-0.8%
11	21%	6.7	24.3%	41%	Dime+	12%	7.2	9.0%	12%	Dime+	1%	9.1	49.6%	21	8%	6.0	-3.9%
22	10%	5.7	18.1%	75%	Goal Line	2%	4.6	75.9%	74%	Goal Line	1%	0.6	-128.9%	611	3%	6.0	7.7%
13	9%	6.5	14.6%	64%	Big	2%	4.4	-38.6%	75%					612	2%	2.4	-44.8%
														13	2%	1.0	-67.4%

Strategic Tendencies

Run/Pass		Rk	Formation		Rk	Pass Rush		Rk	Secondary		Rk	Strategy		Rk
Runs, first half	44%	2	Form: Single Back	69%	28	Rush 3	3.9%	25	4 DB	26%	19	Play Action	30%	9
Runs, first down	55%	7	Form: Empty Back	4%	31	Rush 4	72.0%	9	5 DB	72%	5	Offensive Motion	35%	22
Runs, second-long	46%	1	Form: Multi Back	26%	2	Rush 5	18.6%	19	6+ DB	1%	31	Avg Box (Off)	6.87	2
Runs, power sit.	58%	12	Pers: 3+ WR	22%	32	Rush 6+	5.4%	16	Man Coverage	27%	28	Avg Box (Def)	6.36	30
Runs, behind 2H	32%	7	Pers: 2+ TE/6+ OL	56%	2	Edge Rusher Sacks	67.7%	7	CB by Sides	87%	7	Offensive Pace	30.08	10
Pass, ahead 2H	36%	31	Pers: 6+ OL	0%	28	Interior DL Sacks	18.8%	19	S/CB Cover Ratio	23%	24	Defensive Pace	30.11	8
Run-Pass Options	2%	29	Shotgun/Pistol	31%	32	Second Level Sacks	13.5%	22	DB Blitz	7%	26	Go for it on 4th	1.92	5

The Vikings led the league with 11.2 average yards after the catch on passes behind/at the line of scrimmage, but they were average with 4.1 average yards after the catch on other passes. ✎. A connected stat: the Vikings were second in the league with 41 running back screens and led the league with 10.6 yards per pass on these plays. Their 72.3% DVOA was second behind New England. ✎. For the third straight year, Minnesota ranked in the top five of both yards per pass (5.1) and DVOA (-28.0%) allowed when blitzing. ✎. The Vikings tied for the smallest gap between where their two safeties made their average play, suggesting interchangeable safeties instead of more-defined roles as free and strong safety. They were also near the bottom of the league in this metric in 2018. ✎. Minnesota benefited from a league-low 101 opponent penalties, including declined and offsetting.

Passing

Player	DYAR	DVOA	Plays	NtYds	Avg	YAC	C%	TD	Int
K.Cousins	795	14.3%	476	3375	7.1	5.8	69.3%	26	6
S.Mannion	-5	-15.2%	21	126	6.0	5.5	57.1%	0	1

Rushing

Player	DYAR	DVOA	Plays	Yds	Avg	TD	Fum	Suc
D.Cook	183	9.3%	250	1135	4.5	13	3	49%
A.Mattison	24	-2.2%	100	462	4.6	1	1	38%
M.Boone	35	9.0%	49	273	5.6	4	0	51%
A.Abdullah	6	0.5%	23	115	5.0	0	0	26%
K.Cousins	-9	-19.8%	18	71	3.9	1	1	–
C.Ham	-20	-49.8%	7	17	2.4	0	0	43%
S.Diggs*	44	103.1%	5	61	12.2	0	0	–
T.Brooks-James	-17	-79.2%	8	7	0.9	0	0	13%

Receiving

Player	DYAR	DVOA	Plays	Ctch	Yds	Y/C	YAC	TD	C%
S.Diggs*	272	24.0%	95	63	1130	17.7	4.7	6	67%
A.Thielen	103	15.4%	48	30	418	13.9	3.9	6	63%
O.Johnson	49	0.9%	45	31	294	9.5	2.2	3	69%
L.Treadwell*	53	31.7%	16	9	184	20.4	6.3	1	56%
T.Sharpe	157	45.1%	34	25	329	13.2	2.3	4	74%
K.Rudolph	118	26.9%	48	39	367	9.4	4.9	6	81%
I.Smith	-39	-18.5%	47	36	311	8.6	3.8	2	77%
T.Conklin	-14	-27.9%	10	8	58	7.3	2.3	0	80%
D.Cook	144	29.2%	63	53	519	9.8	11.2	0	84%
C.Ham	6	-10.1%	26	17	149	8.8	7.4	1	65%
A.Abdullah	12	-4.4%	21	15	88	5.9	5.3	1	71%
A.Mattison	18	21.2%	12	10	82	8.2	7.4	0	83%

Offensive Line

Player	Pos	Age	GS	Snaps	Pen	Sk	Pass	Run	Player	Pos	Age	GS	Snaps	Pen	Sk	Pass	Run
Garrett Bradbury	C	25	16/16	1005	8	4.0	14	10	Riley Reiff	LT	32	15/15	889	8	7.0	19	4
Brian O'Neill	RT	25	15/15	983	7	1.0	9	6	Josh Kline*	RG	31	13/13	742	3	0.0	7	5
Pat Elflein	LG	26	15/15	935	8	5.5	16	9	Dakota Dozier	RG	29	16/4	367	2	2.0	5	5

Year	Yards	ALY	Rank	Power	Rank	Stuff	Rank	2nd Lev	Rank	Open Field	Rank	Sacks	ASR	Rank	Press	Rank	F-Start	Cont.
2017	3.98	3.96	19	67%	10	21%	19	1.11	17	0.77	13	27	4.4%	6	36.1%	29	11	27
2018	4.29	4.09	23	58%	30	21%	25	1.16	23	1.02	9	40	6.1%	9	34.1%	27	14	31
2019	4.67	4.60	7	68%	11	16%	5	1.24	13	1.04	6	28	6.7%	14	29.9%	16	14	24
2019 ALY by direction:		Left End 5.25 (3)			Left Tackle: 4.22 (18)			Mid/Guard: 4.06 (24)			Right Tackle: 5.06 (3)			Right End: 5.32 (6)				

Minnesota had respectable offensive line rankings a year ago—seventh in adjusted line yards and 14th in adjusted sack rate. However, remember that those stats also reflect the scheme and abilities of the quarterback and running backs. The Vikings ranked 19th in blown blocks, in large part due to two interior line starters ranking outside the top 80 in snaps per blown block. That sieve of an interior line really came back to bite them in their divisional-round loss. ✎. Josh Kline was the team's best interior lineman, but he was a victim of the salary-cap purge. Dakota Dozier filled in when Kline missed action last season, but last year's fourth-round pick Dru Samia has more upside and may win the starting role. ✎. Pat Elflein ranked 89th out of 106 interior linemen with a blown block every 37.4 snaps. He was competent enough in Minnesota's new zone-blocking run game, but he was an absolute sieve in pass protection. Elflein has never been the same since fracturing his ankle during the 2017 NFC Championship Game. ✎. Garrett Bradbury replaced Elflein at center as a rookie and struggled; he ranked 82nd in snaps per blown block. Like Elflein, Bradbury was particularly poor in pass protection—Kirk Cousins praised him for his communication and pre-snap reads, but he was too often just beaten by stronger linemen. ✎. The Vikings do have options if they just can't stomach Elflein anymore. Riley Reiff was a potential cap cut, but he's back and could move from left tackle to left guard. That's a temporary stopgap, as Reiff's due nearly $14 million in 2021, but he remains an adequate player, albeit one trending downwards. ✎. Moving Reiff would have been easier had the Vikings capitalized on their pursuit of new 49ers tackle Trent Williams. Instead, they drafted Ezra Cleveland (Boise State) in the second round. Cleveland's a perfect fit for Minnesota's zone-blocking scheme, but he needs to get more consistent to become a starter; he's more a project for 2021 than a Day 1 left tackle.   Right tackle is the one spot on the line with no questions, as Brian O'Neill took a big step forward in his second season, ranking fifth among right tackles at 61.4 snaps per blown block.

Defensive Front

Defensive Line	Age	Pos	G	Snaps	Plays	TmPct	Rk	Stop	Dfts	BTkl	Runs	St%	Rk	RuYd	Rk	Sack	Hit	Hur	Dsrpt
						Overall						vs. Run				Pass Rush			
Shamar Stephen	29	DT	15	588	23	2.8%	84	16	3	0	17	65%	81	2.8	72	1.0	1	6	2
Linval Joseph*	32	DT	13	559	44	6.2%	36	28	10	2	37	62%	84	2.9	83	3.0	3	6	0
Jaleel Johnson	26	DT	16	410	29	3.3%	--	15	7	1	23	48%	--	3.4	--	3.5	1	4	0
Michael Pierce	28	DT	14	489	35	5.6%	38	26	7	2	31	71%	69	2.0	29	0.5	2	12	1

Edge Rushers	Age	Pos	G	Snaps	Plays	TmPct	Rk	Stop	Dfts	BTkl	Runs	St%	Rk	RuYd	Rk	Sack	Hit	Hur	Dsrpt
						Overall						vs. Run				Pass Rush			
Danielle Hunter	26	DE	16	897	70	8.0%	7	46	25	5	55	56%	80	3.0	69	14.5	7	59	1
Everson Griffen*	33	DE	15	863	42	5.1%	42	33	16	7	25	80%	21	2.2	34	8.0	16	40	1
Stephen Weatherly*	26	DE	16	424	24	2.7%	--	17	8	2	21	67%	--	2.4	--	3.0	7	19	0
Ifeadi Odenigbo	26	DE	16	372	23	2.6%	--	17	12	3	13	54%	--	4.2	--	7.0	9	15	0

Linebackers	Age	Pos	G	Snaps	Plays	TmPct	Rk	Stop	Dfts	BTkl	Runs	St%	Rk	RuYd	Rk	Sack	Hit	Hur	Tgts	Suc%	Rk	AdjYd	Rk	PD	Int
						Overall						vs. Run				Pass Rush				vs. Pass					
Eric Kendricks	28	MLB	15	962	122	14.8%	23	65	21	11	78	56%	56	3.4	24	0.5	2	10	44	66%	5	5.6	25	12	0
Anthony Barr	28	OLB	14	944	83	10.8%	48	41	14	4	40	68%	18	3.6	29	1.5	6	15	30	47%	46	7.3	49	4	1
Eric Wilson	26	OLB	16	383	57	6.5%	--	25	9	4	36	39%	--	5.1	--	3.0	2	3	15	67%	--	6.2	--	0	0

Year	Yards	ALY	Rank	Power	Rank	Stuff	Rank	2nd Level	Rank	Open Field	Rank	Sacks	ASR	Rank	Press	Rank
2017	3.56	3.99	13	55%	5	19%	26	0.91	2	0.33	2	37	6.3%	18	31.1%	13
2018	4.05	4.60	24	66%	17	16%	25	1.09	6	0.48	5	50	9.3%	2	32.0%	9
2019	4.39	4.60	25	49%	1	16%	25	1.13	12	0.71	14	48	8.2%	5	30.4%	16

2019 ALY by direction:	Left End: 4.47 (25)	Left Tackle: 5.24 (31)	Mid/Guard: 4.4 (16)	Right Tackle: 5.04 (29)	Right End: 4.62 (18)

Minnesota had the best tackle rate in the NFL—only 91 broken tackles allowed, with a broken tackle on just 7.7% of plays. The Vikings have ranked first or second in each of the last three seasons.   The Vikings lost more than 35% of their individual pass pressures this offseason, mostly from the departures of Everson Griffen and Stephen Weatherly.   Danielle Hunter has improved his rank in quarterback hurries every season of his career, hitting the top five in 2019. Hunter's one of four players to be in the top 10 in hurries in each of the last two seasons—and he's three years younger than any of the others (Cam Jordan, DeMarcus Lawrence, and Aaron Donald).   Ifeadi Odenigbo's 15 pass pressures came on only 372 defensive snaps. He won't keep that efficiency level up when he becomes an every-down player, but that's still a promising success rate.   Although he's coming off of a down year, Michael Pierce was the best pure run-stuffer available in free agency. Conditioning issues last offseason might have contributed to early-season struggles; there's reason to expect him to return to his fantastic 2018 and earlier form this season.   Eric Kendricks bounced back from a poor 2018, ending up as arguably one of the top five linebackers in football in both pass coverage and run defense. He set career highs in both success rate in coverage and run stop rate last season.   While Minnesota ranked first in DVOA against tight ends, that was very matchup-dependent. Kendricks, Trae Waynes, and Harrison Smith each had success rates over 55% when covering tight ends. Anthony Barr and Anthony Harris? 33% or worse.   Eric Wilson was significantly better than Ben Gedeon last season, to the point where Gedeon's roster spot is now in jeopardy. That being said, Wilson's 39% stop rate against the run is not acceptable for an every-down linebacker; it would have ranked second-worst in the league among outside linebackers had he had enough snaps to qualify.   Fourth-round pick Troy Dye (Oregon) surrendered 27 broken tackles over the last two seasons and is coming off of a torn meniscus; this will likely be a redshirt year for him.   The Vikings also grabbed a pair of fourth-rounders on the defensive line: James Lynch (Baylor) and D.J. Wonnum (South Carolina). Of the two, Wonnum's more likely to make an impact as a rotational pass-rusher, though he could stand to add some mass and strength to battle NFL-caliber tackles. Lynch is an undersized 3-tech with a surprisingly solid inside pass-rushing move.

Defensive Secondary

Secondary	Age	Pos	G	Snaps	Plays	TmPct	Rk	Stop	Dfts	BTkl	Runs	St%	Rk	RuYd	Rk	Tgts	Tgt%	Rk	Dist	Suc%	Rk	AdjYd	Rk	PD	Int
						Overall						vs. Run							vs. Pass						
Harrison Smith	31	SS	15	984	96	11.6%	18	35	19	10	31	35%	50	6.8	36	26	6.3%	54	8.2	65%	8	3.7	4	11	3
Anthony Harris	29	FS	14	922	71	9.2%	45	21	9	3	33	24%	66	7.0	40	21	5.4%	63	12.0	48%	47	7.7	40	11	6
Xavier Rhodes*	30	CB	15	807	69	8.4%	37	25	12	7	12	67%	11	3.2	9	62	18.2%	59	11.4	32%	85	9.8	76	6	0
Trae Waynes*	28	CB	14	782	66	8.6%	48	33	10	8	12	75%	8	1.3	1	78	23.6%	13	11.4	47%	63	7.6	43	8	1
Mackensie Alexander*	27	CB	13	541	41	5.7%	--	19	8	1	9	44%	--	5.7	--	42	18.4%	--	10.5	52%	--	6.0	--	5	1
Mike Hughes	23	CB	14	505	52	6.8%	71	15	7	8	7	14%	82	9.9	75	64	30.0%	1	11.8	47%	66	7.2	37	9	1
Andrew Sendejo*	33	SS	15	395	43	6.1%	--	17	9	7	15	40%	--	5.8	--	13	7.5%	--	9.5	46%	--	9.3	--	4	3
Jayron Kearse*	26	FS	15	275	33	4.0%	--	18	6	2	14	57%	--	4.0	--	19	16.4%	--	11.9	74%	--	4.0	--	6	1
Holton Hill	23	CB	8	150	13	3.0%	--	4	2	2	4	50%	--	5.0	--	8	12.6%	--	13.1	38%	--	8.1	--	1	0

Year	Pass D Rank	vs. #1 WR	Rk	vs. #2 WR	Rk	vs. Other WR	Rk	WR Wide	Rk	WR Slot	Rk	vs. TE	Rk	vs. RB	Rk
2017	4	-13.1%	9	-22.2%	5	-3.5%	15	-4.9%	13	-15.3%	7	-24.2%	2	-37.6%	1
2018	5	-23.8%	3	-20.0%	6	-11.4%	9	-33.9%	1	-4.6%	11	22.6%	30	12.5%	27
2019	7	5.4%	21	-13.9%	6	17.0%	24	15.3%	28	-7.0%	7	-46.4%	1	-9.3%	11

There isn't a better safety duo in the league than Anthony Harris and Harrison Smith. The Vikings made sure they kept them together by using the franchise tag on Harris this offseason; even in a cap-strapped year, Harris was too valuable to let loose. You could make the argument that Harris and Smith are the best two safeties in the entire league. ◕ The Vikings better hope Harris and Smith both stay healthy. They do not have another safety with any NFL experience on the roster. ◕ A cardboard cut-out with a "please do not throw it here" sign would have been more effective than Xavier Rhodes last season, so it's no surprise that Minnesota used their second first-round pick on Jeff Gladney out of TCU. Per SIS, Gladney allowed a 38% completion rate last year and a 33% completion rate in 2018, which is a little better than third-overall pick Jeff Okudah. Of course, Okudah is 6-foot-1; Gladney is 5-foot-10, which is an issue, but his cover skills pass even the closest inspection. ◕ Trae Waynes is gone too, so the Vikings will need to have two new starting corners for 2020. Gladney will play second banana to Mike Hughes, who ranked 66th out of 85 qualified corners in success rate and was targeted more frequently than any of them when he was on the field. ◕ Holton Hill had a strong rookie season in 2018 and will be looking to replicate that as the slot corner in 2020. He missed half of last season, however, serving two consecutive four-game bans for violating the PED and substance-abuse policies. ◕ With 2,098 cornerback snaps leaving the team this offseason, the Vikings needed some warm bodies to fill up their depth chart. Along with Gladney, the draft brought in third-rounder Cameron Dantzler (Mississippi State) and fifth-rounder Harrison Hand (Temple), each of whom have a chance to make a splash on a depleted depth chart. Dantzler was targeted only 28 times last season, so opposing defenses knew to stay away; he should enter the starting lineup sooner rather than later. Hand led Temple with three interceptions so he has some playmaking ability, but his technique and movement skills need significant work.

Special Teams

Year	DVOA	Rank	FG/XP	Rank	Net Kick	Rank	Kick Ret	Rank	Net Punt	Rank	Punt Ret	Rank	Hidden	Rank
2017	-0.9%	18	-3.1	20	-5.0	26	-2.6	21	2.9	17	3.1	8	-4.2	19
2018	-0.9%	19	-15.2	32	-1.5	23	1.2	10	5.8	8	5.3	5	-11.4	29
2019	0.8%	14	4.1	10	0.0	18	-1.4	19	6.9	6	-5.7	31	-2.8	20

2019 saw the Vikings put up positive FG/XP value for the first time since 2015. Dan Bailey jumped from 75.0% to 93.1% in field goal accuracy in what is either a return to form for the kicker after two years of struggles or yet another data point showing that field goal accuracy is inconsistent from year to year. ◕ The swap from Matt Wile to Britton Colquitt was a net positive for the Vikings, as Colquitt put up Minnesota's highest punt value since Mitch Berger in 1999. ◕ Not so positive of a switch: Marcus Sherels to Mike Hughes as a punt returner. Hughes averaged just 7.4 yards per return and ended a six-year string of positive punt return value for the franchise. The Vikings have a couple of options to throw back there if they're unhappy with Hughes' performance. Ameer Abdullah has never returned punts but isn't terrible as a kick returner. More promising might be fifth-round receiver K.J. Osborn, who was a reliable return option for both Miami and Buffalo (the Hurricanes and Bulls, not the Dolphins and Bills).

New England Patriots

2019 Record: 12-4	**Total DVOA:** 30.8% (2nd)	**2020 Mean Projection:** 8.5 wins	**On the Clock (0-4):** 7%
Pythagorean Wins: 13.1 (2nd)	**Offense:** 4.1% (11st)	**Postseason Odds:** 54.8%	**Mediocrity (5-7):** 28%
Snap-Weighted Age: 28.6 (1st)	**Defense:** -25.5% (1st)	**Super Bowl Odds:** 7.5%	**Playoff Contender (8-10):** 42%
Average Opponent: -5.8% (32nd)	**Special Teams:** 1.2% (11st)	**Proj. Avg. Opponent:** -0.5% (21st)	**Super Bowl Contender (11+):** 24%

2019: The end of an era.

2020: Superman swoops in to replace Tom Brady and save the Patriots.

No amount of bidding farewell can do the Tom Brady era any justice. Six Super Bowl rings, 14 Pro Bowls (10 of them in a row, at that), three MVPs, a host of NFL career records—everything there was to accomplish, Brady did it in his 20 years with the Patriots. He was the point man for the dynasty to end all dynasties. Every quarterback for the rest of the sport's lifespan will be chasing Brady.

"Inevitable" is the only way to capture the Patriots' suffocating run of dominance with Brady. Our projections have placed the Patriots in the top five for total DVOA every season since 2007. In all but four of those seasons, the Patriots did indeed finish in the top five for total DVOA, and they never once slipped outside of the top 10. We, both Football Outsiders and any halfway informed football fan, always expected the Patriots to be elite and they always were. In the years to come, the Patriots may still be a force to reckon with and regular favorites to win the ever-troubled AFC East, but the looming feeling that the Patriots were inevitable goes as Brady goes.

As the Patriots stumbled into their first Brady-less offseason in decades, the possibilities for the GOAT's replacement seemed endless. Many expected the Patriots to pursue Andy Dalton, who eventually signed with the Dallas Cowboys for $3 million, or trade for someone along the lines of Derek Carr. Before Ryan Tannehill re-signed with the Titans, he was floated as an option to fill in for Brady. Even Jameis Winston and Cam Newton, though both more aggressive than what Bill Belichick prefers in a quarterback, were mentioned in discussions about possible Patriots starters. When none of that came to fruition by late April, the assumption was that they would make a move on draft weekend. That option bore no action either. Through months of inaction, it seemed as though Belichick was handing his vote of confidence to 2019 fourth-round pick Jarrett Stidham.

What a disaster that would have been. Assuming Stidham was going to be the starting quarterback, the Patriots offense was projected outside of the top 20 in DVOA, well below their norm. In addition to problems across the rest of the offense—we'll get to that in a moment—Stidham had unimpressive college metrics. There also isn't much history of mid-round picks such as Stidham successfully starting in Year 2 despite having no rookie starting experience.

Since 2000, 17 players selected between the third and fifth round started more than four games in their second NFL sea-son. Of those 17, only Mike McMahon of the 2002 Lions entered the year as the Week 1 starter after having started fewer than four games as a rookie. McMahon lost all four starts before being benched in favor of Joey Harrington. Over the next four years, McMahon started just seven more games (all with the Eagles in 2005) before being pushed to the CFL. The only other somewhat comparable player in recent memory is Trevor Siemian, who was a seventh-round pick in 2015 rather than a mid-rounder. The Broncos handed Siemian the keys to be the Week 1 starter in 2016 when they quickly realized in training camp that rookie first-round pick Paxton Lynch was not going to be ready. Siemian is now an unsigned free agent coming off a couple of years as a decent backup.

Yet true to form, Belichick waited until the final hour to make the savvy move that every non-Patriots fan feared. On June 28, the slim chance of Newton stepping in for Brady became a reality. The former MVP signed a one-year, $1.75-million deal that could ramp up to nearly $8 million through a handful of incentives. Bringing in Newton at the $20 million price tag Teddy Bridgewater got from the Panthers would have been a nice deal for the Patriots, but this? Less than $10 million for a former MVP who was in top form when he was last healthy in 2018? Only Belichick could get away with such outrageous theft.

A healthy Cam Newton changes what is possible for a post-Brady future. Dalton, Carr, Winston, etc., are far from bad quarterbacks, but none have quite the same pedigree or ceiling as Newton. With Joe Burrow and Tua Tagovailoa expected to be drafted well before the Patriots got a shot at them, as they were, there was no clear star option in the draft, either. Newton was the only available quarterback with trajectory-changing star power.

Aside from Newton's general wealth of talent, it works in the Patriots' favor that Newton's most recent season of full play was a closer approximation to what he will be asked to do in New England than any of his previous seasons were. From 2011 to 2017, Newton played in offenses that emphasized play-action, shot plays, and intermediate route combinations intended to target the area outside the numbers. Carolina's dropback passing game for much of Newton's career revolved around deep drops in the pocket with little to no checkdown or underneath options to speak of, instead leaving Newton to be his own checkdown as a runner. Yes, Newton himself had

2020 Patriots Schedule

Week	Opp.	Week	Opp.	Week	Opp.
1	MIA	7	SF	13	at LAC
2	at SEA	8	at BUF	14	at LAR (Thu.)
3	LV	9	at NYJ (Mon.)	15	at MIA
4	at KC	10	BAL	16	BUF (Mon.)
5	DEN	11	at HOU	17	NYJ
6	BYE	12	ARI		

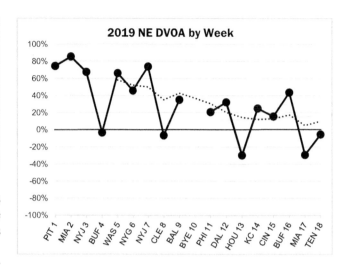

2019 NE DVOA by Week

a characteristic handful of misfires each game. But Newton's completion percentage and overall efficiency suffered more often than not because he was playing in aggressive offenses with minimal wide receiver talent.

The 2018 version of Newton and the Panthers passing offense was a different beast. While shot plays and play-action were present, the passing offense shifted more towards deception via shifts and motion, spacing in the quick game, and trust in running back Christian McCaffrey to carry the burden of the offense as a heavily used checkdown option. Newton's 2018 average depth of target of 7.4 yards was down from his 2016 and 2017 marks of 11.0 yards and 8.9 yards, respectively. Save for the use of Newton's legs, the overarching theme of Carolina's offense that year was not terribly different from the theme of some of New England's offense with Brady. Many of New England's recent offenses have leaned toward heavier personnel sets, whereas the Panthers did not have that luxury, but a good chunk of the pass concepts and ideas were similar. So was the lingo, as Norv Turner comes from the same Erhardt-Perkins offensive tree as Josh McDaniels.

Carolina's offensive renovations helped quell Newton's recurring issue of posting a low completion percentage. Even with a shoulder injury slowing him down over the second half of 2018, Newton finished the year with a career-high 67.9% completion rate. His previous high was 61.7% in 2013. In kind, Newton also finished with his career best in Completion Percentage Over Expected. Newton's MVP campaign netted a lukewarm +0.4% completion rate over expected, followed by bottom-three finishes in 2016 and 2017. The +1.9% completion rate over expected Newton posted in 2018 was good for 13th in the league and tied with MVP Patrick Mahomes. Through the first half of the season, before he hurt his shoulder, Newton was in the top 10 of passing DVOA at 13.2%. This would also have been a career high.

This is all before delving into what Newton provides as a runner. Be it zone reads, counter reads, or run-pass options that involve a quarterback run, Newton can be the key that unlocks a part of the run game previously out of Belichick and McDaniels' reach. Some experimentation with option football during Jacoby Brissett's pair of starts in 2016 is all Belichick has ever shown in terms of a quarterback-centric run game. That being said, Newton probably will not be the driving force for a run-heavy offense. Seeing as Newton's health is a priority, especially coming off of last year's foot injury, and Belichick is a thoughtful coach, it is more than likely that current Newton does not get the volume as a runner that, say, 2015 or

2016 Newton would have gotten. Rather, Belichick should be looking to use Newton as a runner almost exclusively in high-leverage situations (short yardage, red zone, goal line, etc.) instead of as a key feature for the offense at large.

With all that Newton provides through both the air and ground, it comes as no surprise that substituting him for Stidham dramatically changes the outlook for the Patriots offense. Having an offense geared towards Newton's safety and newfound passing identity is only part of the puzzle, though. Newton will have to call on his experience in making up for middling skill talent from his Carolina days, which our projections expect him to do. Josh McDaniels remaining on staff to call plays will be a plus for Newton, but each position group on offense needs questions answered.

New England's pass-catching corps has concerns all up and down the depth chart. The healthy return of slot star Julian Edelman is a welcomed boost, but he does not solve New England's issues with wide receiver play on the outside. 2019 first-round pick N'Keal Harry was woefully underwhelming for most of his rookie year. Jakobi Meyers surprised as an undrafted rookie contributor, but projecting him as more than a role player moving forward is a hair optimistic. Trading for Mohammed Sanu midway through last year did not provide the results the team was looking for either, although an ankle injury is partly to blame. Sanu is primarily a "big" slot receiver whose ideal route tree somewhat overlaps with Edelman's. If none of the non-Edelman receivers can step up, the unit will again be a speed-deficient disaster, and even a positive outlook for the group still comes without any meaningful speed to threaten down the field unless the Patriots coax a dramatic transformation out of Newton's former Panthers teammate Damiere Byrd.

Despite all the resources thrown at tight end in this year's draft, there is no telling if the Patriots have actually found a solution yet. Third-round selection Devin Asiasi (UCLA) fits the mold of a "move" tight end the Patriots have been looking for, while Dalton Keene (Virginia Tech), another third-round selection, is a perfect Belichickian hybrid fullback/tight end, but rookie tight ends rarely make a noticeable impact.

Since 2000, just 13 tight ends have earned over 500 yards receiving in their rookie season. Six of those 13 were top-50 picks, which neither Asiasi or Keene were. For further perspective, 14 tight ends cleared 500 receiving yards just last season, yet Denver's Noah Fant was the only rookie to do so. Fant was not particularly efficient in getting there either. Denver's first-round tight end finished just 28th in both DYAR and DVOA, putting him right around average among 47 qualifiers at the position. Even the best tight end prospects are far from a guarantee to be average, let alone good, as rookies.

Granted, with the Patriots' leading receiver at tight end last season being 39-year-old Benjamin Watson and his 173 yards, there is more room for improvement on this team than most others, but rookie tight ends are still just that. Keene may be somewhat of an exception in that he is more of a blocker and chess piece anyway, so perhaps his value is never going to show in receiving numbers, but that only serves to drive home the idea that this year's young tight ends may not immediately give the passing offense the help it needs.

Running back is the deepest position on the Patriots offense, but feel free to insert a typical Twitter argument about how much running backs matter here. That's before we get to Sony Michel's chronic knee problems or his offseason foot surgery.

For the offensive line, the biggest question is not personnel but rather coaching, because of the retirement of Dante Scarnecchia. Not many position coaches deserve a clear spot in Canton, but not many have made the clear impact Scar has.

Scarnecchia has been critical in helping the Patriots maintain top-class offensive line play for the past two decades without having too many elite talents at his disposal. Scarnecchia has a gift for developing projects and getting the most out of players, which is often only evident once those players venture away from his guidance to play for other teams.

Despite all these imperfections, Newton and the coaching staff should be enough to keep the offense in or close to the NFL's top 10, even if they don't reach elite Kansas City territory. Where our numbers break from the pack is in projecting the Patriots defense. Many analysts still hold the Patriots defense in high regard for the upcoming season. Who can blame them for their optimism? The Patriots just pulled off one of the most dominant defensive seasons in years right after a 2018 postseason in which they nearly shut out the best offense in the league in the Super Bowl. Losing a few starters in the front seven can't be that bad, right?

Wrong. Perhaps in different circumstances losing a few starters may not be catastrophic, but this particular group of names which the Patriots are losing is littered with top-tier players at their respective positions. The Patriots are hemorrhaging one of the most valuable groups of defenders (per Approximate Value) in two decades without replacing them with any notable veterans (Table 1). This is not your standard

Table 1. Biggest Net AV Over Replacement Loss on Defense, 2003-2020

Team	Year	Net AV Change	DVOA Y-1	Rk	DVOA	Rk	Change	Players Added	Players Lost
NE	2020	-34	-25.5%	1	--	--	--	NONE	J.Collins (12), K.Van Noy (10), D.Shelton (9), D.Harmon (2), E.Roberts (1)
TB	2009	-32	-10.7%	6	8.0%	25	18.6%	NONE	D.Brooks (8), G.Adams (6), P.Buchanon (5), K.Carter (5), J.Haye (4), C.June (4)
BAL	2019	-27	-13.1%	3	-12.7%	4	0.4%	E.Thomas (est. 7)*	C.J.Mosley (12), T.Suggs (7), B.Urban (6), E.Weddle (6), Z.Smith (3)
NYJ	2013	-24	-4.2%	9	-5.6%	12	-1.3%	D.Landry (3)	B.Scott (7), L.Landry (5), Y.Bell (4), S.Pouha (4), B.Thomas (4), M.Devito (3)
CAR	2010	-23	-12.8%	6	-1.1%	16	11.7%	NONE	J.Peppers (12), D.Lewis (5), C.Harris (4), N.Diggs (2)
PHI	2003	-20	-11.2%	4	3.0%	17	14.2%	M.Coleman (4), N.Wayne (6)	H.Douglas (14), S.Barber (8), L.Kirkland (6), B.Bishop (2)
SF	2015	-20	-10.1%	5	9.9%	27	20.0%	S.Wright (2)	J.Smith (5), P.Cox (4), C.Culliver (4), R.McDonald (4), C.Borland (3), D.Skuta (2)
ARI	2017	-19	-13.6%	3	-12.7%	4	0.9%	A.Bethea (3), K.Dansby (2), J.Jones (2)	C.Campbell (13), K.Minter (5), M.Cooper (3), T.Jefferson (3), D.J.Swearinger (2)
CAR	2006	-18	-14.2%	2	-10.9%	4	3.3%	K.Lucas (6), M.Kemoeatu (5), R.Howard (1)	W.Witherspoon (7), B.Buckner (6), K.Lucas (6), M.McCree (5), B.Short (5), R.Manning (1)
CAR	2016	-17	-18.4%	2	-5.3%	10	13.1%	P.Soliai (2)	J.Norman (12), J.Allen (3), R.Harper (3), C.Tillman (1)
SD	2013	-17	2.0%	18	17.5%	32	15.5%	D.Freeney (3), D.Cox (2)	Q.Jammer (5), S.Phillips (5), T.Spikes (4), A.Cason (3), V.Martin (2), A.Bigby (1), A.Franklin (1), D.Williams (1)
CLE	2011	-17	1.7%	18	4.2%	22	2.6%	D.Patterson (1)	K.Coleman (5), A.Elam (4), M.Roth (4), E.Barton (3), D.Bowens (1), E.Wright (1)
CLE	2003	-17	-5.1%	10	-1.9%	14	3.2%	NONE	E.Holmes (5), D.Hambrick (4), D.Rudd (4), D.Bush (2), C.Fuller (2)
AVERAGE (except NE)		*-9.1%*	*7.2*		*-0.6%*	*15.6*	*8.5%*		

*Thomas had only 2 AV in 2018 due to injury; for our projections, we estimated him at 10 AV to match what he earned in his last two full seasons.

offseason turnover of talent. Barring some surprises, New England's defensive front is going to take a major step back.

Inside linebacker Jamie Collins and outside linebacker Kyle Van Noy are the Patriots' two most valuable losses, as well as the two players least likely to have their roles filled to the fullest right away. As awkward as Collins' stint in Cleveland was before his return to New England last season, Collins was a monster in his one year back under Belichick's guidance. In addition to being an excellent coverage piece, a good chunk of Collins' prowess is rooted in his "educated guessing" as a gap shooter against the run. Precious few linebackers in the NFL have the downhill speed, side-to-side coordination, and instant trigger that Collins does. Every now and again, Collins' gambling looks foolish, but it worked like a charm for most of last year and was devastating for opposing offenses when it did. Through limited action early in his career, Ja'Whaun Bentley, a 2018 fifth-round pick assumed to take over for Collins, has played with nowhere near the same proficiency in that area. None of the Patriots' late-round picks or UDFAs at the position look to be up to par either.

Van Noy's vacancy presents a similar predicament, albeit with better rookie resources thrown at it. Though Van Noy himself was a low-cost project some years ago, he was groomed into a do-it-all weapon on the perimeter. Van Noy could attack the outside, move around the line as a twist/stunt piece, set the edge in run defense, and occasionally drop back into coverage (though that happened less and less with each passing season in New England). Even if there are players better than him in each individual area, not many edge defenders can wear as many hats as he did in New England and perform at a high level. Belichick threw a pair of Day 2 draft picks at the position on players who fit the role (Michigan's Josh Uche and Alabama's Anfernee Jennings), but assuming rookies can perform in Belichick's intricate defense as though Van Noy never left is generous.

The firestorm of regression goes beyond just losing a few key players, though. The Patriots are also running up against massive turnover regression—a burden that weighs on most defenses which seemingly fall from excellent to ordinary in the blink of an eye. More specifically, interception regression and, in turn, coverage regression are breathing down Belichick's neck headed into the new season.

Regular Football Outsiders readers may recognize Table 2 as the interception regression chart from last year's Chicago Bears chapter, now with the Bears' and Patriots' figures from 2019 tacked on. The Bears, as expected, saw their interception rate dramatically fall. Sustaining league-high interception rates just is not realistic. One can hope the Patriots follow in the footsteps of other all-time great secondaries such as the Legion of Boom and Denver's No Fly Zone, but even if we assume the Patriots' secondary is as talented and cohesive as those units, it is no guarantee that they will continue picking off passes at an ungodly rate, especially considering how much weaker New England's front is about to be. In fact, some of that regression already hit during last season. The Patriots picked off 19 passes in the first eight games compared to just six over the final eight games. The 2020 season is more likely to look like that second half of last season than the first half.

The Patriots secondary will no longer have the luxury of a league-best pressure rate. While there is some argument to be made that New England's secondary aided the pass rush more than the pass rush aided the secondary, the Patriots are losing their most productive pass-rusher by far in Van Noy. Even under the assumption that the Patriots secondary can boost the pass rush again, the pass rush will certainly take a hit without its most productive member returning.

Additionally, New England's defense will no longer have the ever-steady insurance policy of Brady on the other side of the ball. Brady and the offense were not the helping hand last year they had been for the previous two decades, but they rarely turned the ball over and forced their own defense into bad spots. In turn, the Patriots' defense had the most favorable field position in the league. Maybe that is a self-fulfilling prophecy considering the Patriots defense also set up the offense with the league's best field position, but since we can tie that in part to the amount of turnovers the Patriots defense produced, that should take a step back as the turnover rate does.

There are two reasons the Patriots may yet fight off regression and still field a top-10 defensive unit in 2020. Relying on Belichick's track record and ingenuity is an obvious part of the equation, but the other is that the Patriots have an unmatched pool of cornerback talent with effectively zero personnel turnover from last season. The team's top four cornerbacks are all returning to the lineup, while 2019 second-round pick Joejuan Williams now has the experience under his belt to potentially step into a bigger role. New England's third and fourth cornerbacks, Jonathan Jones and J.C. Jackson, would be better than all but a handful of teams' starters at the position. Belichick would prefer to lean toward man coverages with any reasonably talented cornerback group, but the fact that he has four cornerbacks who excel in man coverage—five if Williams develops—is a cheat code.

In part because of the cornerbacks' raw talent and free safety

Table 2. Interception Per Drive Leaders, 2008-2019

Team	Year	Int/Drive	Int/Dr over Avg	Int/Dr Y+1	Rank Y+1
CLE	2008	14.0%	5.8%	5.5%	29
GB	2009	16.3%	7.3%	13.2%	2
NE	2010	14.3%	5.6%	13.1%	2
GB	2011	17.4%	8.8%	9.8%	9
CHI	2012	12.5%	4.4%	11.0%	4
SEA	2013	15.6%	7.2%	7.9%	18
SF	2014	13.5%	5.6%	5.1%	27
CAR	2015	12.4%	4.8%	9.1%	7
KC	2016	10.3%	3.0%	9.2%	10
BAL	2017	11.6%	4.1%	6.9%	20
CHI	2018	14.8%	7.3%	5.7%	27
NE	**2019**	**13.4%**	**6.0%**	--	--
AVERAGE		*13.9%*	*5.8%*	*8.8%*	*14.1*

Devin McCourty's exceptional football IQ, Belichick can vigorously drill the importance of divider leverage into his cornerbacks' technique. In short, divider leverage is the idea that there is an invisible line on the field (around the painted numbers, though it changes slightly depending on where the ball is snapped). Versus inside stems and routes, the cornerback plays outside leverage to help funnel throws toward the centerfielding safety. Conersely, outside stems and routes force the cornerback to play inside leverage and go one-on-one while using the boundary as help rather than the deep safety, allowing the safety to help elsewhere and shift the numbers advantage. Divider leverage is certainly not a Belichick exclusive. Every defense makes use of it. No defense is better at executing it properly right now, though. Since there is such little turnover in the Patriots secondary and five of the team's top six defensive backs have been in the system for more than one season (veteran corner Jason McCourty being the exception), it is plenty fair to expect the starting lineup to maintain their excellent technique.

Nonetheless, technique is only part of the equation, and it can be nullified by injuries to top players or an aging cornerback losing a touch of speed. Turnover and coverage regression is no joke. A drop in turnover rate alone will hurt the coverage unit, let alone any other factors.

Belichick should not be expected to replace more than 30 points in AV over replacement without missing a beat. His genius can only reach so far. Belichick's track record and the roster's immense cornerback talent are reasons to believe that

our statistical projections are overstating just how much this defense is coming back to earth. But while Belichick should be the one coach capable of avoiding complete disaster, a fall from grace to some degree is nearly inescapable.

In large part because of the addition of Newton, the Patriots are now aiming to maintain a happy middle ground between the dominant days of old and the potential disaster that could have followed Brady's departure. The defense's projected step back and an offense no longer being expected to be elite combine to knock the Patriots off their pedestal atop the NFL, but their AFC East crown is still waiting for them. Their path to winning the division just may not look as convincing as it usually does. Instead of the standard 12- to 14-win stranglehold, the Patriots may only squeak out the division title with 10 wins. Not since 2009, Brady's first year back from his ACL injury, have the Patriots won the division with fewer than 11 wins.

A nine- or 10-win season topped off by a division title is as much as any team could reasonably hope for after losing a franchise cornerstone. And if Newton has a strong season, the Patriots should be able to keep him for the long term; they're currently up against the cap for 2020 but rank in the top five for cap space in 2021. The day that Brady would eventually leave had been a dreaded thought for the past five years or so, but now that it is here, the Patriots look to have made it out the other end in good shape. Typical Belichick.

Derrik Klassen

2019 Patriots Stats by Week

Wk	vs.	W-L	PF	PA	YDF	YDA	TO	Total	Off	Def	ST
1	PIT	W	33	3	465	308	+1	75%	69%	0%	6%
2	at MIA	W	43	0	379	184	+3	86%	8%	-91%	-14%
3	NYJ	W	30	14	381	105	-1	68%	18%	-51%	-2%
4	at BUF	W	16	10	224	375	+3	-3%	-39%	-44%	-8%
5	at WAS	W	33	7	442	223	+1	66%	11%	-46%	9%
6	NYG	W	35	14	427	213	+2	46%	-8%	-58%	-5%
7	at NYJ	W	33	0	323	154	+5	74%	-2%	-68%	8%
8	CLE	W	27	13	318	310	+3	-6%	-11%	-20%	-16%
9	at BAL	L	20	37	342	372	0	35%	27%	5%	14%
10	BYE										
11	at PHI	W	17	10	298	255	+1	21%	-6%	-12%	15%
12	DAL	W	13	9	282	321	+1	32%	-13%	-51%	-6%
13	at HOU	L	22	28	448	276	-1	-29%	-2%	24%	-3%
14	KC	L	16	23	278	346	+1	25%	-5%	-39%	-9%
15	at CIN	W	34	13	291	315	+5	16%	-14%	-18%	11%
16	BUF	W	24	17	414	268	-1	44%	37%	0%	7%
17	MIA	L	24	27	352	389	-2	-29%	-9%	32%	12%
18	TEN	L	13	20	307	272	-1	-5%	-14%	-3%	6%

Trends and Splits

	Offense	Rank	Defense	Rank
Total DVOA	4.1%	11	-25.5%	1
Unadjusted VOA	6.0%	10	-28.5%	1
Weighted Trend	-0.6%	15	-16.8%	4
Variance	6.2%	9	11.8%	31
Average Opponent	1.3%	24	-5.5%	32
Passing	14.8%	14	-33.8%	1
Rushing	-2.7%	15	-14.0%	6
First Down	4.5%	10	-28.8%	1
Second Down	6.8%	10	8.4%	25
Third Down	-1.0%	19	-72.0%	1
First Half	-1.9%	15	-24.7%	1
Second Half	11.5%	7	-26.4%	1
Red Zone	-2.3%	18	-37.1%	1
Late and Close	9.6%	9	-19.8%	5

Five-Year Performance

Year	W-L	Pyth W	Est W	PF	PA	TO	Total	Rk	Off	Rk	Def	Rk	ST	Rk	Off AGL	Rk	Def AGL	Rk	Off Age	Rk	Def Age	Rk	ST Age	Rk
2015	12-4	11.7	10.9	465	315	+7	22.6%	6	15.4%	5	-3.3%	12	3.9%	5	60.5	28	36.5	20	27.2	12	25.9	27	25.9	18
2016	14-2	12.8	11.9	441	250	+12	24.9%	1	20.8%	2	-1.8%	16	2.3%	8	51.8	25	9.4	1	27.3	7	26.6	14	26.3	9
2017	13-3	12.0	11.0	458	296	+6	22.6%	6	27.3%	1	10.9%	31	6.3%	3	37.0	18	26.7	11	27.7	3	26.3	15	26.7	3
2018	11-5	10.8	10.0	436	325	+10	14.2%	7	14.5%	5	0.4%	16	0.1%	16	40.0	18	35.2	18	28.5	1	27.2	5	27.9	1
2019	12-4	13.1	12.3	420	225	+21	30.8%	2	4.1%	11	-25.5%	1	1.2%	11	69.7	30	11.4	1	29.3	1	28.2	1	27.9	1

2019 Performance Based on Most Common Personnel Groups

NE Offense					NE Offense vs. Opponents					NE Defense				NE Defense vs. Opponents			
Pers	Freq	Yds	DVOA	Run%	Pers	Freq	Yds	DVOA	Run%	Pers	Freq	Yds	DVOA	Pers	Freq	Yds	DVOA
11	55%	5.8	6.5%	31%	Base	24%	5.0	5.2%	64%	Base	15%	5.8	9.9%	11	59%	4.9	-35.0%
21	15%	5.3	17.9%	51%	Nickel	52%	5.1	-6.6%	37%	Nickel	42%	4.6	-28.7%	12	20%	4.6	-17.0%
12	13%	4.9	1.0%	69%	Dime+	23%	6.7	42.8%	14%	Dime+	41%	4.8	-40.4%	10	5%	6.3	-18.0%
10	6%	6.1	43.7%	5%	Goal Line	1%	0.7	17.1%	100%	Goal Line	1%	0.6	4.3%	2.	5%	3.6	-44.9%
20	6%	4.4	-1.4%	16%						Big	1%	6.3	20.7%	13	3%	6.5	32.3%
22	3%	3.3	-17.8%	55%										612	2%	5.3	9.1%

Strategic Tendencies

Run/Pass		Rk	Formation		Rk	Pass Rush		Rk	Secondary		Rk	Strategy		Rk
Runs, first half	37%	17	Form: Single Back	66%	30	Rush 3	16.4%	5	4 DB	15%	30	Play Action	24%	16
Runs, first down	53%	10	Form: Empty Back	10%	8	Rush 4	53.6%	30	5 DB	43%	27	Offensive Motion	63%	2
Runs, second-long	21%	28	Form: Multi Back	24%	4	Rush 5	22.5%	12	6+ DB	41%	4	Avg Box (Off)	6.65	8
Runs, power sit.	78%	3	Pers: 3+ WR	66%	16	Rush 6+	7.5%	10	Man Coverage	55%	2	Avg Box (Def)	6.47	22
Runs, behind 2H	32%	9	Pers: 2+ TE/6+ OL	19%	30	Edge Rusher Sacks	44.6%	26	CB by Sides	54%	31	Offensive Pace	27.69	1
Pass, ahead 2H	54%	4	Pers: 6+ OL	2%	17	Interior DL Sacks	26.1%	12	S/CB Cover Ratio	24%	23	Defensive Pace	32.72	32
Run-Pass Options	2%	28	Shotgun/Pistol	52%	27	Second Level Sacks	29.3%	5	DB Blitz	11%	15	Go for it on 4th	1.39	17

This was the third straight year that the Patriots ranked first or second in situation-neutral pace. Whether that continues without Tom Brady around remains to be seen. ● The Patriots are not listening to the analytics people when they talk about running against light boxes. The Patriots were once again high in running against heavy boxes. They ranked first in 2018 and then sixth last year, with 37% of runs coming against boxes of eight or more. However, also for the second straight year, the Patriots' run DVOA was basically the same either way. ● New England used six linemen on 27 plays but never once passed the ball in those sets. These plays only gained 2.3 yards on average with -28.9% DVOA. ● The Patriots were one of three teams that used play-action on over 10% of third-down passes. (Indianapolis and Philadelphia were the others.) ● New England was fourth in the league with 37 running back screens and had a league-leading 102.7% DVOA on these plays with 9.8 yards per pass. ● The Patriots ranked second by running 11.5% of their plays without a tight end or sixth lineman in the personnel. They had an excellent 22.8% DVOA on these plays. ● The Patriots defense is one of the best at tackling nearly every year, and in 2019 their total of 86 broken tackles was the lowest in the league. ● The Patriots had the best defensive DVOA in the league against both short passes (up to 15 air yards) and deep passes (16 or more air yards). They also had the best defensive DVOA when there was no pass pressure, as the only defense with negative DVOA without pressure. With pressure, the Patriots ranked seventh. ● Was there anything that the Patriots pass defense couldn't stop? Actually, yes: the play-action pass. The Patriots ranked tenth in DVOA against play-action passes and had the league's biggest gap between defense of play-action passes (9.6%) and defense of other pass plays (-43.1%). However, this is not a tendency that tends to carry over from year to year. ● The Patriots were once again among the league's least-penalized teams, tied for 30th in 2019 after ranking 26th in 2018. Their defense also benefited from a league-high 75 penalties by opposing offenses.

Passing

Player	DYAR	DVOA	Plays	NtYds	Avg	YAC	C%	TD	Int
T.Brady*	550	2.4%	639	3830	6.0	5.0	61.3%	24	8
C.Newton	19	-8.0%	94	529	5.6	4.1	56.8%	0	1
B.Hoyer	-175	-53.1%	70	332	4.7	4.5	53.8%	4	4

Rushing

Player	DYAR	DVOA	Plays	Yds	Avg	TD	Fum	Suc
S.Michel	23	-6.4%	247	912	3.7	7	2	49%
J.White	-1	-9.0%	67	263	3.9	1	0	42%
R.Burkhead	85	22.2%	65	302	4.6	3	0	52%
B.Bolden	34	39.5%	15	68	4.5	3	0	53%
T.Brady*	32	22.0%	11	46	4.2	3	0	-
J.Edelman	12	-13.9%	8	27	3.4	0	0	-
N.Harry	30	62.7%	5	49	9.8	0	0	-
D.Harris	-5	-74.0%	4	12	3.0	0	0	0%
C.Newton	-48	-230.2%	5	-2	-0.4	0	2	-

Receiving

Player	DYAR	DVOA	Plays	Ctch	Yds	Y/C	YAC	TD	C%
J.Edelman	48	-8.6%	153	100	1117	11.2	3.2	6	65%
P.Dorsett*	46	-2.1%	54	29	397	13.7	2.7	5	54%
M.Sanu	-75	-32.5%	47	26	207	8.0	2.7	1	55%
J.Meyers	61	5.9%	41	26	359	13.8	4.4	0	63%
J.Gordon*	10	-9.0%	36	20	287	14.4	6.7	1	56%
N.Harry	-25	-26.1%	24	12	105	8.8	3.5	2	50%
A.Brown*	-1	-14.0%	8	4	56	14.0	1.8	1	50%
D.Byrd	30	-4.6%	46	32	359	11.2	4.7	1	70%
B.Watson*	3	-5.2%	24	17	173	10.2	4.9	0	71%
M.LaCosse	-5	-10.8%	19	13	131	10.1	3.5	1	68%
R.Izzo	36	56.4%	9	6	114	19.0	8.3	1	67%
J.White	142	14.8%	95	72	645	9.0	7.4	5	76%
R.Burkhead	37	4.0%	38	27	279	10.3	8.5	0	71%
S.Michel	-9	-21.3%	20	12	94	7.8	10.1	0	60%
B.Bolden	52	69.5%	11	9	111	12.3	6.6	1	82%
D.Vitale	13	3.3%	12	7	97	13.9	8.0	0	58%

Offensive Line

Player	Pos	Age	GS	Snaps	Pen	Sk	Pass	Run	Player	Pos	Age	GS	Snaps	Pen	Sk	Pass	Run
Joe Thuney	LG	28	16/16	1147	0	1.0	7	3	Marshall Newhouse*	LT	32	15/9	735	3	4.5	19	2
Shaq Mason	RG	27	15/15	1074	4	1.0	10	9	Isaiah Wynn	LT	25	8/8	503	3	1.5	13	3
Ted Karras*	C	27	15/15	1046	3	1.0	13	8	James Ferentz*	C/RG	31	15/2	205	0	1.0	9	1
Marcus Cannon	RT	32	15/15	1014	3	6.5	28	9									

Year	Yards	ALY	Rank	Power	Rank	Stuff	Rank	2nd Lev	Rank	Open Field	Rank	Sacks	ASR	Rank	Press	Rank	F-Start	Cont.
2017	4.43	5.05	1	65%	14	16%	3	1.35	2	0.60	20	35	6.4%	13	27.0%	7	13	29
2018	4.24	5.03	3	58%	29	16%	4	1.19	21	0.63	25	21	3.8%	1	22.9%	1	16	31
2019	3.90	4.49	9	65%	17	21%	24	1.19	16	0.49	28	28	5.3%	5	24.7%	2	11	28

2019 ALY by direction:	Left End 3.31 (26)	Left Tackle: 4.60 (9)	Mid/Guard: 4.72 (6)	Right Tackle: 3.96 (20)	Right End: 5.17 (7)

Offensive line coach Dante Scarnecchia retired (again) following the 2019 season. Scarnecchia's initial retirement through 2014 and 2015 did not lead to immediate collapse—the Patriots still finished second in adjusted sack rate in 2014—but the unit fell apart after a full year without Scarnecchia, plummeting to 18th in adjusted sack rate in 2015. ◆ Starting center David Andrews is set to return to action after missing all of last season battling blood clots in his lungs. Andrews had the best year of his career in 2018, ranking seventh among centers in snaps per blown block. Ted Karras, who started in Andrews' place last year, was a much worse 27th in snaps per blown block in 2019. Without Andrews, New England fell to 24th in stuff rate after two seasons in the top five. Given how critical the center is to setting blocking adjustments, it would make sense that losing their starting center resulted in more blocking breakdowns up front. ◆ Do not let the lack of Pro Bowl or All-Pro selections fool you: the Patriots were smart to franchise tag left guard Joe Thuney. For two seasons in a row, Thuney has ranked first among left guards and top five among all interior offensive linemen in snaps per blown block. ◆ Left tackle Isaiah Wynn was firmly mediocre last season, but the hope is that a bill of good health can turn that around. Wynn is now more than a full year removed from the Achilles injury that ended his 2018 rookie season before it started and has now had an offseason to fully recover from the toe injury that sidelined him for the first half of last year. ◆ Not a single Patriots offensive lineman committed more than two false starts all season. Oddly enough, wide receiver Julian Edelman tied right tackle Marcus Cannon for most false starts on the team. Likewise, no Patriots offensive linemen committed more than three holding penalties, with Karras and right guard Shaq Mason tying for the team lead.

Defensive Front

Defensive Line	Age	Pos	G	Snaps	Plays	TmPct	Rk	Stop	Dfts	BTkl	Runs	St%	Rk	RuYd	Rk	Sack	Hit	Hur	Dsrpt
						Overall							vs. Run				Pass Rush		
Lawrence Guy	30	DT	16	539	61	8.1%	5	46	9	2	55	75%	51	2.3	46	3.0	2	9	0
Danny Shelton*	27	DT	16	508	61	8.1%	5	43	6	3	56	68%	75	2.8	75	3.0	4	11	0
Adam Butler	26	DT	16	483	29	3.8%	65	28	13	3	16	94%	2	1.9	27	6.0	1	13	5

Edge Rushers	Age	Pos	G	Snaps	Plays	TmPct	Rk	Stop	Dfts	BTkl	Runs	St%	Rk	RuYd	Rk	Sack	Hit	Hur	Dsrpt
						Overall							vs. Run				Pass Rush		
Kyle Van Noy*	29	OLB	15	832	59	8.3%	8	39	16	5	43	63%	76	3.2	75	6.5	11	46	3
John Simon	30	DE	16	492	47	6.2%	24	33	11	3	33	73%	51	2.3	40	4.0	3	15	3
Chase Winovich	25	DE	16	296	20	2.6%	--	15	9	2	9	67%	--	4.4	--	5.5	3	20	0
Shilique Calhoun	28	DE	15	272	9	1.3%	--	4	1	3	6	33%	--	4.8	--	0.0	3	14	0
Deatrich Wise	26	DE	14	232	26	3.9%	--	14	4	1	20	50%	--	4.4	--	2.0	10	13	0
Brandon Copeland	29	OLB	12	340	37	6.1%	45	27	11	10	24	75%	39	2.1	30	1.5	1	4	0

Linebackers	Age	Pos	G	Snaps	Plays	TmPct	Rk	Stop	Dfts	BTkl	Runs	St%	Rk	RuYd	Rk	Sack	Hit	Hur	Tgts	Suc%	Rk	AdjYd	Rk	PD	Int
						Overall							vs. Run				Pass Rush				vs. Pass				
Jamie Collins*	31	OLB	16	833	86	11.4%	34	60	29	16	47	77%	6	3.1	12	7.0	2	19	17	53%	28	5.5	21	7	3
Dont'a Hightower	30	OLB	15	736	74	10.4%	45	40	15	6	39	59%	44	3.7	35	5.5	6	28	15	40%	56	7.3	47	4	0
Ja'Whaun Bentley	24	ILB	16	287	39	5.2%	--	27	5	2	26	77%	--	2.6	--	0.0	1	7	13	46%	--	6.4	--	1	0
Elandon Roberts*	26	ILB	16	210	29	3.8%	--	17	2	1	20	70%	--	3.4	--	1.0	2	4	7	57%	--	7.0	--	1	0

Year	Yards	ALY	Rank	Power	Rank	Stuff	Rank	2nd Level	Rank	Open Field	Rank	Sacks	ASR	Rank	Press	Rank
2017	4.69	4.51	31	62%	15	16%	30	1.28	29	0.95	28	42	7.1%	10	27.5%	30
2018	4.79	4.67	26	67%	18	16%	24	1.31	23	0.91	19	30	5.0%	30	33.0%	6
2019	4.06	3.99	6	60%	10	18%	20	1.00	5	0.68	13	47	7.7%	8	37.1%	1
2019 ALY by direction:		Left End: 4.36 (20)			Left Tackle: 2.68 (1)			Mid/Guard: 4.19 (11)			Right Tackle: 4.2 (14)			Right End: 3.61 (12)		

The New England Patriots were one of just two teams to improve in rank in all five run defense categories (ALY, Power, Stuff, Second-Level, and Open-Field). The Tampa Bay Buccaneers were the other. While plenty of other units were better overall, the Patriots' boost in play across the board went a long way. ◗ In true Bill Belichick fashion, the Patriots are replacing a solid starter, Danny Shelton, with a bargain-bin buy, Beau Allen. The former Buc played sparingly in 2019, but his 85% stop rate in 2018 ranked 12th in the league. Allen also ranked 18th in stop rate and 13th in average rushing gain allowed as part of the Eagles' Super Bowl roster in 2017. ◗ Just when Kyle Van Noy had fully hit his stride as a Patriot, the team opted not to retain him. Van Noy's 46 hurries in 2019 were the most in his six-year career, nearly doubling the 28 he had posted the year before. Additionally, Van Noy has increased his hurry total every season since his second year in the league. ◗ Out goes Van Noy, in comes Michigan second-round pick Josh Uche. Uche fits the hybrid role in New England's scheme as someone who can play on the edge as a long-armed run defender as well as a lightning-fast pass-rusher, while also being able to play off the ball and chase like a traditional linebacker. Many of Uche's best pass-rush reps in college involved an inside countermove he set up with a quick jab step outside. ◗ Alabama third-round pick Anfernee Jennings does not share the same versatility as Uche, but he does provide a much stronger presence in the run game. Though lacking in speed and flexibility, Jennings packs a hell of a punch when he engages and has the raw strength to bully his way into rushing lanes as well as collapse the pocket. He is the exact kind of player who serves as a nice building block for Belichick's defense, but is never a featured star. ◗ Among players from last year's squad, 2019 third-round pick Chase Winovich is best positioned to make up for Van Noy's lost production. Winovich racked up 20 hurries on just 296 total snaps, good for about 6.8% of his snaps. Van Noy's 46 hurries on 832 snaps comes out to just 5.5%. Granted, Winovich was used intentionally on passing downs more often, so his numbers are skewed to some degree, but it is promising that he could affect the quarterback so often in a limited rookie sample.

Defensive Secondary

Secondary	Age	Pos	G	Snaps	Plays	TmPct	Rk	Stop	Dfts	BTkl	Runs	St%	Rk	RuYd	Rk	Tgts	Tgt%	Rk	Dist	Suc%	Rk	AdjYd	Rk	PD	Int
						Overall						vs. Run							vs. Pass						
Stephon Gilmore	30	CB	16	973	74	9.8%	11	30	22	7	11	27%	71	9.7	74	86	21.5%	27	12.3	57%	24	6.4	15	20	6
Devin McCourty	33	FS	16	968	64	8.5%	42	25	11	8	27	41%	38	9.0	57	23	5.8%	56	9.7	70%	5	5.0	9	7	5
J.C. Jackson	25	CB	16	696	46	6.1%	66	22	10	5	8	25%	72	12.3	82	58	20.3%	39	12.7	72%	2	4.0	1	10	5
Duron Harmon*	29	SS	16	669	27	3.6%	73	10	6	4	9	44%	30	6.0	30	10	3.6%	72	14.8	60%	17	9.2	58	5	2
Patrick Chung	33	SS	13	653	54	8.8%	54	23	2	7	25	52%	12	4.6	10	35	13.1%	8	8.5	46%	56	7.4	36	3	0
Jonathan Jones	27	CB	15	633	58	8.2%	43	25	14	5	11	64%	18	8.5	68	63	24.3%	10	12.6	59%	17	7.1	32	8	0
Jason McCourty	33	CB	12	482	45	7.9%	69	28	13	2	9	67%	11	4.1	18	44	22.2%	23	11.8	73%	1	5.1	5	6	1
Terrence Brooks	28	SS	15	280	25	3.5%	--	12	4	1	9	67%	--	4.1	--	14	12.2%	--	8.1	43%	--	8.1	--	3	1
Adrian Phillips	28	SS	7	282	32	9.5%	--	9	3	5	14	29%	--	4.9	--	9	9.8%	--	4.2	56%	--	5.1	--	0	0

Year	Pass D Rank	vs. #1 WR	Rk	vs. #2 WR	Rk	vs. Other WR	Rk	WR Wide	Rk	WR Slot	Rk	vs. TE	Rk	vs. RB	Rk
2017	21	18.9%	26	4.9%	19	6.8%	22	-4.9%	14	24.2%	29	-11.6%	8	10.1%	22
2018	13	0.0%	16	-6.1%	12	-17.4%	5	-14.0%	7	-2.5%	15	-12.8%	8	9.5%	22
2019	1	-34.5%	1	-49.9%	1	-40.1%	1	-46.3%	2	-38.4%	1	-10.6%	7	3.5%	21

For the second year in a row, a Patriots cornerback led the league in coverage success rate. Stephon Gilmore's 67% success rate topped the league in 2018, while Jason McCourty's 73% success rate took the crown in 2019. ✎ With cornerback J.C. Jackson placing second in cornerback coverage success rate, the Patriots were the only team in the league last year to feature two cornerbacks in the top 10. And though Gilmore wasn't in that group, he was still the Defensive Player of the Year. ✎ The more defensive backs New England had on the field last season, the better they were. Going from base to nickel to dime personnel, the Patriots' DVOA improved from 9.9% to -28.7% to -40.4%. Among defenses with at least 5% usage for all three personnel categories, no other defense showed the same progressive improvement the Patriots did, and many of them performed progressively worse the more defensive backs they had on the field. ✎ Do-it-all safety Patrick Chung hit a decline last season. After posting a coverage success rate of 55% or better while allowing fewer than 7 yards per target in both 2017 and 2018, Chung's success rate fell to 46% while allowing 7.4 yards per target in 2019. ✎ In turn, the Patriots spent their first 2020 draft pick on Lenoir-Rhyne safety Kyle Dugger early in the second round. Dugger's 6-foot-2 and 220-pound frame is a bit bigger than Chung's, but the former Division II safety shows the same positional flexibility that Chung did in his prime. Dugger can fill in as a linebacker in or near the box, cover in the slot, and hold his own as a split-field defender in deep coverage. ✎ Don't forget about 2019 second-round pick Joejuan Williams, even though he faced just seven targets as a rookie. At Vanderbilt, Williams played press-man coverage all over the field, including covering tight ends when called upon.

Special Teams

Year	DVOA	Rank	FG/XP	Rank	Net Kick	Rank	Kick Ret	Rank	Net Punt	Rank	Punt Ret	Rank	Hidden	Rank
2017	6.3%	3	8.9	6	8.4	1	6.4	4	8.2	4	-0.6	18	13.1	3
2018	0.1%	16	0.1	17	-8.7	32	5.3	5	4.5	10	-0.6	17	8.5	8
2019	1.2%	11	-9.7	30	5.0	7	-0.9	15	10.5	3	1.2	11	6.9	4

Four different kickers attempted at least one field goal for the Patriots last season, and six missed extra point attempts tied Indianapolis for the most in the league. ✎ Fifth-round kicker Justin Rohrwasser (Marshall) showed massive improvement as a redshirt senior. After finishing 1-for-5 beyond 40 yards in 2018, Rohrwasser went 7-for-8 beyond 40 yards in 2019 with a long of 53 yards. ✎ The weird hiccup where the Patriots had the worst kickoff coverage in the league in 2018 turned out not to be a long-term trend. Instead, the Pats were back to their usual spot as one of the best teams on both kickoff and punt coverage. Based on our metrics, the Patriots finished fourth in covering both kickoff returns and punt returns. Rookie Jake Bailey handled both punts and kickoffs and added gross positive value on both. ✎ Running back Brandon Bolden was thrust into kick return duties for the first time in his eight-year career last season but was the first Patriots kick returner to have negative value since Cyrus Jones in 2016. Undrafted running back J.J. Taylor (Arizona) is a candidate to replace Bolden. Though undersized at 5-foot-6 and 185 pounds, Taylor averaged 24.1 yards per return and scored one touchdown on 41 kick return attempts in college. ✎ The Patriots' four blocked punts aren't included in their special teams DVOA rating because blocked punts are "non-repeatable" plays where past performance doesn't usually correlate to future results, but they played a critical role in close wins over the Bills and Cowboys. Don't expect to see another four of them in 2020.

New Orleans Saints

2019 Record: 13-3	Total DVOA: 29.3% (4th)	2020 Mean Projection: 10.5 wins	On the Clock (0-4): 1%
Pythagorean Wins: 10.9 (6th)	Offense: 21.4% (4th)	Postseason Odds: 80.0%	Mediocrity (5-7): 10%
Snap-Weighted Age: 26.6 (8th)	Defense: -4.3% (11st)	Super Bowl Odds: 26.6%	Playoff Contender (8-10): 35%
Average Opponent: -1.6% (22nd)	Special Teams: 3.6% (3rd)	Proj. Avg. Opponent: 0.2% (12nd)	Super Bowl Contender (11+): 54%

2019: "No way a pass interference no-call ends our season again."

2020: *The Last Chance*, starring Drew Brees and Sean Payton.

tick to sports?

The Saints are making that impossible. Over the past year, they've been connected to numerous controversies and crises.

In January, a lawsuit claimed the Saints advised the Archdiocese of New Orleans on how to handle sexual abuse accusations. The team acknowledged it provided public relations help but maintained that its involvement was "minimal." In June, however, Jenny Ventras of *Sports Illustrated* wrote that multiple executives had worked with the church and for longer than the team had suggested.

In March, the Saints became the first NFL team hit by the coronavirus when head coach Sean Payton announced he had tested positive. His case was relatively mild—he passed the time in quarantine by tweeting diagrams of his favorite plays out of empty backfield formations—and he made a full recovery.

In May, Drew Brees set off a firestorm when he reasserted his position on kneeling during the national anthem, telling Yahoo Finance that he "will never agree with anybody disrespecting the flag of the United States of America." At best, he failed to read the room. After the killing of unarmed Black man George Floyd, protests over police brutality had gripped the nation. At worst, he deliberately mischaracterized fellow NFL players' peaceful demonstrations. Players who took a knee or raised a fist during the anthem never intended to disrespect the flag, and they had been clear on that point.

Brees had not been listening. In 2019, *The New Orleans Advocate* won a Pulitzer Prize for its reporting on Louisiana's Jim Crow-era law that allowed juries to convict defendants without reaching a unanimous verdict. The newspaper's coverage led to the drafting and ultimately the passage of an amendment to the state constitution. Two prominent names to publicly campaign for the amendment: Brees' teammates Demario Davis and Benjamin Watson.

The backlash was swift. The most emotional rebuke came from safety Malcolm Jenkins, whom the Saints signed to a multi-year deal during the offseason, in part for his leadership. During his six seasons in Philadelphia, Jenkins pushed hard for criminal justice reform. He participated in a ride-along with a police officer. He visited a prison. He met with lawmakers. In a tearful post to Instagram, Jenkins told Brees, "We need help. And what you're telling us is, don't ask for help that way. Ask for it a different way. I can't listen to it when you ask that way."

Brees apologized twice the next day, first in written form and then in a video. "I'm sorry," he said. "I will do better, and I will be a part of the solution. I am your ally." When Tweeter-in-Chief Donald Trump, a vociferous critic of kneelers, weighed in and said Brees should not have apologized, Brees stood firm. "We can no longer use the flag to turn people away or distract them from the real issues that face our Black communities," he replied. It was a first step toward proving his words were more than lip service, and his teammates took notice.

And so now the Saints face an inflection point. Brees' original remarks managed to do what three straight excruciating playoffs losses couldn't: divide the locker room. Many of his teammates have since accepted his apology, and Jenkins has said he and Brees have had constructive conversations. Healing, however, is a process. It requires work. It requires commitment. The civil unrest sweeping the country isn't going away. Brees will have to show that he has his teammates' backs every step of the way, and if he succeeds, he just might bring the locker room closer than it had been before. How he and the Saints navigate the turmoil could very well determine the course of their season.

Otherwise, this is, from top to bottom, one of the most complete teams in football, and it should be in the Super Bowl picture once again. The one glaring need the Saints did have—a receiver to pair with Michael Thomas—they fixed by signing Emmanuel Sanders. What does Sanders bring to the offense that it didn't already have? In a word: optionality. New Orleans has been far too dependent on Thomas. His 185 targets last season were one-third of the team's total and 23 shy of Rob Moore's record of 208, set back in 1997. Granted, it's hard to find much fault with the frequency, given that Thomas caught just about every pass thrown his way. His 80.5% catch rate led the NFL and his 149 catches broke the single-season record. In the Saints' past three playoff losses, however, they weren't able to feed him the ball early and often, and the offense sputtered.

Sanders, who can line up outside, inside, and even in the backfield on occasion, gives the Saints the efficiency and versatility at receiver they've lacked since they traded Brandin Cooks to the Patriots after the 2016 season. Last season, Sanders ranked 22nd in DYAR (188) and 25th in DVOA (10.5%).

2020 Saints Schedule

Week	Opp.	Week	Opp.	Week	Opp.
1	TB	7	CAR	13	at ATL
2	at LV (Mon.)	8	at CHI	14	at PHI
3	GB	9	at TB	15	KC
4	at DET	10	SF	16	MIN (Fri./Xmas)
5	LAC (Mon.)	11	ATL	17	at CAR
6	BYE	12	at DEN		

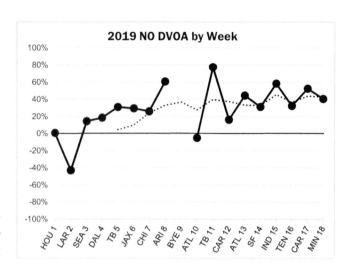

Though those numbers might not scream difference-maker, Sanders was just that for the 49ers. After seven weeks, they were 6-0 but ranked just 14th in pass DVOA at 19.3%. Over the final 10 weeks, San Francisco was the NFL's seventh-most efficient pass offense (26.6% DVOA).

Last we saw Sanders, he had broken through the Chiefs' double-coverage late in Super Bowl LIV. He was open for a potential go-ahead touchdown, but Jimmy Garoppolo's pass sailed about 5 yards beyond his reach. It was an especially cruel twist because weeks earlier San Francisco had executed a similar play in a similar situation. Against the Rams in Week 16, with the score tied at 31 and the 49ers facing third-and-16, Garoppolo and Sanders connected for a 46-yard gain that set up a game-winning field goal. A loss would have radically reshaped San Francisco's path through the playoffs. No first-round bye. No home-field advantage. It would have reshaped New Orleans' path, too, handing the Saints a first-round bye.

Sanders' performance in such situations was instrumental in the 49ers' transformation from a below-average passing offense on late downs (-13.0% DVOA through seven weeks) to an above-average one (34.4% DVOA over the final 10 weeks). His 32.8% DVOA on third and fourth downs ranked 12th among all receivers (minimum 10 catches). That late-down reliability could be the key to the Saints avoiding another postseason disappointment. Study their offense in their last three playoff losses and a pattern emerges: ineffectiveness on third and fourth down. Brees completed about half of his passes, averaged about 4 yards per attempt, and threw one touchdown and one interception. Thomas was a non-factor on third downs in those three games, catching one of three targets for 19 yards.

The rest of the offense hasn't changed much. First-round draft pick Cesar Ruiz replaces Larry Warford at right guard, though New Orleans could put him at center and kick Erik McCoy over to guard. Receiver-turned-running back Ty Montgomery joins a backfield that features Alvin Kamara, who said he played "on one leg" much of last season, and Latavius Murray. Third-round draft pick Adam Trautman, arguably this year's top tight end prospect, provides depth behind Jared Cook.

Brees is still Brees. Despite missing five games last season because of a thumb injury, he was as sharp as ever. At 40 years old, he led the league in DVOA for the first time in his 19-year career. His average depth of target (aDOT) and completion percentage over expectation (CPOE)—statistics that can sometimes foreshadow a decline—have been relatively

stable. He did experience a drop in aDOT last season, from 7.6 yards to 6.7, but it wasn't out of the ordinary for Brees. His aDOT in 2017 was 6.7. As for CPOE, he led the league last season (8.5%) by our CPOE formula. He also led the league in 2017 and 2018.

If Brees were to miss time again, the Saints can make do, even after losing Teddy Bridgewater to the Panthers in free agency. Former Buccaneers starter Jameis Winston and jack-of-all-trades Taysom Hill are capable fill-ins. Winston probably would get the first crack at starting; he already has completed more passes to Saints players (10) than Hill (seven).

Given New Orleans' talent, depth, and continuity on offense, a fourth consecutive top-five finish in DVOA seems like a safe bet, and one backed by our projections. If the defense is merely competent, the road back to the playoffs should be a smooth one. That is not the standard, however. The standard is the Super Bowl, and a first-round bye and homefield advantage certainly would make it easier to get there.

Like on offense, there are a lot of familiar faces on defense. Even the new guy, Malcolm Jenkins, is a familiar face. He played in New Orleans from 2009 to 2013 and was a two-time defensive captain during that stint. He replaces former second-round draft pick Vonn Bell. Though he's seven years older, he should be an upgrade in pass coverage. In each of the past four seasons, he bested Bell in success rate and yards per pass, and last season it wasn't particularly close. The Saints won't ask him to play centerfield, though. That's not his strength. Instead, they'll take advantage of his versatility and have him play inside and match up against slot receivers, tight ends, and running backs. And then there are the things we can't chart, such as the pre-snap guidance he gives his teammates. They could use the direction. They suffered more than an occasional lapse last season, allowing 25 pass plays of 30 or more yards, tied for fifth-most. "We're a lot more successful when you've got guys—not just me—but when you've got a cast of guys that can really manipulate the defense based on what they see, based on what they study, and put teammates in the right position to make plays," he said during a March press conference.

The defense finished last season just outside the top 10 in DVOA, but there's no reason to think that it won't be at least as good again this fall, outside of the Football Outsiders axiom that projecting defensive performance is a bit of a crapshoot. It's not as if the Saints' success was a fluke. They weren't an outlier in terms of health (they suffered 35.1 adjusted games lost, which ranked 17th) or takeaways (they forced a turnover on 12.7% of drives, which ranked 13th). They might not rack up 51 sacks again (third; about a quarter of them were of the non-pressure variety), but that's unlikely to be their downfall given the depth and playmaking ability they possess at every level.

It's almost unfair. Up front, New Orleans has three starting-caliber edge rushers (Cameron Jordan, Marcus Davenport, and Trey Hendrickson) and three starting-caliber defensive tackles (Sheldon Rankins, David Onyemata, and Malcom Brown). There are some question marks at linebacker, where Kiko Alonso and Alex Anzalone are coming off injuries, but no one's overlooking a group that includes All-Pro Demario Davis. Besides, the Saints rarely will be in their "base" defense (16.4% of the time last season, the fourth-lowest rate). And the secondary? It might be the deepest unit in the NFL. Two-time Pro Bowler Marshon Lattimore and late-season pickup Janoris Jenkins will man the outside, while P.J. Williams, Patrick Robinson *and* C.J. Gardner-Johnson will compete for snaps at nickelback.

All the pieces are in place, but they won't be for long. Brees is playing season-to-season, and if and when he retires, he already has a broadcasting gig lined up. But he's not the only major contributor the Saints stand to lose after this season. Demario Davis, Jared Cook, and Sheldon Rankins can become free agents. So can Marcus Williams, Alvin Kamara, and Trey Hendrickson, members of the 2017 draft class that helped New Orleans extend its Super Bowl window. The team's two first-rounders from that class, Lattimore and Ryan Ramczyk, are under contract for one more season but are in line for significant raises. The Saints literally can't afford to keep their core together.

What a run it has been. The Saints have won 146 games since Brees and Payton arrived in 2006, fourth-most in the NFL during that span. Only one of those 146, however, has been a Super Bowl, and that was more than a decade ago. It's incredible to think that after all they've accomplished over the past 14 seasons, they still have much to prove.

Thomas Bassinger

2019 Saints Stats by Week

Wk	vs.	W-L	PF	PA	YDF	YDA	TO	Total	Off	Def	ST
1	HOU	W	30	28	510	414	0	1%	26%	33%	7%
2	at LAR	L	9	27	244	380	0	-43%	-36%	13%	6%
3	at SEA	W	33	27	265	514	0	15%	6%	9%	17%
4	DAL	W	12	10	266	257	+2	19%	-22%	-36%	4%
5	TB	W	31	24	457	252	-1	31%	41%	2%	-8%
6	at JAX	W	13	6	326	226	+1	29%	-4%	-28%	5%
7	at CHI	W	36	25	424	252	+2	26%	43%	-12%	-28%
8	ARI	W	31	9	510	237	-1	61%	34%	-37%	-11%
9	BYE										
10	ATL	L	9	26	310	317	+1	-5%	-22%	-11%	6%
11	at TB	W	34	17	328	334	+4	78%	48%	-22%	8%
12	CAR	W	34	31	418	351	0	16%	25%	13%	4%
13	at ATL	W	26	18	279	348	+3	44%	13%	-26%	5%
14	SF	L	46	48	465	516	0	31%	43%	30%	18%
15	IND	W	34	7	424	205	0	58%	46%	-9%	4%
16	at TEN	W	38	28	377	397	+1	33%	38%	19%	14%
17	at CAR	W	42	10	379	329	+3	53%	37%	-10%	6%
18	MIN	L	20	26	324	362	-1	41%	24%	-11%	6%

Trends and Splits

	Offense	Rank	Defense	Rank
Total DVOA	21.4%	4	-4.3%	11
Unadjusted VOA	22.3%	4	-5.3%	9
Weighted Trend	27.8%	2	-6.7%	11
Variance	7.5%	19	5.0%	9
Average Opponent	0.3%	19	0.2%	14
Passing	43.8%	3	1.7%	13
Rushing	0.1%	10	-14.3%	5
First Down	30.6%	1	-6.0%	9
Second Down	19.1%	4	5.7%	23
Third Down	5.8%	13	-14.9%	7
First Half	14.4%	5	-8.9%	9
Second Half	28.9%	3	-0.3%	13
Red Zone	26.7%	6	-10.5%	10
Late and Close	26.6%	3	-14.4%	7

Five-Year Performance

Year	W-L	Pyth W	Est W	PF	PA	TO	Total	Rk	Off	Rk	Def	Rk	ST	Rk	Off AGL	Rk	Def AGL	Rk	Off Age	Rk	Def Age	Rk	ST Age	Rk
2015	7-9	6.4	5.2	408	476	+2	-18.7%	28	10.5%	7	26.1%	32	-3.2%	26	19.0	3	35.6	19	28.2	4	26.5	20	26.7	4
2016	7-9	8.3	8.6	469	454	-3	-1.9%	21	15.4%	6	14.6%	31	-2.6%	27	22.5	5	59.0	25	28.3	2	26.8	11	27.0	4
2017	11-5	11.1	13.4	448	326	+7	30.7%	1	21.6%	2	-7.9%	8	1.2%	15	32.6	16	66.4	29	27.5	6	24.9	31	25.7	21
2018	13-3	11.5	11.1	504	353	+9	20.5%	4	15.9%	4	-2.9%	11	1.7%	9	28.0	9	22.4	8	28.2	3	25.3	29	26.6	7
2019	13-3	10.9	12.8	458	341	+15	29.3%	4	21.4%	4	-4.3%	11	3.6%	3	23.2	8	35.1	18	27.5	5	25.8	21	26.5	6

2019 Performance Based on Most Common Personnel Groups

NO Offense					NO Offense vs. Opponents					NO Defense					NO Defense vs. Opponents			
Pers	Freq	Yds	DVOA	Run%	Pers	Freq	Yds	DVOA	Run%	Pers	Freq	Yds	DVOA		Pers	Freq	Yds	DVOA
11	50%	6.1	24.6%	26%	Base	33%	6.4	31.8%	55%	Base	16%	5.1	-34.6%		11	68%	5.8	8.8%
12	15%	7.0	54.5%	32%	Nickel	56%	6.2	26.9%	30%	Nickel	64%	5.6	2.7%		12	13%	5.6	-3.7%
21	15%	6.1	16.6%	44%	Dime+	9%	5.2	3.3%	12%	Dime+	19%	5.6	4.9%		21	6%	3.6	-82.3%
621	4%	4.4	6.6%	88%	Goal Line	1%	0.9	-27.5%	64%	Goal Line	1%	1.8	-37.5%		10	6%	4.9	-24.6%
612	4%	6.9	27.9%	71%	Big	1%	3.4	8.0%	75%						22	2%	4.4	-16.9%
611	4%	5.7	15.6%	63%														

Strategic Tendencies

Run/Pass		Rk	Formation		Rk	Pass Rush		Rk	Secondary		Rk	Strategy		Rk
Runs, first half	33%	26	Form: Single Back	75%	27	Rush 3	11.6%	10	4 DB	16%	29	Play Action	20%	28
Runs, first down	48%	17	Form: Empty Back	8%	18	Rush 4	58.8%	24	5 DB	64%	11	Offensive Motion	35%	20
Runs, second-long	22%	24	Form: Multi Back	17%	8	Rush 5	22.8%	11	6+ DB	19%	14	Avg Box (Off)	6.64	9
Runs, power sit.	62%	5	Pers: 3+ WR	53%	27	Rush 6+	6.8%	11	Man Coverage	31%	20	Avg Box (Def)	6.48	20
Runs, behind 2H	27%	20	Pers: 2+ TE/6+ OL	33%	10	Edge Rusher Sacks	60.0%	13	CB by Sides	67%	24	Offensive Pace	31.63	23
Pass, ahead 2H	51%	10	Pers: 6+ OL	15%	3	Interior DL Sacks	18.0%	21	S/CB Cover Ratio	27%	12	Defensive Pace	29.91	6
Run-Pass Options	2%	30	Shotgun/Pistol	54%	25	Second Level Sacks	22.0%	13	DB Blitz	14%	8	Go for it on 4th	1.56	14

Our sparkling projection for 2020 comes despite the regression that the Saints will likely see in turnover margin. They had the league's best rate of recovering fumbles at 70%. Of course, recovery rate matters less when you barely fumble the ball in the first place: New Orleans had only six fumbles on offense, recovering five. ◈ The Saints threw 33% of their time to the No. 1 receiver (Michael Thomas), the highest rate in the league, but 10% of the time to the No. 2 receiver (Ted Ginn), the lowest rate in the league. ◈ The Saints led the league with 41.3% DVOA when running on second-and-long; their 6.7 yards per carry ranked second behind Baltimore. ◈ Given Sean Payton's ability to manipulate defenses, it's a bit surprising that Saints running backs ran against heavy boxes (eight or more) on 43% of runs, second in the league behind Tennessee. But the Saints were actually better in DVOA on these runs, 5.8% DVOA compared to -7.0% DVOA on other running back carries. ◈ Payton has been one of the most aggressive coaches on fourth down in NFL history, but it's interesting to see that he has stayed in place while the league has moved forward. Payton's Aggressiveness Index number has stayed around 1.5, but that has meant a middle-of-the-pack ranking for the last couple years as the league as a whole gets more aggressive on fourth downs. ◈ The New Orleans defense was third with just 94 broken tackles, trailing only New England and Minnesota. ◈ New Orleans was tied with Minnesota for the fewest penalty yards earned by opponents (713). The Saints themselves were one of the league's most penalized teams, fifth with 147 flags and seventh with 1,023 yards.

Passing

Player	DYAR	DVOA	Plays	NtYds	Avg	YAC	C%	TD	Int
D.Brees	1316	39.8%	385	2882	7.5	5.3	75.5%	27	4
T.Bridgewater*	340	15.3%	208	1283	6.2	5.6	68.2%	9	2
T.Hill	6	4.2%	7	46	6.6	4.0	50.0%	0	0
J.Winston	57	-9.8%	674	4769	7.1	4.9	61.3%	33	30

Rushing

Player	DYAR	DVOA	Plays	Yds	Avg	TD	Fum	Suc
A.Kamara	81	3.1%	171	802	4.7	5	3	52%
L.Murray	125	10.7%	146	637	4.4	5	0	60%
T.Hill	7	-7.5%	27	156	5.8	1	0	-
T.Bridgewater*	-19	-32.7%	15	44	2.9	0	0	-
D.Washington	15	39.8%	8	60	7.5	0	0	63%
Z.Line*	3	-3.1%	7	20	2.9	0	0	71%
J.Winston	53	12.6%	41	264	6.4	1	0	-

Receiving

Player	DYAR	DVOA	Plays	Ctch	Yds	Y/C	YAC	TD	C%
M.Thomas	538	23.9%	185	149	1727	11.6	3.9	9	81%
T.Ginn*	22	-7.7%	56	30	421	14.0	1.6	2	54%
T.Smith	135	53.6%	25	18	234	13.0	6.4	5	72%
T.Hill	140	65.5%	22	19	234	12.3	7.8	6	86%
D.Harris	-14	-47.1%	6	6	24	4.0	6.2	0	100%
E.Sanders	188	10.5%	97	66	869	13.2	3.6	5	68%
J.Cook	205	37.7%	65	43	705	16.4	5.8	9	66%
J.Hill	-6	-9.8%	35	25	226	9.0	6.4	3	71%
A.Kamara	83	1.6%	97	81	533	6.6	6.9	1	84%
L.Murray	19	-5.6%	43	34	235	6.9	8.4	1	79%
Z.Line*	-16	-50.9%	10	6	36	6.0	7.5	0	60%

Offensive Line

Player	Pos	Age	GS	Snaps	Pen	Sk	Pass	Run	Player	Pos	Age	GS	Snaps	Pen	Sk	Pass	Run
Erik McCoy	C	23	16/16	1077	8	0.0	8	7	Andrus Peat	LG	27	10/10	586	3	2.5	14	3
Ryan Ramczyk	RT	26	16/16	1077	6	2.5	13	5	Nick Easton	LG	28	10/6	415	3	0.0	3	3
Larry Warford*	RG	29	15/15	989	6	2.0	13	13	Will Clapp	RG/C	25	14/3	313	3	2.0	6	1
Terron Armstead	LT	29	15/15	951	6	0.0	17	3	James Hurst	LT	29	16/2	196	0	1.0	2	5

Year	Yards	ALY	Rank	Power	Rank	Stuff	Rank	2nd Lev	Rank	Open Field	Rank	Sacks	ASR	Rank	Press	Rank	F-Start	Cont.
2017	5.11	4.93	2	69%	7	15%	1	1.30	3	1.37	1	20	4.0%	2	20.9%	1	6	23
2018	4.60	5.19	2	70%	9	14%	1	1.28	14	0.77	21	20	4.4%	3	23.9%	3	11	24
2019	4.56	4.92	1	67%	13	16%	4	1.27	11	0.80	15	25	4.7%	3	23.7%	1	14	33
2019 ALY by direction:			Left End 4.40 (11)			Left Tackle: 4.36 (14)			Mid/Guard: 5.25 (1)			Right Tackle: 4.85 (7)			Right End: 4.28 (16)		

The Saints ranked third in adjusted sack rate, the fifth straight season they've ranked in the top seven. Since 2006, the beginning of the Drew Brees-Sean Payton era, they've never ranked lower than 12th. Brees led the league in sack rate (3.1%) for the third time in his career. He posted his best rate, however, in 2008 (2.0%). ⚫ After Ronnie Stanley and Orlando Brown of the Ravens, Terron Armstead and Ryan Ramczyk can make the argument that they're the best tackle tandem in football. Together, they allowed just 2.5 sacks because of blown blocks, tied with Stanley and Brown for the lowest total in the NFL (minimum 600 snaps each). ⚫ Ramczyk had the stronger season. He averaged 59.8 snaps per blown block, which ranked ninth among all tackles. ⚫ Armstead shed the injury-prone label, playing in 15 games for the first time in his seven seasons. The one game he missed — the Thanksgiving night game against the Falcons — was a road game in a short week. From 2016 to 2018, he missed 21 games. Armstead was bound to regress after allowing only one blown block in 2018, but he took a bigger step back than expected. He averaged 47.6 snaps per blown block, which ranked 15th among left tackles and 27th among all tackles. ⚫ Left guard Andrus Peat signed a multi-year deal that could keep him in a Saints uniform through 2024. His salary cap hit this season is the 16th-highest among left guards, but in 2021 it will be the second-highest. ⚫ Interior lineman Cesar Ruiz won plaudits from draftniks for his all-around athletic skill set, which fits either zone or power blocking. After selecting the Michigan alum in the first round, New Orleans released right guard Larry Warford, who had been invited to the Pro Bowl in each of his three seasons with the Saints. Ruiz might get a look at center but without a normal offseason of work is probably better suited to play at right guard for now. It's not as if New Orleans is hurting at center. As a rookie, Erik McCoy played in all 16 games and allowed the fewest blown blocks on the team.

Defensive Front

Defensive Line	Age	Pos	G	Snaps	Plays	TmPct	Rk	Stop	Dfts	BTkl	Runs	St%	Rk	RuYd	Rk	Sack	Hit	Hur	Dsrpt
David Onyemata	28	DT	15	577	33	4.5%	52	26	10	5	27	78%	34	2.4	54	3.0	7	12	0
Malcom Brown	26	DT	16	503	33	4.2%	52	24	7	4	27	74%	53	3.1	88	2.0	2	7	1
Shy Tuttle	25	DT	16	347	22	2.8%	--	18	6	1	16	75%	--	1.9	--	2.0	2	8	3
Sheldon Rankins	26	DT	10	329	10	2.0%	96	8	2	0	6	83%	19	2.8	79	2.0	3	13	0
Margus Hunt	33	DT	16	456	17	2.1%	93	10	1	5	15	60%	87	3.2	91	0.0	0	6	0

Edge Rushers	Age	Pos	G	Snaps	Plays	TmPct	Rk	Stop	Dfts	BTkl	Runs	St%	Rk	RuYd	Rk	Sack	Hit	Hur	Dsrpt
Cameron Jordan	31	DE	16	894	56	7.1%	14	43	22	6	33	64%	74	2.8	57	15.5	8	67	4
Marcus Davenport	24	DE	13	547	31	4.8%	59	25	14	1	21	81%	19	3.6	84	6.0	10	32	1
Trey Hendrickson	26	DE	13	411	18	2.8%	89	16	7	2	10	90%	5	0.9	5	4.5	6	27	0
Mario Edwards	26	DE	14	299	8	1.2%	--	6	3	0	5	60%	--	4.0	--	3.0	0	9	0

Linebackers	Age	Pos	G	Snaps	Plays	TmPct	Rk	Stop	Dfts	BTkl	Runs	St%	Rk	RuYd	Rk	Sack	Hit	Hur	Tgts	Suc%	Rk	AdjYd	Rk	PD	Int
Demario Davis	31	OLB	16	1006	122	15.5%	16	75	23	7	57	65%	23	4.1	52	4.0	6	20	46	67%	3	3.4	2	12	1
A.J. Klein*	29	OLB	15	766	69	9.4%	54	41	12	12	36	69%	14	3.9	39	2.5	2	4	36	53%	31	8.1	56	2	1
Kiko Alonso	30	MLB	13	290	32	5.0%	--	20	5	4	18	78%	--	2.7	--	0.0	2	8	13	46%	--	5.6	--	1	0
Craig Robertson	32	OLB	15	193	23	3.1%	--	11	4	3	8	63%	--	1.3	--	1.0	1	2	13	31%	--	7.5	--	1	1

Year	Yards	ALY	Rank	Power	Rank	Stuff	Rank	2nd Level	Rank	Open Field	Rank	Sacks	ASR	Rank	Press	Rank
2017	4.11	4.10	17	66%	21	21%	13	1.08	11	0.80	22	42	7.8%	6	32.3%	8
2018	3.22	3.61	2	57%	3	24%	6	0.87	1	0.40	3	49	8.7%	4	31.2%	13
2019	3.65	3.94	5	58%	5	21%	8	0.95	3	0.51	4	51	7.7%	9	36.2%	2

2019 ALY by direction:	Left End: 4.64 (30)	Left Tackle: 3.7 (8)	Mid/Guard: 3.68 (5)	Right Tackle: 4.02 (12)	Right End: 5.53 (28)

From 1988 through 1992, the Saints had an Ironhead. Since 2011, they've had an iron man. Cameron Jordan is one of three players (not counting long snappers) to play in every game in each of the past nine seasons. The others are quarterback Philip Rivers and cornerback Brandon Carr. ✎ Paced by Jordan's league-leading 67 quarterback hurries, New Orleans generated pressure on 36.2% of dropbacks. Only New England (37.1%) generated pressure at a higher rate. Jordan's 15.5 sacks were a career high and ranked third in the NFL. ✎ After Alex Okafor became a free agent, 2018 first-round draft pick Marcus Davenport assumed a starting role. He came on strong late, recording three sacks and two forced fumbles in Weeks 12 and 13. The next week he suffered a season-ending Lisfranc injury. Defensive line coach Ryan Nielsen said in June that Davenport has been "busting his butt" and "really putting the work in to come back in the best shape that he's ever been in." That sounds as if he'll be questionable come Week 1. Then again, isn't everyone? If Davenport isn't at full strength, 2017 third-round draft pick Trey Hendrickson is a more than viable option. ✎ Sheldon Rankins was in the midst of a breakout season in 2018 when he ruptured his Achilles during the playoffs. The injury cost him the first five games of last season, and when he returned he wasn't the quite the same pass-rusher. He recorded a sack or hit once every 66 snaps; the season before, he did so once every 43 snaps. ✎ David Onyemata is another recent mid-round draft pick that has paid major dividends. He filled in while Rankins was out, and his performance earned him a multi-year contract worth up to $27 million. Not bad for a guy who hadn't even seen a football game until 2011, when he left Nigeria for Winnipeg, Canada. ✎ Since joining the Saints in 2018, Demario Davis has 22 tackles for loss, second on the team after Jordan. Pass coverage is where he really shined last season. He broke up 12 passes, tied with Eric Kendricks and Luke Kuechly for most in the NFL among linebackers.

Defensive Secondary

Secondary	Age	Pos	G	Snaps	Plays	TmPct	Rk	Stop	Dfts	BTkl	Runs	St%	Rk	RuYd	Rk	Tgts	Tgt%	Rk	Dist	Suc%	Rk	AdjYd	Rk	PD	Int
Marcus Williams	24	FS	15	971	66	8.9%	44	28	12	10	25	36%	49	10.2	64	22	5.1%	65	11.5	55%	29	8.4	51	13	4
Eli Apple*	25	CB	15	954	62	8.4%	35	16	4	4	12	25%	72	8.3	66	64	15.2%	77	12.1	53%	38	8.6	61	4	0
Vonn Bell*	26	SS	13	893	91	14.2%	14	38	17	11	37	59%	4	4.9	13	31	7.9%	37	11.9	45%	58	9.0	55	5	1
Marshon Lattimore	24	CB	14	836	71	10.3%	23	30	13	6	13	54%	28	7.0	54	82	22.2%	24	12.4	55%	30	7.4	40	14	1
P.J. Williams	27	CB	14	815	45	6.5%	75	23	9	8	14	79%	4	3.3	10	54	15.0%	79	10.9	50%	55	8.0	52	4	1
Chauncey Gardner-Johnson	23	SS	16	552	54	6.9%	55	32	16	5	19	68%	2	2.7	1	30	12.3%	11	9.1	63%	10	6.5	24	8	1
Malcolm Jenkins	33	SS	16	1035	86	11.4%	16	42	17	12	36	50%	15	7.4	44	40	8.9%	24	9.8	55%	25	7.1	30	8	0
Janoris Jenkins	32	CB	15	998	77	9.5%	24	33	13	13	17	65%	16	3.8	13	67	15.9%	72	13.4	52%	43	7.2	38	16	5
D.J. Swearinger	29	SS	9	497	52	12.0%	57	17	4	11	30	43%	33	6.0	28	20	9.4%	19	11.3	30%	70	10.1	66	3	0

Year	Pass D Rank	vs. #1 WR	Rk	vs. #2 WR	Rk	vs. Other WR	Rk	WR Wide	Rk	WR Slot	Rk	vs. TE	Rk	vs. RB	Rk
2017	5	-19.1%	6	0.6%	18	-21.8%	5	-31.6%	2	7.9%	16	-17.0%	6	-5.5%	12
2018	22	17.7%	30	28.4%	31	-16.4%	6	13.5%	27	5.6%	20	-22.2%	4	19.8%	29
2019	13	-6.3%	11	-4.6%	11	10.1%	22	-9.7%	14	9.9%	20	-7.8%	8	-3.2%	16

We've seen some wild swings in the Saints' pass defense DVOA in recent seasons. They ranked 30th in 2016, fifth in 2017, 22nd in 2018, and 13th in 2019. ✎ Last season's rebound coincided with that of Marshon Lattimore. He struggled mightily in 2018, ranking 72nd out of 79 cornerbacks in success rate and 77th in yards per pass allowed. Last year, that improved to 30th and 40th, respectively. He drew some exceptionally tough assignments, too, facing DeAndre Hopkins, Amari Cooper, Mike Evans (twice), and Julio Jones (also twice). ✎ New Orleans will have a new Week 1 starter opposite Lattimore: Janoris Jenkins. The Saints claimed him late last season after the Giants released him following an exchange on Twitter in which he called a fan a "retard." He was scheduled to earn $11.25 million this season, but New Orleans reworked his contract to lower his cap hit to $4.05 million. ✎ Jenkins replaces Eli Apple, another Giants castoff. His 12 pass interference penalties over the past two seasons led the league. ✎ When the NFL announced a two-game suspension of nickelback P.J. Williams in mid-October, New Orleans tapped fourth-round rookie C.J. Gardner-Johnson, not veteran Patrick Robinson. He didn't disappoint. He was a factor down the field and behind the line of scrimmage. No other rookie recorded at least six tackles for loss and eight passes defensed, putting Gardner-Johnson in select company with Darius Leonard (2018), Kwon Alexander (2015), C.J. Mosley (2014), and Tyrann Mathieu (2013). ✎ The signing of Malcolm Jenkins marks the second straight offseason in which the Saints have reacquired a defensive back they once drafted in the first round (they signed Robinson in 2018). Who's next? Kenny Vaccaro? Alex Molden?

Special Teams

Year	DVOA	Rank	FG/XP	Rank	Net Kick	Rank	Kick Ret	Rank	Net Punt	Rank	Punt Ret	Rank	Hidden	Rank
2017	1.2%	15	-0.9	17	-0.3	20	5.6	5	6.5	7	-5.0	28	10.3	4
2018	1.7%	9	6.8	6	-0.9	19	-0.2	13	5.3	9	-2.4	19	23.5	1
2019	3.6%	3	8.4	4	-7.0	31	3.1	9	4.9	10	9.0	2	6.8	5

The Saints finished third in special teams DVOA, their best finish since 2004. 🏈 One of the forces behind New Orleans' improvement was undrafted free agent-turned-All-Pro Deonte Harris, who led the NFL in combined return yardage (982). One more kick return and he likely would have become the first Saints player since Darren Sproles to amass 1,000 return yards. 🏈 Wil Lutz produced the most field goal/extra point value of any New Orleans kicker since John Carney in 2002. He has been perfect on field goals inside 40 yards in each of the past two seasons (31-of-31). Lutz was average in gross kickoff value, but the Saints kickoff coverage unit allowed more value in returns than any other team, leading to their poor finish in net kickoff value. 🏈 Thomas Morstead is entering his 12th season with the Saints. Sam Koch is the only punter who has been with his original team longer (he is entering his 15th season with the Ravens). Morstead finished last season 10th in net punting value and seventh in gross punting value. He has finished in the top eight in gross punting value for four straight seasons. 🏈 New Orleans has not had a punt blocked since 2011, the longest active streak in the NFL. 🏈 Saints opponents' punts traveled an average of 43.7 yards, the third-lowest average in the league. As if they needed the help.

New York Giants

2019 Record: 4-12	Total DVOA: -17.4% (27th)	2020 Mean Projection: 7.0 wins	On the Clock (0-4): 17%
Pythagorean Wins: 5.3 (27th)	Offense: -7.3% (23rd)	Postseason Odds: 28.8%	Mediocrity (5-7): 42%
Snap-Weighted Age: 26.2 (23rd)	Defense: 10.4% (27th)	Super Bowl Odds: 2.0%	Playoff Contender (8-10): 32%
Average Opponent: -1.1% (19th)	Special Teams: 0.3% (17th)	Proj. Avg. Opponent: 0.5% (9th)	Super Bowl Contender (11+): 9%

2019: "I tried to make ramen in the coffee pot and I broke everything." —Andy Dwyer

2020: "Never half-ass two things. Whole-ass one thing." —Ron Swanson

The Dave Gettleman era for the New York Giants has been based around the idea a team could both rebuild and win at the same time. After two years of that strategy, the Giants found themselves having done a poor job rebuilding and an even worse job winning.

During an interview after the regular season, Gettleman admitted trying to straddle the line between winning and rebuilding was "a miscalculation." But the mea culpa came with few other details. It was an admission of guilt without stating anything specifically done wrong. It's not as if every move the Giants have made has been a complete failure, but few of those moves ever fit together into one coherent plan to build a long-term successful football team.

Gettleman has shown an ability to bring in good players, but one of his biggest problems is how those players were valued and acquired. It's not breaking new ground to point out faults in the selection of Saquon Barkley with the second overall pick in 2018; or the trade of Odell Beckham for what turned into Jabrill Peppers, Dexter Lawrence, and Oshane Ximines; or the Nate Solder contract; or the selection of Daniel Jones sixth overall; or the Alec Ogletree trade; or the signing of Jonathan Stewart; or the short-lived Patrick Omameh experiment; or that a team short on talent never once traded back in the draft to acquire more picks. But it doesn't help that moves like these have continued to pile up without any signs of slowing down, even after realizing the "miscalculation." We're only nine months removed from a 2-6 team trading its third-round pick for a half-year of Leonard Williams and three months removed from doubling down on that trade with a $16.1-million franchise tag.

Part of the Gettleman conundrum is that the trade technically worked. The Giants' run defense was sixth in DVOA (-18.3%) over the second half of the season after Williams was added to the roster. But they had already been good enough there over the first half of the season without him (-10.6% DVOA, 16th) and the improvement in that area did little to make the whole team better.

The Giants now enter the 2020 season with a roster still made up of many of the players acquired during the rebuild-and-win phase and the organization has potentially backed itself into a similar corner with its front office and coaching staff dynamic.

After two seasons and nine wins, Pat Shurmur was fired as the team's head coach, but Gettleman was retained as general manager. Though he was kept in place, Gettleman wasn't allowed off the hook completely. In a postseason press conference, owner John Mara stated Gettleman "does know the batting average has got to increase going forward. We need to win more games, and Dave knows that."

That, too, is part of the problem. For as easy as Gettleman has been as a target with both his words and actions—he's basically a walking meme generator between his analytics typing, "generational talent," and "computer folk"—the ownership has been just as culpable for the current rut that has seen the team rank 20th or worse in DVOA three times over the past five seasons, including picks within the top six in each of the past three drafts.

Over the past few seasons, Giants ownership has tried hard to project the illusion of stability while creating more instability in the process. This is a team that held on to Tom Coughlin for a year or two too long and refused to do anything that would potentially undermine a ride off into the sunset for Eli Manning before his contract expired after the 2019 season, despite the aging quarterback ranking 20th or worse in DVOA and DYAR in each season since 2016. After making the effort to keep the 38-year-old around in 2019 for $23 million, Manning only got four starts. He was benched for Daniel Jones by Week 3 after two losses but got two late-season starts, including a farewell home win in Week 15 against the Miami Dolphins. That at least gave the Giants and Manning the last chapter both wanted in the midst of another lost season.

So after a two-year effort that all the major players admitted was poorly planned and executed, ownership allowed that GM to be a significant voice in the room for the hiring process of a new head coach. As a result, the Giants will enter the 2020 season with a general manager on a "win-now" mandate and a first-year head coach set to take over a roster that is again projected to finish as a bottom-five team in the league. It's a marriage set up with conflicting motivations for the sake of presenting some form of stability.

The coaching search eventually landed on New England Patriots special teams coordinator and wide receivers coach Joe Judge. Judge, like many first-time head coaches, brings a lot of unknown, and his introduction was a little shaky at first. His intense introductory press conference where he referenced a team that would fit the blue-collar nature of the area (that area

2020 Giants Schedule

Week	Opp.	Week	Opp.	Week	Opp.
1	PIT (Mon.)	7	at PHI (Thu.)	13	at SEA
2	at CHI	8	TB (Mon.)	14	ARI
3	SF	9	at WAS	15	CLE
4	at LAR	10	PHI	16	at BAL
5	at DAL	11	BYE	17	DAL
6	WAS	12	at CIN		

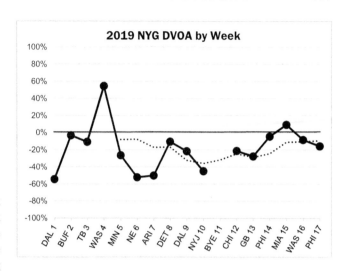

2019 NYG DVOA by Week

... New York City) and spouted off football guy clichés went well for some and felt forced for others. His insistence on not mentioning any player by name for the first three months he had the job also felt like it veered dangerously close to the long-beaten path of former Bill Belichick assistants doing their best Belichick impressions once they got a head job of their own.

Still, there are things to like about Judge as a head coaching candidate. The hiring of a special teams coordinator piggy-backs on the success of John Harbaugh. It's the one coaching position outside of head coach that deals with players on both sides of the ball and has the added responsibility of having to consistently adjust to available personnel on a given week. It should be seen as just as much of a stepping stone to a head coaching position as the offensive or defensive coordinator role. Judge, for his part, was a successful special teams coordinator. Over his five seasons in charge of New England's special teams, the Patriots never ranked lower than 16th in DVOA, with three top-eight finishes and two in the top five. He also got the rub from Belichick, who trusted him with added duties as the wide receivers coach on top of his coordinator role in 2019.

Judge takes over a team with a young quarterback he did not have a hand in selecting, yet nothing will shape the seasons of both the general manager and head coach more than the development of Daniel Jones in Year 2. Jones had a stellar first start in Week 3 against the Tampa Bay Buccaneers, which featured a number of impressive throws and a come-from-behind rushing touchdown to take the lead with 1:21 remaining. But for the remainder of the season, Jones played very much like an overmatched rookie. He finished the year 31st in DYAR and 30th in DVOA. Few rookies are ever actually good during their first pro seasons, but there are concerns for a quarterback many already believed to be overdrafted with the sixth overall pick last season.

Most will point out the fumbling issue as the biggest thing Jones needs to correct in his second season—he fumbled a league-leading 18 times as a rookie—but that stems from a larger issue with pocket presence. Dating back to his time at Duke, Jones showed a habit of locking on to his first read often and becoming oblivious to pressure around him. Occasionally that led to miraculous completions with a defender on top of him, which can describe more than a few throws against the Buccaneers, but more often it led to sacks and fumbles when the quarterback was not prepared to get hit. Combine Jones's lack of awareness with a leaky offensive line—a left tackle,

specifically—and the potential for disaster was there.

As an extension of that issue, the longer Jones stayed in the pocket, the worse the passing game performed. On 0-/1-step drops that allowed the ball to get the ball out quickly on a first read, Jones was one of the best quarterbacks in the league, with a league-high 7.4 yards per attempt. But on 3-step drops, Jones fell to 6.3 yards per attempt. On 5-step drops, where deeper passes typically occur, Jones had a league-worst 5.5 yards per attempt (Table 1).

Table 1. Daniel Jones by Dropback Type, 2019

Dropback	YPA	TD Rate	INT Rate	Sack Rate
0/1 steps	7.4	6.2%	1.5%	4.4%
3 steps	6.3	5.3%	2.9%	10.4%
5 steps	5.5	1.9%	5.7%	7.0%

A study by John Shirley of Sports Info Solutions showed quarterbacks do tend to improve on deeper drops with more experience. But there are still questions for Jones and the Giants, such as how much that will improve in Year 2 and if the improvement on deeper drops will be enough to offset what will likely be some decline in performance on those 0-/1-step drops.

All of this matters more because of the offense the Giants will install for 2020. Jason Garrett is now the offensive coordinator after his 10-year run as head coach of the Cowboys. Garrett started as the Cowboys' offensive coordinator in 2007 before he was bumped up to head coach in 2010, but he hasn't called plays since 2012 when he was stripped of those duties. Add that to how we just saw the Cowboys' offense improve dramatically last season when Kellen Moore took over and modernized the scheme and there's a lot to still be learned about what the 2020 version of offensive coordinator and playcaller Jason Garrett looks like.

What we do know is Garrett favors a vertical offense that is likely to ask Jones to take those deeper drops and throw down the field more often. Jones wasn't afraid of deep passes in 2019, a stark difference from the checkdown machine Eli Manning became over his final seasons, but he wasn't particularly successful at them, either. Only 28.8% of Jones's passes that traveled at least 20 yards down the field were completed, a rate that ranked 25th among 30 quarterbacks with at least 25 such attempts.

Jones showed a hyper-aggressiveness on these throws despite the coverage which, like his performance in the pocket, covered the entire spectrum of possible outcomes. Per Next Gen Stats, Jones threw into tight windows (a yard or fewer of separation) on 22.4% of his attempts, the third-highest rate among qualified quarterbacks. This led to a lot of low-percentage throws that weren't completed often but looked incredible when they worked. Despite Jones having a near-league-worst completion rate of his deep attempts, he had a 17.3% touchdown rate on those throws, which trailed only Jimmy Garoppolo and Patrick Mahomes.

Many teams around the league have figured out the best way to defeat tight windows is to avoid them almost entirely, as the league average rate of throws into tight windows has decreased each season since Next Gen started tracking in 2015. Teams have done this by either creating a scheme that emphasizes spacing or valuing skill position players who can consistently create separation. In cases like the Chiefs, it's both. The problem with the Giants is they don't appear set to embrace either of those philosophies. Garrett has never been a "scheme them open" type of offensive mind and the Giants' current receivers aren't going to be springing themselves free down the field often. Last season the Giants built their receiving corps around helping both Manning and Jones with yards after the catch rather than deep separation. That's still how the position is set up after the team declined to add any notable receivers to the group through the draft or free agency.

Fifth-round rookie Darius Slayton was a surprise breakout and the closest thing the Giants had to a deep threat last season, but much of his production came on spectacular plays in contested catch situations; his two deep touchdown receptions against the Lions come to mind. It's hard to project those types of plays continuing from year-to-year without an improvement in separation that could make some of those catches easier for both the passer and receiver.

The pairing of Sterling Shepard and Golden Tate overlaps in skill set as players who perform better from the slot, but neither did that particularly well in 2019. Tate had -6.5% DVOA from the slot and Shepard was just barely above average at 0.4%. 91% of Tate's targets came when he was lined up inside, as did 66% of Shepard's.

Shepard moved outside more when he was on the field with Tate (mostly unsuccessfully, with -28.0% DVOA on wide targets) but the problem was that duo wasn't on the field together as often as the Giants would have hoped. Between Tate's suspensions and various injuries to Shepard, Evan Engram, and Saquon Barkley, the Giants' offense was never at full strength. They suffered 49.0 adjusted games lost on that side of the ball, more than 20 other teams, and played just one game with Tate, Shepard, and Engram on the field together—a Week 5 28-10 home loss to the Minnesota Vikings. Of course, Barkley missed that game and the Giants got a combined 14 carries for 49 yards between Jon Hilliman, Wayne Gallman, and Eli Penny.

Barkley was banged up for part of the year and that sapped some of the explosiveness he showed during his rookie season. Unable to run at full strength, Barkley didn't produce big plays as frequently. In 2018, Barkley had a league-leading 16 rushes that gained 20 or more yards, five more than the next group of four backs who tied with 11. In 2019, he was still one of the best big-play threats on the ground, but he dropped to eight such runs (still fifth-most).

But even with a less-than-100% Barkley, the Giants didn't see a drop-off in their rushing efficiency and actually improved from -6.5%% DVOA in 2018 to -5.0% in 2019.

If there is a silver lining to the offense for 2020, it's that the intended skill position starters should be on the field together more often. That has to be the hope because, after the expected starters, the Giants still don't have much quality depth to fill in. Dion Lewis was signed as a free agent to back up Barkley, but the Giants' fourth wide receiver this season might be Corey Coleman off a torn ACL.

While the Giants left the offense mostly alone during the offseason, they continued to turn over the defense. A majority of the available cap space was used to add to that side of the ball, but many of the players brought in were just used to replace those lost, and it's unclear how many of them will be significant upgrades. Leonard Williams stays on a crowded defensive line. Blake Martinez replaces the released and disappointing Alec Ogletree. James Bradberry will take over for Janoris Jenkins. It's likely the biggest upgrade on the defense comes from their second-round pick, Alabama safety Xavier McKinney, who will replace Antoine Bethea and give the Giants more versatility in the defensive backfield.

New defensive coordinator Patrick Graham's philosophy reads like the profile of any new defensive coordinator: he wants to be multiple and aggressive. Any "What Does Patrick Graham Bring to the Giants?" articles could be copy-and-paste jobs of what was written when former defensive coordinator James Bettcher came on board. Bettcher eventually had to water down his defense given the players available. Time will tell if Graham will become hamstrung by the same issues. Graham and Brian Flores did some good things with a lack of talent on Miami's defensive roster last year, but it was still a unit that finished last in the league with one of the worst defensive DVOA ratings we've ever tracked.

On top of the issues regarding on-field performance, the Giants had to deal with significant issues off the field this offseason. Last year's first-round pick DeAndre Baker was arrested in May on four counts of armed robbery and four counts of aggravated assault with a firearm. While the legal process is ongoing, the Giants asked Baker to stay away from virtual team activities. This comes after the Giants traded back up in the first round to make Baker the first cornerback selected in the 2019 draft. His rookie year on the field came with its own struggles and reports came in after the season that Baker slept through meetings while he struggled to pick up the defense.

Then in June, kicker Aldrick Rosas was arrested for a hit and run accident where the police report noted Rosas was driving in excess of 100 miles per hour when he T-boned another vehicle before he fled the scene. The police also believed alcohol was involved in the incident. Rosas had previously been arrested for a DUI in 2016 before he was in the NFL.

All of this brings an added layer to Gettleman's roster construction. He made changing locker room culture the main focus when he was hired by the Giants and a reason to jettison some of the players he inherited from the previous regime, such as Odell Beckham. Of course, a winning culture is created best by winning, and that's not what the Giants have done lately. The GM is on notice and a new head coach has been brought in to help fix the problem.

The Giants now need to figure out what stage of the rebuild they're in to truly assess their expectations on the season and how it will be viewed. Are they in Year 3 of Gettleman or Year 1 of Judge? What exactly is going to differentiate the two? Wins aren't likely to come often in 2020, and if the batting average on offseason moves does not improve enough, the Giants could find themselves once again split between being a team making an effort to get better or just trying to give off the appearance of one.

Dan Pizzuta

2019 Giants Stats by Week

Wk	vs.	W-L	PF	PA	YDF	YDA	TO	Total	Off	Def	ST
1	at DAL	L	17	35	470	494	-2	-54%	-8%	45%	-1%
2	BUF	L	14	28	370	388	-2	-3%	16%	26%	7%
3	at TB	W	32	31	384	499	-1	-11%	13%	25%	1%
4	WAS	W	24	3	389	176	0	55%	-17%	-77%	-5%
5	MIN	L	10	28	211	490	0	-26%	-7%	22%	2%
6	at NE	L	14	35	213	427	-2	-52%	-33%	-2%	-21%
7	ARI	L	21	27	263	245	-3	-50%	-43%	-1%	-7%
8	at DET	L	26	31	370	375	+1	-10%	2%	10%	-3%
9	DAL	L	18	37	271	429	-1	-21%	-22%	10%	11%
10	at NYJ	L	27	34	281	294	-2	-45%	-19%	23%	-3%
11	BYE										
12	at CHI	L	14	19	243	335	+1	-21%	-20%	4%	3%
13	GB	L	13	31	335	322	-3	-28%	-18%	16%	6%
14	at PHI	L	17	23	255	418	+1	-4%	-16%	-4%	8%
15	MIA	W	36	20	412	384	-2	9%	9%	7%	8%
16	at WAS	W	41	35	552	361	0	-8%	42%	39%	-12%
17	PHI	L	17	34	397	400	-2	-16%	-17%	10%	12%

Trends and Splits

	Offense	Rank	Defense	Rank
Total DVOA	-7.3%	23	10.4%	27
Unadjusted VOA	-8.8%	24	8.4%	23
Weighted Trend	-8.8%	23	9.3%	24
Variance	4.4%	4	7.2%	23
Average Opponent	-1.2%	10	-2.1%	25
Passing	-4.7%	26	31.3%	31
Rushing	-5.0%	18	-14.0%	7
First Down	-5.6%	22	7.1%	23
Second Down	-14.0%	27	15.9%	27
Third Down	-0.3%	18	8.6%	21
First Half	-3.9%	20	10.8%	29
Second Half	-10.4%	24	10.0%	25
Red Zone	4.3%	12	17.4%	29
Late and Close	-33.0%	32	17.9%	31

Five-Year Performance

Year	W-L	Pyth W	Est W	PF	PA	TO	Total	Rk	Off	Rk	Def	Rk	ST	Rk	Off AGL	Rk	Def AGL	Rk	Off Age	Rk	Def Age	Rk	ST Age	Rk
2015	6-10	7.5	7.4	420	442	+7	-7.1%	20	-1.8%	19	10.7%	30	5.4%	2	66.4	31	85.6	32	26.2	22	27.0	13	26.5	8
2016	11-5	8.8	9.8	310	284	-2	9.6%	8	-6.0%	22	-14.5%	2	1.2%	11	27.9	11	24.6	7	26.3	22	25.9	27	26.2	13
2017	3-13	4.0	4.4	246	388	-3	-22.3%	30	-9.1%	23	5.7%	24	-7.5%	32	59.0	26	36.4	17	26.5	23	26.0	20	25.6	24
2018	5-11	6.9	7.9	369	412	+2	0.0%	15	1.3%	13	5.8%	24	4.5%	3	32.6	14	18.5	7	26.9	14	26.1	21	26.0	12
2019	4-12	5.3	4.0	341	451	-17	-17.4%	27	-7.3%	23	10.4%	27	0.3%	17	49.0	21	23.6	5	26.7	17	26.0	20	25.4	26

2019 Performance Based on Most Common Personnel Groups

NYG Offense					NYG Offense vs. Opponents					NYG Defense					NYG Defense vs. Opponents			
Pers	Freq	Yds	DVOA	Run%	Pers	Freq	Yds	DVOA	Run%	Pers	Freq	Yds	DVOA	Pers	Freq	Yds	DVOA
11	73%	6.0	3.3%	24%	Base	18%	4.0	-33.0%	59%	Base	18%	5.1	-3.0%	11	56%	6.6	23.2%
12	17%	3.9	-22.6%	52%	Nickel	68%	5.9	7.0%	29%	Nickel	63%	5.8	6.6%	12	23%	5.1	-7.3%
21	5%	4.9	-14.0%	52%	Dime+	13%	5.4	-30.0%	11%	Dime+	18%	7.7	52.0%	21	6%	7.1	24.7%
22	1%	6.1	34.1%	71%	Goal Line	1%	0.3	36.1%	83%	Goal Line	1%	0.2	-15.2%	13	4%	2.5	-36.6%
611	1%	3.2	-46.4%	67%										22	3%	5.4	-14.1%

Strategic Tendencies

Run/Pass		Rk	Formation		Rk	Pass Rush		Rk	Secondary		Rk	Strategy		Rk
Runs, first half	36%	20	Form: Single Back	88%	6	Rush 3	4.9%	22	4 DB	18%	28	Play Action	22%	23
Runs, first down	42%	29	Form: Empty Back	5%	24	Rush 4	66.7%	13	5 DB	63%	13	Offensive Motion	32%	23
Runs, second-long	28%	13	Form: Multi Back	7%	24	Rush 5	19.1%	18	6+ DB	18%	16	Avg Box (Off)	6.57	15
Runs, power sit.	56%	17	Pers: 3+ WR	74%	6	Rush 6+	9.3%	5	Man Coverage	32%	16	Avg Box (Def)	6.70	8
Runs, behind 2H	24%	27	Pers: 2+ TE/6+ OL	21%	27	Edge Rusher Sacks	54.2%	18	CB by Sides	81%	14	Offensive Pace	29.82	8
Pass, ahead 2H	50%	12	Pers: 6+ OL	2%	19	Interior DL Sacks	31.9%	9	S/CB Cover Ratio	26%	15	Defensive Pace	29.70	4
Run-Pass Options	8%	10	Shotgun/Pistol	73%	7	Second Level Sacks	13.9%	21	DB Blitz	13%	11	Go for it on 4th	2.21	3

The Giants had a horrific league-low -44.6% DVOA when running against heavy boxes of eight or more. Unfortunately, Saquon Barkley can't call his own audibles. ● For the second straight year, the Giants were far better running the ball from shotgun formations. They gained 5.3 yards per carry (5.8% DVOA) on runs from shotgun, compared to 3.5 yards per carry (-28.5% DVOA) on runs with the quarterback under center. ● The Giants were 29th in the NFL with just 100 broken tackles, just one year after they finished third in the league and Barkley led all players with 94 broken tackles on his own. ● New York had the league's second-highest gap in DVOA performance between plays from shotgun (4.5% DVOA, 14th) and plays with the quarterback under center (-33.1% DVOA, 30th). ● The Giants gained 5.8 yards per play on RPOs, the highest average among the 18 teams that used them at least 5% of the time. ● Giants opponents ran 35 screens, close to the NFL high, and the Giants allowed a terrible 10.9 yards per pass with 91.1% DVOA on these plays. ● Although the Giants used a lot of defensive back blitzes, they weren't very good at them, allowing 34.8% DVOA which ranked 30th in the NFL. ● The Giants ranked fourth against the run on third downs but 26th against the pass.

Passing

Player	DYAR	DVOA	Plays	NtYds	Avg	YAC	C%	TD	Int
D.Jones	-256	-19.2%	498	2733	5.5	4.9	61.9%	24	12
E.Manning*	-38	-15.0%	153	983	6.4	4.6	62.3%	6	5
C.McCoy	-114	-73.8%	33	80	2.4	1.9	66.7%	0	1

Rushing

Player	DYAR	DVOA	Plays	Yds	Avg	TD	Fum	Suc
S.Barkley	84	0.4%	217	1003	4.6	6	0	44%
D.Jones	45	7.9%	40	283	7.1	2	4	-
J.Hilliman	-32	-32.9%	30	91	3.0	1	1	43%
W.Gallman	-9	-15.5%	29	111	3.8	2	1	41%
E.Penny	-22	-40.1%	15	39	2.6	0	0	47%
J.Allen*	8	10.5%	10	36	3.6	1	0	60%
S.Shepard	50	156.5%	6	72	12.0	0	0	-
D.Lewis	-26	-20.7%	54	209	3.9	0	1	46%

Receiving

Player	DYAR	DVOA	Plays	Ctch	Yds	Y/C	YAC	TD	C%
G.Tate	71	-2.0%	86	49	676	13.6	5.8	6	58%
D.Slayton	148	9.6%	84	48	740	15.4	4.0	8	57%
S.Shepard	30	-8.1%	83	57	576	10.1	3.1	3	69%
C.Latimer*	45	0.0%	42	24	300	12.5	2.9	2	57%
B.Fowler*	-21	-20.3%	36	23	193	8.4	1.3	0	64%
R.Shepard*	-29	-56.3%	8	3	25	8.3	4.3	0	38%
E.Engram	-37	-15.7%	68	44	467	10.6	5.7	3	65%
K.Smith	-52	-25.8%	42	31	268	8.6	2.9	3	74%
R.Ellison*	-57	-38.8%	28	18	167	9.3	4.6	1	64%
S.Barkley	-37	-22.8%	73	52	438	8.4	8.4	2	71%
W.Gallman	14	6.0%	15	11	102	9.3	9.5	1	73%
D.Lewis	3	-11.9%	32	25	164	6.6	7.7	1	78%

Offensive Line

Player	Pos	Age	GS	Snaps	Pen	Sk	Pass	Run	Player	Pos	Age	GS	Snaps	Pen	Sk	Pass	Run
Will Hernandez	LG	25	16/16	1081	4	0.0	7	8	Mike Remmers*	RT	31	14/14	881	5	3.5	13	7
Nate Solder	LT	32	16/16	1023	5	12.0	40	2	Nick Gates	RT/RG	25	16/3	294	0	0.5	7	1
Kevin Zeitler	RG	30	15/15	1004	2	1.5	6	6	Cameron Fleming	LT	28	14/3	259	4	1.5	8	0
Jon Halapio*	C	29	15/15	991	5	1.5	8	8									

Year	Yards	ALY	Rank	Power	Rank	Stuff	Rank	2nd Lev	Rank	Open Field	Rank	Sacks	ASR	Rank	Press	Rank	F-Start	Cont.
2017	4.02	4.06	15	50%	29	17%	6	1.02	24	0.68	18	34	5.8%	10	25.5%	5	13	20
2018	4.69	3.90	29	69%	10	21%	24	1.10	25	1.60	1	47	7.4%	20	30.7%	17	17	29
2019	4.25	3.96	25	58%	26	20%	19	1.10	24	0.99	8	43	7.1%	17	33.4%	27	8	34

2019 ALY by direction: Left End 3.09 (29)   Left Tackle: 3.75 (23)   Mid/Guard: 3.90 (26)   Right Tackle: 4.11 (16)   Right End: 4.82 (11)

As a whole, the Giants' line was above average (12th) in snaps per blown block, but left tackle Nate Solder had a league-high 40 blown blocks on pass plays and finished second in the league with 12 sacks allowed. He was beaten both quickly off the line and late in the play. He will remain a liability in a more vertical offense that should ask him to hold blocks longer than he did over the past two seasons. ◥ Fourth overall pick Andrew Thomas was one of the best overall college tackles in 2019, with the versatility to play on the left or the right. He'll likely start his career on the right side, but projects to be the long-term left tackle once the team moves on from Solder. Over the past three seasons, Thomas was called for holding just twice. ◥ The best addition for the line in 2019 was guard Kevin Zeitler, who remained one of the better players in the league at his position with the fourth-best snaps per blown block rate among right guards. ◥ Second-year left guard Will Hernandez quadrupled his blown block total on run plays from his rookie year (two to eight), part of a slight sophomore slump, though his pass protection was similar to 2018. ◥ There's no favorite for the starting center job. Jon Halapio was the starter for most of the season but did not receive a tender from the team after he tore his Achilles in Week 17. He also lost most of the 2018 season to a broken ankle. Spencer Pulley, the only natural center on the roster, was part of a below-average rotation in 2018 and lost the job to a returning Halapio to start 2019. Nick Gates started two games at tackle last season and acted as the third-string center in practice, the first time he snapped in his career. He'll also be in play to start at center. Fifth-round pick Shane Lemieux, a guard at Oregon, has worked on snapping since getting drafted but has no previous experience at the position.

Defensive Front

Defensive Line	Age	Pos	G	Snaps	Plays	Overall TmPct	Rk	Stop	Dfts	BTkl	Runs	vs. Run St%	Rk	RuYd	Rk	Pass Rush Sack	Hit	Hur	Dsrpt
Leonard Williams	26	DE	15	749	49	6.1%	25	37	12	4	42	74%	55	2.3	48	0.5	18	36	2
Dexter Lawrence	23	DE	16	717	40	4.6%	44	33	11	1	32	81%	25	2.0	31	2.5	6	18	2
Dalvin Tomlinson	26	DT	16	606	49	5.7%	25	42	17	3	43	88%	8	1.3	8	3.5	5	11	0
B.J. Hill	25	DE	16	504	36	4.2%	55	33	8	0	33	91%	5	1.6	15	1.0	1	11	0
Olsen Pierre*	29	DT	9	177	8	1.7%	--	7	3	2	4	100%	--	1.0	--	2.0	0	3	0
Austin Johnson	26	DT	16	326	24	2.8%	--	18	2	1	22	77%	--	2.5	--	0.0	2	5	1

Edge Rushers	Age	Pos	G	Snaps	Plays	Overall TmPct	Rk	Stop	Dfts	BTkl	Runs	vs. Run St%	Rk	RuYd	Rk	Pass Rush Sack	Hit	Hur	Dsrpt
Markus Golden*	29	OLB	16	939	71	8.2%	4	50	26	11	52	67%	68	3.1	70	10.0	15	45	0
Lorenzo Carter	25	OLB	15	739	49	6.1%	34	36	14	6	33	67%	69	2.9	63	4.5	10	20	4
Oshane Ximines	24	OLB	16	512	24	2.8%	79	18	9	2	15	67%	69	2.8	54	4.5	6	16	2
Kyler Fackrell	29	OLB	16	422	19	2.4%	87	11	6	4	8	38%	91	4.6	90	1.0	8	27	1

Linebackers	Age	Pos	G	Snaps	Plays	Overall TmPct	Rk	Stop	Dfts	BTkl	Runs	vs. Run St%	Rk	RuYd	Rk	Pass Rush Sack	Hit	Hur	Tgts	vs. Pass Suc%	Rk	AdjYd	Rk	PD	Int
Alec Ogletree*	29	ILB	13	867	86	12.3%	42	43	17	18	36	64%	27	3.2	16	1.0	2	12	26	46%	48	5.4	17	6	1
David Mayo	27	ILB	16	645	82	9.5%	46	54	12	11	58	76%	7	3.2	14	2.0	0	1	18	56%	20	4.2	7	2	0
Deone Bucannon*	28	ILB	14	247	26	3.5%	--	10	2	2	13	46%	--	3.8	--	0.0	1	3	6	33%	--	8.7	--	0	0
Ryan Connelly	25	OLB	4	195	22	10.2%	84	16	6	2	15	80%	3	1.5	1	1.0	0	2	2	100%	--	2.5	--	2	2
Blake Martinez	26	ILB	16	1035	157	19.7%	2	73	20	17	98	53%	68	4.4	67	3.0	0	6	40	38%	57	7.1	45	2	1

Year	Yards	ALY	Rank	Power	Rank	Stuff	Rank	2nd Level	Rank	Open Field	Rank	Sacks	ASR	Rank	Press	Rank
2017	4.22	4.30	23	53%	4	22%	12	1.23	22	0.79	21	27	4.9%	30	29.0%	25
2018	4.25	4.38	18	64%	12	20%	13	1.21	16	0.85	17	30	4.9%	31	30.8%	16
2019	3.96	4.02	7	59%	9	21%	11	1.16	17	0.71	15	36	6.3%	23	28.6%	23
2019 ALY by direction:		Left End: 4.05 (16)			Left Tackle: 4.2 (14)			Mid/Guard: 4.36 (14)			Right Tackle: 3.86 (8)			Right End: 2.93 (7)	

Spilt between the Jets and Giants, Leonard Williams gave a typical Leonard Williams season. There was a lot of pressure, few sacks, and fine play against the run—a luxury on a rebuilding team to some, a third-round pick and $16 million for others. ◥ Dexter Lawrence was drafted in the first round to be the big run-stuffer, but Dalvin Tomlinson played the nose more often and was significantly more productive against the run with a little pass rush mixed in. ◥ B.J. Hill was the interior lineman hurt the most by the addition of Williams, though even before the trade, Hill had not looked as explosive as in his impressive rookie season. ◥ Markus Golden finished the season seventh in quarterback hits and 11th in total defeats. While many of his sacks and hits came late in the down opposed to early wins off the line, Golden was often the Giants' only real threat of a pass rush. Golden is a free agent but without a deal early on, the Giants used the rare UFA tender, which would keep him on the team if he does not reach another agreement before July 22. ● While teams have gotten better at figuring out "tweeners," there has been little development for Lorenzo Carter as a pass-rusher after Year 2. The Giants hired Kevin Sheerer as inside linebackers coach this offseason and he was the outside linebackers coach at Georgia when Carter played for the Bulldogs. There has been some talk of moving Carter inside where his raw athleticism could play better. ● Dave Gettleman has said the team can scheme pass rush this season and that responsibility will fall on defensive coordinator Patrick Graham. However, Graham comes from the Belichick tree that has embraced rushing three at a high rate. The Dolphins rushed three 20% of the time under Graham last season, second-most in the league. ● No position has hurt the Giants more than off-ball linebacker over the past decade. After getting out of the Alec Ogletree contract, the Giants signed a carbon copy in Blake Martinez. Both are players who struggle in coverage and can put up high-volume, low-impact tackle numbers cleaning up plays after long gains. Martinez was last seen as Kyle Shanahan's preferred target in the NFC Championship Game.

Defensive Secondary

Secondary	Age	Pos	G	Snaps	Plays	Overall TmPct	Rk	Stop	Dfts	BTkl	Runs	St%	Rk	RuYd	Rk	Tgts	Tgt%	Rk	Dist	Suc%	Rk	AdjYd	Rk	PD	Int
Antoine Bethea*	36	FS	16	1132	116	13.5%	5	30	12	17	57	25%	64	9.9	61	26	6.3%	53	13.5	23%	73	15.4	73	6	1
Janoris Jenkins*	32	CB	15	998	77	9.5%	24	33	13	13	17	65%	16	3.8	13	67	15.9%	72	13.4	52%	43	7.2	38	16	5
Deandre Baker	23	CB	16	994	69	8.0%	33	31	8	6	22	59%	26	6.0	38	73	20.2%	42	13.8	52%	46	9.1	70	8	0
Jabrill Peppers	25	SS	11	725	81	13.7%	34	42	15	9	47	55%	8	5.4	18	22	8.3%	32	8.4	55%	28	5.7	17	5	1
Grant Haley	24	CB	15	430	43	5.3%	--	24	5	3	15	93%	--	1.8	--	24	15.3%	--	13.0	38%	--	9.1	--	0	0
Julian Love	22	SS	15	412	38	4.7%	70	22	13	5	21	71%	1	2.9	2	20	13.3%	6	6.2	60%	15	3.6	2	3	1
Michael Thomas*	30	SS	16	306	43	5.0%	--	19	14	4	13	62%	--	4.8	--	18	16.1%	--	10.1	33%	--	10.6	--	3	0
Corey Ballentine	24	CB	13	303	27	3.9%	--	8	0	1	4	25%	--	8.3	--	35	31.7%	--	12.3	40%	--	10.0	--	2	0
Sam Beal	24	CB	6	291	27	8.4%	--	9	3	3	7	57%	--	4.6	--	19	17.9%	--	14.9	42%	--	7.0	--	1	0
James Bradberry	27	CB	15	1038	77	10.0%	16	22	9	8	20	20%	77	10.5	80	75	19.5%	49	14.9	52%	48	6.9	26	12	3

Year	Pass D Rank	vs. #1 WR	Rk	vs. #2 WR	Rk	vs. Other WR	Rk	WR Wide	Rk	WR Slot	Rk	vs. TE	Rk	vs. RB	Rk
2017	19	-2.8%	13	42.4%	32	-17.3%	6	2.8%	22	8.9%	17	-0.4%	15	-2.8%	15
2018	26	15.0%	26	-18.8%	7	20.0%	28	-18.7%	4	30.3%	30	3.1%	18	-14.6%	6
2019	31	32.8%	32	-2.2%	15	37.2%	32	-6.4%	16	48.2%	32	6.1%	20	12.8%	24

James Bradberry, a second-round pick under Gettleman in Carolina, came over in free agency to be the No. 1 corner. Bradberry is a versatile outside corner for both zone and man, whose charting stats undersell his level of play by virtue of matching up against the likes of Julio Jones, Mike Evans, and Michael Thomas twice each season in the NFC South. After adjusting for opponent, Carolina ranked in the top 10 of DVOA covering No. 1 receivers each of the last two years. ● DeAndre Baker's rookie season was a disaster and it only got worse over the offseason. Baker was routinely out of position or playing zone when the rest of the defense was in man. There were rumors of work habit concerns when he came out of Georgia and there was little done in 2019 to quell those on or off the field. ● 2018 Supplemental third-rounder Sam Beal flashed at the end of the season as a starter after Janoris Jenkins was waived. Beal has only played six games in two seasons but may be forced to be a starter opposite Bradberry, pending Baker's legal issues. ● Julian Love didn't play defense regularly until Week 12 but was the standout of the 2019 draft class. Love played well in the box, at deep safety, and at slot corner during his rookie season and he could find a starter's worth of snaps bouncing around the secondary in 2020. ● Picking an uber-athletic small-school prospect in the sixth round is good process. Having so little depth in the secondary that he has to play as a raw rookie is a bad result. Opposing offenses picked on Corey Ballentine whenever he was on the field. Among 145 cornerbacks with at least 100 pass snaps, only Atlanta's Jamar Taylor was targeted more often per snap than Ballentine. ● The slot position is wide-open and could be an open competition between Grant Haley, the 2018 UDFA who fell out of favor with the previous coaching staff throughout the 2019 season, and 2020 fourth-round pick Darnay Holmes of UCLA. Holmes improved his yards per target allowed each year at UCLA but SIS scouts described him as "more of an athlete playing corner." Just 10% of his snaps came in the slot last season. ● Alabama's Xavier McKinney should immediately slot in as a do-it-all safety with the range and instincts to cover all responsibilities at the position. ● Jabrill Peppers showed his best play comes when he's within 20 yards of the line of scrimmage. With Love and McKinney on the team, Peppers could play even closer to the box this season.

Special Teams

Year	DVOA	Rank	FG/XP	Rank	Net Kick	Rank	Kick Ret	Rank	Net Punt	Rank	Punt Ret	Rank	Hidden	Rank
2017	-7.5%	32	-12.2	30	-0.8	22	-3.5	23	-16.5	32	-4.5	26	-3.5	17
2018	4.5%	3	11.5	2	5.3	2	2.2	7	9.6	2	-5.8	29	-16.5	31
2019	0.3%	17	-9.7	29	5.7	4	0.5	13	2.5	13	2.4	8	-2.7	19

The Giants turned the special teams around over the past two seasons under Thomas McGaughey. He was kept as special teams coordinator, but Joe Judge's experience in that area should also help. ● Over his first three years in the NFL, Aldrick Rosas has been the model of year-to-year kicker inconsistency and another example of why teams shouldn't fall for an out-of-nowhere peak season. After a stellar 2018 when Rosas hit 97% of both his field goals and extra points, he dropped back to his rookie season levels, connecting on 71% of his field goals and 90% of extra points in 2019. This inconsistency is one reason the Giants should have no problem letting go of Rosas after his offseason hit-and-run arrest. As of press time, however, they have not made any move to cut Rosas or bring in other kickers. ● Riley Dixon remained an above-average punter for the second straight season, but the punt coverage was not as good as it was in 2018. ● The Giants struggled to find solid kick returners last season before Cody Latimer took the role during the second half of the season. He was allowed to leave in free agency, and both Corey Ballentine and Darius Slayton were below-average returners on a small sample of returns, just 10 and 9 respectively. Corey Coleman was re-signed after a torn ACL forced him to miss all of 2019. He was ninth in kick return value in 2018 and could take over that role again. ● The team also had problems finding a regular punt returner. Golden Tate led the team with just 10 returns though he was 11th in the league in punt return value. His long return was just 17 yards, but he made steady gains. ● Jabrill Peppers was a standout with the Browns in 2018 but returned just four punts for the Giants last season, though that came with a long of 40 yards. ● The Giants will miss special teams ace Michael Thomas, a team captain who signed with the Texans this offseason. Cody Core could take a bigger role on special teams, as he was outstanding as a punt gunner last season.

New York Jets

2019 Record: 7-9	Total DVOA: -15.6% (26th)	2020 Mean Projection: 7.4 wins	On the Clock (0-4): 13%
Pythagorean Wins: 5.6 (25th)	Offense: -24.8% (31st)	Postseason Odds: 35.9%	Mediocrity (5-7): 39%
Snap-Weighted Age: 26.4 (17th)	Defense: -5.8% (10th)	Super Bowl Odds: 2.7%	Playoff Contender (8-10): 36%
Average Opponent: -3.4% (28th)	Special Teams: 3.4% (4th)	Proj. Avg. Opponent: 0.0% (14th)	Super Bowl Contender (11+): 12%

2019: Out Indefinitely—Mononucleosis.

2020: A surprisingly good defense may not matter if the third-year quarterback can't take a big leap forward. Yes, the Jets are now the poor man's Buffalo Bills.

Remember when Sam Darnold contracted mono before Week 2? And when Trevor Siemian, Luke Falk, and David Fales had to fill in for him and did so in disastrous fashion? How about when Darnold made his return to action, only to get obliterated by the New England Patriots on Monday Night Football? Of course you do! The Jets' 1-7 start to the year was so tragic, so farcical, so inherently *Jets*-ian that it could not possibly be forgotten. It was the particular kind of bad that made for excellent television—so long as you are not a Jets fan, that is.

As clear as the memories of New York's struggles were, that floundering iteration of the 2019 Jets is all anyone can recall. It is easy to forget how well the rest of the year went for them. The team had been effectively eliminated from the playoffs with their 1-7 start, so the spotlight was turned away from them, but the Jets went on a 6-2 run to close out the year and finish at 7-9. Granted, the back half of their schedule was a relative stroll in the park, but wins over the Oakland Raiders and Pittsburgh Steelers were both plenty respectable dubs which nobody who saw their first half of the season would have predicted them to win.

Do not get us wrong: a 7-9 record is nothing to get excited over. The Jets still missed the postseason and have nothing meaningful to show for their late-season surge. That said, a 7-9 record does lend to the idea that perhaps the Jets were better than we thought they were. When you hear the words "2019 Jets," do you think of a competitive, near-.500 team? Perhaps if their developing, second-year quarterback had not contracted a month-long sickness, the team could have been in the playoff hunt.

In part because of his compromised immune system, Darnold finds himself in a peculiar spot among young quarterbacks. There is no clear answer on who Darnold is, nor is the 2020 offensive depth chart primed to give us that answer. Division rival Josh Allen, for example, may not yet have proved he is a franchise quarterback, but the Buffalo Bills' offensive roster is stocked in a way that will almost certainly give us that answer in 2020. With Darnold's top wideouts looking like Breshad Perriman (a worse Robby Anderson), Jamison Crowder, and rookie Denzel Mims, it is more than likely Darnold will once again be slinging it around to a below-average receiving unit behind an offensive line that still has question marks across the board.

To this point in his career, the numbers do not favor Darnold, either. As highlighted in the Bills chapter with respect to Allen (page 23), hardly any quarterbacks who post a negative DYAR figure in each of their first two seasons become quality NFL starters. Of the 13 quarterbacks to do so since 2004, Alex Smith is the only real, clear success case, and there are one or two other fringe cases at best. Additionally, Darnold's adjusted net yards per attempt through two seasons is just 5.37, which falls a hair short of the 5.50 benchmark also highlighted in the Bills chapter.

Driving home the side-by-side comparison with Allen even further, a good chunk of hope for Darnold rests upon the idea that he improved over the back half of last year. In theory, Darnold can build on that progress and improve even further in 2020, but there is precious little evidence that second-half success in one season converts into sustained success the following season. As is the case with just about everything in Darnold's skill set and career profile, however, there is hope that Darnold can defy clear trends, in this case because of the nature of last year's first-half disaster.

Darnold's season-opener versus Buffalo was not good. On 45 dropbacks, Darnold completed 28 passes for 175 yards, one touchdown, and zero interceptions. It was not a catastrophic performance, but he was not pulling his weight. Darnold, in peak 22-year-old fashion, missed the next three games recovering from mononucleosis—an "injury" that provided us one of the best GIFs of the year, which featured Darnold dramatically pointing through the television screen with an "Out Indefinitely—Mononucleosis" graphic plastered next to him. Over that span, Darnold also missed out on having a full, healthy bye week. With Darnold being out for those four weeks, he did not get a complete first half of the year to compare to his eventual second half.

Darnold's return was a surprising upset over the Cowboys in Week 6, but then he ran into a buzzsaw. The following week's game came against the New England Patriots, whose defense through the first 10 or so weeks of the year was among the most dominant and turnover-heavy units the league has ever seen. Facing that defense after having just missed a month of play, while having to play behind a disastrous offensive line with limited talent in the pass-catcher department, was a recipe for one of the most embarrassing quarterback performances of the year. Darnold threw four interceptions and

2020 Jets Schedule

Week	Opp.	Week	Opp.	Week	Opp.
1	at BUF	7	BUF	13	LV
2	SF	8	at KC	14	at SEA
3	at IND	9	NE (Mon.)	15	at LAR (Sat.)
4	DEN (Thu.)	10	at MIA	16	CLE (Sat.)
5	ARI	11	BYE	17	at NE
6	at LAC	12	MIA		

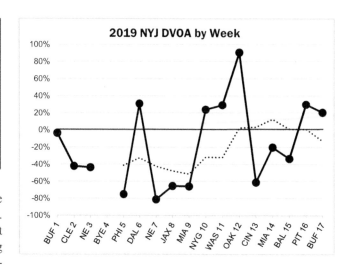

2019 NYJ DVOA by Week

earned a putrid 86 passing yards on 32 attempts. When the clock hit zeroes, he had posted a quarterback rating of 3.6. Three-point-six! There are only three other games in the past five seasons in which a quarterback earned a passer rating worse than 10.0 with at least 15 passing attempts: Nathan Peterman's unforgettable implosion against the Baltimore Ravens in 2018, decrepit Peyton Manning's midseason collapse against the Kansas City Chiefs in 2015, and Marcus Mariota's final start of 2019 against the Denver Broncos in Week 6.

Between Darnold's rusty stretch of games and the three starts which the Jets' backup quarterbacks had to make, the passing offense posted one of the worst first halves of a season in a decade. At -50.5% DVOA, the Jets' passing offense was the worst in the league through the first nine weeks by about -36.0% and was the third-worst passing offense in Weeks 1 to 9 since 2010. Only the 2018 Bills (Peterman game, Allen's rookie year) and the 2011 Jaguars (Blaine Gabbert rookie year) were worse over the last decade.

Over the final eight games, things turned around. Darnold and the Jets passing offense were average or slightly above. The team earned the 18th passing offense per DVOA from Week 10 on, while Darnold's 7.59 adjusted yards per attempt over the final eight games ranked ninth in the league over that span. (Strength of schedule explains some of the gap in rank here.) It is entirely possible that Darnold would have played about at the same level through the first eight games as he did the final eight games if he had been healthy and not had to waste a month's worth of work rehabilitating his immune system and regaining weight to get into playing shape. If Darnold and the passing offense could have hung around 20th in the league during the first eight games of the year, the Jets probably pick up an extra win or two. A tough AFC wild-card race may have kept the Jets out of the playoffs regardless, but at the very least, that would have solidified them in the conversation rather than allowing us to discard them once they got to 1-7.

So what, then, do we do with Football Outsiders' finding that second-half success does not necessarily carry over to the following season? The optimistic fan will frame Darnold's second half not as random improvement but as a more legitimate representation of what he would look like playing to his standard level within the context of the Jets' current offense. Of course, Darnold is not the only quarterback whose season has been sunk by factors largely out of his control.

Anything more stable than the complete disaster Darnold endured in September and October of last season should yield decent results. And do not get it twisted, Darnold has many

improvements to make on his own that have nothing to do with context. He still tends to let games snowball out of hand with his excessive aggression, he too often bypasses free yards underneath, and his deep ball needs to connect more often than it does right now. Being an unfinished product is nothing out of the ordinary for a 23-year-old quarterback, though. Darnold just needs his environment to be more conducive to his growth. The bad news is that the required environment probably will not manifest in the Meadowlands in 2020. Betting on a lack of turbulence from an Adam Gase-led Jets organization, especially one with this much offensive turnover, is wishful thinking.

What Darnold may lack in support from the offense, however, the defense is primed to make up for. Even last year, it was not just Darnold and the offense that led the Jets on their late-season run. The defense turned things up a notch, going from a perfectly average 16th place in DVOA during Weeks 1 to 9 to placing seventh in DVOA through Weeks 10 to 17. For a number of reasons, our projections say there's a good chance that New York's defense will climb higher into the top 10 this season.

The Jets led the NFL in adjusted games lost on defense, including the loss of big-money free-agent linebacker C.J. Mosley for almost the entire season. They fielded an edge-rusher unit without a single name recognizable to the average fan. They trotted out a bunch of unproven no-names at the cornerback position. They traded away Leonard Williams midseason. And still, the Jets defense made off fairly well for themselves in 2019. Their run defense stayed near the top of the league throughout the season, while the secondary slowly but surely showed improvement as youngsters found their footing.

The Jets did not stumble into success with turnover luck, either. The Jets were one of only two teams to finish in the top 10 in defensive DVOA despite a below-average rate of turnovers per drive (Chicago was the other).

More than anything else, it was quality coaching that propelled the Jets defense forward. It's nice to have a small handful of stars such as All-Pro safety Jamal Adams and rookie Quinnen Williams, but the Jets defensive depth chart was made up of a bunch of Madden random-generator names. The inconvenient truth is that Gregg Williams is among the best defensive coordinators in the league. For as much as Williams should never be allowed to live down Bountygate and should be constantly memed on for being part of the 0-16 Cleveland Browns, his 2018 Browns defense was quietly a good unit and he did an excellent job of working with the Jets' talent, or lack thereof, in 2019. His defense is more than just sending his free safety to colonize Mars.

Not many defensive coordinators love a good ol'-fashioned fire zone blitz like Williams does. A fire zone blitz, while it can be executed many ways, is a five-man pressure package with three deep zone defenders and three underneath zone defenders in coverage. The Jets finished sixth in five-man rush rate last season as well as 21st in man coverage, both of which highlight Williams' fire zone tendencies (Table 1). Fire zone blitzes are effective in any defensive scheme for any number of reasons, especially those which are good at mixing and disguising which five players are coming (as Williams is), but they were a particularly effective and necessary tool for a Jets defense lacking talent off the edge. Granted, the Jets have not had a clear stud edge rusher since John Abraham in the mid-2000s, but the lack of pass-rushing prowess was really pronounced last season. Not a single defense in the NFL earned a smaller percentage of their sacks from edge defenders than the Jets.

Table 1. Gregg Williams Blitz Tendencies, 2015-2019

Year	Team	Rush 5	Rk	Rush 5+	Rk	DB Blitz	Rk	Second-Level Sacks	Rk
2015	STL	29%	6	41%	5	21%	1	23%	19
2016	LAR	26%	8	36%	6	17%	1	16%	17
2017	CLE	29%	2	38%	2	16%	1	38%	3
2018	CLE	24%	7	37%	2	11%	9	37%	4
2019	NYJ	26%	6	30%	7	16%	3	30%	4

On the one hand, it is encouraging the Jets retained the coach who cooked up pressure without real edge threats. On the other hand, it would have been nice to address the edge position over the offseason, yet the Jets hardly did as much. Jordan Jenkins and Terrell Basham are a near lock to start Week 1 as New York's edge duo again, with Harvey Langi serving as the third option. If such a prop were out there, we would have bet a hefty amount of money heading into the offseason on the Jets *not* intentionally rolling with those three as their top guys for a second straight year.

The only real addition the Jets made to inspire competition among the group is third-round pick Jabari Zuniga—a strong, explosive pass-rusher out of Florida whose production was middling and technique is still terribly raw. Zuniga is not the type of player who should be expected to contribute right away, which more or less means the Jets are opting into another season of poor pass rush off the edge. As we go to press, a number of veteran options are still on the market: Everson Griffen, Ezekiel Ansah, Jabaal Sheard, and even Jadeveon

Clowney. Yet it feels as though the Jets would have made a move by this point if they really wanted to make one. Even assuming Williams' mad scientist blitz packages continue to yield good results, not having a go-to pass-rusher is objectively bad.

However, odd as it sounds of a unit without a legit pass-rushing ace, the Jets' front is not what is keeping them from being an elite defense. The Jets' run defense was excellent last year even without Mosley, and inserting him into the lineup upon his return to health will only solidify that strength. All of the line's key contributors are returning too. Leonard Williams is the only player to start Week 1 in 2019 and not be back for 2020. Considering the Jets are only adding talent up front rather than losing it, they should be in pretty good shape barring another catastrophic string of injuries.

Uncertainty litters the back end of the defense instead. The secondary is set to be improved over their middling 2019 form, but just how much they will improve relies on a number of potentially volatile factors. Jamal Adams is the team's most versatile, impactful defensive back—a linebacker, slot cover man, and blitzing menace all wrapped into one safety—but he has demanded a new contract and may be donning a different uniform by the time this gets to readers. Adams' situation is far and away the most worrisome issue in the Jets secondary right now, but there is really nothing to do but wait and see if Adams forces the front office's hand. The cornerback room, however, has an endless flow of questions needing to be answered.

2018 free-agent signing Trumaine Johnson imploded last season, as did his partner on the opposite end of the field, Daryl Roberts. Both players were above a 55% coverage success rate in 2018, yet neither earned higher than a 50% success rate in 2019. Johnson was benched early in the season and then lost the second half of the year to an ankle injury. Even the Jets' "third" starting outside cornerback, Nate Hairston, posted a horrific 34% success rate. The failures of those three outshined the limited but promising samples provided by Blessuan Austin, a 2019 sixth-round pick, and Arthur Maulet, a 2017 UDFA with the Saints who made his way to New York last season.

Of the two promising young guns, Austin is more likely to nab the starting spot opposite free-agent signing Pierre Desir, who is coming to New York after two seasons in Indianapolis. Desir is a tall, well-built cornerback whose best clips come within 10 yards of the line of scrimmage. He excels in press coverage and in zone assignments rather than in man coverage. The younger Austin is a bit more spry and capable of keeping up in man coverage, but he shares Desir's favor for zone coverage assignments where he can use his eyes and keep plays in front of him more often. Considering the Jets were already a zone-heavy team under Williams, that should only continue with the new pair of starting cornerbacks.

The overwhelming concern with this new duo, though, is that they are not direct solutions for the Jets' issues against the deep pass. Part of the problem is that the cornerbacks in Williams' scheme do not get real help from the deep safeties, who are asked to play 18 yards off the ball, gain depth at the snap, and play to prevent the absolute worst plays from happening down the middle, rather than trying to actively shut down 12- to 20-yard throws. As such, the corners are often left to their own devices in that range because they do not really get to play with safety leverage the way traditional single-high defenses can. Being that neither Austin nor Desir are particularly fast players or adept in shutting down deep threats, it would not be terribly surprising to find the Jets ranking in the bottom 10 in deep pass DVOA again. Lucky for the Jets, our projections expect the secondary as a whole to be improved, which should play into how well they defend against deep passes.

There is something cruel about the Jets being on their way to their best defensive performance in five years just as Tom Brady exits the division, yet not having a capable enough offense to capitalize on it. As was the case for the last eight games last year, the defense should keep the Jets in every game; it is merely a matter of whether or not the offense can piece together a few coherent scoring drives on a given day.

The longer you look at the Jets' offense depth chart and our projections for them, the gloomier the outlook for them becomes.

Wasted defenses at the hands of incompetent offenses is a familiar nightmare for the Jets. When Rex Ryan's defenses went on a run of four consecutive top-10 finishes in DVOA, the offense never once finished higher than 16th and instead finished outside the top-20 three times. In 2012, specifically, the Jets finished ninth in defensive DVOA, 30th in offensive DVOA, and 27th in overall DVOA, netting them a 6-10 record; all of those marks are right around where our projections expect them to be for 2020. At least the 2012 Jets had the excuse of a defensive head coach and an already-maligned quarterback to blame for their lopsided team dynamic. The 2020 Jets, with Gase calling the offense and a talented quarterback behind center, have no such excuse.

Derrik Klassen

2019 Jets Stats by Week

Wk	vs.	W-L	PF	PA	YDF	YDA	TO	Total	Off	Def	ST
1	BUF	L	16	17	223	370	+3	-3%	-1%	-7%	-10%
2	CLE	L	3	23	262	375	0	-42%	-50%	-12%	-4%
3	at NE	L	14	30	105	381	+1	-44%	-49%	2%	7%
4	BYE										
5	at PHI	L	6	31	128	265	-2	-75%	-85%	-6%	4%
6	DAL	W	24	22	382	399	-1	31%	19%	-5%	7%
7	NE	L	0	33	154	323	-5	-81%	-93%	-14%	-2%
8	at JAX	L	15	29	213	389	-2	-65%	-63%	7%	4%
9	at MIA	L	18	26	321	316	-1	-66%	-49%	29%	13%
10	NYG	W	34	27	294	281	+2	24%	2%	-14%	7%
11	at WAS	W	34	17	400	225	-1	29%	18%	-21%	-10%
12	OAK	W	34	3	401	208	+1	91%	31%	-54%	5%
13	at CIN	L	6	22	271	277	0	-61%	-44%	24%	7%
14	MIA	W	22	21	374	362	0	-20%	-33%	-4%	9%
15	at BAL	L	21	42	310	430	-2	-33%	-4%	36%	7%
16	PIT	W	16	10	259	260	+1	30%	-10%	-30%	10%
17	at BUF	W	13	6	271	309	+2	21%	-14%	-36%	-2%

Trends and Splits

	Offense	Rank	Defense	Rank
Total DVOA	-24.8%	31	-5.8%	10
Unadjusted VOA	-21.3%	31	-8.2%	8
Weighted Trend	-17.8%	29	-6.9%	9
Variance	14.0%	30	5.6%	14
Average Opponent	0.1%	18	-3.6%	27
Passing	-21.6%	32	7.9%	18
Rushing	-23.5%	31	-24.5%	2
First Down	-17.0%	28	-18.9%	4
Second Down	-23.0%	32	-1.6%	13
Third Down	-42.7%	31	13.1%	24
First Half	-18.5%	29	0.6%	16
Second Half	-32.2%	32	-12.2%	5
Red Zone	-30.1%	30	-2.1%	15
Late and Close	-18.6%	26	-8.1%	11

Five-Year Performance

Year	W-L	Pyth W	Est W	PF	PA	TO	Total	Rk	Off	Rk	Def	Rk	ST	Rk	Off AGL	Rk	Def AGL	Rk	Off Age	Rk	Def Age	Rk	ST Age	Rk
2015	10-6	10.0	9.7	387	314	+6	12.4%	9	1.6%	14	-13.8%	5	-2.9%	25	46.5	24	12.1	1	28.5	1	27.1	9	26.6	6
2016	5-11	4.4	4.6	275	409	-20	-32.4%	32	-21.9%	31	3.7%	21	-6.8%	32	67.1	29	42.6	18	27.5	6	26.4	19	26.0	19
2017	5-11	5.6	5.2	298	382	-4	-17.2%	26	-10.3%	25	3.9%	18	-3.0%	25	37.7	19	9.0	4	27.1	13	25.6	27	25.9	13
2018	4-12	5.3	5.9	333	441	-10	-14.7%	25	-19.5%	29	3.3%	21	8.1%	1	47.2	23	23.2	9	26.4	19	26.0	23	26.0	13
2019	7-9	5.6	6.4	276	359	-4	-15.6%	26	-24.8%	31	-5.8%	10	3.4%	4	76.4	31	83.7	32	27.1	9	25.7	23	26.5	5

2019 Performance Based on Most Common Personnel Groups

NYJ Offense					NYJ Offense vs. Opponents					NYJ Defense					NYJ Defense vs. Opponents			
Pers	Freq	Yds	DVOA	Run%	Pers	Freq	Yds	DVOA	Run%	Pers	Freq	Yds	DVOA		Pers	Freq	Yds	DVOA
11	66%	4.9	-21.0%	28%	Base	16%	3.8	-26.0%	73%	Base	19%	3.8	-27.6%		11	58%	5.5	-1.5%
12	10%	3.4	-53.2%	66%	Nickel	63%	5.0	-13.9%	34%	Nickel	77%	5.6	-1.7%		12	21%	5.2	-8.9%
13	6%	4.4	-2.0%	80%	Dime+	20%	4.7	-52.7%	18%	Dime+	3%	9.1	75.9%		21	8%	5.0	-10.7%
10	5%	6.5	5.7%	29%	Goal Line	0%	-1.0	-125.9%	100%	Goal Line	1%	-0.2	-19.0%		10	3%	7.2	52.7%
21	4%	5.2	-19.6%	43%											22	2%	3.4	-41.3%
20	4%	3.9	-39.4%	21%											20	2%	4.7	-34.3%

Strategic Tendencies

Run/Pass		Rk	Formation		Rk	Pass Rush		Rk	Secondary		Rk	Strategy		Rk
Runs, first half	39%	12	Form: Single Back	81%	14	Rush 3	14.7%	6	4 DB	19%	24	Play Action	25%	15
Runs, first down	47%	21	Form: Empty Back	8%	16	Rush 4	55.2%	27	5 DB	77%	2	Offensive Motion	30%	29
Runs, second-long	35%	5	Form: Multi Back	10%	16	Rush 5	25.9%	6	6+ DB	3%	24	Avg Box (Off)	6.59	14
Runs, power sit.	42%	30	Pers: 3+ WR	75%	3	Rush 6+	4.2%	21	Man Coverage	31%	21	Avg Box (Def)	6.77	4
Runs, behind 2H	27%	21	Pers: 2+ TE/6+ OL	19%	28	Edge Rusher Sacks	35.7%	32	CB by Sides	84%	10	Offensive Pace	30.60	16
Pass, ahead 2H	50%	13	Pers: 6+ OL	3%	14	Interior DL Sacks	34.3%	6	S/CB Cover Ratio	14%	31	Defensive Pace	30.13	9
Run-Pass Options	5%	18	Shotgun/Pistol	67%	17	Second Level Sacks	30.0%	4	DB Blitz	16%	3	Go for it on 4th	1.17	24

Adam Gase took the Jets from 25th in using three or more wide receivers (59%) to third (75%). ⬦ The Jets ranked 30th in the NFL with just 95 broken tackles. ⬦ New York's offense, ranked 31st in DVOA overall, improved to 11th in goal-to-go situations. ⬦ Gregg Williams did not big-blitz as much as he usually does. After his last few defenses had ranked in the top five for sending six or more pass-rushers, the Jets were only 21st. ⬦ The Jets had a big gap between defense in man coverage (8.4 yards per pass, 45.8% DVOA) and zone coverage (6.7 yards per pass, 15.2% DVOA). ⬦ The Jets benefited from a league-high 45 dropped passes (8.4%), seven more than any other team.

Passing

Player	DYAR	DVOA	Plays	NtYds	Avg	YAC	C%	TD	Int
S.Darnold	-290	-20.4%	475	2819	5.9	5.4	62.2%	19	13
L.Falk*	-314	-72.3%	89	320	3.6	5.6	64.4%	0	3
T.Siemian*	-64	-157.6%	8	-14	-1.8	3.7	50.0%	0	0
J.Flacco	-144	-18.8%	287	1635	5.7	5.3	65.8%	6	5

Rushing

Player	DYAR	DVOA	Plays	Yds	Avg	TD	Fum	Suc
L.Bell	-76	-16.6%	246	790	3.2	3	0	42%
B.Powell*	-22	-18.6%	59	229	3.9	0	0	37%
T.Montgomery*	-27	-30.4%	32	103	3.2	0	0	38%
S.Darnold	-7	-20.1%	15	70	4.7	2	2	-
J.Adams	-19	-92.9%	8	12	1.5	0	0	25%
F.Gore	-50	-15.2%	166	599	3.6	3	0	45%
J.Flacco	1	-9.3%	7	24	3.4	0	0	-

Receiving

Player	DYAR	DVOA	Plays	Ctch	Yds	Y/C	YAC	TD	C%
J.Crowder	9	-11.8%	122	78	833	10.7	4.5	6	64%
R.Anderson*	66	-4.2%	96	52	779	15.0	3.7	5	54%
D.Thomas*	25	-7.4%	58	36	433	12.0	4.7	1	62%
V.Smith	-14	-18.0%	31	17	225	13.2	6.2	0	55%
B.Berrios	-2	-15.2%	13	6	115	19.2	14.5	0	46%
B.Perriman	155	16.5%	69	36	645	17.9	3.5	6	52%
R.Griffin	45	8.4%	41	34	320	9.4	5.2	5	83%
D.Brown	6	0.4%	11	7	72	10.3	3.0	1	64%
R.Travis	-29	-70.7%	6	4	51	12.8	7.8	0	67%
L.Bell	3	-13.2%	78	66	461	7.0	6.7	1	85%
T.Montgomery*	-26	-41.6%	17	13	90	6.9	7.2	0	76%
B.Powell*	-47	-93.6%	12	7	33	4.7	6.4	0	58%
F.Gore	4	-9.6%	16	13	100	7.7	6.8	0	81%

Offensive Line

Player	Pos	Age	GS	Snaps	Pen	Sk	Pass	Run	Player	Pos	Age	GS	Snaps	Pen	Sk	Pass	Run
Brandon Shell*	RT	28	15/11	823	4	6.0	14	3	Tom Compton*	RG	31	13/5	367	2	2.5	11	4
Kelvin Beachum*	LT	31	13/13	816	9	4.0	11	6	Ryan Kalil*	C	35	7/7	354	5	0.5	2	3
Alex Lewis	LG	28	15/12	777	6	3.0	12	2	Kelechi Osemele*	LG	31	3/3	191	1	0.5	3	4
Jonotthan Harrison	C	29	16/10	687	3	1.0	7	10	Connor McGovern	C	27	16/16	1024	0	1.5	5	7
Brian Winters	RG	29	9/9	541	2	4.5	8	4	George Fant	LT	28	16/7	476	1	0.0	7	4
Chuma Edoga	RT	23	8/8	431	6	7.0	11	2									

Year	Yards	ALY	Rank	Power	Rank	Stuff	Rank	2nd Lev	Rank	Open Field	Rank	Sacks	ASR	Rank	Press	Rank	F-Start	Cont.
2017	3.96	3.40	29	48%	31	26%	29	1.03	23	1.04	5	47	8.6%	27	32.2%	22	14	27
2018	4.05	3.59	32	61%	26	26%	32	1.05	28	1.06	6	37	6.7%	18	32.4%	21	21	28
2019	3.29	3.80	31	69%	8	21%	25	0.91	30	0.17	32	52	9.2%	30	39.8%	32	8	21
2019 ALY by direction:			Left End 4.62 (7)			Left Tackle: 2.80 (31)			Mid/Guard: 3.88 (27)			Right Tackle: 3.80 (22)			Right End: 3.02 (29)			

The Jets are one of just two teams to place in the bottom five in adjusted line yards in each of the past three seasons (the Chicago Bears are the other). With that kind of consistently poor performance, it is no wonder the Jets are rolling with at least two new Week 1 starters in 2020. A full-time switch to center last year did wonders for Connor McGovern. A center/guard flex player for the Denver Broncos, McGovern took over as the starting center in place of Matt Paradis and finished the year ninth in snaps per blown blocks among centers, sandwiched right between Matt Skura (Ravens) and Alex Mack (Falcons). The year prior, when McGovern was at right guard, he finished 24th in snaps per blown block at his position. Finally, one of the Seahawks' offensive line experiments paid off—just in time for him to move on to a different team. George Fant, who played more often as a sixth offensive lineman than as a starting tackle, ranked a perfectly average 16th in snaps per blown blocks in 2019. The previous time Fant played enough to qualify was in 2016, when he started 10 games and finished dead last among left tackles in snaps per blown block. If nothing else, Fant is a good placeholder at left tackle for first-round pick Mekhi Becton (Louisville), who may need some time to develop. Becton is a gargantuan tackle at 6-foot-7 and 364 pounds, but he moves with the grace of a player 50 pounds lighter while still packing as strong a punch as one would expect of a man that size. However, Becton played in a college offense that did not often feature traditional dropback pass sets due to the offense constantly rolling out or making use of play-action and RPOs. It may take some time for Becton to familiarize himself with an offense that will use traditional dropback pass sets far more often than he is used to. Fourth-round guard Cameron Clark (UNC-Charlotte) is perhaps a cheap swing at what the Jets wanted in Kelechi Osemele, who is no longer with the team. Clark has long arms, massive hands, and plays with a mean streak that makes the most of his mighty mitts.

Defensive Front

Defensive Line	Age	Pos	G	Snaps	Plays	Overall TmPct	Rk	Stop	Dfts	BTkl	Runs	vs. Run St%	Rk	RuYd	Rk	Pass Rush Sack	Hit	Hur	Dsrpt
Kyle Phillips	23	DE	15	558	39	5.1%	41	28	13	2	30	73%	57	0.4	2	1.5	4	16	0
Quinnen Williams	23	DT	13	521	29	4.4%	68	26	11	4	24	88%	10	1.0	5	2.5	4	18	1
Steve McLendon	34	DT	16	470	35	4.3%	48	27	11	1	29	79%	29	1.4	11	2.5	5	10	0
Henry Anderson	29	DE	13	460	24	3.7%	79	16	4	0	20	75%	48	2.1	35	1.0	11	18	0
Folorunso Fatukasi	25	DE	14	394	28	4.0%	73	25	9	0	25	92%	4	0.6	3	1.0	2	6	1
Nathan Shepherd	27	DE	9	234	11	2.4%	--	10	6	3	7	100%	--	-0.1	--	2.0	6	11	0
Jordan Willis	25	DE	9	166	7	1.5%	--	6	3	1	5	100%	--	1.0	--	1.0	2	7	0

Edge Rushers	Age	Pos	G	Snaps	Plays	Overall TmPct	Rk	Stop	Dfts	BTkl	Runs	vs. Run St%	Rk	RuYd	Rk	Pass Rush Sack	Hit	Hur	Dsrpt
Tarell Basham	26	OLB	16	602	34	4.2%	55	30	9	5	20	95%	2	1.4	10	2.0	3	26	5
Jordan Jenkins	26	OLB	14	579	35	4.9%	51	29	16	3	19	79%	25	2.6	47	8.0	5	17	2
Brandon Copeland*	29	OLB	12	340	37	6.1%	45	27	11	10	24	75%	39	2.1	30	1.5	1	4	0

Linebackers	Age	Pos	G	Snaps	Plays	TmPct	Rk	Stop	Dfts	BTkl	Runs	St%	Rk	RuYd	Rk	Sack	Hit	Hur	Tgts	Suc%	Rk	AdjYd	Rk	PD	Int
												vs. Run				Pass Rush				vs. Pass				
Neville Hewitt	27	ILB	12	779	77	12.7%	47	37	18	12	45	53%	67	4.9	76	3.0	5	9	34	50%	35	6.1	34	5	2
James Burgess	26	ILB	10	672	83	16.4%	40	54	20	13	36	86%	1	1.6	2	0.5	0	4	32	66%	6	5.1	12	5	1
Blake Cashman	24	ILB	7	434	41	11.6%	76	20	7	4	20	75%	8	2.4	5	0.5	2	8	16	44%	51	8.5	60	1	0

Year	Yards	ALY	Rank	Power	Rank	Stuff	Rank	2nd Level	Rank	Open Field	Rank	Sacks	ASR	Rank	Press	Rank
2017	3.67	3.77	6	70%	24	22%	8	0.93	4	0.66	12	28	5.8%	25	30.0%	18
2018	4.31	4.28	13	55%	2	22%	10	1.25	19	0.87	18	39	6.7%	21	28.1%	24
2019	3.16	3.00	1	52%	3	31%	1	1.01	6	0.56	7	35	6.2%	26	30.4%	17
2019 ALY by direction:		Left End: 3.42 (8)			Left Tackle: 3.35 (6)			Mid/Guard: 3.23 (2)			Right Tackle: 2.36 (2)			Right End: 1.63 (1)	

The Jets finished No. 1 in adjusted line yards and No. 2 in run defense DVOA despite dealing away Leonard Williams at midseason. And how much did the Williams trade affect things? The Jets' run defense DVOA in Weeks 1 to 8 was -24.5%. The Jets' run defense DVOA in Weeks 9 to 17, after the trade, was also -24.5%. ◥ Quinnen Williams was not head-and-shoulders above the rest of last year's rookie defensive tackles in the pass game, but he was the most well-rounded of the class. Williams was tied for second among rookie tackles with 18 hurries, and he had the best run stop rate and average yards on run plays. ◥ The Jets already had two linebackers rank top-ten in stop rate and now they will be getting back their best linebacker, C.J. Mosley, from injury. In Mosley's final year with the Ravens in 2018, he finished top-20 in stop rate while also holding his own in coverage with a 51% success rate. If Mosley is even 90% of who he was in 2018, his return to the field will be a boon for an already impressive Jets front seven. ◥ Despite a poor adjusted sack rate for three years running, the only notable addition the Jets made on the edge was third-round pick Jabari Zuniga (Florida). At the NFL combine, Zuniga flew in the 40-yard dash with a 4.64s time (84th percentile) and leaped to a 127-inch broad jump (94th percentile) at a rocked-up 6-foot-3 and 264 pounds. After showing promise early in his college career, Zuniga never really took that major step forward, though, and he has long been a player with more flash than substance. Maybe defensive line coach Andre Carter can instill some consistency in Zuniga's game.

Defensive Secondary

Secondary	Age	Pos	G	Snaps	Plays	TmPct	Rk	Stop	Dfts	BTkl	Runs	St%	Rk	RuYd	Rk	Tgts	Tgt%	Rk	Dist	Suc%	Rk	AdjYd	Rk	PD	Int
						Overall						vs. Run						vs. Pass							
Marcus Maye	27	FS	16	1110	70	8.7%	40	18	6	8	37	24%	65	8.9	56	19	4.3%	69	19.4	53%	34	11.4	70	7	1
Jamal Adams	25	SS	14	978	81	11.4%	25	48	24	5	38	63%	3	4.8	12	26	6.7%	48	8.4	58%	23	5.9	20	7	1
Brian Poole	28	CB	14	766	63	8.9%	39	28	10	9	19	42%	45	3.8	15	50	16.5%	67	11.2	68%	4	4.8	3	5	1
Darryl Roberts*	30	CB	13	727	67	10.2%	29	15	5	6	12	17%	80	10.0	76	64	22.2%	25	10.0	44%	72	7.2	35	6	1
Nate Hairston	26	CB	11	400	27	4.9%	--	8	3	8	8	38%	--	6.9	--	29	18.3%	--	10.8	34%	--	10.0	--	3	1
Blessuan Austin	24	CB	7	394	29	8.2%	--	15	5	4	8	50%	--	9.4	--	24	15.4%	--	10.8	54%	--	6.7	--	4	0
Arthur Maulet	27	CB	12	355	38	6.3%	--	22	7	9	10	60%	--	3.4	--	31	22.0%	--	9.4	55%	--	7.2	--	2	1
Trumaine Johnson*	30	CB	7	321	27	7.6%	--	11	4	0	4	75%	--	3.5	--	22	17.3%	--	12.9	50%	--	8.6	--	2	1
Pierre Desir	30	CB	12	694	61	10.1%	45	21	8	8	9	44%	44	7.0	54	60	23.2%	17	14.4	43%	76	9.8	75	11	3

Year	Pass D Rank	vs. #1 WR	Rk	vs. #2 WR	Rk	vs. Other WR	Rk	WR Wide	Rk	WR Slot	Rk	vs. TE	Rk	vs. RB	Rk
2017	22	21.1%	28	-7.0%	13	-26.7%	2	13.7%	28	-15.0%	8	-7.4%	9	13.3%	26
2018	19	11.5%	24	-3.5%	14	9.7%	23	-10.5%	10	21.1%	27	7.8%	20	-13.4%	7
2019	18	8.7%	24	16.9%	27	1.0%	18	18.0%	31	4.6%	13	-5.1%	12	-13.0%	5

No qualifying free/strong safety tandem had a higher discrepancy in average depth of target than Marcus Maye and Jamal Adams. Adams' depth of target was within a reasonable range of many other strong safeties, but Maye's 19.4 average depth of target was the second-deepest among all safeties (thanks, Gregg Williams). Only Rayshawn Jenkins (Chargers) had a deeper average depth of target, though the Chargers had no qualifying strong safety. Adams also played a major pass-rushing role and led all NFL defensive backs with both 6.5 sacks and 16 hurries. ◥ Do not expect free-agent cornerback signing Pierre Desir to fix New York's secondary. After a decent year in 2018, Desir reverted back to journeyman form in 2019. In fact, 2018 was the only season in which Desir earned more than ten targets and maintained a success rate better than 50%. In 2019, 2017, and 2015—the only other seasons he earned more than ten targets—he failed to post a success rate better than 50%. ◥ A number of veterans will compete to play opposite Desir, including former Colts Quincy Wilson and Nate Hairston as well as journeyman Arthur Maulet. The best choice may be second-year corner Blessaun Austin, who fell to the sixth round of last year's draft because of college knee injuries but showed good press and ball skills early in his Rutgers career. He mostly played well when starting in Weeks 11 to 16 of last season, but a blown coverage assignment got him benched for the final game of the year. ✎ Coverage volatility was surely a factor, but perhaps all nickelback Brian Poole needed to jump-start his career was a change in scenery. After three seasons of producing a success rate of 46% or worse with the Falcons, Poole dominated last year. Poole was one of six cornerbacks to finish top ten in both success rate and yards per target, joining Marlon Humphrey (Ravens), D.J. Hayden (Jaguars), Troy Hill (Rams), J.C. Jackson (Patriots), and Jason McCourty (Patriots). ✎ Third-round pick Ashtyn Davis (Cal) is unlikely to start, but he can be a great third safety as the league experiments with more three-safety lineups. Though not an elite single-high safety (few are, to be fair), Davis has enough range in centerfield to make it work and has the man coverage skills to match up with slot receivers and tight ends. If nothing else, Davis will serve as a nice backup this year before taking over for Maye in 2021, assuming the Jets drafted Davis to avoid paying Maye when his contract expires after 2020. ✎ Before an ankle injury derailed his 2019 season, fifth-round pick Bryce Hall (Virginia) was considered a borderline first-round talent. That was likely a bit lofty to begin with, but Hall does have the length and ball skills to be a solid No. 2 cornerback in the same mold as players such as Akhello Witherspoon and Rasul Douglas.

Special Teams

Year	DVOA	Rank	FG/XP	Rank	Net Kick	Rank	Kick Ret	Rank	Net Punt	Rank	Punt Ret	Rank	Hidden	Rank
2017	-3.0%	25	2.8	13	3.9	9	-3.4	22	-6.0	23	-12.2	32	5.8	7
2018	8.1%	1	10.3	4	5.1	4	13.6	2	2.7	14	8.8	1	0.8	14
2019	3.4%	4	-4.8	24	6.5	1	0.6	12	10.1	4	4.7	4	1.3	16

Lachlan Edwards posted a positive gross punting value in each of the past three seasons, but his rookie contract expired after 2019. So the Jets made a money decision and used a sixth-round pick on Texas A&M's Braden Mann, the first punter off the board in late April and one of just two punters to be drafted. With no other punter on the roster, Mann is the assumed starter. Mann's 51.0 net yards per punt as a junior in 2018 were the highest mark of any college punter since at least 2009. ✎ After a mediocre year from Sam Ficken, the Jets brought in former Dallas kicker Brett Maher to compete for the starting spot. Maher scored on just five of last year's 13 attempts from 40 or more yards for the Cowboys, however, compared to Ficken nailing 10 of his 17 attempts from that range. Right on to the Jets for sparking competition, but Maher probably will not be the immediate upgrade they are looking for. ✎ Wide receiver Vyncint Smith did all the heavy lifting for the Jets' kick return group. Of the Jets' three qualifying returners—the other two being running backs Ty Montgomery and Trenton Cannon—only Smith had positive return value (2.4 points). ✎ A few teams had a punt returner finish in the top-10 in return points in both 2018 and 2019, but the Jets were one of just two teams to do it with a different player each year. Andre Roberts topped the league with 10.2 points in 2018, while Braxton Berrios followed up in 2019 with a fifth-place 4.7 return points. ✎ Those cold, windy winters in the Meadowlands do the Jets no favors. Neither did their road schedule in 2019. We estimate that the Jets lost -7.8 points of special teams value due to weather and venue, the lowest mark of any team in three years.

Philadelphia Eagles

2019 Record: 9-7	**Total DVOA:** 6.6% (11st)	**2020 Mean Projection:** 8.5 wins	**On the Clock (0-4):** 7%
Pythagorean Wins: 8.8 (11th)	**Offense:** 2.6% (14th)	**Postseason Odds:** 51.9%	**Mediocrity (5-7):** 28%
Snap-Weighted Age: 27.2 (2nd)	**Defense:** -4.0% (12nd)	**Super Bowl Odds:** 7.0%	**Playoff Contender (8-10):** 42%
Average Opponent: -3.3% (27th)	**Special Teams:** 0.0% (19th)	**Proj. Avg. Opponent:** -0.1% (15th)	**Super Bowl Contender (11+):** 23%

2019: Carson Wentz's postseason concussion was one injury too many for a remarkably resilient Eagles team.

2020: Second-round quarterback Jalen Hurts rounds out an even deeper roster for 2020—depth which has already been tested this offseason.

The more time passes, the more the Eagles' Super Bowl LII win seems like a singular experience. It came on the heels of the team's messy divorce with prodigy-turned-patsy Chip Kelly. It came despite the season-ending ACL injury to franchise quarterback and presumed competitive keystone Carson Wentz as backup Nick Foles substituted with uncharacteristic brilliance. And it relied on unsustainable efficiency on third downs and in the red zone, and on innovative but emulatable play calling that included run-pass options, the Philly Special, and a heavy reliance on play-action passes and attempted fourth-down conversions.

Since that magical season, the Eagles have settled into consecutive good-but-not-great seasons with 9-7 records and playoff berths but no deep postseason runs. It's easy to read the results as confirmation that the things that made the 2017 Eagles special no longer set them apart in a copycat league.

There is plenty of statistical evidence that is the case. Doug Pederson's Eagles have gone for 24 to 29 fourth downs on offense in each of his four years with the team. That was good enough for first place in football in his first three seasons, but in 2019, it was fourth most. And where the Eagles were one of just four teams with 20 or more offensive fourth-down attempts in 2016 and one of just six such teams in 2017, they were one of 11 such teams in 2019. More than a third of the league has become as aggressive as they are.

The Eagles also continued their heavy reliance on run-pass options in 2019, using them on 12% of their plays. But that rate was the same that the Cardinals had with new head coach Kliff Kingsbury, himself an innovative playcaller and emblem of the league's increasing willingness to apply college concepts to the pro game. And their rate trailed those of the Bears (15%) under head coach Matt Nagy—Pederson's eventual successor as offensive coordinator of Andy Reid's Chiefs—and the Chiefs (20%) under coaching-tree patriarch Reid himself.

Patrick Mahomes earned one of the two MVP trophies that have been awarded since Wentz nearly won one in the Eagles' Super Bowl season. He has finished in the top three in passing DVOA in each of the last two seasons and is the consensus choice for best quarterback in football. It follows logic that his Chiefs would win the Super Bowl if they and every other team adopted each other's best plays and strategic decisions. But if the major takeaway of the 2019 Chiefs is the inevitability of

talent, then that lesson should star Reid as well as Mahomes. Reid is the head coach who could never win the big one until his winning of the big one made it clear for everyone that he always could. Reid's Chiefs have finished above .500 in all seven of his seasons with the team and reached 11 or more wins five times. The year before Reid got to Kansas City, the team finished last in DVOA; they've finished 10th or better every year since. And if the 2017 Eagles show that teams cannot sustain winning on the foundation of specific strategies that other teams can copy, then Reid deserves praise as much for his leadership and roster management that led to perennial contention as he does for his eventual Super Bowl victory.

Frequent Football Outsiders readers likely understand that the narratives that take root in the public consciousness do not always hold up to statistical scrutiny. But even they may not recognize some worldviews as propped up by narratives, in particular when those narratives are less cliché than Reid's perceived lack of clutchness.

Reid's Chiefs are a foil for Pederson's Eagles, but not because Reid has sustained his team's success around a Super Bowl win where the Eagles have not. They are a foil because Pederson's Eagles have been every bit as successful as Reid's Chiefs, but poor injury luck, poor clustering luck, and a shorter team tenure make that fact more difficult to see.

Pederson joined the Eagles before the 2016 season, kicking off a new era for the team that is clearly demarcated from the one before it under Chip Kelly. Kelly continued to gain power in the organization throughout his three-year stint with the team, which included taking over football operations from Howie Roseman. Roseman regained his general manager position in 2016 and hired Pederson, and together they traded up for and drafted Wentz.

The Eagles' 13 wins in their Super Bowl season are four more than they've produced in the best of their other three seasons with the Pederson-Roseman-Wentz triumvirate. But that results-based metric undersells how consistently excellent they've been as a franchise. They've finished in the top half of the league in DVOA all four seasons, and their cumulative Pythagorean win total of 38.3 is seventh best in the league (Table 1), just 4.4 expected wins behind Reid's Chiefs and ahead of teams with better reputations of sustained excellence such as the Steelers (37.8, eighth), Seahawks (37.1, ninth), and Packers (32.5, 14th).

2020 Eagles Schedule

Week	Opp.	Week	Opp.	Week	Opp.
1	at WAS	7	NYG (Thu.)	13	at GB
2	LAR	8	DAL	14	NO
3	CIN	9	BYE	15	at ARI
4	at SF	10	at NYG	16	at DAL
5	at PIT	11	at CLE	17	WAS
6	BAL	12	SEA (Mon.)		

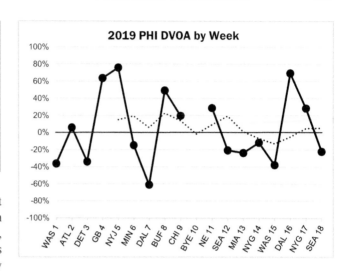

Good in-game strategy has been a part of the Eagles' recent success, but like the Chiefs, they can also credit their position in the upper tiers of team excellence to their strong leadership, roster management, and flexibility. And, in fact, the Eagles have endured more adversity to their team-building than any other successful team in recent seasons, a circumstance that should have spotlighted their virtue but tends to be lost in the bottom line of the extra losses it creates.

That adversity started with Wentz's injury in 2017. And while it is true that Foles' subsequent play that winter was an outlier from his established career standard, his 761 career DYAR entering the season made him one of the best backup quarterbacks in the league. His two-year, $11-million contract certainly paid him as one of the best backups.

No one injury can hurt a team more than one to the starting quarterback, but it would be hard to argue that the combined impact of the injuries the Eagles suffered in 2018 and 2019 wasn't greater than that of Wentz's injury the year before. The Eagles led football with 117.0 adjusted games lost in 2018. On offense, that cost them deep threat Mike Wallace early in the season. He suffered a fractured fibula early in Week 2 that ended his season and eventually his career. The team didn't have a direct skills replacement for Wallace, but they had quality offensive depth thanks to a perceived luxury second-round draft selection of tight end Dallas Goedert. Goedert became a lineup staple alongside tight end star Zach Ertz. Wentz saw his average depth of throw decline from 10.2 yards the year before to just 8.0 yards as the offense morphed to fit its suddenly common 12 personnel, but he continued to excel with 8.1% passing DVOA.

The Eagles' total of 84.4 adjusted games lost in 2019 was only the 12th highest in football, but their injuries clustered to test their depth to an outrageous degree. Wallace's field-stretching replacement, former and now two-time Eagles receiver DeSean Jackson, followed his eight-catch, 154-yard (re-) debut with a core muscle injury that landed him on injured reserve and held him to just one target the rest of the season. Presumed No. 1 receiver Alshon Jeffery lasted just half of the year, suffering calf, hip, and foot injuries that effectively limited him to eight games as a real contributor. The Eagles lost backup receivers such as Nelson Agholor and pass-catching running backs like Darren Sproles and Corey Clement for extended stretches. Ertz only missed one game, but he battled through a broken rib and lacerated kidney in the team's playoff game, a decision one imagines he only made because of the team's myriad other injuries and the stakes of the contest.

Wentz fielded the bulk of the praise for the team's perseverance through its many offensive injuries and rally from a 5-7 record to win their final four games, make the playoffs, and eliminate the division-rival Cowboys in the process. And it's hard to compete with Wentz's incredible distinction of being the first quarterback in NFL history to throw for 4,000 yards without having a single of his receivers reach 500 yards for the season. But Roseman and Pederson deserve as much credit for finding capable players to fill the team's injury voids and for changing the team's approach to fit their different strengths at various points of the season.

Miles Sanders, Boston Scott, Greg Ward, Deontay Burnett, Goedert, and Joshua Perkins started the season as either backups, practice-squad players, or unwanted free agents. But the Eagles still managed an incredible 28.9% DVOA on those players' 231 collective targets from Wentz. The Eagles seemed to see in Scott, Ward, and Burnett value that other teams couldn't, perhaps because of Scott's short height of 5-foot-6 and Ward and Burnett's light weight at 190 and 186 pounds, respectively. And although Goedert and Sanders had the obvious talent that motivated the team's second-round selections of them in 2018 and 2019, the Eagles could afford those luxury picks because of their willingness to trade out of the first round in 2018, netting them the extra second-round pick that became Sanders.

Table 1. Most Pythagorean Wins, 2016-2019

Team	W-L Record	Pyth Wins	Dif
NE	50-14	48.7	+1.3
BAL	41-23	43.3	-2.3
KC	46-18	42.7	+3.3
NO	44-20	41.8	+2.2
MIN	39-24-1	39.6	-0.1
DAL	40-24	38.9	+1.1
PHI	**38-26**	**38.3**	**-0.3**
PIT	41-22-1	37.8	+3.7
SEA	40-23-1	37.1	+3.4
LAC	31-33	36.6	-5.6

Somehow, the Eagles fared even worse with their defensive injury luck the last two seasons, but they and defensive coordinator Jim Schwartz rose to that challenge because of a similar commitment to quality depth and flexibility. They had the third-most (25.7) and most (31.3) adjusted games lost on the defensive line in 2018 and 2019 with Derek Barnett missing most of the former season with a torn rotator cuff, Malik Jackson and Hassan Ridgeway missing most of the latter season with Lisfranc and ankle injuries, and Timmy Jernigan missing parts of both seasons with back and foot injuries. Schwartz responded by playing non-traditional groups of his best remaining defensive linemen, frequently putting Michael Bennett, Brandon Graham, and Vinny Curry inside the tackles to rush the passer from the interior of the line. That kept their defensive pressure rate up around 30% each of the last two seasons, and they still thrived with their resulting undersized defensive lines in run defense. Thanks in large part to five-time Pro Bowl defensive tackle Fletcher Cox, the team finished sixth and third with 3.93 and 3.44 adjusted line yards allowed in 2018 and 2019.

The Eagles have been similarly snake-bitten in their defensive backfield, where a rash of injuries has challenged their depth from presumed starters Ronald Darby and Jalen Mills to backups-turned-starters Avonte Maddox, Sidney Jones, Cre'von LeBlanc, and Orlando Scandrick. At their low point, the Eagles held onto a Week 4 win over the Packers in Green Bay last season down to just two healthy corners, one of whom, Craig James, had been on the team's practice squad earlier that week. James secured that victory on just his third ever defensive snap, jumping the slant route of Marquez Valdes-Scantling—whom Aaron Rodgers undoubtedly targeted because of James' inexperience and late insertion from the bench—and tipping an interception to teammate Nigel Bradham.

James didn't see a ton of work after his game-saving play, but the team's more heavily used backups Maddox, Jones, and Rasul Douglas all excelled in 2019, finishing the season with between 56% and 67% coverage success rates. Expected top corners Darby and Mills ended up with the team's bottom coverage success rates of 48% each. That's an especially surprising low rate for Darby, who had finished the three seasons prior with a coverage success rate of 57% or better. Perhaps his various knee, hamstring, and hip injuries had taken their toll. But either way, the team could let him leave for the Redskins in free agency this offseason because they had identified and developed starting-capable backups and because they conserved the resources to trade for and extend cornerback Darius Slay, who made the last three Pro Bowls for the Lions in seasons with excellent coverage success rates of 57%, 59%, and 53%.

That cornerback arc embodies the approach the Eagles take with their entire roster. As injuries hit their primary and secondary options at corner, they could survive them because they had added Jones, Douglas, and Maddox on Day 2 and 3 of the drafts in 2017 and 2018 before they needed them. They did the same with Goedert and Sanders, who became critical pass-catchers following injuries to several of the team's wide receivers in 2019. And they are poised to do the same with left

tackle Andre Dillard, the team's first-round draft pick from 2019 who had the luxury to learn as primarily a backup in his rookie season but should start in 2020 now that long-time starter Jason Peters has become a free agent.

That is also the approach that makes sense of the team's second-round draft selection of quarterback Jalen Hurts this year. But that's certainly not the public perception of the pick. Informed by the Packers' unexpected trade up and selection of Jordan Love in the first round, many viewed the Hurts selection as an indictment of Wentz, although probably more for Wentz's spotty health track record than his play or the personality conflicts that seem to drive the tension between Aaron Rodgers and the Packers' coaches and front office.

In truth, the Eagles' decision to draft Hurts follows the same logic that had the team pay up for their backup Foles in recent seasons. And if Wentz's injuries have been a motivating factor, they have likely just underscored the Eagles' pre-existing philosophy that their backup quarterback should be viewed as a second quarterback, a player who will likely play and therefore needs to be capable of leading the team.

Foles was an expensive second quarterback that the Eagles could afford because Wentz was on his inexpensive rookie deal. The Eagles are an often overlooked example of a team whose young-quarterback cost savings allowed them to spend more on the rest of their roster and reach the Super Bowl, the same as Colin Kaepernick's 49ers and Russell Wilson's Seahawks before them and Jared Goff's Rams and Mahomes' Chiefs after them. Now that Wentz has signed an extension and will see his cap hit balloon from $8.4 million last year to $18.7 million this year and $34.7 million in 2021, the Eagles need their second quarterback to be a lot less expensive than his value to the team would otherwise necessitate.

With his own wage scale-limited rookie contract, Hurts fits that bill perfectly. And beyond his potential to become a starting-caliber NFL quarterback, Hurts fits the Eagles' current roster perfectly. His athleticism will give him a chance to contribute to the team even when Wentz is healthy—and as a ploy to reduce Wentz's snap count and hopefully keep him healthy more often. And Hurts' graceful response to his Alabama championship-game benching for Tua Tagovailoa—a not totally dissimilar fate to that of Wentz with his injury replacement Foles—makes him a backup the Eagles can trust will not bristle from a non-starting role and disrupt their team chemistry.

Hurts should restore the quality quarterback depth the Eagles had in Foles and needed after Wentz's playoff concussion last year but didn't have, while Hurts' rookie contract allows the team the financial flexibility to fill their roster holes with capable veterans like Slay. Even with Wentz's escalating cap hit, the Eagles still have one of the best and deepest rosters in the league and are one of the top teams in our mean win forecast.

Originally, the Eagles had a similar win projection to their division-rival Cowboys, but then right guard Brandon Brooks tore his Achilles tendon this offseason. He is a major loss for the team. Not only had he made three straight Pro Bowls, but he had several years of experience playing next to returning starters Jason Kelce and Lane Johnson on the offensive line, where stability tends to be critical. But the Eagles shouldn't fear that injury or their projected disadvantage to Dallas. No team survives an NFL season according to their preseason script, and the Eagles have had—and appear again in 2020 to have—the most and best contingency plans. Those should help them survive other teams copying their strategies and injuries to players at pretty much any position. And they should sooner or later show the world that the Eagles, like the Chiefs, are one of the few consistently excellent teams in the sport.

Scott Spratt

2019 Eagles Stats by Week

Wk	vs.	W-L	PF	PA	YDF	YDA	TO	Total	Off	Def	ST
1	WAS	W	32	27	436	398	0	-36%	29%	70%	5%
2	at ATL	L	20	24	286	367	0	6%	-18%	-21%	3%
3	DET	L	24	27	373	287	-2	-34%	-5%	3%	-26%
4	at GB	W	34	27	336	491	+2	64%	50%	0%	14%
5	NYJ	W	31	6	265	128	+2	76%	8%	-66%	1%
6	at MIN	L	20	38	400	447	-1	-15%	5%	25%	5%
7	at DAL	L	10	37	283	402	-3	-61%	-63%	-2%	0%
8	at BUF	W	31	13	371	253	0	49%	31%	-26%	-8%
9	CHI	W	22	14	373	164	+1	20%	12%	-14%	-7%
10	BYE										
11	NE	L	10	17	255	298	-1	29%	15%	-16%	-2%
12	SEA	L	9	17	344	348	-3	-21%	-32%	-13%	-1%
13	at MIA	L	31	37	386	409	0	-24%	-2%	25%	3%
14	NYG	W	23	17	418	255	-1	-12%	-17%	0%	5%
15	at WAS	W	37	27	415	352	0	-38%	3%	43%	2%
16	DAL	W	17	9	431	311	+1	70%	27%	-44%	-1%
17	at NYG	W	34	17	400	397	+2	29%	9%	-15%	5%
18	SEA	L	9	17	282	382	0	-22%	-32%	-1%	9%

Trends and Splits

	Offense	Rank	Defense	Rank
Total DVOA	2.6%	14	-4.0%	12
Unadjusted VOA	4.8%	12	-3.9%	10
Weighted Trend	-0.2%	14	-4.7%	14
Variance	7.4%	18	10.8%	30
Average Opponent	1.4%	25	-2.0%	24
Passing	11.8%	17	5.6%	16
Rushing	-0.7%	13	-18.5%	4
First Down	6.1%	9	7.3%	24
Second Down	-11.6%	25	-26.0%	1
Third Down	18.4%	7	8.4%	20
First Half	-6.2%	22	-1.1%	15
Second Half	11.9%	6	-7.0%	8
Red Zone	27.5%	5	-0.2%	17
Late and Close	21.7%	5	-2.1%	17

Five-Year Performance

Year	W-L	Pyth W	Est W	PF	PA	TO	Total	Rk	Off	Rk	Def	Rk	ST	Rk	Off AGL	Rk	Def AGL	Rk	Off Age	Rk	Def Age	Rk	ST Age	Rk
2015	7-9	6.7	6.8	377	430	-5	-11.2%	22	-10.1%	26	3.0%	17	1.9%	10	22.7	5	27.3	12	27.2	11	26.7	15	26.9	2
2016	7-9	9.0	9.9	367	331	+6	14.4%	5	-5.5%	20	-12.4%	4	7.5%	2	20.4	3	17.7	4	27.0	11	26.9	9	27.0	3
2017	13-3	12.0	11.1	457	295	+11	23.4%	5	10.1%	8	-12.3%	5	0.9%	16	29.0	13	24.4	9	27.1	12	26.9	9	26.4	7
2018	9-7	8.5	8.0	367	348	-9	-0.1%	16	-0.3%	16	0.0%	15	0.2%	15	46.0	22	71.0	31	27.9	5	27.6	3	25.5	26
2019	9-7	8.8	9.2	385	354	-3	6.6%	11	2.6%	14	-4.0%	12	0.0%	19	30.3	10	54.1	29	27.8	3	27.2	4	25.6	21

2019 Performance Based on Most Common Personnel Groups

PHI Offense					PHI Offense vs. Opponents					PHI Defense					PHI Defense vs. Opponents			
Pers	Freq	Yds	DVOA	Run%	Pers	Freq	Yds	DVOA	Run%	Pers	Freq	Yds	DVOA	Pers	Freq	Yds	DVOA
12	46%	5.4	6.2%	33%	Base	23%	4.6	-1.3%	49%	Base	20%	5.6	-12.9%	11	63%	5.9	4.9%
11	41%	5.3	0.9%	35%	Nickel	66%	5.7	6.2%	37%	Nickel	48%	5.7	-2.2%	12	13%	3.9	-51.2%
612	4%	5.6	33.8%	90%	Dime+	10%	5.1	28.0%	11%	Dime+	26%	5.9	8.9%	21	9%	6.2	7.1%
13	3%	2.2	-11.6%	47%	Goal Line	0%	0.8	80.8%	80%	Goal Line	1%	1.3	-3.5%	13	4%	7.4	13.0%
21	3%	7.7	36.1%	45%						Big	4%	4.0	-47.2%	22	3%	4.7	-19.9%

Strategic Tendencies

Run/Pass		Rk	Formation		Rk	Pass Rush		Rk	Secondary		Rk	Strategy		Rk
Runs, first half	37%	16	Form: Single Back	93%	1	Rush 3	3.0%	29	4 DB	20%	22	Play Action	31%	7
Runs, first down	48%	18	Form: Empty Back	5%	26	Rush 4	75.9%	5	5 DB	48%	23	Offensive Motion	32%	25
Runs, second-long	26%	21	Form: Multi Back	2%	29	Rush 5	11.4%	30	6+ DB	26%	8	Avg Box (Off)	6.51	22
Runs, power sit.	58%	14	Pers: 3+ WR	41%	31	Rush 6+	9.8%	4	Man Coverage	36%	9	Avg Box (Def)	6.83	1
Runs, behind 2H	31%	11	Pers: 2+ TE/6+ OL	57%	1	Edge Rusher Sacks	58.1%	14	CB by Sides	84%	11	Offensive Pace	30.81	17
Pass, ahead 2H	51%	11	Pers: 6+ OL	6%	7	Interior DL Sacks	17.4%	24	S/CB Cover Ratio	21%	27	Defensive Pace	29.54	3
Run-Pass Options	12%	3	Shotgun/Pistol	72%	8	Second Level Sacks	24.4%	9	DB Blitz	14%	6	Go for it on 4th	2.06	4

The Eagles were one of just two teams in 2019 that did not have 11 personnel as their most common personnel grouping, using 12 personnel more often. The Eagles threw 39% of passes to tight ends, one of the five highest rates since 1985 (see table in the Baltimore chapter, page 16). They also threw a league-low 8% of passes to "other wide receivers" besides the top two. ◐ Philadelphia averaged 9.6 yards after the catch on passes thrown at or behind the line of scrimmage, fifth in the NFL. They averaged 2.9 yards after the catch on passes thrown past the line of scrimmage, 31st. ◐ Philadelphia's 28.9% DVOA with six linemen was the highest in the league among the 17 teams that used six linemen on at least 2.5% of plays. ◐ The Eagles offense ranked 22nd in the first half of games, but sixth in DVOA after halftime. ◐ The Eagles were one of three teams that used play-action on over 10% of third-down passes. (Indianapolis and New England were the others.) ◐ The Philadelphia defense had the league's biggest gap between man and zone coverage. With man coverage, they allowed 5.9 yards per pass with -1.8% DVOA. With zone coverage, they allowed 8.1 yards per pass with 48.9% DVOA.

Passing

Player	DYAR	DVOA	Plays	NtYds	Avg	YAC	C%	TD	Int
C.Wentz	476	0.1%	645	3788	5.9	4.7	64.0%	27	6

Rushing

Player	DYAR	DVOA	Plays	Yds	Avg	TD	Fum	Suc
M.Sanders	14	-6.6%	179	818	4.6	3	2	45%
J.Howard*	113	14.2%	119	525	4.4	6	0	53%
B.Scott	85	22.2%	61	245	4.0	5	1	52%
C.Wentz	56	6.1%	52	242	4.7	1	3	-
D.Sproles*	-4	-14.3%	17	66	3.9	0	0	41%
J.Ajayi*	-15	-34.2%	10	30	3.0	0	0	40%

Receiving

Player	DYAR	DVOA	Plays	Ctch	Yds	Y/C	YAC	TD	C%
A.Jeffery	50	-4.2%	73	43	490	11.4	2.7	4	59%
N.Agholor*	-123	-35.0%	69	39	363	9.3	3.4	3	57%
G.Ward	-20	-19.0%	40	28	254	9.1	3.5	1	70%
J.Arcega-Whiteside	1	-12.3%	22	10	169	16.9	1.6	1	45%
M.Hollins*	-41	-37.1%	22	10	125	12.5	3.3	0	45%
J.Matthews*	-28	-43.5%	12	4	33	8.3	1.8	0	33%
D.Jackson	47	41.6%	10	9	159	17.7	1.7	2	90%
M.Goodwin	36	7.4%	21	12	186	15.5	2.8	1	57%
Z.Ertz	27	-4.3%	135	88	916	10.4	2.9	6	65%
D.Goedert	30	-2.1%	87	58	607	10.5	5.8	5	67%
J.Perkins	4	-2.0%	13	9	87	9.7	2.9	1	69%
M.Sanders	121	20.0%	63	50	509	10.2	8.3	3	79%
B.Scott	67	29.0%	26	24	204	8.5	11.4	0	92%
J.Howard*	17	6.7%	14	10	69	6.9	6.9	1	71%
D.Sproles*	-30	-63.4%	10	6	24	4.0	4.2	0	60%

Offensive Line

Player	Pos	Age	GS	Snaps	Pen	Sk	Pass	Run	Player	Pos	Age	GS	Snaps	Pen	Sk	Pass	Run
Jason Kelce	C	33	16/16	1184	3	0.8	11	9	Lane Johnson	RT	30	12/12	774	5	1.5	8	4
Isaac Seumalo	LG	27	16/16	1182	6	4.7	18	11	Halapoulivaati Vaitai*	RT	27	16/3	481	5	3.0	15	5
Brandon Brooks	RG	31	16/16	1065	2	1.5	6	3	Andre Dillard	LT	25	16/4	346	1	5.3	20	3
Jason Peters*	LT	38	13/13	885	9	2.5	17	5									

Year	Yards	ALY	Rank	Power	Rank	Stuff	Rank	2nd Lev	Rank	Open Field	Rank	Sacks	ASR	Rank	Press	Rank	F-Start	Cont.
2017	4.52	3.85	22	64%	16	21%	21	1.30	4	1.14	3	36	6.2%	12	34.4%	26	16	28
2018	4.12	4.14	19	62%	25	21%	26	1.28	15	0.61	27	40	6.7%	17	26.0%	7	18	30
2019	4.36	4.34	14	76%	3	18%	13	1.17	18	0.78	16	37	6.4%	11	28.6%	10	15	31

2019 ALY by direction: Left End 4.44 (9)   Left Tackle: 3.70 (24)   Mid/Guard: 5.19 (2)   Right Tackle: 3.76 (23)   Right End: 2.88 (30)

The offensive line was the one Eagles unit that didn't suffer significant injuries in 2019. Presumed starters Jason Peters, Isaac Seumalo, Jason Kelce, Brandon Brooks, and Lane Johnson started 73 of a possible 80 games and provided above-average pass protection and run-blocking that enabled an otherwise injury-decimated offense to remain afloat. 🏈 The Eagles won't have that luxury in 2020 after Brooks tore his Achilles tendon this offseason. He will miss the entire year. The team still has Kelce and Johnson and their combined six Pro Bowl and four All-Pro selections to anchor the right side of their line, but Brooks also made the Pro Bowl in each of the last three seasons. And his absence will also disrupt the unit's continuity, which can often be as important to a team's blocking as the talent of its individual blockers. Third-year utility lineman Matt Pryor is the most likely replacement for Brooks, at least to start the season. 🏈 The Brooks injury is particularly distressing because of the Eagles' uncertainty at left tackle and left guard. While not the All-Pro producer that he was in his prime, Peters enjoyed a slow decline that nevertheless may have culminated in a below-average season of 40.2 snaps per blown block at 37 years old in 2019. The Eagles planned for Peters' free agency a year ahead of time, selecting left tackle Andre Dillard in the first round of the 2019 draft. Dillard should take over for Peters in 2020, but his 15.0 snaps per blown block as a part-time player as a rookie was the second-worst rate among tackles with 300 or more snaps and is concerning. 🏈 Seumalo has established a higher floor than Dillard with consecutive seasons of nine or more starts and between 40 and 55 snaps per blown block, but those rates still fall in the bottom half of qualified guards. Meanwhile, if Seumalo struggles or a second starter on the line suffers an injury, the team does not have much experience behind them. Fourth-round rookie tackle Jack Driscoll is the team's only offensive line selection other than Dillard in the first five rounds of the four most recent drafts. The Eagles may view Driscoll as insurance for Seumalo or Pryor despite his position at Auburn, as a 33-inch wingspan may necessitate Driscoll's transition to guard despite his excellent size and speed for the outside.

Defensive Front

Defensive Line	Age	Pos	G	Snaps	Plays	Overall TmPct	Rk	Stop	Dfts	BTkl	Runs	vs. Run St%	Rk	RuYd	Rk	Pass Rush Sack	Hit	Hur	Dsrpt
Fletcher Cox	30	DT	16	815	42	5.6%	29	31	15	8	32	69%	74	2.4	52	3.5	10	24	0
Timmy Jernigan*	28	DT	10	281	10	2.1%	95	10	4	0	7	100%	1	0.1	1	2.0	2	8	0
Anthony Rush	24	DT	9	152	11	2.6%	--	10	3	0	8	100%	--	-0.3	--	0.0	0	3	2
Javon Hargrave	27	DT	16	692	58	6.8%	15	40	12	6	52	67%	76	3.1	90	4.0	2	28	1

Edge Rushers	Age	Pos	G	Snaps	Plays	Overall TmPct	Rk	Stop	Dfts	BTkl	Runs	vs. Run St%	Rk	RuYd	Rk	Pass Rush Sack	Hit	Hur	Dsrpt
Brandon Graham	32	DE	16	793	49	6.5%	23	43	23	10	33	85%	10	0.4	3	8.5	8	37	0
Derek Barnett	24	DE	14	715	30	4.5%	58	23	12	5	20	80%	21	2.4	45	6.5	16	26	2
Vinny Curry*	32	DE	16	397	27	3.6%	--	22	7	1	15	93%	--	2.3	--	5.0	8	25	1
Josh Sweat	23	DE	16	353	20	2.6%	--	16	10	0	13	77%	--	1.2	--	4.0	7	16	2

Linebackers	Age	Pos	G	Snaps	Plays	Overall TmPct	Rk	Stop	Dfts	BTkl	Runs	vs. Run St%	Rk	RuYd	Rk	Pass Rush Sack	Hit	Hur	vs. Pass Tgts	Suc%	Rk	AdjYd	Rk	PD	Int
Nigel Bradham*	31	MLB	12	733	65	11.5%	60	33	11	10	27	63%	32	3.3	21	0.0	1	5	21	43%	53	5.6	24	5	1
Nathan Gerry	25	OLB	16	629	77	10.2%	41	50	15	18	37	84%	2	2.4	6	2.5	2	8	25	56%	19	4.2	6	5	2
Kamu Grugier-Hill*	26	OLB	10	304	22	4.7%	83	11	6	6	14	57%	50	3.7	33	0.0	1	2	9	56%	--	6.9	--	0	0
Zach Brown*	31	OLB	6	275	31	10.9%	81	19	4	2	18	78%	4	2.6	7	0.0	0	2	10	40%	--	7.3	--	2	0
T.J. Edwards	24	MLB	16	115	22	2.9%	--	14	1	1	18	72%	--	3.3	--	0.0	0	0	4	75%	--	2.3	--	0	0

Year	Yards	ALY	Rank	Power	Rank	Stuff	Rank	2nd Level	Rank	Open Field	Rank	Sacks	ASR	Rank	Press	Rank
2017	3.35	2.99	1	55%	6	29%	2	0.88	1	0.83	23	38	6.3%	19	32.2%	9
2018	4.56	3.93	6	62%	8	26%	2	1.22	17	1.44	32	44	6.5%	26	29.7%	19
2019	3.72	3.44	3	67%	22	26%	3	1.00	4	0.87	23	43	7.0%	17	30.6%	14
2019 ALY by direction:		Left End: 3.8 (13)			Left Tackle: 2.86 (2)			Mid/Guard: 3.44 (3)			Right Tackle: 3.79 (7)			Right End: 3.32 (9)	

With veteran safety Malcolm Jenkins now with the Saints, All-Pro defensive tackle Fletcher Cox is the unquestioned leader of the Eagles defense. That's something he demonstrated on the field in 2019 with strong totals of 31 stops, 15 defeats, and 24 hurries as he led an injury-limited defensive front to its fourth straight season in the top six of adjusted line yards. It's also something he demonstrated off the field, hosting workouts for his defensive line teammates at his home in Houston this offseason during the quarantine. 🏈 After losing Malik Jackson and Timmy Jernigan for much of last season, the Eagles added to their defensive line depth by signing former Steelers defensive tackle Javon Hargrave. Hargrave has steadily improved in his four

NFL seasons, culminating in career highs in tackles, stops, defeats, and hurries in 2019, besting Cox in all of those categories. It's unclear whether defensive coordinator Jim Schwartz will be able to play Cox, Jackson, and Hargrave together in 2020, but he has become known for his willingness to move his defensive ends into the interior. Perhaps he will do the opposite next season. At 32 years old, Brandon Graham is the elder statesman of the Eagles' pass rush, but he continued to set the pace for the team's defensive ends with 37 hurries in 2019. Derek Barnett returned for a full season after a 2018 shoulder injury but again failed to crack 30 hurries. The team could use a breakout for the former first-rounder in 2020 since they lost position-flexible Vinny Curry in free agency and didn't replace him with another free agent or top draft pick. Former fourth-rounders Josh Sweat and Shareef Miller could be heavy rotation members as well. Miller in fact predicted a 10-sack season for himself on Twitter, so go ahead and put that in pen. Linebacker was an underwhelming unit for the Eagles even before they let Nigel Bradham and Kamu Grugier-Hill walk in free agency. Their departures leave the team with incumbent starter Nathan Gerry—whose 29.0% broken tackle rate was tied for third-worst among linebackers with 50 or more attempted tackles—and the mostly unproven Duke Riley and T.J. Edwards. The Eagles passed on potential plug-and-play linebackers Josh Uche and Zack Baun to select quarterback Jalen Hurts in the second round, so they'll have to hope that Davion Taylor (third round, Colorado) and Shaun Bradley (sixth round, Temple) can outperform their draft slots. Interestingly, Taylor, Bradley, and the veterans Gerry and Riley all ran sub-4.6s 40-yard dashes at their respective combines. Speed seems to be the common element in the Eagles' offseason additions on both sides of the ball.

Defensive Secondary

Secondary	Age	Pos	G	Snaps	Plays	TmPct	Rk	Stop	Dfts	BTkl	Runs	St%	Rk	RuYd	Rk	Tgts	Tgt%	Rk	Dist	Suc%	Rk	AdjYd	Rk	PD	Int
Malcolm Jenkins*	33	SS	16	1035	86	11.4%	16	42	17	12	36	50%	15	7.4	44	40	8.9%	24	9.8	55%	25	7.1	30	8	0
Rodney McLeod	30	FS	16	1033	80	10.6%	21	32	8	14	36	47%	24	5.6	22	25	5.6%	60	9.0	60%	16	7.1	31	6	2
Rasul Douglas	25	CB	16	591	45	6.0%	68	23	10	6	13	62%	21	3.8	14	52	20.4%	38	16.8	58%	21	8.7	67	10	0
Avonte Maddox	24	CB	12	527	57	10.1%	46	25	12	5	11	18%	79	9.0	69	52	22.8%	19	10.7	56%	28	6.9	24	10	0
Ronald Darby*	26	CB	11	522	48	9.2%	58	21	7	9	10	50%	34	9.0	69	59	26.2%	4	16.1	47%	62	10.6	82	11	2
Jalen Mills	26	CB	9	511	48	11.3%	58	17	4	4	15	40%	50	5.1	28	48	21.7%	26	14.6	48%	61	8.7	64	7	1
Sidney Jones	24	CB	12	300	29	5.1%	--	20	10	3	3	67%	--	2.0	--	30	23.2%	--	11.3	67%	--	6.3	--	8	2
Darius Slay	29	CB	14	871	59	7.9%	50	20	6	5	8	25%	72	12.6	83	76	20.3%	40	15.2	53%	42	7.8	47	13	2
Nickell Robey-Coleman	28	CB	16	714	42	5.0%	--	22	16	12	9	67%	--	3.3	--	42	16.0%	--	10.0	55%	--	6.5	--	7	0
Will Parks	26	FS	14	555	33	4.5%	71	15	4	8	16	50%	15	3.7	3	30	14.8%	4	11.8	63%	9	5.8	19	2	1

Year	Pass D Rank	vs. #1 WR	Rk	vs. #2 WR	Rk	vs. Other WR	Rk	WR Wide	Rk	WR Slot	Rk	vs. TE	Rk	vs. RB	Rk
2017	8	-15.8%	7	-48.5%	1	5.9%	21	-12.1%	7	-25.4%	1	0.7%	17	-6.1%	10
2018	15	0.0%	15	6.5%	22	-2.7%	16	8.1%	25	-6.6%	9	-16.1%	7	11.2%	24
2019	16	2.2%	16	6.4%	21	-2.1%	17	-6.5%	15	15.4%	23	-5.2%	11	-10.2%	9

The loss of three-time Pro Bowler Malcolm Jenkins will leave a void in the Eagles secondary, but it's hard to argue that the team didn't improve there overall after trading for and extending cornerback Darius Slay. Slay's 53% coverage success rate in 2019 was a three-year low for him, but it still beat the rates of the Eagles' 2019 starters Ronald Darby and Jalen Mills by 5% each. With Darby and Mills frequently injured, backups-turned-starters Avonte Maddox, Rasul Douglas, and Sidney Jones made strong cases for permanent starter roles with success rates above 55%. Maddox will likely draw the starting assignment alongside Slay, although Douglas or Jones could also start, especially if Maddox's 5-foot-9 stature causes coverage issues against bigger receivers. Philadelphia's other offseason cornerback addition is appropriately named nickelback Nickell Robey-Coleman, who you may remember for his uncalled defensive pass interference on Tommylee Lewis in the 2019 NFC Championship Game between the Rams and Saints. The Eagles filled Jenkins' roster spot with former Broncos safety Will Parks. Replacing Jenkins would be a tough ask of the historically part-time player, but he will have help in the form of the former corner Mills, who the team retained and plans to convert to safety in 2020. Adding experience to the position will be Rodney McLeod, who has been a starter for the team the last four years and posted excellent 56% and 60% coverage success rates in his two most recent healthy seasons.

Special Teams

Year	DVOA	Rank	FG/XP	Rank	Net Kick	Rank	Kick Ret	Rank	Net Punt	Rank	Punt Ret	Rank	Hidden	Rank
2017	0.9%	16	3.9	11	-0.8	21	0.6	12	3.4	14	-2.5	22	0.8	12
2018	0.2%	15	-0.5	19	3.1	7	-2.6	23	6.4	6	-5.3	28	-6.7	24
2019	0.0%	19	3.8	11	-3.6	25	-2.3	23	5.0	9	-3.1	24	-13.5	32

The Eagles ran in two or more return touchdowns in 2014, 2015, and 2016, but have not managed a single return touchdown in the three years since. That's a one-sentence explanation of how the team saw its perennial top-10 special teams unit become a perennial middle-of-the-pack one. ◥ Not coincidentally, 2016 was Darren Sproles' last healthy year and Josh Huff's last year with the team, period. They've tried a number of players at punt and kick returner since with little luck. Even breakout offensive players Miles Sanders and Boston Scott failed to excel in their stints as kick returners in 2019. ◥ Things could change for the Eagles in 2020 following their run on speedy receivers in the draft. Fifth- and sixth-round selections John Hightower and Quez Watkins have college return experience and track-star speed. Hightower literally ran track at his junior college before transferring to Boise State, and Watkins ran the second-fastest 40-yard dash (4.35 seconds) among receivers at this year's combine. ◥ The team's net kick value dropped from 2018, but that was the fault of the coverage team rather than kicker Jake Elliott. Elliott improved from third-best in 2018 to No. 1 last season in gross kickoff value. ◥ He may not have an All-Pro selection like his countrymate Michael Dickson, but punter Cameron Johnston looks like another excellent Australian import. His 48.1 and 46.4 average yards per punt in 2018 and 2019 landed him in the top eight at the position. ◥ Philadelphia's high rating in "hidden" special teams comes from opponents being particularly strong last year on both field goals and gross punt distance.

Pittsburgh Steelers

2019 Record: 8-8	Total DVOA: -5.4% (18th)	2020 Mean Projection: 9.0 wins	On the Clock (0-4): 5%
Pythagorean Wins: 7.6 (18th)	Offense: -25.3% (32nd)	Postseason Odds: 58.6%	Mediocrity (5-7): 23%
Snap-Weighted Age: 26.4 (16th)	Defense: -18.4% (3rd)	Super Bowl Odds: 9.0%	Playoff Contender (8-10): 42%
Average Opponent: 1.5% (10th)	Special Teams: 1.5% (8th)	Proj. Avg. Opponent: -2.1% (31st)	Super Bowl Contender (11+): 30%

2019: The worst offense in the NFL is almost dragged to the playoffs by one of the best defenses in the NFL.

2020: Big Ben's last hurrah, or was 2019 just a bump in the road?

" I know where Ben [Roethlisberger] is, where he's been in his career, and I've never worried about his conditioning," Steelers general manager Kevin Colbert told *The Pittsburgh Tribune-Review* in May. Questions arose when Jay Glazer of The Athletic characterized Roethlisberger's offseason plan as "doing one yoga session, playing golf, and drinking some beer."

Roethlisberger suffered an elbow injury in Week 2's game against Seattle and missed the rest of the season. He had surgery to reattach three tendons and was essentially characterized by media jokesters as the lost McCrary Twin. The Steelers have been quite steadfast in their insistence that Roethlisberger will be prepared and ready for this season. Mike Tomlin told *First Take* in February that he had "no hesitation" that Roethlisberger would be ready for Week 1. The Steelers stuck with Mason Rudolph and Devlin Hodges as backups despite the fact that players like Jameis Winston and Cam Newton were free agents long past the NFL draft. They are unified behind the idea that Roethlisberger will be what he was before the injury.

The history of quarterbacks over 35 years old that have had a year of 100 or fewer pass attempts since 2000 suggests that caution may be more warranted. It's a 13-quarterback list

Table 1: Low-Attempt Starting Quarterbacks over 35, 2000-2019

Player	Year	Age	Team	GS	Att	Prior Career AV	Future Career AV
Randall Cunningham	2001	38	BAL	2	89	134	0
Vinny Testaverde	2002	39	NYJ	4	83	125	17
Steve Beuerlein	2003	38	DEN	2	63	83	0
Chris Chandler	2004	39	STL	2	62	102	0
Rich Gannon	2004	39	OAK	3	68	120	0
Damon Huard	2008	35	KC	3	81	20	0
Brad Johnson	2008	40	DAL	3	78	90	0
Charlie Batch	2010	36	PIT	2	49	34	2
Kerry Collins	2011	39	IND	3	98	111	0
Charlie Batch	2012	38	PIT	2	70	37	0
Michael Vick	2015	35	PIT	3	66	113	0
Derek Anderson	2018	35	BUF	2	70	22	0
Matt Moore	2019	35	KC	2	91	19	—
Ben Roethlisberger	**2019**	**37**	**PIT**	**2**	**62**	**186**	—

in which exactly one quarterback ever entered a season as a starter again (Table 1).

Now, yes, Roethlisberger has had a more distinguished career than these players, but that's because Roethlisberger is a likely Hall of Famer. There are some very good quarterbacks on this list who played a long, long time, some who started Super Bowls. Once they hit Roethlisberger's age and took a major injury, only Vinny Testaverde made it back to the field as a starter. You may remember the fabled 2004 season in which Testaverde started 15 games for the Cowboys, leading them to a 5-10 record at 41 years old and leading the league in interceptions with a 32-year-old Keyshawn Johnson as his main target. The 2004 Cowboys were basically a 1998 Jets sequel that came out five years too late.

What we're talking about Pittsburgh relying on Roethlisberger to do here, then, is essentially unprecedented in recent NFL history. Even if we expand our view a little and look at other Hall of Famers, most of them take that season and are done. Steve Young, Bob Griese, and Bart Starr all had that season and never played again. Johnny Unitas did something approximating what the Steelers are asking Roethlisberger to do at 36 years old, in 1969, He was coming off a five-game, 32-attempt season in 1968. If your eyes glazed over that, 1968 is the year when the Jets upset the Colts in Super Bowl III. To tell the tale from a 1997 *Baltimore Sun* column, Unitas had "the flexor and pronator muscles torn from their track by the intensity of a hit" that he took in the final game of 1968's preseason. He actually came back from the injury to play in the second half of Super Bowl III. Unitas played two more solid seasons with a lower volume than in his prime, winning Super Bowl V, then became a part-timer.

So even if the Steelers believe that they can trust in 16 games of Roethlisberger, it can absolutely be characterized as a risk that they didn't make more of an effort to secure a solid backup. It goes without saying that the kind of production the Steelers get out of Roethlisberger could be one of the great turning points of the NFL season this year. If they get 2018 vintage Roethlisberger and pair him with the defense they got last season after trading for Minkah Fitzpatrick, this could be one of the best teams in the AFC. If they go right back to the hellscape that was inflicted on them by their backup quarterbacks in 2019, this team will be fighting for its playoff life every week.

2020 Steelers Schedule					
Week	Opp.	Week	Opp.	Week	Opp.
1	at NYG (Mon.)	7	at BAL	13	WAS
2	DEN	8	BYE	14	at BUF
3	HOU	9	at DAL	15	at CIN (Mon.)
4	at TEN	10	CIN	16	IND
5	PHI	11	at JAX	17	at CLE
6	CLE	12	BAL (Thu.)		

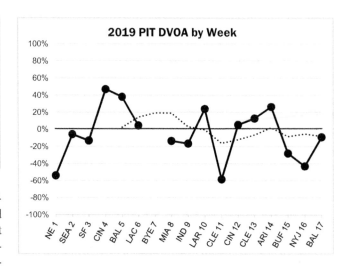

2019 PIT DVOA by Week

Because while it has dawned on folks that Pittsburgh's offense was bad without Roethlisberger, it hasn't really seemed to hit the public consciousness how bad it was and how it changed the entire operation. They saw the quick lead Pittsburgh jumped out to against the Chargers in Week 6 on Sunday Night Football and assumed that the rest of the season played out that easily. Pittsburgh threw for more than 200 yards as a team just three times from Week 2 on, and two of them were against bottom-three DVOA Bengals and Dolphins defenses. Overall, the Steelers had one of the five greatest one-year drops in offensive DVOA ever measured (Table 2).

Table 2. Biggest Year-to-Year Offensive Declines by DVOA, 1986-2019

Year	Team	Year N-1	Rank	Year N	Rank	Change	Year N+1	Rank
2010	ARI	6.8%	13	-35.6%	31	-42.4%	-18.4%	28
2005	NYJ	20.8%	4	-19.8%	31	-40.6%	5.6%	12
2006	SEA	28.5%	1	-11.2%	27	-39.7%	6.6%	11
2019	**PIT**	**13.8%**	**6**	**-25.3%**	**32**	**-39.1%**	—	—
2006	OAK	-0.6%	15	-37.0%	32	-36.4%	-18.0%	28
1991	PHI	11.1%	6	-24.6%	26	-35.7%	10.5%	5
2013	NYG	12.8%	7	-22.0%	31	-34.9%	-0.3%	15
2010	CAR	-2.0%	20	-35.8%	32	-33.8%	18.2%	4
2015	DAL	16.8%	4	-15.6%	31	-32.5%	19.9%	3
2006	DEN	26.9%	2	-4.8%	18	-31.7%	9.5%	8

Rudolph was one of two qualifying quarterbacks last year to have a negative DVOA on throws against zone coverage at -2.6%. (Kyle Allen was the other.) Duck Hodges had a DVOA of -11.2% against zone coverage. Hodges, in particular, was regarded as such a liability that opposing defenses played man coverage against him on just 22% of his pass dropbacks, which would have been the lowest rate among qualifying quarterbacks in the NFL. In 2018, Roethlisberger had a 44.8% DVOA against zone coverage and teams played more man against him than they did against all but three other qualifying starting quarterbacks. Some of the change there is the drop-off from Antonio Brown to the other underneath receivers that Pittsburgh used in 2020, but neither Rudolph nor Hodges acquitted themselves well in extended trials. Rudolph threw three picks against zone coverage in a ghastly loss to the

Browns on Thursday Night Football that will be remembered more for helmet-swinging. Hodges threw four picks against zone against the Bills in Week 15 in a game with huge playoff implications that the Steelers lost by seven points. A careful watch of the Steelers games with either of these two quarterbacks starting—and I plead that you don't do this to yourself—shows a real lack of ability to diagnose a defense. Plays where JuJu Smith-Schuster is jumping up and down because he wasn't targeted on a slant to the wide side of the field that was open, plays where a first read was locked on to a little too long, plays where underneath defenders that weren't accounted for before the snap undercut routes. The difference between Roethlisberger's mind for the game and those of Rudolph and Hodges was quite evident.

How did that inconsistency manifest itself? Teams stacked the box and dared the Steelers to beat simple zones and the backup quarterbacks simply couldn't do it. They faced the fourth-highest average number of players in the box in the NFL, at 6.76. In 2018, that average box number was 6.16, 20th in the NFL. Pittsburgh used more throws behind the line of scrimmage than any NFL team in 2018 and had a 21.1% DVOA on those throws. In 2019? They finished fourth in the NFL in throws behind the line of scrimmage but had a -2.0% DVOA on those throws. It was a disappointing season for a number of Steelers receivers, particularly Smith-Schuster, James Washington, and Jaylen Samuels. Every receiver the Steelers threw to behind the line of scrimmage more than 10 times finished with a negative DVOA, and as a team they finished with -196 DYAR on those throws. When you watch some of the quick throws that this team ran out of empty sets last year with Rudolph and compare them to Roethlisberger's 2018 tape, it accentuates how much pre-snap adjustments can mean for a spacing offense.

Thus, Pittsburgh was able to remain competitive in 2019 solely because of their defense, which suddenly spiked with the offseason additions of linebacker Devin Bush and cornerback Steven Nelson followed by the in-season acquisition of Minkah Fitzpatrick from the Dolphins for a first-round pick. While certain aspects of Pittsburgh's defense have been good for a while, like the monster pass rush that has finished No. 1 in adjusted sack rate for three straight years, the defense prior to 2019 had a few specific holes in coverage that opponents could attack. The mitigating factors were always the poor cornerback play and an inability to adjust as a defense to throws over the middle. You could reliably set your watch to Artie Burns giving up big plays and Pittsburgh not having a real backup plan for that. As for the throws over the middle, the Chargers memorably carved up the Steelers in base personnel in a 2018 game where Keenan Allen was targeted *19* times, catching 14 passes for 148 yards and a score. Sports Info Solutions marked 11 of those 19 throws as uncovered or covered by a linebacker.

In 2019, the Steelers had just 36 throws *total* where SIS marked a linebacker as the main coverage player, and only 19 where a linebacker was the main coverage player against a wide receiver. Bush's speed in a vacuum made throws over the middle a lot less viable, and once Fitzpatrick came aboard those throws were all but erased by the range that the pair demonstrated. "If I was in the middle of the field, they weren't going to be throwing it into the middle of the field," Fitzpatrick told Steelers.com after the season. "If I was in the half, they weren't going to be targeting that area. Wherever I was, I don't know if it was game plan, or just decision-making by the quarterback, but I did realize a difference." Table 3 shows just how much instant impact Bush and Fitzpatrick made. Both are still young, and there should be a lot of hope that they can build on that performance even further.

Meanwhile, Nelson was stunningly competent. He was

Table 3. Pittsburgh's Defensive Improvement, 2018-2019

Category	2018		2019	
	DVOA	Rk	DVOA	Rk
Defense DVOA	-0.9%	13	-18.4%	3
Run Defense DVOA	-13.1%	8	-20.3%	3
Pass Defense DVOA	7.5%	17	-16.5%	3
Short Middle DVOA	14.9%	22	-18.5%	2
Deep Middle DVOA	76.9%	28	11.4%	11

somewhat of an overlooked free-agent signing given how bad the Chiefs pass defense was in 2018, but Nelson had a 60% success rate for the Steelers that almost mirrored the 59% he had in 2018 with the Chiefs. Joe Haden and Mike Hilton were never really problems and remained solid in 2019 with better support over the middle of the field and no sieve on the outside. (The Steelers did have a bit of a problem with slot receivers in 2019, but they shut down both running backs and tight ends.)

There's some regression coming for the defense and the loss of Javon Hargrave to the Eagles will likely be felt to some extent. (Chris Wormley, who came from the Ravens in a rare interdivisional trade, is not an equal replacement.) But if you believe in Roethlisberger to be healthy and good next season, it's hard to see the Steelers as anything but a good team and our projections certainly mirror that attitude.

Nonetheless, there is a deep floor for this offense that can't be completely ignored. Roethlisberger is 38, James Conner and Smith-Schuster are heading into the final year of their rookie deals, and the offensive line lost Ramon Foster and B.J. Finney. The three anchors of the line are over 30 now; Matt Feiler, one of two younger starters, will be a free agent after this season. Only Diontae Johnson really showed much promise in last season's lost offense. There is a dark potential future where Pittsburgh winds up having to totally start over on offense next season as they deal with cap concerns potentially arising from COVID-19, injuries, and age.

However, that is just one of many potential futures. And even as regression threatens some of the defense's gains last season, the Steelers will likely remain pretty competitive this season with a weak projected schedule. The question is more if they'll reprise last year's all-defense/no-offense role, or if they'll reclaim the spot among the AFC's elite that they've had for most of the Roethlisberger Era. The sword of Damocles dangling over an old superstar quarterback can fall at any time. It finally fell for the Patriots last year. The question that guides the franchise as things stand is simply: How much more does Ben have to give?

Rivers McCown

2019 Steelers Stats by Week

Wk	vs.	W-L	PF	PA	YDF	YDA	TO	Total	Off	Def	ST
1	at NE	L	3	33	308	465	-1	-54%	-8%	42%	-4%
2	SEA	L	26	28	261	425	+1	-6%	7%	15%	2%
3	at SF	L	20	24	239	436	+3	-13%	-14%	-8%	-8%
4	CIN	W	27	3	326	175	+1	47%	6%	-36%	6%
5	BAL	L	23	26	269	277	+1	38%	-19%	-63%	-6%
6	at LAC	W	24	17	256	348	+2	5%	-6%	-8%	2%
7	BYE										
8	MIA	W	27	14	394	230	+3	-13%	-24%	-16%	-6%
9	IND	W	26	24	273	328	+1	-16%	-33%	-2%	15%
10	LAR	W	17	12	273	306	+2	24%	-27%	-60%	-8%
11	at CLE	L	7	21	236	293	-4	-58%	-65%	-8%	-1%
12	at CIN	W	16	10	338	244	+1	6%	-39%	-30%	14%
13	CLE	W	20	13	323	279	+1	13%	-17%	-19%	11%
14	at ARI	W	23	17	275	236	+1	27%	-21%	-34%	14%
15	BUF	L	10	17	229	261	-3	-28%	-52%	-19%	5%
16	at NYJ	L	10	16	260	259	-1	-43%	-50%	0%	7%
17	at BAL	L	10	28	168	304	0	-9%	-31%	-42%	-20%

Trends and Splits

	Offense	Rank	Defense	Rank
Total DVOA	-25.3%	32	-18.4%	3
Unadjusted VOA	-22.8%	32	-17.5%	3
Weighted Trend	-33.6%	32	-24.3%	1
Variance	4.1%	3	7.1%	22
Average Opponent	-1.0%	11	0.0%	16
Passing	-18.3%	30	-16.5%	3
Rushing	-22.3%	30	-20.3%	3
First Down	-22.7%	30	-25.2%	2
Second Down	-21.7%	31	-25.7%	2
Third Down	-36.6%	29	7.9%	19
First Half	-25.8%	32	-14.9%	5
Second Half	-24.7%	30	-22.0%	2
Red Zone	-48.3%	32	-17.4%	6
Late and Close	-18.2%	25	-27.7%	2

Five-Year Performance

Year	W-L	Pyth W	Est W	PF	PA	TO	Total	Rk	Off	Rk	Def	Rk	ST	Rk	Off AGL	Rk	Def AGL	Rk	Off Age	Rk	Def Age	Rk	ST Age	Rk
2015	10-6	10.7	10.8	423	319	+2	21.3%	7	17.3%	3	-3.8%	11	0.1%	18	42.7	23	23.0	7	28.2	5	27.0	11	26.2	14
2016	11-5	9.9	10.2	399	327	+5	17.1%	4	12.5%	7	-4.7%	11	-0.1%	16	34.7	15	26.4	9	27.1	9	26.5	15	25.7	23
2017	13-3	10.6	11.3	406	308	+2	27.1%	3	17.6%	3	-6.4%	9	3.1%	9	13.8	6	14.8	6	27.4	7	25.7	23	25.9	14
2018	9-6-1	9.7	9.2	428	360	-11	11.2%	9	13.8%	6	-0.9%	13	-3.5%	27	24.4	7	14.1	3	27.9	6	26.2	18	26.1	10
2019	8-8	7.6	7.3	289	303	+8	-5.4%	18	-25.3%	32	-18.4%	3	1.5%	8	30.6	11	30.0	15	27.0	11	26.1	19	25.9	16

2019 Performance Based on Most Common Personnel Groups

PIT Offense					PIT Offense vs. Opponents					PIT Defense				PIT Defense vs. Opponents			
Pers	Freq	Yds	DVOA	Run%	Pers	Freq	Yds	DVOA	Run%	Pers	Freq	Yds	DVOA	Pers	Freq	Yds	DVOA
11	65%	5.6	-18.7%	28%	Base	28%	4.3	-15.6%	62%	Base	29%	4.3	-27.4%	11	57%	5.1	-11.5%
612	10%	3.3	-23.3%	83%	Nickel	51%	5.3	-21.5%	34%	Nickel	51%	5.0	-12.9%	12	14%	4.3	-37.7%
12	10%	4.7	-11.5%	27%	Dime+	19%	5.7	-16.0%	9%	Dime+	18%	5.4	-10.8%	21	12%	5.2	-7.7%
611	5%	4.0	-6.6%	71%	Goal Line	1%	-0.7	-16.0%	83%	Goal Line	0%	-0.5	-21.3%	20	6%	5.3	10.1%
621	2%	4.2	-35.2%	89%	Big	1%	2.4	-56.9%	86%	Big	2%	4.2	-45.5%	22	3%	2.5	-62.4%
00	2%	2.3	-58.1%	0%										10	2%	5.3	-52.6%
WC	2%	4.4	-60.8%	69%										611	2%	5.4	2.6%

Strategic Tendencies

Run/Pass		Rk	Formation		Rk	Pass Rush		Rk	Secondary		Rk	Strategy		Rk
Runs, first half	38%	14	Form: Single Back	86%	10	Rush 3	8.4%	14	4 DB	29%	13	Play Action	14%	32
Runs, first down	53%	9	Form: Empty Back	8%	15	Rush 4	57.6%	26	5 DB	51%	21	Offensive Motion	42%	12
Runs, second-long	30%	9	Form: Multi Back	5%	27	Rush 5	32.2%	2	6+ DB	18%	15	Avg Box (Off)	6.76	4
Runs, power sit.	55%	19	Pers: 3+ WR	68%	13	Rush 6+	1.8%	31	Man Coverage	32%	19	Avg Box (Def)	6.40	29
Runs, behind 2H	25%	24	Pers: 2+ TE/6+ OL	31%	13	Edge Rusher Sacks	50.0%	24	CB by Sides	92%	3	Offensive Pace	32.33	29
Pass, ahead 2H	46%	20	Pers: 6+ OL	20%	2	Interior DL Sacks	33.0%	7	S/CB Cover Ratio	22%	25	Defensive Pace	30.91	21
Run-Pass Options	4%	20	Shotgun/Pistol	76%	6	Second Level Sacks	17.0%	17	DB Blitz	13%	10	Go for it on 4th	1.23	23

Stuck with backup quarterbacks, Pittsburgh changed a number of tendencies significantly. The Steelers ran the ball much more often than in 2018 despite being behind in games more often and facing more men in the box (from 20th to fourth). They used six offensive linemen more than three times as often as in 2018 and used empty backfields less than half as often. They also slowed down in situation-neutral pace (from 11th to 29th). ◗ Pittsburgh had just 3.6 yards per play and -18.9% DVOA with six offensive linemen on the field. Only Seattle used six linemen more often. ◗ Pittsburgh had just 3.4 yards per play and ranked 29th with -27.5% DVOA out of empty-backfield formations. ◗ Once again, we need to explore the Pittsburgh Steelers' relationship with the play-action pass because the trend gets curiouser and curiouser. In general, if you separate it from overall passing performance, we haven't found much year-to-year consistency in which teams are most and least efficient using play-action. But in 2019, for the fifth straight year, Pittsburgh was at the bottom of the league for using play-action and had a reverse split: the Steelers were better without play-action even though almost every NFL team is better at passing with play-action.

Pittsburgh on Play-Action, 2015-2019

Year	PA Pct	Rank	Yds (w/PA)	DVOA (w/PA)	Yds (no PA)	DVOA (no PA)	Yds Dif	DVOA Dif
2015	14%	31	8.3	3.6%	7.7	39.0%	+0.6	-35.4%
2016	14%	32	8.3	12.7%	6.9	33.7%	+1.4	-21.0%
2017	11%	32	6.6	31.5%	7.6	37.8%	-0.9	-6.2%
2018	12%	32	7.0	9.0%	7.2	30.0%	-0.2	-21.0%
2019	14%	32	3.8	-39.5%	6.1	-11.4%	-2.4	-28.1%

Note: includes scrambles and defensive pass interference.

This trend was apparent through two different offensive coordinators, so we wondered whether it was just related to Ben Roethlisberger himself. Does he just have an unconvincing play fake, or really dislike play-action passes? Well, last year we got to see the Steelers with two other quarterbacks instead of Roethlisberger and the trend continued. The same reverse split existed, just worse in every way: worse with play-action and worse without it. ◗ OK, not quite. Roethlisberger and Mason Rudolph were both much worse with play-action in 2019. Devin Hodges had fewer yards per pass with play-action (6.0 to 5.0) but a higher DVOA (6.5% to -20.4%). However, his play-action passes weren't exactly field-stretchers: he had an average depth of target of just 3.3 yards on 22 play-action attempts, with only one pass going over 10 yards downfield. ◗ One other strange thing about the Steelers and play-action: they were the only team in the league to use play-action more often on second down (19%) than on first down (18%). ◗ The Steelers benefited from a league-high 1,118 penalty yards by opponents. This was the second straight year the Steelers led the league in opposing penalty yards even though there generally isn't a strong year-to-year correlation in this metric.

Passing

Player	DYAR	DVOA	Plays	NtYds	Avg	YAC	C%	TD	Int
M.Rudolph	-225	-23.0%	298	1632	5.5	5.3	62.4%	13	9
D.Hodges	-122	-22.1%	175	944	5.4	5.7	63.3%	5	8
B.Roethlisberger	69	5.4%	64	338	5.3	5.5	56.5%	0	1

Rushing

Player	DYAR	DVOA	Plays	Yds	Avg	TD	Fum	Suc
J.Conner	-13	-11.3%	115	464	4.0	4	1	45%
B.Snell	-14	-11.7%	108	426	3.9	2	1	49%
J.Samuels	-64	-32.6%	66	175	2.7	1	0	39%
K.Whyte	21	18.1%	25	122	4.9	0	0	40%
T.Edmunds	-29	-36.9%	22	92	4.2	0	0	32%
M.Rudolph	0	-12.5%	13	49	3.8	0	0	-
D.Hodges	-16	-34.5%	12	79	6.6	0	1	-
T.Brooks-James*	-17	-79.2%	8	7	0.9	0	0	13%
D.Watt	*10*	*9.2%*	*7*	*10*	*1.4*	*1*	*0*	*86%*

Receiving

Player	DYAR	DVOA	Plays	Ctch	Yds	Y/C	YAC	TD	C%
D.Johnson	26	-8.9%	91	58	680	11.7	5.2	5	64%
J.Washington	156	11.2%	80	44	735	16.7	4.2	3	55%
J.Smith-Schuster	8	-11.3%	71	42	552	13.1	5.3	3	59%
J.Holton*	-70	-66.1%	16	4	21	5.3	3.5	0	25%
D.Moncrief*	-71	-76.3%	15	4	18	4.5	0.8	0	27%
R.Switzer	-41	-55.3%	11	8	27	3.4	2.1	0	73%
T.Jones*	-12	-29.9%	10	4	61	15.3	2.8	0	40%
D.Cain	46	57.5%	6	5	72	14.4	2.2	0	83%
V.McDonald	-83	-32.4%	55	38	273	7.2	4.5	3	69%
N.Vannett*	10	2.7%	17	13	128	9.8	4.8	0	76%
E.Ebron	*21*	*-1.1%*	*52*	*31*	*375*	*12.1*	*5.0*	*3*	*60%*
J.Samuels	17	-8.9%	57	47	305	6.5	7.8	1	82%
J.Conner	75	21.2%	38	34	251	7.4	8.8	3	89%
Tr.Edmunds	6	2.1%	7	6	48	8.0	7.0	0	86%

Offensive Line

Player	Pos	Age	GS	Snaps	Pen	Sk	Pass	Run	Player	Pos	Age	GS	Snaps	Pen	Sk	Pass	Run
David DeCastro	RG	30	16/16	1016	4	2.0	8	9	Maurkice Pouncey	C	31	13/13	790	4	0.0	5	4
Matt Feiler	RT	28	16/16	1016	3	6.5	15	3	B.J. Finney*	C	29	16/4	335	0	1.0	2	2
Alejandro Villanueva	LT	32	16/16	1016	10	2.0	18	0	Zach Banner	OT	27	14/1	222	2	0.0	0	2
Ramon Foster*	LG	34	14/14	840	2	0.0	8	4	Stefen Wisniewski	LG	31	11/2	208	0	0.0	1	1

Year	Yards	ALY	Rank	Power	Rank	Stuff	Rank	2nd Lev	Rank	Open Field	Rank	Sacks	ASR	Rank	Press	Rank	F-Start	Cont.
2017	4.07	4.36	7	65%	12	17%	5	1.22	10	0.48	27	24	3.9%	1	22.7%	2	14	26
2018	4.36	4.44	15	71%	5	16%	5	1.20	20	0.80	19	24	4.4%	4	23.2%	2	8	28
2019	3.74	3.84	30	54%	27	23%	31	1.05	26	0.52	26	32	6.6%	12	30.0%	17	19	31

2019 ALY by direction:	Left End 4.37 (12)	Left Tackle: 3.44 (26)	Mid/Guard: 4.06 (23)	Right Tackle: 3.29 (26)	Right End: 3.15 (28)

The low blown block numbers don't totally match the story for Maurkice Pouncey, who lost a step last season and simply couldn't reach a lot of the guys he should have blocked. He's still well-respected as a teammate and as the man making the line calls, and plenty of great linemen played well into their 30s, but he'll want to reverse that trend fast. ☙ Alejandro Villanueva has been one of the sport's great bargains over the last five seasons, in which the Steelers have paid him just $24 million. He's a pending free agent at season's end, and heading on 32 years old; remember, he didn't start in the NFL until age 27 because of time spent in the military. Villanueva is yet another Steelers player who might not return in 2021 if things don't break right. ☙ David DeCastro has made the Pro Bowl in five consecutive seasons and was named first-team All-Pro in 2015 and 2017. He has lived up to the first-round billing and is the linchpin of the line at this point. ☙ Signed in the offseason for a modest two-year, $2.9-million pact, Stefen Wisniewski combines surprisingly strong play with the inability to stay healthy or in the starting lineup long enough to be recognized for it. Into his 30s now, Wisniewski is here to keep the seat warm for 2020 fourth-rounder Kevin Dotson (Louisiana), an All-American with a pure power approach that worked well in college. Dotson was the first player off the board in this year's draft who didn't go to the NFL combine. ☙ Right tackle Matt Feiler is yet another successful UDFA who stepped into the starting lineup after Marcus Gilbert was injured and hasn't missed a beat. Feiler also played a fine game at guard against the Rams as the Steelers were trying to find an answer for Aaron Donald's athleticism, in a game in which Donald had just four tackles and a sack. Feiler is another free agent-to-be at season's end. Chuwuma Okorafor is also mentioned in the left guard derby; he was inactive all of last season except when he played right tackle in Feiler's place in that Rams game. ☙ The beneficiary of all those guard options is Zach Banner, who showed some promise in a limited sample last year and could slide into the starting lineup for a bigger sample size if Okorafor remains more of a vision than a player.

Defensive Front

Defensive Line	Age	Pos	G	Snaps	Plays	TmPct	Rk	Stop	Dfts	BTkl	Runs	St%	Rk	RuYd	Rk	Sack	Hit	Hur	Dsrpt
						Overall						vs. Run				Pass Rush			
Cameron Heyward	31	DE	16	885	89	10.4%	1	66	26	6	68	71%	70	2.8	72	9.0	13	32	5
Javon Hargrave*	27	DT	16	692	58	6.8%	15	40	12	6	52	67%	76	3.1	90	4.0	2	28	1
Tyson Alualu	33	DE	16	440	42	4.9%	37	32	11	3	34	74%	56	2.2	42	1.0	2	10	2
Stephon Tuitt	27	DE	6	282	22	6.9%	85	18	8	4	17	82%	24	1.2	6	3.5	3	7	0
Chris Wormley	27	DE	16	457	35	4.9%	38	26	6	2	29	72%	61	2.3	49	1.5	4	5	3

Edge Rushers	Age	Pos	G	Snaps	Plays	TmPct	Rk	Stop	Dfts	BTkl	Runs	St%	Rk	RuYd	Rk	Sack	Hit	Hur	Dsrpt
						Overall						vs. Run				Pass Rush			
Bud Dupree	27	OLB	16	997	69	8.1%	5	53	25	10	52	71%	55	1.9	22	11.5	8	30	3
T.J. Watt	26	OLB	16	952	63	7.4%	11	56	36	9	34	85%	8	1.4	11	14.5	20	47	6

Linebackers	Age	Pos	G	Snaps	Plays	TmPct	Rk	Stop	Dfts	BTkl	Runs	St%	Rk	RuYd	Rk	Sack	Hit	Hur	Tgts	Suc%	Rk	AdjYd	Rk	PD	Int
						Overall						vs. Run				Pass Rush				vs. Pass					
Devin Bush	22	ILB	16	905	113	13.2%	27	67	18	13	73	64%	24	4.0	45	1.0	1	4	43	60%	10	6.0	28	4	2
Mark Barron*	31	ILB	15	766	85	10.6%	44	37	12	9	42	40%	80	5.2	77	3.0	0	6	46	57%	17	5.7	26	3	1
Vince Williams	31	ILB	14	401	55	7.4%	70	39	11	8	36	78%	4	2.2	3	2.5	6	10	10	50%	--	8.3	--	1	0

Year	Yards	ALY	Rank	Power	Rank	Stuff	Rank	2nd Level	Rank	Open Field	Rank	Sacks	ASR	Rank	Press	Rank
2017	4.47	3.96	12	82%	31	20%	18	1.31	30	1.04	30	56	9.8%	1	34.3%	4
2018	4.04	4.24	12	69%	22	19%	17	1.17	11	0.63	8	52	9.3%	1	34.5%	2
2019	3.89	4.12	11	76%	31	20%	15	1.15	14	0.44	1	54	9.7%	1	34.4%	5
2019 ALY by direction:			Left End: 1.75 (1)			Left Tackle: 3.91 (10)			Mid/Guard: 4.19 (10)			Right Tackle: 3.52 (6)			Right End: 5.93 (29)	

One of the most taken-for-granted players in the NFL is Cam Heyward. When the conversation about best pass-rushers in the NFL takes place, Heyward is often forgotten because he never picked up more than 7.5 sacks in his first six years in the NFL. Over the last three years, he has 29.0. He has not registered below 28 hurries in a season in any of those three years, and he does it while playing stellar run defense as well. ● Speaking of dominant pass-rushers, T.J. Watt now has 34.5 sacks, 15 forced fumbles, and 18 passes defensed in his first three seasons while averaging 33 hurries a year. Scouts who downplayed his breakout junior season and watched him fall almost to the end of the first round are going to have to take the L on this one. ● Stephon Tuitt's torn pectoral muscle gave the world more Tyson Alualu than they ever dreamt of, with the former surprise top-10 Jaguars pick playing fairly well at 3-4 end. The Steelers would probably prefer a healthy Tuitt, at least unless Gene Smith is suddenly on staff. ● Chris Wormley never really grew beyond a secondary role on the Baltimore front, so it was a very curious move to pick him up. Wormley could play nose tackle or end for this team, but with Javon Hargrave off to Philadelphia, nose tackle is the real hole. Steelers general manager Kevin Colbert told reporters in April that "my assumption is he'll still be used as a defensive end." Daniel McCullers is the long-time incumbent backup at the spot. The Steelers also spent a seventh-round draft pick on Nebraska tackle Carlos Davis, a 320-pounder with a discus background and a 4.82s 40-yard dash at the combine. Alualu has been mentioned as a possibility at nose too. ● Bud Dupree's first good season after mostly wiggling between competence and bust over the first four years of his rookie deal led the Steelers to slap the franchise tag on him and try to figure it out later. Dupree has had seasons this solid by pure hurries before, but this was the first time he ever converted so many of them to sacks. The Steelers spent a top-100 pick on Alex Highsmith (Charlotte) to push Dupree. Highsmith bumped up from three sacks to 14 in his senior season after being moved from 4-technique to the outside, and Colbert said "We all think this kid isn't anywhere near where he might be somewhere down the road." He'll get at least one year to learn. ● Despite the high cost of the trade up, it's hard to call Devin Bush's rookie season anything but a success. He was impressive in pass coverage and competent against the run. If he can improve his zone coverage and lose a few broken tackles next year, he'll be well on his way to Pro Bowl consideration. ● Mark Barron remains unsigned as we go to press, leaving the other middle linebacker position to veteran Vince Williams, whom the Steelers mostly kept on the sideline last year because they weren't convinced he could cover. 2019 sixth-rounder Ulysees Gilbert III was a small-school athletic marvel who ran up his Akron pro day. He may get a shot if the Steelers don't sign anyone else.

Defensive Secondary

Secondary	Age	Pos	G	Snaps	Plays	Overall TmPct	Rk	Stop	Dfts	BTkl	Runs	vs. Run St%	Rk	RuYd	Rk	Tgts	vs. Pass Tgt%	Rk	Dist	Suc%	Rk	AdjYd	Rk	PD	Int
Joe Haden	31	CB	16	1074	82	9.6%	13	37	19	12	24	42%	46	5.5	32	76	19.0%	56	12.5	58%	20	5.7	8	17	5
Minkah Fitzpatrick	24	FS	16	1065	77	9.0%	38	27	15	10	33	33%	53	8.3	49	19	4.8%	66	14.5	42%	66	10.2	68	9	5
Terrell Edmunds	23	SS	16	1055	107	12.5%	12	41	15	14	59	46%	29	6.0	27	35	8.9%	25	11.1	46%	57	10.2	67	3	0
Steven Nelson	27	CB	15	1030	69	8.6%	31	25	7	8	21	38%	56	7.3	59	62	16.2%	69	13.9	60%	15	6.6	20	8	1
Mike Hilton	26	CB	16	687	73	8.5%	26	53	15	13	24	88%	2	3.0	6	46	18.0%	61	11.2	52%	45	8.7	65	11	1
Cameron Sutton	25	CB	16	269	21	2.5%	--	11	8	2	2	100%	--	5.0	--	26	26.0%	--	8.6	58%	--	4.9	--	5	1

Year	Pass D Rank	vs. #1 WR	Rk	vs. #2 WR	Rk	vs. Other WR	Rk	WR Wide	Rk	WR Slot	Rk	vs. TE	Rk	vs. RB	Rk
2017	7	4.3%	17	-10.9%	10	17.5%	25	-10.7%	8	21.7%	28	-34.6%	1	12.5%	23
2018	17	-6.0%	10	2.4%	19	10.8%	25	-6.8%	17	10.0%	22	25.5%	31	1.6%	15
2019	3	4.2%	19	-15.8%	5	20.4%	26	-30.5%	3	20.9%	29	-25.3%	3	-36.7%	3

The weak link in this unit at this point is Terrell Edmunds, a physical marvel who can play a solid box safety, but just isn't a great coverage player. He was a first-round pick, and he will continue to get opportunities—he might be a Mark Barron/Deone Bucannon type player who fits better as a linebacker—but so far there has not been a lot of optimism on the All-22. ● Replacing Sean Davis with Fitzpatrick was, it turns out, a pretty big upgrade. Moreover, because Fitzpatrick was a 2018 rookie, he's under contract at extremely reasonable rates for the next two seasons and the Steelers will have a fifth-year option. Giving up a first-round pick when you are as long-term bereft at quarterback as Pittsburgh looked last year is not nothing, but the Steelers did well for themselves here. ● Steven Nelson sure feels a lot like a spiritual successor to Brent Grimes, another small-ish corner who got passed around team-to-team because he didn't look like teams wanted an outside corner to look. ● Neither

Joe Haden nor Mike Hilton has had a seasonal success rate below 50% yet in a Steelers jersey. Haden is 31 with two years left on his deal. Pittsburgh will probably need to prioritize outside corner in next year's draft, but he has absolutely been worth the cost of investment as a late-camp free-agent signing back in 2017. Hilton is heading towards free agency for the first time and will play out this year on an RFA tender. Former third-rounder Cameron Sutton was mostly a bust in his first two seasons, but finally showed a little something last year and could be in line to replace Hilton in both the short and long term. ● The lead backup safety at this point is probably Jordan Dangerfield, but 2020 sixth-rounder Antoine Brooks (Maryland) could be a passable box safety or dime linebacker.

Special Teams

Year	DVOA	Rank	FG/XP	Rank	Net Kick	Rank	Kick Ret	Rank	Net Punt	Rank	Punt Ret	Rank	Hidden	Rank
2017	3.1%	9	8.4	7	5.2	7	1.3	10	3.3	15	-2.9	24	-8.0	28
2018	-3.5%	27	-11.0	30	3.7	6	-4.2	28	-5.5	26	-0.5	16	1.2	12
2019	1.5%	8	10.7	2	5.4	5	-5.5	31	-9.1	28	5.9	3	-3.6	22

Apparently over what ailed him in 2018, Chris Boswell won a training camp fight for his job and stuck in a career-high 93.5% of his field goals while making every extra point. Boswell restructured his contract to help create space for Bud Dupree's franchise tag in March. ● Incumbent punter Jordan Berry is joined in camp by undrafted rookie Corliss Waitman, who is absolutely an NBA2K Create-a-Player, out of South Alabama. Our metrics have Berry as more or less an average punter for the last three years; Pittsburgh's negative value on net punting comes from poor coverage teams. Waitman is a left-footed punter, so we can only hope he inspires an eight-minute dissertation from Bill Belichick at some point. ● Diontae Johnson was explosive on punt returns last year. The Steelers will have to hope they can keep using him for that because their other in-house options just aren't great. Ryan Switzer hasn't had a positive value on kickoff returns or punt returns in the last two seasons. Kerrith Whyte has all the tools to be a good returner but didn't deliver on that promise when returning kickoffs last season. ● Derek Watt led the NFL with 13 return stops and was tied for the lead with 16 special teams tackles for the Chargers last season. Now he'll get to join brother T.J. in Pittsburgh.

San Francisco 49ers

2019 Record: 13-3	Total DVOA: 27.9% (5th)	2020 Mean Projection: 8.4 wins	On the Clock (0-4): 7%
Pythagorean Wins: 12.0 (3rd)	Offense: 7.2% (7th)	Postseason Odds: 48.2%	Mediocrity (5-7): 29%
Snap-Weighted Age: 26.1 (26th)	Defense: -19.7% (2nd)	Super Bowl Odds: 6.3%	Playoff Contender (8-10): 42%
Average Opponent: 0.5% (12th)	Special Teams: 1.0% (12th)	Proj. Avg. Opponent: 0.3% (11st)	Super Bowl Contender (11+): 22%

2019: Everything comes together until the final 10 minutes of the season.

2020: Beware the Plexiglass, my son; the jaws that bite, the claws that catch!

The Jimmy Garoppolo era did not start out as planned for the 49ers, as their extremely well-compensated young quarterback missed the majority of his first full season in San Francisco with an injury. Preseason optimism for 2019 surrounded Garoppolo's return to Kyle Shanahan's offensive scheme. San Francisco fans were hoping for a turnaround due to major improvement on the offensive side, potentially leading to a playoff berth. Little did they know that their defense would morph from comfortably below average to being one of the very best units in the entire league. The offense took the expected step forward to complement that massive uptick on defense, and the end result was a Super Bowl appearance along with a top-five finish in DVOA one year after ranking 30th league-wide.

Getting Garoppolo back from his ACL injury was a significant help on the offensive side of the ball. In 2018, without their preferred signal-caller, San Francisco only managed to post a positive single-game offensive DVOA in three games as they struggled to a bottom-six finish for the season. It's safe to say that in 2019 the 49ers did not have that problem. With Garoppolo starting all 16 games for the first time in his career, the 49ers ranked seventh overall in offensive DVOA at 7.2%. After not posting a single game above 20.0% offensive DVOA in 2018, San Francisco had four such games in 2019, including three above 40.0%.

It took a few years for San Francisco's hiring of Kyle Shanahan to take hold on offense, but it finally paid off in 2019. Shanahan's offenses have a reputation of taking some time to really get rolling, and in the 49ers' case, it took getting Garoppolo in place for a full year to make that happen. The 49ers under Shanahan try to create favorable matchups by playing out of run-heavy personnel groupings to keep opponents in base defense. They take advantage of the versatility presented by players such as tight end George Kittle and fullback Kyle Juszczyk to threaten teams in the passing game. Only the Vikings faced base defenses at a higher frequency, and former Shanahan mentor Gary Kubiak (Shanahan served as his offensive coordinator in Houston for two years) had a major influence on Minnesota's offensive approach. San Francisco led the league in DVOA from 21 personnel (two running backs, one tight end) among the 11 teams that used that personnel grouping on more than 10% of their snaps and finished a hair behind the Ravens in yards per play. Shanahan deserves a lot

of credit for his team's offensive success by virtue of his ability to create matchup problems and easy throws to make his quarterback's life easier, and he leveraged that into a six-year contract extension in June that would keep him in San Francisco through 2025.

For as much as the offense improved a massive amount from 2018 to 2019, the defense's leap from being comfortably below average to one of the two best units in the league was much more impressive and the driving force behind San Francisco's surprise Super Bowl run. Sure, drafting Ohio State pass-rusher Nick Bosa with the second overall pick was likely to help matters, but we doubt even the most optimistic 49ers fans would have expected the world-beating unit that locked teams down week after week.

Bosa burst onto the scene in style as a rookie, racking up 9.0 sacks along with 16 hits and *62* hurries, third in the NFL. Adding Bosa to a defensive line room already filled with highly pedigreed pass-rushers allowed the 49ers to send wave after wave of players in pursuit of terrified quarterbacks. Arik Armstead had a breakout season playing on his fifth-year option and turned that into a hefty new contract; after spending much of the early part of his career shuffling back and forth between defensive tackle and defensive end, Armstead moved to more of a wide-9 role in 2019. This allowed him more freedom to get after the quarterback, and Armstead took advantage of his pass-rush opportunities in a major way.

Fellow former first-round pick DeForest Buckner was his usual disruptive self on the interior, posting 51 stops on top of another strong year rushing the passer. With Bosa, Armstead, and Buckner wreaking havoc, you almost might forget about offseason addition Dee Ford, who joined the 49ers via trade from Kansas City and inked a massive contract extension in the process. Ford's first season in San Francisco was marred by injuries, preventing him from making a major impact, but it's hard to say that the team truly missed him with how deep their pass-rush unit was.

Despite all the praise bestowed upon those pass-rushers, San Francisco's coverage group was not about to let them have all the fun. On the occasions where the opposing quarterback was not under pressure, he often did not have an appealing option to target. On one side, you had Richard Sherman, who finished seventh league-wide in yards per pass allowed in coverage to go with 11 passes defensed and three intercep-

2020 49ers Schedule

Week	Opp.	Week	Opp.	Week	Opp.
1	ARI	7	at NE	13	BUF (Mon.)
2	at NYJ	8	at SEA	14	WAS
3	at NYG	9	GB (Thu.)	15	at DAL
4	PHI	10	at NO	16	at ARI (Sat.)
5	MIA	11	BYE	17	SEA
6	LAR	12	at LAR		

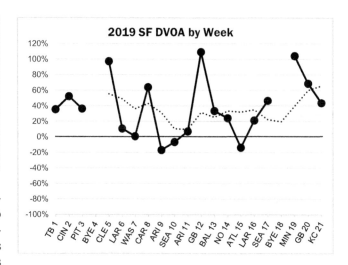

2019 SF DVOA by Week

tions. On the other, Emmanuel Moseley and Ahkello Witherspoon split time but neither was by any means a safe choice to throw against. Jaquiski Tartt and Jimmie Ward made for a formidable safety duo that complemented each other's strengths well; Tartt was a force in the run game while Ward served as the free safety in the eraser role.

Want to throw underneath? Good luck with that too. Linebackers Fred Warner, Kwon Alexander, and Dre Greenlaw were next to impossible to throw on, with second-year pro Warner establishing himself as one of the very best coverage linebackers in the league. Warner allowed a mere 4.7 yards per pass at middle linebacker, good for fourth in the NFL, and finished with nine passes defensed. The former third-round pick from BYU is only entering his third season in the league and should be a headache for opposing offenses for years to come.

All that talent on the defensive side of the ball led to an improvement from 5.7% to -19.7% in defensive DVOA, a difference of 25.4%. Add that to the 22.5% leap San Francisco made on offense, and the end result was a team that went from the bottom five in overall team DVOA to the top five in just one season. There is no denying that the 49ers were a force to be reckoned with in 2019, with a deserved Super Bowl appearance at the end of the year. However, the natural question that arises when a team makes such a large improvement is whether this change will stick. With that in mind, we will turn to our old friend the Plexiglass Principle to examine whether we can expect these improvements to stick around.

For those unfamiliar, the Plexiglass Principle was a term originally coined by baseball statistician Bill James, and it states that teams that improve or decline significantly in one season have a tendency to fall back towards their previous level of performance. To get a better idea of a comparable historical baseline for these teams, we listed all the teams from 1986 through 2019 that improved by at least 15% DVOA on both offense and defense along with their change in overall DVOA and wins in the subsequent year (Table 1). It isn't a long list.

Unsurprisingly, when a team makes such a significant leap in both offensive and defensive DVOA, the end result is a major improvement in overall DVOA, with the smallest amount of improvement "only" 29.4% for the 2014 Packers. The teams that made these major leaps on both sides of the ball fall into a few different categories. The 2004 Steelers, 2012 Broncos, and 2014 Packers made the leap from the muddled mediocre middle to legitimate Super Bowl contenders by virtue of an upgrade at quarterback, courtesy of drafting Ben Roethlisberger, signing Peyton Manning as a free agent, and having a whole season of healthy Aaron Rodgers. Conversely, the 1987 Colts and 2007 Buccaneers were dreadful the preceding seasons before making a leap to comfortably above average, and the 2010 Lions went from being historically terrible to just slightly below average.

San Francisco sticks out here as being the only team with improvements on both sides of the ball of at least 20.0%, resulting in their massive leap of 48.6% in overall DVOA. The

Table 1: 15.0% or Greater DVOA Increases on Both Sides of the Ball, 1986-2019

Year	Team	W-L Y-1	Off DVOA Change	Def DVOA Change	Total DVOA Change	W-L	Off DVOA Change Y+1	Def DVOA Change Y+1	Total DVOA Change Y+1	W-L Y+1
1987*	IND	3-13	+19.6%	-15.8%	+39.9%	7-5	+6.7%	+12.0%	-8.4%	9-7
2004	PIT	6-10	+22.5%	-18.0%	+39.1%	15-1	-4.3%	+5.3%	-10.4%	11-5
2007	TB	4-12	+21.9%	-15.7%	+37.6%	9-7	-6.3%	+1.0%	-8.2%	9-7
2010	DET	2-14	+27.6%	-15.0%	+50.5%	6-10	+7.9%	-11.0%	+11.1%	10-6
2012	DEN	8-8	+32.0%	-15.4%	+48.3%	13-3	+11.4%	+13.6%	-3.9%	13-3
2013	KC	2-14	+28.1%	-19.7%	+57.6%	11-5	+2.0%	+8.1%	-7.1%	9-7
2014	GB	8-7-1	+16.0%	-15.4%	+29.4%	12-4	-22.4%	-6.3%	-13.4%	10-6
2019	**SF**	**4-12**	**+22.5%**	**-25.4%**	**+48.6%**	**13-3**	--	--	--	--

1987 stats do not include strikebreaker games.

2004 Steelers and 2013 Chiefs came close to the 20.0% improvement mark on defense, so perhaps it makes sense that they both saw a nine-win increase year-over-year, much like San Francisco. The remainder of the teams on this list saw the bulk of their improvement come from the offensive side of the ball and just barely snuck over the 15.0% threshold on defense.

The 2004 Steelers and 2013 Chiefs still remained in the top ten in overall DVOA the following year, but they did see a clear decline in wins and overall DVOA. The only team that saw an increase in overall DVOA the following season was the 2010 Lions, which makes sense given that Matthew Stafford was starting to come into his own in his first fully healthy season as a starter and that the team saw continued improvement from its defense.

There is no one great comparable team for the 49ers here, as the macro-level circumstances are at least slightly different in each situation. Pittsburgh's defense went from being about average to the top three in 2004 alongside Roethlisberger's debut season. Kansas City was in its first season coached by Andy Reid and had just traded for a veteran quarterback in Alex Smith. Neither of these two line up perfectly with San Francisco given that Kyle Shanahan had been the head coach for two years prior to 2019 and that the defense went from atrocious to one of the best in the league. Those Chiefs are probably the closest fit given that they had been terrible on both offense and defense in 2012, and they definitely took a step back the following season despite remaining a frequent playoff participant for the rest of the Alex Smith era at quarterback. The 2014 team finished with nine wins but missed the playoffs on a wild-card tiebreaker with the Chargers in a tough AFC West.

We can also look at San Francisco's improvement on offense and defense separately. From 1986 to 2018, 39 different offenses improved their offensive DVOA by 20.0% to 25.0%. These 39 offenses dropped the following year by an average of -9.2%. Fifteen different defenses improved their defensive DVOA by -22.5% to -27.5%. Those 15 defenses saw their DVOA go up (i.e., get worse) the following year by an average of 8.7%.

It's safe to say that there is not a great historical precedent for maintaining this level of improvement, and the 49ers may need to hang on to most of it to keep their grip on the NFC West with the Seahawks, Rams, and ascendant Cardinals fighting for the throne. The defense is almost certainly going to take a step back, but it remains a very talented unit and should hold on to a top-10 rank even after trading away DeForest Buckner. The outlook for the offense is not quite so sunny after losing some key contributors, and we expect them to drop back toward the middle of the pack.

Another season of continued improvement from Garoppolo could certainly help the 49ers outperform their current projection; he ranked 11th in DYAR in his first fully healthy season as a starting quarterback, though it is fair to wonder how much more room for improvement there actually is for a player who turns 29 in November. It seems at times like Garoppolo is just getting his feet wet, having only started 26 games in his ca-

reer, but he is entering his seventh season in the NFL at this point.

Shanahan's offensive wizardry should provide a baseline level of performance if he has his preferred starter under center, but his scheme and skill in play-sequencing alone is no guarantee that the 49ers will see sustained success on offense. It was only a year ago that many regarded Rams head coach Sean McVay as the best offensive mind in the league, but injuries on the offensive line and unimpressive play from quarterback Jared Goff dragged Los Angeles' offense down to league-average in 2019.

The 49ers still have superstar Kittle at tight end, but the rest of the receiving corps leaves a bit to be desired. Deebo Samuel showed promise as a rookie, both as a receiver and as a runner taking end arounds and sweeps, but with the departure of Emmanuel Sanders in free agency, the 49ers will be relying on a largely unproven group to carry more of the load. They may not even be able to count on Samuel early in the season, as he suffered a Jones fracture while working out in the offseason; because of his surgery to repair the fracture, he may have to miss the first month of 2020. It remains to be seen whether Garoppolo can carry an offense to sustained success, and the youth of San Francisco's receiver room will likely add to the degree of difficulty in 2020. First-round pick Brandon Aiyuk will have a chance to make an early impression, but Playmaker Score was not a huge fan of his as a prospect.

On the defensive side of the ball, San Francisco managed to retain almost all of their starters with the major exception of Buckner, whose trade to the Colts provided the 49ers with the necessary cap space to keep Armstead as well as the first-round pick used to select Buckner's replacement in South Carolina defensive tackle Javon Kinlaw. Other than Buckner, the band is back together and seems poised to be a fearsome unit yet again.

It may not be for long though. Defensive backs Sherman, Tartt, Witherspoon, Moseley, and K'Waun Williams are all entering the final years of their contracts in 2020, though it should be noted that Moseley is scheduled to be a restricted free agent whom San Francisco will likely be able to bring back. Defensive linemen Solomon Thomas and D.J. Jones are also slated for free agency. With the aforementioned Kittle in need of an extension and stud coverage linebacker Warner eligible for one as well, it seems likely that San Francisco will be seeing some major changes in the defensive backfield come season's end.

The 49ers made an impressive run to the Super Bowl last year, holding a 10-point lead in the fourth quarter before Patrick Mahomes happened. Their march to Miami was made even more stunning by just how much they improved from 2018 to 2019. However, that 2019 Super Bowl run may be as far as this 49ers core group gets unless they can make it back this season because the breakup of this defense in free agency is looming over the horizon. And with San Francisco's expected regression on the offensive side of the ball, returning to the Super Bowl may not be in the cards for 2020 either.

Carl Yedor

2019 49ers Stats by Week

Wk	vs.	W-L	PF	PA	YDF	YDA	TO	Total	Off	Def	ST
1	at TB	W	31	17	256	295	+2	36%	-3%	-39%	0%
2	at CIN	W	41	17	571	316	0	52%	46%	-13%	-7%
3	PIT	W	24	20	436	239	-3	37%	14%	-19%	4%
4	BYE										
5	CLE	W	31	3	446	180	+4	97%	16%	-92%	-11%
6	at LAR	W	20	7	331	157	-1	11%	-14%	-32%	-8%
7	at WAS	W	9	0	283	154	0	1%	-27%	-27%	2%
8	CAR	W	51	13	388	230	+2	64%	13%	-46%	5%
9	at ARI	W	28	25	411	357	0	-17%	11%	32%	4%
10	SEA	L	24	27	302	336	+1	-6%	-42%	-42%	-6%
11	ARI	W	36	26	442	266	0	7%	8%	8%	7%
12	GB	W	37	8	339	198	+1	109%	50%	-50%	9%
13	at BAL	L	17	20	331	283	0	34%	13%	-24%	-4%
14	at NO	W	48	46	516	465	0	24%	37%	5%	-8%
15	ATL	L	22	29	313	290	-1	-14%	-12%	9%	8%
16	LAR	W	34	31	334	395	-1	21%	-3%	-2%	22%
17	at SEA	W	26	21	398	348	0	47%	42%	-5%	-1%
18	BYE										
19	MIN	W	27	10	308	147	0	104%	19%	-84%	2%
20	GB	W	37	20	354	358	+3	69%	53%	3%	19%
21	KC	L	20	31	351	397	0	44%	22%	-23%	-1%

Trends and Splits

	Offense	Rank	Defense	Rank
Total DVOA	7.2%	7	-19.7%	2
Unadjusted VOA	7.1%	8	-17.7%	2
Weighted Trend	4.4%	8	-15.2%	5
Variance	6.9%	12	8.8%	28
Average Opponent	-0.1%	16	0.7%	13
Passing	24.2%	8	-26.3%	2
Rushing	-0.3%	12	-12.0%	11
First Down	14.7%	5	-14.5%	6
Second Down	-3.5%	17	-21.4%	4
Third Down	8.4%	10	-26.8%	2
First Half	10.4%	7	-22.4%	2
Second Half	4.1%	14	-16.8%	3
Red Zone	1.3%	15	-10.7%	9
Late and Close	5.1%	13	-29.9%	1

Five-Year Performance

Year	W-L	Pyth W	Est W	PF	PA	TO	Total	Rk	Off	Rk	Def	Rk	ST	Rk	Off AGL	Rk	Def AGL	Rk	Off Age	Rk	Def Age	Rk	ST Age	Rk
2015	5-11	3.8	4.1	238	387	-5	-27.5%	32	-14.0%	28	9.9%	27	-3.6%	27	56.7	27	24.5	9	27.7	6	25.4	32	25.1	31
2016	2-14	3.9	4.6	309	247	-5	-19.6%	28	-7.2%	23	12.1%	28	-0.3%	17	38.4	20	57.8	24	27.0	13	26.2	22	26.1	17
2017	6-10	6.6	6.7	331	383	-3	-8.4%	20	-3.0%	19	8.3%	26	2.9%	11	23.8	8	69.8	32	27.3	9	25.4	29	25.8	18
2018	4-12	5.6	4.8	342	435	-25	-20.7%	30	-15.4%	27	5.7%	23	0.3%	14	54.4	26	42.8	25	26.7	17	25.1	30	25.2	30
2019	13-3	12.0	12.0	479	310	+4	27.9%	5	7.2%	7	-19.7%	2	1.0%	12	49.5	22	46.4	26	27.0	14	25.2	31	25.8	19

2019 Performance Based on Most Common Personnel Groups

SF Offense					SF Offense vs. Opponents					SF Defense					SF Defense vs. Opponents			
Pers	Freq	Yds	DVOA	Run%	Pers	Freq	Yds	DVOA	Run%	Pers	Freq	Yds	DVOA	Pers	Freq	Yds	DVOA
11	42%	6.4	17.1%	28%	Base	49%	6.2	11.1%	59%	Base	28%	4.6	-14.5%	11	65%	4.8	-25.7%
21	27%	6.9	24.3%	55%	Nickel	38%	6.4	16.0%	37%	Nickel	70%	4.9	-23.5%	12	21%	5.3	-1.0%
12	21%	4.8	-30.3%	59%	Dime+	11%	6.0	-2.7%	19%	Dime+	1%	4.4	3.7%	21	4%	4.2	-43.9%
22	8%	7.1	44.7%	74%	Goal Line	0%	0.5	38.1%	50%	Goal Line	0%	1.0	92.0%	10	3%	4.9	3.5%
13	1%	7.2	20.7%	62%	Big	1%	2.9	-1.1%	69%					22	2%	3.0	-32.0%
23	1%	0.6	45.7%	80%										611	2%	4.4	-10.4%

Strategic Tendencies

Run/Pass		Rk	Formation		Rk	Pass Rush		Rk	Secondary		Rk	Strategy		Rk
Runs, first half	40%	9	Form: Single Back	58%	32	Rush 3	2.1%	30	4 DB	28%	16	Play Action	32%	4
Runs, first down	59%	3	Form: Empty Back	7%	22	Rush 4	78.6%	3	5 DB	70%	7	Offensive Motion	70%	1
Runs, second-long	36%	3	Form: Multi Back	35%	1	Rush 5	16.6%	25	6+ DB	1%	29	Avg Box (Off)	6.93	1
Runs, power sit.	59%	8	Pers: 3+ WR	42%	30	Rush 6+	2.6%	27	Man Coverage	20%	29	Avg Box (Def)	6.64	13
Runs, behind 2H	39%	1	Pers: 2+ TE/6+ OL	31%	14	Edge Rusher Sacks	63.5%	9	CB by Sides	91%	4	Offensive Pace	31.36	20
Pass, ahead 2H	42%	28	Pers: 6+ OL	0%	30	Interior DL Sacks	21.9%	17	S/CB Cover Ratio	25%	19	Defensive Pace	30.63	16
Run-Pass Options	3%	25	Shotgun/Pistol	45%	30	Second Level Sacks	14.6%	20	DB Blitz	7%	24	Go for it on 4th	1.06	28

Kyle Shanahan cares not for your analysis that suggests running the ball against lighter boxes. Only 12% of San Francisco runs came against a light box of six or fewer, the lowest rate in the league, while 41% of runs came against a heavy box of eight or more. (Part of the reason: the 49ers had 52% of their runs with two backs in the backfield; no other offense was above 40%.) And there was a significant impact on the 49ers running game from the box count. Those runs against light boxes gained 6.3 yards per carry with 20.6% DVOA. For seven men in the box, those numbers were 5.2 yards and 9.9% DVOA. For eight or more, the numbers were 4.0 yards and -16.4% DVOA. ● San Francisco ranked first in DVOA on passes to the left and fourth on passes to the middle, but only 26th on passes to the right. ● The 49ers led the league with 6.6 average yards after the catch, which broke down to 5.2 on passes past the line of scrimmage (first in the NFL) and 10.5 on passes at or behind the line of scrimmage (third). This was the second straight year the 49ers led the NFL in average yards after the catch (7.0 in 2018). ● San Francisco finished sixth in broken tackles even though no 49ers running back finished in the NFL's top 30 in this metric. However, George Kittle led all tight ends with 27 and Deebo Samuel led all wide receivers with 28. ● San Francisco's high use of 12 personnel was directly connected to the injury to fullback Kyle Juszczyk, with two-thirds of their 12-personnel usage coming in the four games he missed. And in turn, their struggles in this personnel group were a major reason their offense dropped to -0.5% DVOA from Weeks 6 to 9. In the other regular-season games, they used 11 personnel on 42% of plays, 21 personnel on 36% of plays, and 12 personnel on just 9% of plays. ● San Francisco was one of three teams that never used six offensive linemen. However, the 49ers were first in the league with 12.6% of plays coded as max protect (seven or more blockers with at least two more blockers than pass-rushers). ● The San Francisco defense faced 62 wide receiver or tight end screens, while no other defense was above 43. The 49ers' 6.7% DVOA on these plays was a little bit worse than the NFL average. However, the 49ers had the best defense in the league against running back screens: -80.6% DVOA. ● They didn't do it much, but the 49ers led the NFL with -76.1% DVOA and just 3.4 yards allowed per play when they blitzed a defensive back. ● For a forward-thinking young head coach, Kyle Shanahan is distinctly conservative on fourth downs, ranking 27th or lower in Aggressiveness Index for three straight years.

Passing

Player	DYAR	DVOA	Plays	NtYds	Avg	YAC	C%	TD	Int
J.Garoppolo	724	10.8%	513	3727	7.3	6.6	69.4%	27	13

Rushing

Player	DYAR	DVOA	Plays	Yds	Avg	TD	Fum	Suc
R.Mostert	191	26.8%	137	772	5.6	8	1	53%
T.Coleman	-38	-15.3%	137	544	4.0	6	0	39%
M.Breida*	33	-1.8%	123	623	5.1	1	2	46%
J.Wilson	39	20.3%	27	105	3.9	4	0	52%
J.Garoppolo	-9	-18.0%	24	65	2.7	1	2	-
D.Samuel	111	107.6%	14	159	11.4	3	0	-
G.Kittle	1	-32.4%	5	22	4.4	0	0	-

Receiving

Player	DYAR	DVOA	Plays	Ctch	Yds	Y/C	YAC	TD	C%
D.Samuel	121	7.3%	81	57	802	14.1	8.3	3	70%
E.Sanders*	117	13.4%	53	36	502	13.9	3.3	3	68%
K.Bourne	130	25.7%	44	30	358	11.9	4.1	5	68%
D.Pettis	-29	-28.1%	24	11	109	9.9	2.1	2	46%
M.Goodwin*	36	7.4%	21	12	186	15.5	2.8	1	57%
R.James	54	64.5%	10	6	165	27.5	17.2	1	60%
T.Benjamin	-84	-78.9%	16	6	30	5.0	3.2	0	38%
G.Kittle	187	18.9%	107	85	1053	12.4	7.1	5	79%
R.Dwelley	-21	-21.1%	22	15	91	6.1	2.7	2	68%
T.Coleman	23	0.0%	30	21	180	8.6	9.7	1	70%
K.Juszczyk	98	47.6%	24	20	239	12.0	7.9	1	83%
R.Mostert	62	39.3%	22	14	180	12.9	11.1	2	64%
M.Breida*	39	19.5%	22	19	120	6.3	6.7	1	86%

Offensive Line

Player	Pos	Age	GS	Snaps	Pen	Sk	Pass	Run	Player	Pos	Age	GS	Snaps	Pen	Sk	Pass	Run
Laken Tomlinson	LG	28	16/16	1085	5	2.5	10	8	Daniel Brunskill	RT/RG	26	14/7	483	1	1.5	7	3
Mike Person*	RG	32	14/14	961	2	1.5	7	9	Joe Staley*	LT	36	7/7	445	2	1.5	6	5
Weston Richburg	C	29	13/13	858	4	0.0	2	6	Ben Garland	C	32	9/3	237	1	0.5	2	2
Mike McGlinchey	RT	25	12/12	795	6	5.5	13	2	Tom Compton	RG	31	13/5	367	2	2.5	11	4
Justin Skule	LT	24	15/8	556	6	5.0	13	3									

Year	Yards	ALY	Rank	Power	Rank	Stuff	Rank	2nd Lev	Rank	Open Field	Rank	Sacks	ASR	Rank	Press	Rank	F-Start	Cont.
2017	4.13	4.20	10	62%	20	23%	25	1.24	7	0.76	14	43	6.8%	18	31.3%	17	22	28
2018	4.84	4.56	10	68%	16	19%	18	1.47	3	1.13	5	48	8.0%	22	31.9%	19	25	37
2019	4.80	4.53	8	67%	13	20%	20	1.32	7	1.16	3	36	6.9%	15	26.0%	5	18	25

2019 ALY by direction:	Left End 5.19 (4)	Left Tackle: 3.97 (21)	Mid/Guard: 4.46 (14)	Right Tackle: 4.53 (11)	Right End: 4.84 (10)

Longtime starting left tackle Joe Staley hung up the cleats after an injury-shortened 2019 season. Normally when you lose a 13-year starter at a position as important as left tackle, there will be cause for concern. Not exactly the case for San Francisco, as they were able to swing a trade on draft weekend for former Washington star Trent Williams. Williams had a falling out with Washington due to how the team handled a cancerous growth on his head, forcing them to deal him away. Going from 2019's worst NFC team to its best NFC team is probably the change of scenery he had in mind. ✏ Lining up opposite Williams will be third-year right tackle Mike McGlinchey, who excelled in run blocking in his second season with only two blown run blocks on the year. ✏ Veteran center Weston Richburg finished third among centers in snaps per blown block while serving as a key component of San Francisco's run-heavy attack. Unfortunately for the 49ers, Richburg tore his patellar tendon late in the season, so he may not be ready for the start of 2020. In that event, Ben Garland will continue filling in for Richburg, as he did at the end of 2019. ✏ Former undrafted free agent Daniel Brunskill impressed when playing at a variety of spots along the line. He'll be competing for the starting right guard job vacated by incumbent Mike Person's release. Brunskill will have to beat out veteran Tom Compton (ex-Jets) for the job. ✏ Rounding out the starting offensive line is left guard Laken Tomlinson, who was the only lineman to start every game for the 49ers last year. Tomlinson had a solid yet unspectacular year at guard and managed to cut down on his penalties after holding the dubious distinction of leading all guards in false starts in 2018. ✏ Colton McKivitz, a fifth-round rookie from West Virginia, will serve as depth at both tackle and guard in his rookie season. The four-year starter enters the league as a developmental prospect best suited for right tackle.

Defensive Front

Defensive Line	Age	Pos	G	Snaps	Plays	Overall TmPct	Rk	Stop	Dfts	BTkl	Runs	vs. Run St%	Rk	RuYd	Rk	Pass Rush Sack	Hit	Hur	Dsrpt
DeForest Buckner*	26	DT	16	824	62	7.8%	8	51	17	2	47	77%	44	3.0	84	7.5	6	25	4
Sheldon Day*	26	DT	16	330	14	1.8%	--	10	2	2	10	80%	--	2.5	--	1.0	1	7	0
D.J. Jones	25	DT	11	307	23	4.2%	81	18	9	1	21	76%	45	2.4	56	2.0	0	4	0

Edge Rushers	Age	Pos	G	Snaps	Plays	Overall TmPct	Rk	Stop	Dfts	BTkl	Runs	vs. Run St%	Rk	RuYd	Rk	Pass Rush Sack	Hit	Hur	Dsrpt
Nick Bosa	23	DE	16	789	48	6.0%	27	35	20	4	32	72%	54	2.0	25	9.0	16	62	2
Arik Armstead	27	DE	16	788	55	6.9%	15	46	22	5	35	74%	45	2.1	32	10.0	7	28	2
Solomon Thomas	25	DE/DT	16	428	21	2.6%	83	16	4	4	15	73%	49	1.7	18	2.0	5	9	1
Dee Ford	29	DE	11	232	14	2.6%	--	14	10	2	4	100%	--	2.3	--	6.5	1	7	1
Ronald Blair	27	DE	9	201	21	4.7%	--	16	11	3	18	72%	--	2.2	--	3.0	0	5	0
Kerry Hyder	29	DE	16	447	17	2.1%	90	12	3	3	15	73%	49	2.5	46	1.0	3	28	0

Linebackers	Age	Pos	G	Snaps	Plays	Overall TmPct	Rk	Stop	Dfts	BTkl	Runs	vs. Run St%	Rk	RuYd	Rk	Pass Rush Sack	Hit	Hur	vs. Pass Tgts	Suc%	Rk	AdjYd	Rk	PD	Int
Fred Warner	24	MLB	16	1000	125	15.7%	13	63	19	17	63	56%	61	4.1	55	3.0	2	6	45	67%	4	4.7	9	9	1
Dre Greenlaw	23	OLB	16	730	89	11.2%	36	37	12	6	50	38%	82	5.5	80	1.0	2	4	14	57%	14	5.2	13	2	1
Kwon Alexander	26	OLB	8	368	38	9.6%	79	20	7	8	19	47%	76	3.5	28	0.5	0	1	12	67%	--	4.3	--	4	1

Year	Yards	ALY	Rank	Power	Rank	Stuff	Rank	2nd Level	Rank	Open Field	Rank	Sacks	ASR	Rank	Press	Rank
2017	3.82	4.09	15	64%	17	22%	9	1.05	8	0.62	10	30	5.0%	29	29.4%	23
2018	4.08	4.39	19	61%	6	17%	21	1.19	12	0.59	6	37	6.9%	18	29.9%	18
2019	4.23	4.16	13	50%	2	20%	14	1.29	23	0.67	12	48	9.0%	2	30.8%	13

2019 ALY by direction:	Left End: 3.97 (15)	Left Tackle: 3.64 (7)	Mid/Guard: 4.33 (12)	Right Tackle: 4.84 (27)	Right End: 3.03 (8)

Arik Armstead's breakout year and Nick Bosa's instant impact as a rookie helped mitigate the lack of production from another former first-round defensive lineman in Solomon Thomas. The 49ers chose not to exercise the fifth-year option on his rookie contract, so Thomas will need to make an impact fast to cash in on free agency come springtime. Armstead and Bosa were so disruptive (81 combined run stops, 90 combined hurries, and 19.0 combined sacks) that the 49ers barely needed Dee Ford to see the field. It is fair to wonder just how dominant San Francisco's defense would have been had they all been healthy. With DeForest Buckner off to Indianapolis, rookie first-round defensive tackle Javon Kinlaw will have to step into the void early on. The former South Carolina Gamecocks star earned high marks for his explosiveness from draft analysts and should be a good fit as a one-gap defensive tackle for San Francisco. Sheldon Day followed Buckner to Indianapolis in free agency after being mostly a rotational piece at defensive tackle in 2019. With the emergence of young nose tackle D.J. Jones, the 49ers did not need to make a major effort to bring back Day. Jones suffered a season-ending ankle injury in December and missed the playoffs, but he should be full-go in 2020. Ronald Blair will still be around as defensive line depth alongside new acquisition Kerry Hyder, who is reuniting with defensive line coach Kris Kocurek after the two spent time together in Detroit. Kwon Alexander joined San Francisco on an expensive deal and did not have the first season he hoped for after tearing a pectoral muscle. Alexander was strong against the run but overall was upstaged by Fred Warner's coming-out party. Warner was a nightmare for opposing offenses in coverage with a success rate of 67% on four times the number of targets Alexander faced. Someone had to be the third linebacker for the 49ers and that duty fell to 2019 fifth-rounder Dre Greenlaw. The youngster from Arkansas was no superstar and had some issues against the run, but the 49ers are going to need starters on cheap contracts to try to keep their studs. Greenlaw seems like he should fit the bill.

Defensive Secondary

Secondary	Age	Pos	G	Snaps	Plays	TmPct	Rk	Stop	Dfts	BTkl	Runs	St%	Rk	RuYd	Rk	Tgts	Tgt%	Rk	Dist	Suc%	Rk	AdjYd	Rk	PD	Int
Richard Sherman	32	CB	15	911	72	9.7%	22	30	11	7	20	45%	42	6.6	45	49	16.1%	71	11.2	53%	39	5.6	7	11	3
Jimmie Ward	29	FS	13	819	68	10.5%	41	25	13	4	31	26%	62	11.9	71	18	6.6%	51	11.9	72%	4	5.1	11	8	0
Jaquiski Tartt	28	SS	12	689	46	7.7%	64	21	9	5	27	48%	22	5.6	23	16	7.0%	46	15.5	75%	2	2.0	1	2	0
K'Waun Williams	29	CB	15	615	53	7.1%	55	30	14	9	20	65%	15	3.8	12	35	17.1%	65	6.8	57%	23	7.0	29	2	2
Emmanuel Moseley	24	CB	16	589	51	6.4%	57	20	6	4	12	50%	34	6.3	42	47	23.9%	12	12.7	62%	9	6.3	14	8	1
Ahkello Witherspoon	25	CB	10	565	37	7.5%	84	17	6	9	8	38%	57	4.5	22	48	25.5%	5	13.4	54%	34	7.8	45	9	1
Marcell Harris	26	SS	13	340	39	6.0%	--	17	4	7	19	47%	--	5.7	--	10	8.8%	--	10.5	60%	--	6.7	--	5	0

Year	Pass D Rank	vs. #1 WR	Rk	vs. #2 WR	Rk	vs. Other WR	Rk	WR Wide	Rk	WR Slot	Rk	vs. TE	Rk	vs. RB	Rk
2017	28	21.1%	27	-1.6%	16	30.7%	32	17.3%	30	20.2%	27	-19.5%	5	13.2%	24
2018	27	4.8%	19	18.5%	26	36.9%	31	-9.9%	11	36.7%	32	9.6%	21	5.7%	19
2019	2	-9.0%	10	-2.8%	13	-15.8%	7	-22.0%	8	3.6%	11	-33.4%	2	-63.8%	1

The 49ers were very tough to throw on when targeting wide receivers in 2019, but they were definitely your best bet if you were trying to identify an area where you might have a slightly favorable matchup in the passing game. San Francisco ranked second in DVOA against opposing tight ends and first against running backs, but they were "only" above average against teams' No. 2 targets. Richard Sherman may not be quite as dominant as he was in his youth, but the decorated veteran proved he still had some gas in the tank in 2019. Teams still targeted each of San Francisco's other primary cornerbacks more frequently despite his advancing age and averaged their fewest yards per pass against San Francisco's corners when choosing Sherman. He is entering the final year of his deal in 2020 and seems likely to cash in again as a free agent. Ahkello Witherspoon has not lived up to expectations opposite Sherman since being drafted in the third round, losing his starting role as an outside corner to Emmanuel Moseley by season's end. Unfortunately for Witherspoon, he did not have the chance to simply bump inside to the nickel role because of K'Waun Williams. Strong safety Jaquiski Tartt was a heat-seeking missile against the run and not too shabby in pass coverage as well. In his fifth year with the 49ers, Tartt finished first among safeties in yards per pass allowed and second in success rate. Rounding out the group was free safety Jimmie Ward, who started the most games of his career just in time to lock down a solid three-year deal. It was by no means a megadeal, but it does give him some job security for the first time in his career. Ward and Tartt both missed a handful of games, which gave Marcell Harris a chance to see some playing time in his second season in the league. The former sixth-rounder took advantage of his opportunities and finished with more passes defensed than Tartt on half the snaps.

Special Teams

Year	DVOA	Rank	FG/XP	Rank	Net Kick	Rank	Kick Ret	Rank	Net Punt	Rank	Punt Ret	Rank	Hidden	Rank
2017	2.9%	11	14.2	2	3.0	10	-6.4	32	3.6	13	0.0	16	4.9	10
2018	0.3%	14	6.6	7	-0.4	17	1.7	8	0.0	17	-6.4	30	3.6	10
2019	1.0%	12	-5.7	27	0.5	16	1.3	10	6.4	7	2.4	9	-5.9	24

San Francisco's field goal kicking took a nosedive during the 2019 season after being a point of strength for the previous two years. Robbie Gould started the season in a major slump before suffering an injury in Week 9, forcing the 49ers to turn to rookie Chase McLaughlin during his absence. Upon Gould's return to health, he managed to pull it together, missing only two combined kicks over the team's final eight games (including playoffs). San Francisco is going with Gould again in 2020 while McLaughlin found his way to Indianapolis after the 49ers waived him late in the season. ● The 49ers drafted punter Mitch Wishnowsky in the fourth round in 2019, and they were likely hoping for a better performance out of the former Ray Guy Award winner. Wishnowsky finished in the bottom ten among qualified punters in points of field position value from punts only. He did not impress on kickoffs either, so the early returns have not been promising. ● The punt return unit was much improved, and diminutive speedster Richie James likely had a lot to do with that. James did not have very many chances to return punts as a rookie in 2018 (due in large part to San Francisco's defensive woes), but with more opportunities in 2019, he made much more of an impact. For James, continued impact in the return game may be necessary to keep a hold on his roster spot. 2020 first-round wide receiver Brandon Aiyuk may have some chances to get involved in the return game too, so that job may not belong to James by default.

Seattle Seahawks

2019 Record: 11-5	Total DVOA: 13.5% (8th)	2020 Mean Projection: 8.7 wins	On the Clock (0-4): 6%
Pythagorean Wins: 8.2 (14th)	Offense: 17.1% (5th)	Postseason Odds: 52.9%	Mediocrity (5-7): 26%
Snap-Weighted Age: 26.6 (10th)	Defense: 2.6% (18th)	Super Bowl Odds: 7.3%	Playoff Contender (8-10): 42%
Average Opponent: 4.8% (2nd)	Special Teams: -1.0% (20th)	Proj. Avg. Opponent: -1.2% (27th)	Super Bowl Contender (11+): 26%

2019: "In Russ We Trust" can only take you so far.

2020: We still trust the quarterback. It's the defense we're worried about.

Five years have passed since the Butler did it. Five years ago, Russell Wilson's goal-line pass was intercepted by Malcolm Butler, taking a Lombardi Trophy out of Seattle and delivering it to Foxborough. It was the most decisive play in Super Bowl history, the biggest mistake at the worst time in the annals of America's biggest sporting event. It was a loss so devastating, so painful, that it left everyone involved wondering whether the quarterback or his team would be able to recover. Well, the quarterback has done just fine, thank you very much. The team? That's another story.

In the five years since the Butler interception, Wilson has shown remarkable resilience, shaking off his error and becoming one of the NFL's best quarterbacks. He has completed 65% of his passes for nearly 20,000 yards. Only Tom Brady has won more games; only Derek Carr has led more fourth-quarter comebacks. And in a bit of karmic retribution, Wilson has shown why his coaches trusted him to throw at the goal line with a championship at stake, delivering a league-high 155 touchdown passes and running in eight more scores to boot. His advanced statistics have been tremendous as well; his 4,620 combined passing and rushing DYAR are in the top five over the last five seasons.

It's consistency that really sets Wilson apart. Even at his worst in 2016, when he fought through an ankle injury and finished below replacement level as a runner, he still passed

well enough to post 568 combined DYAR. That's not a terribly significant number in a single season; 17 quarterbacks topped 500 combined DYAR in 2019. To do it every year for half a decade, however, is extremely rare. Wilson, Drew Brees, and Tom Brady are the only quarterbacks to hit 500 DYAR in each of the last five years. Even if we look just at the last four years, Matt Ryan is the only name we add to that list.

As good as Wilson has been, however, what does Seattle have to show for it? The Seahawks have just one division title since 2014 and have yet to return to the Super Bowl; in fact, they haven't even gotten back to the NFC Championship Game. Shouldn't a team with a quarterback this good be winning more often?

We catalogued every team since 1985 that had one quarterback top 500 combined DYAR five years in a row. We omitted quarterbacks who changed teams (or vice versa) because we wanted to measure the benefits of having a franchise passer in place—if you've already got your quarterback, you can devote resources to building around him instead of replacing him. We broke longer streaks into overlapping chunks. For example, Drew Brees has topped 500 DYAR in each of his 14 seasons in New Orleans, the longest streak since 1985 (and that doesn't even count his last two years in San Diego, because he switched teams), but we broke that down into 10 overlapping five-year stretches.

We found 81 franchises that qualified, which works out to two or three active streaks in a given year. Of those 81 teams:
- 34 (42%) won at least one Super Bowl; nine (11%) won two or more.
- 46 (57%) reached at least one Super Bowl; 20 (25%) reached two or more.
- 65 (80%) reached at least one conference championship game; 44% reached two or more.

The 2015-2019 Seattle Seahawks are in that 20% of teams that failed to reach the conference championship game despite elite quarterback play (Table 1). If it's any consolation to Wilson and Seattle fans, there have been a few better quarterbacks whose teams have accomplished less in the past 35 years. Wilson's Seahawks have the best winning percentage in this table, and they're tied with Brees' Saints with three playoff wins (though it took New Orleans three more years to get them). Still, given the brevity of this list over three-plus decades, it's fair to say that Wilson has been wasted. The questions now

Table 1. Consecutive 500-DYAR Seasons, QBs on One Team, No CCGs, 1985-2019

Quarterback	Team	Seasons	Years	W-L	Pct	Missed Playoffs	Playoff W-L
Dan Marino	MIA	6	1986-1991	50-45	0.526	5	1-1
Warren Moon	HOIL	5	1988-1992	49-31	0.613	0	2-5
Dan Marino	MIA	5	1994-1998	46-34	0.575	1	2-4
Brett Favre	GB	8	1998-2005	76-52	0.594	3	2-5
Peyton Manning	IND	5	1998-2002	42-38	0.525	2	0-3
Matt Schaub	HOU	5	2008-2012	45-35	0.563	3	2-2
Drew Brees	NO	8	2010-2017	74-54	0.578	4	3-4
Ben Roethlisberger	PIT	5	2011-2015	49-31	0.613	2	1-3
Russell Wilson	**SEA**	**5**	**2015-2019**	**50-29-1**	**0.631**	**1**	**3-4**

220

2020 Seahawks Schedule

Week	Opp.	Week	Opp.	Week	Opp.
1	at ATL	7	at ARI	13	NYG
2	NE	8	SF	14	NYJ
3	DAL	9	at BUF	15	at WAS
4	at MIA	10	at LAR	16	LAR
5	MIN	11	ARI (Thu.)	17	at SF
6	BYE	12	at PHI (Mon.)		

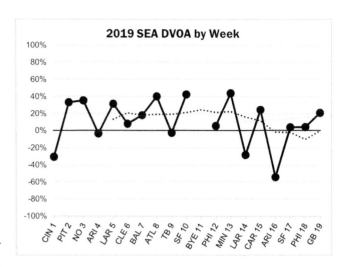

2019 SEA DVOA by Week

become how and why, and what can Seattle do to ensure he won't be wasted again in 2020?

Ask any Seahawks fan what their team does wrong and you'll get three quick answers: Pete Carroll's coaching staff runs the ball too often and is too conservative on fourth downs, while John Schneider has let the best defenders from the Super Bowl teams walk out the door with no adequate replacements. Let's examine whether those claims are fair, in the long term and in 2019:

- The Seahawks have run the ball on 46% of offensive plays since 2015. Only the Bills have run more often, and if your quarterbacks were Tyrod Taylor and Josh Allen, you would call for a lot of handoffs too. Many of those runs actually started as pass plays—the Bills and Seahawks rank one-two in scrambles over the past five years—but even if we count scrambles as pass plays, Seattle has still run the ball 40% of the time, ninth most. (The Bills remain at No. 1.) Most of the teams in the top 10 have run so often because they couldn't pass very well. The Seahawks have called all those runs despite averaging 6.9 net yards per dropback, even accounting for the many sacks Wilson has taken. Only one team in the top 10 in run rate has averaged more net yards per pass: the New England Patriots, who have run so often in part because they have been killing clock in a league-high 62 wins.

- Since the Super Bowl loss to New England, Seattle has gone for it on fourth down only 10% of the time, the lowest rate in the league. That doesn't change much when we look only at situations where going for it would be more likely, such as in short yardage (they have gone for it 32% of the time, 27th), or when they are losing (16%, 31st), or in opponents' territory (17%, 29th).

- And yes, the Legion of Boom that obliterated Peyton Manning's Broncos in the Super Bowl is long gone. Granted, there was nowhere to go but down from that dominant performance, but seven years later the Seahawks have done little to stop the bleeding. Seattle's defensive DVOA has gotten worse every season since winning the Super Bowl.

In 2019, each of those trends continued. Including scrambles, Seattle ran the ball 46% of the time last year, sixth most in the league and exactly matching their rate over the past five years (without scrambles, they fall to 41% and seventh place). Only Denver had a lower Aggressiveness Index. And the

ever-declining defense officially transitioned from a strength to a weakness; their DVOA of 7.2% was 23rd in the league. It's that last number that is most worrisome, because there's not going to be a quick fix. Carroll could wake up tomorrow and order offensive coordinator Brian Schottenheimer to start passing more, but there's no similar obvious move Schottenheimer's counterpart Ken Norton Jr. could make to get things turned around.

While some of the biggest stars from Seattle's Super Bowl defenses (Michael Bennett, Richard Sherman, Earl Thomas) have been making key contributions elsewhere, the Seahawks have been busy squandering high draft picks. They have taken 11 players in the first and second round in the past six years, and also traded a second-rounder for Sheldon Richardson. That's a dozen players who should theoretically be forming the backbone of the current Seahawks roster, but only two of them—wide receiver DK Metcalf and defensive tackle Jarran Reed—are likely to be starters in 2020.

That talent drain has mostly been felt on defense, where the Seahawks essentially played the 2019 season without the benefit of a nickelback. Seattle used a base defense 69% of the time, nearly twice as often as the next team (Arizona at 38%). As you might expect, opponents tried to exploit that by targeting Seattle's linebackers, who faced a league-high 130 targets in coverage. K.J. Wright led the position with 56 targets; Bobby Wagner was tied for fifth with 49. This left the team relying on zone coverage so their linebackers would not be isolated against wideouts. That in turn left Seattle relying on a four-man pass rush, a task at which they were woefully inadequate, finishing last in the league in pressure rate.

Now, here's the funny thing: it worked. Seattle allowed -3.4% DVOA and 6.0 yards per play from base defense, compared to 30.4% DVOA and 7.0 yards per play from nickel. Even when opponents had three or more wide receivers on the field, Seattle allowed 5.9 yards per play and -7.3% DVOA from base defense. There's no specific matchup where the Seahawks suffered, either; they finished 12th or better in coverage against No. 1, No. 2, and "other" wide receivers. They were much better against receivers split wide than they had been in prior seasons, and they were in the middle of the pack against receivers out of the slot.

In fact, leaguewide over the last couple of seasons, it seems that playing base defense against three or more wide receivers is not a serious problem for most teams that do it. Back in 2017, we were shocked at how much base defense Gregg Williams and the Cleveland Browns played against 11 personnel. It appeared to be a terrible decision that helped contribute to the Browns finishing 16th that year in defensive DVOA, including 26th against the pass. But let's look instead at the entire league over the last three years, instead of the 2017 Browns or 2019 Seahawks specifically.

Defenses remain in base on only 5% of snaps with three or more wide receivers on the field, according to numbers from 2017 to 2019. But defenses allow fewer yards per play from base (5.43) than from nickel (5.72) or dime (6.00) personnel. Once we account for down and distance, we get DVOA ratings that are closer but show a similar split, with -0.5% DVOA for base, 1.8% DVOA for nickel, and 2.5% for dime.

This probably doesn't mean that base personnel is actually *better* against three or more wide receivers. There's some selection bias here, where the teams that play base defense against three or more wide receivers are mostly the teams where the linebackers are good enough to stay on the field against three or more wide receivers. But it does suggest that teams should put their best players on the field whenever possible, no matter what their position. Even when the offense spreads things out with more receivers, a Pro Bowl-quality linebacker may be a better choice than a subpar cornerback. Certainly that was the case for the 2019 Seahawks, where the two linebackers were the best players on the defense.

Nevertheless, the use of this much base defense was apparently a reaction to the secondary personnel more than a specific strategic change related to Wright and Wagner. Jamar Taylor was signed to play nickel corner, but he was picked on so frequently Seattle opted to keep third linebacker Mychal Kendricks on the field instead. (Taylor was cut in November and later played three games for Atlanta.) We suspect the Seahawks will go back to using more nickel in 2020. They used nickel more than base in every season from 2014 to 2018. Several times this offseason, Carroll has indicated he'd like to use more nickel this fall; the coach has suggested Ugo Amagi, Marquise Blair, or Tre Flowers as nickelback candidates. But where does that leave Jordyn Brooks, the Texas Tech linebacker they drafted 27th overall? He may be the odd man out as a rookie, which doesn't seem like an efficient use of a first-round pick.

It is defense which has hurt Seattle most in their last four playoff losses—their average offensive DVOA in those games was 15%, while their average defensive DVOA was 8%. (Remember, positive DVOA means worse defense.) They especially struggled in the first half. The Seahawks trailed at halftime of these four losses by a combined margin of 81-19. Opposing quarterbacks completed more than 70% of their passes in the first half of those games and topped 8.0 yards per throw with five touchdowns and no interceptions. Seattle also gave up nearly 5.0 yards per carry and four more touchdowns on the ground. Wilson tried to work his fourth-quarter magic and the Seahawks outscored those opponents 70-38 in the second halves of those games, but by then the damage had been done.

We saw a lot of these weaknesses play out in the divisional-round loss to Green Bay last season. Despite losing Chris Carson and Rashaad Penny to injury, Seattle exhausted an entire first-quarter drive by giving twice-retired Marshawn Lynch three handoffs and then punting on fourth-and-1 from their own 42. The defense gave up touchdowns on four straight drives as the Packers took a 28-10 lead in the third quarter. Seattle still rallied and had a chance to go ahead on their last drive, but Carroll opted to punt on fourth-and-11. Wilson never got the ball back because the defense surrendered a pair of third-down conversions and Green Bay ran out the clock.

There are signs of life in that defense, starting with a couple of trades that revitalized the secondary. The first of those came last October, when the Seahawks got safety Quandre Diggs and a seventh-round pick from Detroit for the low price of a fifth-rounder. They proceeded to win five of his seven starts, four of them against playoff teams. This offseason, they traded another fifth-round pick to Washington for cornerback Quinton Dunbar. Dunbar has limited experience, with only 25 starts in five NFL seasons, but he has played well—he averaged exactly 7.5 yards allowed per pass in both 2017 and 2018, on 30-plus targets each season, then just 6.7 yards allowed last year. Assuming Dunbar's legal issues (discussed later in the chapter) don't affect his status, his presence should allow Seattle to re-join the modern era of the NFL and field five-plus defensive backs more often than not. Simple regression also suggests they'll have a better pass rush this year, if only because it can't get any worse.

But make no mistake, this is Wilson's team now. The good news is that he'll have plenty of weapons. Chris Carson, the NFL's 2019 tackle-breaking king, will return, and the depth chart at running back could go four-deep behind him. If tight end Will Dissly is healthy, he could team with the hyper-efficient Tyler Lockett and prime athletic specimen DK Metcalf as the best targets Wilson has ever seen. That's not even acknowledging the offseason whispers that Josh Gordon could return from his latest suspension, or that Seattle might take a chance on Antonio Brown.

This is all cause for cautious optimism. The Seahawks are our slight favorites to win the NFC West. The schedule is favorable—they play the floundering AFC East and NFC East divisions, and they get last year's other NFC wild-card team, Minnesota, at home. The tougher games are going to be within the division, and that's really where Seattle has struggled the most lately. In the past five seasons, they have the best record in the NFC West at 50-29-1, going 34-16 (.680) against teams outside the division, but 16-13-1 (.550) against the 49ers, Cardinals, and Rams. And while the Seahawks have been consistent, winning nine to 11 games each season, one of their rivals usually finds itself in an upswing and takes the division title, and the home game that goes with it. Since 2015, Arizona, L.A., and San Francisco each have at least one season with a dozen losses but also at least one season with at least 13 wins.

The challenge for the Seahawks is to get to 13 wins themselves. Otherwise, we may be back here next year talking about teams that wasted their quarterbacks for six-plus years.

Vincent Verhei

2019 Seahawks by Week

Wk	vs.	W-L	PF	PA	YDF	YDA	TO	Total	Off	Def	ST
1	CIN	W	21	20	232	429	+2	-31%	-29%	5%	4%
2	at PIT	W	28	26	425	261	-1	33%	56%	21%	-2%
3	NO	L	27	33	514	265	0	35%	44%	-5%	-14%
4	at ARI	W	27	10	340	321	+1	-3%	-8%	-5%	-1%
5	LAR	W	30	29	429	477	+1	31%	50%	18%	-1%
6	at CLE	W	32	28	454	406	+3	8%	16%	-8%	-16%
7	BAL	L	16	30	347	340	-2	18%	-2%	-22%	-3%
8	at ATL	W	27	20	322	510	+3	40%	52%	20%	8%
9	TB	W	40	34	492	418	0	-3%	48%	34%	-17%
10	at SF	W	27	24	336	302	-1	43%	-11%	-47%	7%
11	BYE										
12	at PHI	W	17	9	348	344	+3	6%	-18%	-25%	-1%
13	MIN	W	37	30	444	354	+1	44%	30%	-6%	8%
14	at LAR	L	12	28	308	455	+1	-28%	1%	29%	-1%
15	at CAR	W	30	24	428	414	+2	24%	26%	3%	1%
16	ARI	L	13	27	224	412	-1	-54%	-47%	10%	3%
17	SF	L	21	26	348	398	0	4%	24%	29%	8%
18	at PHI	W	17	9	382	282	0	4%	-3%	-8%	0%
19	at GB	L	23	28	375	344	0	21%	33%	12%	1%

Trends and Splits

	Offense	Rank	Defense	Rank
Total DVOA	17.1%	5	2.6%	18
Unadjusted VOA	11.3%	6	2.8%	19
Weighted Trend	11.3%	6	0.6%	17
Variance	10.1%	27	4.9%	8
Average Opponent	-4.2%	3	0.8%	12
Passing	42.9%	4	3.8%	15
Rushing	2.7%	6	1.0%	26
First Down	13.3%	7	18.4%	29
Second Down	23.1%	3	-11.9%	7
Third Down	14.1%	9	-6.4%	14
First Half	15.4%	4	3.1%	21
Second Half	18.7%	4	2.2%	18
Red Zone	34.4%	3	9.7%	23
Late and Close	26.5%	4	-6.0%	14

Five-Year Performance

Year	W-L	Pyth W	Est W	PF	PA	TO	Total	Rk	Off	Rk	Def	Rk	ST	Rk	Off AGL	Rk	Def AGL	Rk	Off Age	Rk	Def Age	Rk	ST Age	Rk
2015	10-6	11.8	12.5	423	277	+7	38.1%	1	18.7%	1	-15.2%	4	4.2%	3	23.5	8	22.5	6	25.9	25	27.0	12	26.3	12
2016	10-5-1	9.8	9.1	354	292	+1	8.0%	11	-2.6%	16	-10.6%	5	-0.1%	15	23.2	6	17.0	3	25.7	29	27.2	7	26.4	8
2017	9-7	9.0	8.5	366	332	+8	3.8%	14	2.0%	14	-3.8%	13	-2.0%	20	55.1	24	49.5	26	26.1	29	27.0	8	25.8	20
2018	10-6	10.1	8.9	428	347	+16	6.7%	12	8.8%	9	-0.1%	14	-2.2%	24	31.5	12	31.3	14	27.2	11	25.5	27	25.8	16
2019	11-5	8.2	10.8	405	398	+12	13.5%	8	17.1%	5	2.6%	18	-1.0%	20	31.5	12	25.0	8	27.2	8	26.6	12	25.3	28

2019 Performance Based on Most Common Personnel Groups

SEA Offense					SEA Offense vs. Opponents					SEA Defense				SEA Defense vs. Opponents			
Pers	Freq	Yds	DVOA	Run%	Pers	Freq	Yds	DVOA	Run%	Pers	Freq	Yds	DVOA	Pers	Freq	Yds	DVOA
11	62%	5.9	20.8%	30%	Base	26%	5.7	13.7%	58%	Base	69%	6.0	-3.4%	11	45%	6.2	2.6%
12	11%	6.5	43.5%	39%	Nickel	63%	6.1	28.5%	37%	Nickel	27%	7.0	30.4%	12	32%	6.0	-3.1%
611	11%	5.1	-1.8%	71%	Dime+	10%	5.7	0.7%	14%	Dime+	3%	4.0	-113.2%	21	7%	5.5	-26.1%
610	6%	6.0	34.5%	70%	Goal Line	1%	0.3	3.4%	86%	Goal Line	1%	1.1	17.3%	10	5%	6.7	39.8%
612	3%	3.9	-3.5%	80%	Big	1%	3.1	31.5%	75%					22	4%	7.0	28.2%
10	3%	6.9	64.2%	33%										13	2%	10.8	67.4%

Strategic Tendencies

Run/Pass		Rk	Formation		Rk	Pass Rush		Rk	Secondary		Rk	Strategy		Rk
Runs, first half	41%	3	Form: Single Back	91%	3	Rush 3	3.2%	28	4 DB	69%	1	Play Action	29%	10
Runs, first down	50%	13	Form: Empty Back	7%	21	Rush 4	73.2%	7	5 DB	27%	31	Offensive Motion	35%	21
Runs, second-long	26%	20	Form: Multi Back	2%	28	Rush 5	17.7%	21	6+ DB	3%	23	Avg Box (Off)	6.51	23
Runs, power sit.	67%	4	Pers: 3+ WR	72%	7	Rush 6+	5.9%	14	Man Coverage	19%	30	Avg Box (Def)	6.70	9
Runs, behind 2H	31%	13	Pers: 2+ TE/6+ OL	33%	12	Edge Rusher Sacks	55.6%	15	CB by Sides	94%	2	Offensive Pace	31.79	24
Pass, ahead 2H	45%	22	Pers: 6+ OL	22%	1	Interior DL Sacks	13.0%	29	S/CB Cover Ratio	31%	5	Defensive Pace	30.63	17
Run-Pass Options	4%	22	Shotgun/Pistol	71%	10	Second Level Sacks	31.5%	2	DB Blitz	8%	21	Go for it on 4th	0.86	31

For the second straight year, Seattle not only led the league in use of six-lineman sets but was above-average in both DVOA (10.9%) and yards per play (5.3) on these plays. ❧ Seattle led the league with 47% of passes going to the left side. The Seahawks were 31st in percentage of passes to the middle (19%) and 30th in passes to the right (33%). As far as efficiency, the Seahawks passing game ranked sixth to the left, second to the middle, and first to the right. ❧ In 2018, Seattle ranked 30th in DVOA on passes behind or at the line of scrimmage, but in 2019 the Seahawks improved to rank No. 1 in DVOA on those passes. By comparison, the Seahawks ranked No. 1 in DVOA on passes past the line of scrimmage in 2018, and No. 2 on those passes in 2019. ❧ The Seahawks used just 19 wide receiver or tight end screens, compared to an NFL average of 29, but had a league-best 91.0% DVOA on these plays with 7.8 yards per pass. ❧ Seattle will run the ball out of shotgun more than almost any other team, with running back carries as 30% of their shotgun plays. That was No. 2 behind Baltimore, but that number is a bit deceiving because many of those Baltimore "shotgun" plays were actually the pistol formation. Seattle ran even more out of shotgun the year before: 40% of shotgun plays in 2018. ❧ The Seahawks defense was much stronger in man coverage (5.8 yards per pass, -18.9% DVOA) than zone coverage (7.9 yards per pass, 30.7% DVOA). ❧ Seattle was ninth in defensive DVOA against passes on third down but 27th against runs on third down.

Passing

Player	DYAR	DVOA	Plays	NtYds	Avg	YAC	C%	TD	Int
R.Wilson	1265	24.3%	561	3788	6.8	5.1	66.5%	31	5

Rushing

Player	DYAR	DVOA	Plays	Yds	Avg	TD	Fum	Suc
C.Carson	130	1.9%	278	1235	4.4	7	6	57%
R.Penny	115	32.4%	65	370	5.7	3	1	57%
R.Wilson	33	-0.3%	60	342	5.7	3	3	-
C.Prosise*	-41	-49.6%	23	72	3.1	1	1	39%
T.Homer	21	19.8%	18	114	6.3	0	0	56%
M.Lynch*	-1	-10.5%	12	34	2.8	1	0	33%
C.Hyde	54	-3.3%	245	1086	4.4	6	4	52%

Receiving

Player	DYAR	DVOA	Plays	Ctch	Yds	Y/C	YAC	TD	C%
T.Lockett	317	24.6%	110	82	1057	12.9	3.7	8	75%
DK.Metcalf	105	0.6%	100	58	900	15.5	4.8	7	58%
D.Moore	19	-5.5%	34	17	301	17.7	7.5	2	50%
J.Brown*	21	-3.1%	28	16	220	13.8	3.7	2	57%
M.Turner*	62	24.5%	22	15	245	16.3	6.7	1	68%
J.Gordon	42	42.1%	11	7	139	19.9	2.3	0	64%
P.Dorsett	46	-2.1%	54	29	397	13.7	2.7	5	54%
J.Hollister	25	-0.8%	59	41	349	8.5	4.1	3	69%
W.Dissly	74	36.0%	27	23	262	11.4	3.0	4	85%
L.Willson	7	2.2%	10	8	79	9.9	4.8	0	80%
G.Olsen	4	-6.5%	82	52	597	11.5	3.9	2	63%
C.Carson	57	8.9%	47	37	266	7.2	8.6	2	79%
T.Homer	-6	-21.7%	13	11	56	5.1	5.5	0	85%
C.Prosise*	22	16.6%	12	10	76	7.6	6.6	0	83%
R.Penny	37	45.4%	11	8	83	10.4	11.4	1	73%
C.Hyde	-36	-50.3%	16	10	42	4.2	5.1	0	63%

Offensive Line

Player	Pos	Age	GS	Snaps	Pen	Sk	Pass	Run	Player	Pos	Age	GS	Snaps	Pen	Sk	Pass	Run
Germain Ifedi*	RT	26	16/16	1124	13	3.5	18	8	Justin Britt*	C	29	8/8	513	1	1.5	6	5
Mike Iupati	LG	33	16/15	1029	9	2.0	8	8	George Fant*	LT	28	16/7	476	1	0.0	7	4
D.J. Fluker*	RG	29	14/14	876	7	3.3	17	6	Jamarco Jones	RG	24	15/3	322	1	0.3	6	3
Duane Brown	LT	35	12/12	807	2	1.5	8	8	Brandon Shell	RT	28	15/11	823	4	6.0	14	3
Joey Hunt	C	26	14/8	621	3	2.8	12	5	B.J. Finney	C	29	16/4	335	0	1.0	2	2

Year	Yards	ALY	Rank	Power	Rank	Stuff	Rank	2nd Lev	Rank	Open Field	Rank	Sacks	ASR	Rank	Press	Rank	F-Start	Cont.
2017	3.30	3.18	31	55%	27	30%	32	0.97	28	0.54	21	43	8.1%	25	36.9%	30	20	29
2018	4.64	4.50	12	71%	5	17%	8	1.30	10	0.85	15	51	10.4%	30	35.7%	30	20	26
2019	4.61	4.32	16	68%	10	18%	9	1.33	6	0.93	13	48	7.9%	24	36.6%	30	16	28
2019 ALY by direction:		Left End 5.37 (2)			Left Tackle: 4.30 (16)			Mid/Guard: 3.87 (29)			Right Tackle: 4.79 (8)			Right End: 5.09 (8)				

Seattle's statistics in this section must always be viewed through the prism of Russell Wilson, whose tendency to scramble around in search of big plays inevitably leads to more pressures than almost any other quarterback. The Seahawks allowed a dozen sacks to an untouched rusher, four more than any other team, and 13 more that were marked as coverage sacks or failed scrambles. Still, though this was no longer one of the worst lines in the league, there was room for improvement. So now this unit is undergoing a major overhaul. ❧ The changes began when the Seahawks opted not to re-sign tackles Germain Ifedi and George Fant, who eventually left town for the Bears and Jets, respectively. Seattle didn't make any major acquisitions to the line, opting for a crap-against-the-wall methodology instead. (Hey, it worked for Buffalo last year.) They signed a bevy of second- and third-rate free agents and used a third-round draft pick on a lineman in hopes that one or two of these players might win a starting job, even though none of them are certain to. Then, just after the draft, Seattle released two incumbent starters, right guard D.J. Fluker and center Justin Britt. (Fluker was quickly snapped up by the Ravens; Britt remained unsigned as of press time.) So the Seahawks will have at least three new starters up front, possibly four. ✎ Duane Brown remains entrenched at left tackle. Left guard Mike Iupati was re-signed in April, late in free agency but before the draft. Nothing's for sure, but it's a good sign for him that he was re-acquired even though Seattle had other options at the position. Among other incumbents, Joey Hunt filled in for the injured Britt, starting the last 10 games including the playoffs, but he had the worst blown block rate of any qualifying center last season. The Seahawks also have a slew of younger veterans—Phil Haynes, Jamarco Jones, Ethan Pocic, and Jordan Roos—who have thus far failed to secure starting roles. ✎ Two veteran acquisitions played enough to qualify for our tables here. Brandon Shell started for the Jets for two years, but spent last season bouncing from the field to the bench and back. B.J. Finney started 13 games over the last four years for the Steelers; he'll compete with Hunt and Roos for the center position. ✎ Seattle also added a pair of former first-round picks, neither of whom has started since 2017. Guard Chance Warmack began his career with Tennessee in 2013, then spent two years in Philadelphia before taking last year off to heal from assorted injuries. Tackle Cedric Ogbuehi spent four years Cincinnati and last year in Jacksonville, where he appeared in 14 games with no starts. ✎ The final candidate for Seattle's line: Damien Lewis, a third-round pick out of LSU. At 6-foot-2 and 327 pounds, Lewis had a habit of bulldozing SEC defenders on running plays, but his lack of agility made him less impressive in pass protection. Just the kind of blocker the Seahawks like.

Defensive Front

Defensive Line	Age	Pos	G	Snaps	Plays	TmPct	Rk	Stop	Dfts	BTkl	Runs	St%	Rk	RuYd	Rk	Sack	Hit	Hur	Dsrpt
						Overall							vs. Run				Pass Rush		
Poona Ford	25	DT	15	518	33	4.4%	57	29	9	3	28	89%	7	1.4	10	0.5	2	7	2
Jarran Reed	28	DT	10	493	28	5.6%	72	21	5	5	20	75%	48	2.9	81	2.0	5	10	1
Al Woods*	33	DT	14	459	32	4.5%	59	23	7	2	29	76%	46	1.7	18	1.0	1	10	1

Edge Rushers	Age	Pos	G	Snaps	Plays	TmPct	Rk	Stop	Dfts	BTkl	Runs	St%	Rk	RuYd	Rk	Sack	Hit	Hur	Dsrpt
						Overall							vs. Run				Pass Rush		
Jadeveon Clowney*	27	DE	13	624	34	5.2%	54	29	15	4	24	88%	6	0.9	6	3.0	10	41	2
Quinton Jefferson*	27	DE	14	602	28	4.0%	64	23	8	5	21	76%	34	1.9	24	3.5	8	21	6
Rasheem Green	23	DE	16	562	28	3.5%	64	22	9	5	19	74%	48	2.3	39	4.0	1	11	2
Branden Jackson	28	DE	15	426	22	2.9%	81	17	5	2	14	79%	26	3.4	81	2.0	1	9	3
Ezekiel Ansah*	31	DE	11	347	19	3.4%	88	13	7	6	7	86%	7	1.9	21	2.5	6	12	2
Bruce Irvin	33	OLB	13	623	37	5.5%	46	29	17	4	26	69%	64	2.7	49	8.5	9	23	0
Benson Mayowa	29	DE	15	316	14	1.9%	--	11	10	0	3	33%	--	5.3	--	7.0	5	18	0

Linebackers	Age	Pos	G	Snaps	Plays	TmPct	Rk	Stop	Dfts	BTkl	Runs	St%	Rk	RuYd	Rk	Sack	Hit	Hur	Tgts	Suc%	Rk	AdjYd	Rk	PD	Int
						Overall						vs. Run				Pass Rush					vs. Pass				
Bobby Wagner	30	MLB	16	1080	165	20.4%	1	76	21	10	88	57%	51	4.6	71	3.0	3	7	49	35%	63	8.1	57	6	1
K.J. Wright	31	OLB	16	1021	143	17.7%	5	72	24	10	69	57%	54	4.4	66	0.0	1	3	56	52%	32	6.5	36	11	3
Mychal Kendricks*	30	OLB	14	664	75	10.6%	49	42	10	16	40	53%	69	4.8	74	3.0	0	7	20	55%	23	10.4	65	4	1

Year	Yards	ALY	Rank	Power	Rank	Stuff	Rank	2nd Level	Rank	Open Field	Rank	Sacks	ASR	Rank	Press	Rank
2017	4.01	4.10	18	67%	22	18%	27	1.00	7	0.75	18	39	6.6%	15	30.9%	14
2018	4.55	4.55	22	58%	5	19%	19	1.28	20	0.91	20	43	7.3%	14	28.9%	21
2019	4.28	4.36	21	67%	22	20%	12	1.21	20	0.82	21	28	5.1%	30	24.0%	32
2019 ALY by direction:		Left End: 4.49 (27)			Left Tackle: 4.75 (25)			Mid/Guard: 4.77 (27)			Right Tackle: 3.18 (5)			Right End: 3.79 (13)	

Look, it's impossible to write this section accurately until we know for sure whether Jadeveon Clowney is playing in Seattle, or in Tennessee, or in Cleveland, or just becoming a full-time quarantiner and refusing to leave his basement until a vaccine has been developed. Maybe we'll just leave this part blank for now, and after Clowney signs somewhere we'll update the book and you could buy it again? No? OK. Well, Clowney's return would change everything. He was much more effective than his 3.0 sacks would indicate—he was in the top 20 in hurries despite drawing more double-teams than most any defender in the league—but for now we'll assume that he's gone. That leaves Seattle with a lot of candidates to start at their two edge rusher spots and no guarantees. ✎ Let's start with the holdovers. In addition to Rasheem Green and Branden Jackson, there's also L.J. Collier, whom you may have forgotten was a first-round draft pick just one year ago. Collier's rookie year was a disaster, limited to 152 defensive snaps and zero sacks in 11 games. Shaquem Griffin also had zero sacks in the regular season, but he did have three hits and eight hurries in only 96 defensive snaps, and he had a big third-down sack of Aaron Rodgers in the playoff loss to Green Bay. He's also 227 pounds and missing a hand, so he'll likely never be an every-down player. ❧ The new/old faces are Bruce Irvin and Benson Mayowa, Seahawks teammates in 2013 who have since played for the Raiders, Falcons, Panthers, Cowboys, and Cardinals. They combined for 15.5 sacks last season, which sounds great, but it was an anomaly—Irvin only averaged 6.7 sacks in the five years prior while Mayowa only averaged 2.6. ❧ The new/new faces are a pair of draftees, second-rounder Darrell Taylor (Tennessee) and fifth-rounder Alton Robinson (Syracuse). Taylor goes 6-foot-4 and 267 pounds, while Robinson is 6-foot-3 and 264; that makes them virtual clones of each other, and also Nick Bosa. Taylor quietly finished third in SackSEER rating in this year's class, mainly because he had seven passes defensed to go along with his 19.5 sacks in Knoxville. Robinson's SackSEER rating is high for a fifth-rounder; his 4.69s 40, 35-inch vertical, and 7.32s 3-cone time were all in the top five for defensive linemen at this year's combine. ❧ The rest of the front seven is a bit more straightforward. Jarran Reed signed a two-year, $23-million contract in March, ensuring that he would return next to Poona Ford at defensive tackle. Reed missed the first six games of the year due to a domestic violence suspension concerning a 2017 incident for which he was never charged nor arrested. If he can continue to stay out of trouble, he has demonstrated he has a high ceiling, with 10.5 sacks in 2018. That year was the outlier, however—he has only 5.0 sacks in his other three seasons. ❧ Bobby Wagner and K.J. Wright will return at linebacker. Jordyn Brooks, Seattle's first-round draft pick out of Texas Tech, likely projects as a weakside linebacker this year before taking over Wagner in the middle in later seasons. Wright, who had shoulder surgery this offseason, would move to the strong side for the first time in his career. Irvin may also play some off-ball linebacker on early downs.

Defensive Secondary

Secondary	Age	Pos	G	Snaps	Plays	TmPct	Rk	Stop	Dfts	BTkl	Runs	St%	Rk	RuYd	Rk	Tgts	Tgt%	Rk	Dist	Suc%	Rk	AdjYd	Rk	PD	Int
						Overall							vs. Run					vs. Pass							
Tre Flowers	25	CB	15	998	88	11.6%	5	25	10	16	21	33%	66	9.5	73	89	22.5%	20	10.0	47%	64	7.9	48	8	3
Bradley McDougald	30	SS	15	962	76	10.0%	33	30	15	10	30	43%	33	5.5	21	45	11.8%	13	13.1	58%	22	7.0	29	6	2
Shaquill Griffin	25	CB	14	943	78	11.0%	12	32	12	10	21	62%	20	5.6	33	74	19.8%	45	12.0	51%	51	6.4	16	13	0
Quandre Diggs	27	FS	10	621	44	8.7%	66	13	6	15	24	21%	68	8.8	52	8	3.3%	74	12.3	63%	12	5.6	15	3	3
Tedric Thompson*	25	FS	6	397	21	6.9%	--	4	2	5	5	20%	--	12.0	--	14	8.9%	--	14.1	43%	--	12.4	--	2	2
Delano Hill	25	SS	12	303	23	3.8%	--	3	2	9	8	25%	--	9.6	--	3	2.5%	--	29.0	67%	--	15.0	--	0	0
Akeem King*	28	CB	13	271	19	2.9%	--	4	1	0	5	20%	--	7.4	--	19	17.7%	--	14.2	53%	--	7.6	--	2	0
Marquise Blair	23	FS	14	238	26	3.7%	--	9	4	4	9	33%	--	8.0	--	12	12.7%	--	6.8	50%	--	6.3	--	1	0
Jamar Taylor*	30	CB	12	224	24	4.0%	--	6	5	3	3	33%	--	12.7	--	30	36.1%	--	10.5	40%	--	6.8	--	3	0
Quinton Dunbar	28	CB	11	620	45	7.4%	80	25	14	1	13	31%	67	8.5	67	54	24.8%	8	11.9	59%	16	6.7	22	8	4

Year	Pass D Rank	vs. #1 WR	Rk	vs. #2 WR	Rk	vs. Other WR	Rk	WR Wide	Rk	WR Slot	Rk	vs. TE	Rk	vs. RB	Rk
2017	3	0.9%	16	38.9%	31	-5.3%	14	20.2%	31	0.8%	13	-23.9%	3	-33.0%	2
2018	14	13.1%	25	4.6%	20	-10.3%	10	18.8%	30	-3.7%	14	-12.3%	10	-3.7%	13
2019	15	-2.9%	12	-5.6%	10	-9.6%	11	-27.8%	5	5.9%	16	3.3%	17	-9.4%	10

The youth movement that brought an end to the Legion of Boom didn't always go smoothly, but the Seahawks secondary has certainly gotten younger; their oldest projected starter, Bradley McDougald, doesn't turn 30 until November. ❧ McDougald and cornerbacks Shaquill Griffin and Tre Flowers were rocks in the defensive backfield last year; each started at least 14 games at his respective position. The free safety slot, however, was a revolving door, with four different players starting there throughout the year. Hopefully, the trade for Quandre Diggs will solidify that position in 2020 and beyond. ❧ Shortly after Seattle traded for Quinton Dunbar, he and the Giants' Deandre Baker were accused of a phenomenally stupid crime: robbing people at gunpoint at a party where *everyone there knew their names and faces*. Dunbar has pled not guilty, the league has yet to suspend him, and the Seahawks are moving forward as if he will be starting at right cornerback this fall, with Flowers moving into the slot. ❧ Flowers' main competition will be Ugo Amadi, a fourth-round pick out of Oregon last year. Amadi only played 76 snaps on defense, but he also played 246 snaps on special teams and led the Seahawks in tackles on coverage. Carroll said in March that the nickel job was "really Ugo's to lose," but that was before the trade for Dunbar. ❧ Carroll has also mentioned another rookie last season, second-rounder Marquise Blair, as a candidate for nickelback duties. Virtually all of the Utah product's action in 2019, including all three of his starts, came at safety.

Special Teams

Year	DVOA	Rank	FG/XP	Rank	Net Kick	Rank	Kick Ret	Rank	Net Punt	Rank	Punt Ret	Rank	Hidden	Rank
2017	-2.0%	20	-7.6	27	3.0	11	8.1	3	-13.4	31	0.1	15	-7.5	26
2018	-2.2%	24	-0.8	20	-6.6	30	1.4	9	-2.2	20	-2.7	22	-1.7	18
2019	-1.0%	20	-0.1	18	-0.9	20	-2.1	22	-1.2	20	-0.5	15	4.9	10

Behold the tepid, room-temperature mediocrity of Seattle's kicking game. The Seahawks and Chargers were the only teams to finish with negative value in all five facets of our special teams ratings, but Seattle was much better than L.A. in each department and finished in the low to mid 20s overall for the third year in a row. ✎ Michael Dickson suffered a sophomore slump; he was second in the NFL with a 48.2-yard gross average in 2018 but fell to 20th at 45.1 last year. His coverage team usually played well—led by Ugo Amadi, Seattle made 25 stops on punt returns, tied with Arizona for most of the league—but they did allow Deonte Harris of the Saints to return one 53 yards for a touchdown. ✎ Jason Myers was perfect on field goals within 40 yards but only hit 6-of-11 from outside that distance. He also missed four extra points. As usual, he was strong on kickoffs, but Seattle's kick coverage team gave that value away. ✎ Tyler Lockett's punt return average has gotten worse in each of his five NFL seasons, bottoming out at 5.1 yards in 2019. His 19.9-yard average on kickoff returns was also the worst of his career. But Seattle made no move to replace him, so he'll probably remain the primary man in both categories this season.

Tampa Bay Buccaneers

2019 Record: 7-9	Total DVOA: 1.4% (14th)	2020 Mean Projection: 8.9 wins	On the Clock (0-4): 5%
Pythagorean Wins: 8.2 (13rd)	Offense: -7.3% (22nd)	Postseason Odds: 55.7%	Mediocrity (5-7): 24%
Snap-Weighted Age: 25.8 (28th)	Defense: -11.5% (5th)	Super Bowl Odds: 9.1%	Playoff Contender (8-10): 43%
Average Opponent: -0.9% (18th)	Special Teams: -2.8% (27th)	Proj. Avg. Opponent: 1.2% (5th)	Super Bowl Contender (11+): 28%

2019: Jameis Winston is Jameis Winston.

2020: How much longer can Tom Brady be Tom Brady?

When the Buccaneers were on their way to London for their Week 6 game against the Panthers, there was still time.

Tampa Bay was 2-3 but had won twice as road underdogs, once in Carolina against the Panthers and once in Los Angeles against the defending NFC champion Rams. Jameis Winston had been Jameis Winston—spectacularly good and incomprehensibly bad but overall reliably unreliable. Through five weeks, he had been as good of a passer (8.3 yards per attempt, 11 touchdowns, five interceptions, 5.0% DVOA) as future MVP Lamar Jackson (7.9 yards per attempt, 11 touchdowns, five interceptions, 5.6% DVOA). There was hope that, in his first season under head coach Bruce Arians, he would improve.

It's usually hyperbolic to point to any single game and suggest that it changed the course of NFL history, but a reasonable case can be made for the Buccaneers-Panthers game in Week 6. When Tampa Bay walked into Tottenham Hotspur Stadium, Winston was firmly entrenched as their quarterback. Six turnovers and one demoralizing 37-26 loss later, the Buccaneers began to waver. Devotion had turned to doubt.

Winston has had a lot of ghastly games since he entered the NFL in 2015—he has thrown multiple interceptions a league-high 25 times—but this stinker came at a particularly bad time. Throw five interceptions in Carolina? No big deal, it's an hour-and-a-half flight back to Tampa. Throw five interceptions *in London*? It's a 13-hour flight back, leaving coaches plenty of time to think.

Winston never did win back their trust and went on to become the first quarterback in three decades to throw 30 interceptions in a season. The last quarterback to do so also was drafted No. 1 overall by Tampa Bay: Vinny Testaverde. As bad as that seems, it still doesn't fully convey the extent of Winston's self-destruction. Put another way, he was responsible for 7.3% of the interceptions thrown in the NFL last year, the highest share in a season during the Super Bowl era.

On a related note, the Buccaneers had the worst average opponent starting field position in the league. After a Winston interception, opponents took over inside the Tampa Bay 40-yard line 14 times. No other defense faced such a situation more than nine times. Add Winston's NFL-record seven pick-sixes, and that's how you end up with a team that allowed the fourth-most points despite featuring a top-five defense by DVOA.

For years, the Buccaneers had denied the truth about Winston. They made excuses. He needed better weapons. He needed a better coach. He needed a better defense. By the end of 2019, they had addressed those weaknesses. When Falcons linebacker Deion Jones returned an interception for a touchdown during overtime in Week 17, he didn't just close out Tampa Bay's season. He rendered a verdict: Winston was not the victim of a bad situation; he was the cause.

Before, the Buccaneers could tolerate Winston's interceptions. If those interceptions cost them games, well, they could live with a few losing seasons. That changed when they hired Arians in January 2019. The interceptions started costing them something more precious than games: time.

Arians, who turns 68 in October, doesn't have time to waste.

Which brings us to Tom Brady. Perhaps you've heard of him. Three-time MVP award-winner. Six-time Super Bowl champion. Four-time Super Bowl MVP award-winner. He, too, is running out of time. This is his age-43 season, but that doesn't concern the Buccaneers. In March, they signed him to a two-year contract that has a base value of $50 million. That was not a hallucinatory event. That really did happen.

Brady's decision to leave New England for Tampa surprised even the Buccaneers. Arians and general manager Jason Licht figured they would have to make an aggressive pitch. Instead, when they called Brady on the first day of the new league year, he did most of the talking. "It was almost like a recruitment on his part, telling us why it would make sense for him to come to Tampa Bay," Licht said on ESPN's *Get Up*.

Brady and the Buccaneers are an odd pairing. Why would the winningest quarterback of all time choose to play for the losingest NFL franchise of all time? The Pro Bowl receivers? A more relaxed head coach? The weather? The lack of a state income tax? The proximity to assisted living facilities?

More likely: a market never materialized, or as ESPN's Dianna Russini put it in the days before Brady became a free agent, "Brady's interest in other teams outweighs the amount of teams that are interested." Tampa Bay, however, was infatuated. It proclaimed its adoration for Brady like Michael Scott blurted "That's what she said" jokes. The Buccaneers, desperate to become relevant again after a 12-year playoff drought, were willing to give Brady the thing he wanted most and the thing the Patriots weren't willing to give: time, in the form of a commitment beyond 2020.

2020 Buccaneers Schedule

Week	Opp.	Week	Opp.	Week	Opp.
1	at NO	7	at LV	13	BYE
2	CAR	8	at NYG (Mon.)	14	MIN
3	at DEN	9	NO	15	at ATL
4	LAC	10	at CAR	16	at DET (Sat.)
5	at CHI (Thu.)	11	LAR (Mon.)	17	ATL
6	GB	12	KC		

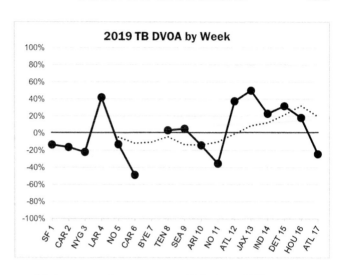

2019 TB DVOA by Week

As Brady begins his next chapter, he has plenty to prove. That he can win without Bill Belichick. That he can compete into his mid-40s. That he can lead a different team to the Super Bowl. But he has even more to sell. Resistance bands. Protein powders. Recovery pajamas. "Immunity" capsules. After all, he's more than a quarterback now. He's a pseudoscience pitchman, Gwyneth Paltrow in a football jersey. Sure, he could retire, spare his body another 100 or so hits and focus on expanding his TB12 lifestyle business. But who wants to listen to a *retired* football player talk about exercise, diet, and nutrition? The longer he plays—and plays at a high level—the easier it is for him to claim that his methods truly have extended his playing career. Every snap builds his brand's credibility.

It's a curious fit from a football standpoint, too. Though Brady and Arians might downplay their philosophical differences, make no mistake, Brady does not share Arians' "no risk it, no biscuit" mentality. "Football, to me, is about throwing the ball to the guy that is open," he said at his introductory news conference. "If he is open deep, that is where you throw it, and if he's open short, you throw it there."

That's not how Arians rolls. From his book, *The Quarterback Whisperer*: "I constantly told Andrew (Luck) to take a shot if the defense appeared vulnerable based on its pre-snap formation. 'If it's third-and-3 and you got T.Y. (Hilton) on a deep route, then throw the f-cking ball to T.Y.,' I'd tell Andrew. 'I don't care that we only need 3 yards. Throw the ball to T.Y.'"

Heck, they even have different views on hydration.

Brady, from his book, *The TB12 Method*: "Reduce or eliminate your intake of caffeine, soda, and alcohol. All three can be dehydrating."

Arians' motto: "Win or lose, we booze."

Can Brady and Arians adapt to each other? "We'll probably meet in the middle," Arians told NFL.com. Meeting in the middle won't be enough. Arians will need to see Brady as the quarterback that he is (a quarterback in decline), not the quarterback he has been (the greatest quarterback of all time). The grim reaper comes for us all, no matter how much elderberry syrup and larch tree extract we consume.

In what has become an annual Football Outsiders tradition, let's review the warning signs that we're on the precipice of Bradymaggedon. Last season, he posted:

- his lowest touchdown total (24) since 2006.
- the lowest touchdown rate (3.9) of his career.
- his lowest completion rate (60.8%) since 2013.

- his lowest yards per attempt (6.6) since 2002.
- his lowest yards per completion (10.9) since 2008.
- his lowest passer rating (88.0) since 2013.
- his lowest DYAR (550) since 2001, his first season as a starter.
- the lowest DVOA (2.4%) of his career.

Drill deeper into Brady's DYAR and DVOA numbers (Table 1), and you'll notice a striking decline in his efficiency during the second half of the season, though that might be more interesting than meaningful. Football Outsiders research has found, time and again, that full-season performance is more predictive than half-season performance. But we're also in uncharted territory, and we know that an older quarterback's performance can decline suddenly. What stands out about Brady's drop-off last season is that he fell from an above-average quarterback to a below-average quarterback. It was the first time that Brady had a below-average DVOA in the second half of the season since 2002. In fact, his second-half DYAR (-25) and DVOA (-12.6%) were nearly identical to Winston's (-32 DYAR, -12.6% DVOA).

Table 1. Tom Brady's Passing DVOA Splits, 2010-2019

Year	Overall	Weeks 1-9	Weeks 10-17	Difference
2010	46.7%	28.1%	67.8%	+39.7%
2011	41.4%	34.0%	49.4%	+15.4%
2012	35.1%	39.2%	30.2%	-9.0%
2013	10.9%	-2.1%	26.4%	+28.5%
2014	18.1%	23.1%	11.2%	-11.9%
2015	19.5%	34.5%	2.6%	-31.9%
2016	33.4%	56.5%	22.9%	-33.6%
2017	27.8%	32.6%	22.6%	-10.0%
2018	15.4%	11.0%	21.7%	+10.7%
2019	2.4%	12.8%	-12.6%	-25.4%

We could brush aside Brady's statistical decline by blaming it on a weak supporting cast. He had Josh Gordon for only a short time (six games) and Antonio Brown for an even shorter time (24 snaps). The Patriots were one of only three teams (the Eagles and Bengals were the others) to not have a wide receiver crack the top 50 in DYAR. In fact, the team leader in receiving DYAR was running back James White. At the same time, Brady was not as accurate as he had been in the past. His rate of on-target throws (72.9%) ranked 29th, according to Sports Info Solutions. Winston's on-target rate was 72.1%. An aberration? No. It marked the third straight season in which Brady's on-target rate declined. In 2016, it was more than 10 percentage points higher.

It's possible that Brady, instead of taking a sack or forcing a pass into tight coverage, throws the ball to places where no player can get to it, particularly when he doesn't trust his receiver to make a contested catch. Even so, his completion percentage over expectation statistics, which account for the difficulty of passes, suggest that he is indeed missing his spots more often. Like his on-target rate, his completion percentage over expectation has fallen in each of the past three seasons, from 2.7% above expectation in 2016 to 3.1% *below expectation* in 2019.

Maybe Brady isn't elevating the players around him anymore. Maybe now he needs players to elevate him, or at least help him hold off further decline. In that sense, he's in the right place. In Chris Godwin and Mike Evans, the Buccaneers boast arguably the best receiver tandem in the NFL, better than Julio Jones-Calvin Ridley in Atlanta, Amari Cooper-Michael Gallup in Dallas, and Odell Beckham Jr.-Jarvis Landry in Cleveland. Last season, Godwin and Evans combined for 2,490 yards and 17 touchdowns and finished second and sixth, respectively, in receiving DYAR.

To borrow a catchphrase from the late Billy Mays, Tampa's most famous pitchman pre-Brady: but wait … there's more! The roster features not just one, but two tight ends who are a season removed from finishing in the top six in DYAR at their positions: Rob Gronkowski, whom the Buccaneers lured out of retirement a month after signing Brady, and former first-round draft pick O.J. Howard. Cameron Brate is still here, too. He was a top-five tight end by DYAR in 2016 and 2017. Even nose tackle Vita Vea is a red-zone threat (he caught a touchdown pass in a Week 11 win over the Falcons).

What will the Buccaneers offense look like this season? It depends on how much you believe Arians' "meet in the middle" comment or on what his definition of "middle" is. Our educated guess is that Brady won't chuck the ball down the field with reckless abandon like Yosemite Jameis did last season. Winston's average depth of target of 10.9 yards ranked second in the league (Matthew Stafford's aDOT was 11.3 yards). He threw more than 60% of his passes beyond 5 yards of the line of scrimmage. Brady's aDOT of 7.9 yards ranked 27th. He threw only 49% of his passes beyond 5 yards of the line of scrimmage. To head off the "but he had a weak supporting cast" rebuttal once more: even in 2018, with Gronkowski, Brady's aDOT of 8.2 yards ranked 18th. He threw half of his passes within 5 yards of the line of scrimmage then, too. And the Patriots' offense was not based on making up for short throwing distance with yards after the catch. New England, like Tampa Bay, was around the league average in yards after the catch last season.

What changes will come before the ball leaves Brady's hand? We'll likely see the Buccaneers move at a quicker pace. Arians' offenses consistently have been around the league average in situation-neutral pace. Brady's offenses have been No. 1 or close to it. Count on more pre-snap chicanery, too. Arians said this offseason that he's eager to see Brady run "our audible system, our check-with-me stuff, where the quarterback puts us in the best plays. We didn't do a lot of that— we did some of it last year, not a lot of it. That's something he's very comfortable with."

Keep an eye on Tampa Bay's play-action pass rate. If we see a surge, that will be a tell-tale sign that this is Brady's offense. Though the Buccaneers had tremendous success off play-action last season, averaging 10.4 yards per pass and posting a 58.9% DVOA (vs. 6.6 yards per pass and a -6.2% DVOA on all other pass plays), they seldom used it. Their 18.2% rate ranked 30th, which is typical of Arians' offenses. Going back to his stint as head coach of the Cardinals from 2013 to 2017, Arizona ranked 26th, 27th, 21st, 31st, and 28th.

As for Brady, play-action has been one of the staples of his game. Though the Patriots' frequency (24.5%) slipped last season to league average, they've long been among the top 10 in yards per play and DVOA. As recently as 2018, they ranked fourth in play-action rate (30.7%), first in yards per play (9.8) and first in DVOA (76.4%). One other notable difference between Tampa Bay and New England: when the Buccaneers used play-action last season, they did so to set up deep passes; Brady attacked at the intermediate level, targeting receivers on in-breaking (crossers and digs) and seam routes.

Fortunately for Brady, the Buccaneers don't need him to carry the team. Tampa Bay has a defense now. The 49ers' defensive turnaround received much national attention, but the Buccaneers' turnaround was even more dramatic, at least in terms of DVOA. Tampa Bay jumped from 32nd in 2018 (14.8%) to fifth (-11.5%) thanks in large part to the stingiest run defense (-30.5% DVOA) we've seen since the 2015 Jets. The architects of that unit: Todd Bowles, now the Buccaneers defensive coordinator, and Kacy Rodgers, now the Buccaneers defensive line coach.

Tampa Bay's pass defense was credible in its own right, posting a -0.3% DVOA, which ranked 12th. Much of that improvement, however, came during the second half of the season. From Week 12 on, the Buccaneers allowed the third-lowest completion percentage (55.4%), the third-fewest touchdown passes (five) and the third-lowest passer rating (70.5). They also recorded the most sacks (25) and second-most takeaways (13). Granted, that stretch included games against Gardnick Minfoles, Jacoby Brissett, and David Blough, who sounds more like a late-season callup from the Toledo Mud Hens than a starting NFL quarterback. But even after adjusting for those opponents, Tampa Bay's pass defense was the league's best by DVOA (-36.3%). In other words, over a six-week span, the Buccaneers pass defense rivaled the Patriots.

What happened? One popular theory is that the turnaround coincided with the release of cornerback Vernon Hargreaves, the team's 2016 first-round draft pick. Tampa Bay benched him during a Week 10 win over Arizona and waived him two days later. The move cleared room for a pair of rookies—Sean Murphy-Bunting, who moved to nickel cornerback, and Jamel Dean, who took over at outside cornerback. But it wasn't just addition by subtraction that triggered the improvement. In 2018, the Buccaneers defense suffered injuries to a near record-breaking degree. In just its secondary alone, Tampa Bay accumulated 46.4 adjusted games lost, the second-most we've ever measured. Last season, the Buccaneers' luck turned. The secondary's total adjusted games lost in 2019: 1.6!

So how much of Tampa Bay's defensive turnaround is likely to stick? This is where we remind you about the Plexiglass Principle, which states that teams that significantly improve in a season are likely to experience some degree of decline the next season. Consider the greatest defensive turnarounds of the past 10 seasons (Table 2). The 2019 Buccaneers are high on the list. The next season, some fell from great to good and some from good to bad, but most declined. Defense isn't consistent from season to season.

There are a few reasons why Tampa Bay could beat this trend.

- Continuity: The Buccaneers managed to keep their defense mostly intact, retaining three key starters who could have departed via free agency—NFL sack leader Shaquil Barrett (franchise tag), Jason Pierre-Paul (two-year contract), and Ndamukong Suh (one-year contract). In all, 10 of their 11 projected starters were starters last season, and incoming safety Antoine Winfield Jr., a second-round draft pick, should be an upgrade.
- Youth: By snap-weighted age, Tampa Bay had the ninth-youngest defense last season (25.6 years) and the youngest secondary (23.8 years).
- Rest: Imagine what this unit can do now that it won't have to constantly run back onto the field after an interception.

Our projections see the defense regressing, but less than you might expect. The Buccaneers might not be a top-five unit again, but top 10 is realistic. Pair that with a quarterback who isn't going to throw games away in the first quarter and that should be enough to get Tampa Bay past the velvet rope and into Club Playoffs for the first time since the George W. Bush administration. Brady was 30 years old then. Gronkowski was 18 and a freshman at the University of Arizona.

The Buccaneers, however, are still the Buccaneers, a franchise that has long lacked a clear and consistent vision, a franchise that would like to be the Patriots but doesn't know how. And so they're looking to Brady and hoping that some of that mystique will rub off on them. Thing is, there is no such mystique. There is a formula, and New England has been hiding it in plain view the whole time. Tampa Bay just isn't following it.

The Patriots are the Patriots because of what they do before a pass is thrown, before a ball is snapped, before a play is called. The not-so-secret secret to their sustained success is their salary-cap management. They don't allocate a large percentage of their cap to expensive players. This season, they will spend 22.3% of their cap on high-cost players (players who will earn more than $9.8 million), the sixth-lowest percentage in the NFL, according to OverTheCap.com. Instead, they'll allocate more to middle-income players (30.1%, third-most) and low-cost players (22.3%, fourth-most). They don't beat you with star power. They beat you because the 53rd man on their roster is better than the 53rd man on your roster.

In terms of cap allocation, the Buccaneers are the anti-Patriots. More than half of their cap (57.2%) is tied up in expensive players (Tom Brady, Mike Evans, Shaquil Barrett, Donovan Smith, Jason Pierre-Paul, Ali Marpet, Lavonte David, and Ryan Jensen), second to only the Super Bowl champion Chiefs. They'll allocate 8.4% of their dollars to middle-income players (fifth lowest) and 11.5% to low-cost players (eighth-lowest). Though Tampa Bay has the frontline talent to

Table 2. Biggest Year-to-Year Improvements in Defensive DVOA, 2010-2019

Year	Team	Year N-1	Rk	Year N	Rk	Change	Year N+1	Rk	Improve?
2011	JAX	17.7%	32	-11.3%	5	-29.0%	11.7%	28	No
2011	HOU	17.5%	31	-9.5%	6	-27.0%	-14.2%	4	Yes
2019	**TB**	**14.8%**	**32**	**-11.5%**	**5**	**-26.3%**	—	—	—
2019	NE	0.4%	16	-25.5%	1	-25.9%	—	—	—
2019	SF	5.7%	23	-19.7%	2	-25.4%	—	—	—
2016	NYG	10.7%	30	-14.5%	2	-25.2%	5.7%	24	No
2018	CHI	-1.5%	14	-26.0%	1	-24.5%	-7.2%	8	No
2013	BUF	10.6%	27	-13.8%	4	-24.4%	-15.5%	2	Yes
2017	NO	14.6%	31	-7.9%	8	-22.5%	-2.9%	11	No
2013	NO	14.8%	32	-5.8%	10	-20.6%	13.1%	31	No
2013	KC	13.0%	30	-6.7%	9	-19.7%	1.3%	19	No
2011	SEA	12.0%	29	-7.1%	10	-19.1%	-14.5%	2	Yes
2012	CAR	15.8%	32	-3.1%	11	-18.9%	-15.7%	3	Yes
2019	PIT	-0.9%	13	-18.4%	4	-17.5%	—	—	—
2015	NYJ	3.5%	21	-13.8%	5	-17.3%	3.7%	21	No
2016	SD	10.4%	28	-6.8%	7	-17.2%	-4.7%	12	No

compete, the lack of depth could be its undoing. That's especially true in this season when otherwise healthy players may randomly disappear for weeks at a time because of positive COVID-19 tests.

The Buccaneers could absorb an injury at tight end or in the secondary, but they're perilously thin everywhere else. The backup quarterback is Blaine Gabbert. His job last season was to be as nonthreatening as possible to Winston. He succeeded. The receivers behind Godwin and Evans, a mix of late-round draft picks and undrafted free agents, have started a grand total of four games. Brady likes to throw to his running backs, but Ronald Jones, Dare Ogunbowale, and rookie Ke'Shawn Vaughn are all works-in-progress. Tampa Bay's top offensive lineman off the bench is veteran Joe Haeg, and it's a good

thing he can play tackle and guard because after him the Buccaneers are down to practice-squaders. In the defensive front, the falloff is more severe. The backup to Vita Vea is sixth-round rookie Khalil Davis, and the primary backup edge rusher is Anthony Nelson, who as a rookie last season played less than 15% of Tampa Bay's defensive snaps.

This boom-or-bust strategy might work this season, but it's not sustainable. Soon, the Buccaneers will find themselves in the situation the Patriots have chosen to avoid: overpaying a declining quarterback at the expense of addressing other weaknesses. There's not enough alkalizing green juice in the world to change that.

Thomas Bassinger

2019 Buccaneers Stats by Week

Wk	vs.	W-L	PF	PA	YDF	YDA	TO	Total	Off	Def	ST
1	SF	L	17	31	295	256	-2	-13%	-36%	-31%	-8%
2	at CAR	W	20	14	289	352	+1	-16%	-18%	-7%	-5%
3	NYG	L	31	32	499	384	+1	-22%	5%	15%	-12%
4	at LAR	W	55	40	464	518	+3	42%	45%	7%	4%
5	at NO	L	24	31	252	457	+1	-13%	-8%	12%	7%
6	CAR	L	26	37	407	268	-6	-49%	-42%	6%	-1%
7	BYE										
8	at TEN	L	23	27	389	246	-3	3%	-22%	-20%	6%
9	at SEA	L	34	40	418	492	0	5%	17%	15%	3%
10	ARI	W	30	27	457	417	-1	-14%	-28%	-4%	10%
11	NO	L	17	34	334	328	-4	-35%	-32%	5%	2%
12	at ATL	W	35	22	446	337	0	38%	16%	-30%	-8%
13	at JAX	W	28	11	315	242	+3	50%	-15%	-70%	-5%
14	IND	W	38	35	542	309	-3	23%	26%	4%	2%
15	at DET	W	38	17	495	295	+2	32%	8%	-32%	-9%
16	HOU	L	20	23	435	229	-3	18%	-31%	-56%	-7%
17	ATL	L	22	28	329	373	-2	-24%	-16%	-16%	-24%

Trends and Splits

	Offense	Rank	Defense	Rank
Total DVOA	-7.3%	22	-11.5%	5
Unadjusted VOA	-6.0%	21	-11.5%	6
Weighted Trend	-8.6%	22	-17.2%	3
Variance	6.3%	10	6.6%	20
Average Opponent	2.8%	30	2.3%	6
Passing	5.1%	18	-0.3%	12
Rushing	-13.4%	26	-30.5%	1
First Down	-3.4%	18	-5.5%	10
Second Down	-3.6%	18	-16.5%	5
Third Down	-21.5%	27	-15.9%	6
First Half	-2.7%	18	-18.8%	3
Second Half	-12.2%	25	-4.5%	10
Red Zone	0.5%	16	-25.3%	4
Late and Close	-30.8%	31	-9.5%	9

Five-Year Performance

Year	W-L	Pyth W	Est W	PF	PA	TO	Total	Rk	Off	Rk	Def	Rk	ST	Rk	Off AGL	Rk	Def AGL	Rk	Off Age	Rk	Def Age	Rk	ST Age	Rk
2015	6-10	6.0	6.7	342	417	-5	-9.1%	21	-1.1%	17	3.3%	18	-4.7%	30	41.9	22	37.4	21	25.9	27	25.9	28	26.2	16
2016	9-7	7.6	7.2	354	369	+2	-3.0%	22	-4.1%	19	-2.9%	13	-1.8%	20	75.9	30	49.1	20	25.7	28	26.2	21	25.8	22
2017	5-11	6.7	6.2	335	382	-1	-12.0%	23	5.2%	11	11.7%	32	-5.5%	29	25.4	9	55.3	27	26.2	27	27.0	7	25.9	12
2018	5-11	6.4	5.5	396	464	-18	-13.0%	24	5.9%	12	14.8%	32	-4.1%	28	14.3	3	91.4	32	26.3	22	26.5	12	25.6	22
2019	7-9	8.2	7.1	458	449	-13	1.4%	14	-7.3%	22	-11.5%	5	-2.8%	27	17.0	6	22.5	4	26.2	25	25.6	24	25.5	22

2019 Performance Based on Most Common Personnel Groups

TB Offense					TB Offense vs. Opponents					TB Defense				TB Defense vs. Opponents			
Pers	Freq	Yds	DVOA	Run%	Pers	Freq	Yds	DVOA	Run%	Pers	Freq	Yds	DVOA	Pers	Freq	Yds	DVOA
11	61%	6.5	4.5%	24%	Base	29%	5.0	-13.2%	56%	Base	29%	5.2	-10.4%	11	59%	5.3	-13.6%
12	20%	5.7	-4.8%	50%	Nickel	50%	6.5	-2.2%	29%	Nickel	66%	5.4	-11.4%	12	18%	5.3	-7.2%
611	6%	5.2	-30.8%	69%	Dime+	19%	6.7	19.2%	8%	Dime+	2%	5.7	-78.6%	21	7%	5.8	-0.3%
02	3%	4.4	-7.6%	0%	Goal Line	1%	0.5	-7.0%	50%	Goal Line	1%	1.4	-21.4%	10	4%	4.7	-55.3%
612	2%	5.8	6.0%	58%	Big	1%	2.1	-82.7%	33%	Big	2%	5.2	11.7%	22	3%	6.3	1.3%
13	2%	3.0	-24.2%	38%										13	3%	5.0	-31.7%
10	2%	6.5	-26.6%	15%										611	2%	7.1	-5.0%

Strategic Tendencies

Run/Pass		Rk	Formation		Rk	Pass Rush		Rk	Secondary		Rk	Strategy		Rk
Runs, first half	32%	31	Form: Single Back	84%	11	Rush 3	5.8%	20	4 DB	29%	12	Play Action	18%	30
Runs, first down	47%	19	Form: Empty Back	10%	9	Rush 4	54.4%	28	5 DB	66%	8	Offensive Motion	43%	11
Runs, second-long	14%	32	Form: Multi Back	6%	26	Rush 5	29.1%	3	6+ DB	2%	27	Avg Box (Off)	6.61	12
Runs, power sit.	52%	20	Pers: 3+ WR	67%	15	Rush 6+	10.7%	3	Man Coverage	37%	7	Avg Box (Def)	6.60	14
Runs, behind 2H	22%	29	Pers: 2+ TE/6+ OL	35%	8	Edge Rusher Sacks	74.5%	2	CB by Sides	68%	22	Offensive Pace	30.53	15
Pass, ahead 2H	49%	16	Pers: 6+ OL	8%	5	Interior DL Sacks	13.8%	27	S/CB Cover Ratio	25%	22	Defensive Pace	27.93	1
Run-Pass Options	5%	17	Shotgun/Pistol	53%	26	Second Level Sacks	11.7%	26	DB Blitz	13%	12	Go for it on 4th	1.24	22

Both the Arians offense and the recent Brady offenses use less shotgun than is currently prevalent around the league. The Bucs were 26th in shotgun rate last year, the Patriots 27th. ✎ Tampa Bay's offense led the league with 17 sacks tagged as "blitz/overall pressure" while Tom Brady's Patriots were tied at the bottom of the league with just two. ✎ Tampa Bay used play-action a league-average 39% of the time on first down, but a league-low 10% of the time on second down. ✎ Probably connected: Tampa Bay ran on just 24% of second downs, the lowest rate in the league, including just 14% of second-and-longs. ✎ Tampa Bay was 22nd in offensive DVOA but only third in the rate of three-and-outs per drive. ✎ The Buccaneers defense ranked third in DVOA against short passes (up to 15 yards through the air) after ranking 31st in this metric the year before. ✎ In a connected stat, the Bucs led the league in DVOA on passes at or behind the line of scrimmage. This came in large part from preventing yards after the catch; they allowed an average of just 6.6, while every other team in the league was at 7.3 or above. ✎ Tampa Bay had the league's second-largest gap in defensive DVOA between plays with pressure (-85.1% DVOA, third in the NFL) and plays without pressure (40.5% DVOA, 20th).

Passing

Player	DYAR	DVOA	Plays	NtYds	Avg	YAC	C%	TD	Int
J.Winston*	57	-9.8%	674	4769	7.1	4.9	61.3%	33	30
T.Brady	550	2.4%	639	3830	6.0	5.0	61.3%	24	8

Rushing

Player	DYAR	DVOA	Plays	Yds	Avg	TD	Fum	Suc
R.Jones	43	-2.3%	172	724	4.2	6	2	45%
P.Barber*	-140	-29.8%	154	470	3.1	7	1	40%
J.Winston*	53	12.6%	41	264	6.4	1	0	-
D.Ogunbowale	-28	-50.4%	11	17	1.5	2	0	36%
T.Brady	32	22.0%	11	46	4.2	3	0	-

Receiving

Player	DYAR	DVOA	Plays	Ctch	Yds	Y/C	YAC	TD	C%
C.Godwin	415	32.8%	121	86	1333	15.5	6.7	9	71%
M.Evans	301	18.0%	118	67	1157	17.3	3.8	8	57%
B.Perriman*	155	16.5%	69	36	645	17.9	3.5	6	52%
J.Watson	20	-2.3%	26	15	159	10.6	0.9	2	58%
S.Miller	-5	-15.5%	26	13	200	15.4	2.8	1	50%
B.Wilson*	-35	-55.7%	11	3	35	11.7	1.0	0	27%
C.Brate	-3	-8.0%	55	36	311	8.6	2.5	4	65%
O.Howard	37	3.2%	53	34	459	13.5	4.4	1	64%
D.Ogunbowale	31	-2.9%	46	35	286	8.2	5.9	0	76%
R.Jones	47	9.2%	40	31	309	10.0	9.5	0	78%
P.Barber*	17	0.3%	24	16	115	7.2	7.4	1	67%

Offensive Line

Player	Pos	Age	GS	Snaps	Pen	Sk	Pass	Run	Player	Pos	Age	GS	Snaps	Pen	Sk	Pass	Run
Ryan Jensen	C	29	16/16	1159	3	0.0	6	11	Alex Cappa	RG	25	13/13	886	3	2.0	14	7
Ali Marpet	LG	27	16/16	1159	5	1.0	9	5	Earl Watford*	RG	30	15/4	330	3	0.0	3	3
Donovan Smith	LT	27	15/15	1075	8	3.0	17	2	Josh Wells*	LT/RT	29	13/2	205	4	3.0	9	1
Demar Dotson*	RT	35	15/15	1065	10	2.0	14	6									

Year	Yards	ALY	Rank	Power	Rank	Stuff	Rank	2nd Lev	Rank	Open Field	Rank	Sacks	ASR	Rank	Press	Rank	F-Start	Cont.
2017	3.53	4.06	16	65%	12	20%	17	0.93	31	0.41	30	40	6.5%	16	30.5%	14	18	34
2018	3.55	3.78	31	64%	22	25%	30	1.06	27	0.49	29	41	6.6%	15	31.4%	18	14	40
2019	3.59	4.00	23	53%	30	23%	30	0.94	28	0.55	24	47	7.6%	22	29.2%	11	19	29
2019 ALY by direction:				Left End 3.37 (23)			Left Tackle: 3.55 (25)			Mid/Guard: 4.28 (19)			Right Tackle: 3.12 (28)			Right End 3.46 (22)		

Other than Joe Burrow going to Cincinnati at No. 1 and Chase Young going to Washington at No. 2, the most predictable move of the first round of April's NFL draft was the Buccaneers taking an offensive tackle. After three of the consensus top four offensive tackles came off the board, an antsy Jason Licht traded a fourth-round pick to San Francisco to move up a spot to No. 13 and take Tristan Wirfs. In his three seasons in Iowa's pro-style offense, Wirfs started 33 games, 29 at right tackle and four at left. In Tampa Bay, he'll take over for Demar Dotson, who had been the team's starting right tackle for most of the past decade. The 320-pound Wirfs brings not only exceptional speed to the line (his 4.85s 40-yard dash time at the combine was the best among offensive linemen) but also impressive power. Before he was a teenager, he was hitting baseballs from home plate to the neighboring municipal pool. ✎ On the left side, much-maligned Donovan Smith enters what is essentially a contract year. He is signed through 2021, but this is the last season his salary is guaranteed. He had a sneaky-good 2019, his best season yet in pass protection. He averaged 56.6 snaps per blown block, which ranked fifth among left tackles. In 2018, he ranked 25th in that same metric. ✎ The Buccaneers were one of five teams last season to have four linemen play at least 1,000 snaps. They're the only team to have four linemen play that many snaps in consecutive seasons. Smith has played at least 1,000 snaps in each of his five seasons. After an offseason without team-sanctioned in-person workouts, Tampa Bay's continuity could prove to be a greater advantage than usual. ✎ Tom Brady can overcome edge pressure; it's the pressure up the middle that frustrates him the most. With left guard Ali Marpet and center Ryan Jensen anchoring the interior, that shouldn't be an issue. ✎ Right guard Alex Cappa, a 2018 third-round draft pick, was inconsistent in his first season as a starter, allowing the most blown blocks on the team and ranking 81st among 106 interior linemen in blown blocks per snap. If he doesn't improve, he could lose snaps to Joe Haeg, who spent the past four seasons in Indianapolis.

Defensive Front

Defensive Line	Age	Pos	G	Snaps	Plays	Overall TmPct	Rk	Stop	Dfts	BTkl	Runs	vs. Run St%	Rk	RuYd	Rk	Pass Rush Sack	Hit	Hur	Dsrpt
Ndamukong Suh	33	DE	16	903	45	5.4%	30	39	13	4	33	85%	14	1.8	24	2.5	13	30	3
Vita Vea	25	DT	16	769	38	4.5%	46	29	9	6	30	77%	43	1.7	19	2.5	11	29	5
William Gholston	29	DE	16	507	40	4.8%	42	32	11	2	36	78%	34	1.5	14	1.0	6	12	3
Rakeem Nunez-Roches	27	DE	16	301	9	1.1%	--	7	2	0	9	78%	--	1.7	--	0.0	2	3	0

Edge Rushers	Age	Pos	G	Snaps	Plays	Overall TmPct	Rk	Stop	Dfts	BTkl	Runs	vs. Run St%	Rk	RuYd	Rk	Pass Rush Sack	Hit	Hur	Dsrpt
Shaquil Barrett	28	OLB	16	917	57	6.8%	18	45	29	2	25	76%	35	1.1	8	19.5	18	55	3
Carl Nassib*	27	OLB	14	656	34	4.6%	56	27	15	6	24	83%	13	0.9	4	6.0	6	24	0
Jason Pierre-Paul	31	OLB	10	599	29	5.6%	66	26	13	6	14	100%	1	0.9	7	8.5	7	29	4

Linebackers	Age	Pos	G	Snaps	Plays	Overall TmPct	Rk	Stop	Dfts	BTkl	Runs	vs. Run St%	Rk	RuYd	Rk	Pass Rush Sack	Hit	Hur	vs. Pass Tgts	Suc%	Rk	AdjYd	Rk	PD	Int
Lavonte David	30	ILB	16	1160	129	15.4%	17	80	30	13	61	57%	49	3.0	11	1.0	6	20	52	79%	1	3.5	3	7	1
Devin White	22	ILB	13	844	94	13.8%	35	52	18	15	47	62%	37	5.3	78	2.5	3	4	28	57%	16	7.5	52	3	1
Kevin Minter	30	ILB	16	290	31	3.7%	--	21	4	5	16	88%	--	2.4	--	0.0	2	10	14	50%	--	6.8	--	2	0

Year	Yards	ALY	Rank	Power	Rank	Stuff	Rank	2nd Level	Rank	Open Field	Rank	Sacks	ASR	Rank	Press	Rank
2017	4.18	4.16	20	62%	13	21%	14	1.19	21	0.84	24	22	4.3%	32	24.8%	32
2018	4.59	4.36	15	71%	24	23%	8	1.45	29	1.04	24	38	8.0%	8	25.0%	31
2019	3.02	3.14	2	62%	11	29%	2	0.81	1	0.45	2	47	6.7%	20	32.9%	7

2019 ALY by direction:	Left End: 3.21 (6)	Left Tackle: 4.24 (15)	Mid/Guard: 3.01 (1)	Right Tackle: 3.15 (4)	Right End: 2.24 (4)

The Buccaneers defensive front remains mostly the same. After Tampa Bay retained Shaquil Barrett, Jason Pierre-Paul, and Ndamukong Suh, Carl Nassib was the odd man out. The Raiders offered him a generous multi-year deal that will pay him $7.75 million this season. If he saves all of it and lives off his earnings from the Browns and Buccaneers, it'll double in seven years, per his financial advice on *Hard Knocks*. If it doubles every seven years for the next 42 years, he'll have half a billion dollars in retirement. Save your money, kids (but keep buying the *Football Outsiders Almanac*). 🏈 Here's a way to triple your money in a year: lead the league in sacks and finish in the top 10 in hits and hurries. Barrett, who earned $5 million last season on a one-year deal, will earn more than $15 million this season under the franchise tag. 🏈 Thanks in part to Barrett, Tampa Bay's defensive pressure rate surged last season to 32.9%, which ranked seventh. They had ranked last and next-to-last in the previous two seasons. 🏈 Related: the Buccaneers became blitz-happy under Todd Bowles. They rushed five or more defenders 39.8% of the time, up from 24.0% the season before. 🏈 After suffering a career-threatening neck fracture in a May car crash, the ever-resilient Pierre-Paul returned to the field in Week 8. Despite missing half a season, he generated a total of 44.5 sacks, hits, and hurries, almost as many as in 2018 (48.5). The Buccaneers haven't been able to draft and develop edge rushers, so they had little choice but to pay the 31-year-old top dollar to return. He's scheduled to earn $12.5 million in each of the next two seasons. 🏈 Vita Vea is a star in the making. He was known as a tough, space-eating run defender when he came into the league in 2018, and now he is showing promise as a pass-rusher too. He tied Aaron Donald with 11 quarterback hits, second among interior linemen trailing only Chris Jones. 🏈 Oh, by the way, the perennially underrated Lavonte David recorded 30 defeats (third-most among linebackers) for the second straight year and sixth time in his eight seasons.

Defensive Secondary

Secondary	Age	Pos	G	Snaps	Plays	TmPct	Rk	Stop	Dfts	BTkl	Runs	St%	Rk	RuYd	Rk	Tgts	Tgt%	Rk	Dist	Suc%	Rk	AdjYd	Rk	PD	Int
Carlton Davis	24	CB	14	965	78	10.7%	17	42	14	8	10	80%	3	3.1	8	101	23.5%	15	12.1	57%	22	6.1	10	19	1
Jordan Whitehead	23	SS	14	953	77	10.5%	35	36	17	14	37	51%	14	3.9	5	39	9.2%	22	11.9	54%	33	9.5	61	9	1
Sean Murphy-Bunting	23	CB	16	702	51	6.1%	64	20	11	8	8	38%	57	4.4	21	53	17.0%	66	11.4	43%	75	7.8	46	8	3
Mike Edwards	24	FS	15	637	51	6.5%	62	25	12	11	15	40%	39	6.8	37	24	8.5%	31	7.3	54%	31	7.8	42	6	0
Andrew Adams	28	FS	14	627	48	6.6%	65	12	7	4	19	37%	47	8.9	54	12	4.3%	70	12.6	33%	67	9.3	60	3	1
Jamel Dean	24	CB	13	374	38	5.6%	--	23	11	4	5	20%	--	9.2	--	43	25.8%	--	11.7	63%	--	6.1	--	17	2
M.J. Stewart	25	CB	10	330	37	7.1%	--	13	2	3	4	100%	--	2.5	--	34	23.1%	--	7.7	47%	--	6.7	--	2	0

Year	Pass D Rank	vs. #1 WR	Rk	vs. #2 WR	Rk	vs. Other WR	Rk	WR Wide	Rk	WR Slot	Rk	vs. TE	Rk	vs. RB	Rk
2017	31	0.9%	15	8.4%	21	21.0%	27	2.5%	21	14.6%	22	6.1%	22	13.3%	25
2018	30	16.0%	29	25.1%	29	-1.4%	18	-11.2%	9	28.7%	29	21.1%	28	2.2%	16
2019	12	3.7%	17	2.2%	18	-20.0%	6	-4.2%	18	-2.8%	8	10.7%	27	-49.0%	2

The Buccaneers have drafted seven defensive backs since 2017. Only the Vikings have drafted more (eight). 🏈 Licht has favored taller defensive backs, but in the second round of this year's draft, he couldn't pass on Antoine Winfield Jr., who is short (5-foot-9) but tough. Scouts laud his instincts, physicality, and playmaking ability. Given his range—he can play deep safety, cover slot receivers and tackle like a linebacker—he should thrive in Bowles' aggressive defense. When he was three years old, his father, then a cornerback for the Bills, intercepted Tom Brady. 🏈 Maybe Winfield can help Tampa Bay shore up its defense against deep passes, which was one of the few areas last season in which the team took a step back. Left, middle, right—it didn't matter. The Buccaneers' 58.3% DVOA against deep passes ranked 29th. 🏈 The status of safety Justin Evans, a 2017 second-round draft pick, remains a mystery. He sustained what the team classified as a turf-toe injury late in the 2018 season. He missed offseason activities, had a procedure in June, was activated after the preseason, then suffered an Achilles tendon injury and ultimately landed on injured reserve. 🏈 Tampa Bay has insurance in case Winfield isn't ready to start right away and/or Evans' injuries continue to linger. Mike Edwards, Andrew Adams, D'Cota Dixon, and Jordan Whitehead are viable options. When Evans couldn't play last season, it was Whitehead who saw more playing time. He struggled in pass coverage (he allowed two touchdowns in a Week 5 loss to the Saints) but was effective at rushing the quarterback. His 14 hurries were second to only Jamal Adams among NFL defensive backs. 🏈 Though he played in only 14 games, Carlton Davis was targeted an NFL-high 101 times. The second-year cornerback held his own, though. He posted a better yards per pass average and success rate than

Defensive Player of the Year Stephon Gilmore. Gilmore led the league with 20 passes defensed, but Davis was right behind 19 and rookie teammate Jamel Dean had 17. ◔ The Buccaneers' "base" defense features five defensive backs (they used that grouping two-thirds of the time last season); in that configuration, Davis and Dean man the outside while Sean Murphy-Bunting covers the slot receiver. ◔ As a rookie in 2018, M.J. Stewart played nickel cornerback. After the season, Tampa Bay said it was moving him to safety. That experiment ended during training camp. For now, he's the Buccaneers' fourth cornerback.

Special Teams

Year	DVOA	Rank	FG/XP	Rank	Net Kick	Rank	Kick Ret	Rank	Net Punt	Rank	Punt Ret	Rank	Hidden	Rank
2017	-5.5%	29	-13.2	31	-14.4	32	-0.6	16	0.2	18	0.3	14	-1.2	14
2018	-4.1%	28	-12.9	31	1.7	12	-2.2	20	-2.9	23	-4.0	26	-8.3	25
2019	-2.8%	27	-3.7	22	4.7	9	-4.4	29	-3.6	22	-6.9	32	-11.3	30

The Buccaneers have had eight straight seasons of below-average special teams play, and given the top-heavy construction of this roster, they likely will extend that streak. ◔ There are three certainties in life: death, taxes, and the Buccaneers missing field goals and extra points. Matt Gay, whom Tampa Bay drafted in the fifth round, missed 13 kicks last season. Only 47-year-old Adam Vinatieri missed more. Gay's most notable miss came in a Week 3 loss to the Giants. In the final seconds, the Buccaneers reached the New York 9-yard line, but before Jameis Winston could take a knee to center the ball between the hashmarks, they drew a delay-of-game penalty. Afterward, Bruce Arians said it was intentional. "I just took it on purpose," he said. "That field goal is easier back 5 yards." Gay's kick drifted wide right by the width of a football. ◔ In March 2019, Tampa Bay made Bradley Pinion one of the NFL's highest-paid punters. He finished 22nd in net punting value and 30th in gross punting value. However, he was much better on kickoffs, finishing third in the league in gross kickoff value. ◔ As bad as the Buccaneers' kicking situations were, their return games were worse. They were the only team to finish in the bottom five in both kick return and punt return value. Among their specialists, running back T.J. Logan was the only one to post a positive value, but only on punt returns. Logan missed the final four games of last season because of a broken thumb. He'll be in the mix for returns again, though he'll have to hold off running back Raymond Calais (on kick returns) and safety Antoine Winfield Jr. (on punt returns). ◔ Maybe the Buccaneers can't solve their own kicking problems, but they should at least have better luck with opposing special teams in 2020. Last year, opposing placekickers were worth an estimated 11.3 points over average, the highest figure in the league. They missed just one extra point and went 37-of-42 on field goals with no misses from within 40 yards. Opponents also were strong on punts, tied for second in the NFL with an average of 47.0 gross yards per punt.

Tennessee Titans

2019 Record: 9-7	**Total DVOA:** 8.1% (9th)	**2020 Mean Projection:** 8.1 wins	**On the Clock (0-4):** 9%
Pythagorean Wins: 9.9 (8th)	**Offense:** 12.6% (6th)	**Postseason Odds:** 45.6%	**Mediocrity (5-7):** 32%
Snap-Weighted Age: 26.4 (18th)	**Defense:** 1.0% (16th)	**Super Bowl Odds:** 4.7%	**Playoff Contender (8-10):** 40%
Average Opponent: -3.9% (29th)	**Special Teams:** -3.5% (29th)	**Proj. Avg. Opponent:** -1.3% (28th)	**Super Bowl Contender (11+):** 19%

2019: The dreadnought rains fire on an unsuspecting AFC.

2020: I Can't Believe It's A Chapter About Regression!

"*Best of all, even a below-average player at backup quarterback is significantly better than what the Titans have had in a number of years. Ryan Tannehill, you're all set to become the most popular man in Nashville, with the possibility some team will make an eight-figure mistake in your favor next offseason. Just don't screw it up.*"

Ryan Tannehill's player comment in *Football Outsiders Almanac 2019* was dead-on prescient outside of the fact that it technically wound up being a nine-figure mistake. The Titans signed Tannehill to a four-year, $118-million deal after the season, ignoring a quarterback market that included Tom Brady, Philip Rivers, Teddy Bridgewater, Cam Newton, Jameis Winston, and others.

While it is an obvious feel-good story for a player who had been trapped in the depressing quagmire of the post-Parcells Dolphins, Tannehill's star rose in a way that is simply not compatible with what we previously knew about him. Rich Gannon is the easy comparison for "older quarterback who needed a new team and system to succeed," but Gannon a) became a better player at an older age and b) also only had about 1,100 passing attempts in his twenties. Tannehill had just south of 3,000 passes with the Dolphins, and this is despite missing the entirety of the 2017 season and only being a part-time starter in 2018. Usually with that much exposure to the league, something important pops out about a player's ability to be a franchise quarterback. Tannehill was a breakout quarterback pick for his last three seasons in Miami, and definitely showed an accurate and impressive arm and deep ball, but never put it all together. If you listened to the people who go throw-by-throw over an NFL season like former FO writer Cian Fahey, you knew that there was redeemable upside in Tannehill that wasn't reached by Tony Sparano or Adam Gase.

And all of that was expressed in a breakout 2019 season in which Tannehill, starting 10 games, led the Titans to the playoffs and rolled them over the Patriots and Ravens before succumbing to the eventual Super Bowl champs in Arrowhead. Tannehill finished fifth in passing DVOA and first in yards per attempt behind a play-action-heavy offense that accentuated his strengths and downplayed his processing speed and poor pocket presence. (Even in a great year for Tannehill, the Titans finished dead last in adjusted sack rate allowed behind what is generally considered a solid offensive line.)

The list of quarterbacks who have finished in the top 10 among qualified DVOA leaders in the last 10 years without reaching the top 10 in any of their first three years in the NFL is a murderer's row of regression (Table 1). Now, granted, there are a lot of journeymen quarterbacks on this list who had no previous starting experience, but even if you narrow the look to players with a lot of early experience that suddenly became good, there's not a lot of signs for optimism. Andy Dalton, Joe Flacco, and Alex Smith were all limited quarterbacks who needed managing by the very best minds in the games or sublime surrounding casts to reach the performance of their best years.

Table 1. QB Breakout Seasons, 2010-2019

Player	Team	Year	DVOA	Rk	DVOA Y+1	Change	Positive Qualified DVOA Years After Breakout
Alex Smith	SF	2012	14.8%	9	-3.7%	-18.5%	4
Josh McCown	CHI	2013	32.1%	4	-41.9%	-74.0%	0
Joe Flacco	BAL	2014	15.5%	8	-10.5%	-26.0%	1
Andy Dalton	CIN	2015	31.7%	2	7.6%	-24.1%	2
Tyrod Taylor	BUF	2015	9.8%	8	-2.1%	-11.9%	0
Brian Hoyer	CHI	2016	19.4%	4	-16.7%	-36.1%	0
Case Keenum	MIN	2017	28.1%	1	-12.7%	-40.8%	0
Ryan Fitzpatrick	TB	2018	16.8%	6	1.3%	-15.5%	1
Ryan Tannehill	**TEN**	**2019**	**28.0%**	**5**	--	--	--
Teddy Bridgewater	**NO**	**2019**	**15.3%**	**9**	--	--	--

And thus, despite what Tannehill did last season, we are pretty skeptical that he has turned the page and become someone who will be competing for DVOA crowns going forward. That doesn't mean he can't be a productive player, and it doesn't mean that he isn't a good fit for this offense. But at $29.5 million per season, with $62 million in guarantees that effectively force him on to the books for three seasons in a row, Tannehill is being paid like a top-10 quarterback. It's almost all speculation at this point, but any sort of COVID-19 reduction on the salary cap in future years based on a decline in revenue could very much make this a franchise-crippling contract.

At the same time Tannehill was leading the Titans' pass-

2020 Titans Schedule

Week	Opp.	Week	Opp.	Week	Opp.
1	at DEN (Mon.)	7	BYE	13	CLE
2	JAX	8	at CIN	14	at JAX
3	at MIN	9	CHI	15	DET (Sat.)
4	PIT	10	IND (Thu.)	16	at GB
5	BUF	11	at BAL	17	at HOU
6	HOU	12	at IND		

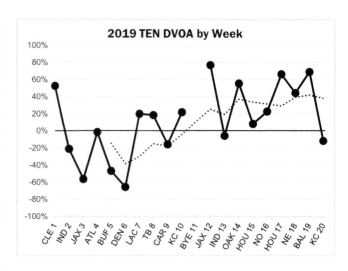

2019 TEN DVOA by Week

ing game to new heights, the Tennessee running game was also hitting on all cylinders, with Derrick Henry exploding in the second half of the year for the second straight season. In 2018, it was easier to write off as a small-sample fluke because it was almost entirely a one-month thing—Henry ran for 625 yards in December of the 2018 season and 434 in the three months before it. As of Week 8 in 2019, the Titans had a -13.8% rushing DVOA, and Henry had -11 DYAR. From Weeks 9 to 17, Henry had a 22.2% rushing DVOA as a pure workhorse back and Tannehill contributed 92 DYAR of his own on 19 high-efficiency totes as the Titans became a dominant ground attack. Henry had 157 carries to Dion Lewis' 37 over that stretch. After two years where every objective outside observer watched him play and wondered how the Titans failed to get him more involved—particularly over a washed-up DeMarco Murray in 2017—Henry finally led the league in carries, rushing yardage, and rushing touchdowns.

That this came right at the same time they suddenly had one of the best quarterback seasons in the NFL fall right into their laps was actually kind of devastating for the Titans. There's no way any rational analysis would suggest that they should make Henry a top-dollar running back. Paying the top of the running back market is essentially that clip of Tobias Funke from *Arrested Development* answering his wife on the question of whether open relationships work: "No, it never does, these people somehow delude themselves into thinking it might, but … but it might work for us." Henry told *The Rich Eisen Show* that Ezekiel Elliott's six-year, $90-million deal was "the floor." The Titans responded by doing the only rational thing they could: franchise-tagging Henry and giving Tannehill a ton of leverage instead.

At the core of the ascent for both Henry and Tannehill last year was first-year offensive coordinator Arthur Smith, someone who came in with almost no coordinating experience. Smith barely budged Tennessee's play-action pass percentage—it went from 29% in 2018 to 31% in 2019—but the changes he made massively boosted its effectiveness. Second-round pick A.J. Brown dominated over the middle of the field in his rookie season with the holes generated by sucking in the underneath linebackers. Given free space in the open field, Brown averaged 15.1 yards *after the catch* on his 31 play-action targets. From Weeks 9 through 17, that number jumped to 16.7 as defenses faced a Henry that they couldn't stop and had to play their run keys even more aggressively.

Of course, Tannehill's deep ball and his ability to make reads from a less-hurried pocket also meshed very well with

the play-action focus, and so the Titans led the league in play-action yards per play by almost a full yard, 11.2 to 10.4 over the second-place Bucs. To find another season where play-action passing cracked 11.0 yards per dropback for a team, you have to go back to the 2013 Broncos, who had 11.1. The highest figure in our database belongs to the 2009 Texans at 11.7 yards per dropback, but the Titans did have the largest gap we've ever measured, with their net yards per pass dropping in half to 5.6 without play-action. The Titans led the NFL in play-action DVOA as well, with a 67.2% figure. That's a little less of a historical outlier, but still puts them in terrific company over the years we've got data for. The issue is that for most of these teams, that extreme play-action spike was not repeatable (Table 2).

Table 2. Play-Action DVOA over 60%, 2011-2019

Team	Year	PA DVOA	PA DVOA Y+1	PA Rate	PA Rate Y+1	Offensive DVOA	Offensive DVOA Y+1
SD	2014	90.3%	27.3%	8%	10%	7.0%	0.9%
DEN	2013	89.7%	33.9%	25%	23%	33.5%	20.0%
SD	2016	83.9%	40.5%	17%	18%	-3.2%	10.6%
SD	2013	81.2%	90.3%	12%	8%	23.1%	7.0%
NE	2018	76.4%	32.0%	31%	24%	14.5%	4.1%
BUF	2015	72.3%	28.5%	17%	21%	9.8%	10.7%
NE	2011	72.0%	55.7%	16%	24%	31.9%	30.8%
ARI	2015	70.7%	35.1%	17%	15%	15.7%	-6.0%
MIN	2017	69.0%	40.3%	30%	21%	12.0%	-1.3%
TEN	**2019**	**67.2%**	--	**31%**	--	**12.6%**	--
TB	2016	67.0%	36.4%	22%	21%	-4.1%	5.2%
WAS	2012	66.7%	-13.0%	42%	27%	15.3%	-10.0%
NO	**2019**	**63.9%**	--	**20%**	--	**21.4%**	--
LAC	2018	63.1%	38.2%	22%	21%	20.7%	3.8%
DET	2011	61.0%	9.1%	14%	16%	7.1%	12.3%
DET	2017	60.6%	24.5%	20%	18%	4.4%	-5.2%
ATL	2011	60.3%	44.1%	17%	17%	6.1%	6.1%
GB	2014	60.0%	-10.8%	24%	16%	24.7%	2.2%
AVG (except 2019)		*71.5%*	*32.0%*			*13.7%*	*5.7%*

That table tells us so, so much about Philip Rivers. Anyway, the Titans will likely be a good play-action team in 2020. They were a good play-action team in 2017, and an average one in 2018. But teams that have their play-action passes work out as well as the Titans did last season tend to be a lot closer to average than good in the following season. To overcome this regression, the Titans are going to need better production from a defense that has been generally mediocre since Mike Vrabel took over in 2018.

There were some major changes on defense this offseason that were curiously addressed by the Titans. Dean Pees retired after two seasons and wasn't ever replaced, with Vrabel the odds-on favorite to call plays over new inside linebackers coach and former Washington defensive coordinator Jim Haslett. "If I were a fan of Tennessee," Pees told Nashville's *Midday 180 Show*, "I would have the utmost confidence that [Vrabel] was going to be able to handle it one way or the other going forward." Vrabel's one year coordinating a defense in Houston was a disaster—the Texans finished 25th in pass defense DVOA and allowed the most points in the league—but he was also dealt a hand without J.J. Watt for all but five games and thus mostly given a pass for that.

After drafting Jeffery Simmons in the first round last year and giving him some space to recover from the ACL he tore at the combine, the Titans plugged Simmons in at midseason and were happy enough with the results to move on from long-time stalwart Jurrell Casey. Casey was traded to the Broncos for nothing but a 2020 seventh-round pick despite finishing second on the team in hurries to Harold Landry. While Simmons showed some flashes last season, his numbers were not really on Casey's level and it takes some projected improvement for him to fully replace Casey. There was a lot of speculation in the offseason about this potentially being a Jadeveon Clowney landing spot because Vrabel coached him in Houston, but as things currently stand the Titans' No. 2 edge rusher is Falcons washout Vic Beasley. The Titans don't really have a true 1A rusher, and though they'll presumably get more games played from No. 1 corner Adoree' Jackson this year, the non-Kevin Byard talent on that side of the roster is rather limited. It's hard to find a lot of scenarios outside of a Simmons breakout that lead to this team improving on last season's 16th-place defensive DVOA finish.

The Titans are right in the thick of the AFC playoff hunt according to our projections, with a mean projection that would put them back into the postseason. If we could guarantee that the Titans got the same sort of empirical results as they did last year, it would be easy to forecast them as AFC South champions, if not a top-of-the-AFC contender. They still get to carry a fairly weak schedule. With Tannehill projected to be a little more like the Ryan Tannehill we've seen over the course of his career, our Titans forecast centers more around an average offense.

It remains to be seen if Tannehill's monster season will be a pyrrhic victory for the Titans, but in the short term, he should at least keep them in the thick of things. That's more than they could get from Marcus Mariota.

Rivers McCown

2019 Titans Stats by Week

Wk	vs.	W-L	PF	PA	YDF	YDA	TO	Total	Off	Def	ST
1	at CLE	W	43	13	339	346	+3	53%	19%	-28%	5%
2	IND	L	17	19	243	288	+2	-21%	-8%	8%	-5%
3	at JAX	L	7	20	340	292	-1	-56%	-28%	22%	-6%
4	at ATL	W	24	10	365	422	+1	-2%	-6%	4%	8%
5	BUF	L	7	14	252	313	+1	-47%	-21%	-2%	-27%
6	at DEN	L	0	16	204	270	-2	-66%	-72%	-12%	-5%
7	LAC	W	23	20	403	365	0	20%	15%	-2%	3%
8	TB	W	27	23	246	389	+3	18%	4%	-9%	6%
9	at CAR	L	20	30	431	370	-2	-16%	22%	16%	-22%
10	KC	W	35	32	371	530	0	22%	38%	14%	-2%
11	BYE										
12	JAX	W	42	20	471	369	-1	77%	76%	10%	11%
13	at IND	W	31	17	292	391	+1	-6%	-7%	0%	1%
14	at OAK	W	42	21	552	355	0	55%	57%	-4%	-6%
15	HOU	L	21	24	432	374	+1	8%	8%	-7%	-7%
16	NO	L	28	38	397	377	-1	23%	47%	17%	-7%
17	at HOU	W	35	14	467	301	+1	66%	57%	-9%	-1%
18	at NE	W	20	13	272	307	+1	44%	21%	-19%	5%
19	at BAL	W	28	12	300	530	+3	69%	27%	-41%	1%
20	at KC	L	24	35	295	404	0	-12%	22%	38%	4%

Trends and Splits

	Offense	Rank	Defense	Rank
Total DVOA	12.6%	6	1.0%	16
Unadjusted VOA	16.6%	5	0.1%	17
Weighted Trend	24.6%	3	1.7%	20
Variance	14.1%	31	1.7%	1
Average Opponent	3.1%	31	-0.8%	22
Passing	29.7%	6	11.0%	21
Rushing	7.3%	5	-12.6%	9
First Down	18.0%	3	10.1%	26
Second Down	18.0%	5	-6.2%	10
Third Down	-9.1%	21	-5.9%	15
First Half	-9.5%	26	1.8%	17
Second Half	33.0%	2	0.2%	16
Red Zone	31.2%	4	12.1%	26
Late and Close	27.8%	2	-1.1%	18

Five-Year Performance

Year	W-L	Pyth W	Est W	PF	PA	TO	Total	Rk	Off	Rk	Def	Rk	ST	Rk	Off AGL	Rk	Def AGL	Rk	Off Age	Rk	Def Age	Rk	ST Age	Rk
2015	3-13	4.8	4.4	299	423	-14	-26.6%	31	-15.7%	32	7.1%	23	-3.8%	28	38.3	20	25.8	10	25.6	29	26.5	18	25.7	24
2016	9-7	8.1	8.7	381	378	0	3.5%	15	10.8%	9	6.4%	24	-1.0%	19	20.7	4	13.1	2	26.2	24	27.0	8	26.2	14
2017	9-7	7.4	7.6	334	356	-4	-5.7%	18	-2.2%	18	5.0%	21	1.6%	13	10.8	5	16.6	7	26.5	22	26.9	10	26.8	2
2018	9-7	8.2	7.7	310	303	-1	-4.9%	20	-5.1%	22	0.6%	19	0.8%	13	29.4	10	35.3	20	26.2	23	26.4	14	26.6	6
2019	9-7	9.9	9.3	402	331	+6	8.1%	9	12.6%	6	1.0%	16	-3.5%	29	19.7	7	23.9	6	26.7	18	26.3	17	26.0	13

2019 Performance Based on Most Common Personnel Groups

TEN Offense					TEN Offense vs. Opponents						TEN Defense					TEN Defense vs. Opponents			
Pers	Freq	Yds	DVOA	Run%	Pers	Freq	Yds	DVOA	Run%		Pers	Freq	Yds	DVOA		Pers	Freq	Yds	DVOA
11	52%	6.0	16.7%	27%	Base	40%	6.8	17.1%	61%		Base	20%	6.3	15.0%		11	63%	5.6	-0.5%
12	29%	7.2	25.9%	58%	Nickel	46%	6.1	19.6%	35%		Nickel	54%	5.5	-1.5%		12	20%	6.2	6.2%
13	8%	5.9	-16.8%	50%	Dime+	12%	6.3	7.0%	8%		Dime+	26%	5.9	-4.8%		21	7%	5.3	7.3%
21	4%	6.5	5.9%	76%	Goal Line	1%	0.9	49.2%	67%		Goal Line	1%	0.2	-6.2%		13	3%	7.2	-22.2%
22	3%	6.8	48.8%	76%	Big	1%	10.8	93.4%	100%							22	3%	6.4	17.0%

Strategic Tendencies

Run/Pass		Rk	Formation		Rk	Pass Rush		Rk	Secondary		Rk	Strategy		Rk
Runs, first half	40%	11	Form: Single Back	77%	21	Rush 3	19.6%	3	4 DB	20%	23	Play Action	31%	5
Runs, first down	56%	5	Form: Empty Back	5%	27	Rush 4	63.2%	19	5 DB	54%	18	Offensive Motion	56%	4
Runs, second-long	30%	11	Form: Multi Back	18%	7	Rush 5	13.6%	28	6+ DB	26%	9	Avg Box (Off)	6.76	5
Runs, power sit.	62%	6	Pers: 3+ WR	53%	25	Rush 6+	3.7%	22	Man Coverage	33%	15	Avg Box (Def)	6.56	17
Runs, behind 2H	32%	6	Pers: 2+ TE/6+ OL	43%	3	Edge Rusher Sacks	53.6%	21	CB by Sides	82%	13	Offensive Pace	31.25	19
Pass, ahead 2H	33%	32	Pers: 6+ OL	2%	20	Interior DL Sacks	22.6%	15	S/CB Cover Ratio	21%	28	Defensive Pace	31.15	25
Run-Pass Options	4%	21	Shotgun/Pistol	51%	29	Second Level Sacks	23.8%	11	DB Blitz	14%	7	Go for it on 4th	1.27	20

One important thing about the Titans offense is that it had to stay on schedule. The Titans were third in offensive DVOA on first down and fifth on second down. They were also second on third-and-short. But the Titans dropped to 28th on third downs with 3 or more yards to go. Even after Ryan Tannehill took over at quarterback, the Titans ranked 19th in offensive DVOA for these situations. ● Tennessee receivers were tied for the league low with just 16 drops. ● Tennessee ran against heavy boxes (eight or more) on 44% of carries, the highest figure in the league. But the Titans had only a slightly lower DVOA on those runs. In fact, the Titans' lowest DVOA came on runs against lighter boxes of six or fewer, and they gained just 4.3 yards per carry on those runs compared to 4.9 yards per carry against boxes of seven or more. ● The Titans were near the league lead with 11.1 average yards after the catch on passes behind or at the line of scrimmage, which helped them finish second in average YAC overall at 6.2. The Titans ranked fourth in DVOA on passes behind or at the line of scrimmage, and first in passes past the line of scrimmage. ● Tennessee was dead last with -36.9% DVOA out of empty-backfield formations. ● Tennessee was second with 166 broken tackles and led the league with broken tackles on 15.1% of all offensive plays. Derrick Henry finished fifth in the league with 69 but A.J. Brown was also fourth among wide receivers with 20 and Jonnu Smith was third among tight ends with 17. ● The Titans offense ranked 26th in the league before halftime but second in the league after halftime. ● Tennessee blitzed much less than the previous season, dropping from 27.2% to 17.3% in how often they sent five or more pass-rushers. However, the rate of defensive back blitzes went up slightly. Defensive back blitzes were much more effective than other blitzes. The Titans allowed 5.5 yards per pass with -5.5% DVOA when blitzing a defensive back. They allowed 7.5 yards with 18.4% DVOA on other blitzes. ● The Tennessee "CB by Sides" number would be much lower if we based it on Logan Ryan, who in many ways was Tennessee's top cornerback but moved around the field as the slot corner when the Titans went to nickel or dime.

Passing

Player	DYAR	DVOA	Plays	NtYds	Avg	YAC	C%	TD	Int
R.Tannehill	773	28.0%	315	2529	8.0	6.1	71.0%	22	6
M.Mariota*	-62	-17.0%	183	1031	5.6	6.4	60.5%	7	2

Rushing

Player	DYAR	DVOA	Plays	Yds	Avg	TD	Fum	Suc
D.Henry	192	6.7%	303	1542	5.1	16	5	50%
D.Lewis*	-26	-20.7%	54	209	3.9	0	1	46%
R.Tannehill	82	48.9%	25	201	8.0	4	0	-
M.Mariota*	-2	-13.7%	23	130	5.7	0	1	-
D.Dawkins	-13	-35.7%	11	26	2.4	0	0	36%

Receiving

Player	DYAR	DVOA	Plays	Ctch	Yds	Y/C	YAC	TD	C%
A.Brown	251	26.2%	84	52	1051	20.2	8.9	8	62%
C.Davis	99	5.4%	69	43	601	14.0	5.0	2	62%
A.Humphries	84	11.7%	47	37	374	10.1	3.2	2	79%
T.Sharpe*	157	45.1%	34	25	329	13.2	2.3	4	74%
K.Raymond	33	21.0%	12	9	170	18.9	1.6	1	75%
D.Jennings*	-19	-52.5%	6	2	17	8.5	7.0	0	33%
J.Smith	91	25.6%	44	35	439	12.5	7.8	3	80%
D.Walker*	0	-7.1%	31	21	215	10.2	3.1	2	68%
A.Firkser	31	13.0%	24	14	204	14.6	5.1	1	58%
M.Pruitt	31	47.9%	8	6	90	15.0	10.8	1	75%
D.Lewis*	3	-11.9%	32	25	164	6.6	7.7	1	78%
D.Henry	46	21.8%	24	18	206	11.4	13.1	2	75%

Offensive Line

Player	Pos	Age	GS	Snaps	Pen	Sk	Pass	Run	Player	Pos	Age	GS	Snaps	Pen	Sk	Pass	Run
Jack Conklin*	RT	26	16/16	957	7	2.8	18	5	Taylor Lewan	LT	29	12/12	730	10	1.5	8	4
Rodger Saffold	LG	32	16/16	953	3	7.8	14	6	Jamil Douglas	RG/C	28	15/5	399	2	2.0	8	2
Ben Jones	C	31	15/15	941	3	1.3	8	7	Dennis Kelly	LT	30	15/4	360	2	2.5	9	4
Nate Davis	RG	24	13/12	743	8	5.0	15	14									

Year	Yards	ALY	Rank	Power	Rank	Stuff	Rank	2nd Lev	Rank	Open Field	Rank	Sacks	ASR	Rank	Press	Rank	F-Start	Cont.
2017	4.00	3.85	23	60%	23	23%	24	1.09	21	0.90	9	35	6.4%	14	24.5%	4	12	36
2018	4.25	4.33	17	67%	17	19%	17	1.15	24	0.83	18	47	10.2%	29	25.7%	5	13	24
2019	4.83	4.65	4	73%	5	18%	15	1.36	3	1.05	5	56	11.2%	32	28.6%	9	20	34

2019 ALY by direction: Left End 5.05 (5) Left Tackle: 4.74 (7) Mid/Guard: 4.41 (17) Right Tackle: 4.39 (14) Right End: 5.72 (3)

Taylor Lewan has tightened up his play over the last two years. After a 2017 season where he allowed 5.5 sacks, he has allowed just 3.5 sacks the last two seasons despite playing with a couple of pretty sack-prone quarterbacks. He's still heavily penalized (29 flags over the last three seasons), but the five-year, $80-million extension he signed in 2018 has aged well so far. ◈ To replace Jack Conklin at right tackle, the Titans tabbed Georgia's Isaiah Wilson in the first round. Wilson's testing left some room to be desired as he put up an 8.26s 3-cone drill time and a 5.07s short shuttle time that were both in the bottom 10 percentile among drafted tackles since 2000. But Wilson is also 6-foot-6, 350 pounds of vortex. College teams almost had to go around him to get any pressure on Jake Fromm. Swing tackle Dennis Kelly has gotten plenty of work the last two seasons and should be an acceptable starter if Wilson needs some time to learn. ◈ Year 1 of Rodger Saffold in Tennessee had a rough start—nine of his blown blocks and six of his allowed sacks came in the first five weeks of the season. To put that in perspective, Saffold allowed just one sack in all of 2018. He was much better after Tannehill took over and the Titans probably don't regret this contract yet. That was a scary first month, though. ◈ Opposite Saffold was the weak link in this line, 2019 third-rounder Nate Davis. Almost all of Davis' blown assignments came with moving parts: zone, pitch, or lead plays made up 10 of his blown run blocks. It was a rocky first year, but the Titans didn't add any real competition to the mix. Jamil Douglas is the only backup guard with NFL experience, and he's at just 907 snaps over the last five years. ◈ Manning the pivot is Ben Jones, who had been an absolute steal on the four-year, $17.5-million deal that lured him away from the Texans. He signed a two-year extension just before last season at $18 million total compensation for two years. Charters assigned Jones with just 34 blown blocks over the last three seasons in Nashville.

Defensive Front

Defensive Line	Age	Pos	G	Snaps	Plays	TmPct	Rk	Stop	Dfts	BTkl	Runs	St%	Rk	RuYd	Rk	Sack	Hit	Hur	Dsrpt
						Overall						*vs. Run*					*Pass Rush*		
Jurrell Casey*	31	DE	14	722	44	5.9%	34	38	11	5	36	86%	12	1.8	22	5.0	5	20	0
DaQuan Jones	29	DT	16	688	45	5.3%	32	36	6	4	38	84%	17	2.0	34	1.0	2	14	3
Austin Johnson*	26	DT	16	326	24	2.8%	--	18	2	1	22	77%	--	2.5	--	0.0	2	5	1
Jeffery Simmons	23	DE	9	318	33	6.9%	61	24	6	2	29	69%	73	2.5	60	2.0	0	4	1
Jack Crawford	32	DT	16	436	27	3.4%	74	20	7	2	18	83%	19	2.2	40	0.5	5	9	1

Edge Rushers	Age	Pos	G	Snaps	Plays	TmPct	Rk	Stop	Dfts	BTkl	Runs	St%	Rk	RuYd	Rk	Sack	Hit	Hur	Dsrpt
						Overall						*vs. Run*					*Pass Rush*		
Harold Landry	24	OLB	16	961	68	8.0%	6	47	19	13	47	70%	59	2.7	51	9.0	6	38	0
Kamalei Correa	26	OLB	16	439	34	4.0%	--	25	8	0	22	68%	--	3.2	--	5.0	2	9	1
Reggie Gilbert	27	OLB	11	300	19	3.3%	--	13	3	1	14	71%	--	1.9	--	1.0	2	8	1
Cameron Wake*	38	OLB	9	198	5	1.1%	--	4	3	1	1	0%	--	4.0	--	2.5	8	18	0
Sharif Finch*	25	OLB	8	182	13	3.1%	--	8	4	0	8	63%	--	2.0	--	2.0	0	6	0
Vic Beasley	28	DE	16	774	44	5.6%	37	35	18	7	27	78%	28	2.9	59	8.0	4	25	1

Linebackers	Age	Pos	G	Snaps	Plays	TmPct	Rk	Stop	Dfts	BTkl	Runs	St%	Rk	RuYd	Rk	Sack	Hit	Hur	Tgts	Suc%	Rk	AdjYd	Rk	PD	Int
						Overall						*vs. Run*				*Pass Rush*				*vs. Pass*					
Rashaan Evans	25	ILB	16	966	111	13.1%	28	61	24	17	67	72%	10	2.6	8	2.5	5	12	24	25%	67	9.2	62	0	0
Jayon Brown	25	ILB	14	841	112	15.1%	26	56	14	14	57	51%	72	4.5	70	1.0	2	7	38	55%	21	5.2	15	8	1
Wesley Woodyard*	34	ILB	15	328	42	5.3%	--	20	5	5	20	70%	--	2.5	--	1.0	1	0	15	40%	--	9.3	--	1	0

Year	Yards	ALY	Rank	Power	Rank	Stuff	Rank	2nd Level	Rank	Open Field	Rank	Sacks	ASR	Rank	Press	Rank
2017	3.44	4.07	14	65%	20	20%	22	0.94	5	0.23	1	43	6.9%	12	31.4%	12
2018	4.29	4.82	28	64%	13	16%	23	1.19	13	0.64	9	39	6.7%	22	27.6%	26
2019	4.01	4.09	9	63%	13	18%	18	1.03	7	0.76	17	43	7.1%	14	25.1%	30

2019 ALY by direction: Left End: 4.53 (28)   Left Tackle: 4.98 (27)   Mid/Guard: 4.19 (9)   Right Tackle: 3.86 (9)   Right End: 2.18 (3)

Two years into Harold Landry's career, the Titans haven't really gotten a stellar season yet. He has gotten a fair amount of sacks and (especially) hurries, but he hasn't been a great edge-setter and certainly hasn't yet lived up to the talk that he might have been the steal of the 2018 draft. Lotta ballgame left, of course, but Tennessee would love to see him blossom into a true No. 1 edge rusher right about now. ◗ On the other edge the Titans appear set to rotate Kamalei Correa on run downs with Vic Beasley on pass downs. That seems to be a good use of the skill sets of each. Beasley will never be the player NFL media thought he might be after his rookie season, but it's not like the Dan Quinn Falcons ran some sort of mastermind defense that got him free looks either. Fourteen of Beasley's 24 pressures and 5.0 of his 7.0 sacks came after Raheem Morris took over defensive play calls in Week 9. Reggie Gilbert is a solid backup edge who should get some looks mixed in as well. ◗ Rashaan Evans can really hit, but he struggled in coverage last year. The Titans finished below-average in DVOA allowed to both tight ends and running backs. Jayon Brown was better as a pass defender, and even more successful in 2018 when he had fewer coverage snaps defending wideouts. (Don't let the Saints scheme Michael Thomas as the man Brown is covering.) It should be a priority going forward for the Titans to find a replacement for Evans on passing downs, whether that's 2019 sixth-rounder David Long Jr. or someone off the board entirely. ◗ Next to Jeffery Simmons, DaQuan Jones is a good run-stuffer with enough power to occasionally find pass pressure, and the Titans have replaced Austin Johnson with Jack Crawford, who is coming off a down year in Atlanta after a six-sack 2018. The other competition for a spot is fifth-rounder Larell Murchison (North Carolina State), who was a stout run defender for the Wolfpack despite his small size (6-foot-2, 297 pounds). That could get Murchison some snaps early on, but he needs to develop some better pass-rush ability to ever be more than that.

Defensive Secondary

Secondary	Age	Pos	G	Snaps	Plays	TmPct	Rk	Stop	Dfts	BTkl	Runs	St%	Rk	RuYd	Rk	Tgts	Tgt%	Rk	Dist	Suc%	Rk	AdjYd	Rk	PD	Int
												vs. Run							vs. Pass						
Logan Ryan*	29	CB	16	1114	131	15.5%	1	67	23	13	39	64%	17	3.7	11	83	19.1%	53	12.4	53%	40	7.9	51	18	4
Kevin Byard	27	FS	16	1114	88	10.4%	22	24	15	6	36	28%	59	9.9	62	30	6.9%	47	10.9	47%	52	8.9	54	9	5
Kenny Vaccaro	29	SS	16	1078	84	9.9%	27	37	15	10	39	46%	27	5.7	24	28	6.7%	50	10.7	50%	42	8.3	47	5	1
Tramaine Brock*	32	CB	14	761	55	7.1%	62	25	11	14	15	47%	40	4.9	26	47	16.2%	68	9.9	49%	58	8.3	59	5	0
Malcolm Butler	30	CB	9	590	41	8.6%	82	18	10	3	6	67%	11	2.8	4	40	17.4%	64	15.6	50%	54	7.9	50	9	2
Adoree' Jackson	25	CB	11	583	51	8.8%	67	27	8	8	9	78%	5	3.0	7	41	18.1%	60	12.2	51%	52	7.3	39	6	0
Amani Hooker	22	FS	16	337	13	1.5%	--	4	4	4	1	0%	--	20.0	--	11	8.4%	--	7.1	55%	--	4.4	--	0	0
LeShaun Sims*	27	CB	14	336	31	4.2%	--	11	0	7	12	33%	--	5.3	--	26	19.9%	--	14.2	54%	--	7.0	--	2	0
Tye Smith	27	CB	9	212	23	4.8%	--	5	4	0	3	33%	--	8.0	--	16	19.4%	--	12.6	38%	--	8.0	--	0	0
Johnathan Joseph	36	CB	14	632	64	9.0%	36	28	11	10	5	40%	50	10.0	76	70	26.7%	2	13.5	50%	57	8.6	62	13	1

Year	Pass D Rank	vs. #1 WR	Rk	vs. #2 WR	Rk	vs. Other WR	Rk	WR Wide	Rk	WR Slot	Rk	vs. TE	Rk	vs. RB	Rk
2017	24	-8.1%	11	29.2%	28	-0.3%	17	0.1%	18	9.5%	18	10.1%	24	28.0%	32
2018	21	5.8%	20	26.1%	30	5.3%	21	8.5%	26	19.2%	26	-10.6%	11	-31.6%	2
2019	21	19.5%	29	-39.4%	2	25.3%	30	9.5%	24	-0.9%	9	4.4%	19	12.1%	23

It has become popular to crap on Malcolm Butler's contract and he has created some high-profile blowups in both 2018 and 2019 (including Week 3's outing against the Jaguars where he allowed 121 yards as the main coverage player and was posterized by DJ Chark), but considering he has mostly been an outside corner the last two years, he's probably not quite as bad as that perception. The real issue for the Titans last year was the broken wrist that cost him half a season, because their backup corner options were not great. ◖ With depth an issue, the Titans added long-time Texans corner Johnathan Joseph to the cornerback room. Joseph has lost three steps at this point, but he's still an incredibly smart zone corner who can make some big plays when properly spotted. It's just hard to leave him on an island all game. ◖ LSU corner Kristian Fulton was regarded as a steal by several draftniks after sliding into the second round. He can play press man, and he was a big difference-maker for the Tigers against Alabama and Clemson last season as he strangled Jerry Jeudy, Henry Ruggs, and Tee Higgins. He clearly has the talent to start sooner rather than later. ◖ One of the big keys to Tennessee's upset of the Chiefs in Arrowhead in Week 10 was Adoree' Jackson giving them someone who could at least hang with Tyreek Hill's speed. Hill got one 39-yarder in man coverage against Jackson, but in sum the Chiefs threw at Jackson 14 times and got just 91 yards out of it. Jackson is two years from free agency, but if he's healthy when he gets there, he'll be a very rich man. ◖ Speaking of very rich men, Kevin Byard continues to be an impact safety against both the run and the pass, and his versatility is an important factor in most of the Titans' coverage disguises because he can hang in the box, at slot corner, or at his nominal role at free safety. ◖ Kenny Vaccaro has essentially become a journeyman at this point but had a nice season as a surprise pass-rusher (do this more, Vrabel!) and stayed relatively healthy for the first time since 2015. Amani Hooker, who had some big fans in the draft community, had a decent year as the third safety and the odds of him getting some more snaps due to a nagging Vaccaro injury are fairly high.

Special Teams

Year	DVOA	Rank	FG/XP	Rank	Net Kick	Rank	Kick Ret	Rank	Net Punt	Rank	Punt Ret	Rank	Hidden	Rank
2017	1.6%	13	0.6	15	2.9	12	0.8	11	3.0	16	0.7	13	-5.8	22
2018	0.8%	13	-1.8	21	-7.2	31	13.6	1	2.3	15	-2.8	23	-5.6	23
2019	-3.5%	29	-14.9	32	-2.9	23	-2.9	27	5.1	8	-1.7	19	6.3	6

Over the past three years, our metrics have Brett Kern's punts adding 24.2 points of gross estimated field-position value. Only Washington's Tress Way is anywhere near that amount. Kern deservedly signed a three-year extension in 2019 and there has been no sign of decline at age 34. ◖ Woe to all who kicked for the Titans in 2019, as a big part of their increase in fourth-down attempts was a lack of faith in their kickers. Ryan Succop made just one of six tries before heading to IR with a knee injury, and he was released after the season. Incumbent Greg Joseph, the fourth kicker the Titans settled on last year, attempted no field goals in two regular-season games with the team, though he did make one in the playoffs. He'll compete for the job with UDFA rookie Tucker McCann, who definitely sounds like he should have been a first-round MLB pick. McCann also spent some time punting at Missouri during his senior season. Most players who appeal to our inner Marie Kondo roster optimist side don't wind up doing well enough at one of those things to be worth it, but, hey, versatility helps. ◖ The Titans don't have anyone on the roster with strong return numbers after losing Darius Jennings to the Chargers. Kalif Raymond was below average last year on kickoffs while Adam Humphries was below average on punt returns. Adoree' Jackson has plus-plus breakaway speed but is mostly a "break glass in case of emergency" returner.

Washington Redskins

2019 Record: 3-13	**Total DVOA:** -25.6% (30th)	**2020 Mean Projection:** 6.0 wins	**On the Clock (0-4):** 29%
Pythagorean Wins: 3.7 (31st)	**Offense:** -20.4% (30th)	**Postseason Odds:** 17.2%	**Mediocrity (5-7):** 45%
Snap-Weighted Age: 26.0 (27th)	**Defense:** 7.9% (24th)	**Super Bowl Odds:** 0.7%	**Playoff Contender (8-10):** 22%
Average Opponent: 0.2% (16th)	**Special Teams:** 2.7% (7th)	**Proj. Avg. Opponent:** 0.1% (13rd)	**Super Bowl Contender (11+):** 5%

2019: Dwayne Haskins stumbles from team savior to scapegoat.

2020: Can Haskins transform from goat to GOAT (or at least capable NFL starter)?

They haven't reached the comedy-of-error levels of the Bears and Browns, but the Redskins have been mired in an extended quarterback search since their incredible three-decade run from the mid-'60s to the mid-'90s with Pro Bowl passers Sonny Jurgensen, Billy Kilmer, Joe Theismann, and Mark Rypien and very few off-years in between. In the 25 years since, several of their quarterbacks sparked optimism. Patrick Ramsey and Jason Campbell were late first-round picks who exhausted almost all of their rookie contracts before the team decided they weren't long-term solutions. Kirk Cousins outlasted his rookie deal by two franchise tags but, in the end, wasn't the answer the Redskins wanted. Fellow 2012 draft pick Robert Griffin III may well have been that player in an alternate reality where he didn't tear his ACL and LCL. His rookie season to that point was phenomenal. His 16.6% passing DVOA ranked seventh among the 38 quarterbacks who threw 200 or more passes that season. And that says nothing of his incredible productivity as a rusher.

If Dwayne Haskins sparked optimism, it was short-lived. The team certainly celebrated when he fell to them at the 15th overall pick in the 2019 draft. Reportedly their guy, Haskins looked like an exceptional relative value to the sixth pick of their division rival Giants, Daniel Jones, whom many scouts did not consider a first-round talent. But it was a disconcerting sign that Haskins failed to beat out journeyman quarterback Case Keenum to start the season in an era of football when many top quarterback prospects play and even succeed immediately in the NFL. And Haskins' performance when he finally did find the field was more alarming. He offset the 12 completions he threw in his first two appearances in Weeks 4 and 8 with about as many combined interceptions (four) and sacks (four). He finally threw a touchdown in his second start in Week 11, but that game also started a streak of four starts with a completion percentage below 60%. By the end of the season, Haskins had compiled a -42.0% passing DVOA that landed him in the company of the worst rookie starters in recent league history (Table 1).

Table 1. Worst Passing DVOA, Rookies, 2008-2019

Player	Year	Team	DVOA
Jared Goff	2016	LAR	-74.8%
Josh Rosen	2018	ARI	-53.7%
Jimmy Clausen	2010	CAR	-48.0%
Blaine Gabbert	2011	JAX	-46.5%
Dwayne Haskins	**2019**	**WAS**	**-42.0%**
Blake Bortles	2014	JAX	-40.7%
Matthew Stafford	2009	DET	-36.6%
Josh Allen	2018	BUF	-35.9%
DeShone Kizer	2017	CLE	-34.5%
Christian Ponder	2011	MIN	-31.5%

Minimum 5 games started

Jared Goff and Matthew Stafford are the slow career starters that every bad rookie quarterback hangs his hopes on, but they look like the two exceptions on a list full of many more infamous busts. The Cardinals, Browns, and Panthers replaced highly drafted rookie starters Josh Rosen, DeShone Kizer, and Jimmy Clausen with top overall picks Kyler Murray, Baker Mayfield, and Cam Newton the very next year. Blaine Gabbert and Christian Ponder lasted longer, but the Jaguars and Vikings were the last ones to know that their young quarterbacks couldn't cut it in the NFL. Blake Bortles and Josh Allen teased and continue to tease greater potential, but any optimism for them stemmed and stems from their stronger rushing efficiency. Haskins may be mobile within the pocket, but he is a traditional pocket passer.

Even a Redskins front-office employee with rose-colored glasses would not have wanted Haskins' career to start the way that it did. And I'm sure many of them considered whether the team should follow the blueprint the Cardinals, Browns, and Panthers provided in recent seasons. With the second pick

Right before publication of this year's Almanac, Washington announced it will finally retire the Redskins team name and logo. As full supporters of a name change, Football Outsiders hoped to include the new name throughout this book. Unfortunately, the timing of publication didn't make that possible, and rather than potentially add confusion by referring to the team by a new name that hadn't been set in stone, we decided to call the team its old name for one last year.

2020 Redskins Schedule

Week	Opp.	Week	Opp.	Week	Opp.
1	PHI	7	DAL	13	at PIT
2	at ARI	8	BYE	14	at SF
3	at CLE	9	NYG	15	SEA
4	BAL	10	at DET	16	CAR
5	LAR	11	CIN	17	at PHI
6	at NYG	12	at DAL (Thu.)		

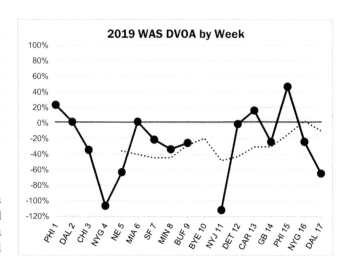

2019 WAS DVOA by Week

earned in part because of Haskins' poor play, the Redskins could easily have taken a mulligan at the position in 2020 and drafted another new franchise quarterback in Tua Tagovailoa or Justin Herbert. Instead, they stuck with Haskins and will have to hope that he can defy long apparent odds.

Football Outsiders isn't optimistic that they can do so. We project the Redskins to have the worst overall DVOA in 2020 and the second-fewest mean wins. But that projection is weighted down by an offensive projection that isn't just the worst in football, but is a negative outlier. And I believe that projection and Haskins' poor rookie statistics paint a bleaker picture of his and the Redskins' chances to quickly become competitive than the reality of those chances.

In true Outsiders' fashion, that dissonance springs from sample-size considerations. Haskins only made seven starts as a rookie, tied with Goff for the fewest among the quarterbacks in Table 1. Stafford made 10 starts in his rookie season, tied for the second-fewest. Every player in that bottom 10 had a bad rookie season, but there is a surprisingly big difference between poor passing efficiency over seven to 10 career starts and over 13 to 15 career starts. To wit, a chart of Haskins' cumulative passing DVOA by career start illustrates that his upward trajectory of performance as a rookie has him comfortably within the bounds of the cumulative passing DVOA

of the quarterbacks who entered football since 2008 and went on to make two or more Pro Bowls (Figure 1).

(A quick aside: I used a cutoff of two or more Pro Bowls as a shorthand to summarily capture the kind of quarterback one would expect a team to believe in as a franchise player. Since 2008, that chosen benchmark includes Patrick Mahomes, Deshaun Watson, Dak Prescott, Derek Carr, Andrew Luck, Russell Wilson, Andy Dalton, Matt Ryan, Cousins, Newton, and Goff. We also granted an exception to include Stafford—who has just one Pro Bowl—based on the nearly $100-million guaranteed second contract the Lions gave him in 2017. Before you dismiss this argument because of his presence on Table 1, keep reading to discover that Stafford's own career trajectory perfectly illustrates Haskins' upside.)

Goff and Stafford were not better performers as rookies than Rosen, Gabbert, Bortles, and Kizer. But they produced their dismal rookie efficiencies over several fewer games. By the time Goff and Stafford reached the 13 starts the least prolific of that latter quartet started in their rookie seasons, they had

Figure 1

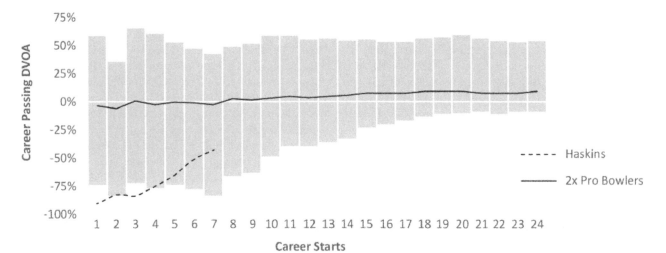

Dwayne Haskins' Career Passing DVOA Trajectory

improved to -33.0% and -28.6% cumulative career DVOA, respectively. By 15 starts, they were up to -22.9% and -19.2% cumulative DVOA. Those rates had Goff and Stafford about as close to Andrew Luck (-5.1%) as they were to the bottom 10 rookies. By 24 career starts, Goff and Stafford had caught up to several other eventual two-time Pro Bowlers with -3.4% and -9.1% career DVOA.

Haskins has work to do to realize a career rebound similar to those of Goff and Stafford, but at least so far, he has followed their leads. Haskins put himself in a big hole with poor performances in relief in Weeks 4 and 8 and in his first start in Week 9 that added up to a -91.1% DVOA. But since then, his cumulative DVOA consistently improved as Haskins turned in single-game passing DVOA rates of -72.6%, -88.4%, -42.7%, -13.8%, 43.7%, and 44.7% in order. His combined 44.0% DVOA over his last two starts before an ankle injury ended his season one week early was fifth-best of the quarterbacks who started in Weeks 15 and 16, trailing just Lamar Jackson (77.0%), Drew Brees (68.1%), Mahomes (54.0%), and Jones (47.1%).

It should strike you as silly to compare Haskins to MVPs like Jackson, Brees, and Mahomes based on their respective performances over just two weeks. But what I want to impress is that it is similarly misguided to draw conclusions after half of a season. Most quarterbacks who have slow starts to their careers fail—which is why our projections for the Redskins offense are as bad as they are—but some of them with similar trajectories over similar small samples do not. If the team likes what they see from Haskins' development beyond his performances in his handful of career games, then they are justified in their decision to stick with him for his sophomore season.

Quarterback play is a keystone for the competitiveness of most teams, but that seems especially true for a young Redskins team whose roster is more talented than it was productive in 2019. That starts on the offensive line, which finished 31st in football with a 9.8% adjusted sack rate. If that finish seems odd for a line anchored by three-time Pro Bowlers Brandon Scherff and Donald Penn, that's because it is. The 2019 Redskins exemplified the reality that quarterbacks are often more responsible for sacks than their pass protectors. Haskins suffered a 12.7% adjusted sack rate that was twice as bad as veteran teammate Keenum's 6.3% rate. If Haskins improves in 2020, then the line's numbers should as well.

At the skill positions, sophomore receiver Terry McLaurin is one of the most valuable assets in football. He dramatically overachieved on his third-round draft status last year with an 18.9% DVOA, the second best of rookie receivers with 50 or more targets behind just A.J. Brown (26.2%). And while the other incumbent receivers expected to see big 2020 target shares had below-average DVOA rates last season, much of their inefficiency can be attributed to their quarterbacks as well. When targeted with an accurate pass, Kelvin Harmon had just two drops against 30 receptions, good for a strong 6.3% drop rate that was better than that of his more-lauded teammate McLaurin. Steven Sims dropped an untenable five of his 39 catchable targets but did lead the team and finished in the highest quartile of regularly targeted wide receivers in

the league with 5.1 average yards after the catch.

Sims did his best work as a rookie as a kick returner, where he trailed only Cordarrelle Patterson with 819 return yards that he accumulated on an excellent 25.6 yards per return. But Sims' ability to make players miss on special teams foretells a chance that he could contribute explosive plays on offense. It is a career path a number of eventual star receivers including Tyreek Hill and Steve Smith have followed. As an undrafted free agent, Sims does not share their pedigree. But former and current players around the team such as Clinton Portis and McLaurin have expressed optimism for such a skills translation, the former on his *26 Minutes* podcast and the latter in an interview with Redskins.com editor Kyle Stackpole in which he said that Sims made a "big jump" this offseason and that "you can tell his feet are so clean."

If Portis and McLaurin prove correct, then Sims would address a major shortcoming of last year's team. Haskins performed particularly poorly on deep passes thrown 16 or more yards in the air with a -74.8% DVOA. No other quarterback finished with a negative DVOA on 30 or more such attempts.

Players attached to the organization may not be the most trustworthy scouts, but if Harmon and Sims fail to become plus contributors, 2020 draft and post-draft additions Antonio Gandy-Golden and Thaddeus Moss still might. At 6-foot-4 and 223 pounds and 6-foot-2 and 250 pounds, Gandy-Golden and Moss add size that could help the team in the red zone to complement a No. 1 receiver in McLaurin who excels because of his route-running.

The Redskins have more uncertainty at running back than at receiver but are similarly talented at the position. Behind 35-year-old veteran Adrian Peterson—who is not a lock to make the 2020 roster—Derrius Guice and Bryce Love offer immense potential with substantial risk. More productive in college than even their second- and fourth-round draft pedigrees would suggest, both players have suffered major knee injuries in recent years that put their NFL futures in doubt. In limited work between knee injuries in 2019, Guice did tease the potential that made him a Day 2 draft pick in the first place. His 15.7% rushing DVOA was much better than Peterson's -4.1% rate, and his 32.7% broken tackle rate would have placed him first among running backs with 100 or more touches if he had the touch volume to qualify himself. But even if Guice and Love can't contribute in 2020, the team's additions of third-round rookie Antonio Gibson and free-agent receiving back J.D. McKissic offer versatility that can create defensive mismatches and importantly limit Peterson's offensive plays to the carries between the tackles he is best suited to handle.

New head coach Ron Rivera may not be a transformer of Haskins' short-term prospects the way Sean McVay was for Goff, but with his own strengths, Rivera could author a similar overall team renaissance as the Rams enjoyed in 2017. Prior to their injury-related collapses the last two seasons, Rivera's Panthers had finished in the upper half of teams in defensive DVOA for six straight seasons. And despite a bottom-10 DVOA finish in 2019, the Redskins defense is rich with talent so that Rivera and defensive coordinator Jack Del Rio have a chance to find immediate success.

The Redskins' defensive talent is concentrated in the defensive line. That unit already stood out in 2019 with a No. 4 adjusted sack rate of 8.3% and four players—Matt Ioannidis, Ryan Kerrigan, Jonathan Allen, and Montez Sweat—who finished with 19 or more pass pressures, a distinction shared by just 12 other teams and bested by just three teams. That foursome is back with the team in 2020 and joined by No. 2 overall pick Chase Young, whose 98.3% SackSEER rating comfortably leads this year's class and offers him comps of great pass-rushers of past and present such as Dwight Freeney and Myles Garrett. The unit's talent and youth make the Washington defense one of the best bets to be 2020's version of last year's 49ers and Buccaneers, whose defenses made dramatic jumps from bottom-10 to top-five efficiencies in just one year.

Our more conservative, middle-of-the-pack defensive projection reflects the holes the Redskins defense has in the second and third levels. Linebacker Jon Bostic was a great story in 2019, ascending from his release from the Steelers following their drafting of Devin Bush to start and call plays for the Redskins and eventually lead them with a career-high 105 tackles. But Bostic's age of 29 and 21.5% broken tackle rate likely make him a short-term solution. Fifth-round sophomore Cole Holcomb (14.7% broken tackle rate) and former first-round pick Reuben Foster offer greater upside but also have greater risk, in particular Foster, whose own devastating knee injury prior to the 2019 season makes him even less likely to play in 2020 than Guice and Love and threatens his NFL career.

The team's secondary is lacking in even that long-shot upside. Former first-team All-Pro safety Landon Collins buoys the team's run defense with continued excellent tackling—he has a stellar 14.7% broken tackle rate since Sports Info Solutions started charting the stat in 2015. But no one on the team provides equivalent plus production in coverage. Former expensive free-agent addition Josh Norman declined precipitously in recent seasons, culminating in a 38% coverage success rate in 2019 that was the second worst of 89 qualified cornerbacks. The team released him this offseason. Presumed 2020 starters Ronald Darby (48%), Fabian Moreau (44%), and Kendall Fuller (35%) ranged from not much better to even

worse in 2019, all three finishing with rates that landed them in the bottom third of qualified corners (or would have, if they had enough targets to qualify). And without a cornerback draft pick from the first six rounds in either of the last two years, the Redskins have limited options to replace any of those players who fail to bounce back in 2020.

With possible major holes on both sides of the ball, it's easy to see how the Redskins project so poorly. However, potential dramatic improvements at quarterback and for an already effective defensive front could hide some of those weaknesses and unlock the untapped potential of players with more talent than production so far in their careers. The 2020 Redskins aren't like the 2017 Browns, 2018 Bills, and 2019 Dolphins who shared their distinction of a last-place DVOA projection and went on to win just 11 of 48 combined games. They're more like the 2014 Rams and 2019 49ers, teams that had invested numerous first-round picks in the defensive front and were waiting for the talent to gel. Sometimes, like the 2014 Rams, those teams go 6-10. Sometimes, like last year's 49ers, those teams take dramatic leaps forward. If the Redskins fall in that latter camp, they could compete for a playoff berth this season.

Washington fans have been burned by hope before. And more likely than not, Haskins will sabotage the team's 2020 season with poor play commensurate with his rookie passing inefficiency, no matter its sample size and trajectory. But whatever the results, the Redskins seem to have turned a corner with their process. It may not be Haskins, but some quarterback should be able to lead the Redskins' young foundation to future relevance. In the worst-case scenario of his continued poor play, Haskins may even prove to be the vanguard of that new franchise quarterback, losing enough games to earn the Redskins another top pick like Rosen, Kizer, and Clausen did for their teams before him. Rivera could likely stomach one more year of losing if it landed him a top quarterback prospect like he once drafted in Newton. And with potential generational talents such as Trevor Lawrence and Trey Lance poised to light up whatever version of college football we get this fall, I think Redskins fans could do the same.

Scott Spratt

2019 Redskins Stats by Week

Wk	vs.	W-L	PF	PA	YDF	YDA	TO	Total	Off	Def	ST
1	at PHI	L	27	32	398	436	0	23%	49%	27%	2%
2	DAL	L	21	31	255	474	+1	2%	16%	19%	4%
3	CHI	L	15	31	356	298	-4	-34%	-20%	15%	1%
4	at NYG	L	3	24	176	389	0	-106%	-119%	-3%	9%
5	NE	L	7	33	223	442	-1	-63%	-49%	13%	0%
6	at MIA	W	17	16	311	271	+2	2%	-15%	-26%	-9%
7	SF	L	0	9	154	283	0	-21%	-29%	-20%	-12%
8	at MIN	L	9	19	216	434	-1	-33%	-31%	10%	7%
9	at BUF	L	9	24	243	268	0	-25%	-18%	-5%	-12%
10	BYE										
11	NYJ	L	17	34	225	400	+1	-112%	-65%	43%	-4%
12	DET	W	19	16	230	364	+2	-1%	-59%	-29%	29%
13	at CAR	W	29	21	362	278	+2	16%	6%	-12%	-2%
14	at GB	L	15	20	262	341	0	-24%	-18%	8%	1%
15	PHI	L	27	37	352	415	0	47%	39%	10%	18%
16	NYG	L	35	41	361	552	0	-24%	19%	50%	7%
17	at DAL	L	16	47	271	517	-1	-65%	-47%	21%	3%

Trends and Splits

	Offense	Rank	Defense	Rank
Total DVOA	-20.4%	30	7.9%	24
Unadjusted VOA	-18.4%	29	7.3%	22
Weighted Trend	-20.6%	31	6.9%	23
Variance	18.0%	32	5.1%	11
Average Opponent	-1.3%	9	-0.7%	21
Passing	-17.2%	29	15.9%	24
Rushing	-12.7%	25	-0.5%	24
First Down	-27.0%	32	-3.7%	12
Second Down	8.6%	8	4.8%	22
Third Down	-55.3%	32	33.5%	31
First Half	-23.1%	31	1.9%	18
Second Half	-17.5%	27	13.9%	29
Red Zone	-20.2%	26	7.6%	21
Late and Close	-21.1%	27	10.0%	27

Five-Year Performance

Year	W-L	Pyth W	Est W	PF	PA	TO	Total	Rk	Off	Rk	Def	Rk	ST	Rk	Off AGL	Rk	Def AGL	Rk	Off Age	Rk	Def Age	Rk	ST Age	Rk
2015	9-7	8.2	7.8	388	379	+5	-0.3%	15	1.9%	12	5.4%	21	3.2%	6	60.6	29	64.9	31	25.9	26	27.1	7	26.0	17
2016	8-7-1	8.3	9.7	396	383	0	9.5%	9	15.8%	5	6.8%	25	0.4%	13	27.8	10	70.2	31	27.1	8	27.4	4	26.1	15
2017	7-9	6.8	7.2	342	388	-4	-0.6%	16	-3.1%	20	-4.9%	11	-2.4%	22	69.4	31	69.3	31	27.1	15	26.3	16	25.3	26
2018	7-9	5.7	6.0	281	359	+7	-18.6%	29	-19.5%	28	1.7%	20	2.5%	8	86.6	31	9.1	1	28.4	2	26.2	19	25.1	32
2019	3-13	3.7	4.5	266	435	+1	-25.6%	30	-20.4%	30	7.9%	24	2.7%	7	81.9	32	49.1	28	27.1	10	25.5	28	25.1	30

2019 Performance Based on Most Common Personnel Groups

WAS Offense					WAS Offense vs. Opponents						WAS Defense					WAS Defense vs. Opponents			
Pers	Freq	Yds	DVOA	Run%	Pers	Freq	Yds	DVOA	Run%		Pers	Freq	Yds	DVOA		Pers	Freq	Yds	DVOA
11	69%	4.9	-16.1%	25%	Base	22%	5.4	-19.3%	68%		Base	34%	5.1	-1.9%		11	56%	6.3	18.3%
12	10%	6.3	-7.9%	58%	Nickel	53%	5.1	-12.4%	32%		Nickel	59%	6.2	16.7%		12	22%	5.6	2.5%
612	4%	5.7	5.6%	97%	Dime+	22%	4.9	-18.6%	14%		Dime+	6%	7.0	-2.1%		21	10%	5.4	-10.5%
611	3%	6.9	7.3%	70%	Goal Line	2%	1.2	-10.6%	71%		Goal Line	1%	-0.3	-45.0%		13	6%	4.6	-2.2%
10	3%	4.6	-50.6%	31%	Big	1%	4.5	-13.9%	100%		Big	1%	1.8	-53.1%		22	2%	2.9	-21.6%

Strategic Tendencies

Run/Pass		Rk	Formation		Rk	Pass Rush		Rk	Secondary		Rk	Strategy		Rk
Runs, first half	41%	6	Form: Single Back	86%	9	Rush 3	18.8%	4	4 DB	34%	4	Play Action	22%	22
Runs, first down	56%	6	Form: Empty Back	5%	25	Rush 4	58.6%	25	5 DB	59%	16	Offensive Motion	45%	9
Runs, second-long	28%	16	Form: Multi Back	9%	21	Rush 5	17.5%	22	6+ DB	6%	19	Avg Box (Off)	6.63	10
Runs, power sit.	41%	32	Pers: 3+ WR	74%	4	Rush 6+	5.0%	17	Man Coverage	34%	13	Avg Box (Def)	6.68	10
Runs, behind 2H	30%	14	Pers: 2+ TE/6+ OL	25%	20	Edge Rusher Sacks	40.2%	29	CB by Sides	78%	16	Offensive Pace	33.03	31
Pass, ahead 2H	39%	30	Pers: 6+ OL	13%	4	Interior DL Sacks	48.9%	2	S/CB Cover Ratio	28%	11	Defensive Pace	30.50	14
Run-Pass Options	5%	15	Shotgun/Pistol	62%	20	Second Level Sacks	10.9%	27	DB Blitz	7%	23	Go for it on 4th	1.37	18

As befits Adrian Peterson's reputation for preferring standard handoffs, Washington had the league's biggest negative gap between DVOA on runs from shotgun (-28.8%, 3.4 yards per carry) and DVOA on runs from under center (-7.2%, 4.7 yards per carry). Furthermore, there was a similar gap in the passing game, where Washington had -23.5% DVOA and 4.8 net yards per pass from shotgun but 3.6% DVOA and 8.2 net yards per pass with the quarterback under center. ◆ Washington was the only defense in the league that allowed fewer yards per play to play-action passes (5.7) compared to other pass plays (7.0). ◆ Washington's defense led the league with 15 coverage sacks; no other defense had more than 11. Overall, a league-leading 41% of Washington sacks were what we might call "non-pressure sacks," a combination of sacks marked coverage sack or failed scramble. ◆ Washington had the largest gap between the average play made by the free safety (Monte Nicholson, 14.4 yards) and the average play made by the strong safety (Landon Collins, 6.1 yards). Carolina, if you're curious, was roughly league average in this metric. ◆ The listed Aggressiveness Index number belongs to Bill Callahan; Jay Gruden had an AI of 0.00 in his five games, as all of Washington's fourth-down attempts through Week 5 came while losing in the second half by double digits.

Passing

Player	DYAR	DVOA	Plays	NtYds	Avg	YAC	C%	TD	Int
C.Keenum*	51	-8.1%	260	1565	6.0	5.0	65.3%	11	5
D.Haskins	-443	-42.0%	232	1148	4.9	5.2	58.9%	7	7
C.McCoy*	-114	-73.8%	33	80	2.4	1.9	66.7%	0	1
K.Allen	-395	-22.4%	536	2916	5.4	5.4	62.2%	17	16

Rushing

Player	DYAR	DVOA	Plays	Yds	Avg	TD	Fum	Suc
A.Peterson	39	-4.1%	211	900	4.3	5	2	47%
D.Guice	42	15.7%	42	245	5.8	2	0	50%
C.Thompson*	3	-6.4%	37	138	3.7	0	0	38%
W.Smallwood*	-4	-13.2%	22	81	3.7	0	0	23%
D.Haskins	-8	-20.9%	17	98	5.8	0	2	-
S.Sims	28	29.4%	9	85	9.4	1	0	-
C.Keenum*	-12	-36.8%	6	16	2.7	1	2	-
P.Barber	-140	-29.8%	154	470	3.1	7	1	40%
J.McKissic	23	6.5%	38	205	5.4	0	0	47%
K.Allen	4	-9.0%	25	108	4.3	2	1	-

Receiving

Player	DYAR	DVOA	Plays	Ctch	Yds	Y/C	YAC	TD	C%
T.McLaurin	237	18.9%	93	58	919	15.8	3.7	7	62%
S.Sims	-53	-24.6%	56	34	310	9.1	5.1	4	61%
T.Quinn	-118	-44.8%	47	26	198	7.6	2.3	1	55%
K.Harmon	33	-2.8%	44	30	365	12.2	3.1	0	68%
P.Richardson*	4	-11.3%	42	28	245	8.8	1.8	2	67%
C.Latimer	45	0.0%	42	24	300	12.5	2.9	2	57%
J.Sprinkle	-21	-15.7%	40	26	241	9.3	3.5	1	65%
V.Davis*	-28	-29.6%	19	10	123	12.3	8.0	1	53%
H.Hentges	4	-2.7%	14	8	103	12.9	5.9	1	57%
L.Thomas	-21	-18.9%	28	16	173	10.8	4.8	1	57%
C.Thompson*	34	-2.1%	58	42	378	9.0	8.0	0	72%
A.Peterson	-1	-14.9%	23	17	142	8.4	9.5	0	74%
W.Smallwood*	6	-5.4%	13	9	64	7.1	5.6	0	69%
D.Guice	29	48.3%	9	7	79	11.3	12.3	1	78%
J.McKissic	12	-8.2%	42	34	233	6.9	7.0	1	81%
P.Barber	17	0.3%	24	16	115	7.2	7.4	1	67%

Offensive Line

Player	Pos	Age	GS	Snaps	Pen	Sk	Pass	Run	Player	Pos	Age	GS	Snaps	Pen	Sk	Pass	Run
Ereck Flowers*	LG	26	16/16	960	5	1.5	13	2	Wes Martin	RG	24	9/5	295	3	0.5	9	1
Donald Penn*	LT	37	16/15	906	11	6.5	21	8	Tony Bergstrom*	C/OT	34	16/6	232	1	1.0	3	0
Morgan Moses	RT	29	16/16	881	11	6.5	15	7	Wes Schweitzer	LG/RG	27	15/7	711	5	2.0	12	6
Chase Roullier	C	27	15/14	851	1	2.5	5	5	Cornelius Lucas	RT	29	16/8	516	0	1.5	6	2
Brandon Scherff	RG	29	11/11	661	9	2.5	8	2									

Year	Yards	ALY	Rank	Power	Rank	Stuff	Rank	2nd Lev	Rank	Open Field	Rank	Sacks	ASR	Rank	Press	Rank	F-Start	Cont.
2017	3.65	3.86	21	55%	27	20%	15	1.04	22	0.45	28	41	7.7%	24	34.9%	27	16	25
2018	4.16	3.96	26	76%	2	23%	28	1.24	19	0.93	13	44	8.5%	24	32.7%	23	24	19
2019	4.36	4.28	18	61%	22	19%	17	1.14	20	0.89	14	50	9.8%	31	30.7%	21	20	29
2019 ALY by direction:			Left End 3.61 (22)			Left Tackle: 4.25 (17)			Mid/Guard: 4.66 (9)			Right Tackle: 4.06 (19)			Right End: 3.93 (20)			

Aforementioned three-time Pro Bowlers Brandon Scherff and Donald Penn weren't equally effective in 2019. Scherff was his usual excellent self. He blew fewer than 2.0% of his attempted blocks according to Sports Info Solutions and earned that third Pro Bowl berth despite missing five games with elbow and shoulder injuries. He'll remain in Washington in 2020 on a franchise tag that pays him $15 million. In contrast, Penn blew 3.4% of his attempted blocks after landing below 2.0% in each of his three previous seasons. The Redskins were comfortable letting the 37-year-old left tackle depart in free agency. He remains unsigned but has indicated he is not ready to retire. ◆ Penn may be a candidate to return to the Redskins this season after the Trent Williams drama culminated in his being traded to the 49ers for draft picks. Williams had made the Pro Bowl every season since 2012 before he sat out all of 2019 because of a dispute he had with the team over possible medical malpractice. Without Williams, the Redskins are left with a pair of right tackles in Cornelius Lucas and Morgan Moses, a 2018 third-round draft pick with just two career starts in Geron Christian, and a 2019 fourth-round draft pick in Saahdiq Charles to potentially start at maybe the most important position on the line. ● Despite an obvious lack of NFL experience as an incoming rookie, Charles did start for his LSU teams the last three seasons. He likely would have been drafted earlier than Day 3 if he hadn't been suspended for six games in 2019 for an unknown-to-the-public disciplinary issue. ● The Redskins helped revive former left tackle Ereck Flowers' career by sliding him to left guard in his one year in Washington in 2019. He excelled in that new role, blowing just 1.6% of his attempted blocks, and earned a new $20-million guaranteed contract from the Dolphins. But unlike at left tackle, the Redskins have a clear path forward at left guard after signing former Falcons lineman Wes Schweitzer. Schweitzer was a bit of a sieve in 2019 as a part-time player but had a miniscule 0.6% blown block rate in 12 starts in 2018.

Defensive Front

Defensive Line	Age	Pos	G	Snaps	Plays	TmPct	Rk	Stop	Dfts	BTkl	Runs	St%	Rk	RuYd	Rk	Sack	Hit	Hur	Dsrpt
					Overall							vs. Run					Pass Rush		
Matt Ioannidis	26	DE	16	839	64	7.2%	11	45	13	7	53	66%	77	2.9	82	8.5	7	29	1
Da'Ron Payne	23	DT	15	766	58	7.0%	17	43	8	3	48	79%	30	2.8	77	2.0	4	10	2
Jonathan Allen	25	DE	15	730	68	8.2%	9	44	16	3	56	59%	91	4.0	97	6.0	3	20	1
Tim Settle	23	DT	15	317	14	1.7%	--	14	3	2	11	100%	--	1.9	--	2.0	3	7	0

Edge Rushers	Age	Pos	G	Snaps	Plays	TmPct	Rk	Stop	Dfts	BTkl	Runs	St%	Rk	RuYd	Rk	Sack	Hit	Hur	Dsrpt
					Overall							vs. Run					Pass Rush		
Montez Sweat	24	OLB	16	729	52	5.9%	31	39	14	5	34	68%	66	3.0	67	7.0	6	19	2
Ryan Kerrigan	32	OLB	12	652	25	3.8%	77	18	11	6	16	56%	81	2.2	33	5.5	7	22	1
Ryan Anderson	26	OLB	16	565	42	4.7%	43	28	10	1	27	70%	57	2.9	59	4.0	8	14	0

Linebackers	Age	Pos	G	Snaps	Plays	TmPct	Rk	Stop	Dfts	BTkl	Runs	St%	Rk	RuYd	Rk	Sack	Hit	Hur	Tgts	Suc%	Rk	AdjYd	Rk	PD	Int
					Overall							vs. Run					Pass Rush				vs. Pass				
Jon Bostic	29	ILB	16	1042	107	12.1%	31	55	17	14	60	55%	64	4.2	57	1.0	5	8	40	45%	49	6.8	41	2	1
Cole Holcomb	24	ILB	16	725	101	11.4%	33	53	12	11	65	63%	31	4.2	56	1.0	1	7	27	37%	58	8.2	58	1	0
Shaun Dion Hamilton	25	ILB	16	392	47	5.3%	--	23	9	5	27	48%	--	3.8	--	1.0	1	4	10	70%	--	5.1	--	2	1
Thomas Davis	37	OLB	16	816	114	14.8%	19	59	11	19	69	58%	47	3.9	38	1.0	0	2	32	56%	18	6.0	32	2	0
Kevin Pierre-Louis	29	ILB	14	215	35	4.8%	--	24	8	2	18	72%	--	2.8	--	0.0	2	10	12	83%	--	3.0	--	3	1

Year	Yards	ALY	Rank	Power	Rank	Stuff	Rank	2nd Level	Rank	Open Field	Rank	Sacks	ASR	Rank	Press	Rank
2017	4.49	4.91	32	74%	27	15%	31	1.23	23	0.71	16	42	8.1%	4	36.7%	1
2018	4.57	4.97	29	76%	28	16%	26	1.37	26	0.71	11	46	7.6%	11	31.3%	12
2019	4.71	4.85	29	64%	16	16%	26	1.22	21	0.95	27	46	8.3%	4	26.1%	29

2019 ALY by direction:	Left End: 4.56 (29)	Left Tackle: 5.38 (32)	Mid/Guard: 4.91 (30)	Right Tackle: 3.94 (11)	Right End: 5.36 (27)

With Jack Del Rio's plan to shift the defensive front from the 3-4 base they've played for the last 10 years to a base 4-3, the Redskins had a question at defensive end even before the team used its second overall pick on pass-rusher Chase Young. Now it appears that two of Matt Ioannidis, Ryan Kerrigan, and Montez Sweat will be demoted to overqualified non-starters in what should nevertheless be one of the best pass-rushing rotations in football. ● At 310 pounds, Ioannidis in particular seems equipped to slide inside the tackles to rush the passer from the interior in obvious passing situations. However, the Redskins will likely not want to rely on rusher-heavy lines in 2020 as often as the division rival Eagles have in recent seasons. Natural defensive tackles Jonathan Allen and Da'Ron Payne were first-round picks by the team in 2017 and 2018 and were excellent pass- and run-defenders, respectively, in 2019. Allen was one of the four Redskins defenders with 19 or more hurries last season, and Payne led the unit with a 79% run stop rate. ● Going from two off-ball linebackers to three only exacerbates the team's weakness at the position. Thomas Davis, a longtime Ron Rivera player in Carolina, and holdover Jon Bostic bring veteran leadership, but their 24.7% and 21.5% respective broken tackle rates from 2019 suggest their best playing days may be behind them. At the very least, Davis should be a capable safety net for presumed weakside starter Cole Holcomb, whose excellent 14.7% broken tackle rate exceeded reasonable expectations for a fifth-round rookie. ● The team's most interesting defensive front dilemma is at strongside linebacker. Former sixth-rounder Shaun Dion Hamilton excelled with a 14.3% broken tackle rate as a sub package player in 2019, but his relatively small stature makes him an odd fit at the position, and his history of serious knee injuries at Alabama may restrict him to a part-time role throughout his NFL career. Instead, the Redskins may try Ryan Anderson in the role. The 2017 second-rounder spent last season as a pass-rushing linebacker and is even less of a natural fit as a 4-3 linebacker. But Anderson is an exceptional athlete whose versatility has spurred myriad contributions as a pass-rusher, special-teamer, and even lead blocker at fullback. One can imagine that the defensive brain trust of Rivera and Del Rio would just want Anderson on the field and could embrace positionless defensive football to make it happen.

Defensive Secondary

Secondary	Age	Pos	G	Snaps	Plays	TmPct	Rk	Stop	Dfts	BTkl	Runs	St%	Rk	RuYd	Rk	Tgts	Tgt%	Rk	Dist	Suc%	Rk	AdjYd	Rk	PD	Int
						Overall						vs. Run							vs. Pass						
Landon Collins	26	SS	15	1070	120	14.4%	4	58	18	14	73	55%	9	4.3	8	48	12.8%	10	9.6	48%	45	6.9	28	4	0
Montae Nicholson*	25	FS	13	886	65	9.0%	52	12	8	13	30	10%	74	14.3	74	23	7.4%	42	10.7	48%	46	5.0	8	4	2
Fabian Moreau	26	CB	12	673	49	7.4%	--	20	11	10	10	20%	--	8.4	--	41	17.3%	--	11.1	44%	--	9.3	--	5	3
Quinton Dunbar*	28	CB	11	620	45	7.4%	80	25	14	1	13	31%	67	8.5	67	54	24.8%	8	11.9	59%	16	6.7	22	8	4
Josh Norman*	33	CB	12	612	46	6.9%	79	14	3	6	11	36%	61	11.9	81	40	18.6%	58	16.9	38%	84	11.1	84	6	1
Jimmy Moreland	25	CB	14	478	46	5.9%	--	14	4	9	13	38%	--	5.3	--	22	13.1%	--	8.8	36%	--	7.2	--	4	0
Ronald Darby	26	CB	11	522	48	9.2%	58	21	7	9	10	50%	34	9.0	69	59	26.2%	4	16.1	47%	62	10.6	82	11	2
Kendall Fuller	25	CB	11	507	51	9.0%	--	19	6	5	21	38%	--	7.3	--	23	12.3%	--	10.5	35%	--	9.0	--	2	0

Year	Pass D Rank	vs. #1 WR	Rk	vs. #2 WR	Rk	vs. Other WR	Rk	WR Wide	Rk	WR Slot	Rk	vs. TE	Rk	vs. RB	Rk
2017	6	-20.1%	5	31.2%	29	-23.0%	4	6.5%	25	-18.0%	4	-6.5%	10	-23.0%	4
2018	11	3.9%	18	-7.2%	10	13.8%	26	17.8%	29	-9.3%	4	-17.4%	6	-6.1%	12
2019	24	-10.5%	9	43.4%	32	12.2%	23	-13.6%	11	34.9%	31	23.6%	31	-3.9%	15

If you're wondering why the Redskins signed Ronald Darby and Kendall Fuller as likely starting corners after their poor 2019 seasons with 48% and 35% coverage success rates, look no further than their uninspiring incumbent options. Since his All-Pro 2015 season with a 62% coverage success rate, Josh Norman steadily declined to 57%, 49%, 54%, and 38% success rates in the four years since. Last year, his 11.1 allowed yards per target was more than double his 5.2-yard rate from 2015. Meanwhile, seventh-round rookie Jimmy Moreland (36%) and midseason pick-up Aaron Colvin (30%) were even worse, and 2018 sixth-round pick Simeon Thomas was suspended in December for violating the league's substance-abuse policy and faces an uncertain future with the team. ● Curiously for a team bereft of quality defensive backs, the Redskins traded their one plus cover corner over a significant target volume from 2019, Quinton Dunbar, to the Seahawks for a fifth-round draft pick in March. That move may have been financially motivated with Dunbar entering the final year of his contract, or it may have been health-motivated since Dunbar ended each of the last two seasons on injured reserve with leg and hamstring issues. ● Montae Nicholson played extensively at free safety in 2019 but was released this offseason after a team tenure mired with its own series of off-the-field incidents. To replace him, the Redskins will likely choose between Sean Davis and Troy Apke. Davis was a three-year starter with the Steelers before a shoulder injury limited him to one game in 2019. That injury likely made him an inexpensive option with a one-year deal that has just $2 million guaranteed. Despite that small number, Davis is the likely starter. Apke was a fourth-round draft pick in 2018 who played sparingly in 2019 except when he filled in for an injured Nicholson in a rain-drenched Week 7 game against the 49ers. Apke was very productive with an interception, pass deflection, and six tackles in that start. Seventh-rounder Kamren Curl out of Arkansas could also be a factor at the position.

Special Teams

Year	DVOA	Rank	FG/XP	Rank	Net Kick	Rank	Kick Ret	Rank	Net Punt	Rank	Punt Ret	Rank	Hidden	Rank
2017	-2.4%	22	-1.6	18	6.9	3	-4.1	28	-7.8	25	-5.5	29	-7.3	25
2018	2.5%	8	9.2	5	2.8	9	-3.0	24	6.1	7	-2.5	20	-1.1	17
2019	2.7%	7	1.2	15	2.5	11	6.8	3	4.8	11	-1.8	20	1.0	17

Steven Sims was the Redskins' breakout special teams player in 2019, leading the league with 32 kickoff returns and putting up an efficient 25.6-yard average on those returns. Most notably, Sims provided one of the highlights of the year: after muffing a kick on the Redskins' 5-yard line—and thereby being unable to recover and take a knee for a touchback—in the team's Week 12 game against the Lions, he picked up the ball, stayed on his feet after an attempted ankle-tackle at the 10-yard line, and then wove through the rest of the Lions' special teams would-be tacklers for a 91-yard score. Sims figures to be the team's primary returner again in 2020 even as he will likely see his workload expand on offense. ● Beyond Sims, the Redskins have and should continue to have a stable and mostly successful special teams unit. Kicker Dustin Hopkins has converted between 81% and 89% of his attempted field goals in each of his five career seasons. Punter Tress Way has bookended his six-year career with league-leading 47.5- and 49.6-yards-per-punt averages, the latter of which landed him a Pro Bowl berth in 2019. Although the team was only 11th in net kickoff and net punt value, Hopkins ranked fourth in gross kickoff value and Way ranked first in gross punt value.

Quarterbacks

On the following pages, we provide the last three years of statistics for the top two quarterbacks on each team's depth chart, as well as a number of other quarterbacks who played significant time in 2019. Each quarterback who is currently on a roster also gets a 2020 projection from our KUBIAK fantasy football projection system, explained further in the Statistical Toolbox at the front of the book.

It is difficult to accurately project statistics for a 162-game baseball season, but it is exponentially more difficult to accurately project statistics for a 16-game football season because of the small size of the data samples involved. With that in mind, we ask that you consider the listed projections not as a prediction of exact numbers, but the mean of a range of possible performances. What's important is not so much the exact number of yards and touchdowns we project, but whether or not we're projecting a given player to improve or decline. Along those same lines, rookie projections will not be as accurate as veteran projections due to lack of data.

Our quarterback projections look a bit different than our projections for the other skill positions. At running back and wide receiver, second-stringers see plenty of action, but, at quarterback, either a player starts or he does not start. We recognize that, when a starting quarterback gets injured in Week 8, you don't want to grab your *Football Outsiders Almanac* to find out if his backup is any good only to find that we've projected that the guy will throw 12 passes this year. Therefore, each year we project all quarterbacks to start all 16 games. If Tom Brady goes down in November, you can look up Blaine Gabbert, divide the stats by 16, and get an idea of what we think he will do in an average week (and then, if you are a Tampa Bay fan, pass out). There are full-season projections for the top two quarterbacks on all 32 depth charts. You'll find projections which incorporate the possibility of injury in the fantasy appendix on page 459.

The first line of each quarterback table contains biographical data—the player's name, height, weight, college, draft position, birth date, and age. Height and weight are the best data we could find; weight, of course, can fluctuate during the offseason. **Age** is very simple: the number of years between the player's birth year and 2020, but birthdate is provided if you want to figure out exact age.

Draft position gives draft year and round, with the overall pick number with which the player was taken in parentheses. In the sample table, it says that Dak Prescott was chosen in the

first round of the 2016 NFL draft, with the 135th overall pick. Undrafted free agents are listed as "FA" with the year they came into the league, even if they were only in training camp or on a practice squad.

To the far right of the first line is the player's Risk variable for fantasy football in 2020, which measures the likelihood of the player hitting his projection. The default rating for each player is Green. As the risk of a player failing to hit his projection rises, he's given a rating of Yellow or, in the worst cases, Red. The Risk variable is not only based on age and injury probability, but how a player's projection compares to his recent performance as well as our confidence (or lack thereof) in his offensive teammates.

Next, we give the last three years of player stats. The majority of these statistics are passing numbers, although the final five columns on the right are the quarterback's rushing statistics.

The first few columns after the year and team the player played for are standard numbers: games and games started (**G/GS**), offensive **Snaps**, pass attempts (**Att**), pass completions (**Cmp**), completion percentage (**C%**), passing yards (**Yds**), passing touchdowns (**TD**). These numbers are official NFL totals and therefore include plays we leave out of our own metrics, such as clock-stopping spikes, and omit plays we include in our metrics, such as sacks and aborted snaps. (Other differences between official stats and Football Outsiders stats are described in the "Statistical Toolbox" introduction at the front of the book.)

The exception among these standard stats is new this year: **CPOE**, or Completion Percentage Over Expectation. The probability of a pass completion is calculated on each play based on numerous factors such as down and distance and location of the pass. There are multiple models of CPOE around the Internet and the numbers in our book come from our model, which removes passes that are marked "Thrown Away," "Batted Down," "Quarterback Hit in Motion," or "Miscommunication." In 2019, Drew Brees' actual completion percentage was 8.5% higher than his expected completion percentage, the best difference in the league. Dwayne Haskins was last at -6.7%.

The column for interceptions contains two numbers, representing the official NFL total for interceptions (**Int**) as well as our own metric for adjusted interceptions (**Adj**). For example, if you look at our sample table, Dak Prescott had 11

Dak Prescott					Height: 6-2		Weight:238		College: Mississippi State			Draft: 2016/4 (135)			Born: 29-Jul-1993			Age: 27			Risk: Green
Year	Tm	G/GS	Snaps	Att	Cmp	C%	CPOE	Yds	TD	INT/Adj	FUM	ASR	NY/P	Rk	DVOA	Rk	DYAR	Rk	Runs	Yds	TD	DVOA	DYAR	QBR
2017	DAL	16/16	1053	490	308	62.9%	1.0%	3324	22	13/17	4	6.4%	6.3	18	-0.2%	17	375	17	57	357	6	46.9%	167	66.7
2018	DAL	16/16	1071	526	356	67.7%	0.9%	3885	22	8/12	12	9.7%	6.1	26	-8.1%	26	112	25	75	305	6	2.0%	45	57.8
2019	DAL	16/16	1124	596	388	65.1%	1.2%	4902	30	11/17	6	4.3%	7.7	3	27.1%	6	1541	1	52	277	3	15.6%	71	70.2
2020	DAL			573	376	65.7%		4670	27	10	9		7.3		14.5%				57	279	4	30.0%		

| 2018: | 50% Short | 35% Mid | 8% Deep | 7% Bomb | aDOT: 7.6 (26) | YAC: 5.3 (18) | ALEX: -1.0 | 2019: | 39% Short | 41% Mid | 12% Deep | 7% Bomb | aDOT: 9.7 (6) | YAC: 4.8 (29) | ALEX: 2.3 |

interceptions and 17 adjusted interceptions in 2019. Adjusted interceptions use game charting data to add dropped interceptions, plays where a defender most likely would have had an interception but couldn't hold onto the ball. Then we remove Hail Mary passes and interceptions thrown on fourth down when losing in the final two minutes of the game. We also remove "tipped interceptions," when a perfectly catchable ball deflected off the receiver's hands or chest and into the arms of a defender.

Overall, adjusted interception rate is higher than standard interception rate, so most quarterbacks will have more adjusted interceptions than standard interceptions. On average, a quarterback will have one additional adjusted interception for every 120 pass attempts. Once this difference is accounted for, adjusted interceptions are a better predictor of next year's interception total than standard interceptions.

The next column is fumbles (**FUM**), which adds together all fumbles by this player, whether turned over to the defense or recovered by the offense (explained in the essay "Pregame Show"). Even though this fumble total is listed among the passing numbers, it includes all fumbles, including those on sacks, aborted snaps, and rushing attempts. By listing fumbles and interceptions next to one another, we're giving readers a general idea of how many total turnovers the player was responsible for.

Next comes Adjusted Sack Rate (**ASR**). This is the same statistic you'll find in the team chapters, only here it is specific to the individual quarterback. It represents sacks plus intentional grounding calls per pass play (total pass plays = pass attempts + sacks) adjusted based on down, distance, and strength of schedule. For reference, the NFL average was 6.7% in 2017, 7.1% in 2018, and 7.0% in 2019.

The next two columns are Net Yards per Pass (**NY/P**), a standard stat but a particularly good one, and the player's rank (**Rk**) in Net Yards per Pass for that season. Net Yards per Pass consists of passing yards minus yards lost on sacks, divided by total pass plays.

The four columns remaining in passing stats give our advanced metrics: **DVOA** (Defense-Adjusted Value Over Average) and **DYAR** (Defense-Adjusted Yards Above Replacement), along with the player's rank in both. These metrics compare each quarterback's passing performance to league-average or replacement-level baselines based on the game situations that quarterback faced. DVOA and DYAR are also adjusted based on the opposing defense. The methods used to compute these numbers are described in detail in the "Statistical Toolbox" introduction at the front of the book. The important distinctions between them is that DVOA is a rate statistic, while DYAR is a cumulative statistic. Thus, a higher DVOA means more value per pass play, while a higher DYAR means more aggregate value over the entire season.

To qualify for a ranking in Net Yards per Pass, passing DVOA, and passing DYAR in a given season, a quarterback must have had 200 pass plays in that season. 35 quarterbacks ranked for 2017, 34 for 2018, and 34 for 2019.

The final five columns contain rushing statistics, starting with **Runs**, rushing yards (**Yds**), and rushing touchdowns (**TD**). Once again, these are official NFL totals and include kneeldowns, which means you get to enjoy statistics such as Matt Schaub rushing three times for -3 yards. The final two columns give **DVOA** and **DYAR** for quarterback rushing, which are calculated separately from passing. Rankings for these statistics, as well as numbers that are not adjusted for defense (YAR and VOA) can be found on our website, FootballOutsiders.com.

The last number listed is the Total **QBR** metric from ESPN Stats & Information. Total QBR is based on the expected points added by the quarterback on each play, then adjusts the numbers to a scale of 0-100. There are four main differences between Total QBR and DVOA:

- Total QBR incorporates information from game charting, such as passes dropped or thrown away on purpose.
- Total QBR splits responsibility on plays between the quarterback, his receivers, and his blockers. Drops, for example, are more on the receiver, as are yards after the catch, and some sacks are more on the offensive line than others.
- Total QBR has a clutch factor which adds (or subtracts) value for quarterbacks who perform best (or worst) in high-leverage situations.
- Total QBR combines passing and rushing value into one number and differentiates between scrambles and planned runs.

The italicized row of statistics for the 2020 season is our 2020 KUBIAK projection, as detailed above. Again, in the interest of producing meaningful statistics, all quarterbacks are projected to start a full 16-game season, regardless of the likelihood of them actually doing so.

The final line below the KUBIAK projection represents data on how far the quarterback throws his passes. First, we break down charted passes based on distance: **Short** (5 yards or less), **Mid** (6 to 15 yards), **Deep** (16 to 25 yards), and **Bomb** (26 or more yards). These numbers are based on distance in the air only and include both complete and incomplete passes. Passes thrown away or tipped at the line are not included, nor are passes on which the quarterback's arm was hit by a defender while in motion. We also give average depth of target (**aDOT**) and average yards after catch (**YAC**) with the rank in parentheses for the 34 quarterbacks who qualify. The final number listed here is **ALEX**, which stands for Air Less EXpected, and measures the distance of each quarterback's average third-down throw compared to how many yards were needed for a first down. Aaron Rodgers' ALEX of 4.1 means his average third-down pass was thrown 4.1 yards deeper than the sticks, the highest in the league; Teddy Bridgewater had the lowest ALEX at -1.4.

A number of third- and fourth-string quarterbacks are briefly discussed at the end of the chapter in a section we call "Going Deep."

Top 20 QB by Passing DYAR (Total Value), 2019

Rank	Player	Team	DYAR
1	Dak Prescott	DAL	1541
2	Patrick Mahomes	KC	1320
3	Drew Brees	NO	1316
4	Russell Wilson	SEA	1265
5	Lamar Jackson	BAL	1261
6	Derek Carr	OAK	1064
7	Kirk Cousins	MIN	795
8	Aaron Rodgers	GB	794
9	Matthew Stafford	DET	776
10	Ryan Tannehill	TEN	773
11	Jimmy Garoppolo	SF	724
12	Deshaun Watson	HOU	722
13	Philip Rivers	LAC	714
14	Matt Ryan	ATL	712
15	Jared Goff	LAR	552
16	Tom Brady	NE	550
17	Carson Wentz	PHI	476
18	Ryan Fitzpatrick	MIA	432
19	Jacoby Brissett	IND	414
20	Teddy Bridgewater	NO	340

Minimum 200 passes

Top 20 QB by Passing DVOA (Value per Pass), 2019

Rank	Player	Team	DVOA
1	Drew Brees	NO	39.8%
2	Lamar Jackson	BAL	34.9%
3	Patrick Mahomes	KC	30.0%
4	Matthew Stafford	DET	28.8%
5	Ryan Tannehill	TEN	28.0%
6	Dak Prescott	DAL	27.1%
7	Russell Wilson	SEA	24.3%
8	Derek Carr	OAK	18.7%
9	Teddy Bridgewater	NO	15.3%
10	Kirk Cousins	MIN	14.3%
11	Jimmy Garoppolo	SF	10.8%
12	Deshaun Watson	HOU	9.5%
13	Aaron Rodgers	GB	9.0%
14	Matt Ryan	ATL	7.0%
15	Philip Rivers	LAC	6.6%
16	Jacoby Brissett	IND	2.6%
17	Tom Brady	NE	2.4%
18	Jared Goff	LAR	2.0%
19	Ryan Fitzpatrick	MIA	1.3%
20	Carson Wentz	PHI	0.1%

Minimum 200 passes

Brandon Allen

Height: 6-2 Weight: 209 College: Arkansas Draft: 2016/6 (201) Born: 5-Sep-1992 Age: 28 Risk: N/A

Year	Tm	G/GS	Snaps	Att	Cmp	C%	CPOE	Yds	TD	INT/Adj	FUM	ASR	NY/P	Rk	DVOA	Rk	DYAR	Rk	Runs	Yds	TD	DVOA	DYAR	QBR
2019	DEN	3/3	180	84	39	46.4%	-12.9%	515	3	2/4	0	9.1%	4.9	--	-30.5%	--	-115	--	10	39	0	41.2%	21	38.1

2019: 54% Short   23% Mid   18% Deep   5% Bomb   aDOT: 8.1 (--)   YAC: 6.0 (--)   ALEX: 0.7

Allen had never thrown a regular-season pass in three NFL seasons when he replaced an injured Joe Flacco while rookie Drew Lock was still coming back from a hand ailment last November. Allen game-managed a win over the self-destructing Browns, then rapidly deteriorated against better opponents. His 10-of-25 for 82 yards performance (with one interception and four sacks) against Buffalo made it clear that, ready or not, Lock's time had come. Allen left Arkansas in 2016 as an immobile looks-the-part prospect with ordinary traits, which explains how he landed on Denver's bench. If he takes the field in 2020, the team he plays for is in deep trouble.

Josh Allen

Height: 6-5 Weight: 237 College: Wyoming Draft: 2018/1 (7) Born: 21-May-1996 Age: 24 Risk: Yellow

Year	Tm	G/GS	Snaps	Att	Cmp	C%	CPOE	Yds	TD	INT/Adj	FUM	ASR	NY/P	Rk	DVOA	Rk	DYAR	Rk	Runs	Yds	TD	DVOA	DYAR	QBR
2018	BUF	12/11	719	320	169	52.8%	-8.3%	2074	10	12/16	8	8.4%	5.3	33	-35.9%	33	-534	33	89	631	8	33.3%	192	52.0
2019	BUF	16/16	1010	461	271	58.8%	-2.4%	3089	20	9/12	14	8.2%	5.8	28	-11.8%	28	-21	28	109	510	9	6.5%	100	47.3
2020	BUF			523	314	60.0%		3620	20	11	14		6.1		-11.1%				109	601	8	29.5%		

2018: 44% Short   26% Mid   19% Deep   11% Bomb   aDOT: 11.1 (2)   YAC: 5.6 (11)   ALEX: 3.6   2019: 42% Short   34% Mid   15% Deep   9% Bomb   aDOT: 9.7 (4)   YAC: 5.0 (26)   ALEX: 3.4

There will not be any excuses left for Allen following the 2020 season. With continuity across the board on a solid Bills offensive depth chart, now bolstered by the addition of wide receiver Stefon Diggs, Allen has every tool available to him to succeed. One encouraging sign for the young quarterback is that he should continue to get the coverage looks a player like him wants: man coverage. Allen's defining traits as a passer are his physical tools—he's better suited to beat man and tight windows rather than outwit defenses in zone coverage. In each of the past two seasons, Allen faced man coverage exactly 43% of the time, a figure that ranked eighth in 2018 and first in 2019. Allen posted higher DVOA numbers versus man coverage in each season, too. In turn, Allen has also posted 292 rushing DYAR over the past two seasons in part because man coverage is more conducive to a quarterback being able to run as the defensive backs have their backs turned. That said, even a stable, bolstered roster and the assumption that Allen will face desired coverages does not mean he will make the mental strides and deep-passing improvements required to send him into the upper echelon of quarterbacks.

Kyle Allen

Height: 6-3   Weight:211   College: Houston   Draft: 2018/FA   Born: 8-Mar-1996   Age: 24   Risk: Green

Year	Tm	G/GS	Snaps	Att	Cmp	C%	CPOE	Yds	TD	INT/Adj	FUM	ASR	NY/P	Rk	DVOA	Rk	DYAR	Rk	Runs	Yds	TD	DVOA	DYAR	QBR
2018	CAR	2/1	68	31	20	64.5%	3.0%	266	2	0/0	0	-0.7%	8.6	--	67.4%	--	158	--	5	19	1	52.8%	19	95.7
2019	CAR	13/12	897	489	303	62.0%	-1.1%	3322	17	16/26	13	9.0%	5.5	32	-22.4%	32	-395	33	32	106	2	-9.0%	4	36.4
2020	WAS			524	334	63.7%		3815	19	15	12		6.3		-15.7%				45	160	3	2.7%		

2018: 50% Short   30% Mid   7% Deep   13% Bomb   aDOT: 10.4 (--)   YAC: 4.6 (--)   ALEX: 4.2   2019: 51% Short   30% Mid   13% Deep   7% Bomb   aDOT: 8.5 (19)   YAC: 5.4 (12)   ALEX: 2.2

There is no forgetting Allen's evisceration of the Arizona Cardinals in Week 3. On 26 attempts, Allen completed 19 passes for 261 yards, four touchdowns, and zero interceptions. The nature of some of Allen's scores via broken plays or phenomenal YAC efforts suggested the success would not last, but his ensuing meltdown was a rough watch. From that game on, Allen threw just 12 touchdowns to 16 interceptions and earned -482 DYAR, quite firmly solidifying himself as the worst non-rookie starter in the league. The silver lining for Allen's woes is that much of his negative production came while under pressure, which can be a volatile stat year over year. Allen's 32.0% DVOA without pressure was only about 12.0% below average, while his -123.4% DVOA under pressure was third worst in the league. For all his flaws, Allen did prove he has the baseline accuracy and trigger needed to be a competent backup. Let's just hope he does not need to start 12 games again.

Matt Barkley

Height: 6-2   Weight:234   College: USC   Draft: 2013/4 (98)   Born: 8-Sep-1990   Age: 30   Risk: Green

Year	Tm	G/GS	Snaps	Att	Cmp	C%	CPOE	Yds	TD	INT/Adj	FUM	ASR	NY/P	Rk	DVOA	Rk	DYAR	Rk	Runs	Yds	TD	DVOA	DYAR	QBR
2018	BUF	1/1	73	25	15	60.0%	0.1%	232	2	0/1	0	3.7%	8.6	--	56.0%	--	109	--	3	-2	0	-97.9%	-11	87.0
2019	BUF	2/0	81	51	27	52.9%	-9.4%	359	0	3/3	3	3.8%	6.7	--	-52.0%	--	-122	--	2	-4	0	-157.5%	-10	9.5
2020	BUF			539	320	59.3%		3702	20	15	12		6.1		-15.3%				44	73	1	-23.9%		

2018: 36% Short   32% Mid   24% Deep   8% Bomb   aDOT: 12.4 (--)   YAC: 5.1 (--)   ALEX: 4.4   2019: 46% Short   35% Mid   13% Deep   7% Bomb   aDOT: 8.7 (--)   YAC: 5.8 (--)   ALEX: 1.4

Since entering the NFL in 2013, Barkley has posted exactly one good game in 14 tries as a spot starter. Thankfully for the Bills, that one good start was during Barkley's first year with the team back in 2018, when he took over in Week 10 for an injured Josh Allen and trashed the Jets with two touchdowns and no interceptions. His pair of relief appearances in 2019 did not go nearly as well. Through his 53 qualifying dropbacks, Barkley got considerably worse with each passing down, going from a -10.1% DVOA on first down pass plays to a catastrophic -147.9% DVOA on third- and fourth-down pass plays. By season's end, Barkley may be pushed down the depth chart in favor of fourth-round rookie Jake Fromm.

David Blough

Height: 6-1   Weight:205   College: Purdue   Draft: 2019/FA   Born: 31-Jul-1995   Age: 25   Risk: Green

Year	Tm	G/GS	Snaps	Att	Cmp	C%	CPOE	Yds	TD	INT/Adj	FUM	ASR	NY/P	Rk	DVOA	Rk	DYAR	Rk	Runs	Yds	TD	DVOA	DYAR	QBR
2019	DET	5/5	321	174	94	54.0%	-9.4%	984	4	6/8	1	7.5%	4.7	--	-19.5%	--	-101	--	8	31	0	-7.7%	2	32.1
2020	DET			561	302	53.9%		3483	21	16	7		5.4		-22.5%				45	174	2	8.5%		

2019: 50% Short   30% Mid   12% Deep   8% Bomb   aDOT: 8.9 (--)   YAC: 3.5 (--)   ALEX: 1.7

The nation woke up on Thanksgiving morning, tuned in to the annual Lions game, and saw … David Blough under center? And balling out? The undrafted rookie out of Purdue carved out a place in NFL lore with a 22-for-38, 280-yard, two-touchdown day, good for a DVOA of 30.5%. While the Lions came up just short in a 24-20 loss to Chicago, it's a story he'll be able to tell his grandkids, and a trivia fact that will come up every Thanksgiving when a backup is forced into action. He also should be lauded for a willingness to throw downfield—he had 34 attempts marked as "deep" over the last five weeks of the season, 10th most in the league. Of course, Blough had a -31.4% DVOA in all non-Thanksgiving games and had no other statistical saving graces. With the Lions signing Chase Daniel, there's a good chance Blough doesn't even make the Lions' roster in 2020. But he'll always have Turkey Day.

Tom Brady

| | Height: 6-4 | Weight:225 | College: Michigan | | Draft: 2000/6 (199) | Born: 3-Aug-1977 | Age: 43 | Risk: Yellow |

Year	Tm	G/GS	Snaps	Att	Cmp	C%	CPOE	Yds	TD	INT/Adj	FUM	ASR	NY/P	Rk	DVOA	Rk	DYAR	Rk	Runs	Yds	TD	DVOA	DYAR	QBR
2017	NE	16/16	1118	581	385	66.3%	3.6%	4577	32	8/13	7	6.4%	7.4	6	27.8%	2	1595	1	25	28	0	-12.2%	0	67.4
2018	NE	16/16	1092	570	375	65.8%	0.0%	4355	29	11/12	4	3.8%	7.1	8	15.4%	7	1034	8	23	35	2	18.1%	30	70.6
2019	NE	16/16	1142	613	373	60.8%	-3.8%	4057	24	8/14	4	5.2%	6.1	21	2.4%	17	550	16	26	34	3	22.0%	32	53.7
2020	TB			613	387	63.2%		4899	28	10	5		7.1		10.0%				27	45	2	-1.6%		

2018: 50% Short 32% Mid 12% Deep 6% Bomb aDOT: 8.2 (18) YAC: 5.7 (10) ALEX: 2.8 2019: 51% Short 32% Mid 11% Deep 7% Bomb aDOT: 7.9 (27) YAC: 5.0 (24) ALEX: 1.0

OTAs: Canceled. Training camp: Who knows? As you might have heard (cue the piano music), these are uncertain times. For Brady and the Buccaneers, the fallout from the pandemic would seem to put them at a distinct disadvantage. Fewer practices. Fewer interactions with coaches. Fewer opportunities for Brady to scowl at receivers when they're not where he expects them to be. "You know, football is a very coordinated game," Brady said in October. "Everybody needs to be thinking the same thing, reacting the same way, anticipating in the same way, in order for it to be successful. That's why us being out there as a unit is very important—practicing, executing in practice so you can build confidence. Confidence builds trust, and the trust leads to good execution when you're out on the field."

With access to team facilities restricted, Brady did the next best thing: he invited a handful of his teammates to work out at Berkeley Preparatory School in Tampa, coronavirus be damned. Early on, center Ryan Jensen received a lesson in towel strategy. He learned Brady doesn't like sweaty butts, so before games he stuffs a towel down the back of his center's pants.

As was the case before last season, it's difficult to predict what's ahead for Brady. No quarterback in NFL history has passed for 1,000 yards after turning 43. This could be the end. Or not. Uncertain times indeed. As he prepares to climb the Stairway to Seven, this much is clear: in Mike Evans, Chris Godwin, Rob Gronkowski, and O.J. Howard, he has a supporting cast he can trust. Chemistry won't be an issue. Nor will swamp ass.

Drew Brees

| | Height: 6-0 | Weight:209 | College: Purdue | | Draft: 2001/2 (32) | Born: 15-Jan-1979 | Age: 41 | Risk: Green |

Year	Tm	G/GS	Snaps	Att	Cmp	C%	CPOE	Yds	TD	INT/Adj	FUM	ASR	NY/P	Rk	DVOA	Rk	DYAR	Rk	Runs	Yds	TD	DVOA	DYAR	QBR
2017	NO	16/16	1034	536	386	72.0%	7.6%	4334	23	8/12	5	4.0%	7.5	3	27.4%	3	1390	3	33	12	2	-5.6%	6	59.0
2018	NO	15/15	978	489	364	74.4%	8.5%	3992	32	5/7	5	4.0%	7.6	3	36.7%	2	1631	2	31	22	4	29.0%	43	80.8
2019	NO	11/11	646	378	281	74.3%	8.5%	2979	27	4/10	0	3.6%	7.5	5	39.8%	1	1316	3	9	-4	1	70.9%	14	71.7
2020	NO			559	407	72.8%		4420	29	8	4		7.1		21.7%				18	24	1	-1.3%		

2018: 55% Short 26% Mid 14% Deep 5% Bomb aDOT: 7.6 (27) YAC: 5.0 (25) ALEX: 0.1 2019: 57% Short 29% Mid 11% Deep 4% Bomb aDOT: 6.7 (33) YAC: 5.3 (15) ALEX: 0.8

When Brees' late-2018 swoon evoked memories of Peyton Manning's late-2014 swoon, we warned not to extrapolate from such a small sample. Turns out, it wasn't meaningful. Despite missing five games because of a freak thumb injury he suffered in Week 2, Brees went on to have one of the best seasons of his career, posting highs in touchdown rate (7.1%), passer rating (116.3), and DVOA (39.8%). And his December? No one—not even league MVP Lamar Jackson—was better. Over the first 13 weeks, Brees threw 12 touchdown passes and four interceptions, resulting in a 18.2% DVOA. Over the final four weeks, he threw 15 touchdown passes and no interceptions, resulting in a 76.3% DVOA. His average depth of target stayed about the same.

The lesson here is that a season has its ebbs and flows, its peaks and valleys. What happens in December doesn't necessarily carry over to even January, let alone September. Take Brett Favre's penultimate season as a counterpoint to Manning's. His DVOA over the first 13 weeks of 2009: 34.7%. His DVOA over the final four weeks: 33.7%. His DVOA the next season: -23.1%. Same for Carson Palmer; he showed no signs of slowing down late in 2015, and yet he was a below-average quarterback in 2016 and 2017. Predictions about an older quarterback's demise often are no more reliable than broken clocks. They're bound to be right—eventually.

Teddy Bridgewater

| | Height: 6-2 | Weight:215 | College: Louisville | | Draft: 2014/1 (32) | Born: 10-Nov-1992 | Age: 28 | Risk: Yellow |

Year	Tm	G/GS	Snaps	Att	Cmp	C%	CPOE	Yds	TD	INT/Adj	FUM	ASR	NY/P	Rk	DVOA	Rk	DYAR	Rk	Runs	Yds	TD	DVOA	DYAR	QBR
2017	MIN	1/0	9	2	0	0.0%	-75.2%	0	0	1/0	0	-0.2%	0.0	--	-493.2%	--	-68	--	3	-3	0	--	--	0.0
2018	NO	5/1	71	23	14	60.9%	-3.3%	118	1	1/1	0	8.6%	4.4	--	-39.7%	--	-46	--	11	5	0	-58.4%	-13	33.6
2019	NO	9/5	408	196	133	67.9%	2.2%	1384	9	2/1	1	6.4%	6.2	16	15.3%	9	340	20	28	31	0	-32.7%	-19	48.9
2020	CAR			597	394	66.0%		4499	28	10	7		6.6		4.6%				53	100	1	-21.6%		

2018: 57% Short 29% Mid 14% Deep 0% Bomb aDOT: 6.7 (--) YAC: 3.8 (--) ALEX: 1.0 2019: 58% Short 31% Mid 6% Deep 6% Bomb aDOT: 6.2 (34) YAC: 5.6 (9) ALEX: -1.4

We've criticized the conservative nature that has left Bridgewater with the third-lowest average depth of throw (7.2 yards) and tied him for the lowest ALEX on third and fourth downs (-0.7) since he entered the league in 2014. But it may not be fair to broadly paint Bridgewater with an Alex Smith brush. It makes sense that head coach Mike Zimmer asked Bridgewater to be conservative in his rookie and sophomore seasons for his defensive-minded Vikings teams, and then Bridgewater suffered his devastating knee injury. Since then, Bridgewater barely played before 2019, when he again could justifiably be asked to play conservatively as a short-term fill-in for Drew Brees on a talent-rich Saints team. Perhaps Bridgewater will be allowed to open things up for the first time for his new offense in Carolina. He has hardly been dreadful when he has attempted deep and bomb throws of 16 or more air yards. His career DVOA on those throws of 46.8% would have landed him 25th of the 34 passers in 2019 with 200 or more total attempts, ahead of a few good or at least promising passers such as Carson Wentz (32.8%), Daniel Jones (25.6%), or Jared Goff (20.7%).

Jacoby Brissett

Height: 6-4   Weight:235   College: North Carolina State   Draft: 2016/3 (91)   Born: 11-Dec-1992   Age: 28   Risk: Green

Year	Tm	G/GS	Snaps	Att	Cmp	C%	CPOE	Yds	TD	INT/Adj	FUM	ASR	NY/P	Rk	DVOA	Rk	DYAR	Rk	Runs	Yds	TD	DVOA	DYAR	QBR
2017	IND	16/15	989	469	276	58.8%	-2.7%	3098	13	7/11	8	9.8%	5.5	29	-14.4%	27	-105	28	63	260	4	-13.7%	-4	39.6
2018	IND	4/0	18	4	2	50.0%	1.6%	2	0	0/0	0	1.2%	0.5	--	-70.3%	--	-16	--	7	-7	0	--	--	100.0
2019	IND	15/15	961	447	272	60.9%	-2.6%	2942	18	6/8	7	5.8%	5.9	24	2.6%	16	414	19	56	228	4	10.1%	57	50.1
2020	IND			523	326	62.4%		3582	23	8	9		6.1		-2.6%				65	261	4	18.2%		

2018: 67% Short   0% Mid   0% Deep   33% Bomb   aDOT: 9.3 (–)   YAC: 0.5 (–)   ALEX: 18.0   2019:   51% Short   30% Mid   13% Deep   6% Bomb   aDOT: 8.4 (21)   YAC: 5.6 (10)   ALEX: -0.3

Brissett has started almost two full seasons as an injury replacement for Andrew Luck. The first of those was far less than ideal: the Colts traded for Brissett ahead of Week 1 in 2017, and despite barely having the time to learn the offense he started every game from Week 2 onwards. 2019 was probably a truer reflection of Brissett's actual ability; he is the type of quarterback who is ideally suited to a backup role but probably miscast as a starter. Solid and dependable but conservative to a fault, he avoids making big mistakes but also struggles to make big plays, which is why in 32 career starts he has thrown very few touchdowns (32) or interceptions (15). His numbers were buoyed by success on third downs, when his DVOA jumped to 23.4%, versus -0.8% on first down and -12.3% on second down.

Brissett's decision-making remains slow even in his fourth year as a pro. As noted in the Colts chapter, he had the second-longest average time to throw in 2019 per NFL Next Gen Stats. He suffered less of a drop-off than most other quarterbacks when pressured, but he was pressured on just over a third of his pass attempts, the sixth-highest rate among qualifying quarterbacks. That pressure only resulted in half as many sacks in 2019 as in 2017, but he still fumbled six times on just 25 sacks (his other fumble came on a rushing attempt). Brissett is exactly the type of player any team would love to have as their backup but be looking to replace immediately if he was their starter—which, as it turns out, is exactly how his Colts career has gone over the past two offseasons.

Joe Burrow

Height: 6-3   Weight:221   College: Louisiana State   Draft: 2020/1 (1)   Born: 10-Dec-1996   Age: 24   Risk: Green

Year	Tm	G/GS	Snaps	Att	Cmp	C%	CPOE	Yds	TD	INT/Adj	FUM	ASR	NY/P	Rk	DVOA	Rk	DYAR	Rk	Runs	Yds	TD	DVOA	DYAR	QBR
2020	CIN			572	352	61.5%		4143	24	14	11		6.4		-8.3%				60	343	3	21.7%		

We covered what you need to know about Burrow on the field in the Bengals chapter, so here are some interesting tidbits from the personal file: ✎ He has been living at home in Athens, Ohio, during the pandemic, and sleeping in his *Star Wars*-themed bedroom. ✎ His football idol is not a Bengals or Browns player but Drew Brees. ✎ He met his girlfriend, Olivia Holzmacher, while at Ohio State. When he transferred to LSU, she stuck with him, perhaps knowing he was fated to one day return to Ohio, given the state of the state's football elevens. ✎ Burrow is fabled for his Ohio roots, but he was actually born in Ames, Iowa. His dad, Jimmy Burrow, was an assistant coach at Iowa State, though he had been fired by the time Joe was born to his second wife. The Burrows stayed in Iowa so Joe's older stepbrothers could finish high school there. ✎ The family also lived in the college towns of Lincoln, Nebraska and Fargo, North Dakota before settling in Athens, when Jimmy Burrow was hired as defensive coordinator at Ohio University. ✎ In case you are wondering about his athletic ability, Burrow was an all-state basketball player in high school and a star defensive back (to go with his quarterback duties) on the football team. ✎ The hoop skills are apparently genetic—one of Burrow's grandmothers once scored 82 points in a single high school basketball game. ✎ His favorite treats are caramel apple suckers, whatever those are. ✎ After dedicating his Heisman Trophy speech to the hungry and disadvantaged in Athens, the local community food bank was deluged with donations totaling over half a million dollars. It isn't known how many caramel apple suckers were donated. ✎ The Athens High School football stadium has been renamed for Burrow.

Now if the Bengals are one day moved to rename Paul Brown Stadium in favor of Joey B., surely the disastrous 2019 season will have been well worth suffering through.

Derek Carr Height: 6-3 Weight: 210 College: Fresno State Draft: 2014/2 (36) Born: 3/28/1991 Age: 29 Risk: Red

Year	Tm	G/GS	Snaps	Att	Cmp	C%	CPOE	Yds	TD	INT/Adj	FUM	ASR	NY/P	Rk	DVOA	Rk	DYAR	Rk	Runs	Yds	TD	DVOA	DYAR	QBR
2017	OAK	15/15	937	515	323	62.7%	-1.6%	3496	22	13/19	8	4.3%	6.6	14	9.7%	13	709	12	23	66	0	-66.5%	-35	46.7
2018	OAK	16/16	1034	553	381	68.9%	3.4%	4049	19	10/20	12	8.6%	6.3	21	-1.0%	22	392	21	24	47	1	-0.3%	8	48.9
2019	OAK	16/16	1014	513	361	70.4%	6.1%	4054	21	8/9	7	6.0%	7.2	9	18.7%	8	1064	6	27	82	2	-60.6%	-49	62.2
2020	LV			539	375	69.5%		4186	24	9	8		6.9		11.6%				24	74	1	4.5%		

2018: 56% Short 30% Mid 10% Deep 4% Bomb aDOT: 7.1 (33) YAC: 5.2 (19) ALEX: 0.3 2019: 61% Short 23% Mid 12% Deep 4% Bomb aDOT: 6.8 (32) YAC: 5.9 (4) ALEX: 1.3

You may see Carr's 70.4% completion rate and think, "I bet that includes lots of checkdowns, dink-and-dunks, and throws in front of the sticks on third-and-long." Well, yes and no. Carr's ALEX of -1.9 on all downs ranked 29th in the NFL, and his average depth of target (6.8 yards) ranked 32nd, so he did throw lots of passes in front of the sticks. But his successful completion rate of 52.7% ranked fifth in the NFL, so he wasn't just playing dink-and-punt. Carr completed 73.2% of his passes for 8.1 yards per attempt on first downs, and the Raiders offense did a fine job remaining on down-and-distance schedule last year, so Carr accumulated a fine success rate and achieved high offensive efficiency without having to throw downfield that much. Much of the credit should go to Jon Gruden's game-planning and offensive design, but Carr also deserves credit for operating effectively within structure despite a weak receiving corps.

Carr's 2020 improvement will amount to naught, of course, if Gruden prefers Marcus Mariota or simply decides to stir the pot at quarterback as we have expected him to do for the last two years. Carr's best chance of continued employment as a franchise quarterback rests with the possibility that he has now aged into Gruden's preferred "heady journeyman" demographic.

Kirk Cousins Height: 6-3 Weight: 202 College: Michigan State Draft: 2012/4 (102) Born: 19-Aug-1988 Age: 32 Risk: Green

Year	Tm	G/GS	Snaps	Att	Cmp	C%	CPOE	Yds	TD	INT/Adj	FUM	ASR	NY/P	Rk	DVOA	Rk	DYAR	Rk	Runs	Yds	TD	DVOA	DYAR	QBR
2017	WAS	16/16	1012	540	347	64.3%	1.5%	4093	27	13/20	13	7.7%	6.5	16	-0.6%	18	395	16	49	179	4	-2.3%	21	52.3
2018	MIN	16/16	1051	606	425	70.1%	5.4%	4298	30	10/13	9	6.1%	6.2	23	2.7%	20	595	13	44	123	1	-13.2%	-2	62.0
2019	MIN	15/15	982	444	307	69.1%	6.2%	3603	26	6/8	10	7.0%	7.2	8	14.3%	10	795	7	31	63	1	-19.8%	-9	58.4
2020	MIN			512	362	70.6%		3929	27	8	8		6.8		9.7%				27	65	1	-5.0%		

2018: 57% Short 27% Mid 9% Deep 7% Bomb aDOT: 7.6 (28) YAC: 4.6 (31) ALEX: 1.0 2019: 55% Short 25% Mid 11% Deep 9% Bomb aDOT: 8.0 (24) YAC: 5.8 (5) ALEX: 2.3

One of the big questions Cousins faces in 2020 is whether or not he'll be able to continue his deep-ball success without Stefon Diggs bailing out some inaccurate throws. Cousins had an 100.8% DVOA last season on passes over 15 yards downfield, and only Patrick Mahomes has more deep touchdowns over the past two seasons than Cousins' 17, per John Kinsley's Deep Ball Project. Cousins doesn't air the ball out all that often—his average depth of target of 8.0 yards ranked 24th out of 34 among qualified passers—but it has been an effective component of his game ever since he arrived in Minnesota. However, 31 of Cousins' 86 deep shots headed Diggs' way last season; take those out and his deep ball DVOA drops to 58.1%, just below league average. Neither Adam Thielen nor Justin Jefferson really replicate Diggs' skill set there, so Cousins will have a higher degree of difficulty on his deep shots in 2020.

Andy Dalton Height: 6-2 Weight: 220 College: TCU Draft: 2011/2 (35) Born: 29-Oct-1987 Age: 33 Risk: Green

Year	Tm	G/GS	Snaps	Att	Cmp	C%	CPOE	Yds	TD	INT/Adj	FUM	ASR	NY/P	Rk	DVOA	Rk	DYAR	Rk	Runs	Yds	TD	DVOA	DYAR	QBR
2017	CIN	16/16	941	496	297	59.9%	-0.6%	3320	25	12/16	4	7.3%	5.8	23	-8.6%	24	87	24	38	99	0	11.3%	24	41.1
2018	CIN	11/11	627	365	226	61.9%	-3.1%	2566	21	11/13	1	5.8%	6.3	20	5.2%	17	404	19	16	99	0	11.9%	14	61.9
2019	CIN	13/13	927	528	314	59.5%	-3.7%	3494	16	14/21	8	6.7%	5.8	27	-10.6%	26	19	26	32	73	4	-7.7%	7	40.1
2020	DAL			525	328	62.5%		3953	22	12	9		6.7		3.0%				55	172	4	17.5%		

2018: 48% Short 34% Mid 12% Deep 6% Bomb aDOT: 8.5 (17) YAC: 5.1 (23) ALEX: 1.1 2019: 47% Short 37% Mid 10% Deep 6% Bomb aDOT: 8.6 (18) YAC: 4.9 (27) ALEX: 1.2

For years with the Bengals, Dalton was the sum of the parts around him. He was rarely a quarterback who was able to make those around him better, but put him on the 2015 Bengals and you can get a top-five season in DVOA. Now Dalton eases into the role of high-end veteran backup with the Cowboys. He's the perfect player you hope can string together a few passable games if the starter gets hurt. The quality is much more palatable at $3 million than relying on it as a starter for $16 million.

Chase Daniel

	Height: 6-0		Weight:229		College: Missouri				Draft: 2009/FA			Born: 7-Oct-1986			Age: 34			Risk: Green					

Year	Tm	G/GS	Snaps	Att	Cmp	C%	CPOE	Yds	TD	INT/Adj	FUM	ASR	NY/P	Rk	DVOA	Rk	DYAR	Rk	Runs	Yds	TD	DVOA	DYAR	QBR
2017	NO	1/0	5	0	0	--	--	0	0	0/0	0	--	--	--	--	--	--	--	3	-2	0	--	--	--
2018	CHI	5/2	148	76	53	69.7%	0.8%	515	3	2/3	4	10.7%	5.6	--	-37.9%	--	-152	--	13	3	0	-107.0%	-26	29.6
2019	CHI	3/1	131	64	45	70.3%	0.7%	435	3	2/2	0	9.8%	5.5	--	-13.2%	--	-9	--	6	6	0	-38.3%	-10	57.6
2020	DET			526	355	67.5%		4128	27	13	8		6.9		3.8%				45	112	1	-8.5%		

2018: 45% Short   36% Mid   13% Deep   6% Bomb   aDOT: 8.6 (--)   YAC: 3.2 (--)   ALEX: -3.9   2019:   55% Short   30% Mid   11% Deep   5% Bomb   aDOT: 6.9 (--)   YAC: 3.0 (--)   ALEX: -1.3

Every year, our Chase Daniel comment is about how he gets paid a ton of money to do very little, and this year won't be an exception. Daniel has now made $34.3 million in the NFL, and he just signed a three-year, $13-million contract with the Lions. He has seven career passing touchdowns. To be fair, six of those seven scores did come in the last two years, in seasons that would have ranked 29th and 34th in passing DVOA had he thrown enough passes to qualify. Daniel's Week 4 win over Minnesota saw him put up a 32.0% DVOA, the first positive performance he has had since Week 17 of 2013. There's precious little evidence that Daniel would be able to keep the ship afloat should Matthew Stafford go down with an injury again in 2020, and one out-of-character game against Minnesota should not alter your opinion of Daniel as a sub-replacement player content with dumping the ball off to running backs and tight ends in limited mop-up work.

Sam Darnold

	Height: 6-3		Weight:225		College: USC				Draft: 2018/1 (3)			Born: 5-Jun-1997			Age: 23			Risk: Green					

Year	Tm	G/GS	Snaps	Att	Cmp	C%	CPOE	Yds	TD	INT/Adj	FUM	ASR	NY/P	Rk	DVOA	Rk	DYAR	Rk	Runs	Yds	TD	DVOA	DYAR	QBR
2018	NYJ	13/13	810	414	239	57.7%	-4.7%	2865	17	15/21	5	6.7%	6.0	27	-15.2%	30	-110	30	44	138	1	0.2%	23	48.4
2019	NYJ	13/13	853	441	273	61.9%	0.5%	3024	19	13/15	11	7.2%	6.0	23	-20.4%	31	-290	32	33	62	2	-20.1%	-7	43.6
2020	NYJ			542	345	63.6%		3974	23	15	9		6.4		-8.6%				30	80	1	-5.2%		

2018: 40% Short   39% Mid   14% Deep   6% Bomb   aDOT: 9.4 (7)   YAC: 5.4 (16)   ALEX: 1.1   2019:   49% Short   27% Mid   17% Deep   6% Bomb   aDOT: 8.9 (13)   YAC: 5.4 (13)   ALEX: 2.5

Playing to each end of the extremes is the name of the game for Darnold. On one play, Darnold will thread a beautiful ball into a nonexistent window while under pressure, only to drill a linebacker in the face mask while throwing from a clean pocket on the following play. The talent and foundation is there for Darnold, but he stills feels a year or two away from having things click. No metric shines a spotlight on that volatility brighter than Darnold's DVOA splits when throwing against man coverage versus zone. At -20.5%, Darnold was by far the worst performer in the league against man coverage and one of just two qualifying quarterbacks to post a negative DVOA rating (the other being Gardner Minshew), yet his 41.3% DVOA versus zone coverages was comfortably above average. True to his inconsistencies, Darnold's splits the previous season were actually flipped in those two areas, though not quite as extreme in either direction. Perhaps related to his man coverage struggles, Darnold was also a trainwreck on third and fourth downs, which was not the case during his rookie year. In 2019, Darnold posted an awful -33.6% DVOA on those plays. The good news is third- and fourth-down play is unstable, so he has a decent chance to be much better in 2020, but it is not like the Jets' roster inspires hope that will happen.

Jeff Driskel

	Height: 6-4		Weight:235		College: Louisiana Tech				Draft: 2016/6 (207)			Born: 23-Apr-1993			Age: 27			Risk: Green					

Year	Tm	G/GS	Snaps	Att	Cmp	C%	CPOE	Yds	TD	INT/Adj	FUM	ASR	NY/P	Rk	DVOA	Rk	DYAR	Rk	Runs	Yds	TD	DVOA	DYAR	QBR
2018	CIN	9/5	372	176	105	59.7%	-6.0%	1003	6	2/8	4	9.4%	4.5	--	-16.4%	--	-61	--	25	130	2	-2.8%	10	31.6
2019	DET	3/3	223	105	62	59.0%	-4.4%	685	4	4/5	1	9.8%	5.6	--	-24.2%	--	-91	--	22	151	1	37.0%	52	47.9
2020	DEN			525	313	59.6%		3587	20	13	9		6.0		-13.5%				73	432	4	21.9%		

2018: 48% Short   30% Mid   15% Deep   7% Bomb   aDOT: 8.5 (--)   YAC: 4.8 (--)   ALEX: -2.0   2019:   46% Short   33% Mid   15% Deep   6% Bomb   aDOT: 8.7 (--)   YAC: 4.7 (--)   ALEX: -1.6

Make a copy of a copy of Patrick Mahomes and you may get Drew Lock. Make a few more copies of copies until things get rather blurry and you arrive at Driskel, an athletic, scatter-armed, danger-to-himself-and-others type capable of looking competent (and a little exciting) for short relief stretches. Driskel is an odd choice as Lock's backup: mop-up relief duties for the Bengals and Lions proved that he is just good enough to keep an offense barely functional, making him neither a challenger nor a mentor nor an insurance policy. If Denver's goal was to find an inexpensive backup quarterback who would make Lock look like Mahomes by comparison, they did a heck of a job.

Luke Falk

Height: 6-4 Weight: 215 College: Washington State Draft: 2018/6 (199) Born: 28-Dec-1994 Age: 26 Risk: N/A

Year	Tm	G/GS	Snaps	Att	Cmp	C%	CPOE	Yds	TD	INT/Adj	FUM	ASR	NY/P	Rk	DVOA	Rk	DYAR	Rk	Runs	Yds	TD	DVOA	DYAR	QBR
2019	NYJ	3/2	154	73	47	64.4%	-3.6%	416	0	3/4	2	17.5%	3.6	--	-72.3%	--	-314	--	0	0	0	--	--	8.9

2019: 63% Short 22% Mid 12% Deep 3% Bomb aDOT: 5.8 (--) YAC: 5.6 (--) ALEX: -0.4

A sixth-round pick for the Tennessee Titans in 2018, Falk got his first pair of NFL starts in 2019. They were ugly. The only quarterback with more than 10 pass attempts last season to put out a worse DVOA than Falk's -72.3% was Colt McCoy, who posted a grotesque -73.8% DVOA on 33 attempts. Falk was particularly bad on third and fourth downs: on 31 dropbacks, Falk converted just five first downs while throwing three interceptions and taking six sacks. The former Washington State signal-caller could hook up somewhere as a backup, but his chances to be a starting quarterback in the league are virtually gone.

Ryan Finley

Height: 6-4 Weight: 207 College: North Carolina State Draft: 2019/4 (104) Born: 26-Dec-1994 Age: 26 Risk: Green

Year	Tm	G/GS	Snaps	Att	Cmp	C%	CPOE	Yds	TD	INT/Adj	FUM	ASR	NY/P	Rk	DVOA	Rk	DYAR	Rk	Runs	Yds	TD	DVOA	DYAR	QBR
2019	CIN	3/3	196	87	41	47.1%	-18.5%	474	2	2/5	4	10.5%	4.0	--	-59.8%	--	-290	--	10	77	0	35.4%	22	23.5
2020	CIN			529	287	54.2%		3352	18	12	14		5.5		-23.2%				50	315	2	19.3%		

2019: 45% Short 39% Mid 12% Deep 4% Bomb aDOT: 8.7 (--) YAC: 5.0 (--) ALEX: 1.0

If anyone can speak to the meaninglessness of preseason football, it is Finley. The fourth-round pick was, by all accounts, horrible in training camp, but was strong in August, going 47-of-64 for 414 yards with three touchdowns and a 99.3 passer rating. But when he got his shot in the games that count, he threw it away, with three horrendous performances that forced Cincy to reinstall Andy Dalton as starter. Now, three games with a bad team does not a career make (or break), but the weakness of Finley's arm makes Chad Pennington look like John Elway. The Bengals have committed to Finley for 2020 as the backup, but he should be thinking less about taking over for Joe Burrow and more about holding off third-stringer Jake Dolegala.

Ryan Fitzpatrick

Height: 6-2 Weight: 228 College: Harvard Draft: 2005/7 (250) Born: 24-Nov-1982 Age: 38 Risk: Red

Year	Tm	G/GS	Snaps	Att	Cmp	C%	CPOE	Yds	TD	INT/Adj	FUM	ASR	NY/P	Rk	DVOA	Rk	DYAR	Rk	Runs	Yds	TD	DVOA	DYAR	QBR
2017	TB	6/3	299	163	96	58.9%	-1.8%	1103	7	3/3	0	5.2%	6.3	--	17.3%	--	307	--	15	78	0	17.5%	17	54.4
2018	TB	8/7	428	246	164	66.7%	3.4%	2366	17	12/14	4	5.5%	8.8	1	16.8%	6	473	15	36	152	2	15.9%	40	63.7
2019	MIA	15/13	885	502	311	62.0%	-0.6%	3529	20	13/15	9	7.4%	6.2	19	1.3%	19	432	18	54	243	4	2.2%	33	66.5
2020	MIA			602	367	61.0%		4326	25	16	9		6.3		-8.3%				61	276	4	18.5%		

2018: 40% Short 33% Mid 17% Deep 10% Bomb aDOT: 10.6 (3) YAC: 5.3 (17) ALEX: 1.9 2019: 41% Short 40% Mid 13% Deep 7% Bomb aDOT: 9.4 (7) YAC: 4.0 (34) ALEX: 4.0

Fitzpatrick was better than you remember he was last season. Given the Miami Dolphins were tanking from the get-go and Josh Rosen's run as the starting quarterback made us all turn our eyes away from the Dolphins offense, there is hardly any blaming someone for skipping right over the rest of their season. When Fitzpatrick took over the reins, though, Miami's passing offense earned the 15th-best DVOA rating from Week 10 onward. Fitzpatrick's 53.3% DVOA when not pressured was slightly above league average, which suggests his success was not a product of good fortune. Coverage design did not factor into Fitzpatrick's success one way or the other either. Fitzpatrick's DVOA rating vs. man coverages was 37.5%, while his DVOA rating vs. zone coverage was nearly identical at 36.3%. Only Giants quarterback Daniel Jones had a smaller difference between the two. For however long the Dolphins need Fitzpatrick to hold down the fort for Tua Tagovailoa, the team will be in good hands.

Joe Flacco

Height: 6-6 Weight:245 College: Delaware Draft: 2008/1 (18) Born: 16-Jan-1985 Age: 35 Risk: Red

Year	Tm	G/GS	Snaps	Att	Cmp	C%	CPOE	Yds	TD	INT/Adj	FUM	ASR	NY/P	Rk	DVOA	Rk	DYAR	Rk	Runs	Yds	TD	DVOA	DYAR	QBR
2017	BAL	16/16	1027	549	352	64.1%	-1.0%	3141	18	13/17	6	4.5%	5.2	33	-19.3%	30	-301	32	25	54	1	37.0%	24	43.0
2018	BAL	9/9	641	379	232	61.2%	-1.8%	2465	12	6/11	3	4.3%	6.1	25	5.4%	16	429	18	19	45	0	2.9%	13	57.4
2019	DEN	8/8	537	262	171	65.3%	2.3%	1822	6	5/6	8	9.7%	5.8	29	-18.8%	29	-144	29	12	20	0	-9.3%	1	48.7
2020	NYJ			526	333	63.3%		3745	19	11	11		6.2		-9.8%				27	68	1	-11.9%		

2018: 46% Short 32% Mid 14% Deep 8% Bomb aDOT: 9.5 (6) YAC: 4.4 (33) ALEX: 1.7 2019: 56% Short 28% Mid 10% Deep 6% Bomb aDOT: 7.3 (29) YAC: 5.3 (17) ALEX: -0.3

Flacco finished 33rd in the NFL in failed completion rate at 29.8% and 32nd in ALEX on all downs, his average throw traveling 2.1 yards in front of the first-down marker. Flacco completed 16 passes on third downs with 4-6 yards to go but netted just eight first downs on those completions, which is practically Failed Completion Self-Parody. Even John Elway and his ball control-obsessed coaches grew weary of Flacco's endless checkdowns to the flat, leaving the former Super Bowl MVP with nowhere else to go but the Jets, where Adam Gase never met a 3-yard shallow drag on third-and-4 that he didn't like. If anything happens to Sam Darnold—injury, megamono, poltergeist, Gase deciding that he doesn't like Darnold's haircut—Flacco could have Jay Cutler's 2017 season: 190 yards per game, 19 touchdowns, 11 interceptions, lotsa dumpoffs. If that floats your boat, more power to you.

Nick Foles

Height: 6-6 Weight:243 College: Arizona Draft: 2012/3 (88) Born: 20-Jan-1989 Age: 31 Risk: Yellow

Year	Tm	G/GS	Snaps	Att	Cmp	C%	CPOE	Yds	TD	INT/Adj	FUM	ASR	NY/P	Rk	DVOA	Rk	DYAR	Rk	Runs	Yds	TD	DVOA	DYAR	QBR
2017	PHI	7/3	212	101	57	56.4%	-4.8%	537	5	2/2	6	5.4%	4.8	--	-28.5%	--	-114	--	11	3	0	-123.1%	-19	28.0
2018	PHI	5/5	357	195	141	72.3%	2.6%	1413	7	4/5	4	4.4%	6.8	13	-5.4%	25	74	26	9	17	0	-2.7%	5	67.4
2019	JAX	4/4	188	117	77	65.8%	2.4%	736	3	2/3	2	7.1%	5.5	--	-21.3%	--	-77	--	4	23	0	26.7%	7	33.6
2020	CHI			525	341	64.8%		3764	22	12	9		6.3		-6.9%				56	214	3	4.5%		

2018: 60% Short 24% Mid 10% Deep 6% Bomb aDOT: 7.0 (34) YAC: 5.2 (20) ALEX: -0.3 2019: 55% Short 23% Mid 12% Deep 10% Bomb aDOT: 8.6 (--) YAC: 4.6 (--) ALEX: 1.8

Foles has been consistently better picking apart man defenses than solving zones throughout his career. Last season, he had a 66.1% DVOA against man, which would have ranked sixth in the league if he had thrown enough passes to qualify, but his -28.4% DVOA against zone would have been last by a country mile. This isn't a recent or sample-size issue phenomenon; he was last in the league against zone defenses in 2018 in Philadelphia as well, and those issues will probably follow him to Chicago. His 2018 improvement under pressure also vanished last season, and it's worth noting that Foles has been significantly below league average with rushers in his face in his three seasons with either Matt Nagy or John DeFilippo—confusion and disguise are the ways to defend against a Foles-led offense. Foles excels when he can make short, quick throws to easily identified targets with room to run; his accuracy and decision-making in those situations alone gives him a leg up in his battle with Mitch Trubisky. He's just a player who needs help from his system and his teammates to put up solid numbers, rather than someone who is going to lift an offense around him.

Blaine Gabbert

Height: 6-4 Weight:235 College: Missouri Draft: 2011/1 (10) Born: 15-Oct-1989 Age: 31 Risk: Green

Year	Tm	G/GS	Snaps	Att	Cmp	C%	CPOE	Yds	TD	INT/Adj	FUM	ASR	NY/P	Rk	DVOA	Rk	DYAR	Rk	Runs	Yds	TD	DVOA	DYAR	QBR
2017	ARI	5/5	345	171	95	55.6%	-6.0%	1086	6	6/9	7	10.6%	5.1	--	-26.4%	--	-189	--	22	82	0	-36.0%	-21	30.7
2018	TEN	8/3	211	101	61	60.4%	-6.8%	626	4	4/7	0	5.7%	5.4	--	-35.5%	--	-154	--	6	0	0	39.6%	8	28.4
2020	TB			525	326	62.0%		4015	25	13	8		6.8		0.8%				57	235	2	10.5%		

2018: 55% Short 30% Mid 13% Deep 2% Bomb aDOT: 7.2 (--) YAC: 4.9 (--) ALEX: 0.5

When Bruce Arians took over as head coach of the Buccaneers, he immediately designated Jameis Winston as his starter, reasoning that the back-and-forth between Winston and Ryan Fitzpatrick during the 2018 season hurt both quarterbacks. "If we have a guy, he's our guy," he said. You knew he meant it because he brought Gabbert to Tampa Bay as a backup. Gabbert was so good at ensuring that Winston didn't have to look over his shoulder that he dislocated his own during the Buccaneers' third preseason game. Though the injury ultimately ended his season, it did not end his time in Tampa Bay. The Buccaneers re-signed him to a one-year, $1.2-million deal to back up Tom Brady.

Jimmy Garoppolo

Height: 6-2 | Weight:225 | College: Eastern Illinois | Draft: 2014/2 (62) | Born: 11-Feb-1991 | Age: 29 | Risk: Green

Year	Tm	G/GS	Snaps	Att	Cmp	C%	CPOE	Yds	TD	INT/Adj	FUM	ASR	NY/P	Rk	DVOA	Rk	DYAR	Rk	Runs	Yds	TD	DVOA	DYAR	QBR
2017	2TM	6/5	353	178	120	67.4%	4.1%	1560	7	5/8	1	3.2%	8.2	--	39.1%	--	598	--	15	11	1	-8.8%	2	80.5
2018	SF	3/3	197	89	53	59.6%	-5.4%	718	5	3/3	4	11.3%	6.1	--	-12.5%	--	-9	--	8	33	0	-48.2%	-14	29.9
2019	SF	16/16	1079	476	329	69.1%	1.2%	3978	27	13/17	10	7.0%	7.3	6	10.8%	11	724	11	46	62	1	-18.0%	-9	58.8
2020	SF			484	325	67.1%		3828	27	13	9		7.0		5.1%				42	63	1	-21.8%		

2018: 43% Short   39% Mid   11% Deep   7% Bomb   aDOT: 9.5 (--)   YAC: 6.9 (--)   ALEX: -1.9   2019: 53% Short   33% Mid   10% Deep   3% Bomb   aDOT: 6.8 (31)   YAC: 6.6 (1)   ALEX: -0.1

Garoppolo was blitzed on 38% of plays, more than any other quarterback in the league. His performance steadily declined with more pass-rushers, from 8.0 net yards per play with four pass-rushers to 7.6 net yards per play with five and then 6.3 net yards per play with six. When turning up the heat on Garoppolo, teams had to make sure to keep him contained in the pocket, as his DVOA nearly doubled when he got outside; there is definitely an asymmetric split here, though, because Garoppolo attempted nearly 87% of his passes from inside the pocket.

Mike Glennon

Height: 6-7 | Weight:225 | College: North Carolina State | Draft: 2013/3 (73) | Born: 12-Dec-1989 | Age: 31 | Risk: Green

Year	Tm	G/GS	Snaps	Att	Cmp	C%	CPOE	Yds	TD	INT/Adj	FUM	ASR	NY/P	Rk	DVOA	Rk	DYAR	Rk	Runs	Yds	TD	DVOA	DYAR	QBR
2017	CHI	4/4	264	140	93	66.4%	-0.7%	833	4	5/7	6	5.4%	5.0	--	-37.1%	--	-231	--	4	4	0	-114.7%	-13	21.9
2018	ARI	2/0	26	21	15	71.4%	7.8%	174	1	0/0	0	5.0%	7.5	--	45.4%	--	73	--	0	0	0	--	--	76.4
2019	OAK	2/0	23	10	6	60.0%	5.0%	56	1	0/0	3	0.6%	5.6	--	-20.2%	--	-6	--	2	0	0	-262.0%	-9	23.7
2020	JAX			524	329	62.8%		3693	23	11	13		6.2		-9.8%				42	128	1	-6.5%		

2018: 40% Short   45% Mid   10% Deep   5% Bomb   aDOT: 8.9 (--)   YAC: 5.6 (--)   ALEX: -8.3   2019: 22% Short   44% Mid   22% Deep   11% Bomb   aDOT: 12.1 (--)   YAC: 3.0 (--)   ALEX: -2.7

A largely forgotten free-agent backup, Glennon's name appeared in headlines this offseason when former teammate Akiem Hicks singled him out as an example of the league's mistreatment of Colin Kaepernick. That is a little unfair to him: Glennon's stint in Chicago was the worst of his career, but he has otherwise been mostly an acceptable backup-level quarterback. He joined the Jaguars following the draft after passing unsigned through the initial wave of free agency. He won't threaten to take Gardner Minshew's job in Jacksonville, but under the tutelage of Jay Gruden he shouldn't completely crash the Jaguars offense if he has to play for a game or two. That's an acceptable fit for an acceptable player.

Jared Goff

Height: 6-4 | Weight:223 | College: California | Draft: 2016/1 (1) | Born: 14-Oct-1994 | Age: 26 | Risk: Green

Year	Tm	G/GS	Snaps	Att	Cmp	C%	CPOE	Yds	TD	INT/Adj	FUM	ASR	NY/P	Rk	DVOA	Rk	DYAR	Rk	Runs	Yds	TD	DVOA	DYAR	QBR
2017	LAR	15/15	937	477	296	62.1%	0.6%	3804	28	7/10	8	5.4%	7.4	4	24.0%	5	1125	6	28	51	1	-20.6%	-6	52.0
2018	LAR	16/16	1064	561	364	64.9%	2.9%	4688	32	12/18	12	5.5%	7.5	5	17.0%	5	1114	6	43	108	2	-11.8%	0	66.4
2019	LAR	16/16	1120	626	394	62.9%	-0.3%	4638	22	16/20	10	3.7%	6.9	12	2.0%	18	552	15	33	40	2	-36.7%	-32	48.5
2020	LAR			598	392	65.5%		4478	25	14	9		6.7		4.8%				29	58	1	-5.2%		

2018: 45% Short   34% Mid   14% Deep   7% Bomb   aDOT: 9.0 (11)   YAC: 5.8 (7)   ALEX: -0.3   2019: 49% Short   33% Mid   14% Deep   4% Bomb   aDOT: 7.9 (26)   YAC: 5.7 (8)   ALEX: 1.8

Goff is the sort of quarterback who amplifies the state of the offense around him. When given open targets and room to move, he has the arm talent to hit receivers in stride anywhere on the field. He also has underrated mobility—his DVOA rose by 23.6% when he left the pocket, the second-biggest improvement behind Jameis Winston. Under pressure, however, he has a habit of floating passes off his back foot, and tight coverage exposes his tendency to throw wide of his mark. As a result, he looked every bit the franchise passer the Rams need him to be against lesser competition but completely overwhelmed by the stronger defenses in the NFL. He played four games against teams ranked 25th or worse in pass defense DVOA (the Bengals, the Falcons, and the Cardinals twice) and ripped them to shreds, completing 64% of his passes for an 8.9-yard average with 10 total touchdowns, no interceptions or fumbles, only two sacks, and a DVOA of 30.6%. However, when he played four games against teams ranked fourth or better (the Patriots, the Ravens, and the 49ers twice), they ate him alive, holding him below a 60% completion rate with 5.8 yards pass, two touchdowns, 10 sacks, five interceptions, a half-dozen fumbles, and a DVOA of -27.8%.

Goff comes off as a likeable guy—he spent his quarantine teaming up with Andrew Whitworth to donate two million meals to Los Angeles families, and he also grew a moustache so he now looks like Ryan Gosling in *Nice Guys* instead of Ryan Gosling in *Drive*. He's got a long way to go to live up to his mega-contract, but it would be good for the league if he could pull it off.

Will Grier   Height: 6-1   Weight:220   College: West Virginia   Draft: 2019/3 (100)   Born: 3-Apr-1995   Age: 25   Risk: Green

Year	Tm	G/GS	Snaps	Att	Cmp	C%	CPOE	Yds	TD	INT/Adj	FUM	ASR	NY/P	Rk	DVOA	Rk	DYAR	Rk	Runs	Yds	TD	DVOA	DYAR	QBR
2019	CAR	2/2	87	52	28	53.8%	-7.6%	228	0	4/6	1	10.0%	3.2	--	-60.6%	--	-180	--	7	22	0	-71.8%	-23	2.5
2020	CAR			538	311	57.8%		3537	21	16	10		5.7		-18.9%				42	154	1	1.2%		

2019:   64% Short   11% Mid   13% Deep   13% Bomb   aDOT: 10.0 (--)   YAC: 6.4 (--)   ALEX: -0.5

If there was a question of whether quarterback Kyle Allen was the primary reason the Panthers had fallen into a six-game losing streak in the second half of 2019, Grier answered it with his own dreadful play in two starts in Weeks 16 and 17. Grier never had much of a chance, taking six sacks behind a bad Panthers line that finished fourth-worst in football with an 8.6% adjusted sack rate. Had he qualified, Grier's personal 10.0% ASR would have been second-highest at the position, ahead of only Redskins quarterback Dwayne Haskins. As a first-round pick, Haskins can survive a rookie season with a -42.0% passing DVOA. But as a third-rounder, Grier may not survive his slow career start. In addition to their new starter Teddy Bridgewater, the Panthers signed XFL standout Phillip "P.J." Walker, who quarterbacked new head coach Matt Rhule's Temple teams from 2013 to 2016. Despite that Day 2 selection just a year ago, Grier may not even make the 2020 roster of a team whose new coaching staff would have no reason to be embarrassed by cutting him.

Robert Griffin   Height: 6-2   Weight:213   College: Baylor   Draft: 2012/1 (2)   Born: 12-Feb-1990   Age: 30   Risk: Green

Year	Tm	G/GS	Snaps	Att	Cmp	C%	CPOE	Yds	TD	INT/Adj	FUM	ASR	NY/P	Rk	DVOA	Rk	DYAR	Rk	Runs	Yds	TD	DVOA	DYAR	QBR
2018	BAL	3/0	21	6	2	33.3%	-26.9%	21	0	0/1	0	-0.9%	3.5	--	-11.4%	--	0	--	0	0	0	--	--	2.2
2019	BAL	7/1	141	38	23	60.5%	-4.3%	225	1	2/3	0	10.6%	4.8	--	-5.9%	--	14	--	20	70	0	-6.6%	5	52.8
2020	BAL			514	312	60.7%		3539	21	14	10		6.1		-9.1%				141	549	3	-15.9%		

2018:   40% Short   20% Mid   20% Deep   20% Bomb   aDOT: 10.8 (--)   YAC: 13 (--)   ALEX: 4.5   2019:   46% Short   40% Mid   6% Deep   9% Bomb   aDOT: 7.5 (--)   YAC: 3.7 (--)   ALEX: 1.4

Griffin got to start the season finale, his first start since 2016, and handed the ball off well enough to lead the Ravens to a meaningless win over Pittsburgh. Good for him. When RG3 was signed by Baltimore it seemed he was merely there to give Lamar Jackson advice on What Not To Do in order to stay in the NFL and be effective. If indeed that's true, mission accomplished. While he is hardly a Nick Foles-level backup, Griffin has found a niche with the Ravens, a stunning twist given where he was four years ago.

Dwayne Haskins   Height: 6-4   Weight:230   College: Ohio State   Draft: 2019/1 (15)   Born: 3-May-1997   Age: 23   Risk: Green

Year	Tm	G/GS	Snaps	Att	Cmp	C%	CPOE	Yds	TD	INT/Adj	FUM	ASR	NY/P	Rk	DVOA	Rk	DYAR	Rk	Runs	Yds	TD	DVOA	DYAR	QBR
2019	WAS	9/7	442	203	119	58.6%	-6.7%	1365	7	7/6	6	12.7%	5.0	34	-42.0%	34	-443	34	20	101	0	-20.9%	-8	26.4
2020	WAS			501	313	62.5%		3604	17	14	10		6.3		-17.1%				40	191	1	4.9%		

2019:   43% Short   38% Mid   12% Deep   6% Bomb   aDOT: 8.9 (15)   YAC: 5.2 (19)   ALEX: 0.2

From a production standpoint, Haskins' rookie season was not quite the disaster we saw from Josh Rosen or Jared Goff, but it was not meaningfully better. Haskins finished worst in the league in DYAR, DVOA, and QBR. Likewise, Haskins was the only quarterback among 34 qualifiers to score a negative DVOA without pressure. Granted, he just barely crossed into the red at -0.1%, but no other quarterback was even below 20.0%. Over his final three starts, though, Haskins started to sharpen up. He completed 47 of 70 pass attempts for 564 yards, five touchdowns, and just one interception, though his alarmingly high sack rate did stay about the same. In the film from those games, Haskins proved he could cycle through multiple reads effectively and find the correct targets, which was his defining trait coming out of college. Accuracy, mechanics, and pocket management still need work, but Haskins showed more than his year-long stats suggest and could be in for a nice season if one or two of Washington's young pass-catchers step up.

Chad Henne

Chad Henne — Height: 6-3 Weight:222 College: Michigan Draft: 2008/2 (57) Born: 2-Jul-1985 Age: 35 Risk: Green

Year	Tm	G/GS	Snaps	Att	Cmp	C%	CPOE	Yds	TD	INT/Adj	FUM	ASR	NY/P	Rk	DVOA	Rk	DYAR	Rk	Runs	Yds	TD	DVOA	DYAR	QBR
2017	JAX	2/0	23	2	0	0.0%	-77.6%	0	0	0/1	0	-1.3%	0.0	--	-87.5%	--	-10	--	5	-5	0	--	--	3.0
2018	KC	1/0	13	3	2	66.7%	-9.6%	29	0	0/0	0	3.9%	9.7	--	38.8%	--	11	--	1	3	0	-51.8%	-2	71.8
2020	KC			523	325	62.2%		3987	27	14	10		6.9		7.3%				45	170	2	13.4%		

2018:   67% Short   33% Mid   0% Deep   0% Bomb   aDOT: 6.0 (--)   YAC: 7.5 (--)   ALEX: 3.0

Henne has thrown just five passes in the last five NFL seasons. My, how time flies! It seems like only yesterday that he was winning a starting job away from Blaine Gabbert. But no, that was two Jacksonville quarterbacks-of-the-future ago. Henne suffered an ankle injury in the preseason last year and landed on IR for the first half of the season. He returned to back up Matt Moore during the Patrick Mahomes crisis and ended up earning a Super Bowl ring for clipboard duties. If we told you that Henne was one of the Bears offensive assistant coaches instead of Mahomes' primary backup, you might have believed us, and it's hard to imagine that a 35-year-old with two layers of rust and a 58:63 career touchdown-to-interception ratio has much to offer as a backup quarterback for a Super Bowl team. But remember that 35-year-old Moore completed 64.8% of his passes, threw four touchdowns, and engineered a win in this offense, a few months after taking a job as a scouting intern. So anything is possible.

Justin Herbert

Justin Herbert — Height: 6-6 Weight:237 College: Oregon Draft: 2020/1 (6) Born: 10-Mar-1998 Age: 22 Risk: Green

Year	Tm	G/GS	Snaps	Att	Cmp	C%	CPOE	Yds	TD	INT/Adj	FUM	ASR	NY/P	Rk	DVOA	Rk	DYAR	Rk	Runs	Yds	TD	DVOA	DYAR	QBR
2020	LAC			525	326	62.0%		3836	25	13	11		6.5		-3.1%				61	246	3	4.9%		

Per Derrik Klassen's charting data, Herbert's adjusted accuracy rate of 73.1% ranked sixth among the nine top quarterback prospects in this class, below Jalen Hurts and Jacob Eason, two prospects not known as pinpoint passers. But Herbert's adjusted accuracy under pressure of 61.3% ranked second below Joe Burrow. Those splits jibe with Herbert's late-season change-of-perception: he went from a guy who puts up gaudy numbers but makes too many errant throws to a field general able to make tough throws, runs, and decisions that didn't stand out on the stat sheet. It's encouraging to see some objective evidence that Herbert is cooler than expected under fire.

Taysom Hill

Taysom Hill — Height: 6-2 Weight:221 College: Brigham Young Draft: 2017/FA Born: 23-Aug-1990 Age: 30 Risk: Green

Year	Tm	G/GS	Snaps	Att	Cmp	C%	CPOE	Yds	TD	INT/Adj	FUM	ASR	NY/P	Rk	DVOA	Rk	DYAR	Rk	Runs	Yds	TD	DVOA	DYAR	QBR
2018	NO	16/4	181	7	3	42.9%	-11.0%	64	0	1/1	1	14.4%	7.6	--	-40.8%	--	-19	--	37	196	2	-7.1%	12	43.5
2019	NO	16/5	242	6	3	50.0%	4.1%	55	0	0/0	0	14.4%	6.6	--	4.2%	--	6	--	27	156	1	-7.5%	7	83.9
2020	NO			8	6	73.8%		65	0	0	1		8.2		22.8%				32	191	1	26.8%		

2018:   33% Short   17% Mid   17% Deep   33% Bomb   aDOT: 19.7 (--)   YAC: 6.0 (--)   ALEX: 0.0   2019:   0% Short   67% Mid   33% Deep   0% Bomb   aDOT: 12.3 (--)   YAC: 4.0 (--)   ALEX: 0.0

Hill is sticking around as the Saints' quarterback/running back/fullback/receiver/tight end/kick returner/punt gunner/Superdome valet manager through at least 2021. In April, New Orleans signed him to a two-year deal that has a base value of $21 million and includes $16 million in guaranteed money. His 2021 salary-cap number, as of now, is the fifth-largest on the team. Does the contract portend a larger role, potentially as the successor to Drew Brees? The Saints' signing of Jameis Winston was a curious way of showing Hill that they're confident he can take over. If Brees suffers an injury again this season and has to miss multiple games, you would think that Winston (2,548 career passes) becomes the full-time starter, not Hill (15 career passes, including the playoffs).

Hill's projection is the only one for a quarterback that is for actual playing time rather than 16 starts. It includes 14 catches for 108 yards and a touchdown. ESPN announced its fantasy leagues will be counting Hill as a tight end this season, just in case you're in a really, really deep league where every team starts three tight ends.

Devlin Hodges

Devlin Hodges — Height: 6-1 Weight:210 College: Samford Draft: 2019/FA Born: 12-Apr-1996 Age: 24 Risk: Green

Year	Tm	G/GS	Snaps	Att	Cmp	C%	CPOE	Yds	TD	INT/Adj	FUM	ASR	NY/P	Rk	DVOA	Rk	DYAR	Rk	Runs	Yds	TD	DVOA	DYAR	QBR
2019	PIT	8/6	385	160	100	62.5%	2.4%	1063	5	8/7	5	9.5%	5.6	--	-22.1%	--	-122	--	21	68	0	-34.5%	-16	30.1
2020	PIT			488	319	65.3%		3614	19	16	12		6.5		-8.2%				40	144	1	1.9%		

2019:   57% Short   23% Mid   8% Deep   12% Bomb   aDOT: 7.9 (--)   YAC: 5.7 (--)   ALEX: -1.4

Quack. Duck Hodges came out of nowhere to start games for the Pittsburgh Steelers last season, and given that fact, we think the Steelers got about what they bargained for. Hodges created a lot of sacks behind a good offensive line, had poor accuracy, and had the kind of process flaws that you'd expect from an undrafted free agent from Samford who was thrust into the starting lineup. If he starts games in 2020, it will be monumentally disappointing. The big story of Hodges' offseason was finding a fawn in a forest while hunting, which is an interesting place to find Mason Rudolph.

Brian Hoyer

Height: 6-2   Weight:215   College: Michigan State   Draft: 2009/FA   Born: 13-Oct-1985   Age: 35   Risk: Green

Year	Tm	G/GS	Snaps	Att	Cmp	C%	CPOE	Yds	TD	INT/Adj	FUM	ASR	NY/P	Rk	DVOA	Rk	DYAR	Rk	Runs	Yds	TD	DVOA	DYAR	QBR
2017	2TM	11/6	381	211	123	58.3%	-7.2%	1287	4	4/8	3	7.7%	5.2	34	-16.7%	28	-80	27	9	4	1	-96.7%	-29	31.9
2018	NE	5/0	27	2	1	50.0%	-28.3%	7	0	0/0	0	-3.2%	3.5	--	-41.8%	--	-3	--	11	-8	0	32.7%	3	0.5
2019	IND	4/1	131	65	35	53.8%	-12.9%	372	4	4/4	2	7.5%	4.7	--	-53.1%	--	-175	--	8	2	0	-68.5%	-6	16.3
2020	NE			524	303	57.8%		3266	22	15	10		5.5		-14.1%				42	58	1	-20.0%		

2018: 50% Short 50% Mid 0% Deep 0% Bomb   aDOT: 2.0 (--)   YAC: 10.0 (--) ALEX: -15.0   2019: 45% Short 27% Mid 23% Deep 5% Bomb aDOT: 9.1 (--)   YAC: 4.5 (--) ALEX: -0.3

As is the natural progression of things, Brian Hoyer has once again found himself back in New England. Hoyer is not the young, reasonably capable backup he once was though. While Hoyer put up a decent run as a backup and spot starter from 2013 to 2015, Hoyer has gone 1-11 in his four seasons since then, earning just 6.5 yards per attempt. Hoyer most recently picked up a paycheck with the Indianapolis Colts, throwing 65 passes and starting one game in relief of an injured Jacoby Brissett. He is probably still in the top half of NFL backups, but there should be no concern over him pushing Cam Newton or Jarrett Stidham for the starting job this year.

Brett Hundley

Height: 6-3   Weight:226   College: UCLA   Draft: 2015/5 (147)   Born: 15-Jun-1993   Age: 27   Risk: Green

Year	Tm	G/GS	Snaps	Att	Cmp	C%	CPOE	Yds	TD	INT/Adj	FUM	ASR	NY/P	Rk	DVOA	Rk	DYAR	Rk	Runs	Yds	TD	DVOA	DYAR	QBR
2017	GB	11/9	622	316	192	60.8%	-0.9%	1836	9	12/12	4	9.1%	4.8	35	-28.3%	34	-396	34	36	270	2	40.3%	100	41.2
2019	ARI	3/0	40	11	5	45.5%	-22.4%	49	0	0/0	0	16.5%	2.9	--	-62.3%	--	-43	--	7	41	0	44.7%	17	79.2
2020	ARI			525	319	60.7%		3415	21	11	9		5.6		-13.2%				64	388	2	22.9%		

2019: 45% Short 27% Mid 9% Deep 18% Bomb aDOT: 10.4 (--)   YAC: 6.8 (--) ALEX: 6.0

Hundley moved from Seattle to Arizona in 2019 to take on the backup role behind Kyler Murray and only saw action in three games. In two of those games, Hundley attempted only one pass, but in Week 16 against Seattle, he filled in for Murray to help Arizona take the air out of the ball in the second half on the way to the team's final win of the season. Hundley has the look of a career backup at this point, and even then, teams should not be counting on him to make a difference in the event that he has to step in for an extended period of time. His only starting experience came in 2017 after Aaron Rodgers went down, and he finished second-to-last among all qualified passers in both DYAR and DVOA, ahead of only DeShone Kizer on a winless Browns team.

Jalen Hurts

Height: 6-1   Weight:222   College: Oklahoma   Draft: 2020/2 (53)   Born: 7-Aug-1998   Age: 22   Risk: Green

Year	Tm	G/GS	Snaps	Att	Cmp	C%	CPOE	Yds	TD	INT/Adj	FUM	ASR	NY/P	Rk	DVOA	Rk	DYAR	Rk	Runs	Yds	TD	DVOA	DYAR	QBR
2020	PHI			525	315	60.0%		3676	23	14	15		6.1		-12.0%				115	630	5	9.3%		

Just how will the Eagles deploy Hurts as a rookie? The shortened offseason will likely delay the deployment of special packages designed around his skill set, but Philadelphia will be doing themselves a disservice if they don't figure out a way to get Hurts into the game around the goal line. Hurts led all players in college football with 17 red zone touchdowns last year—not quarterbacks but all players period. He should be a serious threat on RPOs, with or without Carson Wentz in the backfield with him. As a passer, he's a work in progress but with plenty of upside. Our own Derrik Klassen had him third in the class with a 74.5% adjusted accuracy rate in charting; however, 5.9% of his passes required his receivers to make adjustments, the highest in the class. There's a lot to like, but it's probably for the best that he'll start his career as a backup and occasional package player.

Lamar Jackson Height: 6-2 Weight:212 College: Louisville Draft: 2018/1 (32) Born: 7-Jan-1997 Age: 23 Risk: Yellow

Year	Tm	G/GS	Snaps	Att	Cmp	C%	CPOE	Yds	TD	INT/Adj	FUM	ASR	NY/P	Rk	DVOA	Rk	DYAR	Rk	Runs	Yds	TD	DVOA	DYAR	QBR
2018	BAL	16/7	585	170	99	58.2%	-5.5%	1201	6	3/6	12	10.2%	6.0	--	-9.2%	--	24	--	147	695	5	-27.2%	-112	45.2
2019	BAL	15/15	987	401	265	66.1%	2.4%	3127	36	6/6	9	5.6%	7.2	10	34.9%	2	1261	5	176	1206	7	20.5%	273	81.8
2020	BAL			471	300	63.7%		3613	29	9	12		6.8		7.7%				180	1067	7	5.1%		

2018: 35% Short 49% Mid 10% Deep 5% Bomb aDOT: 9.1 (--) YAC: 5.2 (--) ALEX: 0.2 2019: 45% Short 34% Mid 12% Deep 9% Bomb aDOT: 9.2 (8) YAC: 5.1 (20) ALEX: 1.8

Here's a look at how Jackson's incredible season carrying the ball stacks up historically:

Best Single-Season Rushing DYAR, Quarterbacks, 1985-2019

Name	Year	Team	DYAR	DVOA	Runs	Yards	Avg	TD	FUM
Randall Cunningham	1990	PHI	297	44.8%	105	949	9.04	5	3
Lamar Jackson	**2019**	**BAL**	**273**	**20.5%**	**156**	**1,229**	**7.88**	**7**	**7**
Russell Wilson	2014	SEA	269	43.7%	97	872	8.99	6	4
Michael Vick	2006	ATL	261	35.2%	119	1,038	8.72	2	4
Michael Vick	2004	ATL	241	29.7%	106	919	8.67	3	2
Randall Cunningham	1986	PHI	220	60.5%	63	540	8.57	5	0
Steve McNair	1998	TEN	214	49.2%	66	573	8.68	4	1
Daunte Culpepper	2000	MIN	209	39.5%	72	490	6.81	7	0
Donovan McNabb	2002	PHI	200	50.4%	57	469	8.23	6	1
Randall Cunningham	1988	PHI	196	31.7%	82	633	7.72	6	3
Michael Vick	2010	PHI	192	29.0%	90	681	7.57	9	3
Josh Allen	2018	BUF	192	33.3%	81	638	7.88	8	3
Kneeldowns excluded.									

Jackson broke an amazing 55 tackles (54 of them on running plays), more than twice as many as Josh Allen, the next quarterback on the list. Another sign of his mobility: he was hit on just 6.7% of dropbacks that didn't result in sacks.

Meanwhile, Jackson had an amazing season as a passer. Here is some statistical evidence because, you know, that's what we do here: only Russell Wilson and Deshaun Watson threw a higher percentage of their passes from outside the pocket, but Jackson's DVOA on those throws was higher (the only quarterback better than Jackson was Ryan Tannehill). Jackson's DVOA on passes in the pocket was the best in the league and put him light years ahead of Wilson, Watson, and every other quarterback except second-place Drew Brees (Jackson 58.2%, Brees 57.6%). Brees was the only passer to rate higher in DVOA out of shotgun sets (including pistol), and Jackson was under center on just 14 snaps, by far the fewest of any qualifying quarterback. To no one's shock, Jackson was nigh-unstoppable in the red zone, posting an insanely high 89.9% DVOA, so far ahead of the other quarterbacks they needed the Hubble telescope to spot him.

It will be a difficult job for Jackson to replicate his MVP season, though even a slight downgrade would still translate into a helluva campaign. What's left is to win a playoff game, the lone donut hole on a resume that otherwise is sweeter than a whole rack of Krispy Kremes.

Daniel Jones Height: 6-5 Weight:220 College: Duke Draft: 2019/1 (6) Born: 27-May-1997 Age: 23 Risk: Green

Year	Tm	G/GS	Snaps	Att	Cmp	C%	CPOE	Yds	TD	INT/Adj	FUM	ASR	NY/P	Rk	DVOA	Rk	DYAR	Rk	Runs	Yds	TD	DVOA	DYAR	QBR
2019	NYG	13/12	826	459	284	61.9%	-2.4%	3027	24	12/18	18	7.8%	5.5	31	-19.2%	30	-256	31	45	279	2	7.9%	45	53.6
2020	NYG			591	361	61.1%		4045	25	13	17		6.0		-12.2%				50	298	2	18.9%		

2019: 52% Short 30% Mid 10% Deep 8% Bomb aDOT: 8.2 (22) YAC: 4.9 (28) ALEX: 0.7

Only Ryan Fitzpatrick had a higher percentage of dropbacks that ended with a quarterback hit than Daniel Jones. Only Sam Darnold was under pressure at a higher rate. Few quarterbacks fared worse when under pressure, especially against the blitz. Jones only saw five or more rushers on 22% of his dropbacks, but he dropped to -20.1% DVOA on those plays, opposed to 9.4% against a four-man rush. Against six or more rushers, Jones had -54.4% DVOA. For a quarterback who was so good at getting the ball out on quick drops, extra rushers really messed up Jones' timing. When things were clear, Jones still had his struggles. The rookie tended to play like an aggressive gunslinger without the requisite arm to pull off that type of mentality, which led to some good and awful plays. From a clean pocket, Jones had the fifth-highest touchdown rate (6.4%) but also the third-highest interception rate (3.4%).

Case Keenum

| | | Height: 6-1 | | Weight:215 | | College: Houston | | | Draft: 2012/FA | | Born: 17-Feb-1988 | | Age: 32 | | Risk: Green |

Year	Tm	G/GS	Snaps	Att	Cmp	C%	CPOE	Yds	TD	INT/Adj	FUM	ASR	NY/P	Rk	DVOA	Rk	DYAR	Rk	Runs	Yds	TD	DVOA	DYAR	QBR
2017	MIN	15/14	1017	481	325	67.6%	5.1%	3547	22	7/10	1	4.0%	7.1	8	28.1%	1	1293	4	40	160	1	58.3%	76	69.7
2018	DEN	16/16	1073	586	365	62.3%	-2.7%	3890	18	15/17	11	6.3%	5.9	29	-12.7%	28	-63	29	26	93	2	31.2%	40	46.9
2019	WAS	10/8	460	247	160	64.8%	-1.5%	1707	11	5/8	6	6.3%	6.0	22	-8.1%	23	51	24	9	12	1	-36.8%	-12	43.5
2020	CLE			525	338	64.4%		3811	21	12	12		6.4		-4.9%				40	124	3	5.8%		

2018: 55% Short   28% Mid   10% Deep   7% Bomb   aDOT: 7.8 (23)   YAC: 4.9 (27)   ALEX: 0.1   2019:   51% Short   32% Mid   13% Deep   4% Bomb aDOT: 7.1 (30)   YAC: 5.0 (23)   ALEX: -1.3

Keenum in career pass attempts under center: 62.4% completion rate, 19 touchdowns, eight picks, 8.9 adjusted yards per attempt. Keenum's career pass attempts when his team is trailing with less than four minutes to go: 54.0% completion rate, nine touchdowns, eight picks, 5.1 adjusted yards per attempt. That about sums it up. Keenum has become one of the most highly valued backup quarterbacks in the land by virtue of good work with good game scripts and well-defined, easy reads. The second he goes beyond his first read or is asked to make a difficult throw, the true colors come through. Now on his fourth team in four years, Keenum will provide a high-floor backup for an offensive scheme of which he previously showed a lot of command in Minnesota … which is a very academic way of saying "if Baker Mayfield gets hurt, this guy can beat the Bengals."

Drew Lock

| | | Height: 6-4 | | Weight:228 | | College: Missouri | | | Draft: 2019/2 (42) | | Born: 10-Nov-1996 | | Age: 24 | | Risk: Yellow |

Year	Tm	G/GS	Snaps	Att	Cmp	C%	CPOE	Yds	TD	INT/Adj	FUM	ASR	NY/P	Rk	DVOA	Rk	DYAR	Rk	Runs	Yds	TD	DVOA	DYAR	QBR
2019	DEN	5/5	307	156	100	64.1%	-1.3%	1020	7	3/4	3	4.2%	6.2	--	2.2%	--	138	--	18	72	0	-10.9%	1	48.2
2020	DEN			534	317	59.3%		3640	22	12	10		5.9		-12.4%				58	247	1	-2.4%		

2019:   55% Short   31% Mid   11% Deep   3% Bomb aDOT: 7.1 (--)   YAC: 5.5 (--)   ALEX: 1.3

Lock completed 69.1% of his passes for 7.6 yards per attempt, six touchdowns, and zero interceptions in first halves of games, but 58.5% of his passes for 5.3 yards per attempt, one touchdown, and three interceptions in second halves. He has a gunslinger reputation, but his 14% deep-and-bomb attempt rate and 55% short pass rate reveal that he spent much of last December dinking and dunking.

There's a lot of other circumstantial evidence that Lock performed well within the rookie quarterback guardrails (scripted plays, on schedule, playing with the lead, shorter throws, etc.) but would have gotten into trouble if asked to do more than manage some narrow wins over weak opponents and aid in one of the Texans' regularly scheduled self-destructions. There's nothing wrong with a rookie quarterback only being good at rookie quarterback stuff, but the stat splits are a reminder of how brief Lock's late-season appearance was, how much we don't know about him, and how quickly his career could go in either direction once opponents get a book on him.

Jordan Love

| | | Height: 6-4 | | Weight:224 | | College: Utah State | | | Draft: 2020/1 (26) | | Born: 2-Nov-1998 | | Age: 22 | | Risk: Green |

Year	Tm	G/GS	Snaps	Att	Cmp	C%	CPOE	Yds	TD	INT/Adj	FUM	ASR	NY/P	Rk	DVOA	Rk	DYAR	Rk	Runs	Yds	TD	DVOA	DYAR	QBR
2020	GB			525	314	59.8%		3718	23	13	12		6.3		-6.9%				64	261	3	12.2%		

2018 Jordan Love was a top-tier passer—9.4 adjusted yards per attempt with 32 touchdowns and six interceptions. Had that Love come out in this year's draft, QBASE would have projected him with 420 DYAR, just a rung down from the top of the class. Instead, his 2019 season at Utah State was highly concerning. He ranked eighth out of the nine major quarterbacks in adjusted accuracy, including the worst accuracy in the 6- to 10-yard area at just 67%, and 23% of his passes went to players behind the line of scrimmage, the most in the class. Love has an astounding arm, and the confidence, smoothness, and poise you're looking for in a quarterback prospect, but those didn't translate into results last season. He needs to work on his field vision and the speed of his reads, but that might be something that just comes with time and familiarity with a system. He's a project, in other words. Love needed to go to a team willing to wait for a few years to smooth out his inconsistencies and allow him to develop. Sitting behind Aaron Rodgers definitely counts.

Patrick Mahomes

Height: 6-3 Weight:230 College: Texas Tech Draft: 2017/1 (10) Born: 17-Sep-1995 Age: 25 Risk: Green

Year	Tm	G/GS	Snaps	Att	Cmp	C%	CPOE	Yds	TD	INT/Adj	FUM	ASR	NY/P	Rk	DVOA	Rk	DYAR	Rk	Runs	Yds	TD	DVOA	DYAR	QBR
2017	KC	1/1	63	35	22	62.9%	-3.7%	284	0	1/1	0	5.8%	7.3	--	11.7%	--	54	--	7	10	0	9.2%	4	64.8
2018	KC	16/16	1032	580	383	66.0%	1.9%	5097	50	12/21	9	5.4%	8.1	2	39.9%	1	2031	1	60	272	2	3.0%	39	81.6
2019	KC	14/14	889	484	319	65.9%	2.7%	4031	26	5/10	3	4.3%	7.8	2	30.0%	3	1320	2	43	218	2	28.1%	66	76.3
2020	KC			571	376	65.8%		4795	33	9	8		7.6		24.4%				67	340	4	28.6%		

| 2018: | 47% Short | 31% Mid | 13% Deep | 10% Bomb | aDOT: 9.3 (9) | YAC: 6.8 (2) | ALEX: 4.5 | 2019: | 47% Short | 30% Mid | 15% Deep | 8% Bomb | aDOT: 9.0 (12) | YAC: 6.1 (2) | ALEX: 1.5 |

Mahomes isn't just beginning to set new statistical benchmarks for NFL quarterbacks. He's also a trailblazer when it comes to how franchise quarterbacks handle social media.

Quarterbacks of the Manning-Brady-Brees era didn't engage much on Twitter, Instagram, etc., though Brady eventually cultivated an "I'm just an ordinary family man" online persona with the help of his team of filmmakers and brand managers. Russell Wilson followed Brady's "half of a celebrity power couple" approach, while other quarterbacks mostly used their social networking presence as a promotional arm of their team's front office and/or their charitable foundation. Most quarterback accounts, if they exist at all, are safe, calculated, impersonal, and dull, which makes sense for individuals whose every facial expression and utterance is scrutinized by an entire industry and millions of fans. A quarterback who takes a social media misstep, from the legitimately foolish (Baker Mayfield's tiresome media feuds) to the overbaked (Cam Newton's weird fonts) to the absurd (Lamar Jackson trading virtual high-fives with the president), runs the risk of causing an avoidable headache for himself.

Mahomes comes across as chatty and affable online, able to comment on the latest memes and converse with teammates/fans about non-football topics without causing red alerts on the daytime talk shows (even during the quarantine, when we were hungry to talk about ANYTHING). He was chosen as the first player to proclaim "Black Lives Matter" on the viral video which made the rounds in June, and it was reportedly his prominence which prompted the NFL to rethink its position (or at least its messaging) on social justice and racial issues. In short, Mahomes is #Relatable, which has little to do with what we do here at *Football Outsiders Almanac* but everything to do with how younger fans engage the NFL. The league needs young stars who come across as regular 20-something bros without getting into beefs or causing distractions. Mahomes is navigating a new course for quarterbacks who also want to publicly look, act, and sound like real people.

Oh yeah, he's also going to throw for, like, 4,800 yards and totally dominate the league again this year.

Eli Manning

Height: 6-5 Weight:218 College: Mississippi Draft: 2004/1 (1) Born: 3-Jan-1981 Age: 40 Risk: N/A

Year	Tm	G/GS	Snaps	Att	Cmp	C%	CPOE	Yds	TD	INT/Adj	FUM	ASR	NY/P	Rk	DVOA	Rk	DYAR	Rk	Runs	Yds	TD	DVOA	DYAR	QBR
2017	NYG	15/15	1018	571	352	61.6%	-3.4%	3468	19	13/17	11	5.6%	5.5	28	-8.2%	23	117	23	12	26	1	-15.1%	-1	43.8
2018	NYG	16/16	1010	576	380	66.0%	-1.0%	4299	21	11/15	7	7.5%	6.3	19	-2.5%	24	337	22	15	20	1	-7.4%	4	51.8
2019	NYG	4/4	252	147	91	61.9%	0.9%	1042	6	5/8	3	4.6%	6.6	--	-15.0%	--	-38	--	4	7	0	11.6%	3	34.4

| 2018: | 55% Short | 25% Mid | 12% Deep | 7% Bomb | aDOT: 7.8 (24) | YAC: 5.7 (9) | ALEX: -0.5 | 2019: | 48% Short | 34% Mid | 11% Deep | 7% Bomb | aDOT: 8.5 (--) | YAC: 4.6 (--) | ALEX: 2.3 |

The Eli Manning era for the New York Giants officially ended with the quarterback's retirement this offseason. His legacy is a complicated one, one that will be highly debated until his case is officially brought up in the Hall of Fame discussion. There are the two Super Bowl wins, but Manning was never among the best quarterbacks in the NFL—he peaked at ninth in DVOA twice (2008 and 2011) and usually hovered around the top 15. The only "black ink" on Manning's Pro Football Reference page comes from leading the league in interceptions three times.

The decline over the past few seasons also tanked his win-loss record. His final home win in Week 15 against the Miami Dolphins brought Manning's career record to a most fitting 117-117. But thanks to his peak and longevity, Manning put up 165 Career AV (42nd all-time) and every Hall of Fame-eligible player to hit that mark has been elected to the Hall.

If Manning *is* going to make the Hall of Fame, he might have to sneak in on the first ballot in front of logjams at other positions because, in the next few seasons, we're likely to see the retirements of Tom Brady, Drew Brees, Philip Rivers, Ben Roethlisberger, and eventually Aaron Rodgers and Matt Ryan—all names that will complicate Manning's path to the small five-man class each year.

Sean Mannion

Height: 6-6　Weight:231　College: Oregon State　Draft: 2015/3 (89)　Born: 25-Apr-1992　Age: 28　Risk: Green

Year	Tm	G/GS	Snaps	Att	Cmp	C%	CPOE	Yds	TD	INT/Adj	FUM	ASR	NY/P	Rk	DVOA	Rk	DYAR	Rk	Runs	Yds	TD	DVOA	DYAR	QBR
2017	LAR	5/1	102	37	22	59.5%	-9.6%	185	0	0/0	2	8.3%	4.1	--	-66.6%	--	-141	--	9	-2	0	-33.0%	-6	14.4
2018	LAR	3/0	36	3	2	66.7%	-20.9%	23	0	0/0	0	-1.8%	7.7	--	66.0%	--	10	--	7	-9	0	40.8%	4	6.4
2019	MIN	3/1	54	21	12	57.1%	-3.4%	126	0	2/1	1	1.0%	6.0	--	-15.2%	--	-5	--	6	-5	0	-352.9%	-21	24.8
2020	MIN		516	336		65.2%		3721	23	14	10		6.4		-5.7%				41	37	1	-29.0%		

2018: 100% Short　0% Mid　0% Deep　0% Bomb　aDOT: -3.3 (--)　YAC: 13.5 (--)　ALEX: -14.5　2019: 71% Short　24% Mid　0% Deep　6% Bomb　aDOT: 7.6 (--)　YAC: 5.5 (--)　ALEX: -4.8

Mannion doubled his career starts last season. He now has two, both of which produced negative DVOA. The Vikings re-signed Mannion not because he was the best backup quarterback available, but because he was cheap and knew the system, which are significant positive attributes for a team butting against the salary cap and facing a reduced offseason program due to COVID-19. Kirk Cousins has never missed a game due to injury, and the Vikings are betting big he won't this fall either, as they have one of the worst backup situations in the league.

Marcus Mariota

Height: 6-4　Weight:222　College: Oregon　Draft: 2015/1 (2)　Born: 30-Oct-1993　Age: 27　Risk: Yellow

Year	Tm	G/GS	Snaps	Att	Cmp	C%	CPOE	Yds	TD	INT/Adj	FUM	ASR	NY/P	Rk	DVOA	Rk	DYAR	Rk	Runs	Yds	TD	DVOA	DYAR	QBR
2017	TEN	15/15	945	453	281	62.0%	0.8%	3232	13	15/17	2	5.3%	6.4	17	-3.3%	20	236	19	60	312	5	35.6%	114	54.9
2018	TEN	14/13	775	331	228	68.9%	2.5%	2528	11	8/10	9	11.6%	6.1	24	-8.5%	27	65	27	64	357	2	15.1%	86	55.5
2019	TEN	7/6	367	160	95	59.4%	-4.9%	1203	7	2/3	3	13.6%	5.7	--	-17.0%	--	-62	--	24	129	0	-13.7%	-2	33.7
2020	LV		525	345		65.6%		3894	23	10	10		6.6		4.1%				72	399	2	10.2%		

2018: 52% Short　30% Mid　12% Deep　7% Bomb　aDOT: 8.1 (21)　YAC: 5.6 (12)　ALEX: 1.6　2019: 48% Short　37% Mid　10% Deep　5% Bomb　aDOT: 7.4 (--)　YAC: 6.4 (--)　ALEX: 0.2

Mariota's average depth of target of 7.4 yards would have ranked 29th in the NFL last season if he had qualified as a starter. He ranked a respectable 21st in that category as a starter in 2018 with an average depth of target of 8.1 air yards per intended target. He's not the checkdown specialist he's sometimes caricatured as, but passes more than 15 yards down the field and toward the sidelines require all the oomph he's got, and defenses now respond accordingly.

Mariota might have held onto his starting job in Tennessee if he were an efficient short passer, but his sack rates remained above 11% for two straight years despite playing behind a well-regarded offensive line, and his completion rate sagged to below league average last season (after hovering close to league average in 2016 and 2017). So Mariota became a dink-and-dunker without the benefits. That makes him, to use the technical term, a "bad starting quarterback," which the Titans figured out when they finally stopped twisting their offense into knots to hide the deficiency of his pea-shooter arm and let Ryan Tannehill stretch defenses a little more frequently. Jon Gruden may see Rich Gannon in Mariota, and Mariota could still revive his career as designer knockoff Alex Smith, but at some point we'll have to forget about the guy we saw at Oregon and accept that Mariota is the injury-riddled, faded prospect we saw in Tennessee for the last three years.

Baker Mayfield

Height: 6-1　Weight:215　College: Oklahoma　Draft: 2018/1 (1)　Born: 14-Apr-1995　Age: 25　Risk: Green

Year	Tm	G/GS	Snaps	Att	Cmp	C%	CPOE	Yds	TD	INT/Adj	FUM	ASR	NY/P	Rk	DVOA	Rk	DYAR	Rk	Runs	Yds	TD	DVOA	DYAR	QBR
2018	CLE	14/13	906	486	310	63.8%	0.4%	3725	27	14/14	7	5.5%	7.0	11	8.1%	14	628	12	39	131	0	-28.6%	-20	53.9
2019	CLE	16/16	1058	534	317	59.4%	-2.8%	3827	22	21/23	6	7.1%	6.2	17	-9.8%	25	48	25	28	141	3	21.9%	48	52.4
2020	CLE		519	319		61.4%		3733	27	17	7		6.4		-7.4%				36	157	2	19.9%		

2018: 44% Short　29% Mid　19% Deep　9% Bomb　aDOT: 9.7 (4)　YAC: 5.5 (14)　ALEX: 1.8　2019: 44% Short　33% Mid　15% Deep　8% Bomb　aDOT: 8.9 (14)　YAC: 5.7 (6)　ALEX: 1.6

College empirical scouting models have, for the better part of the last 25 years, run into a problem dealing with a quarterback on a statistically good-to-great college offense that is on the cutting edge. Mayfield dominated our QBASE system, as we talked about plenty over the past two seasons. QBASE said there were only three quarterbacks more likely to produce star seasons: Philip Rivers, Carson Palmer, and Donovan McNabb. Mayfield has two of the five highest passing efficiency ratings in NCAA history. The only problem is that two of the other top 10 are Kyler Murray and Jalen Hurts, also both at Oklahoma, in the years succeeding Mayfield. QBASE has tried to account for this by adding adjustments for passing defenses played and the quality of teammates, and it has always ruled out lower-round prospects in the eyes of scouts because if you ran those numbers, you'd get a ton of messy data from ho-hum Bowling Green quarterbacks with four good spread offense seasons. Mayfield's projection was always a unique one because a) traditionally, transfer quarterbacks have not been top prospects, and b) separating Lincoln Riley's offense from what his quarterbacks have produced is not something that is easily sussed out by a model. Mayfield still has time to restore the promise his 2018 season brought, but the fact that this was a rocky road in and of itself probably should be a little less surprising than it was thought to be 12 months ago. Now, let's all get set for 100 more insurance commercials of which one is actually funny. (It's the one with the low battery smoke alarm, by the way.)

AJ McCarron

Height: 6-3 Weight:220 College: Alabama Draft: 2014/5 (164) Born: 13-Sep-1990 Age: 30 Risk: Green

Year	Tm	G/GS	Snaps	Att	Cmp	C%	CPOE	Yds	TD	INT/Adj	FUM	ASR	NY/P	Rk	DVOA	Rk	DYAR	Rk	Runs	Yds	TD	DVOA	DYAR	QBR
2017	CIN	3/0	26	14	7	50.0%	-13.2%	66	0	0/0	0	5.5%	3.8	--	-11.1%	--	0	--	0	0	0	--	--	21.3
2018	OAK	2/0	12	3	1	33.3%	24.2%	8	0	0/0	1	24.6%	0.3	--	-157.0%	--	-30	--	3	-2	0	-118.4%	-12	0.4
2019	HOU	2/1	69	37	21	56.8%	0.1%	225	0	1/1	0	12.1%	4.3	--	-43.6%	--	-96	--	5	39	1	48.3%	19	25.5
2020	HOU			530	329	62.1%		4027	22	12	7		6.6		-3.4%				37	169	2	21.6%		

2018: 0% Short 100% Mid 0% Deep 0% Bomb aDOT: 7.0 (--) YAC: 1.0 (--) ALEX: 0.0 2019: 58% Short 23% Mid 13% Deep 6% Bomb aDOT: 8.7 (--) YAC: 6.2 (--) ALEX: 3.0

McCarron has now accumulated enough name recognition to continue getting chances. Alabama starting quarterback, playoff starting quarterback, guy whom Hue Jackson almost traded a high-round pick for—these are a lot of signs to the average fan that McCarron should be taken a bit more credibly as a starting option than he has been. But McCarron has underwhelmed at every level, and his biggest knockout factor remains his complete inability to handle the pass rush that his process generates. He was sacked five times in his sparse amount of attempts last year, and is now at 19 sacks in 192 career NFL dropbacks. He was sacked five times in the fourth preseason game he played against the Bears in 2018, when he was with the Bills. The more chances he gets, the more McCarron proves that the only games he belongs in are those fourth preseason games. But, good news, he's got another one-year deal with the Texans that values him much more highly than that!

Colt McCoy

Height: 6-1 Weight:212 College: Texas Draft: 2010/3 (85) Born: 5-Sep-1986 Age: 34 Risk: Green

Year	Tm	G/GS	Snaps	Att	Cmp	C%	CPOE	Yds	TD	INT/Adj	FUM	ASR	NY/P	Rk	DVOA	Rk	DYAR	Rk	Runs	Yds	TD	DVOA	DYAR	QBR
2017	WAS	1/0	4	0	0	--	--	0	0	0/0	0	--	--	--	--	--	--	--	0	0	0	--	--	--
2018	WAS	3/2	100	54	34	63.0%	1.4%	372	3	3/4	1	10.9%	5.8	--	-40.8%	--	-119	--	10	63	0	48.3%	30	41.5
2019	WAS	1/1	59	27	18	66.7%	0.1%	122	0	1/2	2	16.9%	2.4	--	-73.8%	--	-114	--	2	14	0	90.1%	9	13.9
2020	NYG			524	322	61.4%		3517	21	13	12		5.9		-13.7%				60	307	2	7.3%		

2018: 37% Short 39% Mid 16% Deep 8% Bomb aDOT: 9.7 (--) YAC: 4.4 (--) ALEX: 3.7 2019: 52% Short 36% Mid 4% Deep 8% Bomb aDOT: 6.9 (--) YAC: 1.9 (--) ALEX: -3.7

McCoy only got one start in 2019 and he got the short straw of options, facing the New England Patriots. McCoy was sacked six times on 33 dropbacks despite trying as hard as possible to get the ball out quickly—he released the ball at an average of 2.44 seconds per Next Gen Stats. He also had an interception and no touchdowns on 27 attempts. And yet, he still provides the best backup option the Giants have rostered in some time.

Gardner Minshew

Height: 6-1 Weight:225 College: Washington State Draft: 2019/6 (178) Born: 16-May-1996 Age: 24 Risk: Green

Year	Tm	G/GS	Snaps	Att	Cmp	C%	CPOE	Yds	TD	INT/Adj	FUM	ASR	NY/P	Rk	DVOA	Rk	DYAR	Rk	Runs	Yds	TD	DVOA	DYAR	QBR
2019	JAX	14/12	920	470	285	60.6%	-4.0%	3271	21	6/10	13	7.0%	6.1	20	-5.0%	22	193	22	67	344	0	8.1%	48	42.6
2020	JAX			563	352	62.6%		3942	25	9	13		6.2		-7.1%				69	342	1	-2.7%		

2019: 50% Short 32% Mid 11% Deep 7% Bomb aDOT: 7.7 (28) YAC: 5.4 (14) ALEX: 2.0

The surprise rookie star of the first half of the season, Minshew was thrust into action in Week 1 following the collarbone injury to preferred starter Nick Foles. He performed wildly better than expectations, his passing statistics even comparing favorably with No. 1 overall pick Kyler Murray. Minshew had the best passing yards, touchdowns, yards per attempt, completion percentage, and interception rate of any rookie starting quarterback in Jaguars history, though Byron Leftwich had a higher DVOA in 2003.

Yet for all that success, the Jaguars benched Minshew when Foles returned from injured reserve. Minshew did later reclaim the starting job, but his passing DVOA during his second stint fell to -21.4%, compared to 4.5% for the first half. Though he declined in most advanced statistics in the second half, the biggest difference was his performance on second down:

Gardner Minshew on Second Down, First Half vs. Second Half

	Avg Yds to Go	Plays	Yds/Play	Comp%	FD/TD Rate	Success Rate	DVOA
Weeks 1-9	9.4	111	6.6	63.6%	41%	49%	25.9%
Weeks 13-17	8.3	54	3.6	50.0%	22%	31%	-29.1%

Despite having on average fewer yards to go for a first down, Minshew's success rate and first-down rate dropped precipitously. He became more conservative, throwing a larger share of his passes to running back Leonard Fournette in the second half rather than Dede Westbrook and DJ Chark as he did in the first. That trend was less exaggerated on first and third down, but the target share still tilted in Fournette's direction. Yet despite the shorter passes, Minshew still completed them at a lower rate during his second stint.

It remains to be seen whether Minshew's second-half struggles were a result of defenses adjusting to what they now had on tape, a rise in the quality of opposing defenses, or simply a blip from which he can recover. Also, for all his success at avoiding interceptions, only four quarterbacks fumbled more often on pass plays. With Foles now replaced by journeyman Mike Glennon, Minshew's job should be secure for this season at least. What happens in 2020 will determine how secure it remains beyond that.

Matt Moore
Height: 6-3   Weight:219   College: Oregon State   Draft: 2007/FA   Born: 9-Aug-1984   Age: 36   Risk: Green

Year	Tm	G/GS	Snaps	Att	Cmp	C%	CPOE	Yds	TD	INT/Adj	FUM	ASR	NY/P	Rk	DVOA	Rk	DYAR	Rk	Runs	Yds	TD	DVOA	DYAR	QBR
2017	MIA	4/2	203	127	78	61.4%	-0.2%	861	4	5/5	0	9.2%	5.8	--	-16.1%	--	-41	--	3	9	0	-51.2%	-8	37.7
2019	KC	6/2	171	91	59	64.8%	3.7%	659	4	0/1	2	7.8%	6.1	--	15.5%	--	172	--	5	-1	0	-67.0%	-2	55.4
2020	KC			551	358	65.1%		4159	24	9	10		6.8		12.4%				40	112	1	3.9%		

2019:   53% Short   29% Mid   12% Deep   6% Bomb   aDOT: 7.2 (--)   YAC: 4.9 (--)   ALEX: -0.7

Moore was scouting for the Dolphins and coaching high school football last season until the Chiefs signed him to back up Patrick Mahomes when Chad Henne was unavailable. He mopped up a lopsided win over the Broncos, led the Chiefs to a win over the Vikings, and threw two touchdown passes in a narrow loss to the Packers before Mahomes' nigh-miraculous return. Moore also played well in relief stints for the Dolphins down the playoff stretch in 2016 and in 2017, yet he has never acquired a Josh McCown cachet as a mentor for hire. Moore re-signed with the Chiefs on July 10.

Nick Mullens
Height: 6-1   Weight:210   College: Southern Mississippi   Draft: 2017/FA   Born: 21-Mar-1995   Age: 25   Risk: Green

Year	Tm	G/GS	Snaps	Att	Cmp	C%	CPOE	Yds	TD	INT/Adj	FUM	ASR	NY/P	Rk	DVOA	Rk	DYAR	Rk	Runs	Yds	TD	DVOA	DYAR	QBR
2018	SF	8/8	519	274	176	64.2%	1.4%	2277	13	10/12	2	6.3%	7.5	6	4.2%	18	286	24	18	-16	0	-118.6%	-43	54.9
2019	SF	1/0	7	0	0	--	--	0	0	0/0	0	--	--	--	--	--	--	--	3	-3	0	--	--	--
2020	SF			556	359	64.6%		4359	27	14	7		7.0		3.9%				36	64	1	-13.4%		

2018:   47% Short   38% Mid   13% Deep   2% Bomb   aDOT: 7.4 (31)   YAC: 7.0 (1)   ALEX: 0.1

After comfortably outperforming former second-stringer C.J. Beathard in 2018 as a fill-in for an injured Jimmy Garoppolo, Mullens spent his second season on San Francisco's active roster firmly nailed to the bench, only taking seven snaps all year long. In 2018, Mullens performed like an average NFL quarterback; for a guy who started the season on the practice squad, that was everything the 49ers could have hoped for. He even outperformed most of the 2018 first-round picks at quarterback, finishing comfortably ahead of Josh Allen, Josh Rosen, and Sam Darnold in DYAR and DVOA. With Mullens still around, the 49ers have to be happy with their current backup quarterback situation in the event that Garoppolo goes down with an injury; given Garoppolo's history, that seems like an important contingency plan to have.

Kyler Murray
Height: 5-10   Weight:207   College: Oklahoma   Draft: 2019/1 (1)   Born: 7-Aug-1997   Age: 23   Risk: Yellow

Year	Tm	G/GS	Snaps	Att	Cmp	C%	CPOE	Yds	TD	INT/Adj	FUM	ASR	NY/P	Rk	DVOA	Rk	DYAR	Rk	Runs	Yds	TD	DVOA	DYAR	QBR
2019	ARI	16/16	1025	542	349	64.4%	0.5%	3722	20	12/15	5	8.2%	5.9	26	-3.1%	21	305	21	93	544	4	8.5%	87	55.7
2020	ARI			557	369	66.1%		4094	26	12	7		6.4		0.4%				81	470	3	23.6%		

2019:   54% Short   27% Mid   11% Deep   8% Bomb   aDOT: 7.9 (25)   YAC: 5.3 (18)   ALEX: 1.5

After one season, it looks like the 2019 first overall pick made the right call in choosing football over baseball. While he did not step into the league as an immediately above-average starter, Murray still showed a lot to build on. One area where he could use a bit of work is his performance outside the pocket, which seems a bit counterintuitive based on how effective he was when scrambling at the University of Oklahoma. Murray went from a roughly average quarterback inside the pocket to one of the five worst qualified passers outside of it. This presented a bit of a problem because Murray left the pocket at the fifth-highest rate among qualified starters. His struggles outside the pocket can largely be attributed to sacks, because when sacks and scrambles are removed, his out-of-pocket DVOA jumped from -38.5% to -3.2%.

Cam Newton

Height: 6-5	Weight:245	College: Auburn	Draft: 2011/1 (1)	Born: 11-May-1989	Age: 31	Risk: Yellow

Year	Tm	G/GS	Snaps	Att	Cmp	C%	CPOE	Yds	TD	INT/Adj	FUM	ASR	NY/P	Rk	DVOA	Rk	DYAR	Rk	Runs	Yds	TD	DVOA	DYAR	QBR
2017	CAR	16/16	1063	492	291	59.1%	-3.2%	3302	22	16/16	9	7.2%	6.0	21	-6.9%	21	141	21	139	754	6	6.5%	120	47.7
2018	CAR	14/14	885	471	320	67.9%	1.9%	3395	24	13/17	6	6.6%	6.4	18	-1.4%	23	321	23	101	488	4	2.7%	71	55.9
2019	CAR	2/2	146	89	50	56.2%	-5.4%	572	0	1/1	2	6.1%	5.6	--	-8.0%	--	19	--	5	-2	0	-230.2%	-48	21.1
2020	NE			528	339	64.2%		3590	20	11	11		6.1		-2.4%				110	489	5	7.0%		

2018:   49% Short   35% Mid   13% Deep   4% Bomb   aDOT: 7.4 (30)   YAC: 5.4 (15)   ALEX: 1.1   2019:   37% Short   48% Mid   7% Deep   9% Bomb   aDOT: 9.3 (--)   YAC: 4.1 (--)   ALEX: -0.5

The nightmare of all non-Patriots fans materialized the moment Newton signed with New England in late June. Newton's mostly absent 2019 season made it easy to forget the player he was before his foot injury sidelined him. In 2018, before a shoulder injury hampered him down the stretch (see a theme here?), Newton was on another MVP-caliber run and had the Panthers offense flying with the fifth-best DVOA rating through Week 9. Over those eight games (Carolina had an early bye), Newton threw 15 touchdowns to just four interceptions while completing over 67% of his passes. He earned 480 DYAR through those eight games, which would have put him on pace to exceed the 630 DYAR he earned during his 2015 MVP campaign. All of this success was in part because the Panthers offense finally enabled Newton as a quick-game passer, particularly via running backs. If there is anything Bill Belichick and Josh McDaniels can guarantee for Newton, it is help in the passing game via running backs.

Dak Prescott

Height: 6-2	Weight:238	College: Mississippi State	Draft: 2016/4 (135)	Born: 29-Jul-1993	Age: 27	Risk: Green

Year	Tm	G/GS	Snaps	Att	Cmp	C%	CPOE	Yds	TD	INT/Adj	FUM	ASR	NY/P	Rk	DVOA	Rk	DYAR	Rk	Runs	Yds	TD	DVOA	DYAR	QBR
2017	DAL	16/16	1053	490	308	62.9%	1.0%	3324	22	13/17	4	6.4%	6.3	18	-0.2%	17	375	17	57	357	6	46.9%	167	66.7
2018	DAL	16/16	1071	526	356	67.7%	0.9%	3885	22	8/12	12	9.7%	6.1	26	-8.1%	26	112	25	75	305	6	2.0%	45	57.8
2019	DAL	16/16	1124	596	388	65.1%	1.2%	4902	30	11/17	6	4.3%	7.7	3	27.1%	6	1541	1	52	277	3	15.6%	71	70.2
2020	DAL			573	376	65.7%		4670	27	10	9		7.3		14.5%				57	279	4	30.0%		

2018:   50% Short   35% Mid   8% Deep   7% Bomb   aDOT: 7.6 (26)   YAC: 5.3 (18)   ALEX: -1.0   2019:   39% Short   41% Mid   12% Deep   7% Bomb   aDOT: 9.7 (6)   YAC: 4.8 (29)   ALEX: 2.3

Prescott now has two top-five DYAR finishes in four years. Yes, some people have expressed concern about how Prescott would play if he wasn't playing in such a positive offensive environment, but it doesn't seem like that's in the realm of possibility with the current Dallas roster. Few quarterbacks played better when the situation was ideal, either. On non-play-action passes from a clean pocket, Prescott had the league's third-highest yards per attempt (8.6) and the second-lowest interception rate (0.7%). Much of Prescott's year-to-year improvement came in the pocket. Prescott's DVOA in the pocket shot up from 1.2% in 2018 to 45.6% in 2019. But also, no quarterback handled pressure better than Prescott. His 6.1 yards per play with pressure led the league, and only Lamar Jackson and Patrick Mahomes had a higher DVOA.

Philip Rivers

Height: 6-5	Weight:228	College: North Carolina State	Draft: 2004/1 (4)	Born: 8-Dec-1981	Age: 39	Risk: Green

Year	Tm	G/GS	Snaps	Att	Cmp	C%	CPOE	Yds	TD	INT/Adj	FUM	ASR	NY/P	Rk	DVOA	Rk	DYAR	Rk	Runs	Yds	TD	DVOA	DYAR	QBR
2017	LAC	16/16	1028	575	360	62.6%	1.6%	4515	28	10/16	8	4.3%	7.5	2	26.1%	4	1412	2	18	-2	0	-97.2%	-10	57.4
2018	LAC	16/16	964	508	347	68.3%	2.0%	4308	32	12/16	2	6.1%	7.6	4	27.2%	3	1316	3	18	7	0	-96.5%	-55	70.2
2019	LAC	16/16	1044	591	390	66.0%	2.9%	4615	23	20/26	8	6.3%	7.1	11	6.6%	15	714	13	12	29	0	-41.9%	-10	48.6
2020	IND			600	399	66.5%		4480	27	16	7		6.6		6.7%				16	38	0	1.0%		

2018:   53% Short   28% Mid   11% Deep   7% Bomb   aDOT: 8.2 (20)   YAC: 6.1 (6)   ALEX: 1.7   2019:   48% Short   29% Mid   15% Deep   8% Bomb   aDOT: 9.0 (10)   YAC: 5.5 (11)   ALEX: 2.0

The sixth-most productive passer of all time in both yards and touchdowns, Rivers departed the Chargers this offseason as the holder of franchise records in pretty much every major passing statistic except interceptions, where he ranks third. Rivers has never missed a start since taking over from Drew Brees in 2006, has thrown for over 4,000 yards in 11 of the past 12 seasons, and has at various times led the league in completion percentage, yards, touchdowns, and yards per attempt (for three straight years) over that period. Yet for all his historic production, many fans would argue that Rivers feels like a fringe Hall of Fame player and the least successful of the Big Three quarterbacks (himself, Eli Manning, and Ben Roethlisberger) from the 2004 draft. A lot of that has do with his playoff record: his Chargers teams only made the playoffs six times in his 14 seasons as the starting quarterback, only won five games across those six appearances, and only made a single AFC Championship Game, which they lost without scoring a touchdown. Last season, despite being preseason darlings and many people's dark horse in the AFC (including ours) the Chargers went 5-11—their third season in the past five years with five or fewer wins.

Rivers has showing signs of aging, especially late in recent seasons, but he was rarely the problem with the Chargers in 2019 or any year prior. He has posted positive passing DVOA in 13 of his 14 seasons as a starter, finishing in the top 10 eight times and No. 1 twice. Though his personal DVOA was lower in 2019, the Chargers still ranked among the top 10 in passing DVOA. Where Rivers did struggle was the red zone: only seven starting quarterbacks had a lower DVOA than Rivers in that area of the field, and only two of those (Baker Mayfield and Sam Darnold) are guaranteed starting jobs next season. He also threw too many interceptions, especially the nine he threw while trailing in the fourth quarter (a figure only eclipsed, as most interception stats were, by Jameis Winston's 11). This Colts team, playing against a significantly weaker schedule, should put Rivers in that position less often, and Rivers had the best completion rate of his career when Frank Reich was his quarterbacks coach in San Diego.

Aaron Rodgers

Height: 6-2		Weight:225			College: California				Draft: 2005/1 (24)			Born: 2-Dec-1983			Age: 37			Risk: Yellow			

Year	Tm	G/GS	Snaps	Att	Cmp	C%	CPOE	Yds	TD	INT/Adj	FUM	ASR	NY/P	Rk	DVOA	Rk	DYAR	Rk	Runs	Yds	TD	DVOA	DYAR	QBR
2017	GB	7/7	418	238	154	64.7%	2.8%	1675	16	6/6	1	8.3%	6.0	22	7.8%	14	334	18	24	126	0	48.7%	55	62.6
2018	GB	16/16	1013	597	372	62.3%	-0.1%	4442	25	2/8	6	8.0%	6.3	22	8.1%	12	817	9	43	269	2	18.4%	66	60.6
2019	GB	16/16	1082	569	353	62.0%	0.1%	4002	26	4/6	4	6.5%	6.2	18	9.0%	13	794	8	46	183	1	35.9%	61	50.4
2020	GB			579	363	62.6%		4300	27	7	7		6.6		7.8%				46	201	1	13.0%		

2018:	47% Short	30% Mid	15% Deep	8% Bomb	aDOT: 9.1 (10)	YAC: 5.7 (8)	ALEX: 4.5	2019:	49% Short	27% Mid	14% Deep	11% Bomb	aDOT: 9.1 (9)	YAC: 5.7 (7)	ALEX: 4.1

The Packers need to figure out a way to connect on their deep shots in 2020. Rodgers' air yards dropped from 9.1 yards on all attempts to 5.6 yards on completions alone. That was the second biggest drop-off in the league; Rodgers' length on attempts put him in league with the Patrick Mahomes and Lamar Jacksons of the world, while his completions had him sandwiched between Case Keenum and Jimmy Garoppolo. Rodgers' bomb percentage hit 11% last season, the highest mark in his career; only Jameis Winston threw more passes 25 or more yards downfield. That's exciting, but only 17 of those 59 deep shots actually were completed, putting Rodgers outside the top 20 in completion percentage. The lack of success isn't all on Rodgers' receivers, either; 22 of those deep shots were charted as either overthrown or underthrown, compared to just five that were dropped or miscommunications. If Rodgers can find a way to connect on a few more of those shot plays, it would add a new dimension to Green Bay's offense.

Ben Roethlisberger

Height: 6-5		Weight:240			College: Miami (Ohio)				Draft: 2004/1 (11)			Born: 2-Mar-1982			Age: 38			Risk: Yellow			

Year	Tm	G/GS	Snaps	Att	Cmp	C%	CPOE	Yds	TD	INT/Adj	FUM	ASR	NY/P	Rk	DVOA	Rk	DYAR	Rk	Runs	Yds	TD	DVOA	DYAR	QBR
2017	PIT	15/15	1038	561	360	64.2%	2.3%	4251	28	14/18	3	3.6%	7.4	5	21.8%	8	1270	5	28	47	0	-2.1%	6	63.2
2018	PIT	16/16	1086	675	452	67.0%	0.4%	5129	34	16/20	7	4.4%	7.1	9	14.5%	8	1204	5	31	98	3	37.8%	62	71.8
2019	PIT	2/2	96	62	35	56.5%	-11.1%	351	0	1/2	1	3.1%	5.3	--	5.4%	--	69	--	1	7	0	26.2%	2	27.1
2020	PIT			626	389	62.2%		4616	26	14	9		6.5		-1.5%				24	82	1	13.8%		

2018:	54% Short	28% Mid	10% Deep	8% Bomb	aDOT: 8.0 (22)	YAC: 6.2 (3)	ALEX: 1.4	2019:	56% Short	24% Mid	6% Deep	13% Bomb	aDOT: 9.5 (--)	YAC: 5.5 (--)	ALEX: 3.3

Well, obviously we don't have much to say about last season. It's kind of funny that the Miami (Ohio) quarterback who came of age with the 2004 and 2005 Steelers where he attempted less than 300 passes a year ended his 2018 season with a league-high 675 attempts and was well on pace to reach that figure again in 2019 before the elbow injury. It's probably fair to say that Roethlisberger was already beginning to decline a bit from his impressive 2014/2015 peak: he has always been a little interception-prone for a top quarterback, but it has become more noticeable as teams begin to implement safer passes as base concepts. Given the schedule and his surrounding cast, that KUBIAK projection may be a bit conservative despite age-related decline.

Josh Rosen

| | | Height: 6-4 | | Weight:226 | | College: UCLA | | | | Draft: 2018/1 (10) | | | Born: 10-Feb-1997 | | | Age: 23 | | | Risk: Green |

Year	Tm	G/GS	Snaps	Att	Cmp	C%	CPOE	Yds	TD	INT/Adj	FUM	ASR	NY/P	Rk	DVOA	Rk	DYAR	Rk	Runs	Yds	TD	DVOA	DYAR	QBR
2018	ARI	14/13	781	393	217	55.2%	-7.2%	2278	11	14/17	10	10.0%	4.5	34	-53.7%	34	-1145	34	23	138	0	25.2%	23	26.1
2019	MIA	6/3	200	109	58	53.2%	-10.9%	567	1	5/7	1	12.7%	3.8	--	-63.0%	--	-409	--	3	13	0	-23.7%	-2	18.4
2020	MIA			562	319	56.9%		3552	18	18	12		5.5		-24.4%				45	242	1	12.4%		

2018: 46% Short   32% Mid   14% Deep   8% Bomb   aDOT: 8.8 (14)   YAC: 4.5 (32)   ALEX: -0.7   2019: 50% Short   30% Mid   9% Deep   12% Bomb   aDOT: 9.0 (--)   YAC: 5.5 (--)   ALEX: 7.7

It's not over until it's over, but Rosen's career is looking rather doomed. After an all-time terrible rookie year with the Arizona Cardinals, Rosen earned just a few starts with the Miami Dolphins last season before promptly being sent back to the sidelines in favor of Ryan Fitzpatrick. There is some argument to be made that the Dolphins' offensive depth chart was not good enough to help Rosen, which is fair, but Fitzpatrick performed just fine. Moreover, the offense when Rosen was on the field was reduced to RPOs (run-pass options), a heavy dose of screens, and relatively simple dropback concepts, whereas Fitzpatrick was trusted enough to operate a much fuller offense. There is no denying Rosen has been dealt a bad hand, but the flashes of promise have been few and far between and there is zero degree of consistency to cling to.

Mason Rudolph

| | | Height: 6-5 | | Weight:235 | | College: Oklahoma State | | | | Draft: 2018/3 (76) | | | Born: 17-Jul-1995 | | | Age: 25 | | | Risk: Green |

Year	Tm	G/GS	Snaps	Att	Cmp	C%	CPOE	Yds	TD	INT/Adj	FUM	ASR	NY/P	Rk	DVOA	Rk	DYAR	Rk	Runs	Yds	TD	DVOA	DYAR	QBR
2019	PIT	10/8	534	283	176	62.2%	-1.1%	1765	13	9/9	4	5.7%	5.5	30	-23.0%	33	-225	30	21	42	0	-12.5%	0	34.4
2020	PIT			551	341	62.0%		3780	24	15	8		6.0		-8.6%				41	100	1	-6.7%		

2019: 55% Short   23% Mid   10% Deep   12% Bomb   aDOT: 8.7 (16)   YAC: 5.3 (16)   ALEX: -0.2

Checkdown Machine and Guy Who Was Definitely A *Degrassi* Villain at Some Point Mason Rudolph has the deep ball. That was something that was clear at Oklahoma State. But it's one thing to have it and one thing to be able to use it effectively in the NFL, as players like Joe Flacco and Josh Allen have found out. Rudolph's deep-pass DVOA of 4.0% was the worst of any quarterback with more than 25 deep throws besides Dwayne Haskins. It was largely an accuracy issue, as he completed just 17 of 57 deep attempts, which goes against the grain of a lot of what was written about Rudolph's deep accuracy coming out of college. When you combine the empty-carb dumpoffs with no big-play nourishment, you have a resume that leaves a team quarterback-hungry. Rudolph also had the biggest gap of any qualifying quarterback between his VOA (-17.5%) and DVOA, which means he played badly against a rather easy schedule of opponents. He will have another year to learn behind Ben Roethlisberger, but nothing we saw last year should make Steelers fans feel like they have an answer-in-waiting.

Matt Ryan

| | | Height: 6-4 | | Weight:217 | | College: Boston College | | | | Draft: 2008/1 (3) | | | Born: 17-May-1985 | | | Age: 35 | | | Risk: Green |

Year	Tm	G/GS	Snaps	Att	Cmp	C%	CPOE	Yds	TD	INT/Adj	FUM	ASR	NY/P	Rk	DVOA	Rk	DYAR	Rk	Runs	Yds	TD	DVOA	DYAR	QBR
2017	ATL	16/16	1026	529	342	64.7%	2.7%	4095	20	12/9	4	4.8%	7.2	7	19.1%	9	1084	7	32	143	0	43.4%	54	63.7
2018	ATL	16/16	1048	608	422	69.4%	3.5%	4924	35	7/11	10	6.7%	7.1	7	18.2%	4	1232	4	33	125	3	33.9%	68	68.2
2019	ATL	15/15	1087	616	408	66.2%	3.2%	4466	26	14/18	9	6.8%	6.3	15	7.0%	14	712	14	34	147	1	18.1%	38	57.6
2020	ATL			635	427	67.3%		4877	30	13	9		6.8		10.9%				27	116	1	16.4%		

2018: 47% Short   33% Mid   13% Deep   7% Bomb   aDOT: 9.0 (12)   YAC: 5.1 (22)   ALEX: 0.8   2019: 49% Short   33% Mid   12% Deep   6% Bomb   aDOT: 8.6 (17)   YAC: 4.0 (33)   ALEX: 2.5

As the Falcons recede to a boring competence over the back nine of his career, Ryan seems destined to fade from memory in favor of the generational quarterbacks of his era such as Tom Brady and Drew Brees. But that isn't totally fair to Ryan. He has finished in the top 10 in passing DVOA in nine of his 12 seasons, and while his 2016 MVP campaign was spoiled by the team's historic collapse in the Super Bowl, Ryan is near the bottom of potential scapegoats for that loss. It's easy to imagine what Ryan's reputation could have been with better defensive play in the fourth quarter of that one game. We would likely think of Ryan much like we think of Brees; Brees' Saints have been victims of many more head-scratching losses than Ryan's Falcons, but the former's ring from the 2009 season weighs heavier in the balance. And while both Ryan and Brees enjoy the comforts and inflated stats of a home dome, Brees has relied disproportionally on his to compile his incredible resume. Starting with his 2016 MVP season, Ryan has authored a nearly identical road DVOA of 17.7% to Brees' rate away from the Superdome (20.3%).

Matt Schaub

Height: 6-6 | Weight:245 | College: Virginia | Draft: 2004/3 (90) | Born: 25-Jun-1981 | Age: 39 | Risk: Green

Year	Tm	G/GS	Snaps	Att	Cmp	C%	CPOE	Yds	TD	INT/Adj	FUM	ASR	NY/P	Rk	DVOA	Rk	DYAR	Rk	Runs	Yds	TD	DVOA	DYAR	QBR
2018	ATL	3/0	12	7	5	71.4%	-2.9%	20	0	0/0	1	-0.9%	2.9	--	-114.3%	--	-52	--	1	0	0	--	--	65.5
2019	ATL	6/1	103	67	50	74.6%	10.4%	580	3	1/3	1	5.2%	8.4	--	37.6%	--	217	--	3	-3	0	--	--	78.9
2020	ATL			548	356	65.0%		4044	24	11	10		6.5		0.7%				49	94	2	-13.9%		

2018: 43% Short   57% Mid   0% Deep   0% Bomb   aDOT: 4.6 (--)   YAC: 1.6 (--)   ALEX: 0.0   2019: 46% Short   40% Mid   14% Deep   0% Bomb   aDOT: 7.4 (--)   YAC: 5.3 (--)   ALEX: -0.7

Schaub's job as Matt Ryan's backup quarterback in Atlanta was starting to look as cushy as Jim Sorgi's used to be behind Peyton Manning in Indianapolis. In his first three seasons with the Falcons, Schaub threw just 10 passes. But it's much harder to be an iron man in football than it is in other sports, and after Ryan suffered an ankle injury in Week 7 last season, Schaub was called upon in a couple of games that the Falcons desperately needed to win. He couldn't quite deliver those victories, but despite his recent bench-warming and advanced age of 38 years old, Schaub did remind the world the he is a capable passer. In fact, every team would happily take Schaub's 2019 stat line from their starter. Obviously, Schaub wouldn't be able to sustain that stellar efficiency over multiple games, but he likely won't have to; Ryan has missed just three starts in his 12-year professional career. Schaub will likely spend the full 2020 season on the bench, but now he has a retort for anyone who scoffs at his $2-million annual salary.

Geno Smith

Height: 6-3 | Weight:221 | College: West Virginia | Draft: 2013/2 (39) | Born: 10-Oct-1990 | Age: 30 | Risk: Green

Year	Tm	G/GS	Snaps	Att	Cmp	C%	CPOE	Yds	TD	INT/Adj	FUM	ASR	NY/P	Rk	DVOA	Rk	DYAR	Rk	Runs	Yds	TD	DVOA	DYAR	QBR
2017	NYG	2/1	66	36	21	58.3%	-4.3%	212	1	0/0	2	8.6%	5.3	--	-41.4%	--	-83	--	4	12	0	6.4%	4	34.5
2018	LAC	5/0	32	4	1	25.0%	-27.4%	8	0	0/0	1	16.8%	-1.0	--	-282.0%	--	-49	--	8	2	0	45.4%	3	0.8
2020	SEA			526	320	60.8%		3796	24	11	9		6.3		-2.6%				51	197	2	11.2%		

2018: 50% Short   50% Mid   0% Deep   0% Bomb   aDOT: 2.0 (--)   YAC: 11.0 (--)   ALEX: -11.0

Smith returns to Seattle for another year in one of the cushiest jobs in sports: Seahawks backup quarterback. In the eight years since Russell Wilson was drafted, his backups have thrown a total of 47 passes, none of them coming in the last three years. No backup has even taken the field since 2017, when Austin Davis played exactly five snaps and took one knee. Smith, sometimes considered a failed quarterback, will earn over a million dollars this year and may not play any more than you or I will. We should all be so lucky to fail so badly.

Matthew Stafford

Height: 6-3 | Weight:220 | College: Georgia | Draft: 2009/1 (1) | Born: 7-Feb-1988 | Age: 32 | Risk: Yellow

Year	Tm	G/GS	Snaps	Att	Cmp	C%	CPOE	Yds	TD	INT/Adj	FUM	ASR	NY/P	Rk	DVOA	Rk	DYAR	Rk	Runs	Yds	TD	DVOA	DYAR	QBR
2017	DET	16/16	1035	565	371	65.7%	2.2%	4446	29	10/18	11	7.6%	7.0	11	14.9%	11	1004	10	29	98	0	0.2%	11	61.7
2018	DET	16/16	1053	555	367	66.1%	-1.5%	3777	21	11/16	6	6.4%	5.9	28	-0.8%	21	396	20	25	71	0	1.9%	12	54.0
2019	DET	8/8	558	291	187	64.3%	2.2%	2499	19	5/7	5	6.0%	7.7	4	28.8%	4	776	9	20	66	0	-40.1%	-19	69.6
2020	DET			574	368	64.2%		4452	30	11	8		6.8		4.5%				32	107	1	3.1%		

2018: 59% Short   27% Mid   9% Deep   6% Bomb   aDOT: 7.2 (32)   YAC: 5.5 (13)   ALEX: 1.3   2019: 41% Short   32% Mid   15% Deep   12% Bomb   aDOT: 11.3 (1)   YAC: 4.8 (30)   ALEX: 3.0

Among the many positive notes from Stafford's half-season was a dramatic improvement in his failed completions (completions that failed to hit the benchmark for a successful play, such as 2-yard gains on third-and-10). Stafford ranked fourth in the league with a 19.8% failed completion rate, and his completion percentage jumps from 17th in the league to eighth when you only count successful completions. This is a big change from 2018, when 28.6% of his completions failed to gain significant yardage; his 105 failures that season are the 19th most in our database (since 2006). The Lions' passing game had gotten conservative in the final years of the Jim Bob Cooter era; Darrell Bevell has allowed Stafford to open things up.

Jarrett Stidham

Height: 6-3 | Weight:214 | College: Auburn | Draft: 2019/4 (133) | Born: 8-Aug-1996 | Age: 24 | Risk: Yellow

Year	Tm	G/GS	Snaps	Att	Cmp	C%	CPOE	Yds	TD	INT/Adj	FUM	ASR	NY/P	Rk	DVOA	Rk	DYAR	Rk	Runs	Yds	TD	DVOA	DYAR	QBR
2019	NE	3/0	15	4	2	50.0%	-11.2%	14	0	1/1	0	19.7%	1.4	--	-306.6%	--	-68	--	2	-2	0	--	--	0.1
2020	NE			525	314	59.8%		3420	21	14	10		5.8		-9.4%				43	115	2	-1.4%		

2019: 50% Short   50% Mid   0% Deep   0% Bomb   aDOT: 5.3 (--)   YAC: 2.5 (--)   ALEX: -4.5

The New England Patriots spent the offseason trying to convince us (and perhaps themselves) that they have struck gold on another Day 3 quarterback, but nothing Jarrett Stidham's college days suggest that is the case. Our own Derrik Klassen has charted the top 10 or so quarterbacks per draft class dating back to 2016, 48 quarterbacks in total. Stidham's 62.4% adjusted accuracy ranks 42nd out of 48, which drops to 46th when adjusting for the standard deviation in accuracy for each class (meaning Stidham was that much worse relative to his class). That 46th-place spot sandwiches Stidham between Davis Webb and Nate Stanley. Furthermore, 34.2% of Stidham's charted passes were behind the line of scrimmage, which was by far the most in his class. Though Stidham did finish his rookie preseason with a 67.8% completion rate and four touchdowns to just one interception, that limited sample of play versus mostly backups and practice-squad players is not enough to wash away an entire collegiate career. The signing of Cam Newton at the end of June put Stidham's grip on the starting job in serious jeopardy, to say the least.

Tua Tagovailoa

| | | | | Height: 6-0 | | Weight:217 | | College: Alabama | | | | Draft: 2020/1 (5) | | | Born: 2-Mar-1998 | | | Age: 22 | | Risk: Yellow |

Year	Tm	G/GS	Snaps	Att	Cmp	C%	CPOE	Yds	TD	INT/Adj	FUM	ASR	NY/P	Rk	DVOA	Rk	DYAR	Rk	Runs	Yds	TD	DVOA	DYAR QBR
2020	MIA		524	311	59.4%			3648	22	13	8		6.1		-10.3%				30	159	1	20.7%	

Perhaps more so than any other rookie quarterback, Tagovailoa is going to require a massive overhaul from his team's offense, or he will have to make a sizeable adjustment himself. Our own Derrik Klassen charted 46.2% of Tagovailoa's pass attempts being play-action or RPOs, by far the highest rate in the class. Conversely, Miami ranked 29th in play-action rate at around 18% last season while only sprinkling in a few RPOs during Josh Rosen's brief stint as the starting quarterback. Granted, Tagovailoa was a stud on third downs in college and posted the highest explosive-play rate in the class, so there is reason to believe his playmaking and overall command outweigh some of his incompleteness as a player. With veteran Ryan Fitzpatrick still in town, Tagovailoa may even be afforded the luxury of sitting on the bench for a month or two, or possibly the entire season, to learn the ropes without the pressure of having to win games.

Ryan Tannehill

| | | | | Height: 6-4 | | Weight:207 | | College: Texas A&M | | | | Draft: 2012/1 (8) | | | Born: 27-Jul-1988 | | | Age: 32 | | Risk: Yellow |

Year	Tm	G/GS	Snaps	Att	Cmp	C%	CPOE	Yds	TD	INT/Adj	FUM	ASR	NY/P	Rk	DVOA	Rk	DYAR	Rk	Runs	Yds	TD	DVOA	DYAR	QBR
2018	MIA	11/11	580	274	176	64.2%	-0.7%	1979	17	9/16	5	12.0%	5.5	32	-20.8%	32	-186	31	32	145	0	34.9%	39	35.0
2019	TEN	12/10	651	286	201	70.3%	7.7%	2742	22	6/5	6	9.8%	8.1	1	28.0%	5	773	10	43	185	4	48.9%	82	62.2
2020	TEN			461	300	65.1%		3797	25	10	9		7.2		5.2%				55	230	3	17.8%		
2018:	54% Short		27% Mid		9% Deep		10% Bomb		aDOT: 8.6 (16)		YAC: 6.1 (5)		ALEX: 0.9		2019:		41% Short		37% Mid		14% Deep		9% Bomb	aDOT: 10.1 (3)	YAC: 6.1 (3)	ALEX: 2.9

The Titans chapter digs deep on a few of our regression favorites, but here's another we cut for space. In Tannehill's career, on third-and-10 or longer, he has taken 38 sacks in 336 dropbacks and has an adjusted yards per attempt of just 3.91. Last year, he took just three sacks in 34 dropbacks in third-and-10-plus situations, and his adjusted yards per attempt went up to 9.55. One thing that we've literally never seen is what the average Ryan Tannehill season looks like in an offense that maximizes him like this Titans one does. Is that a top-15 quarterback? Is it a top-20 quarterback? Is it Alex Smith, or is it more like another quarterback who benefited from a lot of play-action passing back in the day, Matt Schaub? Even as we accept that Tannehill will have to regress somewhere, the question of where that somewhere is has a lot of meaning going forward for the Titans—especially since they're locked into this for three years.

Tyrod Taylor

| | | | | Height: 6-1 | | Weight:215 | | College: Virginia Tech | | | | Draft: 2011/6 (180) | | | Born: 3-Aug-1989 | | | Age: 31 | | Risk: Red |

Year	Tm	G/GS	Snaps	Att	Cmp	C%	CPOE	Yds	TD	INT/Adj	FUM	ASR	NY/P	Rk	DVOA	Rk	DYAR	Rk	Runs	Yds	TD	DVOA	DYAR	QBR
2017	BUF	15/14	931	420	263	62.6%	0.2%	2799	14	4/4	4	10.2%	5.6	26	-7.0%	22	121	22	84	427	4	20.8%	110	52.7
2018	CLE	4/3	185	85	42	49.4%	-12.5%	473	2	2/2	3	13.3%	3.9	--	-53.5%	--	-264	--	16	125	1	-6.8%	4	29.1
2019	LAC	8/0	32	6	4	66.7%	-5.0%	33	1	0/0	0	-1.6%	5.5	--	59.3%	--	23	--	10	7	0	-48.0%	-8	3.1
2020	LAC			524	322	61.4%		3681	23	8	11		6.2		-1.4%				96	387	3	-4.8%		
2018:	48% Short		19% Mid		23% Deep		11% Bomb		aDOT: 11.1 (--)		YAC: 4.7 (--)		ALEX: 0.5		2019:		50% Short		33% Mid		17% Deep		0% Bomb	aDOT: 5.3 (--)	YAC: 4.8 (--)	ALEX: 1.7

Taylor threw five passes while mopping up the Chargers' 45-10 win over the Jaguars and played a few snaps to finish the 30-10 win over the Dolphins last season. The rest of his production (such as it was) came in a Wildcat role, and many of his official rushes were simply kneels. Taylor started for the Bills when Anthony Lynn was running backs coach and later offensive coordinator, and he may well open the season as the Chargers' starter. Taylor got a raw deal when the Bills pushed him out in favor of Nathan Peterman in a blatant effort by the Sean McDermott regime to promote "their guy," no matter how unprepared he was. That said, he peaked in 2015 and grew less effective as defenses adjusted to both his game and read-option tactics in general, and the fact that he made the least of a golden opportunity in Cleveland (Hue Jackson would have started him all year simply to flex his authority if Taylor had been effective at all) cancels out his Bills experience to some degree. Taylor still has value as a pesky, scrambling spot starter, but his primary role in Los Angeles is to be a fairly low hurdle for Justin Herbert to vault on his way to franchise quarterback status.

Mitchell Trubisky Height: 6-2 Weight:215 College: North Carolina Draft: 2017/1 (2) Born: 20-Aug-1994 Age: 26 Risk: Red

Year	Tm	G/GS	Snaps	Att	Cmp	C%	CPOE	Yds	TD	INT/Adj	FUM	ASR	NY/P	Rk	DVOA	Rk	DYAR	Rk	Runs	Yds	TD	DVOA	DYAR	QBR
2017	CHI	12/12	726	330	196	59.4%	-3.7%	2193	7	7/8	10	8.7%	5.5	27	-16.8%	29	-119	29	41	248	2	9.7%	32	29.2
2018	CHI	14/14	929	434	289	66.6%	0.7%	3223	24	12/16	6	5.1%	6.7	15	3.6%	19	448	17	68	421	3	22.9%	114	72.8
2019	CHI	15/15	960	516	326	63.2%	-3.7%	3138	17	10/15	5	7.0%	5.3	33	-11.0%	27	5	27	48	193	2	-17.6%	-12	39.5
2020	CHI			568	355	62.5%		3824	23	12	8		5.9		-10.6%				64	303	3	12.8%		

2018: 46% Short   31% Mid   12% Deep   10% Bomb   aDOT: 9.3 (8)   YAC: 4.9 (28)   ALEX: 2.7   2019: 50% Short   30% Mid   14% Deep   6% Bomb   aDOT: 8.2 (23)   YAC: 4.3 (32)   ALEX: 1.5

In positive news, Trubisky has seemed to fix the issues he had throwing to his left, setting a career high with a 14.3% DVOA in that direction—progress! Of course, he ended up with the third-worst DVOA in the league throwing to his *right* in 2019, clocking in at -19.1%, because it just has to be one step forward, one step back for Trubisky's NFL career. While his struggles to the left had been accuracy- and mechanics-related, his struggles to the right last season are a symptom of his checkdown-itis; he led the league with 51 failed completions to the right side of the field. The reason? Tarik Cohen lined up on the right side of the field significantly more often than the left, and would naturally leak out to that side as a safety valve target, one Trubisky was ever so happy to hit early and often. Trubisky had -169 DYAR throwing to Cohen in the short right, the worst total for any quarterback to any player in any area of the field by 63 DYAR. The only quarterbacks with a higher failed completion percentage than Trubisky in 2019 were either rookies or lost their jobs halfway through the season.

Deshaun Watson Height: 6-2 Weight:221 College: Clemson Draft: 2017/1 (12) Born: 14-Sep-1995 Age: 25 Risk: Yellow

Year	Tm	G/GS	Snaps	Att	Cmp	C%	CPOE	Yds	TD	INT/Adj	FUM	ASR	NY/P	Rk	DVOA	Rk	DYAR	Rk	Runs	Yds	TD	DVOA	DYAR	QBR
2017	HOU	7/6	464	204	126	61.8%	1.5%	1699	19	8/8	3	8.5%	7.7	1	23.1%	7	497	14	36	269	2	29.3%	70	81.3
2018	HOU	16/16	1093	505	345	68.3%	3.7%	4165	26	9/14	9	11.6%	6.8	14	9.5%	11	737	10	99	551	5	7.8%	95	63.8
2019	HOU	15/15	1026	495	333	67.3%	2.6%	3852	26	12/17	10	8.1%	6.7	14	9.5%	12	722	12	82	413	7	9.9%	77	68.7
2020	HOU			542	360	66.3%		4401	27	11	12		7.1		4.9%				95	496	7	30.8%		

2018: 44% Short   38% Mid   12% Deep   6% Bomb   aDOT: 8.9 (13)   YAC: 5.1 (21)   ALEX: -0.3   2019: 54% Short   27% Mid   9% Deep   10% Bomb   aDOT: 9.0 (11)   YAC: 5.0 (22)   ALEX: 1.2

Circumstances around Watson are a hurricane. He is the calm, unblinking, eye. The Texans have overhauled their offensive line and their receiving corps, and have come up with a few different game plans in a few games. But Watson wound up with a 9.5% DVOA for the second straight season, completed about the same number of passes, and remained a plus runner and scrambler who takes too many sacks. Generally, not much has changed in his statistical output over the last two years outside of trading some intermediate throws for some short ones in 2019. Forcibly divorced from DeAndre Hopkins, Watson responded on Twitter with a Drake song lyric noting that "iconic duos rip and split at the seams," which was good for some cryptic offseason speculation. The reality of the situation is that Watson is set to become a very, very rich man, and no great NFL quarterback really leaves in free agency absent wild extenuating circumstances such as injuries or management rifts. The only question left is if he has another level to his game that can carry a Texans offense that, on paper, looks a little worse than last year's at the skill positions.

Carson Wentz Height: 6-5 Weight:237 College: North Dakota State Draft: 2016/1 (2) Born: 30-Dec-1992 Age: 28 Risk: Yellow

Year	Tm	G/GS	Snaps	Att	Cmp	C%	CPOE	Yds	TD	INT/Adj	FUM	ASR	NY/P	Rk	DVOA	Rk	DYAR	Rk	Runs	Yds	TD	DVOA	DYAR	QBR
2017	PHI	13/13	879	440	265	60.2%	-0.8%	3296	33	7/13	9	6.1%	6.9	12	23.8%	6	1047	8	64	299	0	6.7%	52	75.9
2018	PHI	11/11	724	401	279	69.6%	2.7%	3074	21	7/11	9	7.8%	6.6	16	8.1%	13	545	14	34	93	0	-6.8%	7	64.2
2019	PHI	16/16	1169	607	388	63.9%	-0.5%	4039	27	7/16	16	6.5%	5.9	25	0.1%	20	476	17	62	243	1	6.1%	56	60.8
2020	PHI			584	370	63.4%		4254	27	9	14		6.4		-1.8%				55	208	1	-2.6%		

2018: 47% Short   36% Mid   10% Deep   8% Bomb   aDOT: 8.2 (19)   YAC: 5.0 (24)   ALEX: 0.5   2019: 48% Short   33% Mid   12% Deep   7% Bomb   aDOT: 8.4 (20)   YAC: 4.7 (31)   ALEX: 2.7

Howie Roseman said that the Eagles want to feature more of a downfield passing attack in 2020, which would be nice to see—in his 2017 MVP candidate season, Wentz had an aDOT of 10.4, third-best in the league, but that has fallen to a below-average 8.2 and 8.4 in the past two years. Going shorter was smarter last season, as Wentz ranked 27th in DVOA at 35.7% and 28th in success rate at 39% when going deep; everyone below him were either rookies, backups, Sam Darnold, or Josh Allen. Adding Jalen Reagor and some other speed racers at wideout will certainly help, as having an open receiver downfield would be a new experience for Wentz, but it's important to remember that Wentz has now been outside the top 15 in deep passing DVOA for two straight years, and we've heard this song and dance about opening up the offense before.

Russell Wilson

Height: 5-11 | Weight:215 | College: Wisconsin | Draft: 2012/3 (75) | Born: 29-Nov-1988 | Age: 32 | Risk: Green

Year	Tm	G/GS	Snaps	Att	Cmp	C%	CPOE	Yds	TD	INT/Adj	FUM	ASR	NY/P	Rk	DVOA	Rk	DYAR	Rk	Runs	Yds	TD	DVOA	DYAR	QBR
2017	SEA	16/16	1063	553	339	61.3%	2.2%	3983	34	11/15	14	8.1%	6.1	20	2.9%	15	530	13	95	586	3	28.9%	154	58.3
2018	SEA	16/16	1069	427	280	65.6%	5.1%	3448	35	7/11	10	10.4%	6.6	17	11.3%	10	673	11	67	376	0	23.3%	83	65.6
2019	SEA	16/16	1124	516	341	66.1%	4.9%	4110	31	5/7	8	7.9%	6.8	13	24.3%	7	1265	4	75	342	3	-0.3%	33	69.8
2020	SEA			507	343	67.7%		4193	28	7	8		7.3		17.6%				76	388	2	13.9%		

| 2018: | 45% Short | 31% Mid | 13% Deep | 11% Bomb | aDOT: 9.7 (5) | YAC: 4.9 (26) | ALEX: 2.8 | 2019: | 43% Short | 35% Mid | 11% Deep | 11% Bomb | aDOT: 9.7 (5) | YAC: 5.1 (21) | ALEX: 3.7 |

This offseason revealed the human side of the NFL's most robotic quarterback. After Seattle was knocked out of the playoffs, Wilson said the Seahawks needed to re-sign Jadeveon Clowney and "get a few other players on the defense," and that he would like the freedom to use a hurry-up offense earlier in games. For many quarterbacks, asking for more talent on defense and more chances to throw the ball would be pretty standard offseason fare. For Wilson—who had devoted eight years of press conferences to praising every member of the Seahawks organization and throwing out a few bumper-sticker positivity slogans—it was revolutionary. As Mike Salk of 710 AM radio in Seattle put it: "Who was that guy? That's not Russell Wilson! That can't be Russ, he said actual things!"

Then came the deaths of Ahmaud Arbery. And Breonna Taylor. And George Floyd. When Wilson spoke at an online press conference on June 3, he opened with a six-minute monologue, moving back and forth from sadness to anger to fear. He talked about being the descendant of slaves, the lessons his father taught him about being Black in America, and his worries about the country in which his children will grow. "I don't even want to talk about football right now. I don't even know what that looks like right now," he said. "None of that matters. I can't compare football to life." For the next 30 minutes he led Seattle media members through a difficult discussion on race relations in America. He went even further when hosting the ESPYs a few weeks later, demanding justice and better leadership and calling his white teammates and friends to action: "Don't just listen. Help."

On the field, Wilson is a known commodity. Two or three times a game, he will take a sack most other quarterbacks would have avoided; far more often, he will take your breath away with a perfect deep ball, a scramble for a first down on third-and-long, or improv skills that remain unparalleled. Off the field, he's a changing man in a changing world, using his platform to work towards an achievement far more important than any trophy.

Jameis Winston

Height: 6-4 | Weight:231 | College: Florida State | Draft: 2015/1 (1) | Born: 6-Jan-1994 | Age: 27 | Risk: Green

Year	Tm	G/GS	Snaps	Att	Cmp	C%	CPOE	Yds	TD	INT/Adj	FUM	ASR	NY/P	Rk	DVOA	Rk	DYAR	Rk	Runs	Yds	TD	DVOA	DYAR	QBR
2017	TB	13/13	795	442	282	63.8%	4.5%	3504	19	11/19	15	7.0%	7.1	10	14.3%	12	779	11	33	135	1	-21.7%	-14	48.2
2018	TB	11/9	688	378	244	64.6%	0.7%	2992	19	14/19	7	7.4%	7.0	10	6.9%	15	470	16	49	281	1	4.7%	37	68.6
2019	TB	16/16	1149	626	380	60.7%	0.7%	5109	33	30/40	12	7.6%	7.2	7	-9.0%	24	92	23	59	250	1	12.6%	53	53.7
2020	NO			515	351	68.2%		3957	23	20	11		6.9		0.8%				63	287	2	11.9%		

| 2018: | 33% Short | 43% Mid | 17% Deep | 7% Bomb | aDOT: 11.1 (1) | YAC: 3.7 (34) | ALEX: 3.2 | 2019: | 38% Short | 36% Mid | 15% Deep | 11% Bomb | aDOT: 10.9 (2) | YAC: 5.0 (25) | ALEX: 2.2 |

The Buccaneers didn't make a decision about Jameis Winston. He made it for them. Coach Bruce Arians considered benching him after a horrendous October, during which the Bucs lost all three games and Winston turned the ball over 10 times. He stuck with him, in part because he didn't have a better option. Blaine Gabbert was on injured reserve, and backup Ryan Griffin had never thrown a pass during a regular-season game.

Winston bounced back some, but the final two games of the season sealed his fate. The first five drives of Tampa Bay's Week 16 game against Houston: interception return for a touchdown, interception, blocked field goal, field goal, interception. "Those turnovers in December made us look to see if there was something better behind Door No. 2," Arians said, via the *Tampa Bay Times*.

Now a backup to Drew Brees in New Orleans, Winston won't feel the pressure of having to carry a franchise. "I actually have a Hall of Fame quarterback that I'm learning from, opposed to trying to learn by myself, or use Google," he said.

John Wolford Height: 6-1   Weight:199   College: Wake Forest   Draft: 2018/FA   Born: 16-Oct-1995   Age: 25   Risk: Green

Year	Tm	G/GS	Snaps	Att	Cmp	C%	CPOE	Yds	TD	INT/Adj	FUM	ASR	NY/P	Rk	DVOA	Rk	DYAR	Rk	Runs	Yds	TD	DVOA	DYAR QBR
2020	LAR			526	327	62.3%		3649	22	13	14		6.2		-5.4%				89	378	4	5.5%	

A four-year starter at Wake Forest, Wolford set Demon Deacons records with 3,192 yards and 29 touchdowns in 2017. He went undrafted in 2018 and failed to stick with Jets, but then thrived the following spring for the Arizona Hotshots, leading the AAF with 14 touchdown passes and twice earning Offensive Player of the Week honors. After that league folded, he joined the Rams but underwhelmed in his first NFL action, completing only 57% of his throws with a 5.7-yard average in the preseason last year. With Blake Bortles out of Los Angeles, Wolford is the slim favorite over undrafted rookies Josh Love and Bryce Perkins for the backup job behind Jared Goff.

Logan Woodside Height: 6-1   Weight:213   College: Toledo   Draft: 2018/7 (249)   Born: 27-Jan-1995   Age: 25   Risk: Green

Year	Tm	G/GS	Snaps	Att	Cmp	C%	CPOE	Yds	TD	INT/Adj	FUM	ASR	NY/P	Rk	DVOA	Rk	DYAR	Rk	Runs	Yds	TD	DVOA	DYAR QBR
2020	TEN			525	313	59.5%		3771	21	14	11		6.2		-12.8%				43	184	2	11.9%	

There's "playing with fire" and there's "we've let the quarterback depth get so low that Football Outsiders have moved Logan Woodside into the main player comments section." Woodside latched on in the Alliance of American Football in 2019, doing very general Logan Woodside things: he completed 58.3% of his passes for seven touchdowns and seven picks, and he took 17 sacks in 192 dropbacks. Back at Western Kentucky, the biggest bugaboo on Woodside was his inability to deal with pressure in the pocket effectively; that has become a bit of a knockout factor for some scouts, so he was way below where his best throws would have placed him on many boards. The Titans signed him after the AAF folded and carried him on the practice squad all season. When your starting quarterback has a devastating ACL injury and a shoulder capsule injury on his recent resume, it's a good idea to have a better backup than this. Colin Kaepernick would be a perfect fit for this team.

Going Deep

C.J. Beathard, SF: Beathard enters the final year of his rookie contract as the third-string quarterback behind Jimmy Garoppolo and Nick Mullens. The 2019 season was the first in which Beathard did not start any games after filling in for parts of both 2017 and 2018 without much success (career DVOA: -23.7%). Mullens outplayed Beathard in 2018, and after suffering a preseason injury in 2019, Beathard never had a real shot at the backup job. Beathard was reportedly the subject of trade talks during last season, so it's possible that he ends up on the move.

Blake Bortles, FA: Bortles played exactly 11 offensive snaps in 2019, spread out over three separate games. In the closing minutes against Arizona in Week 13, he went to hand off, but when Darrell Henderson slipped, Bortles kept the ball and hit the turf for a 10-yard loss. It was the biggest loss on a running play without a fumbled snap or handoff for any quarterback last year. Bortles is unsigned, but he's still only 28. Just three years ago he made the top 16 in passing DYAR and DVOA and was playing in the AFC Championship Game. It's hard to believe there's not a good place in the NFL for him.

Tim Boyle, GB: Boyle, a 2018 undrafted free agent out of Eastern Kentucky, saw his first NFL action last season, going 3-for-4 and picking up a DPI against the 49ers late in Green Bay's Week 12 blowout loss. With a DVOA of 37.4%, Boyle would have ranked fourth in the league if our attempt threshold for the leaderboards was three. That will probably also be the *last* NFL action of his career; Jordan Love is obviously going to make the squad, and the Packers haven't kept three quarterbacks on the roster since 2016.

Ben DiNucci, DAL: DiNucci, a seventh-round pick, spent his past two seasons with James Madison after he transferred from Pitt following his redshirt sophomore season. He was one of the most productive FCS quarterbacks in 2019, finishing sixth in yards per attempt (9.1) and 12th in passing yards (3,441). He can also scoot, with 569 yards and seven touchdowns added on the ground last season.

Joshua Dobbs, JAX: Since being drafted in the fourth round in 2017 by the Steelers, Dobbs has thrown only 12 passes in his first three NFL seasons. He was dealt to Jacksonville last year immediately following Nick Foles' injury. Now seemingly supplanted as Gardner Minshew's backup by Mike Glennon, Dobbs may have to outduel sixth-round pick Jake Luton just to make the practice squad.

Jacob Dolegala, CIN: The pride of the Central Connecticut State Blue Devils was a surprise year-long member of the Bengals active roster in 2019, a sign that the team thought highly enough of the strong-armed if raw prospect to not risk exposure to the practice squad. This season's bump in roster size only increases the likelihood that Jake the Snake gets a crack at the backup job. If only the Bengals could combine Dolegala's physical traits with Ryan Finley's mental makeup…

Jacob Eason, IND: Widely touted as a likely Day 2 pick out of the University of Washington, Eason somewhat surprisingly fell to the fourth round despite prototypical physical attributes, including starting-caliber arm strength. His major weaknesses are accuracy under pressure and pocket mobility, which the Colts as currently constructed are theoretically well-placed to mitigate. Still, he is a raw player who needs a lot of work. Eason is currently the only quarterback the Colts have under contract for 2021, but any talk of him being the heir to Philip Rivers' spot is wildly premature.

David Fales, NYJ: Wherever Adam Gase goes, David Fales follows. Gase first paired up with Fales when he became the offensive coordinator for the Bears in 2015, where Fales had been drafted the year before as a sixth-round pick. Since then, Fales has bummed around the league almost in tandem with Gase, serving as the coach's preferred reserve quarterback with three different teams (Bears, Dolphins, Jets). However, through all those stops, Fales has only once thrown more than five passes in a season. In 2017, Gase's last year with the Dolphins, Fales started in Week 17 and completed 29-of-42 passes for a measly 6.3 yards per attempt but a surprisingly high 3.7% DVOA. If Joe Flacco's neck isn't ready for Week 1, Fales will probably be the backup to Sam Darnold. He might even stick on the roster all season since he has such an intimate understanding of Gase' system and how the coach wants the quarterback room to operate.

Jake Fromm, BUF: History will forget how close Fromm was to being one of the most decorated college quarterbacks of the modern era. Alas, Fromm never did win that elusive national championship. He ultimately pieced together a lackluster junior year before deciding he had nothing further to prove at the college level. Fromm is a more aggressive passer than he gets credit for, with 18.5% of his passes (via Derrik Klassen's charting) traveling further than 20 yards, the second-highest rate in the class. Fromm also finished third in the class in red zone accuracy at 66.0%. Though Fromm, a fifth-round pick, is limited in physical ability, he shows the processing and mindset to be a capable backup and spot starter.

Garrett Gilbert, CLE: Kyle Allen's spiritual predecessor in big-name Texas football transfers, Gilbert bombed badly enough at Texas to transfer to SMU, where he was drafted despite completing more than 60% of his passes just once in five seasons. Gilbert kicked around practice squads for a few years and wound up in the Alliance, where he led the AAF with 2,152 yards and 13 touchdowns in eight games. He still completed just 60.6% of those passes. Gilbert relieved Baker Mayfield on Monday Night Football last season and completed none of his three passes. Turning 29 before the season, he's a fringe NFL quarterback and essentially has always been one.

Anthony Gordon, SEA: After starting his collegiate career at City College of San Francisco, Gordon transferred to Washington State. He only started one year in the Pac-12, but what a year it was: he led the nation in completions and pass attempts, while only Joe Burrow threw for more yards or touchdowns, and only Jordan Love threw more interceptions. Gordon signed with Seattle after the draft and was briefly the top backup behind Russell Wilson, but he was bumped back to Going Deep when the Seahawks re-signed Geno Smith.

Ryan Griffin, TB: Moonlight Griffin finally got his chance. On December 11, 2019, more than four years after the Buccaneers claimed the quarterback (not the tight end) off waivers, he walked onto the field during a regular-season game for the first time. In temporary relief of Jameis Winston, who suffered a thumb injury, Griffin completed two of four passes for 18 yards. He will earn $945,000 in base salary this season, about as much as Winston ($952,000), despite having thrown 2,544 fewer passes.

Chad Kelly, IND: Still more famous for being Uncle Jim's nephew than for any of his own achievements, Kelly has been much more of an off-field headache than an on-field presence since the Broncos made him 2017's Mr. Irrelevant. Denver released him after he was arrested (and later convicted) of criminal trespassing, and he spent much of 2019 on the Colts practice squad. A similar fate probably awaits him in 2020.

Josh Love, LAR: The other Love in the class of 2020, Josh Love was a walk-on at San Jose State and developed to the point where he won Mountain West Offensive Player of the Year in 2019 in a senior season highlighted by 22 touchdowns with just eight interceptions. He's unathletic but was lauded by scouts for his ability to play in the pocket under pressure. Since he's only competing with other UDFAs, he's got a reasonable chance to end up as the Rams' backup this season.

Jake Luton, JAX: Some NFL teams sure do love tall quarterbacks. The Jaguars added Mike Glennon as their backup shortly after drafting Mike Glennon Lite in the sixth round out of Oregon State. Luton is tall but scrawny, smart but inaccurate, and had a great touchdown-to-interception ratio but a reputation for checking down, and down, and down again. His smarts give him a chance to stick as a long-term backup, which would be a solid outcome for a sixth-round pick.

Cole McDonald, TEN: There's something comforting about a Hawaiian spread quarterback showing up in Going Deep. McDonald was dinged for his lack of awareness of underneath defenders for the Rainbow Warriors—he has thrown 24 picks in his last 27 starts. This is not at all a bad situation to wind up in for McDonald, though, with Ryan Tannehill not exactly dominating with the longest track record of success and only Logan Woodside in front of him on the depth chart. There are flashes of a good deep ball with McDonald and he has enough option experience to do well with Tennessee's power-run/play-action game.

Alex McGough, HOU: A 2018 seventh-round pick by Seattle, McGough has been on three different NFL practice squads and is now the No. 3 quarterback for Houston. He has some mobility and can put zip on the ball when needed, but his mechanics were iffy coming out of Florida International.

Trace McSorley, BAL: McSorley's is a famous, classic NYC Irish ale house, opened in 1854 by immigrants fleeing the potato famine. In 1940 the pub was rediscovered by a new generation of sots thanks to a memorable article in *The New Yorker*, written by the fabled Joseph Mitchell. In 1986, a women's restroom was at last installed in the dank interior. On Sundays the place is packed with customers sipping Guinness and Harp and watching non-Gaelic football. Alas, Trace McSorley has yet to appear on a field and receive the *"Faugh A Ballagh!"* war chant from the pickled clientele. Barring a most unfortunate injury to Lamar Jackson and another in a series of injuries to Robert Griffin, he isn't likely to anytime soon. The boys in the bar won't notice.

James Morgan, NYJ: Even as a fourth-round pick, which is no cheap investment, Morgan may be on the outside looking in at the Jets roster. With Sam Darnold and Joe Flacco one and two on the depth chart, Morgan will compete with long-time Adam Gase backup David Fales. The good news for Morgan's case is that his low interception rate and fairly conservative play style meshes well with Gase as a playcaller. Granted, Morgan's subpar 58% completion rate does not mesh so well, but perhaps a year or two of NFL coaching rather than Group of Five collegiate coaching can iron out Morgan's fundamentals just enough to unlock his physical tools.

Bryce Perkins, LAR: Perkins' college career bounced from Arizona State to Arizona Western College to two years as the starter for Virginia. He's a dual-threat quarterback with over 200 rushing attempts in each of those two seasons (that includes sacks, since these are official college numbers). Perkins combines exciting athletic highs with inaccurate lows. Since he's only competing with other UDFAs, he's got a reasonable chance to end up as the Rams' backup this season.

Cooper Rush, NYG: In four years at Central Michigan (2013-2016), Rush was among the top five passers in the country with 90 touchdowns, tied with Deshaun Watson and just behind Patrick Mahomes. He also threw 55 interceptions, eight more than anyone else. The Cowboys cut him this offseason after three years as the Dallas backup, and he signed with the Giants to reunite with Jason Garrett.

Brett Rypien, DEN: By decree of Lord Elway, the third-string Broncos quarterback role shall be filled by the nephew of a successful former NFL quarterback. If said nephew gets involved in a little intoxicated home invasion, another nephew must take his place. The order of succession goes from Chad Kelly to Brett Rypien to whatever nephews can be located to fill the void until such time as Arch Manning reaches the age of ascendency.

Alex Smith, WAS: A healthy Smith would likely be the best Redskins quarterback in 2020. He enjoyed a career-best 18.3% DVOA season just three years ago in Kansas City, and even his subsequent -13.5% DVOA in 2018 in Washington easily beat the rates of his teammates Dwayne Haskins (-42.0%) and Kyle Allen (-22.4%) in 2019. But Smith's devastating leg injury in November of 2018 may have ended his playing career, and even if he can fully recover, he better fits a rebuilding Redskins team as a mentor to Haskins than as a stopgap starter.

Nate Stanley, MIN: Stanley checks a lot of the boxes you're looking for in a seventh-round backup prospect. He has experience in pro system at Iowa, he has the arm strength you need to hit intermediate and deep passes, and perhaps most importantly for Minnesota, he's best when working out of play-action. Buyer beware, however—his 66% adjusted accuracy was the worst of any quarterback our Derrik Klassen charted this year, and he especially struggles with the deep ball and in the red zone. He also has shown no ability to handle pressure and struggles when coming off of his first read. Still, the physical traits are there to give him a kick of the tires.

Tommy Stevens, NO: As the draft was winding down, the Panthers were talking to Stevens about signing him as an undrafted free agent. When Saints coach Sean Payton got word, he jumped back into the seventh round and drafted the quarterback. Teams usually don't fight over quarterbacks who throw interceptions at 3.1% clip, so what's the appeal? Payton sees a bit of Taysom Hill in Stevens. At Mississippi State last season, Stevens rushed for 490 yards and four touchdowns on 67 non-sack carries (7.3 yards per play). "We know the role," Payton told *The Athletic*. "We invented the role."

Easton Stick, LAC: Stick was the Chargers' fifth-round pick out of North Dakota State last year. He's a scrambling pepperpot with a decent arm but a hinky delivery which the coaching staff presumably spent last season ironing out. The Chargers could hypothetically start the 2020 season with Tyrod Taylor starting in a Ravens-flavored offense, Stick backing him up, and Justin Herbert soaking up wisdom through a headset. It's not a very likely scenario, so Stick may have to do his best (yawn) Taysom Hill impersonation if he hopes to see the field.

Nate Sudfeld, PHI: The Eagles have become famous for their consideration of and reliance on second quarterbacks, and Sudfeld became the heir apparent to Nick Foles for that role when he set the NFL completion percentage record for a career debut (83%) in late 2017 and threw five touchdowns, including a 63-yarder to Shelton Gibson, in the subsequent preseason. He likely would have played the bulk of Philadelphia's playoff game against the Seahawks last season if he hadn't broken his wrist in the preseason. Now, with the drafting of Jalen Hurts, he may have missed his chance.

Jordan Ta'amu, KC: Ta'amu was the Ole Miss quarterback in 2018, when their receiving corps featured A.J. Brown (now with the Titans), DK Metcalf (Seahawks), DaMarkus Lodge (Bengals practice squad) and tight end Dawson Knox (Bills). He threw just 19 touchdown passes that year. Needless to say, he went undrafted. He spent a few weeks in Texans camp, then ended up as the starting quarterback for the XFL's St. Louis Battlehawks. He's listed as the No. 3 quarterback for the Chiefs, but Andy Reid will probably call Matt Moore out of retirement again before he gives Ta'amu a meaningful start. In fact, he did.

Clayton Thorson, DAL: Though Northwestern did not boast immense talent on offense, it's hard to make a case for Thorson based a senior season with just 5.6 net yards per attempt (including sacks). Philadelphia cut their fifth-round pick at the end of last year's preseason and he spent the year on the Dallas practice squad.

Phillip Walker, CAR: The Panthers were a little bit too successful in 2019 to earn a pick that could get them Joe Burrow, Tua Tagovailoa, or Justin Herbert, the three presumed franchise quarterbacks in the 2020 class. But new head coach Matt Rhule may trust his former Temple quarterback Walker to be that sort of high-ceiling asset. Walker set most of Temple's passing records in his four seasons at the school, then emerged as an NFL prospect in the now-defunct XFL in early 2020, throwing 15 touchdowns in five games and displaying the athleticism that is increasingly important for the position in the modern game.

Running Backs

In the following section we provide the last three years of statistics, as well as a 2020 KUBIAK projection, for every running back who either played a significant role in 2019 or is expected to do so in 2020.

The first line contains biographical data—each player's name, height, weight, college, draft position, birth date, and age. Height and weight are the best data we could find; weight, of course, can fluctuate during the offseason. **Age** is very simple, the number of years between the player's birth year and 2020, but birthdate is provided if you want to figure out exact age.

Draft position gives draft year and round, with the overall pick number with which the player was taken in parentheses. In the sample table, it says that Todd Gurley was chosen in the 2015 NFL draft in the first round with the 10th overall pick. Undrafted free agents are listed as "FA" with the year they came into the league, even if they were only in training camp or on a practice squad.

To the far right of the first line is the player's Risk for fantasy football in 2020. As explained in the quarterback section, the standard is for players to be marked Green. Players with higher than normal risk are marked Yellow, and players with the highest risk are marked Red. Players who are most likely to match or surpass our forecast—primarily second-stringers with low projections but also some particularly strong break-out candidates—are marked Blue. Risk is not only based on age and injury probability, but how a player's projection compares to his recent performance as well as our confidence (or lack thereof) in his offensive teammates.

Next we give the last three years of player stats. First come games played and games started (**G/GS**). Games played is the official NFL total and may include games in which a player appeared on special teams but did not carry the ball or catch a pass. We also have a total of offensive **Snaps** for each season. The next four columns are familiar: **Runs**, rushing yards (**Yds**), yards per rush (**Yd/R**) and rushing touchdowns (**TD**).

The entry for fumbles (**FUM**) includes all fumbles by this running back, no matter whether they were recovered by the offense or defense. Holding onto the ball is an identifiable skill; fumbling it so that your own offense can recover it is not. (For more on this issue, see the essay "Pregame Show" in the front of the book.) This entry combines fumbles on both carries and receptions. Fumbles on special teams are not included. (That's particularly important for Jalen Richard of Oakland, who fumbled seven times on special teams in 2017.)

The next four columns give our advanced metrics for rushing: **DVOA** (Defense-Adjusted Value Over Average) and **DYAR** (Defense-Adjusted Yards Above Replacement), along with the player's rank (**Rk**) in both. These metrics compare every carry by the running back to a league-average baseline based on the game situations in which that running back carried the ball. DVOA and DYAR are also adjusted based on the opposing defense. The methods used to compute these numbers are described in detail in the "Statistical Toolbox" introduction in the front of the book. The important distinctions between them is that DVOA is a rate statistic, while DYAR is a cumulative statistic. Thus, a higher DVOA means more value per play, while a higher DYAR means more aggregate value over the entire season.

To qualify for ranking in rushing DVOA and DYAR, a running back must have had 100 carries in that season. Last year, 45 running backs qualified to be ranked in these stats, compared to 47 backs in 2018 and 2017.

Numbers without opponent adjustment (YAR and VOA) can be found on our website, FootballOutsiders.com.

Success Rate (**Suc%**), listed along with rank, represents running back consistency as measured by successful running plays divided by total running plays. (The definition for success is explained in the "Statistical Toolbox" introduction in the front of the book.) A player with high DVOA and a low Success Rate mixes long runs with plays on which he was stuffed at or behind the line of scrimmage. A player with low DVOA and a high Success Rate generally gets the yards needed, but rarely gets more. The league-average Success Rate in 2019 was 48%. Success Rate is not adjusted for the defenses a player faced.

We also give a total of broken tackles (**BTkl**) according to charting from Sports Info Solutions. This total includes broken tackles on both runs and receptions. Please note that SIS marked broken tackles roughly 10% less often in 2018 than in either 2017 or 2019.

New this year is yards after contact (**YafC**), which measures how many yards a runner gained after making contact with any defensive player.

The shaded columns to the right of yards after contact give data for each running back as a pass receiver. Receptions (**Rec**) counts passes caught, while Passes (**Pass**) counts total passes thrown to this player, complete or incomplete. The next four columns list receiving yards (**Yds**), receiving touchdowns (**TD**), catch rate (**C%**), yards per catch (**Yd/C**), and

Todd Gurley			Height: 6-1		Weight: 224		College: Georgia				Draft: 2015/1 (10)			Born: 3-Aug-1994			Age: 26		Risk: Yellow

Year	Tm	G/GS	Snaps	Runs	Yds	TD	Yd/R	FUM	DVOA	Rk	DYAR	Rk	Suc%	Rk	BTkl	YafC	Pass	Rec	Yds	TD	C%	Yd/C	YAC	DVOA	Rk	DYAR	Rk
2017	LAR	15/15	794	279	1305	13	4.7	5	13.9%	4	268	2	53%	5	79	2.8	87	64	788	6	74%	12.3	12.3	35.9%	7	236	2
2018	LAR	14/14	825	256	1251	17	4.9	1	23.6%	1	366	1	57%	4	42	3.0	81	59	580	4	73%	9.8	9.9	6.9%	20	98	12
2019	LAR	15/15	805	223	857	12	3.8	3	-2.4%	25	58	21	48%	26	40	2.5	49	31	207	2	63%	6.7	6.3	-13.8%	40	0	40
2020	ATL			220	890	9	4.0	2	1.6%								58	41	318	2	71%	7.8		-6.5%			

average yards after the catch (**YAC**).

Our research has shown that receivers bear some responsibility for incomplete passes, even though only their catches are tracked in official statistics. Catch rate represents receptions divided by all intended passes for this running back. The average NFL running back caught 77% of passes in 2019. Unfortunately, we don't have room to post the best and worst running backs in receiving plus-minus, but you'll find the top 10 and bottom 10 running backs in this metric listed in the statistical appendix.

Finally we have receiving DVOA and DYAR, which are entirely separate from rushing DVOA and DYAR. To qualify for ranking in receiving DVOA and DYAR, a running back must have 25 passes thrown to him in that season. There are 50 players ranked for 2019, 53 for 2018, and 62 players ranked for 2017.

The italicized row of statistics for the 2020 season is our 2020 KUBIAK projection as explained further in the Statistical Toolbox at the front of the book. Be aware that projections account for the possibility of injury so workload projections may seem low for the top players.

It is difficult to accurately project statistics for a 162-game baseball season, but it is exponentially more difficult to accurately project statistics for a 16-game football season. Consider

Top 20 RB by Rushing DYAR (Total Value), 2019

Rank	Player	Team	DYAR
1	Ezekiel Elliott	DAL	324
2	Christian McCaffrey	CAR	278
3	Mark Ingram	BAL	257
4	Aaron Jones	GB	207
5	Kenyan Drake	2TM	202
6	Derrick Henry	TEN	192
7	Raheem Mostert	SF	191
8	Dalvin Cook	MIN	183
9	Nick Chubb	CLE	162
10	Chris Carson	SEA	130
11	Gus Edwards	BAL	126
12	Josh Jacobs	OAK	126
13	Latavius Murray	NO	125
14	Jordan Howard	PHI	113
15	Marlon Mack	IND	102
16	Phillip Lindsay	DEN	94
17	Joe Mixon	CIN	90
18	Saquon Barkley	NYG	84
19	Alvin Kamara	NO	81
20	Devin Singletary	BUF	75

Minimum 100 carries.

Top 20 RB by Rushing DVOA (Value per Rush), 2019

Rank	Player	Team	DVOA
1	Raheem Mostert	SF	26.8%
2	Mark Ingram	BAL	19.8%
3	Kenyan Drake	2TM	19.7%
4	Ezekiel Elliott	DAL	16.5%
5	Christian McCaffrey	CAR	14.9%
6	Jordan Howard	PHI	14.2%
7	Aaron Jones	GB	12.0%
8	Gus Edwards	BAL	11.8%
9	Latavius Murray	NO	10.7%
10	Dalvin Cook	MIN	9.3%
11	Derrick Henry	TEN	6.7%
12	Nick Chubb	CLE	4.5%
13	Devin Singletary	BUF	3.7%
14	Josh Jacobs	OAK	3.5%
15	Alvin Kamara	NO	3.1%
16	Chris Carson	SEA	1.9%
17	Phillip Lindsay	DEN	1.9%
18	Marlon Mack	IND	1.0%
19	Saquon Barkley	NYG	0.4%
20	Joe Mixon	CIN	-0.9%

Minimum 100 carries.

Top 10 RB by Receiving DYAR (Total Value), 2019

Rank	Player	Team	DYAR
1	Christian McCaffrey	CAR	386
2	Austin Ekeler	LAC	320
3	Mark Ingram	BAL	145
4	Dalvin Cook	MIN	144
5	James White	NE	142
6	Duke Johnson	HOU	125
7	Miles Sanders	PHI	121
8	David Johnson	ARI	114
9	Jamaal Williams	GB	103
10	Ezekiel Elliott	DAL	99

Minimum 25 passes.

Top 10 RB by Receiving DVOA (Value per Pass), 2019

Rank	Player	Team	DVOA
1	Mark Ingram	BAL	74.6%
2	Kyle Juszczyk	SF	47.6%
3	Austin Ekeler	LAC	38.8%
4	Christian McCaffrey	CAR	34.8%
5	Dalvin Cook	MIN	29.2%
6	David Johnson	ARI	29.2%
7	Boston Scott	PHI	29.0%
8	Jamaal Williams	GB	27.4%
9	Duke Johnson	HOU	24.6%
10	James Conner	PIT	21.2%

Minimum 25 passes.

the listed projections not as a prediction of exact numbers, but the mean of a range of possible performances. What's important is less the exact number of yards we project, and more which players are projected to improve or decline. Actual performance will vary from our projection less for veteran starters and more for rookies and third-stringers, for whom we must base our pro-

jections on much smaller career statistical samples. Touchdown numbers will vary more than yardage numbers.

Finally, in a section we call "Going Deep," we briefly discuss lower-round rookies, free-agent veterans, and practice-squad players who may play a role during the 2020 season or beyond.

Ameer Abdullah
Height: 5-9   Weight: 203   College: Nebraska   Draft: 2015/2 (54)   Born: 13-Jun-1993   Age: 27   Risk: Green

Year	Tm	G/GS	Snaps	Runs	Yds	TD	Yd/R	FUM	DVOA	Rk	DYAR	Rk	Suc%	Rk	BTkl	YafC	Pass	Rec	Yds	TD	C%	Yd/C	YAC	DVOA	Rk	DYAR	Rk
2017	DET	14/11	378	165	552	4	3.3	2	-10.0%	37	-9	36	35%	47	26	2.1	35	25	162	1	71%	6.5	5.8	1.7%	30	33	32
2018	2TM	10/0	17	1	1	0	1.0	0	-138.7%	--	-4	--	0%	--	1	2.0	4	3	28	0	75%	9.3	9.3	22.6%	--	8	--
2019	MIN	16/0	137	23	115	0	5.0	0	0.5%	--	6	--	26%	--	6	1.9	21	15	88	1	71%	5.9	5.3	-4.4%	--	12	--
2020	MIN			19	84	1	4.4	0	2.2%								8	6	46	0	75%	7.7		0.9%			

Abdullah hasn't seen any significant offensive action since joining the Vikings in mid-2018; with 23 rushing attempts and 23 kick returns, he might as well be listed as a returner on the depth chart. Even in the two-and-a-half games Dalvin Cook missed at the end of the season, Abdullah received 15 carries to Mike Boone's 41; he is an afterthought in the offense. If Cook does end up holding out, Abdullah might carve out some work in a rotation, but he's probably the fifth option in the Minnesota backfield. Even his kickoff returns aren't a saving grace; he ended up with -0.8 points of kick return value last season.

Cam Akers
Height: 5-11   Weight: 212   College: Florida State   Draft: 2020/2 (52)   Born: 22-Jun-1999   Age: 21   Risk: Green

Year	Tm	G/GS	Snaps	Runs	Yds	TD	Yd/R	FUM	DVOA	Rk	DYAR	Rk	Suc%	Rk	BTkl	YafC	Pass	Rec	Yds	TD	C%	Yd/C	YAC	DVOA	Rk	DYAR	Rk
2020	LAR			140	600	4	4.3	1	2.7%								26	20	145	1	77%	7.3		-4.6%			

The reason for pessimism for Akers is his lack of explosive plays in college. In three years at Florida State, he averaged only 4.9 yards per carry, next to last among all runners in this year's BackCAST class. But the reason for optimism is his rare combination of size and speed—his 4.47s 40 at the combine buoyed him to a top-five BackCAST projection and a top-three Speed Score of 108.7. In addition, he has adequate receiving ability and better-than-adequate throwing ability, completing five of his eight pass attempts for the Seminoles for 97 yards. Akers will compete with veterans Malcolm Brown and Darrell Henderson for playing time, but the Rams wouldn't have made him their first draft pick this year if they didn't think he could contribute right away.

Ryquell Armstead
Height: 5-11   Weight: 220   College: Temple   Draft: 2019/5 (140)   Born: 30-Oct-1996   Age: 24   Risk: Green

Year	Tm	G/GS	Snaps	Runs	Yds	TD	Yd/R	FUM	DVOA	Rk	DYAR	Rk	Suc%	Rk	BTkl	YafC	Pass	Rec	Yds	TD	C%	Yd/C	YAC	DVOA	Rk	DYAR	Rk
2019	JAX	16/1	152	35	108	0	3.1	0	-26.0%	--	-23	--	29%	--	6	2.1	24	14	144	2	58%	10.3	8.0	19.3%	--	48	--
2020	JAX			18	67	1	3.7	0	-8.1%								11	8	67	0	73%	8.4		-5.0%			

As a fifth-round rookie out of Temple, Armstead recorded only 35 carries and 24 targets in a backfield dominated as usual by Leonard Fournette. Armstead's putrid rushing DVOA would have ranked No. 45 of 46 qualifiers if he had enough carries to make the leaderboard, but his receiving DVOA would have tied Joe Mixon for No. 13. Some offseason rumors have the Jaguars cutting Fournette to save his $4.1-million salary and rolling out Armstead as the primary back; though not impossible, that seems a stretch. More likely, he could compete with Chris Thompson for receiving work and spell Fournette in the rushing game in a role akin to Kapri Bibbs in Washington. At the very least, he is the first back off the bench if Fournette gets hurt. He'll have to improve on his 2019 performance if he hopes to take over the starting role next time out.

Kalen Ballage
Height: 6-2   Weight: 230   College: Arizona State   Draft: 2018/4 (131)   Born: 22-Dec-1995   Age: 25   Risk: Green

Year	Tm	G/GS	Snaps	Runs	Yds	TD	Yd/R	FUM	DVOA	Rk	DYAR	Rk	Suc%	Rk	BTkl	YafC	Pass	Rec	Yds	TD	C%	Yd/C	YAC	DVOA	Rk	DYAR	Rk
2018	MIA	12/0	92	36	191	1	5.3	1	1.0%	--	16	--	42%	--	2	4.4	11	9	56	0	82%	6.2	8.4	-39.6%	--	-17	--
2019	MIA	12/6	256	74	135	3	1.8	0	-33.9%	--	-75	--	32%	--	5	1.3	24	14	63	0	58%	4.5	6.2	-66.6%	--	-65	--
2020	MIA			12	38	0	3.2	0	-16.3%								5	3	25	0	60%	8.3		-5.9%			

Some day Ballage will make his natural transition to H-back, but today is not that day. For now, Ballage is still masquerading as a running back—the kind that was primarily used as a Wildcat quarterback in college and still does not look comfortable in traditional formations, either under center or in shotgun, heading into Year 3 of his pro career. Given his size and thickness, it makes sense that Ballage is neither an agile nor particularly explosive back. Where Ballage does win is when afforded a sliver of space in the open field. With just a few steps, Ballage can kick into high gear and rip off a home run. Ballage stunted on the Vikings as a rookie in 2018 with one of those home run dashes for a 75-yard score, but in part because of Miami's atrocious offensive line, he never really got the chance to do so in 2019. With the team bringing in players such as Matt Breida and Jordan Howard, as well as rookie late-round pick Malcolm Perry, it seems Ballage is drifting further toward the fringes of the running back rotation.

Peyton Barber

Height: 5-11   Weight: 225   College: Auburn   Draft: 2016/FA   Born: 27-Jun-1994   Age: 26   Risk: Green

Year	Tm	G/GS	Snaps	Runs	Yds	TD	Yd/R	FUM	DVOA	Rk	DYAR	Rk	Suc%	Rk	BTkl	YafC	Pass	Rec	Yds	TD	C%	Yd/C	YAC	DVOA	Rk	DYAR	Rk
2017	TB	16/4	254	108	423	3	3.9	2	4.4%	15	63	19	57%	3	16	2.3	19	16	114	0	84%	7.1	7.1	-11.1%	--	3	--
2018	TB	16/16	616	234	871	5	3.7	1	-12.4%	38	-37	41	44%	36	44	2.3	29	20	92	1	69%	4.6	3.2	-35.1%	53	-34	53
2019	TB	16/7	347	154	470	6	3.1	1	-29.8%	45	-140	45	40%	43	17	2.0	24	16	115	1	67%	7.2	7.4	0.3%	--	17	--
2020	WAS			3	11	0	3.7	0	-14.4%								0	0	0	0	0%	0.0		0.0%			

Not many backs in the league have earned as much work while being largely unproductive as Barber has. Since 2017, 26 running backs have earned at least 450 carries. Barber's 3.56-yard average ranks dead-last in that group and he is one of just six running backs to be below four yards per carry. He also played the easiest schedule of any qualifying running back last season, with an eight-point gap between his VOA (-21.1%) and DVOA. In theory, the value in a tough, balanced runner like Barber is that he can be a stable force on first down, but he has never actually been that. In the past three seasons, Barber's best DVOA rating on first down is 1.7% in 2018; he posted negative figures in both 2017 and 2019. Barber now enters a loaded backfield with a clear one-two punch and a handful of viable depth players who could push him off the roster entirely.

Saquon Barkley

Height: 5-11   Weight: 233   College: Penn State   Draft: 2018/1 (2)   Born: 9-Feb-1997   Age: 23   Risk: Green

Year	Tm	G/GS	Snaps	Runs	Yds	TD	Yd/R	FUM	DVOA	Rk	DYAR	Rk	Suc%	Rk	BTkl	YafC	Pass	Rec	Yds	TD	C%	Yd/C	YAC	DVOA	Rk	DYAR	Rk
2018	NYG	16/16	853	261	1307	11	5.0	0	3.3%	18	127	14	41%	40	94	3.2	121	91	721	4	75%	7.9	8.4	-0.7%	28	86	13
2019	NYG	13/13	737	217	1003	6	4.6	1	0.4%	19	84	18	44%	38	55	3.1	73	52	438	2	71%	8.4	8.4	-22.8%	45	-37	46
2020	NYG			263	1192	9	4.5	1	9.7%								77	55	456	2	71%	8.3		1.1%			

The key to Saquon Barkley's success has been getting him into space, and that was clear in 2019 when he struggled with some injuries and didn't always play at 100%. On runs from shotgun, Barkley had 19.6% DVOA, which was the third-highest mark among 28 running backs with at least 50 such carries. However, his success rate was just 16th, which points to some of his boom-or-bust type runs. In tighter spaces, when Barkley had to rely more heavily on the offensive line, the results were much worse. He had -45.2% DVOA on 11 third- or fourth-down carries with just a 36% success rate. In the red zone, Barkley's DVOA was -16.8%, which was 28th of 35 backs with at least 20 carries. That was still an improvement on his 2018 results: a -27.1% DVOA on 50 red zone carries. Inside the 5, Barkley finished with just one touchdown on eight runs, which placed him among the worst backs in touchdowns vs expectation.

Le'Veon Bell

Height: 6-1   Weight: 225   College: Michigan State   Draft: 2013/2 (48)   Born: 18-Feb-1992   Age: 28   Risk: Yellow

Year	Tm	G/GS	Snaps	Runs	Yds	TD	Yd/R	FUM	DVOA	Rk	DYAR	Rk	Suc%	Rk	BTkl	YafC	Pass	Rec	Yds	TD	C%	Yd/C	YAC	DVOA	Rk	DYAR	Rk
2017	PIT	15/15	945	321	1291	9	4.0	3	7.9%	11	214	5	49%	11	79	2.5	106	85	655	2	80%	7.7	8.0	2.5%	29	101	11
2019	NYJ	15/15	798	245	789	3	3.2	1	-16.6%	44	-76	44	42%	40	55	2.3	78	66	461	1	85%	7.0	6.7	-13.2%	39	3	39
2020	NYJ			228	813	5	3.6	1	-8.9%								68	54	392	2	79%	7.3		-0.6%			

Bell's 2019 season is the perfect summation of the idea that the offensive line means more to the run game than the running back does. When you turn on the game film, Bell was still dashing and dodging defenders with his sixth-sense spatial awareness and sudden movements. As an individual, the former All-Pro looked like a plenty capable running back. However, the Jets' offensive line finished with an abysmal 3.80 adjusted line yards, second-worst in the league. Good rushing lanes seldom opened up for Bell, on top of the Jets' passing game being nothing of note, so the handsomely paid running back finished with one of the worst success rates in the league as he was smothered by opposing defenses week in, week out. Given Bell's advancing age for a running back and the Jets' offensive line still being a question mark despite some new additions, it is unlikely we ever see the Steelers version of Bell again.

Giovani Bernard   Height: 5-9   Weight: 205   College: North Carolina   Draft: 2013/2 (37)   Born: 22-Nov-1991   Age: 29   Risk: Yellow

Year	Tm	G/GS	Snaps	Runs	Yds	TD	Yd/R	FUM	DVOA	Rk	DYAR	Rk	Suc%	Rk	BTkl	YafC	Pass	Rec	Yds	TD	C%	Yd/C	YAC	DVOA	Rk	DYAR	Rk
2017	CIN	16/2	486	105	458	2	4.4	0	3.4%	16	48	24	40%	40	22	2.4	60	43	389	2	72%	9.0	10.0	-10.3%	41	11	40
2018	CIN	12/4	329	56	211	3	3.8	0	-1.6%	--	16	--	41%	--	10	2.1	48	35	218	0	73%	6.2	6.5	-11.8%	37	5	37
2019	CIN	16/2	457	53	170	0	3.2	2	-33.5%	--	-52	--	32%	--	11	2.0	43	30	234	0	70%	7.8	7.3	-38.5%	48	-55	49
2020	CIN			50	187	2	3.7	1	-8.0%								39	29	234	1	74%	8.1		-2.1%			

Once upon a time, Bernard was a third-down conversion machine, but those days are long gone, to the point that his DVOA on the money down was a scandalous -65.8% on nine carries and almost exactly as awful (-65.6%) on 15 passes. It used to be the case that the issue was defenses keying on Gio on third down; now it seems more of a "swept up in Cincy's horrid offense" problem. A rethink of his usage might do wonders—or, perhaps, a change of scenery. There is a strong whiff of "what if?" that adheres to Bernard; he should have approximated Darren Sproles' career, but it never really happened.

Reggie Bonnafon   Height: 6-0   Weight: 215   College: Louisville   Draft: 2018/FA   Born: 4-Jan-1996   Age: 25   Risk: Green

Year	Tm	G/GS	Snaps	Runs	Yds	TD	Yd/R	FUM	DVOA	Rk	DYAR	Rk	Suc%	Rk	BTkl	YafC	Pass	Rec	Yds	TD	C%	Yd/C	YAC	DVOA	Rk	DYAR	Rk
2019	CAR	16/0	69	16	116	1	7.3	0	15.2%	--	14	--	38%	--	1	1.5	9	6	57	0	67%	9.5	8.7	14.9%	--	13	--
2020	CAR			21	97	1	4.6	0	9.1%								9	7	58	0	78%	8.3		2.9%			

Any NFC South rivals who wanted to be cheeky could point to Bonnafon as a reason to call Panthers star Christian Mc-Caffrey a system running back. McCaffrey almost never comes off the field, but Bonnafon did manage to scrape together tremendous efficiencies in limited action last year; his rushing DVOA was even better than McCaffrey's excellent rate of 14.9%. Bonnafon's 59-yard touchdown against the Jaguars in Week 5 will likely prove to be his career highlight. He went undrafted out of Louisville, where he spent most of his college career backing up non-prospect Brandon Radcliff and being outproduced on the ground by his quarterback Lamar Jackson when he did play. Bonnafon broke just one tackle on his 22 offensive touches in 2019. He could play in 2020 if McCaffrey suffered an injury; the Panthers spent all of their draft capital on defense, which leaves Bonnafon as the presumptive backup. But whatever his small-sample success, Bonnafon has provided little real reason to believe that he would excel in the NFL with an extended look.

Mike Boone   Height: 5-10   Weight: 206   College: Cincinnati   Draft: 2018/FA   Born: 30-Jun-1995   Age: 25   Risk: Green

Year	Tm	G/GS	Snaps	Runs	Yds	TD	Yd/R	FUM	DVOA	Rk	DYAR	Rk	Suc%	Rk	BTkl	YafC	Pass	Rec	Yds	TD	C%	Yd/C	YAC	DVOA	Rk	DYAR	Rk
2018	MIN	8/0	36	11	47	0	4.3	0	-4.2%	--	2	--	36%	--	0	3.7	3	2	1	0	67%	0.5	2.5	-105.0%	--	-15	--
2019	MIN	16/2	82	49	273	3	5.6	0	9.0%	--	35	--	51%	--	10	3.1	4	3	17	0	75%	5.7	8.7	-10.6%	--	1	--
2020	MIN			17	79	1	4.6	0	9.0%								3	2	18	0	67%	9.0		-0.4%			

In Week 17, Boone racked up 148 yards and a touchdown, good for 48 DYAR, the second-best rushing day for any Vikings running back in 2019. Of course, that was a meaningless game against Chicago, with the Vikings already locked into a wild-card slot and the Bears long since eliminated from contention. It also was exceptionally frustrating for fantasy football fans, who grabbed Boone in Week 16 for their championships after Dalvin Cook's injury, only to see him lay a 28-yard egg. While Boone has a solid athletic profile, he's just a replacement-level player at the moment.

Lynn Bowden   Height: 5-11   Weight: 204   College: Kentucky   Draft: 2020/3 (80)   Born: 14-Oct-1997   Age: 23   Risk: Green

Year	Tm	G/GS	Snaps	Runs	Yds	TD	Yd/R	FUM	DVOA	Rk	DYAR	Rk	Suc%	Rk	BTkl	YafC	Pass	Rec	Yds	TD	C%	Yd/C	YAC	DVOA	Rk	DYAR	Rk
2020	LV			58	261	2	4.5	1	4.6%								18	15	116	0	83%	7.7		5.4%			

Bowden, an option quarterback in high school, began his Kentucky career as a slot receiver and Wildcat (the play package, not the school nickname) quarterback, catching 67 passes as a sophomore in 2018. He moved to option quarterback to quell a crisis midway through last season and ended up leading Kentucky in rushing (1,468 yards, 7.9 yards per carry, 13 touchdowns) and receiving (30-348-1) while finishing second in passing with 460 yards. The Raiders list Bowden as a running back and will give him an opportunity to be a more dynamic alternative to Jalen Richard as their change-up back as well as possibly a Taysom Hill-type role. You'll probably get used to hearing that last bit by the time you get to the end of this year's player comments.

Matt Breida

Height: 5-10 | Weight: 190 | College: Georgia Southern | Draft: 2017/FA | Born: 28-Feb-1995 | Age: 25 | Risk: Yellow

Year	Tm	G/GS	Snaps	Runs	Yds	TD	Yd/R	FUM	DVOA	Rk	DYAR	Rk	Suc%	Rk	BTkl	YafC	Pass	Rec	Yds	TD	C%	Yd/C	YAC	DVOA	Rk	DYAR	Rk
2017	SF	16/0	310	105	465	2	4.4	1	13.0%	5	87	15	47%	16	12	1.9	37	21	180	1	59%	8.6	7.3	-4.8%	37	16	37
2018	SF	14/13	364	153	814	3	5.3	1	1.3%	23	58	23	46%	30	28	2.4	31	27	261	2	87%	9.7	8.7	44.8%	2	105	10
2019	SF	13/5	259	123	623	1	5.1	2	-1.8%	22	33	25	46%	31	16	2.3	22	19	120	1	86%	6.3	6.7	19.5%	--	39	--
2020	MIA			98	457	2	4.7	1	4.5%								47	36	263	1	77%	7.3		-7.7%			

Players such as Alvin Kamara, Tarik Cohen, and Christian McCaffrey are the first guys you think of when you hear about running backs split out wide, but Breida fits right into the mold. Over the last three years, 30% of his targets have come from a wide receiver position (slot or wide), and he led all running backs at 39% in 2018. A small, explosive running back, Breida is at his absolute best when given space to work with. Whether that is outside zone carries in the run game or quick passes, Breida's blazing 4.39s 40-yard dash speed rests in the back of every defense's mind whenever he touches the ball. As is the case with many home-run backs, Breida also strikes out a lot. Breida has never cleared a 47% rushing success rate in his three-year career, which is startling for someone who played all three of those seasons in a rushing offense as wonderfully designed as Kyle Shanahan's. As was his role in San Francisco, Breida is primed in Miami to be the speedy changeup to the slower, steadier Jordan Howard. The good news for Breida is that Howard is the only real threat to his carries. Myles Gaskin and Day 3 rookie Malcolm Perry are the only players on the roster who fit Breida's archetype, but neither should be pushing for Breida's workload.

Malcolm Brown

Height: 5-11 | Weight: 222 | College: Texas | Draft: 2015/FA | Born: 15-May-1993 | Age: 27 | Risk: Green

Year	Tm	G/GS	Snaps	Runs	Yds	TD	Yd/R	FUM	DVOA	Rk	DYAR	Rk	Suc%	Rk	BTkl	YafC	Pass	Rec	Yds	TD	C%	Yd/C	YAC	DVOA	Rk	DYAR	Rk
2017	LAR	11/1	150	63	246	1	3.9	1	-6.9%	--	4	--	33%	--	13	2.2	11	9	53	0	82%	5.9	6.6	-24.6%	--	-7	--
2018	LAR	12/0	123	43	212	0	4.9	0	9.7%	--	36	--	67%	--	7	3.0	7	5	52	1	71%	10.4	7.8	43.5%	--	23	--
2019	LAR	14/1	226	69	255	5	3.7	0	-0.1%	--	25	--	46%	--	16	2.2	6	2	16	0	33%	8.0	3.5	-71.9%	--	-19	--
2020	LAR			75	294	3	3.9	0	-0.8%								18	14	97	1	78%	6.9		-4.2%			

If Brown gains precisely 31 yards on his first three runs this season, his career numbers will be at an even 200 carries with an average gain of 4.0 yards on the nose. He has made only two starts in the regular season—both against San Francisco—and failed to rush for 100 total yards between them. To put it kindly, these are modest figures for a running back entering his sixth NFL season. Brown will enter training camp as the most accomplished runner in the Rams backfield, but he has probably already hit his ceiling. If he struggles out of the gate, he could quickly lose playing time to youngsters Darrell Henderson and Cam Akers.

Rex Burkhead

Height: 5-10 | Weight: 215 | College: Nebraska | Draft: 2013/6 (190) | Born: 2-Jul-1990 | Age: 30 | Risk: Red

Year	Tm	G/GS	Snaps	Runs	Yds	TD	Yd/R	FUM	DVOA	Rk	DYAR	Rk	Suc%	Rk	BTkl	YafC	Pass	Rec	Yds	TD	C%	Yd/C	YAC	DVOA	Rk	DYAR	Rk
2017	NE	10/3	196	64	264	5	4.1	1	10.5%	--	56	--	53%	--	14	2.0	36	30	254	3	83%	8.5	6.1	33.7%	8	102	8
2018	NE	8/4	151	57	186	0	3.3	2	-8.2%	--	1	--	40%	--	14	2.4	20	14	131	1	70%	9.4	8.6	-9.1%	--	5	--
2019	NE	13/1	264	65	302	3	4.6	1	22.2%	--	85	--	52%	--	14	3.1	38	27	279	0	71%	10.3	8.5	4.0%	21	37	23
2020	NE			60	242	2	4.0	1	0.1%								30	24	206	1	80%	8.6		12.4%			

In three seasons with the Patriots, Burkhead has never been the team's best running back at any one thing, but he can do a little bit of everything. Burkhead has been third in carries and second in targets (among running backs) in each of his three years on the team. He is the filler for any blank spaces the offense might have. In 2017 and 2019, the two New England seasons in which he had the targets to qualify, Burkhead earned just over 30% of his targets from a wide receiver spot. Only Chicago's Tarik Cohen had a higher percentage of such targets in 2019. Burkhead's quality pass-catching and capable ball-carrying make him the preferred early-down option over teammate James White. Between 2018 and 2019, 86% of Burkhead's 180 touches were on first or second down, compared to 74% of White's. Meanwhile, Burkhead's red zone workload continues to decrease. Since 2017, Burkhead's red zone carries has dropped from 17 to two to zero. Burkhead posted a positive DVOA and 50%-plus success rate in the red zone in 2017, so it is tough to say why his work there has been cut out of the offense. Unless 2019 third-round pick Damien Harris explodes onto the scene, it is fair to assume Burkhead will maintain the same role he has for the past few seasons.

Chris Carson Height: 5-11 Weight: 222 College: Oklahoma State Draft: 2017/7 (249) Born: 16-Sep-1994 Age: 26 Risk: Yellow

Year	Tm	G/GS	Snaps	Runs	Yds	TD	Yd/R	FUM	DVOA	Rk	DYAR	Rk	Suc%	Rk	BTkl	YafC	Pass	Rec	Yds	TD	C%	Yd/C	YAC	DVOA	Rk	DYAR	Rk
2017	SEA	4/3	152	49	208	0	4.2	0	7.0%	--	33	--	43%	--	21	2.7	8	7	59	1	88%	8.4	6.6	34.9%	--	26	--
2018	SEA	14/14	454	247	1151	9	4.7	3	3.9%	17	133	12	51%	15	61	3.0	24	20	163	0	83%	8.2	8.2	21.2%	--	43	--
2019	SEA	15/15	736	278	1230	7	4.4	7	1.9%	16	130	10	57%	3	78	3.3	47	37	266	2	79%	7.2	8.6	8.9%	18	57	18
2020	SEA			224	947	7	4.2	4	0.2%								43	34	255	1	79%	7.5		-0.9%			

The defining play of Carson's season came in the third quarter of Week 9 against Tampa Bay. He took a handoff up the gut and slipped through the grasp of two defensive linemen near the line of scrimmage, then powered past a pair of safeties, one of whom had a perfect angle from the deep middle of the field. Many NFL running backs might have scored after breaking four tackles, but Carson was chased down from behind by linebacker Devin White, who swatted the ball out of Carson's hands and out of bounds. And that's everything you need to know about Carson in 2019: he led the NFL in broken tackles, but he also fumbled seven times, more than any non-quarterback. Add in Carson's lack of top-end speed (that play against Tampa Bay was his only run of more than 25 yards) and you're left with something like a butterfingered Ironhead Heyward. The good news is that Carson hasn't fumbled nearly so frequently in the past, so hopefully he won't put the ball on the turf very often in 2020. Carson's season ended with a fractured hip in Week 16, but he was able to avoid surgery and the Seahawks said after the draft that they expected him to available for Week 1.

Nick Chubb Height: 5-11 Weight: 225 College: Georgia Draft: 2018/2 (35) Born: 27-Dec-1995 Age: 25 Risk: Green

Year	Tm	G/GS	Snaps	Runs	Yds	TD	Yd/R	FUM	DVOA	Rk	DYAR	Rk	Suc%	Rk	BTkl	YafC	Pass	Rec	Yds	TD	C%	Yd/C	YAC	DVOA	Rk	DYAR	Rk
2018	CLE	16/9	395	192	996	8	5.2	0	1.1%	24	80	18	50%	19	47	4.3	29	20	149	2	69%	7.5	9.1	-4.6%	30	14	32
2019	CLE	16/16	728	298	1494	8	5.0	3	4.5%	12	162	9	45%	37	74	3.5	49	36	278	0	73%	7.7	8.8	-15.3%	41	-4	41
2020	CLE			258	1236	9	4.8	2	13.8%								31	23	184	1	74%	8.0		0.3%			

The second-most startling thing about Chubb's season is the gap between him and the rest of the league in yards after contact. Chubb averaged 3.54 according to SIS charting, a sizeable gap over second-place Chris Carson at 3.26. However, the *most* startling thing about Chubb's season is that his statistical output in the red zone was terrible. He rushed 51 times for just 89 yards once the Browns got down there, and only seven of those carries were touchdowns or first downs, so it's not like that artificially held the numbers down. His DVOA of -39.8% on red zone runs was lower than every back with at least 20 carries besides Frank Gore and Leonard Fournette. Eighteen of those runs went for zero or less yards. What that means is that outside the red zone, Chubb averaged 5.6 yards per carry. (The NFL average for running backs lst year was 4.6 yards per carry.) In 2018, Chubb had 57 yards on 26 carries—still at -13.4% DVOA—in the red zone. If Chubb is to hit his high fantasy football expectations, this has to change. For what it's worth, Kevin Stefanski's main back in 2019, Dalvin Cook, had a 20.0% DVOA on 47 red zone totes last year.

Speaking of those high expectations, Chubb averaged 15.8 fantasy points per game in the first eight games of last season, but 11.6 fantasy points per game in the final eight games. Kareem Hunt matters.

Tarik Cohen Height: 5-6 Weight: 191 College: North Carolina A&T Draft: 2017/4 (119) Born: 26-Jul-1995 Age: 25 Risk: Yellow

Year	Tm	G/GS	Snaps	Runs	Yds	TD	Yd/R	FUM	DVOA	Rk	DYAR	Rk	Suc%	Rk	BTkl	YafC	Pass	Rec	Yds	TD	C%	Yd/C	YAC	DVOA	Rk	DYAR	Rk
2017	CHI	16/4	360	87	370	2	4.3	2	-6.8%	--	6	--	46%	--	33	2.1	71	53	353	1	75%	6.7	5.9	-30.6%	58	-64	61
2018	CHI	16/7	495	99	444	3	4.5	3	-12.9%	--	-17	--	44%	--	37	1.7	91	71	725	5	78%	10.2	7.3	21.3%	6	184	4
2019	CHI	16/11	543	64	213	0	3.3	1	-17.2%	--	-23	--	42%	--	22	1.6	104	79	456	3	76%	5.8	5.4	-20.1%	43	-36	45
2020	CHI			57	218	2	3.8	1	-7.5%								78	60	417	2	77%	7.0		-5.2%			

Cohen finished near the very bottom of the running back receiving leaderboards in both DYAR and DVOA, as he led the league with 41 failed receptions, making him one of the least efficient players in football last season. This is not entirely his fault, however; Cohen had 51 DYAR on pass attempts at or beyond the line of scrimmage, which ranked 21st among running backs. But no back in football lost more DYAR on passes behind the line, where Cohen's -92 DYAR and -45.4% DVOA challenge some all-time records. Some backs are good enough to turn screens and checkdowns into positive yardage; Cohen took a bad situation and made the worst out of it. With either Mitch Trubisky or all-time failed completions leader Nick Foles under center, expect more failed screens, curls, and flats in 2020.

Tevin Coleman   Height: 6-1   Weight: 210   College: Indiana   Draft: 2015/3 (73)   Born: 16-Apr-1993   Age: 27   Risk: Yellow

Year	Tm	G/GS	Snaps	Runs	Yds	TD	Yd/R	FUM	DVOA	Rk	DYAR	Rk	Suc%	Rk	BTkl	YafC	Pass	Rec	Yds	TD	C%	Yd/C	YAC	DVOA	Rk	DYAR	Rk
2017	ATL	15/3	425	156	628	5	4.0	1	-6.5%	31	14	32	40%	39	31	2.6	39	27	299	3	69%	11.1	8.1	41.2%	4	121	6
2018	ATL	16/14	580	167	800	4	4.8	2	-6.4%	30	14	30	43%	37	26	2.4	44	32	276	5	73%	8.6	8.6	17.2%	10	77	16
2019	SF	14/11	392	137	544	6	4.0	0	-15.3%	43	-38	41	39%	44	19	2.1	30	21	180	1	70%	8.6	9.7	0.0%	24	23	30
2020	SF			130	519	4	4.0	1	0.0%								29	22	195	1	76%	8.9		7.5%			

Coleman reunited with Kyle Shanahan, his former offensive coordinator in Atlanta, after joining the 49ers as a free agent in 2019. He stepped into the starting role for a run-heavy offense right away, though he dealt with a handful of injuries throughout the year that limited his overall production. Coleman did not offer a ton as a receiver when he wasn't catching screen passes on first down, but between San Francisco's run-heavy approach and the many second-half leads the 49ers needed to salt away, he did not have to do much more than that. Late in the year, an injury opened the door for Raheem Mostert to take on a larger role, and as a result, Coleman will be battling for opportunities again in another crowded San Francisco backfield in 2020.

James Conner   Height: 6-1   Weight: 233   College: Pittsburgh   Draft: 2017/3 (105)   Born: 5-May-1995   Age: 25   Risk: Red

Year	Tm	G/GS	Snaps	Runs	Yds	TD	Yd/R	FUM	DVOA	Rk	DYAR	Rk	Suc%	Rk	BTkl	YafC	Pass	Rec	Yds	TD	C%	Yd/C	YAC	DVOA	Rk	DYAR	Rk
2017	PIT	14/0	68	32	144	0	4.5	0	10.2%	--	20	--	53%	--	4	2.4	1	0	0	0	0%	0.0	0.0	-130.7%	--	-7	--
2018	PIT	13/12	718	215	973	12	4.5	4	2.3%	21	99	16	49%	24	56	2.8	71	55	497	1	77%	9.0	10.0	15.2%	11	112	9
2019	PIT	10/10	334	116	464	4	4.0	1	-11.3%	38	-13	37	45%	35	33	2.3	38	34	251	3	89%	7.4	8.8	21.2%	10	75	14
2020	PIT			231	1007	8	4.4	3	3.0%								65	53	432	2	82%	8.2		13.6%			

"When healthy," Mike Tomlin added at the end of a description of Conner as a "featured guy and proven runner" to *The Pittsburgh Tribune-Review*. That's pretty much the gist of Conner's 2019 season, which saw him fight through thigh, shoulder, ankle, knee, and quad injuries. Conner's 2019 season was a game of Operation! gone wrong. This is truly a player with a limitless number of possibilities where what happens this year will play an enormous role in his future. Conner will hit free agency at 26. If he does so with a good, healthy year, he'll have proven himself to be a good three-down or head-of-committee back. If he trends closer to what he did last year, he may never have a starting job again. The 2018 broken tackle rate is a great indicator that he can play. But NFL running backs who can't stay healthy are rarely considered worth the time investment. Our KUBIAK projection favors the idea that Conner will be a workhorse starter again as he was in 2018.

Dalvin Cook   Height: 5-10   Weight: 210   College: Florida State   Draft: 2017/2 (41)   Born: 10-Aug-1995   Age: 25   Risk: Yellow

Year	Tm	G/GS	Snaps	Runs	Yds	TD	Yd/R	FUM	DVOA	Rk	DYAR	Rk	Suc%	Rk	BTkl	YafC	Pass	Rec	Yds	TD	C%	Yd/C	YAC	DVOA	Rk	DYAR	Rk
2017	MIN	4/4	169	74	354	2	4.8	1	7.4%	--	48	--	55%	--	23	2.8	16	11	90	0	69%	8.2	9.5	-19.0%	--	-5	--
2018	MIN	11/10	490	133	615	2	4.6	2	-13.7%	41	-27	38	41%	41	42	2.8	49	40	305	2	82%	7.6	9.3	2.1%	26	45	24
2019	MIN	14/14	615	250	1135	13	4.5	4	9.3%	10	183	8	49%	23	68	2.7	63	53	519	0	84%	9.8	11.2	29.2%	5	144	4
2020	MIN			252	1076	10	4.3	4	2.6%								74	59	484	1	80%	8.2		5.8%			

At time of writing, Cook is still threatening to hold out for the 2020 season unless a contract extension can get done. The problem here isn't Cook, who has been highly productive when healthy and took his game to another level in Gary Kubiak's system. The problem is whether any running back is worth the ten-digit annual figure Cook is reportedly asking for. We've seen teams regret handing large extensions to star running backs before—see Todd Gurley and David Johnson for examples 1A and 1B. Statistically, the Vikings were better with Cook on the field last season, in both the running and passing game, but be careful about using that stat too much, as it includes the team's utter collapse in Week 16 against Green Bay which was due to more than just Cook being out. In addition, while Cook was a positive asset in the receiving game last season, he shouldn't be confused for a Christian McCaffrey type, running receiver routes. Add all the evidence together, and Cook deserves to be paid more than his rookie contract is currently giving him, but there has yet to be a running back who has been worth the figures that Cook and his agents are suggesting. A rock and a hard place situation for the Vikings.

AJ Dillon

| | Height: 6-0 | Weight: 250 | College: Boston College | Draft: 2020/2 (62) | Born: 2-May-1998 | Age: 22 | Risk: Blue |

Year	Tm	G/GS	Snaps	Runs	Yds	TD	Yd/R	FUM	DVOA	Rk	DYAR	Rk	Suc%	Rk	BTkl	YafC	Pass	Rec	Yds	TD	C%	Yd/C	YAC	DVOA	Rk	DYAR	Rk
2020	GB		73	290	2	4.0	1	-1.3%									14	10	83	1	71%	8.3		-1.3%			

In most years, Dillon's Speed Score of 117.3 would have led the combine; running a 4.53s 40-yard dash at 247 pounds is no mean feat. People Dillon's size are not supposed to move that fast. There were 17 running backs in the NFL who clocked in at 240 pounds last year, and 15 of them were fullbacks. Sixteen of them combined for 74 yards; the other was Derrick Henry. Dillon's unlikely to be Henry; he takes too many hits and lacks some of that top-end explosiveness, averaging just 5.2 yards per attempt against college competition. With no receiving skills to speak of, he'll be a two-down back subbed out in passing situations, and will likely become Green Bay's leading rusher in 2021 when Aaron Jones' rookie contract expires.

J.K. Dobbins

| | Height: 5-9 | Weight: 209 | College: Ohio State | Draft: 2020/2 (55) | Born: 17-Dec-1998 | Age: 22 | Risk: Green |

Year	Tm	G/GS	Snaps	Runs	Yds	TD	Yd/R	FUM	DVOA	Rk	DYAR	Rk	Suc%	Rk	BTkl	YafC	Pass	Rec	Yds	TD	C%	Yd/C	YAC	DVOA	Rk	DYAR	Rk
2020	BAL		124	565	4	4.6	1	5.7%									9	8	62	0	89%	7.8		3.7%			

J'Kaylin Dobbins will be an interesting study in collegiate usage affecting pro production. In three seasons in Columbus, Dobbins racked up 725 carries and 71 receptions, a massive workload, even more than Christian McCaffrey at Stanford (not counting CMC's return touches). Of course, he was incredibly productive on all those touches, rushing for nearly 4,500 yards (including 2003 yards in 2019), and is just 21 years old. And McCaffrey has turned out all right…

Dobbins didn't run at the combine, and his pro day was wiped away by COVID-19, so gauging his Speed Score isn't possible. He scored 43 touchdowns at Ohio State, many of them on breakaway runs (including a 68-yard sprint in the NCAA semifinal against Clemson), and Dobbins laid down a 4.45s 40 at an all-star combine coming out of high school. He's plenty athletic, and strong, and has all the makings of a quality NFL starter, especially in the run-heavy attack in Baltimore, where Lamar Jackson and Mark Ingram (for now) will allow Dobbins to ease into the league and not become an immediate bell cow back. It isn't known if tire tread can be regrown, but Dobbins is in an ideal position to find out.

Kenyan Drake

| | Height: 6-1 | Weight: 211 | College: Alabama | Draft: 2016/3 (73) | Born: 26-Jan-1994 | Age: 26 | Risk: Green |

Year	Tm	G/GS	Snaps	Runs	Yds	TD	Yd/R	FUM	DVOA	Rk	DYAR	Rk	Suc%	Rk	BTkl	YafC	Pass	Rec	Yds	TD	C%	Yd/C	YAC	DVOA	Rk	DYAR	Rk
2017	MIA	16/6	477	133	644	3	4.8	2	-11.3%	39	-14	38	44%	25	39	3.3	48	32	239	1	67%	7.5	6.7	-19.1%	52	-13	52
2018	MIA	16/7	545	120	535	4	4.5	2	4.7%	16	58	22	45%	33	41	2.4	74	53	477	5	73%	9.0	7.8	14.0%	12	123	8
2019	2TM	14/10	622	170	817	8	4.8	2	19.7%	3	202	5	51%	16	34	2.3	68	50	345	0	74%	6.9	8.5	-7.9%	33	23	29
2020	ARI			209	947	6	4.5	3	4.6%								74	57	433	2	77%	7.6		-0.4%			

Prior to 2019, Drake had never managed to take control over a starting job in the NFL, and with the Dolphins tanking, he ended up getting traded to Arizona after the Cardinals were hit with a slew of running back injuries. Faced with an excellent opportunity, Drake took it and (literally) ran with it, performing well enough that he made David Johnson expendable. In his eight starts in Arizona, Drake was a highly efficient runner on all three downs and earned a transition tag contract for his performance. While he is seeking a long-term deal, the Cardinals may be looking for him to prove that his 2019 showing was no fluke before they ink an extension.

Chase Edmonds Height: 5-9   Weight: 210   College: Fordham   Draft: 2018/4 (134)   Born: 13-Apr-1996   Age: 24   Risk: Green

Year	Tm	G/GS	Snaps	Runs	Yds	TD	Yd/R	FUM	DVOA	Rk	DYAR	Rk	Suc%	Rk	BTkl	YafC	Pass	Rec	Yds	TD	C%	Yd/C	YAC	DVOA	Rk	DYAR	Rk
2018	ARI	16/0	198	60	208	2	3.5	1	-18.9%	--	-27	--	45%	--	14	2.1	23	20	103	0	87%	5.2	6.1	-27.7%	--	-19	--
2019	ARI	13/2	209	60	303	4	5.1	0	31.7%	--	84	--	40%	--	10	2.6	21	12	105	1	57%	8.8	8.8	-15.3%	--	-2	--
2020	ARI			63	271	1	4.3	1	0.6%								20	14	115	1	70%	8.2		-5.2%			

Edmonds had an opportunity to seize control of the Arizona starting running back slot in place of an injured David Johnson, but shortly after entering the starting lineup, he suffered an injury of his own. This provided some of the impetus behind the trade for Kenyan Drake, and lo and behold, Drake stepped in and grabbed a hold of the starting job ahead of Edmonds. With Drake playing on the transition tag now, Edmonds is stuck as the backup again and will likely have to hope for some injury luck in order to take on a larger role in the backfield. He looked plenty capable in limited time in 2019, so it may just be a matter of getting another chance.

Gus Edwards Height: 6-1   Weight: 235   College: Rutgers   Draft: 2018/FA   Born: 13-Apr-1995   Age: 25   Risk: Green

Year	Tm	G/GS	Snaps	Runs	Yds	TD	Yd/R	FUM	DVOA	Rk	DYAR	Rk	Suc%	Rk	BTkl	YafC	Pass	Rec	Yds	TD	C%	Yd/C	YAC	DVOA	Rk	DYAR	Rk
2018	BAL	11/6	286	137	718	2	5.2	0	13.9%	9	130	13	63%	1	19	2.6	2	2	20	0	100%	10.0	8.5	69.1%	--	10	--
2019	BAL	16/1	402	133	711	2	5.3	2	11.8%	8	126	11	56%	6	23	3.1	7	7	45	0	100%	6.4	6.4	24.7%	--	15	--
2020	BAL			19	95	1	5.0	0	10.9%								2	2	14	0	100%	7.0		1.1%			

The bruising, 238-pound Edwards got the lion's share of third- and fourth-down carries but didn't do much with them (1.7% DVOA). On the other hand, when he toted it on first-and-10 he was good, with a better DVOA (25.0%) than Mark Ingram, albeit on half as many carries. More surprising still was Edwards' performance on the goal line—he was stopped shy of paydirt on all eight of his carries inside the five, by far the most carries without scoring of any back in the league. Edwards had a fantastic 2019 overall and continues to be part of the plan in Baltimore, but the drafting of J.K. Dobbins should encourage Gus to remember that running backs in the NFL come and go with the wind.

Clyde Edwards-Helaire Height: 5-7   Weight: 207   College: Louisiana State   Draft: 2020/1 (32)   Born: 11-Apr-1999   Age: 21   Risk: Green

Year	Tm	G/GS	Snaps	Runs	Yds	TD	Yd/R	FUM	DVOA	Rk	DYAR	Rk	Suc%	Rk	BTkl	YafC	Pass	Rec	Yds	TD	C%	Yd/C	YAC	DVOA	Rk	DYAR	Rk
2020	KC			162	722	5	4.5	1	7.5%								48	36	295	2	75%	8.2		8.4%			

When the analytics-friendly Chiefs selected a running back at the end of the first round, it inspired a bit of apoplexy among the denizens of analytics Twitter. The subset of analytics Twitter known as Football Outsiders readers was probably even more surprised, since Edwards-Helaire had a negative BackCAST projection. The biggest issue is Edwards-Helaire's unimpressive size-speed combination. He ran a 4.60s 40-yard dash at 207 pounds; the best drafted running back who ever recorded a 40 of 4.60 seconds or worse with a weight under 210 pounds was probably Ahmad Bradshaw, and the rest of the list is mostly washouts such as Javon Ringer, Storm Johnson, and Travis Stephens.

What's the case for Edwards-Helaire? First of all, BackCAST's blind spot is broken tackles, since it is built on over 20 years of data and we only have collegiate broken tackle stats for the last couple years. Kareem Hunt, for example, was a big BackCAST miss for this reason. Edwards-Helaire was tied for second in FBS with 35 broken tackles per 100 touches according to Sports Info Solutions charting. Edwards-Helaire may be small but he's got a bowling ball frame reminscent of Maurice Jones-Drew that allows him to gain yardage between the tackles. His vision to explode through creases fits the zone-heavy run scheme that Kansas City likes to use. The other reason to the Chiefs to favor Edwards-Helaire is his ability as a receiver. He has smooth hands and the ability to make plays in space, and Andy Reid historically loves running backs with those abilities. (Brian Westbrook might ring a bell.) There has been some research that suggests that while there's very little difference between running backs, what difference there is comes mostly in the passing game. That's good for Edwards-Helaire's value and goes a long way towards explaining the pick. On the other hand, value in the passing game includes pass protection, and blocking is an area where Edwards-Helaire really struggles.

The moral of the story: Edwards-Helaire is a perfect fit for the team he's joining and will probably put up very impressive numbers in one of the league's best offenses. We still wouldn't have chosen a running back with our first-round pick.

Austin Ekeler   Height: 5-10   Weight: 200   College: Western State   Draft: 2017/FA   Born: 17-May-1995   Age: 25   Risk: Yellow

Year	Tm	G/GS	Snaps	Runs	Yds	TD	Yd/R	FUM	DVOA	Rk	DYAR	Rk	Suc%	Rk	BTkl	YafC	Pass	Rec	Yds	TD	C%	Yd/C	YAC	DVOA	Rk	DYAR	Rk
2017	LAC	16/0	197	47	260	2	5.5	2	22.7%	--	59	--	55%	--	23	3.2	35	27	279	3	77%	10.3	9.3	27.1%	12	84	16
2018	LAC	14/3	348	106	554	3	5.2	1	4.9%	15	59	21	52%	13	39	3.8	53	39	404	3	74%	10.4	10.5	30.3%	4	131	7
2019	LAC	16/8	609	132	557	3	4.2	3	-10.0%	35	-8	35	45%	32	62	2.8	108	92	993	8	85%	10.8	10.2	38.8%	3	320	2
2020	LAC			177	749	6	4.2	2	0.9%								84	65	565	3	77%	8.7		11.3%			

Ekeler lined up primarily at running back during Melvin Gordon's holdout, then returned to his more traditional role when Gordon returned, playing about a dozen snaps in the slot or split wide and 15-25 in the backfield per game. He should see more snaps in the backfield with Gordon gone this year, though both Justin Jackson and rookie Joshua Kelley are capable of doing nearly everything Gordon could do, only cheaper and with less name recognition.

Ezekiel Elliott   Height: 6-0   Weight: 228   College: Ohio State   Draft: 2016/1 (4)   Born: 22-Jul-1995   Age: 25   Risk: Green

Year	Tm	G/GS	Snaps	Runs	Yds	TD	Yd/R	FUM	DVOA	Rk	DYAR	Rk	Suc%	Rk	BTkl	YafC	Pass	Rec	Yds	TD	C%	Yd/C	YAC	DVOA	Rk	DYAR	Rk
2017	DAL	10/10	591	242	983	7	4.1	1	11.1%	8	205	7	57%	2	42	2.9	38	26	269	2	68%	10.3	10.0	-11.2%	43	5	43
2018	DAL	15/15	890	304	1434	6	4.7	6	2.9%	20	149	9	50%	18	46	3.0	95	77	567	3	81%	7.4	7.5	-3.2%	29	52	20
2019	DAL	16/16	941	301	1357	12	4.5	3	16.5%	4	324	1	56%	4	54	2.6	71	54	420	2	76%	7.8	7.3	12.6%	16	99	10
2020	DAL			275	1202	9	4.4	3	4.8%								65	50	381	2	77%	7.6		-1.3%			

Even with the more modern and progressive offense they ran in 2019, the Cowboys gave Elliott a ton of work early in the game. Elliott had a league-leading 88 carries in the first quarter and league-leading 92 carries in the second quarter. The next closest back in the second quarter was Joe Mixon with 70. His 180 first-half carries were 31 more than Nick Chubb at No. 2. Elliott had his fewest carries (56) and lowest first-down rate (21.4%) in fourth quarters.

Throughout the game, Elliott had a ton of high-leverage carries, and he delivered. He led the league with 61 attempts in the red zone, and his 18.6% DVOA was seventh-highest among 35 backs with 20 or more carries. He also had 35.0% DVOA and a 76% success rate on third- and fourth-down carries. No player (quarterbacks included) with at least 20 third-down carries had a higher first down rate than Elliott's 72.7%. The next highest was 63.3%.

Darrynton Evans   Height: 5-11   Weight: 200   College: Appalachian State   Draft: 2020/3 (93)   Born: 9-Jul-1998   Age: 22   Risk: Blue

Year	Tm	G/GS	Snaps	Runs	Yds	TD	Yd/R	FUM	DVOA	Rk	DYAR	Rk	Suc%	Rk	BTkl	YafC	Pass	Rec	Yds	TD	C%	Yd/C	YAC	DVOA	Rk	DYAR	Rk
2020	TEN			72	318	2	4.4	1	3.8%								34	27	231	1	79%	8.6		11.8%			

With Dion Lewis released, the Titans needed a new receiving back and appear to be projecting Evans into that role. Evans played well on gap runs at Appalachian State and was explosive when he actually did get to the open field. There were many 20-plus-yard runs in his boxscores. His vision behind the line is a little more sketchy as zone blocking seemed to give him problems and he was not forcing broken tackles in bushels. This is a prime depth chart to be drafted to because Derrick Henry is on a franchise tag and nobody else is all that threatening. But unless Evans has a David Johnson-type rookie season, it's going to be hard for the Titans to not entrench him as a committee back or worse next year.

Leonard Fournette   Height: 6-0   Weight: 228   College: Louisiana State   Draft: 2017/1 (4)   Born: 18-Jan-1995   Age: 25   Risk: Yellow

Year	Tm	G/GS	Snaps	Runs	Yds	TD	Yd/R	FUM	DVOA	Rk	DYAR	Rk	Suc%	Rk	BTkl	YafC	Pass	Rec	Yds	TD	C%	Yd/C	YAC	DVOA	Rk	DYAR	Rk
2017	JAX	13/13	564	268	1040	9	3.9	2	2.1%	17	115	11	44%	26	55	2.3	48	36	302	1	75%	8.4	8.5	7.2%	18	58	21
2018	JAX	8/8	280	133	439	5	3.3	0	-9.3%	32	-4	33	47%	26	17	2.1	26	22	185	1	85%	8.4	9.7	9.6%	17	37	26
2019	JAX	15/15	918	265	1152	3	4.3	1	-8.6%	34	0	34	42%	39	56	2.9	101	76	522	0	76%	6.9	7.2	-17.0%	42	-17	42
2020	JAX			244	986	8	4.0	1	1.1%								62	45	339	1	73%	7.5		-6.6%			

Fournette's 2019 season is a great example of the difference between fantasy value and actual value. In fantasy terms, despite only three touchdowns, Fournette's career-high 76 receptions and 1,674 scrimmage yards made 2019 the most valuable PPR season of his career. In the real world, he had his second consecutive season with negative rushing DVOA, and his 101 pass targets produced negative receiving value for the first time. Fournette is due almost $4.2 million in 2020 and the team has already declined his fifth-year option, which has led to speculation that he could be a cap casualty, but the mostly likely scenario is that he plays out his rookie deal as the workhorse back then moves on in the ensuing free agency.

For 2020 at least, that is good news for fantasy owners. Jay Gruden loves a workhorse back: he has coaxed 260-plus carries and 1,000-plus yards out of four different lead backs in his nine seasons as an offensive coordinator or head coach, which would be right in line with Fournette's previous healthy seasons. As long as he can stay healthy and engaged, Fournette should be one of fantasy football's most valuable commodities, almost regardless of what else happens around him in Jacksonville. There's no guarantee that will translate to increased real-world value, but the chances of the starting running back's advanced statistics mattering for the 2020 Jaguars are already slim.

Devonta Freeman   Height: 5-8   Weight: 206   College: Florida State   Draft: 2014/4 (103)   Born: 15-Mar-1992   Age: 28   Risk: N/A

Year	Tm	G/GS	Snaps	Runs	Yds	TD	Yd/R	FUM	DVOA	Rk	DYAR	Rk	Suc%	Rk	BTkl	YafC	Pass	Rec	Yds	TD	C%	Yd/C	YAC	DVOA	Rk	DYAR	Rk
2017	ATL	14/14	552	196	865	7	4.4	4	1.5%	18	89	14	51%	9	59	2.4	47	36	317	1	77%	8.8	6.8	23.6%	13	102	10
2018	ATL	2/2	67	14	68	0	4.9	0	-6.9%	--	1	--	50%	--	2	1.9	7	5	23	0	71%	4.6	4.0	-109.8%	--	-30	--
2019	ATL	14/14	675	184	656	2	3.6	3	-11.1%	37	-19	39	41%	41	38	2.0	70	59	410	4	84%	6.9	5.8	-0.9%	25	51	19

Freeman personifies the sabermetric wisdom to never give a big contract to a running back. Between 2015 and 2017, he was one of the best and most elusive backs in football. He finished top five in total broken tackles in the former two seasons, and on a smaller touch volume in the latter, he broke a tackle on a career high 25.4% of his touches, the eighth-best rate for backs with 150 or more touches that season. But in the two years since, Freeman has suffered knee, groin, and foot injuries that have limited him to 16 of a possible 32 games, and declined to 10.5% and 15.6% broken-tackle rates. He was released this offseason just halfway through the five-year, $41.3-million extension he signed three years ago. Freeman is still just 28 years old, and he can point to injuries as a reason for his poor performance the last two seasons. But he produced a worse rushing DVOA (-15.7%) prior to his foot injury in Week 10 last season when he was ostensibly healthy than he did after it (-4.4%). Perhaps he can find a one-year deal as part of a time share to reestablish himself, but likely most teams would sooner place their uncertain bets at the position on cost-controlled recent draft picks.

Royce Freeman   Height: 6-0   Weight: 238   College: Oregon   Draft: 2018/3 (71)   Born: 24-Feb-1996   Age: 24   Risk: Green

Year	Tm	G/GS	Snaps	Runs	Yds	TD	Yd/R	FUM	DVOA	Rk	DYAR	Rk	Suc%	Rk	BTkl	YafC	Pass	Rec	Yds	TD	C%	Yd/C	YAC	DVOA	Rk	DYAR	Rk
2018	DEN	14/8	308	130	521	5	4.0	1	-6.8%	31	10	31	46%	29	31	2.8	20	14	72	0	70%	5.1	4.2	-32.2%	--	-20	--
2019	DEN	16/0	513	132	496	3	3.8	0	-11.0%	36	-12	36	41%	42	22	2.1	50	43	256	1	86%	6.0	6.0	-10.1%	36	10	36
2020	DEN			23	86	1	3.7	0	-7.6%								9	8	43	0	89%	5.4		-5.5%			

The 230-plus-pound Freeman has rushed 22 times for 31 yards and seven touchdowns inside the 10-yard line over the last two seasons. The 190-ish-pound Phillip Lindsay has rushed 27 times for 53 yards and 11 touchdowns in the same situations. There's overwhelming evidence that big backs are no more useful in short-yardage and goal-to-go situations than small backs, and while there's undoubtedly some selection bias in the data (tiny backs who aren't trusted to run the ball at the 1-yard line are never asked to, while the big guys are given more low-success-rate opportunities), Freeman's inability to prove himself a better battering ram than Lindsay was a missed opportunity for him, career-wise. Melvin Gordon will replace Freeman as the thunder to Lindsay's lightning, and there shouldn't be many touches available for the third running back in the revamped and reloaded Broncos offense.

Wayne Gallman   Height: 6-0   Weight: 210   College: Clemson   Draft: 2017/4 (140)   Born: 1-Oct-1994   Age: 26   Risk: Green

Year	Tm	G/GS	Snaps	Runs	Yds	TD	Yd/R	FUM	DVOA	Rk	DYAR	Rk	Suc%	Rk	BTkl	YafC	Pass	Rec	Yds	TD	C%	Yd/C	YAC	DVOA	Rk	DYAR	Rk
2017	NYG	13/1	325	111	476	0	4.3	3	-5.2%	29	15	31	50%	10	31	3.0	48	34	193	1	71%	5.7	5.9	-14.6%	48	-2	48
2018	NYG	15/1	155	51	176	1	3.5	2	7.3%	--	30	--	39%	--	12	2.1	22	14	89	0	64%	6.4	5.8	-63.8%	--	-47	--
2019	NYG	10/2	167	29	110	2	3.8	1	-15.5%	--	-9	--	41%	--	5	1.7	15	11	102	1	73%	9.3	9.5	6.0%	--	14	--
2020	NYG			8	31	0	3.9	0	-4.2%								2	2	14	0	100%	7.0		-3.2%			

Gallman would be a perfect committee back on almost any other team in the NFL, but he has been buried behind Saquon Barkley and will now likely fall behind Dion Lewis on the Giants' depth chart. Gallman had his chance for a start in Weeks 4 and 5 with Barkley injured but was forced to leave Week 5 with a concussion after just two carries in the first quarter. He struggled upon his return—he didn't get a carry in Week 13 and was a healthy scratch from Week 14 through the end of the regular season.

Myles Gaskin Height: 5-10 Weight: 205 College: Washington Draft: 2019/7 (234) Born: 15-Feb-1997 Age: 23 Risk: Green

Year	Tm	G/GS	Snaps	Runs	Yds	TD	Yd/R	FUM	DVOA	Rk	DYAR	Rk	Suc%	Rk	BTkl	YafC	Pass	Rec	Yds	TD	C%	Yd/C	YAC	DVOA	Rk	DYAR	Rk
2019	MIA	7/0	125	36	133	1	3.7	0	-10.3%	--	-3	--	42%	--	8	3.0	12	7	51	0	58%	7.3	6.6	-32.9%	--	-14	--
2020	MIA			9	37	0	4.1	0	-5.4%								3	2	17	0	67%	8.5		-2.3%			

The silver lining for Gaskin is that his 42% rushing success rate was not the worst on the team. However, that relative success did not earn him any brownie points with the Dolphins offensive staff. He still finished fifth among the team's running backs in carries; even Ryan Fitzpatrick ran more often. Likewise, Gaskin finished fifth in receptions among the team's running backs, so it is not as though Gaskin was making up for his middling rushing on passing downs. With a new one-two punch of Jordan Howard and Matt Breida in town, Gaskin will surely be barred from major carries in 2020 the same as he was in 2019.

Antonio Gibson Height: 6-0 Weight: 228 College: Memphis Draft: 2020/3 (66) Born: 23-Jun-1998 Age: 22 Risk: Green

Year	Tm	G/GS	Snaps	Runs	Yds	TD	Yd/R	FUM	DVOA	Rk	DYAR	Rk	Suc%	Rk	BTkl	YafC	Pass	Rec	Yds	TD	C%	Yd/C	YAC	DVOA	Rk	DYAR	Rk
2020	WAS			30	129	1	4.3	0	-0.6%								28	23	187	1	82%	8.1		7.6%			

Washington's third-round pick is part running back, part wide receiver, and 100% playmaker. In college, Gibson did not break out until his senior season, but when he did, the results were nuclear. Gibson earned 369 yards on 33 carries and 735 receiving yards on just 38 receptions, giving him bonkers yards per play figures. Memphis' offense used him as a deep threat, YAC monster, jet sweep weapon, and more. Though not the sharpest route-runner or polished runner, Gibson's raw speed and athleticism in small areas make him a nightmare for defenses once the ball is in his hands. He led Sports Info Solutions charting with 38 broken tackles per 100 touches. Gibson is currently listed as a running back after technically being a wide receiver in college, but look for the rookie to find playing time in both roles, presumably with some unique deployment.

Melvin Gordon Height: 6-1 Weight: 215 College: Wisconsin Draft: 2015/1 (15) Born: 13-Apr-1993 Age: 27 Risk: Yellow

Year	Tm	G/GS	Snaps	Runs	Yds	TD	Yd/R	FUM	DVOA	Rk	DYAR	Rk	Suc%	Rk	BTkl	YafC	Pass	Rec	Yds	TD	C%	Yd/C	YAC	DVOA	Rk	DYAR	Rk
2017	LAC	16/16	750	284	1105	8	3.9	1	-6.8%	33	21	29	40%	41	73	2.5	83	58	476	4	70%	8.2	8.5	3.0%	28	76	18
2018	LAC	12/12	524	175	885	10	5.1	1	20.8%	3	210	5	53%	9	55	3.2	66	50	490	4	76%	9.8	10.7	5.5%	22	72	19
2019	LAC	12/11	433	162	612	8	3.8	4	-7.5%	33	8	32	51%	15	37	2.1	55	42	296	1	76%	7.0	7.6	-7.3%	32	19	31
2020	DEN			177	719	7	4.1	3	-1.4%								49	40	262	2	82%	6.6		-4.3%			

Gordon began last season with one of the most ill-advised holdouts in NFL history, then rushed 36 times for 91 yards (2.5 yards per carry) in his first three games after the holdout because it's hard to break tackles or elude defenders with your tail tucked between your legs. Gordon has only played one full 16-game season in his career for various reasons and only cracked the 4.0-yards-per-carry barrier in 2018, so his name and reputation have always been out-of-scale to his accomplishments. He worked his way back up to a notch above replacement level as a committee back last season, and he should be able to sustain both that role and performance level in Denver.

Frank Gore Height: 5-9 Weight: 212 College: Miami Draft: 2005/3 (65) Born: 14-May-1983 Age: 37 Risk: Yellow

Year	Tm	G/GS	Snaps	Runs	Yds	TD	Yd/R	FUM	DVOA	Rk	DYAR	Rk	Suc%	Rk	BTkl	YafC	Pass	Rec	Yds	TD	C%	Yd/C	YAC	DVOA	Rk	DYAR	Rk
2017	IND	16/16	555	261	961	3	3.7	3	-2.3%	23	66	18	44%	23	41	2.5	38	29	245	1	76%	8.4	9.5	4.1%	25	35	31
2018	MIA	14/14	330	156	722	0	4.6	1	5.7%	14	86	17	50%	19	28	2.6	16	12	124	1	75%	10.3	9.6	35.4%	--	49	--
2019	BUF	16/8	381	166	599	2	3.6	0	-15.2%	42	-50	43	45%	36	16	2.3	16	13	100	0	81%	7.7	6.8	-9.6%	--	4	--
2020	NYJ			80	305	3	3.8	0	-3.3%								14	11	84	0	79%	7.6		-2.6%			

In signing with the Jets this offseason, Frank Gore earned himself the third of four stones in the AFC East Infinity Gauntlet. The everlasting running back is coming off a year with the Bills in which he served as the bridge to 2019 third-round pick

Devin Singletary. Gore saw 106 carries over the first eight games of the season before his workload was cut nearly in half to 60 carries over the final eight games of the year. What is more telling, however, is Gore's situational use. Gore carried the ball just 25 times for a measly 78 yards out of shotgun and pistol formations, while Singletary nearly tripled that amount of carries with 67 carries for 286 yards. Thankfully for Gore, the Jets' shotgun usage in 2019 was right around league average. Le'Veon Bell is a much more capable shotgun back anyway, so Gore should not have to shoulder the load in those situations. More than likely, Gore will just be a short-yardage and under-center specialist for the Jets, same as he was with the Bills.

Derrius Guice

		Height: 5-11		Weight: 225			College: Louisiana State				Draft: 2018/2 (59)			Born: 21-Jun-1997			Age: 23		Risk: Red

Year	Tm	G/GS	Snaps	Runs	Yds	TD	Yd/R	FUM	DVOA	Rk	DYAR	Rk	Suc%	Rk	BTkl	YafC	Pass	Rec	Yds	TD	C%	Yd/C	YAC	DVOA	Rk	DYAR	Rk
2019	WAS	5/1	98	42	245	2	5.8	0	15.7%	--	42	--	50%	--	16	4.6	9	7	79	1	78%	11.3	12.3	48.3%	--	29	--
2020	WAS			135	629	5	4.7	1	8.4%								22	17	158	1	77%	9.3		12.2%			

Talent has never been the issue for Guice, who missed all of his rookie campaign with an ACL injury he suffered in a pre-season game. Guice's 2019 season was slimmed down due to injury as well. Not only did a torn meniscus in Week 1 keep Guice out for the next 10 weeks, but an MCL sprain towards the end of the season put him on injured reserve for a second time. Through 42 carries in Guice's five healthy games, he earned more than five yards per carry and finished with a 50% success rate, both of which were the best marks among the team's running backs. If Guice can bounce back from last year's injuries with at least 90% of the burst and balance that made him a star coming out of college, he should be able to supplant Adrian Peterson for the starting position.

Todd Gurley

		Height: 6-1		Weight: 224			College: Georgia				Draft: 2015/1 (10)			Born: 3-Aug-1994			Age: 26		Risk: Yellow

Year	Tm	G/GS	Snaps	Runs	Yds	TD	Yd/R	FUM	DVOA	Rk	DYAR	Rk	Suc%	Rk	BTkl	YafC	Pass	Rec	Yds	TD	C%	Yd/C	YAC	DVOA	Rk	DYAR	Rk
2017	LAR	15/15	794	279	1305	13	4.7	5	13.9%	4	268	2	53%	5	79	2.8	87	64	788	6	74%	12.3	12.3	35.9%	7	236	2
2018	LAR	14/14	825	256	1251	17	4.9	1	23.6%	1	366	1	57%	4	42	3.0	81	59	580	4	73%	9.8	9.9	6.9%	20	98	12
2019	LAR	15/15	805	223	857	12	3.8	3	-2.4%	25	58	21	48%	26	40	2.5	49	31	207	2	63%	6.7	6.3	-13.8%	40	0	40
2020	ATL			220	890	9	4.0	2	1.6%								58	41	318	2	71%	7.8		-6.5%			

Gurley has jumped to the front of the line of examples of ill-advised running back contract extensions. His extension hadn't even kicked in when he broke down during the Rams' Super Bowl push at the end of the 2018 season. He quickly became the primary hindrance as the Rams attempted to tighten their belts while retaining their Super Bowl core—an effort that Gurley himself couldn't survive despite leaving nearly $18 million of dead cap across 2020 and 2021 after his release this offseason. But for all the forward-looking fear of Gurley's apparent knee arthritis, that extension seems to have misjudged what Gurley—or likely any running back—could contribute based on their skill set alone. Gurley's production has always ebbed and flowed with the team around him. In 2017 and 2018, he produced excellent rushing DVOA rates for teams that finished third and first with 4.70 and 5.49 adjusted line yards. But in 2016 and 2019, he fell to -14.4% and -2.4% rushing DVOA rates for teams with lesser blocking of 3.66 and 4.27 adjusted line yards, 29th and 19th in the league, respectively. Those trends may reveal that Gurley was never as great a talent as the production in his best seasons would suggest, but they also could be good news for a Falcons team that signed him to an inexpensive one-year deal. If recent offensive line draft picks Chris Lindstrom and Kaleb McGary can return the team to its former exceptional run-blocking, then perhaps Gurley can bounce back to at least close to his peak efficiency.

Darrell Henderson

		Height: 5-8		Weight: 208			College: Memphis				Draft: 2019/3 (70)			Born: 19-Aug-1997			Age: 23		Risk: Yellow

Year	Tm	G/GS	Snaps	Runs	Yds	TD	Yd/R	FUM	DVOA	Rk	DYAR	Rk	Suc%	Rk	BTkl	YafC	Pass	Rec	Yds	TD	C%	Yd/C	YAC	DVOA	Rk	DYAR	Rk
2019	LAR	13/0	95	39	147	0	3.8	0	-11.6%	--	-5	--	46%	--	15	3.1	6	4	37	0	67%	9.3	9.3	-8.1%	--	2	--
2020	LAR			130	528	3	4.1	1	-1.0%								31	22	165	1	71%	7.5		-9.3%			

The first significant action of Henderson's career came in Week 6 against San Francisco. He entered the game in the second quarter and promptly reeled off runs of 22, 14, and 4 yards. One would have expected that to spark a productive November and December, but after Malcolm Brown killed the drive with consecutive carries for no gain on third and fourth down, Henderson lost a yard on just three carries the rest of the game, injured his ankle, and eventually landed on injured reserve. In the end, more than a quarter of Henderson's yardage as a rookie came on that one possession. In his rookie season, Henderson rarely showed the game-breaking speed that helped him average more than 8 yards per carry at Memphis and made him the standout prospect of our 2019 BackCAST projections. But that speed makes him the best bet to replace Todd Gurley as the home-run threat in L.A.'s backfield in 2020.

Derrick Henry   Height: 6-3   Weight: 247   College: Alabama   Draft: 2016/2 (45)   Born: 4-Jan-1994   Age: 27   Risk: Green

Year	Tm	G/GS	Snaps	Runs	Yds	TD	Yd/R	FUM	DVOA	Rk	DYAR	Rk	Suc%	Rk	BTkl	YafC	Pass	Rec	Yds	TD	C%	Yd/C	YAC	DVOA	Rk	DYAR	Rk
2017	TEN	16/2	411	176	744	5	4.2	1	-1.2%	21	56	22	48%	15	45	3.0	17	11	136	1	65%	12.4	11.8	23.6%	--	31	--
2018	TEN	16/12	401	215	1059	12	4.9	1	23.1%	2	281	2	51%	16	55	3.6	18	15	99	0	83%	6.6	7.7	-18.0%	--	-4	--
2019	TEN	15/15	602	303	1540	16	5.1	5	6.7%	11	192	6	50%	17	69	3.2	24	18	206	2	75%	11.4	13.1	21.8%	--	46	--
2020	TEN			290	1409	10	4.9	3	12.8%								31	25	219	1	81%	8.8		14.7%			

A superstar in the 1970s NFL, Henry did a phenomenal job last year of breaking tackles despite unattractive box situations. Henry faced a box of eight men or more on a league-leading 45.2% of his carries last year according to Sports Info Solutions charting. Everyone knows he's a battering ram, and his success in that context is highly abnormal. Henry offers a stylistic zig that's hard for teams to zag with when they've been built to deal with spread passing for five years and have 230-pound linebackers trying to deal with someone who can literally run them over. With the franchise tag slapped on him this offseason, Henry will hit free agency again next year at 27. Assuming he plays well and doesn't get tagged again, it would be one of the more fascinating free agency cases. There are plenty of coaches who still operate like they want a back like Henry, but there are also a very limited number of general managers willing to pay for a running back. Which side wins out? And does COVID-19 play a role in determining that winner by shrinking the cap?

Brian Hill   Height: 6-1   Weight: 219   College: Wyoming   Draft: 2017/5 (156)   Born: 9-Nov-1995   Age: 25   Risk: Green

Year	Tm	G/GS	Snaps	Runs	Yds	TD	Yd/R	FUM	DVOA	Rk	DYAR	Rk	Suc%	Rk	BTkl	YafC	Pass	Rec	Yds	TD	C%	Yd/C	YAC	DVOA	Rk	DYAR	Rk
2017	2TM	7/0	19	11	37	0	3.4	0	6.7%	--	6	--	36%	--	3	2.8	2	2	36	0	100%	18.0	16.0	96.6%	--	12	--
2018	ATL	10/0	66	20	157	0	7.9	1	-10.8%	--	-2	--	50%	--	7	5.6	2	1	9	0	50%	9.0	5.0	-82.6%	--	-5	--
2019	ATL	12/2	238	78	323	2	4.1	0	-4.1%	--	14	--	44%	--	9	2.9	14	10	69	1	71%	6.9	5.4	16.5%	--	23	--
2020	ATL			30	125	1	4.2	0	-0.1%								11	9	60	0	82%	6.7		-7.5%			

The small-sample warrior Hill was never meant to play on offense in 2019 despite an average of 7.9 yards per carry the year before—which was appropriate given that his -10.8% DVOA on those 20 carries was likely more predictive. But after Devonta Freeman and Ito Smith went down with respective foot and head injuries, Hill did play and even started a pair of games. The results? A modest 4.1 yards per carry and -4.1% rushing DVOA, both of which better matched his previous DVOA than his previous yards per carry average. Regression can be cruel that way. Hill started in relief over power back Qadree Ollison because of his relative versatility, which he did showcase somewhat with a 16.5% receiving DVOA on 14 targets. But Hill also dropped two of his 11 catchable targets, and his overall 10.2% broken-tackle rate was seventh-lowest of the 64 backs with 75 or more combined touches. Hill could get playing time again in 2020 behind Smith and new starter Todd Gurley given their injury histories, but there is little reason to consider the former fifth-rounder Hill as any more than a temporary fill-in.

Justice Hill   Height: 5-10   Weight: 198   College: Oklahoma State   Draft: 2019/4 (113)   Born: 14-Nov-1997   Age: 23   Risk: Green

Year	Tm	G/GS	Snaps	Runs	Yds	TD	Yd/R	FUM	DVOA	Rk	DYAR	Rk	Suc%	Rk	BTkl	YafC	Pass	Rec	Yds	TD	C%	Yd/C	YAC	DVOA	Rk	DYAR	Rk
2019	BAL	16/0	193	58	225	2	3.9	0	-2.6%	--	13	--	36%	--	11	1.8	15	8	70	0	53%	8.8	10.1	-3.4%	--	9	--
2020	BAL			55	220	2	4.0	0	-3.5%								28	21	178	1	75%	8.5		1.8%			

The selection of J.K. Dobbins pushes Hill further down the depth chart, but he was never really supposed to be a standard three-downs running back in the first place. He's a third-down scatback, best used catching passes as a mismatch against linebackers. Yet he had 36 carries on first down last year (0.2% DVOA) and 19 more on second down (-10.8% DVOA). We think he'll be used in more of a receiving role this season.

Nyheim Hines

Height: 5-9   Weight: 198   College: North Carolina State   Draft: 2018/4 (104)   Born: 12-Nov-1996   Age: 24   Risk: Green

Year	Tm	G/GS	Snaps	Runs	Yds	TD	Yd/R	FUM	DVOA	Rk	DYAR	Rk	Suc%	Rk	BTkl	YafC	Pass	Rec	Yds	TD	C%	Yd/C	YAC	DVOA	Rk	DYAR	Rk
2018	IND	16/4	499	85	314	2	3.7	1	-11.8%	--	-12	--	46%	--	21	2.4	81	63	425	2	78%	6.7	5.5	3.5%	23	79	15
2019	IND	16/2	341	52	199	2	3.8	1	8.4%	--	38	--	52%	--	14	2.0	58	44	320	0	76%	7.3	7.2	-21.5%	44	-24	43
2020	IND			38	152	1	4.0	1	-3.3%								69	54	454	3	78%	8.4		13.6%			

Hines' contribution as both a runner and a receiver dropped in 2019 with Marlon Mack staying slightly healthier, which tells us what we need to know about Hines' place in the Colts backfield. Worse, the team used a second-round pick on Wisconsin rusher Jonathan Taylor, likely relegating Hines to third on the depth chart for rushing workload. However, Hines remains the primary passing-down back, which is a role that has been highly productive for Philip Rivers in the past—we all know about Darren Sproles, Danny Woodhead, and more recently Austin Ekeler, but Ronnie Brown and even Branden Oliver had productive seasons in that role for the Chargers as well. Hines has never been close to their efficiency, but he was significantly more effective with Andrew Luck at quarterback than with Jacoby Brissett. A return to his 2018 workload is probably too much to ask, but a return to his 2018 efficiency would make him a very useful component of Rivers' arsenal.

Travis Homer

Height: 5-10   Weight: 201   College: Miami   Draft: 2019/6 (204)   Born: 7-Aug-1998   Age: 22   Risk: Green

Year	Tm	G/GS	Snaps	Runs	Yds	TD	Yd/R	FUM	DVOA	Rk	DYAR	Rk	Suc%	Rk	BTkl	YafC	Pass	Rec	Yds	TD	C%	Yd/C	YAC	DVOA	Rk	DYAR	Rk
2019	SEA	16/1	84	18	114	0	6.3	0	19.8%	--	21	--	56%	--	3	1.8	13	11	56	0	85%	5.1	5.5	-21.7%	--	-6	--
2020	SEA			8	33	0	4.1	0	-3.9%								4	3	21	0	75%	7.0		-0.7%			

The first carry of Homer's career was a 29-yard gain on a fake punt in Week 13 against Minnesota; take away that play and his DVOA plummets to a mundane 2.3%. He didn't get another carry until after Rashaad Penny tore his ACL. With Penny and Chris Carson injured, Homer got 14 carries in two playoff games and produced all of 25 yards. Between Carson, Penny, and the offseason additions of Carlos Hyde and DeeJay Dallas, Homer will have a difficult time getting carries in 2020, but he was one of Seattle's top special-teamers, so his job should still be safe this fall.

Jordan Howard

Height: 6-0   Weight: 224   College: Indiana   Draft: 2016/5 (150)   Born: 2-Nov-1994   Age: 26   Risk: Green

Year	Tm	G/GS	Snaps	Runs	Yds	TD	Yd/R	FUM	DVOA	Rk	DYAR	Rk	Suc%	Rk	BTkl	YafC	Pass	Rec	Yds	TD	C%	Yd/C	YAC	DVOA	Rk	DYAR	Rk
2017	CHI	16/16	578	276	1122	9	4.1	1	5.8%	14	160	10	42%	35	42	2.9	32	23	125	0	72%	5.4	6.7	-53.3%	61	-60	60
2018	CHI	16/15	624	250	935	9	3.7	2	-11.1%	36	-28	40	50%	17	26	2.3	27	20	145	0	74%	7.3	6.4	-21.9%	50	-13	49
2019	PHI	10/4	283	119	525	6	4.4	0	14.2%	6	113	14	53%	8	15	2.7	14	10	69	1	71%	6.9	6.9	6.7%	--	17	--
2020	MIA			179	717	6	4.0	1	0.0%								41	29	214	1	71%	7.4		-12.2%			

The glory days of 2016, when Howard gained 1,313 rushing yards on 5.2 yards per carry, are unlikely to show again, but Howard can still be an effective early-down back. Howard not only has the balance and power often required of early-down "tone setters," but the vision and surprisingly smooth transitions between rushing lanes to excel in zone schemes. Howard was at his best in Chicago when executing outside zone runs, whereas his days in Philly went well in part because of a strong dose of inside zone from single-back formations. As the "thunder" in Chicago's running back pair in 2018, Howard put up a solid 51% success rate on 141 first-down runs, which was considerably better than teammate Tarik Cohen. Howard quietly took it up a notch in 2019, getting to a 58% success rate on 78 first-down rushing attempts. Reliable and hard-nosed as he is, Howard also posted the best red zone rushing DVOA in the league last season after doing fairly well in that regard in 2018. Howard is not the most threatening long-speed runner in the league, nor is he a particularly valuable pass-catcher, but the stability he can provide is rivaled by few, even if he is not a household name. If nothing else, Howard is an exponential upgrade over what the Dolphins rolled out last year.

Kareem Hunt   Height: 5-11   Weight: 216   College: Toledo   Draft: 2017/3 (86)   Born: 6-Aug-1995   Age: 25   Risk: Blue

Year	Tm	G/GS	Snaps	Runs	Yds	TD	Yd/R	FUM	DVOA	Rk	DYAR	Rk	Suc%	Rk	BTkl	YafC	Pass	Rec	Yds	TD	C%	Yd/C	YAC	DVOA	Rk	DYAR	Rk
2017	KC	16/16	670	272	1327	8	4.9	1	11.9%	6	222	4	47%	18	89	3.1	63	53	455	3	84%	8.6	7.8	15.6%	14	102	9
2018	KC	11/11	503	181	824	7	4.6	0	9.1%	11	134	11	55%	7	54	3.2	35	26	378	7	74%	14.5	13.0	79.4%	1	198	1
2019	CLE	8/3	313	43	179	2	4.2	1	7.9%	--	26	--	53%	--	34	2.7	44	37	285	1	84%	7.7	7.5	14.2%	15	71	16
2020	CLE			81	343	2	4.2	1	2.2%								59	46	393	2	78%	8.5		10.0%			

Admitting that his release from the Chiefs "still hurts [him] to this day," in a January traffic stop, Hunt's offseason got off to a rocky start, but he remains a big part of the Browns offense and perhaps the most valuable handcuff back in the NFL right now. In just eight games, Hunt drew 44 targets and continued to show elite production while serving as a changeup for Nick Chubb. Hunt participated in the receiving room's virtual meetings this offseason and, in an optimistic scenario, might even serve as the team's third receiver this year per wide receivers coach Chad O'Shea. Hunt remains a great back; he also remains just enough of a domestic violence pariah to be underpaid for his work despite his talent. He's heading into free agency after the year and pretty much no result would surprise us.

Carlos Hyde   Height: 6-0   Weight: 229   College: Ohio State   Draft: 2014/2 (57)   Born: 20-Sep-1990   Age: 30   Risk: Yellow

Year	Tm	G/GS	Snaps	Runs	Yds	TD	Yd/R	FUM	DVOA	Rk	DYAR	Rk	Suc%	Rk	BTkl	YafC	Pass	Rec	Yds	TD	C%	Yd/C	YAC	DVOA	Rk	DYAR	Rk
2017	SF	16/16	783	240	938	8	3.9	2	-7.4%	35	12	33	44%	27	52	2.8	89	59	350	0	67%	5.9	5.4	-22.4%	53	-43	58
2018	2TM	14/7	385	172	571	5	3.3	2	-11.0%	35	-18	36	39%	42	28	2.4	16	10	33	0	63%	3.3	5.9	-73.3%	--	-51	--
2019	HOU	16/14	538	245	1070	6	4.4	4	-3.3%	26	54	22	52%	13	34	2.3	16	10	42	0	63%	4.2	5.1	-50.3%	--	-36	--
2020	SEA			77	295	2	3.8	1	-4.1%								20	15	108	1	75%	7.2		-6.2%			

In the three regular-season games where Bill O'Brien ran Carlos Hyde into 8-man boxes over 30% of the time, Hyde ran 48 times for 104 yards. That's pretty much the gist of his season, which started with a bang (38 DYAR in Weeks 1 and 2) and ended with a whimper as Houston's offense became incredibly predictable. Hyde is a good zone runner who follows his blocks and reads well, gets past arm tackles at the line of scrimmage, and has absolutely no breakaway speed. If he busts a long run, that is the defense's fault. After rejecting a two-year contract from the Texans early in the offseason, Hyde languished until he was signed by the Seahawks after the draft. Hyde will be the Rashaad Penny insurance for a year.

Mark Ingram   Height: 5-9   Weight: 215   College: Alabama   Draft: 2011/1 (28)   Born: 21-Dec-1989   Age: 31   Risk: Yellow

Year	Tm	G/GS	Snaps	Runs	Yds	TD	Yd/R	FUM	DVOA	Rk	DYAR	Rk	Suc%	Rk	BTkl	YafC	Pass	Rec	Yds	TD	C%	Yd/C	YAC	DVOA	Rk	DYAR	Rk
2017	NO	16/12	571	230	1124	12	4.9	3	11.2%	7	193	8	49%	12	56	2.9	71	58	416	0	82%	7.2	8.7	-10.7%	42	13	39
2018	NO	12/6	350	138	645	6	4.7	3	2.9%	19	71	20	57%	3	24	2.9	27	21	170	1	78%	8.1	7.4	-18.8%	46	-7	43
2019	BAL	15/15	511	202	1018	10	5.0	2	19.8%	2	257	3	60%	1	46	2.7	29	26	247	5	90%	9.5	8.5	74.6%	1	145	3
2020	BAL			180	840	8	4.7	2	11.0%								26	21	169	1	81%	8.0		9.2%			

Ingram's middle name is Valentino, and boy, did the Ravens fall hard for their free-agent pickup, one of the most impactful of any 2019 offseason acquisition. If he was lost a bit in the hoopla around Lamar Jackson, Ingram's value was noticeable in the playoff loss to Tennessee, when a calf injury limited him to six ineffectual carries. It feels like the smart fantasy play would be to assume a slight-to-fair reduction in Baltimore's rushing rates, but presumably that would apply more to Jackson than Ingram.

Justin Jackson   Height: 6-0   Weight: 200   College: Northwestern   Draft: 2018/7 (251)   Born: 22-Apr-1996   Age: 24   Risk: Blue

Year	Tm	G/GS	Snaps	Runs	Yds	TD	Yd/R	FUM	DVOA	Rk	DYAR	Rk	Suc%	Rk	BTkl	YafC	Pass	Rec	Yds	TD	C%	Yd/C	YAC	DVOA	Rk	DYAR	Rk
2018	LAC	13/1	149	50	206	2	4.1	0	-6.0%	--	6	--	56%	--	20	2.4	19	15	135	0	79%	9.0	10.1	29.9%	--	37	--
2019	LAC	7/0	95	29	200	0	6.9	0	34.9%	--	50	--	62%	--	9	4.9	11	9	22	0	82%	2.4	4.2	-74.9%	--	-33	--
2020	LAC			92	456	2	5.0	1	11.6%								29	21	158	1	72%	7.5		-8.9%			

Jackson rushed 18 times for 142 yards (7.9 yards per carry) in three September games while Melvin Gordon was holding out, which provided a neat illustration of why Gordon's holdout was so foolish. He then suffered a calf injury and missed two months while Gordon returned and spent weeks slowly working his way back to replacement level. Jackson and Joshua Kelley will battle to join Austin Ekeler in the Chargers running back committee. They may end up sharing the duties. Either way, the Chargers should be set at running back, and all at highly affordable prices.

Josh Jacobs

Height: 5-10		**Weight:** 220		**College:** Alabama						**Draft:** 2019/1 (24)		**Born:** 11-Feb-1998			**Age:** 22		**Risk:** Yellow								

Year	Tm	G/GS	Snaps	Runs	Yds	TD	Yd/R	FUM	DVOA	Rk	DYAR	Rk	Suc%	Rk	BTkl	YafC	Pass	Rec	Yds	TD	C%	Yd/C	YAC	DVOA	Rk	DYAR	Rk
2019	OAK	13/13	469	242	1150	7	4.8	1	3.5%	14	126	12	51%	14	68	3.0	27	20	166	0	74%	8.3	9.2	4.6%	20	28	27
2020	LV			250	1130	7	4.5	1	7.4%								53	42	345	1	79%	8.2		6.7%			

Jacobs broke tackles on 26.0% of his touches, the highest rate of any player with more than 250 touches and second to Austin Ekeler (28.4%) among players with 200 or more touches. He broke all those tackles despite playing through a fractured shoulder for several weeks before getting shelved for the final two games. Mike Mayock said in March that Jacobs is expected to play a major role in the passing game this season. All signs point to a productive year for a rugged young runner, but you know the drill: if Jacobs was already grinning-and-bearing major injuries to stay on the field as a rookie, he's likely to have the shelf life of a ripe avocado.

David Johnson

Height: 6-1		**Weight:** 224		**College:** Northern Iowa						**Draft:** 2015/3 (86)		**Born:** 16-Dec-1991			**Age:** 29		**Risk:** Yellow								

Year	Tm	G/GS	Snaps	Runs	Yds	TD	Yd/R	FUM	DVOA	Rk	DYAR	Rk	Suc%	Rk	BTkl	YafC	Pass	Rec	Yds	TD	C%	Yd/C	YAC	DVOA	Rk	DYAR	Rk
2017	ARI	1/1	46	11	23	0	2.1	2	-100.3%	--	-40	--	18%	--	5	2.5	9	6	67	0	67%	11.2	7.7	-33.0%	--	-9	--
2018	ARI	16/16	749	258	940	7	3.6	3	-12.6%	40	-42	42	38%	43	45	2.2	76	50	446	3	66%	8.9	7.7	-17.1%	43	-13	50
2019	ARI	13/9	445	94	345	2	3.7	1	-10.8%	--	-9	--	43%	--	14	2.0	47	36	370	4	77%	10.3	6.3	29.2%	6	114	8
2020	HOU			222	822	7	3.7	2	-4.9%								50	35	311	2	70%	8.9		0.6%			

The secretly weird part of the DeAndre Hopkins trade is that it's hard to understand what David Johnson adds to the Texans roster. His best skill is his ability as a receiving back, to the point where he has made multiple downfield catches in his healthiest seasons. But the Texans traded a third-round pick for Duke Johnson and already weren't using him enough last year. David Johnson rushed for 3.9 and 3.8 yards per carry the last two years on zone rushes, the primary focus of the Bill O'Brien Texans run game. Carlos Hyde ran for 4.4 yards per carry on zone rushes last year. With a long-term back injury and healthy inactive status in Arizona last year, most reporter and insider talk about Johnson was focused on what the Cardinals would have to give up to be rid of him. Johnson has the third-highest average guarantee per year on his contract and, on a rational team, would have been threatened with a "paycut or release" ultimatum. All that said, he's definitely going to get carries; if you are a volume-based fantasy football drafter, it's hard to ignore Johnson and a Texans offensive line that has been a major focal point. Just, you know, don't mistake that for Johnson actually being good at football anymore.

Duke Johnson

Height: 5-9		**Weight:** 210		**College:** Miami						**Draft:** 2015/3 (77)		**Born:** 23-Sep-1993			**Age:** 27		**Risk:** Green								

Year	Tm	G/GS	Snaps	Runs	Yds	TD	Yd/R	FUM	DVOA	Rk	DYAR	Rk	Suc%	Rk	BTkl	YafC	Pass	Rec	Yds	TD	C%	Yd/C	YAC	DVOA	Rk	DYAR	Rk
2017	CLE	16/0	565	82	348	4	4.2	3	15.7%	--	90	--	53%	--	51	2.4	94	74	693	3	80%	9.4	8.6	6.7%	19	110	7
2018	CLE	16/2	459	40	201	0	5.0	1	7.2%	--	24	--	50%	--	20	3.6	62	47	429	3	76%	9.1	8.0	12.9%	14	103	11
2019	HOU	16/2	531	83	410	2	4.9	1	-2.0%	--	21	--	48%	--	35	3.1	62	44	410	3	71%	9.3	8.2	24.6%	9	125	6
2020	HOU			76	362	2	4.8	1	8.4%								51	37	316	2	73%	8.5		6.3%			

Johnson got a fair contract (three years, $15.6 million) from the Browns, and that's about all the respect he has ever received. He's an excellent receiving back who has outshined more-heralded teammates any time he has been given consistent touches. His third-and-16 reception that converted to a first down was one of the key points of Houston's playoff comeback against the Bills. Did the Texans reform their offense to give him more screens? Nope! They've run exactly six running back screens in each of the last two seasons. Did they give him an opportunity for more snaps? Nope! They traded for David Johnson. Duke will just be over here quietly doing great work, as always, waiting for someone other than fantasy football Twitter to realize it.

Kerryon Johnson   Height: 5-11   Weight: 212   College: Auburn   Draft: 2018/2 (43)   Born: 30-Jun-1997   Age: 23   Risk: Yellow

Year	Tm	G/GS	Snaps	Runs	Yds	TD	Yd/R	FUM	DVOA	Rk	DYAR	Rk	Suc%	Rk	BTkl	YafC	Pass	Rec	Yds	TD	C%	Yd/C	YAC	DVOA	Rk	DYAR	Rk
2018	DET	10/7	346	118	641	3	5.4	1	17.5%	5	124	15	53%	12	35	2.6	39	32	213	1	82%	6.7	8.3	-4.8%	31	20	30
2019	DET	8/7	281	113	403	3	3.6	1	-13.7%	41	-26	40	52%	11	18	2.3	15	10	127	1	67%	12.7	11.6	29.3%	--	39	--
2020	DET			134	554	5	4.1	1	0.9%								45	35	263	1	78%	7.5		-0.9%			

Johnson's numbers collapsed after his very strong rookie season, both in terms of DVOA and in traditional stats like yards per carry, going from 5.4 to a woeful 3.6 in 2019. His receiving workload plummeted too, with the addition of J.D. McKissic eating into Johnson's value as a pass-catcher. The one area in which Johnson was consistent from 2018 to 2019 was health, as he once again missed half the season with a knee injury. These concerns led to the Lions drafting both D'Andre Swift and Jason Huntley. Johnson will still have a role in the rotation, but you don't select two running backs if you aren't expecting them to earn significant playing time.

Ty Johnson   Height: 5-10   Weight: 208   College: Maryland   Draft: 2019/6 (186)   Born: 17-Sep-1997   Age: 23   Risk: Green

Year	Tm	G/GS	Snaps	Runs	Yds	TD	Yd/R	FUM	DVOA	Rk	DYAR	Rk	Suc%	Rk	BTkl	YafC	Pass	Rec	Yds	TD	C%	Yd/C	YAC	DVOA	Rk	DYAR	Rk
2019	DET	16/1	318	63	273	0	4.3	1	3.5%	--	28	--	44%	--	8	2.5	31	24	109	0	77%	4.5	3.9	-40.2%	50	-45	47
2020	DET			8	35	0	4.4	0	0.9%								2	2	11	0	100%	5.5		-3.8%			

Bob Quinn explicitly said that Johnson will be in competition with fifth-round pick Jason Huntley after the draft, which doesn't bode particularly well for last year's sixth-round pick. Johnson actually led the Lions in running back snaps last season, though it doesn't help his argument for a roster slot that he immediately lost his starting role to Bo Scarbrough when Detroit brought him off the practice squad. Johnson excelled in the preseason, but simply couldn't get things going for most of the year. Johnson earned 41 DYAR in the last two games of the season, so at least he ended the year in a high note. He'll have to keep that momentum going to keep a spot on the 53-man roster.

Aaron Jones   Height: 5-9   Weight: 208   College: Texas-El Paso   Draft: 2017/5 (182)   Born: 2-Dec-1994   Age: 26   Risk: Green

Year	Tm	G/GS	Snaps	Runs	Yds	TD	Yd/R	FUM	DVOA	Rk	DYAR	Rk	Suc%	Rk	BTkl	YafC	Pass	Rec	Yds	TD	C%	Yd/C	YAC	DVOA	Rk	DYAR	Rk
2017	GB	12/4	236	81	448	4	5.5	0	31.3%	--	143	--	53%	--	15	2.9	18	9	22	0	50%	2.4	3.3	-75.4%	--	-60	--
2018	GB	12/8	376	133	728	8	5.5	1	17.1%	7	146	10	55%	6	34	2.7	35	26	206	1	74%	7.9	8.5	2.2%	25	33	27
2019	GB	16/16	676	236	1084	16	4.6	3	12.0%	7	207	4	56%	5	54	2.6	68	49	474	3	72%	9.7	8.9	-5.1%	29	35	24
2020	GB			212	937	8	4.4	2	7.7%								65	48	388	3	74%	8.1		5.6%			

Jones had a 49.5% rushing DVOA in the red zone, best among all players with at least 25 carries; with production like that, it's not surprising that Jones set the franchise single-season record with 23 touchdowns (postseason included). It's unlikely that he'll approach touchdown numbers like that again, but it's not like that was the only part of his game with value. The fact that his success rate actually improved after being given a bigger workload in 2019 bodes very well for his continued success, even if the Packers have yet to treat him like a true bell cow back. It's also notable that Jones is having great success despite being something of a square peg in a round hole in Matt LaFleur's system. Jones' 51.5% rushing DVOA out of the shotgun was best in the league (minimum 40 carries) but the Packers operated more under center under LaFleur's leadership.

Ronald Jones   Height: 5-11   Weight: 208   College: USC   Draft: 2018/2 (38)   Born: 3-Aug-1997   Age: 23   Risk: Yellow

Year	Tm	G/GS	Snaps	Runs	Yds	TD	Yd/R	FUM	DVOA	Rk	DYAR	Rk	Suc%	Rk	BTkl	YafC	Pass	Rec	Yds	TD	C%	Yd/C	YAC	DVOA	Rk	DYAR	Rk
2018	TB	9/0	90	23	44	1	1.9	0	-24.3%	--	-15	--	30%	--	3	2.0	9	7	33	0	78%	4.7	6.0	-42.4%	--	-15	--
2019	TB	16/9	422	172	724	6	4.2	3	-2.3%	24	43	23	45%	33	43	3.1	40	31	309	0	78%	10.0	9.5	9.2%	17	47	20
2020	TB			195	788	5	4.0	2	-2.8%								49	35	315	1	71%	9.0		0.4%			

After what was essentially a redshirt rookie season, Jones turned in a decent sophomore campaign. At midseason, he emerged as the Buccaneers' primary ballcarrier and went on to become the team's first running back to gain 1,000 yards from scrimmage since Doug Martin in 2015. He flashed some explosiveness, too. In 2018, he didn't have a single run of at least 10 yards. In 2019, he had 20, or 11.6% of his carries. He wasn't reliable as a pass-catcher or pass-blocker, though, so he ceded snaps to Dare

Ogunbowale. Expect to see a similar arrangement early this season, with Jones being featured on early downs and Ogunbowale splitting snaps on passing downs with rookie Ke'Shawn Vaughn.

Kyle Juszczyk

Height: 6-1 | Weight: 240 | College: Harvard | Draft: 2013/4 (130) | Born: 23-Apr-1991 | Age: 29 | Risk: Green

Year	Tm	G/GS	Snaps	Runs	Yds	TD	Yd/R	FUM	DVOA	Rk	DYAR	Rk	Suc%	Rk	BTkl	YafC	Pass	Rec	Yds	TD	C%	Yd/C	YAC	DVOA	Rk	DYAR	Rk
2017	SF	14/10	397	7	31	0	4.4	2	21.3%	--	12	--	57%	--	6	2.4	42	33	315	1	79%	9.5	6.3	3.7%	27	41	28
2018	SF	16/14	662	8	30	0	3.8	2	-86.7%	--	-29	--	38%	--	6	1.5	41	30	324	1	73%	10.8	5.8	18.7%	8	76	18
2019	SF	12/12	396	3	7	0	2.3	0	-49.0%	--	-7	--	33%	--	1	3.0	24	20	239	1	83%	12.0	7.9	47.6%	2	98	11
2020	SF			5	15	1	3.0	0	7.3%								27	21	194	1	78%	9.2		9.7%			

Juszczyk shattered records for the most money given to a fullback when San Francisco originally signed him as a free agent, but head coach Kyle Shanahan values the versatility that Juszczyk brings to the offense a great deal. Juszczyk is much more skilled than the average fullback as a receiver, though he saw fewer targets in 2019 than he had since his rookie year in 2013. Even though he is known for his receiving ability, he's an effective run-blocker as well, finishing 2019 with only one blown run block. Entering his contract year in 2020, Juszczyk will need to continue putting that versatility on display in order to lock up another long-term deal. Considering how much praise Shanahan has expressed regarding his play, he may not have to look far to find that contract.

Alvin Kamara

Height: 5-10 | Weight: 215 | College: Tennessee | Draft: 2017/3 (67) | Born: 25-Jul-1995 | Age: 25 | Risk: Green

Year	Tm	G/GS	Snaps	Runs	Yds	TD	Yd/R	FUM	DVOA	Rk	DYAR	Rk	Suc%	Rk	BTkl	YafC	Pass	Rec	Yds	TD	C%	Yd/C	YAC	DVOA	Rk	DYAR	Rk
2017	NO	16/3	464	120	728	8	6.1	1	44.5%	1	255	3	53%	6	66	3.6	100	81	826	5	81%	10.2	8.5	36.4%	6	278	1
2018	NO	15/13	657	194	883	14	4.6	0	18.5%	4	238	3	58%	2	43	2.4	105	81	709	4	77%	8.8	7.9	19.4%	7	197	2
2019	NO	14/9	636	171	797	5	4.7	4	3.1%	15	81	19	52%	12	56	2.6	97	81	533	1	84%	6.6	6.9	1.6%	23	83	13
2020	NO			203	892	8	4.4	3	5.4%								95	76	523	2	80%	6.9		-0.7%			

Kamara became the first Saints running back since Deuce McAllister to gain 1,300 yards from scrimmage in three straight seasons. While productive, he wasn't as efficient as he had been in 2017 (when he led the league in rushing DVOA) or 2018. Knee and ankle injuries likely contributed. By his own admission he was playing at 75% health. In fact, before he sat out New Orleans' Week 7 and 8 games, his rushing DVOA had cratered to -3.3%. He returned in Week 10 after the Saints' bye and from then on posted a 9.7% DVOA. He might have experienced some bad scoring luck, too. During his first two seasons, he scored a touchdown once every 23 touches. Last season, he scored once every 42. He didn't score at all from Week 4 through Week 15.

Kamara will earn $2.1 million this season, a steal for a player who has been not only New Orleans' top running back but also their No. 2 receiver. Carolina already has locked up Kamara's 2017 draftmate Christian McCaffrey, signing him in April to a four-year extension that has a new-money average of $16 million. Kamara surely wants a comparable commitment, but the Saints don't have much salary-cap breathing room. They're already $30 million over next season's projected cap.

Joshua Kelley

Height: 5-11 | Weight: 219 | College: UCLA | Draft: 2020/4 (112) | Born: 20-Nov-1997 | Age: 23 | Risk: Green

Year	Tm	G/GS	Snaps	Runs	Yds	TD	Yd/R	FUM	DVOA	Rk	DYAR	Rk	Suc%	Rk	BTkl	YafC	Pass	Rec	Yds	TD	C%	Yd/C	YAC	DVOA	Rk	DYAR	Rk
2020	LAC			46	195	1	4.2	0	0.3%								11	8	64	0	73%	8.0		-2.0%			

Kelley rushed for 2,303 yards and 24 rushing touchdowns in two seasons in Chip Kelly's Bruins offense. He then performed well at both the Senior Bowl and the combine, demonstrating usefulness as a receiver as well as a running back. Kelley is the perfect back to draft in the fourth round and stick in a rotation with another late-round pick (Justin Jackson) and a reliable-but-still-affordable all-purpose veteran (Austin Ekeler) for three years. And that appears to be what the Chargers plan to do.

Patrick Laird

Height: 6-0 | Weight: 205 | College: California | Draft: 2019/FA | Born: 17-Aug-1995 | Age: 25 | Risk: Green

Year	Tm	G/GS	Snaps	Runs	Yds	TD	Yd/R	FUM	DVOA	Rk	DYAR	Rk	Suc%	Rk	BTkl	YafC	Pass	Rec	Yds	TD	C%	Yd/C	YAC	DVOA	Rk	DYAR	Rk
2019	MIA	15/4	292	62	168	1	2.7	0	-23.0%	--	-34	--	29%	--	11	1.9	30	23	204	0	77%	8.9	7.7	8.6%	19	39	22
2020	MIA			4	14	0	3.5	0	0.0%								5	4	32	0	80%	8.0		0.0%			

The Miami Dolphins had so many running backs last year. None of them were good. Laird, an undrafted free agent out of Cal, was among that group. Though he did become somewhat of a cult hero in fantasy football communities looking for the cheapest scoring options, largely for his two-touchdown game in Week 13, Laird was not an effective reality football player. Laird put up a putrid 29% success rate through 62 carries, a mark that would have been worst in the league by almost 10% if he had hit the 100-carry qualifying threshold. In similar fashion, Laird was one of just three players in the league with more than 50 carries, yet fewer than 3.0 yards per carry. As the roster stands now, Laird is Miami's fifth running back at best, and may be sixth if rookie Malcolm Perry (a former Navy quarterback) can comfortably make a quick transition to the position.

Dion Lewis   Height: 5-8   Weight: 195   College: Pittsburgh   Draft: 2011/5 (149)   Born: 27-Sep-1990   Age: 30   Risk: Yellow

Year	Tm	G/GS	Snaps	Runs	Yds	TD	Yd/R	FUM	DVOA	Rk	DYAR	Rk	Suc%	Rk	BTkl	YafC	Pass	Rec	Yds	TD	C%	Yd/C	YAC	DVOA	Rk	DYAR	Rk
2017	NE	16/8	404	180	896	6	5.0	0	27.6%	2	273	1	56%	4	60	3.1	35	32	214	3	91%	6.7	7.0	32.0%	10	90	12
2018	TEN	16/7	600	155	517	1	3.3	1	-20.1%	43	-69	43	34%	47	53	2.2	67	59	400	1	88%	6.8	8.1	-9.8%	35	15	31
2019	TEN	16/1	379	54	209	0	3.9	1	-20.7%	--	-26	--	46%	--	25	2.5	32	25	164	1	78%	6.6	7.7	-11.9%	38	3	38
2020	NYG			35	133	1	3.8	0	-6.9%								16	12	91	0	75%	7.6		-5.7%			

Lewis lost his job to Derrick Henry in Tennessee, and while he'll be the primary backup for the Giants, that's a team that hasn't used the primary backup often to replace Saquon Barkley. Lewis' fit in Tennessee was always odd as he was often used like a more traditional running back, often in front of Henry. Lewis could now see a role closer to how he was used in New England as a situational pass-heavy back.

Phillip Lindsay   Height: 5-8   Weight: 190   College: Colorado   Draft: 2018/FA   Born: 24-Jul-1994   Age: 26   Risk: Yellow

Year	Tm	G/GS	Snaps	Runs	Yds	TD	Yd/R	FUM	DVOA	Rk	DYAR	Rk	Suc%	Rk	BTkl	YafC	Pass	Rec	Yds	TD	C%	Yd/C	YAC	DVOA	Rk	DYAR	Rk
2018	DEN	15/8	453	192	1037	9	5.4	0	17.3%	6	203	6	49%	22	36	2.2	47	35	241	1	74%	6.9	8.5	-10.4%	36	9	36
2019	DEN	16/16	516	224	1011	7	4.5	0	1.9%	17	94	16	50%	19	45	2.4	48	35	196	0	73%	5.6	6.9	-39.7%	49	-69	50
2020	DEN			125	560	3	4.5	1	5.1%								39	30	185	1	77%	6.2		-14.3%			

Lindsay's -69 receiving DYAR ranked dead last among qualifiers in 2019. On first downs, he caught 11 passes for a miserable 32 yards on 16 targets (2.9 yards per catch, 2.0 yards per play). Lindsay was the target for many quick swing passes, predictable screens, and emergency checkdowns on first downs, some of them thrown over his head out of bounds or at his back. From a skills perspective, Lindsay is a capable receiver who should bounce back in a more functional offense.

Lindsay has only rushed 20-plus times in a game once in two seasons as a featured back: he went 21-81-2 in Week 3 against the Packers last season. Melvin Gordon will leech away more goal-line opportunities than Royce Freeman did, but if you are hoping that a 190-pound committee back will be a steady source of fantasy touchdowns, that's on you.

Marlon Mack   Height: 6-0   Weight: 210   College: South Florida   Draft: 2017/4 (143)   Born: 7-Mar-1996   Age: 24   Risk: Yellow

Year	Tm	G/GS	Snaps	Runs	Yds	TD	Yd/R	FUM	DVOA	Rk	DYAR	Rk	Suc%	Rk	BTkl	YafC	Pass	Rec	Yds	TD	C%	Yd/C	YAC	DVOA	Rk	DYAR	Rk
2017	IND	14/0	310	93	358	3	3.8	1	-6.9%	--	6	--	41%	--	23	2.8	33	21	225	1	64%	10.7	13.5	9.2%	16	38	29
2018	IND	12/10	445	195	908	9	4.7	2	16.8%	8	216	4	54%	8	27	2.6	26	17	103	1	65%	6.1	7.2	-21.3%	49	-10	48
2019	IND	14/12	517	247	1091	8	4.4	0	1.0%	18	102	15	52%	10	39	2.3	17	14	82	0	82%	5.9	5.7	-18.5%	--	-4	--
2020	IND			182	790	6	4.3	1	5.5%								37	28	234	1	76%	8.4		5.8%			

Running back roles on the Colts are about as clearly defined as you will find anywhere. Mack is the leading rusher, a former fourth-round pick whose workload and production has increased in each of his first three years. He finally broke the 1,000-yard threshold in 2019, but as his rushing load has increased his already limited receiving load has declined. Second-round rookie Jonathan Taylor threatens to take away some of Mack's carry share, and Mack simply doesn't have the involvement in the passing game to make up for it. He should continue to be an effective pounder with Philip Rivers under center, and he may find a few extra targets out of the backfield, but he is unlikely to be the major beneficiary of Rivers' arrival, and his replacement appears to have already been added to the roster.

Alexander Mattison
Height: 5-11 Weight: 221 College: Boise State Draft: 2019/3 (102) Born: 19-Jun-1998 Age: 22 Risk: Blue

Year	Tm	G/GS	Snaps	Runs	Yds	TD	Yd/R	FUM	DVOA	Rk	DYAR	Rk	Suc%	Rk	BTkl	YafC	Pass	Rec	Yds	TD	C%	Yd/C	YAC	DVOA	Rk	DYAR	Rk
2019	MIN	13/0	200	100	462	1	4.6	1	-2.2%	23	24	27	38%	45	16	2.7	12	10	82	0	83%	8.2	7.4	21.2%	--	18	--
2020	MIN			107	462	4	4.3	1	2.9%								27	22	174	1	81%	7.9		4.4%			

Mattison averaged more yards per carry than Dalvin Cook and faced loaded boxes more frequently than his backfield mate, which are some impressive stats for a rookie. Less impressive was his 38% success rate, the worst in the league in 2019. Players with decent DVOA and poor success rate generally mix big plays with getting stuffed at the line, and that's more or less the case here—49% of Mattison's carries gained 2 or fewer yards, but his average carry that got past that initial front went for 8.6 yards. For Cook, those numbers were 42% and 7.3. Mattison was billed as the low-variance guy who would pick up what was blocked for him; that was very much not the case in 2019.

Christian McCaffrey
Height: 5-11 Weight: 205 College: Stanford Draft: 2017/1 (8) Born: 7-Jun-1996 Age: 24 Risk: Green

Year	Tm	G/GS	Snaps	Runs	Yds	TD	Yd/R	FUM	DVOA	Rk	DYAR	Rk	Suc%	Rk	BTkl	YafC	Pass	Rec	Yds	TD	C%	Yd/C	YAC	DVOA	Rk	DYAR	Rk
2017	CAR	16/10	757	117	435	2	3.7	1	-6.2%	30	11	34	45%	22	47	2.1	113	80	651	5	71%	8.1	7.4	5.7%	21	128	5
2018	CAR	16/16	965	219	1098	7	5.0	4	9.6%	10	167	7	55%	5	63	2.7	124	107	867	6	86%	8.1	8.0	11.5%	15	183	5
2019	CAR	16/16	1056	287	1387	15	4.8	1	14.9%	5	278	2	47%	28	73	2.0	142	116	1005	4	82%	8.7	8.5	34.8%	4	386	1
2020	CAR			267	1217	10	4.6	2	11.3%								94	81	655	3	86%	8.1		23.2%			

McCaffrey never comes off the field because of his receiving prowess, but he deserves consideration as one of the best backs in football because of his evolution as a runner. Combined with the Panthers offensive line improvements from 3.79 adjusted line yards in 2017 to 4.55 and 4.30 the last two years, and McCaffrey has landed among the positional leaders in yards per carry and rushing DVOA in 2018 and 2019. McCaffrey excelled in 2019 despite playing the hardest schedule of any qualifying running back, with a big gap between his rushing VOA (7.5%, ranked 12th) and DVOA (14.9%, ranked fifth). If only he could have faced the Panthers' own horrible run defense.

LeSean McCoy
Height: 5-11 Weight: 210 College: Pittsburgh Draft: 2009/2 (53) Born: 12-Jul-1988 Age: 32 Risk: N/A

Year	Tm	G/GS	Snaps	Runs	Yds	TD	Yd/R	FUM	DVOA	Rk	DYAR	Rk	Suc%	Rk	BTkl	YafC	Pass	Rec	Yds	TD	C%	Yd/C	YAC	DVOA	Rk	DYAR	Rk
2017	BUF	16/16	722	287	1138	6	4.0	3	-10.8%	38	-26	41	43%	32	61	2.5	78	59	448	2	77%	7.6	6.9	-1.8%	33	48	24
2018	BUF	14/13	490	161	514	3	3.2	0	-26.2%	45	-109	46	37%	45	34	2.0	46	34	238	0	74%	7.0	8.5	-24.5%	51	-26	52
2019	KC	13/9	299	101	465	4	4.6	3	-4.1%	28	20	29	49%	25	17	1.8	35	28	181	1	82%	6.5	8.1	-32.2%	46	-34	44

Shady's career is likely over; his value as a receiver has evaporated over the last three years, and his yards per rush dropped steadily from 5.35 in September to 2.95 last December. McCoy now has 11,071 career rushing yards, and 18 of the 21 players ahead of him are either active (Frank Gore, Adrian Peterson) or in the Hall of Fame. Unfortunately, the three who are not (Corey Dillon, Steven Jackson, and Fred Taylor) are very comparable to Shady, as are several of the backs just below him (Ricky Watters, Jamal Lewis, Marshawn Lynch, and others). Shady won just one rushing title (2013) and has a nondescript postseason record, further hurting his Hall candidacy when stacked up against players like Lewis or Lynch. This is all a nice way of saying that Shady is not a Hall of Famer. That won't stop folks on Twitter from declaring him a First Ballot Sure-Fire Hall of Famer (and Anyone Who Disagrees is an Idiot) on the day he officially retires. Hey, we do what we can.

Anthony McFarland
Height: 5-9 Weight: 198 College: Maryland Draft: 2020/4 (124) Born: 4-Mar-1999 Age: 21 Risk: Green

Year	Tm	G/GS	Snaps	Runs	Yds	TD	Yd/R	FUM	DVOA	Rk	DYAR	Rk	Suc%	Rk	BTkl	YafC	Pass	Rec	Yds	TD	C%	Yd/C	YAC	DVOA	Rk	DYAR	Rk
2020	PIT			46	195	1	4.2	0	-0.2%								8	7	53	0	88%	7.6		3.5%			

The ultimate dream of drafting someone like McFarland is that they do an impersonation of Chris Johnson. McFarland is 5-foot-8, 208 pounds, with a 4.44s 40-yard dash at the combine, and was one of the lone victims of this year's COVID-shortened anonymous scout season when one of them told The Athletic's Bob McGinn that McFarland's character was "absolutely terrible." With a history of dings and some indecisiveness between the tackles, expectations are probably best set as a passing-down committee back for now. He'll have to beat Jaylen Samuels out.

Jerick McKinnon   Height: 5-9   Weight: 209   College: Georgia Southern   Draft: 2014/3 (96)   Born: 5-Mar-1992   Age: 28   Risk: Blue

Year	Tm	G/GS	Snaps	Runs	Yds	TD	Yd/R	FUM	DVOA	Rk	DYAR	Rk	Suc%	Rk	BTkl	YafC	Pass	Rec	Yds	TD	C%	Yd/C	YAC	DVOA	Rk	DYAR	Rk
2017	MIN	16/1	528	150	570	3	3.8	2	-12.7%	40	-24	40	43%	28	43	2.8	68	51	421	2	75%	8.3	9.0	-0.4%	31	48	23
2020	SF			43	169	1	3.9	0	-3.7%								8	6	51	0	75%	8.5		1.6%			

McKinnon signed a four-year deal with the 49ers two years ago. He has yet to play a down for them, having torn his ACL in the team's last training camp practice before the 2018 season, then suffering a setback in his recovery and missing all of 2019 as well. San Francisco didn't exactly miss McKinnon last season, as their running back meeting room resembled a clown car at times, but Kyle Shanahan viewed McKinnon as his Devonta Freeman type when he signed him, and may still be holding out hope that Jet can play a role. However, as of press time, McKinnon has yet to resume cutting on his injured knee, making his availability for the start of 2020 questionable as well. Presumably, at some point McKinnon will touch the ball in red and gold. We think. Possibly.

J.D. McKissic   Height: 5-10   Weight: 195   College: Arkansas State   Draft: 2016/FA   Born: 15-Aug-1993   Age: 27   Risk: Green

Year	Tm	G/GS	Snaps	Runs	Yds	TD	Yd/R	FUM	DVOA	Rk	DYAR	Rk	Suc%	Rk	BTkl	YafC	Pass	Rec	Yds	TD	C%	Yd/C	YAC	DVOA	Rk	DYAR	Rk
2017	SEA	13/1	296	46	187	1	4.1	0	8.2%	--	31	--	51%	--	8	2.2	47	34	266	2	74%	7.8	5.5	3.9%	26	49	22
2018	SEA	5/0	9	3	8	0	2.7	0	-38.3%	--	-3	--	33%	--	0	0.3	1	0	0	0	0%	0.0	0.0	-171.3%	--	-1	--
2019	DET	16/3	262	38	205	0	5.4	0	6.5%	--	23	--	47%	--	14	3.1	42	34	233	1	81%	6.9	7.0	-8.2%	34	12	35
2020	WAS			26	116	1	4.5	0	3.5%								24	18	154	1	75%	8.6		4.1%			

Every other year, McKissic wiggles his way into a contributing position. In 2016 and 2018, McKissic hardly touched the ball, yet he earned over 70 touches for more than 400 yards in both 2017 and 2019. Unfortunately, if that rather arbitrary rollercoaster of production is to mean anything, 2020 is an off year for McKissic. More meaningful than McKissic's odd production trends is that 2020 will be his first season away from offensive coordinator Darrell Bevell, with whom he spent three seasons in Seattle as well as last year in Detroit. McKissic probably will not earn the No. 3 spot over rookie Antonio Gibson, but the No. 4 spot on the back end of the rotation should be within his reach.

Sony Michel   Height: 5-11   Weight: 215   College: Georgia   Draft: 2018/1 (31)   Born: 17-Feb-1995   Age: 25   Risk: Yellow

Year	Tm	G/GS	Snaps	Runs	Yds	TD	Yd/R	FUM	DVOA	Rk	DYAR	Rk	Suc%	Rk	BTkl	YafC	Pass	Rec	Yds	TD	C%	Yd/C	YAC	DVOA	Rk	DYAR	Rk
2018	NE	13/8	320	209	931	6	4.5	1	-2.7%	26	58	24	53%	11	23	2.4	11	7	50	0	64%	7.1	7.1	-18.4%	--	-3	--
2019	NE	16/14	422	247	912	7	3.7	2	-6.4%	29	23	28	49%	22	30	2.4	20	12	94	0	60%	7.8	10.1	-21.3%	--	-9	--
2020	NE			178	681	7	3.8	1	-1.8%								21	15	126	1	71%	8.4		-4.4%			

The mocking of Bill Belichick for selecting a running back in the first round was somewhat muzzled when the Patriots won the Super Bowl during Michel's rookie season, when he shouldered the load of the rushing offense. In 2020, however, critics of all volumes got the ammo they needed to criticize the pick once again. Michel posted negative DVOA splits on each individual down, and was particularly mediocre on first down. Michel logged 147 first-down runs, yet came away with just a 47% success rate on 3.79 yards per carry, both down from his 49% success rate and 4.91 yards per carry in 2018. It is not like Michel made up any of that lost rushing value through the air, either. Michel earned just 20 targets on the season and posted a supremely mediocre 55% success rate. Moreover, a foot injury may hold Michel on the sideline for at least the start of the season. Given Michel already looked a hair slower in 2019 than in 2018, further decline of his lower-body health could spell bad news. Hopefully this year's unique, more reserved offseason and preseason allow him the rest he needs to return at full capacity.

Lamar Miller   Height: 5-10   Weight: 220   College: Miami   Draft: 2012/4 (97)   Born: 25-Apr-1991   Age: 29   Risk: N/A

Year	Tm	G/GS	Snaps	Runs	Yds	TD	Yd/R	FUM	DVOA	Rk	DYAR	Rk	Suc%	Rk	BTkl	YafC	Pass	Rec	Yds	TD	C%	Yd/C	YAC	DVOA	Rk	DYAR	Rk
2017	HOU	16/13	757	238	888	3	3.7	1	-2.8%	25	57	21	45%	21	34	2.3	45	36	327	3	80%	9.1	8.2	42.7%	2	134	4
2018	HOU	14/14	619	210	973	5	4.6	1	-5.3%	28	28	27	44%	35	28	2.7	35	25	163	1	71%	6.5	6.8	-19.9%	47	-10	45

A devastating preseason injury that led to a torn ACL and MCL in Dallas has combined with Miller's age (29) and COVID-19 (inability to make medical visits easily and safely) to limit Miller to an NFL after-thought. Even after the draft, there has been almost no news of him working out for teams or otherwise drawing interest. Miller didn't produce as much as was probably hoped when he was given a clear starting shot in Houston—likely because Bill O'Brien ran more zone than he should have with a back like Miller—but he was productive and it wouldn't be totally unsurprising for him to resurface once he's able to prove he's healthy.

Joe Mixon

Height: 6-1 Weight: 220 College: Oklahoma Draft: 2017/2 (48) Born: 24-Jul-1996 Age: 24 Risk: Green

Year	Tm	G/GS	Snaps	Runs	Yds	TD	Yd/R	FUM	DVOA	Rk	DYAR	Rk	Suc%	Rk	BTkl	YafC	Pass	Rec	Yds	TD	C%	Yd/C	YAC	DVOA	Rk	DYAR	Rk
2017	CIN	14/7	385	178	626	4	3.5	3	1.0%	19	68	17	41%	37	22	2.5	35	30	287	0	89%	9.6	10.9	-6.8%	38	13	38
2018	CIN	14/13	596	237	1168	8	4.9	0	6.4%	13	154	8	49%	23	46	2.7	55	43	296	1	78%	6.9	7.7	-15.3%	41	-5	42
2019	CIN	16/15	661	278	1137	5	4.1	0	-0.9%	20	90	17	46%	30	71	2.8	45	35	287	3	78%	8.2	9.5	19.3%	13	86	12
2020	CIN			240	986	8	4.1	1	3.2%								57	45	346	2	79%	7.7		4.5%			

Through eight frustrating games in 2019, Mixon had just 320 yards rushing on 101 carries, an almost unfathomable level of ineptitude for a back of Mixon's quality. The splits in some of those games were excruciating—six carries, 10 yards in the opener against Seattle; eight carries for 10 yards in Week 6 vs. Baltimore; 10 carries for 2 (!) yards the following Sunday against the Jags. The stats didn't tell the whole story; one had to see Mixon work miracles just to fight back to the line of scrimmage week after week to truly appreciate how the Bengals offensive line was letting him down. Then the coaching staff scrapped the incumbent zone-based blocking scheme in favor of a "pin and pull" system, and Mixon got back to being Mixon, putting up 817 yards on 177 carries. In the first eight weeks of the year, Mixon had -58 DYAR and a -22.0% DVOA. After the Bengals' Week 9 bye, he had 147 DYAR and an 11.2% DVOA. The fact that Mixon somehow got over 1,000 yards (and comfortably) given his horrendous start was about the lone bright spot in Cincinnati's season. He's also a strong receiver, one of just five backs to post a double-digit YAC in his catches out of the backfield (10.2), and it seems incumbent upon Zac Taylor and his staff to utilize Mixon more in the passing game.

Mixon is the next running back up in the "Never pay for that position!" team-building Twitter wars. One extenuating circumstance that is unique to Mixon is the residual good feeling he maintains towards the Bengals, who drafted him under controversial circumstances after his horrible assault in college. Both sides were rewarded. Mix has been a straight-A character guy as a pro and is one of the most popular players on the team. None of that means anything to his agent, of course, and Mixon regularly hands out social media likes anytime a fellow back gets paid, so if he is inclined to offer Cincy a discount, it will likely be a modest one.

David Montgomery

Height: 5-10 Weight: 222 College: Iowa State Draft: 2019/3 (73) Born: 7-Jun-1997 Age: 23 Risk: Green

Year	Tm	G/GS	Snaps	Runs	Yds	TD	Yd/R	FUM	DVOA	Rk	DYAR	Rk	Suc%	Rk	BTkl	YafC	Pass	Rec	Yds	TD	C%	Yd/C	YAC	DVOA	Rk	DYAR	Rk
2019	CHI	16/8	625	242	889	6	3.7	2	-13.0%	40	-46	42	46%	29	53	1.9	35	25	185	1	71%	7.4	6.2	-5.5%	30	15	34
2020	CHI			228	838	8	3.7	2	-6.4%								32	25	180	1	78%	7.2		-6.2%			

Montgomery's rookie season wasn't *all* terrible. He did have 45 broken tackles on runs, sixth-most in the league, so that aspect of his game did translate. The problem was that he didn't end up doing much after breaking those tackles; his 1.92 yards after contact per attempt was third worst among qualifying backs. Broken tackles are great, but you need to then turn those opportunities into big plays, and Montgomery's subpar athleticism let him down as a rookie. The Bears are committed to feeding Montgomery the rock, so he'll have a chance to bounce back in 2020, but the fears about his lack of speed and explosiveness were very much realized last year.

Ty Montgomery

Height: 6-0 Weight: 216 College: Stanford Draft: 2015/3 (94) Born: 22-Jan-1993 Age: 27 Risk: Green

Year	Tm	G/GS	Snaps	Runs	Yds	TD	Yd/R	FUM	DVOA	Rk	DYAR	Rk	Suc%	Rk	BTkl	YafC	Pass	Rec	Yds	TD	C%	Yd/C	YAC	DVOA	Rk	DYAR	Rk
2017	GB	8/5	274	71	273	3	3.8	0	2.8%	--	37	--	49%	--	12	2.2	31	23	173	1	74%	7.5	9.3	-3.7%	35	19	35
2018	2TM	13/0	264	41	188	1	4.6	1	0.9%	--	17	--	57%	--	13	2.6	40	25	235	0	63%	9.4	8.5	-14.1%	40	-1	40
2019	NYJ	16/2	149	32	103	0	3.2	0	-30.4%	--	-27	--	38%	--	1	1.7	17	13	90	0	76%	6.9	7.2	-41.6%	--	-26	--
2020	NO			9	37	0	4.1	0	-2.9%								4	3	19	0	75%	6.3		-2.7%			

The road for Montgomery since his surprising 2016 season has been rocky, to say the least. From 2017 to 2019, Montgomery's carries have dropped each year, going from 71 in 2017 to just 32 with the Jets in 2019. Montgomery has also played for three different teams over that span (Packers, Ravens, Jets) and is currently without a team heading into the 2020 season. Seeing as Montgomery did not have the hands or route-running skills to succeed at wide receiver, his conversion to running back still makes sense in hindsight, but he has yet to develop the nuance of this position either. Montgomery's kick return success alone will likely net him a job by the time the season rolls around, but do not look for him to get many touches out of the backfield.

Zack Moss

Height: 5-9 | Weight: 222 | College: Utah | Draft: 2020/3 (86) | Born: 15-Dec-1997 | Age: 23 | Risk: Green

Year	Tm	G/GS	Snaps	Runs	Yds	TD	Yd/R	FUM	DVOA	Rk	DYAR	Rk	Suc%	Rk	BTkl	YafC	Pass	Rec	Yds	TD	C%	Yd/C	YAC	DVOA	Rk	DYAR	Rk
2020	BUF			99	390	3	3.9	1	-4.8%								12	9	71	0	75%	7.9		-3.3%			

The Buffalo Bills are replacing Frank Gore, but they are not replacing the archetype. Moss is a tough, downhill runner who can be the steak to Devin Singletary's sizzle. Injuries sapped Moss of some of his athletic dominance through the years, which is part of why he did not go higher in the draft, but he makes up for it through impeccable vision, patience at the line of scrimmage, and a veteran-like decisiveness when presented with cloudy reads at the second level. Moss also sports fantastic balance through contact, thanks in part to his short, thick frame. Over his four-year career at Utah, Moss earned the school record for career rushing yards (4,067) by almost 1,000 yards more than the previous record holder. He also ranks 10th in career rushing yards among all Pac-12 players. Long runs will come few and far between with Moss, but his ability to squeeze the most out of ordinary rushing plays and shoulder the load of a run-heavy offense will be valuable for Bills offense constantly looking for stability to help counterbalance quarterback Josh Allen.

Raheem Mostert

Height: 5-10 | Weight: 197 | College: Purdue | Draft: 2015/FA | Born: 9-Apr-1992 | Age: 28 | Risk: Yellow

Year	Tm	G/GS	Snaps	Runs	Yds	TD	Yd/R	FUM	DVOA	Rk	DYAR	Rk	Suc%	Rk	BTkl	YafC	Pass	Rec	Yds	TD	C%	Yd/C	YAC	DVOA	Rk	DYAR	Rk
2017	SF	11/0	15	6	30	0	5.0	1	-49.6%	--	-11	--	50%	--	0	1.0	--	0	0	0	--	0.0	--	--	--	--	--
2018	SF	9/0	89	34	261	1	7.7	1	19.4%	--	40	--	65%	--	5	3.9	7	6	25	0	86%	4.2	7.3	-32.1%	--	-6	--
2019	SF	16/0	370	137	772	8	5.6	1	26.8%	1	191	7	53%	9	30	2.9	22	14	180	2	64%	12.9	11.1	39.3%	--	62	--
2020	SF			208	975	5	4.7	2	9.2%								30	23	200	1	77%	8.7		8.0%			

A late bloomer by almost every definition, Mostert appeared in all 16 games last season for the first time since entering the league in 2015 as an undrafted free agent. Prior to 2019, Mostert had never exceeded 35 carries in a season, and he began the year buried on the depth chart behind Tevin Coleman and Matt Breida. Coleman spent much of 2019 banged up and Breida had his own injury issues and a fumbling problem, which finally opened the door for Mostert to truly shine late in the year. Safe to say, he did so swimmingly, leading all running backs in rushing DVOA. Between his highly efficient performance on the season as well as his 220 yards in the NFC Championship Game, it appears that Mostert has finally earned a starting role on his seventh NFL team as he enters his age-28 season. San Francisco likes to rotate its runners, so he may not get all the carries to himself. But at this point, he probably doesn't mind that much.

Latavius Murray

Height: 6-3 | Weight: 230 | College: Central Florida | Draft: 2013/6 (181) | Born: 21-Feb-1991 | Age: 29 | Risk: Blue

Year	Tm	G/GS	Snaps	Runs	Yds	TD	Yd/R	FUM	DVOA	Rk	DYAR	Rk	Suc%	Rk	BTkl	YafC	Pass	Rec	Yds	TD	C%	Yd/C	YAC	DVOA	Rk	DYAR	Rk
2017	MIN	16/11	421	216	842	8	3.9	1	-2.3%	24	59	20	44%	23	34	2.3	17	15	103	0	88%	6.9	8.3	-11.6%	--	2	--
2018	MIN	16/6	461	140	578	6	4.1	0	-4.2%	27	25	29	46%	31	18	2.7	26	22	141	0	85%	6.4	5.2	-7.5%	33	9	35
2019	NO	16/8	442	146	637	5	4.4	0	10.7%	9	125	13	60%	2	34	2.5	43	34	235	1	79%	6.9	8.4	-5.6%	31	19	32
2020	NO			130	528	4	4.1	0	2.2%								16	12	88	0	75%	7.3		-7.1%			

When Alvin Kamara missed a pair of games midseason, Murray filled in capably. His 307 yards from scrimmage (averaging 5 yards per touch) and four touchdowns resulted in a career-best 10.7% DVOA. He was particularly useful in short-yardage situations (1-3 yards to go), producing more value than Kamara (7.1% DVOA vs. -6.0% DVOA). Given Kamara's workload (527 touches the past two seasons, ninth-most) and the Saints' frequent use of multiple-back formations, Murray is a worthy handcuff.

Dare Ogunbowale

Dare Ogunbowale Height: 5-10 Weight: 205 College: Wisconsin Draft: 2017/FA Born: 4-May-1994 Age: 26 Risk: Green

Year	Tm	G/GS	Snaps	Runs	Yds	TD	Yd/R	FUM	DVOA	Rk	DYAR	Rk	Suc%	Rk	BTkl	YafC	Pass	Rec	Yds	TD	C%	Yd/C	YAC	DVOA	Rk	DYAR	Rk
2019	TB	16/0	367	11	17	2	1.5	1	-50.4%	--	-28	--	36%	--	8	1.4	46	35	286	0	76%	8.2	5.9	-2.9%	27	31	26
2020	TB			9	37	0	4.1	0	-1.4%								38	27	231	1	71%	8.6		-3.3%			

Ogunbowale, who started his NFL career as an undrafted free agent with the Texans in 2017, finally saw some meaningful playing time last season. He became the running back the Buccaneers trusted most in passing situations and led the backfield in targets and catches. Though he proved to be the team's best blocking back, that wasn't a high bar—Ronald Jones was a total liability. With the addition of third-round draft pick Ke'Shawn Vaughn, Ogunbowale will have to fight for snaps once again, but given the frequency with which Tom Brady targets his running backs, don't let him slip off your radar just yet.

Rashaad Penny Height: 5-11 Weight: 220 College: San Diego State Draft: 2018/1 (27) Born: 2-Feb-1996 Age: 24 Risk: Red

Year	Tm	G/GS	Snaps	Runs	Yds	TD	Yd/R	FUM	DVOA	Rk	DYAR	Rk	Suc%	Rk	BTkl	YafC	Pass	Rec	Yds	TD	C%	Yd/C	YAC	DVOA	Rk	DYAR	Rk
2018	SEA	14/0	180	85	419	2	4.9	0	8.9%	--	56	--	40%	--	12	2.6	12	9	75	0	75%	8.3	8.1	8.3%	--	12	--
2019	SEA	10/0	152	65	370	3	5.7	1	32.4%	--	115	--	57%	--	8	2.6	11	8	83	1	73%	10.4	11.4	45.4%	--	37	--
2020	SEA			53	260	1	4.9	1	12.2%								16	13	103	1	81%	7.9		4.5%			

In limited action, Penny looked every bit like a first-round running back in 2019. Had he played enough to qualify, he would have led the league in rushing DVOA, and his receiving DVOA would have been in the top five as well. In a remarkable if probably meaningless stat, the Seahawks went 8-0 in games where Penny got at least one carry. Unfortunately, he didn't get a carry in the Week 14 loss to the Rams because he tore his ACL on a screen pass in the first quarter. Pete Carroll described the injury as "more than just a normal ACL tear" following Penny's surgery. Though the Seahawks remain hopeful that he will eventually make a full recovery, all signs say that Penny will begin 2020 on the PUP list and miss the first six games of the year.

Adrian Peterson Height: 6-1 Weight: 220 College: Oklahoma Draft: 2007/1 (7) Born: 21-Mar-1985 Age: 35 Risk: Red

Year	Tm	G/GS	Snaps	Runs	Yds	TD	Yd/R	FUM	DVOA	Rk	DYAR	Rk	Suc%	Rk	BTkl	YafC	Pass	Rec	Yds	TD	C%	Yd/C	YAC	DVOA	Rk	DYAR	Rk
2017	2TM	10/7	300	156	529	2	3.4	3	-21.9%	46	-85	46	40%	42	32	2.6	19	11	70	0	58%	6.4	5.0	-35.7%	--	-23	--
2018	WAS	16/16	481	251	1042	7	4.2	3	-6.0%	29	26	28	47%	28	56	3.0	26	20	208	1	77%	10.4	10.1	22.3%	5	50	21
2019	WAS	15/15	407	211	898	5	4.3	3	-4.1%	27	39	24	47%	27	45	2.5	23	17	142	0	74%	8.4	9.5	-14.9%	--	-1	--
2020	WAS			116	473	3	4.1	1	-1.0%								21	16	143	1	76%	8.9		6.7%			

With 211 carries in 2019, Peterson crossed an elite threshold with regards to running back longevity. Peterson is now just the eighth running back since the AFL-NFL merger to earn at least 200 carries in 10 individual seasons, matching LaDainian Tomlinson, Jerome Bettis, Barry Sanders, and Walter Payton. It is unlikely Peterson gets to 14 seasons as Emmitt Smith did—the 11 of Curtis Martin or 12 of Frank Gore are more realistic targets—but the fact that Peterson is still kicking in 2020 is impressive enough. At this point, though, Peterson is not much more than mediocre despite what his heavy workload suggests. In each of the past three seasons, Peterson has ranked outside the top 20 in DYAR, including a second-to-last finish in 2017. Perhaps this is the season Derrius Guice remains healthy enough to push Peterson for the starting job.

Tony Pollard Height: 6-0 Weight: 210 College: Memphis Draft: 2019/4 (128) Born: 30-Apr-1997 Age: 23 Risk: Blue

Year	Tm	G/GS	Snaps	Runs	Yds	TD	Yd/R	FUM	DVOA	Rk	DYAR	Rk	Suc%	Rk	BTkl	YafC	Pass	Rec	Yds	TD	C%	Yd/C	YAC	DVOA	Rk	DYAR	Rk
2019	DAL	15/0	204	86	455	2	5.3	1	11.6%	--	71	--	52%	--	26	4.0	20	15	107	1	75%	7.1	9.0	-2.7%	--	12	--
2020	DAL			69	326	1	4.7	1	7.3%								23	18	134	1	78%	7.4		-3.4%			

Pollard was a change-of-pace back and often came in as the closer. He had as many rushing attempts with the lead in the fourth quarter as Ezekiel Elliott (35), but blew him out of the water with 229 yards to Elliott's 156, thanks mostly to a few big plays in Week 15 against the Rams. With the Cowboys nursing a big lead, Pollard had runs of 33 and 44 yards in the fourth quarter. He also had a 25-yard run earlier in that game during the second quarter.

There's no doubting Pollard's big-play ability, but he was rarely put in position to work off that in the passing game. His aDOT came behind the line of scrimmage on each down, and only seven of his 20 targets came when lined up in the slot or outside. Even those plays had a total of -17 air yards.

Bilal Powell

Height: 5-10   Weight: 204   College: Louisville   Draft: 2011/4 (126)   Born: 27-Oct-1988   Age: 32   Risk: N/A

Year	Tm	G/GS	Snaps	Runs	Yds	TD	Yd/R	FUM	DVOA	Rk	DYAR	Rk	Suc%	Rk	BTkl	YafC	Pass	Rec	Yds	TD	C%	Yd/C	YAC	DVOA	Rk	DYAR	Rk
2017	NYJ	15/10	401	178	772	5	4.3	1	-14.8%	42	-43	43	35%	45	36	2.4	33	23	170	0	70%	7.4	7.0	-30.4%	57	-30	56
2018	NYJ	7/7	208	80	343	0	4.3	2	-19.9%	--	-34	--	44%	--	8	2.2	18	11	110	1	61%	10.0	7.6	-14.4%	--	-1	--
2019	NYJ	13/1	168	59	229	0	3.9	0	-18.6%	--	-22	--	37%	--	6	2.2	12	7	33	0	58%	4.7	6.4	-93.6%	--	-47	--

It is incredible that Powell remained with the Jets for nine seasons as nothing more than a solid role player. That is no knock on him—that kind of career would be envied by many—but that caliber of player tends to bounce around a bit. At age 32, Powell has finally found himself looking for a new team. Part of Powell's value for so long was that he was a plus in the passing game, but with Le'Veon Bell being the team's lead back, there was no need for a pass-catching role player the way there had been in previous seasons. In turn, Powell earned just 12 targets on the season, which matched his drop to just 59 carries. His 66 total touches were the fewest he had earned since 2014. As recyclable as running backs seem to be, it is tough to imagine Powell will last the whole 2020 season without a job, but his days of being meaningful contributor appear to be gone.

Jalen Richard

Height: 5-8   Weight: 207   College: Southern Mississippi   Draft: 2016/FA   Born: 15-Oct-1993   Age: 27   Risk: Green

Year	Tm	G/GS	Snaps	Runs	Yds	TD	Yd/R	FUM	DVOA	Rk	DYAR	Rk	Suc%	Rk	BTkl	YafC	Pass	Rec	Yds	TD	C%	Yd/C	YAC	DVOA	Rk	DYAR	Rk
2017	OAK	16/1	219	56	275	1	4.9	1	-1.4%	--	15	--	38%	--	10	2.3	36	27	256	1	75%	9.5	9.0	33.3%	9	86	14
2018	OAK	16/1	413	55	259	1	4.7	2	-20.3%	--	-28	--	45%	--	27	3.2	81	68	607	0	84%	8.9	7.3	17.4%	9	138	6
2019	OAK	16/0	305	39	145	0	3.7	1	-3.6%	--	8	--	46%	--	7	1.1	43	36	323	0	84%	9.0	6.6	2.7%	22	39	21
2020	LV			25	102	1	4.1	1	-1.7%								36	30	242	0	83%	8.1		11.5%			

Richard's rushing production has fallen in each of his four NFL seasons, yet he retained a role as an adequate-if-unspectacular third-down back, even when Josh Jacobs proved capable of catching passes as a rookie. The Raiders expect to use Jacobs more often as a receiver this season. They are also listing all-purpose weapon Lynn Bowden as a running back, and added Devontae Booker to the payroll in the offseason for some reason, so Richard could be the odd man out of the committee. But he has survived numerous lineup changes in the past.

Jaylen Samuels

Height: 6-0   Weight: 225   College: North Carolina State   Draft: 2018/5 (165)   Born: 20-Jul-1996   Age: 24   Risk: Green

Year	Tm	G/GS	Snaps	Runs	Yds	TD	Yd/R	FUM	DVOA	Rk	DYAR	Rk	Suc%	Rk	BTkl	YafC	Pass	Rec	Yds	TD	C%	Yd/C	YAC	DVOA	Rk	DYAR	Rk
2018	PIT	14/3	228	56	256	0	4.6	0	-1.3%	--	17	--	52%	--	11	2.3	29	26	199	3	90%	7.7	8.3	36.4%	3	79	14
2019	PIT	14/4	369	66	175	1	2.7	1	-32.6%	--	-64	--	39%	--	9	2.0	57	47	305	1	82%	6.5	7.8	-8.9%	35	17	33
2020	PIT			14	51	0	3.6	0	-9.3%								25	19	153	1	76%	8.1		4.1%			

In the five 2019 games where Jaylen Samuels got seven or more carries, he rushed for 32, 29, 26, 16, and 10 yards. Or, to put it another way, in 2018's win against the Patriots in which Samuels took 19 carries for 142 yards, he outgained his five best games of 2019 combined. As with James Conner, Samuels also suffered from multiple injuries over the course of the season, including issues with his knee and groin. It is still worth considering the idea that Samuels is an effective third-down back in spite of his numbers last season, because a lot of what the Steelers did got compressed. But it is also worth considering that one more year like this will probably put Samuels into the C.J. Prosise memory hole of "that guy had one great game versus the Patriots ... what happened to him after that?"

Miles Sanders

Height: 5-11   Weight: 211   College: Penn State   Draft: 2019/2 (53)   Born: 1-May-1997   Age: 23   Risk: Green

Year	Tm	G/GS	Snaps	Runs	Yds	TD	Yd/R	FUM	DVOA	Rk	DYAR	Rk	Suc%	Rk	BTkl	YafC	Pass	Rec	Yds	TD	C%	Yd/C	YAC	DVOA	Rk	DYAR	Rk
2019	PHI	16/11	626	179	818	3	4.6	2	-6.6%	30	14	30	45%	34	36	2.8	63	50	509	3	79%	10.2	8.3	20.0%	12	121	7
2020	PHI			224	981	7	4.4	2	3.3%								56	44	383	2	79%	8.7		13.1%			

Many narratives of Sanders' season consist simply of "Sanders turned it on in the second half," and that's not entirely wrong—but it's really more accurate to say that Sanders had four four-week seasons as a rookie. In Weeks 1-4, Sanders was dreadful, with a -36.8% rushing DVOA and -54 DYAR. As a result, Sanders found himself on the pine more often than not in Weeks 5-8, gathering just 21 carries and 14 targets over that time span, 20 fewer touches than any other four-week period. A 65-yard scamper in Week 8, however, got him back onto the field on rushing downs once more, and he delivered with a 4.2% DVOA and a 52% success rate from Weeks 9-13, his most productive rushing period of the season. But as injuries piled up and Sanders was leaned on more and more, his efficiency went down, with just a -0.2% DVOA over the last four weeks of the season, despite averaging 15.8 carries per game over that time period. This all adds up to progress over the course of the year, but the Eagles are really betting on a four-game sample size of effective play on the ground as they make Sanders their undisputed RB1 entering 2020.

Bo Scarbrough

Height: 6-1   Weight: 235   College: Alabama   Draft: 2018/7 (236)   Born: 29-Sep-1996   Age: 24   Risk: Blue

Year	Tm	G/GS	Snaps	Runs	Yds	TD	Yd/R	FUM	DVOA	Rk	DYAR	Rk	Suc%	Rk	BTkl	YafC	Pass	Rec	Yds	TD	C%	Yd/C	YAC	DVOA	Rk	DYAR	Rk
2019	DET	6/5	171	89	377	1	4.2	1	-5.7%	--	10	--	56%	--	10	2.6	4	1	5	0	25%	5.0	8.0	-74.2%	--	-14	--
2020	DET			48	200	1	4.2	0	-0.9%								4	4	24	0	100%	6.0		-1.4%			

After failing to see the field as a rookie, Scarbrough found himself promoted from the practice squad to the role of starting running back in November as the rest of the Lions' depth chart was injured or poor. Given the situation he found himself in, Scarbrough handled himself quite well—opposing defenses weren't exactly quaking in their boots about Jeff Driskel and David Blough, so a -1.2% DVOA in those four weeks as Detroit's primary running back is fairly impressive. Scarbrough's issue with making the roster in 2020 is his complete lack of contribution as a receiver; only Benny Snell had more rushes than Scarbrough did among backs with six or fewer targets in the passing game.

Boston Scott

Height: 5-6   Weight: 203   College: Louisiana Tech   Draft: 2018/6 (201)   Born: 27-Apr-1995   Age: 25   Risk: Green

Year	Tm	G/GS	Snaps	Runs	Yds	TD	Yd/R	FUM	DVOA	Rk	DYAR	Rk	Suc%	Rk	BTkl	YafC	Pass	Rec	Yds	TD	C%	Yd/C	YAC	DVOA	Rk	DYAR	Rk
2019	PHI	11/2	187	61	245	5	4.0	2	22.2%	--	85	--	52%	--	17	1.9	26	24	204	0	92%	8.5	11.4	29.0%	7	67	17
2020	PHI			90	367	3	4.1	1	-1.1%								38	30	248	1	79%	8.3		10.5%			

Scott went from practice-squad afterthought to crucial stretch-run contributor in 2019, and his performance in December was exemplary. His 58 DYAR and 24.4% DVOA down the stretch both were in the top 10 for all running backs over the last four weeks of the season; all in all, he ended up leading the Eagles in rushing DYAR in five games. Scott's emergence as a quality reserve likely emboldened the Eagles into letting Jordan Howard and Corey Clement go; while Miles Sanders will be the go-to guy in Philly's backfield, Scott's December probably earned him nine or 10 touches a week. Not bad for a guy who didn't make final roster cuts last year.

Devin Singletary

Height: 5-7   Weight: 203   College: Florida Atlantic   Draft: 2019/3 (74)   Born: 3-Sep-1997   Age: 23   Risk: Yellow

Year	Tm	G/GS	Snaps	Runs	Yds	TD	Yd/R	FUM	DVOA	Rk	DYAR	Rk	Suc%	Rk	BTkl	YafC	Pass	Rec	Yds	TD	C%	Yd/C	YAC	DVOA	Rk	DYAR	Rk
2019	BUF	12/8	540	151	775	2	5.1	4	3.7%	13	75	20	50%	21	42	2.4	41	29	194	2	71%	6.7	6.7	-35.2%	47	-47	48
2020	BUF			199	932	4	4.7	3	3.6%								61	45	349	2	74%	7.8		-4.4%			

The thinking behind Buffalo's backfield last year was that Frank Gore would be the stable producer who allowed Singletary's streaky, explosive style to shine. In reality, Singletary was both more explosive and efficient than Gore. Singletary earned a 50% success rate with seven rushes of at least 20 yards, whereas Gore only put up a 45% success rate with four rushes of at least 20 yards. Even on first down, theoretically the down a team would most want their stable back to produce, Singletary earned a 52% success rate to Gore's 45%. As last season rolled on, the coaching staff started to realize Gore's ineffectiveness and began favoring Singletary regardless of down, distance, or game situation, which was clearly the right call. Now the Bills have third-round pick Zack Moss to fill Gore's old role, hopefully giving the Bills the one-two punch with Singletary that they were aiming for originally.

Ito Smith

Height: 5-9   Weight: 195   College: Southern Mississippi   Draft: 2018/4 (126)   Born: 11-Sep-1995   Age: 25   Risk: Green

Year	Tm	G/GS	Snaps	Runs	Yds	TD	Yd/R	FUM	DVOA	Rk	DYAR	Rk	Suc%	Rk	BTkl	YafC	Pass	Rec	Yds	TD	C%	Yd/C	YAC	DVOA	Rk	DYAR	Rk
2018	ATL	14/0	311	90	315	4	3.5	1	-13.4%	--	-19	--	48%	--	20	2.4	32	27	152	0	84%	5.6	5.9	-17.7%	45	-8	44
2019	ATL	7/0	153	22	106	1	4.8	0	13.7%	--	27	--	55%	--	9	2.3	14	11	87	0	79%	7.9	6.5	-14.7%	--	-1	--
2020	ATL			74	301	3	4.1	1	1.4%								28	22	155	1	79%	7.0		-6.0%			

At just 5-foot-9 and 195 pounds, Smith never made complete sense as a skill-for-skill replacement of Tevin Coleman in Atlanta. But the quick Smith has teased his receiving potential, dropping just one of his 39 catchable targets in his first two seasons—even if his receiving DVOAs of -17.7% and -14.7% in 2018 and 2019 would suggest otherwise. Smith makes sense as a complement to the bigger Todd Gurley in 2020 if the Falcons are willing to split their work according to their skill sets as opposed to by drive the way they did with Coleman and Devonta Freeman. And Smith has the potential for more workload given the declining health of Gurley's knees.

Benny Snell

Height: 5-10   Weight: 224   College: Kentucky   Draft: 2019/4 (122)   Born: 27-Feb-1998   Age: 22   Risk: Green

Year	Tm	G/GS	Snaps	Runs	Yds	TD	Yd/R	FUM	DVOA	Rk	DYAR	Rk	Suc%	Rk	BTkl	YafC	Pass	Rec	Yds	TD	C%	Yd/C	YAC	DVOA	Rk	DYAR	Rk
2019	PIT	13/2	171	108	426	2	3.9	1	-11.7%	39	-14	38	49%	24	17	2.9	4	3	23	0	75%	7.7	7.3	-13.2%	--	0	--
2020	PIT			48	189	2	3.9	0	-3.7%								9	8	55	0	89%	6.9		3.7%			

From Week 6 on, Snell was essentially the Steelers' early-down back whenever James Conner couldn't cut it or got injured mid-game, finishing with some respectable yardage totals and five separate games of 16 or more rushes. He is completely invisible as a receiver, but Snell was a battering ram with a lot of momentum at Kentucky. In the event of another season of Conner injuries, he would probably be first in line for a major portion of the workload. And remember, this is under a head coach who has a preference for having a feature back. Sneaky handcuff for the deeper leagues, and a good waiver wire pick-up waiting to happen if Ben Roethlisberger stays healthy.

D'Andre Swift

Height: 5-9   Weight: 215   College: Georgia   Draft: 2020/2 (35)   Born: 14-Jan-1999   Age: 21   Risk: Green

Year	Tm	G/GS	Snaps	Runs	Yds	TD	Yd/R	FUM	DVOA	Rk	DYAR	Rk	Suc%	Rk	BTkl	YafC	Pass	Rec	Yds	TD	C%	Yd/C	YAC	DVOA	Rk	DYAR	Rk
2020	DET			191	810	5	4.2	2	0.7%								49	38	289	1	78%	7.6		0.8%			

While Swift was generally considered the top running back prospect in the draft—to the point where it was a mild upset when Clyde Edwards-Helaire went before him—BackCAST only had him in fourth place. The big penalty Swift had in the model was his lack of a workload in college; he found himself competing with current practice-squad player Elijah Holyfield for playing time. When Swift did see the field, however, he looked like an NFL starter already. His cutback ability is phenomenal, his vision is fantastic, and he has enough receiving chops to be a three-down back, even if that isn't his calling card. He's not going to provide explosive plays down after down, but he's the kind of guy who can squeeze an extra yard out of plays on a consistent basis.

Jonathan Taylor

Height: 5-10   Weight: 226   College: Wisconsin   Draft: 2020/2 (41)   Born: 19-Jan-1999   Age: 21   Risk: Green

Year	Tm	G/GS	Snaps	Runs	Yds	TD	Yd/R	FUM	DVOA	Rk	DYAR	Rk	Suc%	Rk	BTkl	YafC	Pass	Rec	Yds	TD	C%	Yd/C	YAC	DVOA	Rk	DYAR	Rk
2020	IND			165	743	5	4.5	1	5.9%								23	19	152	1	83%	8.0		11.1%			

Behold the new record-holder for the highest BackCAST projection ever (since 1998). Scouting reports from Taylor's time at Wisconsin are filled with glowing reviews of his combination of size and speed, a combination reflected in the 10th-highest running back Speed Score we've ever recorded. Taylor rushed for over 1,900 yards in all three of his seasons in Madison, showing off vision, patience, acceleration, speed, strength, and durability. That's a heck of a combination for a young back, but there are also three consistent red flags: his high fumble rate, his lack of proven ability as a receiver, and his 900-carry workload in college. If Taylor can hold onto the ball consistently in the NFL, he is a perfect fit as a foil for (and possible successor to) Marlon Mack. He begins as Mack's backup, but most observers expect him to eat into Mack's carry total pretty much immediately.

Chris Thompson
Height: 5-8   Weight: 195   College: Florida State   Draft: 2013/5 (154)   Born: 20-Oct-1990   Age: 30   Risk: Red

Year	Tm	G/GS	Snaps	Runs	Yds	TD	Yd/R	FUM	DVOA	Rk	DYAR	Rk	Suc%	Rk	BTkl	YafC	Pass	Rec	Yds	TD	C%	Yd/C	YAC	DVOA	Rk	DYAR	Rk
2017	WAS	10/1	338	64	294	2	4.6	1	-4.9%	--	9	--	42%	--	29	2.5	54	39	510	4	72%	13.1	12.2	67.3%	1	223	3
2018	WAS	10/0	308	43	178	0	4.1	1	-30.7%	--	-35	--	30%	--	15	1.8	56	41	268	1	75%	6.5	5.3	-17.3%	44	-10	46
2019	WAS	11/0	317	37	138	0	3.7	1	-6.4%	--	3	--	38%	--	11	2.0	58	42	378	0	72%	9.0	8.0	-2.1%	26	34	25
2020	JAX			33	136	1	4.1	1	-1.5%								37	28	219	1	76%	7.8		-2.5%			

Thompson followed his former head coach, Jay Gruden, to Jacksonville this offseason, after playing almost his entire career for Gruden in Washington. Thompson bounced on and off the practice squad in his first couple of years before carving out an effective role as a pass-catching back in Gruden's offense. Thompson's 2017 season, when he had over 800 scrimmage yards and led all running backs in receiving DYAR despite only playing 10 games, was the most productive of his career. Otherwise, he has usually been an effective matchup weapon, good for about 40 or 50 yards per game mostly as a receiver. He may eat into Leonard Fournette's target total, but Thompson has only reached 300 rushing yards once in his seven-year career so he should not be a threat to Fournette's status in the rushing game.

Darwin Thompson
Height: 5-8   Weight: 200   College: Utah State   Draft: 2019/6 (214)   Born: 12-Feb-1997   Age: 23   Risk: Green

Year	Tm	G/GS	Snaps	Runs	Yds	TD	Yd/R	FUM	DVOA	Rk	DYAR	Rk	Suc%	Rk	BTkl	YafC	Pass	Rec	Yds	TD	C%	Yd/C	YAC	DVOA	Rk	DYAR	Rk
2019	KC	12/0	108	37	128	1	3.5	0	1.6%	--	16	--	58%	--	7	2.2	10	9	43	0	90%	4.8	6.9	-34.8%	--	-12	--
2020	KC			10	38	0	3.8	0	-4.2%								2	1	10	0	50%	10.0		-2.2%			

Eleven of Thompson's 37 carries (and his lone touchdown) last season came in one fourth-quarter drive of a game the Chiefs won 40-9 over the Raiders. In fact, 22 of his runs came in fourth quarters, 34 of them with the Chiefs leading, and 32 of them in December, when Darrell Williams and LeSean McCoy were unavailable or limited. A clearer statistical picture of "late-game carries-eater in blowouts" has rarely been painted. Thompson was useful on special teams and fits the Chiefs rusher/receiver profile, so he could stick as the No.3 back in the Damien Williams/Clyde Edwards-Helaire committee. But that back's role may be limited to "late-game carries eater in blowouts."

Ke'Shawn Vaughn
Height: 5-10   Weight: 218   College: Vanderbilt   Draft: 2020/3 (76)   Born: 4-May-1997   Age: 23   Risk: Green

Year	Tm	G/GS	Snaps	Runs	Yds	TD	Yd/R	FUM	DVOA	Rk	DYAR	Rk	Suc%	Rk	BTkl	YafC	Pass	Rec	Yds	TD	C%	Yd/C	YAC	DVOA	Rk	DYAR	Rk
2020	TB			169	713	5	4.2	2	0.6%								38	29	237	1	76%	8.2		3.6%			

In March, Buccaneers coach Bruce Arians said he would "love to have a pass-catching back," which was an honest assessment of need and an admission that the team didn't have confidence in Ronald Jones as an every-down back. A month later, Arians got what he wanted when Tampa Bay drafted Vaughn in the third round. Our BackCAST system approves. His +30.9% score—which means he is projected to gain 30.9% more yards than the "average" drafted running back—ranked seventh in this class.

In producing back-to-back 1,000-yard rushing seasons at Vanderbilt, Vaughn showed balance and power as a runner. He ranked fifth in the FBS in broken tackles per 100 touches (31) and fourth in yards after contact per attempt (3.5), according to Sports Info Solutions. He showed some upside as a pass-catcher in his two seasons with the Commodores, hauling in 41 passes for 440 yards. Someone in your fantasy league will draft him too early and ultimately become impatient and drop him. That's when you can swoop in and add him just as his role starts to increase.

Mark Walton
Height: 5-10   Weight: 200   College: Miami   Draft: 2018/4 (112)   Born: 29-Mar-1997   Age: 23   Risk: N/A

Year	Tm	G/GS	Snaps	Runs	Yds	TD	Yd/R	FUM	DVOA	Rk	DYAR	Rk	Suc%	Rk	BTkl	YafC	Pass	Rec	Yds	TD	C%	Yd/C	YAC	DVOA	Rk	DYAR	Rk
2018	CIN	14/0	93	14	34	0	2.4	0	-21.8%	--	-10	--	36%	--	2	1.6	8	5	41	0	63%	8.2	9.6	-40.1%	--	-10	--
2019	MIA	7/4	200	53	201	0	3.8	1	6.7%	--	33	--	45%	--	8	2.2	21	15	89	0	71%	5.9	7.1	-39.1%	--	-28	--

Believe it or not, Walton was Miami's most effective back last season. Now, the competition was not stiff by any means, and stating his relative success is not a call for him to earn any more touches than he did, but at least someone in that backfield appeared competent. Walton was the only runner on the team to post positive DVOA ratings on both first and second down. The same can not be said of his pass-catching, but it is not like any of Miami's other backs were really outshining him in that regard. Walton was cut this offseason after a domestic violence arrest.

DeAndre Washington Height: 5-8   Weight: 210   College: Texas Tech   Draft: 2016/5 (143)   Born: 22-Feb-1993   Age: 27   Risk: Green

Year	Tm	G/GS	Snaps	Runs	Yds	TD	Yd/R	FUM	DVOA	Rk	DYAR	Rk	Suc%	Rk	BTkl	YafC	Pass	Rec	Yds	TD	C%	Yd/C	YAC	DVOA	Rk	DYAR	Rk
2017	OAK	15/0	223	57	153	2	2.7	2	-33.1%	--	-55	--	40%	--	23	2.0	45	34	197	1	76%	5.8	4.9	-13.6%	46	1	46
2018	OAK	10/0	70	30	115	0	3.8	1	-19.6%	--	-16	--	55%	--	4	2.6	1	1	9	0	100%	9.0	7.0	144.7%	--	8	--
2019	OAK	16/3	273	108	387	3	3.6	0	-7.0%	32	7	33	50%	19	23	1.9	41	36	292	0	88%	8.1	6.8	21.1%	11	74	15
2020	KC			7	24	0	3.4	0	-5.3%								5	4	28	0	80%	7.0		-0.9%			

Washington and Jalen Richard spent four years splitting the rotational carries behind Latavius Murray, then Marshawn Lynch, then Josh Jacobs. Washington went 54-215-2 (4.0 yards per carry) as a runner and caught 16 passes for 119 yards in three December starts when Jacobs was hurt last year. That's what replacement-level running back performance looks like when given lots of touches, folks. Washington is now in a crowded Chiefs backfield, where he will try to push past Darwin Thompson and whichever D. Williams wasn't awesome in the Super Bowl for a roster spot.

James White Height: 5-10   Weight: 205   College: Wisconsin   Draft: 2014/4 (130)   Born: 3-Feb-1992   Age: 28   Risk: Green

Year	Tm	G/GS	Snaps	Runs	Yds	TD	Yd/R	FUM	DVOA	Rk	DYAR	Rk	Suc%	Rk	BTkl	YafC	Pass	Rec	Yds	TD	C%	Yd/C	YAC	DVOA	Rk	DYAR	Rk
2017	NE	14/4	384	43	171	0	4.0	0	-9.3%	--	-1	--	51%	--	10	2.0	72	56	429	3	78%	7.7	6.1	6.4%	20	86	13
2018	NE	16/3	600	94	425	5	4.5	0	1.6%	--	42	--	47%	--	14	1.5	123	87	751	7	71%	8.6	7.6	13.5%	13	194	3
2019	NE	15/1	493	67	263	1	3.9	0	-9.0%	--	-1	--	42%	--	20	2.1	95	72	645	5	76%	9.0	7.4	14.8%	14	142	5
2020	NE			46	185	2	4.0	0	1.1%								53	42	356	2	79%	8.5		14.9%			

There is not much Bill Belichick loves more than a pass-catching specialist at running back. For the past five seasons, White has filled the role to near perfection. His role is taken to the extreme, too. Not once in the previous past five seasons has White received more carries than receptions (let alone targets). White especially shines on third and fourth downs, as should be the case for a truly elite pass-catching back. In each of the past three years, White has posted a DVOA rating on those downs higher than 14.8%. That figure has also risen in each of the past three seasons, topping out at 35.1% DVOA on 41 such targets in 2019. As well as he played last year and with no real competition being added to contest his spot, White will continue to be Belichick's quick-game star.

Jordan Wilkins Height: 6-1   Weight: 217   College: Mississippi   Draft: 2018/5 (169)   Born: 18-Jul-1994   Age: 26   Risk: Green

Year	Tm	G/GS	Snaps	Runs	Yds	TD	Yd/R	FUM	DVOA	Rk	DYAR	Rk	Suc%	Rk	BTkl	YafC	Pass	Rec	Yds	TD	C%	Yd/C	YAC	DVOA	Rk	DYAR	Rk
2018	IND	16/3	198	60	336	1	5.6	2	15.0%	--	61	--	58%	--	9	2.4	17	16	85	0	94%	5.3	6.6	-47.8%	--	-34	--
2019	IND	14/1	178	51	307	2	6.0	0	20.9%	--	64	--	57%	--	13	3.2	11	7	43	0	64%	6.1	4.6	-31.5%	--	-9	--
2020	IND			19	93	1	4.9	0	14.3%								4	4	29	0	100%	7.3		1.9%			

A 2018 draftee who has enjoyed a role as a situational back and occasional rushing-down sub for Marlon Mack, Wilkins has been highly efficient when called on as a rusher, but he has been bumped down the depth chart by the arrival of Jonathan Taylor. His path to playing time is more obstructed now than it was in the past two seasons, and those two seasons still amounted to an average of only four carries per game.

Damien Williams Height: 5-11   Weight: 224   College: Oklahoma   Draft: 2014/FA   Born: 3-Apr-1992   Age: 28   Risk: Yellow

Year	Tm	G/GS	Snaps	Runs	Yds	TD	Yd/R	FUM	DVOA	Rk	DYAR	Rk	Suc%	Rk	BTkl	YafC	Pass	Rec	Yds	TD	C%	Yd/C	YAC	DVOA	Rk	DYAR	Rk
2017	MIA	11/4	195	46	181	0	3.9	0	-22.7%	--	-25	--	28%	--	20	1.8	28	20	155	1	71%	7.8	7.7	12.2%	15	44	27
2018	KC	16/3	207	50	256	4	5.1	1	26.4%	--	79	--	62%	--	9	2.2	24	23	160	2	96%	7.0	9.3	33.9%	--	74	--
2019	KC	11/6	368	111	498	5	4.5	1	-6.8%	31	8	31	50%	18	40	3.2	37	30	213	2	81%	7.1	7.7	-3.7%	28	24	28
2020	KC			123	519	4	4.2	1	4.8%								43	33	262	2	77%	7.9		8.4%			

Williams went 46-196-4 (4.3 yards per carry) and 11-94-2 (8.6 yards per catch) in the postseason last year, with a near-MVP caliber performance (133 total yards, two touchdowns, 11 first downs rushing or receiving) in the Super Bowl. Those high-profile performances may have inflated perceptions of his importance to the Chiefs offense. Williams only cracked 20 total touches in one regular-season game last year and produced several stat-lines in the vicinity of nine carries for 8 yards. Andy Reid knows a gutsy committee back when he sees one and will rotate Williams with Clyde Edwards-Helaire and others instead of getting carried away with Williams' touches and targets. Fantasy gamers expecting weekly repeats of the Super Bowl are almost guaranteed to be disappointed.

Darrel Williams   Height: 5-11   Weight: 229   College: Louisiana State   Draft: 2018/FA   Born: 15-Apr-1995   Age: 25   Risk: N/A

Year	Tm	G/GS	Snaps	Runs	Yds	TD	Yd/R	FUM	DVOA	Rk	DYAR	Rk	Suc%	Rk	BTkl	YafC	Pass	Rec	Yds	TD	C%	Yd/C	YAC	DVOA	Rk	DYAR	Rk
2019	KC	12/0	199	41	141	3	3.4	1	-15.7%	--	-15	--	56%	--	7	1.3	19	15	167	1	79%	11.1	11.9	38.9%	--	57	--
2020	KC			0	0	0	0.0	0	0.0%								0	0	0	0	0%	0.0		0.0%			

The other "Da.Williams" in the Chiefs offense rushed nine times for 62 yards in Week 3 against the Ravens and had a 52-yard catch-and-scamper against the Texans, but struggled in most weeks to find a regular role in the Chiefs running back rotation before missing December and the playoffs with a hamstring injury. Williams was given trials as both a goal-line back (seven carries for 10 yards and three touchdowns inside the 10-yard line, with two plunge touchdowns against the Lions) and a third-down back (7-91-1 as a receiver on third downs) based on who else was available in the Chiefs backfield last year, but right now the Chiefs' running back depth chart is so packed that we don't even have a KUBIAK projection for him.

Jamaal Williams   Height: 6-0   Weight: 213   College: BYU   Draft: 2017/4 (134)   Born: 3-Apr-1995   Age: 25   Risk: Green

Year	Tm	G/GS	Snaps	Runs	Yds	TD	Yd/R	FUM	DVOA	Rk	DYAR	Rk	Suc%	Rk	BTkl	YafC	Pass	Rec	Yds	TD	C%	Yd/C	YAC	DVOA	Rk	DYAR	Rk
2017	GB	16/7	443	153	556	4	3.6	0	7.4%	12	108	12	48%	14	23	2.1	34	25	262	2	74%	10.5	10.2	29.9%	11	84	17
2018	GB	16/8	523	121	464	3	3.8	0	1.7%	22	52	25	45%	32	21	2.2	41	27	210	0	66%	7.8	8.5	-9.3%	34	11	33
2019	GB	14/2	385	107	460	1	4.3	0	-1.5%	21	31	26	53%	7	25	2.5	45	39	253	5	87%	6.5	7.2	27.4%	8	103	9
2020	GB			26	105	1	4.0	0	-1.5%								29	22	164	1	76%	7.5		-3.8%			

Williams does not dilly-dally with the ball in his hands. Per Next Gen Stats, Williams averaged just 2.55 seconds behind the line of scrimmage on his carries, the fastest back to the line in the league. Williams' primary skill is quickly finding and hitting a hole; it's what allows him to have a good success rate despite finishing with a negative rushing DVOA for the first time in his career. Williams will pick up what the offensive line blocks for him, but not much else. What might keep him both in the rotation and on the roster is his receiving chops, as Williams bounced back from a poor 2018. Williams led all running backs with 80 receiving DYAR in the red zone—a lack of explosiveness in space doesn't matter as much when you're catching the ball in the end zone to begin with.

Jonathan Williams   Height: 6-0   Weight: 217   College: Arkansas   Draft: 2016/5 (156)   Born: 2-Feb-1994   Age: 26   Risk: N/A

Year	Tm	G/GS	Snaps	Runs	Yds	TD	Yd/R	FUM	DVOA	Rk	DYAR	Rk	Suc%	Rk	BTkl	YafC	Pass	Rec	Yds	TD	C%	Yd/C	YAC	DVOA	Rk	DYAR	Rk
2018	2TM	3/0	18	3	0	0	0.0	0	-104.7%	--	-14	--	0%	--	0	0.7	1	1	1	0	100%	1.0	0.0	-138.8%	--	-7	--
2019	IND	9/1	101	49	235	1	4.8	0	2.0%	--	21	--	53%	--	18	3.7	5	5	59	0	100%	11.8	12.8	67.2%	--	22	--

A journeyman who has bounced around teams for years, Williams set career highs in yards and carries with the Colts in 2019 and even earned his first career start. However, almost all of that production came during late November and early December while Marlon Mack was hurt. Outside that period, he had only two snaps on offense and no carries or targets. Currently an unsigned free agent at press time.

T.J. Yeldon   Height: 6-1   Weight: 223   College: Alabama   Draft: 2015/2 (36)   Born: 2-Oct-1993   Age: 27   Risk: Green

Year	Tm	G/GS	Snaps	Runs	Yds	TD	Yd/R	FUM	DVOA	Rk	DYAR	Rk	Suc%	Rk	BTkl	YafC	Pass	Rec	Yds	TD	C%	Yd/C	YAC	DVOA	Rk	DYAR	Rk
2017	JAX	10/0	230	49	253	2	5.2	2	-6.7%	--	4	--	43%	--	13	2.3	41	30	224	0	73%	7.5	6.3	-9.9%	40	8	42
2018	JAX	14/5	507	104	414	1	4.0	1	-12.5%	39	-17	35	48%	25	19	2.5	79	55	487	4	71%	8.9	8.0	3.0%	24	76	17
2019	BUF	6/0	154	17	63	0	3.7	1	-11.4%	--	-2	--	53%	--	4	2.9	15	13	124	0	87%	9.5	9.2	8.8%	--	18	--
2020	BUF			25	98	1	3.9	0	-5.4%								10	8	58	0	80%	7.3		-0.6%			

If nothing else, Yeldon is firmly the No. 3 back in Buffalo. Devin Singletary will take the lead and rookie Zack Moss will likely assume the change-up role, but nobody past those two can really contest Yeldon for carries. Yeldon is an awkward runner in that he shows phenomenal balance, yet a stark lack of power; impressive side-to-side burst, yet very little speed to threaten explosive plays. What Yeldon lacks as a runner, however, he makes up for as a pass-catcher. In 2018, the last time Yeldon earned enough targets to qualify, he saw 72 targets from running back alignments, which was sixth-most in the league. He earned a solid 9.8% DVOA rating on those targets. Yeldon is not the best or flashiest back, but he covers enough of the bases and is a perfect No. 3 in a backfield such as Buffalo's.

Going Deep

Josh Adams, NYJ: After earning a fair amount of playing time in the Philadelphia Eagles' desolate running back rotation as a rookie in 2018 (120-511-3, -11.0% DVOA), Adams was relegated to practice squad duties for much of the 2019 season as a member of the New York Jets. Adams was pulled up to the active roster in early November, but only earned carries in two games, in both of which he handled exactly four carries for exactly 6 yards. A tall, bulky runner at 6-foot-2 and 225-pounds, Adams has neither the speed or flexibility to function well at his size and is not quite as well-balanced and tough as a back his size should be. It would be no surprise to see Adams back on the practice squad.

Rodney Anderson, CIN: Anderson's sad story contributed to Cincinnati's horrible summer of injuries. The Oklahoma star who put up 201 yards in the 2018 Rose Bowl fought his way back from a torn ACL to wow the team in camp and make a scintillating preseason debut, gaining 51 yards on just four catches. Then he blew out the same ACL again in the preseason finale (incredibly, his fourth season-ending injury in five years), making Rodney the Tyler Eifert of running backs. Anderson is by all accounts a great person and something of a Renaissance man, so his life after football should be replete, but he is rehabbing like mad for yet another crack at finishing a season without being carried off on a stretcher. As a producer his output will surely be limited at best, but as an inspiration he could be exemplary.

Eno Benjamin, ARI: The rookie seventh-round pick from Arizona State goes from being a workhorse in Tempe to the likely third-stringer in Glendale. A highly touted recruit coming out of high school, it was a surprise when Benjamin fell all the way to the seventh round in the draft; his five fumbles in 2019 may have been part of the reason why.

Brandon Bolden, NE: Somehow, some way, Bolden always finds himself taking snaps for the New England Patriots. Since 2012, Bolden has taken at least one carry for the Patriots in every season except for 2018, when he played for the Dolphins and handled all of eight carries for them. A short, thick running back, Bolden is best served as a short-yardage back and checkdown option in the passing game. Five of Bolden's 16 carries in 2019 were taken in the red zone, four of which he converted for a successful gain.

Devontae Booker, LV: Devontae Booker's yards from scrimmage dropped from 877 to 544 to 458 to 66 as the Broncos offensive talent level went from AAF-caliber to respectable over the last four seasons. That left Booker to go to the retirement home for replacement-level players. The Raiders have plenty of all-purpose back and kick return options, so there is no reason for them to give a 28-year-old a second look except that Jon Gruden and Mike Mayock obsessively collect veterans for unknown reasons.

Raymond Calais, TB: Calais posted the third-fastest 40-yard dash time (4.42s) among running backs at the NFL combine, but at 5-foot-8 and 188 pounds, he'll have to work to shake the track star label, which will be difficult given that he actually was a track star in high school. Though he rushed for 886 yards on just 117 carries last season at the University of Louisiana, the seventh-round draft pick's clearest path to securing a roster spot is as a kick returner. He's up to the task. He made the all-Sun Belt team as a specialist, averaging 28.5 yards on 19 returns. He'll have to beat out incumbent T.J. Logan.

Trenton Cannon, NYJ: Only a kickoff returner in 2019, Cannon made it through just five weeks of the season before being sidelined by a foot injury. As a rookie in 2018, Cannon managed a putrid 37% success rate on 38 carries. Though Cannon also caught 17 balls in limited action, his receiving skills were not enough to get him more playing time. Considering the Jets invested a few draft picks and free-agent signings to solve the running back position, one has to imagine Cannon's only role on the team will continue to be on special teams, if he remains on the active roster at all.

DeeJay Dallas, SEA: This Seahawks fourth-round pick was a committee back at Coral Gables, splitting time in the Miami backfield with Cam'ron Harris and current Seahawks teammate Travis Homer. He never rushed for even 700 yards in a season, and he followed that lack of production with a mediocre outing at the combine. BackCAST, as you can imagine, was not impressed, giving him a score of -28.9%. Dallas started at Miami as a wide receiver, and his hands may be his best asset—he caught 28 passes in college with only one drop. He did deal with fumbles at one point, but seems to have overcome that issue after working with a sports psychiatrist—he had four fumbles in the first nine games of 2018, but never fumbled again in 14 more games in a Hurricanes uniform. He also has experience returning both punts and kickoffs, taking a punt back for a house call against Pittsburgh in 2018. Dallas projects as a third-down back this season, battling Homer and Carlos Hyde for playing time behind Chris Carson as Rashaad Penny recovers from his torn ACL.

Mike Davis, CAR: By traditional measurements, Davis looked like an effective runner for the 2018 Seahawks, averaging 4.6 yards on a career-best 112 carries. But DVOA paints a darker picture of his value. Even in that best season, Davis peaked at a modest 9.0% rushing DVOA. He has been well below average in four other career seasons, and teams seem to believe the broader trend if his recent journeyman status is any indication. Davis may be the No. 2 back on the Panthers ahead of Reggie Bonnafon, Jordan Scarlett, and Rodney Smith, but Christian McCaffrey's dominance of the team's touches makes that distinction moot barring an injury.

Dalyn Dawkins, TEN: Brian Dawkins' nephew has been promoted and demoted from the Titans to the practice squad a grand total of nine times and signed to two futures contracts in two offseasons. At a listed 5-foot-7, 183 pounds, Dawkins typecasts well as a scatback and had 79 total receptions in four years at Colorado State and Purdue. With Dion Lewis on the go, the Titans would appear to have an empty slot at passing-down back. Until or unless that is filled externally, Dawkins would appear to be the best option for the job despite just 11 career NFL touches.

Kenneth Dixon, NYJ: Many moons ago, Dixon was a mid-round darling of the NFL draft and fantasy football community. A three-down back in theory, Dixon had the agility and balance to be a menace in space. Alas, knee injuries took control of Dixon's NFL career from the get-go, most recently forcing him to miss the entire 2019 season. In Dixon's last year of play in 2018, he finished with a 57% rushing success rate on 60 carries as Baltimore's third-leading rusher. Ideally, Dixon can slot in as an emergency third-down back behind Le'Veon Bell.

Trey Edmunds, PIT: Undrafted out of Maryland, Edmunds was pilfered by the Steelers from New Orleans as a practice-squad stash at last cuts in 2018. Last season he had a 12-carry, 73-yard game against Indianapolis in Week 9 that briefly inspired fantasy football hope. That hope dimmed as the Steelers drafted Anthony McFarland to add to the current room of James Conner, Benny Snell, and Jaylen Samuels. Edmunds is more likely to be fighting for a roster spot than carries at this point.

David Fluellen, FA: Last offseason, Fluellen made it a point to put on weight. "They are all encouraging me, especially the offensive line," he told Titans.com. "Those guys are big eaters, so they are making sure my weight is right so I can be ready to go." Used more as an H-back than a true runner, Fluellen contributes on special teams and has 27 offensive snaps in the last three seasons. If a pandemic weren't going around, we'd like to think someone would affectionately call him The Big Sick.

C.J. Ham, MIN: We generally don't do player comments for fullbacks, but most fullbacks aren't C.J. Ham. Ham and Kyle Juszczyk were the only two fullbacks to get enough pass targets to be ranked in receiving DYAR and DVOA, making him a larger part of Minnesota's offense than your average big thumper—24 of his 55 career touches came last season. Those targets got him just 6 DYAR and -10.1% DVOA, but they also got him a four-year deal worth up to $12.3 million. The Vikings had the second-most snaps with two running backs on the field last season, so expect 2020 to feature a steady diet of Ham.

Damien Harris, NE: From 2010 to 2019, 53 running backs were drafted in the second or third round; 49 of those players had more runs in their rookie season than the four carries Harris had last year, all of which came during the blowout win over the New York Jets on Monday night. With few changes or additions to the Patriots backfield, Harris' path toward snaps is neither clearer nor cloudier than before. Perhaps a year of development will be enough to push him into the rotation in 2020. He's known for his vision and power rather than agility and speed.

Dontrell Hilliard, CLE: Hilliard is one of just 10 running backs since 2000 to rush at least five times, catch at least five balls, return more than 100 yards of punts, and return more than 400 yards of kickoffs in a single season. The other nine: Chad Morton in 2000 and 2003; C.J. Spiller in 2010; Brian Mitchell in 2000 and 2001; Dexter McCluster in 2010; Jalen Richard in 2016; Leon Washington in 2007, 2008, 2010, and 2011; Tarik Cohen in 2017; Darren Sproles from each year of 2007 to 2012; and Brian Westbrook in 2003. It goes without saying that Hilliard is the least successful player on that list. It also speaks to how rare it is that the backup running back has this skill set when, if you remove the running back requirement, the number of qualifying seasons suddenly jumps to 59. Hilliard is no threat to Kareem Hunt or Nick Chubb but shall remain a useful NFL player in spite of that.

Jon Hilliman, NYG: It's hard to find playing time backing up Saquon Barkley and it's harder to find playing time backing up the guy backing up Saquon Barkley. Hilliman, a 2019 undrafted free agent from Rutgers, bounced off and on the practice squad and worked his way to 30 carries for just 91 yards and a -32.9% DVOA along with a mighty three receptions for 1 yard. Eleven of those carries and 38 of those yards came during an injury-forced start against the Patriots in Week 6. However, he didn't get on the field from Week 7 on.

Wes Hills, DET: Hills was a December call-up from the practice squad, scoring two touchdowns in his one appearance. That put him just one score behind Kerryon Johnson for the team lead in rushing touchdowns, which goes a long way to explaining why the Lions used both second- and fifth-round picks on running backs in the 2020 draft. Hills was a long shot to make the roster before the draft; now he'll have to scrap to keep his spot on the practice squad.

Buddy Howell, HOU: The recipient of some clock-killing touches as the Texans ran out a meaningless Week 17 game, Howell is a great special-teamer who has shown some burst in the preseason. Howell's upside is probably a stop-gap fill-in lead back à la Alfred Blue, and he had only 10 career receptions in 472 touches in college. Good depth and good on special teams, probably not any fantasy upside lurking here.

Jason Huntley, DET: After taking a more traditional back in the second round, the Lions doubled down on running backs in Round 5 with Huntley, a tiny (5-foot-9, 193-pound) scatback out of New Mexico State. Huntley averaged 7.1 yards per rush in 2019, is a potential receiving threat out of the slot, and returned three kicks for touchdowns in 2018. His size is a real black mark, however—he's a non-factor in pass protection, takes a lot of punishment, and fumbled five times a year ago. A gadget player more than a traditional back.

D'Ernest Johnson, CLE: "We were chasing the birds, really," Johnson said. "That's what we were doing. So we'd go out deep out there and look for birds. I didn't even know birds be out that far." That's straight from ClevelandBrowns.com's seminal D'Ernest Johnson article "D'Ernest Johnson's path to the NFL included time spent out to sea," which explains that after getting released by the Saints in 2018 training camp, Johnson worked out of Key West fishing for mahi-mahi. Johnson played in the Alliance of American Football and caught enough attention to get a job with the Browns, eventually challenging to become a returner/receiving back specialist. Johnson backed up Marlon Mack at South Florida for three years before getting his shot. He and Dontrell Hilliard are probably battling for one roster spot.

Bryce Love, WAS: Love looked like he might follow in the NFL footsteps of Stanford predecessor Christian McCaffrey when he ran for 2,118 yards and 19 touchdowns and finished as the Heisman runner-up as a junior in 2017. But since then, he has been limited by myriad injuries (including an ACL tear in his college finale) that dropped him into the fourth round of the draft and cost him the entire 2019 season. If Love can recover his health for 2020, he has some hope of an NFL role, because presumed Redskins starter Derrius Guice has had similar trouble with injuries and Adrian Peterson is 35 years old.

Ryan Nall, CHI: Nall is a big (239 pounds), physical back who was nicknamed "Wrecking Nall" at Oregon State, where he also showed some talent as a receiver (career 10.1 yards per reception). He had an impressive 54.2% BackCAST but went undrafted. Last year he got just two carries for eight yards, but an injury to David Montgomery might mean some real playing time because Tarik Cohen plays such a specialized role in the offense and wouldn't necessarily take over Montgomery's carries.

Qadree Ollison, ATL: A fifth-round draft pick last year, Ollison got more run than expected as a rookie after Falcons starter Devonta Freeman suffered a foot sprain. Ollison's production mirrored the expectations for a 232-pound power back. His rate of four touchdowns on 22 carries suggests a possible niche role as a goal-line back, but his -11.1% DVOA suggests he may never see a more expansive role on offense.

Devine Ozigbo, JAX: Ozigbo initially signed for the Saints as a 2019 undrafted free agent out of Nebraska, but was claimed by the Jaguars on waivers on September 1. Primarily a power back, he had nine carries and five targets on 29 offensive snaps for Jacksonville but played 27% of special teams snaps. That kicking game contribution may be what saves his roster spot; he appears to be fourth, at best, among the tailback options.

La'Mical Perine, NYJ: Somewhere between the skill sets of Le'Veon Bell and Frank Gore sits La'Mical Perine. As Florida's leading rusher and third-leading receiver last season, Perine echoes some of the do-it-all nature Bell provides as well as the hard-nosed running style of Gore. Perine was more of a battering ram in the run game and a safety net in the pass game than he was a dynamic weapon in either, though. That said, Perine is a fresh face on whom the team just spent a fourth-round pick, so it would be no surprise for him to slide right into the No. 3 role.

Troymaine Pope, LAC: Pope has bounced around various practice squads (Seahawks three separate times, Jets, Colts, Texans, Chargers) since 2016. All 10 of his 2019 carries (for 20 yards) came in the Week 3 30-10 victory over the Dolphins, when Melvin Gordon was still waiting by a phone that might as well have been deactivated and Justin Jackson was out with a calf injury. Pope stuck as a special-teamer for the rest of the year and could retain a role as a third running back; players who survive multiple trips to the practice squad across three years usually have traits that help them endear themselves to coaches.

C.J. Prosise, FA: In four NFL seasons, Prosise has played 25 games and missed 44 including the playoffs. From top to bottom, he has missed time with (deep inhale) shoulder, arm, hand, abdominal, groin, hip, hamstring, and ankle injuries, and has landed on season-ending injured reserve each of the past three years. He survived in the NFL long enough to see his rookie contract expire, but he's unlikely to sign a second deal.

Jordan Scarlett, CAR: Carolina drafted Scarlett out of Florida in last year's fifth round, and he got four carries as a rookie for nine yards. The Panthers don't really use backup running backs, and if they do use one, it will be Reggie Bonnafon or Mike Davis. Scarlett is a pure power back who doesn't do much as a receiver, and he can't even vulture goal-line carries; that's what fullback Alex Armah is for.

Wendell Smallwood, FA: Smallwood had a brief career renaissance in 2018 when injuries to Eagles starters Jay Ajayi and Darren Sproles promoted him to a role as the team's primary receiving back, and he produced a stellar 11.2% receiving DVOA. But even in that career-best season, Smallwood barely beat average as a rusher (6.5% DVOA), and he followed that with a return to his established standard as a negative contributor on his carries (-15.5%) in his lone season with the Redskins. He is currently a free agent, and his greater history of modest productivity suggests any future NFL opportunities will be as a backup or short-term fill-in.

Dwayne Washington, NO: Washington's biggest play of the 2019 season came on Monday Night Football in Week 15, when he deflected a Colts punt early in the first quarter. He also rushed eight times for 60 yards, but each of those carries came during the fourth quarter of blowout wins. He'll likely be limited to special teams again this season, especially after the Saints added Ty Montgomery to a backfield that already includes Alvin Kamara and Latavius Murray.

Kerrith Whyte, PIT: Boom/bust back with a killer athletic profile (4.37s 40-yard dash and a 42-inch vertical jump at his pro day), Whyte was the college teammate who sometimes siphoned action away from Buffalo's Devin Singletary. As far as rookie years for low-round picks go, not a bad one at all. Whyte was signed on to the Steelers active roster from Chicago's practice squad and saw consistent work in four of six games (25 carries for 122 yards, 18.1% DVOA) while also contributing on kick-offs. Whyte isn't exactly polished as a receiver just yet, but he's got the home-run speed that coaches love.

Trayveon Williams, CIN: By the time you read this, Williams will be a first-time father. Perhaps his newborn will get a chance to see Daddy actually touch the ball, something he didn't do in an injury-hit 2019 (though he was a special teams regular). A tough inside runner with excellent pass-blocking skills, Williams might have a place in the NFL if he can ever display his worth on the field. He was second in his draft class with a 57.3% BackCAST projection.

Jeffery Wilson, SF: Wilson's primary role was as a special-teamer, but during Tevin Coleman's injury-related absence, he was able to get on the field for some goal-line work, driving Matt Breida fantasy owners nuts by punching in four touchdowns in two games. Despite Breida's departure to Miami, Wilson still has an uphill climb to playing time in a crowded 49ers backfield featuring Coleman, Jerick McKinnon, and late-season starter Raheem Mostert.

Wide Receivers

In the following two sections we provide the last three years of statistics, as well as a 2020 KUBIAK projection, for every wide receiver and tight end who either played a significant role in 2019 or is expected to do so in 2020.

The first line contains biographical data—each player's name, height, weight, college, draft position, birth date, and age. Height and weight are the best data we could find; weight, of course, can fluctuate during the off-season. **Age** is very simple, the number of years between the player's birth year and 2020, but birth date is provided if you want to figure out exact age.

Draft position gives draft year and round, with the overall pick number with which the player was taken in parentheses. In the sample table, it says that Stefon Diggs was chosen in the 2015 NFL draft with the 146th overall pick in the fifth round. Undrafted free agents are listed as "FA" with the year they came into the league, even if they were only in training camp or on a practice squad.

To the far right of the first line is the player's Risk for fantasy football in 2020. As explained in the quarterback section, the standard is for players to be marked Green. Players with higher than normal risk are marked Yellow, and players with the highest risk are marked Red. Players who are most likely to match or surpass our forecast—primarily second-stringers with low projections but also some particularly strong breakout candidates—are marked Blue. Risk is not only based on age and injury probability, but how a player's projection compares to his recent performance as well as our confidence (or lack thereof) in his offensive teammates.

Next we give the last three years of player stats. Note that rushing stats are not included for receivers, but that any receiver with at least five carries last year will have his 2019 rushing stats appear in his team's chapter.

Next we give the last three years of player stats. First come games played and games started (**G/GS**). Games played represents the official NFL total and may include games in which a player appeared on special teams but did not play wide receiver or tight end. We also have a total of offensive **Snaps** for each season. Receptions (**Rec**) counts passes caught, while Passes (**Pass**) counts passes thrown to this player, complete or incomplete. Receiving yards (**Yds**) and touchdowns (**TD**) are the official NFL totals for each player. New this year is End Zone Targets (**EZ**), which counts how often a player was targeted while in the end zone.

Catch rate (**C%**) includes all passes listed in the official

play-by-play with the given player as the intended receiver, even if those passes were listed as "Thrown Away," "Batted Down," or "Quarterback Hit in Motion." The average NFL wide receiver has caught between 58% and 63% of passes over the last five seasons; tight ends caught between 64% and 68% of passes over the last five seasons.

Plus/minus (**+/-**) is a metric that we introduced in *Football Outsiders Almanac 2010*. It estimates how many passes a receiver caught compared to what an average receiver would have caught, given the location of those passes. Unlike simple catch rate, plus/minus does not consider passes listed as "Thrown Away," "Batted Down," "Quarterback Hit in Motion," or "Miscommunication." Player performance is compared to a historical baseline of how often a pass is caught based on the pass distance, the distance required for a first down, and whether it is on the left, middle, or right side of the field. Note that plus/minus is not scaled to a player's target total.

Drops (**Drop**) list the number of dropped passes according to charting from Sports Info Solutions. Our totals may differ from the drop totals kept by other organizations. Yards per catch (**Yd/C**) is a standard statistic.

Next you'll find each player's average depth of target (**aDOT**). This is the average distance beyond the line of scrimmage on all throws to this player, not counting passes listed as "Thrown Away," "Batted Down," or "Quarterback Hit in Motion." Long-ball specialists will rank high in this category (Mike Williams of the Chargers had a 17.7 aDOT, most of any qualifying wide receiver) while players who see a lot of passes on slots and screens will rank low (Miami's Albert Wilson was lowest at 5.3 aDOT).

Next we list yards after catch (**YAC**), rank (**Rk**) in yards after catch, and **YAC+.** YAC+ is similar to plus-minus; it estimates how much YAC a receiver gained compared to what we would have expected from an average receiver catching passes of similar length in similar down-and-distance situations. This is imperfect—we don't specifically mark what route a player runs, and obviously a go route will have more YAC than a comeback—but it does a fairly good job of telling you if this receiver gets more or less YAC than other receivers with similar usage patterns. We also give a total of broken tackles (**BTkl**) according to Sports Info Solutions charting.

The next four columns include our main advanced metrics for receiving: **DVOA** (Defense-Adjusted Value Over Average) and **DYAR** (Defense-Adjusted Yards Above Replace-

Stefon Diggs				Height: 6-0		Weight: 191		College: Maryland				Draft: 2015/5 (146)			Born: 29-Nov-1993			Age: 27		Risk: Green	
Year	Tm	G/GS	Snaps	Pass	Rec	Yds	TD	EZ	C%	+/-	Drop	Yd/C	aDOT	Rk	YAC	Rk	YAC+	BTkl	DVOA	Rk	DYAR	Rk	Use	Rk	Slot
2017	MIN	14/14	781	95	64	849	8	9	67%	+6.8	5	13.3	11.9	41	4.7	30	+0.3	9	24.7%	5	295	9	21.4%	25	40%
2018	MIN	15/14	874	149	102	1021	9	13	68%	+9.7	3	10.0	9.1	61	4.3	42	-0.7	24	-12.0%	66	8	64	26.7%	8	42%
2019	MIN	15/15	783	95	63	1130	6	8	67%	+9.0	4	17.9	15.6	9	4.7	28	+0.1	12	24.0%	7	272	10	22.9%	20	38%
2020	BUF			104	60	791	4		58%			13.2							-5.0%						

320

ment), along with the player's rank in both. These metrics compare every pass intended for a receiver and the results of that pass to a league-average baseline based on the game situations in which passes were thrown to that receiver. DVOA and DYAR are also adjusted based on the opposing defense and include Defensive Pass Interference yards on passes intended for that receiver. The methods used to compute these numbers are described in detail in the "Statistical Toolbox" introduction in the front of the book. The important distinction between them is that DVOA is a rate statistic, while DYAR is a cumulative statistic. Thus, a higher DVOA means more value per pass play, while a higher DYAR means more aggregate value over the entire season. Numbers without opponent adjustment (YAR and VOA) can be found on our website, FootballOutsiders.com.

To qualify for ranking in YAC, receiving DVOA, or receiving DYAR, a wide receiver must have had 50 passes thrown to him in that season. We ranked 81 wide receivers in 2019, 84 in 2018, and 86 in 2017. Tight ends qualify with 25 targets in a given season; we ranked 48 tight ends in 2019, 49 in 2018, and 51 in 2017.

The final columns measure each player's role in his offense. Usage rate (**Use**) measures each player's share of his team's targets, adjusted for games played. Green Bay's Davante Adams was targeted on 23.8% of his team's targets, but he also missed four games. Adjusting for those missing games gives Adams a usage rate of 31.7%, a more accurate assessment of his workload. The final column shows the percentage of each player's targets that came when he lined up in the **Slot** (or at tight end). Randall Cobb of the Dallas Cowboys saw 99% of

his targets from the slot, the highest rate in the league; the Seahawks' DK Metcalf had the lowest rate of slot targets at 17%. Tight ends have an additional column listing how frequently they were split **Wide**, from a high of 18% (the Rams' Gerald Everett) to a low of 0% (lots of guys).

"Slot" and "Wide" here are defined based on where the players are lined up in relation to the field, not based on where they are lined up in relation to other receivers. For example, if three wide receivers are in a trips bunch that is tight to the formation, all three receivers are marked as "slot" even if no other receiver is further out wide on that same side of the formation.

The italicized row of statistics for the 2020 season is our 2020 KUBIAK projection as explained further in the Statistical Toolbox at the front of the book. Be aware that projections account for the possibility of injury so workload projections may seem low for the top players.

It is difficult to accurately project statistics for a 162-game baseball season, but it is exponentially more difficult to accurately project statistics for a 16-game football season. Consider the listed projections not as a prediction of exact numbers, but as the mean of a range of possible performances. What's important is less the exact number of yards we project, and more which players are projected to improve or decline. Actual performance will vary from our projection less for veteran starters and more for rookies and third-stringers, for whom we must base our projections on much smaller career statistical samples. Touchdown numbers will vary more than yardage numbers. Players facing suspension or recovering from injury have those missed games taken into account.

Top 20 WR by DYAR (Total Value), 2019

Rank	Player	Team	DYAR
1	Michael Thomas	NO	538
2	Chris Godwin	TB	415
3	Amari Cooper	DAL	324
4	Tyler Lockett	SEA	317
5	Calvin Ridley	ATL	310
6	Mike Evans	TB	301
7	Julio Jones	ATL	299
8	DeVante Parker	MIA	283
9	Kenny Golladay	DET	279
10	Stefon Diggs	MIN	272
11	A.J. Brown	TEN	251
12	Tyreek Hill	KC	237
13	Terry McLaurin	WAS	237
14	Mike Williams	LAC	235
15	Michael Gallup	DAL	233
16	Keenan Allen	LAC	232
17	DeAndre Hopkins	HOU	224
18	Cooper Kupp	LAR	205
19	John Brown	BUF	205
20	Tyrell Williams	OAK	204

Minimum 50 passes.

Top 20 WR by DVOA (Value per Pass), 2019

Rank	Player	Team	DVOA
1	Chris Godwin	TB	32.8%
2	Calvin Ridley	ATL	30.6%
3	Tyrell Williams	OAK	27.2%
4	A.J. Brown	TEN	26.2%
5	Kenny Stills	HOU	24.7%
6	Tyler Lockett	SEA	24.6%
7	Stefon Diggs	MIN	24.0%
8	Michael Thomas	NO	23.9%
9	Tyreek Hill	KC	22.4%
10	Amari Cooper	DAL	22.3%
11	Mike Williams	LAC	20.6%
12	Terry McLaurin	WAS	18.9%
13	Kenny Golladay	DET	18.0%
14	Mike Evans	TB	18.0%
15	Breshad Perriman	TB	16.5%
16	Adam Thielen	MIN	15.4%
17	DeVante Parker	MIA	14.9%
18	Allen Lazard	GB	14.6%
19	Michael Gallup	DAL	13.5%
20	Marvin Jones	DET	11.8%

Minimum 50 passes.

A few low-round rookies, guys listed at seventh on the depth chart, and players who are listed as wide receivers but really only play special teams are briefly discussed at the end of the chapter in a section we call "Going Deep."

Two notes regarding our advanced metrics: We cannot yet fully separate the performance of a receiver from the performance of his quarterback. Be aware that one will affect the other. In addition, these statistics measure only passes thrown to a receiver, not performance on plays when he is not thrown the ball, such as blocking and drawing double teams.

Davante Adams Height: 6-1   Weight: 215   College: Fresno State   Draft: 2014/2 (53)   Born: 12/24/1992   Age: 28   Risk: Green

Year	Tm	G/GS	Snaps	Pass	Rec	Yds	TD	EZ	C%	+/-	Drop	Yd/C	aDOT	Rk	YAC	Rk	YAC+	BTkl	DVOA	Rk	DYAR	Rk	Use	Rk	Slot
2017	GB	14/14	776	117	74	885	10	10	63%	+4.7	6	12.0	10.1	59	4.5	35	+0.1	23	10.3%	25	215	15	23.8%	13	32%
2018	GB	15/15	954	169	111	1386	13	18	66%	+5.0	5	12.5	11.2	44	4.3	43	-0.5	10	6.1%	30	246	16	29.3%	4	32%
2019	GB	12/12	695	127	83	997	5	13	65%	+0.3	8	12.0	10.5	51	4.7	31	-0.1	5	0.6%	43	139	31	31.7%	2	48%
2020	GB			141	91	1187	7		65%			13.0							6.2%						

Adams is on a 34-game streak with at least four receptions, stretching all the way back to October of 2017. All other Packers have combined for 73 four-catch games in that time period, with none doing it more than a dozen times, so Adams' massive usage isn't anything new. It's worth noting that his DVOA dropped for the third consecutive year, and most of his other stats slipped in 2019 as well, but that's in large part due to being the focal point of the passing game to an almost ludicrous extent. Adams still had more than 100 DYAR on third and fourth downs, and the third-most DYAR in the league on go/fly routes; he knows a thing or two about big plays in the clutch.

Nelson Agholor Height: 6-0   Weight: 198   College: USC   Draft: 2015/1 (20)   Born: 24-May-1993   Age: 27   Risk: Green

Year	Tm	G/GS	Snaps	Pass	Rec	Yds	TD	EZ	C%	+/-	Drop	Yd/C	aDOT	Rk	YAC	Rk	YAC+	BTkl	DVOA	Rk	DYAR	Rk	Use	Rk	Slot
2017	PHI	16/10	813	95	62	768	8	7	65%	+2.1	8	12.4	10.6	54	4.9	24	-0.2	12	6.7%	33	141	32	16.8%	54	92%
2018	PHI	16/16	985	97	64	736	4	4	66%	+2.0	4	11.5	10.5	48	5.5	17	-0.2	11	-21.8%	77	-69	78	16.2%	56	78%
2019	PHI	11/10	706	69	39	363	3	6	57%	-1.4	4	9.3	11.8	41	3.4	62	-2.0	8	-35.0%	79	-123	80	16.7%	59	83%
2020	LV			5	3	39	0		60%			13.0							2.5%						

Agholor was called upon to be the Eagles' top receiver for much of last season and was categorically not up to the challenge. His two drops in the Week 2 loss to the Falcons (in an otherwise productive 8-107-0 game) became the stuff of viral video history when an Eagles fan took a break in the televised tale of how he rescued babies from a burning building to rip the receiver. ("We were catching them, unlike Agholor.") Things went downhill from there before Agholor joined the rest of the team's receivers and running backs on the injury list. Agholor was a hero of the Eagles' Super Bowl run but is best suited to a slot role in an offense full of RPOs and quick throws. He could be very effective in an offense in which Henry Ruggs and Tyreek Williams keep the safeties on their heels, allowing Agholor to work in space against the opponent's sixth- or seventh-best defensive back. But right now that role belongs to Hunter Renfrow.

Brandon Aiyuk Height: 6-0   Weight: 206   College: Arizona State   Draft: 2020/1 (25)   Born: 17-Mar-1998   Age: 22   Risk: Blue

Year	Tm	G/GS	Snaps	Pass	Rec	Yds	TD	EZ	C%	+/-	Drop	Yd/C	aDOT	Rk	YAC	Rk	YAC+	BTkl	DVOA	Rk	DYAR	Rk	Use	Rk	Slot
2020	SF			63	41	554	3		65%			13.5							7.9%						

Aiyuk spent two years in junior college before joining the Sun Devils for his junior season. In his first year in the desert, he was overshadowed by 2019 first-round receiver N'Keal Harry, but Aiyuk took advantage of Harry's departure to take over the leading role as a senior and put up a healthy 18.3 yards per reception. San Francisco thought highly enough of Aiyuk to trade up and go get him, and with impressive 2019 rookie Deebo Samuel recovering from a Jones fracture, Aiyuk may have a chance to really solidify himself in the San Francisco receiver pecking order. Our Playmaker Score projections were not a huge fan of Aiyuk's, but time will tell whether he can justify San Francisco's move up to pick him.

Keenan Allen

Height: 6-2   Weight: 211   College: California   Draft: 2013/3 (76)   Born: 27-Apr-1992   Age: 28   Risk: Green

Year	Tm	G/GS	Snaps	Pass	Rec	Yds	TD	EZ	C%	+/-	Drop	Yd/C	aDOT	Rk	YAC	Rk	YAC+	BTkl	DVOA	Rk	DYAR	Rk	Use	Rk	Slot
2017	LAC	16/15	897	159	102	1393	6	14	64%	+8.3	8	13.7	9.8	65	4.9	25	+0.7	16	16.5%	14	378	3	28.3%	6	54%
2018	LAC	16/14	794	136	97	1196	6	8	71%	+7.2	4	12.3	8.9	68	4.2	45	-0.3	9	18.1%	15	320	9	27.0%	7	64%
2019	LAC	16/16	944	149	104	1199	6	12	70%	+8.5	5	11.5	10.2	55	3.5	59	-0.7	11	7.3%	28	232	16	25.7%	10	63%
2020	LAC			121	74	890	6		61%			12.0							-2.5%						

Allen caught 41 passes on 65 targets for 392 yards (a meager 9.6 yards per catch) and one touchdown in the eight games from the Chargers' Week 4 win over the Dolphins to their Week 11 loss to the Chiefs. That averages out to about five catches for 49 yards on eight targets each week, hardly Allen-worthy production. A hamstring injury limited him for part of that span, but he and Philip Rivers also appeared to be stuck in a rut, with Allen running lots of short shake routes in the middle of the field and Rivers pump-faking and waiting for Allen to get open, often after making multiple adjustments at the line. It sure looked at times as if Rivers didn't trust the play call at all and just decided that he and Allen would figure something out on the fly. Allen's numbers rebounded a bit later in the season, but using him exclusively as a possession safety valve is like using a Mercedes E Class as a golf cart.

Geronimo Allison

Height: 6-3   Weight: 202   College: Illinois   Draft: 2016/FA   Born: 18-Jan-1994   Age: 26   Risk: Green

Year	Tm	G/GS	Snaps	Pass	Rec	Yds	TD	EZ	C%	+/-	Drop	Yd/C	aDOT	Rk	YAC	Rk	YAC+	BTkl	DVOA	Rk	DYAR	Rk	Use	Rk	Slot
2017	GB	15/2	343	39	23	253	0	3	59%	-1.6	4	11.0	7.9	--	5.2	--	+0.3	3	-15.0%	--	-8	--	7.7%	--	44%
2018	GB	5/4	241	30	20	303	2	3	67%	+1.3	2	15.2	12.9	--	5.3	--	+1.0	4	16.8%	--	66	--	15.4%	--	23%
2019	GB	16/6	654	55	34	287	2	6	62%	-3.1	7	8.4	7.8	74	3.2	66	-2.2	2	-35.8%	80	-98	79	10.1%	77	82%
2020	DET			11	7	81	1		64%			11.6							-4.7%						

After flashing in limited action in 2018, Allison was second from the bottom on our DVOA tables last season. He was, at least, a little less terrible in the slot, with his DVOA improving to -26.3%; that places him 26th out of the 29 qualified receivers who spent at least two-thirds of their time in the slot. Allison is now battling with Quintez Cephus for the fourth receiver role in Detroit and will have to show some of his pre-2018 hamstring injury form in order to earn even that much.

Danny Amendola

Height: 5-11   Weight: 185   College: Texas Tech   Draft: 2008/FA   Born: 2-Nov-1985   Age: 35   Risk: Yellow

Year	Tm	G/GS	Snaps	Pass	Rec	Yds	TD	EZ	C%	+/-	Drop	Yd/C	aDOT	Rk	YAC	Rk	YAC+	BTkl	DVOA	Rk	DYAR	Rk	Use	Rk	Slot
2017	NE	15/8	569	86	61	659	2	2	71%	+6.9	3	10.8	8.2	76	3.4	62	-0.9	6	8.4%	29	138	34	15.4%	61	97%
2018	MIA	15/15	682	79	59	575	1	1	75%	+5.1	1	9.7	7.4	78	3.9	53	-1.3	2	-6.2%	55	38	55	19.1%	36	91%
2019	DET	15/10	656	97	62	678	1	4	64%	-2.2	6	10.9	8.9	66	3.3	64	-0.9	6	-10.2%	64	18	64	18.6%	47	88%
2020	DET			71	47	543	4		66%			11.6							4.1%						

Amendola with Matthew Stafford: 43 DYAR, 0.3% DVOA. Amendola without Stafford: -25 DYAR, -19.0% DVOA. Amendola's season-long numbers were down, but that's simply an issue of quarterback quality; his performance with a healthy quarterback mirrored his high points in the middle of 2018 before he got hurt. If both he and his quarterback manage to stay healthy for a full season, Amendola could still be a useful player at age 35. You should expect his targets to drop off, however; his 97 targets in 2019 were his highest total since 2012, and a healthy T.J. Hockenson could end up eating away at some of those short outs that Amendola typically racks up.

Robby Anderson

Height: 6-3   Weight: 190   College: Temple   Draft: 2016/FA   Born: 9-May-1993   Age: 27   Risk: Green

Year	Tm	G/GS	Snaps	Pass	Rec	Yds	TD	EZ	C%	+/-	Drop	Yd/C	aDOT	Rk	YAC	Rk	YAC+	BTkl	DVOA	Rk	DYAR	Rk	Use	Rk	Slot
2017	NYJ	16/15	812	116	63	941	7	15	56%	-3.4	7	14.9	12.9	34	4.4	38	-0.3	7	-0.1%	47	113	41	23.1%	15	33%
2018	NYJ	14/9	682	94	50	752	6	14	53%	+0.3	1	15.0	16.4	4	3.6	61	-0.6	3	-11.8%	65	6	66	21.2%	28	32%
2019	NYJ	16/15	944	96	52	779	5	10	54%	-2.3	2	15.0	15.6	10	3.7	53	-0.8	4	-4.2%	53	66	52	20.0%	39	21%
2020	CAR			92	54	815	6		59%			15.1							4.0%						

The optimism that Anderson could ride the momentum of his 2018 December (384 yards, three touchdowns, and a 6.4% DVOA) and Sam Darnold's Year 2 improvements to a breakout 2019 season were quickly dashed when Darnold developed mono and missed a month at the start of the year. Still, it's not fair to hang Anderson's production plateau entirely on Darnold's health. Anderson had similar -4.0% and -5.7% DVOA rates with and without Darnold in 2019; his better traditional statistics were pretty much all a result of a greater volume of targets in Darnold's healthy weeks. Now 27 years old, the four-year veteran Anderson has a dwindling chance for a full breakout. That's especially true now that he has joined his former Temple head coach Matt Rhule in Carolina, where quarterback Teddy Bridgewater has avoided the deep attempts that are Anderson's specialty like the plague.

JJ Arcega-Whiteside

Height: 6-2   Weight: 225   College: Stanford   Draft: 2019/2 (57)   Born: 31-Dec-1996   Age: 24   Risk: Blue

Year	Tm	G/GS	Snaps	Pass	Rec	Yds	TD	EZ	C%	+/-	Drop	Yd/C	aDOT	Rk	YAC	Rk	YAC+	BTkl	DVOA	Rk	DYAR	Rk	Use	Rk	Slot
2019	PHI	16/5	492	22	10	169	1	3	45%	-1.0	1	16.9	17.8	--	1.6	--	-2.3	0	-12.3%	--	1	--	3.6%	--	41%
2020	PHI			26	14	184	1		54%			13.1							-12.0%						

Arcega-Whiteside's rookie year was a disappointment, but that's at least in part due to the multiple lower-body injuries he had to fight through the entire way; he was never truly healthy after September. Still, injured or not, JJAW was at least active for all 16 games, making his 10 catches for 169 yards a truly nightmarish number for a second-round pick. Other high draftees have floundered due to injury or being unable to make the active roster, but only one other rookie this millennium—Michael Jenkins in 2004—was drafted in the first two rounds, played a full season, and still had 10 or fewer receptions. JJAW flashed enough in preseason for there to still be some hope that he turns things around, but the Eagles' heavy investment in the receiver position this offseason may limit his opportunities.

Cole Beasley

Height: 5-8   Weight: 174   College: Southern Methodist   Draft: 2012/FA   Born: 26-Apr-1989   Age: 31   Risk: Green

Year	Tm	G/GS	Snaps	Pass	Rec	Yds	TD	EZ	C%	+/-	Drop	Yd/C	aDOT	Rk	YAC	Rk	YAC+	BTkl	DVOA	Rk	DYAR	Rk	Use	Rk	Slot
2017	DAL	15/4	576	63	36	314	4	3	57%	-1.3	2	8.7	7.9	79	3.4	60	-0.4	1	-16.9%	74	-22	73	14.0%	69	88%
2018	DAL	16/4	713	87	65	672	3	5	75%	+5.1	2	10.3	7.5	77	3.3	71	-1.1	5	2.1%	38	100	41	16.9%	50	89%
2019	BUF	15/10	747	106	67	778	6	2	63%	-2.9	6	11.6	8.4	68	5.0	21	+0.8	4	1.3%	41	112	37	23.3%	19	89%
2020	BUF			69	46	491	3		67%			10.7							0.2%						

If there were any one player to define what a true, full-time slot receiver looks like, it just might be Cole Beasley. Only two players in the entire league earned a higher percentage of their targets from the slot in each of the last three seasons than Beasley: Cooper Kupp and Danny Amendola. Beasley has not seen fewer than 88% of his targets from the slot in any of the past four seasons. In his first year with Buffalo, however, Beasley's role from the slot changed a bit. Beasley hit his highest marks in usage (23.3%) and average depth of target (8.4) since entering the league in 2015, signaling that he was used as more of an intermediate weapon than purely a safety blanket underneath. With Stefon Diggs now added to the lineup to pull some attention away from the middle of the field, Beasley could be set up for a career year.

Odell Beckham

Height: 5-11   Weight: 198   College: Louisiana State   Draft: 2014/1 (12)   Born: 5-Nov-1992   Age: 28   Risk: Green

Year	Tm	G/GS	Snaps	Pass	Rec	Yds	TD	EZ	C%	+/-	Drop	Yd/C	aDOT	Rk	YAC	Rk	YAC+	BTkl	DVOA	Rk	DYAR	Rk	Use	Rk	Slot
2017	NYG	4/2	212	41	25	302	3	4	61%	+0.3	6	12.1	12.9	--	2.6	--	-1.5	4	3.5%	--	57	--	28.3%	--	9%
2018	NYG	12/12	716	124	77	1052	6	21	62%	+1.7	3	13.7	12.2	30	4.1	50	-0.8	18	2.5%	37	151	27	29.5%	3	44%
2019	CLE	16/15	1017	133	74	1035	4	13	56%	-5.5	9	14.0	13.2	27	4.4	38	-0.3	8	-5.4%	56	79	46	26.6%	6	30%
2020	CLE			110	63	877	6		57%			13.9							-3.0%						

While the system around him crumbled, it's also fair to say that Beckham's hernia injury devastated his season. Beckham looked downright slow last season, and it didn't ever feel like he could push into his breaks the same way he could when he was in New York. Where that leaves him for 2020 is anyone's guess—Beckham's the kind of pick where if you nail it in the third round you win your fantasy football league. However, if a second straight year of this kind of play comes to pass, Beckham will transition from asset to liability, and the hot take columns about how Dave Gettleman bailed on him at just the right time will propagate the portion of the media that believes in body language and boat trips as major sections of a player's story. It's worth noting that Stefon Diggs only had 94 targets in Kevin Stefanski's offense last year. The Vikings were kind of a game-script outlier, but Beckham may have a few targets shaved off his usual totals as well if that kind of distribution continues.

Kendrick Bourne

Height: 6-1 Weight: 203 College: Eastern Washington Draft: 2017/FA Born: 4-Aug-1995 Age: 25 Risk: Green

Year	Tm	G/GS	Snaps	Pass	Rec	Yds	TD	EZ	C%	+/-	Drop	Yd/C	aDOT	Rk	YAC	Rk	YAC+	BTkl	DVOA	Rk	DYAR	Rk	Use	Rk	Slot
2017	SF	11/0	283	34	16	257	0	5	47%	-1.0	1	16.1	11.0	--	7.1	--	+2.7	3	-9.7%	--	8	--	8.2%	--	48%
2018	SF	16/8	606	67	42	487	4	3	63%	+0.5	4	11.6	9.0	67	3.5	65	-0.4	4	-4.5%	51	42	52	12.8%	74	52%
2019	SF	16/0	475	44	30	358	5	5	68%	+0.1	3	11.9	9.3	--	4.1	--	+0.3	6	25.7%	--	130	--	9.4%	--	78%
2020	SF			34	21	272	2		62%			13.0							1.6%						

Bourne took advantage of rookie Jalen Hurd's injury and second-year pro Dante Pettis' inability to live up to expectations in order to play almost half the team's snaps. This still represented a step back for the former undrafted free agent, but Bourne's experience in head coach Kyle Shanahan's system helped him stay on the field ahead of some of his more highly drafted peers. While Bourne did not have the same starting role as he did in 2018, he took on a much larger role on special teams and ended up receiving a second-round tender in restricted free agency, suggesting that San Francisco definitely sees him as a valuable part of the team in 2020.

Tyler Boyd

Height: 6-2 Weight: 203 College: Pittsburgh Draft: 2016/2 (55) Born: 15-Nov-1994 Age: 26 Risk: Green

Year	Tm	G/GS	Snaps	Pass	Rec	Yds	TD	EZ	C%	+/-	Drop	Yd/C	aDOT	Rk	YAC	Rk	YAC+	BTkl	DVOA	Rk	DYAR	Rk	Use	Rk	Slot
2017	CIN	10/1	307	32	22	225	2	1	69%	+1.2	2	10.2	6.9	--	4.1	--	-0.5	1	19.5%	--	76	--	10.3%	--	97%
2018	CIN	14/14	773	108	76	1028	7	4	70%	+7.4	6	13.5	9.8	55	5.5	17	+0.6	5	24.1%	4	305	12	22.9%	21	82%
2019	CIN	16/15	1001	148	90	1046	5	3	61%	-3.4	5	11.6	9.8	62	3.9	48	-0.9	16	-12.4%	68	3	67	25.2%	12	77%
2020	CIN			102	67	782	4		66%			11.7							-0.1%						

If you look at Cincinnati's wideout performance by down splits, there are exactly two in positive DVOA. One is Boyd's 3.7% on third/fourth downs (45 targets), which, in the context of the Bengals' passing horror show, is something of a miracle. Boyd was also the only Bengals pass-catcher with more than two targets to post a positive red zone DVOA (15.4%). Boyd is one of the few Bengals whose 2020 projection doesn't come with high injury risk or caveats about "if this or that happens." He's rock-solid, and should only be better after a quarterback upgrade.

Miles Boykin

Height: 6-4 Weight: 220 College: Notre Dame Draft: 2019/3 (93) Born: 12-Oct-1996 Age: 24 Risk: Green

Year	Tm	G/GS	Snaps	Pass	Rec	Yds	TD	EZ	C%	+/-	Drop	Yd/C	aDOT	Rk	YAC	Rk	YAC+	BTkl	DVOA	Rk	DYAR	Rk	Use	Rk	Slot
2019	BAL	16/11	433	22	13	198	3	5	59%	+2.0	1	15.2	17.2	--	0.9	--	-2.3	0	16.2%	--	50	--	5.2%	--	23%
2020	BAL			54	32	444	4		59%			13.9							0.6%						

Boykin, a third-round pick from Notre Dame a year ago, caught a touchdown pass in his debut for the Ravens, then turned to blocking as the team threw the ball less and less. He shined knocking defensive backs around, but would naturally prefer to catch passes in front of and behind them. All the physical traits that made Boykin a Day 2 draft choice—6-foot-4, 200-pound pound frame, strong hands—remain, but his experience as a professional route-runner necessarily lagged with a lack of rookie reps. Should Baltimore open up its passing attack in 2020, Boykin will be a major part of it.

A.J. Brown

Height: 6-0 Weight: 226 College: Mississippi Draft: 2019/2 (51) Born: 30-Jun-1997 Age: 23 Risk: Green

Year	Tm	G/GS	Snaps	Pass	Rec	Yds	TD	EZ	C%	+/-	Drop	Yd/C	aDOT	Rk	YAC	Rk	YAC+	BTkl	DVOA	Rk	DYAR	Rk	Use	Rk	Slot
2019	TEN	16/11	695	84	52	1051	8	5	62%	+0.8	2	20.2	13.2	26	8.9	1	+4.4	20	26.2%	4	251	11	19.4%	43	40%
2020	TEN			94	57	939	5		61%			16.5							4.6%						

It's early, and we don't want to throw too much on anyone for fear of Michael Clayton-ing them, but Brown's rookie season is a hell of a lot for the Titans to build on. He played outside a vast majority of the time, defeated press coverage often, and was extremely dynamic in the open field when the Titans schemed him there with play-action passes. Brown had the highest YAC+ (yards after catch over expectation) of any qualifying receiver we've measured since 2006. He blew previous records away: Greg Jennings was the only receiver who had ever put up a mark over +3.0 with more than 75 targets. The only area where Brown seemed to have struggles was on the deeper end of the route spectrum—and what he did to make up for the fact that he wasn't winning those routes decisively was simply to box out corners and make highlight-reel catches all season anyway. A lot of the shine went to Ryan Tannehill and Derrick Henry, but don't overlook just how important Brown's phenomenal rookie year was in creating Tennessee's offensive explosion.

Antonio Brown   Height: 5-10   Weight: 185   College: Central Michigan   Draft: 2010/6 (195)   Born: 10-Jul-1988   Age: 32   Risk: N/A

Year	Tm	G/GS	Snaps	Pass	Rec	Yds	TD	EZ	C%	+/-	Drop	Yd/C	aDOT	Rk	YAC	Rk	YAC+	BTkl	DVOA	Rk	DYAR	Rk	Use	Rk	Slot
2017	PIT	14/14	888	163	101	1533	9	19	62%	+12.0	6	15.2	14.3	17	4.8	27	+0.1	29	20.1%	11	430	1	32.3%	2	21%
2018	PIT	15/15	998	168	104	1297	15	24	62%	-4.2	2	12.5	11.1	46	4.7	34	-0.3	17	1.7%	41	191	19	26.4%	10	38%
2019	NE	1/0	24	8	4	56	1	4	50%	-1.0	0	14.0	11.5	--	1.8	--	-0.9	0	-14.0%	--	-1	--	21.3%	--	50%

For the moment, Brown is without a contract, but as unpredictable as the past 18 months have been with regards to his playing status, there is no telling when his next deal may come. Perhaps the unique preparation restrictions of this season will lend to a team bringing in Brown's talent out of desperation. The last time Brown played a full season in 2018, he led the league in touchdowns after having led the league in receiving yards the season before. From 2014 to 2018, Brown earned the receiving DYAR crown twice and never fell below 19th. Chances are Brown has not suddenly lost the talent that made him one of the best. It is just a matter of whether or not any team wants to deal with the backlash and headache that comes with him.

John Brown   Height: 5-11   Weight: 179   College: Pittsburg St. (KS)   Draft: 2014/3 (91)   Born: 4-Mar-1990   Age: 30   Risk: Yellow

Year	Tm	G/GS	Snaps	Pass	Rec	Yds	TD	EZ	C%	+/-	Drop	Yd/C	aDOT	Rk	YAC	Rk	YAC+	BTkl	DVOA	Rk	DYAR	Rk	Use	Rk	Slot
2017	ARI	10/5	491	55	21	299	3	7	38%	-6.4	2	14.2	17.0	3	2.8	73	-0.8	1	-24.4%	83	-51	83	15.3%	62	39%
2018	BAL	16/15	757	97	42	715	5	15	43%	-11.2	6	17.0	16.9	2	3.8	56	-0.5	1	-12.2%	67	4	67	18.1%	42	51%
2019	BUF	15/15	934	115	72	1060	6	5	63%	+4.6	5	14.7	14.6	12	3.0	73	-1.2	13	11.0%	23	205	19	25.0%	14	34%
2020	BUF			94	54	806	5		57%			14.9							-1.1%						

Brown had been cast almost exclusively as a deep threat up until last season. While he very much is one, Brown had arguably the best year of his career in 2019 while catching passes from one of the worst deep passers in the league. Rather than fall by the wayside, which would not have been much of a surprise given his poor 2018 season in Baltimore, Brown found success as an intermediate threat. Nearly half of his targets were in the middle of the field, whereas just 37% of his targets were in that area in his breakout 2015 season. In the previous three seasons—the worst three seasons by DYAR of Brown's career, excluding his rookie year—44% to 52% of Brown's targets came in the middle of the field. Brown was particularly effective on first down, when every passing concept should be available to the offense. His 43 targets and 28.3% DVOA on first-down targets were each the highest marks on the team, while his 74% catch rate on first down was the best mark on the team among players with at least 15 such targets. While the addition of Stefon Diggs may relieve Brown of some of his duties as an intermediate-area receiver, it is a blessing for Josh Allen that Brown established himself so well as an extra intermediate option while still posing a dangerous deep threat.

Marquise Brown   Height: 5-9   Weight: 170   College: Oklahoma   Draft: 2019/1 (25)   Born: 4-Jun-1997   Age: 23   Risk: Green

Year	Tm	G/GS	Snaps	Pass	Rec	Yds	TD	EZ	C%	+/-	Drop	Yd/C	aDOT	Rk	YAC	Rk	YAC+	BTkl	DVOA	Rk	DYAR	Rk	Use	Rk	Slot
2019	BAL	14/11	571	71	46	584	7	10	65%	+1.3	3	12.7	12.1	37	4.9	22	-0.4	6	4.2%	35	98	42	19.6%	41	63%
2020	BAL			82	50	651	5		61%			13.0							0.7%						

A rather convincing case can be made that after just one good but hardly remarkable season, "Hollywood" is already the best wideout the Ravens have ever drafted. (OK, Torrey Smith was good, so was Brandon Stokley, though both were gone after their rookie deals in Baltimore.) That's more of an indictment of the team's ability to pick receivers than it is a compliment to Brown, but 'Wood did explode onto the scene with a 147-yard, two-touchdown debut before slowing considerably as the season went on. Brown's ability to stretch defenses is a unique one in Baltimore, though his diminutive size meant he saw less action as a blocker, thus tipping opponents when he was on the field that a pass was likely coming. On another team Brown could be a superstar in the making. On the Ravens he is more of a one-trick pony, if an important one.

Damiere Byrd

Height: 5-9   Weight: 180   College: South Carolina   Draft: 2015/FA   Born: 27-Jan-1993   Age: 27   Risk: Green

Year	Tm	G/GS	Snaps	Pass	Rec	Yds	TD	EZ	C%	+/-	Drop	Yd/C	aDOT	Rk	YAC	Rk	YAC+	BTkl	DVOA	Rk	DYAR	Rk	Use	Rk	Slot
2017	CAR	8/3	191	17	10	105	2	2	59%	-0.9	1	10.5	8.4	--	6.1	--	+1.8	1	-13.0%	--	0	--	6.8%	--	53%
2018	CAR	8/0	44	2	1	8	0	0	50%	-0.1	0	8.0	12.5	--	1.0	--	-2.9	0	-25.3%	--	-2	--	0.7%	--	50%
2019	ARI	11/3	461	46	32	359	1	1	70%	+2.3	0	11.2	10.0	--	4.7	--	-0.4	7	-4.6%	--	30	--	12.7%	--	11%
2020	NE			20	12	161	1		60%			13.4							2.4%						

Arizona's offense was so desperate for talent last season that Damiere Byrd caught nearly three times as many passes in 2019 alone than he did in his previous three seasons with the Carolina Panthers. Byrd was not just feasting on Arizona's lack of talent, though. Though his first-down numbers were middling, Byrd earned positive DVOA marks on second down as well as third-/fourth-down targets, seeing about equal volume of targets in all three splits. Of the five wide receivers with at least 20 targets on the team, only Byrd and Larry Fitzgerald showed positive DVOA in two of the three down-related splits. Byrd is a deep threat at heart, though, and the Arizona offense did not allow him to express that as often as one might think. In New England, Byrd may be able to pick up where Phillip Dorsett left off.

Parris Campbell

Height: 6-0   Weight: 205   College: Ohio State   Draft: 2019/2 (59)   Born: 16-Jul-1997   Age: 23   Risk: Yellow

Year	Tm	G/GS	Snaps	Pass	Rec	Yds	TD	EZ	C%	+/-	Drop	Yd/C	aDOT	Rk	YAC	Rk	YAC+	BTkl	DVOA	Rk	DYAR	Rk	Use	Rk	Slot
2019	IND	7/3	200	24	18	127	1	1	75%	+1.3	1	7.1	8.1	--	5.9	--	-0.5	5	-73.4%	--	-104	--	11.0%	--	63%
2020	IND			58	39	415	3		67%			10.6							0.1%						

During his rookie season, Parris Campbell averaged only 7.1 yards per catch while catching 75% of his passes. That puts him in rare company: per Pro Football Reference, only two wide receivers have ever averaged under 8.0 yards per catch on at least 20 targets with such a high catch rate. The other was Ryan Switzer, who averaged 7.0 yards per catch with the 2018 Steelers. Both players, unsurprisingly, had very poor receiving DVOA. At that rate, with enough targets to qualify, Campbell would have endangered Tavon Austin's record for worst receiving DYAR on record. He fumbled twice on just 18 receptions, and those fumbles came at the end of two of his three longest plays. Campbell has elite speed and ridiculous agility, but he is underdeveloped as a route-runner and doesn't yet have a clear position in the regular offense. Campbell should see a larger role as the Colts' slot receiver this season, but Michael Pittman does knock him down a spot on the depth chart.

DJ Chark

Height: 6-4   Weight: 198   College: Louisiana State   Draft: 2018/2 (61)   Born: 23-Sep-1996   Age: 24   Risk: Green

Year	Tm	G/GS	Snaps	Pass	Rec	Yds	TD	EZ	C%	+/-	Drop	Yd/C	aDOT	Rk	YAC	Rk	YAC+	BTkl	DVOA	Rk	DYAR	Rk	Use	Rk	Slot
2018	JAX	11/0	291	32	14	174	0	3	44%	-4.7	2	12.4	10.3	--	3.2	--	-1.5	1	-47.4%	--	-90	--	8.8%	--	34%
2019	JAX	15/14	864	118	73	1008	8	12	62%	+1.8	4	13.8	11.9	39	4.3	39	-0.3	14	1.9%	38	134	32	22.8%	21	50%
2020	JAX			103	62	875	6		60%			14.1							-0.2%						

Chark went directly from barely-used rookie to No. 1 target in his second year, and the 23-year-old looked immediately like he belonged in that role. Middling advanced statistics belie a player who was productive at every spot—Chark had over 500 yards from both the slot and outside receiver positions—and who could run the entire route tree as a top target. His first career 1,000-yard season continued the Jaguars' reputation for developing second-round wideouts, and fully a quarter of Gardner Minshew's passing yards came targeting Chark. He already looks like one of the best young receivers in the league, and as close to a sure thing as this Jaguars offense possesses.

Chase Claypool

Height: 6-4   Weight: 229   College: Notre Dame   Draft: 2020/2 (49)   Born: 7-Jul-1998   Age: 22   Risk: Green

Year	Tm	G/GS	Snaps	Pass	Rec	Yds	TD	EZ	C%	+/-	Drop	Yd/C	aDOT	Rk	YAC	Rk	YAC+	BTkl	DVOA	Rk	DYAR	Rk	Use	Rk	Slot
2020	PIT			29	18	254	1		62%			14.1							3.2%						

The Notre Dame receiver was talked up as a potential tight end convert because he is huge for a wideout, but he didn't live up to that standard of physical domination in college and his releases and routes have all the subtlety of a Chuck Norris movie right now. The Steelers have been wildly successful at drafting wideouts, so we tend to give them a little benefit of the doubt. Kevin Colbert told Pro Football Talk in May that Claypool is "a 6-foot-4, 230-pound receiver that can get deep, and quite honestly we didn't have that threat last year. We didn't have that tall receiver that can just outrun coverage. We've always had that in the past with Nate Washington, Mike Wallace, or Martavis Bryant. Again, that was very attractive to us in the long term. In the short term we know Chase will be a special teams contributor right out of the gate." With no development, Claypool is probably looking at a Devin Funchess sort of career. But from that line about "short-term" in Colbert's quote, it's clear the Steelers think they can make more out of him.

Randall Cobb

Randall Cobb			Height: 5-10		Weight: 192		College: Kentucky				Draft: 2011/2 (64)			Born: 22-Aug-1990			Age: 30			Risk: Yellow				

Year	Tm	G/GS	Snaps	Pass	Rec	Yds	TD	EZ	C%	+/-	Drop	Yd/C	aDOT	Rk	YAC	Rk	YAC+	BTkl	DVOA	Rk	DYAR	Rk	Use	Rk	Slot
2017	GB	15/14	742	93	66	653	4	3	72%	+4.1	1	9.9	5.8	86	6.2	8	+0.4	9	-6.0%	62	48	61	17.7%	47	76%
2018	GB	9/6	466	61	38	383	2	4	62%	-3.3	4	10.1	8.4	71	6.2	6	+0.1	5	-22.1%	78	-45	76	17.7%	46	90%
2019	DAL	15/6	727	83	55	828	3	4	66%	+0.9	10	15.1	9.9	61	6.0	7	+1.5	16	5.4%	33	119	35	15.2%	63	98%
2020	HOU			61	42	548	3		69%			13.0							12.2%						

When you look at Randall Cobb's numbers last season, and you see some of the previous context in that box, you start to understand how a team could be fooled into thinking he's a good slot receiver. The problem lies in the context. Cobb's DVOA looks solid, but it was the lowest of any non-Jason Witten core receiver in the Dallas offense. Per NFL Next Gen Stats, Cobb was given more cushion than any receiver the Cowboys had last season, at an average of 6.2 yards. He was handily out-produced by every other Packers receiver that got full-time work in 2018. He was empirically less effective than any non-Lance Kendricks receiver that got playing time with the Packers in 2017. Cobb has missed games in every season since 2014. With the Texans, who desperately need an underneath receiver who can win one-on-one with the absence of DeAndre Hopkins, Cobb is going to be forecast into a role that he hasn't really filled since 2016, if we're being honest with ourselves, and he's going to have to replace literally the league's best receiver at dealing with tight coverage. This is going to create some pretty fantasy football lines, but the real-life fit has a lot of downside potential.

Keelan Cole

Keelan Cole			Height: 6-1		Weight: 194		College: Kentucky Wesleyan				Draft: 2017/FA			Born: 20-Apr-1993			Age: 27			Risk: Green			

Year	Tm	G/GS	Snaps	Pass	Rec	Yds	TD	EZ	C%	+/-	Drop	Yd/C	aDOT	Rk	YAC	Rk	YAC+	BTkl	DVOA	Rk	DYAR	Rk	Use	Rk	Slot
2017	JAX	16/6	755	83	42	748	3	6	51%	-1.9	6	17.8	13.3	30	7.0	3	+2.5	6	-7.4%	66	35	65	16.0%	55	54%
2018	JAX	16/11	687	70	38	491	1	4	54%	-4.8	8	12.9	10.2	51	3.6	60	-0.7	1	-21.3%	76	-48	77	13.5%	67	51%
2019	JAX	16/1	380	35	24	361	3	2	69%	+2.4	1	15.0	11.0	--	4.1	--	-0.7	1	24.8%	--	105	--	6.3%	--	67%
2020	JAX			16	10	133	1		63%			13.3							-0.4%						

After a surprise rookie campaign that promised much, Cole's usage and production has decreased in each subsequent season. The emergence of Dede Westbrook in 2018 pushed Cole out of his favored slot role, forcing him to stake a claim on the outside. He lost his starting job midway through 2018 and has since been effectively the team's fourth receiver. That has occasionally been a valuable role, including three games over 60 yards and three scores in 2019, and his snap count increased considerably in the second half of last season. Cole also had the highest DVOA of any Jaguars receiver, and he was the only Jaguars player to have positive receiving DVOA in the red zone and on each of first, second, and third down. However, the addition of Laviska Shenault is likely to drop Cole back down the pecking order in 2020.

Cole did make a Week 17 cameo as an effective returner, which if sustained could rescue a spot on the game day roster. Even if that happens, he looks set to begin the season as the fifth of five active wideouts in an offense that, even at its peak, supported three productive pass-catchers.

Chris Conley

Chris Conley			Height: 6-3		Weight: 205		College: Georgia				Draft: 2015/3 (76)			Born: 25-Oct-1992			Age: 28			Risk: Green			

Year	Tm	G/GS	Snaps	Pass	Rec	Yds	TD	EZ	C%	+/-	Drop	Yd/C	aDOT	Rk	YAC	Rk	YAC+	BTkl	DVOA	Rk	DYAR	Rk	Use	Rk	Slot
2017	KC	5/5	293	16	11	175	0	2	69%	+1.8	0	15.9	14.4	--	4.1	--	-0.1	0	27.2%	--	50	--	9.6%	--	13%
2018	KC	16/13	802	52	32	334	5	10	62%	-3.1	5	10.4	9.0	64	4.4	39	+0.1	4	-1.0%	47	48	50	9.5%	83	66%
2019	JAX	16/14	880	90	47	775	5	4	52%	-4.4	5	16.5	14.3	18	5.1	17	+1.1	9	-2.7%	50	68	50	15.9%	61	22%
2020	JAX			56	32	465	3		57%			14.5							-3.3%						

In his first season in Jacksonville, Conley had the third-most DYAR (44) among all receivers on broken plays, which says something about the rapport he has with Gardner Minshew. However, Conley was barely above replacement level on the rest of his targets mainly due to his -13.8% DVOA on first down. Despite that, 2019 was his most productive year as a professional and he seems clearly entrenched as the second outside receiver in Jacksonville. Conley had the highest DVOA of any Jaguars starting receiver on second and third down (backup Keelan Cole had higher DVOA on all three downs, but on just 36 total targets), possibly because he had the team's highest average depth of target on all three downs.

Brandin Cooks Height: 5-10 Weight: 183 College: Oregon State Draft: 2014/1 (20) Born: 25-Sep-1993 Age: 27 Risk: Yellow

Year	Tm	G/GS	Snaps	Pass	Rec	Yds	TD	EZ	C%	+/-	Drop	Yd/C	aDOT	Rk	YAC	Rk	YAC+	BTkl	DVOA	Rk	DYAR	Rk	Use	Rk	Slot
2017	NE	16/15	1058	114	65	1082	7	12	57%	+2.1	8	16.6	16.5	4	3.5	57	-1.3	8	14.9%	17	258	13	20.0%	34	29%
2018	LAR	16/16	989	117	80	1204	5	6	68%	+9.1	1	15.1	14.0	19	4.3	41	-1.0	9	21.5%	12	318	10	21.7%	26	70%
2019	LAR	14/14	716	72	42	583	2	3	58%	+2.5	4	13.9	14.3	17	4.0	44	-1.0	3	0.0%	46	71	49	13.5%	67	63%
2020	*HOU*			*73*	*49*	*761*	*3*		*67%*			*15.5*							*12.5%*						

Acquired for a second-round pick to try to mitigate the DeAndre Hopkins disaster, Cooks has never done particularly well against man or press coverage and is more speed merchant than complete receiver. The "buyer beware" signs are strong: he has incurred five NFL concussions, he had just one game with more than 75 receiving yards last year, and the Rams were willing to take an NFL-record $21.8-million cap hit to move on from him. That does not mean that he can't be a good fit for some of what the Bill O'Brien offense brings to Houston—Cooks definitely has a long track record prior to last season of empirical success, and the move could be termed a buy-low if not for the fact Houston gave up a lot. The Texans are going to need to mandate zone coverage a lot more if they want to find a way to make Cooks more effective. Or, perhaps they can trade Cooks for something—just as every team that has ever had his rights so far has done.

Amari Cooper Height: 6-1 Weight: 211 College: Alabama Draft: 2015/1 (4) Born: 17-Jun-1994 Age: 26 Risk: Green

Year	Tm	G/GS	Snaps	Pass	Rec	Yds	TD	EZ	C%	+/-	Drop	Yd/C	aDOT	Rk	YAC	Rk	YAC+	BTkl	DVOA	Rk	DYAR	Rk	Use	Rk	Slot
2017	OAK	14/12	710	95	48	680	7	7	51%	-7.6	9	14.2	12.2	38	6.0	11	+1.6	6	-9.1%	68	27	67	19.8%	36	42%
2018	2TM	15/15	838	107	75	1005	7	9	70%	+6.4	5	13.4	9.9	53	5.5	15	+1.2	13	8.7%	27	187	20	21.9%	25	31%
2019	DAL	16/16	850	119	79	1189	8	9	66%	+6.2	6	15.1	13.1	28	3.0	72	-1.0	6	22.3%	10	324	3	20.6%	34	29%
2020	*DAL*			*112*	*72*	*1032*	*6*		*64%*			*14.3*							*9.1%*						

Few receivers are better route-runners than Amari Cooper, and that can put defensive backs in a poor position. That's especially true when Cooper sets them up with a double move. It's small sample size, but Cooper led the league with 167 yards on five double-move targets (four receptions).

Still, Cooper's biggest issue is consistency. He can have huge games like Week 5's 226-yard explosion against Green Bay, but also no-show like his 12-target, four-reception, 24-yard game against the Eagles in Week 16. Cooper had as many games with 100 or more receiving yards last season as he did with 30 or fewer (four each). With Michael Gallup and CeeDee Lamb on the field, Cooper won't have the pressure to take over, but with a new $100-million contract, the Cowboy also aren't paying him to be a boom-or-bust option.

Keke Coutee Height: 5-11 Weight: 180 College: Texas Tech Draft: 2018/4 (103) Born: 14-Jan-1997 Age: 23 Risk: Green

Year	Tm	G/GS	Snaps	Pass	Rec	Yds	TD	EZ	C%	+/-	Drop	Yd/C	aDOT	Rk	YAC	Rk	YAC+	BTkl	DVOA	Rk	DYAR	Rk	Use	Rk	Slot
2018	HOU	6/2	267	41	28	287	1	0	68%	-2.5	3	10.3	5.1	--	7.5	--	+1.1	2	-10.5%	--	7	--	21.9%	--	73%
2019	HOU	9/4	350	36	22	254	0	1	61%	-2.7	3	11.5	7.7	--	6.4	--	+1.6	3	-25.5%	--	-37	--	12.3%	--	67%
2020	*HOU*			*19*	*14*	*164*	*1*		*74%*			*11.7*							*10.4%*						

A popular breakout pick last season after bursting onto the scene with an 11-catch, 109-yard game against the Colts in Week 4, Coutee was publicly slagged by wide receivers coach John Parry for not showing enough at practice. At times, Coutee seemed to be running the wrong routes during games (memorably, Deshaun Watson's deep interception near the end of the first half of Week 6's game in Arrowhead) and that led the Texans to phase him out of the offense. He played just 98 offensive snaps that mattered after Week 7, along with some extra playing time in a Week 17 contest that was meaningless for the Texans. Coutee, on talent, should be the kind of player that can thrive and make someone like Randall Cobb redundant. But the Texans have essentially no confidence in him at this point and he has tumbled all the way down to fifth on the depth chart. Sometimes a player like this is traded for a bargain price, sometimes they're released—whichever team they wind up with is essentially their last chance. Coutee absolutely has the talent to be on the field. He's going to have to work on impressing his coaches more to use it.

Jamison Crowder
Height: 5-9   Weight: 177   College: Duke   Draft: 2015/4 (105)   Born: 17-Jun-1993   Age: 27   Risk: Green

Year	Tm	G/GS	Snaps	Pass	Rec	Yds	TD	EZ	C%	+/-	Drop	Yd/C	aDOT	Rk	YAC	Rk	YAC+	BTkl	DVOA	Rk	DYAR	Rk	Use	Rk	Slot
2017	WAS	15/6	674	103	66	789	3	5	64%	+1.4	8	12.0	7.5	80	5.6	12	+0.6	5	-4.5%	57	64	55	20.3%	30	89%
2018	WAS	9/7	428	49	29	388	2	1	59%	-1.1	2	13.4	10.2	52	7.0	4	+1.6	4	-6.2%	54	23	56	18.0%	43	84%
2019	NYJ	16/12	815	122	78	833	6	5	64%	-3.4	7	10.7	8.0	73	4.5	34	-0.4	17	-11.8%	66	9	65	24.4%	15	85%
2020	NYJ			96	61	669	4		64%			11.0							-3.3%						

Crowder has been on the decline since his breakout 2016 season. In each of the three years since, his DVOA has fallen progressively; he ranked just 66th among qualifying receivers in 2019. Oddly enough, last season also saw Crowder earn a whopping 122 targets, the most of his career and good for 16th in the NFL. Crowder's 8.0-yard average depth of target was his second-highest mark since 2016. The only season over that span in which Crowder posted a higher average depth of target was in 2018, when his 10.2-yard depth of target was heavily skewed by 11% of his passes that were categorized as bombs. Crowder has never seen more than 5% of his targets count as bombs in any other season, and only 1% of his targets counted as such in 2019. Given all the uncertainty in the Jets' receiver room, Crowder is set up to have another decent, high-volume season.

Corey Davis
Height: 6-3   Weight: 209   College: Western Michigan   Draft: 2017/1 (5)   Born: 11-Jan-1995   Age: 25   Risk: Green

Year	Tm	G/GS	Snaps	Pass	Rec	Yds	TD	EZ	C%	+/-	Drop	Yd/C	aDOT	Rk	YAC	Rk	YAC+	BTkl	DVOA	Rk	DYAR	Rk	Use	Rk	Slot
2017	TEN	11/9	516	65	34	375	0	2	52%	-4.8	2	11.0	11.7	43	3.1	67	-1.4	10	-30.2%	85	-88	85	19.4%	38	28%
2018	TEN	16/16	872	112	65	891	4	9	58%	-2.7	5	13.7	11.2	43	4.1	49	-0.8	10	-1.2%	48	104	40	27.1%	6	62%
2019	TEN	15/11	733	69	43	601	2	3	62%	+1.9	3	14.0	12.5	35	5.0	19	+0.8	17	5.4%	34	99	41	17.5%	57	63%
2020	TEN			61	36	504	3		59%			14.0							-0.4%						

Corey Davis fits a very specific niche we like to call "small-market receivers who never blew up like we expected them to." The way it works is that we don't watch the games they play in because the team usually isn't nationally relevant; the players themselves don't tend to have huge enough fantasy roles to get that community interested; and any national media who would answer why these players have stagnated are instead assigned to a piece that an editor thinks someone would actually read. Davis has flashed the ability to take over a game by beating Stephon Gilmore like a drum, but he has dealt with a lot of injuries and has averaged just 7.0 (2018) and 6.9 (2019) yards per target against man coverage. There's very little that Davis does as a deep receiver that matters against man coverage. He has just one catch that went for more than 25 yards over the past two years against man, and that was on a ball that only went 13 yards. Despite all that, the talent is still there for him to be more than he has been: he's a hell of a blocker, he did a great job breaking tackles last year, and he has shown a lot of skill working the underneath game. He's just never going to be the guy people thought he was at No. 5 overall. With another great wideout class coming next year, though, Tennessee declined his fifth-year option. Someone will make an honest No. 2 receiver out of him and we'll be able to move past the "failed expectations" part of his career.

Stefon Diggs
Height: 6-0   Weight: 191   College: Maryland   Draft: 2015/5 (146)   Born: 29-Nov-1993   Age: 27   Risk: Green

Year	Tm	G/GS	Snaps	Pass	Rec	Yds	TD	EZ	C%	+/-	Drop	Yd/C	aDOT	Rk	YAC	Rk	YAC+	BTkl	DVOA	Rk	DYAR	Rk	Use	Rk	Slot
2017	MIN	14/14	781	95	64	849	8	9	67%	+6.8	5	13.3	11.9	41	4.7	30	+0.3	9	24.7%	5	295	9	21.4%	25	40%
2018	MIN	15/14	874	149	102	1021	9	13	68%	+9.7	3	10.0	9.1	61	4.3	42	-0.7	24	-12.0%	66	8	64	26.7%	8	42%
2019	MIN	15/15	783	95	63	1130	6	8	67%	+9.0	4	17.9	15.6	9	4.7	28	+0.1	12	24.0%	7	272	10	22.9%	20	38%
2020	BUF			104	60	791	4		58%			13.2							-5.0%						

Good news: per DYAR, Diggs was the most valuable wide receiver on go/fly routes last season, putting up 154 DYAR on 15 such plays. The bad news: Diggs is now paired with one of the worst deep-ball passers in the league in Josh Allen. There is no doubt a player of Diggs' quality will be a boon for the Bills offense, but it is quite sad that arguably his best trait will be muzzled to some degree due to quarterback play. Something that does bode well for Diggs' fit in Buffalo, however, is his move towards being an outside wide receiver. In each of the past three seasons, Diggs' percentage of targets in the slot has remained under 45%, after 69% of his targets as rookie in 2016 came from there. Seeing as Cole Beasley will almost exclusively be Buffalo's slot receiver, Diggs' steady push towards being more of an outside receiver helps ensure that the Bills' top receivers each fit a specific role in the offense.

Phillip Dorsett

Height: 5-10		Weight: 192		College: Miami						Draft: 2015/1 (29)				Born: 5-Jan-1993				Age: 28			Risk: Green			

Year	Tm	G/GS	Snaps	Pass	Rec	Yds	TD	EZ	C%	+/-	Drop	Yd/C	aDOT	Rk	YAC	Rk	YAC+	BTkl	DVOA	Rk	DYAR	Rk	Use	Rk	Slot
2017	NE	15/2	377	18	12	194	0	0	67%	+2.9	1	16.2	18.2	--	5.7	--	+1.0	2	21.6%	--	45	--	3.2%	--	56%
2018	NE	16/2	399	42	32	290	3	4	76%	+3.0	1	9.1	10.5	--	3.1	--	-1.1	3	5.4%	--	56	--	7.4%	--	29%
2019	NE	14/4	567	54	29	397	5	5	54%	-3.4	1	13.7	14.6	13	2.7	75	-1.3	0	-2.1%	49	46	56	10.8%	74	40%
2020	SEA			24	16	218	1		67%			13.6							14.1%						

More than 20% of Dorsett's targets last season were bombs that traveled more than 25 yards beyond the line of scrimmage, putting him in the top ten in that category. And he excelled on those plays, with a catch rate of 40% and a DVOA of 86.9% (average rates for a wide receiver: 33% catch rate, 27.2% DVOA). Granted, we're talking a tiny sample size here of only five catches plus a pair of DPIs, but imagine being a deep-ball specialist and going from the second wideout for a 42-year-old Tom Brady to the third option (at best) for Russell Wilson in the prime of his career. Dorsett probably won't catch as many passes this year as he did in 2019, but he could still have a longer, better highlight reel.

Devin Duvernay

Height: 5-11		Weight: 210		College: Texas						Draft: 2020/3 (92)				Born: 12-Sep-1997				Age: 23			Risk: Green			

Year	Tm	G/GS	Snaps	Pass	Rec	Yds	TD	EZ	C%	+/-	Drop	Yd/C	aDOT	Rk	YAC	Rk	YAC+	BTkl	DVOA	Rk	DYAR	Rk	Use	Rk	Slot
2020	BAL			38	26	315	2		68%			12.1							8.0%						

Duvernay possesses a unique combination of traits. On the pro side, he has tremendous speed and good hands. A major negative: he is hopelessly stiff due to extremely tight hips. (Devin won't be asked to be an Elvis impersonator anytime soon.) That leaves his ceiling as a slot receiver somewhat up in the air. If Lamar Jackson can get him the ball in space, Double-D is tough to capture, but getting him the ball in the first place may be problematic, as he won't be faking out too many pro slot corners. Just in case, the Ravens went for another slot type from a Texas program, James Proche of SMU, and it wouldn't be a shock if the latter is the better pro.

Julian Edelman

Height: 5-10		Weight: 200		College: Kent State						Draft: 2009/7 (232)				Born: 22-May-1986				Age: 34			Risk: Green			

Year	Tm	G/GS	Snaps	Pass	Rec	Yds	TD	EZ	C%	+/-	Drop	Yd/C	aDOT	Rk	YAC	Rk	YAC+	BTkl	DVOA	Rk	DYAR	Rk	Use	Rk	Slot
2018	NE	12/12	747	108	74	850	6	5	69%	+1.3	8	11.5	7.9	75	4.7	30	+0.1	10	1.7%	42	122	35	25.5%	13	82%
2019	NE	16/13	1009	153	100	1117	6	6	65%	-1.7	11	11.2	9.7	64	3.2	68	-1.1	9	-8.6%	62	48	55	26.3%	8	84%
2020	NE			109	69	724	4		63%			10.5							-3.4%						

As we have seen for years on end, Edelman is arguably the league's most dangerous slot receiver when given even a sliver of space to operate. That space was not there at all in 2019, however, and Edelman suffered for it. Edelman's -4.5% DVOA from slot positions in 2019, where he saw 86% of his targets, was one of the lowest marks of his career and on par with his middling 2016 season. It's not as if Edelman's role out of the slot changed a whole lot either. Edelman is best on short in-/out-breaking routes as well as option routes that give him the choice to do both based on leverage. Vertical routes are not really his niche. In turn, Edelman led the league in both out routes (37) as well as dig routes (23). Edelman himself was not really the problem, though. It is fair to assume that if any of New England's young outside receivers can break out and draw some attention away from the middle of the field, Edelman will find success again.

Bryan Edwards

Height: 6-3		Weight: 215		College: South Carolina						Draft: 2020/3 (81)				Born: 13-Nov-1998				Age: 22			Risk: Green			

Year	Tm	G/GS	Snaps	Pass	Rec	Yds	TD	EZ	C%	+/-	Drop	Yd/C	aDOT	Rk	YAC	Rk	YAC+	BTkl	DVOA	Rk	DYAR	Rk	Use	Rk	Slot
2020	LV			23	16	197	1		70%			12.3							11.4%						

Edwards, one of the Raiders' third-round picks, was a four-year regular in the South Carolina offense. He ended his career with 234 career receptions, the most in program history (more than Alshon Jeffery, Sterling Sharpe, or Deebo Samuel, among others). He's nimble and creative when releasing off the line; that, coupled with his 6-foot-3 frame, makes him an inviting target on short run-pass options. He has the sneaky speed to slip past defenders on longer routes, and while he isn't elusive, he's a determined runner on screens and reverses who will drag defenders for a few yards. Edwards lacks the pure speed and explosiveness to be more than a No. 2 or No. 3 receiver at the NFL level, but he could develop into a Nelson Agholor type. The Raiders already have Agholor, of course, so Edwards may start his career by pushing Zay Jones off the bottom of the depth chart and waiting his turn as a fourth or fifth receiver.

Alex Erickson Height: 6-0   Weight: 195   College: Wisconsin   Draft: 2016/FA   Born: 6-Nov-1992   Age: 28   Risk: Green

Year	Tm	G/GS	Snaps	Pass	Rec	Yds	TD	EZ	C%	+/-	Drop	Yd/C	aDOT	Rk	YAC	Rk	YAC+	BTkl	DVOA	Rk	DYAR	Rk	Use	Rk	Slot
2017	CIN	16/0	187	16	12	180	1	0	75%	+2.3	0	15.0	11.8	--	3.3	--	-0.7	0	31.1%	--	54	--	3.2%	--	88%
2018	CIN	16/6	364	29	20	167	0	3	69%	+0.0	2	8.4	9.8	--	3.8	--	-1.9	0	-16.4%	--	-8	--	5.8%	--	61%
2019	CIN	16/6	628	78	43	529	0	4	55%	-6.9	3	12.3	9.0	65	5.3	14	+0.7	8	-22.0%	76	-55	77	13.0%	70	58%
2020	CIN			10	6	71	0		60%			11.8							-3.2%						

Erickson is reminiscent of Brian Finneran, an undrafted free agent whose special teams excellence allowed him to stay on rosters (mostly in Atlanta) and from thence build a strong career as a wideout. The snag is, when injuries gave Erickson a shot to play more than usual in 2019, he didn't take advantage. Worse, the extra duty affected his special teams—he lost over 4 yards per punt return from his 2018 average, and had kickoff return duties taken away from him altogether. As ever, Erickson is on the roster bubble, and this year it will take an extra-strong summer for him to make the team (and of course, if there is a training camp/preseason at all it will possibly be truncated, making his job that much tougher).

Mike Evans Height: 6-5   Weight: 231   College: Texas A&M   Draft: 2014/1 (7)   Born: 21-Aug-1993   Age: 27   Risk: Green

Year	Tm	G/GS	Snaps	Pass	Rec	Yds	TD	EZ	C%	+/-	Drop	Yd/C	aDOT	Rk	YAC	Rk	YAC+	BTkl	DVOA	Rk	DYAR	Rk	Use	Rk	Slot
2017	TB	15/15	884	136	71	1001	5	20	52%	-2.6	7	14.1	14.2	19	1.7	85	-2.0	4	1.2%	42	149	27	24.6%	12	39%
2018	TB	16/16	940	138	86	1524	8	16	62%	+10.3	6	17.7	15.8	6	3.3	70	-1.0	6	26.3%	3	420	4	22.3%	24	29%
2019	TB	13/13	810	118	67	1157	8	18	57%	+1.1	7	17.3	15.8	6	3.8	49	-0.5	3	18.0%	14	301	6	25.1%	13	25%
2020	TB			128	73	1173	8		57%			16.1							1.8%						

Because Evans has played in relative obscurity since 2014, you might not know that he is building a Hall of Fame-caliber resume. Playing with Tom Brady should help with the obscurity part. Evans has gained 1,000 receiving yards in each of his first six seasons. Only one other player has done that, and his name is Randy Moss. A seventh straight season would be a record. Assuming a 16-game season, KUBIAK likes Evans' chances. It's also worth noting how far along he has come as a receiver. Early in his career, his production was tied to volume. Over his first four seasons, he never ranked higher than 21st in receiving DVOA. In 2018 and 2019, he ranked third and 14th, respectively.

Larry Fitzgerald Height: 6-3   Weight: 225   College: Pittsburgh   Draft: 2004/1 (3)   Born: 31-Aug-1983   Age: 37   Risk: Green

Year	Tm	G/GS	Snaps	Pass	Rec	Yds	TD	EZ	C%	+/-	Drop	Yd/C	aDOT	Rk	YAC	Rk	YAC+	BTkl	DVOA	Rk	DYAR	Rk	Use	Rk	Slot
2017	ARI	16/16	1074	161	109	1156	6	11	68%	+7.1	5	10.6	8.6	75	3.7	47	-1.1	8	-1.3%	50	147	28	27.2%	10	81%
2018	ARI	16/16	872	112	69	734	6	11	62%	-1.4	2	10.6	9.5	58	3.0	76	-1.7	12	-15.3%	71	-23	72	23.6%	18	89%
2019	ARI	16/16	903	109	75	804	4	7	69%	+3.7	2	10.7	8.4	69	4.6	32	-0.9	12	-2.0%	48	90	44	20.6%	32	86%
2020	ARI			69	45	500	4		65%			11.1							2.5%						

The future Hall of Fame receiver appears to be nearing the end of the road, but that does not mean he is completely running on empty. Kliff Kingsbury and Kyler Murray helped squeeze some more production out of the aging star after a nightmare season for everyone involved with the Arizona offense in 2018. Fitzgerald was a sure-handed option on early downs for the young Murray, but he finished well below average in DVOA on third downs. With all the young talent in Arizona's receiver room, Fitzgerald will likely have a mentor role on the team as long as he wants one. The Cardinals love to use personnel groupings of three and four wide receivers, so there are plenty of reps to go around for Fitzgerald and others.

Isaiah Ford

Height: 6-2   Weight: 195   College: Virginia Tech   Draft: 2017/7 (237)   Born: 9-Feb-1996   Age: 24   Risk: Green

Year	Tm	G/GS	Snaps	Pass	Rec	Yds	TD	EZ	C%	+/-	Drop	Yd/C	aDOT	Rk	YAC	Rk	YAC+	BTkl	DVOA	Rk	DYAR	Rk	Use	Rk	Slot
2018	MIA	1/0	13	1	0	0	0	0	0%	-0.8	0	--	6.0	--	--	--	--	0	-115.4%	--	-8	--	3.6%	--	100%
2019	MIA	8/0	224	35	23	244	0	2	66%	+0.3	1	10.6	8.3	--	3.7	--	-0.4	4	-11.7%	--	3	--	11.7%	--	44%
2020	MIA			6	3	43	0		50%			14.3							-1.3%						

Through their offensive turmoil, the Dolphins toyed around with a number of complementary receivers to go alongside DeVante Parker. Ford, who contributed close to nothing in his first two seasons, stepped up as one of Miami's wide receiver experiments. While his work in the red zone was a disaster (-44.8% DVOA and 2.5 yards per pass), Ford made some noise as an underneath tool. Only seven of Ford's 35 targets came on third down, which is a bit odd considering end-of-the-roster guys do not tend to get much usage early in the series.

Bennie Fowler

Height: 6-1   Weight: 212   College: Michigan State   Draft: 2014/FA   Born: 10-Jun-1991   Age: 29   Risk: N/A

Year	Tm	G/GS	Snaps	Pass	Rec	Yds	TD	EZ	C%	+/-	Drop	Yd/C	aDOT	Rk	YAC	Rk	YAC+	BTkl	DVOA	Rk	DYAR	Rk	Use	Rk	Slot
2017	DEN	16/4	575	56	29	350	3	6	52%	-5.3	4	12.1	10.2	57	3.7	50	-0.1	3	-9.8%	69	12	70	10.0%	82	77%
2018	NYG	10/5	370	27	16	199	1	3	59%	-1.2	1	12.4	9.9	--	4.8	--	+0.5	6	-18.4%	--	-12	--	7.4%	--	46%
2019	NYG	8/2	341	36	23	193	0	1	64%	+2.5	2	8.4	11.3	--	1.3	--	-2.3	1	-20.3%	--	-21	--	12.1%	--	56%

Fowler was a fill-in at wide receiver in 2018 and stuck around just long enough to fill in again when suspension and injuries hit the Giants' receiving corps in 2019. Fowler added little value, though, with negative DVOA on every down. Fowler's special teams snaps even disappeared, dropping from 21% to 3%. With little depth at the position, the Giants chose to bring back Corey Coleman off a torn ACL rather than re-sign Fowler, who still remains a free agent.

Will Fuller

Height: 6-0   Weight: 184   College: Notre Dame   Draft: 2016/1 (21)   Born: 16-Apr-1994   Age: 26   Risk: Red

Year	Tm	G/GS	Snaps	Pass	Rec	Yds	TD	EZ	C%	+/-	Drop	Yd/C	aDOT	Rk	YAC	Rk	YAC+	BTkl	DVOA	Rk	DYAR	Rk	Use	Rk	Slot
2017	HOU	10/10	530	50	28	423	7	5	56%	+1.7	2	15.1	17.4	2	3.5	56	-0.7	0	17.6%	12	126	35	15.6%	59	42%
2018	HOU	7/7	375	45	32	503	4	5	71%	+6.0	0	15.7	16.3	--	5.2	--	+0.6	4	34.6%	--	180	--	21.5%	--	40%
2019	HOU	11/11	580	71	49	670	3	9	69%	+7.8	4	13.7	14.6	14	4.5	37	-0.5	2	1.8%	39	82	45	20.1%	36	63%
2020	HOU			88	59	814	5		67%			13.8							11.2%						

Welcome to one of the most frustrating players in recent memory for projection systems around the world. The Texans freed up a ton of targets. Fuller has talent worthy of No. 1 receiver money and, in theory, should be the clear No. 1 option on this offense. Also, he has frequent injury issues and they are the soft-tissue kind that aren't easy to explain away as random chance. When he gets injured, the Texans lose so much big-play ability that it negatively impacts the entire offense: they had a 35.4% pass offense DVOA in games where Fuller played at least 20 snaps last season, but a -8.5% passing DVOA in games where he didn't. He's on his fifth-year option, the Texans haven't really made any attempt to extend him, and they've surrounded him with three other capable receivers because he can't stay healthy. Fuller is so good that he simultaneously is hard to ignore and hard to count on.

Devin Funchess

Height: 6-4   Weight: 225   College: Michigan   Draft: 2015/2 (41)   Born: 21-May-1994   Age: 26   Risk: Yellow

Year	Tm	G/GS	Snaps	Pass	Rec	Yds	TD	EZ	C%	+/-	Drop	Yd/C	aDOT	Rk	YAC	Rk	YAC+	BTkl	DVOA	Rk	DYAR	Rk	Use	Rk	Slot
2017	CAR	16/16	853	112	63	840	8	11	56%	-2.0	4	13.3	13.4	26	4.5	36	+0.2	3	6.8%	32	168	21	22.8%	16	38%
2018	CAR	14/12	622	79	44	549	4	8	56%	-2.0	7	12.5	13.0	22	1.7	84	-1.9	1	-10.5%	62	13	61	16.4%	54	39%
2019	IND	1/1	36	5	3	32	0	1	60%	-0.3	0	10.7	9.8	--	2.0	--	-2.1	0	-7.6%	--	2	--	16.0%	--	0%
2020	GB			56	33	449	3		59%			13.6							-1.4%						

Funchess' only successful season was 2017; can the Packers use any of the lessons from that year to try to revive his career? Well, Funchess that year had the league's best DVOA on dig routes at 58.4%; that's the route that typically generates the most DVOA and DYAR in football. Green Bay didn't throw a lot of digs last season—just 20, with Geronimo Allison leading the way with seven. Funchess has never had that success again, but his route-running is his No. 1 aspect; you could imagine him finding some success as a deep threat with his precise cuts. To contribute, however, he'll have to find a way to hold onto footballs; Funchess has always had a problem with drops thanks to poor hands and poor technique. It seems more likely than not that 2017 was a fluke season where Funchess' hands didn't let him down as often as usual, but he's worth a kick of the tires to see if he can contribute now that he's fully healthy.

Taylor Gabriel

Height: 5-7   Weight: 167   College: Abilene Christian   Draft: 2014/FA   Born: 17-Feb-1991   Age: 29   Risk: N/A

Year	Tm	G/GS	Snaps	Pass	Rec	Yds	TD	EZ	C%	+/-	Drop	Yd/C	aDOT	Rk	YAC	Rk	YAC+	BTkl	DVOA	Rk	DYAR	Rk	Use	Rk	Slot
2017	ATL	16/4	540	51	33	378	1	5	65%	+0.2	2	11.5	10.3	56	6.6	6	+0.8	7	-8.0%	67	18	68	9.9%	84	48%
2018	CHI	16/11	830	93	67	688	2	5	72%	+5.4	2	10.3	11.9	32	3.2	72	-2.3	6	-10.2%	61	19	59	18.6%	38	48%
2019	CHI	9/7	458	48	29	353	4	6	60%	-1.4	2	12.2	11.6	--	2.7	--	-1.7	1	-5.8%	--	24	--	14.9%	--	46%

Beware overpaying for one season, and beware of small sample sizes. Gabriel was a monster in 2016 with Matt Ryan and Kyle Shanahan, leading the league with a 33.7% DVOA and with a 1.9 YAC+. Outside the confines of Shanahan's offense, Gabriel has never come within spitting distance of those numbers. In fairness to Gabriel, however, none of his playcallers since have used him in the same way he was used in Atlanta. In 2016, Gabriel was in the slot 71% of the time; he has been in the slot less than half the time in every season since. The Bears cut Gabriel for salary reasons and for ineffective play; maybe a team in need of a slot receiver will give Gabriel another chance to do what he's actually good at.

Russell Gage

Height: 6-0   Weight: 184   College: Louisiana State   Draft: 2018/6 (194)   Born: 22-Jan-1996   Age: 24   Risk: Green

Year	Tm	G/GS	Snaps	Pass	Rec	Yds	TD	EZ	C%	+/-	Drop	Yd/C	aDOT	Rk	YAC	Rk	YAC+	BTkl	DVOA	Rk	DYAR	Rk	Use	Rk	Slot
2018	ATL	15/0	60	10	6	63	0	0	60%	-1.1	2	10.5	10.5	--	3.2	--	-1.8	0	-24.2%	--	-9	--	1.7%	--	10%
2019	ATL	16/4	527	74	49	446	1	3	66%	-1.5	4	9.1	7.1	80	3.1	71	-1.5	13	-14.1%	70	-8	70	11.2%	73	76%
2020	ATL			70	48	538	4		69%			11.2							4.6%						

Gage has the pedigree and skill set of a player one might expect to spend the bulk of his NFL career on special teams. But after the Falcons traded away Mohamed Sanu to the Patriots last season, Gage became an offensive fixture in their three-receiver sets. Gage's poor results fail to inspire confidence in his chances to contribute next season, but his overall DVOA was weighted down by a -31.6% figure when he was split out wide. In the slot, Gage produced a much more palatable -8.1% DVOA, and he spent the bulk (76%) of his time there last year and should again in 2020. That gives Gage a real chance to become a featured part of the Falcons passing attack.

Michael Gallup

Height: 6-1   Weight: 200   College: Colorado State   Draft: 2018/3 (81)   Born: 4-Mar-1996   Age: 24   Risk: Green

Year	Tm	G/GS	Snaps	Pass	Rec	Yds	TD	EZ	C%	+/-	Drop	Yd/C	aDOT	Rk	YAC	Rk	YAC+	BTkl	DVOA	Rk	DYAR	Rk	Use	Rk	Slot
2018	DAL	16/8	739	68	33	507	2	6	49%	-5.7	1	15.4	14.3	16	5.2	23	-0.1	2	-14.3%	68	-9	68	13.4%	69	16%
2019	DAL	14/12	853	113	66	1107	6	5	58%	-1.8	10	16.8	12.9	32	5.0	20	+1.1	10	13.5%	19	233	15	22.6%	24	19%
2020	DAL			94	59	903	5		63%			15.3							7.0%						

Gallup took to the Cowboys' No. 2 receiver role and ran with it. He showed the ability to both run after the catch with short passes and win deeper down the field. He was among the most valuable receivers on both drags (second in DYAR) and posts (third). Gallup had as many 100-yard receiving games as Amari Cooper and added two more with 98 yards. Only 19% of Gallup's targets came from the slot, but he had an impressive 27.3% DVOA on those 22 passes. With slot-only option Randall Cobb gone and CeeDee Lamb added to the mix, the Cowboys will have the ability to rotate all three top receivers into the slot more often, which could help Gallup take advantage of more two-way goes and run-after-the-catch opportunities, which helped with his top finish on drag routes. Four receptions, 80 yards, and two touchdowns came on drag routes from the slot.

Ted Ginn

Height: 5-11   Weight: 180   College: Ohio State   Draft: 2007/1 (9)   Born: 12-Apr-1985   Age: 35   Risk: Green

Year	Tm	G/GS	Snaps	Pass	Rec	Yds	TD	EZ	C%	+/-	Drop	Yd/C	aDOT	Rk	YAC	Rk	YAC+	BTkl	DVOA	Rk	DYAR	Rk	Use	Rk	Slot
2017	NO	15/10	617	70	53	787	4	5	76%	+10.0	2	14.8	12.6	36	5.4	14	+0.1	9	34.8%	2	259	12	14.0%	68	59%
2018	NO	5/3	197	30	17	209	2	4	57%	-0.4	2	12.3	16.6	--	2.8	--	-1.7	3	-21.6%	--	-21	--	18.3%	--	53%
2019	NO	16/9	620	56	30	421	2	7	54%	-1.2	5	14.0	16.0	5	1.6	81	-2.3	0	-7.7%	60	22	63	10.1%	78	35%
2020	CHI			36	18	272	2		50%			15.1							-11.5%						

Ginn's 16.0 aDOT was fifth in the league last season, as he played his part as the dedicated deep-ball target for the Saints, the team with the *lowest* aDOT last season. Technically, Ginn did not have the most deep targets for New Orleans last season; Michael Thomas pipped him to the line, 23 to 22. But just 12.2% of Thomas' targets were deep; 38.6% of Ginn's were, and it's not like he was running a ton of underneath crossing routes without being targeted, either. Ginn still has his speed, being clocked at over 20 MPH on multiple plays in 2019, but he's no longer a threat with the ball in his hands, finishing dead last in YAC+. He needs a clean release to run downfield to be useful; he'll be a borderline WR4 in 2020 at best.

Chris Godwin

Height: 6-1   Weight: 209   College: Penn State   Draft: 2017/3 (84)   Born: 27-Feb-1996   Age: 24   Risk: Green

Year	Tm	G/GS	Snaps	Pass	Rec	Yds	TD	EZ	C%	+/-	Drop	Yd/C	aDOT	Rk	YAC	Rk	YAC+	BTkl	DVOA	Rk	DYAR	Rk	Use	Rk	Slot
2017	TB	16/2	449	55	34	525	1	6	62%	+2.4	2	15.4	13.4	27	5.0	23	+0.8	7	20.5%	10	138	33	9.1%	86	44%
2018	TB	16/5	717	95	59	842	7	15	62%	+1.2	1	14.3	11.9	33	4.2	46	+0.1	10	1.3%	43	105	39	15.5%	60	49%
2019	TB	14/14	957	121	86	1333	9	9	71%	+11.6	1	15.5	10.6	49	6.7	4	+2.0	19	32.8%	1	415	2	22.5%	25	82%
2020	TB			121	77	1091	6		64%			14.2							7.3%						

Before the season, Buccaneers coach Bruce Arians predicted Godwin would be "close to a 100-catch guy." It seemed like a broad proclamation at the time. After all, Godwin had yet to catch 100 passes in his career. Had he not missed the final two games of last season because of a hamstring injury, he might have proven Arians right. He was remarkably efficient, too. The last receiver to see more than 120 targets and post a better DVOA than Godwin's 32.8% was Randall Cobb in 2014 (35.7%). Like Cobb, Godwin did most of his damage from the slot, catching 63 passes for 1,092 yards and seven touchdowns.

From 1998 to 2000, Vikings teammates Randy Moss and Cris Carter each posted three consecutive 1,000-yard seasons. It's not inconceivable for Godwin and Mike Evans to accomplish the same in Tampa Bay. One season down...

Kenny Golladay

Height: 6-4   Weight: 213   College: Northern Illinois   Draft: 2017/3 (96)   Born: 3-Nov-1993   Age: 27   Risk: Green

Year	Tm	G/GS	Snaps	Pass	Rec	Yds	TD	EZ	C%	+/-	Drop	Yd/C	aDOT	Rk	YAC	Rk	YAC+	BTkl	DVOA	Rk	DYAR	Rk	Use	Rk	Slot
2017	DET	11/5	477	48	28	477	3	4	58%	+0.7	1	17.0	14.9	--	6.5	--	+1.5	2	21.9%	--	130	--	12.4%	--	33%
2018	DET	15/13	904	119	70	1063	5	13	59%	-0.5	5	15.2	12.9	23	5.0	25	+0.7	10	13.3%	21	250	15	23.2%	19	46%
2019	DET	16/16	957	116	65	1190	11	15	56%	+1.0	6	18.3	15.7	7	4.7	30	+0.6	7	18.0%	13	279	9	21.1%	30	45%
2020	DET			110	68	1137	8		62%			16.7							8.5%						

Golladay with Matthew Stafford: 172 DYAR, 23.5% DVOA. Golladay without Stafford: 107 DYAR, 12.1% DVOA. Golladay was the only Lions receiver to put up a positive DVOA without Stafford last season. 2019 saw Babytron go from an effective secondary receiver behind Marvin Jones to a legitimate top threat in his own right. Golladay has taken to Darrell Bevell's deep-shot philosophy like a fish to water, finishing second in the league with 249 DYAR on deep passes; he should be in the conversation right next to the Stefon Diggses, Mike Williamses, and Mike Evanses as one of the league's premier deep threats. He also pulled all this off while making a lot of contested catches; he had a league-low 1.9 yards of separation on his targets according to NFL Next Gen Stats. It wouldn't kill the Lions to try to find a way to scheme Golladay into some open space every now and again.

Josh Gordon

Height: 6-3   Weight: 225   College: Baylor   Draft: 2012/2 (SUP)   Born: 12-Apr-1991   Age: 29   Risk: N/A

Year	Tm	G/GS	Snaps	Pass	Rec	Yds	TD	EZ	C%	+/-	Drop	Yd/C	aDOT	Rk	YAC	Rk	YAC+	BTkl	DVOA	Rk	DYAR	Rk	Use	Rk	Slot
2017	CLE	5/5	259	42	18	335	1	4	43%	-2.5	1	18.6	17.2	--	6.8	--	+2.2	4	-7.8%	--	16	--	23.1%	--	38%
2018	2TM	12/12	633	71	41	737	4	8	58%	-0.4	6	18.0	14.9	11	6.4	5	+2.3	9	20.4%	14	193	18	17.7%	45	26%
2019	2TM	11/7	464	47	27	426	1	3	57%	-1.0	2	15.8	11.7	--	5.5	--	+0.2	5	2.2%	--	53	--	12.7%	--	31%

Gordon started the first six games for the Patriots before going on IR with a knee injury. Just as he was prepared to return to the field, New England surprisingly waived him. Seattle claimed him and got him on the field for 136 snaps before he received the sixth suspension of his NFL career for substance abuse and/or performance-enhancing drugs. In that limited time, he showed once again why teams keep giving him chances—his between-the-fingertips diving catch for a gain of 58 yards against Carolina was one of the best plays of Seattle's season. Gordon's agent claimed in June that the wide receiver suffered a relapse after the death of his brother; shortly thereafter, Gordon applied to be reinstated, and if he gets his wish he will be an unrestricted free agent. The new CBA, which eliminates suspensions for marijuana use, would seem to be a point in his favor. Gordon has been training in the Seattle area and the Seahawks would probably be the favorites to sign him if he gets his seventh chance at glory, but at this point his health as a human being is a more pressing concern than his status as a football player.

Jakeem Grant
Height: 5-7   Weight: 169   College: Texas Tech   Draft: 2016/6 (186)   Born: 30-Oct-1992   Age: 28   Risk: Red

Year	Tm	G/GS	Snaps	Pass	Rec	Yds	TD	EZ	C%	+/-	Drop	Yd/C	aDOT	Rk	YAC	Rk	YAC+	BTkl	DVOA	Rk	DYAR	Rk	Use	Rk	Slot
2017	MIA	16/0	132	23	13	203	2	3	61%	-0.2	2	15.6	10.5	--	11.4	--	+5.8	9	22.1%	--	60	--	4.0%	--	21%
2018	MIA	10/2	282	34	21	268	2	0	62%	-0.4	2	12.8	8.5	--	6.7	--	+1.3	3	-4.6%	--	21	--	12.7%	--	31%
2019	MIA	10/2	219	33	19	164	0	0	58%	-0.2	2	8.6	12.4	--	4.6	--	-1.5	2	-33.1%	--	-52	--	8.6%	--	61%
2020	MIA			15	9	120	1		60%			13.3							2.9%						

Grant is one of those players who is not a meaningful contributor at his actual position, but is such a valuable return man that he is well worth a roster spot anyway. His speed and short-area quickness is absolutely devastating and usually good for one electric score a year, but his legitimate receiver skills—route-running, hands, toughness through contact—are lacking. As a kick returner, however, that speed and quickness get to shine. Though he was relieved of punt return duties in 2019 in favor of Preston Williams, Marcus Sherels, and Trevor Davis, Grant returned a punt return for a touchdown in 2018 while also placing third in our punt return value metric that season. With Williams stepping into a presumably bigger role at wide receiver, perhaps Grant will take on punt return duties again. Grant's minimal role as a gadget wide receiver will almost certainly remain the same, though.

A.J. Green
Height: 6-4   Weight: 210   College: Georgia   Draft: 2011/1 (4)   Born: 31-Jul-1988   Age: 32   Risk: Red

Year	Tm	G/GS	Snaps	Pass	Rec	Yds	TD	EZ	C%	+/-	Drop	Yd/C	aDOT	Rk	YAC	Rk	YAC+	BTkl	DVOA	Rk	DYAR	Rk	Use	Rk	Slot
2017	CIN	16/16	857	143	75	1078	8	16	52%	-1.3	6	14.4	13.9	23	4.0	44	+0.2	11	-6.4%	63	73	49	29.7%	3	25%
2018	CIN	9/9	457	77	46	694	6	13	60%	-1.2	4	15.1	12.7	24	3.5	64	-0.4	4	12.4%	23	155	24	26.1%	11	47%
2020	CIN			103	58	833	5		56%			14.4							-3.5%						

Missing 18 consecutive games to leg injuries is never auspicious, and it is even more ominous for wide receivers on the wrong side of 30. Green has been a special player when healthy, giving some hope that if he can actually dress out for games he can regain most of what he was, which is better than a large percentage of wideouts. Green's contractual future is likewise murky; he will play 2020 on the franchise tag, seeking to ensure teams (including his own) that he can still bring it. After years and years of chasing Andy Dalton's errant throws, Green now gets to play with the hyper-accurate Joe Burrow. The Bengals also drafted another young flier, Tee Higgins, to understudy Adriel Jeremiah. There is every reason to believe an energized AJG has a Comeback Player of the Year-level campaign in him. There is also every reason to believe Green's time in Cincy will come to an end after the 2020 season. Which probably makes a decent season followed by a new contract to stay with the Bengals the most likely outcome.

DaeSean Hamilton
Height: 6-1   Weight: 206   College: Penn State   Draft: 2018/4 (113)   Born: 10-Mar-1995   Age: 25   Risk: Green

Year	Tm	G/GS	Snaps	Pass	Rec	Yds	TD	EZ	C%	+/-	Drop	Yd/C	aDOT	Rk	YAC	Rk	YAC+	BTkl	DVOA	Rk	DYAR	Rk	Use	Rk	Slot
2018	DEN	14/5	471	46	30	243	2	2	65%	-0.9	1	8.1	8.5	--	2.3	--	-2.3	0	-18.1%	--	-20	--	9.4%	--	77%
2019	DEN	16/2	660	52	28	297	1	2	54%	-4.6	4	10.6	8.3	70	4.6	33	-0.2	2	-18.0%	74	-21	72	10.6%	75	85%
2020	DEN			14	8	90	1		57%			11.3							-16.3%						

Hamilton spent the first half of last year as the Broncos' No. 3 receiver, usually operating out of the slot. After Emmanuel Sanders was traded, Hamilton shared the nominal starting job with Tim Patrick but still played primarily a slot role. He offers little except a well-built target on short underneath routes and could be pushed off the back of the Broncos' depth chart by the influx of fresh receiver talent.

KJ Hamler   Height: 5-9   Weight: 176   College: Penn State   Draft: 2020/2 (46)   Born: 8-Jul-1999   Age: 21   Risk: Green

Year	Tm	G/GS	Snaps	Pass	Rec	Yds	TD	EZ	C%	+/-	Drop	Yd/C	aDOT	Rk	YAC	Rk	YAC+	BTkl	DVOA	Rk	DYAR	Rk	Use	Rk	Slot
2020	DEN			49	27	334	2		55%			12.4							-11.4%						

Hamler went 56-904-8 as a fun-sized 5-foot-9, 178-pound receiver for Penn State last season, with some rushing and kickoff and punt return production sprinkled in. The profile screams "slot receiver," but the tape suggests that Hamler would be better off as a vertical threat up the sideline, and the Broncos haven't really known what to do with a pure slot receiver since Wes Welker left town. There's a chance that Hamler helps the Broncos offensive achieve critical mass, but at least an equal chance that he maxes out as a return man who runs a few reverses. The good news is that Hamler is penciled in as a fourth-to-seventh option in the offense; a few years ago, the Broncos would have expected him to contribute right away.

Mecole Hardman   Height: 5-10   Weight: 187   College: Georgia   Draft: 2019/2 (56)   Born: 12-Mar-1998   Age: 22   Risk: Blue

Year	Tm	G/GS	Snaps	Pass	Rec	Yds	TD	EZ	C%	+/-	Drop	Yd/C	aDOT	Rk	YAC	Rk	YAC+	BTkl	DVOA	Rk	DYAR	Rk	Use	Rk	Slot
2019	KC	16/5	479	41	26	538	6	0	63%	+1.5	1	20.7	11.3	--	11.2	--	+5.3	12	44.1%	--	181	--	7.6%	--	60%
2020	KC			51	31	506	3		61%			16.3							7.6%						

Hardman looked like a Tyreek Hill Expansion Pack when the Chiefs drafted him out of Georgia, and he turned out to be exactly that. Hardman had some productive games when Hill was out with a clavicle injury (4-61-1 in Week 2 against the Raiders, 2-97-1 in Week 3 over the Ravens, 4-79-0 in the Week 5 loss to the Colts), then settled into the role of kickoff returner/speedster off the bench when Hill returned. It's hard to see Hardman's role in a crowded offense expanding much as long as Hill is healthy, but he's an insurance policy for the whole offense: if Hill goes down, opponents will still have to account for a dangerous lid-lifter on every snap. Expect him to get overdrafted in your fantasy league because of the upside.

Kelvin Harmon   Height: 6-2   Weight: 213   College: North Carolina State   Draft: 2019/6 (206)   Born: 15-Dec-1996   Age: 24   Risk: Green

Year	Tm	G/GS	Snaps	Pass	Rec	Yds	TD	EZ	C%	+/-	Drop	Yd/C	aDOT	Rk	YAC	Rk	YAC+	BTkl	DVOA	Rk	DYAR	Rk	Use	Rk	Slot
2019	WAS	16/8	493	44	30	365	0	4	68%	+2.0	2	12.2	11.6	--	3.1	--	-1.1	3	-2.8%	--	33	--	9.3%	--	45%
2020	WAS			59	36	457	2		61%			12.7							-4.9%						

The entire online NFL draft community was stunned when Harmon lasted until the sixth round in 2019. To some, Harmon was a top-five wide receiver in the class and worth a Day 2 pick, yet NFL teams made it clear they did not feel the same. As a rookie, Harmon wedged himself into an odd purgatory, neither fully validating his online supporters nor invalidating NFL teams letting him slide as far as he did. Through Week 9, Harmon hardly saw the field and earned just nine targets as Paul Richardson took snaps ahead of him. From Week 10 and on, following a season-ending injury to Richardson, Harmon stepped up as a competent fill-in by snagging 22 of 35 targets for nearly 300 yards. With Washington's receiver room a bit more crowded as free agent Cody Latimer and fourth-round pick Antonio Gandy-Golden enter the mix, Harmon will have to take a major step forward to be more than the reliable spot starter he was as a rookie.

N'Keal Harry   Height: 6-4   Weight: 225   College: Arizona State   Draft: 2019/1 (32)   Born: 17-Dec-1997   Age: 23   Risk: Green

Year	Tm	G/GS	Snaps	Pass	Rec	Yds	TD	EZ	C%	+/-	Drop	Yd/C	aDOT	Rk	YAC	Rk	YAC+	BTkl	DVOA	Rk	DYAR	Rk	Use	Rk	Slot
2019	NE	7/5	220	24	12	105	2	4	50%	-3.2	1	8.8	9.6	--	3.5	--	-0.6	8	-26.1%	--	-25	--	9.5%	--	25%
2020	NE			74	44	556	3		59%			12.6							-1.9%						

Harry got off to a slow start in New England, both literally and figuratively. The rookie did not take a snap until Week 11, leaving him with just seven regular-season appearances. In those seven games, he never eclipsed three receptions or 29 yards. His playoff performance against the Tennessee Titans was even more disastrous. Against a solid pair of cornerbacks, seven targets went Harry's way, yet he came down with just two of them for a whopping 21 yards. Above all else, Harry's issue as a rookie (and in college) was that he could not get off the line of scrimmage quickly enough to win reps early, but also did not show the crisp route-running or raw speed to break away later. The entirety of his game feels sluggish right now, which is unfortunate for a player who shows clear strengths in winning at the catch point and being a bully-style YAC guy. Hopefully another offseason of technique and speed training gives Harry the tools he needs to take the next step.

Rashard Higgins

Height: 6-1   Weight: 198   College: Colorado State   Draft: 2016/5 (172)   Born: 7-Oct-1994   Age: 26   Risk: Green

Year	Tm	G/GS	Snaps	Pass	Rec	Yds	TD	EZ	C%	+/-	Drop	Yd/C	aDOT	Rk	YAC	Rk	YAC+	BTkl	DVOA	Rk	DYAR	Rk	Use	Rk	Slot
2017	CLE	15/4	664	51	27	312	2	4	55%	-1.5	2	11.6	9.6	69	5.3	16	+0.7	9	-23.1%	82	-41	81	9.4%	85	92%
2018	CLE	13/1	483	53	39	572	4	4	74%	+7.6	3	14.7	11.6	38	3.7	57	-1.0	3	22.3%	11	143	28	11.6%	76	57%
2019	CLE	10/1	177	11	4	55	1	2	36%	-2.6	0	13.8	11.1	--	2.3	--	-0.6	0	-27.0%	--	-11	--	3.3%	--	64%
2020	CLE			13	8	107	1		62%			13.4							-0.5%						

Higgins had two catches for 46 yards in the season-opening loss to the Titans, then did not play a real role for the Browns again until Antonio Callaway was released following Week 9. In that next month of playing time, Higgins played 113 snaps and was targeted exactly five times. He was then phased out of the offense entirely for more of a look at Damion Ratley. What Higgins does appear to have is a real connection with Baker Mayfield when he's an honest part of the game plan. He's tentatively expected to be the third receiver this year, though with the extra multiple-tight end sets, that doesn't exactly mean a huge boost in playing time. Don't expect speed, but Higgins can be a successful underneath receiver.

Tee Higgins

Height: 6-4   Weight: 215   College: Clemson   Draft: 2020/2 (33)   Born: 18-Jan-1999   Age: 21   Risk: Green

Year	Tm	G/GS	Snaps	Pass	Rec	Yds	TD	EZ	C%	+/-	Drop	Yd/C	aDOT	Rk	YAC	Rk	YAC+	BTkl	DVOA	Rk	DYAR	Rk	Use	Rk	Slot
2020	CIN			58	33	445	3		57%			13.5							-6.2%						

You can call him "Tee" for the sake of expedience, but he will always be Tamaurice Higgins to us. By whatever name, his 27 touchdowns in 37 games tied a couple of fair wideouts, Sammy Watkins and DeAndre Hopkins, for the Clemson program record. Higgins was used across the formation in college, with success in the slot and outside the numbers, and his high 65% catch rate and radius showed up no matter where he lined up. He put up far better YAC numbers than his 6-foot-4 frame would indicate—he isn't an explosive athlete, but he runs strong and with excellent balance. His drawbacks are a lack of straight-line speed and an inability to regularly defeat press coverage off the line. Presuming the other wideouts in Cincy remain healthy and active, Higgins should flourish as a mismatch rover; if he's suddenly the team's biggest threat, he could struggle.

Tyreek Hill

Height: 5-10   Weight: 185   College: West Alabama   Draft: 2016/5 (165)   Born: 1-Mar-1994   Age: 26   Risk: Green

Year	Tm	G/GS	Snaps	Pass	Rec	Yds	TD	EZ	C%	+/-	Drop	Yd/C	aDOT	Rk	YAC	Rk	YAC+	BTkl	DVOA	Rk	DYAR	Rk	Use	Rk	Slot
2017	KC	15/13	779	106	75	1183	7	6	72%	+10.0	3	15.8	11.7	44	6.1	9	+0.4	19	23.6%	7	304	8	21.4%	24	42%
2018	KC	16/16	905	137	87	1479	12	11	64%	+8.3	8	17.0	15.3	10	6.1	8	+0.5	19	23.8%	6	387	5	24.0%	17	59%
2019	KC	12/12	567	89	58	860	7	4	65%	+4.6	3	14.8	12.9	33	4.8	24	-0.2	13	22.4%	9	237	12	20.9%	31	58%
2020	KC			108	69	1074	7		64%			15.6							13.1%						

Hill on third downs in 2019: 20 receptions on 27 targets, 317 yards, 15.9 yards per catch, a 74.1% catch rate, three touchdowns, and 19 first downs. That's a sick split, and it's a reminder that Hill has become much more than a bombs-screens-reverses specialist: he can generate big plays and first downs in high-leverage situations where the defense is doing everything it can to stop him.

T.Y. Hilton

Height: 5-10   Weight: 183   College: Florida International   Draft: 2012/3 (92)   Born: 14-Nov-1989   Age: 31   Risk: Yellow

Year	Tm	G/GS	Snaps	Pass	Rec	Yds	TD	EZ	C%	+/-	Drop	Yd/C	aDOT	Rk	YAC	Rk	YAC+	BTkl	DVOA	Rk	DYAR	Rk	Use	Rk	Slot
2017	IND	16/16	926	109	57	966	4	7	52%	-0.9	5	16.9	13.4	28	5.3	15	+0.7	3	-3.8%	56	75	48	23.2%	14	68%
2018	IND	14/14	763	120	76	1270	6	8	63%	-0.4	3	16.7	11.8	34	6.0	9	+1.0	8	23.4%	8	359	7	22.4%	23	50%
2019	IND	10/10	485	68	45	501	5	4	66%	+0.5	2	11.1	10.1	56	4.7	26	-0.2	4	1.6%	40	76	47	22.7%	22	52%
2020	IND			106	68	933	5		64%			13.7							4.9%						

A calf injury and subsequent aggravation limited Hilton to 10 appearances in 2019, the first time in his career that he has failed to play at least 14 games. Even beyond the absences, however, Hilton recorded career lows in yards per reception and yards per game mostly due to the three substandard games he played while still hobbled by the calf strain. At 30, Hilton should still have a few good years in him, so there seems little reason to worry about the career-worst season. Also, Hilton's worst three years in DVOA have all been those of which Andrew Luck missed at least half due to injury. In between those seasons, he has two finishes in the top eight of DYAR and the top 12 of DVOA. A healthy Hilton is clearly the Colts' top receiver.

DeAndre Hopkins

Height: 6-1 Weight: 212 College: Clemson Draft: 2013/1 (27) Born: 6-Jun-1992 Age: 28 Risk: Green

Year	Tm	G/GS	Snaps	Pass	Rec	Yds	TD	EZ	C%	+/-	Drop	Yd/C	aDOT	Rk	YAC	Rk	YAC+	BTkl	DVOA	Rk	DYAR	Rk	Use	Rk	Slot
2017	HOU	15/15	1027	174	96	1378	13	24	55%	-1.7	5	14.4	13.2	31	3.7	49	-0.2	9	13.3%	22	367	4	37.0%	1	20%
2018	HOU	16/16	1084	163	115	1572	11	20	71%	+14.2	1	13.7	11.6	40	3.4	69	-0.9	10	22.6%	10	455	2	33.0%	1	33%
2019	HOU	15/15	1000	150	104	1165	7	11	69%	+7.5	5	11.2	10.2	54	3.7	54	-1.0	17	6.2%	31	224	17	30.8%	3	52%
2020	ARI			145	96	1209	7		66%			12.6							7.3%						

Another year, another highly productive season for one of the league's best wide receivers. Hopkins finished out his tenure with the Texans by earning first-team All-Pro honors, though he was not quite as dominant as he had been in years past. Houston moved him all over the field, resulting in a near-even split between targets out wide and targets from the slot or in tight. His DVOA on those passes was almost identical, with only a 0.5% gap between those two marks. Houston responded to another strong year by dealing him to Arizona when he requested a new contract, though his relationship with head coach Bill O'Brien had reportedly deteriorated to a significant degree as well. Regardless of Houston's motivation, Hopkins steps into an Arizona unit that, while promising, could use a dose of star power to help out the young Kyler Murray. Per Over the Cap, since Hopkins signed his most recent contract, the receiver market has increased to the point that his deal only represents the ninth-largest by average money per year.

Adam Humphries

Height: 5-11 Weight: 195 College: Clemson Draft: 2015/FA Born: 24-Jun-1993 Age: 27 Risk: Yellow

Year	Tm	G/GS	Snaps	Pass	Rec	Yds	TD	EZ	C%	+/-	Drop	Yd/C	aDOT	Rk	YAC	Rk	YAC+	BTkl	DVOA	Rk	DYAR	Rk	Use	Rk	Slot
2017	TB	16/3	684	83	61	631	1	1	73%	+4.7	2	10.3	7.1	81	4.6	33	-0.6	8	5.1%	36	112	42	13.8%	70	83%
2018	TB	16/10	781	105	76	816	5	5	72%	+0.6	3	10.7	6.4	84	5.5	20	+0.5	6	6.7%	28	152	26	16.7%	52	84%
2019	TEN	12/3	390	47	37	374	2	2	79%	+4.3	1	10.1	7.5	--	3.2	--	-1.5	4	11.7%	--	84	--	14.4%	--	98%
2020	TEN			51	37	382	3		73%			10.3							7.6%						

Humphries missed real time to injury for essentially the first time in his NFL career, but the biggest factor in limiting his production was Tennessee's decisive game-script wins. Humphries was the $8-million rock that keeps negative game scripts away. (Lisa, Doug Marrone would like to buy your rock.) If Humphries is healthy, he'll probably get more of a role this year, but A.J. Brown's breakout has probably capped his highest ceilings closer to 80 targets than 100.

Jalen Hurd

Height: 6-4 Weight: 227 College: Baylor Draft: 2019/3 (67) Born: 23-Jan-1996 Age: 24 Risk: Yellow

Year	Tm	G/GS	Snaps	Pass	Rec	Yds	TD	EZ	C%	+/-	Drop	Yd/C	aDOT	Rk	YAC	Rk	YAC+	BTkl	DVOA	Rk	DYAR	Rk	Use	Rk	Slot
2020	SF			29	18	242	2		62%			13.4							2.7%						

Hurd missed his entire rookie season recovering from a stress fracture in his back. While he was out, fellow 2019 rookie Deebo Samuel impressed, but now Samuel is dealing with an injury of his own. Unfortunately for Hurd, San Francisco added even more youth at wide receiver in the form of first-round pick Brandon Aiyuk, so he will have to scratch and claw for all the opportunities he gets this season. His Playmaker Score was fairly lukewarm coming out of college, but it is worth noting that he spent three years at Tennessee as a running back before transferring to Baylor his senior year and moving to wide receiver. With how Kyle Shanahan used Samuel in the running game in 2019, it would not be surprising if Hurd were used in a similar role if Samuel has to miss serious time.

Allen Hurns

Height: 6-3 Weight: 195 College: Miami Draft: 2014/FA Born: 12-Nov-1991 Age: 29 Risk: Green

Year	Tm	G/GS	Snaps	Pass	Rec	Yds	TD	EZ	C%	+/-	Drop	Yd/C	aDOT	Rk	YAC	Rk	YAC+	BTkl	DVOA	Rk	DYAR	Rk	Use	Rk	Slot
2017	JAX	10/8	537	56	39	484	2	4	70%	+5.5	1	12.4	10.1	60	4.5	34	+0.5	7	20.6%	9	149	26	17.3%	50	82%
2018	DAL	16/7	452	35	20	295	2	4	57%	+1.7	1	14.8	12.2	--	3.9	--	-0.1	2	-9.3%	--	9	--	6.7%	--	29%
2019	MIA	14/7	527	47	32	416	2	3	68%	+1.0	4	13.0	10.8	--	3.0	--	-1.4	3	5.2%	--	64	--	8.9%	--	81%
2020	MIA			44	27	358	2		61%			13.3							2.2%						

The highs of 2015 continue to elude Allen Hurns with each passing year. Since then, Hurns has never caught more than three touchdowns in a year and has only crossed the 100-DYAR threshold once. At his best, Hurns was a short-to-intermediate bully who worked best on slants, curls, and in/out routes that could convert into yards after the catch. From 2016 through 2019, however, Hurns' yards after catch has progressively dropped from 6.0 to 3.0. Additionally, Hurns' season only really picked up because he had to fill in for an injured Preston Williams. Through his first seven appearances while Williams was in the lineup, Hurns saw just 15 targets, but he earned 27 targets in the seven games without Williams. Assuming Williams remains healthy in 2020, expect Hurns to be a role player and nothing more.

Andy Isabella Height: 5-9 Weight: 190 College: Massachusetts Draft: 2019/2 (62) Born: 18-Nov-1996 Age: 24 Risk: Green

Year	Tm	G/GS	Snaps	Pass	Rec	Yds	TD	EZ	C%	+/-	Drop	Yd/C	aDOT	Rk	YAC	Rk	YAC+	BTkl	DVOA	Rk	DYAR	Rk	Use	Rk	Slot
2019	ARI	15/1	160	13	9	189	1	1	69%	+0.3	0	21.0	6.3	--	15.6	--	+9.3	4	33.4%	--	44	--	2.6%	--	46%
2020	ARI			18	11	161	1		61%			14.6							3.9%						

Isabella had a disappointing rookie campaign as he struggled to see the field behind more experienced but less pedigreed receivers. Isabella's full-season statistics are inflated by an admittedly impressive 88-yard touchdown he scored against the 49ers. As Larry Fitzgerald continues to get older, Isabella will have the chance to take on more responsibility in his second season. But with DeAndre Hopkins now in the fold, Isabella will be stuck as the fourth option at best until he can eclipse Fitzgerald.

DeSean Jackson Height: 5-10 Weight: 175 College: California Draft: 2008/2 (49) Born: 1-Dec-1986 Age: 34 Risk: Red

Year	Tm	G/GS	Snaps	Pass	Rec	Yds	TD	EZ	C%	+/-	Drop	Yd/C	aDOT	Rk	YAC	Rk	YAC+	BTkl	DVOA	Rk	DYAR	Rk	Use	Rk	Slot
2017	TB	14/13	610	90	50	668	3	9	56%	+2.2	2	13.4	16.4	5	3.8	46	-0.3	1	1.6%	41	105	45	17.8%	45	43%
2018	TB	12/10	453	74	41	774	4	6	55%	+1.3	2	18.9	19.5	1	4.4	38	-0.2	3	12.2%	25	153	25	16.4%	53	32%
2019	PHI	3/3	67	10	9	159	2	1	90%	+2.7	1	17.7	14.1	--	1.7	--	-2.6	1	41.6%	--	47	--	9.6%	--	64%
2020	PHI			59	40	680	4		68%			17.0							15.4%						

Jackson was going to be the deep threat that added an element of verticality to Philadelphia's offense, and it worked wonders … in Week 1. Jackson had 66 DYAR on his three deep shots that week—and then that was it, as he injured his groin in Week 2 and then his abdomen when he returned in Week 9. The worst part is, Jackson still was the team's leading wideout in DYAR on deep passes, which perhaps says more about Alshon Jeffery and Nelson Agholor than it does about Jackson. When healthy, Jackson is still a blazing-fast and productive deep threat, but he has now missed 19 games over the last three seasons. There's a reason the Eagles went out and added Jalen Reagor and Marquise Goodwin this offseason; this time, all their eggs won't be in Jackson's fragile basket.

Justin Jefferson Height: 6-1 Weight: 202 College: Louisiana State Draft: 2020/1 (22) Born: 16-Jan-1999 Age: 21 Risk: Green

Year	Tm	G/GS	Snaps	Pass	Rec	Yds	TD	EZ	C%	+/-	Drop	Yd/C	aDOT	Rk	YAC	Rk	YAC+	BTkl	DVOA	Rk	DYAR	Rk	Use	Rk	Slot
2020	MIN			64	42	561	4		66%			13.4							8.2%						

In the Minnesota chapter, we already discussed how Jefferson will have to adjust to being used on the outside more in the pros. The other issue he'll need to work on is the crispness and complexity of his routes. LSU used a lot of bunch and trips formations to help Jefferson get lost in the crowd, and when he was one-on-one, he had trouble beating physical coverage. That being said, when he's open, the ball sticks to his hands; he may be the best natural pass-catcher of any of the first-round receivers this year.

Van Jefferson Height: 6-2 Weight: 197 College: Florida Draft: 2020/2 (57) Born: 26-Jul-1996 Age: 24 Risk: Green

Year	Tm	G/GS	Snaps	Pass	Rec	Yds	TD	EZ	C%	+/-	Drop	Yd/C	aDOT	Rk	YAC	Rk	YAC+	BTkl	DVOA	Rk	DYAR	Rk	Use	Rk	Slot
2020	LAR			30	18	230	1		60%			12.8							-0.5%						

Jefferson's selection in the second round was a bit of a head-scratcher. In two years at Mississippi and two more at Florida, he maxed out at 657 yards in a season and never ranked better than 13th in the SEC in that category. And Jefferson seems to have less room for development than most wideouts in the draft—he's old for a rookie, he's small, and he enters the pros close to a finished product best known for his route-running and fundamentals. His father Shawn Jefferson was an NFL wide receiver—

he played for 13 years and reached the Super Bowl with the Chargers—and currently is a receivers coach for Adam Gase and the New York Jets. The younger Jefferson has been absorbing that knowledge his entire life; is there that much more he can learn from the Rams' coaching staff? Jefferson goes into training camp as the team's fourth wideout, but that's a bigger role in L.A. than it is on many other clubs, so he'll get his chances to make an impact.

Alshon Jeffery

Height: 6-3 — Weight: 218 — College: South Carolina — Draft: 2012/2 (45) — Born: 14-Feb-1990 — Age: 30 — Risk: Red

Year	Tm	G/GS	Snaps	Pass	Rec	Yds	TD	EZ	C%	+/-	Drop	Yd/C	aDOT	Rk	YAC	Rk	YAC+	BTkl	DVOA	Rk	DYAR	Rk	Use	Rk	Slot
2017	PHI	16/16	927	120	57	789	9	18	48%	-7.6	4	13.8	14.2	21	3.4	59	-0.4	3	-1.2%	49	108	43	21.8%	22	36%
2018	PHI	13/13	771	92	65	843	6	10	71%	+6.5	4	13.0	11.6	39	4.1	47	-0.5	11	21.1%	13	251	14	19.7%	33	39%
2019	PHI	10/10	504	73	43	490	4	6	59%	-2.0	4	11.4	11.6	43	2.7	76	-1.5	3	-4.2%	52	50	54	19.4%	42	28%
2020	PHI			54	31	383	2		57%			12.4							-9.0%						

Jeffery is coming off of a Lisfranc injury, the worst possible variation on a broken foot for a wide receiver. He went down in December without contact and, as of press time, still doesn't have a timetable for his return. The Eagles still hope that he'll be ready for action right off the bat, with Jeffery and DeSean Jackson starting before rookie Jalen Reagor is ready, but that all depends on how the 30-year-old's foot holds out. Jeffery's biggest asset to the Eagles is that he's *not* competing with one of the many speedsters Philly added this offseason; he's the big outside option, with only J.J. Arcega-Whiteside really competing with him for that role in the offense. If JJAW had produced a promising rookie season, perhaps the Eagles would have moved on from Jeffery. Instead, last year's team leader among wideouts in DYAR and DVOA will be counted on once more.

Jerry Jeudy

Height: 6-1 — Weight: 192 — College: Alabama — Draft: 2020/1 (15) — Born: 24-Apr-1999 — Age: 21 — Risk: Green

Year	Tm	G/GS	Snaps	Pass	Rec	Yds	TD	EZ	C%	+/-	Drop	Yd/C	aDOT	Rk	YAC	Rk	YAC+	BTkl	DVOA	Rk	DYAR	Rk	Use	Rk	Slot
2020	DEN			83	46	614	3		55%			13.3							-8.4%						

Jeudy caught 155 passes for 2,478 yards and 24 touchdowns in his final two seasons at Alabama, but he was the second receiver selected from his own program in April's draft because Henry Ruggs' 4.27s combine 40-yard dash made NFL executives drool. Jeudy has plenty of speed and is a far better route-runner than either Ruggs or Oklahoma's CeeDee Lamb, who was also selected before him. Jeudy should establish himself as the Broncos' No. 2 receiver while Ruggs and Lamb are still being used as screen-reverse-bomb package guys by their teams, and Jeudy could start seeing more targets than Courtland Sutton as the season wears on; Jeudy is better suited to shorter routes, while Sutton may be most effective as a vertical boundary threat. Jeudy and Sutton give the Broncos a receiving tandem which could be on par with Demaryius Thomas and Emmanuel Sanders in their prime. Drew Lock ain't Peyton Manning by a long stretch, but at least he has some weapons to work with.

Diontae Johnson

Height: 5-10 — Weight: 181 — College: Toledo — Draft: 2019/3 (66) — Born: 5-Jul-1996 — Age: 24 — Risk: Green

Year	Tm	G/GS	Snaps	Pass	Rec	Yds	TD	EZ	C%	+/-	Drop	Yd/C	aDOT	Rk	YAC	Rk	YAC+	BTkl	DVOA	Rk	DYAR	Rk	Use	Rk	Slot
2019	PIT	16/12	666	91	59	680	5	2	64%	+2.6	5	11.5	10.0	59	5.2	16	+0.2	22	-8.9%	63	26	61	18.6%	48	33%
2020	PIT			98	61	758	5		62%			12.4							-1.0%						

Keep in mind that because JuJu Smith-Schuster was often a slot player, Johnson had to play the vast majority of his snaps outside, negating easy looks. That makes his rookie numbers a bit more impressive, as he had by far the highest catch rate amongst the main Steelers wideouts and displayed the quick lateral movement to shake open on a number of occasions against top-flight corners such as Richard Sherman, Marcus Peters, and Patrick Peterson. Johnson had more broken tackles than many NFL running backs had on a much lower number of touches. If Ben Roethlisberger can stay healthy, Johnson has sky-high fantasy football potential and should be higher on radars than he currently appears to be. However, it should be noted that his core muscle offseason surgery still had not been completely cleared by team doctors as of a late-May conference call.

KeeSean Johnson   Height: 6-1   Weight: 199   College: Fresno State   Draft: 2019/6 (174)   Born: 9-Oct-1996   Age: 24   Risk: Green

Year	Tm	G/GS	Snaps	Pass	Rec	Yds	TD	EZ	C%	+/-	Drop	Yd/C	aDOT	Rk	YAC	Rk	YAC+	BTkl	DVOA	Rk	DYAR	Rk	Use	Rk	Slot
2019	ARI	10/4	378	42	21	187	1	2	50%	-5.2	2	8.9	9.9	--	2.0	--	-2.1	1	-45.6%	--	-105	--	12.5%	--	7%
2020	ARI			8	5	61	0		63%			12.2							-0.7%						

The last of three receivers drafted by Arizona in 2019, Johnson leapfrogged both his fellow draftees for playing time in his first season. Johnson saw a decent amount of playing time considering his draft status and unimpressive receiving production when on the field for the Cardinals, likely due to his playbook knowledge and his willingness to help out in run blocking. Johnson struggled in a major way as a receiver across all three downs and was not much of a factor in the red zone when targeted. We expect him to fall on the depth chart this year, at least behind Andy Isabella and possibly farther.

Olabisi Johnson   Height: 6-0   Weight: 203   College: Colorado State   Draft: 2019/7 (247)   Born: 17-Mar-1997   Age: 23   Risk: Green

Year	Tm	G/GS	Snaps	Pass	Rec	Yds	TD	EZ	C%	+/-	Drop	Yd/C	aDOT	Rk	YAC	Rk	YAC+	BTkl	DVOA	Rk	DYAR	Rk	Use	Rk	Slot
2019	MIN	16/6	547	45	31	294	3	8	69%	+3.0	1	9.5	9.6	--	2.2	--	-1.6	1	0.9%	--	49	--	10.2%	--	61%
2020	MIN			37	26	308	2		70%			11.8							10.6%						

The surgeon general suggests only taking Bisi Johnson in small doses. DYAR is a counting stat, so most players' top days will come when they get fed the ball over and over again. Not Johnson—Johnson had three games with just one target, and those were three of his top five single-game performances, while the two games in which he received nine targets combined for -11 DYAR and a -20.1% DVOA. You could do worse as a third or fourth target, certainly, but Johnson's biggest moments in 2019 were when he was able to get matched up against a third or fourth cornerback and make a play. Still, an average DVOA for a seventh-round pick is a successful season in anyone's book.

Tyler Johnson   Height: 6-2   Weight: 205   College: Minnesota   Draft: 2020/5 (161)   Born: 25-Aug-1998   Age: 22   Risk: Green

Year	Tm	G/GS	Snaps	Pass	Rec	Yds	TD	EZ	C%	+/-	Drop	Yd/C	aDOT	Rk	YAC	Rk	YAC+	BTkl	DVOA	Rk	DYAR	Rk	Use	Rk	Slot
2020	TB			14	9	119	1		64%			13.2							3.4%						

Receivers drafted in the fifth round rarely make an immediate impact. From 2010 through 2019, teams chose 38 receivers in the fifth round. A third of them didn't catch a pass during their rookie seasons. The last one the Buccaneers drafted, Justin Watson, caught one pass for 5 yards in 2018 and has been relegated to the "Going Deep" section of this chapter. Every now and then, though, someone surprises—Kenny Stills in 2013, Stefon Diggs in 2015, Tyreek Hill in 2016, and Hunter Renfrow and Darius Slayton last season.

Will Johnson be next? Our Playmaker Score suggests he has a better chance than most. As noted in *The SIS Football Rookie Handbook 2020*, Johnson is an intelligent player who can reliably read coverages and identify blitzers, a trait that gives him the inside track to becoming Tom Brady's new favorite slot receiver. What he lacks in straight-line speed, he makes up for in his ability to make contested catches. When Tampa Bay's not in 12 personnel, look for No. 18.

Julio Jones   Height: 6-3   Weight: 220   College: Alabama   Draft: 2011/1 (6)   Born: 8-Feb-1989   Age: 31   Risk: Green

Year	Tm	G/GS	Snaps	Pass	Rec	Yds	TD	EZ	C%	+/-	Drop	Yd/C	aDOT	Rk	YAC	Rk	YAC+	BTkl	DVOA	Rk	DYAR	Rk	Use	Rk	Slot
2017	ATL	16/16	766	148	88	1444	3	19	59%	+3.1	8	16.4	14.2	20	5.5	13	+1.1	17	13.7%	18	313	7	28.7%	4	51%
2018	ATL	16/16	818	170	113	1677	8	10	66%	+10.1	6	14.8	14.5	14	4.0	51	-0.4	13	15.9%	17	382	6	28.2%	5	43%
2019	ATL	15/15	834	157	99	1394	6	11	63%	+4.5	5	14.1	12.6	34	3.5	61	-0.7	10	11.6%	21	299	7	25.6%	11	49%
2020	ATL			145	98	1339	7		68%			13.7							11.5%						

Jones is basically the perfect wide receiver. At 6-foot-3 and 220 pounds, he can win over the top and by bullying smaller cornerbacks. With a 4.39s 40, he can run past most others. He has produced an above-average receiving DVOA all nine seasons of his professional career, including now four straight years at 10.0% or better. And the bizarre end zone inefficiency that became one of the major narratives of the Falcons' Super Bowl hangover—Jones scored just three touchdowns and caught just two of 19 end zone targets in 2017—was clearly either a fluke or a vestige of poor play calling by then-offensive coordinator Steve Sarkisian. In the two years since, Jones has caught 9 of 20 end zone targets (plus a 32-yard DPI) and reasserted himself as one of the league's best fantasy football receivers beyond his consistent status as one of the league's best real football receivers. Jones fell 6 yards shy of pushing his already-NFL-record five straight seasons of 1,400 or more receiving yards to six, but that is clearly not a sign of any skill decline. Still just 31 years old, Jones should gracefully finish the four remaining years on his current Falcons contract barring a Calvin Johnson-like exit from the sport. I suppose that if football is that easy for you, it's easier to lose interest.

Marvin Jones Height: 6-2 Weight: 198 College: California Draft: 2012/5 (166) Born: 12-Mar-1990 Age: 30 Risk: Green

Year	Tm	G/GS	Snaps	Pass	Rec	Yds	TD	EZ	C%	+/-	Drop	Yd/C	aDOT	Rk	YAC	Rk	YAC+	BTkl	DVOA	Rk	DYAR	Rk	Use	Rk	Slot
2017	DET	16/16	1005	107	61	1101	9	18	57%	+2.8	1	18.0	16.0	7	3.2	66	-1.2	11	33.8%	3	395	2	19.9%	35	21%
2018	DET	9/9	538	62	35	508	5	13	56%	-0.6	1	14.5	15.5	9	3.1	74	-0.6	3	15.7%	18	142	29	20.5%	30	23%
2019	DET	13/11	837	91	62	779	9	9	68%	+6.0	5	12.6	13.4	24	1.7	80	-2.1	6	11.8%	20	180	24	20.6%	33	66%
2020	DET			91	58	787	6		64%			13.6							7.1%						

Jones with Matthew Stafford: 157 DYAR, 21.7% DVOA. Jones without Stafford: 21 DYAR, -5.0% DVOA. Obviously some of the reason for the lower DYAR total without Stafford was the ankle injury that prematurely ended Jones' season. You'll note that Jones' DVOA dropped more without Stafford than either Kenny Golladay or Danny Amendola, the other two receivers who had 25 targets both with and without the Lions' starting quarterback. The difference comes almost entirely down to the Week 12 nightmare against Washington, where Jeff Driskel tried to force the ball to Jones every other play, with terrible results. Take out that week, and Jones actually had the highest receiving DVOA on the team post-Stafford; he's not quite ready to give up the spot as Detroit's top receiver to Golladay just yet. It should be noted that his YAC+ was third-worst in the league; he has never been particularly special with the ball in his hands, but last season was unusually poor for him.

Zay Jones Height: 6-2 Weight: 200 College: East Carolina Draft: 2017/2 (37) Born: 30-Mar-1995 Age: 25 Risk: Green

Year	Tm	G/GS	Snaps	Pass	Rec	Yds	TD	EZ	C%	+/-	Drop	Yd/C	aDOT	Rk	YAC	Rk	YAC+	BTkl	DVOA	Rk	DYAR	Rk	Use	Rk	Slot
2017	BUF	15/10	793	74	27	316	2	13	36%	-11.8	3	11.7	13.1	32	2.3	81	-1.4	1	-35.2%	86	-131	86	16.8%	53	32%
2018	BUF	16/15	941	102	56	652	7	10	55%	-6.2	4	11.6	12.5	27	2.5	82	-1.9	3	-15.5%	72	-22	71	21.4%	27	57%
2019	2TM	15/9	643	45	27	216	0	4	60%	-1.3	1	8.0	11.1	--	2.9	--	-1.7	0	-38.6%	--	-91	--	9.3%	--	65%
2020	LV			3	2	22	0		67%			11.0							0.9%						

A former draftnik favorite (but Playmaker Score bust pick) who washed out of Buffalo after a variety of on- and off-field issues early last season, Jones got an extended audition as a nominal starter for the Raiders in the second half of the year. Most of Jones' production, such as it was, came on quick outs, short stop routes from bunch formations, and other plays that any practice squad-caliber receiver could execute, with a few "why not?" bombs mixed in that didn't amount to much. Nelson Agholor does all the things Jones can do, only much better. Unlikely to make the final roster.

Christian Kirk Height: 5-11 Weight: 200 College: Texas A&M Draft: 2018/2 (47) Born: 18-Nov-1996 Age: 24 Risk: Green

Year	Tm	G/GS	Snaps	Pass	Rec	Yds	TD	EZ	C%	+/-	Drop	Yd/C	aDOT	Rk	YAC	Rk	YAC+	BTkl	DVOA	Rk	DYAR	Rk	Use	Rk	Slot
2018	ARI	12/7	542	68	43	590	3	4	63%	-0.5	3	13.7	9.8	54	5.3	22	-0.1	3	-1.8%	49	57	49	19.2%	35	48%
2019	ARI	13/13	804	108	68	709	3	6	63%	+1.6	2	10.4	10.9	45	4.2	40	-0.9	8	-5.1%	55	67	51	25.9%	9	52%
2020	ARI			96	63	727	5		66%			11.5							2.7%						

After serving as one of the lone bright spots in Arizona's disastrous 2018 season, Kirk stepped into the No. 1 role for the Cardinals in 2019. He may have been a bit miscast as a primary target, but he was definitely the Cardinals' most reliable option at receiver in the red zone. Kirk also faced the toughest schedule of any receiver as determined by the largest gap between his VOA (-9.8%) and DVOA (-5.1%). He will not have nearly the same pressure on him now that DeAndre Hopkins is in town, and he will still have plenty of opportunities to see his share of targets in Arizona's version of the Air Raid. Kirk does not turn 24 until well into the season; his future is definitely promising. He's a receiver KUBIAK loves much more than conventional wisdom (i.e. ADP).

Cooper Kupp

Height: 6-2   Weight: 208   College: Eastern Washington   Draft: 2017/3 (69)   Born: 15-Jun-1993   Age: 27   Risk: Yellow

Year	Tm	G/GS	Snaps	Pass	Rec	Yds	TD	EZ	C%	+/-	Drop	Yd/C	aDOT	Rk	YAC	Rk	YAC+	BTkl	DVOA	Rk	DYAR	Rk	Use	Rk	Slot
2017	LAR	15/6	740	92	62	869	5	7	65%	+3.3	7	14.0	9.8	66	6.0	10	+1.7	15	24.8%	4	272	10	19.4%	39	94%
2018	LAR	8/8	439	55	40	566	6	4	73%	+3.9	1	14.2	7.4	79	7.6	2	+2.2	8	23.8%	7	158	23	19.9%	31	100%
2019	LAR	16/14	905	134	94	1161	10	7	70%	+4.4	5	12.4	7.4	76	5.7	11	+1.0	12	7.1%	30	205	18	22.0%	27	92%
2020	LAR			113	81	990	6		72%			12.2							13.5%						

Kupp rebounded nicely from the torn ACL that ended his 2018 season prematurely. His efficiency took a hit, especially in yards after the catch, but he played a bigger part in the L.A. offense than ever before and capitalized with career highs in all of his counting stats. Most of his production came in the first half of the year. After a seven-catch, 220-yard performance against the Bengals in Week 8, Kupp had outstanding season totals of 58 catches, 792 yards, and five touchdowns at the midpoint. He only put up a 36-369-5 statline after L.A.'s bye in Week 9, but he remained a consistent scoring threat in the second half, finding the end zone in each of the Rams' final five games. In an otherwise uneven season, what didn't change was Kupp's effectiveness on third downs. Though he had negative DVOAs on both first and second down, his third-down DVOA was an outstanding 31.9%, and his 29 third-down conversions were tied with Julio Jones for most in the league.

CeeDee Lamb

Height: 6-2   Weight: 198   College: Oklahoma   Draft: 2020/1 (17)   Born: 8-Apr-1999   Age: 21   Risk: Green

Year	Tm	G/GS	Snaps	Pass	Rec	Yds	TD	EZ	C%	+/-	Drop	Yd/C	aDOT	Rk	YAC	Rk	YAC+	BTkl	DVOA	Rk	DYAR	Rk	Use	Rk	Slot
2020	DAL			81	50	724	4		62%			14.5							5.0%						

The Cowboys certainly didn't need a wide receiver, but when a talent like CeeDee Lamb is still available with the 17th overall pick, it's nearly impossible to pass up. Lamb might be the most well-rounded receiver prospect in the draft class, a class that he led in Playmaker Score. Lamb had 1,237 yards as Oklahoma's top target. He led this class in yards per target (14.3), yards after the catch per reception (11.2), and yards per route run (3.9). His YAC was helped some by Lincoln Riley's scheme, but he wasn't just some shallow catch-and-run receiver. His 12.1 aDOT was well above the class average.

Jarvis Landry

Height: 5-11   Weight: 196   College: Louisiana State   Draft: 2014/2 (63)   Born: 11/28/1992   Age: 28   Risk: Green

Year	Tm	G/GS	Snaps	Pass	Rec	Yds	TD	EZ	C%	+/-	Drop	Yd/C	aDOT	Rk	YAC	Rk	YAC+	BTkl	DVOA	Rk	DYAR	Rk	Use	Rk	Slot
2017	MIA	16/16	932	161	112	987	9	10	70%	+1.8	7	8.8	6.4	83	4.4	37	-0.7	15	-4.9%	59	98	46	27.3%	9	76%
2018	CLE	16/14	957	149	81	976	4	11	54%	-7.9	6	12.0	11.7	36	3.4	67	-1.6	9	-22.2%	79	-111	83	26.6%	9	75%
2019	CLE	16/16	998	138	83	1174	6	8	60%	-0.3	3	14.1	10.3	52	5.3	15	+0.5	23	4.1%	36	182	23	26.6%	7	77%
2020	CLE			102	61	814	5		60%			13.3							-0.5%						

Patient Zero of the current Browns analytics-versus-scouts debate, Landry was not completely in the toilet as he had been in 2018. He's always been more of a volume player that provided some missed tackles but otherwise was an extension of the run game. In Landry's six NFL seasons, his career-high in DVOA is 4.8%. He's a shifty zone buster who—despite improvement last year—doesn't handle man coverage well enough to be a part of a game plan against it. Projecting him to a Kevin Stefanski offense is kind of tricky because this kind of player didn't really exist last year for the Vikings. If the Browns take a lot of leads, Landry might be held under 110 targets for the first time in his career. If the Browns take Stefanski's best screen game principles for backs and tight ends and let Landry run them, maybe he has his highest-efficiency season ever.

Cody Latimer

Height: 6-2   Weight: 215   College: Indiana   Draft: 2014/2 (56)   Born: 10-Oct-1992   Age: 28   Risk: Red

Year	Tm	G/GS	Snaps	Pass	Rec	Yds	TD	EZ	C%	+/-	Drop	Yd/C	aDOT	Rk	YAC	Rk	YAC+	BTkl	DVOA	Rk	DYAR	Rk	Use	Rk	Slot
2017	DEN	11/1	376	31	19	287	2	3	61%	+2.4	1	15.1	11.6	--	3.4	--	-0.7	1	21.9%	--	88	--	8.1%	--	61%
2018	NYG	6/2	209	16	11	190	1	2	69%	+2.7	0	17.3	19.9	--	2.1	--	-3.0	0	19.7%	--	40	--	7.3%	--	25%
2019	NYG	15/10	373	42	24	300	2	2	57%	+0.0	2	12.5	12.3	--	2.9	--	-1.0	1	0.0%	--	45	--	7.7%	--	31%
2020	WAS			5	3	43	0		60%			14.3							-1.8%						

Latimer will never live up to his second-round draft pedigree but over the past couple seasons he has established himself as a capable fourth or fifth receiver for teams looking for a bit of depth on the outside. After a combined 16 receptions from 2014 to 2016, Latimer earned himself 54 receptions from 2017 to 2019, almost half of which he caught last season with the Giants after a run of injuries to their receiving corps. Latimer now joins a Washington team in desperate need of someone to step up across from Terry McLaurin on the outside. He will compete with Kelvin Harmon and rookie Antonio Gandy-Golden for snaps.

Allen Lazard

Height: 6-5   Weight: 227   College: Iowa State   Draft: 2018/FA   Born: 11-Dec-1995   Age: 25   Risk: Green

Year	Tm	G/GS	Snaps	Pass	Rec	Yds	TD	EZ	C%	+/-	Drop	Yd/C	aDOT	Rk	YAC	Rk	YAC+	BTkl	DVOA	Rk	DYAR	Rk	Use	Rk	Slot
2018	GB	1/0	1	1	1	7	0	0	100%	+0.3	0	7.0	7.0	--	0.0	--	-3.6	0	-2.6%	--	1	--	2.6%	--	100%
2019	GB	16/3	484	52	35	477	3	8	67%	+4.0	5	13.6	13.9	22	3.7	51	-0.4	2	14.6%	18	118	36	9.7%	81	72%
2020	GB			72	47	639	4		65%			13.6							9.0%						

The $64,000 question is whether or not Lazard can keep up his top-20 DVOA rate with what should be a healthy increase in targets, as the Packers are comfortable keeping him as their secondary wideout. The historical evidence is … complicated, but players who had 40 to 60 targets one year and then saw their workload increase by at least 20 targets the next have seen their DVOA actually improve by 2.8%. It's noisy data, for sure, and there are plenty of examples of players who have wilted when asked to do more, but the move isn't a statistically improbable one. We'd still be more comfortable with Lazard as a third-option downfield threat rather than an every-down contributor, but Lazard played like a low-tier starting-quality receiver ever since he worked his way into the rotation in Week 6.

Tyler Lockett

Height: 5-10   Weight: 182   College: Kansas State   Draft: 2015/3 (69)   Born: 28-Sep-1992   Age: 28   Risk: Green

Year	Tm	G/GS	Snaps	Pass	Rec	Yds	TD	EZ	C%	+/-	Drop	Yd/C	aDOT	Rk	YAC	Rk	YAC+	BTkl	DVOA	Rk	DYAR	Rk	Use	Rk	Slot
2017	SEA	16/8	692	71	45	555	2	8	63%	+2.5	1	12.3	12.7	35	4.2	42	-1.0	8	-3.4%	54	48	60	13.2%	71	68%
2018	SEA	16/14	908	70	57	965	10	9	81%	+17.7	0	16.9	15.9	5	3.7	58	-1.5	7	66.3%	1	464	1	18.5%	39	58%
2019	SEA	16/16	1010	110	82	1057	8	14	75%	+13.6	4	12.9	13.0	29	3.7	55	-1.1	4	24.6%	6	317	4	22.4%	26	83%
2020	SEA			96	66	933	6		69%			14.1							16.9%						

There may not be a receiver in the league with a bigger gap between his advanced statistics and his fantasy numbers than Lockett. In the past two seasons, he has ranked 13th and 16th among wideouts in PPR scoring, but he has dominated our DVOA and DYAR leaderboards. His 2019 usage rate was nearly identical to that of Tampa Bay's Chris Godwin (22.5%), but while Godwin was playing in Tampa Bay's pass-heavy scheme, Lockett was plying his trade in Brian Schottenheimer's ground-based attack. That limited his opportunities, but Lockett still maximized his efficiency. This was best exemplified from Week 4 to Week 7, when Lockett averaged less than 60 yards per game and only scored twice despite a 90% catch rate (!) and 13.2 yards per reception. Lockett had a legitimate slump late in the year—from Week 10 until the end of the regular season, he averaged only 41 yards per game with two touchdown catches and a DVOA of -5.8%—and it looked like rookie DK Metcalf may have taken over as Seattle's top receiver. But Lockett rebounded in the playoffs, catching 13 of 18 passes for 198 yards and a touchdown, good for a DVOA of 36.3%.

Isaiah McKenzie

Height: 5-8   Weight: 173   College: Georgia   Draft: 2017/5 (172)   Born: 9-Apr-1995   Age: 25   Risk: Green

Year	Tm	G/GS	Snaps	Pass	Rec	Yds	TD	EZ	C%	+/-	Drop	Yd/C	aDOT	Rk	YAC	Rk	YAC+	BTkl	DVOA	Rk	DYAR	Rk	Use	Rk	Slot
2017	DEN	11/0	131	13	4	29	0	1	31%	-2.6	0	7.3	16.9	--	2.5	--	-3.6	4	-66.8%	--	-50	--	3.4%	--	85%
2018	2TM	8/1	225	30	18	179	0	2	60%	-2.6	1	9.9	7.7	--	4.2	--	-1.5	3	-23.8%	--	-25	--	12.3%	--	90%
2019	BUF	15/8	454	39	27	254	1	3	69%	-1.7	2	9.4	4.3	--	7.6	--	+0.4	5	-21.0%	--	-24	--	8.5%	--	67%
2020	BUF			21	14	134	1		67%			9.6							-4.2%						

Nobody on the Bills roster is hurting more from the Stefon Diggs acquisition than McKenzie. Without a standout No. 3 receiver on the team, McKenzie assumed the role for most of last year with mixed results. McKenzie proved himself to be a reliable quick-game and early-down receiver, earning himself a 69% catch rate, but wasn't much of a threat down the field. 62% of McKenzie's targets came in the "short" area of the field, which is up from last season's 52%. With Diggs now on the team, McKenzie's watch as the outside receiver opposite John Brown in three-receiver sets is over.

Terry McLaurin Height: 6-0 Weight: 210 College: Ohio State Draft: 2019/3 (76) Born: 15-Apr-1996 Age: 24 Risk: Green

Year	Tm	G/GS	Snaps	Pass	Rec	Yds	TD	EZ	C%	+/-	Drop	Yd/C	aDOT	Rk	YAC	Rk	YAC+	BTkl	DVOA	Rk	DYAR	Rk	Use	Rk	Slot
2019	WAS	14/14	784	93	58	919	7	12	62%	+3.3	5	15.8	14.3	19	3.7	52	-0.3	6	18.9%	12	237	13	23.3%	18	34%
2020	WAS			104	62	880	4		60%			14.2							-4.6%						

Many suspected McLaurin to find an early connection with his former college quarterback Dwayne Haskins, but hardly anyone foresaw McLaurin setting the league on fire from the start. Eleven wide receivers were drafted before McLaurin in 2019, yet only Tennessee's A.J. Brown (a second-round pick) earned more yards. McLaurin's rookie production is not impressive just within the context of his peers, but also considering his own previous production. McLaurin never earned more than 701 receiving yards in a season at Ohio State and only finished with 1,251 yards in his college career. McLaurin was particularly dominant on early downs as an intermediate-to-deep threat for Washington. McLaurin earned positive DVOA marks on first- and second-down plays with an average depth of target over 14 yards on each down. Given the sharp route-running and soft hands McLaurin showed on film in addition to his impressive numbers, look for him to be the engine of Washington's passing offense for years to come.

DK Metcalf Height: 6-4 Weight: 230 College: Mississippi Draft: 2019/2 (64) Born: 14-Dec-1997 Age: 23 Risk: Green

Year	Tm	G/GS	Snaps	Pass	Rec	Yds	TD	EZ	C%	+/-	Drop	Yd/C	aDOT	Rk	YAC	Rk	YAC+	BTkl	DVOA	Rk	DYAR	Rk	Use	Rk	Slot
2019	SEA	16/15	940	100	58	900	7	21	58%	-1.1	7	15.5	13.0	31	4.8	25	+0.3	13	0.6%	44	105	39	20.2%	35	17%
2020	SEA			94	59	958	6		63%			16.2							11.0%						

In the wild-card round, Metcalf exploited a banged-up Eagles secondary for 160 receiving yards, an all-time rookie playoff record. He added 59 more in the loss to Green Bay; his two-game total of 219 was the most for any rookie in the postseason since Austin Collie had 241 in three games with the Colts in 2009. Add in Metcalf's impressive regular-season numbers and this freight train of a receiver became just the 18th rookie to top 1,100 yards. (The list also includes A.J. Brown, who was Metcalf's teammate at Ole Miss before starring for the Tennessee Titans.) Most of Metcalf's predecessors went on to enjoy long, productive careers, but it's worrisome that one of the exceptions—the 6-foot-5, 245-pound Kelvin Benjamin—was even bigger than Metcalf. One cannot live on freakish size and speed alone; Metcalf will need to refine his route-running and hands if he's going to continue to thrive in the NFL. One area where Metcalf could certainly improve is the red zone. The Seahawks gave him plenty of opportunities to score—Metcalf led the league in end zone targets—but his DVOA inside the 20 was a disappointing -13.0%.

Jakobi Meyers Height: 6-2 Weight: 200 College: North Carolina State Draft: 2019/FA Born: 9-Nov-1996 Age: 24 Risk: Green

Year	Tm	G/GS	Snaps	Pass	Rec	Yds	TD	EZ	C%	+/-	Drop	Yd/C	aDOT	Rk	YAC	Rk	YAC+	BTkl	DVOA	Rk	DYAR	Rk	Use	Rk	Slot
2019	NE	15/1	420	41	26	359	0	3	63%	+2.9	3	13.8	11.2	--	4.4	--	-0.4	5	5.9%	--	61	--	7.8%	--	67%
2020	NE			31	19	237	1		61%			12.5							1.4%						

Three rookie wide receivers made the Patriots active roster last season: first-round draftee N'Keal Harry, UDFA Gunner Olszewski, and Meyers. Meyers led the trio in every statistical category aside from touchdowns. With the team struggling to find outside receiver production, Meyers stepped up as an intermediate threat with quality route-running and a knack for getting his hands on the ball, no matter where or how. Though not an explosive player, Meyers was the only receiver on the team to earn a positive DVOA rating on first, second, and third/fourth down. Meyers' middling athletic profile likely puts a ceiling on his game, but if he can take a step forward following a solid rookie season, he could blossom into a reliable No. 2 type of receiver for the Patriots.

Anthony Miller Height: 5-11 Weight: 199 College: Memphis Draft: 2018/2 (51) Born: 9-Oct-1994 Age: 26 Risk: Green

Year	Tm	G/GS	Snaps	Pass	Rec	Yds	TD	EZ	C%	+/-	Drop	Yd/C	aDOT	Rk	YAC	Rk	YAC+	BTkl	DVOA	Rk	DYAR	Rk	Use	Rk	Slot
2018	CHI	15/4	576	54	33	423	7	8	61%	-2.0	4	12.8	11.8	35	5.2	24	+0.4	4	3.9%	36	71	46	11.4%	77	82%
2019	CHI	16/7	704	85	52	656	2	7	61%	-2.5	4	12.6	10.3	53	4.2	42	-0.9	4	-7.6%	59	34	58	14.8%	66	88%
2020	CHI			70	43	540	3		61%			12.6							-3.8%						

Rather than being the breakout season some fans were hoping for, Miller floundered a bit as a sophomore. Both his average depth of target and his YAC+ dropped, though you can blame both of those pretty squarely on Mitch Trubisky's step backwards. Bears fans like to point out Miller's hot streak to end the season, when he averaged nearly six receptions and 72 yards per game before injuring his shoulder in Week 17. Those certainly aren't bad numbers, but they only resulted in a 5.5% DVOA; the Bears finished against a very weak slate of defenses, including three of the bottom 10 in the league. His best game by our numbers was actually his 3-for-3, 67-yard day against the Chargers in Week 8 before Taylor Gabriel went down.

Scott Miller   Height: 5-11   Weight: 174   College: Bowling Green   Draft: 2019/6 (208)   Born: 31-Jul-1997   Age: 23   Risk: Blue

Year	Tm	G/GS	Snaps	Pass	Rec	Yds	TD	EZ	C%	+/-	Drop	Yd/C	aDOT	Rk	YAC	Rk	YAC+	BTkl	DVOA	Rk	DYAR	Rk	Use	Rk	Slot
2019	TB	10/2	180	26	13	200	1	4	50%	-0.3	0	15.4	17.9	--	2.8	--	-1.9	0	-15.5%	--	-5	--	6.7%	--	40%
2020	TB			13	7	101	1		54%			14.4							-3.8%						

In 2019, the Buccaneers drafted the diminutive Miller during the sixth round hoping he would develop into a field-stretching slot receiver. Thing is, it's hard to develop into a slot receiver when Chris Godwin already is the slot receiver. Buried on the depth chart, Miller played more than 20 snaps in only three of his 10 games. When Breshad Perriman became a free agent, it seemed as if Miller would be in line for a larger role. Then Tampa Bay drafted Tyler Johnson.

Denzel Mims   Height: 6-3   Weight: 207   College: Baylor   Draft: 2020/2 (59)   Born: 10-Oct-1997   Age: 23   Risk: Blue

Year	Tm	G/GS	Snaps	Pass	Rec	Yds	TD	EZ	C%	+/-	Drop	Yd/C	aDOT	Rk	YAC	Rk	YAC+	BTkl	DVOA	Rk	DYAR	Rk	Use	Rk	Slot
2020	NYJ			72	45	604	3		63%			13.4							1.7%						

Finally, Sam Darnold is paired with a "go get it" wide receiver. Mims is the big-bodied, sure-handed sideline menace Darnold has been looking for. At 6-foot-3 and 207 pounds, Mims has the size of a prototypical boundary threat. At the NFL combine in February, Mims blew away the competition. His 4.38s 40-yard dash alone was enough to get the chatter going, but Mims solidified his stunning athletic ability by clearing the 80th percentile in the vertical jump, broad jump, and 3-cone drill. The silky smooth movement skills show up on his college film, too. As a yards-after-catch threat, Mims proved himself to have quite the throttle as soon as the ball hit his hands. More impressive, however, is Mims' gravity-defying play near the sideline—he shows the coordination and awareness to pluck the ball out of the air with ease while somehow keeping both feet in bounds. Outward displays of athletic ability are going to be where Mims has to win early on, though. Mims' route tree at Baylor was rudimentary and left too much room for imagination as to what his route-running will look like in the NFL. Right away, Mims is set to be an inconsistent big-play threat, but the right development path could push him towards being one of the NFL's best in a few seasons. However, one negative for Mims' development: he stayed in school through his senior year, and most of the best receivers in the NFL came out of school as juniors.

D.J. Moore   Height: 5-11   Weight: 215   College: Maryland   Draft: 2018/1 (24)   Born: 14-Apr-1997   Age: 23   Risk: Green

Year	Tm	G/GS	Snaps	Pass	Rec	Yds	TD	EZ	C%	+/-	Drop	Yd/C	aDOT	Rk	YAC	Rk	YAC+	BTkl	DVOA	Rk	DYAR	Rk	Use	Rk	Slot
2018	CAR	16/10	732	82	55	788	2	6	67%	+1.2	1	14.3	8.6	70	7.7	1	+2.2	27	4.1%	35	109	38	15.4%	61	35%
2019	CAR	15/15	925	135	87	1175	4	7	64%	+3.6	3	13.5	11.6	42	4.5	36	+0.3	17	3.2%	37	167	25	24.0%	17	26%
2020	CAR			112	77	947	5		69%			12.3							8.9%						

At 5-foot-11 and 215 pounds, Moore does not look like a No. 1 receiver, especially now that he'll have to stand next to the 6-foot-3 Robby Anderson in Carolina. But Moore is a No. 1 receiver because he plays with a similar attitude to Panthers Hall of Honor member Steve Smith. Statistically, that attitude is best captured by Moore's 5.8 average yards after the catch since he entered the league in 2018, tied for the fourth-highest among the 60 wide receivers with 75 or more receptions in that time. The other four players in that group include two slot receivers in Cooper Kupp (6.3) and Randall Cobb (6.0) and two big-play Chiefs receivers in Sammy Watkins (5.9) and Tyreek Hill (5.8), whose typical target character likely influences their success. Moore saw 73% of his targets in 2019 when he lined up out wide, but he nevertheless averaged a relatively low 11.6-yard target depth. You could not make a more perfect receiver in a laboratory for new Panthers quarterback Teddy Bridgewater, whose career 7.2-yard average depth of target is tied for the third-lowest among quarterbacks with 1,000 or more attempts since 2014.

David Moore

Height: 6-0   Weight: 215   College: East Central (OK)   Draft: 2017/7 (226)   Born: 15-Jan-1995   Age: 25   Risk: Green

Year	Tm	G/GS	Snaps	Pass	Rec	Yds	TD	EZ	C%	+/-	Drop	Yd/C	aDOT	Rk	YAC	Rk	YAC+	BTkl	DVOA	Rk	DYAR	Rk	Use	Rk	Slot
2018	SEA	16/7	620	53	26	445	5	14	49%	-3.5	1	17.1	15.6	7	3.6	62	-1.2	5	-7.4%	57	20	58	12.9%	72	4%
2019	SEA	14/1	318	34	17	301	2	9	50%	-1.7	2	17.7	14.6	--	7.5	--	+2.3	8	-5.5%	--	19	--	7.8%	--	24%
2020	SEA			16	11	167	1		69%			15.2							18.5%						

A one-trick pony, but it's a hell of a trick: Moore has averaged 17.3 yards on his 43 NFL catches, and 24.6 yards on his seven touchdowns. The Seahawks re-signed their deep-ball specialist to a one-year, $2.1-million contract, but he will need to fight off free-agent signee Phillip Dorsett to hold on to the No. 3 receiver job.

DeVante Parker

Height: 6-3   Weight: 216   College: Louisville   Draft: 2015/1 (14)   Born: 20-Jan-1993   Age: 27   Risk: Yellow

Year	Tm	G/GS	Snaps	Pass	Rec	Yds	TD	EZ	C%	+/-	Drop	Yd/C	aDOT	Rk	YAC	Rk	YAC+	BTkl	DVOA	Rk	DYAR	Rk	Use	Rk	Slot
2017	MIA	13/12	678	96	57	670	1	9	59%	+0.4	3	11.8	12.5	37	3.7	51	-1.0	3	-11.0%	70	12	69	20.0%	32	14%
2018	MIA	11/7	411	48	24	309	1	3	52%	-3.1	1	12.9	13.6	--	3.9	--	-1.1	2	-26.6%	--	-52	--	15.8%	--	15%
2019	MIA	16/14	914	128	72	1202	9	11	56%	+0.1	4	16.7	14.4	15	3.7	56	-0.4	9	14.9%	17	283	8	21.4%	28	40%
2020	MIA			108	62	994	6		57%			16.0							1.0%						

After five seasons, first-round "bust" DeVante Parker finally bloomed into the stud No. 1 wide receiver Dolphins fans have been waiting for. Parker earned career-bests across the board in 2019 and made his first ever appearance in the DYAR top 10, situated between Julio Jones and Kenny Golladay. A number of factors contributed to Parker's rise, but one of them was his newfound success out of the slot. Less than 15% of Parker's targets in 2017 and 2018 came from the slot, which was among the lowest rates in the league in each season. In 2019, however, Parker's slot target percentage skyrocketed to 40%. He earned a 24.4% DVOA rating on 58 slot targets. Parker's most effective route on the season, either from the slot or outside, was the deep post; Parker earned 80 DYAR on seven post routes in 2019, fourth-best in the league. That kind of post dominance would be welcomed by any quarterback, but first-round rookie Tua Tagovailoa will especially love it, seeing as deep posts litter his highlight reel from Alabama. If the Dolphins offense as a whole can be even mediocre instead of worst in the league, Parker's breakout will get the national spotlight it deserves.

Zach Pascal

Height: 6-2   Weight: 214   College: Old Dominion   Draft: 2017/FA   Born: 18-Dec-1994   Age: 26   Risk: Green

Year	Tm	G/GS	Snaps	Pass	Rec	Yds	TD	EZ	C%	+/-	Drop	Yd/C	aDOT	Rk	YAC	Rk	YAC+	BTkl	DVOA	Rk	DYAR	Rk	Use	Rk	Slot
2018	IND	16/4	527	46	27	268	2	4	59%	-2.8	2	9.9	8.9	--	3.0	--	-1.4	2	-20.5%	--	-28	--	7.1%	--	48%
2019	IND	16/13	809	72	41	607	5	8	57%	-3.6	3	14.8	11.8	40	5.8	8	+1.6	6	8.4%	26	121	33	15.0%	64	60%
2020	IND			22	14	194	1		64%			13.9							4.3%						

The Colts used Pascal in the slot 60% of the time, and he was far more effective when deployed this way. His catch rate when split wide was a terrible 37%, but he caught 69% of his passes from the slot and averaged 6.9 yards after the catch. He was also Jacoby Brissett's favorite third-down target, where he averaged 10.1 yards and recorded 19.3% DVOA on 29 targets. Pascal may be the Colts receiver who benefited most from Jacoby Brissett, but he has plenty to offer Philip Rivers in a role not dissimilar to Dontrelle Inman or Tyrell Williams on the Chargers in 2016 and 2017, respectively. A 57% catch rate won't cut it though, so the team should focus on getting Pascal those slot targets to make best use of his skill set.

Tim Patrick

Height: 6-4   Weight: 212   College: Utah   Draft: 2017/FA   Born: 23-Nov-1993   Age: 27   Risk: Green

Year	Tm	G/GS	Snaps	Pass	Rec	Yds	TD	EZ	C%	+/-	Drop	Yd/C	aDOT	Rk	YAC	Rk	YAC+	BTkl	DVOA	Rk	DYAR	Rk	Use	Rk	Slot
2018	DEN	16/4	393	41	23	315	1	2	56%	-1.9	2	13.7	10.7	--	4.9	--	+0.1	0	-17.6%	--	-16	--	7.2%	--	44%
2019	DEN	8/2	290	31	16	218	0	2	52%	-2.2	2	13.6	10.7	--	2.4	--	-1.7	3	-7.8%	--	11	--	12.6%	--	52%
2020	DEN			24	13	177	1		54%			13.6							-9.6%						

Patrick missed the first half of last season with a broken hand and a shoulder injury, then had a few productive games down the stretch. He started a few late-season 2018 games when Emmanuel Sanders was injured and also played well. Thanks to those two late-season surges, 30 of Patrick's 39 career receptions have come in December. Patrick is a lean 6-foot-4 matchup headache with an off-brand version of Courtland Sutton's skill set. As the No. 3 or No. 4 receiver in a passing game that will feature the tight ends and running backs a lot, he won't get many opportunities. Unless someone gets hurt in December, at least.

Breshad Perriman   Height: 6-2   Weight: 215   College: Central Florida   Draft: 2015/1 (26)   Born: 10-Sep-1993   Age: 27   Risk: Yellow

Year	Tm	G/GS	Snaps	Pass	Rec	Yds	TD	EZ	C%	+/-	Drop	Yd/C	aDOT	Rk	YAC	Rk	YAC+	BTkl	DVOA	Rk	DYAR	Rk	Use	Rk	Slot
2017	BAL	11/3	387	35	10	77	0	3	29%	-7.8	3	7.7	14.4	--	0.5	--	-4.0	0	-71.8%	--	-158	--	9.0%	--	22%
2018	CLE	10/2	218	25	16	340	2	4	64%	+2.2	0	21.3	18.4	--	4.7	--	-0.4	1	36.6%	--	97	--	7.1%	--	28%
2019	TB	14/4	652	69	36	645	6	11	52%	+1.3	0	17.9	17.4	2	3.5	60	-1.1	3	16.5%	15	155	29	13.1%	68	34%
2020	NYJ			84	48	796	5		57%			16.6							-0.9%						

A failed early-career stint in Baltimore earned Perriman the first-round bust label, and rightly so, but the 4.24s speedster quietly seemed to find his footing with the Buccaneers last season. While not the most productive receiver himself, Perriman's speed and ability to stretch the field is such that the Bucs' other talented wide receivers—namely Mike Evans and Chris Godwin—were afforded space over the middle that they may not have seen otherwise. Plenty of players such as Ted Ginn Jr., Marquise Goodwin, and Taylor Gabriel have filled similar roles as effective field-stretchers without being major producers themselves. Where Perriman did produce in 2019, however, was on broken plays. Three Bucs placed in the top five for DYAR on broken plays, which checks out given Jameis Winston's quarterback style, but Perriman topped the bunch with 83 DYAR on five broken plays. Though broken-play production feels like it would be unstable, Perriman is now paired up with Sam Darnold, so the potential for chaos is still very much alive. Perriman's deep-threat ability and knack for finding work on broken plays comes as a huge welcome for the Jets with Robby Anderson now out the door. Anderson and Perriman effectively fill the same role, though it is fair to say Anderson is better established as a consistent producer than Perriman is right now. This is the perfect chance for Perriman to prove himself for good, though, given the barren nature of the Jets' receiving group.

Michael Pittman   Height: 6-4   Weight: 220   College: USC   Draft: 2020/2 (34)   Born: 5-Oct-1997   Age: 23   Risk: Green

Year	Tm	G/GS	Snaps	Pass	Rec	Yds	TD	EZ	C%	+/-	Drop	Yd/C	aDOT	Rk	YAC	Rk	YAC+	BTkl	DVOA	Rk	DYAR	Rk	Use	Rk	Slot
2020	IND			87	57	765	4		66%			13.4							7.0%						

Pittman recorded 1,275 yards as USC's No. 1 receiver in his senior year, and the 6-foot-4 target fits the physical profile Philip Rivers loves in his top receivers. Strong at the catch point, Pittman has good ball skills and the toughness to make catches regardless of impending contact. He lacks top-end speed, as might be expected for a player his size, but he understands how to use his body to shield the ball and his wingspan gives him a massive catch radius. If he can transfer his college ability to the professional game, Pittman should establish himself very quickly as a red zone and third-down target. He has the ability to go straight into the starting lineup opposite T.Y. Hilton, and a clear path to do exactly that.

Trey Quinn   Height: 6-0   Weight: 202   College: Southern Methodist   Draft: 2018/7 (256)   Born: 7-Dec-1995   Age: 25   Risk: Green

Year	Tm	G/GS	Snaps	Pass	Rec	Yds	TD	EZ	C%	+/-	Drop	Yd/C	aDOT	Rk	YAC	Rk	YAC+	BTkl	DVOA	Rk	DYAR	Rk	Use	Rk	Slot
2018	WAS	3/2	107	10	9	75	1	1	90%	+2.1	0	8.3	7.3	--	1.9	--	-2.1	0	14.9%	--	22	--	10.8%	--	90%
2019	WAS	12/6	442	47	26	198	1	3	55%	-5.8	2	7.6	7.0	--	2.3	--	-2.3	1	-44.8%	--	-118	--	13.3%	--	93%
2020	WAS			46	29	325	1		63%			11.2							-6.2%						

For whatever reason, Quinn and quarterback Dwayne Haskins could never get on the same page last season. Miscommunications and misunderstandings about route timings or route breaks were littered throughout their film catalog. Quinn's stat line suffered greatly for it. Among receivers with 10 to 49 targets last season, Quinn's -118 DYAR was the worst mark by a comfortable margin. Quinn stayed on the field partly because Washington lacked receiver talent, partly because of his versatility as a blocker from the slot. Quinn can function similarly to Cooper Kupp from the Rams, often blocking on zone runs his way or crack-blocking on runs designed to go outside of him. With a non-Shanahan style offense on the way in Washington, though, it is tough to predict how Quinn's new role will shake out.

Jalen Reagor   Height: 5-11   Weight: 195   College: Texas Christian   Draft: 2020/1 (21)   Born: 1-Jan-1999   Age: 22   Risk: Blue

Year	Tm	G/GS	Snaps	Pass	Rec	Yds	TD	EZ	C%	+/-	Drop	Yd/C	aDOT	Rk	YAC	Rk	YAC+	BTkl	DVOA	Rk	DYAR	Rk	Use	Rk	Slot
2020	PHI			65	38	476	3		58%			12.5							-7.5%						

Get Reagor the ball in space and watch him fly. Reagor might be the best receiver in this year's class at running with the ball in his hands; he had multiple punt return touchdowns last season at TCU and was good for one or two end arounds per game as well. With his 4.47s speed and quick acceleration, Reagor's going to be a serious threat right off the bat on vertical routes, sprinting downfield and daring the defense to come with him. The issue is that he's not a complete receiver quite yet; his route-running needs work, he has trouble in traffic, and he really benefitted from soft coverage in college. It will take a clever play-caller, unafraid to bust out the gadget plays, to get the most out of Reagor as a rookie. Reagor will be helped enormously if the rest of the Eagles' offense is healthy enough for him to play a supporting role in 2019 as he continues to develop his undeniable athleticism into a complete package.

Hunter Renfrow   Height: 5-10   Weight: 185   College: Clemson   Draft: 2019/5 (149)   Born: 21-Dec-1995   Age: 25   Risk: Green

Year	Tm	G/GS	Snaps	Pass	Rec	Yds	TD	EZ	C%	+/-	Drop	Yd/C	aDOT	Rk	YAC	Rk	YAC+	BTkl	DVOA	Rk	DYAR	Rk	Use	Rk	Slot
2019	OAK	13/4	445	71	49	605	4	5	69%	+3.4	6	12.3	7.2	78	6.1	6	+1.8	14	7.9%	27	112	38	17.6%	56	97%
2020	LV			77	54	592	4		70%			11.0							8.8%						

It's almost surreal that Renfrow caught 49 passes last season. He looks and runs like a 5-foot-10, 185-pound tight end, with none of the lateral quickness you would expect from a Julian Edelman cosplayer. He's a slow-footed route-runner and tiny target, and while his hands are sticky on contested catches, a few easy receptions bounced off his chest. Yet Renfrow was often open, with the defense sometimes appearing to forget to cover him on deep routes, as if they mistook him for a young camera-man who strayed onto the field. Renfrow is the player your cranky father-in-law creates for himself in *Madden*, right down to the receding hairline, with 99 ratings in all the awareness-and-pluck categories. Both Jon Gruden and Mike Mayock have strong father-in-law tendencies, and Renfrow indeed has awareness and pluck, so he should still play a significant role in the Raiders' offense, despite the influx of larger receivers who can run fast.

Josh Reynolds   Height: 6-3   Weight: 196   College: Texas A&M   Draft: 2017/4 (117)   Born: 16-Feb-1995   Age: 25   Risk: Green

Year	Tm	G/GS	Snaps	Pass	Rec	Yds	TD	EZ	C%	+/-	Drop	Yd/C	aDOT	Rk	YAC	Rk	YAC+	BTkl	DVOA	Rk	DYAR	Rk	Use	Rk	Slot
2017	LAR	16/1	280	24	11	104	1	5	46%	-3.9	0	9.5	7.4	--	3.1	--	-0.4	1	-31.0%	--	-35	--	4.6%	--	79%
2018	LAR	16/8	611	53	29	402	5	12	55%	-1.6	2	13.9	11.7	37	4.4	37	+0.4	4	1.9%	40	62	48	9.6%	82	79%
2019	LAR	16/2	490	43	21	326	1	4	49%	-5.5	1	15.5	10.8	--	6.6	--	+1.6	6	-16.1%	--	-11	--	7.0%	--	65%
2020	LAR			47	29	407	2		62%			14.0							4.7%						

Reynolds' rises and falls in the Los Angeles lineup are as regular and predictable as California sunshine—and just like the sun setting into the Pacific, when Reynolds disappears, he vanishes entirely. As a rookie, he had eight catches in one three-game stretch but only three catches in his other 13 games. In 2018, he followed a catchless four games with seven catches in four games, two more catchless contests, and finally 30 catches in nine games including the playoffs to end the season. In 2019, it was more of the same with two catches in his first seven games and then 19 receptions in his last nine. He has only started 11 games in his career, but following the trade of Brandin Cooks, the Rams are counting on him not just to be a full-time starter but also to spend less time in the slot and more time split wide. This could be the last chance Reynolds gets under the sun.

Paul Richardson   Height: 6-0   Weight: 180   College: Colorado   Draft: 2014/2 (45)   Born: 4/13/1992   Age: 28   Risk: N/A

Year	Tm	G/GS	Snaps	Pass	Rec	Yds	TD	EZ	C%	+/-	Drop	Yd/C	aDOT	Rk	YAC	Rk	YAC+	BTkl	DVOA	Rk	DYAR	Rk	Use	Rk	Slot
2017	SEA	16/13	816	80	44	703	6	7	55%	-2.3	6	16.0	15.4	10	2.8	72	-1.4	5	13.4%	20	161	23	15.4%	60	35%
2018	WAS	7/4	368	35	20	262	2	2	57%	-1.5	0	13.1	13.8	--	2.3	--	-2.0	1	4.1%	--	48	--	17.1%	--	56%
2019	WAS	10/6	412	42	28	245	2	4	67%	+0.9	2	8.8	9.6	--	1.8	--	-2.4	3	-11.3%	--	4	--	14.6%	--	60%

Various shoulder, knee, and hamstring injuries may have sealed Richardson's fate in Washington even before the team drafted quarterback Dwayne Haskins in 2019. But if his rookie passing splits were any indication, Haskins didn't help. Richardson earned his five-year, $40-million contract with the Redskins in part on the strength of his ability to go deep. He had five catches in 2017 on passes that traveled between 35 and 45 yards in the air. But in Richardson's first year in Washington, the hyper-conservative Alex Smith threw Richardson mostly screens and comebacks, and in Richardson's second year, Haskins produced a dreadful -86.0% DVOA on his bomb attempts thrown 26 or more yards down the field. It was the worst rate of any quarterback with 10 or more such attempts. The trajectory of the Redskins' current rebuild wouldn't fit with Richardson's potential late-20s peak anyway, but if Haskins can't throw a quality deep ball, then Richardson could not have fit in any alternate timelines. The Redskins released Richardson this offseason to reduce his substantial cap hit. And with his injuries and modest production from recent seasons, Richardson may be staring at the end of his NFL career.

Calvin Ridley

Height: 6-1 | Weight: 190 | College: Alabama | Draft: 2018/1 (26) | Born: 20-Dec-1994 | Age: 26 | Risk: Green

Year	Tm	G/GS	Snaps	Pass	Rec	Yds	TD	EZ	C%	+/-	Drop	Yd/C	aDOT	Rk	YAC	Rk	YAC+	BTkl	DVOA	Rk	DYAR	Rk	Use	Rk	Slot
2018	ATL	16/5	644	92	64	821	10	5	70%	+3.9	9	12.8	10.6	47	5.7	13	+0.7	5	10.2%	26	167	21	15.3%	63	49%
2019	ATL	13/10	732	93	63	866	7	8	68%	+8.3	3	13.7	14.1	21	2.2	78	-1.9	6	30.6%	2	310	5	17.8%	53	32%
2020	ATL			112	75	944	6		67%			12.6							9.0%						

With 31-year-old teammate Julio Jones under contract for four more years and showing no signs of an imminent decline, Ridley may need until his own 30s to escape from Jones' long shadow. But Ridley deserves praise today, however good his circumstances are. He may not be the athletic marvel of his 6-foot-3, 220-pound teammate, but Ridley is exceptionally versatile. In 2019, he finished top 10 at the position with a 26.9% DVOA from the slot and a 34.3% DVOA out wide among the players with at least 30 targets from those positions. Jones can't boast that same distinction despite qualifying for both lists. Only Michael Thomas and the criminally underrated Tyrell Williams share Ridley's honor.

Seth Roberts

Height: 6-2 | Weight: 195 | College: West Alabama | Draft: 2014/FA | Born: 22-Feb-1991 | Age: 29 | Risk: Green

Year	Tm	G/GS	Snaps	Pass	Rec	Yds	TD	EZ	C%	+/-	Drop	Yd/C	aDOT	Rk	YAC	Rk	YAC+	BTkl	DVOA	Rk	DYAR	Rk	Use	Rk	Slot
2017	OAK	15/7	752	65	43	455	1	4	66%	+1.2	5	10.6	10.0	61	2.5	79	-2.0	2	-5.8%	61	34	66	12.5%	74	92%
2018	OAK	15/7	571	64	45	494	2	5	70%	+3.0	3	11.0	9.1	62	4.7	32	-0.7	4	4.7%	33	86	45	13.0%	71	97%
2019	BAL	16/0	558	35	21	271	2	3	60%	-1.3	1	12.9	9.6	--	3.3	--	-0.1	4	10.4%	--	62	--	8.2%	--	17%
2020	CAR			27	18	218	1		67%			12.1							8.6%						

Roberts caught fewer than half as many balls for the 2019 Ravens as he did for the 2018 Raiders, ceding the bulk of his customary underneath work to tight ends Mark Andrews, Hayden Hurst, and Nick Boyle on a team that spent most of its time running the ball in any case. But things could change for Roberts in 2020. His new team, the Panthers, features a new Joe Brady offense with a new quarterback in Teddy Bridgewater who has traditionally been one of the least aggressive quarterbacks in football. That could be bad news for speedy second and third receivers Robby Anderson and Curtis Samuel and good news for Roberts, who in that personal best season of 2018 saw 62 of his 64 targets come in the slot and was a positional leader with +3.0 receiving plus/minus. No other backup Panthers receiver has notable NFL experience, so don't be surprised if Roberts enjoys a new best career season at age 29.

Allen Robinson

Height: 6-2 | Weight: 220 | College: Penn State | Draft: 2014/2 (61) | Born: 8/24/1993 | Age: 27 | Risk: Green

Year	Tm	G/GS	Snaps	Pass	Rec	Yds	TD	EZ	C%	+/-	Drop	Yd/C	aDOT	Rk	YAC	Rk	YAC+	BTkl	DVOA	Rk	DYAR	Rk	Use	Rk	Slot
2017	JAX	1/1	3	1	1	17	0	0	100%	+0.6	0	17.0	15.0	--	2.0	--	-2.2	0	123.1%	--	12	--	3.0%	--	0%
2018	CHI	13/12	765	94	55	754	4	11	59%	-2.0	2	13.7	12.0	31	3.9	52	-0.4	9	-4.8%	52	62	47	24.3%	15	52%
2019	CHI	16/15	1025	154	98	1147	7	14	64%	+0.4	4	11.7	11.3	44	2.6	77	-1.9	9	0.4%	45	165	26	27.9%	4	65%
2020	CHI			124	74	933	5		60%			12.6							-5.1%						

Just once, we'd like to see Robinson have a season with a good quarterback, so we could get a baseline for how much better his somewhat average numbers would be if anyone could throw the ball in his ZIP code; the only season where Robinson's quarterback had a positive DVOA was 2018, when Mitch Trubisky's hit 3.6%. Robinson continues to be targeted in crucial situations at an incredible rate, with almost half of the Bears' third-down passes to wide receivers headed his way, but his DVOA of 1.0% isn't exactly what the Bears are paying for. Neither was his 9.1% DVOA in the red zone, where he had 23 of Chicago's 47 receiver targets. Some of the blame surely goes to the quarterback and some goes to a lack of other quality threats around him; the defense could tee off on Robinson all day long. The biggest Robinson-related concern was his drop in YAC+. While his game has never been about turning short passes upfield, there's a line between "not great at YAC" and "terrible YAC"; ranking 77th out of 81 qualified receivers is on the wrong side of that line. A more accurate passing performance would help with a lot of these issues.

Demarcus Robinson Height: 6-1   Weight: 203   College: Florida   Draft: 2016/4 (126)   Born: 21-Sep-1994   Age: 26   Risk: Green

Year	Tm	G/GS	Snaps	Pass	Rec	Yds	TD	EZ	C%	+/-	Drop	Yd/C	aDOT	Rk	YAC	Rk	YAC+	BTkl	DVOA	Rk	DYAR	Rk	Use	Rk	Slot
2017	KC	16/8	586	39	21	212	0	4	54%	-1.8	3	10.1	11.0	--	2.0	--	-2.0	0	-16.9%	--	-14	--	7.7%	--	51%
2018	KC	16/5	419	33	22	288	4	4	67%	+0.6	1	13.1	12.1	--	5.3	--	+0.0	4	13.5%	--	68	--	5.8%	--	45%
2019	KC	16/10	743	55	32	449	4	6	58%	-1.4	1	14.0	13.3	25	3.2	67	-1.1	9	1.0%	42	61	53	10.1%	79	45%
2020	KC			33	22	296	2		67%			13.5							11.9%						

Robinson went 6-172-2 with Tyreek Hill injured in Week 2 against the Raiders, then slowly slid toward decoy status when Hill returned and Mecole Hardman took on increased duties. There were mumblings that Robinson would cash in as a free agent, but his reputation as a player who struggles with the finer points of the offense must have preceded him, and he returned to the Chiefs after finding no takers. Robinson has spent three seasons as a fast guy who does most of his damage when the defense just runs out of available bodies in coverage against the Chiefs. He'll resume that role this season.

John Ross Height: 5-11   Weight: 194   College: Washington   Draft: 2017/1 (9)   Born: 27-Nov-1995   Age: 25   Risk: Yellow

Year	Tm	G/GS	Snaps	Pass	Rec	Yds	TD	EZ	C%	+/-	Drop	Yd/C	aDOT	Rk	YAC	Rk	YAC+	BTkl	DVOA	Rk	DYAR	Rk	Use	Rk	Slot
2017	CIN	3/1	17	2	0	0	0	0	0%	-0.9	0	0.0	23.0	--	0.0	--	+0.0	0	-105.6%	--	-14	--	2.1%	--	50%
2018	CIN	13/10	601	58	21	210	7	7	36%	-13.3	6	10.0	14.2	18	2.8	78	-1.5	4	-33.3%	84	-96	81	13.5%	68	32%
2019	CIN	8/8	410	56	28	506	3	1	50%	-4.6	7	18.1	15.6	8	7.1	3	+2.3	5	-4.5%	54	36	57	18.9%	45	54%
2020	CIN			64	33	546	4		52%			16.5							-10.4%						

The Bengals have already declined Ross' fifth-year option, meaning unless he has a monster breakout season (or accepts a small deal with no other offer out there), this is likely it for him in Cincinnati. The tantalizing traits and moments remain—in the 19 games Ross has actually started, he has nine touchdowns, and last year he had over 18 yards per catch. But the flaws are there, too—aside from the injuries, his career catch rate is an abominable 42%. Fans dream of Ross streaking under perfectly placed passes from Joe Burrow and providing the game-breaking plays he was drafted so highly to make. But as the late Dolores O'Riordan sang, "In all my dreams, it's never quite as it seems."

Henry Ruggs Height: 5-11   Weight: 188   College: Alabama   Draft: 2020/1 (12)   Born: 24-Jan-1999   Age: 21   Risk: Yellow

Year	Tm	G/GS	Snaps	Pass	Rec	Yds	TD	EZ	C%	+/-	Drop	Yd/C	aDOT	Rk	YAC	Rk	YAC+	BTkl	DVOA	Rk	DYAR	Rk	Use	Rk	Slot
2020	LV			72	45	636	3		63%			14.1							6.3%						

A total of 11 wide receivers have posted 40-yard dash times of 4.3 seconds or faster at the combine since 2000: Ruggs, Dri Archer, Yamon Figurs, Jacoby Ford, Marquise Goodwin, Darrius Heyward-Bey, Jerome Mathis, J.J. Nelson, John Ross, Donte' Stallworth, and the "other" Mike Thomas. (Tyreek Hill, you may recall, was not invited to the combine, and including pro day workouts takes us straight into the Wild Wild West of suspicious data points). Stallworth is the closest thing to a star on that list, and even he was never a true No. 1 wideout. The rest are a mix of sporadic big-play threats (Goodwin, Ford, Nelson, perhaps Ross), special-teamers of various stripes (Heyward-Bey, Mathis, Figurs) and all-purpose threats who enjoyed little (Thomas) to no (Archer) NFL success. Michael Irvin floated some "maybe receivers can just be TOO fast to be useful" nonsense after Ruggs' 4.28s combine result, but the problem with many of the fastest receivers to enter the NFL is that many would not have been college starters if they ran in the 4.45s range because they couldn't run a route, take a hit, or so forth. That was not a problem with Ruggs.

Curtis Samuel

Height: 5-11 Weight: 195 College: Ohio State Draft: 2017/2 (40) Born: 11-Aug-1996 Age: 24 Risk: Green

Year	Tm	G/GS	Snaps	Pass	Rec	Yds	TD	EZ	C%	+/-	Drop	Yd/C	aDOT	Rk	YAC	Rk	YAC+	BTkl	DVOA	Rk	DYAR	Rk	Use	Rk	Slot
2017	CAR	9/4	226	26	15	115	0	1	58%	-2.1	2	7.7	11.0	--	3.4	--	-2.3	4	-18.3%	--	-12	--	9.9%	--	71%
2018	CAR	13/8	466	65	39	494	5	9	60%	-2.2	3	12.7	12.3	29	2.8	77	-1.7	14	-5.4%	53	39	54	14.9%	65	24%
2019	CAR	16/15	970	105	54	627	6	10	51%	-6.0	7	11.6	15.3	11	2.8	74	-1.5	7	-15.1%	71	-21	73	17.9%	52	34%
2020	CAR			84	48	610	5		57%			12.7							-3.6%						

Samuel has been in the league for three seasons now, but it still isn't completely clear what he can be in the NFL. A hybrid running back/receiver in college, Samuel has seen his carry volume double each of the last two seasons with no decline in his efficiency. In 2019, his 54.2% rushing DVOA on 19 carries was the highest of any player with 15 carries or more. But as a receiver, Samuel has struggled to find his niche. There was some pre-draft optimism that he could work from the slot like Percy Harvin, a player with a similar skill set, did in his prime. But Samuel has produced -40.1% and -15.3% receiving DVOA from the slot the last two seasons, and in 2019 he dropped seven of 62 catchable targets, an 11% drop rate that would preclude him from having success in a role that demands consistency. Perhaps that is why Samuel has been a frequent name in trade rumors this offseason, especially after the Panthers added new head coach Matt Rhule's former Temple product Robby Anderson, who at 6-foot-3 and with a similar-to-Samuel 4.36s 40-yard dash time from the combine is a more natural fit as a deep threat.

Deebo Samuel

Height: 5-11 Weight: 214 College: South Carolina Draft: 2019/2 (36) Born: 15-Jan-1996 Age: 24 Risk: Red

Year	Tm	G/GS	Snaps	Pass	Rec	Yds	TD	EZ	C%	+/-	Drop	Yd/C	aDOT	Rk	YAC	Rk	YAC+	BTkl	DVOA	Rk	DYAR	Rk	Use	Rk	Slot
2019	SF	15/11	728	81	57	802	3	5	70%	+1.6	8	14.1	7.6	75	8.3	2	+2.4	28	7.3%	29	121	34	18.1%	51	66%
2020	SF			78	52	660	4		67%			12.7							6.8%						

Samuel did most of his damage out of the slot, finishing with the third-largest gap between DVOA on targets out of the slot and DVOA on targets out wide. Samuel also led the league in rushing DYAR by wide receivers, serving as a serious weapon on end arounds as a counter to San Francisco's bread and butter in the run game. His rookie season was absolutely a success, but unfortunately for Samuel, he suffered a Jones fracture in June that could keep him from being ready by the start of the season. Samuel complemented the 49ers' running game very effectively as a rookie, but if he rushes back too quickly from his injury, his sophomore year could be a struggle.

Emmanuel Sanders

Height: 5-11 Weight: 180 College: Southern Methodist Draft: 2010/3 (82) Born: 17-Mar-1987 Age: 33 Risk: Yellow

Year	Tm	G/GS	Snaps	Pass	Rec	Yds	TD	EZ	C%	+/-	Drop	Yd/C	aDOT	Rk	YAC	Rk	YAC+	BTkl	DVOA	Rk	DYAR	Rk	Use	Rk	Slot
2017	DEN	12/11	635	91	47	555	2	6	51%	-7.1	6	11.8	11.0	50	3.6	54	-0.6	7	-18.2%	75	-40	79	22.0%	21	39%
2018	DEN	12/12	658	99	71	868	4	4	73%	+6.8	5	12.2	9.7	56	4.3	44	-1.3	10	2.0%	39	113	36	23.1%	20	68%
2019	2TM	17/16	859	97	66	869	5	8	68%	+3.7	2	13.2	10.8	46	3.6	58	-0.6	6	10.5%	24	188	22	20.1%	38	67%
2020	NO			80	61	772	5		76%			12.7							24.9%						

The NFL can move to a 17-game regular season as soon as 2021, but Sanders has been there, done that. After seven games, Denver traded him to San Francisco, where he played another 10 to become the ninth player in league history to play in 17 regular-season games. With the 49ers, Sanders enjoyed a modest revival. Over the first seven weeks, he had a 6.9% DVOA. Over the final 10, he had a 13.4% DVOA. San Francisco's offense as a whole experienced a greater bump—from pedestrian to potent—and came a pass away from winning the Super Bowl. In New Orleans, Sanders might not be able to avoid another playoff heartbreak, but Drew Brees definitely isn't going to overthrow him.

Mohamed Sanu

Height: 6-2 Weight: 215 College: Rutgers Draft: 2012/3 (83) Born: 22-Aug-1989 Age: 31 Risk: Green

Year	Tm	G/GS	Snaps	Pass	Rec	Yds	TD	EZ	C%	+/-	Drop	Yd/C	aDOT	Rk	YAC	Rk	YAC+	BTkl	DVOA	Rk	DYAR	Rk	Use	Rk	Slot
2017	ATL	15/15	756	96	67	703	5	7	70%	+4.3	6	10.5	8.0	77	3.7	53	-0.6	8	10.7%	24	179	18	20.0%	33	78%
2018	ATL	16/16	830	94	66	838	4	4	70%	+1.7	2	12.7	8.2	73	6.1	7	+0.8	9	6.4%	29	141	30	15.8%	58	84%
2019	2TM	15/12	769	89	59	520	2	5	66%	-2.5	5	8.8	8.0	72	3.3	65	-1.3	6	-17.0%	73	-30	74	15.4%	62	76%
2020	NE			47	30	300	2		64%			10.0							-3.2%						

By almost any measure, Sanu had a career-worst season in 2019, but it did not start off that way. In seven games with the Falcons, Sanu grabbed 33 balls for 313 yards and a touchdown, more or less keeping pace with his career averages. He also caught nearly 80% of his passes over that span. In eight games after being traded to New England, however, Sanu caught just 26 of his 47 targets (55%) for 207 yards and a touchdown, most of which was well below his norm. Part of the issue was Sanu's role as a big slot receiver was muzzled in terms of average depth of target. Not once in any of Sanu's full seasons in Atlanta did he have more than 45% of his passes in the short area, yet 55% of his plays in 2019 were in the short area—a number that very well could have been higher if he spent the whole year in New England's constipated offense. The situation around Sanu will need to open up in order for him to rediscover himself as a big slot threat over the middle.

Tajae Sharpe			Height: 6-2		Weight: 194		College: Massachusetts			Draft: 2016/5 (140)				Born: 23-Dec-1994		Age: 26		Risk: Green	
Year	Tm	G/GS	Snaps	Pass	Rec	Yds	TD	EZ	C%	+/-	Drop	Yd/C	aDOT	Rk	YAC	Rk	YAC+	BTkl	DVOA	Rk	DYAR	Rk	Use	Rk	Slot
2018	TEN	16/13	592	47	26	316	2	8	55%	-2.5	1	12.2	10.9	--	3.2	--	-1.2	1	-4.9%	--	30	--	11.1%	--	85%
2019	TEN	15/6	444	34	25	329	4	4	74%	+4.9	0	13.2	15.1	--	2.3	--	-1.6	1	45.1%	--	157	--	8.6%	--	57%
2020	MIN			13	9	117	1		69%			13.0							14.4%						

Much like the rest of the Titans' offense, Sharpe's numbers drastically improved once Ryan Tannehill took over from Marcus Mariota, with his DVOA jumping from 16.0% to 54.5%. Mind you, even those Mariota numbers would have represented the best season of Sharpe's career. The addition of A.J. Brown and Adam Humphries cut into Sharpe's workload, and the need for him to work at all in the short game; his 15.1 aDOT would have ranked 12th had he had enough targets to qualify, and his 74% catch rate would have been third in the league. There is a reason, mind you, that the Titans cut his workload and felt fine with letting him go in the offseason—don't expect his rather fluky combination of a high catch rate with a high depth of target to be the norm going forward. Sharpe may actually get the most value in Minnesota's run-happy offense thanks to his willingness to work in the running game; he did some solid blocking for Derrick Henry down the stretch. That might be enough to give him the leg up in the race for the Vikings' third receiver slot.

Laviska Shenault			Height: 6-1		Weight: 227		College: Colorado			Draft: 2020/2 (42)				Born: 5-Oct-1998		Age: 22		Risk: Green	
Year	Tm	G/GS	Snaps	Pass	Rec	Yds	TD	EZ	C%	+/-	Drop	Yd/C	aDOT	Rk	YAC	Rk	YAC+	BTkl	DVOA	Rk	DYAR	Rk	Use	Rk	Slot
2020	JAX			34	21	278	2		62%			13.2							-2.1%						

Often described/decried as another toolsy "offensive weapon" type, Shenault had a productive college career as a receiver at Colorado but also battled injuries far too frequently. A shifty, sure-handed player who often made big plays after the catch, he has been compared to Cordarrelle Patterson and Percy Harvin—two players who had their moments in the NFL, but who ultimately had no true position in a professional offense. He may enjoy some initial success from the slot or as a returner, but he needs to refine and develop his craft as a receiver and to prove that he can withstand the physicality of the NFL. If he can do all of that, he has tremendous potential due to his outstanding athletic ability. If he cannot, the history books are littered with prospects who have struggled to make the transition from college offensive weapon to NFL receiver.

Sterling Shepard			Height: 5-10		Weight: 201		College: Oklahoma			Draft: 2016/2 (40)				Born: 10-Feb-1993		Age: 27		Risk: Red	
Year	Tm	G/GS	Snaps	Pass	Rec	Yds	TD	EZ	C%	+/-	Drop	Yd/C	aDOT	Rk	YAC	Rk	YAC+	BTkl	DVOA	Rk	DYAR	Rk	Use	Rk	Slot
2017	NYG	11/10	688	84	59	731	2	3	70%	+4.5	6	12.4	8.8	72	5.0	21	+0.6	6	4.9%	37	120	37	20.1%	31	89%
2018	NYG	16/16	936	107	66	872	4	12	62%	-2.6	7	13.2	10.2	50	4.7	33	-0.1	9	-0.9%	46	97	42	18.5%	40	69%
2019	NYG	10/10	608	83	57	576	3	7	69%	+1.6	3	10.1	9.9	60	3.1	70	-1.2	8	-8.1%	61	30	60	22.6%	23	65%
2020	NYG			98	61	684	4		62%			11.2							-4.9%						

Without Odell Beckham, Shepard was expected to take over as the Giants' No. 1 receiver, or at least he had the opportunity for that role. But migraine and concussion issues caused him to miss six games and set career lows nearly across the board. With Golden Tate on board, Shepard was expected to play more on the outside, but Shepard played heavily in the slot during Tate's four-game suspension to start the season and continued to play there throughout the remainder of the year. Shepard was much better in the slot (0.4% DVOA) than on the outside (-28.0%), but he was never able to settle into a productive role on the offense. Shepard did have one standout aspect: running the ball, especially early in the season on jet sweeps and end arounds.

He had two carries for 22 yards in Week 3, a 23-yard carry in Week 4, and a 22-yard carry once he returned from injury in Week 11. His 156.5% DVOA was first among receivers with at least five carries.

Steven Sims

| | Height: 5-10 | Weight: 176 | College: Kansas | | | Draft: 2019/FA | | Born: 31-Mar-1997 | | Age: 23 | | Risk: Green |

Year	Tm	G/GS	Snaps	Pass	Rec	Yds	TD	EZ	C%	+/-	Drop	Yd/C	aDOT	Rk	YAC	Rk	YAC+	BTkl	DVOA	Rk	DYAR	Rk	Use	Rk	Slot
2019	WAS	16/2	314	56	34	310	4	8	61%	-1.8	5	9.1	7.2	77	5.1	18	-0.5	8	-24.6%	78	-53	75	12.5%	71	78%
2020	WAS			40	24	282	1		60%			11.8							-9.7%						

A UDFA out of Kansas last year, Sims surprised the masses with a respectable rookie campaign. Though he did not put up any stunning numbers to suggest he is the NFL's next undrafted star receiver, he did find a way to make himself the second-most targeted receiver on Washington's roster, mostly through his performance over the final five games. 259 of Sim's 310 yards came in the final five games. Sim's 5-foot-10 frame would not lead you to believe it, but he shined as a red zone threat. He caught six of 10 red zone targets and posted an 18.0% DVOA, the highest rating on the team. Quarterback Dwayne Haskins also seemed to lean on Sims the longer a series dragged on. Sims earned 12 targets on first down, 19 on second down, and a whopping 28 on third/fourth down. Sims is unlikely to blossom into a heavy contributor, but if he can iron out his game just a bit and be a solid fourth or fifth wide receiver for Washington, that is a win for a UDFA signing.

Darius Slayton

| | Height: 6-1 | Weight: 190 | College: Auburn | | | Draft: 2019/5 (171) | | Born: 12-Jan-1997 | | Age: 23 | | Risk: Green |

Year	Tm	G/GS	Snaps	Pass	Rec	Yds	TD	EZ	C%	+/-	Drop	Yd/C	aDOT	Rk	YAC	Rk	YAC+	BTkl	DVOA	Rk	DYAR	Rk	Use	Rk	Slot
2019	NYG	14/9	709	84	48	740	8	6	57%	+2.0	3	15.4	14.1	20	4.0	45	-0.2	5	9.6%	25	148	30	16.5%	60	21%
2020	NYG			88	51	747	6		58%			14.6							0.8%						

Slayton was the only Giants player who could run further than 10 yards down the field, or at least that's how the Giants treated him. Slayton led the team with a 14.1-yard aDOT and 25.5% of the team's air yards. From the moment Daniel Jones stepped on the field, the quarterback and fifth-round rookie had a connection—mostly from playing on the second team together all through training camp. Slayton was Jones' favorite target partly through that connection, and partly because he was the healthiest receiver throughout the season.

So many of Slayton's catches came down the field in a contested situation with a defender draped all over him. That doesn't say great things about his separation ability at the top of routes. There's a chance Slayton has a Mike Williams-like ability to win a majority of contested catches, but that's something you'd rather see from someone built like Williams and not your 190-pound receiver who ran a 4.39s 40 at the combine.

JuJu Smith-Schuster

| | Height: 6-1 | Weight: 215 | College: USC | | | Draft: 2017/2 (62) | | Born: 22-Nov-1996 | | Age: 24 | | Risk: Yellow |

Year	Tm	G/GS	Snaps	Pass	Rec	Yds	TD	EZ	C%	+/-	Drop	Yd/C	aDOT	Rk	YAC	Rk	YAC+	BTkl	DVOA	Rk	DYAR	Rk	Use	Rk	Slot
2017	PIT	14/7	707	79	58	917	7	4	73%	+8.1	2	15.8	9.9	63	6.7	5	+2.2	8	37.3%	1	317	6	15.3%	63	59%
2018	PIT	16/13	960	167	111	1426	7	14	67%	+3.1	5	12.8	9.0	63	5.8	11	+0.7	12	4.4%	34	235	17	24.8%	14	65%
2019	PIT	12/12	580	71	42	552	3	6	59%	-2.8	6	13.1	10.0	58	5.3	13	+0.2	4	-11.3%	65	8	66	19.7%	40	74%
2020	PIT			106	67	859	5		63%			12.8							2.4%						

Freed from the Antonio Brown/Ben Roethlisberger ecosystem, Smith-Schuster struggled with the extra attention, catching just 23 of 39 targets against man coverage for 340 yards. Smith-Schuster is a zone-buster who operates best out of the slot, and that kind of player needs an outside receiver who can shift some matchups away from him to really thrive. Roethlisberger should be back, and Diontae Johnson has a chance to be that outside receiver. Smith-Schuster's fantasy rebound potential certainly remains intriguing if Roethlisberger is able to make it 16 games.

Tre'Quan Smith

Height: 6-2   Weight: 210   College: Central Florida   Draft: 2018/3 (91)   Born: 7-Jan-1996   Age: 25   Risk: Green

Year	Tm	G/GS	Snaps	Pass	Rec	Yds	TD	EZ	C%	+/-	Drop	Yd/C	aDOT	Rk	YAC	Rk	YAC+	BTkl	DVOA	Rk	DYAR	Rk	Use	Rk	Slot
2018	NO	15/7	567	44	28	427	5	7	64%	+2.8	2	15.3	11.7	--	4.1	--	+0.1	2	22.7%	--	126	--	9.0%	--	55%
2019	NO	11/6	464	25	18	234	5	3	72%	+0.9	2	13.0	7.8	--	6.4	--	+2.8	8	53.6%	--	135	--	6.7%	--	69%
2020	NO			34	23	307	2		68%			13.3							13.8%						

Smith will have to earn his way onto the field this season, a fast fall from a year ago when he was a breakout candidate. Ankle injuries derailed his development last season, costing him five games. The time away took a toll on him, he told NOLA.com. "You want to be there, but then your mind is in a different place," he said. "You can't help it but to get down on yourself." Still, he showed flashes of potential, catching all four of his red zone targets for touchdowns. With the more versatile Emmanuel Sanders in the fold, Smith isn't likely to see much of an uptick in volume. He might even have to fight off the dynamic Deonte Harris.

Willie Snead

Height: 5-11   Weight: 205   College: Ball State   Draft: 2014/FA   Born: 17-Oct-1992   Age: 28   Risk: Green

Year	Tm	G/GS	Snaps	Pass	Rec	Yds	TD	EZ	C%	+/-	Drop	Yd/C	aDOT	Rk	YAC	Rk	YAC+	BTkl	DVOA	Rk	DYAR	Rk	Use	Rk	Slot
2017	NO	11/7	259	16	8	92	0	0	50%	-1.1	1	11.5	7.6	--	4.0	--	-1.2	1	-31.0%	--	-23	--	4.4%	--	81%
2018	BAL	16/10	821	95	62	651	1	1	65%	+0.1	5	10.5	9.0	66	4.5	36	-0.3	9	-9.8%	60	21	57	17.6%	47	91%
2019	BAL	16/11	688	46	31	339	5	4	67%	+1.3	3	10.9	9.0	--	4.1	--	-0.0	6	12.4%	--	88	--	10.8%	--	93%
2020	BAL			28	18	220	2		64%			12.2							4.3%						

Snead made good use of his 31 catches in 2019, scoring on five of them. He was also strong on second downs, with a 35.3% DVOA, but nowhere close to that on the other downs. The competition in the Baltimore receiver room was Kleenex-soft in 2019. The fact the team drafted two slot receivers to compete with Snead speaks volumes about his long-term viability.

Kenny Stills

Height: 6-1   Weight: 202   College: Oklahoma   Draft: 2013/5 (144)   Born: 22-Apr-1992   Age: 28   Risk: Blue

Year	Tm	G/GS	Snaps	Pass	Rec	Yds	TD	EZ	C%	+/-	Drop	Yd/C	aDOT	Rk	YAC	Rk	YAC+	BTkl	DVOA	Rk	DYAR	Rk	Use	Rk	Slot
2017	MIA	16/16	942	105	58	847	6	10	55%	+1.0	4	14.6	15.2	12	2.7	75	-1.4	4	0.4%	44	107	44	18.0%	43	54%
2018	MIA	15/15	745	64	37	553	6	6	58%	+0.9	3	14.9	16.5	3	3.5	63	-0.6	4	12.6%	22	127	33	15.7%	59	54%
2019	HOU	13/5	604	55	40	561	4	4	73%	+5.4	3	14.0	10.6	50	3.6	57	-1.5	1	24.7%	5	162	27	13.0%	69	69%
2020	HOU			50	33	467	3		66%			14.2							13.1%						

A throw-in from the Laremy Tunsil trade who was likely on his way to being cut or traded for a low-round pick, Stills dialed it back to 2014 with a top-five receiving DVOA for the first time since being dealt away from New Orleans. The Dolphins locked into their idea of Stills being primarily a deep receiver: in four years in Miami, Stills' short-target percentage never rose above 24%. In Houston last year, it was 44%. *Logic Will Break Your Heart*, as some other Stills once sang, and that has kind of been the calling card of this Stills' career. It didn't make a lot of sense that the Saints traded him. It didn't make a lot of sense that the Dolphins didn't utilize him underneath to emphasize Jarvis Landry. It currently doesn't make a lot of sense that the Texans appear to be squeezing him out of a role by acquiring Brandin Cooks after a productive season. Stills remains a solid wideout on the WR2/3 cusp who provides real value downfield. Someone might find that out before his NFL clock starts ticking into the 30s.

Courtland Sutton

Height: 6-4   Weight: 216   College: Southern Methodist   Draft: 2018/2 (40)   Born: 10-Oct-1995   Age: 25   Risk: Green

Year	Tm	G/GS	Snaps	Pass	Rec	Yds	TD	EZ	C%	+/-	Drop	Yd/C	aDOT	Rk	YAC	Rk	YAC+	BTkl	DVOA	Rk	DYAR	Rk	Use	Rk	Slot
2018	DEN	16/9	819	84	42	704	4	17	50%	-5.9	9	16.8	14.3	17	3.9	54	-0.5	5	1.3%	44	95	44	15.4%	62	25%
2019	DEN	16/14	942	124	72	1112	6	12	58%	+1.1	6	15.4	12.4	36	4.9	23	+0.6	18	5.7%	32	189	21	26.9%	5	43%
2020	DEN			115	61	895	5		53%			14.7							-8.9%						

Sutton's catch rate and yards per catch by month: September (Joe Flacco at quarterback): 71% and 14.1; October (Flacco): 59% and 19.3; November (Brandon Allen): 44% and 17.8; December (Drew Lock): 55% and 12.7. Flacco threw enough I-formation, play-action heave-ho bombs to Sutton, mixed in with typical Flacco throws in front of the sticks on third down, to make the numbers look good early in the season. Allen uncorked a couple of dump-and-chase bombs (with Sutton making some spectacular catches in traffic) but did little else. Lock lacked timing, accuracy, and comfort when throwing further than 10 yards downfield to Sutton, but benefited from more quick screens and "help the rookie out" play calls.

Sutton has spent his first two seasons proving that he can be a bad quarterback's best friend with his one-handed end zone catches and ability to leap in front of two defenders to turn an underthrown gopher ball into a big play. If Lock can make better use of Sutton's services than he did last year, it will provide a huge statistical boost to both players. And of course, if Lock becomes more accurate and reliable while Sutton helps cover up a mistake here and there, it will benefit all parties in the long term.

Auden Tate   Height: 6-5   Weight: 228   College: Florida State   Draft: 2018/7 (253)   Born: 3-Feb-1997   Age: 23   Risk: Green

Year	Tm	G/GS	Snaps	Pass	Rec	Yds	TD	EZ	C%	+/-	Drop	Yd/C	aDOT	Rk	YAC	Rk	YAC+	BTkl	DVOA	Rk	DYAR	Rk	Use	Rk	Slot
2018	CIN	7/0	77	12	4	35	0	1	33%	-3.8	1	8.8	10.2	--	0.5	--	-3.3	0	-65.0%	--	-48	--	5.1%	--	25%
2019	CIN	12/10	666	80	40	575	1	8	50%	-8.3	3	14.4	12.0	38	3.4	63	-1.0	6	-13.4%	69	-5	69	18.8%	46	41%
2020	CIN			10	6	78	0		60%			13.0							-0.4%						

Tate is supposed to be a red zone weapon, given his height and penchant for the spectacular grab, but his efficiency inside the 20 was horrid, with a -47.3% DVOA on a team-high 14 targets. The return of A.J. Green and the drafting of Tee Higgins knock Tate way down the depth chart.

Golden Tate   Height: 5-10   Weight: 197   College: Notre Dame   Draft: 2010/2 (60)   Born: 2-Aug-1988   Age: 32   Risk: Green

Year	Tm	G/GS	Snaps	Pass	Rec	Yds	TD	EZ	C%	+/-	Drop	Yd/C	aDOT	Rk	YAC	Rk	YAC+	BTkl	DVOA	Rk	DYAR	Rk	Use	Rk	Slot
2017	DET	16/12	791	120	92	1003	5	1	77%	+8.6	3	10.9	6.0	85	6.8	4	+1.2	23	9.7%	27	204	16	20.9%	27	80%
2018	2TM	15/7	606	114	74	795	4	3	66%	-3.6	9	10.7	6.7	80	5.7	12	+0.6	29	-27.8%	81	-134	84	20.8%	29	86%
2019	NYG	11/10	629	86	49	676	6	4	58%	-5.1	4	13.8	10.0	57	5.8	9	+1.1	12	-2.0%	47	71	48	21.3%	29	91%
2020	NYG			87	53	643	3		61%			12.1							-3.0%						

Tate's first season with the Giants began with a four-game suspension for violating the league's substance abuse policy and it didn't get much better. There was still the catch-and-run ability—Tate had the sixth-highest yards after the catch above expectation—but much of that needed to be created in open space. SIS charted Tate with just three broken tackles on receptions all season.

In Week 10 against the Jets, Tate took a screen 61 yards for a touchdown. On four other screen receptions (six targets), he had 17 yards.

One place where Tate brought value was in the red zone. He only had nine targets in that area, but his 38.9% DVOA was the ninth highest among 89 players with at least eight targets.

Trent Taylor   Height: 5-8   Weight: 181   College: Louisiana Tech   Draft: 2017/5 (177)   Born: 30-Apr-1994   Age: 26   Risk: Green

Year	Tm	G/GS	Snaps	Pass	Rec	Yds	TD	EZ	C%	+/-	Drop	Yd/C	aDOT	Rk	YAC	Rk	YAC+	BTkl	DVOA	Rk	DYAR	Rk	Use	Rk	Slot
2017	SF	15/1	491	60	43	430	2	3	72%	+1.8	4	10.0	6.9	82	4.3	41	+0.0	7	11.4%	23	114	40	10.8%	79	84%
2018	SF	14/0	321	40	26	215	1	2	65%	-3.0	2	8.3	6.0	--	4.0	--	-0.9	1	-19.4%	--	-21	--	9.2%	--	90%
2020	SF			16	11	124	1		69%			11.3							6.0%						

Taylor was poised to be San Francisco's starting slot receiver entering 2019, but a foot injury that eventually required five separate procedures kept him out for the entire season. Entering the final year of his rookie contract, Taylor will have to beat out several younger receivers for targets if he wants to make a real impact for the 49ers in 2020 ahead of free agency. Taylor's most productive season came as a rookie in 2017, and he will have to improve on that output to justify a major free-agent outlay come next spring.

Adam Thielen   Height: 6-2   Weight: 200   College: Minnesota State   Draft: 2013/FA   Born: 22-Aug-1990   Age: 30   Risk: Green

Year	Tm	G/GS	Snaps	Pass	Rec	Yds	TD	EZ	C%	+/-	Drop	Yd/C	aDOT	Rk	YAC	Rk	YAC+	BTkl	DVOA	Rk	DYAR	Rk	Use	Rk	Slot
2017	MIN	16/16	1034	142	91	1276	4	13	64%	+8.1	6	14.0	10.9	52	4.9	26	+0.1	11	10.1%	26	261	11	27.5%	7	60%
2018	MIN	16/16	1011	153	113	1373	9	11	74%	+16.6	2	12.2	9.7	57	3.7	59	-0.7	5	15.2%	19	341	8	25.7%	12	70%
2019	MIN	10/10	443	48	30	418	6	7	63%	+2.0	3	13.9	13.0	30	3.9	46	-0.0	4	15.4%	16	103	40	17.7%	55	58%
2020	MIN			99	68	912	6		69%			13.4							13.1%						

You never want a receiver entering his 30s to come down with a soft tissue ailment, but hopefully Thielen's bad hamstring, which cost him six games last season, won't become a recurring issue. Before the hamstring injury, Thielen had a DVOA of 29.2%; that fell to -60.1% as he rushed back at the end of the year before rebounding in the playoffs. With Stefon Diggs out of town, expect Thielen's targets to skyrocket; per ESPN, Thielen was targeted 25.1% of the time over the past three years when Diggs was off the field. The question is whether or not Thielen can make the most of those targets without his long-time partner in crime; Thielen will be the focus of both the Vikings' passing game and their opponents' coverage scheme, so he'll likely get fewer plays matched up against overwhelmed slot corners and linebackers.

Demaryius Thomas
Height: 6-3   Weight: 225   College: Georgia Tech   Draft: 2010/1 (22)   Born: 25-Dec-1987   Age: 33   Risk: N/A

Year	Tm	G/GS	Snaps	Pass	Rec	Yds	TD	EZ	C%	+/-	Drop	Yd/C	aDOT	Rk	YAC	Rk	YAC+	BTkl	DVOA	Rk	DYAR	Rk	Use	Rk	Slot
2017	DEN	16/16	886	140	83	949	5	9	59%	-1.8	10	11.4	10.9	51	3.6	55	-0.7	10	0.2%	46	146	29	26.2%	11	34%
2018	2TM	15/15	764	89	59	677	5	8	66%	+1.4	6	11.5	10.4	49	4.7	31	-0.6	5	0.9%	45	96	43	18.2%	41	47%
2019	2TM	11/10	469	58	36	433	1	3	62%	-0.6	6	12.0	10.7	48	4.7	27	+0.5	3	-7.4%	58	25	62	17.7%	54	57%

Thomas has gone the way of Dez Bryant. A tall, once-athletic X-receiver, Thomas used to be among the league's best YAC and intermediate threats, showing off both the ability to separate and bully at the catch point. As Thomas ages into his 30s, however, the athleticism he used to rely on no longer shines in the same way, leaving him to be a role player at best. Thomas in 2019 was not the automatic yardage on first down that he used to be. In fact, Thomas caught just 50% of his targets and posted a -54.5% DVOA on first downs, which was much worse than both his 2017 and 2018 first-down production. With Thomas' age has also come a change in usage. Back in 2016, Thomas saw just 29% of his targets from the slot. That number has climbed in each season since then, finally coming out to 57% in 2019. Considering he no longer has the speed to threaten deep, it makes sense that Thomas has transitioned more toward being a big slot receiver. If a team signs Thomas this preseason, expect to find him playing in the slot more often than not.

Michael Thomas
Height: 6-3   Weight: 212   College: Ohio State   Draft: 2016/2 (47)   Born: 3-Mar-1993   Age: 27   Risk: Green

Year	Tm	G/GS	Snaps	Pass	Rec	Yds	TD	EZ	C%	+/-	Drop	Yd/C	aDOT	Rk	YAC	Rk	YAC+	BTkl	DVOA	Rk	DYAR	Rk	Use	Rk	Slot
2017	NO	16/14	851	149	104	1245	5	6	70%	+14.9	3	12.0	9.8	67	4.1	43	-0.5	14	15.0%	16	330	5	28.3%	5	52%
2018	NO	16/16	927	147	125	1405	9	8	85%	+24.2	3	11.2	8.0	74	4.1	48	-0.0	18	23.1%	9	442	3	29.6%	2	59%
2019	NO	16/15	959	185	149	1725	9	7	81%	+24.9	3	11.6	8.1	71	3.9	47	-0.2	12	23.9%	8	538	1	33.2%	1	48%
2020	NO			137	108	1228	6		79%			11.4							21.3%						

After signing Thomas to a record-breaking extension ($61 million in guarantees, most ever for a non-quarterback offensive player), the Saints made sure they got their money's worth. Drew Brees threw to Thomas an NFL-high 185 times, and he caught 80.5% of the targets. In other words, defenses knew, with a high degree of confidence, that the ball was going to Thomas, and they still couldn't stop him. He caught at least eight passes and gained 89 yards in all but three games. Yes, about half of his 149 catches came from the slot, but he was historically efficient. Thomas is the 16th receiver since 1985 to see at least 185 targets in a season. The other 15 had an average DVOA of 4.9%, and an average rank of 36. Thomas' DVOA of 23.9% ranked eighth.

Most Targets in a Single Season, 1985-2019

Player	Year	Team	Pass	Rec	C%	Yards	Yd/Rec	DVOA	Rank
Rob Moore	1997	ARI	208	97	46.6%	1,584	16.3	0.0%	44
Herman Moore	1995	DET	206	123	59.7%	1,686	13.7	12.6%	14
Marvin Harrison	2002	IND	205	143	69.8%	1,722	12.0	17.3%	13
Calvin Johnson	2012	DET	204	122	59.8%	1,964	16.1	14.7%	20
Julio Jones	2015	ATL	203	136	67.0%	1,871	13.8	8.5%	34
Isaac Bruce	1995	STL	199	119	59.8%	1,781	15.0	16.2%	11
Cris Carter	1995	MIN	197	122	61.9%	1,371	11.2	4.9%	38
Reggie Wayne	2012	IND	195	106	54.4%	1,355	12.8	-6.8%	63
Antonio Brown	2015	PIT	193	136	70.5%	1,834	13.5	19.7%	9
Brandon Marshall	2012	CHI	192	118	61.5%	1,508	12.8	1.0%	46
DeAndre Hopkins	2015	HOU	192	111	57.8%	1,521	13.7	4.8%	31
Sterling Sharpe	1993	GB	189	112	59.3%	1,274	11.4	-0.9%	40
Cris Carter	1994	MIN	188	122	64.9%	1,256	10.3	-14.2%	59
Randy Moss	2002	MIN	185	106	57.3%	1,347	12.7	-3.9%	59
Michael Thomas	**2019**	**NO**	**185**	**149**	**80.5%**	**1,725**	**11.6**	**23.9%**	**8**

His Twitter handle is @Cantguardmike. We detect no lies.

Laquon Treadwell Height: 6-2   Weight: 215   College: Mississippi   Draft: 2016/1 (23)   Born: 14-Jun-1995   Age: 25   Risk: Green

Year	Tm	G/GS	Snaps	Pass	Rec	Yds	TD	EZ	C%	+/-	Drop	Yd/C	aDOT	Rk	YAC	Rk	YAC+	BTkl	DVOA	Rk	DYAR	Rk	Use	Rk	Slot
2017	MIN	16/7	502	35	20	200	0	2	57%	+0.9	2	10.0	13.2	--	2.9	--	-1.9	0	-18.2%	--	-15	--	6.9%	--	11%
2018	MIN	15/7	543	53	35	302	1	0	66%	-2.0	6	8.6	6.4	82	3.4	66	-1.4	4	-19.1%	75	-27	74	9.8%	81	33%
2019	MIN	13/1	176	16	9	184	1	0	56%	+0.6	0	20.4	12.9	--	6.3	--	+2.3	3	31.7%	--	53	--	4.4%	--	63%
2020	ATL			25	16	200	1		64%			12.5							3.4%						

Treadwell failed to outlive his rookie deal with the Vikings, and he didn't provide anything close to first-round predecessor Cordarrelle's Patterson's silver lining of exceptional kickoff returning. After three seasons of DVOA well below average, Treadwell did flip the script to 31.7% in 2019—but he accomplished that as a rarely-used offensive option on the strength of three catches of 58, 36, and 26 yards that are embarrassingly the longest of his four-year career. The Falcons will have to hope that a change of scenery will help Treadwell finally realize his potential.

Marquez Valdes-Scantling Height: 6-4   Weight: 207   College: South Florida   Draft: 2018/5 (174)   Born: 10-Oct-1994   Age: 26   Risk: Green

Year	Tm	G/GS	Snaps	Pass	Rec	Yds	TD	EZ	C%	+/-	Drop	Yd/C	aDOT	Rk	YAC	Rk	YAC+	BTkl	DVOA	Rk	DYAR	Rk	Use	Rk	Slot
2018	GB	16/10	692	73	38	581	2	6	52%	-5.6	3	15.3	12.5	26	5.6	14	+0.2	4	-11.3%	63	8	63	12.4%	75	56%
2019	GB	16/10	556	56	26	452	2	8	46%	-3.4	2	17.4	17.2	3	5.8	10	+0.0	3	-15.5%	72	-13	71	10.5%	76	45%
2020	GB			47	24	372	2		51%			15.5							-8.5%						

A 46% catch rate simply will not cut it in the NFL, no matter how deep your average target is. Marquez Valdes-Scantling's receiving +/- actually improved a little bit last season due to his increased usage on shots down the field, but a complete lack of chemistry with Aaron Rodgers has made the MVS catch a rare and beautiful thing. His -9.0 receiving plus-minus is the second worst in the league over the last two seasons for players with at least 100 targets, as well as the worst result for any Packers wideout stretching back to 2006, when our data begins. It should be noted, however, that MVS was battling injuries in the second half of last season. His first half splits saw him with a DVOA of 3.2% and a catch rate of 56%—not great, but nowhere near the -61.0% and 24%, respectively, he saw over the second half of the season. Could the hamstring, ankle, and knee injuries have sapped his play to that extent, even while not causing him to actually miss any time? They certainly didn't help, but MVS kept losing playing time even as he got off the injury report, playing just six offensive snaps in the playoffs. Year 3 is a make-or-break season for Valdes-Scantling's NFL future.

Greg Ward

Height: 5-11   Weight: 190   College: Houston   Draft: 2017/FA   Born: 12-Jul-1995   Age: 25   Risk: Green

Year	Tm	G/GS	Snaps	Pass	Rec	Yds	TD	EZ	C%	+/-	Drop	Yd/C	aDOT	Rk	YAC	Rk	YAC+	BTkl	DVOA	Rk	DYAR	Rk	Use	Rk	Slot
2019	PHI	7/3	310	40	28	254	1	3	70%	+1.6	0	9.1	7.0	--	3.5	--	-0.9	3	-19.0%	--	-20	--	15.0%	--	75%
2020	PHI			5	3	30	0		60%			10.0							-3.9%						

Ward's 2019 stat line is incomplete. It's missing the 22 catches for 214 yards Ward put up for the San Antonio Commanders in the AAF, as the ex-Houston Cougars quarterback left his spot on Philadelphia's practice squad to get some actual in-game experience. It would be nice to say that his stint in the short-lived minor league was what finally gave him the chance to make his NFL debut, but it had more to do with the collapse of the Eagles' depth chart. A pair of really bad games against Miami and New York (five receptions on 12 targets for 39 yards with a dropped touchdown) kept Ward in the negative DYAR for the season, but he honestly didn't play that poorly for a practice-squad project pushed into action; Ward was often the only receiver left standing, and certainly the only one Carson Wentz trusted late in December. Don't be shocked if he parlays his performance into a spot on this year's active roster, possibly backing up Jalen Reagor in the slot.

James Washington

Height: 5-11   Weight: 213   College: Oklahoma State   Draft: 2018/2 (60)   Born: 2-Apr-1996   Age: 24   Risk: Green

Year	Tm	G/GS	Snaps	Pass	Rec	Yds	TD	EZ	C%	+/-	Drop	Yd/C	aDOT	Rk	YAC	Rk	YAC+	BTkl	DVOA	Rk	DYAR	Rk	Use	Rk	Slot
2018	PIT	14/6	526	38	16	217	1	2	42%	-4.7	2	13.6	17.0	--	3.3	--	-1.2	1	-25.1%	--	-37	--	6.3%	--	45%
2019	PIT	15/10	649	80	44	735	3	6	55%	+0.2	6	16.7	16.4	4	4.2	41	-0.5	2	11.2%	22	156	28	18.3%	50	48%
2020	PIT			101	48	802	3		48%			16.7							-18.0%						

There's really not a nice way to put "James Washington played poorly enough that the Steelers spent a second-round pick on Chase Claypool" into this comment. Here's a wild split for you: against man coverage, Washington caught 13 of 28 targets. In the two games against the Browns, Washington had five catches for 146 yards dealing with man coverage. Against every other team's man coverage, he had eight catches for 76 yards. A lot of his biggest plays against man were on fade routes. Washington has the speed and separation to be a good outside receiver and appears to have successfully ducked under the radar in Pittsburgh—if he plays 800 snaps next season it will probably be the best year of his career. But between the drops and the Claypool pick, it's also easy to read into the situation and understand that the Steelers might not believe in him as a long-term fixture. Still, a potential post-hype sleeper is in here.

Sammy Watkins

Height: 6-1   Weight: 211   College: Clemson   Draft: 2014/1 (4)   Born: 14-Jun-1993   Age: 27   Risk: Yellow

Year	Tm	G/GS	Snaps	Pass	Rec	Yds	TD	EZ	C%	+/-	Drop	Yd/C	aDOT	Rk	YAC	Rk	YAC+	BTkl	DVOA	Rk	DYAR	Rk	Use	Rk	Slot
2017	LAR	15/14	776	70	39	593	8	8	56%	+3.4	3	15.2	15.5	9	4.7	28	+0.8	2	24.1%	6	216	14	15.0%	65	47%
2018	KC	10/9	459	55	40	519	3	1	73%	+3.8	1	13.0	9.0	65	6.0	10	+1.2	14	24.1%	5	161	22	16.3%	55	57%
2019	KC	14/13	744	90	52	673	3	5	58%	-4.8	4	12.9	9.7	63	5.7	12	+0.9	14	-12.3%	67	3	68	18.3%	49	65%
2020	KC			79	51	685	5		65%			13.4							10.3%						

Ty Dunne's May portrait of Watkins on Bleacher Report painted an interesting picture of the receiver as a person. Watkins' metaphysical beliefs about demons, astral planes, and looming "end times" (as told to Dunne in winter, before Watkins had even heard of coronavirus) could fill an entire series of Facebook documentaries, and they are well beyond the scope of this little segment. But Watkins did reveal that he partied non-stop early in his career, which explains his inconsistency, his injuries (his workout habits stunk), and the Bills' dissatisfaction with him. Andy Reid's ability to handle players with personality quirks clearly benefited Watkins, as did an offense where he could escape the spotlight: he spoke during Super Bowl week about how content he was to be a role player. The Chiefs restructured his contract to retain him, so they will once again have a former fourth overall pick, still in his mid-20s, operating as the third option in their passing game and frequently drawing single-coverage from No. 2 cornerbacks.

Dede Westbrook

Height: 6-0　Weight: 176　College: Oklahoma　Draft: 2017/4 (110)　Born: 21-Nov-1993　Age: 27　Risk: Green

Year	Tm	G/GS	Snaps	Pass	Rec	Yds	TD	EZ	C%	+/-	Drop	Yd/C	aDOT	Rk	YAC	Rk	YAC+	BTkl	DVOA	Rk	DYAR	Rk	Use	Rk	Slot
2017	JAX	7/5	386	51	27	339	1	1	53%	-2.0	2	12.6	12.0	39	3.7	52	-1.2	3	-21.5%	79	-35	76	22.2%	20	39%
2018	JAX	16/9	805	102	66	717	5	6	66%	+0.4	8	10.9	8.7	69	5.4	21	+0.4	12	-15.7%	73	-25	73	19.4%	34	92%
2019	JAX	15/11	757	101	66	660	3	6	65%	-4.0	6	10.0	7.1	79	4.7	29	-0.9	14	-21.8%	75	-73	78	19.0%	44	80%
2020	JAX			85	53	548	3		62%			10.3							-10.2%						

Westbrook continued to feature as the Jaguars' primary slot receiver, a role in which the former fourth-round pick has already amassed 1,700 career yards, but he also continued to have dreadful advanced statistics. Westbrook has ranked among the bottom dozen wideouts in the DYAR table in each of his three seasons, and he was the only Jaguars starter to have negative DVOA on each of first, second, and third/fourth down. For the past two seasons, 175 of his 202 targets have come from the slot, and he has, at least, been more effective on those slot targets than split wide, but his DVOA splits are negative no matter what way you slice them. Westbrook appears to be the Jaguars starter most immediately threatened by recent draftee Laviska Shenault, and he will need to improve his efficiency substantially to hold on to his playing time over the next season or two.

Mike Williams

Height: 6-4　Weight: 218　College: Clemson　Draft: 2017/1 (7)　Born: 4-Oct-1994　Age: 26　Risk: Green

Year	Tm	G/GS	Snaps	Pass	Rec	Yds	TD	EZ	C%	+/-	Drop	Yd/C	aDOT	Rk	YAC	Rk	YAC+	BTkl	DVOA	Rk	DYAR	Rk	Use	Rk	Slot
2017	LAC	10/1	234	23	11	95	0	5	48%	-2.8	2	8.6	9.7	--	1.0	--	-3.0	0	-18.0%	--	-10	--	6.8%	--	20%
2018	LAC	16/5	622	66	43	664	10	13	65%	+4.9	2	15.4	14.7	13	2.7	79	-1.1	8	39.2%	2	262	13	13.2%	70	51%
2019	LAC	15/15	850	90	49	1001	2	13	54%	+1.1	2	20.4	17.7	1	3.8	50	-0.8	3	20.6%	11	235	14	17.1%	58	43%
2020	LAC			93	50	798	6		54%			16.0							-4.0%						

Williams is outrunning two curses: the Curse of the Chargers First-Round Picks (which erased much of his rookie season) and The Curse of Being Named Mike Williams. Past Mike Williamses who disappointed include:
- The Bills' first-round pick in 2002, a tackle whose weight reportedly grew beyond the 400-pound range before he slimmed back down to the mid-300s for a modest comeback.
- The Lions' first-round pick in 2005, a king-sized wide receiver who was essentially the Devin Funchess of the mid-2000s.
- The Buccaneers' fourth-round pick in 2010 who had a strong rookie season, then faded. Hey, becoming Josh Freeman's favorite target seemed like a sound career move at the time.

There have been a few other players named Mike Williams, most of them not noteworthy. The best Mike Williams in NFL history was a first-round Chargers draft pick in 1975 who started at cornerback for the great Don Coryell/Dan Fouts teams of the early 1980s. So maybe the Chargers First-Round Pick and Being Named Mike Williams curses actually cancel each other out! Only time will tell. For now, Williams has settled in as the designated deep threat in the Chargers offense. Williams' efficiency will drop significantly going from a near-Hall of Famer to either a rookie or a longtime backup, but KUBIAK thinks his usage will stay high, which means we have him as very underrated by ADP.

Preston Williams

Height: 6-5　Weight: 218　College: Colorado State　Draft: 2019/FA　Born: 27-Mar-1997　Age: 23　Risk: Blue

Year	Tm	G/GS	Snaps	Pass	Rec	Yds	TD	EZ	C%	+/-	Drop	Yd/C	aDOT	Rk	YAC	Rk	YAC+	BTkl	DVOA	Rk	DYAR	Rk	Use	Rk	Slot
2019	MIA	8/7	412	60	32	428	3	8	53%	-2.3	4	13.4	14.4	16	1.9	79	-1.8	3	-5.9%	57	32	59	20.1%	37	19%
2020	MIA			75	42	586	4		56%			14.0							-3.8%						

A slew of off-field issues pushed Williams out of draft weekend in 2019. Williams would have been a Day 2 talent otherwise, but ended up signing with the Miami Dolphins, a team desperately in need of receiving talent last offseason. From Week 1, Williams was a valuable piece of the Dolphins offense. Williams caught at least four passes in six of eight performances prior to a season-ending ACL injury. A tall, thick wide receiver in a similar mold to Brandon Marshall or Alshon Jeffery, Williams was especially effective in the red zone for Miami, earning the highest DVOA rating on the team among players with at least five targets in that area. Considering Williams' skill set has some overlap with DeVante Parker's, the Dolphins will need one of their slot or tight end threats to step it up in order to round out the group, but it feels like the team has a strong one-two combo for hopeful franchise quarterback Tua Tagovailoa.

Tyrell Williams Height: 6-4 Weight: 205 College: Western Oregon Draft: 2015/FA Born: 12-Feb-1992 Age: 28 Risk: Green

Year	Tm	G/GS	Snaps	Pass	Rec	Yds	TD	EZ	C%	+/-	Drop	Yd/C	aDOT	Rk	YAC	Rk	YAC+	BTkl	DVOA	Rk	DYAR	Rk	Use	Rk	Slot
2017	LAC	16/15	852	69	43	728	4	3	62%	+2.2	4	16.9	14.3	16	7.7	1	+2.6	6	15.4%	15	150	25	12.0%	75	56%
2018	LAC	16/10	761	65	41	653	5	7	63%	+1.2	2	15.9	12.6	25	4.8	29	-0.0	3	12.3%	24	128	32	12.8%	73	62%
2019	OAK	14/12	743	64	42	651	6	8	66%	+3.5	5	15.5	13.5	23	4.5	35	+0.1	4	27.2%	3	204	20	14.9%	65	49%
2020	LV			57	37	576	4		65%			15.6							14.2%						

Williams is a useful but limited deep threat whose statistics have been remarkably stable for three seasons, despite moving from the Chargers to the Raiders and briefly being thrust into the go-to receiver role in the Antonio Brown aftermath. Each year, he produces catch rates in the low-60% range, yards per catch hovering a little above 15, and yards per game in the low- to mid-40s. Five of Williams's six touchdowns came in the first five weeks of last season, but his production dipped slightly in the second half of the year as Hunter Renfrow began to assume a larger offensive role. Williams and Henry Ruggs give the Raiders two vertical No. 2 receiver types without a true No. 1. But if they create space for Renfrow, Darren Waller and others to work underneath, the Raiders might be happy with two guys catching three or four passes for 45 to 60 yards each and every week.

Albert Wilson Height: 5-9 Weight: 195 College: Georgia State Draft: 2014/FA Born: 12-Jul-1992 Age: 28 Risk: Green

Year	Tm	G/GS	Snaps	Pass	Rec	Yds	TD	EZ	C%	+/-	Drop	Yd/C	aDOT	Rk	YAC	Rk	YAC+	BTkl	DVOA	Rk	DYAR	Rk	Use	Rk	Slot
2017	KC	13/7	538	62	42	554	3	2	68%	+0.5	7	13.2	6.3	84	7.5	2	+1.5	13	21.4%	8	167	22	14.5%	67	71%
2018	MIA	7/3	232	35	26	391	4	1	74%	+0.8	1	15.0	7.0	--	12.9	--	+6.5	13	10.8%	--	63	--	18.1%	--	46%
2019	MIA	13/4	441	62	43	351	1	0	69%	-1.0	6	8.2	5.3	81	4.2	43	-1.2	17	-23.7%	77	-53	76	12.4%	72	81%
2020	MIA			56	37	362	2		66%			9.8							-2.4%						

Ever since Wilson entered the league in 2012, yards after catch have been his meal ticket. A short, spry receiver with ample route-running skills, Wilson always found work in the short to intermediate area and did well to maximize his chances. Wilson's YAC took a hit in 2019, though. Prior to 2019, Wilson had never earned less than 4.8 average yards after the catch and only had one season in which he dipped below 6.0 yards. Last season, however, Wilson only managed 4.2 average yards after the catch. That lack of YAC production was accentuated by a lack of deep targets—only 2% of his targets came on deep bombs, the lowest mark of his career. If Wilson is going to get back on track, it will be by finding success on first down again. In both 2017 and 2018, Wilson posted positive DVOA marks on first-down targets, yet he fell well into the negatives (-47.5%) in 2019.

Robert Woods Height: 6-0 Weight: 193 College: USC Draft: 2013/2 (41) Born: 10-Apr-1992 Age: 28 Risk: Green

Year	Tm	G/GS	Snaps	Pass	Rec	Yds	TD	EZ	C%	+/-	Drop	Yd/C	aDOT	Rk	YAC	Rk	YAC+	BTkl	DVOA	Rk	DYAR	Rk	Use	Rk	Slot
2017	LAR	12/11	649	85	56	781	5	5	66%	+4.4	4	13.9	10.6	53	5.2	19	+0.3	6	13.4%	21	172	20	22.4%	19	84%
2018	LAR	16/16	1041	130	86	1219	6	9	66%	+4.1	3	14.2	11.3	42	4.9	27	+0.1	11	17.5%	16	316	11	24.3%	16	85%
2019	LAR	15/15	1009	139	90	1134	2	4	65%	+2.4	4	12.6	8.6	67	6.4	5	+0.7	12	-4.0%	51	94	43	24.2%	16	67%
2020	LAR			121	79	1032	5		65%			13.1							6.8%						

See how Woods' average depth of target plummeted last year? That's partly because the Rams loved to put him in the backfield; his 17 carries produced 103 yards and 59 DYAR. They also threw him 13 passes out of the backfield; no other wideout had more than five such targets. Oddly, these theoretically safe plays had quite a boom-or-bust nature; he caught 11 of them for 100 yards, but that was split between 73 yards on three catches and 27 yards on the other eight, four of which went backwards. His DVOA was -20.1% on backfield passes, compared to 4.3% on 93 targets in the slot and -13.8% on 32 targets split wide. Rookie running back Cam Akers had 69 catches at Florida State; perhaps the Rams will let him handle the screen game, freeing Woods to run more of the curls, outs, and deep crossing routes that produced the bulk of his success last year.

Jarius Wright Height: 5-10 Weight: 191 College: Arkansas Draft: 2012/4 (118) Born: 25-Nov-1989 Age: 31 Risk: N/A

Year	Tm	G/GS	Snaps	Pass	Rec	Yds	TD	EZ	C%	+/-	Drop	Yd/C	aDOT	Rk	YAC	Rk	YAC+	BTkl	DVOA	Rk	DYAR	Rk	Use	Rk	Slot
2017	MIN	16/0	256	25	18	198	2	2	72%	+2.0	0	11.0	8.2	--	4.9	--	-0.3	1	29.0%	--	84	--	4.9%	--	96%
2018	CAR	16/6	528	59	43	447	1	3	73%	+2.5	2	10.4	6.4	83	4.6	35	-0.4	11	-15.1%	70	-12	69	10.9%	79	87%
2019	CAR	16/9	703	58	28	296	0	3	48%	-8.4	6	10.6	10.7	47	3.2	69	-1.3	4	-39.6%	81	-124	81	9.8%	80	80%

Nearly forgotten former Vikings receiver Jarius Wright enjoyed a renaissance on the 2018 Panthers, catching 43 of 59 targets for 447 yards. He thrived on third and fourth downs, where he caught 12 passes to move the chains, tied for the team lead with Christian McCaffrey and double the total of the next highest team receiver. When Greg Olsen landed on injured reserve with a broken foot, Wright became one of Cam Newton's most trusted second-half targets. But Newton missed most of 2019 with his own foot injury, and although Wright's target total remained virtually unchanged, his number of catches fell by 15. Poor quarterbacking was no doubt a contributor, but Wright also dropped six of his 36 catchable balls. A 17% drop rate is an unattractive quality for a slot receiver whose job is to consistently convert modest gains, and it's probably why Wright has yet to find a new team for 2020.

Going Deep

Marcell Ateman, LV: Ateman is a big, slow-footed, high-character receiver who caught a 36-yard bomb up the sideline in Week 7 against the Packers and had a 20-yard reception ripped from his hands for a fumble in Week 17 against the Broncos. He could hang around the league for a while as a special teams gunner, but something will have gone very wrong if he has an offensive role in Las Vegas this season.

Tavon Austin, FA: Every year one team looks at what Tavon Austin should bring to the table and declares he'll have a big role on the offense. Then Austin gets on the field and those plans quickly disintegrate. After seven years of inefficient screens, swings, and reverses, teams have found they can get better versions of those plays elsewhere. Dallas even tried to use him as a more downfield receiver in 2019, albeit in a limited role. His 13.9-yard average depth of target on seven first-down targets produced a -29.3% DVOA.

Reggie Begelton, GB: Belgeton spent the last three seasons playing for the Calgary Stampeders of the CFL. He broke out last season with 102 receptions for 1,444 yards and 10 touchdowns on his way to being named an All-Star. He's only the fifth player in CFL history to record 100 receptions in a season. He's fairly elusive with the ball in space; 519 of those yards came after the catch. With the Packers not taking a receiver in the draft, Begelton has a real chance to not only earn a roster spot but possibly push for some playing time, as well. *C'est parti.*

Travis Benjamin, SF: Benjamin had a season to forget with the Chargers in 2019, recording only six catches in five games before going on injured reserve with a quad injury. After the Chargers let him go in the offseason, Benjamin found his way to San Francisco, where he will have an opportunity to try to take over Marquise Goodwin's old role as a space-creating deep threat. Unfortunately for Benjamin, the 49ers' receiver room is crowded with young players who theoretically should have more upside than the 30-year-old veteran.

Braxton Berrios, NYJ: More than half of Berrios' receiving yards on the season were earned on a single 69-yard play versus a poor Oakland Raiders secondary. Aside from that catch, Berrios earned just 46 yards on 12 targets through the rest of the season (-15.2% DVOA). Berrios, a short slot receiver, was initially drafted by the New England Patriots in 2018, but never played a regular-season offensive snap for them. The good news for Berrios in 2020, though, is that most of the New York Jets' wide receiver additions were not slot players, so his competition as the backup behind Jamison Crowder did not get much stiffer.

Christian Blake, ATL: Blake has worked his way up from humble beginnings, going undrafted out of Northern Illinois but then excelling on the Falcons' practice squad. He made his way to the team's NFL roster in 2019 after the Mohamed Sanu trade and is one of a small handful of their possible 2020 receivers with any relevant NFL experience. That may be enough to earn him a roster spot, but his 11 career catches do not seem to portend a lengthy professional future.

Jaron Brown, FA: Brown opened the season as a starter for Seattle, but after getting 24 targets in his first seven games, he had only four in his last seven as he was largely limited to special teams. He finished at 16-220-2 with -3.1% DVOA. Now 30 years old and three years removed from his only career 100-yard game, Brown remains available for any team in desperate need of a veteran wideout.

Hakeem Butler, ARI: One of Playmaker Score's favorite wide receiver prospects in 2019, Butler struggled during the Cardinals' offseason program last year and ended up missing the season on injured reserve with a hand injury. With DeAndre Hopkins now in the fold in the desert, it will be tough for Butler to carve out a major role while competing for opportunities behind Hopkins, the ageless Larry Fitzgerald, Christian Kirk, and fellow 2019 rookie Andy Isabella.

Deon Cain, PIT: Our Top 25 prospects list had a lot of disappointments last year, and Cain was yet another of them. Cain couldn't seize a role on a relatively wide-open Colts depth chart that eventually led to Zach Pascal fantasy relevance, and the Steelers signed him off Indy's practice squad. Cain still has the size and speed that made him a potential outside receiver coming out of the draft, but he failed to make due on that promise despite torching the league through three preseason games. The Steelers don't figure to have many available targets, but Cain could lurk around the end of the roster like Darrius Heyward-Bey used to.

DeAndre Carter, HOU: A fringe 53-man returner who has seen a decent chunk of time on offense as a try-harder, Carter combines 5-foot-8 size and solid speed. He's fumble-prone (eight fumbles in 30 games), doesn't have great hands, and has had some routes over the past couple years in Houston where he literally fell down into the catch. However, he's one of Bill O'Brien's Guys, so he faces no real competition for his job in 2020 and stands to gain a lot of playing time if Kenny Stills, Will Fuller, or Brandin Cooks gets hurt. Given the histories involved, it should not shock anyone if Carter winds up with 75 targets this year. (2019: 11-of-14 passes with 162 yards, 0 touchdowns, and 21.8% DVOA.)

Quintez Cephus, DET: This fifth-round rookie rose to the occasion against the toughest competition at Wisconsin last season—seven catches for 122 yards against Ohio State in the Big Ten title game, seven more receptions and some highlight-reel catches against Oregon in the Rose Bowl. That Cephus is a budding superstar, but that Cephus didn't always show up; he has plenty of two-reception, 20-ish-yard games dotting his resume. Built like a tight end, Cephus has potential as a possession receiver at the next level, but he lacks speed and his route-running needs some polishing if he's going to contribute.

Tyrie Cleveland, DEN: Cleveland, drafted in the seventh round by the Broncos, is a size/speed prospect and former top recruit out of Texas who caught just 79 passes in four seasons as a contributor to the Florida offense, with a meager 25-351-1 in his final season. He has a reputation as a hustling special-teamer, which may help him cling to the back of what is suddenly a loaded Broncos receiver depth chart.

Corey Coleman, NYG: Coleman missed the 2019 season with a torn ACL. The former first-round pick has never lived up to his draft status but continues to stick on the back end of rosters with special teams ability. In 2018, Coleman averaged 26 yards on 23 kickoff returns in eight games for the Giants. Coleman could be in line to return as the kickoff return specialist and potentially work his way into the rotation as the WR4 on a lacking depth chart.

Pharoh Cooper, CAR: The Panthers are thin at receiver behind starters D.J. Moore, Robby Anderson, and Curtis Samuel, and that could offer Cooper his first extensive work on offense in what will become a five-year career in 2020. But regardless of his offensive limitations, Cooper remains in demand because of his special teams play. He earned first-team All-Pro distinctions in his sophomore season in 2017 because of his league-leading 27.4-yard kickoff return average and second-place 932 kickoff return yards, 399 punt return yards, and 12.5 yards per punt return, and he should return some combination of kicks and punts for the Panthers this season.

Cody Core, NYG: A 2016 sixth-round pick, Core has developed into a special teams ace without much production in the receiving department. For the Giants last season, Core played at least 60% of the special teams snaps in all 16 games. He only played more than 10 offensive snaps in a game twice and finished the year with just three receptions and 28 yards on five targets, though his 1.1% DVOA made him one of two Giants receivers to finish positive in that statistic. With the fourth receiver spot open, Core could be an injury away from more playing time.

Isaiah Coulter, HOU: This fifth-round rookie brings size (6-foot-1) and long speed (4.45s 40-yard dash at 198 pounds). A small-schooler from Rhode Island with 1,039 yards in 12 games last season, he was roundly dinged for attention to detail in routes and ability to get off press coverages by major draft media and draftniks. Coulter's a developmental X receiver; if he improves his weaknesses, he's got a chance to stick for a while. If he continues to have the same issues, he's probably not enough to stick at the end of the roster without being an ace special-teamer.

Gabriel Davis, BUF: Quarterback Josh Allen has yet to figure out how to complete deep passes, but that has not stopped the Bills from trying to find him downfield threats. Even without Central Florida's starting quarterback in 2019, fourth-round pick Gabriel Davis finished the season with a whopping 17.2 yards per catch and 9.5 yards per target. His middling 55% catch rate is more a reflection of his vertical route tree than his actual ability, but it does still serve to highlight the kind of player Davis is. If the Bills can find a purely vertical role for Davis, he may be able to contribute as a rookie.

Quartney Davis, MIN: Davis became one of the most sought-after players in undrafted free agency, earning $100,000 guaranteed from the Vikings. Davis is a bundle of size and athleticism—a 4.54s 40 and a 35.5-inch vertical jump are very respectable numbers, and he's big for a slot receiver at 6-foot-1. What he isn't is someone who produces on the field, with just 99 receptions and 1,201 yards in a two-year career at Texas A&M. The Vikings are gambling that his lack of big plays was due to the Aggies' poor quarterback situation, and that time with an NFL team can help translate his promise into production.

Trevor Davis, CHI: Davis is unlikely to contribute much to the Bears' receiving corps; he has just 16 receptions in a four-year NFL career. But the speed that made him a YAC threat in college has generally made him a solid punt and kickoff returner, which is what he'll have to do to make Chicago's roster. Last season was a significant down year in that department for Davis, who ended up with negative value on both kickoffs and punts as he shuffled from team to team; he'll need to bounce back to his 2017 form to have a chance.

Josh Doctson, NYJ: Every year is supposed to be the year the uber-talented Doctson puts it all together, but every year he disappoints. Injuries aside—he missed virtually all of 2019 due to a hamstring issue—Doctson simply has yet to become the red zone threat he was billed to be as a prospect. Doctson hauled in just seven catches in 25 red zone targets in 2017 and 2018 in Washington. With a wide-open competition for targets on the New York Jets depth chart, however, there has never been a better opportunity for Doctson to rise to the occasion and establish himself as a legit wide receiver.

Keelan Doss, LV: Doss, an undrafted rookie from Cal-Davis last season, was a Hard Knocks star and ended up catching 11-of-14 passes for 133 yards, 0 touchdowns, and 11.6% DVOA. He is likely to fall off the back of the Raiders depth chart now that the team has upgraded its receiver corps but has the size/speed package to latch on elsewhere.

Quincy Enunwa, NYJ: Once upon a time, Enunwa seemed like the most promising receiver on the Jets roster, but he's been able to stay healthy in only one season (2016) since he was drafted in 2014. The neck injury he suffered in Week 1 cost him most of last season and it will cost him all of 2020 as well, and he may never play again. Don't expect him to retire though; he would be giving up a guaranteed $6 million in 2020 and a $4.1-million injury guarantee for 2021.

Antonio Gandy-Golden, WAS: At 6-foot-4 and 220 pounds with 22 bench press reps at the combine, Gandy-Golden is one of the biggest and strongest receivers in this year's class. He used those physical tools to put up tremendous college production, including 1,000 yards and 10 touchdowns in each of his last three seasons. But NFL defenses have different kinds of athletes than Gandy-Golden saw at Liberty against either FBS or FCS opponents—the Flames changed conference affiliations in the middle of his career. Even with his physical gifts, Gandy-Golden will need to refine his route-running to outperform his fourth-round draft selection.

Marquise Goodwin, PHI: The former Olympic long jumper barely saw the field in 2019 for the 49ers after Week 6, and with a crowded receiver room moving forward, San Francisco saw fit to ship him off to Philadelphia for a swap of sixth-round picks. Speed has always been Goodwin's specialty, and he should serve as injury insurance for fellow deep threat DeSean Jackson and rookie Jalen Reagor. Philadelphia would likely need a major run of injuries at wide receiver (in other words, like in 2019) for Goodwin to see much volume in their passing game.

Marvin Hall, DET: Hall had seven receptions in 2019. They went for 13, 21, 34, 39, 47, 49, and 58 yards, with 108.2% DVOA. His average target came 27.6 yards downfield, more than anyone else with at least three targets last season. I suppose if you're going to do one thing, catching bombs is something that will at least get you on the highlight reel. A poor man's Marquise Goodwin, Hall's only real strength is running fast in a straight line, a strength from which the Lions squeezed every drop last season.

Justin Hardy, FA: At 5-foot-10 and 192 pounds, Hardy has the prototypical size of an NFL slot receiver. But he never emerged as a consistent offensive weapon in that role, peaking in his five-year Falcons run at 21 catches and 221 yards in a season despite playing in an offense equipped to highlight such a player. Sixth-rounder Russell Gage lapped Hardy's career bests as he passed him on the team's depth chart in just his second season in 2019. Now Hardy is a free agent; coming off of seasons with -12.8% and -8.5% DVOA rates, he could struggle to find work beyond a special teams role.

Deonte Harris, NO: In about nine months, the pride of Worcester's Assumption College went from undrafted free agent to Saints punt returner to All-Pro. He averaged 9.4 yards per return, which ranked fourth, and was one of six players to return a punt for a touchdown. He also tied for the league lead in plays that sparked an Xavier Rhodes sideline meltdown. In the Vikings-Saints wild-card game, Harris juked Rhodes out of the broadcast picture to haul in a 50-yard bomb from Taysom Hill. With Ted Ginn Jr.'s departure, could New Orleans look to him as a deep threat?

John Hightower, PHI: With Darren Sproles' retirement and Miles Sanders' and Boston Scott's likely impending increases in offensive touches, the Eagles needed some new special teams talent. Their selections of Hightower and Quez Watkins in the fifth and sixth rounds suggest the team's belief that they can become impact contributors. Hightower ran track at a junior college, and his 4.43s speed helped him average 23.3 yards per kickoff return in two seasons after he transferred to Boise State. In time, it could help him snag a few deep targets on offense, although his current lack of a route tree makes him a longshot to inherit DeSean Jackson's starting job.

K.J. Hill, LAC: Hill caught 187 passes for 19 touchdowns in three seasons as one of Ohio State's primary slot targets. He then impressed at the Senior Bowl, showing a deft ability to get open on short passes. Hill's combine results were disappointing, however, and he slipped to the sixth round while another slot receiver from the Big Ten named KJ (Hamler) rose up the draft boards despite being both tiny and less productive than Hill. Don't be surprised if Hill shines as a possession target, taking away some of the targets on shallow drags that Keenan Allen received so Allen can handle more worthy assignments.

Isaiah Hodgins, BUF: While fellow Buffalo draft pick Gabriel Davis is a deep threat, sixth-round selection Isaiah Hodgins is more of a possession receiver with just a dash of big-play ability. Hodgins was one of just six players with at least 85 catches and 13 touchdowns last season, putting him in elite company with fellow draftees CeeDee Lamb and Justin Jefferson. A middling combine performance, particularly his 4.61s 40-yard dash, sunk the Oregon State product's draft stock a bit, but a player of his size and reliability has a chance to develop into a tall, true X-receiver that the Bills have been missing for years.

Mack Hollins, MIA: On December 1, Hollins played six offensive snaps for the Philadelphia Eagles against the Miami Dolphins. A week later, Hollins suited up for the Dolphins, playing 10 offensive snaps. That is the extent to which Hollins has done anything interesting since helping the Eagles with a midseason surge during their 2017 Super Bowl run. A tall, relatively fast receiver, Hollins is more than likely just insurance for DeVante Parker and Preston Williams, both of whom sport similar builds. (2019: 10-for-23, 125 yards, 0 touchdowns, and -30.0% DVOA.)

Dontrelle Inman, FA: Once upon a time, third-year receiver Dontrelle Inman had 58 receptions for 810 yards on 97 targets for the San Diego Chargers. He has since bounced around between Chicago, San Diego again, and Indianapolis, and hasn't even reached half of either figure in any subsequent season. Now 30 and without a team, Inman may catch on somewhere as a depth option—maybe even back in Indianapolis with former teammate Philip Rivers—but his days as a starter appear done.

Richie James, SF: By the end of 2019, James had been more or less relegated to just a return man, and in an incredibly crowded 49ers receiver room, sustained success on punt and kickoff returns may be the only thing keeping him on the roster. James posted an incredibly efficient 64.5% receiving DVOA on 10 targets in 2019, but it's hard to foresee much of a role in the passing game for the former seventh-round pick moving forward.

Jauan Jennings, SF: San Francisco's seventh-round pick from Tennessee was the Volunteers' leading target in his senior season. Jennings was a bright spot on an otherwise unimpressive offense that finished 98th in the NCAA in points per game and 84th in offensive FEI. He does not look to have much of a path to offensive playing time as a rookie, but there is potential for him to develop into more down the road as an outside receiver.

Collin Johnson, JAX: At 6-foot-6, Johnson is startlingly tall for a wide receiver, and he is probably defined more by that attribute than anything else. That said, his 2,624 career receiving yards at Texas were fifth-most in team history and his 177 yards in the Big 12 Championship Game set the all-time record for that fixture, so he is evidently more than just a pair of stilts. He does, however, have a lengthy injury history that probably resulted in a lower draft position (fifth round) than his play merited.

Marcus Johnson, IND: 2019 was Johnson's most productive season as a professional, bringing his first career starts and his first double-digit target and reception totals. That still amounted to only 17 catches on 33 targets, though (277 yards, 2 touchdowns, and 3.7% DVOA). Displaced down the depth chart by second-round pick Michael Pittman and threatened from below by sixth-rounder Dezmon Patmon, Johnson's snap count looks set to drop precipitously assuming the players around him can stay broadly healthy.

Jake Kumerow, GB: While Kumerow received a lot of preseason hype a year ago, he was essentially nonexistent last season, finishing eighth in targets on a team that needed every warm body available at wideout. Kumerow did at least make the most of his 21 targets, finishing with 12 catches, 219 yards, and a touchdown with a 20.1% DVOA. That DVOA put him well above Geronimo Allison and Marquez Valdes-Scantling, each of whom had more than two and a half times as many targets as Kumerow.

Marqise Lee, NE: Just as it seemed Lee was figuring things out, a 2018 ACL injury and 2019 shoulder injury derailed the "second contract" portion of his career. The last time Lee played a (mostly) full season, he led the Jaguars with a 49.0% DVOA on 20 first-down targets. The question now is whether or not Lee can overcome nearly two full years of injury and surgery to return to that level.

Darnell Mooney, CHI: The third-fastest receiver at the combine, fifth-round rookie Mooney averaged 14.9 yards per reception and 8.1 yards per target at Tulane last season. His speed was put to good use both in the catch-and-run game and by running past cornerbacks to catch deep bombs. The trouble is, Mooney's just 5-foot-10, 176 pounds, and the next pass he catches cleanly will be his first. His ceiling is a Tyreek Hill-type threat with the ball; at the moment, he's Ted Ginn with worse hands.

K.J. Osborn, MIN: Osborn's numbers at Miami weren't overly impressive—50 receptions for 547 yards were enough to lead the team, but didn't even put him in the top 20 in the ACC. Miami was likely using him wrong, however; Osborn was significantly more productive when he was a slot receiver at Buffalo from 2016 to 2018. He's an acceptable depth possession receiver, but where he has a chance to shine is as a punt returner, as he averaged 15.9 yards per return last season. That special teams value should be enough to earn him a roster spot as a fifth-round rookie.

Dezmon Patmon, IND: Patmon's scouting reports are reminiscent of short-lived Colts receiver Devin Funchess, another tall wideout who does not play up to either his size or strength. If he did, Patmon's physical profile would be imposing: 6-foot-4, 225 pounds, but still able to log a 4.48s 40 time, he has all the physical attributes necessary to make an impact as an outside receiver. Conversely, his drops, lack of variety in his routes, and lack of physicality at the catch point are the reasons he fell to the sixth round.

Cordarrelle Patterson, CHI: Before 2019, Matt Nagy said that he saw a significant role for Patterson, featuring a diet of jet sweeps, screens, end arounds, and the like. In reality, he received just 28 touches as those promised creative packages never really developed. Patterson remains one of the league's top returners, finishing second in kickoff return value, but expecting anything more out of him is unrealistic.

Andre Patton, LAC: Patton caught just six of 17 passes targeted for him last season, and also lost a fumble after a catch (it was a borderline call, to be fair) against the Vikings. The result was -15.3% DVOA. The low success rate was mostly Philip Rivers' fault, as Patton was the target of many of his worst off-balance flutterballs. But when you're a former undrafted rookie, spend two years on the practice squad, finally get some starts and only catch about one-third of the passes thrown your way, no one is going to blame the borderline Hall of Famer for your shortcomings.

Donovan Peoples-Jones, CLE: The issue with Peoples-Jones is pretty succinct: He profiles as a wide receiver, but there is little evidence he can *play* wide receiver. Peoples-Jones ran a 4.48s 40-yard dash at 212 pounds and had off-the-charts scores in the vertical jump (44 1/2 inches) and broad jump (139 inches). He also finished his junior year with just 438 receiving yards and wasn't used as a runner at all by Michigan. In the short term, he's a dynamic punt returner. In the long-term, he's got starting wideout traits and upside, but not a lot of reasons to believe he'll hit them.

Malcolm Perry, MIA: Following in the footsteps of Keenan Reynolds, Navy's best quarterback in the modern era, was a tall order for Perry, but he lived up to the bill as well as anyone could have asked. Perry trails Reynolds' career-long records at Navy, but his 2,017 rushing yards in 2019 are now etched as the most rushing yards in a single season in school history. Whether the seventh-round pick becomes a running back or a wide receiver (or both) in the NFL is yet to be fully decided, but he has downhill burst to threaten chunk plays whenever he touches the ball. Perry caught 22 passes for 470 yards in 2017 and 2018 as a part-time wide receiver for the Midshipmen.

Dante Pettis, SF: The former second-round pick has struggled to make an impact through two seasons in the NFL. In a young receiver room in 2019, Pettis could not nail down a starting role, and he barely saw any offensive snaps after the midseason acquisition of Emmanuel Sanders. Pettis had an encouraging late-season run in his first year, but after he was clearly passed on the depth chart by 2019 rookie Deebo Samuel, the 49ers drafted wide receiver Brandon Aiyuk in the first round as well. 2020 is a make-or-break year for Pettis.

Byron Pringle, KC: Pringle was a 2018 draft deep-sleeper, a 25-year-old from Kansas State who turned his life around after numerous incidents as a youth. He spent 2018 on IR, then went 6-103-1 in last season's loss to the Colts during Tyreek Hill's injury when the Chiefs receivers took turns putting up huge numbers. Pringle then stuck to the roster as a special-teamer. He can do most of the things that Demarcus Robinson can do, only cheaper. But Robinson's 2020 salary is guaranteed, so Pringle will have to settle for offensive leftovers.

James Proche, BAL: Proche has very strong hands and concentration, which helped him turn in some enormous production in the pass-happy SMU Mustangs offense (over 2,400 yards and 27 touchdowns over the last two seasons). He is like a slower but steadier version of another Baltimore draft choice who likes to line up in the slot, Devin Duvernay. Proche will turn 24 before the season is a month old, but otherwise looks to be a good fit for the Ravens' heavy between-the-hashes attack.

Damion Ratley, CLE: Texas A&M's pro day got Ratley drafted, with a 4.39s 40-yard dash the main instigator of the interest. Ratley was a Blinn College CC transfer who joined the Aggies as a sophomore and had just 47 college catches. He was mostly regarded as a Justin Hunter- or Philip Dorsett-esque long-bombs-only prospect, à la his 46-yard touchdown against the Bengals in Week 17. After two years in Cleveland, he's only 22 catches short of his college total. With a minor trade for Taywan Taylor and Rashard Higgins nipping at Ratley's heels for the No. 3 job, it's an open question if Ratley will match his college reception total.

Kalif Raymond, TEN: Raymond's got one of those Wikipedia pages that has (second stint) notations under the teams he's joined. In four years he has been with four organizations, mostly as a returner. Back at Holy Cross, Raymond popped a 4.34s 40-yard dash at his pro day, which makes him a nice fit on a team that focuses on play-action as much as the Titans do. But at 5-foot-8, 185 pounds, Raymond is mostly just a kick-returning jitterbug. Tennessee's depth chart is real nice for a fourth receiver between Corey Davis' inconsistencies and Adam Humphries not having afterburners, so Raymond might be able to build on last year's nine-catch effort. Don't expect wild fantasy football production, though.

Joe Reed, LAC: Reed, the Chargers' fifth-round pick, went 77-679-7 for an option-heavy Virginia offense in his final season. Reed is built more like a running back than a receiver and did a lot of Deebo Samuel-type stuff for the Cavs: reverses, jet sweeps, screens, shallow crosses, etc. "Deebo Samuel types" are about to become as ubiquitous and annoying as Taysom Hill types, but there's room in the Chargers offense for a burly fourth receiver who can also return kickoffs.

Riley Ridley, CHI: Riley's combination of smooth route-running and poor athleticism did not translate into very much action as a rookie, receiving only 108 offensive snaps and not even being activated until late November. He missed a chunk of training camp, which put him behind the eight-ball early. He did manage a 25.0% DVOA on his seven targets, and he ended the year on a high note with three catches for 54 yards against a resting Minnesota. Ridley will be involved in the dogfight for the last slot on Chicago's wideout depth chart.

Chester Rogers, FA: After spending 2018 in a starting role, Rogers posted the lowest target and reception tallies of his four-year Colts career in 2019, and he was allowed to leave without much fuss in March. He has yet to find a landing spot but has a good chance to catch on as a depth option somewhere as soon as teams are able to resume workouts for free agents.

Devin Smith, DAL: Smith, the former Ohio State deep threat and 2015 second-round pick of the Jets, has never been able to hold on to a consistent role in an offense. Two torn ACLs (actually one ACL torn twice) wiped out most of his first four seasons. He caught three passes for 74 yards with a 51-yard touchdown on a post route against Josh Norman in Week 2 for the Cowboys while the wide receiver rotation was getting worked out, but he didn't play an offensive snap after Week 4.

Vyncint Smith, NYJ: A deep-ball specialist. Smith's initial 15 minutes of fame came as one of Will Fuller's many stand-ins with the Texans. Smith earned just two targets and zero receptions on 64 snaps in a 2018 wild-card game against the Indianapolis Colts. Jets head coach Adam Gase and his conservative offense took some of the wind out of Smith's downfield game, and the rotational receiver ended the season going 17-225-0 with -18.0% DVOA. Smith was nothing of a red zone threat, however, and earned just three targets there for a grand total of 5 yards.

Diontae Spencer, DEN: Spencer earned primary kickoff and punt return duties for the Broncos last year as a 27-year-old, 180-pound, former CFL standout. He also played precisely the role you would expect an aging nifty-shifty guy to play in an offense devoid of talent and creativity. KJ Hamler's arrival makes Spencer redundant and expendable.

Equanimeous St. Brown, GB: St. Brown missed the 2019 season after suffering a high-ankle sprain in Green Bay's third preseason game. That's an injury that usually only costs a player a couple months, so the fact that the Packers went ahead and stuck him on IR that early tells you something about his role in the receiving pecking order there. St. Brown can stretch the field, which makes him relatively unique among the non-Davante Adams receivers in Green Bay. He also put up a respectable -7.2% DVOA as a rookie, albeit on just 36 targets. There's a role for St. Brown in Green Bay this year, but the Packers really need him to be a significant difference-maker.

Freddie Swain, SEA: The play that got Swain drafted might have been his 85-yard punt return touchdown against Colorado State in 2018—the Seahawks haven't taken a punt back to the house since 2015. Of course, Swain only averaged 5.9 yards on his 38 other punt returns at Florida, so we're not talking the second coming of Jacquez Green here. Swain enters the NFL with a reputation for sloppy route-running but enough athletic gifts to warrant a flyer in the sixth round.

Ryan Switzer, PIT: Switzer's a reliable slot receiver with a penchant for high catch rates (career low of 72.7% last year) and the ability to contribute on special teams with both kickoff and punt returns. Switzer doesn't have impressive long speed, but he has short-area burst and separation in spades and should continue to be a part of NFL offenses as long as his 5-foot-8, 185-pound frame can take the pounding. Last year was the first where he missed any real playing time. At 26, there's still time for him to be a bigger part of some team's offense, though it's looking unlikely that'll happen in Pittsburgh.

Malik Turner, FA: Turner's last target in a Seahawks uniform was a dropped pass in the playoffs that would have given Seattle a first down in Green Bay territory with a chance to take a fourth-quarter lead. Instead the drive ended with a punt, and Seattle's season ended shortly thereafter. The Seahawks put an exclusive rights tender on Turner in March, but withdrew it in April, and he remains unsigned.

John Ursua, SEA: Ursua's only catch in his rookie season gave Seattle a first-and-goal at the 1 with a chance to beat the 49ers in Week 17 and win a first-round bye. A few plays later Jacob Hollister was tackled short of the end zone and the Seahawks were a wild-card team instead. Ursua will need to beat out sixth-round rookie Freddie Swain to keep his spot as Seattle's fifth wideout.

Quez Watkins, PHI: Watkins is faster even than his new teammate and competition for kickoff and punt returns, John Hightower. In fact, he was the second fastest receiver in this year's combine, running a 4.35s 40-yard dash that trailed only the 4.27s time of 12th overall pick Henry Ruggs. Speed was the major theme of the Eagles' offseason additions at wide receiver, which also included Round 1 pick Jalen Reagor and former Olympian Marquise Goodwin. It will be interesting to see if the team has bigger plans for Watkins than a special teams role.

Justin Watson, TB: A fifth-round pick from Penn in 2018, Watson saw almost as many targets in the Buccaneers' final two games last season (14) as he had in his previous 26 (15). All it took was the near-total decimation of Tampa Bay's receiving corps (Mike Evans, Chris Godwin, and Scott Miller were sidelined because of injuries). Maybe Watson can carve out a role for himself as Tom Brady's trusty slot receiver, but he'll have to leapfrog Miller and rookie Tyler Johnson on the depth chart.

Duke Williams, BUF: Williams, an undrafted rookie last season, was quiet for most of the year before erupting in the final weeks. 108 of Williams' 166 yards were earned in Week 17 alone, when he caught six passes on 12 targets. Williams also earned 10 targets in the following week's wild-card playoff game, though he caught just four of them for 49 yards. Williams earned the most targets on the team in both of those games. With the Bills trading a first-round pick for Stefon Diggs and spending a fourth-round pick on Gabriel Davis, Williams will not be likely to carry over this same target volume in 2020, but he should still find a role as a depth receiver and red zone target.

Damion Willis, CIN: Willis took advantage of the injuries that struck the receiver corps in Cincinnati to make the opening day roster after signing as an undrafted free agent out of Troy. He caught three balls against Seattle, then spent the rest of the season bouncing to and from the practice squad as the situation demanded. Look for much the same in 2020.

Cedrick Wilson, DAL: Wilson, a 2018 sixth-round pick, spent his rookie season on IR with a torn labrum suffered in training camp. He was put on the practice squad to start 2019 but was promoted in September, though he saw limited action. Wilson's only game with significant playing time came in Week 6 with a six-target, five-catch, 43-yard outing against the Jets. He only had two other targets on the season and finished with a DVOA of -28.2%.

Javon Wims, CHI: A late-season concussion suffered by Taylor Gabriel gave Wims some significant playing time down the stretch, to less than stellar results. Wims finished last in Chicago with -83 receiving DYAR and just a 46% catch rate; his -39.8% DVOA was third worst among receivers with at least 40 targets. Wims is going to have to excel in training camp once again if he's going to save his roster spot.

Brandon Zylstra, CAR: As a former college football and track and field athlete at the small Concordia College in Moorhead, Minnesota, Zylstra had Vikings fans dreaming of another Adam Thielen. Zylstra hasn't touched those extreme heights in his two years in the NFL, but now with the Panthers, he has carved out a role as a special teams player who, as a bonus, produced an efficient 8.4% DVOA on his 12 targets in 2019. As part of an inexperienced bench behind D.J. Moore, Robby Anderson, and Curtis Samuel, Zylstra could see his offensive workload grow somewhat in 2020.

Tight Ends

Top 20 TE by DYAR (Total Value), 2019

Rank	Player	Team	DYAR
1	Darren Waller	OAK	234
2	Jared Cook	NO	205
3	Travis Kelce	KC	203
4	George Kittle	SF	187
5	Hunter Henry	LAC	136
6	Austin Hooper	ATL	130
7	Mark Andrews	BAL	123
8	Kyle Rudolph	MIN	118
9	Jonnu Smith	TEN	91
10	Hayden Hurst	BAL	89
11	Tyler Higbee	LAR	79
12	Darren Fells	HOU	75
13	Will Dissly	SEA	74
14	Foster Moreau	OAK	72
15	Blake Jarwin	DAL	52
16	Ryan Griffin	NYJ	45
17	Jason Witten	DAL	38
18	Jimmy Graham	GB	38
19	O.J. Howard	TB	37
20	Anthony Firkser	TEN	31

Minimum 25 passes.

Top 20 TE by DVOA (Value per Play), 2019

Rank	Player	Team	DVOA
1	Jared Cook	NO	37.7%
2	Will Dissly	SEA	36.0%
3	Foster Moreau	OAK	29.6%
4	Hayden Hurst	BAL	28.1%
5	Kyle Rudolph	MIN	26.9%
6	Jonnu Smith	TEN	25.6%
7	Darren Waller	OAK	22.0%
8	Hunter Henry	LAC	19.0%
9	George Kittle	SF	18.9%
10	Darren Fells	HOU	15.6%
11	Travis Kelce	KC	14.8%
12	Anthony Firkser	TEN	13.0%
13	Austin Hooper	ATL	12.5%
14	Blake Jarwin	DAL	12.1%
15	Mark Andrews	BAL	12.1%
16	Ryan Griffin	NYJ	8.4%
17	Tyler Higbee	LAR	5.5%
18	O.J. Howard	TB	3.2%
19	Jimmy Graham	GB	2.1%
20	Jason Witten	DAL	-0.5%

Minimum 25 passes.

Jordan Akins

Height: 6-4 Weight: 243 College: Central Florida Draft: 2018/3 (98) Born: 19-Apr-1992 Age: 28 Risk: Green

Year	Tm	G/GS	Snaps	Pass	Rec	Yds	TD	EZ	C%	+/-	Drop	Yd/C	aDOT	Rk	YAC	Rk	YAC+	BTkl	DVOA	Rk	DYAR	Rk	Use	Rk	Slot	Wide
2018	HOU	16/6	388	25	17	225	0	1	68%	-0.2	0	13.2	6.9	30	7.2	5	+1.8	4	8.3%	16	24	24	5.0%	47	44%	4%
2019	HOU	16/9	672	55	36	418	2	3	65%	-1.8	3	11.6	7.1	26	6.8	4	+1.9	10	-5.6%	27	6	27	10.6%	30	40%	0%
2020	HOU			30	21	225	2		70%			10.7							1.7%							

It was hard to understand why Akins was never more involved in the offense after his two-touchdown game against the Chargers in Week 3. Well, outside of the fact that Bill O'Brien tight ends are rarely involved in the offense as a general rule. Akins has an interesting backstory—he was once a dream-on-the-tools baseball prospect in the Rangers system, so he's already 28. But obviously, the tools are still there. He puts together a darkly comedic blocking reel, but there are teams that would spread him off the line of scrimmage and make a lot of hay out of it. Akins should settle in for another 30- to 40-target season as Houston's passing-downs tight end, barring a Kahale Warring breakout.

Mark Andrews

Height: 6-5 Weight: 255 College: Oklahoma Draft: 2018/3 (86) Born: 6-Sep-1996 Age: 24 Risk: Green

Year	Tm	G/GS	Snaps	Pass	Rec	Yds	TD	EZ	C%	+/-	Drop	Yd/C	aDOT	Rk	YAC	Rk	YAC+	BTkl	DVOA	Rk	DYAR	Rk	Use	Rk	Slot	Wide
2018	BAL	16/3	414	50	34	552	3	6	68%	+4.3	3	16.2	11.4	4	5.7	17	+1.5	1	36.2%	2	159	4	9.6%	25	51%	8%
2019	BAL	15/4	467	98	64	852	10	13	65%	+1.2	4	13.3	10.8	2	4.5	29	+0.6	9	12.1%	15	123	7	24.5%	2	72%	2%
2020	BAL			84	57	730	6		68%			12.8							17.0%							

Andrews always profiled as a tight end in name only, and last season he was far more of a slot receiver, with 71 of his 98 targets coming when he lined up in that part of the formation. But his high efficiency in the red zone screamed "tight end"—of all receivers with double-digit red zone targets, only the Houston combo of Duke Johnson and Darren Fells posted higher DVOAs than Andrews' 60.8%. Wherever he lines up, Andrews has become Lamar Jackson's favorite wubby, and with Hayden Hurst (who was drafted ahead of Andrews and Jackson in 2018) traded, Andrews should only become more important in the Ravens attack.

Devin Asiasi Height: 6-3 Weight: 257 College: UCLA Draft: 2020/3 (91) Born: 14-Aug-1997 Age: 23 Risk: Blue

Year	Tm	G/GS	Snaps	Pass	Rec	Yds	TD	EZ	C%	+/-	Drop	Yd/C	aDOT	Rk	YAC	Rk	YAC+	BTkl	DVOA	Rk	DYAR	Rk	Use	Rk	Slot	Wide
2020	NE		25	17	185	1		68%			10.9								-2.4%							

The entire Patriots offense lacked speed and athleticism in 2019, but no position was worse in that regard than tight end. Neither Ryan Izzo, ancient Benjamin Watson, nor Matt LaCosse was threatening to blow past anyone. Asiasi, while not quite a Jared Cook-level speedster, is surely an upgrade in the movement department among Patriots tight ends. Asiasi ran a 4.73s 40-yard dash at the NFL combine, which put him in the 63rd percentile. The concern with Asiasi is that it may take time for him to acclimate. Not only do rookie tight ends struggle in general, but Asiasi only produced for one season in college and posted a poor 41% success rate on his catches. Granted, part of that lack of success is tied to UCLA's offense being atrocious all around, but still. Asiasi will need to shatter expectations in order to be the immediate impact player the Patriots need in 2020.

Nick Boyle Height: 6-4 Weight: 270 College: Delaware Draft: 2015/5 (171) Born: 17-Feb-1993 Age: 27 Risk: Green

Year	Tm	G/GS	Snaps	Pass	Rec	Yds	TD	EZ	C%	+/-	Drop	Yd/C	aDOT	Rk	YAC	Rk	YAC+	BTkl	DVOA	Rk	DYAR	Rk	Use	Rk	Slot	Wide
2017	BAL	15/11	696	37	28	203	0	2	76%	+0.5	0	7.3	2.2	51	5.5	15	-0.5	4	-19.3%	45	-32	45	7.0%	42	19%	11%
2018	BAL	16/13	651	37	23	213	0	2	62%	-1.9	1	9.3	3.5	48	6.1	13	+0.8	2	-26.6%	44	-50	43	6.7%	40	19%	0%
2019	BAL	16/15	783	43	31	321	2	3	72%	+0.1	2	10.4	6.4	33	5.2	14	+0.5	2	-0.8%	21	18	26	10.1%	32	14%	0%
2020	BAL			41	27	297	3		66%			11.0							-2.2%							

The former member of the Delaware Fightin' Blue Hens is the blocking tight end that allows Mark Andrews to line up as a wideout in most of Baltimore's formations. It's not as though Boyle is some sort of stone-handed lug, however—he caught 31 of 43 targets in 2019, 13 of them for first downs. He will continue in his well-defined role in 2020, and with Hayden Hurst gone, might even see a slight uptick in passes thrown his way.

Cameron Brate Height: 6-5 Weight: 245 College: Harvard Draft: 2014/FA Born: 3-Jul-1991 Age: 29 Risk: Green

Year	Tm	G/GS	Snaps	Pass	Rec	Yds	TD	EZ	C%	+/-	Drop	Yd/C	aDOT	Rk	YAC	Rk	YAC+	BTkl	DVOA	Rk	DYAR	Rk	Use	Rk	Slot	Wide
2017	TB	16/5	586	77	48	591	6	8	62%	+2.4	4	12.3	9.5	15	3.0	45	-1.2	3	24.7%	8	154	5	12.8%	19	60%	8%
2018	TB	16/2	534	49	30	289	6	7	61%	-2.9	5	9.6	8.4	15	1.7	49	-1.9	1	-6.8%	31	2	31	7.8%	34	53%	12%
2019	TB	16/6	437	55	36	311	4	3	65%	-1.2	3	8.6	7.3	23	2.5	48	-1.6	3	-8.0%	32	-3	32	8.9%	37	49%	4%
2020	TB			16	10	109	1		63%			10.9							-5.0%							

In 2015 and 2016, Brate ranked among the top 10 tight ends in DVOA. His playing time has fallen each season since. In 2016, he played 62.2% of the Buccaneers' offensive snaps. Last season, he played just 37.7%. Barring an injury to Rob Gronkowski or a trade of O.J. Howard—neither of which is a far-fetched possibility—that downward trend is likely to continue. Despite Brate's increasingly limited opportunities, he has remained a reliable red zone target. Since he became a major contributor in 2015, he has scored a team-high 26 touchdowns in the red zone. That's five more than Mike Evans, who has seen 30 more targets.

Trey Burton Height: 6-2 Weight: 238 College: Florida Draft: 2014/FA Born: 29-Oct-1991 Age: 29 Risk: Yellow

Year	Tm	G/GS	Snaps	Pass	Rec	Yds	TD	EZ	C%	+/-	Drop	Yd/C	aDOT	Rk	YAC	Rk	YAC+	BTkl	DVOA	Rk	DYAR	Rk	Use	Rk	Slot	Wide
2017	PHI	15/1	300	31	23	248	5	5	74%	+4.3	1	10.8	9.5	16	1.5	51	-2.0	0	35.0%	3	85	10	5.9%	47	68%	6%
2018	CHI	16/16	860	76	54	569	6	4	71%	+3.1	3	10.5	8.4	16	3.5	42	-1.0	1	-2.7%	27	24	25	14.7%	11	58%	5%
2019	CHI	8/5	291	24	14	84	0	1	58%	-3.7	2	6.0	5.0	--	2.6	--	-2.9	0	-49.1%	--	-65	--	8.4%	--	58%	0%
2020	IND			28	18	176	2		64%			9.8							-10.2%							

Burton is living off the memories of 2017, the only season when he had a positive receiving DVOA and the only year he topped 40 DYAR. Some of Burton's lack of success last season can be blamed on Mitchell Trubisky's regression, but there aren't enough fingers to point to explain away 6.0 yards per reception, the worst figure for any non-running back with at least 20 targets. Fully healthy this year—a back injury kept him from being 100% in 2019—and with a better quarterback throwing him the ball, Burton probably won't finish second-to-last in receiving DYAR once again, but he's best used as a part-time complement in Indianapolis' offense rather than a key contributor.

Jared Cook

Height: 6-5   Weight: 254   College: South Carolina   Draft: 2009/3 (89)   Born: 7-Apr-1987   Age: 33   Risk: Green

Year	Tm	G/GS	Snaps	Pass	Rec	Yds	TD	EZ	C%	+/-	Drop	Yd/C	aDOT	Rk	YAC	Rk	YAC+	BTkl	DVOA	Rk	DYAR	Rk	Use	Rk	Slot	Wide
2017	OAK	16/16	796	86	54	688	2	7	63%	+0.0	5	12.7	9.6	12	3.9	37	-0.6	5	2.1%	19	53	17	15.7%	13	59%	14%
2018	OAK	16/14	770	101	68	896	6	9	67%	+1.8	8	13.2	8.4	17	5.0	24	+0.6	8	13.8%	11	146	5	19.3%	5	36%	18%
2019	NO	14/7	513	65	43	705	9	11	66%	+3.3	4	16.4	10.6	3	5.8	9	+2.4	5	37.7%	1	205	2	13.3%	21	68%	12%
2020	NO			61	42	572	5		69%			13.6							27.0%							

If you drafted Cook last summer, chances are you dropped him around midseason. He started slow—15 catches, 168 yards, and two touchdowns in the Saints' first six games—and then wasn't available the next three weeks (two because of an ankle injury and one because of a bye). Before his Week 10 return, he had a -11.5% receiving DVOA. Then he caught fire, catching 28 passes for 537 yards and seven touchdowns. His 71.4% receiving DVOA over the final eight weeks was the highest of any player at any position (minimum 20 passes). Impressive, but unsustainable. Last season, one out of every five of Cook's catches resulted in a touchdown. Before last season: one out of every 17.

Will Dissly

Height: 6-4   Weight: 267   College: Washington   Draft: 2018/4 (120)   Born: 8-Jul-1996   Age: 24   Risk: Red

Year	Tm	G/GS	Snaps	Pass	Rec	Yds	TD	EZ	C%	+/-	Drop	Yd/C	aDOT	Rk	YAC	Rk	YAC+	BTkl	DVOA	Rk	DYAR	Rk	Use	Rk	Slot	Wide
2018	SEA	4/4	127	14	8	156	2	2	57%	-0.3	1	19.5	10.8	--	11.6	--	+7.4	2	30.6%	--	36	--	13.7%	--	21%	0%
2019	SEA	6/6	256	27	23	262	4	5	85%	+5.5	0	11.4	9.1	12	3.0	42	-1.5	1	36.0%	2	74	13	14.4%	18	30%	7%
2020	SEA			47	34	364	3		72%			10.7							6.5%							

Dissly has already shown the ability to produce at a Pro Bowl-caliber level; he is one of seven tight ends the past two seasons to average at least 13 yards per catch and 40 yards per game. The problem, of course, is that he there have only been ten of those games, as a torn patellar tendon in his rookie year and a torn Achilles last season have robbed him of two-thirds of his career. If Dissly can just do what he has already done for 16 games in 2020, he'll be a fantasy stud—he was fifth among tight ends in fantasy scoring through five games last year. The questions are whether his injuries have robbed him of his athleticism, whether he'll tear a completely different tendon this year, and whether he will lose any playing time to veteran free agent Greg Olsen.

Jack Doyle

Height: 6-6   Weight: 262   College: Western Kentucky   Draft: 2013/FA   Born: 5-May-1990   Age: 30   Risk: Green

Year	Tm	G/GS	Snaps	Pass	Rec	Yds	TD	EZ	C%	+/-	Drop	Yd/C	aDOT	Rk	YAC	Rk	YAC+	BTkl	DVOA	Rk	DYAR	Rk	Use	Rk	Slot	Wide
2017	IND	15/15	909	108	80	690	4	4	74%	+4.0	3	8.6	5.0	50	4.2	33	-0.7	9	-7.5%	29	-2	31	24.3%	2	44%	4%
2018	IND	6/6	332	33	26	245	2	1	79%	+2.3	0	9.4	5.4	43	4.2	36	-0.1	2	-7.4%	33	0	33	13.7%	15	48%	6%
2019	IND	16/16	811	72	43	448	4	7	60%	-4.4	5	10.4	7.2	25	5.0	18	+0.6	1	-6.7%	30	3	30	14.6%	16	46%	3%
2020	IND			61	41	438	3		67%			10.7							0.8%							

While the arrival of Trey Burton from Chicago may have an impact on his perceived value, Doyle has always been a productive part of a strong tight end group during the Frank Reich era. Other than his abbreviated 2018 season, Doyle has reached at least 70 targets, 440 yards, and four touchdowns in every season as a starter. 2019 brought the lowest catch rate of Doyle's career, but that was probably a function of the quarterback: both Doyle and Eric Ebron were at -32.0% DVOA or lower on first down, but both had positive DVOA on third and fourth down, when Jacoby Brissett was also at his most effective. Doyle's 37.3% DVOA on third downs was the highest of any Colts player with at least three such targets, and only Zach Pascal was targeted more often in those critical situations. While nobody will mistake him for Hunter Henry or prime Antonio Gates, Doyle should continue to be a highly valuable player for his new quarterback.

Eric Ebron

	Height: 6-4	Weight: 253	College: North Carolina	Draft: 2014/1 (10)	Born: 10-Apr-1993	Age: 27	Risk: Yellow

Year	Tm	G/GS	Snaps	Pass	Rec	Yds	TD	EZ	C%	+/-	Drop	Yd/C	aDOT	Rk	YAC	Rk	YAC+	BTkl	DVOA	Rk	DYAR	Rk	Use	Rk	Slot	Wide
2017	DET	16/9	552	86	53	574	4	6	62%	-1.7	6	10.8	7.8	32	4.9	25	+0.3	9	2.0%	20	50	18	15.0%	15	47%	10%
2018	IND	16/8	634	110	66	750	13	17	60%	-4.9	8	11.4	9.6	8	3.8	41	-0.4	6	2.0%	22	68	11	17.1%	6	76%	4%
2019	IND	11/2	328	52	31	375	3	5	60%	-1.4	5	12.1	9.8	8	5.0	19	+1.0	3	-1.1%	23	21	25	15.4%	12	73%	4%
2020	PIT			56	38	453	3		68%			11.9							7.1%							

Even the most pessimistic of fantasy projections didn't think Ebron would lose over 50% of his 2018 targets, but those projections were of an Andrew Luck offense rather than a Jacoby Brissett outfit: nobody on the Colts came close to their 2018 target distribution. With Mo Alie-Cox and Jack Doyle more favored in Indy for their blocking, Ebron was allowed to walk, so he washed up with the Steelers as the clear No. 2 tight end to Vance McDonald. Ebron has never lacked for big-play ability and has a body made for posting up small safeties and slot corners, but it comes with drops by the bushel.

Tyler Eifert

	Height: 6-6	Weight: 255	College: Notre Dame	Draft: 2013/1 (21)	Born: 8-Sep-1990	Age: 30	Risk: Red

Year	Tm	G/GS	Snaps	Pass	Rec	Yds	TD	EZ	C%	+/-	Drop	Yd/C	aDOT	Rk	YAC	Rk	YAC+	BTkl	DVOA	Rk	DYAR	Rk	Use	Rk	Slot	Wide
2017	CIN	2/1	104	5	4	46	0	1	80%	+0.8	0	11.5	9.4	--	2.8	--	-4.3	0	11.6%	--	6	--	8.0%	--	60%	0%
2018	CIN	4/2	133	19	15	179	1	3	79%	+3.1	0	11.9	8.2	--	3.6	--	-0.9	1	21.1%	--	36	--	15.6%	--	70%	0%
2019	CIN	16/4	507	63	43	436	3	7	68%	+1.0	4	10.1	8.4	15	2.6	46	-1.4	1	-1.8%	24	22	24	10.6%	29	59%	16%
2020	JAX			46	32	329	3		70%			10.3							-0.8%							

Injuries continued to set the boundaries for Eifert in 2019 even though he played all 16 games for the first time in his seven-year career. He only achieved that on a limited snap count, with only four starts and barely scraping past 500 snaps for the first time since 2015. Those numbers are all still more than the previous two seasons combined. He set a career low in yards per game (discounting the 2017 season when he played just two pain-filled games before back surgery ended his season), yards per target, and yards per reception. His usage was also the lowest it has been in any season with at least two starts; he was targeted a hair short of four times per game.

That would, however, still have been the most productive season for a Jaguars tight end since Julius Thomas in 2015. Jay Gruden loves to incorporate a receiving tight end in his offense, but the similarities between Eifert and Jordan Reed extend to the trainer's room almost as often as the end zone. If Eifert can stay healthy, he has the chance to be a very productive part of this offense. Unfortunately, history is very much against that happening.

Evan Engram

	Height: 6-3	Weight: 240	College: Mississippi	Draft: 2017/2 (23)	Born: 2-Sep-1994	Age: 26	Risk: Yellow

Year	Tm	G/GS	Snaps	Pass	Rec	Yds	TD	EZ	C%	+/-	Drop	Yd/C	aDOT	Rk	YAC	Rk	YAC+	BTkl	DVOA	Rk	DYAR	Rk	Use	Rk	Slot	Wide
2017	NYG	15/11	777	115	64	722	6	9	56%	-7.1	7	11.3	8.5	25	4.7	27	+0.5	7	-8.0%	33	-5	33	20.2%	6	25%	15%
2018	NYG	11/8	475	64	45	577	3	3	70%	-1.8	2	12.8	5.4	42	8.6	3	+2.8	10	4.8%	19	50	19	16.2%	7	54%	2%
2019	NYG	8/6	454	68	44	467	3	3	65%	-4.0	3	10.6	6.0	36	5.7	11	+0.8	2	-15.7%	36	-37	41	22.9%	6	46%	7%
2020	NYG			90	56	630	5		62%			11.3							-3.7%							

Engram's injury issues must be frustrating for coaches. Coaches' usage of Engram is frustrating for literally everyone else. Engram has gone through two staffs that have used him as little more than a drag route option. Only 10 players with at least 43 targets (Next Gen Stats' cutoff) had a lower aDOT than Engram in 2019. Only seven of Engram's 68 targets came more than 15 yards down the field. That's less than half of Jimmy Graham's 2019 total (17). Engram's best play came on a 75-yard touchdown on a deep Y-Cross in Daniel Jones' first start against the Buccaneers in Week 3. But still, his aDOT for that game finished at just 4.5.

Injuries did sap some of Engram's ability. He only played in eight games, and unlike prior years when Engram compensated for short passes with a ton of broken tackles, he broke just two in 2019. If there's one player who should benefit from a more vertical offense under Jason Garrett, it's Engram.

Zach Ertz Height: 6-5   Weight: 250   College: Stanford   Draft: 2013/2 (35)   Born: 10-Nov-1990   Age: 30   Risk: Green

Year	Tm	G/GS	Snaps	Pass	Rec	Yds	TD	EZ	C%	+/-	Drop	Yd/C	aDOT	Rk	YAC	Rk	YAC+	BTkl	DVOA	Rk	DYAR	Rk	Use	Rk	Slot	Wide
2017	PHI	14/13	778	110	74	824	8	9	67%	+4.0	8	11.1	8.0	29	3.4	43	-0.8	4	14.2%	13	154	4	22.3%	4	48%	4%
2018	PHI	16/16	1000	155	116	1163	8	10	74%	+7.7	5	10.0	7.4	27	3.1	46	-1.4	7	1.6%	23	93	8	26.2%	3	65%	4%
2019	PHI	15/15	953	135	88	916	6	9	65%	-2.1	7	10.4	8.8	13	2.9	44	-1.1	8	-4.3%	26	27	22	23.8%	5	59%	4%
2020	PHI			102	70	729	6		69%			10.4							2.4%							

Ertz put up the worst DVOA and DYAR figures of his career last season, but you can put most of the blame there on the injuries the Eagles had at the wideout position; very few tight ends can really shoulder the load as a team's top offensive threat week in and week out. Theoretically, if Jalen Reagor can take the top off the defense, that should give Ertz plenty of room to work over the middle, where few tight ends in the game can match his precise route-running and footwork. Problem is, we said the same thing last season about DeSean Jackson, and, well, stuff happens. Ertz played in-line more in 2019 than he did the year before, and had a higher DVOA working there then he did out of the slot (0.1% to -5.5%); we expect him to continue primarily as a slot receiver as Dallas Goedert continues to excel as the more traditional tight end, but it's something to monitor going forward.

Gerald Everett Height: 6-3   Weight: 240   College: South Alabama   Draft: 2017/2 (44)   Born: 25-Jun-1994   Age: 26   Risk: Green

Year	Tm	G/GS	Snaps	Pass	Rec	Yds	TD	EZ	C%	+/-	Drop	Yd/C	aDOT	Rk	YAC	Rk	YAC+	BTkl	DVOA	Rk	DYAR	Rk	Use	Rk	Slot	Wide
2017	LAR	16/2	299	32	16	244	2	5	50%	-3.3	3	15.3	9.5	14	6.8	6	+1.6	1	-17.0%	44	-20	41	6.2%	45	41%	9%
2018	LAR	16/0	380	50	33	320	3	5	66%	-0.4	0	9.7	6.4	37	4.4	33	+0.0	7	-6.6%	29	2	29	9.1%	27	26%	20%
2019	LAR	13/2	453	60	37	408	2	3	62%	-1.0	1	11.0	8.1	16	4.8	26	+0.3	14	-10.4%	34	-13	34	12.1%	24	51%	18%
2020	LAR			33	23	230	2		70%			10.0							-2.2%							

Everett had seven catches for 136 yards against Seattle in Week 5, the first 100-yard game of his career. It felt like a breakout at the time, but he had only 19 catches for 185 yards the rest of the year as he battled through wrist and knee injuries. Everett is entering the last year of his rookie contract, but he's now the clear second tight end in L.A. following Tyler Higbee's late-season breakout. Everett is going to have a hard time earning a big second contract from the Rams or anyone else.

Noah Fant Height: 6-4   Weight: 249   College: Iowa   Draft: 2019/1 (20)   Born: 20-Nov-1997   Age: 23   Risk: Green

Year	Tm	G/GS	Snaps	Pass	Rec	Yds	TD	EZ	C%	+/-	Drop	Yd/C	aDOT	Rk	YAC	Rk	YAC+	BTkl	DVOA	Rk	DYAR	Rk	Use	Rk	Slot	Wide
2019	DEN	16/11	703	66	40	562	3	8	61%	+0.2	4	14.1	7.9	19	8.3	1	+2.4	8	-5.9%	28	6	28	13.4%	20	23%	6%
2020	DEN			59	38	495	4		64%			13.0							10.5%							

Fant rushed three times on tight end sweeps for -5, -5, and -2 yards. On each occasion, there was an unblocked defender waiting on the backside of the play to wallop Fant before he could turn upfield. We mention this because when you see three rushes for -12 yards on a tight end's stat line (something you probably never saw before in your life before, but play along), you probably assume that he chased down an errant shotgun snap and was charged with a 15-yard loss or something. Nope. The Broncos offense was just so pedestrian last year that not even tight end misdirection plays fooled anyone.

Darren Fells Height: 6-7   Weight: 270   College: California-Irvine   Draft: 2013/FA   Born: 22-Apr-1986   Age: 34   Risk: Green

Year	Tm	G/GS	Snaps	Pass	Rec	Yds	TD	EZ	C%	+/-	Drop	Yd/C	aDOT	Rk	YAC	Rk	YAC+	BTkl	DVOA	Rk	DYAR	Rk	Use	Rk	Slot	Wide
2017	DET	16/13	550	26	17	177	3	3	65%	+0.0	3	10.4	5.3	48	7.2	2	+2.0	2	21.9%	9	48	19	4.5%	50	31%	4%
2018	CLE	16/11	420	12	11	117	3	2	92%	+1.8	0	10.6	4.8	--	6.0	--	+1.1	2	53.9%	--	52	--	2.1%	--	17%	0%
2019	HOU	16/14	759	48	34	341	7	6	71%	+0.3	3	10.0	5.4	42	4.9	21	+1.2	3	15.6%	10	75	12	9.2%	35	20%	0%
2020	HOU			32	21	218	2		66%			10.4							-3.5%							

Signed to a one-year contract when Houston flooded the position with youth, Fells' blocking got him on the field even though he surprisingly led Sports Info Solutions' count of blown blocks by tight ends with 21. He was the beneficiary of a lot of Bill O'Brien's midseason tight end drag option offense, with the result being a few easy walk-in touchdowns. After receiving a two-year deal this offseason, Fells is the safe money to be Houston's blocking/early-down tight end and will probably only see a massive snap decline with an injury or a breakout year from Kahale Warring. Fells' skill set is probably a better fit for a 300- to 500-snap role, because he has real drop issues, but he's a solid second tight end.

Mike Gesicki

Height: 6-6 Weight: 252 College: Penn State Draft: 2018/2 (42) Born: 3-Oct-1995 Age: 25 Risk: Yellow

Year	Tm	G/GS	Snaps	Pass	Rec	Yds	TD	EZ	C%	+/-	Drop	Yd/C	aDOT	Rk	YAC	Rk	YAC+	BTkl	DVOA	Rk	DYAR	Rk	Use	Rk	Slot	Wide
2018	MIA	16/7	400	32	22	202	0	2	69%	+1.1	1	9.2	9.2	10	4.4	33	-0.7	3	-37.3%	47	-70	45	7.5%	37	21%	21%
2019	MIA	16/5	705	89	51	570	5	11	57%	-1.7	0	11.2	10.5	4	3.4	40	-1.1	0	-16.3%	39	-51	45	14.7%	15	39%	4%
2020	MIA			69	43	481	4		62%			11.2							-3.2%							

Gesicki is the perfect young player for a league moving more and more toward tight ends who play like wide receivers. A lean, smooth athlete for the position, Gesicki was at his best last season when allowed to play from slot positions. Only 39% of Gesicki's targets were from the slot in 2019, but he shredded defenses with a 21.8% DVOA rating on those targets, a mark good for 10th out of 48 qualifying tight ends. Gesicki also emerged as a legit red zone threat. After an embarrassing rookie year in that area, Gesicki caught five of his 11 red zone targets for a solid 8.8% DVOA rating. Last but not least on Gesicki's list of promising achievements, SIS did not list him with a single blown block. He is not a people-mover the way George Kittle is, but he has proven himself capable of at least being a useful roadblock play in, play out. If Gesicki's development continues to trend up, he could establish himself among the league's top tight ends (in the sub-Kelce/Kittle area).

Dallas Goedert

Height: 6-5 Weight: 256 College: South Dakota State Draft: 2018/2 (49) Born: 3-Jan-1995 Age: 26 Risk: Green

Year	Tm	G/GS	Snaps	Pass	Rec	Yds	TD	EZ	C%	+/-	Drop	Yd/C	aDOT	Rk	YAC	Rk	YAC+	BTkl	DVOA	Rk	DYAR	Rk	Use	Rk	Slot	Wide
2018	PHI	16/8	524	44	33	334	4	6	75%	+2.4	1	10.1	7.8	20	5.2	22	+0.3	5	5.1%	18	38	21	7.5%	36	29%	7%
2019	PHI	15/9	781	87	58	607	5	7	67%	+2.0	3	10.5	6.2	35	5.8	10	+0.7	9	-2.1%	25	30	21	15.2%	14	43%	3%
2020	PHI			76	51	554	4		67%			10.9							-0.8%							

The Eagles had to lean on 12 personnel down the stretch as their receiving corps was decimated, and Goedert mostly rose to the challenge. Goedert had 36 DYAR over the last five weeks of the season, 11th most among tight ends and well above Zach Ertz's -52 DYAR from the same time period. That's not an arbitrary cutoff, either; it coincides with Goedert's larger role in the passing game. Goedert averaged 4.6 targets per game before those last five weeks, rising to 8.2 over that stretch. It wasn't the most efficient football ever played, with his DVOA only hitting 6.3%, but considering the state of the Eagles' offense in December, that's still an impressive feat.

Jimmy Graham

Height: 6-7 Weight: 265 College: Miami Draft: 2010/3 (95) Born: 24-Nov-1986 Age: 34 Risk: Yellow

Year	Tm	G/GS	Snaps	Pass	Rec	Yds	TD	EZ	C%	+/-	Drop	Yd/C	aDOT	Rk	YAC	Rk	YAC+	BTkl	DVOA	Rk	DYAR	Rk	Use	Rk	Slot	Wide
2017	SEA	16/13	730	96	57	520	10	20	59%	-3.8	7	9.1	7.9	30	3.7	39	-0.4	6	-6.0%	28	9	27	18.0%	10	43%	27%
2018	GB	16/12	795	89	55	636	2	8	62%	+0.7	3	11.6	9.4	9	4.7	28	-0.0	5	-6.6%	30	4	28	14.4%	13	57%	8%
2019	GB	16/10	638	60	38	447	3	9	63%	+0.6	3	11.8	9.9	7	6.5	5	+1.5	7	2.1%	19	38	18	11.4%	25	55%	2%
2020	CHI			35	24	276	2		69%			11.5							3.8%							

Graham still is an above-average slot receiver; his receiving DVOA jumped from -4.3% as an in-line tight end to 11.7% when he lined up in the slot. This has always been the case for Graham, and it has only become more prominent over the last couple of seasons; he hasn't had positive value on passes where he was lined up tight since 2016. The only Bears player to have better value out of the slot last season was Allen Robinson at 12.5%, so there's a chance that Graham could still provide something positive for Chicago in 2020. That being said, there is no way a 34-year-old Graham should be one of the top ten highest-paid players at his position; he is no longer able to physically overwhelm the opposition, and instead gets most of his value by taking advantage of situations where the defense loses track of him. Per Next Gen Stats, Graham's average target came with 3.9 yards of separation, the most space in the NFL.

Ryan Griffin

Height: 6-6   Weight: 255   College: Connecticut   Draft: 2013/6 (201)   Born: 11-Jan-1990   Age: 30   Risk: Yellow

Year	Tm	G/GS	Snaps	Pass	Rec	Yds	TD	EZ	C%	+/-	Drop	Yd/C	aDOT	Rk	YAC	Rk	YAC+	BTkl	DVOA	Rk	DYAR	Rk	Use	Rk	Slot	Wide
2017	HOU	7/6	349	26	13	158	1	3	50%	-2.5	1	12.2	10.3	9	5.6	13	+1.4	1	-11.0%	37	-6	34	11.1%	26	8%	0%
2018	HOU	14/11	743	43	24	305	0	8	56%	-5.3	3	12.7	7.6	24	6.3	8	+1.8	2	-13.5%	38	-18	40	10.1%	24	34%	5%
2019	NYJ	13/13	681	41	34	320	5	2	83%	+4.5	2	9.4	5.5	41	5.2	13	+0.5	3	8.4%	16	45	16	10.1%	33	17%	2%
2020	NYJ			29	21	220	2		72%			10.5							7.5%							

At a glance, Griffin quietly had the best year of his career last season. After years of toiling around as a low-end No. 1 or high-end No. 2 tight end with Houston, Griffin notched career-highs in touchdowns and catch rate in his first year with the Jets. A good chunk of Griffin's production came on first downs. Twenty-four of his 41 targets were on first down, which differs from 2017 when most of his targets were on second down, and 2018 when most of his targets were on third down. Despite all the positive year-end numbers, though, it is tough to sell anyone on the idea that Griffin is breaking out considering half his production came in two games against Jacksonville and Washington. In those two games alone, Griffin earned 175 yards and three touchdowns, while only earning 145 yards and two scores in his other 11 appearances.

Rob Gronkowski

Height: 6-6   Weight: 264   College: Arizona   Draft: 2010/2 (42)   Born: 14-May-1989   Age: 31   Risk: Yellow

Year	Tm	G/GS	Snaps	Pass	Rec	Yds	TD	EZ	C%	+/-	Drop	Yd/C	aDOT	Rk	YAC	Rk	YAC+	BTkl	DVOA	Rk	DYAR	Rk	Use	Rk	Slot	Wide
2017	NE	14/14	905	105	69	1084	8	15	66%	+7.9	3	15.7	12.2	1	5.0	22	+1.0	12	40.4%	2	339	1	21.1%	5	41%	15%
2018	NE	13/11	838	72	47	682	3	8	65%	+1.8	2	14.5	12.4	1	3.9	40	-0.3	5	13.3%	12	98	6	16.1%	8	38%	11%
2020	TB			54	39	521	3		72%			13.4							21.1%							

A retired Gronkowski revealed to NBC News last August that he gets treatments on his head. "No lie, I felt my head, I used to have liquid," he said. "It used to be thicker, like, my head used to be thicker, like a centimeter of liquid in some spots, and you feel it. I'd be like, 'What the heck?' You could put indents in my head, but now, finally, I get the right treatments."

Whaaaaaaat? Why are you coming back, Rob? Sure, we all missed the unrivaled power of your touchdown dance. But your head. Indents, Rob. Indents!

Though a year away from football might have re-energized Gronkowski, he demonstrated a startling lack of awareness and an inability to recover after initial contact during an unsuccessful defense of his WWE 24/7 championship this spring. As he was dancing in the backyard of his Foxborough home, wrestler R-Truth, clumsily disguised as a landscaper, ambushed him and rolled him up with ease for the 1-2-3. Realistically, it's a lot to expect Gronkowski, who has had three back surgeries, to return to even his 2018 level of play.

Hunter Henry

Height: 6-5   Weight: 250   College: Arkansas   Draft: 2016/2 (35)   Born: 7-Dec-1994   Age: 26   Risk: Green

Year	Tm	G/GS	Snaps	Pass	Rec	Yds	TD	EZ	C%	+/-	Drop	Yd/C	aDOT	Rk	YAC	Rk	YAC+	BTkl	DVOA	Rk	DYAR	Rk	Use	Rk	Slot	Wide
2017	LAC	14/13	598	62	45	579	4	10	73%	+5.8	3	12.9	9.2	19	4.2	32	+0.3	1	32.3%	4	165	3	12.4%	23	50%	3%
2019	LAC	12/12	621	76	55	652	5	6	72%	+4.9	3	11.9	10.2	5	2.9	45	-1.1	0	19.0%	8	136	5	17.6%	8	59%	3%
2020	LAC			76	51	571	4		67%			11.2							3.1%							

Henry returned from a 2018 ACL tear and promptly suffered a tibia fracture in the 2019 season opener. He somehow worked his way back by Week 6 and went 25-328-2 in his first four games upon return. His production then dropped and leveled off in the two- to four-catch, 30- to 50-yard range for the rest of the season. A pair of costly drops against the Bears and a slip-and-fall which resulted in a Philip Rivers interception in Week 10 against the Raiders may have cost Henry some targets; Rivers spent much of last season staring down Keenan Allen on shallow crossing routes as if he had lost faith in nearly everyone else. But Rivers is now in Indy, and Henry was franchise-tagged so that he could be part of Justin Herbert's development team. Henry has gobs of talent, of course. But he's entering his fifth NFL season, and we're still waiting for his Travis Kelce/Zach Ertz breakout-type performance.

Christopher Herndon

Height: 6-4   Weight: 252   College: Miami   Draft: 2018/4 (107)   Born: 23-Feb-1996   Age: 24   Risk: Red

Year	Tm	G/GS	Snaps	Pass	Rec	Yds	TD	EZ	C%	+/-	Drop	Yd/C	aDOT	Rk	YAC	Rk	YAC+	BTkl	DVOA	Rk	DYAR	Rk	Use	Rk	Slot	Wide
2018	NYJ	16/12	625	56	39	502	4	3	70%	+3.4	1	12.9	10.5	6	4.7	29	-0.1	4	6.3%	17	50	18	11.1%	22	53%	2%
2019	NYJ	1/0	18	2	1	7	0	0	50%	-0.4	0	7.0	6.0	--	5.0	--	-0.4	0	-57.8%	--	-6	--	6.4%	--	100%	0%
2020	NYJ			50	36	395	3		72%			11.0							8.7%							

Herndon erupted onto the scene as a rookie in 2018, becoming one of just 13 rookie tight ends since 2000 to clear the 500-yard mark. Granted, he only got over the hump by 2 yards, but he was still in rare company. Herndon almost split his work in half between the slot and as an in-line tight end—53% of his targets came from a slot alignment, with a solid 16.3% DVOA. Unfortunately, a hamstring injury ripped Herndon's second season away from him just one game in and we did not get to see him take the next step. If Herndon returns to good health and has developed at least a little bit, he could be a quick fix to the tight end woes that plagued the Jets in his absence last season.

Tyler Higbee

Height: 6-6   Weight: 257   College: Western Kentucky   Draft: 2016/4 (110)   Born: 1-Jan-1993   Age: 28   Risk: Green

Year	Tm	G/GS	Snaps	Pass	Rec	Yds	TD	EZ	C%	+/-	Drop	Yd/C	aDOT	Rk	YAC	Rk	YAC+	BTkl	DVOA	Rk	DYAR	Rk	Use	Rk	Slot	Wide
2017	LAR	16/16	733	45	25	295	1	1	56%	-2.6	2	11.8	10.8	6	3.4	42	-0.9	6	-10.4%	36	-9	36	8.7%	36	24%	7%
2018	LAR	16/16	788	34	24	292	2	3	71%	+1.3	1	12.2	7.0	28	5.7	16	+1.4	4	15.0%	8	54	16	6.2%	42	30%	6%
2019	LAR	15/15	710	89	69	734	3	8	78%	+7.0	2	10.6	6.7	29	5.6	12	+1.1	9	5.5%	17	79	11	15.4%	13	26%	4%
2020	LAR			96	64	697	4		67%			10.9							-0.7%							

Not once in his first 58 NFL games (49 of them starts) did Higbee gain more than 100 yards receiving. Then came last December, when Gerald Everett suffered a knee injury and Higbee transitioned from a blocking specialist and part-time player into a do-it-all threat who almost never left the field. Next thing you know, Higbee had rattled off four 100-yard games in a row, something no tight end had accomplished since Travis Kelce in 2016. Add his 84 yards against Arizona in Week 17 and Higbee finished with 522 yards in five December games. Only 14 other tight ends gained that many yards all season. Higbee was especially dangerous on play-action, averaging 13.9 yards on 30 such catches as opposed to 8.2 yards on 39 catches without a play-fake. Higbee is unlikely to repeat his December outburst, but he remains capable of exploiting defenses who have focused their attention on Robert Woods or Cooper Kupp.

Josh Hill

Height: 6-5   Weight: 250   College: Idaho State   Draft: 2013/FA   Born: 21-May-1990   Age: 30   Risk: Green

Year	Tm	G/GS	Snaps	Pass	Rec	Yds	TD	EZ	C%	+/-	Drop	Yd/C	aDOT	Rk	YAC	Rk	YAC+	BTkl	DVOA	Rk	DYAR	Rk	Use	Rk	Slot	Wide
2017	NO	16/11	588	23	16	125	1	2	74%	-0.5	0	7.8	3.8	--	5.2	--	-0.9	0	-45.1%	--	-56	--	4.3%	--	32%	14%
2018	NO	16/11	652	24	16	185	1	2	67%	-1.7	2	11.6	3.3	--	10.6	--	+3.9	6	0.1%	--	12	--	4.6%	--	29%	8%
2019	NO	16/11	657	35	25	226	3	3	71%	+1.1	1	9.0	5.0	46	6.4	7	+1.1	2	-9.8%	33	-6	33	6.2%	43	12%	9%
2020	NO			20	14	151	1		70%			10.8							4.2%							

Late in the third round of April's draft, the Saints picked Adam Trautman, a tight end out of Dayton. Trautman, a promising pass-catcher but inconsistent blocker, is more likely to replace Jared Cook after this season than Hill, who has been the team's primary blocking tight end since 2013. Though Hill has led New Orleans tight ends in snaps in each of the past three seasons, he hadn't averaged more than two targets per game until last season.

T.J. Hockenson

Height: 6-5   Weight: 248   College: Iowa   Draft: 2019/1 (8)   Born: 3-Jul-1997   Age: 23   Risk: Green

Year	Tm	G/GS	Snaps	Pass	Rec	Yds	TD	EZ	C%	+/-	Drop	Yd/C	aDOT	Rk	YAC	Rk	YAC+	BTkl	DVOA	Rk	DYAR	Rk	Use	Rk	Slot	Wide
2019	DET	12/7	539	59	32	367	2	5	54%	-8.7	2	11.5	7.7	20	6.3	8	+1.8	6	-18.1%	40	-41	44	14.2%	19	62%	5%
2020	DET			64	42	456	3		66%			10.9							-6.5%							

Hockenson with Matthew Stafford: 9 DYAR, -3.9% DVOA. Hockenson without Stafford: -50 DYAR, -48.4% DVOA. While full-season Hockenson was one of the least valuable tight ends in football, his first-half numbers are far more palatable and give reason for hope. Hockenson was inconsistent week-to-week no matter who was under center—his season started with an 131-yard explosion, and ended with the second-worst DYAR total for a tight end in 2019 when he caught six passes on 11 targets for just 18 yards in Week 13—but there were enough flashes to think that he could take a step forward in Year 2. Unfortunately, the ankle injury that prematurely ended his rookie season still isn't 100%, so he may start the year on PUP.

Jacob Hollister | Height: 6-4 | Weight: 245 | College: Wyoming | Draft: 2017/FA | Born: 18-Nov-1993 | Age: 27 | Risk: Green

Year	Tm	G/GS	Snaps	Pass	Rec	Yds	TD	EZ	C%	+/-	Drop	Yd/C	aDOT	Rk	YAC	Rk	YAC+	BTkl	DVOA	Rk	DYAR	Rk	Use	Rk	Slot	Wide
2017	NE	15/1	87	11	4	42	0	2	36%	-1.8	0	10.5	10.1	--	1.3	--	-3.3	0	-58.0%	--	-40	--	2.0%	--	36%	9%
2018	NE	8/1	59	5	4	52	0	0	80%	+0.5	0	13.0	8.2	--	4.0	--	+0.4	0	21.2%	--	10	--	1.8%	--	40%	20%
2019	SEA	11/3	521	59	41	349	3	6	69%	-0.1	1	8.5	6.6	31	4.1	35	-0.5	2	-0.8%	22	25	23	17.5%	9	47%	3%
2020	SEA			3	2	18	0		67%			9.0							-1.1%							

Hollister is best known for the last catch of the 2019 regular season, when he was tackled on fourth down a few inches short of a touchdown that would have given the Seahawks a division title. As it turns out, Hollister specialized in coming up just short of the line to gain—he had eight catches in the regular season and three more in the playoffs that were stopped 1 yard short of a first down. That total of 11 was tied for most in the league with Chicago's Allen Robinson, who caught more than twice as many passes as Hollister did. With free-agent signing Greg Olsen joining a healthy Will Dissly on Seattle's tight end depth chart, there doesn't seem to be much opportunity left for Hollister to almost get where he's going in 2020, but that didn't stop the Seahawks from re-signing him to a one-year, $3.3-million deal in April.

Austin Hooper | Height: 6-4 | Weight: 254 | College: Stanford | Draft: 2016/3 (81) | Born: 29-Oct-1994 | Age: 26 | Risk: Green

Year	Tm	G/GS	Snaps	Pass	Rec	Yds	TD	EZ	C%	+/-	Drop	Yd/C	aDOT	Rk	YAC	Rk	YAC+	BTkl	DVOA	Rk	DYAR	Rk	Use	Rk	Slot	Wide
2017	ATL	16/8	787	65	49	526	3	4	75%	+5.8	4	10.7	6.8	40	5.3	17	+0.4	10	9.4%	14	71	13	12.4%	21	43%	0%
2018	ATL	16/7	809	88	71	660	4	6	81%	+8.1	1	9.3	6.8	32	3.3	44	-1.3	9	2.2%	21	56	15	14.5%	12	47%	7%
2019	ATL	13/10	743	97	75	787	6	8	77%	+8.9	3	10.5	6.6	30	4.4	33	-0.4	13	12.5%	13	130	6	18.2%	7	47%	1%
2020	CLE			72	50	538	5		69%			10.8							7.6%							

After four very solid seasons in Atlanta, where he seemed to become a bigger part of the offense each year, Hooper hit free agency and was a surprisingly popular guy there. The four-year, $42-million deal he pulled from the Browns gives him the highest guaranteed figure of any tight end other than T.J. Hockenson. He has even delivered on things that observers thought he struggled with at Stanford. He caught five seam routes on seven targets for two touchdowns and 104 yards, and his tackle-breaking in the open field has been better than advertised. Hooper gives you just about anything you'd ask for from a tight end. He can block a little, he's got great hands, and he is effective against man coverage and diagnosing holes in zones. He figures to be in line for a good amount of work in a Browns offense that should center around two-tight end sets this year.

O.J. Howard | Height: 6-6 | Weight: 250 | College: Alabama | Draft: 2017/1 (19) | Born: 18-Nov-1994 | Age: 26 | Risk: Yellow

Year	Tm	G/GS	Snaps	Pass	Rec	Yds	TD	EZ	C%	+/-	Drop	Yd/C	aDOT	Rk	YAC	Rk	YAC+	BTkl	DVOA	Rk	DYAR	Rk	Use	Rk	Slot	Wide
2017	TB	14/14	608	39	26	432	6	5	67%	+4.0	1	16.6	11.9	2	5.8	12	+1.5	1	32.2%	5	101	7	7.4%	39	21%	3%
2018	TB	10/8	436	48	34	565	5	2	71%	+3.3	2	16.6	11.7	3	6.1	12	+1.8	4	44.0%	1	169	3	12.2%	17	57%	6%
2019	TB	14/14	793	53	34	459	1	4	64%	+0.1	4	13.5	10.9	1	4.4	32	-0.7	3	3.2%	18	37	19	10.0%	34	26%	2%
2020	TB			43	29	373	2		67%			12.9							8.6%							

After leading all tight ends in receiving DVOA in 2018, Howard looked like a rising star, the next Rob Gronkowski. He fell out of favor quickly during Bruce Arians' first season in Tampa Bay and ended up on the offseason trading block. In February, the Buccaneers discussed sending him to Washington in exchange for offensive tackle Trent Williams.

Though Howard caught as many passes in 2019 as he did in 2018, his efficiency plummeted. His lone touchdown came in Week 10 against the Cardinals, the league's worst defense against tight ends (28.2% DVOA). What happened? Part of the answer is regression. Over his first two seasons, he averaged an unsustainable 16.6 yards per catch, and nearly 20% of his catches resulted in a touchdown. Also, his role changed. Howard lined up in a traditional alignment more often last season, limiting his upside as a receiver.

Even though a healthy Gronkowski probably will eat into some of his targets, Howard's a good bounce-back candidate, especially if the Buccaneers decide to take advantage of his size and move him to the slot or out wide. He struggled last season, but he didn't get shorter.

Hayden Hurst

Height: 6-4		Weight: 245		College: South Carolina			Draft: 2018/1 (25)			Born: 24-Aug-1993			Age: 27			Risk: Green								

Year	Tm	G/GS	Snaps	Pass	Rec	Yds	TD	EZ	C%	+/-	Drop	Yd/C	aDOT	Rk	YAC	Rk	YAC+	BTkl	DVOA	Rk	DYAR	Rk	Use	Rk	Slot	Wide
2018	BAL	12/0	275	23	13	163	1	0	57%	-2.6	0	12.5	7.5	--	5.7	--	+1.0	2	-17.5%	--	-16	--	5.6%	--	30%	13%
2019	BAL	16/4	466	39	30	349	2	4	77%	+3.6	1	11.6	8.7	14	4.9	22	+1.0	3	28.1%	4	89	10	9.2%	36	46%	5%
2020	ATL			75	57	609	4		76%			10.7							12.3%							

Hurst's Jones facture in 2018 only cost him the first month of the regular season, but that was enough time for third-round fellow rookie Mark Andrews to assert himself as the Ravens' top receiving option at tight end. And now, two years after selecting him seven picks before taking star quarterback Lamar Jackson, the Ravens have traded Hurst to the Falcons. It is the trajectory one might expect from a draft bust, but Hurst doesn't look like one of those on the field. He trailed the more prolific Andrews in DYAR in 2019, but Hurst's 28.1% receiving DVOA was much better than Andrews' 12.1%. It was in fact the second-best rate among tight ends with 30 or more targets, trailing only the 37.7% rate of Jared Cook.

In Atlanta, Hurst will have to prove that he can maintain that level of receiving efficiency in an expanded role. The cash-strapped Falcons traded a second-round pick for him because they didn't have the cap space to retain Austin Hooper, whose 97 targets were sixth most among tight ends. Hurst's splits make that a good bet. Beyond his good in-line blocking, Hurst saw 46% of his targets come out of the slot—a nearly identical rate to Hooper (47%)—and finished fourth among positional qualifiers with 6.5 average yards after the catch on his slot receptions.

Blake Jarwin

Height: 6-5		Weight: 260		College: Oklahoma State			Draft: 2017/FA			Born: 16-Jul-1994			Age: 26			Risk: Green								

Year	Tm	G/GS	Snaps	Pass	Rec	Yds	TD	EZ	C%	+/-	Drop	Yd/C	aDOT	Rk	YAC	Rk	YAC+	BTkl	DVOA	Rk	DYAR	Rk	Use	Rk	Slot	Wide
2018	DAL	16/4	387	36	27	307	3	2	75%	+2.1	2	11.4	8.3	18	4.1	37	-0.6	5	24.0%	4	68	12	6.9%	38	58%	0%
2019	DAL	16/7	436	41	31	365	3	2	76%	+2.5	1	11.8	8.0	17	5.1	17	+1.0	3	12.1%	14	52	15	7.0%	40	51%	2%
2020	DAL			51	38	413	3		75%			10.9							10.4%							

Jarwin has flashed at times over the past two seasons, but was always the No. 2 tight end behind someone, which typically made him the fourth or fifth option for targets. Now with Jason Witten in Las Vegas, Jarwin will take over as the top tight end (though he still might be the fourth or fifth option on the field). Last year Jarwin didn't do many of the things a typical tight end does. He was buried in the red zone with just two targets on the season and he was a much better early-down receiver (2.0% DVOA on first down, 35.5% DVOA on second down) than he was a late-down safety net (-15.4% DVOA). With 166 potential targets freed up from the losses of Witten and Randall Cobb, there will be plenty of opportunities for Jarwin to have a bigger role in the passing game.

Travis Kelce

Height: 6-5		Weight: 260		College: Cincinnati			Draft: 2013/3 (63)			Born: 5-Oct-1989			Age: 31			Risk: Green								

Year	Tm	G/GS	Snaps	Pass	Rec	Yds	TD	EZ	C%	+/-	Drop	Yd/C	aDOT	Rk	YAC	Rk	YAC+	BTkl	DVOA	Rk	DYAR	Rk	Use	Rk	Slot	Wide
2017	KC	15/15	875	122	83	1038	8	9	68%	+7.4	7	12.5	9.6	11	4.9	24	+0.2	18	17.0%	12	197	2	24.4%	1	56%	16%
2018	KC	16/16	993	150	103	1336	10	14	69%	+5.0	6	13.0	9.0	11	5.5	18	+1.1	16	11.5%	14	196	2	26.6%	1	66%	8%
2019	KC	16/16	981	136	97	1229	5	10	71%	+11.5	6	12.7	9.3	10	4.2	34	-0.0	19	14.8%	11	203	3	24.3%	3	63%	10%
2020	KC			105	78	966	6		74%			12.4							25.1%							

Kelce caught exactly seven passes in seven games last year, 13 games (counting one playoff game) in the past two years, and 17 in the past three years. Kelce has caught at least five passes in 50 of his 70 regular and postseason games over the last four years. The consistency is remarkable, and there's no sign that Kelce is about to tail off now that he is on the wrong side of 30: he posted three-year highs in catch rate and yards per target last year, and his yards per reception have been about as consistent over the last four years as his catch totals. Tight ends of Kelce's caliber either hit a Gronk wall (and, apparently, bust through it after a year of recuperation in Gronk's case) or slide very slowly from their peaks (think Tony Gonzalez, Jason Witten, Antonio Gates). With no wall in sight, Kelce should be producing seven-catch, 70-something-yard stat lines for years to come.

George Kittle

Height: 6-4   Weight: 250   College: Iowa   Draft: 2017/5 (146)   Born: 9-Oct-1993   Age: 27   Risk: Green

Year	Tm	G/GS	Snaps	Pass	Rec	Yds	TD	EZ	C%	+/-	Drop	Yd/C	aDOT	Rk	YAC	Rk	YAC+	BTkl	DVOA	Rk	DYAR	Rk	Use	Rk	Slot	Wide
2017	SF	15/7	591	63	43	515	2	4	68%	-0.1	7	12.0	7.4	35	6.2	10	+1.6	6	5.6%	17	55	16	11.3%	25	44%	2%
2018	SF	16/16	928	136	88	1377	5	9	65%	-3.9	4	15.6	7.5	25	9.9	1	+4.7	19	15.1%	7	207	1	26.5%	2	40%	4%
2019	SF	14/14	815	107	85	1053	5	7	79%	+9.0	2	12.4	5.9	37	7.1	3	+1.6	27	18.9%	9	187	4	26.1%	1	40%	6%
2020	SF			79	59	735	6		75%			12.5							27.7%							

Kittle is the rare tight end in the modern NFL who is both a fierce run-blocker and an athletic mismatch as a receiver, and it should come as no surprise that he is looking for a market-setting second contract as a result. He did some of his best work in the passing game on first downs, averaging nearly 12.5 yards per target due in large part to a crazy YAC of 11.2 on those plays. While some of this can be attributed to play design, Kittle is also a major pain to bring down in the open field. Kittle and the 49ers were reportedly not particularly close on contract terms when the topic was initially broached in February, so the San Francisco braintrust will likely be stressing until they can find a deal that ultimately works for both parties. After falling to the fifth round in 2017, it makes sense that Kittle wants to blow the previous tight end salary record out of the water.

Cole Kmet

Height: 6-6   Weight: 262   College: Notre Dame   Draft: 2020/2 (43)   Born: 10-Mar-1999   Age: 21   Risk: Green

Year	Tm	G/GS	Snaps	Pass	Rec	Yds	TD	EZ	C%	+/-	Drop	Yd/C	aDOT	Rk	YAC	Rk	YAC+	BTkl	DVOA	Rk	DYAR	Rk	Use	Rk	Slot	Wide
2020	CHI			20	14	154	1		70%			11.0							-1.4%							

While it's easy—and fun, too!—to mock the Bears for their offseason desire to collect every tight end available, as if appealing to the spirit of Ditka would bring good times to the Windy City once again, it's more fair to realize that Kmet doesn't play the same position as free-agent acquisition Jimmy Graham, who has always been a slot receiver in tight end's clothing. Kmet bumps Adam Shaheen at in-line tight end, and ideally replaces Demetrius Harris as the 2020 starter sooner rather than later. At this point, Kmet is a better receiver than blocker; he could stand to bulk up and improve his technique to succeed at the next level. As a receiver, however, he's a solid threat if he can get a clean break off the line: a size mismatch with surprising amounts of speed.

Dawson Knox

Height: 6-4   Weight: 254   College: Mississippi   Draft: 2019/3 (96)   Born: 14-Nov-1996   Age: 24   Risk: Green

Year	Tm	G/GS	Snaps	Pass	Rec	Yds	TD	EZ	C%	+/-	Drop	Yd/C	aDOT	Rk	YAC	Rk	YAC+	BTkl	DVOA	Rk	DYAR	Rk	Use	Rk	Slot	Wide
2019	BUF	15/11	655	50	28	388	2	5	56%	-4.9	7	13.9	9.3	9	5.1	15	+0.3	6	-14.0%	35	-23	38	11.1%	26	22%	12%
2020	BUF			48	28	337	2		58%			12.0							-8.8%							

In two seasons as a steady contributor at Ole Miss, Knox did not score a single touchdown despite catching 39 passes. By Week 3 of 2019, Knox had already scored his first receiving touchdown, marking the beginning of what looks to be a rare but inspiring "better pro than college player" career. Knox fits the mold of an old school in-line tight end who works best when attached to the line of scrimmage. Only 33% of Knox's targets in 2019 came from wideout or slot positions, which was among the bottom third in usage rate at those alignments among tight ends. With the addition of a third top-tier wide receiver in Stefon Diggs this offseason, Knox's already low wide receiver usage may drop further. Knox also adds value in the run game, though. Even with the strains of playing in a run-heavy offense as a rookie, Know blew just three blocks in the run game all year. Do not sit on the edge of your seat waiting for Knox to bloom into an elite pass-catcher, but he has the baseline skills to be effective in both the run and pass game as an in-line player.

Vance McDonald

Height: 6-4   Weight: 267   College: Rice   Draft: 2013/2 (55)   Born: 13-Jun-1990   Age: 30   Risk: Green

Year	Tm	G/GS	Snaps	Pass	Rec	Yds	TD	EZ	C%	+/-	Drop	Yd/C	aDOT	Rk	YAC	Rk	YAC+	BTkl	DVOA	Rk	DYAR	Rk	Use	Rk	Slot	Wide
2017	PIT	10/7	270	24	14	188	1	3	58%	-1.4	3	13.4	8.7	--	6.3	--	+1.9	3	-2.4%	--	7	--	6.4%	--	21%	0%
2018	PIT	15/14	564	72	50	610	4	7	69%	-0.1	2	12.2	5.2	46	7.7	4	+2.3	16	3.6%	20	51	17	11.2%	21	28%	4%
2019	PIT	14/14	702	55	38	273	3	2	69%	-2.5	4	7.2	5.1	45	4.5	31	-0.8	7	-32.4%	47	-83	48	12.5%	23	16%	5%
2020	PIT			29	21	214	1		72%			10.2							1.4%							

Everyone suffered in the quarterback downgrade for Pittsburgh, but McDonald's numbers took a massive hit because of how close to the line of scrimmage his targets generally are. McDonald was a screens-and-curls receiver without a real counterpunch. After Ben Roethlisberger went down in Week 2, McDonald had just 197 yards in the next 14 games, to the point where a "good" boxscore would look something like three catches for 30 yards. All Pittsburgh receivers need a healthy Roethlisberger to raise tides, but there's nobody who needs the quick placement and pre-snap knowledge as badly as McDonald does.

Foster Moreau

Height: 6-4   Weight: 250   College: Louisiana State   Draft: 2019/4 (137)   Born: 6-May-1997   Age: 23   Risk: Green

Year	Tm	G/GS	Snaps	Pass	Rec	Yds	TD	EZ	C%	+/-	Drop	Yd/C	aDOT	Rk	YAC	Rk	YAC+	BTkl	DVOA	Rk	DYAR	Rk	Use	Rk	Slot	Wide
2019	OAK	13/7	378	25	21	174	5	4	84%	+3.7	0	8.3	4.6	47	4.6	27	+0.8	5	29.6%	3	72	14	6.2%	42	8%	4%
2020	LV			16	12	112	1		75%			9.3							-1.1%							

Moreau did everything a team could expect a rookie fourth-round tight end to do last year: he was sure-handed and useful as a receiver (he produced six first downs on seven third-down targets and four touchdowns on four targets inside the 10-yard line) and didn't get obliterated as a blocker. He looks like a serviceable, affordable second tight end with some upside. So of course the Raiders signed Jason Witten to be their second tight end behind Darren Waller. This is how a team which should be rebuilding needlessly clogs its salary-cap ledger and depth chart, folks.

David Njoku

Height: 6-4   Weight: 246   College: Miami   Draft: 2017/1 (29)   Born: 10-Jul-1996   Age: 24   Risk: Yellow

Year	Tm	G/GS	Snaps	Pass	Rec	Yds	TD	EZ	C%	+/-	Drop	Yd/C	aDOT	Rk	YAC	Rk	YAC+	BTkl	DVOA	Rk	DYAR	Rk	Use	Rk	Slot	Wide
2017	CLE	16/5	501	60	32	386	4	9	53%	-4.1	4	12.1	10.4	8	4.7	26	-0.3	3	-9.7%	34	-10	37	10.8%	27	23%	16%
2018	CLE	16/14	871	88	56	639	4	8	64%	-2.9	5	11.4	8.7	13	5.5	19	+0.3	9	-18.1%	41	-63	44	15.8%	9	25%	10%
2019	CLE	4/1	101	10	5	41	1	2	50%	-2.3	3	8.2	6.4	--	3.2	--	-0.7	1	-23.7%	--	-10	--	7.5%	--	40%	20%
2020	CLE			24	15	165	2		63%			11.0							-6.7%							

A wrist injury that sent him to IR and a knee injury that dinged him down the stretch contributed to make Njoku's breakout year one where he was only broken. Three seasons into the league, the Browns have a tight end that doesn't really contribute as a blocker despite his ideal size, hasn't delivered on the above-average talent he has as a receiver, and broke fewer tackles in 2018 than Vance McDonald. Still just 24, there's something to be made of this. The Browns picked up his fifth-year option and will try him in the Irv Smith role in Kevin Stefanski's offense this season. With Harrison Bryant on his heels, nothing after that is guaranteed.

Greg Olsen

Height: 6-5   Weight: 255   College: Miami   Draft: 2007/1 (31)   Born: 11-Mar-1985   Age: 35   Risk: Yellow

Year	Tm	G/GS	Snaps	Pass	Rec	Yds	TD	EZ	C%	+/-	Drop	Yd/C	aDOT	Rk	YAC	Rk	YAC+	BTkl	DVOA	Rk	DYAR	Rk	Use	Rk	Slot	Wide
2017	CAR	7/7	367	38	17	191	1	4	45%	-4.0	0	11.2	10.6	7	2.8	47	-1.0	0	-24.5%	49	-44	49	18.2%	9	63%	3%
2018	CAR	9/9	429	38	27	291	4	5	71%	+2.3	2	10.8	8.8	12	3.1	45	-1.0	0	14.6%	9	57	14	12.6%	16	54%	0%
2019	CAR	14/14	805	82	52	597	2	6	63%	-1.7	3	11.5	9.1	11	3.9	37	-0.4	2	-6.5%	29	4	29	15.5%	11	54%	1%
2020	SEA			49	34	381	3		69%			11.2							9.3%							

With Will Dissly constantly hurt, the Seahawks needed a more reliable option at tight end, so they signed … a 35-year-old who has missed 18 games due to foot and concussion issues over the past three seasons. Olsen's production last year was highly erratic; in four straight games, he had 110 yards against Tampa Bay and 75 yards against Arizona, then 5 yards against Houston and a goose egg against Jacksonville, despite playing more snaps in the latter two than the former. Olsen has been turning down TV contracts for years and appeared as an analyst for XFL games. He will likely spend 2020 teaming with Dissly in an offense built around two-tight end sets, then make his NFL TV debut in 2021.

Kyle Rudolph

Height: 6-6   Weight: 265   College: Notre Dame   Draft: 2011/2 (43)   Born: 9-Nov-1989   Age: 31   Risk: Green

Year	Tm	G/GS	Snaps	Pass	Rec	Yds	TD	EZ	C%	+/-	Drop	Yd/C	aDOT	Rk	YAC	Rk	YAC+	BTkl	DVOA	Rk	DYAR	Rk	Use	Rk	Slot	Wide
2017	MIN	16/16	924	81	57	532	8	8	70%	+5.3	2	9.3	7.6	33	4.0	36	-0.2	6	8.8%	15	88	9	15.1%	14	28%	3%
2018	MIN	16/16	925	82	64	634	4	10	78%	+6.7	1	9.9	6.5	35	3.9	39	-0.7	6	8.6%	15	91	9	13.9%	14	46%	7%
2019	MIN	16/16	807	48	39	367	6	8	81%	+7.3	0	9.4	7.3	24	4.9	23	+0.1	1	26.9%	5	118	8	11.1%	27	6%	0%
2020	MIN			48	37	353	4		77%			9.5							8.4%							

Rudolph was fourth among tight ends with 51 red zone DYAR; a return to form for him after a down year in that part of the field in 2018. He did have his streak of being the Vikings' best receiver on third and fourth downs snapped, but he's the *returning* champion with Stefon Diggs out of town. Rudolph again finished in the top five in receiving plus/minus, and he had zero drops on 50 targets. Rudolph may not produce highlight reel-quality plays on a regular basis, but there are few players in the NFL more consistent and reliable.

Irv Smith

Height: 6-2   Weight: 240   College: Alabama   Draft: 2019/2 (50)   Born: 9-Aug-1998   Age: 22   Risk: Green

Year	Tm	G/GS	Snaps	Pass	Rec	Yds	TD	EZ	C%	+/-	Drop	Yd/C	aDOT	Rk	YAC	Rk	YAC+	BTkl	DVOA	Rk	DYAR	Rk	Use	Rk	Slot	Wide
2019	MIN	16/7	620	47	36	311	2	4	77%	+3.5	2	8.6	5.9	38	3.8	38	-1.5	2	-18.5%	41	-39	42	10.6%	28	40%	4%
2020	MIN			55	41	394	4		75%			9.6							3.0%							

While his DVOA wasn't particularly high—tight ends generally struggle as rookies—Smith was at least sure-handed, with his 77% catch rate ranking eighth among tight ends. Part of that is due to the fact that Smith's average catch came just 4.9 yards down the field, but sure hands are sure hands. He's solid as a blocker, too, and the Vikings grew more and more comfortable with Smith as the year went on. He went from playing about half as many snaps as Kyle Rudolph in Week 1 to being on par or even ahead of him by the end of the year. Smith could be primed for a big sophomore jump.

Jonnu Smith

Height: 6-3   Weight: 248   College: Florida International   Draft: 2017/3 (100)   Born: 22-Aug-1995   Age: 25   Risk: Green

Year	Tm	G/GS	Snaps	Pass	Rec	Yds	TD	EZ	C%	+/-	Drop	Yd/C	aDOT	Rk	YAC	Rk	YAC+	BTkl	DVOA	Rk	DYAR	Rk	Use	Rk	Slot	Wide
2017	TEN	16/13	556	30	18	157	2	3	60%	-1.8	1	8.7	7.2	37	5.3	18	-0.1	4	-30.7%	51	-44	48	6.2%	46	10%	10%
2018	TEN	13/12	610	30	20	258	3	2	67%	-2.0	3	12.9	5.4	44	9.0	2	+3.7	4	-1.8%	26	11	27	8.5%	31	23%	13%
2019	TEN	16/14	718	44	35	439	3	2	80%	+2.7	1	12.5	5.7	40	7.8	2	+2.4	17	25.6%	6	91	9	10.4%	31	36%	7%
2020	TEN			54	39	467	4		72%			12.0							14.5%							

After two seasons of middling production in platoons, Smith exploded in 2020 as the main replacement for Delanie Walker. Smith showcased rare explosiveness for a tight end by creating a ton of big plays without being targeted downfield much. He showed enough that the Titans designed screens for him, and he also had some designed runs that he made a lot of hay with. Smith has become a popular fantasy football sleeper, and while it's probably asking a lot for him to make a huge leap in the receiving pecking order, it shouldn't be a surprise if the Titans decide he deserves more targets based on last year's results.

Kaden Smith

Height: 6-5   Weight: 252   College: Stanford   Draft: 2019/6 (176)   Born: 24-Apr-1997   Age: 23   Risk: Green

Year	Tm	G/GS	Snaps	Pass	Rec	Yds	TD	EZ	C%	+/-	Drop	Yd/C	aDOT	Rk	YAC	Rk	YAC+	BTkl	DVOA	Rk	DYAR	Rk	Use	Rk	Slot	Wide
2019	2TM	9/6	436	42	31	268	3	2	74%	+0.7	1	8.6	5.7	39	2.9	43	-1.9	1	-25.8%	45	-52	46	12.6%	22	20%	0%
2020	NYG			18	13	121	1		72%			9.3							-6.2%							

Smith was a great find for the Giants as a mid-September waiver claim from the 49ers, though he didn't play much until he was thrust into a heavy role in Week 10. From that point on, Smith was 10th among tight ends in targets, eighth in receptions, and 12th in yards. He was a good security blanket for the quarterbacks as his only down with positive DVOA came on third down. There is nothing flashy to Smith's game, but he could be a discount version of fellow Stanford tight end Austin Hooper by doing just enough well to be a plus on the field. More likely, he'll settle back into a second tight end role behind Evan Engram.

Jeremy Sprinkle

Height: 6-5 Weight: 255 College: Arkansas Draft: 2017/5 (154) Born: 10-Aug-1994 Age: 26 Risk: Green

Year	Tm	G/GS	Snaps	Pass	Rec	Yds	TD	EZ	C%	+/-	Drop	Yd/C	aDOT	Rk	YAC	Rk	YAC+	BTkl	DVOA	Rk	DYAR	Rk	Use	Rk	Slot	Wide
2017	WAS	11/5	126	3	2	13	1	1	67%	-0.0	0	6.5	6.7	--	1.5	--	-1.1	0	50.6%	--	11	--	0.8%	--	0%	33%
2018	WAS	16/9	363	9	5	41	1	2	56%	-0.6	0	8.2	6.4	--	4.2	--	+0.4	0	-13.6%	--	-4	--	1.8%	--	13%	0%
2019	WAS	16/13	614	40	26	241	1	2	65%	-3.0	5	9.3	6.5	32	3.5	39	-1.1	2	-15.7%	37	-21	36	8.5%	38	15%	0%
2020	WAS			26	17	180	2		65%			10.6							-6.8%							

For the first time in his three-year career, Sprinkle stepped into a starting role last season after Vernon Davis suffered a year-ending injury in Week 4. Sprinkle's entire NFL career has been spent in Jay Gruden's (and briefly Bill Callahan's in 2019) under-center offense. Being a traditional in-line tight end is all Sprinkle really knows. Of the 44 qualifying tight ends last season, Sprinkle's 15% target share from wide receiver positions was the fifth lowest in the league. Though Sprinkle is not the most dynamic receiver from in-line spots, he is a plenty competent blocker and did well to help facilitate Washington's run game; he only blew two blocks in the run game all year. Without any meaningful free agents or fresh top-100 picks in the mix this offseason, Sprinkle is assumed to be the starter for 2020.

Jace Sternberger

Height: 6-4 Weight: 250 College: Texas A&M Draft: 2019/3 (75) Born: 26-Jun-1996 Age: 24 Risk: Blue

Year	Tm	G/GS	Snaps	Pass	Rec	Yds	TD	EZ	C%	+/-	Drop	Yd/C	aDOT	Rk	YAC	Rk	YAC+	BTkl	DVOA	Rk	DYAR	Rk	Use	Rk	Slot	Wide
2019	GB	6	60	1	0	0	0	1	0%	-0.7	1	--	13.0	--	--	--	--	0	-110.1%	--	-8	--	0.5%	--	0%	0%
2020	GB			44	29	295	2		66%			10.2							-10.0%							

Sternberger is in line to replace Jimmy Graham as the Packers' primary receiving tight end, a big jump for a player with 60 career snaps. Sternberger is a more well-rounded player than Graham was, which means that the Packers can actually count on him to block, but he's likely to be less of a threat in the slot than even the diminished, Green Bay version of Graham. Sternberger's value will come from versatility; he can line up anywhere in the formation and produce, which gives Matt LaFleur and company maximum options.

Ian Thomas

Height: 6-3 Weight: 260 College: Indiana Draft: 2018/4 (101) Born: 6-Jun-1996 Age: 24 Risk: Green

Year	Tm	G/GS	Snaps	Pass	Rec	Yds	TD	EZ	C%	+/-	Drop	Yd/C	aDOT	Rk	YAC	Rk	YAC+	BTkl	DVOA	Rk	DYAR	Rk	Use	Rk	Slot	Wide
2018	CAR	16/6	525	49	36	333	2	3	73%	+1.5	4	9.3	6.3	38	4.4	32	-0.4	1	0.9%	24	27	23	8.9%	29	49%	0%
2019	CAR	16/3	305	30	16	136	1	0	53%	-4.6	3	8.5	7.0	27	4.8	25	+0.8	2	-27.1%	46	-41	43	5.0%	47	50%	3%
2020	CAR			60	42	431	4		70%			10.3							2.0%							

Thomas offered a preview of his potential production for the Panthers in the Decembers of 2018 and 2019 when he averaged 4.0 catches and 38 yards per game as the temporary starter for an injured Greg Olsen. Now Olsen is in Seattle and Thomas has a chance to become a permanent fixture for Matt Rhule's new offense. One could be more optimistic if Thomas hadn't taken a step back from a surprisingly efficient rookie year with underwhelming 53% catch rate and -27.1% DVOA rates in his sophomore season. But Thomas should see more accurate short passes from new quarterback Teddy Bridgewater in 2020, and he has the size and athleticism to stick as a starter.

C.J. Uzomah

Height: 6-6 Weight: 260 College: Auburn Draft: 2015/5 (157) Born: 14-Jan-1993 Age: 27 Risk: Green

Year	Tm	G/GS	Snaps	Pass	Rec	Yds	TD	EZ	C%	+/-	Drop	Yd/C	aDOT	Rk	YAC	Rk	YAC+	BTkl	DVOA	Rk	DYAR	Rk	Use	Rk	Slot	Wide
2017	CIN	14/4	213	15	10	92	1	1	67%	+0.8	1	9.2	5.2	--	5.0	--	+0.7	1	-1.1%	--	7	--	3.4%	--	20%	0%
2018	CIN	16/15	840	65	43	439	3	5	66%	-2.4	4	10.2	7.5	26	4.5	30	+0.0	4	-11.3%	36	-18	39	12.2%	18	47%	2%
2019	CIN	16/16	654	40	27	242	2	3	68%	-1.0	3	9.0	4.3	48	5.0	20	+0.0	2	-19.6%	43	-34	40	6.6%	41	10%	5%
2020	CIN			32	22	219	2		69%			10.0							-4.7%							

Tyler Eifert played all 16 games (for once) in 2019 and was far more effective than Uzomah, but as an indication of how brittle and unreliable Eifert has been, the Bengals re-signed Uzomah and let Eifert walk. Given his lack of use at Auburn, Uzomah's development into a half-decent pro is laudable, but when your top tight end is 40th in DYAR, it figures to be an issue. On the other hand, CJU is generally considered one of the funniest guys ever to grace the Cincy locker room, so worst-case scenario, he should have plenty of material.

Delanie Walker									Height: 6-2		Weight: 248		College: Central Missouri			Draft: 2006/6 (175)		Born: 12-Aug-1984		Age: 36		Risk: N/A	
Year	Tm	G/GS	Snaps	Pass	Rec	Yds	TD	EZ	C%	+/-	Drop	Yd/C	aDOT	Rk	YAC	Rk	YAC+	BTkl	DVOA	Rk	DYAR	Rk	Use	Rk	Slot	Wide
2017	TEN	16/11	744	111	74	807	3	12	67%	+6.7	2	10.9	9.3	17	3.3	44	-1.4	5	-7.6%	32	-3	32	22.8%	3	51%	3%
2018	TEN	1/1	39	7	4	52	0	0	57%	-0.3	0	13.0	6.6	--	5.0	--	+0.7	2	-25.9%	--	-9	--	25.9%	--	57%	14%
2019	TEN	7/4	201	31	21	215	2	2	68%	+0.1	1	10.2	7.9	18	3.1	41	-1.4	1	-7.1%	31	0	31	16.9%	10	72%	3%

It's hard to say this is "it" for any tight end, because as long as their bodies hold together, athletic tight ends can play a long time. Walker's teammate with the 49ers in their glory years, Vernon Davis, is a testament to this. But a Walker ankle injury put him on IR for the second straight season and the Titans released him. Walker had a nice little run from 2013 to 2017 with the Titans, clearing 1,000 yards in his breakout 2015 season. DVOA and DYAR do not historically look back on Walker's Titans career well (276 DYAR in 2015 and 2016, 38 DYAR in the other years combined), but Walker was also stuck on offenses that had Zach Mettenberger and Jake Locker as starters, so that's not a big surprise. Not bad for a four-year, $17.1-million stab in the dark on a tight end who had mostly been a blocker for the Harbaugh 49ers.

Darren Waller									Height: 6-6		Weight: 255		College: Georgia Tech			Draft: 2015/6 (204)		Born: 13-Sep-1992		Age: 28		Risk: Green	
Year	Tm	G/GS	Snaps	Pass	Rec	Yds	TD	EZ	C%	+/-	Drop	Yd/C	aDOT	Rk	YAC	Rk	YAC+	BTkl	DVOA	Rk	DYAR	Rk	Use	Rk	Slot	Wide
2018	OAK	4/0	42	6	6	75	0	0	100%	+1.5	0	12.5	3.2	--	9.3	--	+4.8	1	26.7%	--	15	--	4.5%	--	0%	33%
2019	OAK	16/16	940	117	90	1145	3	7	77%	+9.5	5	12.7	7.6	21	6.4	6	+1.5	15	22.0%	7	234	1	23.9%	4	53%	13%
2020	LV			82	58	680	4		71%				11.7						12.8%							

Waller wasn't used all that often in high-leverage situations. He was targeted 26 times on third and fourth downs and just 11 times (eight receptions, four first downs) on third down with more than 6 yards to go. He was targeted 11 times in the red zone and just four times inside the 10-yard line (with three red zone touchdowns). Hunter Renfrow was targeted more often than Waller on third downs and third-and-long and nearly as often (10 targets) in the red zone, which is significant because Waller was the Raiders' leading receiver and Renfrow looks like an intern who just won a talk-radio "Join the Raiders for a Day" sweepstakes.

As his league-leading (for tight ends) DYAR indicates, Waller wasn't just feasting on short passes in meaningless situations by any means. He just did the vast majority of his damage on first and second downs, usually on the Raiders' side of the 50-yard line (54 of his catches came between the Raiders' 21-yard line and midfield) and early in the game (50-716-1 yards in first halves, 40-429-2 in second halves). But when trying to determine whether a player who came from nowhere at age 27 will continue to perform at a Pro Bowl level or fall back significantly toward the pack, it's worth noting how much of his production came in situations where targets and touches could easily be parsed out to other players.

Jason Witten									Height: 6-6		Weight: 265		College: Tennessee			Draft: 2003/3 (69)		Born: 6-May-1982		Age: 38		Risk: Yellow	
Year	Tm	G/GS	Snaps	Pass	Rec	Yds	TD	EZ	C%	+/-	Drop	Yd/C	aDOT	Rk	YAC	Rk	YAC+	BTkl	DVOA	Rk	DYAR	Rk	Use	Rk	Slot	Wide
2017	DAL	16/16	1050	87	63	560	5	5	72%	+6.5	1	8.9	7.4	36	1.7	50	-2.1	1	-0.4%	24	40	20	17.8%	11	65%	1%
2019	DAL	16/16	851	83	63	529	4	5	76%	+3.7	6	8.4	6.7	28	2.6	47	-1.5	0	-0.5%	20	38	17	14.4%	17	61%	4%
2020	LV			27	18	177	1		67%				9.8						0.4%							

Witten has been inching towards replacement level since 2015, with his targets, receiving yards, and yards per catch decreasing each year, not counting the season he spent punishing our eardrums as a broadcaster. Witten was once a great run blocker but is now no better than the typical second tight end. (He ranked third in the NFL with 13 blown blocks a year ago.) Only the Cowboys' need to give him the living legend treatment, at the expense of developing a replacement—or giving more opportunities to Blake Jarwin, the replacement they finally found—has kept Witten from having the 20-catch, two-touchdown season players of his current caliber typically have, then hanging up the cleats and waiting for Canton to call. That 20-catch season may finally be coming in Las Vegas, where Darren Waller is coming off a 90-catch season and Jon Gruden has no special loyalty to Witten. Then again, Witten could just go 58-995-2 or something, then stick around for another half a decade.

Going Deep

Mo Alie-Cox, IND: This basketball conversion project from Virginia Commonwealth has developed into a pretty good blocker. He catches a few passes every year but clearly comes in third behind Jack Doyle and Trey Burton. (11-93-0, 13.6% DVOA in 2019.)

Dan Arnold, ARI: Arnold is a developmental prospect that the Saints eventually gave up on developing. He was a wide receiver in college at Division III Wisconsin-Platteville so he's not much of a blocker. Arizona picked him up off waivers and started him in Week 17. For the season he caught 8-of-14 passes for 127 yards, 2 touchdowns, and 16.6% DVOA. He won't start over Maxx Williams but may end up leading Arizona tight ends in receiving yardage. It won't be a high number considering how much more 10 personnel the Cardinals use compared to everyone else.

Harrison Bryant, CLE: While Bryant didn't wow anybody at the combine, it's still a bit of a shock that a player who has a chance to be as good of a tight end as he does fell all the way into the fourth round. Bryant offers reasonable blocking, a number of moves to get off coverage, good hands, a history of production (1,004 yards last year, 2,137 for his career), and good size. He won the John Mackey Award as the nation's top tight end in his senior year at Florida Atlantic. His 4.73s 40-yard dash is plenty good for a tight end, but his 30 5/8-inch arms are in the first percentile of all tight ends at the combine since 2000. In Cleveland he'll have what amounts to a redshirt year behind David Njoku and Austin Hooper; Njoku's long-term future in Cleveland is uncertain and Bryant gives the Browns an obvious direction if he develops as expected.

Hunter Bryant, DET: Bryant is a divisive prospect. Some called him the best tight end available in the draft—a big slot receiver type, with strong hands and a whopping 16.4 yards per catch at Washington. Others point to his lack of size and a ton of easy schemed receptions in open space and say he was overrated. In the end, two things led to him going undrafted: a terrible combine (with a 4.74s 40 highlighting some terrible athletic numbers) and a history of knee injuries that limited him to nine games as a freshman and five as a sophomore.

Derek Carrier, LV: Carrier is a veteran special teams ace who gained 27 yards on a nifty fake-punt end around last year and has handled the No. 3 blocking tight end chores adequately at various stops. The Raiders signed Jason Witten to play a similar role this season, only for more money and without the special teams usefulness. Go figure.

Charles Clay, FA: After nine years in the league, Clay is at press time still hoping to catch on with a team for the upcoming season. Clay split reps with Maxx Williams in 2019, and Arizona elected to go with the younger Williams as their lead tight end for 2020. While Clay was slightly more productive and efficient in his limited 2019 opportunities (18-237-1, 45.3% DVOA), neither tight end was much of a focal point in Kliff Kingsbury's passing game. Even if this is the end of the road for the 31-year-old Clay, he's had a much more productive career than the average sixth-round pick.

Tyler Davis, JAX: A developmental tight end who played most of his college ball in Cincinnati but spent his final season at Georgia Tech as a graduate transfer, Davis has the right mix of size and speed for the position and a reputation for the sort of work ethic and tape grinding that throws coaches head over heels in love. He'll have to make his way on special teams at first, but even on a crowded depth chart his intangibles suggest he has as good a chance as any sixth-round pick of making the roster.

Josiah Deguara, GB: If you're looking for an H-back, Deguara was your man in the 2020 draft. At Cincinnati, Deguara was a gritty run-blocker with solid hands and enough athleticism to make some plays in the receiving game leaking out of the backfield; he had over 500 yards last season. He's not a real playmaker, per se, but has a ceiling as the in-line blocking compliment to Jace Sternberger in two-tight end sets once Marcedes Lewis eventually retires.

Ross Dwelley, SF: Dwelley played a major role on special teams early in the year but saw his offensive snaps increase with injuries to fullback Kyle Juszczyk and tight end George Kittle over the course of the year. He caught 15-of-22 passes for 91 yards, 2 touchdowns, and -21.1% DVOA. Entering his third season, the former undrafted free agent from the University of San Diego should have the first crack at the No. 2 tight end role, but rookie Charlie Woerner may be able to compete for snaps there due to his blocking ability.

Anthony Firkser, TEN: Firkser's most memorable play of 2019 is probably the ball Justin Reid knocked out of his hands on the goal line that got returned 90 yards by Whitney Mercilus to set up the Titans losing the AFC South in Week 15. 2018's 95% catch rate proved unsustainable for Firkser, but he has become a reliable outlet receiver for the Titans (14-204-1, 13.0% DVOA in 2019). Firkser became the first Harvard graduate to catch a touchdown in the playoffs and got re-signed to a one-year deal as a fixture in Tennessee's heavier sets. Not bad for someone who barely played until Delanie Walker was lost for the year in Week 6.

Demetrius Harris, CHI: Harris should start the season as Chicago's primary in-line tight end until Cole Kmet is ready to take over the position (the Bears have enough tight ends that you have to get hyper-specific about these sorts of things). Harris has yet to put up a positive DVOA in six professional seasons, but at least he knows the system, having worked with Matt Nagy for four years with the Chiefs. Harris is at least an adequate pass-protector, but the sooner Kmet is ready the better for Chicago.

Jeff Heuerman, DEN: Your classic tough-guy No. 2 or No. 3 tight end. Noah Fant's emergence ensures that Heuerman will remain a depth piece, not the starter as the Broncos asked him to be during their talent drought. (14-114-1, -9.7% DVOA in 2019.)

Brycen Hopkins, LAR: A first-team all-Big Ten selection in his senior season at Purdue, Hopkins joins the Rams as a fourth-round draft pick. He's got speed; his 4.66s 40 was tied for second among tight ends at this year's combine. And he has been productive; his seven touchdown catches in 2019 were tied for most on the Boilermakers and he was second with 61 catches for 830 yards, averaging an impressive 13.6 yards per reception. This fall, however, he looks like strictly a depth player behind Tyler Higbee and Gerald Everett.

Jesse James, DET: James (16-142-0) would not have qualified for our tight end leaderboards if T.J. Hockenson had not gone down with an ankle injury. As it was, James ranked 44th out of 48 tight ends in DVOA at -23.9%. James' magical 2018, when he caught 77% of his passes and ended up third in DVOA and eighth in DYAR among tight ends, is a massive career outlier for a player with limited pass-catching abilities.

Dalton Keene, NE: Third-round pick Dalton Keene is the perfect candidate to surprise as Bill Belichick and Josh McDaniels' do-it-all piece. At Virginia Tech, Keene played all over the formation, including fullback, H-back, in-line tight end, and "jumbo" slot. The positionless pass-catcher also crushed the NFL combine at 6-foot-3 and 254 pounds, running a 4.71s 40-yard dash and a 7.07s three-cone drill. Quarterback woes during Keene's two years as a starter at Virginia Tech limited how well he was able to produce, but it would not be outside the realm of possibility for the Patriots to find a niche role for him right away.

Matt LaCosse, NE: Not that any of New England's tight ends were phenomenal pass-catchers last season, but LaCosse is particularly lacking in that area. LaCosse is neither an especially capable athlete nor someone with great mitts, which leaves him with no real calling card as a receiver. However, he is a skilled blocker, particularly in the run game. The influx of talent New England took in at tight end this offseason likely eats away at LaCosse's playing time, but he should still have a role as a blocker and short-yardage player.

Marcedes Lewis, GB: Lewis hasn't qualified for the tight end leaderboards since coming to Green Bay two years ago, but that's no longer what he's there to do. Lewis is a very solid run-blocking tight end, though he did end up with six blown blocks recorded a year ago. Don't expect him to benefit much from Jimmy Graham's departure; Jace Sternberger will be the one inheriting those pass-catching opportunities. Lewis will keep plugging away in the trenches, as his transition to near-full-time blocker has probably extended his career by years.

Thaddeus Moss, WAS: Moss had an abbreviated college career and NFL audition because of a transfer from North Carolina State to LSU, a medical redshirt, and a fractured foot that prevented his combine participation. Still, it's difficult to believe that the son of NFL Hall of Famer Randy Moss didn't merit a draft pick. The undrafted free agent could be a steal for the Redskins, who lack a play-making tight end after Jordan Reed became a free agent. Moss was an efficient if underutilized receiving option for the national champions with 12.1 yards per catch and a 62% receiving success rate.

Albert Okwuegbunam, DEN: Fourth-round pick Okwuegbunam was a big winner at the combine, where he ran a stunning 4.49s 40 at 258 pounds. However, he didn't look nearly that fast on his tape at Mizzou. A lack of lateral quickness, both off the line and when changing direction, negates Okwuegbunam's straight-line speed. While he's as good of a blocker as your typical college tight end nowadays, typical college tight ends are not very good blockers. Okwuegbenum may be a better track and weight-room athlete than a football player. But if he pans out, opponents are going to have their hands full when he and Noah Fant run vertical routes from two-tight end sets.

Josh Oliver, JAX: Injuries robbed 2019 third-round pick Josh Oliver of the chance to make a meaningful impact during his rookie season: he missed the first six games with hamstring problems, then injured his back in Week 11 and missed the rest of the year. A converted receiver who can run a wide array of routes, Oliver has the potential to be a matchup player and red-zone contributor, but he lacks the blocking skills to be a traditional starting tight end. Though he is currently behind Tyler Eifert on the depth chart, the Jaguars staff is excited about Oliver as a pass target. He will probably give way to others on rushing downs.

James O'Shaughnessy, JAX: After four years as mainly a backup in Kansas City and Jacksonville, O'Shaughnessy finally looked to have made the Jaguars' starting tight end spot his own last year before a torn ACL ended his season in Week 5. He expects to be ready for opening day 2020, but the team has since added Tyler Eifert in free agency to take over that starting role. O'Shaughnessy should be a part of the team's plans, but Eifert and 2019 third-rounder Josh Oliver will probably keep him out of the starting lineup at least for the opening few games.

Donald Parham, LAC: Parham left Stetson University as their all-time leader in every receiving category that really matters, had training camp cups of coffee with Washington and Detroit, spent a few weeks on Washington's practice squad, then ended up with the Dallas Renegades of the XFL, where he was playing well before the world stopped spinning. He was your basic FCS tight end prospect leaving college: bigger and faster than anyone else on the field, but raw as a fresh-caught trout. He's slated to be the primary backup to oft-injured Hunter Henry for the Chargers.

Colby Parkinson, SEA: Despite his towering size (6-foot-7, 255 pounds), Parkinson is more of a slot receiver than a tight end. He scored 11 touchdowns on only 39 catches as a freshman and sophomore at Stanford while averaging nearly 15 yards per catch, but quarterback injuries limited him to one score and a 12.3-yard average as a junior last year. He skipped his senior season and the Seahawks drafted him in the fourth round. He couldn't ask for a better pro passer than Russell Wilson, who loves to toss jump balls to big receivers in one-on-one matchups.

Jared Pinkney, ATL: Pinkney likely would have pulled a Day 2 draft selection if he had left Vanderbilt after his 774-yard junior season. But after productive quarterback Kyle Shurmur graduated, Pinkney reverted to his sub-300-yard standard from his freshman and sophomore seasons and ended up undrafted. Still, the script could flip for Pinkney thanks to a landing spot on the salary cap-strapped Falcons, who could not afford to retain free agent Austin Hooper and have little tight end depth behind their efficient but unproven new starter Hayden Hurst.

Drew Sample, CIN: Sample was a surprising second-round choice in the 2019 draft and did little to justify Cincinnati's faith in him, catching a mere five passes and getting overrun at times as a blocker, which was supposed to be his dominant trait. He did show signs of stronger play right before he injured his ankle in Week 10 and was lost for the remainder of the year. Every writer and coach around the team has indicated Sample's usage and performance is expected to jump in his second season, but Sample has zero history of reliable pass-catching going back to his college days, when he caught just 46 balls in his four years at Washington. Amazingly, that is 17 more than the other Bengals tight end, C.J. Uzomah, caught in his collegiate career.

Dalton Schultz, DAL: This 2018 fourth-round pick out of Stanford is essentially just a sixth blocker at 6-foot-5, 244 pounds. Schultz got offensive snaps in all 16 games last year but still caught just one pass all season. It's hard to see him fitting into Blake Jarwin's role if Jarwin gets injured.

Ricky Seals-Jones, KC: Seals-Jones was one of the worst regulars on one of the league's worst offenses for the Cardinals in 2018. He got a measure of revenge against his old team last year, catching two touchdown passes for the Browns in their 38-24 loss to the Cardinals. (We said it was a "measure" of revenge, not a lot of revenge.) He finished catching 14-of-22 passes for 229 yards, 4 touchdowns, and 10.2% DVOA, although one 59-yard catch against the Ravens skews Seals-Jones' 2019 stats a bit. He's a looks-the-part type of mismatch tight end whose upside is weak tea Eric Ebron. Now in Kansas City, Seals-Jones could well catch 10 passes all season when the defense is napping or otherwise occupied, each one going for 59 yards.

Stephen Sullivan, SEA: Seattle head coach Pete Carroll made it clear that Sullivan, who played both wide receiver and tight end at LSU, would be lining up in the latter slot for the Seahawks, who traded a 2021 sixth-round pick so they could select Sullivan in this year's seventh round. Sullivan has speed (a 4.66s 40 at the combine, tied for second among tight ends) and the Reed Richards-long arms that Carroll craves, but he's very raw—after catching 23 passes as a junior, he only caught a dozen as a senior, and that was with Joe Burrow at quarterback.

Jordan Thomas, HOU: Injured while trying to get recovery reps from a previous injury in the final week of the preseason, Thomas tumbled from presumptive top tight end on the Houston depth chart to a distant third-stringer behind Darren Fells and Jordan Akins. Houston's tight end roster is pretty deep, so even though Thomas has shown something, he might be an end-of-roster cut or trade if Kahale Warring is dealing aces whenever the actual offseason happens. Thomas has good hands, good size, and solid speed for a tight end. He could surprise in a bigger role.

Logan Thomas, WAS: Thomas has never had less competition on his tight end depth chart than he should have on the 2020 Redskins, who let Jordan Reed leave in free agency after multiple concussions derailed his once-promising career and didn't draft a replacement. But if Thomas were going to emerge as an impact receiver, he likely would have done so already in his six-year career. That may not be entirely fair to the one-time quarterback prospect, but his -43.5% and -18.9% receiving DVOA rates in 2018 and 2019—albeit on limited targets—do not inspire confidence.

Robert Tonyan, GB: Tonyan may end up being the odd man out of the Packers' tight end room, though Green Bay liked him enough to bring him back as an exclusive rights free agent. Tonyan's best argument for a roster spot is that both Marcedes Lewis and Josiah Deguara are primarily blockers; Tonyan has 14 receptions over the last two seasons for 177 yards and a positive DVOA in very limited work. The ex-Indiana State receiver might be the Packers' best option as a receiving tight end should something happen to Jace Sternberger.

Adam Trautman, NO: Trautman arrived at Dayton, a non-scholarship FCS school, as a quarterback in 2015. After redshirting as a true freshman, he pitched an idea to his coaches: a move to tight end. That September, he recorded the first reception of his life. He went on to catch another 177 passes, as well as the attention of the Saints, who traded up to draft him during the third round in April. He has plus size, agility (6.78s 3-cone time at the combine, third-fastest among tight ends), and hands (70 catches in 2019), but he's facing a daunting leap in competition, making his trajectory difficult to predict. If he develops into a competent blocker, he has a clear path to significant playing time in 2021. Jared Cook's contract expires after this season.

Nick Vannett, DEN: Vannett was one of the interchangeable tight ends who played major roles in the Seahawks offense during the recent "let's make Russell Wilson boring" era. The Steelers traded for him last year when they were pretending that everything would be just fine after Ben Roethlisberger's injury, and he caught 13 passes as the team burned resources in an almost-successful bid for a wild-card berth. (Final season stats: 17-166-0, 0.9% DVOA.) Vannett could replace Jeff Heuerman as the blocking tight end for the Broncos. Thanks to Denver's revamped offense, that no longer equates to a starting job and featured role.

Kahale Warring, HOU: Houston's third-rounder from the 2019 class, Warring missed the entire season with a concussion and hamstring IR designation. Asked about him in one of his rare media availabilities this offseason, Bill O'Brien noted that it was "[not] ideal for him to not play football last year." Warring has a body to dream on at 6-foot-5, 252 pounds, and he's essentially a true wild card for this team. The San Diego State alum could still blossom into a No. 1 tight end that can block and stretch the seam. He could also be out of the league next year.

Maxx Williams, ARI: Williams may have started 10 games for the Cardinals in 2019, but the tight end was not much of a factor as a receiving threat in Kliff Kingsbury's offense (15-202-1, 30.0% DVOA). With Charles Clay now a free agent, Williams does not have much competition for the starting role, and he may finally be able to deliver on the potential that made him a second-round pick for Baltimore all the way back in 2015. While 2020 will be Williams' sixth year in the NFL, he only just turned 26, so he may still have some room to grow as a player.

Charlie Woerner, SF: A sixth-round pick from Georgia, Woerner will have an opportunity to earn playing time as a blocking tight end for the 49ers in multiple-tight end sets. The run-heavy Bulldogs rarely targeted Woerner in the passing game, leaving him to do a lot of the dirty work as a run-blocker. Woerner's profile is different enough from incumbent backup Ross Dwelley that he may be able to carve out a role as a rookie, but that role would likely not involve the ball coming his way all that often.

2020 Kicker Projections

Listed below are the 2020 KUBIAK projections for kickers. Kicker effectiveness is inconsistent from one year to the next, so the major differentiator between kickers in our fantasy projections is their projected field goal and extra point opportunities that vary based on their offenses, schedules, and other contextual factors. That said, the projections do aim to estimate kicker ranges, which in turn influence the volume of their projected deep field goal attempts.

Kickers are listed with their total fantasy points based on two different scoring systems. For **Pts1**, all field goals are worth three points. For **Pts2**, all field goals up to 39 yards are worth three points, field goals of 40 to 49 yards are worth four points, and field goals over 50 yards are worth five points. Kickers are also listed with a Risk of Green, Yellow, or Red, as explained in the introduction to the section on quarterbacks.

Note that field goal totals below are rounded, but "fantasy points" are based on the actual projections, so the total may not exactly equal (FG * 3 + XP).

Fantasy Kicker Projections, 2020

Kicker	Team	FG	Pct	XP	Pts1	Pts2	Risk
Justin Tucker	BAL	26-30	87.6%	44	124	137	Green
Harrison Butker	KC	26-30	86.2%	43	122	135	Green
Wil Lutz	NO	27-32	84.0%	41	121	135	Green
Younghoe Koo	ATL	27-32	82.4%	40	119	133	Yellow
Matt Prater	DET	26-32	82.7%	40	118	133	Green
Robbie Gould	SF	27-32	82.2%	38	118	130	Green
Greg Zuerlein	DAL	26-33	79.4%	39	117	130	Green
Josh Lambo	JAX	28-32	87.9%	33	116	130	Green
Dan Bailey	MIN	26-31	83.9%	39	116	129	Yellow
Joey Slye	CAR	25-31	82.4%	39	114	128	Red
Ka'imi Fairbairn	HOU	25-30	81.5%	39	114	126	Green
Zane Gonzalez	ARI	26-31	82.9%	35	112	124	Green
Chase McLaughlin	IND	25-31	81.4%	37	112	125	Red
Jason Myers	SEA	24-30	82.1%	38	111	123	Green
Mason Crosby	GB	25-30	83.2%	37	111	123	Green
Randy Bullock	CIN	26-31	83.2%	34	111	123	Green
Chris Boswell	PIT	25-30	83.0%	36	110	122	Green
Matt Gay	TB	25-31	79.8%	36	110	123	Yellow
Michael Badgley	LAC	25-31	81.2%	35	110	122	Green
Brandon McManus	DEN	26-31	83.5%	33	109	122	Green
Austin Seibert	CLE	25-30	82.5%	35	109	121	Yellow

Kicker	Team	FG	Pct	XP	Pts1	Pts2	Risk
Jake Elliott	PHI	25-30	82.2%	35	109	120	Green
Stephen Hauschka	BUF	25-30	81.1%	34	108	120	Yellow
Sam Sloman	LAR	24-32	77.0%	33	107	119	Yellow
Jason Sanders	MIA	24-30	79.1%	34	106	118	Yellow
Eddy Pineiro	CHI	24-31	79.1%	34	106	118	Yellow
Greg Joseph	TEN	22-28	80.7%	38	105	117	Yellow
Dustin Hopkins	WAS	26-31	83.2%	27	105	119	Green
Justin Rohrwasser	NE	24-31	77.2%	33	103	115	Yellow
Daniel Carlson	LV	23-30	76.2%	34	103	114	Yellow
Sam Ficken	NYJ	24-31	77.6%	31	103	116	Yellow
Aldrick Rosas	NYG	23-29	78.4%	33	101	111	Red

Other kickers who may win jobs:

Kicker	Team	FG	Pct	XP	Pts1	Pts2	Risk
Kai Forbath	DAL	27-32	84.7%	38	120	135	Yellow
Elliott Fry	TB	24-31	77.4%	36	107	119	Red
Rodrigo Blankenship	IND	24-31	77.2%	36	107	119	Red
Austin MacGinnis	LAR	24-32	77.0%	33	107	119	Red
Tyler Bass	BUF	23-30	76.3%	33	102	114	Red
Brett Maher	NYJ	23-31	73.8%	33	102	113	Red
Tucker McCann	TEN	21-28	76.8%	37	101	112	Red

2020 Fantasy Defense Projections

Listed below are the 2020 KUBIAK projections for fantasy team defense. The main elements of team defense projections are:

- Schedule strength is very important for projecting fantasy defense.
- Categories used for scoring in fantasy defense have no consistency from year-to-year whatsoever, with the exception of sacks and interceptions.

Fumble recoveries and defensive touchdowns are forecast based on league averages, rather than the team's totals in these categories from a year ago. This is why the 2020 projections may look very different from the fantasy defense values from the 2019 season. Safeties and shutouts are not common enough to have a significant effect on the projections. Team defenses are also projected with a Risk factor of Green, Yellow, Red or Blue.

In addition to projection of separate categories, we also give an overall total based on our generic fantasy scoring formula: one point for a sack, two points for a fumble recovery or interception, and six points for a touchdown. Remember that certain teams (for example, Denver) will score better if your league also gives points for limiting opponents' scoring or yardage. Special teams touchdowns are listed separately and are not included in the fantasy scoring total listed.

Fantasy Team Defense Projections, 2020

Team	Fant Pts	Sack	Int	FR	Def TD	Risk	ST TD	Team	Fant Pts	Sack	Int	FR	Def TD	Risk	ST TD
PIT	107	43.4	14.7	10.9	2.0	Green	0.5	NO	85	40.2	9.9	8.1	1.5	Green	0.7
NE	98	37.3	15.1	9.4	2.0	Red	0.4	CIN	85	34.1	12.1	8.3	1.7	Green	0.6
SF	97	42.0	12.0	10.4	1.8	Green	0.4	TB	84	35.8	10.5	8.7	1.6	Blue	0.4
WAS	92	39.4	12.1	9.1	1.7	Yellow	0.6	DAL	84	36.9	10.4	8.5	1.5	Green	0.4
CLE	92	37.7	12.9	8.9	1.8	Yellow	0.5	IND	84	36.2	11.0	8.1	1.6	Green	0.8
JAX	91	40.5	11.6	8.8	1.7	Yellow	0.7	DEN	82	37.1	11.1	7.0	1.5	Green	0.6
GB	90	39.5	12.3	7.8	1.7	Green	0.4	NYJ	81	30.8	11.9	8.4	1.7	Green	0.6
BUF	89	38.0	12.5	7.9	1.7	Green	0.5	CHI	81	35.1	10.5	8.0	1.5	Blue	0.9
BAL	88	35.6	13.3	7.7	1.8	Green	0.4	LAC	81	33.3	10.6	8.5	1.5	Green	0.6
KC	88	38.6	11.9	7.8	1.6	Green	0.6	ARI	80	33.7	9.8	8.8	1.5	Green	0.5
CAR	88	41.9	11.0	7.3	1.5	Red	0.5	MIA	79	27.0	11.9	8.9	1.7	Green	0.4
LAR	87	40.6	11.1	7.5	1.6	Green	0.5	NYG	78	30.8	11.2	7.8	1.6	Green	0.5
TEN	87	36.8	11.7	8.4	1.7	Green	0.5	LV	78	32.3	10.5	7.7	1.5	Green	0.3
SEA	87	32.1	13.0	9.0	1.8	Green	0.5	HOU	77	30.8	10.4	8.2	1.5	Green	0.4
MIN	87	40.9	10.5	7.9	1.5	Green	0.6	DET	76	32.0	8.9	9.1	1.4	Green	0.6
PHI	87	34.3	12.0	9.1	1.7	Green	0.4	ATL	76	30.7	9.3	8.9	1.4	Green	0.4

Projected Defensive Leaders, 2020

Solo Tackles			Total Tackles			Sacks			Interceptions		
Player	Team	Tkl	Player	Team	Tkl	Player	Team	Sacks	Player	Team	Int
B.Martinez	NYG	148	B.Martinez	NYG	93	A.Donald	LAR	13.4	J.Johnson	LAR	3.6
B.Wagner	SEA	141	D.Leonard	IND	91	C.Jones	ARI	12.9	J.Simmons	DEN	3.6
D.Leonard	IND	140	R.Smith	CHI	90	M.Garrett	CLE	12.6	M.Humphrey	BAL	3.4
R.Smith	CHI	131	B.Baker	ARI	90	D.Hunter	MIN	12.6	M.Peters	BAL	3.2
B.Baker	ARI	127	Z.Cunningham	HOU	87	C.Jordan	NO	12.5	Q.Diggs	SEA	3.1
D.White	TB	126	F.Warner	SF	85	J.Watt	HOU	12.3	M.Williams	NO	3.0
D.Jones	ATL	126	B.Wagner	SEA	85	T.Watt	PIT	12.2	K.Byard	TEN	3.0
Z.Cunningham	HOU	126	D.White	TB	85	V.Miller	DEN	12.0	T.White	BUF	2.9
D.Bush	PIT	123	D.Jones	ATL	84	K.Mack	CHI	11.9	T.Mathieu	KC	2.9
J.Smith	DAL	122	C.Littleton	LV	82	J.Allen	JAX	11.6	J.Bates	CIN	2.9
C.Littleton	LV	121	J.Smith	DAL	82	J.Bosa	LAC	11.5	A.Harris	MIN	2.9
L.Vander Esch	DAL	120	E.Kendricks	MIN	81	S.Barrett	TB	11.5	J.Thornhill	KC	2.8

College Football Introduction and Statistical Toolbox

In the year 2020, making a prediction of any kind with any degree of confidence is more than a bit audacious. As the college football regular season tenuously approaches, the only thing that seems certain is how irregular this season will be. The global coronavirus pandemic interrupted and suspended the sports world back in March, just as most college football programs were initiating their spring practice regimens. Extraordinary new procedures and protocols have been developed to safely bring athletes back to their respective playing fields and courts, and sports leagues have had to modify almost every element of their operations to ensure a restart will not result in another shutdown soon thereafter.

The challenges facing college football's return to competition are especially daunting. Unlike the NFL and other professional sports leagues, there is no central commissioner's office providing leadership and making policy decisions to govern the process. College football conferences, power and non-power alike, have many common interests, but each ultimately organizes its membership under its own set of rules and priorities. Many scheduling arrangements (and if necessary, rescheduling arrangements) are made by the schools themselves. And of course, it's the college part of college football that may be the most complicating factor. Creating a bubble around 18- to 22-year-old student athletes on campus in order to mitigate the risks of the virus and its impact on the season feels at times like an exercise in futility.

Against this backdrop we present our *Football Outsiders Almanac 2020* college football projections. There are no reasonable metrics to employ here that adjust for coronavirus uncertainty. Our team forecasts assume the season will start and conclude on schedule and will be played in full. If our numbers are accurate about anything this year, let's hope first and foremost it's that the sport we love returns as planned.

As uncertain as the particulars of this season may be, the certainty around which teams and programs are best positioned to contend for the College Football Playoff (CFP) remains as strong as ever. LSU exceeded all preseason expectations in their undefeated championship run last fall, but they were by no means a Cinderella story. The Tigers ranked sixth nationally in our preseason forecast in last year's Almanac, based on an excellent recent program performance history, elite recruiting prowess, and strong returning production. Joe Burrow's record-setting quarterback play in a newly dynamic offense was the surprise ingredient that turned a merely strong season into a dream season for LSU, of course. But the key team factors driving our projection model were critical to making that recipe for success possible in the first place.

The consolidation of power at the top of the college football universe wasn't toppled when LSU defeated Alabama and kept the Crimson Tide out of the playoff mix for the first time in CFP history. Alabama ranks No. 1 once again in our preseason projections, boasting a stronger profile for conference and national championship contention this year than last. Ohio State ranks No. 2 and Clemson ranks No. 3. Those three programs along with No. 8 Oklahoma each project to have a better than 25% chance to reach the playoff; no other program has better than an 18% chance of making the 2020 playoff field. There are no surprises here. Over the course of the six-year history of the CFP, those four programs have combined to claim 17 of the 24 total playoff berths and five of the six championships won.

Outside of that group, we'll be keeping a close eye on Georgia especially. The Bulldogs will be carried by the nation's best defense and they have had the recent recruiting prowess and program power to make an LSU-like championship leap forward if the offense steps up. Oregon and Washington should be the best out west, but we're not ruling out USC elevating itself back up into Pac-12 title contention on the strength of its returning production, best among the top 50 teams we've profiled. And though we don't project any of them making a serious surge into the playoff picture, teams such as Texas, Texas A&M, North Carolina, and Nebraska have solid projection factors indicating a positive trajectory forecast for each in 2020.

Though the bones of our projection model have remained in place for several years, we did some work this offseason to revise the calculation and format of our F/+ ratings. The results improved F/+ preseason projection accuracy overall, especially in relationship to the first few weeks of the season. We strive to improve our numbers individually and collectively every year to maximize projection accuracy, but college football is often most fun when it is exceptionally unpredictable. For everyone's sake, let's hope unpredictability this year manifests itself with a slew of wild upsets and fourth-quarter comebacks and not something more serious like an aggravated health crisis. However (and whenever) the season plays out, enjoy *Football Outsiders Almanac* and join us at FootballOutsiders.com for insight and analysis throughout the year.

College Statistics Toolbox

Regular readers of FootballOutsiders.com may be familiar with our college football stats published throughout the year. Others may be learning about our advanced approach to college football stats analysis for the first time by reading this book. In either case, this College Statistics Toolbox section is highly recommended reading before getting into the conference chapters. The stats that form the building blocks for F/+, FEI, and SP+ are constantly being updated and refined.

Each team profile begins with a statistical snapshot, highlighting each team's Mean Wins projection along with projected likelihoods of reaching key performance benchmarks—the chance to claim a division or conference championship, appear in the College Football Playoff, and to meet or exceed total win thresholds. Game-by-game win likelihoods and key projection factors are also provided in the snapshot. These and other stats referenced in our team capsules are explained below.

1. Alabama Crimson Tide (10.2 mean wins)

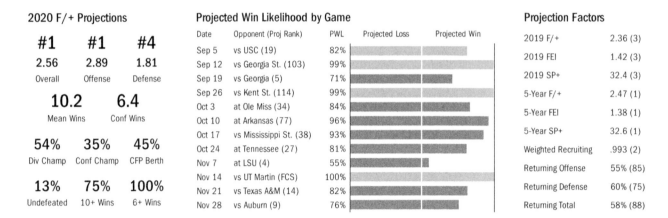

2020 F/+ Projections		
#1	**#1**	**#4**
2.56	2.89	1.81
Overall	Offense	Defense
10.2	**6.4**	
Mean Wins	Conf Wins	
54%	**35%**	**45%**
Div Champ	Conf Champ	CFP Berth
13%	**75%**	**100%**
Undefeated	10+ Wins	6+ Wins

Projected Win Likelihood by Game

Date	Opponent (Proj Rank)	PWL
Sep 5	vs USC (19)	82%
Sep 12	vs Georgia St. (103)	99%
Sep 19	vs Georgia (5)	71%
Sep 26	vs Kent St. (114)	99%
Oct 3	at Ole Miss (34)	84%
Oct 10	at Arkansas (77)	96%
Oct 17	vs Mississippi St. (38)	93%
Oct 24	at Tennessee (27)	81%
Nov 7	at LSU (4)	55%
Nov 14	vs UT Martin (FCS)	100%
Nov 21	vs Texas A&M (14)	82%
Nov 28	vs Auburn (9)	76%

Projection Factors	
2019 F/+	2.36 (3)
2019 FEI	1.42 (3)
2019 SP+	32.4 (3)
5-Year F/+	2.47 (1)
5-Year FEI	1.38 (1)
5-Year SP+	32.6 (1)
Weighted Recruiting	.993 (2)
Returning Offense	55% (85)
Returning Defense	60% (75)
Returning Total	58% (88)

Drive-by-Drive Data

Fremeau Efficiency Index (FEI)

Approximately 20,000 possessions are contested annually in FBS vs. FBS games, an average of 26.6 total game possessions per game. First-half clock-kills and end-of-game garbage drives are filtered out, and the resulting possessions (23.8 per game) are evaluated to determine the success rates of each team's offensive, defensive, and special teams units. Raw possession efficiency rates are adjusted for opponent team unit strength. FEI ratings represent the opponent-adjusted per-possession scoring advantage a team would be expected to have on a neutral field against an average opponent.

Offensive and Defensive FEI

Maximizing success on offensive possessions and minimizing success on opponent possessions begins with an understanding of the value of field position. An average offense facing an average defense may expect to score 2.1 points on average at the conclusion of each drive. If a given drive begins at the offense's own 15-yard line, the average scoring value is only 1.5 points. If it begins at the opponent's 15-yard line, the average scoring value is 4.9 points. Offensive and defensive efficiency is in part a function of the intrinsic value of starting field position.

Drive-ending field position is an important component as well. Touchdowns represent the ultimate goal of an offensive possession, but drives that fall short of the end zone can also add scoring value attributed to the offense. National field goal success rates correlate strongly with proximity of the attempt to the end zone, and an offense that drives deep into opponent territory to set up a chip shot field goal generates more scoring value than one that ends a drive at the edge of or outside field goal range.

The value generated by an offense on a given possession is the difference between the drive-ending value and the value of field position at the start of the drive. Offensive efficiency is the average per-possession value generated or lost by the offense. Defensive efficiency is the average per-possession value generated or lost by the defense. Offensive FEI and Defensive FEI are the opponent-adjusted per-possession values generated or lost by these units, adjusted according to the strength of the opponent defense and offenses faced.

Play-by-Play Data

Success Rates

More than one million plays over the last ten years in college football have been collected and evaluated to determine baselines for success for every situational down in a game. Similar to the success rates that form the basis for DVOA, basic success rates are determined by national standards. The distinction for college football is in defining the standards of success. We use the following determination of a "successful" play:

- First-down success = 50% of necessary yardage
- Second-down success = 70% of necessary yardage
- Third-/Fourth-down success = 100% of necessary yardage

On a per-play basis, these form the standards of efficiency for every offense in college football. Defensive success rates are based on preventing the same standards of achievement.

Equivalent Points and Isolated Points per Play (IsoPPP)

All yards are not created equal. A 10-yard gain from a

team's own 15-yard line does not have the same value as a 10-yard gain that goes from the opponent's 10-yard line into the end zone. Based on expected scoring rates by field position, we calculate a point value for each play in a drive. Equivalent Points (EqPts) are calculated by subtracting the value of the resulting yard line from the initial yard line of a given play. This assigns credit to the yards that are most associated with scoring points, the end goal in any possession.

With EqPts, the game can be broken down and built back up again in a number of ways. Average EqPts per play (PPP) measures consistency and IsoPPP measures EqPts per play on successful plays only as a way to isolate of explosiveness. For the SP+ formula, IsoPPP is used, which allows us to ask two specific questions:

1. How frequently successful are you (consistency)?
2. When you're successful, how successful are you (magnitude)?

The best offenses in the country can maximize both efficiency and explosiveness on a down-by-down basis. Reciprocally, the best defenses can limit both.

SP+

Along with applying extra weight for plays inside the opponent's 40, plus a selection of other field position and turnover factors, success rate and IsoPPP make up the meat of the SP+ formula.

As with the FEI stats discussed above, context matters in college football. Adjustments are made to the unadjusted data with a formula that takes into account a team's production, the quality of the opponent, and the quality of the opponent's opponent. To eliminate the noise of less-informative blowout stats, we filtered the play-by-play data to include only those that took place when the game was "close." This excludes plays where the score margin is larger than 28 points in the first quarter, 24 points in the second quarter, 21 points in the third quarter, or 16 points in the fourth quarter.

The combination of the play-by-play and drive data gives us SP+, a comprehensive measure that represents a team's efficiency and explosiveness as compared to all other teams in college football. SP+ values are calibrated around adjusted scoring averages. Taking a team's percentile ratings and applying it to a normal distribution of points scored in a given season, can give us an interesting, descriptive look at a team's performance in a given season.

Expected Points Added (EPA)

Expected points added (EPA) is a measure of success and explosion on any given play. EPA considers the context of down, distance, yards to the end zone, and game situation to translate the result of every play into a point value. EPA, a descriptive statistic, is the change in point value between the beginning and the end of the play, which allows more granular and precise comparison of team performance across situations; it answers the question in college football, "Given the context, how well did this team perform compared to expectations?" in a single play or even across drives, games, and seasons. Like SP+, EPA accounts for context, weighting the calculations of expected points to emphasize large differences and extreme outliers less than traditional stats, which provides a clearer picture of true team quality. EPA figures for college football are calculated by Meyappan Subbaiah of Zelus Analytics (@msubbaiah1), Saiem Gilani of Tomahawk Nation (@saiemgilani), and Parker Fleming (@statsowar). The figures are available in the cfbscrapR package for the statistical software R; you can find the data, technical documentation, and more information at: https://saiemgilani.github.io/cfbscrapR/.

Combination Data

F/+

Introduced in *Football Outsiders Almanac 2009*, the F/+ rating combines FEI and SP+. There is a clear distinction between the two individual approaches, and merging the two diminishes certain outliers caused by the quirks of each method. The resulting metric is both powerfully predictive and sensibly evaluative.

Projected F/+

Relative to the pros, college football teams are much more consistent in year-to-year performance. Breakout seasons and catastrophic collapses certainly occur, but generally speaking, teams can be expected to play within a reasonable range of their baseline program expectations. For each team statistical profile, we provide thier five-year ratings profile and other projection factors that are included in the formula for the projected FEI and SP+ data that is used to produce the Projected F/+ ratings.

Weighted recruiting ratings are based on a blend of Rivals.com and 247Sports.com recruiting ratings. The weighted percentile rating for each team's last four recruiting classes reflects the potential impact for both recent star-studded classes and the depth of talent for each team. Our returning production data represents the percentage of production that returns to the roster this fall rather than a simple count of players labeled as starters.

Strength of Schedule

Unlike other rating systems, our Strength of Schedule (SOS) calculation is not a simple average of the Projected F/+ data of each team's opponents. Instead, it represents the likelihood that an elite team (typical top-five team) would win every game on the given schedule. The distinction is valid. For any elite team, playing No. 1 Alabama and No. 130 Massachusetts in a two-game stretch is certainly more difficult than playing No. 65 San Diego State and No. 66 Illinois. An average rating might judge these schedules to be equal.

The likelihood of an undefeated season is calculated as the product of individual game projected win likelihoods. Generally speaking, an elite team may have a 75% chance of defeating a team ranked No. 10, an 85% chance of defeating a team ranked No. 20, and a 95% chance of defeating a team ranked No. 40. Combined, the elite team has a 61% likelihood of defeating all three ($0.75 \times 0.85 \times 0.95 = 0.606$).

A lower SOS rating represents a lower likelihood of an elite team running the table, and thus a stronger schedule. For our calculations of FBS versus FCS games, with all due apologies to North Dakota State, et al., the likelihood of victory is 100% in the formula.

Mean Wins and Win Probabilities

To project records for each team, we use Projected F/+ and win likelihood formulas to estimate the likelihood of victory for a given team in its individual games. The probabilities for winning each game are added together to represent the average number of wins the team is expected to tally over the course of its scheduled games. Potential conference championship games and bowl games are not included.

Mean Wins are not intended to represent projected outcomes of specific matchups; rather they are our most accurate forecast for the team's season as a whole. The correlation of mean projected wins to actual wins is 0.69 for all games, 0.61 for conference games.

Win likelihoods are also used to produce the likelihood of each team winning a division or championship. Our College Football Playoff appearance likelihoods are a function of each team's likelihood to go undefeated or finish the season with one loss as well as the strength of the team's conference and overall schedule, factors that the CFP selection committee considers in their process.

The Win Probability tables that appear in each conference chapter are also based on the game-by-game win likelihood data for each team. The likelihood for each record is rounded to the nearest whole percent.

Brian Fremeau and Bill Connelly

NCAA Top 50

1. Alabama Crimson Tide (10.2 mean wins)

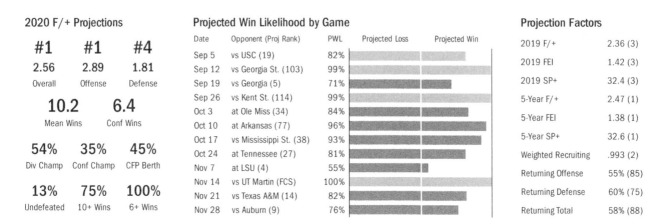

2020 F/+ Projections

#1	#1	#4
2.56	2.89	1.81
Overall	Offense	Defense

10.2	6.4
Mean Wins	Conf Wins

54%	35%	45%
Div Champ	Conf Champ	CFP Berth

13%	75%	100%
Undefeated	10+ Wins	6+ Wins

Projected Win Likelihood by Game

Date	Opponent (Proj Rank)	PWL	Projected Loss	Projected Win
Sep 5	vs USC (19)	82%		
Sep 12	vs Georgia St. (103)	99%		
Sep 19	vs Georgia (5)	71%		
Sep 26	vs Kent St. (114)	99%		
Oct 3	at Ole Miss (34)	84%		
Oct 10	at Arkansas (77)	96%		
Oct 17	vs Mississippi St. (38)	93%		
Oct 24	at Tennessee (27)	81%		
Nov 7	at LSU (4)	55%		
Nov 14	vs UT Martin (FCS)	100%		
Nov 21	vs Texas A&M (14)	82%		
Nov 28	vs Auburn (9)	76%		

Projection Factors

2019 F/+	2.36 (3)
2019 FEI	1.42 (3)
2019 SP+	32.4 (3)
5-Year F/+	2.47 (1)
5-Year FEI	1.38 (1)
5-Year SP+	32.6 (1)
Weighted Recruiting	.993 (2)
Returning Offense	55% (85)
Returning Defense	60% (75)
Returning Total	58% (88)

The 2019 season was a great, lost "what if?" year for the Alabama football program amidst a historically dominant run under head coach Nick Saban. While the team finished 10-2 and whipped Michigan in their bowl game, it seemed that so much more would be achieved. The 2020 NFL draft removed offensive tackle Jedrick Willis, wide receivers Jerry Jeudy and Henry Ruggs, and quarterback Tua Tagovailoa from the Alabama football roster before the first round had even concluded. Alabama's athleticism and talent in the passing game was nearly unheard of, but between a catastrophic hip injury to Tagovailoa and the sudden arrival of an even more potent passing attack in Baton Rouge, they weren't able to make the most of it. Instead the Tide were relegated to SEC West runner-ups and missed both the SEC title game and the playoffs.

Had Tagovailoa not dislocated his hip against Mississippi State, it's likely that the Tide would have defeated Auburn in the Iron Bowl. Even though they had already been beaten convincingly at home by LSU, an Iron Bowl win would have given 'Bama a shot at being selected over Oklahoma as the fourth team in the playoffs. The Tide, even with Tua's injury, finished the season as the nation's second-most efficient offense (.410 EPA/play, +47.5 SP+). In the face of last year's disappointment and the exodus of a substantial amount of NFL talent, the Tide have again reloaded.

Alabama's 2020 class was ranked No. 2 in the nation by 247 Sports and joins a roster built from No. 1 classes in the years 2016, 2017, and 2019. The team also has a fair amount of firepower remaining on offense despite the loss of Tagovailoa and his teammates. In 2020 the Alabama offensive line will boast former 5-star recruits at both tackle positions and four returning starters with a total of 67 starts in Alabama uniforms. They'll pave the way for returning starter and former 5-star recruit Najee Harris at running back (1,224 rushing yards, 13 touchdowns in 2019).

The Tide offense these days heavily involves spread formations that put speed on the perimeter so the quarterback can punish the defense for loading the box with RPOs and play-action. Despite losing Ruggs and Jeudy, the Tide still have Devonta Smith (1,256 receiving yards, 14 touchdowns in 2019) and Jaylen Waddle (560 receiving yards, six touchdowns in 2019) returning on the perimeter along with the two-deep at tight end lead by redshirt senior Miller Forristall.

Given the beef and experience up front combined with the limitations of the COVID-shortened offseason, what might have been an interesting battle at quarterback may end up simpler. Redshirt junior Mac Jones filled in for Tagovailoa in 2019 and threw for 1,503 yards at 10.7 yards per attempt with 14 touchdowns and three interceptions. He has experience in this offensive system and some skins on the wall with wins over Arkansas and Missouri, perhaps slightly offset by his loss against Auburn. Jones has to be the favorite, but the Tide also have 5-star freshman Bryce Young who enrolled in the spring. Whereas Jones is similar to previous Alabama quarterbacks like Jake Coker or AJ McCarron, Young is a 5-foot-11, 185-pound dual threat who offers more explosiveness and possibilities for the offense. If Jones falters, Young's dynamic talent may force its way onto the field.

The Alabama defense is a lesser part of the formula now than in previous years but they're in stronger shape than in 2019 when they had to start true freshmen inside at both linebacker positions and at nose tackle. Throughout their title run, the nose tackle and inside linebacker positions have typically been where Alabama sets themselves apart from other programs, but in 2019 they were young and inexperienced. Saban will get junior linebacker Dylan Moses back from injury to help those rising sophomores and Alabama's trademark dominant box defense will be in better shape.

In the secondary, where the Tide have struggled in the last several years against pro-spread passing attacks (Deshaun Watson's Clemson, Trevor Lawrence's Clemson, Joe Burrow's LSU), they're sending off four starters to the NFL and reloading again. Junior Patrick Surtain figures to slide inside to nickelback to help anchor a unit that replaces starters at nickelback, free safety, and strong safety.

The talent is all there for a typical Alabama season, but there are a number of question marks for Saban's program in Year 14 under his tenure. Can Alabama's still run-centric attack keep up against the nation's top offenses? Will the retooled Alabama secondary be able to check the increasing number of high-level, spread-passing opponents such as LSU, Clemson, Ohio State, and USC? How well can Nick Saban's detailed, complicated schemes on defense take hold in a shortened off-season? Underneath it all is the question of whether the rest of college football has caught up to Alabama's winning formula by matching their recruiting and deploying talent in pro-style passing systems rather than the Tide's spread run game.

2. Ohio State Buckeyes (10.5 mean wins)

2020 F/+ Projections

#2	**#3**	**#3**
2.50	2.54	1.88
Overall	Offense	Defense

10.5	**7.8**
Mean Wins	Conf Wins

68%	**46%**	**55%**
Div Champ	Conf Champ	CFP Berth

17%	**83%**	**100%**
Undefeated	10+ Wins	6+ Wins

Projected Win Likelihood by Game

Date	Opponent (Proj Rank)	PWL	Projected Loss	Projected Win
Sep 5	vs Bowling Green (126)	99%		
Sep 12	at Oregon (13)	70%		
Sep 19	vs Buffalo (82)	99%		
Sep 26	vs Rutgers (113)	99%		
Oct 10	vs Iowa (18)	85%		
Oct 17	at Michigan St. (41)	85%		
Oct 24	at Penn St. (7)	62%		
Oct 31	vs Nebraska (36)	92%		
Nov 7	vs Indiana (37)	92%		
Nov 14	at Maryland (78)	96%		
Nov 21	at Illinois (66)	93%		
Nov 28	vs Michigan (12)	79%		

Projection Factors

2019 F/+	2.66 (1)
2019 FEI	1.66 (1)
2019 SP+	35.4 (1)
5-Year F/+	2.08 (2)
5-Year FEI	1.13 (3)
5-Year SP+	28.5 (2)
Weighted Recruiting	.986 (3)
Returning Offense	65% (66)
Returning Defense	47% (114)
Returning Total	56% (93)

The 2019 Buckeyes were a nice example of the challenges of winning at the highest level with the sort of "spread run game plus elite defense" formula that Alabama has relied on. After using Dwayne Haskins to throw 533 passes for 4,831 yards in 2018, the Buckeyes had to retool in 2019 and pivoted toward emphasizing a powerful offensive line and running back J.K. Dobbins (2,003 rushing yards, 21 touchdowns). That approach paid off, as the Buckeyes led the Big Ten in rushing efficiency (0.214 EPA/rush) and ranked fifth nationally in success rate (50.6%).

With that offense paired with an elite defense lead by first-round NFL talents Chase Young (defensive end) and Jeff Okudah (cornerback), the Buckeyes dominated the Big Ten and headed into the playoffs 13-0. They were lauded by many as being potentially one of the greatest college football teams in recent history. Then they were defeated by Clemson before even reaching LSU, who ended up with a legendary resume of their own. For 2020, the Buckeyes figure to pivot back to an increased focus on the passing game and lean on junior Justin Fields. The former 5-star prospect was considered one of the most talented quarterback recruits in history and he transferred to Ohio State from Georgia rather than waiting behind Jake Fromm.

Fields threw for 3,273 yards at 9.2 yards per attempt in 2019 with 41 touchdowns to just three interceptions. He feasted on Big Ten defenses throwing occasional RPOs or play-action bombs against teams primarily concerned with stopping Dobbins or Fields the runner. For 2020 he'll have left tackle Thayer Munford back to watch his blind side while throwing to Chris Olave (840 receiving yards, 12 touchdowns in 2019) and rising sophomore and former 5-star recruit Garrett Wilson

(432 receiving yards, five touchdowns in 2019). The Buckeye offense is losing some important pieces but could actually become more deadly thanks to growth from Fields and his young receivers. Like elsewhere around the nation, some of this will hinge on how many offseason reps the Buckeye quarterbacks and receivers are able to get with the passing game.

The run game will remain a formidable piece of the puzzle as well. Right guard Wyatt Davis, the threat of Fields' option keepers, and the overall threat of the passing game will open up space for the running backs. The Buckeyes welcomed Oklahoma grad transfer Trey Sermon to help out here. In three years as part of running back committees in Norman, Sermon ran for 2,076 yards at 6.1 yards per carry with 22 touchdowns. He's a power back at 6-foot-0 and 216 pounds that should be able to punish defenses that overcompensate trying to stop Fields from throwing the ball around.

On defense, the Buckeyes could potentially slip as a result of losing their main talents to the NFL and then dismissing rising senior Amir Riep after sexual assault charges in the offseason. Riep was expected to start at slot cornerback, in place of Shaun Wade who's moving to outside cornerback where both of the 2019 starters (Jeff Okudah and Damon Arnette) have moved on to the NFL. Now the Buckeyes will be plugging in new starters at three out of four positions in the secondary, as well as on the defensive line where both tackles are moving on along with Chase Young.

In 2019 the Buckeyes turned heads by playing single-high safety man or zone coverage nearly every snap. With safety/linebacker hybrid Pete Werner (returning in 2020) matching tight ends, Wade matching slot receivers, and then Jordan Fuller over the top it was very difficult for opposing offenses to find matchups and get the ball out in the passing game before Chase Young was tackling their quarterback. The formula is expected to remain the same in 2020 and repeating that success will hinge on how well the new defensive backs come along and whether or not they get high level pass rush from rising sophomore and former 5-star recruit Zach Harrison at defensive end.

In general, repeating as Big Ten champions and playoff contenders will hinge on maximizing the talent of Fields, Olave, and Wilson behind a veteran offensive line.

3. Clemson Tigers (10.8 mean wins)

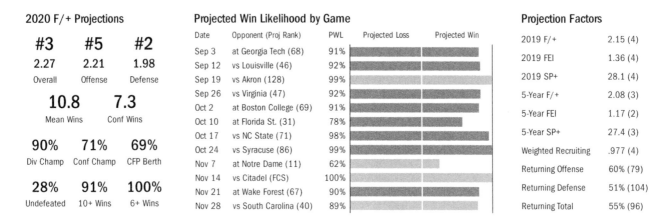

2020 F/+ Projections

#3	#5	#2
2.27	2.21	1.98
Overall	Offense	Defense

10.8	7.3
Mean Wins	Conf Wins

90%	71%	69%
Div Champ	Conf Champ	CFP Berth

28%	91%	100%
Undefeated	10+ Wins	6+ Wins

Projected Win Likelihood by Game

Date	Opponent (Proj Rank)	PWL
Sep 3	at Georgia Tech (68)	91%
Sep 12	vs Louisville (46)	92%
Sep 19	vs Akron (128)	99%
Sep 26	vs Virginia (47)	92%
Oct 2	at Boston College (69)	91%
Oct 10	at Florida St. (31)	78%
Oct 17	vs NC State (71)	98%
Oct 24	vs Syracuse (86)	99%
Nov 7	at Notre Dame (11)	62%
Nov 14	vs Citadel (FCS)	100%
Nov 21	at Wake Forest (67)	90%
Nov 28	vs South Carolina (40)	89%

Projection Factors

2019 F/+	2.15 (4)
2019 FEI	1.36 (4)
2019 SP+	28.1 (4)
5-Year F/+	2.08 (3)
5-Year FEI	1.17 (2)
5-Year SP+	27.4 (3)
Weighted Recruiting	.977 (4)
Returning Offense	60% (79)
Returning Defense	51% (104)
Returning Total	55% (96)

Clemson's toughest challenge heading into the 2019 season was seeing their entire defensive line drafted into the NFL. The Tigers' big victory over Alabama in the 2018 National Championship had hinged not only on their success on offense with Trevor Lawrence throwing the ball but also on their defense playing two deep safeties and holding up Alabama's run game by relying on that star-studded defensive line. They had to adjust in the following playoffs when their retooled defensive line couldn't hold up against Ohio State's running game. Their adjustment was the adoption of a 3-2-6 dime package that locked up the Buckeyes and then became a 3-1-7 against LSU's pro-spread attack in the Championship Game.

In 2020 the Tigers will be older on the defensive line but now must replace most of the secondary that flooded the field with upperclassmen against Ohio State and LSU, including first-round safety/linebacker Isaiah Simmons. Defensive coordinator Brent Venables has shown a real knack for evolving Clemson's approach from year to year in order to make the most of the talent on the roster—the Tigers finished in the top five in defensive EPA/Play (-0.249 EPA/play allowed) and success rate allowed (35.2%) yet again in 2019. This season he may focus on the defensive end tandem of Justin Foster and Xavier Thomas along with hard-charging inside linebacker James Skalski, whose inside blitzes shut down Ohio State and befuddled LSU for nearly half the title game before they adjusted. The Tigers also bring back star cornerback Derion Kendrick and veteran safety Nolan Turner.

The real name of the game during Clemson's amazing run under head coach Dabo Swinney has been offense, particularly throwing to NFL-bound star receivers. Trevor Lawrence is back to lead that effort at quarterback and he'll have receiver Amari Rodgers returning but the Tigers lost Tee Higgins to the NFL and then Justyn Ross was ruled out for the season with a spinal issue. The Tigers will have to usher in the next generation of star outside receivers and may also get some extra punch at tight end with a healthy Braden Galloway. The Tigers relied on J.C. Chalk at tight end in the regular season and he caught just 13 balls all year. In the playoffs they started mixing in the more athletic Galloway and in one playoff game (against LSU) he caught two passes for 60 yards.

Clemson's approach the last few years has been to lean on the run game in the regular season, relying on running back Travis Etienne, who's back after a season with 2,046 total yards (1,614 rushing yards at 7.8 yards per carry) and 23 total touchdowns. When they face higher level opponents in the playoffs they dial up more passing, unleashing a pro-style drop-back attack. The Clemson offensive line successfully quieted Chase Young in the semifinal a year ago but will have to find new starters at four spots to go with star left tackle Jackson Carman.

Trevor Lawrence has been the favorite to be drafted No. 1 in 2021 ever since his freshman season, and he'll have lots of weapons around him to guide one more run at the title. If Clemson can reload at wide receiver and find a new identity on defense then the Tigers look as dangerous as anyone. Their schedule gives them an easier path because traditional ACC powers Virginia Tech, Miami, and Florida State are all in down cycles. The Tigers will play at Notre Dame at midseason and get a taste of playing a nationally competitive roster to help them tune up for another almost inevitable playoff appearance.

4. LSU Tigers (9.4 mean wins)

2020 F/+ Projections

#4	#4	#13
2.06	2.43	1.42
Overall	Offense	Defense

9.4	5.6
Mean Wins	Conf Wins

26%	17%	17%
Div Champ	Conf Champ	CFP Berth

3%	46%	100%
Undefeated	10+ Wins	6+ Wins

Projected Win Likelihood by Game

Date	Opponent (Proj Rank)	PWL	Projected Loss / Projected Win
Sep 5	vs UTSA (123)	99%	
Sep 12	vs Texas (16)	77%	
Sep 19	vs Rice (120)	99%	
Sep 26	vs Ole Miss (34)	85%	
Oct 3	vs Nicholls (FCS)	100%	
Oct 10	at Florida (10)	55%	
Oct 17	at Arkansas (77)	90%	
Oct 24	vs Mississippi St. (38)	86%	
Nov 7	vs Alabama (1)	45%	
Nov 14	vs South Carolina (40)	86%	
Nov 21	at Auburn (9)	54%	
Nov 28	at Texas A&M (14)	61%	

Projection Factors

2019 F/+	2.45 (2)
2019 FEI	1.50 (2)
2019 SP+	33.1 (2)
5-Year F/+	1.73 (4)
5-Year FEI	0.91 (4)
5-Year SP+	24.7 (4)
Weighted Recruiting	.974 (5)
Returning Offense	30% (128)
Returning Defense	54% (92)
Returning Total	42% (127)

The 2019 LSU Tigers have a case as the greatest college football team of all time. They were undefeated overall, beat Alabama and Texas on the road, beat ranked Auburn and Florida teams at home, and finished the season by crushing Georgia (37-10) in the SEC title game and then Oklahoma (50-7) and defending champions Clemson (42-25) in the playoffs to claim their rings. A talented and pressuring defense showed up when it mattered while Joe Burrow won the Heisman by throwing for 5,671 yards at 10.8 yards per attempt with 60 touchdowns and six interceptions. The Tigers accumulated 304.3 expected points added in 2019, more than 30 points higher than the second most-valuable offense.

They embraced aggressive, pro-style spread passing and tempo to a greater degree than any previous college offense at a major program and unleashed absolute hell on defenses all year. New offensive coach Joe Brady helped them mold the Joe Moorhead RPO offense with sections from Sean Payton's pass game playbook at New Orleans (Brady's last stop before LSU) and then parlayed the breakthrough success into the offensive coordinator job for the Carolina Panthers. His offense forced opponents to attempt new sub packages like the 3-2-6 or 3-1-7 in order to hold up against all the matchups the Tigers could create in space from their 11-personnel attack.

On defense they executed defensive coordinator Dave Aranda's three-down, versatile blitzing scheme well enough to finish 13th in defensive FEI. Then Aranda left to be the new head coach for the Baylor Bears.

The 2020 LSU Tigers are not the same team. Burrow is off to the NFL, as are 13 other starters from the 2019 team. Only six starters remain from the championship squad, plus FCS transfer linebacker Jabril Cox, who started for three consecutive North Dakota State championship teams.

Myles Brennan is next in line at quarterback, a redshirt junior who backed up Burrow in 2019 within the same system. He'll benefit from the return of superstar receiver Ja'Marr Chase and Terrace Marshall Jr. who was the No. 5 target behind Chase, tight end Thaddeus Moss (gone), running back Clyde Edwards-Helaire (gone), and slot receiver Justin Jefferson (gone). The Tigers will aim to reload in part by adding tight end Arik Gilbert, a 6-foot-5, 253-pound freshman who was rated as a 5-star recruit and potentially the greatest tight end talent in LSU history. The offensive line returns two starters from the very strong 2019 lineup and will aim to reload from a roster of up-and-coming former blue chips and Harvard grad transfer Liam Shanahan.

The overall approach should remain consistent, even with new offensive coach Scott Linehan. The main question is whether Myles Brennan can execute anywhere near the same level of field generalship and lethality in the passing game as Joe Burrow did.

On defense the Tigers are both changing the staff and the overall approach. Head coach Ed Orgeron hired Bo Pellini to coordinate the defense, as he did under Les Miles at LSU for their national championship run back in 2007. The 2020 Tigers will move to a 4-2-5 base defense and there's excitement and intrigue about how they'll use former 5-star recruit Marcell Brooks with the answer appearing to be as a 210-pound, ultra-athletic inside linebacker.

Thorpe Award winner Grant Delpit is moving on from safety but the always potent Tiger secondary will still include safety JaCoby Stevens (92 tackles, nine TFLs, five sacks, three interceptions) and rising sophomore phenom Derek Stingley (six interceptions, 15 pass breakups) at cornerback. This will be an extraordinarily athletic defense, as is the custom in Baton Rouge.

The schedule will include a home date in week two against the Texas Longhorns, an SEC East draw with a road trip to Florida and home date against South Carolina, and then the Tigers play LSU in Baton Rouge but finish the season with back to back road trips against Auburn and Texas A&M. It's a tough slate, the Tigers normally face one of the tougher schedules in the country.

5. Georgia Bulldogs (9.2 mean wins)

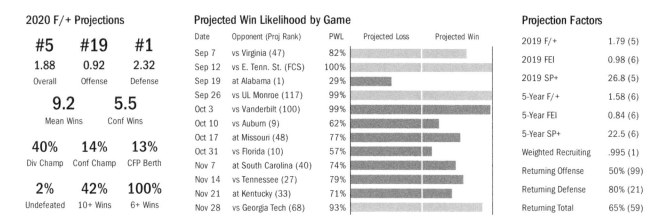

2020 F/+ Projections

#5	#19	#1
1.88	0.92	2.32
Overall	Offense	Defense

9.2	5.5
Mean Wins	Conf Wins

40%	14%	13%
Div Champ	Conf Champ	CFP Berth

2%	42%	100%
Undefeated	10+ Wins	6+ Wins

Projected Win Likelihood by Game

Date	Opponent (Proj Rank)	PWL
Sep 7	vs Virginia (47)	82%
Sep 12	vs E. Tenn. St. (FCS)	100%
Sep 19	at Alabama (1)	29%
Sep 26	vs UL Monroe (117)	99%
Oct 3	vs Vanderbilt (100)	99%
Oct 10	vs Auburn (9)	62%
Oct 17	at Missouri (48)	77%
Oct 31	vs Florida (10)	57%
Nov 7	at South Carolina (40)	74%
Nov 14	vs Tennessee (27)	79%
Nov 21	at Kentucky (33)	71%
Nov 28	vs Georgia Tech (68)	93%

Projection Factors

2019 F/+	1.79 (5)
2019 FEI	0.98 (6)
2019 SP+	26.8 (5)
5-Year F/+	1.58 (6)
5-Year FEI	0.84 (6)
5-Year SP+	22.5 (6)
Weighted Recruiting	.995 (1)
Returning Offense	50% (99)
Returning Defense	80% (21)
Returning Total	65% (59)

The Bulldogs had a relatively disappointing 2019 season despite winning 11 games and competing for their third consecutive SEC Championship. The obvious stains on the season were a 20-17 defeat to a South Carolina team that finished 4-8 and then losing the SEC title game against LSU, 37-10. Despite a top-ten defensive effort (-0.083 EPA/Play ranked seventh nationally and second in the SEC), the Bulldog offense muddled to a 52nd overall ranking on offense (0.114 EPA/Play). Beyond those shortcomings, the Bulldogs were in their third and ultimately final season with quarterback Jake Fromm, who finished 36-7 as their quarterback. With the loss to LSU, the Fromm era concluded without a National Championship. On top of that, by committing to Fromm the Bulldogs helped encourage the transfer of generational talent Justin Fields to Ohio State, which may haunt Georgia fans for years to come.

Beyond losing Jake Fromm to the NFL, the 2020 Bulldogs also have to replace three offensive linemen, running back D'Andre Swift, and tight end Charlie Woerner. Former 5-star recruit and rising junior Cade Mays would have been a cornerstone of the rebuild but instead transferred to divisional rival Tennessee. For all of Georgia's early success under head coach Kirby Smart and Fromm, there's a possibility that a window of opportunity was missed.

But the Bulldogs have already adjusted and reloaded for the 2020 season. To replace Fromm and Fields they took grad transfer quarterback Jamie Newman from Wake Forest as well as USC transfer and former 5-star recruit J.T. Daniels for subsequent seasons. The offensive line has only two returning starters but they were able to get snaps for several key players like prospective left tackle Jamaree Salyer in the bowl game against Baylor. The skill positions boast potential stars at wide receiver and running back in sophomores George Pickens (49 catches for 727 yards, eight touchdowns) and Zamir White

(78 carries for 408 rushing yards in 2019).

Georgia will also be evolving their offensive approach with new coordinator Todd Monken and offensive line coach Matt Luke. Expect the Dawgs to be more spread-oriented, as both coaches have roots in the Air Raid and transfer quarterback Jamie Newman ran an innovative RPO offense at Wake Forest.

On defense things should remain fairly consistent under the watchful eye of head coach Kirby Smart. The Bulldogs ranked third in defensive FEI in 2019, 10th in 2018, and fourth in 2017. Their system has been yielding consistent results and the roster is fairly intact from 2019. All-SEC defensive tackle Tyler Clark is moving on but lead tackler and middle linebacker Monty Rice, edge rusher Azeez Ojulari, and three starting cornerbacks and two safeties are back.

Smart's defensive strategy has often been oriented around building sub packages and his 2017 defense was very comfortable playing in a 3-2-6 dime that hinged on the abilities of linebacker Roquan Smith and defensive back Aaron Davis. The 2020 Bulldogs have loads of experienced defensive backs along with rising young stars in the secondary such as sophomore Tyrique Stevenson, freshman Kelee Ringo, and redshirt sophomore Divaad Wilson. So long as 6-foot-6, 330-pound junior nose tackle Jordan Davis is holding things down up front, Smart will have endless waves of athletes to throw at opponents on defense.

The schedule will be fairly intense. The Bulldogs open with Virginia in Atlanta and two weeks later travel to Tuscaloosa to play Alabama. Then they have their normal date with Auburn, this year taking place in Georgia, and the rivalry game against a strong looking Florida team in Jacksonville coming on the heels of those contests. The SEC East could be more competitive than usual in 2020 so Georgia's high-level recruiting and offensive changes may be necessary just to tread water.

6. Wisconsin Badgers (9.1 mean wins)

2020 F/+ Projections

#6	#10	#6
1.75	1.35	1.64
Overall	Offense	Defense

9.1	6.8
Mean Wins	Conf Wins

65%	21%	16%
Div Champ	Conf Champ	CFP Berth

3%	42%	99%
Undefeated	10+ Wins	6+ Wins

Projected Win Likelihood by Game

Date	Opponent (Proj Rank)	PWL	Projected Loss	Projected Win
Sep 4	vs Indiana (37)	80%		
Sep 12	vs S. Illinois (FCS)	100%		
Sep 19	vs Appalachian St. (35)	80%		
Sep 26	at Michigan (12)	51%		
Oct 3	vs Notre Dame (11)	57%		
Oct 10	vs Minnesota (20)	73%		
Oct 24	at Maryland (78)	86%		
Oct 31	vs Illinois (66)	91%		
Nov 7	at Northwestern (53)	78%		
Nov 14	at Purdue (55)	78%		
Nov 21	vs Nebraska (36)	80%		
Nov 28	at Iowa (18)	60%		

Projection Factors

2019 F/+	1.67 (6)
2019 FEI	1.12 (5)
2019 SP+	20.3 (11)
5-Year F/+	1.38 (11)
5-Year FEI	0.76 (9)
5-Year SP+	18.7 (12)
Weighted Recruiting	.760 (27)
Returning Offense	62% (72)
Returning Defense	81% (17)
Returning Total	72% (34)

The formula of the 2019 Wisconsin Badgers' season may sound familiar. Behind the consistently explosive running threat of Jonathan Taylor (6.3 yards per carry) and the efficient and timely passing of junior Jack Coan, the Badgers started their 2019 campaign 6-0, shutting out four of their opponents, and winning by an average margin of over 30 points. Yet again, the Badgers mixed a ground-and-pound approach with solid offensive line play and a competent passing game to start the season looking like a lock to make their sixth trip to Lucas Oil Stadium as the Big Ten West champions.

A trip to Champaign, Illinois, and a last-second field goal threw that narrative for a loop; the Badgers averaged 3.8 yards per carry and lost to Illinois, followed by a trip to Columbus and a defeat at the hands of Ohio State. The Badgers managed to right the ship, reminding upstart Minnesota who really ran the division in a de facto play-in game, and finished with their first Rose Bowl appearance since 2013. In April, senior linebacker Zack Baun got his due, being selected in the third round of the NFL draft, while the Badger offense lost Taylor (second round), center Tyler Biadasz (fourth), and leading pass-catcher Quintez Cephus (fifth) to the big league.

Despite losing Taylor and Cephus (3,156 combined yards, 33 combined touchdowns, and more than 51% of targets and rushes), the Badgers bring back five of their top six pass-catchers, coupled with sophomore Nakia Watson (331 yards and two touchdowns in 74 rushes), who is primed to fill the vacancy at running back and become the next in a long line of very productive Wisconsin rushers.

The defense will need to replace linebackers Baun and Chris Orr (123 combined tackles, 33.5 TFLs), but junior Jack Sanborn returns, along with all four starting defensive backs. Basing out of a 3-4, the Badgers need the linebackers and secondary to make tackles, but defensive ends Garret Rand (senior, 20 tackles, three TFLs) and Matt Henningsen (junior, 19 tackles, five TFLs) will be anchors on the defensive line.

The Badgers' recruiting class ranked 26th nationally this season, with the standard Wisconsin mix of linebackers and linemen that will need to be developed, although a couple of 4-stars may have an immediate impact: running back Jalen Berger out of New Jersey may see time in the backfield, while linebacker Kaden Johnson from Minnesota will contribute defensively.

Senior quarterback Coan returns for his final year, along with three starting offensive linemen. Coan proved himself an effective passer at the start of the season but struggled with accuracy against the stouter defenses on the schedule (69.6% completion rate on the season, but below 65% against Northwestern, Iowa, and Ohio State.) With the turnover at running back, Coan will have to progress to keep the Badgers at the top of the Big Ten West.

In 2020, the Badgers add Notre Dame and a tricky Appalachian State to the schedule, also facing trips to Ann Arbor, Chicago, and Iowa City. The Badgers have the linemen, they have the defensive secondary, and they have the returning quarterback. Can Paul Chryst leverage that returning quarterback into another Rose Bowl, or even the Badgers' first playoff berth? Will the Badgers be able to fend off upstart programs in their division like Minnesota and Nebraska, while positioning themselves against old staples like Iowa and a potentially revamped Northwestern? Wisconsin's strength of schedule is tough enough that the Badgers might have the luxury of making the playoff with a loss but filling the void of Jonathan Taylor's rushing production on offense will be a tall task. Unlike last year, the Badgers will have a tougher schedule on the front end, and if the Badgers can take advantage of their historically hot starts, they may build enough capital to take a shot at the Big Ten title, and the playoff.

7. Penn State Nittany Lions (9.2 mean wins)

2020 F/+ Projections

#7	#8	#9
1.72	1.38	1.49
Overall	Offense	Defense

9.2	6.5
Mean Wins	Conf Wins

21%	14%	12%
Div Champ	Conf Champ	CFP Berth

2%	44%	100%
Undefeated	10+ Wins	6+ Wins

Projected Win Likelihood by Game

Date	Opponent (Proj Rank)	PWL	Projected Loss	Projected Win
Sep 5	vs Kent St. (114)	99%		
Sep 12	at Virginia Tech (30)	68%		
Sep 19	vs San Jose St. (108)	99%		
Sep 26	vs Northwestern (53)	86%		
Oct 3	at Michigan (12)	50%		
Oct 17	vs Iowa (18)	72%		
Oct 24	vs Ohio St. (2)	38%		
Oct 31	at Indiana (37)	69%		
Nov 7	at Nebraska (36)	69%		
Nov 14	vs Michigan St. (41)	82%		
Nov 21	vs Maryland (78)	93%		
Nov 28	at Rutgers (113)	94%		

Projection Factors

2019 F/+	1.65 (7)
2019 FEI	0.93 (9)
2019 SP+	24.3 (6)
5-Year F/+	1.39 (10)
5-Year FEI	0.72 (11)
5-Year SP+	19.9 (8)
Weighted Recruiting	.943 (11)
Returning Offense	74% (38)
Returning Defense	63% (66)
Returning Total	69% (47)

The Nittany Lions in 2019 faced a similar situation to Wisconsin, as many Big Ten teams do: how to succeed as a really good team in a conference full of really good teams? James Franklin's sixth season in Happy Valley featured his third 10-win campaign and his fourth New Year's Six Bowl (a 53-39 shootout win over Group of 5 champion Memphis), but featured a close loss to Ohio State for the third year in a row. The Nittany Lions found wins last year, going 5-1 in one-score games, and stealing a road win against Iowa, but fell to the Buckeyes and P.J. Fleck's Minnesota on the road.

The Penn State offense was led by the Sean Clifford-KJ Hamler connection. The junior duo connected for 904 yards and 8 touchdowns, averaging an explosive 16.1 yards per catch. Hamler, drafted in the second round by the Denver Broncos, was a deep threat so respected that he freed up plenty of ground for tight end Pat Freiermuth (507 yards and seven touchdowns in 2019), wide receiver Jahan Dotson (488 yards and five touchdowns), and even running back Journey Brown (134 yards on 22 catches, 1 TD) to get involved in the passing game. Journey Brown is a name you ought to know. The Penn State junior rushed for 890 yards on 129 carries last year (6.9 yards per carry) but scored 12 touchdowns on the ground and is poised to be the next great Penn State running back. The offense does lose four starters on the line, and some turnover is to be expected, but the Nittany Lions hired Kirk Ciarrocca away from Minnesota last year to be the new offensive coordinator. Whereas Penn State finished 29th overall in EPA/play last season on offense, Minnesota ranked fifth, suggesting that Ciarrocca's offense in the hands of the senior Clifford may be able to take Penn State's offense from middling to great. The question, of course, then rests on how disruptive the shortened offseason will be for a team working to incorporate a new offensive coordinator.

The defense looks primed to repeat a stellar 2019 performance in 2020. The Nittany Lions allowed -0.082 EPA/play last season, seventh nationally (but just third in their division, one should note), holding eight opponents to 13 or fewer points in 2019. The rushing defense was stout (third nationally at -0.190 EPA/rush allowed), led by sophomore linebacker Micah Parsons (80.5 tackles and 14 TFLs) and senior linebacker Cam Brown (50 tackles, 5.5 TFLs). Brown was selected in the sixth round by the New York Giants, but Parsons returns for 2020, alongside senior defensive end Yetur Gross-Matos (15 TFLs in 2019), who will be playing to improve his own draft stock this season, senior safety LaMont Wade (53 tackles and 5 pass breakups), and senior cornerback Tariq Castro-Fields (41.5 tackles, 8 pass breakups).

Penn State's 2020 schedule is overall light, but their three toughest opponents all fall in consecutive games: the Nittany Lions head to Ann Arbor, then host Iowa and Ohio State during the month of October, before finishing with three of five games against teams coming off losing seasons. As it so often goes with college football's upper middle class, the Nittany Lions' season will rest on the results of their games against Iowa, Michigan, and Ohio State. Penn State returns an able quarterback, some dynamic offensive weapons, and a stifling defense, but will need for all of those elements to coalesce in their three big games in order to reach the playoff.

8. Oklahoma Sooners (9.5 mean wins)

2020 F/+ Projections

#8	#2	#43
1.70	2.66	0.44
Overall	Offense	Defense

9.5	6.8
Mean Wins	Conf Wins

-	47%	27%
Div Champ	Conf Champ	CFP Berth

4%	49%	100%
Undefeated	10+ Wins	6+ Wins

Projected Win Likelihood by Game

Date	Opponent (Proj Rank)	PWL	Projected Loss	Projected Win
Sep 5	vs Missouri St. (FCS)	100%		
Sep 12	vs Tennessee (27)	76%		
Sep 26	at Army (94)	88%		
Oct 3	vs Baylor (25)	75%		
Oct 10	vs Texas (16)	64%		
Oct 17	at Iowa St. (26)	64%		
Oct 24	vs Oklahoma St. (22)	73%		
Oct 31	at TCU (28)	66%		
Nov 7	at West Virginia (61)	80%		
Nov 14	vs Kansas St. (44)	83%		
Nov 21	vs Kansas (110)	99%		
Nov 28	at Texas Tech (56)	78%		

Projection Factors

2019 F/+	1.53 (10)
2019 FEI	0.83 (14)
2019 SP+	22.9 (8)
5-Year F/+	1.72 (5)
5-Year FEI	0.89 (5)
5-Year SP+	24.4 (5)
Weighted Recruiting	.954 (10)
Returning Offense	49% (103)
Returning Defense	70% (47)
Returning Total	59% (82)

Is there a claim too bold regarding Lincoln Riley's offense? For the third straight year, the offensive savant rode a different quarterback through the Big 12 gauntlet, into the playoffs, and to the Heisman ceremony, each time in a slightly different manner than the year before. Alabama graduate transfer Jalen Hurts (3,832 passing yards, 32 touchdowns, 1,451 rushing yards, and 20 rushing touchdowns) plugged right into Riley's system and the Sooners' multiple Air Raid and power rush offense ranked third nationally in efficiency (.338 EPA/play), winning the Big 12 and earning a playoff bid for the third consecutive year. The Sooners' regular season was a bit more of a roller coaster than the previous two years, as seven of their last nine games were one score affairs, including a 34-31 win in Waco that saw Oklahoma down 28-3 early in the second quarter.

The Sooners found themselves victim to Joe Burrow and Joe Brady's LSU passing offense, falling to the Tigers 63-28 in the first round of the playoffs in a game that never felt in reach. That belied some serious improvement on behalf of Oklahoma's defense, thanks to the addition of coordinator Alex Grinch. Grinch, who got his first defensive coordinator job under Mike Leach at Washington State, came to Norman in 2019 with the expectation that he could finally address the one weakness with Riley's teams, defense. And insofar as one defensive coordinator can affect a defense in one offseason, Grinch did. The Sooners finished 33rd in EPA/play (+0.060) on defense, and 24th in EPA/pass (0.131), a huge step up from prior seasons. That improvement came largely on the back of junior linebacker Kenneth Murray (85.5 tackles, 17.5 TFLs, 4 sacks, and 4 pass breakups). The Sooners lost Murray to the NFL draft, but return eight of 10 leading tacklers. Grinch's system is geared towards simplicity, speed, and ruthlessness, and although his 3-4 base defense is familiar to the Sooners, the responsibilities of a hybrid defense require some learning.

Again, the shortened offseason rears its head, but given the dearth of talent Oklahoma has amassed and the returning production, the defensive improvement should continue.

On the offensive side of the ball, Oklahoma for the fourth straight year will need to replace their quarterback—also their top rusher—and their top receiver. At quarterback, breaking the streak of graduate transfers, redshirt freshman Spencer Rattler will take over. Rattler, a 5-star recruit out of Oklahoma, is expected to be another one of Riley's great quarterbacks, although he certainly will need more time to develop than his predecessors. Rattler, as a redshirt freshman, will be the youngest QB starter of a Lincoln Riley offense at Oklahoma, and the Sooners' youngest QB starter since Landry Jones took over for Sam Bradford in 2009. As for who Rattler with share the ball with, rising junior Kennedy Brooks (1,011 yards, 6.5 yards per carry, and 6 touchdowns in 2019) joins him in the backfield, and junior Charleston Rambo (743 yards, 5 touchdowns, 69.4% catch rate) appears to be the primary receiving target, along with the larger-bodied sophomore Jadon Haselwood (19 catches, 272 yards, 1 touchdown).

The Sooners host Tennessee in a potentially challenging non-conference game, and make road trips to Ames, Fort Worth, Morgantown, and Lubbock this season. They'll get rival Oklahoma State in Norman, and face their toughest test against Texas in Dallas, but finish the season with five teams who averaged five wins last season. If the Sooners can take care of business early on against Baylor, Texas, and Oklahoma State, their last five games before the Big 12 championship may provide them a unique opportunity to rest and get Spencer Rattler comfortable in the offense before a high-stakes playoff game. New quarterbacks have never been a concern for Riley, but the question this year is whether the defense will improve enough to push Oklahoma further than the playoff's first round.

9. Auburn Tigers (8.4 mean wins)

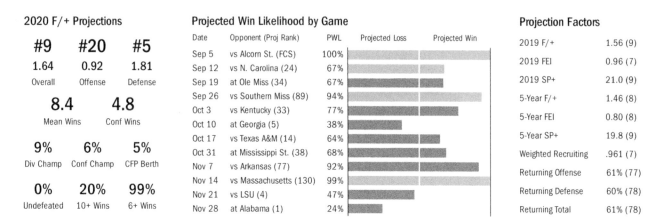

2020 F/+ Projections

#9	#20	#5
1.64	0.92	1.81
Overall	Offense	Defense

8.4	4.8
Mean Wins	Conf Wins

9%	6%	5%
Div Champ	Conf Champ	CFP Berth

0%	20%	99%
Undefeated	10+ Wins	6+ Wins

Projected Win Likelihood by Game

Date	Opponent (Proj Rank)	PWL	Projected Loss	Projected Win
Sep 5	vs Alcorn St. (FCS)	100%		
Sep 12	vs N. Carolina (24)	67%		
Sep 19	at Ole Miss (34)	67%		
Sep 26	vs Southern Miss (89)	94%		
Oct 3	vs Kentucky (33)	77%		
Oct 10	at Georgia (5)	38%		
Oct 17	vs Texas A&M (14)	64%		
Oct 31	at Mississippi St. (38)	68%		
Nov 7	vs Arkansas (77)	92%		
Nov 14	vs Massachusetts (130)	99%		
Nov 21	vs LSU (4)	47%		
Nov 28	at Alabama (1)	24%		

Projection Factors

2019 F/+	1.56 (9)
2019 FEI	0.96 (7)
2019 SP+	21.0 (9)
5-Year F/+	1.46 (8)
5-Year FEI	0.80 (8)
5-Year SP+	19.8 (9)
Weighted Recruiting	.961 (7)
Returning Offense	61% (77)
Returning Defense	60% (78)
Returning Total	61% (78)

Auburn's win totals under Gus Malhzan (since 2013): 12, 8, 7, 8, 10, 8, 9. The Tigers have two 10-win seasons in seven years of Malzahn, partly a product of playing in the daunting SEC West. In 2019, things weren't much different for the Tigers. Heading into the season, Bo Nix won the starting job as a freshman, and he and the Tigers stunned Oregon in Week 1 with a last-second touchdown. The Tigers cruised through their next four games, including a win in College Station against Texas A&M. Sitting at 5-0, Auburn looked like they might be having one of their better years. The Tigers then proceeded to lose to Florida, LSU, and Georgia, knocking them firmly out of national contention. Malhzan beat a Tua-less Alabama, and for that, may have staved off talk about his job security, but this offseason, the Auburn head coach made some changes.

The Tigers finished the season 35th in offensive EPA/play, 29th in rushing and 35th in passing among Power Five schools. No one can blame them for struggling against the eventual national champion LSU and New Year's Six participants Georgia and Florida, but under Gus Mahlzan, a middling offense is a disappointment. For the second straight season, Auburn will have a new offensive coordinator: recently fired Arkansas coach Chad Morris. Morris, the coach most famously credited with developing Tajh Boyd and recruiting Deshaun Watson at Clemson, will take charge of an offense with a lot of youth, but a lot of potential.

Nix (57.6% completion percentage, 2,542 yards, 16 touchdowns) had his moments (see the end of the Oregon game, or all of the Alabama game, for example), but struggled with consistency and moving the ball downfield: his yards per attempt was a meager 6.1 and he threw 6 interceptions. He relied mostly on sophomore Seth Williams as his primary target. Williams, a big-bodied receiver, caught eight of Nix's touch-

down throws and amassed 830 yards on the season. Junior Eli Stove played a nice complement to Williams as a smaller, speedier threat, catching 37 passes for 321 yards and three touchdowns last season. All three players return, plus leading rusher JaTarvious Whitlow (763 yards and 10 touchdowns on 156 rushes), giving Morris plenty of tools to work with in revamping the Auburn offense. The line lost tackle Prince Tega Wanogho to the NFL draft, and three other starters graduated. The skill players will be there, and if the offense can find replacements along the line, Nix's second year could be special.

On the defensive side of the ball, Auburn had some playmakers that handled some of the best offenses in college football: 22nd in the Power Five in EPA/play. Along the way, the Tigers had five top 15 EPA offenses on their schedule. Four Auburn defenders were selected in the 2020 NFL draft, including first-round pick Derrick Brown. The senior tackle had 12.5 TFLs and four sacks in 2019, and filling his production will be tough. The keystone of the 2020 defense will be rising senior K.J. Britt, who had 53 tackles, ten TFLs, and 2.5 sacks last season. He led an Auburn defense that was much more disruptive towards the run (-0.044 EPA/rush) than the pass (0.064 EPA/pass). Britt will be joined in the secondary by five returning defensive backs, including rising junior Roger McCreary, who had 11 pass breakups in 2019. Auburn's defense was at the usual standard of the SEC West's best, and the names will change, but the defense will be the anchor going into 2020.

The Tigers will have another tough schedule in 2020, but such is life for the SEC West and the Tigers, who have perennial rival Georgia from the East. Auburn plays a neutral-site game against a similarly stationed North Carolina, and makes trips to Georgia, Mississippi State, and Alabama while hosting LSU. The Tigers' offense will have to catch up to the defense to survive their schedule and the gauntlet of the SEC West.

10. Florida Gators (9.0 mean wins)

2020 F/+ Projections

#10	#15	#11
1.58	1.14	1.47
Overall	Offense	Defense

9.0	5.4
Mean Wins	Conf Wins

36%	13%	11%
Div Champ	Conf Champ	CFP Berth

3%	38%	100%
Undefeated	10+ Wins	6+ Wins

Projected Win Likelihood by Game

Date	Opponent (Proj Rank)	PWL
Sep 5	vs E. Washington (FCS)	100%
Sep 12	vs Kentucky (33)	76%
Sep 19	vs S. Alabama (119)	99%
Sep 26	at Tennessee (27)	62%
Oct 3	vs S. Carolina (40)	79%
Oct 10	vs LSU (4)	45%
Oct 17	at Ole Miss (34)	65%
Oct 31	vs Georgia (5)	43%
Nov 7	at Vanderbilt (100)	88%
Nov 14	vs Missouri (48)	82%
Nov 21	vs N. Mexico St. (127)	99%
Nov 28	at Florida St. (31)	65%

Projection Factors

2019 F/+	1.61 (8)
2019 FEI	0.88 (11)
2019 SP+	24.0 (7)
5-Year F/+	1.11 (13)
5-Year FEI	0.51 (15)
5-Year SP+	17.2 (13)
Weighted Recruiting	.958 (9)
Returning Offense	63% (67)
Returning Defense	67% (55)
Returning Total	65% (61)

The 2019 Florida Gators lost to eventual national champion LSU and SEC East champion Georgia last season but were undefeated otherwise. Dan Mullen has now won 21 games in his two-year tenure in Gainesville; the Gators had two 10-win seasons in the seven years before Mullen. The Gators' offense ranked 12th in EPA/play in Mullen's second season, 13th in passing EPA. Quarterback Kyle Trask, returning as a senior this fall, replaced starter Felipe Franks after an injury in the Kentucky game, led three fourth-quarter touchdown drives, and never looked back. Trask (2,941 yards, 66.9% completion, 25 touchdowns) became the face of the Gator offense, posting 310 passing yards against LSU and against Virginia in Florida's Orange Bowl win. Trask is in some ways an odd fit for the Florida offense; the former 3-star recruit is more of a pro-style quarterback than Mullen's typical starter, but he ran well at times last year, especially in the red zone (4.3 yards/carry, 4 touchdowns). Trask won't break any rushing records this season, but Mullen is innovative enough to work around that constraint.

For 2020, the Florida Gators faces some turnover; leading rusher La'Mical Perine (676 yards, 5.1 yards/carry, 6 touchdowns rushing, 5 touchdowns receiving in 2019) plays for the New York Jets now, and seniors Van Jefferson and Freddie Swain both were selected in the NFL draft. Jefferson and Swain accounted for about a third of Trask's targets and 13 touchdowns. In the rushing game, rising junior Dameon Pierce will get the bulk of the carries (5.6 yards per carry, 4 touchdowns in 2019). Florida's leader in targets and catches, tight end Kyle Pitts (649 yards on 54 catches, 70.1% catch rate and 5 touchdowns) is back, but five of Trask's top targets have moved on. Trevon Grimes, returning for his senior season, is a big body (6-foot-5, 214 pounds) who will provide a downfield dimension for Mullen's offense. Other names to watch in the passing game are sophomore wide receiver Jacob Copeland, who had 36 targets last year, athlete Kadarius Toney, and running back Pierce, all of whom can fill that speed and space receiver role in Mullen's offense. Tight end Kyle Pitts returns as

Trask's favorite weapon from 2019 (77 targets, 70.1% catch rate, 649 yards).

On the defensive side of the ball, the Gators bring back much more. Defensive coordinator Todd Grantham has had three offseasons to install his 3-4 defense, and eight of the Gators' top ten tacklers return for 2020, all quite familiar with Grantham's scheme. Along the defensive line, rising senior Kyree Campbell looks to disrupt (4 TFLs in 2019). The linebacking core loses both David Reese II and Jonathan Greenard to the NFL and will have to fill those seniors' roles, perhaps the only glaring issue with Florida's defensive personnel this season. In the Grantham defense, the interior linebackers are crucial to defending the rush game: the duo of Reese and Greenard accounted for 22 TFLs, 11.5 sacks, and over 100 tackles. There to take over are James Houston IV, who played as Reese's backup, and returning starter Ventrell Miller (40.5 tackles, 5.5 TFLs, 3 sacks in 2019). In the secondary, three of four starters return: cornerback CJ Henderson was drafted in the first round, but Shawn Davis, Marco Wilson, and Donovan Stiner all look to return. Florida's defense ranked 15th in EPA/play in the Power Five last season and looks to replicate that consistent strength this fall.

Mullen recruited well, boasting two straight top-ten recruiting classes, and players like 5-star defensive tackle Gervon Dexter and 4-star wide receiver Xzavier Henderson look to have an immediate impact, while 2019 recruits like 4-star cornerback Kaiir Elam will have chances to win starting spots outright.

Florida's defense will again be excellent, and returning an experienced quarterback never hurts, but the Gators will have to adapt some new faces on offense to take a step forward in the new SEC East. The Gators face early tests in 2020, hosting Kentucky, traveling to Tennessee, and hosting LSU in their first six games. For better or worse, the nation will know a lot more about Kyle Trask's senior season and Dan Mullen's third year after that trip to Knoxville. The Gators have the talent, they have the coaching, but the path to the SEC Championship Game is much tougher than it was when Florida last made it (2016).

11. Notre Dame Fighting Irish (8.6 mean wins)

2020 F/+ Projections

#11	#12	#15
1.46	1.26	1.26
Overall	Offense	Defense

8.6	-
Mean Wins	Conf Wins

-	-	2%
Div Champ	Conf Champ	CFP Berth

1%	27%	98%
Undefeated	10+ Wins	6+ Wins

Projected Win Likelihood by Game

Date	Opponent (Proj Rank)	PWL	Projected Loss	Projected Win
Sep 5	at Navy (45)	73%		
Sep 12	vs Arkansas (77)	90%		
Sep 19	vs W. Michigan (80)	90%		
Sep 26	vs Wake Forest (67)	82%		
Oct 3	vs Wisconsin (6)	43%		
Oct 10	vs Stanford (50)	80%		
Oct 17	at Pittsburgh (49)	69%		
Oct 31	vs Duke (64)	86%		
Nov 7	vs Clemson (3)	38%		
Nov 14	at Georgia Tech (68)	78%		
Nov 21	vs Louisville (46)	79%		
Nov 28	at USC (19)	54%		

Projection Factors

2019 F/+	1.35 (14)
2019 FEI	0.85 (13)
2019 SP+	17.7 (19)
5-Year F/+	1.34 (12)
5-Year FEI	0.68 (12)
5-Year SP+	19.5 (10)
Weighted Recruiting	.935 (13)
Returning Offense	66% (64)
Returning Defense	51% (102)
Returning Total	59% (83)

The Fighting Irish made a strong showing in 2019 coming off a playoff appearance in 2018. They narrowly lost at Georgia 23-17 early in the year, took a beating at Michigan 45-14 later in the season, but pummeled most everyone else on the schedule and edged out USC 30-27. Then they beat Iowa State convincingly (33-9) in the Camping World Bowl. After the season an evidently turbulent relationship between head coach Brian Kelly and offensive coordinator Chip Long was dissolved and Kelly's former quarterback Tommy Rees was promoted from quarterbacks coach to be the new offensive coordinator.

Reese will coordinate an offense that is short on known, dynamic playmakers after the top two receivers and lead running back departed for the NFL. There aren't any household names yet amongst Notre Dame's skill players or amongst the defense. However, what the Irish do have is one of the most experienced offenses in the entire nation.

It starts at the line of scrimmage, where they bring back third-year starting quarterback Ian Book and five different offensive linemen with at least 13 starts apiece. At receiver the Irish will be promoting redshirt sophomore tight end Tommy Tremble and redshirt senior Javon McKinley, who had four touchdown catches each in 2019. They also welcome Northwestern grad transfer Ben Skowronek, who was a key piece to the Wildcats 2018 Big Ten West title. The Irish tend to have exceptional receivers rising up the ranks and redshirt sophomores Lawrence Keys III and Braden Lenzy are also among the options here.

On defense, there's a bit more for the Irish to sort out but their depth chart has a similar dynamic of featuring older players. The defensive line will include redshirt senior defensive ends Daelin Hayes and Adetokunbo Ogundeji and returning redshirt junior tackles Kurt Hinish and Myron Tagovailoa-Amosa. There's a lot of experience across the group but they need Ogundeji to build on his success at the end of 2019 when he had all three of his sacks in two games and see him emerge as a premier pass-rusher.

Behind the line the Irish return linebackers Jeremiah Owusu-Koramoah and Drew White, the former of whom led the team in tackles with 80, TFLs with 13, and sacks with 5.5. Big safety Kyle Hamilton (6-foot-4, 210 pounds) split time with star junior Alohi Gilman and will now own the free safety position after Gilman departed for the NFL. In limited action Hamilton had 41 tackles, four interceptions, and six pass breakups.

The Irish will pair Hamilton with rising junior Houston Griffith and redshirt senior Shaun Crawford at the nickel. They'll need to establish their cornerback rotation in fall camp. Cornerback is where the Clemson Tigers ultimately took down the Irish in their 2018 playoff matchup. For 2020 Notre Dame will have TaRiq Bracy locking down one side and will look to Crawford, redshirt freshman Isaiah Rutherford, and North Carolina State transfer Nick McCloud to give them depth and options at the other spot.

Overall, there's experience on defense but the major question for Notre Dame will be how much explosive athleticism there is across the unit for when they face top level competition. The schedule will be revelatory in this regard. The Irish open against Navy and will face Wisconsin at Lambeau Field in September, they'll host Stanford in October and Clemson in November, then they'll finish the season against USC on the road. If all the experience on this roster is brought to bear against their opponents then Notre Dame will have a playoff resume. If they can overcome the early schedule, the Clemson game may be one of the biggest games of the season, effectively a quarterfinal game for the playoffs.

12. Michigan Wolverines (8.1 mean wins)

2020 F/+ Projections

#12	#26	#10
1.43	0.82	1.48
Overall	Offense	Defense

8.1	5.8
Mean Wins	Conf Wins

9%	6%	4%
Div Champ	Conf Champ	CFP Berth

1%	16%	96%
Undefeated	10+ Wins	6+ Wins

Projected Win Likelihood by Game

Date	Opponent (Proj Rank)	PWL
Sep 5	at Washington (15)	50%
Sep 12	vs Ball St. (97)	93%
Sep 19	vs Arkansas St. (93)	92%
Sep 26	vs Wisconsin (6)	49%
Oct 3	vs Penn St. (7)	50%
Oct 10	at Michigan St. (41)	66%
Oct 17	at Minnesota (20)	54%
Oct 24	vs Purdue (55)	83%
Nov 7	vs Maryland (78)	89%
Nov 14	at Rutgers (113)	91%
Nov 21	vs Indiana (37)	75%
Nov 28	at Ohio St. (2)	21%

Projection Factors

2019 F/+	1.46 (12)
2019 FEI	0.85 (12)
2019 SP+	20.7 (10)
5-Year F/+	1.55 (7)
5-Year FEI	0.82 (7)
5-Year SP+	21.3 (7)
Weighted Recruiting	.926 (15)
Returning Offense	36% (119)
Returning Defense	49% (110)
Returning Total	43% (125)

Jim Harbaugh has had a reasonably solid run as the head coach of Michigan. The Wolverines have gone 47-19 under Jim Harbaugh over five years, 32-12 in the Big Ten, and 7-8 against their divisional rivals Michigan State, Penn State, and Ohio State. In truth, it's Michigan's 0-5 mark against Ohio State that is tarnishing the overall tenure of Harbaugh. The Wolverines are 7-3 against Michigan State and Penn State over this time.

The Shea Patterson era that was inaugurated when the one-time 5-star recruit transferred in from Ole Miss with two years of eligibility didn't really pan out for Michigan. Uniting him with new offensive coordinator and spread guru Josh Gattis yielded only a 9-4 season in 2019, and now Patterson's eligibility is up. In addition to losing Patterson, Michigan sent 10 players to the NFL draft, including four offensive linemen. Starting tight end Sean McKeon left early and was an undrafted free agent signing for the Dallas Cowboys.

Despite all that, the Wolverines return a tackle that largely limited No. 2 overall pick Chase Young in the rivalry game with Ohio State in Jalen Mayfield. Top receivers Ronnie Bell (48 catches for 758 yards and one touchdown) and Nico Collins (37 catches for 729 yards and seven touchdowns) are back. The returning platoon at running back of Zach Charbonnet and Hassin Haskins combined for 270 carries that yielded 1,348 yards at about five yards per carry and 15 rushing touchdowns. There's some intrigue around the program regarding who will take over at quarterback but it'll likely be redshirt junior Dylan McCaffrey, son of Denver Broncos wide receiver Ed McCaffrey and younger brother to Carolina running back Christian McCaffrey.

Michigan is now in the second year of a new RPO spread offense and is turning to a new generation of offensive starters with more athleticism across the board. The offensive line will be built from long, athletic players with redshirts. New weapons like slot receivers Mike Sainristil or Giles Jackson potentially bring more explosiveness to the equation than the squad has seen in years past.

The Wolverine defense has enjoyed multiple seasons now in which they dominated most of the Big Ten only to be taken completely apart by Ohio State. To help tweak and shore up the strategy and make it more Buckeye-resistant, Michigan added new hires Bob Shoop and Brian Jean-Mary. Shoop was the defensive coordinator at Vanderbilt and Penn State under James Franklin before coaching at Tennessee and Mississippi State. Jean-Mary has been an assistant under Charlie Strong for years and coordinated the South Florida defense. Both will bring a deep, working knowledge of zone coverages and zone blitzing to the man-pressure oriented defensive coordinator Don Brown.

They'll have a lot to work with, including seven returning starters, but will need to find more defensive tackles from their underclassman ranks and work out how to generate a pass rush. Two key departing pieces include weakside ends Josh Uche and Mike Danna and there aren't obvious replacements. Brown may need to brainstorm with Jean-Mary and develop a 3-3-5 scheme that takes advantage of Michigan's abundance of long defensive ends such as Kwity Paye (6-foot-4, 277 pounds, 6.5 sacks in 2019) and Aidan Hutchinson (6-foot-6, 270 pounds, three sacks in 2019).

Michigan is replacing a lot of talented, veteran players but it's possible that they could surprise if new starters like quarterback Dylan McCaffrey or linebacker Michael Barrett take flight in the new schemes. Among the tougher games on the schedule are an opening road trip to Washington, home dates against Wisconsin and Penn State, and road games against Minnesota and Ohio State.

13. Oregon Ducks (8.7 mean wins)

2020 F/+ Projections

#13	#30	#7
1.33	0.71	1.52
Overall	Offense	Defense

8.7	6.4
Mean Wins	Conf Wins

50%	29%	18%
Div Champ	Conf Champ	CFP Berth

1%	27%	99%
Undefeated	10+ Wins	6+ Wins

Projected Win Likelihood by Game

Date	Opponent (Proj Rank)	PWL	Projected Loss	Projected Win
Sep 5	vs N. Dakota St. (FCS)	100%		
Sep 12	vs Ohio St. (2)	30%		
Sep 19	vs Hawaii (99)	92%		
Sep 26	at Colorado (74)	78%		
Oct 3	vs Washington (15)	61%		
Oct 17	at California (51)	69%		
Oct 24	vs Stanford (50)	78%		
Oct 31	at Arizona (81)	79%		
Nov 7	vs USC (19)	63%		
Nov 13	vs Arizona St. (43)	75%		
Nov 21	at Washington St. (42)	64%		
Nov 28	at Oregon St. (76)	79%		

Projection Factors

2019 F/+	1.48 (11)
2019 FEI	0.96 (8)
2019 SP+	19.0 (15)
5-Year F/+	0.72 (27)
5-Year FEI	0.33 (27)
5-Year SP+	11.5 (25)
Weighted Recruiting	.937 (12)
Returning Offense	34% (124)
Returning Defense	81% (18)
Returning Total	57% (89)

The Ducks had a breakthrough season in 2019. They had two major factors driving their success and rise to Pac-12 champions under second-year head coach Mario Cristobal. The first was an offense powered by an offensive line with four seniors, two of which were drafted by the NFL, and four-year starting quarterback and first round draft pick Justin Herbert. The other major factor driving Oregon's rise was a defense that jumped from 43rd in FEI's defensive ratings in 2018 to sixth in 2019.

During the offseason before 2019, Cristobal fired defensive coordinator Jim Leavitt and brought in Andy Avalos from Boise State. Avalos put a big emphasis on getting athletes on the field and particularly on the edge, at times playing small up front while weighting the perimeter with outside linebackers in sub packages. That helped the Ducks hem in opposing rushing attacks, including opponents like Wisconsin, and pressure the passing game with zone blitzes.

Avalos has a lot of key pieces back from the terrific 2019 defense, headlined by rising sophomore defensive end Kayvon Thibodeaux, inside linebacker Isaac Slade-Matautia, and the top six defensive backs.

On offense the Ducks will be retooling. The main weapons, such as running back C.J. Verdell, top receivers Johnny Johnson and Jaylon Reed, are all back. The offensive line will return a top NFL prospect to man the left tackle position in rising junior Penei Sewell but everyone else will be a new starter and Herbert has to be replaced. Toward that end, the Ducks accepted grad transfer Anthony Brown from Boston College. Brown was a three-year starter for the Eagles who threw for 1,250 yards in six games in 2019 at 9.1 yards per attempt with nine touchdowns to two interceptions. He was also adept at executing some of the quarterback option plays that made a difference for the Ducks in 2019 in their postseason wins over Utah for the Pac-12 championship and over Wisconsin in the Rose Bowl. If Brown isn't up for the job, the Ducks have rising sophomore Tyler Shough, a former 4-star recruit from Arizona.

For the most part, Oregon's success in 2020 will hinge on how well they rebuild their offensive line. As it happens, Mario Cristobal was the former offensive line coach for Alabama in the mid-2010s and the Ducks have been recruiting well and have several big blue-chip prospects waiting in the wings.

The schedule has some challenges. The Ducks open against perennial FCS champion North Dakota State, whose quarterback Trey Lance is considered a potential No. 1 pick in 2021. Then they face Ohio State at home. Their Pac-12 rotation will bring Washington, Stanford, and USC all to their home stadium in Eugene, so even if they slip up early against the nonconference slate the Ducks will still have an advantage as they seek another Pac-12 championship.

14. Texas A&M Aggies (8.4 mean wins)

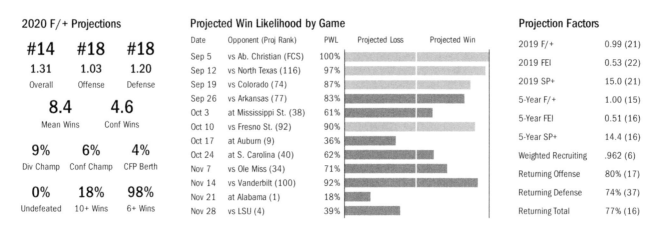

2020 F/+ Projections

#14	#18	#18
1.31	1.03	1.20
Overall	Offense	Defense

8.4	4.6
Mean Wins	Conf Wins

9%	6%	4%
Div Champ	Conf Champ	CFP Berth

0%	18%	98%
Undefeated	10+ Wins	6+ Wins

Projected Win Likelihood by Game

Date	Opponent (Proj Rank)	PWL
Sep 5	vs Ab. Christian (FCS)	100%
Sep 12	vs North Texas (116)	97%
Sep 19	vs Colorado (74)	87%
Sep 26	vs Arkansas (77)	83%
Oct 3	at Mississippi St. (38)	61%
Oct 10	vs Fresno St. (92)	90%
Oct 17	at Auburn (9)	36%
Oct 24	at S. Carolina (40)	62%
Nov 7	vs Ole Miss (34)	71%
Nov 14	vs Vanderbilt (100)	92%
Nov 21	at Alabama (1)	18%
Nov 28	vs LSU (4)	39%

Projection Factors

2019 F/+	0.99 (21)
2019 FEI	0.53 (22)
2019 SP+	15.0 (21)
5-Year F/+	1.00 (15)
5-Year FEI	0.51 (16)
5-Year SP+	14.4 (16)
Weighted Recruiting	.962 (6)
Returning Offense	80% (17)
Returning Defense	74% (37)
Returning Total	77% (16)

The Aggies had a really difficult setup in 2019 that effectively set a ceiling for what anything other than a really high-level team could hope to accomplish. Their schedule took them to Clemson before SEC conference play began, forced them to manage the normal SEC West gauntlet of facing Auburn (at home) and Alabama (at home), and concluded with back to back road trips to Georgia and LSU. Texas A&M came up empty in every single one of those high-profile games, leaving them with a 7-5 regular season devoid of a signature victory for head coach Jimbo Fisher in his second year in College Station.

Beyond the tough schedule, the Aggies also had to replace star running back Trayveon Williams, tight ends Jace Sternberger and Trevor Wood, and center Erik McCoy from the 2018 team on offense and a talented defensive line on defense. Those pieces on offense had been the driving force of a terrific rushing attack and in 2019 the Aggies had to start over, ultimately turning to true freshman running Isaiah Spiller after injury ended the season for Jashaun Corbin.

In 2020 the Aggies will be on firmer footing with five returning offensive linemen having starting experience, star sophomore tight end Jalen Wydermeyer back along with Spiller, and then fourth-year starting quarterback Kellen Mond. The quarterback position is a controversial one at A&M. Mond has had a very inconsistent tenure as a passer and threw 419 passes for 2,897 yards at 6.9 yards per attempt with 20 touchdowns and nine interceptions in 2019. In Texas A&M's five losses, Mond threw for 1,202 yards at 5.9 yards per attempt with six touchdowns and four interceptions. A&M will add 4-star freshman Haynes King to the rotation but it looks like Mond will continue to run the show as a senior in 2020. The team figures to be powered by sophomores from the highly rated 2019 class

such as Wydermeyer, Spiller, tight end Baylor Cupp, wide receiver Dylan Wright, and offensive lineman Kenyon Green.

The Aggies will likely continue to be a largely two-tight end team that emphasizes the run game, play-action to Wydermeyer, and ball control in order to shorten games and protect the defense. That's been the modus operandi under Fisher for the last few seasons and the Aggies will be better suited to execute that strategy with more experience across the tight ends and offensive line.

On defense, A&M had a tough rebuild from 2018, replacing multiple star linemen such as nose tackle Daylon Mack and defensive ends Kingsley Keke and Landis Durham. They reloaded with some younger reinforcements headlined by blue chip tackle DeMarvin Leal and nose guard Bobby Brown. Defensive coordinator John Chavis will be looking for them to make a leap in 2020 to anchor his 4-3 Under defense.

The struggle on this side of the ball for the Aggies is in the secondary, where A&M was revealed to be short on dominant skill athletes against teams like Alabama or LSU. They have Myles Jones back at cornerback, a uniquely tall defensive back at 6-foot-4 who had two interceptions and six pass breakups in 2019. He'll probably be joined by Elijah Blades, a juco transfer who played in spot duty. The safeties had some tough moments but return starters Demani Richards and Leon O'Neal and there are other options as well in sophomore Erick Young and senior Keldrick Carper.

Texas A&M's schedule is lighter outside of the conference with a home date against Colorado serving as the feature matchup. The SEC East draw will include Vanderbilt and South Carolina and then the Aggies will have to travel to Alabama twice to play both Auburn and Alabama before concluding the season at home against LSU.

15. Washington Huskies (8.2 mean wins)

2020 F/+ Projections

#15	#43	#8
1.16	0.38	1.52
Overall	Offense	Defense

8.2	5.9
Mean Wins	Conf Wins

28%	16%	10%
Div Champ	Conf Champ	CFP Berth

0%	19%	98%
Undefeated	10+ Wins	6+ Wins

Projected Win Likelihood by Game

Date	Opponent (Proj Rank)	PWL
Sep 5	vs Michigan (12)	50%
Sep 12	vs Sacramento St. (FCS)	100%
Sep 19	vs Utah St. (95)	89%
Oct 3	at Oregon (13)	39%
Oct 10	vs Oregon St. (76)	85%
Oct 17	at Utah (17)	46%
Oct 23	vs Arizona (81)	85%
Oct 31	at California (51)	65%
Nov 7	vs Stanford (50)	74%
Nov 14	at USC (19)	46%
Nov 21	vs Colorado (74)	85%
Nov 27	at Washington St. (42)	60%

Projection Factors

2019 F/+	1.19 (17)
2019 FEI	0.63 (18)
2019 SP+	18.3 (16)
5-Year F/+	1.41 (9)
5-Year FEI	0.76 (10)
5-Year SP+	19.3 (11)
Weighted Recruiting	.914 (17)
Returning Offense	30% (127)
Returning Defense	74% (39)
Returning Total	52% (104)

The 2019 season proved to be the last for Washington's head coach Chris Petersen. He announced his retirement before facing his former school (Boise State) and assistant (Bryan Harsin) in the bowl game. The Huskies won big, 38-7, and Petersen stepped down as head coach. Washington promoted defensive coordinator Jimmy Lake to replace him.

It wasn't likely to get better for Petersen in 2020. The Huskies lose both tackles, quarterback Jacob Eason, top wide receivers Aaron Fuller and Andrew Baccellia, running back Salvon Ahmed, and star tight end Hunter Bryant from the 2019 offense to graduation and/or the NFL. New head coach Lake started in Washington as the defensive backs coach and was eventually named co-coordinator alongside Pete Kwiatkowski. His offensive staff will be revamped with the hire of John Donovan from the Jacksonville Jaguars to renovate Washington's pro-style offense.

In 2020 the Huskies will essentially be starting over on offense but Donovan will inherit a pair of starting guards along the offensive line and several redshirted replacements rising up the ranks, plus experienced tight ends Cade Otton (32 catches for 344 yards and two touchdowns in 2019) and Jacob Kizer. Running back Richard Newton was the backup to Salvon Ahmed in 2019 and ran for 498 yards at 4.3 yards per carry with 10 rushing touchdowns. The receiving room will retool but quarterback is the main question mark. Donovan will be choosing between big 6-foot-5 Jacob Sirmon, a redshirt sophomore who was Eason's

backup in 2019, or redshirt freshman Dylan Morris.

The offense will primarily be asked to run and protect the football while paired with the Huskies' always stout defense. Washington ranked 16th in defensive FEI in 2019 after sending five starters to the NFL. For 2020 they'll have seven starters back, including star nickelback Elijah Molden (lead tackler with 79, four interceptions, 12 pass breakups) and pass-rushing outside linebackers Joe Tryon (12.5 TFLs, eight sacks) and Ryan Bowman (9.5 TFLs, 6.5 sacks).

Under Lake, the Huskies have become known for their defensive backs and stout defensive line play. The line returns Levi Onwuzurike and will pair him with tackle Tuli Letuligasenoa while moving in younger inside linebackers behind them. Things will hinge on the play of the secondary in Lake's single-high coverage schemes. At corner, the Huskies return Keith Taylor and Trent McDuffie, and at safety they will play a pair of true sophomores in Asa Turner and Cameron Williams who also both played regularly in 2019. It will be a young unit on both sides of the ball in Year 1 for the Lake era.

The schedule opens with a visit from the Michigan Wolverines and then will challenge the young roster with road games against Utah, USC, Oregon, and rival Washington State. It's a brutal slate for a young team under a first-year head coach and the Huskies may have to accept another 7-5 sort of season in order to retool and gain experience before attempting to charge back in 2021.

16. Texas Longhorns (7.8 mean wins)

2020 F/+ Projections

#16	#11	#36
1.11	1.33	0.61
Overall	Offense	Defense

7.8	5.7
Mean Wins	Conf Wins

-	16%	7%
Div Champ	Conf Champ	CFP Berth

0%	13%	93%
Undefeated	10+ Wins	6+ Wins

Projected Win Likelihood by Game

Date	Opponent (Proj Rank)	PWL
Sep 5	vs S. Florida (84)	85%
Sep 12	at LSU (4)	24%
Sep 19	vs UTEP (129)	99%
Oct 3	at Kansas St. (44)	60%
Oct 10	vs Oklahoma (8)	36%
Oct 17	vs W. Virginia (61)	79%
Oct 24	at Texas Tech (56)	67%
Oct 31	vs Baylor (25)	63%
Nov 7	at Kansas (110)	86%
Nov 14	vs TCU (28)	65%
Nov 21	vs Iowa St. (26)	64%
Nov 27	at Oklahoma St. (22)	48%

Projection Factors

2019 F/+	0.94 (22)
2019 FEI	0.60 (20)
2019 SP+	12.0 (26)
5-Year F/+	0.64 (31)
5-Year FEI	0.32 (29)
5-Year SP+	9.6 (32)
Weighted Recruiting	.958 (8)
Returning Offense	66% (62)
Returning Defense	82% (14)
Returning Total	74% (21)

This is going to be a big season for Tom Herman's Texas program. Quarterback Sam Ehlinger announced that Texas was "back" after a 10-4 season in 2018 and a Sugar Bowl victory over Georgia. Then the Longhorns slipped to 8-5 in 2019 with high profile defeats against LSU, Oklahoma, Iowa State, and Baylor along with an embarrassing road loss against a 5-7 TCU team.

For 2020, Texas returns Ehlinger for his senior season after he threw for 3,663 yards with 32 touchdowns and 10 interceptions in 2019 while running for 663 yards and seven more touchdowns. Ehlinger's top receivers Devin Duvernay and Collin Johnson were drafted by the NFL but young targets Brennan Eagles (32 catches for 522 yards, six touchdowns) and Jake Smith (25 catches for 274 yards, six touchdowns) are back. The Longhorns will also supplement them with former 5-star redshirt freshman Jordan Whittington, who was expected to be a major weapon in 2019 before being afflicted by a sports hernia in preseason camp, and Michigan transfer Tarik Black (25 catches for 323 yards, one touchdown in 2019).

Ehlinger will have the benefit of his left tackle Sam Cosmi returning along with two other starters, guard Junior Angilau and right tackle Derek Kerstetter (who's expected to slide inside to center). In the backfield he'll be working alongside the top two tight ends from 2019 and a running back tandem of Keaontay Ingram and Roschon Johnson that combined for 267 carries for 1,502 yards at 5.6 yards per carry with 14 touchdowns. Texas even adds a 5-star recruit, Bijan Robinson of Arizona, to join Ingram and Johnson. To help make sure all of these weapons come together, Herman hired offensive

coordinator Mike Yurcich from Ohio State (formerly of Oklahoma State). The Big 12 has tended to be won in the 2010s by the team with the most potent offense and this should be the strongest Longhorn offensive unit since Colt McCoy was on campus.

Texas' defense was also overhauled after a rough 2019. Herman fired defensive coordinator Todd Orlando and replaced him with his former staff mate at Ohio State Chris Ash, who was fired as the Rutgers head coach during 2019. Ash will be simplifying Texas' 3-3-5/3-2-6, zone-blitzing defense into a 4-2-5 quarters scheme with a fresh emphasis on fundamentals.

Two of the biggest pieces to this puzzle and possible beneficiaries of the defensive changes include rising juniors DeMarvion Overshown and Joseph Ossai. Overshown missed some of 2019 with injury and is a 6-foot-4, 210-pound former safety that Ash and his new defensive staff will be looking to develop into a weakside linebacker. Ossai was Texas' leading tackler in 2019 with 90 tackles, 13.5 TFLs, five sacks, and two interceptions. At 6-foot-4 and 250 pounds Ossai is a natural edge rusher, but Texas moved him to nickel linebacker and weak inside linebacker at various points in the season before finally allowing him to play on the edge in the Alamo Bowl against Utah. In that game Ossai had nine tackles, six of which were tackles for loss and three of which were sacks.

Texas' track record of late has been to bungle their talent and resource advantages but to do so again in 2020 would be their greatest failure to date. It should be possible to fit all the pieces together into a squad that makes a major leap and competes for the Big 12 title and the playoffs.

17. Utah Utes (8.5 mean wins)

2020 F/+ Projections

#17	#25	#25
1.05	0.83	0.96
Overall	Offense	Defense

8.5	6.0
Mean Wins	Conf Wins

45%	19%	12%
Div Champ	Conf Champ	CFP Berth

1%	23%	99%
Undefeated	10+ Wins	6+ Wins

Projected Win Likelihood by Game

Date	Opponent (Proj Rank)	PWL	Projected Loss	Projected Win
Sep 5	vs BYU (60)	78%		
Sep 12	vs Montana St. (FCS)	100%		
Sep 19	at Wyoming (79)	74%		
Sep 26	at California (51)	63%		
Oct 2	vs USC (19)	57%		
Oct 10	at Washington St. (42)	58%		
Oct 17	vs Washington (15)	54%		
Oct 29	at UCLA (62)	67%		
Nov 7	vs Arizona (81)	84%		
Nov 14	vs Oregon St. (76)	83%		
Nov 21	at Arizona St. (43)	58%		
Nov 28	at Colorado (74)	73%		

Projection Factors

2019 F/+	1.46 (13)
2019 FEI	0.91 (10)
2019 SP+	19.5 (12)
5-Year F/+	0.93 (18)
5-Year FEI	0.46 (18)
5-Year SP+	14.1 (17)
Weighted Recruiting	.720 (31)
Returning Offense	48% (105)
Returning Defense	27% (130)
Returning Total	37% (130)

On December 5, 2019, the Utah Utes were one win away from a playoff berth, the crown jewel of Kyle Wittingham's unassumingly sparkling resume. On December 7, the Utah Utes found themselves bound instead for the Alamo Bowl to play a seven-win team from the Big 12's middle class.

It's hard not to see 2019 as a ceiling for the Utes: USC and Washington both had down years, and a favorable home schedule had the Utes representing the South Division at 10-1. A 37-15 loss to Oregon in the Pac-12 Championship relegated Utah to the Alamo Bowl.

It seems a place of privilege to frame an 11-3 season and a top 15 finish as a disappointment, but that is a testament to Kyle Wittingham's job at building and maintaining the Utah program. Wittingham took over for Urban Meyer in 2004, and since then, has won ten games five times, and at least nine games nine times. When Utah left the Mountain West for the Pac-12, the Utes initially struggled, but they have rebounded and rebuilt under Wittingham, maintaining consistent top-40 recruiting classes and winning nine games in five of the last six seasons.

The 2019 Utes represented the top of Utah's recruiting cycle and demonstrated what the Utes could be, nationally, given a core of skill players at their full potential. 2019's offense featured a three-headed monster of seniors: quarterback Tyler Huntley (73.1% completion rate, 19 touchdowns, 3,023 yards), running back Zack Moss (1,735 all-purpose yards, 17 touchdowns, 6.0 yards/carry), and receiver Demari Simpkins (32 catches, 352 yards, 76.2% catch rate, 2 touchdowns). Moss was drafted in the third round, Huntley signed as a free agent with the Baltimore Ravens, and Simpkins graduated, leaving an effectual void in the Ute offense for 2020.

The most obvious fill to that void is South Carolina graduate transfer Jake Bentley. Bentley, a three-year starter in the SEC East, found himself sidelined in 2019 with a foot injury, and looks to plug into Utah's offense as the starting quarterback. Junior Jason Shelley, a former 3-star dual-threat prospect, will compete for the job, but Bentley's experience should win out in the short term. Consider this a positional battle, though, as Tyler Huntley left some large shoes to fill. In the running game, rising junior Devin Brumfield took most of the non-Moss carries last fall (263 yards on 59 carries, two touchdowns), and at 5-foot-10, 218 pounds, matches Moss' body type and playing style well. In a run-heavy Utah offense, though, don't be surprised to see sophomore Jordan Wilmore, a smaller and speedier back, get involved in stretching the field horizontally, as well as the passing game. Tight end Brant Kuithe (44 targets, 602 yards, 6 TDs, 77.3% catch rate) returns for his junior season as a staple of the passing game, whoever the quarterback is. Along the offensive line, the Utes return three of five starters.

On defense, the Utes ranked third in EPA/play in the 2019 season, one of just 19 Power Five teams who held opponents to negative numbers (-0.094), but they lost eight of their top 11 tacklers. The defense will be a shuffle, given substantial loss of production, the short offseason, and the uncertainty at defensive coordinator. Junior Devin Lloyd, the team's leading tackler in 2019 (67.5 tackles, 11.0 TFLs, 6.5 sacks), will be the anchor of the 2020 Utah defense, paired with cornerback Javelin Guidry, the lone returner of an outstanding secondary (-0.061 EPA/pass in 2019). Along the defensive line, Junior Mike Tafua (8.5 TFLs, 3 sacks in 2019) will lead the way.

The Utes host USC and Washington in 2020, along with rival BYU. Their schedule is relatively light outside of those three games—a trip to Berkley to face California should have ramifications for the Pac-12 South's pecking order, and traveling to Arizona State and Colorado in back-to-back weekends to close the season might prove tricky. The Utes have plenty of question marks headed into the 2020 season, and Kyle Wittingham has raised their floor. Replicating the success of 2019 seems possible but will rely on Utah's new offense gelling quickly.

18. Iowa Hawkeyes (7.3 mean wins)

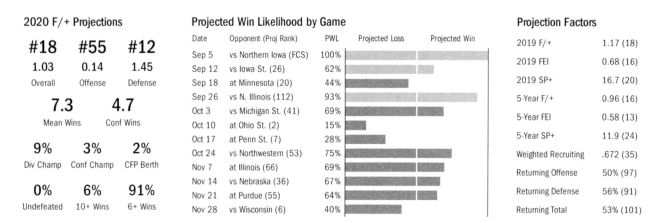

2020 F/+ Projections

#18	#55	#12
1.03	0.14	1.45
Overall	Offense	Defense

7.3	4.7
Mean Wins	Conf Wins

9%	3%	2%
Div Champ	Conf Champ	CFP Berth

0%	6%	91%
Undefeated	10+ Wins	6+ Wins

Projected Win Likelihood by Game

Date	Opponent (Proj Rank)	PWL	Projected Loss	Projected Win
Sep 5	vs Northern Iowa (FCS)	100%		
Sep 12	vs Iowa St. (26)	62%		
Sep 18	at Minnesota (20)	44%		
Sep 26	vs N. Illinois (112)	93%		
Oct 3	vs Michigan St. (41)	69%		
Oct 10	at Ohio St. (2)	15%		
Oct 17	at Penn St. (7)	28%		
Oct 24	vs Northwestern (53)	75%		
Nov 7	at Illinois (66)	69%		
Nov 14	vs Nebraska (36)	67%		
Nov 21	at Purdue (55)	64%		
Nov 28	vs Wisconsin (6)	40%		

Projection Factors

2019 F/+	1.17 (18)
2019 FEI	0.68 (16)
2019 SP+	16.7 (20)
5-Year F/+	0.96 (16)
5-Year FEI	0.58 (13)
5-Year SP+	11.9 (24)
Weighted Recruiting	.672 (35)
Returning Offense	50% (97)
Returning Defense	56% (91)
Returning Total	53% (101)

Iowa finished third in the Big Ten in 2019, 6-3 in conference, with losses at Michigan, to Penn State, and to West Division Champion Wisconsin. They beat unexpected contender Minnesota and were largely responsible for keeping the Gophers out of the Big Ten Championship game. 6-3, third in the division, beating the teams they should and some that they shouldn't; the 2019 season was perfectly emblematic of Kirk Ferentz's Iowa. Ferentz's teams have won nine games in eleven of his 21 seasons in Iowa City.

The 2019 Hawkeyes displayed that remarkable Ferentz consistency, hallmarked by a stifling defense. Iowa ranked 15th in EPA/play on defense (-0.015), 20th against the rush and 18th against the pass. The Hawkeye defense held nine opponents to 20 or fewer points in 2019, led by junior defensive ends A.J. Epenesa (14.5 TFLs, 11.5 sacks) and Chauncey Golston (9.5 TFLs, 36.5 tackles). Epenesa is off to the NFL for 2020, but Golston returns as the anchor of an experienced defensive line that created over 45 havoc plays last season. That line includes junior Daviyon Nixon and seniors Austin Schulte and Zach VanValkenburg. Leading tackler Kristian Welch (65 tackles, 9 TFLs, 3 sacks, 3 pass breakups) leaves a hole at linebacker for the Hawkeyes, likely to be filled by rising junior Djimon Colbert, responsible for 47.5 tackles last season. Given Iowa's recent switch to base out of 4-2-5 on defense, Colbert's role will expand. Backing up Colbert in the secondary, strong safety Dane Belton (26.5 tackles, 2.5 TFLs) will be the flexible linebacker-defensive back hybrid necessary for the 4-2-5. Belton saw some time in that role last season, especially in the second half, but the transition to full-time base 4-2-5 will be tricky, especially with the shortened offseason.

Under senior quarterback Nate Stanley, Iowa's offense was consistent, but not quite good. Iowa's passing offense and rushing offense both ranked in the bottom half of EPA/play (53rd in rushing at -0.021 EPA/rush and 37th in passing at 0.094 EPA/

pass). Stanley, in his final year at Iowa, completed 59.4% of his passes for 2,951 yards and 16 touchdowns. His replacement this year will be rising junior Spencer Petras, who's had two years in the system to learn and should be capable of taking over the offense on Day 1. Petras is in the traditional mold of Iowa quarterbacks: the 6-foot-5, 230-pound quarterback was a 3-star commit out of California known for his pocket passing abilities. Though Stanley is gone, his seven favorite targets return. Two seniors will lead the receiving corps: Ihmir Smith-Marsette (722 yards, 58.7% catch rate, five touchdowns in 2019), along with Brandon Smith (439 yards, 63.8% catch rate, 5 touchdowns in 2019), but the weapons don't end there. Petras will also have productive sophomores Nico Ragaini (59.7% catch rate, 439 yards) and Tyrone Tracy Jr. (55.4% catch rate, 589 yards, three touchdowns) to throw to. There's a satisfying symmetry about Iowa's wide receivers: Smith, Tracy, and Ragaini all have similar bodies for outside receivers, whereas Smith-Marsette provides a nice speed option. One would be remiss to mention Iowa and not focus on the running game. The Hawkeyes return sophomore Tyler Goodson, who averaged 4.8 yards per carry and scored four touchdowns on the season, as well as Mekhi Sargent (4.7 yards.carry, four touchdowns), a bigger back who can complement Goodson's speed game.

Iowa travels to Ohio State, Penn State, and Minnesota this year, three games which will be a tall task for a first-time starting quarterback, but Iowa's defense held Penn State and Minnesota to 17 and 19 points, respectively last season, and looks to be as good if not better in 2020. If the transition to the 4-2-5 allows Iowa to maintain the same consistent defense while adding personnel flexibility, Iowa's offense will have a longer leash to let the new quarterback find rhythm with the experienced receivers. Expect the last game of the season when Iowa hosts Wisconsin to have large ramifications for who moves on to the Big Ten title game.

19. USC Trojans (7.2 mean wins)

2020 F/+ Projections

#19	#7	#41
1.03	1.42	0.47
Overall	Offense	Defense

7.2	5.6
Mean Wins	Conf Wins

33%	14%	7%
Div Champ	Conf Champ	CFP Berth

0%	6%	87%
Undefeated	10+ Wins	6+ Wins

Projected Win Likelihood by Game

Date	Opponent (Proj Rank)	PWL	Projected Loss	Projected Win
Sep 5	vs Alabama (1)	18%		
Sep 12	vs N. Mexico (122)	98%		
Sep 19	at Stanford (50)	60%		
Sep 26	vs Arizona St. (43)	70%		
Oct 2	at Utah (17)	43%		
Oct 10	vs California (51)	74%		
Oct 17	at Arizona (81)	73%		
Oct 31	vs Colorado (74)	83%		
Nov 7	at Oregon (13)	37%		
Nov 14	vs Washington (15)	54%		
Nov 21	at UCLA (62)	67%		
Nov 28	vs Notre Dame (11)	46%		

Projection Factors

2019 F/+	0.80 (25)
2019 FEI	0.38 (30)
2019 SP+	13.1 (22)
5-Year F/+	1.03 (14)
5-Year FEI	0.45 (19)
5-Year SP+	16.2 (14)
Weighted Recruiting	.712 (32)
Returning Offense	77% (25)
Returning Defense	87% (7)
Returning Total	82% (5)

Kedon Slovis went from USC backup to Heisman contender in the course of one season. Rising sophomore Slovis took over for the injured J.T. Daniels in the opening game, and after a rocky loss to BYU, Slovis (71.9% completion rate, 3502 yards, 30 touchdowns in 2019) established himself as one of the premier quarterbacks in college football. The Trojans went on to upset Southern Division rival Utah and won five of their last six regular-season games, not counting a shocking Holiday Bowl loss to Iowa.

Slovis had a great supporting cast, and once he settled in, he made use. Second-round pick Michael Pittman Jr. led the team in targets and touchdowns, but the second- and third-most targeted receivers return: Tyler Vaughns (108 targets, 68.5% catch rate, 912 yards, 6 touchdowns) will be back as a redshirt senior and highly touted draft prospect Amon-Ra St. Brown (1042 yards, 73.3% catch rate, 6 touchdowns) will return for one more year as a junior.

In his second year, offensive coordinator Graham Harrell will have the opportunity to improve an already impressive offense. The Trojans ranked 14th in EPA/play on offense, 10th in EPA/pass (0.280). Eight receivers who caught a touchdown pass in 2019 return for the 2020 season, along with every player who gained a rushing yard last season. Along the offensive line, the Trojans lost first-round pick Austin Jackson and third-round pick Chuma Edoga, meaning new faces will start at both tackle positions, but the Trojans return plenty of experience, including outstanding guard Alijah Vera-Tucker and two-year starter Andrew Vorhees, who was injured all last season and may switch from guard to tackle. Given the turnover, offensive line seems to be the only weak point of a Trojans offense expected to be one of the best in the country.

On the other side of the ball, though, we must confront Clay Helton's recent issue of fielding a competitive defense. In Helton's first two full seasons, the Trojans finished 9th and 24th in SP+ defense, whereas the last two seasons have featured units ranked 34th and 60th. To ameliorate the defensive dropoff, Helton hired former Texas defensive coordinator Todd Orlando to take charge. Orlando, known for his development of talent at Utah State and Houston, comes to USC after a rocky stint at the University of Texas. He brings an aggressive defensive style, one that might fit the style of the Pac-12 well, but his three-down base defense will require some tinkering with the current roster. The defense will turn to junior safeties Talanoa Hufanga (74 tackles, 3.5 sacks, and 3 pass breakups) and Isaiah Pola-Mao (58 tackles, 4 interceptions) to lead the secondary, while linebacker Drake Jackson, a sophomore, will anchor the linebackers. There is good talent and depth along the defensive line, even if it may not align perfectly to Orlando's scheme, as almost the entire rotation returns: 2019 sacks leader Drake Jackson returns for his sophomore season (11.5 TFLs, 5.5 sacks), joined by juniors Marlong Tuipulotu and Jay Tufele (combined 6.5 sacks, 12.5 TFLs, and 64.5 tackles), either of whom can man the nose tackle position.

USC has the right mix of returning talent on offense and some new life on defense for 2020. With a rising star in Slovis, the Trojans are poised to return to the Pac-12 title game after a two-year absence. The pressures of a blue-blood program like USC are evident, as Helton's job security has been a frequent source of discussion, and those rumors are not likely to die this season: the Trojans face a massive test with Alabama in Week 1. The season is bookended by a visit from Notre Dame, and if the Trojans can escape conference play (trips to Oregon and Utah, and hosting Washington), they'll have the strength of schedule capital to make the playoff with one loss. 2020 USC football has the talent and the breathing room to compete for the Pac-12 title and their first playoff berth.

20. Minnesota Golden Gophers (7.8 mean wins)

2020 F/+ Projections

#20	#6	#44
0.99	1.49	0.40
Overall	Offense	Defense

7.8	5.3
Mean Wins	Conf Wins

17%	6%	4%
Div Champ	Conf Champ	CFP Berth

0%	13%	94%
Undefeated	10+ Wins	6+ Wins

Projected Win Likelihood by Game

Date	Opponent (Proj Rank)	PWL	Projected Loss	Projected Win
Sep 3	vs Florida Atlantic (63)	78%		
Sep 12	vs Tenn. Tech (FCS)	100%		
Sep 18	vs Iowa (18)	56%		
Sep 26	vs BYU (60)	77%		
Oct 3	at Maryland (78)	72%		
Oct 10	at Wisconsin (6)	27%		
Oct 17	vs Michigan (12)	46%		
Oct 24	at Illinois (66)	69%		
Oct 31	at Michigan St. (41)	56%		
Nov 7	vs Purdue (55)	75%		
Nov 21	vs Northwestern (53)	74%		
Nov 27	at Nebraska (36)	53%		

Projection Factors

2019 F/+	1.27 (15)
2019 FEI	0.68 (15)
2019 SP+	19.4 (13)
5-Year F/+	0.57 (34)
5-Year FEI	0.25 (35)
5-Year SP+	9.4 (34)
Weighted Recruiting	.641 (41)
Returning Offense	82% (13)
Returning Defense	33% (125)
Returning Total	58% (86)

P.J. Fleck came to Minnesota after a 13-1 season at Western Michigan, where he took the Broncos to the first New Year's Six bowl a MAC team had participated in. Since then, Fleck has improved Minnesota's win total, culminating in an 11-win 2019 campaign. Fleck has brought the recruiting along with him, as well: Minnesota's class ranked 12th in the conference, 59th nationally when he arrived, and the Gophers have signed five blue-chip recruits since, including 2019 all-conference receiver Rashad Bateman. On the shoulders of Bateman (94 targets, 1,219 yards, 11 touchdowns) and Tyler Johnson (117 targets, 73.5% catch rate, 13 touchdowns and 1,318 yards, a fifth-round draft pick), Minnesota found an offensive explosion in 2019. Redshirt junior quarterback Tanner Morgan completed 66% of his passes for 30 touchdowns and 3,253 yards and the Gophers ranked fifth in offensive EPA/play in the Power Five last season, second in EPA/pass. The rushing attack, led by senior Rodney Smith (eight touchdowns, 1,163 yards, 5.1 yards per carry), punished opponents for committing to the pass. Smith signed with the Carolina Panthers an undrafted free agent, but his backfield complement, rising sophomore Mohamed Ibrahim (604 yards, 5.3 yards per carry, seven touchdowns) returns, poised to take the rushing workload.

The looming shadow over the Minnesota offense is the departure of offensive coordinator Kirk Ciarroca. After three successful seasons at Minnesota, Ciarocca took the same job at Penn State for the 2020 season. In Minneapolis to replace him is Mike Sanford Jr., a long-time coach who most recently coached Jordan Love at Utah State. Sanford will share coordinating duties with co-offensive coordinator Matt Simon, so while there will be turnover, the offense has some consistency in terms of philosophy.

On the defensive side of the ball, the Gophers found some consistent success under Joseph Rossi: 20th in EPA/play (0.006), 21st against the rush and 15th against the pass. Defensive back Antoine Winfield Jr., left for the NFL draft, as did linebackers Kamal Martin and Carter Caughlin. Minnesota loses six of seven leading tacklers from 2019. Rising junior Jordan Howden (48.5 tackles, 6 pass breakups) will be the backbone of the secondary and rising junior Coney Durr (10 pass breakups in 2019) will man one of the corner spots. The Gophers will have to replace all three linebackers, and four rotation defensive linemen.

The Gophers had a season far above their expectations—11 wins is their highest total since 2000, and seven conference wins is nearly unimaginable in the modern Big Ten—and ended the season with a convincing upset of SEC West power Auburn, but the year still held twinges of disappointment, as a one-score loss at Iowa and a second-half stall against Wisconsin left the Gophers on the outside looking in at the Big Ten Championship Game. In 2020, the Gophers' schedule is tightly packed in the middle. They'll host Iowa in September and play Wisconsin and Michigan in back-to-back games in October. The question for Minnesota's season will be how seamlessly they can integrate a new offensive coordinator while maintaining defensive strength. They have as much, if not more, offensive experience than all three of those opponents, and the difference between 2-1 and 1-2 in those three games may be the difference between a New Year's Six bowl and a postseason trip to Tampa.

21. Memphis Tigers (8.8 mean wins)

2020 F/+ Projections

#21	#9	#49
0.97	1.38	0.30
Overall	Offense	Defense

8.8	5.4
Mean Wins	Conf Wins

-	26%	1%
Div Champ	Conf Champ	CFP Berth

2%	32%	99%
Undefeated	10+ Wins	6+ Wins

Projected Win Likelihood by Game

Date	Opponent (Proj Rank)	PWL
Sep 5	vs Arkansas St. (93)	86%
Sep 12	at Purdue (55)	63%
Sep 19	vs Houston (58)	76%
Sep 26	at UTSA (123)	93%
Oct 1	at SMU (57)	64%
Oct 16	vs UCF (23)	58%
Oct 24	vs Temple (70)	79%
Oct 31	at Cincinnati (39)	54%
Nov 7	vs S. Florida (84)	83%
Nov 14	at Navy (45)	57%
Nov 21	vs UT Martin (FCS)	100%
Nov 28	at Tulane (73)	70%

Projection Factors

2019 F/+	1.17 (19)
2019 FEI	0.62 (19)
2019 SP+	18.0 (17)
5-Year F/+	0.71 (28)
5-Year FEI	0.37 (23)
5-Year SP+	10.1 (30)
Weighted Recruiting	.371 (70)
Returning Offense	69% (54)
Returning Defense	77% (29)
Returning Total	73% (29)

2019 was Mike Norvell's *magnum opus* at Memphis. In his fourth season, Norvell finally conjured the right mix of offense and defense to take advantage of a wide-open American Athletic Conference and earn the Group of 5's New Year's Six bowl bid. The Tigers employed a ruthless and fast offensive attack (8th in SP+), scoring 35 or more points in 10 games, and the defense did enough to let the offense win shootouts. Their only regular-season loss came in a weird game at Temple, where the Tigers gave up four turnovers in a one-score loss, and they beat Cincinnati twice in a row to end their season and win the conference championship. Norvell went on to take the Florida State job after a stint in Memphis where he won 38 games and went to four straight bowl games, including Memphis' first New Year's Six bowl in program history.

Taking over for Norvell is longtime assistant Ryan Silverfield, who has experience in the NFL with the Detroit Lions and Minnesota Vikings, in addition to his eight years coaching in college. Silverfield is a continuity hire, looking to maintain the success of Norvell's offense in 2020 and develop the defense.

Quarterback Brady White returns for his senior season after a breakout 2019 campaign. White completed 64% of his passes for 4,014 yards and 33 touchdowns, earning second-team All-Conference honors in a year with historical quarterback depth in the AAC. White relied heavily on Antonio Gibson, the third-round 2020 draft pick who averaged 19.3 yards per catch and scored eight touchdowns in 2019. White's preferred target, wide receiver Damonte Coxie (173 targets, 1292 yards, nine touchdowns) is poised for a stellar 2020; the senior Coxie and White are among the more experienced batteries in the AAC. White will also have options to choose from, with senior Sean Dykes taking over for Joey Magnifico at tight end and explosive secondary receivers in senior Pop Williams and junior Calvin Austin (18.5 yards per catch in 2019).

The rushing game will again be driven by rising sophomore Kenneth Gainwell (1,459 yards, thirteen touchdowns,

6.3 yards per carry), who shared duties with the bigger-bodied Patrick Taylor Jr. Taylor signed as an undrafted free agent with the Green Bay Packers, and his probable replacement is Rodrigues Clark, a freshman who saw only 26 carries in 2019, mostly in short-yardage situations. Junior Kylan Watkins, a similar rusher to Gainwell, will help share the rushing load and provide multiple dimensions to Memphis' offense; the Tigers under Norvell have a long history of getting the running backs involved in the passing game, as well, and Watkins provides that level of versatility. The offensive line will return three starters and plenty of depth, providing continuity suggestive of a high ceiling for 2019.

Memphis returns eleven starters on defense, and although the unit struggled relative to Memphis' recent defensive prowess, the Tigers will field a stout 2020 attack. Former Ole Miss coordinator Mike McIntyre takes over as the defensive coordinator this season. The secondary will be led by four-year starter T.J. Carter at cornerback. Carter had a breakout 2017, but since then has been merely good. Senior linebacker JJ Russell is a run-stopping force who can get in the backfield (47 tackles, 5.5 TFLs). Replacing defensive end Bryce Huff will be the biggest challenge for the defense: Huff had 15.5 TFLs and led the team in sacks with 15.5. McIntyre runs a 3-4 base defense; lineman Joseph Dorceus may be able to shift outside and provide pressure for the Tigers.

American Athletic Conference rivals Cincinnati, UCF, and SMU will all compete for the top spot in 2019, and all are similar to Memphis with their experienced quarterbacks and consistent defenses. The AAC West may be tougher than anticipated, as well, with an improving Tulane and Houston, as well as the ever-competitive Navy, even as the Midshipmen replace an excellent quarterback. Still, the Tigers are in the driver's seat for the division in 2020, and Silverfield has continuity in his favor. The floor for Memphis in 2020 is very high, and a repeat of 2019's New Year's Six bowl berth will be within their grasp.

22. Oklahoma State Cowboys (7.8 mean wins)

2020 F/+ Projections

#22	#16	#38
0.93	1.13	0.50
Overall	Offense	Defense

7.8	5.2
Mean Wins	Conf Wins

-	10%	4%
Div Champ	Conf Champ	CFP Berth

0%	13%	94%
Undefeated	10+ Wins	6+ Wins

Projected Win Likelihood by Game

Date	Opponent (Proj Rank)	PWL	Projected Loss	Projected Win
Sep 3	vs Oregon St. (76)	81%		
Sep 12	vs Tulsa (75)	81%		
Sep 19	vs W. Illinois (FCS)	100%		
Oct 3	at TCU (28)	48%		
Oct 10	vs Iowa St. (26)	60%		
Oct 17	at Kansas (110)	83%		
Oct 24	at Oklahoma (8)	27%		
Oct 31	vs Texas Tech (56)	74%		
Nov 7	at Baylor (25)	45%		
Nov 14	vs W. Virginia (61)	76%		
Nov 21	at Kansas St. (44)	56%		
Nov 27	vs Texas (16)	52%		

Projection Factors

2019 F/+	0.66 (31)
2019 FEI	0.41 (27)
2019 SP+	8.7 (36)
5-Year F/+	0.93 (19)
5-Year FEI	0.47 (17)
5-Year SP+	13.6 (19)
Weighted Recruiting	.636 (42)
Returning Offense	75% (34)
Returning Defense	86% (8)
Returning Total	80% (9)

The Oklahoma State Cowboys narrowly missed their 9-3 projection last season but the story coming out of 2019 was not one of underachievement. The Cowboys fielded a 2,000-yard rusher in Chuba Hubbard, redshirt freshman quarterback Spencer Sanders threw for 2,065 yards and rushed for 628 in 10 games before injury, and wide receiver Tylan Wallace had 903 receiving yards and eight touchdowns in just eight games.

Hubbard and Wallace elected to forego the draft and return to Oklahoma State for another year with head coach Mike Gundy. Sanders will also have his No. 2 receiver Dillon Stoner (52 catches for 599 yards, five touchdowns) and No. 3 receiver Braydon Johnson (23 catches for 491 yards, four touchdowns) back. The offensive line will return tackles Dylan Galloway and Teven Jenkins and add West Virginia transfer and former All-Big 12 guard Josh Sills. This has the potential to be one of the most talented offenses yet in a long line of brilliant Oklahoma State offensive units.

The main factor which has prevented Gundy's Cowboys from winning the Big 12 since their 2011 season with Brandon Weeden and Justin Blackmon has been the lack of a top defense. Things are more promising than usual on that end as well. Oklahoma State found a strong backfield trio in 2019 with safety Kolby Harvel-Peel (five sacks, 13 pass breakups), linebacker Malcolm Rodriguez (103 tackles, seven TFLs), and linebacker Amen Ogbongbemiga (100 tackles, 15.5 TFLs, five sacks). In the pass rush, they settled on true freshman Trace Ford at the end of the year and he had three sacks while showing an elite level of explosiveness off the edge.

Third-year defensive coordinator Jim Knowles has tended to play the percentages with their defensive schemes. By moving former safety Rodriguez to linebacker, he gave the defense a base dime identity. Up front he's tended to play four-down structures but with the weakside end, a spot now owned by Ford (6-foot-3, 230 pounds), lining up all over the line and blitzing gaps as a stand-up player. Those moves led to more speed, disguise, and disruption for the 'Pokes. They can be caught and punished for their lack of size, but they can also inflict negative plays and sometimes limit the damage from big plays because of their team speed and subsequent ability to catch and tackle ballcarriers.

This is a strong Cowboy defensive unit, one of the most talented we've seen heading into a season. Their issues a year ago related to success rate in run defense. The Cowboys' base dime defense was not stout enough at the line of scrimmage. They grew stronger down the stretch when Colorado transfer Israel Antwine and rising senior Cameron Murray won jobs along the defensive line and both will be back to anchor the front in 2020.

The schedule isn't particularly tough in the non-conference section, featuring Oregon State and Tulsa as the headline opponents, and the Big 12 schedule worked out favorably. The Cowboys will have to play Oklahoma on the road but they get Texas and Iowa State at home. The context is well situated for an 8-1 or 7-2 finish in Big 12 play and then their first chance at the Big 12 Championship Game since it was reestablished in 2017.

23. Central Florida Knights (8.8 mean wins)

2020 F/+ Projections

#23	#21	#28
0.91	0.88	0.81
Overall	Offense	Defense

8.8	5.6
Mean Wins	Conf Wins

-	30%	1%
Div Champ	Conf Champ	CFP Berth

2%	34%	99%
Undefeated	10+ Wins	6+ Wins

Projected Win Likelihood by Game

Date	Opponent (Proj Rank)	PWL
Sep 4	vs N. Carolina (24)	58%
Sep 12	vs Fl. International (107)	90%
Sep 18	at Georgia Tech (68)	67%
Sep 24	at E. Carolina (104)	81%
Oct 3	vs Tulsa (75)	81%
Oct 16	at Memphis (21)	42%
Oct 24	vs Tulane (73)	79%
Oct 31	at Houston (58)	63%
Nov 7	vs Florida A&M (FCS)	100%
Nov 14	vs Temple (70)	78%
Nov 21	vs Cincinnati (39)	65%
Nov 27	at S. Florida (84)	72%

Projection Factors

2019 F/+	1.12 (20)
2019 FEI	0.51 (25)
2019 SP+	19.1 (14)
5-Year F/+	0.37 (44)
5-Year FEI	0.17 (46)
5-Year SP+	6.4 (44)
Weighted Recruiting	.417 (68)
Returning Offense	67% (61)
Returning Defense	75% (35)
Returning Total	71% (38)

The Knights took a step back in 2019, hampered by their need to start over at quarterback with freshman Dillon Gabriel and compounded by the rise of Luke Fickell's Cincinnati Bearcat program. The Knights had to play both the Bearcats and Temple Owls on the road in 2019 but they smashed the Owls 63-21 and lost to Cincinnati narrowly, 27-24.

After the season, offensive coordinator Jeff Lebby was hired away to help bring the UCF version of the "veer and shoot" offense to Ole Miss, and the Knights made some promotions to piece together a new offensive staff. There will be continuity in both strategy and scheme with Gabriel back at quarterback along with lead running back Otis Anderson and the second and third targets in the passing game, Marlon Williams and Tre Nixon. Top receiver Gabriel Davis left early for the NFL but there's a lot returning overall.

Otis Anderson had 1,000 all-purpose yards, 726 rushing at 6.4 yards per carry with five touchdowns and then 365 receiving with three more touchdowns. The 5-foot-11, 174-pound senior is perhaps the most dangerous weapon returning for the Knights on offense although teammate Nixon had 830 yards and seven touchdowns on just 49 catches. The offensive line returns three starters and although star offensive tackle Jake Brown graduated, both starting guards Cole Schneider (All-

AAC second team) and Parker Boudreaux are back.

On defense the Knights ticked upwards, going from 45th in defensive FEI in 2018 to 27th in 2019. Lead tackler Nate Evans (112 tackles, 13 TFLs) graduated, but the Knights' two other main inside linebackers Eriq Gilyard (77 tackles) and Eric Mitchell (77 tackles, 11 TFLs, three sacks) are back. In the secondary the team returns safeties Antwan Collier, Richie Grant, and Tay Gowan as well as star cornerback Aaron Robinson.

The main losses were up front where Brendon Hayes is gone after 7.5 sacks in 2019, but the line will still be stout in the run game with Kenny Turnier and Kalia Davis back after they combined for 21.5 tackles for loss and 6.5 sacks a year ago. The pass rush will need more from the weakside end position where the Knights bring back junior Randy Charlton and sophomore Tre'mon Morris-Brash. The schedule opens with a premier home game matchup against the surging UNC Tar Heels, then they have road trips in the AAC schedule against potential contenders Memphis, Houston, and South Florida while Temple and Cincinnati are at home.

If quarterback Dillon Gabriel can make a leap, rather than enduring a sophomore slump without Gabriel Davis, the Knights are well positioned to retake the AAC East division and compete for a fifth AAC Conference Championship.

24. North Carolina Tar Heels (8.0 mean wins)

2020 F/+ Projections

#24	#13	#50
0.88	1.21	0.28
Overall	Offense	Defense

8.0	5.2
Mean Wins	Conf Wins

34%	7%	4%
Div Champ	Conf Champ	CFP Berth

0%	15%	95%
Undefeated	10+ Wins	6+ Wins

Projected Win Likelihood by Game

Date	Opponent (Proj Rank)	PWL	Projected Loss	Projected Win
Sep 4	vs UCF (23)	42%		
Sep 12	vs Auburn (9)	33%		
Sep 19	vs James Madison (FCS)	100%		
Sep 26	vs Georgia Tech (68)	77%		
Oct 3	at Virginia (47)	56%		
Oct 10	vs Virginia Tech (30)	62%		
Oct 17	at Duke (64)	65%		
Oct 24	at Miami (29)	48%		
Nov 7	vs Connecticut (125)	99%		
Nov 14	vs Pittsburgh (49)	69%		
Nov 21	at Boston College (69)	67%		
Nov 27	vs NC State (71)	78%		

Projection Factors

2019 F/+	0.64 (32)
2019 FEI	0.32 (34)
2019 SP+	10.3 (30)
5-Year F/+	0.54 (37)
5-Year FEI	0.19 (42)
5-Year SP+	9.6 (33)
Weighted Recruiting	.854 (21)
Returning Offense	87% (9)
Returning Defense	64% (63)
Returning Total	75% (18)

North Carolina made an unexpected leap in 2019 after hiring old head coach Mack Brown (1988-1997), who in turn hired Air Raid offensive coordinator Phil Longo from Ole Miss and zone-blitzing defensive coordinator Jay Bateman from Army. Longo was able to plug in true freshman quarterback Sam Howell into his system with players previously recruited by Larry Fedora to run a spread offense and generate immediate results. Howell threw for 3,641 yards and 38 touchdowns and the Tar Heels' skill talents took off in the new offense.

Running backs Michael Carter and Javonte Williams almost each went over 1,000 rushing yards (1,003 for Carter, 933 for Williams) and combined for eight touchdowns while receivers Dazz Newsome and Dyami Brown both went over 1,000 receiving yards. All four return for the Tar Heels, as does essentially the entire offensive line. The right side of the unit is massive with right guard Marcus McKethan and right tackle Jordan Tucker each measuring in at 6-foot-7 and 330 pounds, and their ability to execute a power run game gave increased potency to Longo's RPOs and spread play-action attack.

The Tar Heels really blasted some teams in the ACC last season and nearly upset Clemson in a 21-20 loss—and they did smash Temple 55-13 in the Military Bowl. The UNC defense had some mixed results in Year 1 under Bateman but his zone-blitzing schemes did turn their linebacker corps into effective weapons at times. Returning linebacker Chazz Surratt had 115 tackles, 15 TFLs, and six sacks while edge linebacker Tomon Fox managed 10 TFLs and seven sacks.

UNC will be able to build on their experience in 2019, along with that of fellow returning linebacker Jeremiah Gemmell, and it's potentially the defense's turn to take a leap as a result of getting back both cornerbacks Storm Duck and Trey Morrison. Blitzing defenses tend to rely on good cornerback play and versatile safeties and the Tar Heels have senior strong safety D.J. Ford back in addition to their cornerbacks. To all that experience in the backfield, the Tar Heels also add transfer defensive backs Kyler McMichael from Clemson and Bryce Watts from Virginia Tech. They ranked a solid 46th nationally in 2019 in third-down conversion defense at 37.2% and could be even better in 2020.

UNC's schedule is tough in the non-conference slate with an opening date on the road against UCF and then a neutral-site game against Auburn in Atlanta. Their respite from that is to play perennial FCS contender James Madison before settling into the ACC schedule. The Tar Heels don't play in Clemson's division but will need to leapfrog Pitt, Virginia, Virginia Tech, and Miami in order to win the Coastal Division and play for a league title.

25. Baylor Bears (7.4 mean wins)

2020 F/+ Projections

#25	#27	#30
0.85	0.77	0.78
Overall	Offense	Defense

7.4	5.0
Mean Wins	Conf Wins

-	8%	3%
Div Champ	Conf Champ	CFP Berth

0%	8%	90%
Undefeated	10+ Wins	6+ Wins

Projected Win Likelihood by Game

Date	Opponent (Proj Rank)	PWL	Projected Loss	Projected Win
Sep 5	vs Ole Miss (34)	55%		
Sep 12	vs Kansas (110)	90%		
Sep 19	vs Incarnate Word (FCS)	100%		
Sep 26	vs Louisiana Tech (87)	82%		
Oct 3	at Oklahoma (8)	25%		
Oct 15	at Texas Tech (56)	61%		
Oct 24	vs TCU (28)	60%		
Oct 31	at Texas (16)	37%		
Nov 7	vs Oklahoma St. (22)	55%		
Nov 14	at Iowa St. (26)	44%		
Nov 21	at W. Virginia (61)	63%		
Nov 28	vs Kansas St. (44)	67%		

Projection Factors

2019 F/+	1.21 (16)
2019 FEI	0.67 (17)
2019 SP+	17.8 (18)
5-Year F/+	0.62 (33)
5-Year FEI	0.28 (33)
5-Year SP+	9.8 (31)
Weighted Recruiting	.597 (46)
Returning Offense	70% (51)
Returning Defense	32% (127)
Returning Total	51% (108)

Matt Rhule's Baylor Bears took a huge step forward between a 7-6 season in 2018 and a 2019 season where they finished at 11-1 before losing the Big 12 Championship Game to Oklahoma in overtime and then going down 26-14 in the Sugar Bowl against Georgia. Matt Rhule parlayed that success into a lucrative head coaching offer from the Carolina Panthers.

The Bears have been a program on the rise for over a decade now and recouped those losses by hiring LSU's defensive coordinator Dave Aranda, fresh off a national championship, and signing former UNC head coach Larry Fedora to be the offensive coordinator. The main challenge for the new staff, beyond getting settled and installing new systems and schemes in the midst of a global pandemic, was replacing nine starters on defense.

One of those two returning players was linebacker Terrel Bernard, who led the team with 112 tackles while adding 9.5 TFLs and 4.5 sacks. The Bears will be able to flank him with a pair of upperclassmen additions after a productive offseason in the transfer market. Middle linebacker Dillon Doyle of Iowa transferred to Baylor when his father, the Hawkeye strength and conditioning coach Chris Doyle, was bought out amidst allegations of making racist comments to Iowa football players over multiple years. Doyle played regularly as a backup for the 2019 Hawkeyes and made 23 tackles and was in line to be the new starting middle linebacker. The Bears also added Arkansas State edge rusher William Bradley-King coming off a season with 13.5 TFLs and 8.5 sacks.

Baylor will still have to overhaul their secondary with four new starters in their base nickel package. Retooling the defensive line may be the real challenge after losing defensive end James Lynch to the NFL. The Big 12's Defensive Player of the Year had 13.5 sacks and with nose tackle Bravvion Roy (5.5 sacks) and James Lockhart (six sacks) helped the Bears to maintain a pass rush on opponents while only rushing three. All three are now gone and will need to be replaced.

On offense the Bears have a lot more to work with, assuming health. The entire offensive line returns, including three different players that have taken snaps at tackle for the Bears in Connor Galvin, Casey Phillips, and Blake Bedier. Although Denzel Mims is now with the New York Jets, the Bears welcome back their other main wide receivers led by Tyquan Thornton who had 45 catches for 782 yards and five touchdowns in 2019. The main concern is the health of senior quarterback Charlie Brewer, who left three of the last four games of the season after hitting his head with at least one confirmed concussion occurring against Oklahoma. If Brewer has further concussion or injury issues the Bears will have to rebuild around Gerry Bohanon or Jacob Zeno. This team has a different ceiling when Brewer is healthy, as the senior has a lot of athleticism and knowhow executing the spread in the Big 12. The Bears were explosive at times in 2019 before cumulative injuries sapped Brewer of arm strength and overall health.

Baylor's schedule is less favorable than 2019 when they faced Iowa State, Oklahoma, and Texas all at home. Those games will all come on the road this season and the Bears also open up the year against Ole Miss in Houston. Aranda and his staff will be up against it trying to get to know their new team and conference while incorporating transfers in time to put together a competitive season in which they face three of the league's four toughest teams on the road.

26. Iowa State Cyclones (7.4 mean wins)

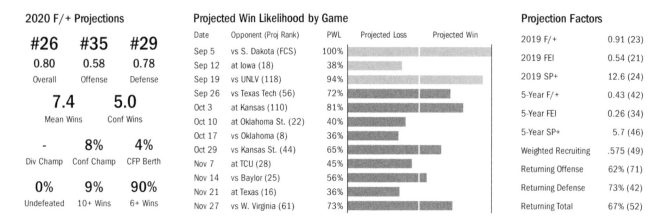

2020 F/+ Projections

#26	#35	#29
0.80	0.58	0.78
Overall	Offense	Defense

7.4	5.0
Mean Wins	Conf Wins

-	8%	4%
Div Champ	Conf Champ	CFP Berth

0%	9%	90%
Undefeated	10+ Wins	6+ Wins

Projected Win Likelihood by Game

Date	Opponent (Proj Rank)	PWL
Sep 5	vs S. Dakota (FCS)	100%
Sep 12	at Iowa (18)	38%
Sep 19	vs UNLV (118)	94%
Sep 26	vs Texas Tech (56)	72%
Oct 3	at Kansas (110)	81%
Oct 10	at Oklahoma St. (22)	40%
Oct 17	vs Oklahoma (8)	36%
Oct 29	vs Kansas St. (44)	65%
Nov 7	at TCU (28)	45%
Nov 14	vs Baylor (25)	56%
Nov 21	at Texas (16)	36%
Nov 27	vs W. Virginia (61)	73%

Projection Factors

2019 F/+	0.91 (23)
2019 FEI	0.54 (21)
2019 SP+	12.6 (24)
5-Year F/+	0.43 (42)
5-Year FEI	0.26 (34)
5-Year SP+	5.7 (46)
Weighted Recruiting	.575 (49)
Returning Offense	62% (71)
Returning Defense	73% (42)
Returning Total	67% (52)

Iowa State has been better than their record suggests for a few years in a row. In 2019, the Cyclones finished 7-6 (5-4 in the Big 12 conference) with four one-score losses. Their defense outpaced their offense, as has been the standard under Matt Campbell, but rising junior Brock Purdy established himself as one of the top quarterbacks in the Big 12 (65.7% completion rate, 27 passing touchdowns, 3,982 yards in 2019). Iowa State in 2019 had a full plate of missed opportunities: a late-game lead blown against Baylor, a late turnover versus Oklahoma State, a failed comeback drive against Iowa, and an abysmal second half at Kansas State. Couple those frustrations with a less-than-memorable Russell Athletic Bowl loss to Notre Dame, and you could wonder about the state of the Iowa State football program.

To do so would be unwise. Campbell's build (not rebuild) at Iowa State has been nothing short of magnificent, even without a win over in-state rival Iowa and two bowl losses. Before Campbell arrived, Iowa State had gone to three bowls in ten years; Campbell has taken the Cyclones to three straight bowls in his first three seasons, the second three-game bowl streak in Iowa State football history. Before Campbell, Iowa State won fewer than seven games in 11 of the previous 16 seasons. Campbell has won eight games twice, and seven in his third season. Campbell has more winning seasons than Iowa State's previous two coaches combined. All that is to say that Matt Campbell, given the history and resources of Iowa State, has brought his program into the modern era.

Second-year coordinator Tom Manning will have some weapons surrounding Purdy for the 2020 season. Sophomore Breece Hall returns (4.9 yards per carry, nine touchdowns, and 898 total yards in 2019), with a substantial amount of hype. The passing game, while certainly bemoaning the loss of senior receiving duo Deshaunte Jones and La'Michael Pettway (8 touchdowns and over 1,500 yards), returns one of the best tight ends in the country, junior Charlie Kolar (78 targets, 65.4% catch rate, 7 touchdowns, 697 yards). Tarique Milton, a

5-foot-10, 183-pound junior will provide a speedy underneath threat for Purdy, while rising sophomore Sean Shaw Jr. will provide some play-making ability in the vertical game. Matt Campbell has traditionally been a run-first coach, as his tenure at Toledo and his year with current NFL running back David Montgomery can attest, but his primary attribute as a coach has been adaptability—last year, with the anchor of Purdy's arm, Iowa State passed more than they had in Campbell's first two seasons (47.7% rush rate on early downs). With the addition of former Northwestern offensive coordinator Mick Mc-Call as running backs coach, though, the Cyclones are turning their attention to rounding out the rushing attack as a more robust complement to Kolar, a tall task considering Iowa State loses three full-time offensive line starters.

Iowa State's defense was very good in 2019, but still a slight step back from the year before. Defensive coordinator Jon Heacock has taken on the tite front defense and thrived, posting defensive efficiency numbers towards the top of the Big 12 conference the last few years. 2017's upset of Oklahoma in Norman proved the defining moment for the Iowa State defense, and since then, Heacock has not disappointed. The Cyclones lose leader Marcel Spears Jr. (UDFA to the Cincinnati Bengals), but linebacker Mike Rose (58 tackles, 9.5 TFLs, 3.5 sacks as a sophomore) will be the leader going into the 2020 season. Rising senior Eyioma Uwazurike and junior Zach Peterson will man the defensive end position. The Cyclones defense returns eight defensive backs with experience; the biggest question mark remains who will fill the hole at nose tackle now that Ray Lima (18.5 tackles, 2.5 TFLs) has moved on to the NFL.

The Cyclones get a favorable slate in 2020, hosting both participants (Oklahoma and Baylor) from the 2019 Big 12 Championship Game in Ames, and the new power vacuum in the Big 12 means the league is there for the taking. With a hard-nosed, flexible defense and a senior quarterback, the Cyclones control their own destiny in the conference.

27. Tennessee Volunteers (6.9 mean wins)

2020 F/+ Projections

#27	#57	#19
0.78	0.13	1.18
Overall	Offense	Defense

6.9	4.0
Mean Wins	Conf Wins

10%	4%	2%
Div Champ	Conf Champ	CFP Berth

0%	3%	83%
Undefeated	10+ Wins	6+ Wins

Projected Win Likelihood by Game

Date	Opponent (Proj Rank)	PWL	Projected Loss	Projected Win
Sep 5	vs Charlotte (111)	89%		
Sep 12	at Oklahoma (8)	24%		
Sep 19	vs Furman (FCS)	100%		
Sep 26	vs Florida (10)	38%		
Oct 3	vs Missouri (48)	67%		
Oct 10	at S. Carolina (40)	50%		
Oct 24	vs Alabama (1)	19%		
Oct 31	at Arkansas (77)	68%		
Nov 7	vs Kentucky (33)	60%		
Nov 14	at Georgia (5)	21%		
Nov 21	vs Troy (90)	82%		
Nov 28	at Vanderbilt (100)	75%		

Projection Factors

2019 F/+	0.55 (37)
2019 FEI	0.19 (47)
2019 SP+	10.8 (29)
5-Year F/+	0.62 (32)
5-Year FEI	0.23 (38)
5-Year SP+	10.7 (27)
Weighted Recruiting	.920 (16)
Returning Offense	68% (59)
Returning Defense	69% (50)
Returning Total	68% (50)

Jeremy Pruitt is coming for your blue-chip recruits. In Pruitt's first two recruiting cycles, the Volunteers ranked 13th (2019) and 10th (2020) nationally, signing two 5-star and 23 4-star recruits. At the time of the writing of this preview, Tennessee's 2021 class ranks third nationally, with a 5-star and nine 4-stars. There are worse strategies to try and win in college football. On the field, as compared to recruiting, Pruitt's tenure in Knoxville has been less productive—the Vols are decisively in the middle of a rebuild. They won five games in 2018 and eight in 2019, and notably rebounded after embarrassing losses to Georgia State and BYU, finishing the season on a six-game winning streak, including a Gator Bowl win over Indiana. Tennessee finished 5-3 in the SEC, after going 2-14 in conference play the two seasons prior.

Tennessee's defense struggled to defend the rush in the 2019 season (0.149 EPA/rush, 58th nationally), allowing 100 rushing yards to nine opponents. On the passing side, the outcomes were slightly better: -0.028 EPA/pass (14th nationally) and seven opponents held under 200 yards. Rising Sophomore Henry To'o had a breakout freshman season, with 52.5 tackles (5 TFLs), and will hold down the linebacker position for the Volunteers. Another tough loss for the Vol defense is safety Nigel Warrior (All-SEC in 2019, with nine pass breakups and four interceptions). Trevon Flowers, a rising junior, will look to fill that role at safety (12.5 tackles, one interception in 2019). The final hole to fill on the defense will be sack leader Darrell Taylor, an edge rusher with 8.5 sacks, 10 TFLs, and 34.5 tackles in 2019. There's a wide-open competition for that spot, including some new recruits, but given the short offseason, look for Quarvaris Crouch to fill that edge role in 2020.

The Volunteer offense struggled with junior quarterback Jarrett Guarantano, ranking in the bottom half of the Power Five teams (36th in EPA/play, 59th in EPA/rush, but 15th in EPA/passing). Guarantano looks to retain his starting job for 2020, especially given the lack of spring football, but former 4-star Kasim Hill has transferred in and might be able to make a play for a starting job in camp. Leading rushers Ty Chandler (655 yards, 4.9 yards/carry, 3 touchdowns) and Eric Gray (4 touchdowns and 539 yards on 101 carries) return; Gray took over in the last game of the regular season, rushing for 246 yards on 9.8 carries against Vanderbilt. For all their rushing struggles, the passing game somewhat developed. Guarantano (2,158 yards on the season, 16 touchdowns, 59.1% completion rate) came on later in the season: 47% of his season total passing yards and 30% of his passing touchdowns came in his last five games. Three of the top receiving targets moved on from Tennessee, leaving senior Josh Palmer (457 yards on 34 receptions in 2019) as the leader of the receiving corps. Transfer Velus Jones Jr., immediately eligible, figures to have an impact on the passing game as well. Pending approval, Nebraska transfer Miles Jones will give Guarantano a slot option as well, rounding out the offensive attack. The Vols' offensive line might be one of the stronger units in the SEC, if not the country, in 2020. Guard Trey Smith unexpectedly announced his return for a senior season, and Georgia transfer Cade Mays should be immediately eligible, taking a unit that allowed three sacks in the last five games to a previously unanticipated level of quality and depth. If the last five games of 2019 are any indication of future performance, the Vols will be moving out of rebuild territory and into contention with the 2020 season.

28. TCU Horned Frogs (7.0 mean wins)

2020 F/+ Projections

#28	#52	#22
0.73	0.15	1.04
Overall	Offense	Defense

7.0	4.9
Mean Wins	Conf Wins

-	7%	3%
Div Champ	Conf Champ	CFP Berth

0%	5%	85%
Undefeated	10+ Wins	6+ Wins

Projected Win Likelihood by Game

Date	Opponent (Proj Rank)	PWL
Sep 5	at California (51)	55%
Sep 12	vs Pr. View A&M (FCS)	100%
Sep 26	at SMU (57)	59%
Oct 3	vs Oklahoma St. (22)	52%
Oct 10	at W. Virginia (61)	60%
Oct 17	vs Kansas St. (44)	64%
Oct 24	at Baylor (25)	41%
Oct 31	vs Oklahoma (8)	34%
Nov 7	vs Iowa St. (26)	55%
Nov 14	at Texas (16)	35%
Nov 21	vs Texas Tech (56)	70%
Nov 28	at Kansas (110)	79%

Projection Factors

2019 F/+	0.54 (39)
2019 FEI	0.36 (33)
2019 SP+	6.7 (43)
5-Year F/+	0.82 (22)
5-Year FEI	0.38 (22)
5-Year SP+	12.5 (23)
Weighted Recruiting	.768 (26)
Returning Offense	61% (75)
Returning Defense	68% (51)
Returning Total	65% (64)

In 2018 and 2019, the TCU Horned Frogs won single-digit games in consecutive seasons for only the second time in Gary Patterson's 20-year career. The 2019 campaign was nothing short of a disappointment. There were no dreams of competing for a Big 12 championship with Kansas State grad transfer Alex Delton slated as the starting QB, but missing out on a bowl still felt like an abject failure. While true freshman Max Duggan eventually—and rightfully—won the starting job and sparked hope in the hearts of Frog faithful everywhere, the loss of senior tackle Lucas Niang to a torn hip labrum sent the offensive line spiraling. Quarterback instability has plagued the Horned Frogs—whereas they started five quarterbacks from 2008-2015, eight different quarterbacks have started a game in the four seasons since.

The 2019 offense was arguably the worst of offensive coordinator Sonny Cumbie's tenure; while the Frogs found success on the ground (+0.153 EPA/rush ranked 12th in the Power Five), the passing game was disastrous (-0.137 EPA/pass, 60th). The Frogs had some powerful moments last season, beating Purdue on the road and upsetting Texas, but lost six games by one score in a fashion suggesting something worse than mere bad luck.

Despite losing wide receiver Jalen Reagor (first round) and tackle Niang (third round) to the NFL, TCU brings back a sizeable chunk of their supporting cast for 2020. The good news: most of their lost production was concentrated in losing both running backs, who carried the ball frequently enough to soak up a large chunk of the total yards and touchdowns. The bad news: who will fill those production gaps is not obvious.

The Frogs bring back a starting quarterback in Max Duggan (53.4% completion rate, 15 touchdowns, 2,077 yards in 2019) who still needs some development but has shown the raw tools and maturity to lead an excellent offense, along with a

running back corps—Darwin Barlow, 5-star Zach Evans, and Daimarqua Foster—every bit as talented as their predecessors (Darius Anderson and Sewo Olonilua, both signed as UDFA, combined for over 1,100 all-purpose yards). In the receiving ranks, junior Taye Barber (29 receptions, 372 yards in 5 games) looks to build on a dynamic second half of the season as he's overcome some injuries, and junior Te'Vailance Hunt will have his opportunity to become an outside playmaker. Nine returning players caught a pass last season, among them tight end Pro Wells, who was pushed into WR roles due to depth issues last season. Adding to this depth of riches at the WR position is 4-star freshman Quentin Johnston out of Temple, Texas, who will pose another deep, athletic threat even as he builds up his frame.

On defense, TCU returns perhaps the best safety tandem in the country. Junior Trevon Moehrig recorded 11 pass break-ups and five interceptions in 2019, and sophomore Ar'Darius Washington recorded 39 tackles and five interceptions. Senior Garret Wallow has become an anchor at the linebacker position. Defensive end will be a question mark for the team, as last year's ends recorded a mere six sacks on the season. Sophomore Ochaun Mathis will look to lead that unit, but if there was a single point of failure for the 2020 TCU defense, it would be defensive end depth.

The Frogs host Oklahoma, Oklahoma State, and Iowa State this season, but make trips to Austin and Waco. For a team which has won six and five regular season games the last two seasons, improvement might be just not losing the games they shouldn't lose. The Frogs have lost to SMU and Kansas in the last two years, and to take a step forward, will need to avoid similar losses in 2020. The bright spot: a young quarterback who will improve, a stacked defense, and a coach who has followed up a down season with double-digit wins five times.

29. Miami Hurricanes (7.7 mean wins)

2020 F/+ Projections

#29	#69	#14
0.68	-0.15	1.30
Overall	Offense	Defense

7.7	4.7
Mean Wins	Conf Wins

23%	5%	3%
Div Champ	Conf Champ	CFP Berth

0%	12%	92%
Undefeated	10+ Wins	6+ Wins

Projected Win Likelihood by Game

Date	Opponent (Proj Rank)	PWL
Sep 5	vs Temple (70)	74%
Sep 12	vs Wagner (FCS)	100%
Sep 17	vs UAB (88)	80%
Sep 26	at Michigan St. (41)	48%
Oct 3	vs Pittsburgh (49)	65%
Oct 9	at Wake Forest (67)	62%
Oct 24	vs N. Carolina (24)	52%
Oct 31	at Virginia (47)	51%
Nov 7	vs Florida St. (31)	57%
Nov 14	at Virginia Tech (30)	44%
Nov 21	at Georgia Tech (68)	62%
Nov 28	vs Duke (64)	72%

Projection Factors

2019 F/+	0.40 (45)
2019 FEI	0.06 (52)
2019 SP+	9.6 (33)
5-Year F/+	0.81 (23)
5-Year FEI	0.31 (31)
5-Year SP+	13.8 (18)
Weighted Recruiting	.927 (14)
Returning Offense	59% (82)
Returning Defense	50% (106)
Returning Total	55% (97)

To say Miami's 2019 was underwhelming would be an understatement. The Hurricanes, and new coach Manny Diaz, came into the season just outside the AP Top 25, with hopes that talent at wide receiver and a little bit of development at quarterback could pair with Diaz's defense and begin the Hurricanes' upswing. Receivers K.J. Osborn and Jeff Thomas played well enough to find spots in the NFL, but the quarterback position played out in more rollercoaster fashion. Four-star freshman Jarren Williams (61.2% completion, 19 touchdowns, 12.9 yards per completion) started out with the job but sat in the middle of the season with turnover issues. Sophomore N'Kosi Perry struggled as he took over, and despite an impressive Williams performance against Louisiville (a school-record six touchdowns), the offense never got started. The Hurricanes finished 81st in SP+ and 40th in Power Five EPA/play.

Hope springs for the Miami offense, though, in Year 2 of the Diaz era. Rising junior Cam'Ron Harris played well as a complement to fourth-round draft pick DeeJay Dallas, averaging 5.1 yards per carry. The offensive line, for all their public struggles last year, will be improved and experienced. These factors alone would improve the Miami offense, but two key additions take Miami from "interesting development project" to "quiet contention" in 2020. First, offensive coordinator Rhett Lashlee comes from SMU to replace Dan Enos in Miami. Lashlee oversaw an SMU offense that finished 30th in SP+ last season, a 70-spot improvement from 2018. Lashlee, a Gus Malzahn disciple, will run a more versatile offense than Miami's 2019, incorporating high-tempo spread concepts and moving away from tight ends and towards having three receivers on the field at all times.

The addition of Lashlee alone would improve Miami's 2020 offense, but there is yet still more. Houston transfer D'Eriq King will man the helm at quarterback this fall, giving the Hurricanes offense a proven starter to run a well-designed offense. King planned to redshirt 2019 as part of Houston coach Dana Holgerson's roster manipulation plan but transferred upon reconsideration. In 2018, King's last full season, the dual threat quarterback passed for 2,928 yards and 36 touchdowns (63.5% completion rate) while rushing for 674 yards and 14 more touchdowns. Couple the wide receiver talent at Miami with a new offensive coordinator and a legitimate dual-threat quarterback? The Hurricanes offense could take great strides forward in 2020.

As far as the defense goes, the Hurricanes lose arguably their top three defenders, but 4-star transfer Quincy Roche provides immediate reinforcement at defensive line. Roche and rising sophomore Gregory Rousseau (41.5 tackles, 15.5 sacks in 2019) will prove one of the better pass-rush duos in the country. The Hurricanes will have to replace all three linebackers, including four-year starter Shaquille Quarterman (selected in the fourth round of the NFL draft). At safety, junior Gurvan Hall Jr. and senior Amari Carter will man the secondary.

Diaz secured the 13th-ranked recruiting class in 2020, second in the ACC, featuring six 4-star recruits, one of those a quarterback for the future. While 2020 has a high ceiling on the field for the Hurricanes, they will only go as far as the limited offensive line will take them. The Hurricanes will host Diaz's almost-team, Temple, and travel to Michigan State, which are both winnable non-conference games. Miami's hopes for contention in the ACC will come down to games against North Carolina and at Virginia in October. With a few weeks under their belts, Lashlee and King might have enough offensive firepower to win both of those games and alter the ACC Coastal race. Given the new hire of Lashlee and the high-level of recruiting, Miami might be able to use 2020 as both a bridge to the future and a path for contention now.

30. Virginia Tech Hokies (7.6 mean wins)

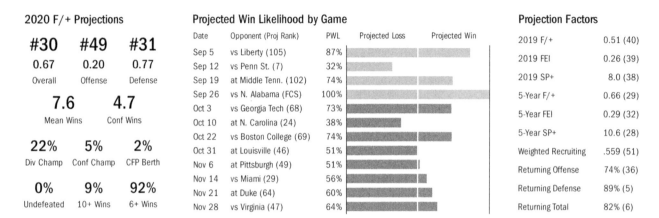

2020 F/+ Projections

#30	#49	#31
0.67	0.20	0.77
Overall	Offense	Defense

7.6	4.7
Mean Wins	Conf Wins

22%	5%	2%
Div Champ	Conf Champ	CFP Berth

0%	9%	92%
Undefeated	10+ Wins	6+ Wins

Projected Win Likelihood by Game

Date	Opponent (Proj Rank)	PWL
Sep 5	vs Liberty (105)	87%
Sep 12	vs Penn St. (7)	32%
Sep 19	at Middle Tenn. (102)	74%
Sep 26	vs N. Alabama (FCS)	100%
Oct 3	vs Georgia Tech (68)	73%
Oct 10	at N. Carolina (24)	38%
Oct 22	vs Boston College (69)	74%
Oct 31	at Louisville (46)	51%
Nov 6	at Pittsburgh (49)	51%
Nov 14	vs Miami (29)	56%
Nov 21	at Duke (64)	60%
Nov 28	vs Virginia (47)	64%

Projection Factors

2019 F/+	0.51 (40)
2019 FEI	0.26 (39)
2019 SP+	8.0 (38)
5-Year F/+	0.66 (29)
5-Year FEI	0.29 (32)
5-Year SP+	10.6 (28)
Weighted Recruiting	.559 (51)
Returning Offense	74% (36)
Returning Defense	89% (5)
Returning Total	82% (6)

Justin Fuentes' 2019 season matched expectations almost perfectly. Uncertainty on offense with some consistency on defense resulted in an 8-4 season, a second-place finish in the ACC Coastal, and a trip to the Belk Bowl. 2019 was also the season where Virginia Tech lost to their in-state rivals, Virginia, for the first time in 16 games. The season was off to a rocky start with a road loss to Boston College and a home blowout at the hands of Duke, but the Hokies made up for that by stealing a win at Miami and slipping by a North Carolina team which had yet to come alive. Down the stretch, Virginia basically beat teams worse than them, and lost to teams better than them, with few surprises.

The offense was lackluster, ranking 54th in EPA/play (-0.021). Quarterback Hendon Hooker (61.1% completion rate, 1,555 passing yards, 13 touchdowns) took over the starting job in week three, yet the offense struggled to find a rhythm. The rushing game struggled, generally, with efficiency, ranking 61st in EPA/rush and 87th in rushing SP+. The passing side of the ball flourished, relatively, as Hooker demonstrated some passing acumen (24th in passing SP+). Senior Damon Hazleton, a 6-foot-2, 215-pound receiver led the team in targets last year, although he struggled with catches (45.6% catch rate). He's a candidate for improvement on that end, al-

though a full circuit of spring ball would have helped. Sophomore Tayvion Robinson and Junior Tre Turner round out a receiving corps which had moderate success and will improve with experience in 2020.

On the defensive side of the ball, Rayshad Ashby returns for a senior season after recording 90.5 tackles in 2019, and he is joined by two of three starting defensive backs—Divine Deable (58.5 tackles, two pass breakups as a junior in 2019) and Chamarri Conner (eight pass breakups as a sophomore, 53.5 tackles). The loss of Reggie Floyd to the draft leaves a lot of defensive production to be made up in the secondary. Along the defensive line, the Hokies return quite a bit of their rotation: rising seniors Emmanuel Belmar and Jarrod Hewitt combined for 13 TFLs and eight sacks, while freshman Norell Pollard contributed three sacks and four TFLs in limited minutes last season.

The schedule presents a challenge for the Hokies: they'll host Penn State, Miami, and Virginia, while travelling to North Carolina and Lousiville. The ACC Coastal is known for turnover at the top of the standings, and Virginia Tech has a returning quarterback with passing chops, but they'll have to steal a few road games to compete for the division title. Whether Hooker takes that next step, whether the defense can replace its star—those are looming questions.

31. Florida State Seminoles (7.0 mean wins)

2020 F/+ Projections

#31	#42	#27
0.66	0.39	0.83
Overall	Offense	Defense

7.0	4.5
Mean Wins	Conf Wins

6%	5%	2%
Div Champ	Conf Champ	CFP Berth

0%	5%	81%
Undefeated	10+ Wins	6+ Wins

Projected Win Likelihood by Game

Date	Opponent (Proj Rank)	PWL	Projected Loss	Projected Win
Sep 5	vs W. Virginia (61)	65%		
Sep 12	vs Samford (FCS)	100%		
Sep 19	at Boise St. (32)	43%		
Oct 3	at NC State (71)	62%		
Oct 10	vs Clemson (3)	22%		
Oct 17	vs Wake Forest (67)	73%		
Oct 24	at Louisville (46)	50%		
Oct 31	vs Pittsburgh (49)	64%		
Nov 7	at Miami (49)	43%		
Nov 14	vs Boston College (69)	73%		
Nov 19	at Syracuse (86)	68%		
Nov 28	vs Florida (10)	35%		

Projection Factors

2019 F/+	0.10 (54)
2019 FEI	0.05 (54)
2019 SP+	1.8 (58)
5-Year F/+	0.87 (21)
5-Year FEI	0.33 (28)
5-Year SP+	14.6 (15)
Weighted Recruiting	.900 (18)
Returning Offense	63% (69)
Returning Defense	83% (9)
Returning Total	73% (27)

Florida State has been a mess since their National Championship in 2013, falling off under Jimbo Fisher before losing the title-winning coach to Texas A&M and struggling to replace him. The Willie Taggart era never got off the ground and after a 9-12 start to his tenure the school fired him midseason and began the search for his replacement. They landed on successful Memphis head coach Mike Norvell, fresh off a 12-1 season that ended with an AAC Championship.

Norvell's rise to prominence at Memphis was the result of a unique approach to the spread offense, utilizing traditional attached tight ends to create extra gaps for the defense but then mixing in spread concepts like RPOs along with play-action. Their 2019 quarterback Brady White threw for over 4,000 yards while lead running back Kenny Gainwell ran for nearly 1,500 yards and 13 touchdowns. Florida State has a number of obstacles preventing them from matching that success and strategy.

The main problem for the Seminoles the last few years has been an atrocious offensive line that allowed quarterback Alex Hornibrook to be sacked 20 times in six games last season and James Blackman to take 27 sacks in 12 appearances. Between the two of them, Florida State had a sack rate of 10%, which was crippling to their ability to keep drives alive and quarterbacks healthy. They hope to benefit from the return of Darius Washington, who was the starting left tackle in 2019 as a true freshman for the first few games before an injury ended his season. Additionally, they welcomed Florida International transfer Devontay Love-Taylor to fill in at guard and help stabilize their interior.

Beyond that, the 'Noles have to replace starting running back Cam Akers and all of their tight ends. They brought in transfer running back Jashaun Corbin from Texas A&M and UCLA tight end Jordan Wilson to help realize Norvell's vision for a tight end-driven run game and balanced offense.

Defensively the 'Noles had mixed results and now have a new coordinator, Adam Fuller, who helped shore up Memphis defense in 2019 and followed Norvell to Tallahassee. Fuller is inheriting a stronger situation on the defensive side with most of the 2019 unit returning intact. His first priority will be making the most of returning star Hamsah Nasirildeen, a 6-foot-4, 212-pound defensive back who led the team with 101 tackles in 2019. Nasirildeen will likely remain as the boundary safety where he can easily drop in on offenses and disrupt plays from around the box as a blitzer or run stopper. The 'Noles have a lot of big disruptive players returning up front including defensive linemen Marvin Wilson and Cory Durden (five sacks apiece in 2019) as well as all three starting linebackers.

Florida State has a pretty tough schedule in 2020: they get Boise State, West Virginia, and Florida in their non-conference slate, share a division with Clemson, and face Miami from the opposite division. They could make major improvements under Norvell and still struggle to have a breakthrough season. Should they get to eight wins, that would be indicative of a strong new process under the new staff.

32. Boise State Broncos (8.9 mean wins)

2020 F/+ Projections

#32	#37	#37
0.65	0.53	0.60
Overall	Offense	Defense

8.9	6.2
Mean Wins	Conf Wins

56%	38%	0%
Div Champ	Conf Champ	CFP Berth

1%	35%	99%
Undefeated	10+ Wins	6+ Wins

Projected Win Likelihood by Game

Date	Opponent (Proj Rank)	PWL	Projected Loss / Projected Win
Sep 5	vs Ga. Southern (85)	78%	
Sep 12	at Air Force (52)	54%	
Sep 19	vs Florida St. (31)	57%	
Sep 25	at Marshall (83)	66%	
Oct 3	vs San Jose St. (108)	87%	
Oct 17	vs Utah St. (95)	81%	
Oct 24	at Hawaii (99)	72%	
Oct 31	vs UNLV (118)	92%	
Nov 6	vs BYU (60)	70%	
Nov 14	at New Mexico (122)	86%	
Nov 21	at Wyoming (79)	66%	
Nov 28	vs Colorado St. (91)	80%	

Projection Factors

2019 F/+	0.56 (36)
2019 FEI	0.32 (35)
2019 SP+	8.1 (37)
5-Year F/+	0.72 (26)
5-Year FEI	0.36 (24)
5-Year SP+	10.5 (29)
Weighted Recruiting	.464 (64)
Returning Offense	54% (86)
Returning Defense	75% (34)
Returning Total	65% (62)

The 2019 season was about as successful as expected for Boise State but it wasn't a particularly smooth ride. Head coach Bryan Harsin balanced playing three quarterbacks over the course of the season and the lead passer was true freshman Hank Bachmeier, who missed multiple games with injuries. Despite the inconsistency at that position, the Broncos found stability in true freshman running back George Holani (192 carries, 1,014 rushing yards, seven touchdowns) and receivers John Hightower (51 catches, 943 yards, eight touchdowns) and Khalil Shakir (63 catches, 872 yards, six touchdowns).

All of those pieces return save for Hightower and four starters from a shaky offensive line. The Boise State coaching staff infused some extra competition at quarterback by taking in USC transfer and former blue-chip recruit Jack Sears. Bachmeier was quite strong up until the bowl game against Washington when he threw two incautious interceptions, but he was only a true freshman. Meanwhile Jack Sears was the loser in a four-way battle for the USC quarterback job that unexpectedly went to true freshman Kedon Slovis.

Whichever of these two quarterbacks wins the job will be well positioned thanks to the return of all their weapons on offense. The ceiling for the unit will depend on developments along the offensive line. Star left tackle Ezra Cleveland departed for the NFL leaving the Broncos with only one returning starter, right tackle John Ujukwu, who now figures to slide over to Cleveland's position.

The Boise defense had a great 2019 despite losing defensive coordinator Andy Avalos, who made dramatic improvements to the Oregon Ducks. They'll return most of the backfield but lose NFL-bound edge rusher Curtis Weaver (19.5 TFLs, 13.5 sacks), senior defensive tackle Chase Hatada (13 TFLs, six sacks), and nose tackle Sonatane Lui (six TFLs, 4.5 sacks), who had to retire due to back injuries. Despite all those departing fixtures, the Boise program has been reloading for years.

The next generation of stars up front will include Demetri Washington, who had four sacks in the last five games and replaces Weaver as the "stud" defensive end, and nose tackle Scale Igiehon who played a lot in 2019. Inside linebackers Riley Whimpey and Benton Wickersham return after finishing first and third on the team in tackles and starting cornerbacks Jalen Walker and Avery Williams are also back.

Boise State has won their division four seasons in a row and twice won the Mountain West, including last season. They recruit at the top of the league and just signed their 10th consecutive class to be ranked No. 1 in the Mountain West by 247 Sports. How their quarterback position shakes out will likely determine their ceiling but the floor is safely set as No. 1 in the Mountain division. They'll play Florida State and BYU in 2020 and we've still yet to see how the playoff selection committee would treat an undefeated Boise team.

33. Kentucky Wildcats (6.9 mean wins)

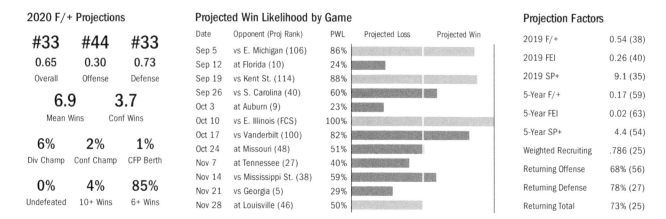

2020 F/+ Projections

#33	#44	#33
0.65	0.30	0.73
Overall	Offense	Defense

6.9	3.7
Mean Wins	Conf Wins

6%	2%	1%
Div Champ	Conf Champ	CFP Berth

0%	4%	85%
Undefeated	10+ Wins	6+ Wins

Projected Win Likelihood by Game

Date	Opponent (Proj Rank)	PWL
Sep 5	vs E. Michigan (106)	86%
Sep 12	at Florida (10)	24%
Sep 19	vs Kent St. (114)	88%
Sep 26	vs S. Carolina (40)	60%
Oct 3	at Auburn (9)	23%
Oct 10	vs E. Illinois (FCS)	100%
Oct 17	vs Vanderbilt (100)	82%
Oct 24	at Missouri (48)	51%
Nov 7	at Tennessee (27)	40%
Nov 14	vs Mississippi St. (38)	59%
Nov 21	vs Georgia (5)	29%
Nov 28	at Louisville (46)	50%

Projection Factors

2019 F/+	0.54 (38)
2019 FEI	0.26 (40)
2019 SP+	9.1 (35)
5-Year F/+	0.17 (59)
5-Year FEI	0.02 (63)
5-Year SP+	4.4 (54)
Weighted Recruiting	.786 (25)
Returning Offense	68% (56)
Returning Defense	78% (27)
Returning Total	73% (25)

In 2019, Kentucky predictably fell off their 2018 pace when they went 9-3 and then won the Citrus Bowl against Penn State. The Wildcats had to replace the 2019 NFL draft's No. 7 overall pick Josh Allen, who had 17 sacks that season. They also had to replace most of their other defensive starters that had united with Allen to produce FEI's 21st-ranked defense. Despite that daunting task, the 2019 Wildcats didn't collapse on defense but only slipped to 40th in defensive FEI. As an overall team they also worked out some ways to improve as an offense.

The story of their 2019 season was Lynn Bowden Jr., a wide receiver who took over at quarterback after a 2-3 start to the season and injuries to the top two quarterbacks. As a full-time Wildcat quarterback, Bowden led the Wildcats to a 6-2 finish in their final eight games. The already zone-option heavy Kentucky offense had Bowden carry the ball 185 times for 1,468 yards at 7.9 yards per carry with 13 rushing touchdowns. Bowden was just drafted by the NFL and Kentucky turns back to 2018 starter Terry Wilson, who's returning from a knee injury. Wilson has been eager to show that the Wildcat offense can also feature more passing at quarterback after he

threw for under 2,000 yards in 2018. Even if he comes back as a healthier and more skilled passer than before, the team returns four starters on the offensive line and running backs Asim Rose and Kavosiey Smoke to continue to run the ball.

Head coach Mark Stoops' defense is in even better shape to make a sharp return from a solid 2019 season. Pass-rushing outside linebackers Jordan Wright (three sacks) and Jamar Watson (6.5 sacks) are back on the edge to help flank 6-foot-4, 361-pound nose tackle Quinton Bohana up the middle. The team's top two tacklers last season were weak inside linebacker DeAndre Square and strong safety Yusuf Corker and they both return as well. Stoops even has the three cornerbacks who played extensively in 2019 returning.

Overall, the formula of mixing a zone-option run game and aggressive defense that has served Kentucky well in recent seasons has all the necessary components to be effective again in 2020. Their schedule will make winning the SEC East a tall order. The Wildcats travel to play Florida on the road in Week 2, draw a road trip to Auburn and host Mississippi State for their West division draw, and conclude their season hosting Georgia before playing rival Louisville on the road.

34. Ole Miss Rebels (6.5 mean wins)

2020 F/+ Projections

#34	#34	#40
0.64	0.63	0.48
Overall	Offense	Defense

6.5	3.2
Mean Wins	Conf Wins

1%	1%	0%
Div Champ	Conf Champ	CFP Berth

0%	2%	73%
Undefeated	10+ Wins	6+ Wins

Projected Win Likelihood by Game

Date	Opponent (Proj Rank)	PWL
Sep 5	vs Baylor (25)	45%
Sep 12	vs SE Missouri St. (FCS)	100%
Sep 19	vs Auburn (9)	33%
Sep 26	at LSU (4)	15%
Oct 3	vs Alabama (1)	16%
Oct 10	at Vanderbilt (100)	72%
Oct 17	vs Florida (10)	35%
Oct 24	vs Connecticut (125)	98%
Nov 7	at Texas A&M (14)	29%
Nov 14	at Arkansas (77)	65%
Nov 21	vs Ga. Southern (85)	78%
Nov 26	vs Mississippi St. (38)	59%

Projection Factors

2019 F/+	0.34 (48)
2019 FEI	0.29 (36)
2019 SP+	2.9 (53)
5-Year F/+	0.80 (24)
5-Year FEI	0.34 (26)
5-Year SP+	12.8 (20)
Weighted Recruiting	.702 (34)
Returning Offense	78% (23)
Returning Defense	64% (61)
Returning Total	71% (35)

The 2019 Rebels had a strange season, handing the keys to their offense to true freshman John Rhys Plumlee at quarterback and struggling to a 2-6 finish in league play before firing their head coach Matt Luke. Plumlee threw for only 910 yards but turned 154 carries into 1,023 rushing yards at 6.6 yards per carry with 12 rushing touchdowns. The Rebels finished the season with a one-point loss to Mississippi State, who also fired their head coach, and lost that contest in a remarkable fashion. Star wide receiver Elijah Moore scored a touchdown that would have set up the Rebels for the game-tying point on the extra point attempt but then incurred an unsportsmanlike penalty when he mimed peeing in the end zone like a dog.

The Rebels were penalized and missed the now more distant extra point attempt, and consequently lost 21-20. The coaching staff was fired and, facing a coaching search at the same time as SEC West rivals Mississippi State and Arkansas, the Rebels hired the colorful Lane Kiffin from Florida Atlantic. Kiffin built an offensive staff that continued to build on his project over the last few years to fuse pro-style concepts with the RPO spread developed by Art Briles and introduced to Kiffin by Kendall Briles.

Kiffin and his staff may be challenged to fuse pro-style passing concepts to an offense that depended so much on the quarterback run game, but there are options. Leading receiver Elijah Moore returns in the slot and the Rebels bring in grad transfer tight end Kenny Yeboah from Temple. Yeboah is more of a receiving tight end who will find it easier to block in a system where the quarterback can read unblocked defensive linemen rather than needing his tight end to block them. The key will be building around the unique ball skills and running abilities of Plumlee, which is made easier by having athletic targets like Moore and Yeboah.

Ole Miss' 2019 defense was solid. LSU and Alabama pushed them past the breaking point, as those units did for most opponents, but the Rebels made strong showings against the rest of the SEC West. Inside linebackers Lakia Henry and Jacquez Jones led the team in tackles as part of a conservative team strategy oriented around sound fundamentals rather than havoc creation up front. The team only forced 16 turnovers though and will need to increase that number in order for a similar strategy to work more effectively in 2020.

The Rebels didn't get a spring practice for Kiffin's staff to settle in or install their new schemes, which surely hurts the effort in 2020 more than for many other teams. Ole Miss will open the season against the Baylor Bears, who are also turning over their staff, at the Texans' NRG Stadium in Houston. The SEC will give them Auburn, at LSU, and Alabama in three successive weeks and they draw Florida at home from the SEC East. As is always the case in the SEC West, a strong team can struggle to win more than six or seven games. Lane Kiffin will likely be eying 2021 as a more favorable year to make a big splash with his new squad.

35. Appalachian State Mountaineers (9.0 mean wins)

2020 F/+ Projections

#35	#33	#42
0.60	0.66	0.46
Overall	Offense	Defense

9.0	6.2
Mean Wins	Conf Wins

65%	39%	0%
Div Champ	Conf Champ	CFP Berth

2%	37%	100%
Undefeated	10+ Wins	6+ Wins

Projected Win Likelihood by Game

Date	Opponent (Proj Rank)	PWL
Sep 5	vs Morgan St. (FCS)	100%
Sep 11	at Wake Forest (67)	60%
Sep 19	at Wisconsin (6)	20%
Sep 26	vs Massachusetts (130)	99%
Oct 7	vs Louisiana (54)	67%
Oct 14	at Ga. Southern (85)	66%
Oct 24	vs Arkansas St. (93)	80%
Oct 31	at UL Monroe (117)	81%
Nov 7	at Texas St. (124)	88%
Nov 14	vs Ga. State (103)	85%
Nov 21	at Coastal Car. (115)	79%
Nov 28	vs Troy (90)	79%

Projection Factors

2019 F/+	0.75 (27)
2019 FEI	0.40 (28)
2019 SP+	11.3 (27)
5-Year F/+	0.55 (36)
5-Year FEI	0.24 (36)
5-Year SP+	8.8 (36)
Weighted Recruiting	.242 (93)
Returning Offense	87% (7)
Returning Defense	53% (95)
Returning Total	70% (42)

Appalachian State is looking for some stability in 2020 after consecutive seasons in which they won 10 or more games but then immediately had their head coach poached by a bigger program. The 2018 Mountaineers lost head man Scott Satterfield to Louisville and replaced him with North Carolina State offensive coordinator Eli Drinkwitz. They went 13-1 and then Drinkwitz was poached by the Missouri Tigers.

So Appalachian State promoted offensive line coach (and former Mountaineer offensive lineman) Shawn Clark to head coach in hopes of maintaining continuity from the program's recent success and stabilizing their future. The offensive line has been a big part of the team's four consecutive Sun Belt titles and Clark will have the whole unit back save for the left tackle. Running back Darrynton Evans is also gone; he left early for the NFL draft after taking 255 carries for 1,480 yards at 5.8 yards per carry with 18 rushing touchdowns.

Running back coach Garrett Riley, younger brother to Oklahoma head coach Lincoln Riley, also left to become the new offensive coordinator at SMU. Backup running back Marcus Williams Jr. takes the top spot now after getting 113 carries for 652 yards in 2019. Despite returning quarterback Zac Thomas and the team's top four wide receivers, running the ball will remain the emphasis at Appalachian State under Clark.

The key to their approach has been an embrace of outside

zone blocking, which is fairly unique in the spread-heavy college game and is a good fit for the Mountaineers' program. Their line is built from players like Baer Hunter, a 6-foot-2, 285-pound converted defensive lineman, and senior center Noah Hannon who's 6-foot-1 and 265 pounds. Shorter, quicker linemen thrive in their stretch blocking schemes.

Quarterback Thomas contributes here as well and had 104 carries for 440 yards and seven touchdowns in 2019. Three of his receivers had over 500 receiving yards as well and Thomas threw for 2,718 yards in 2019 at 7.6 yards per attempt with 28 touchdowns and just six interceptions.

On defense the Mountaineers have to replace their inside linebackers Jordan Fehr (107 tackles) and NFL-bound Akeem Davis-Gaither (101 tackles, 14.5 TFLs, five sacks) as well as starting safeties Josh Thomas and Desmond Franklin. The team returns highly disruptive defensive tackle Demetrius Taylor though, fresh off a season with 13 TFLs and seven sacks. Star cornerback Shaun Jolly who had five interceptions is back, as is his counterpart Shemar Jean-Charles. There's a lot of momentum and talent within the program and the leadership has shown every inclination to keep things rolling along.

36. Nebraska Cornhuskers (6.5 mean wins)

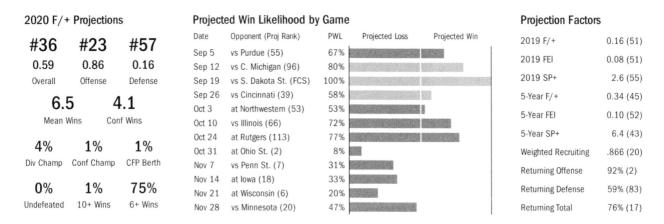

Nebraska fans have been waiting for "next year" for a few seasons now. The Cornhuskers have won 13 games over the last three years, and the shine of recent hire Scott Frost threatens to dim if 2020 is not a demonstrable improvement over his first two years. The Cornhuskers struggled in 2019, finishing 55th in SP+ (41st on offense, 63rd on defense) and losing to Colorado, Indiana, and Purdue along the way, all of which were penciled in as wins before the start of the season. Sophomore quarterback Adrian Martinez was given Heisman odds in 2019, but finished the season with just 1,956 passing yards, 10 touchdowns, and nine interceptions, completing only 59.4% of his passes. He added 756 yards and seven touchdowns on the ground, but Martinez's 2019 was, in a word, underwhelming.

Adding to the quarterback issues, 20 Nebraska players are in the transfer portal, as Frost works to reconfigure his personnel. Frost has shown that he can recruit and develop talent that fits his scheme, both at UCF and in Lincoln. His two recent classes ranked 17th and 20th nationally and included 11 blue-chip recruits. How soon all that program development manifests on the field is a different story, though. Martinez returns with a weight on his shoulders—after a disappointing 2019 and some minor injuries, he will be looking to live up to expectations this fall. In that way, he and Frost share a common fate. Either Martinez pans out as a legitimate college football starter and Frost's Nebraska starts contending, or perhaps both quarterback and coach will look different in the near future. At his best, Marti-

nez is a vibrant dual-threat quarterback, capable of explosive open-field runs and downfield passes. That skill set is the bedrock of Frost's offenses, and so despite rumblings about rising sophomore Luke McCaffrey, Martinez will be the starter unless something goes drastically wrong for the Cornhuskers. The offense returns three of its top five receiving targets, including speedy rising sophomore Wan'Dale Robinson (453 yards, two touchdowns, and a 70.2% catch rate), but the loss of JD Spielman will hurt (five touchdowns, 898 yards). As a rushing threat, Martinez will share carries with returning senior Dedrick Mills (745 yards, 5.2 yards per carry, ten touchdowns). The line returns both tackles and plenty of depth, which will help Martinez both avoid injury and rush more effectively.

On defense, Nebraska loses playmaking cornerback Lamar Jackson (12 pass breakups, three interceptions, 35 tackles), linebacker Mohamed Barry (team-leading 65 tackles, 3.5 TFLs), and defensive lineman Khalil Davis (36 tackles, eleven TFLs, and eight sacks). Replacing production at all three levels may string the defense thin. Linebackers Collin Miller (49 tackles) and JoJo Domann (44 tackles, 2.5 sacks) will be called upon to produce in 2020, and at corner, Cam-Taylor Britt may take over for the departed Jackson.

A lot rides on Nebraska's 2020 season, including Martinez's college career and Frost's timeline for rebuilding. The Cornhuskers have a schedule full of difficult games. Central Michigan won eight games last year, and Cincinnati won the AAC Eastern division. Those potential stumbling blocks in the non-conference schedule look small in comparison to the back half of the schedule. The Huskers finish the season with games against Ohio State, Penn State, Iowa, Wisconsin, and Minnesota in consecutive weeks. A lot has to happen between now and then for the Huskers to continue on their build towards competition in the Big Ten.

37. Indiana Hoosiers (6.7 mean wins)

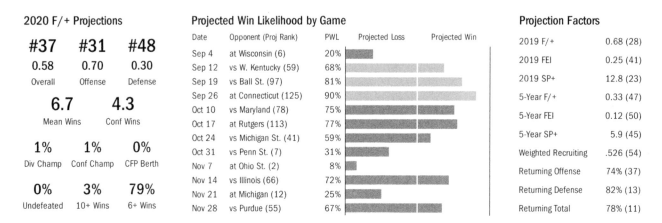

2020 F/+ Projections

#37	#31	#48
0.58	0.70	0.30
Overall	Offense	Defense

6.7	4.3
Mean Wins	Conf Wins

1%	1%	0%
Div Champ	Conf Champ	CFP Berth

0%	3%	79%
Undefeated	10+ Wins	6+ Wins

Projected Win Likelihood by Game

Date	Opponent (Proj Rank)	PWL
Sep 4	at Wisconsin (6)	20%
Sep 12	vs W. Kentucky (59)	68%
Sep 19	vs Ball St. (97)	81%
Sep 26	at Connecticut (125)	90%
Oct 10	vs Maryland (78)	75%
Oct 17	at Rutgers (113)	77%
Oct 24	vs Michigan St. (41)	59%
Oct 31	vs Penn St. (7)	31%
Nov 7	at Ohio St. (2)	8%
Nov 14	vs Illinois (66)	72%
Nov 21	at Michigan (12)	25%
Nov 28	vs Purdue (55)	67%

Projection Factors

2019 F/+	0.68 (28)
2019 FEI	0.25 (41)
2019 SP+	12.8 (23)
5-Year F/+	0.33 (47)
5-Year FEI	0.12 (50)
5-Year SP+	5.9 (45)
Weighted Recruiting	.526 (54)
Returning Offense	74% (37)
Returning Defense	82% (13)
Returning Total	78% (11)

After two 5-7 seasons, Tom Allen's Indiana Hoosiers finally broke through: in 2019, the Hoosiers won eight games, their highest win total since 1993, breaking an eleven-year streak of losing seasons. True freshman quarterback Michael Penix Jr. was injured in his sixth game of the season, disrupting a very productive season (68.8% completion rate, 10 touchdowns, 1,394 yards in six games). Junior Peyton Ramsey took back over the starting job and played well—68.0% completion rate, 13 touchdowns, and 2,454 yards) as Indiana won five conference games and an invite to the Gator Bowl.

Ramsey has since transferred, leaving the offense fully in the hands of Penix for the 2020 season. Leading rusher Stevie Scott III returns, as well as receiver Whop Philyor and tight end Peyton Hendershot. While the Hoosiers will have a new offensive coordinator (newly promoted tight ends coach Nick Sheridan), they should expect to see some consistency on offense under Penix. Indiana finished the season 22nd in offensive SP+ and returns three starters on the offensive line. Dylan Powell, a transfer from Stanford, also figures to play along the offensive line. Indiana's offense in 2019 ran a modern 11-personnel grouping often, preferring to keep the versatile Hendershot on the field at all times. With a solid offensive line, returning playmakers, and a healthy dual-threat Penix, the Indiana offense in 2020 looks to step forward.

The Hoosier defense improved in 2019 as well, with breakout seasons from freshman cornerback Tiawan Mullen (13 pass breakups, 23.5 tackles) and sophomore linebacker Micah McFadden (10 TFLs, 51 tackles). Two Indiana starters graduated, but otherwise, almost their entire defensive rotation returns. The defense finished 43rd in SP+, and the returning production puts the Hoosiers in a spot to build on a surprising 2019 season.

Indiana starts their season with a trip to Camp Randle to face Wisconsin, a tough draw in the cross-divisional games, and will play Penn State, at Ohio State, and at Michigan over the course of 22 days to close out their season. Life is tough in the Big Ten West, and progress incremental, but Indiana will attack that tough schedule with an experienced defense and a dynamic quarterback.

38. Mississippi State Bulldogs (6.3 mean wins)

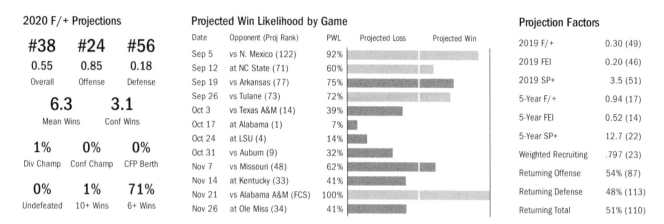

2020 F/+ Projections

#38	#24	#56
0.55	0.85	0.18
Overall	Offense	Defense

6.3	3.1
Mean Wins	Conf Wins

1%	0%	0%
Div Champ	Conf Champ	CFP Berth

0%	1%	71%
Undefeated	10+ Wins	6+ Wins

Projected Win Likelihood by Game

Date	Opponent (Proj Rank)	PWL
Sep 5	vs N. Mexico (122)	92%
Sep 12	at NC State (71)	60%
Sep 19	vs Arkansas (77)	75%
Sep 26	vs Tulane (73)	72%
Oct 3	vs Texas A&M (14)	39%
Oct 17	at Alabama (1)	7%
Oct 24	at LSU (4)	14%
Oct 31	vs Auburn (9)	32%
Nov 7	vs Missouri (48)	62%
Nov 14	at Kentucky (33)	41%
Nov 21	vs Alabama A&M (FCS)	100%
Nov 26	at Ole Miss (34)	41%

Projection Factors

2019 F/+	0.30 (49)
2019 FEI	0.20 (46)
2019 SP+	3.5 (51)
5-Year F/+	0.94 (17)
5-Year FEI	0.52 (14)
5-Year SP+	12.7 (22)
Weighted Recruiting	.797 (23)
Returning Offense	54% (87)
Returning Defense	48% (113)
Returning Total	51% (110)

The Mississippi State Bulldogs narrowly avoided a loss to their in-state rivals to end the season in 2019, thanks to an unsportsmanlike penalty. That Egg Bowl win capped a 6-6 season where things were good at times in Starkville, but never seemed to be as good as they should or could have been. The ensuing month was one of the more chaotic in recent memory: bowl practice fights between players, an uninspiring bowl loss, and ultimately the dismissal of head coach Joe Moorhead. Into all that volatility, though, the Bulldogs brought a head coach who has a history of volatility himself. Mike Leach, and all of his Air Raid reputation, moves from the Pac-12 North to the SEC West.

Along with Leach, the roster will consist of plenty of brand-new faces. Graduate transfer K.J. Costello (3,540 yards, 65.1% completion, 29 touchdowns in 2018) will man the helm of the offense. Costello, appeared in only five games in 2019, but the 2018 All-Pac-12 quarterback will look to rebound in Starkville. However, managing the volume of the Air Raid will present a challenge: Costello, in his career, has thrown about the same amount of passes that Leach's most recent quarterback (Anthony Gordon) did in 2019 alone. Costello has demonstrated accuracy, and the question will be how that accuracy will hold up with a drastic increase in participation and pass rate.

The receiving corps loses four of its top five targets and yards from 2019. The Bulldogs would need to replace over 1,200 yards in the Moorhead offense. With the Leach offense, though, they're going to have to find playmakers to match the pace and frequency of the Air Raid offense: Leach's 2019 offense passed for 5,579 yards, almost twice the yardage 2019 Bulldog starters Tommy Stevens and Garrett Shrader accrued. Osirus Mitchell, a rising senior, will be the anchor of the new Mississippi State passing attack. Mitchell (49 targets, 430

yards, six touchdowns in 2019) will be joined by two key pieces: Alabama transfer Tyrell Shavers and senior running back Kylin Hill (23 targets, 180 yards, 78.3% catch rate). Shavers, a 4-star recruit out of high school, has the body of an NFL receiver and could be a problem for SEC West defenses. Hill was involved plenty in the passing game under Moorhead and has the body and speed to be productive in the passing game. Alabama transfer tackle Scott Lashley will provide depth along the offensive line, as well.

On defense, the Bulldogs lose linebackers Willie Gay and Brian Cole II and cornerback Cameron Dantzler to the NFL draft. Senior Erroll Thompson, who lead the team in tackles last year, will be the lynchpin for new coordinator Zach Arnett, a Rocky Long disciple who joins Leach in Starkville after two outstanding seasons at San Diego State in the same role. Thompson will be productive, as Arnett's defense is a 3-3-5 based on stopping the run and being flexible. Defensive ends Kobe Jones and Marquiss Spencer combined for 50.5 tackles and six sacks in 2019, and in a three-down front will have to adapt to a role change, but they should be productive in 2020 as well. The secondary will be entirely remade, but versatile safety Marcus Murphy could star as a junior.

Success in the SEC West is always a hard concept to define, as the schedule can be prohibitively difficult to manage. The Bulldogs play Texas A&M, Alabama, LSU, and Auburn in the month of October, and 2-2 against that slate would be impressive. Outside of the October gauntlet, Mississippi State gets Kentucky and Missouri from the east, a manageable slate. The Bulldogs have made ten straight bowl games, and that streak doesn't look to be any different. The question isn't whether the Bulldogs will get six wins, it's whether Mike Leach can substantially raise Mississippi State's ceiling given the in-division competition.

39. Cincinnati Bearcats (7.7 mean wins)

2020 F/+ Projections

#39	#60	#26
0.54	0.07	0.84
Overall	Offense	Defense

7.7	4.8
Mean Wins	Conf Wins

-	14%	1%
Div Champ	Conf Champ	CFP Berth

0%	12%	92%
Undefeated	10+ Wins	6+ Wins

Projected Win Likelihood by Game

Date	Opponent (Proj Rank)	PWL
Sep 3	vs Austin Peay (FCS)	100%
Sep 11	vs W. Michigan (80)	75%
Sep 19	at Miami (OH) (101)	71%
Sep 26	at Nebraska (36)	42%
Oct 3	vs S. Florida (84)	76%
Oct 17	at Tulsa (75)	63%
Oct 24	at SMU (57)	55%
Oct 31	vs Memphis (21)	46%
Nov 7	vs Houston (58)	67%
Nov 12	vs E. Carolina (104)	84%
Nov 21	at UCF (23)	35%
Nov 28	at Temple (70)	59%

Projection Factors

2019 F/+	0.66 (30)
2019 FEI	0.39 (29)
2019 SP+	9.1 (34)
5-Year F/+	0.01 (71)
5-Year FEI	-0.06 (74)
5-Year SP+	2.0 (66)
Weighted Recruiting	.571 (50)
Returning Offense	69% (53)
Returning Defense	76% (33)
Returning Total	73% (31)

Luke Fickell was a hot name on the coaching carousel this past offseason. The Cincinnati head coach is coming off two-straight 11-win seasons and a top 40 recruiting class. The Bearcats' only losses in 2019 were to Ohio State (a blowout) and to Memphis, twice, on back-to-back weekends. Fickell's defense, 34th in SP+, held opponents to 24 or fewer points in 10 games last season en route to an East Division championship and a dominating Birmingham Bowl win.

That defense returns all but two starters, led by seniors safety Darrick Forrest (83.5 tackles, three interceptions in 2019) and linebacker Jarell White (49.5 tackles, 7.5 TFLs), who will be the backbone of the multiple 4-3 defense. Senior linebacker Joel Dublanko also performed well in limited time as a backup in 2019 and looks to take over a starting spot. Defensive end positions will all be up for grabs—all four players who saw time at end in 2019 return, and the group combined for 15 sacks last season, led by rising senior Michael Pitts (22.5 tackles, 9 TFLs) who will start again this year. The depth along the line and the returning secondary put the Bearcats in a nice position to maintain their defensive success under Fickell in 2020.

Quarterback Desmond Ridder had a sophomore season that can be described optimistically as a stepping-stone. The rising junior completed 55.1% of his passes for 2,164 yards and 18 touchdowns, but also threw 9 interceptions. He'll re-

tain his starting job and look to improve a passing offense that finished 94th in SP+ in 2019. Replacing top target Josiah Deguara, a senior tight end with 68 targets and seven touchdowns, will be tough, but a trio of tight ends saw time in 2019 and could vie for the job. Look for rising junior Leonard Taylor to take over the role initially (75% catch rate, one touchdown in 2019). Speedy receiver Rashad Medaris (354 yards, two touchdowns) graduates, but rising junior Jayshon Jackson will fill the underneath role this fall. As for a deep threat, junior Alex Pierce is the name to watch. Ridder had success with his legs (7.1 yards per carry and five touchdowns on 116 carries), but leading rusher Michael Warren II opted for the NFL draft in 2020. The void at running back will be tough to fill, but under new Associate Head Coach Dan Enos, the offense should take steps forward and a natural candidate for running back will emerge.

The Bearcats project towards the top of the AAC East again in 2020, and any offensive improvement could help Cincinnati win their first conference championship under Fickell. Games at SMU, UCF, and Temple will be decisive, but look for a Halloween game with Memphis to be the most important matchup this season. Cincinnati met expectations last season and won their division with a struggling offense. Can Dan Enos conjure up some improvement and develop Ridder into the offensive star the Bearcats need?

40. South Carolina Gamecocks (6.0 mean wins)

2020 F/+ Projections

#40	#80	#20
0.52	-0.28	1.11
Overall	Offense	Defense

6.0	3.2
Mean Wins	Conf Wins

3%	1%	1%
Div Champ	Conf Champ	CFP Berth

0%	1%	63%
Undefeated	10+ Wins	6+ Wins

Projected Win Likelihood by Game

Date	Opponent (Proj Rank)	PWL	Projected Loss	Projected Win
Sep 5	vs Coastal Car. (115)	86%		
Sep 12	vs E. Carolina (104)	84%		
Sep 19	vs Missouri (48)	61%		
Sep 26	at Kentucky (33)	40%		
Oct 3	at Florida (10)	22%		
Oct 10	vs Tennessee (27)	50%		
Oct 24	vs Texas A&M (14)	38%		
Oct 31	at Vanderbilt (100)	70%		
Nov 7	vs Georgia (5)	26%		
Nov 14	at LSU (4)	14%		
Nov 21	vs Wofford (FCS)	100%		
Nov 28	at Clemson (3)	11%		

Projection Factors

2019 F/+	0.30 (50)
2019 FEI	0.15 (49)
2019 SP+	4.8 (47)
5-Year F/+	0.33 (48)
5-Year FEI	0.15 (48)
5-Year SP+	5.4 (49)
Weighted Recruiting	.900 (19)
Returning Offense	72% (43)
Returning Defense	72% (43)
Returning Total	72% (32)

South Carolina arguably held the mantle of "best eight-loss team" in 2019. Will Muschamp's squad finished 47th in SP+ but lost eight games against possibly the most difficult schedule in America. Based on SP+ rank, the Gamecocks played No. 3 Alabama, No. 4 Clemson, No. 5 Georgia, No. 7 Florida, plus four teams ranked between 20th and 30th. They went 1-7 against that slate. In 2020, they'll replace Alabama with defending national-champion LSU, taking a trip to Baton Rouge and making a near-impossible schedule that much more difficult. The defense in 2019 was a strong unit, finishing 30th in SP+ and holding opponents to 30 or fewer points in seven games, but the offense fizzled, scoring 25 or fewer points in 10 games. 2019 was Muschamp's second losing season in his four years at South Carolina, and despite efforts to "speed up the offense" last fall, he brings in yet another new offensive coordinator.

Mike Bobo joins the staff after a tenure at Colorado State, and he'll apply his balanced offensive philosophy to South Carolina's erratic 2019 unit. The entire offense rests on the shoulders of rising sophomore Ryan Hillinski (58.1% completion rate, 2,357 yards, 11 touchdowns in 2019), and as far as he goes, the offense will go. Hillinski's receiving corps will be thin; Bryan Edwards moved on to the NFL and replacing the production of the 6-foot-3, 215-pound receiver will be dif-

ficult. The next leading target comes back, rising senior Shi Smith, but Smith's body and skillset fits better as a slot type, so there is a vacuum for an outside threat to step up. Sophomore Xavier Legette or junior OrTre Smith might both fill that role, and 4-star recruits Eric Shaw and Mike Wyman will have opportunities to secure a starting role in their freshman seasons. On the rushing side of the ball, the Gamecocks will look to rising sophomores Deshaun Fenwick and Kevin Harris (237 yards and four touchdowns on 31 carries in 2019) to replace their three leading rushers, all graduated seniors.

Muschamp's defense will again face the unenviable task of dealing with Texas A&M, Florida, Georgia, LSU, and Clemson this season, but playmakers Ernest Jones (78 tackles and five pass breakups as a sophomore in 2019) and a secondary that returns four of five starters will prove up to the usual standards. The Gamecocks have a lighter out-of-conference schedule in 2020: they play Coastal Carolina and East Carolina in addition to their regular rival Clemson, and that relief provides a path to a bowl. Given the schedule and the rise of Florida, Tennessee, and Kentucky in the SEC East, the Gamecocks won't be competing for a division title, but in Hillinski's sophomore season they can right the ship, build the foundations of a functioning offense, and move towards competing for the SEC East title in the next few seasons.

41. Michigan State Spartans (5.8 mean wins)

2020 F/+ Projections

#41	#88	#16
0.48	-0.41	1.21
Overall	Offense	Defense

5.8	3.9
Mean Wins	Conf Wins

1%	1%	0%
Div Champ	Conf Champ	CFP Berth

0%	1%	56%
Undefeated	10+ Wins	6+ Wins

Projected Win Likelihood by Game

Date	Opponent (Proj Rank)	PWL	Projected Loss	Projected Win
Sep 5	vs Northwestern (53)	63%		
Sep 12	at BYU (60)	54%		
Sep 19	vs Toledo (98)	79%		
Sep 26	vs Miami (29)	52%		
Oct 3	at Iowa (18)	31%		
Oct 10	vs Michigan (12)	35%		
Oct 17	vs Ohio St. (2)	15%		
Oct 24	at Indiana (37)	41%		
Oct 31	vs Minnesota (20)	44%		
Nov 14	at Penn St. (7)	18%		
Nov 21	vs Rutgers (113)	85%		
Nov 28	at Maryland (78)	62%		

Projection Factors

2019 F/+	0.49 (41)
2019 FEI	0.28 (38)
2019 SP+	7.2 (42)
5-Year F/+	0.73 (25)
5-Year FEI	0.34 (25)
5-Year SP+	11.1 (26)
Weighted Recruiting	.661 (38)
Returning Offense	43% (112)
Returning Defense	49% (111)
Returning Total	46% (117)

The 2019 season was another disappointment for the Mark Dantonio era of Michigan State football and the all-time winningest Spartan head coach resigned the day before national signing day. There's a lot to unpack about the Spartans' rise and fall under Dantonio but a major factor was certainly the rebuild of Ohio State under Urban Meyer, Penn State under James Franklin, and Michigan under Jim Harbaugh. All three of those East division Big Ten rivals have more resources and brought in higher rated recruiting classes over the latter half of the 2010s while the Spartans struggled with stagnation in offensive development and some diminishing returns to their defensive approach.

Now the Spartans will be run by Mel Tucker, a former Wisconsin defensive back who got his start in coaching as a grad assistant for Michigan State under Nick Saban. Tucker's career continued with some time in the NFL before returning to college and coaching defensive backs for Alabama, then following Kirby Smart to Georgia as a defensive coordinator, and finally serving as the head coach at Colorado for the 2019 season before leaving for Lansing.

Like Dantonio, Tucker's background is in fielding great defenses but his schemes and approach are pretty different from the previous Spartan systems. Tucker has always pursued a Saban-esque, single-high safety pattern-matching system on defense with heavy use of nickel and dime sub packages. His Colorado defenses used a 3-4 scheme. Dantonio's Spar-

tans were known for playing the same 4-3 Over defense with press-quarters on nearly every snap while mixing in ultra-aggressive zone blitzes like their famous double-A gap pressure. Tucker hired Scottie Hazelton, a 4-3 coach with a similar view towards coverages, fresh off a strong run at Kansas State. Hazelton and Tucker retained longtime Dantonio assistant Mike Tressell as the safeties coach and brought back former cornerbacks coach Harlon Barnett. It's likely that they'll ease into a new defensive system rather than completely overhauling Dantonio's famous system but the days of playing a true 4-3 are over.

Things will change on offense as well. The Spartans have been lining up under center and looking to play power football from the I-formation for years and years, despite regular struggles to score and their five-year drought of fielding a 1,000-yard running back. Tucker's offensive coordinator Jay Johnson will aim to transition the old school, pro-style approach of Colorado into a modern "pro-spread" system for Michigan State. They'll still look to run the ball but will play from the shotgun with 11 personnel on the field. Multi-year starting quarterback Brian Lewerke and his top receivers Cody White and Darrell Stewart Jr. are all gone so the Spartans will be facing a total overhaul of personnel and approach.

Between the system overhauls, shortened offseason, and the departure of 12 total starters in a tough division, the Spartans are looking at a tough first year for the new regime.

42. Washington State Cougars (6.9 mean wins)

2020 F/+ Projections

#42	#14	#84
0.46	1.14	-0.36
Overall	Offense	Defense

6.9	4.6
Mean Wins	Conf Wins

10%	6%	3%
Div Champ	Conf Champ	CFP Berth

0%	5%	82%
Undefeated	10+ Wins	6+ Wins

Projected Win Likelihood by Game

Date	Opponent (Proj Rank)	PWL	Projected Loss	Projected Win
Sep 3	at Utah St. (95)	66%		
Sep 12	vs Houston (58)	66%		
Sep 19	vs Idaho (FCS)	100%		
Sep 26	at Oregon St. (76)	61%		
Oct 3	vs California (51)	62%		
Oct 10	vs Utah (17)	42%		
Oct 17	at Stanford (50)	47%		
Oct 31	vs Arizona St. (43)	57%		
Nov 7	at Colorado (74)	61%		
Nov 14	at UCLA (62)	54%		
Nov 21	vs Oregon (13)	36%		
Nov 27	vs Washington (15)	40%		

Projection Factors

2019 F/+	0.60 (33)
2019 FEI	0.24 (43)
2019 SP+	11.1 (28)
5-Year F/+	0.66 (30)
5-Year FEI	0.38 (21)
5-Year SP+	8.3 (38)
Weighted Recruiting	.523 (55)
Returning Offense	36% (121)
Returning Defense	80% (22)
Returning Total	58% (85)

The big news for Washington State this season is that they'll be moving on from the Mike Leach era after his eight years as head coach. The Cougars looked to make the changes from Leach as minimal as possible by hiring Hawaii head coach and run 'n' shoot offensive practitioner Nick Rolovich.

Rolovich's offense is similarly pass-heavy, although not to the same extent as the Mike Leach Air Raid. The 2019 Washington State Cougars' lead running back Max Borghi (who returns) ran the ball 127 times for 817 yards and 11 touchdowns while catching a team-leading 86 passes for 597 more yards and five touchdowns. In contrast, the 2019 Hawaii Rainbow Warriors ran the ball 174 times with lead running back Miles Reed for 908 yards and eight touchdowns while quarterback Cole McDonald added 101 more carries for 383 yards and seven touchdowns.

Hawaii also had three receivers go over 1,000 receiving yards and the fourth managed 913 whereas receptions were more distributed across the Cougar roster. True to his run 'n' shoot and pistol roots, Rolovich involves more running and play-action in his approach than Leach, who only ever ran the ball when the quarterback saw the defense dropping everyone into coverage.

Senior quarterback Anthony Gordon is moving on after throwing for 5,579 yards in place of Gardner Minshew and Leach wasn't recruiting dual-threat quarterbacks so Rolovich will have to continue to develop his RPO plays. The quarterback run schemes that McDonald ran in 2018 and 2019 won't translate with someone like Washington State's 6-foot-4 pocket passer Cammon Cooper, who figures to be next in line. The top three receivers for the 2019 Cougars are moving on but the next generation of Renard Bell, Travell Harris, and Davontaeven Martin also received a lot of targets in 2019.

Leach's teams were never known for defense but they often played it at a reasonably high level. On the other hand, Rolovich's Hawaii teams notoriously gave up 30 points per game as a matter of course. The Cougars return a lot of key pieces from a defense that struggled in 2019, including linebacker Jahad Woods (141 tackles) and safety Skyler Thomas (72 tackles, four interceptions). Former Wyoming defensive coordinator Jake Dickert was hired to shape up the returning starters into a stronger unit.

Learning the new systems will be an obstacle, as it will be for so many other programs that are undergoing transitions or which rely heavily on development. The Cougars will at least be philosophically similar on offense and have the players in the passing game to approach their transition to the new system.

43. Arizona Wildcats (7.1 mean wins)

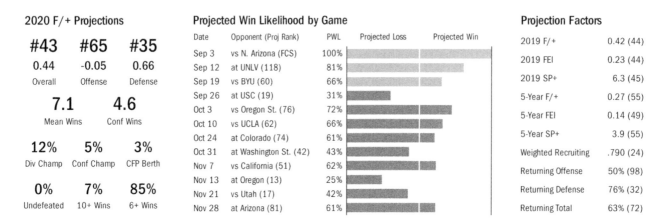

2020 F/+ Projections

#43	#65	#35
0.44	-0.05	0.66
Overall	Offense	Defense

7.1	4.6
Mean Wins	Conf Wins

12%	5%	3%
Div Champ	Conf Champ	CFP Berth

0%	7%	85%
Undefeated	10+ Wins	6+ Wins

Projected Win Likelihood by Game

Date	Opponent (Proj Rank)	PWL	Projected Loss	Projected Win
Sep 3	vs N. Arizona (FCS)	100%		
Sep 12	at UNLV (118)	81%		
Sep 19	vs BYU (60)	66%		
Sep 26	at USC (19)	31%		
Oct 3	vs Oregon St. (76)	72%		
Oct 10	vs UCLA (62)	66%		
Oct 24	at Colorado (74)	61%		
Oct 31	at Washington St. (42)	43%		
Nov 7	vs California (51)	62%		
Nov 13	at Oregon (13)	25%		
Nov 21	vs Utah (17)	42%		
Nov 28	at Arizona (81)	61%		

Projection Factors

2019 F/+	0.42 (44)
2019 FEI	0.23 (44)
2019 SP+	6.3 (45)
5-Year F/+	0.27 (55)
5-Year FEI	0.14 (49)
5-Year SP+	3.9 (55)
Weighted Recruiting	.790 (24)
Returning Offense	50% (98)
Returning Defense	76% (32)
Returning Total	63% (72)

2020 might be a make or break season for Arizona's head coach Kevin Sumlin, assuming that athletic departments like Arizona's have the financial flexibility to make moves with hot seat coaches in the midst of the pandemic. In two years Sumlin's Wildcats have yet to manage a winning season and have gone 6-12 in Pac-12 play with back-to-back losses against rival Arizona State.

Sumlin was hired after Texas A&M removed him as head coach and he brought along his Aggie offensive coordinator Noel Mazzone. Sumlin had some major success recruiting the state of Arizona while the head coach at A&M and one of his early successes at Arizona was to successfully recruit a big (6-foot-6, 225 pounds) quarterback from Houston named Grant Gunnell. With Khalil Tate gone after two struggling seasons, Gunnell is now the guy for Arizona and he had great flashes in 2019. In three starts with a few other appearances, Gunnell threw for 1,239 yards at eight yards per attempt with nine touchdowns and a single interception.

Arizona's top three targets from 2019 all return with Gunnell, including Jamarye Joiner who had 34 catches for a team-leading 552 yards and five touchdowns. The offensive line is also welcoming back several key pieces such as Paiton Fears,

Jordan Morgan, Donovan Laie, and Edgar Burrola. Between those players Arizona will have a lot of the key components necessary to make Noel Mazzone's spread offense hum.

Arizona's defense didn't have a great 2019 season, giving up 30 points or more against most everyone in the conference, but they return all of their main linebackers from the 3-3-5 defense. The roster did take a big hit from the graduation of two safeties while a third, Scottie Young Jr., grad transferred to West Virginia. They'll have to lean extra hard on returning boundary cornerback Lorenzo Burns, who had four interceptions and seven pass breakups in 2019.

The schedule in 2020 is a difficult one, mostly for the conference slate. Their non-conference schedule will take them to Lubbock to play Texas Tech. Within the Pac-12 they play divisional heavyweight Utah on the road, USC at home, and rival Arizona State at home. From the Pac-12 North they drew Oregon at home the week after travelling to play Washington on the road. They'll also host Stanford in Week 2 before their trip to Lubbock. That's a lot of potentially top-25 caliber teams for the Wildcats to navigate so they'll really need a breakthrough with sophomore quarterback Gunnell and their offense.

44. Kansas State Wildcats (6.6 mean wins)

2020 F/+ Projections

#44	#56	#39
0.41	0.14	0.50
Overall	Offense	Defense

6.6	4.1
Mean Wins	Conf Wins

-	3%	1%
Div Champ	Conf Champ	CFP Berth

0%	3%	75%
Undefeated	10+ Wins	6+ Wins

Projected Win Likelihood by Game

Date	Opponent (Proj Rank)	PWL	Projected Loss	Projected Win
Sep 5	vs Buffalo (82)	73%		
Sep 12	vs N. Dakota (FCS)	100%		
Sep 19	vs Vanderbilt (100)	78%		
Sep 26	at W. Virginia (61)	53%		
Oct 3	vs Texas (16)	40%		
Oct 10	vs Kansas (110)	83%		
Oct 17	at TCU (28)	36%		
Oct 29	at Iowa St. (26)	35%		
Nov 7	vs Texas Tech (56)	64%		
Nov 14	at Oklahoma (8)	18%		
Nov 21	vs Oklahoma St. (22)	44%		
Nov 28	at Baylor (25)	34%		

Projection Factors

2019 F/+	0.57 (35)
2019 FEI	0.43 (26)
2019 SP+	6.0 (46)
5-Year F/+	0.42 (43)
5-Year FEI	0.24 (37)
5-Year SP+	5.5 (48)
Weighted Recruiting	.491 (60)
Returning Offense	59% (80)
Returning Defense	63% (67)
Returning Total	61% (76)

The Wildcats wildly overperformed their projections for 2019; they were expected to finish 5-7 but instead went 8-4 and were the only Big 12 team to defeat the Oklahoma Sooners. A major reason for this unexpected success was that new head coach Chris Klieman made considerable changes to a roster that was returning zero scholarship running backs to make his power-I offense a feasible strategy.

K-State welcomed in grad transfer running backs James Gilbert (Ball State) and Jordon Brown (North Carolina) who combined to turn 255 carries into 1,142 rushing yards at 4.5 yards per carry with 17 rushing touchdowns. They maintained a fairly plodding and inexplosive approach on offense that was enabled by quarterback Skylar Thompson's turnover avoidance (five interceptions) and red zone run-game participation (11 rushing touchdowns).

On defense Klieman's staff was able to make the most of a veteran unit on the back end and a defensive line with some star power between defensive tackle Trey Dishon (signed by the Bengals as a UDFA) and defensive end Wyatt Hubert (seven sacks, returns in 2020). They yielded only a 28% conversion rate on third down in 2019 and made great use of a dime package and depth at defensive end to get their defense off the field and get back to their ground-and-pound, clock-killing offense.

For the 2020 season, various components of the strategy may need to be adjusted to generate similar returns. Five seniors that were starters or co-starters along the offensive line graduated from the team and the power run game that was the focus of the team's strategy will be starting over with fresh faces across the line as well as at running back with both grad transfers moving on. Kansas State will welcome back senior quarterback Skylar Thompson and his supporting cast at wide receiver will be young but also faster and more talented than in previous years. They'll need to carry some water for a retooling run game.

The Wildcats don't have an obvious star power on this squad but they do have a number of rising young players stepping into the skill player positions around a senior quarterback and a deep collection of tight ends bolstered by grad transfer Briley Moore-McKinney from Northern Iowa.

On defense things are more promising with six starters returning, mostly in the defensive backfield, and reinforcements coming in the form of junior college transfers along the defensive line and the return of linebacker Mike Hughes who missed the 2019 season. Cornerback A.J. Parker returns after picking off three passes in eight games in 2019, as do cornerback Walter Neil Jr. and nickel Jahron McPherson who helped maintain K-State's effective pass defenses.

The name of the game for defenses in the Big 12, which is dominated by explosive spread offenses, is defending the pass well and then playing well situationally on third down and in the red zone. K-State played well against the pass and on third down but then were often pushed around in the red zone when opponents could get that far. But between their strong pass defense and ball control approach to offense they often avoided the red zone as a defense and gave up only 21.4 points per game. K-State is quietly poised to be pretty competitive once again in the Big 12.

45. Navy Midshipmen (7.4 mean wins)

2020 F/+ Projections

#45	#22	#66
0.41	0.87	-0.06
Overall	Offense	Defense

7.4	4.9
Mean Wins	Conf Wins

-	13%	1%
Div Champ	Conf Champ	CFP Berth

0%	7%	88%
Undefeated	10+ Wins	6+ Wins

Projected Win Likelihood by Game

Date	Opponent (Proj Rank)	PWL
Sep 5	vs Notre Dame (11)	27%
Sep 12	vs Lafayette (FCS)	100%
Sep 19	at Tulane (73)	57%
Sep 26	vs Temple (70)	69%
Oct 3	at Air Force (52)	48%
Oct 17	at E. Carolina (104)	72%
Oct 24	vs Houston (58)	65%
Oct 31	at SMU (57)	51%
Nov 7	vs Tulsa (75)	72%
Nov 14	vs Memphis (21)	43%
Nov 21	at S. Florida (84)	62%
Dec 12	vs Army (94)	71%

Projection Factors

2019 F/+	0.78 (26)
2019 FEI	0.51 (24)
2019 SP+	9.9 (31)
5-Year F/+	0.31 (50)
5-Year FEI	0.20 (41)
5-Year SP+	3.6 (56)
Weighted Recruiting	.148 (124)
Returning Offense	50% (100)
Returning Defense	66% (58)
Returning Total	58% (87)

Navy was one of the highest overachievers relative to last year's forecast. Coming off only the second losing season in head coach Ken Niumatalolo's tenure, we projected them to go 4-8. Instead, Niumatalolo led them all the way back to a 10-2 regular-season record plus a Liberty Bowl win. The defense improved markedly and the flexbone got humming with star athlete Malcolm Perry cemented as the quarterback and boosted by fullback Jamale Carothers (14 rushing touchdowns).

Maintaining their success into 2020 will unquestionably hinge on replacing Malcolm Perry as the quarterback. The captain of their attack had a remarkable 295 carries for 2,017 yards at 6.1 yards per carry with 21 rushing touchdowns in 2019. He also added another 1,084 passing yards and seven touchdowns to three interceptions through the air. When you consider that he measured in at 5-foot-10 and 181 pounds it's truly impressive that he was able to carry such a load playing in the American Athletic Conference, the deepest and most challenging "Group of Five" conference.

The best Navy teams under Niumatalolo resemble the 2019 unit, featuring a quarterback that can handle getting 200 or so carries and do damage off tackle while supplemented by a power runner at fullback that makes the dive option in the triple-option attack work. Jamale Carothers returns to handle that second duty but quarterback will feature an abridged battle in fall camp between Perry Olsen (6-foot-2, 210 pounds) and Jeremiah Boyd (6-foot-0, 225 pounds), both of whom are bigger than Malcolm Perry.

Vegas would probably make Olsen the favorite since he ran a flexbone offense as a quarterback at his Oklahoma high school and got some snaps in 2019. He's the best bet to be able to bring both the run dimension they need as well as the necessary command of the offense to keep their offense ahead ahead of the chains despite missing spring practice.

The defensive surge was largely thanks to a devastating linebacker corps that loses three-fourths of the unit but still features leading tackler Diego Fagot in the middle. Fagot had 100 tackles in 2019, 12 TFLs, and 5.5 sacks. Their 3-4 system is heavy on zone-blitzing with the linebackers and Fagot would regularly get walked down into the A gaps and shoot them at the snap as part of their system. Because Navy's physical requirements for cadets make the accumulation of 280+-pound athletes infeasible, having 240-pound linebackers like Fagot that can help them own the interior gaps is essential.

Niumatalolo has a system and program in place at Navy to keep things rolling year after year. It's a developmental system that will be more badly hurt by the loss of spring practices than a more talent-dependent program but the Midshipmen will have some of the key players in place at their most crucial positions. The AAC around them will be transformed by the departure of Mike Norvell from Memphis to Florida State as well as the likely resurgence of Houston under Dana Holgorsen and the improvement of SMU as well. The East division could be open if Navy can get their triple-option machine humming without as many practices.

46. Louisville Cardinals (6.4 mean wins)

2020 F/+ Projections

#46	#17	#83
0.37	1.12	-0.35
Overall	Offense	Defense

6.4	4.0
Mean Wins	Conf Wins

2%	2%	1%
Div Champ	Conf Champ	CFP Berth

0%	2%	73%
Undefeated	10+ Wins	6+ Wins

Projected Win Likelihood by Game

Date	Opponent (Proj Rank)	PWL	Projected Loss	Projected Win
Sep 3	vs NC State (71)	68%		
Sep 12	at Clemson (3)	9%		
Sep 19	vs Murray St. (FCS)	100%		
Sep 26	vs W. Kentucky (59)	64%		
Oct 3	at Syracuse (86)	61%		
Oct 10	at Boston College (69)	55%		
Oct 24	vs Florida St. (31)	50%		
Oct 31	vs Virginia Tech (30)	50%		
Nov 7	at Virginia (47)	44%		
Nov 14	vs Wake Forest (67)	67%		
Nov 21	at Notre Dame (11)	21%		
Nov 28	vs Kentucky (33)	50%		

Projection Factors

2019 F/+	0.05 (58)
2019 FEI	0.05 (53)
2019 SP+	0.2 (63)
5-Year F/+	0.51 (38)
5-Year FEI	0.16 (47)
5-Year SP+	9.3 (35)
Weighted Recruiting	.631 (43)
Returning Offense	79% (21)
Returning Defense	77% (31)
Returning Total	78% (13)

Scott Satterfield took over a Lousiville program in shambles. Bobby Petrino's second stint at the school went much worse than the first, and since a nine-win season driven by Lamar Jackson's Heisman effort in 2016, the program fell to a rock bottom of 2-10 in 2018. Couple the on-field struggles with a 2019 recruiting class ranking 69th nationally, and the expectations for Satterfield's first season were quite low. He blew those expectations out of the water. The Cardinals, projected to finish at the bottom of the ACC, won eight games, upsetting Wake Forest, and Virginia, and winning the Music City Bowl to cap off an unexpectedly successful first season for Satterfield.

The Cardinals looked very similar to Satterfield's previous offenses, a pistol offense heavy on the run with spread passing principles. Rising sophomore Javian Hawkins racked up 1,525 yards and nine touchdowns on 108 carries last season, and he will again be a focal point of the offense. Junior Hassan Hall, who had 108 rushes and five touchdowns in 2019 will undoubtedly share in the rushing load. The Satterfield offense involves the quarterback in the rush game, and Micale Cunningham averaged 6.3 yards per carry (96 carries, 607 yards, six touchdowns) for the Cardinals last year. Cunningham, a 2,000-yard passer (62.6% completion rate, 22 touchdowns, five interceptions) is the star of the Satterfield offense; the former 4-star recruit is a dynamic rusher and an accurate passer, which gives the Lousiville offense plenty of options for plans of attack, and Satterfield has shown he can innovate well enough to help Cunningham develop into one of the premier quarterbacks in the ACC. Wide receiver Chatarius Atwell will be the primary taget this season (101 targets, 69.3% catch rate, 12 touchdowns in 2019), providing a horizontal and a vertical dimension to the passing game. Offensive line was a limiting factor in 2019, and the loss of tackle Mekhi Becton to the NFL doesn't help, but Satterfield emphasized the line in his 2019 class, and the unit returns three starters and features increased depth.

On defense, the linebacker duo of C.J. Avery and Rodjay Burns will continue to lead a disruptive and versatile unit. Avery has his name on draft boards after a 2019 season with 75.5 tackles and six pass breakups. Cornerback Chandler Jones returns for his junior year with demonstrated ability to matchup versus his opponent's best receiver (10 pass breakups, 41.5 tackles). Along the line, Jared Goldwire returns as the leading tackler, along with Tabarius Peterson, but there will be some questions as to rotation and depth for 2020.

Satterfield showed he could build and maintain success at the FBS level in his tenure at Appalachian State, and 2019 laid the foundation for him to do the same at Lousiville. With a dynamic passer, an innovative offense, and an experienced back seven on defense, the Cardinals will have their chances to disrupt some national contenders (Clemson, Notre Dame) and to continue to progress towards competing on the national scale.

47. Virginia Cavaliers (6.5 mean wins)

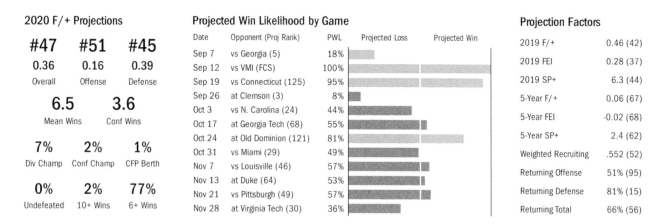

2020 F/+ Projections		
#47	#51	#45
0.36	0.16	0.39
Overall	Offense	Defense

6.5	3.6
Mean Wins	Conf Wins

7%	2%	1%
Div Champ	Conf Champ	CFP Berth

0%	2%	77%
Undefeated	10+ Wins	6+ Wins

Projected Win Likelihood by Game

Date	Opponent (Proj Rank)	PWL
Sep 7	vs Georgia (5)	18%
Sep 12	vs VMI (FCS)	100%
Sep 19	vs Connecticut (125)	95%
Sep 26	at Clemson (3)	8%
Oct 3	vs N. Carolina (24)	44%
Oct 17	at Georgia Tech (68)	55%
Oct 24	at Old Dominion (121)	81%
Oct 31	vs Miami (29)	49%
Nov 7	vs Louisville (46)	57%
Nov 13	at Duke (64)	53%
Nov 21	vs Pittsburgh (49)	57%
Nov 28	at Virginia Tech (30)	36%

Projection Factors

2019 F/+	0.46 (42)
2019 FEI	0.28 (37)
2019 SP+	6.3 (44)
5-Year F/+	0.06 (67)
5-Year FEI	-0.02 (68)
5-Year SP+	2.4 (62)
Weighted Recruiting	.552 (52)
Returning Offense	51% (95)
Returning Defense	81% (15)
Returning Total	66% (56)

In many ways, Virginia's four years under Bronco Mendenhall are a manual for building a program. Mendenhall came into a program that averaged 4.5 wins under their previous coach and has improved every year, culminating in a nine-win 2019 campaign. In that timeframe, Mendenhall has justified his reputation as a development coach, winning 25 games while recruiting zero blue-chip recruits. He's had six draft picks, four of them defensive backs, and it seems the longtime BYU coach has successfully transitioned into the ACC. The Cavaliers had a relatively light slate in 2019, but they took care of business, winning all of their home games, including the program's first victory over in-state rival Virginia Tech in 16 years. The reward for Virginia's six conference wins and ACC Coastal title was unfortunately to face Clemson in the ACC title game, and a 62-17 blowout could've easily put a black mark on a positive season. The Cavaliers refused to end that season on a down note, competing strongly in the Orange Bowl against a Florida team that outmatched them.

Virginia returns 10 starters on a defensive unit that finished 52nd in SP+. 2020 will feature 10 upperclassmen on the defensive side of the ball, a level of experience on defense perhaps unparalleled in the ACC (outside of Clemson). The Cavaliers held opponents to thirty or fewer points in ten games, led by rising senior linebackers Zane Zandier (78.5 tackles, five sacks, five pass breakups in 2019) and Jordan Mack (7.5 sacks, 50.5 tackles). Mendenhall knew coming in that he would have to make some roster tweaks to implement his 3-4 system, but in Year 4, that coalesced. Returning safeties Joey Blount and De'Vante Cross combined for nine pass breakups, five interceptions, and over 100 tackles in 2019, and

corner Nick Grant proved himself a lockdown threat, assuming the role from fifth-round NFL draft pick Bryce Hall. On the defensive line, sophomore Aaron Famui will return at the tackle position. Edge rushing will be a strength, as the Cavaliers return outside linebackers Charles Snowden and Noah Taylor, who combined for 14.5 sacks and 23 TFLs last season. The Cavalier defense will be one of Mendenhall's best, and at the top of the ACC.

The Cavaliers were a balanced team in 2019 (48th in SP+ offense, 52nd in defense), and that offensive attack will look markedly different in 2020. Under senior quarterback Bryce Perkins (1,011 yards rushing, 3,538 yards passing, 33 total touchdowns, 64.5% completion rate), the Virginia offense presented a multiple attack. Hall connected with seniors Joe Reed and Hasise Dubois for 220 targets, 1741 yards and 13 touchdowns in 2019. None of those three players return for 2020. In their stead, Mississippi State transfer Keytaon Thompson will try to replicate Perkins' dual-threat success, and receiver Terrell Jana (103 targets, 886 yards, 71.8% catch rate) will be his primary target. Thompson has two years of eligibility left,and played sparingly as backup. The former 4-star recruit will be at a disadvantage in learning the offense this offseason, but his skill set and experience bode well for success as Perkins' predecessor. Sophomore Wayne Taulapapa returns in the rushing game (473 yards, 4.1 yards/carry, 12 touchdowns) and a nice ground threat complement to Thompson.

Virginia's story this year will be reconciling the abundance of experience on defense with the dramatic loss of production on offense. The quality defense ideally would give the offense time enough to settle in, and enough slack to develop rhythms early in the season, but the Cavaliers face Georgia and Clemson in their first four games of the season. If they can survive that initial rush, they should be able to steadily improve over the course of the season. With Miami and North Carolina ris-ing, a repeat as Coastal Division champions seems unlikely, but the Cavaliers have enough potential to pull off one or two upsets this fall.

48. Missouri Tigers (6.4 mean wins)

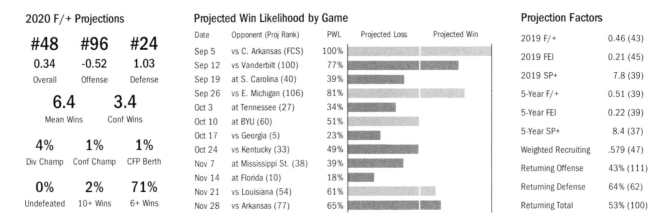

2020 F/+ Projections

#48	#96	#24
0.34	-0.52	1.03
Overall	Offense	Defense

6.4	3.4
Mean Wins	Conf Wins

4%	1%	1%
Div Champ	Conf Champ	CFP Berth

0%	2%	71%
Undefeated	10+ Wins	6+ Wins

Projected Win Likelihood by Game

Date	Opponent (Proj Rank)	PWL	Projected Loss	Projected Win
Sep 5	vs C. Arkansas (FCS)	100%		
Sep 12	vs Vanderbilt (100)	77%		
Sep 19	at S. Carolina (40)	39%		
Sep 26	vs E. Michigan (106)	81%		
Oct 3	at Tennessee (27)	34%		
Oct 10	at BYU (60)	51%		
Oct 17	vs Georgia (5)	23%		
Oct 24	vs Kentucky (33)	49%		
Nov 7	at Mississippi St. (38)	39%		
Nov 14	at Florida (10)	18%		
Nov 21	vs Louisiana (54)	61%		
Nov 28	vs Arkansas (77)	65%		

Projection Factors

2019 F/+	0.46 (43)
2019 FEI	0.21 (45)
2019 SP+	7.8 (39)
5-Year F/+	0.51 (39)
5-Year FEI	0.22 (39)
5-Year SP+	8.4 (37)
Weighted Recruiting	.579 (47)
Returning Offense	43% (111)
Returning Defense	64% (62)
Returning Total	53% (100)

No team missed the mark as much as Missouri did in 2019. Projected for 10 wins, the Tigers lost to Wyoming to start the season. After running through a light first half of the schedule, the 5-1 Tigers lost five straight, including a disappointing trip to Nashville, where Missouri lost to lowly Vanderbilt. A rivalry win against Arkansas saved Missouri from a losing season, but the damage was done—head coach Barry Odom was fired after four seasons in Columbus. Replacing him is former North Carolina State offensive coordinator and Appalachian State head coach Eli Drinkwitz.

Drinkwitz is an offense-first head coach, anchored in a downhill, quarterback power run approach. He relies heavily on play-action and spacing, and he needs a mobile quarterback with a strong arm. He will have that for 2020, as TCU transfer Shawn Robinson will man the starting job. Robinson is a versatile rusher and has the raw talent to be an above-average passer. Robinson struggled with turnovers in his only season starting at TCU, and there are concerns about his accuracy. In 2018, he completed 60.8% of his passes, but at times looked erratic, throwing eight interceptions in seven games. Robinson will fit well in the Drinkwitz offense and is a solid candidate to emerge as an above-average quarterback in the SEC. Returning talent surrounding Robinson is a concern. The Tigers lose 1,400 receiver yards and 15 receiving touchdowns from 2019, but Virginia Tech transfer Damon Hazleton will provide depth. Leading rusher

Larry Rountree III returns for a senior season, so there will be continuity in the rushing game, but between the wide receiver turnover and some instability on the offensive line (four starting spots are undecided), the 2020 offense might be a work in progress.

Rising junior Nick Bolton (8 pass breakups, 84 tackles in 2019) is one of the better coverage linebackers in college football, and he will continue to be the main playmaker on defense. The Tigers return six of eight top tacklers from 2019 on defense, and for defensive coordinator Ryan Walters, that provides plenty of talent to work with. Waters, held over from the Odom administration, is in his second season as defensive coordinator, and will look to improve on a season where the Tigers finished 17th in SP+.

Like so many teams in college football's middle class, the Missouri Tigers have a promising defense and raw tools on offense. The biggest hurdle for Drinkwitz is the lack of spring ball, where he would have the time to install his offense. The Tigers might have a rocky start as they adjust, but an easy front end to the schedule (Central Arkansas, Vanderbilt, South Carolina, and Eastern Michigan) may give them enough time to get the offense functioning properly before they head to Knoxville in October. Missouri should have plenty to make a bowl this season, and perhaps pull off an upset or two, but the Tigers will have trouble competing in a very-deep SEC East with the offensive turnover.

49. Pittsburgh Panthers (6.7 mean wins)

2020 F/+ Projections

#49	#97	#23
0.33	-0.54	1.04
Overall	Offense	Defense

6.7	4.0
Mean Wins	Conf Wins

7%	2%	1%
Div Champ	Conf Champ	CFP Berth

0%	3%	80%
Undefeated	10+ Wins	6+ Wins

Projected Win Likelihood by Game

Date	Opponent (Proj Rank)	PWL	Projected Loss	Projected Win
Sep 5	vs Miami (OH) (101)	78%		
Sep 12	at Marshall (83)	59%		
Sep 19	vs Richmond (FCS)	100%		
Sep 26	vs Duke (64)	65%		
Oct 3	at Miami (29)	35%		
Oct 17	vs Notre Dame (11)	31%		
Oct 24	vs Georgia Tech (68)	67%		
Oct 31	at Florida St. (31)	36%		
Nov 6	vs Virginia Tech (30)	49%		
Nov 14	at N. Carolina (24)	31%		
Nov 21	at Virginia (47)	43%		
Nov 28	vs Syracuse (86)	72%		

Projection Factors

2019 F/+	0.15 (52)
2019 FEI	0.00 (64)
2019 SP+	4.1 (49)
5-Year F/+	0.45 (40)
5-Year FEI	0.18 (44)
5-Year SP+	7.4 (39)
Weighted Recruiting	.606 (45)
Returning Offense	77% (24)
Returning Defense	60% (79)
Returning Total	69% (48)

Few teams could maintain any form of success with a vast gulf between offensive and defensive quality like 2019 Pittsburgh had. The Panthers ranked 60th in offensive EPA/play among Power Five teams and seventh in defensive EPA/play. Pitt went 6-2 in one score games, emblematic of having just enough defense to squeeze by opponents. The season had its peaks—the Panthers ended UCF's 27-game regular season win streak and a solid win against North Carolina—and its valleys—a 28-0 loss at Virginia Tech, a home loss to Boston College. All in all, Pittsburgh's 2019 defensive consistency was enough to mask offensive issues, but the Panthers left wins on the table with their offensive stagnation.

The defense, led by cornerback Dane Jackson (12 pass breakups in 2019), held opponents to twenty or fewer points in six games, and gave up more than thirty points only once. Jackson was selected in the NFL draft, leaving Pitt with some personnel questions on defense for 2020. Rising junior Paris Ford lead the team in tackles last season, and earned a spot on the Thorpe, Nagurski, and Bednarik Awards candidate lists. At safety in Pat Narduzzi's 4-3 cover-4 defense, Ford gets involved in the pass game (11 pass breakups, three interceptions) and the rush game (78.5 tackles, 2.5 TFLs). His counterpart, redshirt senior Damar Hamlin (72 tackles, 10 pass breakups, one interception) will anchor the unit in his fifth season of eligibility. Pitt will replace two of three starters at linebacker, but Cam Bright returns as a staple (51 tackles, 9 TFLs). The defensive line will return an experienced rotation. The Pittsburgh secondary next season will be a source of disruption for ACC offenses.

On offense, Kenny Pickett will enter his senior season without his leading receiver, Maurice Ffrench (125 targets, 850 yards, four touchdowns). Pitt's passing offense ranked 56th in EPA/play in 2019; while Picket was productive (61.6% completion rate, 3,098 yards), he was rarely timely (only 13 touchdowns through the air). Look for senior Taysir Mack (57.3% catch rate, three touchdowns, 736 yards), to take over the bulk of production, along with junior Shocky Jacques-Louis (59.0% catch rate, 348 yards, two touchdowns). In the rushing game Pickett will continue to be involved (4.8 yards per carry on 66 rushes) and leading rusher A.J. Davis returns. The skill talent mostly returns for Pitt's offense; the greater issue will be finding a way to put the pieces together, help Pickett take a step forward, and improve enough to move from a liability into an average unit. With a non-conference game against Notre Dame, trips to North Carolina, Miami, and Florida State, Pitt's defense has the opportunity to affect both the national landscape and the race for the ACC Coastal, if only the offense can progress.

50. Stanford Cardinal (6.2 mean wins)

2020 F/+ Projections

#50	#39	#62
0.32	0.43	0.04
Overall	Offense	Defense

6.2	4.4
Mean Wins	Conf Wins

7%	4%	2%
Div Champ	Conf Champ	CFP Berth

0%	2%	65%
Undefeated	10+ Wins	6+ Wins

Projected Win Likelihood by Game

Date	Opponent (Proj Rank)	PWL
Sep 5	vs William & Mary (FCS)	100%
Sep 12	at Arizona (81)	59%
Sep 19	vs USC (19)	40%
Sep 26	at UCLA (62)	51%
Oct 10	at Notre Dame (11)	20%
Oct 17	vs Washington St. (42)	54%
Oct 24	at Oregon (13)	23%
Oct 30	vs Oregon St. (76)	70%
Nov 7	at Washington (15)	26%
Nov 14	vs Colorado (74)	70%
Nov 21	at California (51)	46%
Nov 28	vs BYU (60)	63%

Projection Factors

2019 F/+	-0.25 (77)
2019 FEI	-0.10 (71)
2019 SP+	-4.7 (88)
5-Year F/+	0.89 (20)
5-Year FEI	0.43 (20)
5-Year SP+	12.7 (21)
Weighted Recruiting	.831 (22)
Returning Offense	71% (45)
Returning Defense	74% (36)
Returning Total	73% (28)

David Shaw has had better years at Stanford. 2019 was Shaw's ninth season in Palo Alto and one of only two seasons where he won fewer than nine games; Stanford's 4-8 record under Shaw was his first losing season as a head coach. The Cardinal lost at home to Cal, Notre Dame, and UCLA last year, and their only road win came at Oregon State. Stanford finished 88th overall in SP+ in 2019, 74th on offense and 87th on defense—all lows for Shaw's tenure. In addition, 14 players have transferred from Stanford or are in the portal.

On offense, senior quarterback Davis Mills returns (65.6% completion, 1,960 yards, and eleven touchdowns in 2019). Mills took over for the injured K.J. Costello, who has since transferred to Mississippi State. True to form, Stanford's most-targeted receiver was a tight end: rising senior Colby Parkinson had 85 targets and 589 yards in 2019. The deep threat was rounded out by Michael Wilson (67.5% catch rate, 673 yards, five touchdowns) and Simi Fehoko (556 yards, 6 touchdowns), both of whom return for 2020. The offensive line will largely be intact for 2020. Standout tackle Andrew Little was drafted in the first round, but Foster Sarell, Drew Dalman, and Walker Little will continue a tradition of quality Stanford offensive lines. The returning passing attack and offensive line stability are positive indicators for Stanford's potential rebound this fall.

Cornerback Paulson Adebo (ten pass breakups, 28 tackles) returns for 2020 to try and improve his draft stock, joined in the secondary by safeties Kendall Williamson (42 tackles, 11.5 TFLs) and Stuart Head (33.5 tackles). The secondary looks to be a strength of the defense, as cornerback Kyu Blu Kelly shone in his freshman season as well. Along the line, junior end Thomas Booker will provide the pass rush (four sacks in 2020).

The Cardinal travel to Notre Dame, Cal, Washington, and Oregon this season, and host USC. Outside of those five games, Stanford has a clear path to a bowl. How they handle the top of the Pac-12 will determine whether 2020 is a small step forward or a return to business for David Shaw and the Stanford Cardinal.

NCAA Win Projections

Projected Win Probabilities For ACC Teams

ACC Atlantic	Overall Wins													Conference Wins								
	12-0	11-1	10-2	9-3	8-4	7-5	6-6	5-7	4-8	3-9	2-10	1-11	0-12	8-0	7-1	6-2	5-3	4-4	3-5	2-6	1-7	0-8
Boston College	-	-	-	2	8	17	23	25	16	7	2	-	-	-	-	3	8	23	29	24	11	2
Clemson	28	40	23	8	1	-	-	-	-	-	-	-	-	48	38	11	3	-	-	-	-	-
Florida State	-	1	4	12	19	25	20	14	4	1	-	-	-	1	7	19	26	28	14	4	1	-
Louisville	-	-	2	6	16	25	24	17	8	2	-	-	-	-	3	10	24	29	21	9	4	-
NC State	-	-	-	3	10	19	24	23	14	6	1	-	-	-	-	2	10	25	30	21	10	2
Syracuse	-	-	-	2	7	14	25	23	18	9	2	-	-	-	-	1	7	17	31	27	14	3
Wake Forest	-	-	-	3	6	16	24	24	19	6	2	-	-	-	1	2	10	22	34	22	8	1
ACC Coastal	12-0	11-1	10-2	9-3	8-4	7-5	6-6	5-7	4-8	3-9	2-10	1-11	0-12	8-0	7-1	6-2	5-3	4-4	3-5	2-6	1-7	0-8
Duke	-	-	-	4	11	20	25	22	12	5	1	-	-	-	1	5	16	24	26	19	8	1
Georgia Tech	-	-	-	-	1	6	14	27	26	19	6	1	-	-	-	2	8	17	30	26	14	3
Miami	-	3	9	18	25	23	14	6	1	1	-	-	-	1	9	19	28	25	12	5	1	-
North Carolina	-	3	12	20	27	22	11	4	1	-	-	-	-	3	14	26	28	18	9	2	-	-
Pittsburgh	-	1	2	9	18	25	25	13	6	1	-	-	-	-	2	8	21	30	23	13	3	-
Virginia	-	-	2	7	17	26	25	16	6	1	-	-	-	-	1	8	17	30	25	14	5	-
Virginia Tech	-	2	7	19	26	24	14	6	2	-	-	-	-	1	7	20	27	25	12	6	2	-

Projected Win Probabilities For American Teams

American	Overall Wins													Conference Wins								
	12-0	11-1	10-2	9-3	8-4	7-5	6-6	5-7	4-8	3-9	2-10	1-11	0-12	8-0	7-1	6-2	5-3	4-4	3-5	2-6	1-7	0-8
Cincinnati	-	3	9	20	23	22	15	7	1	-	-	-	-	1	9	23	30	22	11	3	1	-
East Carolina	-	-	-	1	2	6	13	21	27	21	8	1	-	-	-	1	4	11	24	31	21	8
Houston	-	-	1	4	13	20	23	21	11	6	1	-	-	-	1	7	17	29	26	15	5	-
Memphis	2	9	21	28	23	12	4	1	-	-	-	-	-	5	15	29	26	16	7	2	-	-
Navy	-	1	6	16	24	24	17	9	3	-	-	-	-	2	9	23	27	22	12	4	1	-
SMU	-	1	4	11	23	22	23	12	3	1	-	-	-	-	2	13	23	28	20	10	3	1
South Florida	-	-	-	1	6	11	22	27	21	10	2	-	-	-	1	3	10	22	28	25	9	2
Temple	-	-	1	6	15	23	23	20	9	3	-	-	-	-	1	6	17	29	28	14	5	-
Tulane	-	-	1	3	11	18	25	22	13	6	1	-	-	-	1	5	16	25	29	17	6	1
Tulsa	-	-	1	3	8	19	26	21	15	5	2	-	-	-	1	6	13	27	27	18	7	1
UCF	2	10	22	23	24	12	6	1	-	-	-	-	-	5	19	32	26	13	4	1	-	-

Projected Win Probabilities For Big 12 Teams

Big 12	Overall Wins													Conference Wins								
	12-0	11-1	10-2	9-3	8-4	7-5	6-6	5-7	4-8	3-9	2-10	1-11	0-12	9-0	8-1	7-2	6-3	5-4	4-5	3-6	2-7	1-8	0-9
Baylor	-	1	7	15	25	25	17	7	3	-	-	-	-	1	4	11	20	26	21	12	4	1	-
Iowa State	-	2	7	15	24	26	16	8	2	-	-	-	-	-	3	11	21	30	20	11	3	1	-
Kansas	-	-	-	-	-	1	4	12	24	29	21	9	-	-	-	-	-	1	4	11	29	36	19
Kansas State	-	1	2	7	16	27	22	17	6	1	1	-	-	-	1	3	14	20	28	21	10	3	-
Oklahoma	4	19	26	27	16	6	2	-	-	-	-	-	-	9	23	31	24	10	3	-	-	-	-
Oklahoma State	-	3	10	23	27	20	11	5	1	-	-	-	-	-	4	14	24	30	17	9	2	-
TCU	-	1	4	13	21	26	20	10	4	1	-	-	-	-	3	10	22	27	22	11	4	1	-
Texas	-	3	10	19	25	23	13	5	2	-	-	-	-	1	6	21	30	25	11	5	1	-	-
Texas Tech	-	-	1	4	13	21	28	21	10	2	-	-	-	-	-	2	6	15	28	26	16	6	1
West Virginia	-	-	1	1	5	14	23	26	20	8	2	-	-	-	-	2	4	12	24	29	22	6	1

443

Projected Win Probabilities For Big Ten Teams

Big Ten East	Overall Wins													Conference Wins									
	12-0	11-1	10-2	9-3	8-4	7-5	6-6	5-7	4-8	3-9	2-10	1-11	0-12	9-0	8-1	7-2	6-3	5-4	4-5	3-6	2-7	1-8	0-9
Indiana	-	-	3	8	18	25	25	14	5	1	1	-	-	-	-	3	15	28	29	17	7	1	-
Maryland	-	-	-	-	1	4	15	26	28	18	7	1	-	-	-	-	1	4	11	26	33	19	6
Michigan	1	3	12	24	28	19	9	3	1	-	-	-	-	1	7	21	30	25	12	3	1	-	-
Michigan State	-	-	1	3	9	18	25	23	13	7	1	-	-	-	1	3	10	20	28	24	12	2	-
Ohio State	17	37	29	14	3	-	-	-	-	-	-	-	-	27	39	24	9	1	-	-	-	-	-
Penn State	2	15	27	29	19	6	2	-	-	-	-	-	-	5	17	32	26	14	5	1	-	-	-
Rutgers	-	-	-	-	-	1	3	12	26	28	23	7	-	-	-	-	-	1	4	14	34	32	15
Big Ten West	12-0	11-1	10-2	9-3	8-4	7-5	6-6	5-7	4-8	3-9	2-10	1-11	0-12	9-0	8-1	7-2	6-3	5-4	4-5	3-6	2-7	1-8	0-9
Illinois	-	-	-	2	9	18	26	25	14	5	1	-	-	-	-	-	2	8	22	27	26	12	3
Iowa	-	1	5	15	22	27	21	6	3	-	-	-	-	-	2	8	20	27	25	12	5	1	-
Minnesota	-	3	10	21	26	22	12	5	1	-	-	-	-	-	5	16	24	26	17	9	3	-	-
Nebraska	-	-	1	7	16	26	25	16	7	2	-	-	-	-	-	3	11	23	29	24	8	2	-
Northwestern	-	-	1	3	12	18	25	22	13	5	1	-	-	-	-	1	6	15	26	26	19	6	1
Purdue	-	-	-	1	4	10	20	25	23	12	4	1	-	-	-	1	5	15	26	29	17	6	1
Wisconsin	3	13	26	27	18	9	3	1	-	-	-	-	-	7	22	31	22	13	4	1	-	-	-

Projected Win Probabilities For Conference USA Teams

Conf USA East	Overall Wins													Conference Wins								
	12-0	11-1	10-2	9-3	8-4	7-5	6-6	5-7	4-8	3-9	2-10	1-11	0-12	8-0	7-1	6-2	5-3	4-4	3-5	2-6	1-7	0-8
Charlotte	-	-	-	3	8	18	26	23	15	6	1	-	-	-	1	8	19	30	28	11	2	1
Florida Atlantic	-	2	9	20	25	24	13	5	2	-	-	-	-	3	13	28	29	18	7	2	-	-
Florida International	-	-	1	4	13	22	25	21	11	3	-	-	-	-	1	8	21	26	27	12	4	1
Marshall	-	1	2	6	15	22	22	19	8	4	1	-	-	1	7	19	29	26	13	4	1	-
Middle Tennessee	-	-	1	5	14	23	23	20	10	4	-	-	-	-	2	12	26	28	19	11	2	-
Old Dominion	-	-	-	1	3	7	19	25	21	17	6	1	-	-	-	2	7	16	30	26	15	4
Western Kentucky	-	3	8	17	27	22	16	5	2	-	-	-	-	3	13	27	30	18	7	2	-	-
Conf USA West	12-0	11-1	10-2	9-3	8-4	7-5	6-6	5-7	4-8	3-9	2-10	1-11	0-12	8-0	7-1	6-2	5-3	4-4	3-5	2-6	1-7	0-8
Louisiana Tech	-	1	8	16	23	24	16	9	3	-	-	-	-	2	11	26	31	21	8	1	-	-
North Texas	-	-	-	2	6	15	24	25	19	7	2	-	-	-	2	12	19	27	27	10	3	-
Rice	-	-	-	-	4	9	19	26	25	14	3	-	-	-	-	4	14	25	30	21	5	1
Southern Mississippi	-	-	4	13	23	24	21	11	3	1	-	-	-	1	7	17	33	25	12	4	1	-
UAB	1	2	9	20	28	22	13	4	1	-	-	-	-	2	11	26	31	20	7	3	-	-
UTEP	-	-	-	-	-	-	1	3	11	22	30	24	9	-	-	-	1	3	12	30	36	18
UTSA	-	-	-	-	1	5	15	25	30	18	5	1	-	-	-	1	8	22	31	24	13	1

Projected Win Probabilities For Independent Teams

Independents	Overall Wins												
	12-0	11-1	10-2	9-3	8-4	7-5	6-6	5-7	4-8	3-9	2-10	1-11	0-12
Army	-	1	3	11	22	27	20	11	4	1	-	-	-
BYU	-	-	1	6	12	19	24	20	12	5	1	-	-
Connecticut	-	-	-	-	-	1	7	19	29	29	12	3	-
Liberty	-	-	2	8	20	27	24	13	5	1	-	-	-
Massachusetts	-	-	-	-	-	-	3	8	20	32	27	10	-
Notre Dame	1	9	17	26	24	15	6	2	-	-	-	-	-
New Mexico State	-	-	-	-	1	6	14	26	29	17	7	-	-

Projected Win Probabilities For MAC Teams

MAC East	Overall Wins													Conference Wins								
	12-0	11-1	10-2	9-3	8-4	7-5	6-6	5-7	4-8	3-9	2-10	1-11	0-12	8-0	7-1	6-2	5-3	4-4	3-5	2-6	1-7	0-8
Akron	-	-	-	-	1	3	10	21	30	24	10	1	-	-	-	-	1	8	21	33	29	8
Bowling Green	-	-	-	-	-	2	7	17	28	27	15	4	-	-	-	-	2	11	25	31	24	7
Buffalo	-	1	3	10	18	28	23	11	5	1	-	-	-	2	11	23	29	24	9	2	-	-
Kent State	-	-	-	-	2	10	18	27	26	13	4	-	-	-	2	6	15	30	28	14	4	1
Miami (OH)	-	-	1	7	15	28	23	14	8	3	1	-	-	1	5	16	27	28	16	6	1	-
Ohio	1	4	13	23	27	17	10	4	1	-	-	-	-	5	15	29	29	16	5	1	-	-
MAC West	12-0	11-1	10-2	9-3	8-4	7-5	6-6	5-7	4-8	3-9	2-10	1-11	0-12	8-0	7-1	6-2	5-3	4-4	3-5	2-6	1-7	0-8
Ball State	-	-	1	5	10	23	26	22	8	4	1	-	-	1	4	16	25	28	16	8	2	-
Central Michigan	-	-	1	6	14	22	24	20	9	3	1	-	-	1	4	11	22	26	21	11	3	1
Eastern Michigan	-	-	1	1	5	9	20	27	19	13	4	1	-	-	2	7	18	30	24	14	4	1
Northern Illinois	-	-	-	2	8	14	23	26	18	7	2	-	-	-	2	7	20	27	27	12	5	-
Toledo	-	-	2	9	16	24	24	16	6	3	-	-	-	1	5	17	27	28	14	7	1	-
Western Michigan	-	-	5	11	20	27	19	12	5	1	-	-	-	2	11	24	28	22	10	3	-	-

Projected Win Probabilities For MWC Teams

MWC Mountain	Overall Wins													Conference Wins								
	12-0	11-1	10-2	9-3	8-4	7-5	6-6	5-7	4-8	3-9	2-10	1-11	0-12	8-0	7-1	6-2	5-3	4-4	3-5	2-6	1-7	0-8
Air Force	1	3	9	20	27	20	12	7	1	-	-	-	-	2	14	26	29	20	7	2	-	-
Boise State	1	10	24	26	21	12	5	1	-	-	-	-	-	11	31	32	19	6	1	-	-	-
Colorado State	-	-	2	6	12	24	22	18	12	3	1	-	-	-	2	8	20	31	23	12	3	1
New Mexico*	-	-	-	1	1	7	15	27	28	16	5	-	-	-	-	1	4	9	26	32	21	7
Utah State	-	-	-	3	7	16	24	23	18	7	2	-	-	-	2	7	19	29	25	14	3	1
Wyoming	-	1	2	8	13	24	23	17	8	3	1	-	-	1	5	14	26	27	17	8	2	-
MWC West	12-0	11-1	10-2	9-3	8-4	7-5	6-6	5-7	4-8	3-9	2-10	1-11	0-12	8-0	7-1	6-2	5-3	4-4	3-5	2-6	1-7	0-8
Fresno State	-	-	1	7	15	25	26	17	8	1	-	-	-	-	4	11	25	28	22	8	2	-
Hawaii*	-	1	2	8	15	24	25	15	8	2	-	-	-	-	3	9	19	29	25	13	2	-
Nevada	-	-	1	4	11	21	25	23	11	3	1	-	-	-	2	7	16	25	25	18	6	1
San Diego State	1	1	7	19	26	23	13	7	2	1	-	-	-	4	11	25	29	20	9	2	-	-
San Jose State	-	-	-	3	5	17	25	25	16	7	2	-	-	-	1	4	12	27	28	19	8	1
UNLV	-	-	-	-	-	2	6	15	23	27	17	9	1	-	-	1	4	17	26	30	17	5

*Hawaii and New Mexico will each play 13 regular-season games; for projected overall records, 12-0 means 13-0, 11-1 means 12-1, etc.

Projected Win Probabilities For Pac-12 Teams

Pac 12 North	Overall Wins													Conference Wins									
	12-0	11-1	10-2	9-3	8-4	7-5	6-6	5-7	4-8	3-9	2-10	1-11	0-12	9-0	8-1	7-2	6-3	5-4	4-5	3-6	2-7	1-8	0-9
California	-	-	1	4	12	19	25	20	13	4	2	-	-	-	-	3	8	21	26	22	14	5	1
Oregon	1	10	16	28	23	15	6	1	-	-	-	-	-	5	17	29	26	15	6	2	-	-	-
Oregon State	-	-	-	1	2	10	18	25	24	15	4	1	-	-	-	1	2	10	21	29	24	12	1
Stanford	-	-	2	4	14	23	22	20	10	4	1	-	-	-	1	7	11	27	24	21	7	2	-
Washington	-	5	14	24	28	18	9	2	-	-	-	-	-	1	9	21	30	23	12	3	1	-	-
Washington State	-	1	4	12	18	27	20	12	5	1	-	-	-	-	2	10	18	25	24	14	5	2	-
Pac 12 South	12-0	11-1	10-2	9-3	8-4	7-5	6-6	5-7	4-8	3-9	2-10	1-11	0-12	9-0	8-1	7-2	6-3	5-4	4-5	3-6	2-7	1-8	0-9
Arizona	-	-	-	1	3	10	18	27	24	13	4	-	-	-	-	1	3	9	19	30	23	13	2
Arizona State	-	2	5	13	22	26	17	11	3	1	-	-	-	-	2	7	17	28	26	13	6	1	-
Colorado	-	-	-	-	-	4	12	22	25	21	11	5	-	-	-	1	3	9	19	28	24	13	3
UCLA	-	-	1	5	10	19	23	21	15	5	1	-	-	-	1	4	11	21	26	22	11	4	-
USC	-	1	5	14	23	28	16	9	3	1	-	-	-	2	7	19	25	25	16	5	1	-	-
Utah	1	6	16	28	26	16	6	1	-	-	-	-	-	3	10	23	28	19	12	4	1	-	-

Projected Win Probabilities For SEC Teams

	Overall Wins													Conference Wins								
SEC East	12-0	11-1	10-2	9-3	8-4	7-5	6-6	5-7	4-8	3-9	2-10	1-11	0-12	8-0	7-1	6-2	5-3	4-4	3-5	2-6	1-7	0-8
Florida	3	11	24	28	21	10	3	-	-	-	-	-	-	3	14	29	29	16	7	2	-	-
Georgia	2	13	27	30	19	7	2	-	-	-	-	-	-	3	16	30	29	16	5	1	-	-
Kentucky	-	1	3	10	21	28	22	10	4	1	-	-	-	-	2	7	17	28	29	14	3	-
Missouri	-	-	2	5	14	24	26	19	8	2	-	-	-	-	1	5	14	29	28	16	6	1
South Carolina	-	-	1	3	10	21	28	22	11	4	-	-	-	-	1	2	14	26	30	19	7	1
Tennessee	-	-	3	11	20	27	22	12	4	1	-	-	-	-	2	11	24	31	19	10	3	-
Vanderbilt	-	-	-	-	-	2	9	17	26	26	17	3	-	-	-	-	1	3	11	27	39	19
SEC West	12-0	11-1	10-2	9-3	8-4	7-5	6-6	5-7	4-8	3-9	2-10	1-11	0-12	8-0	7-1	6-2	5-3	4-4	3-5	2-6	1-7	0-8
Alabama	13	31	31	18	5	2	-	-	-	-	-	-	-	16	34	30	17	3	-	-	-	-
Arkansas	-	-	-	-	1	2	12	26	30	21	7	1	-	-	-	-	1	5	16	32	33	13
Auburn	-	4	16	27	29	16	7	1	-	-	-	-	-	1	6	21	31	24	13	3	1	-
LSU	3	17	26	31	16	5	2	-	-	-	-	-	-	6	19	28	28	14	4	1	-	-
Mississippi State	-	-	1	6	14	24	26	20	7	2	-	-	-	-	-	2	10	23	34	20	10	1
Ole Miss	-	-	2	5	15	26	25	18	7	2	-	-	-	-	-	3	11	27	32	20	6	1
Texas A&M	-	4	14	27	28	18	7	2	-	-	-	-	-	1	6	20	32	23	14	4	-	-

Projected Win Probabilities For Sun Belt Teams

	Overall Wins													Conference Wins								
Sun Belt East	12-0	11-1	10-2	9-3	8-4	7-5	6-6	5-7	4-8	3-9	2-10	1-11	0-12	8-0	7-1	6-2	5-3	4-4	3-5	2-6	1-7	0-8
Appalachian State	2	11	24	31	20	9	3	-	-	-	-	-	-	11	32	31	16	8	2	-	-	-
Coastal Carolina	-	-	-	2	6	14	23	26	19	7	3	-	-	-	1	3	12	24	31	20	8	1
Georgia Southern	-	-	2	7	15	25	23	17	8	3	-	-	-	1	5	19	26	28	14	6	1	-
Georgia State	-	-	-	2	6	15	24	26	16	7	3	1	-	-	-	5	17	27	28	16	6	1
Troy	-	1	5	12	21	27	20	10	3	1	-	-	-	1	7	16	28	27	14	6	1	-
Sun Belt West	12-0	11-1	10-2	9-3	8-4	7-5	6-6	5-7	4-8	3-9	2-10	1-11	0-12	8-0	7-1	6-2	5-3	4-4	3-5	2-6	1-7	0-8
Arkansas State	-	-	1	4	13	22	26	21	9	3	1	-	-	1	4	14	31	26	17	6	1	-
Louisiana	1	6	17	29	23	16	6	2	-	-	-	-	-	4	23	30	24	14	4	1	-	-
South Alabama	-	-	-	-	3	7	17	24	26	16	6	1	-	-	1	2	8	22	29	25	11	2
Texas State	-	-	-	-	1	2	8	16	23	27	16	6	1	-	-	-	3	10	24	33	21	9
UL Monroe	-	-	-	1	1	8	18	25	23	17	6	1	-	-	-	3	10	19	31	24	12	1

NCAA F+ Projections

F+: Projected overall F/+

OF+: Projected offensive F/+ with rank

DF+: Projected defensive F/+ with rank

MW: Mean wins

CW: Mean conference wins

Div: Odds of winning division

Conf: Odds of winning conference

CFP: Odds of making College Football Playoff

U: Odds of going undefeated

10+: Odds of winning 10 or more games

6+: Odds of winning 6 or more games

SOS: Strength of schedule (odds of an elite team going undefeated against this schedule) with rank

CSOS: Conference strength of schedule with rank

NCAA Teams, No. 1 to No. 130

Rk	Team	F+	OF+	Rk	DF+	Rk	MW	CW	Div	Conf	CFP	U	10+	6+	SOS	Rk	CSOS	Rk
1	Alabama	2.56	2.89	1	1.81	4	10.2	6.4	54%	35%	45%	13%	75%	100%	0.033	13	0.046	12
2	Ohio State	2.50	2.54	3	1.88	3	10.5	7.8	68%	46%	55%	17%	83%	100%	0.064	31	0.112	35
3	Clemson	2.27	2.21	5	1.98	2	10.8	7.3	90%	71%	69%	28%	91%	100%	0.163	67	0.340	72
4	LSU	2.06	2.43	4	1.42	13	9.4	5.6	26%	17%	17%	3%	46%	100%	0.029	9	0.039	8
5	Georgia	1.88	0.92	19	2.32	1	9.2	5.5	40%	14%	13%	2%	42%	100%	0.034	16	0.043	11
6	Wisconsin	1.75	1.35	10	1.64	6	9.1	6.8	65%	21%	16%	3%	42%	99%	0.062	29	0.118	39
7	Penn State	1.72	1.38	8	1.49	9	9.2	6.5	21%	14%	12%	2%	44%	100%	0.058	26	0.080	24
8	Oklahoma	1.70	2.66	2	0.44	43	9.5	6.8	-	47%	27%	4%	49%	100%	0.102	53	0.136	47
9	Auburn	1.64	0.92	20	1.81	5	8.4	4.8	9%	6%	5%	0%	20%	99%	0.018	2	0.025	1
10	Florida	1.58	1.14	15	1.47	11	9.0	5.4	36%	13%	11%	3%	38%	100%	0.066	33	0.090	27
11	Notre Dame	1.46	1.26	12	1.26	15	8.6	-	-	-	2%	1%	27%	98%	0.065	32	-	-
12	Michigan	1.43	0.82	26	1.48	10	8.1	5.8	9%	6%	4%	1%	16%	96%	0.029	8	0.047	14
13	Oregon	1.33	0.71	30	1.52	7	8.7	6.4	50%	29%	18%	1%	27%	99%	0.087	47	0.195	57
14	Texas A&M	1.31	1.03	18	1.20	18	8.4	4.6	9%	6%	4%	0%	18%	98%	0.038	18	0.040	10
15	Washington	1.16	0.38	43	1.52	8	8.2	5.9	28%	16%	10%	0%	19%	98%	0.086	46	0.126	44
16	Texas	1.11	1.33	11	0.61	36	7.8	5.7	-	16%	7%	0%	13%	93%	0.049	22	0.120	40
17	Utah	1.05	0.83	25	0.96	25	8.5	6.0	45%	19%	12%	1%	23%	99%	0.160	66	0.194	56
18	Iowa	1.03	0.14	55	1.45	12	7.3	4.7	9%	3%	2%	0%	6%	91%	0.025	6	0.032	3
19	USC	1.03	1.42	7	0.47	41	7.2	5.6	33%	14%	7%	0%	6%	87%	0.033	15	0.130	46
20	Minnesota	0.99	1.49	6	0.40	44	7.8	5.3	17%	6%	4%	0%	13%	94%	0.082	43	0.096	30
21	Memphis	0.97	1.38	9	0.30	49	8.8	5.4	-	26%	1%	2%	32%	99%	0.234	82	0.287	67
22	Oklahoma State	0.93	1.13	16	0.50	38	7.8	5.2	-	10%	4%	0%	13%	94%	0.091	50	0.099	31
23	UCF	0.91	0.88	21	0.81	28	8.8	5.6	-	30%	1%	2%	34%	99%	0.247	85	0.360	74
24	North Carolina	0.88	1.21	13	0.28	50	8.0	5.2	34%	7%	4%	0%	15%	95%	0.112	55	0.280	66
25	Baylor	0.85	0.77	27	0.78	30	7.4	5.0	-	8%	3%	0%	8%	90%	0.069	34	0.090	26
26	Iowa State	0.80	0.58	35	0.78	29	7.4	5.0	-	8%	4%	0%	9%	90%	0.075	38	0.114	36
27	Tennessee	0.78	0.13	57	1.18	19	6.9	4.0	10%	4%	2%	0%	3%	83%	0.030	11	0.062	19
28	TCU	0.73	0.15	52	1.04	22	7.0	4.9	-	7%	3%	0%	5%	85%	0.080	42	0.118	38
29	Miami	0.68	-0.15	69	1.30	14	7.7	4.7	23%	5%	3%	0%	12%	92%	0.168	69	0.237	62
30	Virginia Tech	0.67	0.20	49	0.77	31	7.6	4.7	22%	5%	2%	0%	9%	92%	0.142	63	0.239	63
31	Florida State	0.66	0.39	42	0.83	27	7.0	4.5	6%	5%	2%	0%	5%	81%	0.077	40	0.179	55
32	Boise State	0.65	0.53	37	0.60	37	8.9	6.2	56%	38%	0%	1%	35%	99%	0.443	115	0.658	93
33	Kentucky	0.65	0.30	44	0.73	33	6.9	3.7	6%	2%	1%	0%	4%	85%	0.053	23	0.067	21
34	Ole Miss	0.64	0.63	34	0.48	40	6.5	3.2	1%	1%	0%	0%	2%	73%	0.024	5	0.033	5
35	Appalachian State	0.60	0.66	33	0.46	42	9.0	6.2	65%	39%	0%	2%	37%	100%	0.329	97	0.774	115

Rk	Team	F+	OF+	Rk	DF+	Rk	MW	CW	Div	Conf	CFP	U	10+	6+	SOS	Rk	CSOS	Rk
36	Nebraska	0.59	0.86	23	0.16	57	6.5	4.1	4%	1%	1%	0%	1%	75%	0.030	10	0.035	6
37	Indiana	0.58	0.70	31	0.30	48	6.7	4.3	1%	1%	0%	0%	3%	79%	0.036	17	0.040	9
38	Mississippi State	0.55	0.85	24	0.18	56	6.3	3.1	1%	0%	0%	0%	1%	71%	0.023	4	0.028	2
39	Cincinnati	0.54	0.07	60	0.84	26	7.7	4.8	-	14%	1%	0%	12%	92%	0.209	76	0.307	70
40	South Carolina	0.52	-0.28	80	1.11	20	6.0	3.2	3%	1%	1%	0%	1%	63%	0.017	1	0.047	13
41	Michigan State	0.48	-0.41	88	1.21	16	5.8	3.9	1%	1%	0%	0%	1%	56%	0.033	14	0.047	15
42	Washington State	0.46	1.14	14	-0.36	84	6.9	4.6	10%	6%	3%	0%	5%	82%	0.143	64	0.168	54
43	Arizona State	0.44	-0.05	65	0.66	35	7.1	4.6	12%	5%	3%	0%	7%	85%	0.135	62	0.147	52
44	Kansas State	0.41	0.14	56	0.50	39	6.6	4.1	-	3%	1%	0%	3%	75%	0.078	41	0.081	25
45	Navy	0.41	0.87	22	-0.06	66	7.4	4.9	-	13%	1%	0%	7%	88%	0.203	75	0.415	75
46	Louisville	0.37	1.12	17	-0.35	83	6.4	4.0	2%	2%	1%	0%	2%	73%	0.062	28	0.143	50
47	Virginia	0.36	0.16	51	0.39	45	6.5	3.6	7%	2%	1%	0%	2%	77%	0.054	25	0.103	33
48	Missouri	0.34	-0.52	96	1.03	24	6.4	3.4	4%	1%	1%	0%	2%	71%	0.076	39	0.100	32
49	Pittsburgh	0.33	-0.54	97	1.04	23	6.7	4.0	7%	2%	1%	0%	3%	80%	0.128	59	0.208	58
50	Stanford	0.32	0.43	39	0.04	62	6.2	4.4	7%	4%	2%	0%	2%	65%	0.074	37	0.141	49
51	California	0.22	0.19	50	0.22	53	6.0	3.8	4%	2%	1%	0%	1%	61%	0.095	51	0.116	37
52	Air Force	0.20	0.72	29	-0.34	78	7.8	5.2	22%	15%	0%	1%	13%	92%	0.401	109	0.602	85
53	Northwestern	0.18	-1.03	112	1.20	17	5.8	3.5	2%	1%	0%	0%	1%	59%	0.063	30	0.067	20
54	Louisiana	0.15	0.68	32	-0.39	86	8.5	5.6	67%	26%	0%	1%	24%	98%	0.516	121	0.678	97
55	Purdue	0.13	0.40	41	-0.24	73	4.9	3.5	2%	1%	0%	0%	0%	35%	0.048	21	0.079	23
56	Texas Tech	0.10	0.55	36	-0.35	80	6.1	3.5	-	1%	0%	0%	1%	67%	0.091	49	0.095	29
57	SMU	0.07	0.74	28	-0.45	90	6.9	4.0	-	5%	0%	0%	5%	84%	0.281	90	0.348	73
58	Houston	0.06	0.28	45	-0.21	72	6.1	3.6	-	3%	0%	0%	1%	61%	0.149	65	0.232	60
59	Western Kentucky	0.06	-0.60	100	0.74	32	7.7	5.2	30%	18%	0%	0%	11%	93%	0.398	108	0.677	96
60	BYU	0.04	0.03	62	0.09	60	5.9	-	-	-	0%	0%	1%	62%	0.124	57	-	-
61	West Virginia	0.03	-0.18	72	0.12	58	5.4	3.4	-	1%	0%	0%	1%	44%	0.070	36	0.093	28
62	UCLA	0.02	0.40	40	-0.33	77	5.9	4.0	7%	3%	1%	0%	1%	58%	0.173	71	0.216	59
63	Florida Atlantic	-0.02	0.05	61	-0.01	63	7.7	5.3	31%	18%	0%	0%	11%	93%	0.404	110	0.690	102
64	Duke	-0.05	-0.92	108	0.71	34	5.9	3.3	4%	1%	0%	0%	0%	60%	0.134	61	0.239	64
65	San Diego State	-0.08	-1.40	121	1.06	21	7.6	5.1	45%	15%	0%	1%	9%	90%	0.526	124	0.722	107
66	Illinois	-0.11	-0.46	89	0.09	59	5.6	2.9	1%	0%	0%	0%	0%	55%	0.053	24	0.053	16
67	Wake Forest	-0.11	-0.32	85	0.20	54	5.4	3.1	1%	1%	0%	0%	0%	49%	0.087	48	0.165	53
68	Georgia Tech	-0.12	-0.46	90	0.18	55	4.4	2.8	2%	0%	0%	0%	0%	21%	0.031	12	0.124	41
69	Boston College	-0.13	0.14	54	-0.27	75	5.6	2.9	1%	0%	0%	0%	0%	50%	0.116	56	0.139	48
70	Temple	-0.13	-0.57	98	0.36	47	6.4	3.5	-	2%	0%	0%	1%	68%	0.171	70	0.236	61
71	NC State	-0.15	-0.27	79	-0.03	65	5.7	3.1	0%	0%	0%	0%	0%	56%	0.099	52	0.127	45
72	Ohio	-0.16	0.47	38	-0.71	100	8.2	5.4	43%	23%	0%	1%	18%	95%	0.647	130	0.772	114
73	Tulane	-0.17	-0.21	74	-0.02	64	5.7	3.5	-	2%	0%	0%	1%	58%	0.177	73	0.290	68
74	Colorado	-0.28	0.02	63	-0.45	89	4.1	2.8	2%	1%	0%	0%	0%	16%	0.060	27	0.111	34
75	Tulsa	-0.29	-0.09	67	-0.29	76	5.7	3.4	-	2%	0%	0%	1%	57%	0.187	74	0.298	69
76	Oregon State	-0.29	0.14	53	-0.75	103	4.8	3.0	1%	1%	0%	0%	0%	31%	0.084	44	0.125	42
77	Arkansas	-0.30	-0.30	82	-0.35	81	4.2	1.7	0%	0%	0%	0%	0%	15%	0.020	3	0.035	7
78	Maryland	-0.30	-0.30	83	-0.34	79	4.4	2.3	0%	0%	0%	0%	0%	20%	0.027	7	0.032	4
79	Wyoming	-0.31	-0.90	107	0.27	52	6.4	4.3	10%	7%	0%	0%	3%	71%	0.364	102	0.619	88
80	Western Michigan	-0.31	0.23	48	-0.62	96	7.0	5.1	32%	15%	0%	0%	5%	82%	0.349	100	0.842	123
81	Arizona	-0.31	0.27	46	-0.68	99	4.9	2.9	2%	1%	0%	0%	0%	32%	0.104	54	0.125	43
82	Buffalo	-0.33	-0.47	91	0.07	61	6.8	5.0	30%	16%	0%	0%	4%	83%	0.174	72	0.747	110
83	Marshall	-0.34	-0.65	103	-0.07	67	6.3	4.6	17%	10%	0%	0%	3%	68%	0.421	113	0.680	98
84	South Florida	-0.36	-0.82	106	0.27	51	5.2	3.0	-	1%	0%	0%	0%	40%	0.133	60	0.244	65
85	Georgia Southern	-0.39	-0.64	102	-0.15	70	6.5	4.6	14%	9%	0%	0%	2%	72%	0.321	96	0.637	90
86	Syracuse	-0.39	-0.36	87	-0.35	82	5.4	2.7	0%	0%	0%	0%	0%	48%	0.126	58	0.145	51
87	Louisiana Tech	-0.42	-0.35	86	-0.24	74	7.4	5.1	30%	12%	0%	0%	9%	88%	0.535	125	0.822	121
88	UAB	-0.44	-1.13	115	0.36	46	7.8	5.1	32%	13%	0%	1%	12%	95%	0.586	128	0.808	119
89	Southern Mississippi	-0.46	-0.61	101	-0.14	69	7.1	4.7	20%	8%	0%	0%	4%	85%	0.341	99	0.680	99
90	Troy	-0.49	0.11	58	-0.88	106	7.0	4.5	14%	9%	0%	0%	6%	86%	0.410	111	0.612	87

Rk	Team	F+	OF+	Rk	DF+	Rk	MW	CW	Div	Conf	CFP	U	10+	6+	SOS	Rk	CSOS	Rk
91	Colorado State	-0.50	-0.28	81	-0.63	97	6.2	3.9	5%	3%	0%	0%	2%	66%	0.388	106	0.482	76
92	Fresno State	-0.50	-0.26	78	-0.60	95	6.5	4.1	20%	7%	0%	0%	1%	74%	0.368	103	0.692	103
93	Arkansas State	-0.52	0.08	59	-0.87	105	6.1	4.4	22%	9%	0%	0%	1%	66%	0.215	78	0.585	83
94	Army	-0.53	-0.15	68	-0.71	101	7.0	-	-	-	0%	0%	4%	84%	0.373	104	-	-
95	Utah State	-0.53	-0.58	99	-0.36	85	5.5	3.7	5%	3%	0%	0%	0%	50%	0.224	80	0.489	77
96	Central Michigan	-0.57	-0.51	94	-0.39	87	6.2	4.1	13%	6%	0%	0%	1%	67%	0.461	116	0.756	112
97	Ball State	-0.60	-0.31	84	-0.65	98	6.1	4.3	18%	8%	0%	0%	1%	65%	0.290	93	0.704	104
98	Toledo	-0.61	-0.09	66	-0.93	108	6.5	4.5	20%	9%	0%	0%	2%	75%	0.503	120	0.783	117
99	Hawaii	-0.62	0.25	47	-1.28	117	6.5	3.9	15%	5%	0%	0%	3%	75%	0.254	87	0.518	78
100	Vanderbilt	-0.64	-1.07	114	-0.12	68	3.7	1.4	0%	0%	0%	0%	0%	11%	0.046	20	0.061	18
101	Miami (OH)	-0.69	-1.01	111	-0.21	71	6.5	4.4	18%	10%	0%	0%	1%	74%	0.519	122	0.777	116
102	Middle Tennessee	-0.72	-0.02	64	-1.13	112	6.3	4.0	9%	5%	0%	0%	1%	66%	0.523	123	0.738	108
103	Georgia State	-0.86	-0.18	71	-1.14	113	5.4	3.4	3%	2%	0%	0%	0%	47%	0.167	68	0.553	82
104	East Carolina	-0.87	-0.18	73	-1.29	119	4.3	2.3	-	0%	0%	0%	0%	22%	0.225	81	0.317	71
105	Liberty	-0.89	-0.50	93	-0.89	107	6.8	-	-	-	0%	0%	2%	81%	0.469	118	-	-
106	Eastern Michigan	-0.89	-0.17	70	-1.24	115	5.0	3.7	8%	4%	0%	0%	1%	36%	0.362	101	0.676	95
107	Florida International	-0.91	-1.06	113	-0.58	93	6.1	3.7	6%	3%	0%	0%	1%	65%	0.469	117	0.713	105
108	San Jose State	-0.91	-0.25	76	-1.27	116	5.4	3.3	7%	2%	0%	0%	0%	50%	0.240	83	0.518	79
109	Nevada	-0.94	-1.13	116	-0.55	92	6.0	3.6	11%	4%	0%	0%	1%	62%	0.637	129	0.794	118
110	Kansas	-0.94	-0.69	104	-0.99	110	3.3	1.4	-	0%	0%	0%	0%	5%	0.070	35	0.076	22
111	Charlotte	-0.95	-0.22	75	-1.34	120	5.7	3.8	6%	4%	0%	0%	0%	55%	0.396	107	0.654	92
112	Northern Illinois	-0.95	-1.26	118	-0.43	88	5.4	3.7	9%	4%	0%	0%	0%	47%	0.416	112	0.767	113
113	Rutgers	-0.97	-1.39	120	-0.48	91	3.3	1.6	0%	0%	0%	0%	0%	4%	0.045	19	0.054	17
114	Kent State	-1.02	-0.49	92	-1.40	122	4.8	3.7	7%	4%	0%	0%	0%	30%	0.085	45	0.744	109
115	Coastal Carolina	-1.02	-0.52	95	-1.29	118	5.3	3.2	3%	2%	0%	0%	0%	45%	0.430	114	0.587	84
116	North Texas	-1.08	-0.97	110	-1.00	111	5.5	3.9	11%	4%	0%	0%	0%	47%	0.377	105	0.818	120
117	UL Monroe	-1.14	-0.26	77	-1.46	123	4.6	3.0	5%	2%	0%	0%	0%	28%	0.240	84	0.605	86
118	UNLV	-1.31	-0.80	105	-1.37	121	3.3	2.5	2%	1%	0%	0%	0%	8%	0.287	91	0.536	81
119	South Alabama	-1.33	-1.52	123	-0.76	104	4.6	3.0	5%	2%	0%	0%	0%	27%	0.315	94	0.659	94
120	Rice	-1.34	-1.78	127	-0.72	102	4.8	3.3	5%	2%	0%	0%	0%	32%	0.287	92	0.716	106
121	Old Dominion	-1.38	-1.89	128	-0.60	94	4.7	2.7	1%	1%	0%	0%	0%	30%	0.539	127	0.654	91
122	New Mexico	-1.40	-0.96	109	-1.55	125	4.7	2.2	1%	0%	0%	0%	0%	24%	0.256	88	0.519	80
123	UTSA	-1.58	-1.18	117	-1.56	126	4.4	2.9	2%	1%	0%	0%	0%	21%	0.222	79	0.685	101
124	Texas State	-1.62	-1.65	125	-1.18	114	3.6	2.1	1%	1%	0%	0%	0%	11%	0.536	126	0.619	89
125	Connecticut	-1.78	-1.50	122	-1.66	127	3.7	-	-	-	0%	0%	0%	8%	0.278	89	-	-
126	Bowling Green	-1.86	-1.73	126	-1.55	124	3.7	2.2	0%	0%	0%	0%	0%	9%	0.210	77	0.754	111
127	New Mexico State	-1.87	-1.34	119	-1.83	128	4.4	-	-	-	0%	0%	0%	21%	0.318	95	-	-
128	Akron	-1.92	-2.46	130	-0.94	109	4.1	2.0	0%	0%	0%	0%	0%	14%	0.253	86	0.685	100
129	UTEP	-2.42	-1.89	129	-2.24	129	2.2	1.5	0%	0%	0%	0%	0%	1%	0.477	119	0.839	122
130	Massachusetts	-2.49	-1.64	124	-2.76	130	3.0	-	-	-	0%	0%	0%	3%	0.338	98	-	-

FO Rookie Projections

Over the years, Football Outsiders has developed a number of methods for forecasting the NFL success of highly drafted players at various positions. Here is a rundown of those methods and what they say about players drafted in 2020.

Quarterbacks: QBASE

The QBASE (Quarterback Adjusted Stats and Experience) system analyzes the last 21 years of rookie quarterbacks chosen among the top 100 picks of the NFL draft and uses regression analysis to determine which factors helped predict their total passing DYAR in Years 3 through 5 of their careers. (We use these years to account for the fact that many highly drafted quarterbacks may not play regularly until their second or even third seasons.)

The primary factor in QBASE is the quarterback's college performance, analyzed with three metrics: completion rate, yards per attempt adjusted based on touchdowns and interceptions, and team passing SP+ from Bill Connelly's college stats. We then adjust based on strength of schedule and strength of teammates. The latter element gives credit based on the draft-pick value of offensive linemen and receivers drafted in the quarterback's draft year as well as the projected draft position of younger teammates in 2021.

The measurement of past performance is then combined with two other factors: college experience and draft position. The latter factor accounts for what scouts will see but a statistical projection system will not, including personality, leadership, and projection of physical attributes to the next level.

QBASE also looks at the past performance of quarterbacks compared to their projection and, using 50,000 simulations, produces a range of potential outcomes for each prospect: Elite quarterback (over 2,500 DYAR in Years 3 through 5), Upper Tier quarterback (1,500 to 2,500 DYAR), Adequate Starter (500 to 1,500 DYAR), or Bust (less than 500 DYAR in Years 3 through 5).

Here are QBASE projections for quarterbacks chosen in the top 100 picks of the 2020 NFL draft:

Player	College	Tm	Rd	Pick	QBASE	Elite	Upper Tier	Adequate	Bust
Joe Burrow	LSU	CIN	1	1	759	12%	19%	27%	42%
Tua Tagovailoa	ALA	MIA	1	5	653	8%	19%	27%	45%
Justin Herbert	ORE	LAC	1	6	806	13%	18%	25%	43%
Jordan Love	USU	GB	1	26	30	2%	9%	22%	67%
Jalen Hurts	OKLA	PHI	2	53	719	10%	20%	25%	44%

Projections are slightly different from those posted on our website in April because they have been adjusted for each player's actual draft position instead of projected draft position.

Running Backs: BackCAST

BackCAST is Football Outsiders' metric for projecting the likelihood of success for running back prospects in the NFL draft. Historically, a college running back is more likely to succeed at the NFL level if he has a good size/speed combination, gained a high average yards per carry, and represented a large percentage of his college team's running attack. Criteria measured include:

- Weight and 40-yard dash time at the NFL combine. BackCAST uses pro day measurements for prospects that did not run at the combine. For 2020, we made additional estimates for players whose pro days were cancelled due to COVID-19.
- Average yards per rush attempt, with an adjustment for running backs who had fewer career carries than an average drafted running back.
- A measurement of how much each prospect's team used him in the running game during his career relative to an average drafted running back in the same year of eligibility.
- Prospect's receiving yards per game in his college career.

BackCAST considers these factors and projects the degree to which the running back will exceed the NFL production of an "average" drafted running back during his first five years in the NFL. For example, a running back with a 50% BackCAST is projected to gain 50% more yards than the "average" drafted running back. BackCAST also lists each running back's "RecIndex," measuring whether the player is likely to be a ground-and-pound two-down back, more of a receiving back, or something in between. The higher the RecIndex, the better the back is as a receiver.

Here are the BackCAST numbers for running backs drafted in the first three rounds of the 2020 draft, along with the three later-round picks with positive BackCAST ratings.

Player	College	Tm	Rd	Pick	BackCAST	RecIndex
Clyde Edwards-Helaire	LSU	KC	1	32	-36.1%	+0.18
D'Andre Swift	UGA	DET	2	35	53.7%	+0.14
Jonathan Taylor	WIS	IND	2	41	196.9%	-0.21
Cam Akers	FSU	LAR	2	52	51.7%	+0.01
J.K. Dobbins	OSU	BAL	2	55	67.5%	+0.16
AJ Dillon	BC	GB	2	62	111.4%	-0.51
Ke'Shawn Vaughn	VAN	TB	3	76	30.9%	+0.06
Zack Moss	UTAH	BUF	3	86	6.4%	+0.03
Darrynton Evans	APP	TEN	3	93	25.7%	-0.08
Anthony McFarland	UMD	PIT	4	124	39.1%	-0.11
Joshua Kelley	UCLA	LAC	4	112	24.7%	0.00
Eno Benjamin	ASU	ARI	7	222	1.5%	+0.29

Two running backs who played significantly at wide receiver in college, Lynn Bowden and Antonio Gibson, were projected using Playmaker Score instead and are listed in that section.

Edge Rushers: SackSEER

SackSEER is a method that projects sacks for edge rushers, including both 3-4 outside linebackers and 4-3 defensive ends, using the following criteria:

- An "explosion index" that measures the prospect's scores in the 40-yard dash, the vertical jump, and the broad jump in pre-draft workouts.
- Sacks per game, adjusted for factors such as early entry in the NFL draft and position switches during college.
- Passes defensed per game.
- Missed games of NCAA eligibility due to academic problems, injuries, benchings, suspensions, or attendance at junior college.

SackSEER outputs two numbers. The first, SackSEER Rating, solely measures how high the prospect scores compared to players of the past. The second, SackSEER Projection, represents a forecast of sacks for the player's first five years in the NFL. It synthesizes metrics with conventional wisdom by adjusting based on the player's expected draft position (interestingly, not his actual draft position) based on pre-draft analysis at the site NFLDraftScout.com.

Here are the SackSEER numbers for edge rushers drafted in the first three rounds of the 2020 draft, along with the four later-round picks with the highest SackSEER Ratings.

Name	College	Tm	Rnd	Pick	SackSEER Projection	SackSEER Rating
Chase Young	OSU	WAS	1	2	30.7	98.3%
K'Lavon Chaisson	LSU	JAX	1	20	18.5	36.0%
Yetur Gross-Matos	PSU	CAR	2	38	18.0	61.6%
Darrell Taylor	TENN	SEA	2	48	6.5	73.5%
A.J. Epenesa	IOWA	BUF	2	54	23.5	72.4%
Josh Uche	MICH	NE	2	60	2.9	42.7%
Julian Okwara	ND	DET	3	67	13.9	68.8%
Zach Baun	WIS	NO	3	74	12.6	10.1%
Jabari Zuniga	FLA	NYJ	3	79	4.3	66.8%
Terrell Lewis	ALA	LAR	3	84	15.8	72.0%
Anfernee Jennings	ALA	NE	3	87	15.8	61.6%
Jonathan Greenard	FLA	HOU	3	90	6.3	67.0%
Alex Highsmith	CHAR	PIT	3	102	2.8	38.6%
Curtis Weaver	BSU	MIA	5	164	17.9	91.8%
Alton Robinson	SYR	SEA	5	148	5.3	65.9%
Casey Toohill	STAN	PHI	7	233	5.7	65.5%
Jonathan Garvin	MIA	GB	7	242	5.2	63.4%

Wide Receivers: Playmaker Score

Playmaker Score projects success for NFL wide receivers using the following criteria:

- The wide receiver's peak season for receiving yards per team attempt and receiving touchdowns per team attempt.
- Differences between this prospect's peak season and most recent season, to adjust for players who declined in their final college year.
- Rushing attempts per game.
- A binary variable that rewards players who enter the draft as underclassmen.
- A factor that gives a bonus to wideouts who played on the same college team as other receivers who are projected to be drafted.

The final factor is new in Playmaker Score for 2020 and helps boost the stock of receivers whose raw numbers were hurt because they had to split passes with one or more other talented receivers: for example Jerry Jeudy and Henry Ruggs III in this past draft.

Playmaker Score's output represents a forecast of average receiving yards per year in the player's first five seasons, synthesizing metrics with conventional wisdom by adjusting based on the player's expected draft position.

Here are the Playmaker Score numbers for players drafted in the first three rounds of the 2020 draft. Antonio Gibson and Lynn Bowden, drafted as running backs, are listed separately. We also list the highest Playmaker Score numbers for Day 3 picks.

The highest UDFA Playmaker Score belonged to Carolina's Omar Bayless (Arkansas State) at 216. A full explanation of Playmaker Score can be found online.[1]

Name	College	Team	Rnd	Pick	Playmaker Score
Henry Ruggs	ALA	LV	1	12	567
Jerry Jeudy	ALA	DEN	1	15	668
CeeDee Lamb	OKLA	DAL	1	17	690
Jalen Reagor	TCU	PHI	1	21	425
Justin Jefferson	LSU	MIN	1	22	599
Brandon Aiyuk	ASU	SF	1	25	370
Tee Higgins	CLEM	CIN	2	33	417
Michael Pittman	USC	IND	2	34	379
Laviska Shenault	COLO	JAX	2	42	395
KJ Hamler	PSU	DEN	2	46	416
Chase Claypool	ND	PIT	2	49	364
Van Jefferson	FLA	LAR	2	57	96
Denzel Mims	BAY	NYJ	2	59	469
Bryan Edwards	SCAR	LV	3	81	169
Devin Duvernay	TEX	BAL	3	92	308
Antonio Gibson	MEM	WAS	3	66	54
Lynn Bowden	UK	LV	3	80	349
Gabriel Davis	UCF	BUF	4	128	404
Antonio Gandy-Golden	LIB	WAS	4	142	291
Tyler Johnson	MINN	TB	5	161	288
Isaiah Hodgins	ORST	BUF	6	207	260

---

1 https://www.footballoutsiders.com/stat-analysis/2020/playmaker-score-2020.

Top 25 Prospects

Every year, Football Outsiders puts together a list of the NFL's best and brightest young players who have barely played. Eighty percent of draft-day discussion is about first-round picks, and 10% is about the players who should have been first-round picks but instead went in the second round. Particularly if they were quarterbacks.

This list is about the last 10%.

Everybody knows that Chase Young and Joe Burrow are good. There's a cottage industry around the idea of hyping every draft's No. 1 quarterback as a potential superstar. But players don't stop being promising just because they don't make waves in their rookie seasons. This is a list of players who have a strong chance to make an impact in the NFL despite their lack of draft stock and the fact that they weren't immediate NFL starters.

Previous editions of the list have hyped players such as Geno Atkins, Grady Jarrett, Chris Godwin, Tyreek Hill, and Jamaal Charles before they blew up. Last year's list included Mark Andrews, Maurice Hurst, Tracy Walker, and J.C. Jackson.

Most of these lists are heavily dependent on the depth of incoming draft classes. For instance, this year's list doesn't have many edge players, because most of the eligible players either played right away or didn't have the requisite talent. Last year's list was packed with interior linemen. This year is heavier on cornerbacks after a 2019 draft class that was quite strong on the defensive line. We're also going to be focusing more heavily on players with immediate chances to play this year because COVID-19 is going to be shortening the preseason in a material way. We think there will be fewer cases of new players winning jobs in camp.

This is the 14th anniversary of the list. We're still relying on the same things we always do: scouting, statistics, measurables, context, ceiling, expected role, and what we hear from other sources. The goal is to bring your attention to players who are still developing in their second and third seasons, even after the draftniks have forgotten them. It's important to note that this list is not strictly about fantasy football (otherwise, there would be no offensive linemen on it) and it's about career potential, not just the 2020 season.

Here's our full criteria:

- Drafted in the third round or later, or signed as an undrafted free agent.
- Entered the NFL between 2017 and 2019.
- Fewer than 500 career offensive or defensive snaps (except running backs, who are allowed just 300 offensive snaps).
- Have not signed a contract extension (players who have bounced around the league looking for the right spot, however, still qualify for the list).
- Age 26 or younger in 2020.

1 Ifeadi Odenigbo, ER, MIN; Age: 26
Drafted 2017, pick 220; Career snaps: 375

With the Vikings parting with Everson Griffen, it's a pretty clean projection to assume that Odenigbo will be moving into the starting lineup. But in case you want a word from Vikings defensive line coach/co-coordinator Andre Patterson, he told Vikings reporters in a conference call: "I'm excited about Ifeadi to continue to improve as a player. He made great strides last year, and he's a tremendously hard worker. I know he's busting his tail right now ... as a matter of fact, I have to talk to him about not over-training."

Odenigbo's Northwestern roots were as a power player with NFL pass-rush moves and flashes, but also as someone who was essentially platooned by the Wildcats. He led the Big Ten in sacks as a senior anyway with 10 and ran a 4.72s 40-yard dash at the combine. His SackSEER rating of 62.7% was impressive for a low-round pick; Odenigbo had an explosion index of 0.61 and offered a lot of college production.

Over the last five games of last season, Odenigbo notched four of his seven sacks, forced a fumble, and returned another fumble for a 56-yard touchdown. He brought down both Russell Wilson and Aaron Rodgers last year. He may still platoon with a different defender on pure run downs if that section of his game gets off to a poor start, but Odenigbo is on pace to become yet another late-round win on the edge for a Vikings team that already starts 2015 third-rounder Danielle Hunter.

2 Dre'Mont Jones, IDL, DEN; Age: 23
Drafted 2019, pick 71; Career snaps: 284

All Jones did down the stretch was win AFC Defensive Player of the Week with a 2.5-sack, two-tackle for loss demolition against the Lions in Week 16. That about matches the gist of what happened when he played at Ohio State, where he picked up 8.5 sacks and 13 tackles for loss in a dominant junior year that helped him make the easy decision to turn pro.

The Broncos had some turnover inside this offseason, bringing in Jurrell Casey and losing Derek Wolfe and Adam Gotsis. Jones is ticketed for a bigger role this season in that front, though one that may still seem him protected on some snaps as the Broncos have a deep line of solid run-stuffers such as Mike Purcell and DeMarcus Walker. Jones gained the respect of head coach Vic Fangio by playing hurt down the stretch, and Fangio noted in a presser after that Week 16 win over the Lions that "a lot of guys wouldn't have played yesterday with what he had, but he wanted to play. I think that's a good indication of who he is as a guy and he got rewarded with a couple of sacks. Those are the kind of guys you want on your team."

If Jones grows further into his role and learns to run-stuff as well as he can rush, he's on the path to be one of the better interior linemen in the game, and he couldn't pick a better player to learn from in that regard than Casey. If he never learns to do more than that, he'll probably be a pretty good situational pass-rusher à la Nick Fairley or Sheldon Richardson.

3 Preston Williams, WR, MIA; Age: 23
Undrafted free agent, 2019; Career snaps: 404

It had just turned November, the Dolphins were tanking for Tua (turns out they didn't need to), and Preston Williams was somehow the best receiver on the roster. Williams, who went undrafted out of Colorado State mostly because of a college arrest for domestic violence, led the Dolphins to an upset win over the Jets in which he caught five balls for 72 yards and two touchdowns. He also tore his ACL, maintaining his ability to remain under the snap count for this list.

After Williams left, DeVante Parker exploded. Parker had zero games with over 75 receiving yards in the first nine. After Williams left, Parker had five over the last seven, earning a huge contract extension. Between Parker's blow-up and the hiring of new offensive coordinator Chan Gailey, Williams' ability to repeat his early-season play is a bit more in question than some players on this list. Still, the Dolphins didn't pick anyone in one of the deepest receiver drafts in some time, and Williams should have recovered from his injury in time for the 2020 season.

A tall, fast, jump-ball winner, Williams caught just 53% of his passes last year—but in an offense that did not truly hit its stride until after he left. Whether it's Ryan Fitzpatrick or Tagovailoa at quarterback, Williams is the best bet among the receivers on this list to hit in a volume role. That's why he's parked right here.

4 Jamel Dean, CB, TB; Age: 24
Drafted 2019, pick 94; Career snaps: 370

In his first year with Tampa Bay, Dean was one of those odd corners who come in with the nickel package but played outside. Sean Murphy-Bunting would move to the slot, freeing Dean to practice his aggressive press coverage on anyone he can get his hands on. Which, it turned out, was a lot of receivers … after his first game. In Dean's first NFL action against Seattle in Week 9, he allowed 155 yards on targets in his coverage, including 81 alone on two DK Metcalf bombs.

For the entirety of the rest of the season, Dean was targeted 30 times and allowed 107 total yards. That includes holding his targets to zero yards against Arizona, 38 in two games against Atlanta, and 28 against Houston. He also picked off both Deshaun Watson and Kyler Murray.

Scouts liked Dean's size and speed coming out of Auburn but were concerned about his multiple high school and college knee surgeries. Running a 4.3s 40-yard dash at the combine seemed to assuage a lot of those fears. The Bucs were a terrific landing spot for him precisely because of how much aggressive coverage Todd Bowles plays, but anyone who can play outside corner as well as Dean played for the last seven weeks of the season deserves to raise some alarm bells.

5 Chase Winovich, ER, NE; Age: 25
Drafted 2019, pick 77; Career snaps: 291

Winovich told Patrots.com during the 2020 offseason that he saw last season as "challenging," which is an interesting way to describe a year where he had 5.5 sacks off the bench in a part-time role. Winovich is a big winner in New England's tumultuous offseason that saw Jamie Collins, Elandon Roberts, and Kyle Van Noy flee to former Patriots coaches in big-money deals. New England hit the pass rush hard in the draft with Josh Uche in the second round and Anfernee Jennings in the third round, but Winovich is the only upside player they have with much in the way of real experience.

Winovich was an effort rusher at Michigan, finishing with 18.5 sacks in his last three seasons as well as 43 tackles for loss. None of his combine results really stood out for good or ill except for an impressive 6.94s 3-cone drill. His SackSEER was low (36.7%) in part due to a lack of passes defensed in college.

The Patriots figure to break in the rookies slowly in a CO-VID year as long as they have an option, and with the depth chart populated by John Simon and Shilique Calhoun—and maybe a throwback to prospect lists of old in Derek Rivers!—they don't have any impactful pass-rushers with any experience outside of Winovich. He figures to be involved early and often.

6 Miles Boykin, WR, BAL; Age: 24
Drafted 2019, pick 93; Career snaps: 425

Boykin would have been compared physically to Calvin Johnson if he were about 2 inches taller. What happened instead is that Boykin went to the combine and ran a 4.42s 40-yard dash at 220 pounds, then followed that up with 98th-percentile scores in the jumps while showcasing elite skill at just about everything besides the bench press. If the 2019 combine was a show, Boykin was one of the main attractions.

However, he's in a bit of an odd situation. Clearly the Ravens are likely to have him on the field a lot this year. Seth Roberts is gone to Carolina, and both Willie Snead and Devin Duvernay are better suited for the slot. So the path to playing time is clear. The college production shows Boykin as a touchdown machine with 11 scores in 77 career college catches. Playmaker Score (170 yards per season) was not quite as high given a projected fifth-round slot for Boykin, but the combine made his stock soar.

Lamar Jackson is a much more accurate quarterback when targeting the middle of the field right now, and Boykin is mostly going to be a perimeter operator in an offense that already has plenty of mouths to feed. That doesn't mean Boykin won't offer a lot of value: he caught 10 of 15 targets from Jackson on the outside last year for 166 yards. But Boykin could be a better overall player than Preston Williams in 2020, just without the same volume.

7 Bobby Okereke, LB, IND; Age: 24
Drafted 2019, pick 89; Career snaps: 472

Will Okereke beat out Anthony Walker to be the No. 2 linebacker in Indy this year? It seems like a pretty easy transition on paper, but the Colts have offered a ton of praise for Walker's intelligence. Linebackers coach Dave Borgozi certainly expects a breakout, telling Colts.com: "We expect Bobby to make a big jump from Year 1 to Year 2, just in his production, his plays on the ball, interceptions, game-changing plays. Bobby has a lot of ability and we expect him to really have a great season this coming year."

Coming out of Stanford, Okereke caught eyes at the combine with a blazing fast 4.58s 40-yard dash at 239 pounds. Being a good coverage linebacker means a lot in a league that needs as many of them as it can get, and Okereke showed some early aptitude in that area as he allowed just 71 yards on 12 coverage targets after Week 3's firestorm against the Falcons.

If Okereke can improve on run defense quickly heading into the year, he won't give the Colts any choice but to play him. Even if the Colts still do play Walker some, it's likely that Okereke will be the big factor on passing downs. If that pans out as they hope, an Okereke/Darius Leonard tandem could be tough to throw underneath on for many years.

8 Jace Sternberger, TE, GB; Age: 24
Drafted 2019, pick 75; Career snaps: 65

Buried on the bench last year almost inexplicably behind a washed-up Jimmy Graham, Sternberger should finally get some freedom now that the only player on the tight end depth chart with a meaningful role in 2019 is Marcedes Lewis. Sternberger is a rarity: a skill position player that has Matt LaFleur's eye. LaFleur told the team's official website in March that "[Sternberger] has contact courage. He's not afraid to put his face on people. He's a much better blocker than anyone ever thought he was coming out of Texas A&M. I'm just excited for his future."

And while Sternberger showed plenty at Texas A&M with an 832-yard, 10-touchdown outburst in his only real season of work after transferring from Kansas, this placement for him is really more about the opportunity than anything else. The Packers had no reliable targets last year other than Davante Adams—Aaron Jones finished second on the team in targets—so it stands to reason that Sternberger could step right in and fill a gaping No. 2 target role the Packers never properly filled after Jordy Nelson was released.

Sternberger's rookie season did not offer much of a clue about how he would play going forward, as he was mostly utilized as an extra blocker in three-tight end sets, but the pedigree and opportunity combine to tell a story worth being quite optimistic about.

9 Alexander Mattison, RB, MIN; Age: 22
Drafted 2019, pick 102; Career snaps: 197

Simply put: with Dalvin Cook holding out and on the verge of free agency, there are very few players with a better potential future situation than Alexander Mattison. Gary Kubiak's running backs have been putting up 1,000-yard seasons whether they are good or not since before Football Outsiders even existed. The Vikings picked Mattison in the third round despite a number of pundits not having that high of a grade on him, which suggests they hold him in quite high esteem.

Mattison, like Cook, had a pretty mediocre combine that ended with a faceplant on the 40-yard dash at a time of just

4.67 seconds at 221 pounds. That's linebacker speed at defensive back size. But Mattison showed just about everything else you could want from a runner: physicality, quickness, vision, and intelligence. It all led to massive production at Boise State as Mattison saw the field for all 13 games as a freshman.

His first season in Minnesota saw Mattison finish with a respectable 24 DYAR in 100 totes, despite a relatively low success rate of 38%. Mattison averaged 4.6 yards per attempt with no real negative split when running zone plays, but SIS charting charged the Vikings with 11 blown blocks during those 100 attempts, and those 11 carries averaged -1.2 yards. With enough skill to be a competent receiver as well, the Vikings have the ultimate leverage against a Cook holdout: someone who can do the job just as well without a high price tag.

10 Daniel Brunskill, OL, SF; Age: 26
Undrafted free agent, 2017; Career snaps: 476

Mike Person was the 49ers' starting right guard last year, but it was Brunskill who showed time and time again that he belonged on the field. Working at both tackle and guard, Brunskill blew just two blocks that led to sacks—one against Aaron Donald—and showcased some pass-blocking steadiness on a team that needed a lot of it over the course of the season due to various injuries.

Brunskill's time at San Diego State showed a player with enough athleticism to fit a zone scheme: he's a converted tight end that earned a second-team All-Mountain West selection after switching positions right before his senior year though he did play offensive line in high school. The knock on him coming out was a lack of functional strength, which is why he went undrafted. After two years in Atlanta—originally under Kyle Shanahan—Brunskill signed with the 49ers last offseason and picked up seven starts.

Person retired this offseason but the 49ers didn't draft a lineman until the fifth round and only Ben Garland remains as an interior challenger who played last year. That should put the 26-year-old Brunskill in position to become a starter for the first time, and what we saw last year indicates he can handle that well.

11 Hunter Renfrow, WR, LV; Age: 25
Drafted 2019, pick 149; Career snaps: 435

He's the 11th-best prospect because he's only on the field in 11 personnel. See what we did there? Renfrow had always played above his tools at Clemson, and he did so again in his first season with the Raiders when he put up a 7.9% DVOA on the back of a 69% catch rate as a super slot receiver.

Renfrow's combine was the disaster that it was expected to be: he ran a 4.59s 40-yard dash, he weighed in at just 184 pounds, and his hand size, wingspan, and arm length were all in the bottom five percentile of all NFL wideouts since 2000. It didn't really matter, because Renfrow is the rare player who appears to live the Wes Welker lifestyle as well as Welker did. He uses the shifty, quick change of direction to get open underneath, and he knows exactly where to run when he catches the ball.

The upside of a player like this is a weird topic to discuss. There's no physical upside, but Renfrow is the kind of player who can thrive as a big part of a short-passing offense as long as he stays healthy. That's exactly what the Raiders did with him last year, and as long as they're trailing often enough to keep Gruden from using multiple tight ends, they should repeat the same thing this season.

12 Julian Love, DB, NYG; Age: 22
Drafted 2019, pick 108; Career snaps: 409

One of the youngest players on the list, Love was an easy middle-of-the-field pick for the Giants in the middle rounds of the draft, and one of the few players that showed Dave Gettleman recognizing that the passing game exists. Love essentially didn't break the lineup until Week 12 but played almost all the Giants snaps from Week 13 to the end of the season. Over that span, we have Love credited with 21 targets into his coverage, on which he allowed just 72 yards and one touchdown. He moved from cornerback to strong safety to replace the injured Jabrill Peppers.

Coming out of Notre Dame in 2019, Love was regarded as a very safe fit as an NFL slot corner with great coverage instincts. The combine caused his draft stock some damage because he ran just a 4.55s 40-yard dash, and most draftniks have congealed around the notion that anything lower than 4.60 for a corner is generally too slow to ride the NFL ride. That was the main grievance that took him out of the top two rounds despite breaking up 39 passes in his final two seasons for the Irish.

With the selection of Xavier McKinney in the second round, the Giants have the makings of a good nickel or dime set between Love, McKinney, and Peppers. We don't exactly know what Love is going to technically be called, be it safety or corner, but he's going to play in the middle of the field and he's going to cause havoc.

13 Drue Tranquil, LB, LAC; Age: 25
Drafted 2019, pick 130; Career snaps: 380

What Tranquil offered was well-spelled out in college: he's a modern coverage linebacker who doubles as an excellent special-teamer. He finished his career at Notre Dame with three picks and 11 passes defensed, as well as 184 solo tackles. Placed into this role at the NFL level, Tranquil did fairly well in coverage and excelled at special teams. He was named to the PFWA All-Rookie Team as the non-returner/kicker special teams player and finished second on the Chargers in special teams tackles behind Derek Watt.

Where his stock really climbed was (surprise) at the combine, where he ran a 4.57s 40-yard dash at 234 pounds, showed good leaping ability, and had a sub-7s 3-cone drill while completing the bench press 31 times. Tranquil gave up two passes all season that went more than 15 yards: a 47-yard go route to Tyreek Hill in Week 17, and a screen to Jonnu Smith for 35 yards in Week 7. He also added some pretty solid run defense, albeit in a small sample of plays that mostly saw him in on passing downs.

The Chargers added a lot at linebacker this season between first-round pick Kenneth Murray and ex-Bengal Nick Vigil. They also have to decide just how invested they are in Denzel Perryman after three straight years below 400 snaps. At worst, Tranquil will continue to be an ace special-teamer and passing-downs linebacker. At best, he can take the leap up and become a three-down player next to Murray.

14 Justin Jackson, RB, LAC; Age: 25
Drafted 2018, pick 251; Career snaps: 242

Jackson lost a large chunk of last season to a calf injury and missed his opportunity to really solidify a role in the Chargers backfield for this season. When he played, he was wildly effective, finishing with the highest DVOA of any back with more than 20 rushes at 34.9%. In 2018, he recorded a 29.9% receiving DVOA. So the full package has been on display for the last two years, but after Jackson played in just 20 of 32 possible games the Chargers had to spend a draft pick on Josh Kelley to make sure they were set post-Melvin Gordon.

However, with Kelley not getting in any work in front of Anthony Lynn, it's a little harder to believe offensive coordinator Shane Steichen's May proclamation that all three backs would share the load. We believe Jackson will get the first opportunity to be the inside thunder to Austin Ekeler's lightning, and Jackson has shown that he has the talent to seize the role if he plays well off the bat.

Despite power running and tackle-breaking being considered a bit of a weakness of Jackson's game in college, we now have him down for 27 broken tackles in 103 touches, which is a ridiculous rate. We have seen other people lose faith in Jackson, but every time he has been on the field so far, he has made explosive offense happen and it's hard to ignore it.

15 Ja'Whaun Bentley, LB, NE; Age: 24
Drafted 2018, pick 143; Career snaps: 413

We believed that Bentley would get on the field last year and make his presence felt after losing his rookie season to a biceps tear, but instead the Patriots were able to swoop up Jamie Collins in free agency and used him and Kyle Van Noy extensively up the middle with Dont'a Hightower. Bentley instead spent the season mostly as a reserve, playing over 40% of snaps in just three games.

Bentley now finds an almost barren depth chart in front of him with Collins in Detroit and Van Noy and another Patriots backup linebacker, Elandon Roberts, in Miami. Hightower and Bentley are the only middle linebackers from last year's team that played regular-season snaps. The only player New England added in the draft at the position is sixth-rounder Cassh Maluia.

We still like Bentley as a run-stuffer a lot. It's a very small sample size, but he allowed just 49 yards on 12 targets in pass coverage in every game besides New England's Week 4 contest against the Bills. There's little reason to believe he won't be a three-down linebacker this year as long as he proves he can handle passing-down duties. That's a long-term concern, but there's not much in place to challenge him right away in 2020.

16 David Long, CB, LAR; Age: 22
Drafted 2019, pick 79; Career snaps: 109

This is mostly a pick about pedigree, because Long didn't log many snaps last year for a Rams team that primarily used Jalen Ramsey (or Marcus Peters before the trade), Troy Hill, and Nickell Robey-Coleman at cornerback. Robey-Coleman departed for free agency, leaving only Darious Williams as a real challenger for Long as the third corner.

At Michigan, Long was a true outside corner who bullied receivers without much in the way of repercussions, piling up impressive coverage numbers like a few other former Wolverines in the past couple of draft classes. He plays stronger than his 5-foot-11½, 196-pound frame would lead you to believe, which means he can handle some of the tougher matchups outside that the NFL can sometimes present. His horizontal movement is top-notch, which he demonstrated with an absurd 6.45s 3-cone drill time at the combine.

Long's only real taste of major NFL action was in Week 17's finale against the Cardinals, where he played 76% of the snaps. We have him allowing three catches for 42 yards and a touchdown on five targets—not bad, but not great either. We believe that Williams will probably get the first look at snaps, but there's not much track record of NFL success there, and Long's pedigree will probably get him on the field in some way this year between Williams' past, Hill playing on a one-year deal, and Ramsey's contract status being hung up in long negotiations. Long is the best long-term bet of the group, and we expect him to start making that clear this year.

17 Jalen Hurd, WR, SF; Age: 24
Drafted 2019, pick 67; Career snaps: 0

What makes Hurd such a fascinating player is that he's got the classic X receiver body, but he also spent a large majority of his college career as a running back—a running back that started ahead of Alvin Kamara. He spent three years at Tennessee, then transferred to Baylor where, after a year learning the position, he went off for 946 yards on 69 catches as a senior.

So, obviously, you've got a lot of after-the-catch ability here. If Hurd had a bonkers pro day (he didn't work out at the combine) he probably had second-round ability, but he only ran a 4.66s 40-yard dash coming off offseason knee surgery. Hurd then went and caught two touchdowns in the 49ers' first preseason game before a stress fracture in his back later in the preseason cost him his rookie year.

Anybody who plays in a Kyle Shanahan offense that cuts like this should be on your radar, and that was before Deebo Samuel's Jones fracture put his early-season availability into doubt. Jimmy Garoppolo told reporters in June: "When you have a guy like that, it makes quarterbacking very easy." Hurd is the obvious draft value choice to get extended snaps and, if he's used anything like the way the Titans used A.J. Brown last year, he could be an instant hit for fantasy leagues.

18 Amani Oruwariye, CB, DET; Age: 24
Drafted 2019, pick 146; Career snaps: 215

Oruwariye's rookie season mostly came down to the fairly meaningless games the Lions had right around Thanksgiving; he played 76% of the snaps in Week 12 against Washington and got 91% the next week against the Bears. As you would expect from a rookie as physically gifted as Oruwariye who didn't get picked in the first round, the season became a bit of a learning experience. He mixed good games (one pick, 21 yards in five targets against Washington) with mediocre ones (36 yards allowed on three completed targets against the Bears). He did end the season on a high note by picking Aaron Rodgers in the Week 17 upset bid that almost toppled Green Bay out of the No. 2 seed.

Oruwariye has true outside size at 6-foot-2, 205 pounds, and showed proficient speed with a 4.47s 40-yard dash at the combine. Oruwariye's combine performance was by no means noteworthy or dominant, but corners that size are valued as long as they have proficient athleticism and can jam, which Oruwariye demonstrated he could at Penn State.

With Jeff Okudah, Justin Coleman, and Desmond Trufant signed up for next year, Oruwariye will again start the season as the fourth cornerback. But rookie cornerbacks are not always a group that starts well, and Trufant allowed roughly 10 yards per pass attempt last year and has not been the same player since his 2016 pectoral tear. Orwaruiye is going to surface here eventually; the only question is when.

19 Chandon Sullivan, CB, GB; Age: 24
Undrafted free agent, 2018; Career snaps: 437

The Packers never trusted Sullivan with a true starting role outside, but he got playing time in their deeper packages both in the box and at slot cornerback. Sullivan was absolutely lights-out in coverage in this role that mostly saw him on slot receivers, running backs, and tight ends. He allowed five first downs in coverage all season, and no touchdowns. He also allowed a grand total of six completions in his 21 coverage snaps.

Sullivan's draft stock was heavily impacted by his combine, running a 4.60s-flat 40-yard dash that essentially ended any hopes he had of ending up as an outside corner. However, he displayed other athleticism there by placing in the 90th percentile of both the broad and vertical jumps among corners since 2000. Sullivan signed with the Eagles after the draft and made it to their practice squad in 2018. The Packers signed him away after the 2019 season and plugged him into this role, and it worked.

With Tramon Williams leaving as a free agent, the path of least resistance for the Packers is probably using Sullivan as the primary nickel corner, which is a role that wouldn't seem to stretch what he did last year. No new corners were drafted, and 2018 second-rounder Josh Jackson has been a pretty big disappointment in his first two years in the NFL. If Jackson does get corner snaps, of course, Sullivan gets to stay in a familiar role that he excelled at in 2019.

20 Will Dissly, TE, SEA; Age: 24
Drafted 2018, pick 120; Career snaps: 376

Let's lead with the bad: Dissly has finished the season on IR in two of his two years. A torn Achilles ended his 2019 season, and a torn patellar tendon ended his 2018 season. He has played in just 10 of the 32 possible games he could have played in since the Seahawks drafted him.

But when he plays … Dissly caught 23 of 27 targets last year for 262 yards and four scores, finishing second among qualifying players in tight end DVOA at 36.0%. In 2018, he finished with a 30.6% DVOA on 14 pass attempts. He has showcased a natural chemistry with Russell Wilson on the play-action pass and has more evasion than you'd expect in the open field and up the seam for a player who runs as stiffly as he does with the ball.

The Seahawks signed Greg Olsen this offseason to provide some more punch in passing sets, and that may relegate Dissly to more of a complementary role again. But Olsen is no long-term solution at 35, and all Dissly has done is produce when given the opportunity. Health is a skill, which is why Dissly is as low as he is, but he stands a good chance to outproduce the other tight ends on this list if he can remain healthy.

21 Darius Phillips, CB, CIN; Age: 25
Drafted 2018, pick 170; Career snaps: 341

After a phenomenal preseason, Phillips blitzed his way on to the Cincinnati 53-man roster last year for the second straight season on a crowded depth chart that included B.W. Webb, William Jackson III, Darqueze Dennard, Dre Kirkpatrick, and Tony McRae. All Phillips did with his 101 snaps was intercept four different balls while allowing just four completions in 12 attempts.

A small-schooler out of Western Michigan, Phillips caught scouts' eyes by putting on a show against the big boys. He returned a kickoff 100 yards against USC and picked off balls against USC and Michigan State. Phillips was not a big corner at 5-foot-10, 193 pounds, so scouts assumed he would have to play inside and create value on special teams, but he drew enough interest to get a combine invite and the Bengals popped him in the fifth round.

While the Bengals reloaded on corners in free agency, the end result was pretty favorable for Phillips. Trae Waynes and Jackson are likely locks to play, with Mackenzie Alexander as the presumptive third corner ahead of Phillips. Jackson was the only one of the corners ahead of Phillips in the pecking order to return, and defensive coordinator Lou Anarumo seemed enamored with Phillips' finish to last season at the combine, praising his ball skills. There might be more here than meets the eye.

22 Foster Moreau, TE, OAK; Age: 23
Drafted 2019, pick 137; Career snaps: 371

Another player that probably would have avoided this list if not for a knee injury, Moreau was instantly a high-use tight end in an offense that loves tight ends, and he produced early. Moreau was targeted 27 times last season and had a 29.6% DVOA that ranked third-highest in the NFL among tight ends.

Moreau managed 629 receiving yards and six touchdowns in LSU's offense circa Not Joe Brady, but showed off a broad skill set at the NFL combine, running a 4.66s 40-yard dash at 253 pounds, along with an elite 4.11s 20-yard shuttle time.

Moreau was more of a possession receiver at LSU and that continued in the pros—he did not catch a single pass that traveled more than 15 yards. However, only one of his catches came out of a one-tight end set, whereas eight of them came out of three-tight end sets.

With the signing of Jason Witten, Moreau's role for this year is a bit more up in the air than it probably should be. Jon Gruden loves tight ends, but between Moreau, Witten, and Darren Waller, he has a lot of potential pass targets. At the very worst, though, this season can probably be sold as Moreau learning from an all-time great, and he should be a solid tight end going forward.

23 Steven Sims, WR, WAS; Age: 23
Undrafted free agent, 2019; Career snaps: 310

Sims is one of those football stories that might not happen at all in 2020 as we deal with shortened preseason and training camps. Sims was not invited to the combine and didn't show up on many, if any, pre-draft lists we could find. Mel Kiper's wideout list for the 2019 draft went 106 players deep and he didn't mention Sims. It's not a total surprise given Sims' 40-yard dash time at his pro day of 4.5 seconds at 5-foot-10, 176 pounds.

Sims was Kansas' best receiver for the entirety of his career, garnering 30 receptions as a freshman and leaping to a team-high 72 as a sophomore, but his senior season was a mess. Washington thought they were getting a return specialist—and Sims can do that too—when they signed him as an UDFA. What they didn't know was that they'd get someone as versatile and agile in the open field as Sims turned out to be. That's how he ascended the depth chart one peg at a time, until suddenly he was drawing massive target shares in the final three weeks of the season. In those last three weeks, Sims was targeted 31 times and caught four touchdowns.

Washington offensive coordinator Scott Turner named Sims as one of the three players he wants to creatively get the ball to in a conference call with reporters this offseason. Antonio Gibson is a bit of a threat, and while Sims had good results on balls thrown deeper, he had an extremely low aDOT of 4.6. So there's a little bit of a squeeze here, but Sims has already bloomed under pressure several times throughout his career. Our Dan Pizutta claims he is what Tavon Austin would have been like if Austin could play receiver.

24 Amani Hooker, S, TEN; Age: 22
Drafted 2019, pick 116; Career snaps: 332

Another secondary prospect without a set position, Hooker was dominant throughout his final two seasons of eligibility at Iowa, where he broke up nine passes, picked off six, and played a brand of press coverage you don't often see in college. He was a force in the slot when asked to come erase players at the line of scrimmage. He tested well at the combine, putting up 70th percentile or better scores in almost all the agility, jump, and speed drills.

The Titans didn't have much of a plan for him to start in Year 1, but he got consistent playing time in big nickel and dime packages as the deep safety. The only game where

Hooker was targeted more than twice per our numbers was in Week 13 against the Colts, where he allowed just one catch for 12 yards on four targets. His major bugaboo in the playoffs was just covering Tyreek Hill, which as you can see from this list and Hill's statline last year, is something most players have problems with.

For Year 2, the Titans have let Logan Ryan walk and will be counting on rookie Kristian Fulton as their third corner behind Adoree' Jackson and Malcolm Butler. They also have retained Kenny Vaccaro as a starting safety, which comes with its own health concerns because last year was the first time since 2015 that Vaccaro didn't miss a game. The bet here is that Hooker is going to get on the field in some form next season and show enough of what he showed at Iowa that the coaching staff won't be able to relegate him back to the bench.

25 Connor McGovern, OL, DAL; Age: 23
Drafted 2019, pick 90; Career snaps: 0

Not to be confused with the other Connor McGovern, an offensive lineman drafted by the Broncos in 2016—yes, we've somehow got multiple Connor McGoverns in the league—this McGovern was the latest out of the Penn State offensive line factory. While (the Cowboys') McGovern did not play any games last year after an offseason pectoral injury, he's likely to be involved in any sort of Dallas offensive line play going forward following Travis Frederick's retirement.

McGovern is one of those players who seemed to be high on every pre-draft list we could find. He did extremely well at the NFL combine, doing 28 reps in the bench press, run-

ning the 20-yard shuttle in 4.57 seconds, and showing off a broad jump of 112 inches that implied a lot of explosiveness. McGovern played nine of 13 games at right guard as a freshman at Penn State, moved to center as a sophomore, and then switched back to right guard as a junior. He's a good fit for the gap schemes that Dallas likes to run with Ezekiel Elliott. The knock on him was in pass protection.

Dallas has talked up a couple of different versions of the future in the interior of their line. Joe Looney took a few snaps at center, and Dallas has also talked about potentially moving Connor Williams there. They also drafted Wisconsin's Tyler Biadasz in the fourth round. But given how Looney hasn't been deeply impressive in most of his stints, the path of least resistance probably has McGovern starting at either guard or center while Biadasz gets acquainted to the NFL.

Honorable Mention

Blessaun Austin, CB, NYJ
Hakeem Butler, WR, ARI
Blake Cashman, LB, NYJ
Justin Layne, CB, PIT
Harrison Phillips, IDL, BUF
Tony Pollard, RB, DAL
Ben Powers, OL, BAL
Tim Settle, IDL, WAS
Jarrett Stidham, QB, NE
Josh Sweat, ER, PHI

Rivers McCown

Fantasy Projections

Here are the top 270 players according to the KUBIAK projection system, ranked by projected fantasy value (FANT) in 2020. We've used the following generic scoring system:

- 1 point for each 10 yards rushing, 10 yards receiving, or 25 yards passing
- 6 points for each rushing or receiving TD, 4 points for each passing TD
- -2 points for each interception or fumble lost
- Kickers: 1 point for each extra point, 3 points for each field goal
- Team defense: 2 points for a fumble recovery, interception, or safety, 1 point for a sack, and 6 points for a touchdown.

These totals are then adjusted based on each player's listed Risk for 2020:

- Green: Standard risk, no change
- Yellow: Higher than normal risk, value dropped by 5%
- Red: Highest risk, value dropped by 10%
- Blue: Stronger chance of breakout, value increased by 5%

Note that fantasy totals may not exactly equal these calculations, because each touchdown projection is not necessarily a round number. (For example, a quarterback listed with 2 rushing touchdowns may actually be projected with 2.4 rushing touchdowns, which will add 14 fantasy points to the player's total rather than 12.) Fantasy value does not include adjustments for week-to-week consistency.

The projections listed below for quarterbacks differ from those found in the quarterbacks section earlier in the book because they incorporate the possibility of injury and represent 14 or 15 games started rather than representing 16 games started. This puts the quarterback projections in line with the other projections which also incorporate the possibility of injury.

Players are ranked in order based on marginal value of each player, the idea that you draft based on how many more points a player will score compared to the worst starting player at that position, not how many points a player scores overall. We've ranked players in five league configurations:

- Flex Rk: 12 teams, starts 1 QB, 2 RB, 2 WR, 1 FLEX (RB/WR), 1 TE, 1 K, and 1 D.
- 3WR Rk: 12 teams, starts 1 QB, 2 RB, 3 WR, 1 TE, 1 K, and 1 D.
- PPR Rk: 12 teams, starts 1 QB, 2 RB, 2 WR, 1 FLEX (RB/WR), 1 TE, 1 K, and 1 D. Also adds one point per reception to scoring.
- 10-3WR Rk: same as 3WR, but with only 10 teams.
- 10-PPR Rk: same as PPR, but with only 10 teams.

These rankings also reduce the value of kickers and defenses to reflect the general drafting habits of fantasy football players. (We estimated five bench players for each team; for each additional bench spot in your league, move kickers and defenses down 10 to 12 spots.) We urge you to draft using common sense, not a strict reading of these rankings.

The online KUBIAK application featuring these projections is also available at FootballOutsiders.com as part of an FO Plus subscription. These projections can be customized to the rules of any specific league with the ability to save multiple league setups. The online KUBIAK application is updated based on injuries and changing forecasts of playing time during the preseason, and also has a version which includes individual defensive players.

Player	Team	Bye	Pos	Age	PaYd	PaTD	INT	Ru	RuYd	RuTD	Rec	RcYd	RcTD	FL	Fant	Risk	Flex Rk	3WR Rk	PPR Rk	10-3WR Rk	10-PPR Rk
Christian McCaffrey	CAR	13	RB	24				267	1217	10	80	655	3	1	264	Green	1	1	1	1	1
Saquon Barkley	NYG	11	RB	23				263	1192	9	55	456	2	1	229	Green	2	2	2	2	2
Derrick Henry	TEN	7	RB	26				290	1409	10	25	219	1	2	227	Green	3	3	10	3	9
Ezekiel Elliott	DAL	10	RB	25				274	1202	9	50	381	2	2	220	Green	4	4	5	4	5
Dalvin Cook	MIN	7	RB	25				252	1076	10	58	484	1	2	210	Yellow	5	5	7	6	7
Nick Chubb	CLE	9	RB	25				258	1236	9	23	184	1	1	199	Green	6	7	25	9	25
Alvin Kamara	NO	6	RB	25				203	892	8	76	523	2	1	197	Green	7	9	3	10	3
Aaron Jones	GB	5	RB	26				212	937	8	48	388	3	1	196	Green	8	10	13	11	13
Patrick Mahomes	KC	10	QB	25	4529	31	8	63	322	3				4	333	Green	9	6	12	5	10
Joe Mixon	CIN	9	RB	24				240	986	8	45	346	2	0	190	Green	10	12	17	15	17
Lamar Jackson	BAL	8	QB	23	3288	27	8	164	970	6				5	327	Yellow	11	8	14	7	12
Miles Sanders	PHI	9	RB	23				224	981	7	44	383	2	1	184	Green	12	14	20	18	20
Kenyan Drake	ARI	8	RB	26				209	947	6	57	433	2	1	184	Green	13	15	15	19	15
Josh Jacobs	LV	6	RB	22				250	1130	7	42	345	1	1	183	Yellow	14	16	22	20	22
James Conner	PIT	8	RB	25				231	1007	8	53	432	2	2	180	Red	15	20	21	25	21
Leonard Fournette	JAX	7	RB	25				244	986	8	45	339	1	1	178	Yellow	16	22	26	26	26
Todd Gurley	ATL	10	RB	26				220	890	9	41	318	2	1	176	Yellow	17	23	29	27	29

Player	Team	Bye	Pos	Age	PaYd	PaTD	INT	Ru	RuYd	RuTD	Rec	RcYd	RcTD	FL	Fant	Risk	Flex Rk	3WR Rk	PPR Rk	10-3WR Rk	10-PPR Rk
Julio Jones	ATL	10	WR	31				0	0	0	98	1339	7	1	174	Green	18	11	4	8	4
Austin Ekeler	LAC	10	RB	25				177	749	6	65	565	3	1	170	Yellow	19	27	18	30	18
Mike Evans	TB	13	WR	27				0	0	0	73	1173	8	0	166	Green	20	13	16	12	16
Travis Kelce	KC	10	TE	31							78	966	6	1	132	Green	21	24	9	24	14
DeAndre Hopkins	ARI	8	WR	28				0	0	0	96	1209	7	1	163	Green	22	17	8	13	8
Kenny Golladay	DET	5	WR	27				0	0	0	68	1137	8	0	162	Green	23	18	19	14	19
Michael Thomas	NO	6	WR	27				0	0	0	108	1228	6	0	161	Green	24	19	6	16	6
Dak Prescott	DAL	10	QB	27	4425	26	10	54	264	4				4	300	Green	25	26	30	21	28
Davante Adams	GB	5	WR	28				0	0	0	91	1187	7	1	159	Green	26	21	11	17	11
Deshaun Watson	HOU	8	QB	25	4035	25	10	87	455	6				5	298	Yellow	27	28	32	23	30
David Johnson	HOU	8	RB	29				222	822	7	35	311	2	1	158	Yellow	28	32	49	37	48
Chris Carson	SEA	6	RB	26				224	947	7	34	255	1	2	158	Yellow	29	33	50	38	49
David Montgomery	CHI	11	RB	23				228	838	8	25	180	1	1	155	Green	30	36	60	43	60
Tyreek Hill	KC	10	WR	26				5	29	0	69	1074	7	0	153	Green	31	25	24	22	24
Devin Singletary	BUF	11	RB	23				199	932	4	45	348	2	2	153	Yellow	32	37	44	51	44
Le'Veon Bell	NYJ	11	RB	28				228	812	5	54	392	2	1	150	Yellow	33	41	39	53	36
Russell Wilson	SEA	6	QB	32	3904	26	6	71	361	2				4	289	Green	34	30	38	29	34
D'Andre Swift	DET	5	RB	21				190	810	5	38	289	1	1	147	Green	35	46	53	56	52
Raheem Mostert	SF	11	RB	28				208	975	5	23	200	1	1	147	Yellow	36	47	81	58	72
Chris Godwin	TB	13	WR	24				0	0	0	77	1091	6	0	146	Green	37	29	23	28	23
Mark Ingram	BAL	8	RB	31				180	840	8	20	169	1	1	146	Yellow	38	50	87	60	79
Clyde Edwards-Helaire	KC	10	RB	21				162	722	5	36	294	2	1	144	Green	39	55	59	62	59
George Kittle	SF	11	TE	27							59	735	6	0	109	Green	40	40	31	39	38
Matt Ryan	ATL	10	QB	35	4566	28	12	26	108	1				4	281	Green	41	38	46	34	40
Mark Andrews	BAL	8	TE	25							57	730	6	1	106	Green	42	43	35	44	43
Melvin Gordon	DEN	8	RB	27				177	719	7	40	262	2	1	139	Yellow	43	58	67	72	66
Zach Ertz	PHI	9	TE	30							70	729	6	0	106	Green	44	45	27	46	32
Robert Woods	LAR	9	WR	28				10	62	0	79	1032	5	0	139	Green	45	31	28	31	27
Ronald Jones	TB	13	RB	23				195	788	5	35	315	1	1	138	Yellow	46	62	74	73	73
Marlon Mack	IND	7	RB	24				182	790	6	28	234	2	0	137	Yellow	47	64	89	76	81
Amari Cooper	DAL	10	WR	26				0	0	0	72	1032	6	0	136	Green	48	34	34	32	33
Calvin Ridley	ATL	10	WR	26				3	32	0	75	944	7	0	136	Green	49	35	33	33	31
Jordan Howard	MIA	11	RB	26				179	717	6	29	214	1	1	133	Green	50	72	91	78	82
DK Metcalf	SEA	6	WR	23				0	0	0	59	958	6	1	132	Green	51	39	48	35	47
Tyler Lockett	SEA	6	WR	28				8	22	0	66	932	6	0	130	Green	52	42	43	36	42
Ke'Shawn Vaughn	TB	13	RB	23				169	713	5	28	237	1	1	130	Green	53	77	98	82	87
Tyler Higbee	LAR	9	TE	27							64	697	4	0	96	Green	54	63	37	64	46
DeVante Parker	MIA	11	WR	27				0	0	0	62	994	6	0	128	Yellow	55	44	52	40	51
Kyler Murray	ARI	8	QB	23	3765	24	11	75	432	3				3	267	Yellow	56	61	58	54	53
D.J. Moore	CAR	13	WR	23				6	51	0	77	947	5	1	127	Green	57	48	36	41	35
Adam Thielen	MIN	7	WR	30				3	11	0	68	912	6	0	127	Green	58	49	45	42	45
Darren Waller	LV	6	TE	28							58	680	4	0	93	Green	59	68	47	71	55
Cooper Kupp	LAR	9	WR	27				2	8	0	81	990	6	1	125	Yellow	60	51	40	45	37
Odell Beckham	CLE	9	WR	28				4	18	0	63	877	6	0	125	Green	61	52	51	47	50
Allen Robinson	CHI	11	WR	27				0	0	0	74	933	5	0	125	Green	62	53	41	48	39
Keenan Allen	LAC	10	WR	28				5	29	0	74	890	6	0	125	Green	63	54	42	49	41
A.J. Brown	TEN	7	WR	23				0	0	0	57	939	5	0	125	Green	64	56	57	50	57
Drew Brees	NO	6	QB	41	4144	27	8	16	23	1				2	264	Green	65	65	66	59	56
Josh Allen	BUF	11	QB	24	3365	19	10	101	558	8				7	263	Yellow	66	69	68	61	58
DJ Chark	JAX	7	WR	24				0	0	0	62	875	6	0	123	Green	67	57	55	52	54
Tom Brady	TB	13	QB	43	4465	26	9	24	41	2				2	261	Yellow	68	74	71	66	63
Michael Gallup	DAL	10	WR	24				0	0	0	59	903	5	0	119	Green	69	59	64	55	64
Evan Engram	NYG	11	TE	26							56	630	5	0	86	Yellow	70	82	56	87	71
Courtland Sutton	DEN	8	WR	25				0	0	0	61	895	5	1	119	Green	71	60	61	57	61
Jared Cook	NO	6	TE	33							42	572	5	0	85	Green	72	83	77	88	103
Jonathan Taylor	IND	7	RB	21				165	743	5	19	152	1	1	124	Green	73	88	104	91	111
Hayden Hurst	ATL	10	TE	27							57	608	4	0	85	Green	74	84	54	89	67
Austin Hooper	CLE	9	TE	26							50	538	5	0	85	Green	75	85	63	90	85
Aaron Rodgers	GB	5	QB	37	4049	25	6	43	189	1				3	257	Yellow	76	79	76	74	68
Christian Kirk	ARI	8	WR	24				14	127	0	62	727	5	0	116	Green	77	66	65	63	65
Sony Michel	NE	6	RB	25				178	681	7	15	126	1	1	117	Yellow	78	97	125	99	133
Mike Williams	LAC	10	WR	26				3	13	0	50	798	6	0	115	Green	79	67	88	65	93
Robby Anderson	CAR	13	WR	27				0	0	0	54	815	6	1	114	Green	80	70	80	67	83
T.Y. Hilton	IND	7	WR	31				0	0	0	68	932	5	0	114	Yellow	81	71	62	68	62
Hunter Henry	LAC	10	TE	26							51	571	4	0	81	Green	82	93	69	101	92

Player	Team	Bye	Pos	Age	PaYd	PaTD	INT	Ru	RuYd	RuTD	Rec	RcYd	RcTD	FL	Fant	Risk	Flex Rk	3WR Rk	PPR Rk	10-3WR Rk	10-PPR Rk
Joe Burrow	CIN	9	QB	24	3868	22	13	56	320	3				5	253	Green	83	89	83	83	74
Dallas Goedert	PHI	9	TE	25							51	554	4	0	80	Green	84	95	72	106	94
Marvin Jones	DET	5	WR	30				0	0	0	58	787	6	0	113	Green	85	73	75	69	75
Matthew Stafford	DET	5	QB	32	4184	28	10	30	100	1				4	253	Yellow	86	90	86	84	77
Kerryon Johnson	DET	5	RB	23				134	554	5	35	263	1	1	112	Yellow	87	104	102	110	104
Jarvis Landry	CLE	9	WR	28				0	0	0	61	814	5	0	113	Green	88	75	73	70	70
Steelers D	PIT	8	D											0	100	Green	89	103	100	81	76
Damien Williams	KC	10	RB	28				123	519	4	33	262	2	1	111	Yellow	90	106	106	113	112
JuJu Smith-Schuster	PIT	8	WR	24				0	0	0	67	859	5	0	111	Yellow	91	76	70	75	69
Stefon Diggs	BUF	11	WR	27				6	58	0	60	791	4	1	110	Green	92	78	79	77	80
Teddy Bridgewater	CAR	13	QB	28	4173	26	10	49	93	1				3	249	Yellow	93	98	90	95	86
Darius Slayton	NYG	11	WR	23				0	0	0	51	747	6	0	109	Green	94	80	94	79	107
Terry McLaurin	WAS	8	WR	24				0	0	0	62	880	4	0	109	Green	95	81	78	80	78
Gardner Minshew	JAX	7	QB	24	3682	23	8	65	320	1				6	248	Green	96	100	92	98	90
Kareem Hunt	CLE	9	RB	25				81	343	3	46	393	2	0	103	Blue	97	113	96	123	96
Justin Tucker	BAL	8	K	31										0	124	Green	98	114	114	94	91
Cam Akers	LAR	9	RB	21				140	600	4	20	145	1	1	102	Green	99	116	140	126	140
Derrius Guice	WAS	8	RB	23				135	629	5	17	158	1	0	100	Red	100	118	149	131	148
Tevin Coleman	SF	11	RB	27				130	519	4	22	195	1	0	100	Yellow	101	120	142	132	143
Curtis Samuel	CAR	13	WR	24				14	106	0	48	610	5	0	106	Green	102	86	108	85	126
Diontae Johnson	PIT	8	WR	24				3	30	0	60	758	5	1	106	Green	103	87	85	86	89
Daniel Jones	NYG	11	QB	23	3781	24	13	46	278	2				8	245	Green	104	110	97	107	98
Harrison Butker	KC	10	K	25										0	122	Green	105	122	121	100	95
Wil Lutz	NO	6	K	26										0	121	Green	106	125	122	102	97
Jared Goff	LAR	9	QB	26	4276	24	13	28	55	1				4	245	Green	107	111	99	111	99
Emmanuel Sanders	NO	6	WR	33				0	0	0	60	772	6	0	104	Yellow	108	91	93	92	100
Phillip Lindsay	DEN	8	RB	26				125	560	4	30	185	1	0	96	Yellow	109	127	136	143	138
Noah Fant	DEN	8	TE	23							38	495	4	0	71	Green	110	121	110	145	154
Breshad Perriman	NYJ	11	WR	27				3	19	0	48	796	5	0	104	Yellow	111	92	123	93	139
49ers D	SF	11	D											0	91	Green	112	129	129	109	101
Carson Wentz	PHI	9	QB	28	3987	25	9	51	195	1				7	243	Yellow	113	115	101	118	102
John Brown	BUF	11	WR	30				0	0	0	54	806	5	0	103	Yellow	114	94	105	96	123
Michael Pittman	IND	7	WR	23				0	0	0	57	765	4	0	102	Green	115	96	95	97	108
Alexander Mattison	MIN	7	RB	22				107	462	4	22	174	1	1	92	Blue	116	131	151	146	150
Matt Prater	DET	5	K	36										0	118	Green	117	132	133	115	105
Robbie Gould	SF	11	K	38										0	118	Green	118	133	134	117	106
Philip Rivers	IND	7	QB	39	4224	26	15	15	36	0				3	241	Green	119	119	103	122	110
Jonnu Smith	TEN	7	TE	25							39	467	4	0	68	Green	120	128	116	148	157
Greg Zuerlein	DAL	10	K	33										0	117	Green	121	136	137	119	109
Duke Johnson	HOU	8	RB	27				76	362	2	37	316	2	0	89	Green	122	137	132	150	136
Latavius Murray	NO	6	RB	30				130	528	4	12	88	0	0	89	Blue	123	138	176	151	165
Darrell Henderson	LAR	9	RB	23				130	528	3	22	165	1	1	89	Yellow	124	139	170	152	153
Kirk Cousins	MIN	7	QB	32	3725	25	7	26	62	1				4	240	Green	125	126	107	124	114
A.J. Green	CIN	9	WR	32				0	0	0	58	833	5	0	100	Red	126	99	111	103	134
Josh Lambo	JAX	7	K	30										0	116	Green	127	143	139	121	113
Tyler Boyd	CIN	9	WR	26				0	0	0	67	782	4	0	100	Green	128	101	84	104	88
Julian Edelman	NE	6	WR	34				6	35	0	69	724	4	1	100	Green	129	102	82	105	84
Mike Gesicki	MIA	11	TE	25							43	481	4	0	66	Yellow	130	134	117	154	158
James Washington	PIT	8	WR	24				0	0	0	48	802	3	0	99	Green	131	105	130	108	144
Boston Scott	PHI	9	RB	25				90	367	3	30	248	1	0	85	Green	132	146	150	156	149
J.K. Dobbins	BAL	8	RB	22				124	565	4	8	62	0	1	85	Green	133	148	178	157	170
Matt Breida	MIA	11	RB	25				98	456	2	36	263	1	1	85	Yellow	134	149	143	158	145
Ben Roethlisberger	PIT	8	QB	38	4316	24	13	22	76	1				4	238	Yellow	135	130	112	133	116
Ian Thomas	CAR	13	TE	24							42	430	4	0	65	Green	136	140	119	159	160
Rob Gronkowski	TB	13	TE	31							39	521	3	0	65	Yellow	137	141	135	160	167
Justin Jackson	LAC	10	RB	24				92	456	2	21	158	1	0	83	Blue	138	152	174	161	159
Nyheim Hines	IND	7	RB	24				38	152	1	54	454	3	0	83	Green	139	153	113	162	115
CeeDee Lamb	DAL	10	WR	21				0	0	0	50	724	4	0	98	Green	140	107	128	112	142
Ka'imi Fairbairn	HOU	8	K	26										0	114	Green	141	154	147	127	117
Will Fuller	HOU	8	WR	26				0	0	0	59	814	5	0	97	Red	142	108	118	114	137
Younghoe Koo	ATL	10	K	26										0	113	Yellow	143	155	148	128	119
Marquise Brown	BAL	8	WR	23				0	0	0	50	651	5	0	97	Green	144	109	131	116	146
Jack Doyle	IND	7	TE	30							41	438	4	0	64	Green	145	144	124	166	163
Cam Newton	NE	6	QB	31	3366	19	11	103	459	4				5	236	Yellow	146	135	120	144	125
Zane Gonzalez	ARI	8	K	25										0	112	Green	147	158	152	135	121

Player	Team	Bye	Pos	Age	PaYd	PaTD	INT	Ru	RuYd	RuTD	Rec	RcYd	RcTD	FL	Fant	Risk	Flex Rk	3WR Rk	PPR Rk	10-3WR Rk	10-PPR Rk
Bills D	BUF	11	D											0	84	Green	148	159	153	134	120
Tarik Cohen	CHI	11	RB	25				57	218	2	60	417	2	1	80	Yellow	149	163	115	170	118
T.J. Hockenson	DET	5	TE	23							42	456	3	0	63	Green	150	150	126	169	164
Brandin Cooks	HOU	8	WR	27				6	43	0	49	761	3	0	96	Yellow	151	112	144	120	152
Packers D	GB	5	D											0	84	Green	152	162	155	136	122
Chiefs D	KC	10	D											0	83	Green	153	164	157	137	124
Darrynton Evans	TEN	7	RB	22				72	318	2	27	231	1	0	78	Blue	154	167	173	172	156
Bears D	CHI	11	D											0	83	Blue	155	168	158	138	127
Redskins D	WAS	8	D											0	83	Yellow	156	169	159	139	128
Jaguars D	JAX	7	D											0	82	Yellow	157	170	160	140	129
Patriots D	NE	6	D											0	82	Red	158	171	161	141	130
Jason Myers	SEA	6	K	29										0	111	Green	159	172	162	203	176
Vikings D	MIN	7	D											0	82	Green	160	173	163	142	131
Mason Crosby	GB	5	K	36										0	111	Green	161	174	164	209	180
Ravens D	BAL	8	D											0	82	Green	162	176	165	202	175
Bucs D	TB	13	D											0	82	Blue	163	177	166	205	177
Ryan Tannehill	TEN	7	QB	32	3536	23	9	51	214	3				4	234	Yellow	164	145	127	147	135
James White	NE	6	RB	28				46	185	2	42	356	2	0	75	Green	165	180	146	175	147
Adrian Peterson	WAS	8	RB	35				116	473	3	16	143	1	1	75	Red	166	181	185	176	174
Sammy Watkins	KC	10	WR	27				3	22	0	51	685	5	0	94	Yellow	167	117	145	125	155
Eric Ebron	PIT	8	TE	27							38	453	3	0	61	Yellow	168	161	156	174	185
Irv Smith	MIN	7	TE	22							41	394	4	0	60	Green	169	166	138	177	169
Jamison Crowder	NYJ	11	WR	27				0	0	0	61	669	4	0	93	Green	170	123	109	129	132
Deebo Samuel	SF	11	WR	24				9	116	0	52	660	4	0	92	Red	171	124	167	130	161
Blake Jarwin	DAL	10	TE	26							38	413	3	0	59	Green	172	179	154	183	184
Ito Smith	ATL	10	RB	25				74	301	3	22	155	1	0	68	Green	173	188	182	184	171
Baker Mayfield	CLE	9	QB	25	3539	25	16	34	149	2				3	230	Green	174	175	141	165	141
Kyle Rudolph	MIN	7	TE	31							37	353	4	0	56	Green	175	187	171	185	202
Zack Moss	BUF	11	RB	23				99	390	3	9	71	0	0	63	Green	176	194	201	189	208
DeSean Jackson	PHI	9	WR	34				3	21	0	40	680	4	0	87	Red	177	142	194	149	211
Christopher Herndon	NYJ	11	TE	24							36	395	4	0	54	Red	178	190	179	191	227
Tony Pollard	DAL	10	RB	23				69	326	1	18	134	1	0	61	Blue	179	196	193	192	197
Henry Ruggs	LV	6	WR	21				6	46	0	45	636	4	0	86	Yellow	180	147	180	153	190
Greg Olsen	SEA	6	TE	35							34	381	3	0	53	Yellow	181	191	181	195	230
Jimmy Garoppolo	SF	11	QB	29	3627	25	12	39	60	1				4	225	Green	182	189	168	182	151
Allen Lazard	GB	5	WR	25				0	0	0	47	638	4	0	85	Green	183	151	177	155	172
Malcolm Brown	LAR	9	RB	27				75	294	3	14	97	1	0	57	Green	184	201	203	197	212
A.J. Dillon	GB	5	RB	22				73	290	2	10	83	1	0	57	Blue	185	202	209	198	219
Justice Hill	BAL	8	RB	23				55	220	2	21	178	1	0	55	Green	186	204	198	199	204
Rex Burkhead	NE	6	RB	30				60	242	2	24	206	1	0	55	Red	187	205	197	200	203
Sterling Shepard	NYG	11	WR	27				2	24	0	61	684	4	0	84	Red	188	156	169	163	162
Golden Tate	NYG	11	WR	32				0	0	0	53	643	3	0	84	Green	189	157	172	164	166
Frank Gore	NYJ	11	RB	37				80	305	3	11	84	0	0	54	Yellow	190	206	216	204	224
Tyrell Williams	LV	6	WR	28				0	0	0	37	576	4	0	83	Green	191	160	199	167	221
Giovani Bernard	CIN	9	RB	29				50	186	2	29	234	1	0	53	Yellow	192	208	189	211	196
Carlos Hyde	SEA	6	RB	30				77	295	2	15	108	1	1	53	Yellow	193	210	207	212	217
Will Dissly	SEA	6	TE	24							34	364	3	0	50	Red	194	200	191	208	237
Preston Williams	MIA	11	WR	23				0	0	0	42	586	4	0	83	Blue	195	165	187	168	200
Chase Edmonds	ARI	8	RB	24				63	271	2	14	115	1	0	51	Green	196	212	214	219	223
Jerry Jeudy	DEN	8	WR	21				0	0	0	46	614	3	0	82	Green	197	178	186	171	199
Lynn Bowden	LV	6	RB	23				58	260	2	15	116	0	0	50	Green	198	213	213	222	222
Dawson Knox	BUF	11	TE	24							28	337	2	0	48	Green	199	209	202	224	243
Hunter Renfrow	LV	6	WR	25				0	0	0	54	592	4	0	80	Green	200	182	175	173	168
Brandon Aiyuk	SF	11	WR	22				0	0	0	41	554	4	0	80	Blue	201	183	192	178	210
Justin Jefferson	MIN	7	WR	21				0	0	0	42	561	4	0	80	Green	202	184	196	179	215
N'Keal Harry	NE	6	WR	23				6	52	0	44	556	3	0	79	Green	203	185	190	180	206
Denzel Mims	NYJ	11	WR	23				0	0	0	45	604	3	0	79	Blue	204	186	188	181	201
O.J. Howard	TB	13	TE	26							28	373	2	0	45	Yellow	205	214	210	233	251
Rashaad Penny	SEA	6	RB	24				53	260	2	13	102	1	0	43	Red	206	224	227	236	234
Nick Boyle	BAL	8	TE	27							27	297	3	0	45	Green	207	216	218	235	256
Taysom Hill	NO	6	TE	30							14	108	1	1	44	Green	208	217	254	237	266
Chris Thompson	JAX	7	RB	30				33	136	1	28	219	1	0	42	Red	209	226	208	239	218
Antonio Gibson	WAS	8	RB	22				30	129	1	22	187	1	0	42	Green	210	227	217	240	225
Jace Sternberger	GB	5	TE	24							28	294	2	0	44	Blue	211	218	206	238	247
Tyler Eifert	JAX	7	TE	30							32	329	3	0	44	Red	212	220	212	241	252

Player	Team	Bye	Pos	Age	PaYd	PaTD	INT	Ru	RuYd	RuTD	Rec	RcYd	RcTD	FL	Fant	Risk	Flex Rk	3WR Rk	PPR Rk	10-3WR Rk	10-PPR Rk
Jalen Richard	LV	6	RB	27				24	102	1	30	242	1	0	40	Green	213	228	204	242	213
Randy Bullock	CIN	9	K	31										0	111	Green	214	238	222	213	182
Browns D	CLE	9	D											0	82	Yellow	215	237	221	206	178
Titans D	TEN	7	D											0	82	Green	216	240	223	207	179
Rams D	LAR	9	D											0	82	Green	217	241	224	210	181
Jamaal Williams	GB	5	RB	25				26	105	1	22	164	1	0	39	Green	218	229	220	244	231
Seahawks D	SEA	6	D											0	82	Green	219	245	226	216	183
Dan Bailey	MIN	7	K	32										0	110	Yellow	220	247	228	217	186
Chris Boswell	PIT	8	K	29										0	110	Green	221	248	229	221	189
Eagles D	PHI	9	D											0	81	Green	222	250	230	218	187
Dede Westbrook	JAX	7	WR	27				5	30	0	53	548	3	0	75	Green	223	192	184	186	195
Sam Darnold	NYJ	11	QB	23	3722	22	14	28	75	1				4	215	Green	224	219	183	215	173
Saints D	NO	6	D											0	81	Green	225	251	231	220	188
Russell Gage	ATL	10	WR	24				0	0	0	48	538	4	0	75	Green	226	193	195	187	214
Mecole Hardman	KC	10	WR	22				3	8	0	31	506	3	0	75	Blue	227	195	240	188	245
Michael Badgley	LAC	10	K	25										0	110	Green	228	253	234	225	191
Dare Ogunbowale	TB	13	RB	26				9	37	0	27	231	1	0	36	Green	229	230	219	246	228
Bengals D	CIN	9	D											0	81	Green	230	255	236	226	192
Benny Snell	PIT	8	RB	22				48	189	2	8	55	0	0	35	Green	231	231	244	247	241
J.D. McKissic	WAS	8	RB	27				26	116	1	18	154	1	0	35	Green	232	232	232	249	235
Brandon McManus	DEN	8	K	29										0	109	Green	233	256	237	228	194
Joshua Kelley	LAC	10	RB	23				46	195	1	8	64	0	0	34	Green	234	233	245	250	242
Colts D	IND	7	D											0	81	Green	235	257	238	227	193
Danny Amendola	DET	5	WR	35				0	0	0	47	543	4	0	73	Yellow	236	197	205	190	229
Anthony McFarland	PIT	8	RB	21				46	195	1	7	52	0	0	34	Green	237	234	249	252	244
Jake Elliott	PHI	9	K	25										0	109	Green	238	261	239	231	198
John Ross	CIN	9	WR	25				3	10	0	33	546	4	0	73	Yellow	239	198	247	193	258
Anthony Miller	CHI	11	WR	26				0	0	0	43	540	3	0	73	Green	240	199	215	194	233
Jerick McKinnon	SF	11	RB	28				43	169	1	6	51	0	0	32	Blue	241	235	252	254	249
Kyle Juszczyk	SF	11	RB	29				5	15	1	21	194	1	0	31	Green	242	236	235	255	236
Bo Scarbrough	DET	5	RB	26				48	200	1	4	24	0	0	31	Blue	243	239	259	256	254
La'Mical Perine	NYJ	11	RB	22				39	164	1	8	59	0	0	31	Blue	244	242	251	257	248
Damien Harris	NE	6	RB	23				35	145	1	7	59	0	0	30	Blue	245	244	255	259	250
Larry Fitzgerald	ARI	8	WR	37				0	0	0	45	500	4	0	71	Green	246	203	211	196	232
Dion Lewis	NYG	11	RB	30				35	132	1	12	91	0	0	28	Yellow	247	252	250	260	246
Jaylen Samuels	PIT	8	RB	24				14	51	1	19	153	1	0	27	Green	248	254	241	261	239
Randall Cobb	HOU	8	WR	30				0	0	0	42	548	3	0	70	Yellow	249	207	233	201	240
Broncos D	DEN	8	D											0	78	Green	250	266	246	243	207
Darren Fells	HOU	8	TE	34							21	218	2	0	36	Green	251	243	260	262	268
Brian Hill	ATL	10	RB	25				30	125	1	9	60	0	0	25	Green	252	258	261	263	257
Corey Davis	TEN	7	WR	25				0	0	0	36	504	3	0	69	Green	253	211	243	214	255
Cowboys D	DAL	10	D											0	78	Green	254	267	248	245	209
Jimmy Graham	CHI	11	TE	34							24	276	2	0	35	Yellow	255	249	257	264	267
Kenny Stills	HOU	8	WR	28				0	0	0	33	467	3	0	67	Blue	256	215	253	223	259
Ryan Nall	CHI	11	RB	25				27	107	1	5	36	0	0	21	Green	257	262	270	267	263
Reggie Bonnafon	CAR	13	RB	24				20	96	1	7	58	0	0	20	Green	258	263	268	268	261
T.J. Yeldon	BUF	11	RB	27				25	98	1	8	58	0	0	20	Green	259	264	266	269	260
Jets D	NYJ	11	D											0	77	Green	260	268	256	251	216
Drew Lock	DEN	8	QB	24	3405	21	11	54	231	1				5	206	Yellow	261	246	200	248	205
Jordan Akins	HOU	8	TE	28							21	225	2	0	33	Green	262	259	265	265	270
Gerald Everett	LAR	9	TE	26							23	230	2	0	33	Green	263	260	263	266	269
Chargers D	LAC	10	D											0	77	Green	264	269	258	253	220
Miles Boykin	BAL	8	WR	24				0	0	0	32	444	4	0	66	Green	265	221	264	229	264
Ryquell Armstead	JAX	7	RB	24				18	67	1	8	67	0	0	19	Green	266	265	269	270	262
Jalen Reagor	PHI	9	WR	21				0	0	0	38	476	3	0	66	Blue	267	222	242	230	253
Cole Beasley	BUF	11	WR	31				0	0	0	46	491	3	0	65	Green	268	223	225	232	238
Dustin Hopkins	WAS	8	K	30										0	105	Green	269	270	262	258	226
Chris Conley	JAX	7	WR	28				0	0	0	32	465	3	0	65	Green	270	225	267	234	265

Statistical Appendix

Broken Tackles by Team, Offense

Rk	Team	Plays	Plays w/ BTkl	Pct	Total BTkl
1	TEN	870	131	15.1%	166
2	CLE	924	122	13.2%	159
3	KC	934	122	13.1%	147
4	BAL	1009	130	12.9%	168
5	OAK	951	118	12.4%	143
6	SF	955	117	12.3%	141
7	LAC	952	108	11.3%	126
8	IND	966	108	11.2%	124
9	NO	961	107	11.1%	139
10	WAS	827	91	11.0%	104
11	SEA	980	107	10.9%	130
12	DAL	1035	112	10.8%	134
13	MIN	928	99	10.7%	130
14	CIN	986	104	10.5%	125
15	BUF	961	101	10.5%	118
16	PIT	890	92	10.3%	104
17	DEN	901	93	10.3%	111
18	LAR	1020	104	10.2%	130
19	HOU	955	97	10.2%	118
20	PHI	1056	104	9.8%	118
21	JAX	965	93	9.6%	113
22	ATL	1031	98	9.5%	108
23	CAR	1012	96	9.5%	114
24	GB	960	91	9.5%	108
25	ARI	935	88	9.4%	106
26	TB	1018	95	9.3%	112
27	NYJ	889	81	9.1%	95
28	CHI	966	87	9.0%	110
29	NE	1050	94	9.0%	105
30	NYG	964	86	8.9%	100
31	MIA	952	81	8.5%	93
32	DET	966	78	8.1%	91

Play total includes Defensive Pass Interference.

Broken Tackles by Team, Defense

Rk	Team	Plays	Plays w/ BTkl	Pct	Total BTkl
1	MIN	1000	77	7.7%	91
2	NE	887	69	7.8%	86
3	NO	940	78	8.3%	94
4	CHI	972	94	9.7%	107
5	DEN	952	94	9.9%	113
6	GB	947	94	9.9%	114
7	TB	1014	101	10.0%	128
8	DET	1045	105	10.0%	130
9	LAR	988	102	10.3%	130
10	ATL	939	100	10.6%	118
11	PIT	968	105	10.8%	130
12	NYJ	981	107	10.9%	116
13	SF	916	100	10.9%	111
14	MIA	1015	111	10.9%	131
15	DAL	962	106	11.0%	131
16	WAS	1019	113	11.1%	134
17	KC	988	110	11.1%	129
18	CAR	964	108	11.2%	124
19	TEN	999	112	11.2%	128
20	CIN	972	111	11.4%	143
21	OAK	916	105	11.5%	128
22	SEA	974	112	11.5%	137
23	BAL	876	101	11.5%	122
24	NYG	1005	117	11.6%	133
25	IND	925	109	11.8%	128
26	PHI	914	108	11.8%	125
27	BUF	926	110	11.9%	135
28	HOU	974	117	12.0%	141
29	LAC	880	107	12.2%	128
30	ARI	1026	125	12.2%	153
31	CLE	953	125	13.1%	153
32	JAX	932	132	14.2%	158

Play total includes Defensive Pass Interference.

Most Broken Tackles, Defenders

Rk	Player	Team	BTkl	Rk	Player	Team	BTkl	Rk	Player	Team	BTkl
1	J.Bates	CIN	23	6	Q.Williams	JAX	19	14	Z.Cunningham	HOU	17
1	N.Vigil	CIN	23	9	N.Gerry	PHI	18	14	R.Evans	TEN	17
3	S.Williams	CIN	22	9	M.Humphrey	BAL	18	14	B.Martinez	GB	17
4	J.Hicks	ARI	21	9	A.Ogletree	NYG	18	14	F.Warner	SF	17
5	D.Perryman	LAC	20	9	J.Schobert	CLE	18	19	Six tied with		16
6	T.Davis	LAC	19	9	A.Walker	IND	18				
6	D.Jones	ATL	19	14	A.Bethea	NYG	17				

Top 20 Defenders, Broken Tackle Rate

Rk	Player	Team	BTkl	Tkl	Rate
1	S.Barrett	TB	2	41	4.7%
2	C.Littleton	LAR	4	70	5.4%
3	D.Tranquill	LAC	3	43	6.5%
4	J.Allen	WAS	3	41	6.8%
5	R.Melvin	DET	4	54	6.9%
6	A.Barr	MIN	4	53	7.0%
7	E.Apple	NO	4	49	7.5%
7	R.Ya-Sin	IND	4	49	7.5%
9	J.Adams	NYJ	5	61	7.6%
10	K.Fuller	CHI	6	70	7.9%
11	D.Davis	NO	7	80	8.0%
12	J.Ramsey	LAR	4	45	8.2%
13	C.Harris	DEN	4	43	8.5%
14	D.Wilson	KC	5	53	8.6%
15	R.Smith	CHI	6	63	8.7%
16	T.Davis	DEN	7	72	8.9%
17	J.Ward	SF	4	41	8.9%
18	A.Amos	GB	6	60	9.1%
19	D.Hunter	MIN	5	47	9.6%
20	D.Greenlaw	SF	6	56	9.7%

Broken Tackles divided by Broken Tackles + Solo Tackles.
Special teams not included; min. 40 Solo Tackles

Bottom 20 Defenders, Broken Tackle Rate

Rk	Player	Team	BTkl	Tkl	Rate
1	N.Gerry	PHI	18	44	29.0%
1	A.Ogletree	NYG	18	44	29.0%
3	D.Perryman	LAC	20	49	29.0%
4	N.Vigil	CIN	23	57	28.8%
5	M.Kendricks	SEA	16	42	27.6%
6	L.Vander Esch	DAL	15	41	26.8%
7	J.Bates	CIN	23	63	26.7%
8	M.Humphrey	BAL	18	50	26.5%
9	T.Brock	TEN	14	40	25.9%
10	T.Davis	LAC	19	58	24.7%
11	H.Landry	TEN	13	40	24.5%
12	D.Jones	ATL	19	60	24.1%
13	V.Hargreaves	HOU	16	51	23.9%
14	R.McLeod	PHI	14	45	23.7%
15	M.Nicholson	WAS	13	43	23.2%
16	S.Williams	CIN	22	73	23.2%
17	S.Lee	DAL	15	50	23.1%
18	R.Evans	TEN	17	57	23.0%
19	B.Carr	BAL	12	41	22.6%
19	N.Hewitt	NYJ	12	41	22.6%
19	H.Reddick	ARI	12	41	22.6%

Broken Tackles divided by Broken Tackles + Solo Tackles.
Special teams not included; min. 40 Solo Tackles

Most Broken Tackles, Running Backs

Rk	Player	Team	BTkl
1	C.Carson	SEA	78
2	N.Chubb	CLE	74
3	C.McCaffrey	CAR	73
4	J.Mixon	CIN	71
5	D.Henry	TEN	69
6	D.Cook	MIN	68
6	J.Jacobs	OAK	68
8	A.Ekeler	LAC	62
9	L.Fournette	JAX	56
9	A.Kamara	NO	56
11	S.Barkley	NYG	55
11	L.Bell	NYJ	55
13	E.Elliott	DAL	54
13	A.Jones	GB	54
15	D.Montgomery	CHI	53
16	M.Ingram	BAL	46
17	P.Lindsay	DEN	45
17	A.Peterson	WAS	45
19	R.Jones	TB	43
20	D.Singletary	BUF	42

Most Broken Tackles, WR/TE

Rk	Player	Team	BTkl
1	D.Samuel	SF	28
2	G.Kittle	SF	27
3	J.Landry	CLE	23
4	D.Johnson	PIT	22
5	A.Brown	TEN	20
6	C.Godwin	TB	19
6	T.Kelce	KC	19
8	C.Sutton	DEN	18
9	J.Crowder	NYJ	17
9	C.Davis	TEN	17
9	D.Hopkins	HOU	17
9	D.Moore	CAR	17
9	J.Smith	TEN	17
9	A.Wilson	MIA	17
15	T.Boyd	CIN	16
15	R.Cobb	DAL	16
17	D.Waller	OAK	15
18	D.Chark	JAX	14
18	G.Everett	LAR	14
18	H.Renfrow	OAK	14
18	S.Watkins	KC	14
18	D.Westbrook	JAX	14

Most Broken Tackles, Quarterbacks

Rk	Player	Team	Behind LOS	Beyond LOS	BTkl	Rk	Player	Team	Behind LOS	Beyond LOS	BTkl
1	L.Jackson	BAL	1	54	55	6	D.Watson	HOU	2	12	14
2	J.Allen	BUF	1	24	25	8	R.Fitzpatrick	MIA	2	10	12
3	K.Murray	ARI	1	14	15	9	C.Wentz	PHI	1	9	10
3	D.Prescott	DAL	0	15	15	10	G.Minshew	JAX	5	4	9
3	J.Winston	TB	4	11	15	10	A.Rodgers	GB	1	8	9
6	J.Brissett	IND	5	9	14						

Best Broken Tackle Rate, Offensive Players (min. 80 touches)

Rk	Player	Team	BTkl	Touch	Rate
1	K.Hunt	CLE	34	80	42.5%
2	G.Kittle	SF	27	90	30.0%
3	Dam.Williams	KC	40	141	28.4%
4	A.Ekeler	LAC	62	224	27.7%
5	D.Johnson	HOU	35	127	27.6%
6	J.Landry	CLE	23	84	27.4%
7	J.Jacobs	OAK	68	262	26.0%
8	T.Pollard	DAL	26	101	25.7%
9	C.Carson	SEA	78	315	24.8%
10	D.Singletary	BUF	42	180	23.3%
11	J.Mixon	CIN	71	313	22.7%
12	D.Cook	MIN	68	303	22.4%
13	A.Kamara	NO	56	252	22.2%
14	N.Chubb	CLE	74	334	22.2%
15	J.Conner	PIT	33	150	22.0%
16	C.Godwin	TB	19	87	21.8%
17	D.Henry	TEN	69	321	21.5%
18	R.Jones	TB	43	203	21.2%
19	S.Barkley	NYG	55	269	20.4%
20	M.Ingram	BAL	46	228	20.2%

Best Yards After Contract (min. 100 carries)

Rk	Player	Team	YafC
1	N.Chubb	CLE	3.54
2	C.Carson	SEA	3.26
3	Dam.Williams	KC	3.22
4	D.Henry	TEN	3.19
5	S.Barkley	NYG	3.13
6	R.Jones	TB	3.13
7	G.Edwards	BAL	3.10
8	J.Jacobs	OAK	2.96
9	R.Mostert	SF	2.93
10	L.Fournette	JAX	2.86

Worst Yards After Contract (min. 100 carries)

Rk	Player	Team	YafC
1	L.McCoy	KC	1.80
2	D.Washington	OAK	1.90
3	D.Montgomery	CHI	1.92
4	D.Freeman	ATL	1.96
5	C.McCaffrey	CAR	2.03
6	P.Barber	TB	2.04
7	R.Freeman	DEN	2.05
8	M.Gordon	LAC	2.07
9	T.Coleman	SF	2.15
10	L.Bell	NYJ	2.25

Top 20 Defenders, Passes Defensed

Rk	Player	Team	PD
1	S.Gilmore	NE	20
2	C.Davis	TB	19
3	L.Ryan	TEN	18
4	J.Alexander	GB	17
4	J.Dean	TB	17
4	J.Haden	PIT	17
4	T.White	BUF	17
8	J.Jenkins	2TM	16
9	K.King	GB	15
9	J.Simmons	DEN	15
11	C.Awuzie	DAL	14
11	M.Humphrey	BAL	14
11	M.Lattimore	NO	14
11	M.Peters	2TM	14
15	J.Coleman	DET	13
15	G.Conley	2TM	13
15	Sl.Griffin	SEA	13
15	T.Herndon	JAX	13
15	J.Joseph	HOU	13
15	D.Slay	DET	13
15	M.Williams	NO	13

Top 20 Defenders, Defeats

Rk	Player	Team	Dfts
1	T.Watt	PIT	36
2	J.Hicks	ARI	31
3	L.David	TB	30
4	S.Barrett	TB	29
4	J.Collins	NE	29
6	J.Bosa	LAC	28
6	D.Leonard	IND	28
8	J.Smith	DAL	27
9	A.Donald	LAR	26
9	C.Heyward	PIT	26
9	M.Golden	NYG	26
12	B.Baker	ARI	25
12	C.Dunlap	CIN	25
12	B.Dupree	PIT	25
12	D.Fowler	LAR	25
12	D.Hunter	MIN	25
12	G.Jarrett	ATL	25
12	Z.Smith	GB	25
19	7 tied with		24

Top 20 Defenders, Quarterback Hits

Rk	Player	Team	Hits
1	M.Judon	BAL	27
2	Z.Smith	GB	23
3	T.Watt	PIT	20
4	J.Bosa	LAC	19
4	C.Campbell	JAX	19
4	C.Lawson	CIN	19
7	S.Barrett	TB	18
7	J.Watt	HOU	18
7	L.Williams	2TM	18
10	D.Barnett	PHI	16
10	N.Bosa	SF	16
10	E.Griffen	MIN	16
13	T.Flowers	DET	15
13	M.Golden	NYG	15
13	R.Quinn	DAL	15
16	D.Kennard	DET	14
17	J.Allen	JAX	13
17	C.Dunlap	CIN	13
17	C.Heyward	PIT	13
17	C.Jones	KC	13
17	N.Suh	TB	13

Top 20 Defenders, QB Knockdowns (Sacks + Hits)

Rk	Defender	Team	KD
1	M.Judon	BAL	38
1	Z.Smith	GB	38
3	S.Barrett	TB	37
3	T.Watt	PIT	37
5	J.Bosa	LAC	32
6	M.Golden	NYG	30
6	C.Jones	ARI	30
8	E.Griffen	MIN	28
9	N.Bosa	SF	26
9	C.Campbell	JAX	26
9	A.Donald	LAR	26
9	C.Jordan	NO	26
9	R.Quinn	DAL	26
14	D.Hunter	MIN	24
14	C.Lawson	CIN	24
16	J.Allen	JAX	23
16	D.Barnett	PHI	23
16	C.Heyward	PIT	23
16	P.Smith	GB	23
20	5 tied with		22

Full credit for whole and half sacks; includes sacks cancelled by penalty. Does not include strip sacks.

Top 20 Defenders, Hurries

Rk	Defender	Team	Hur
1	C.Jordan	NO	67
2	Z.Smith	GB	66
3	N.Bosa	SF	62
4	D.Hunter	MIN	59
5	S.Barrett	TB	55
6	K.Mack	CHI	53
7	V.Miller	DEN	52
8	D.Lawrence	DAL	50
9	J.Bosa	LAC	49
10	A.Donald	LAR	48
11	T.Flowers	DET	47
11	T.Watt	PIT	47
13	K.Van Noy	NE	46
14	M.Golden	NYG	45
15	C.Campbell	JAX	44
15	M.Judon	BAL	44
17	C.Jones	ARI	43
18	J.Clowney	SEA	41
19	E.Griffen	MIN	40
20	D.Fowler	LAR	39
20	J.Clowney	HOU	34.5
20	B.Graham	PHI	34.5

Top 20 Quarterbacks, QB Knockdowns (Sacks + Hits)

Rk	Player	Team	KD
1	M.Ryan	ATL	137
2	R.Fitzpatrick	MIA	130
3	R.Wilson	SEA	119
4	D.Jones	NYG	112
5	C.Wentz	PHI	111
6	J.Winston	TB	109
7	P.Rivers	LAC	101
8	T.Brady	NE	95
8	D.Prescott	DAL	95
10	A.Rodgers	GB	94
11	D.Watson	HOU	91
12	J.Brissett	IND	89
13	J.Allen	BUF	87
14	J.Garoppolo	SF	83
14	J.Goff	LAR	83
16	K.Allen	CAR	81
17	S.Darnold	NYJ	78
18	B.Mayfield	CLE	74
19	M.Trubisky	CHI	73
20	K.Cousins	MIN	68

Includes sacks cancelled by penalties
Does not include strip sacks or "self sacks" with no defender listed.

Top 20 Quarterbacks, QB Hits

Rk	Player	Team	Hits
1	R.Fitzpatrick	MIA	91
2	M.Ryan	ATL	86
3	D.Prescott	DAL	75
3	C.Wentz	PHI	75
5	D.Jones	NYG	72
6	R.Wilson	SEA	71
7	T.Brady	NE	69
8	P.Rivers	LAC	67
9	J.Brissett	IND	64
10	J.Goff	LAR	63
10	J.Winston	TB	63
12	A.Rodgers	GB	55
13	D.Watson	HOU	51
14	J.Allen	BUF	49
15	S.Darnold	NYJ	43
16	P.Mahomes	KC	42
17	K.Cousins	MIN	41
17	J.Garoppolo	SF	41
19	M.Trubisky	CHI	39
20	K.Allen	CAR	37

Top 10 Quarterbacks, Knockdowns per Pass

Rk	Player	Team	KD	Pct
1	R.Fitzpatrick	MIA	130	22.6%
2	D.Jones	NYG	112	21.1%
3	R.Wilson	SEA	119	19.8%
4	M.Ryan	ATL	137	19.5%
5	D.Haskins	WAS	46	19.1%
6	R.Tannehill	TEN	63	18.9%
7	J.Brissett	IND	89	17.6%
8	J.Allen	BUF	87	16.7%
9	C.Wentz	PHI	111	16.2%
10	C.Keenum	WAS	45	16.0%

Min. 200 passes; includes passes cancelled by penalty

Bottom 10 Quarterbacks in Knockdowns per Pass

Rk	Player	Team	KD	Pct
1	D.Carr	OAK	47	8.4%
2	D.Brees	NO	37	9.1%
3	K.Murray	ARI	62	10.0%
4	A.Dalton	CIN	64	10.9%
5	P.Mahomes	KC	61	10.9%
6	L.Jackson	BAL	52	11.7%
7	B.Mayfield	CLE	74	11.9%
8	J.Goff	LAR	83	12.0%
9	M.Stafford	DET	39	12.1%
10	G.Minshew	JAX	65	12.1%

Min. 200 passes; includes passes cancelled by penalty

Top 10 Most Passes Tipped at Line, Quarterbacks

Rk	Player	Team	Total
1	A.Dalton	CIN	19
2	B.Mayfield	CLE	18
3	R.Fitzpatrick	MIA	15
4	J.Goff	LAR	14
4	P.Rivers	LAC	14
4	M.Ryan	ATL	14
4	C.Wentz	PHI	14
8	K.Allen	PHI	13
8	K.Murray	ARI	13
10	D.Carr	OAK	11
10	J.Winston	TB	11

Top 10 Tipped at the Line, Defenders

Rk	Player	Team	Total
1	S.Harris	DEN	8
2	C.Dunlap	CIN	6
2	C.Jones	ARI	6
4	L.Alexander	BUF	5
4	A.Butler	NE	5
4	D.Fowler	LAR	5
4	C.Heyward	PIT	5
4	T.Watt	PIT	5
9	5 tied with		4

2019 Quarterbacks with and without Pass Pressure

Rank	Player	Team	Plays	Pct Pressure	DVOA with Pressure	Yds with Pressure	DVOA w/o Pressure	Yds w/o Pressure	DVOA Dif	Rank
1	A.Dalton	CIN	579	22.6%	-81.1%	1.7	23.3%	7.2	-104.5%	14
2	D.Brees	NO	391	23.0%	-12.5%	5.2	70.9%	8.2	-83.4%	7
3	T.Bridgewater	NO	221	24.0%	-73.0%	2.3	56.6%	7.2	-129.7%	28
4	T.Brady	NE	656	24.8%	-78.6%	2.0	44.8%	7.7	-123.4%	23
5	D.Carr	OAK	558	25.4%	-34.8%	3.4	47.1%	8.5	-82.0%	6
6	R.Tannehill	TEN	332	25.6%	-45.7%	4.8	93.5%	9.6	-139.2%	30
7	J.Garoppolo	SF	532	25.9%	-81.3%	3.9	63.6%	8.6	-144.9%	31
8	D.Haskins	WAS	246	26.0%	-129.0%	1.3	-0.1%	6.5	-128.9%	27
9	K.Murray	ARI	623	27.8%	-72.6%	2.5	31.2%	7.5	-103.8%	13
10	B.Mayfield	CLE	603	27.9%	-55.5%	2.7	30.7%	7.7	-86.2%	8
11	L.Jackson	BAL	460	28.0%	5.5%	4.8	79.3%	8.6	-73.7%	4
12	M.Trubisky	CHI	580	28.6%	-74.8%	2.7	31.5%	6.4	-106.2%	15
13	C.Wentz	PHI	677	28.8%	-52.8%	4.2	42.1%	6.8	-94.9%	10
14	G.Minshew	JAX	559	29.0%	-78.9%	3.4	43.7%	7.5	-122.6%	21
15	J.Winston	TB	716	29.2%	-79.2%	4.4	45.1%	8.5	-124.3%	24
16	M.Stafford	DET	318	29.2%	-46.3%	3.8	74.8%	9.4	-121.1%	19
17	A.Rodgers	GB	642	29.3%	-30.0%	4.1	41.3%	7.4	-71.2%	2
18	D.Prescott	DAL	644	29.5%	-8.2%	6.1	62.5%	8.4	-70.7%	1
19	K.Allen	CAR	557	29.8%	-123.4%	1.4	32.0%	7.4	-155.4%	33
20	K.Cousins	MIN	489	30.1%	-78.6%	3.1	67.9%	9.0	-146.5%	32
21	M.Rudolph	PIT	315	30.2%	-143.6%	1.9	37.1%	7.6	-180.8%	34
22	J.Flacco	DEN	297	30.3%	-99.3%	2.2	26.4%	7.4	-125.7%	26
23	P.Rivers	LAC	644	30.4%	-54.9%	4.3	55.5%	8.4	-110.3%	16
24	J.Allen	BUF	545	30.8%	-78.6%	3.0	44.7%	7.3	-123.3%	22
25	J.Goff	LAR	663	31.6%	-66.8%	3.9	52.9%	8.2	-119.7%	18
26	P.Mahomes	KC	531	32.2%	-0.5%	5.5	71.0%	9.1	-71.4%	3
27	M.Ryan	ATL	693	32.8%	-70.8%	3.7	53.5%	7.8	-124.3%	25
28	C.Keenum	WAS	267	33.3%	-85.2%	3.6	52.7%	7.3	-137.9%	29
29	J.Brissett	IND	513	33.9%	-49.8%	3.7	38.5%	7.6	-88.3%	9
30	D.Watson	HOU	582	34.0%	-31.6%	4.5	49.7%	7.8	-81.3%	5
31	R.Fitzpatrick	MIA	583	36.2%	-42.8%	4.3	53.3%	7.6	-96.1%	11
32	R.Wilson	SEA	611	36.5%	-17.1%	4.4	83.3%	8.3	-100.3%	12
33	D.Jones	NYG	528	36.6%	-74.7%	2.8	44.7%	7.5	-119.4%	17
34	S.Darnold	NYJ	489	39.6%	-79.9%	3.7	42.3%	7.8	-122.2%	20

Includes scrambles and Defensive Pass Interference. Does not include aborted snaps.
Minimum: 200 passes.

WR: Highest Slot/Wide Ratio of Targets

Rk	Player	Team	Slot	Wide	Slot%
1	R.Cobb	DAL	81	1	99%
2	H.Renfrow	OAK	68	1	99%
3	C.Kupp	LAR	125	11	92%
4	G.Tate	NYG	78	8	91%
5	D.Hamilton	DEN	44	5	90%
6	D.Amendola	DET	85	10	89%
7	C.Beasley	BUF	95	12	89%
8	J.Crowder	NYJ	104	14	88%
9	A.Miller	CHI	74	10	88%
10	L.Fitzgerald	ARI	95	14	87%
11	A.Wilson	MIA	50	8	86%
12	T.Lockett	SEA	93	15	86%
13	J.Edelman	NE	133	23	85%
14	G.Allison	GB	45	8	85%
15	N.Agholor	PHI	57	11	84%
16	J.Wright	CAR	47	10	82%
17	S.Sims	WAS	46	10	82%
18	D.Westbrook	JAX	82	18	82%
19	C.Godwin	TB	100	22	82%
20	M.Sanu	2TM	69	19	78%

Min. 50 passes. Slot includes lined up tight.

WR: Highest Wide/Slot Ratio of Targets

Rk	Player	Team	Slot	Wide	Wide%
1	D.Metcalf	SEA	17	84	83%
2	M.Gallup	DAL	22	93	81%
3	P.Williams	MIA	12	50	81%
4	D.Slayton	NYG	17	65	79%
5	R.Anderson	NYJ	21	79	79%
6	C.Conley	JAX	20	69	78%
7	M.Evans	TB	31	93	75%
8	D.Moore	CAR	36	99	73%
9	A.Jeffery	PHI	21	53	72%
10	A.Cooper	DAL	35	85	71%
11	O.Beckham	CLE	43	98	70%
12	C.Ridley	ATL	30	65	68%
13	D.Johnson	PIT	30	61	67%
14	B.Perriman	TB	24	47	66%
15	J.Brown	BUF	39	76	66%
16	T.McLaurin	WAS	33	63	66%
17	C.Samuel	CAR	37	70	65%
18	T.Ginn	NO	20	37	65%
19	S.Diggs	MIN	36	60	63%
20	P.Dorsett	NE	23	34	60%

Min. 50 passes. Slot includes lined up tight.

Top 10 WR Better Lined Up Wide

Rk	Player	Team	Slot	Wide	Slot	Wide	Dif
1	A.Erickson	CIN	45	31	-34.7%	0.4%	35.0%
2	W.Fuller	HOU	45	27	-10.3%	23.2%	33.5%
3	A.Cooper	DAL	35	85	-0.5%	32.0%	32.5%
4	A.Tate	CIN	35	50	-28.5%	-2.7%	25.8%
5	R.Anderson	NYJ	21	79	-23.6%	1.1%	24.7%
6	D.Moore	CAR	36	99	-13.9%	10.5%	24.4%
7	J.Landry	CLE	108	32	-0.3%	21.5%	21.8%
8	T.Hill	KC	52	33	17.0%	35.5%	18.6%
9	C.Conley	JAX	20	69	-11.0%	1.5%	12.5%
10	J.Jones	ATL	78	81	5.5%	17.5%	12.0%

Min. 20 targets from each position

Top 10 WR Better Lined Up Slot

Rk	Player	Team	Slot	Wide	Slot	Wide	Dif
1	D.Samuel	SF	53	24	35.3%	-46.2%	81.5%
2	J.Ross	CIN	31	24	20.1%	-51.2%	71.2%
3	A.Brown	TEN	34	50	60.3%	3.4%	56.9%
4	P.Dorsett	NE	23	34	31.4%	-23.5%	54.9%
5	A.Jeffery	PHI	21	53	32.2%	-20.0%	52.2%
6	Z.Pascal	IND	45	30	26.4%	-20.4%	46.8%
7	B.Cooks	LAR	45	23	15.7%	-23.0%	38.7%
8	T.Gabriel	CHI	22	26	14.2%	-24.3%	38.5%
9	B.Perriman	TB	24	47	41.1%	3.9%	37.2%
10	M.Evans	TB	31	93	47.9%	11.1%	36.9%

Min. 20 targets from each position

Top 10 TE Highest Rate of Targets from WR Positions (Slot/Wide)

Rk	Player	Team	Tight	Slot	Wide	Back	WR%
1	A.Firkser	TEN	3	21	1	0	88%
2	J.Cook	NO	13	44	8	0	80%
3	E.Ebron	IND	12	38	2	0	77%
4	T.Eifert	CIN	16	38	10	0	75%
4	D.Walker	TEN	8	23	1	0	75%
6	M.Andrews	BAL	23	71	2	2	74%
7	T.Kelce	KC	37	86	14	0	73%
8	G.Everett	LAR	19	31	11	0	69%
9	T.Hockenson	DET	19	36	3	0	67%
10	D.Waller	OAK	41	63	15	0	66%

Min. 25 passes

Top 10 TE Lowest Rate of Targets from WR Positions (Slot/Wide)

Rk	Player	Team	Tight	Slot	Wide	Back	WR%
1	K.Rudolph	MIN	46	3	0	0	6%
2	R.Ellison	NYG	26	2	0	0	7%
3	F.Moreau	OAK	21	2	1	1	12%
4	N.Boyle	BAL	34	6	0	3	14%
5	J.Sprinkle	WAS	34	6	0	0	15%
5	C.Uzomah	CIN	33	4	2	1	15%
7	R.Griffin	NYJ	33	7	1	0	20%
7	K.Smith	NYG	33	8	0	0	20%
9	D.Fells	HOU	35	9	0	2	20%
10	J.Hill	NO	25	4	3	1	21%

Min. 25 passes

Top 10 RB Highest Rate of Targets from WR Positions (Slot/Wide)

Rk	Player	Team	Back	Slot	Wide	Tight	WR%
1	T.Cohen	CHI	57	32	8	6	39%
2	R.Burkhead	NE	25	4	9	0	34%
3	D.Johnson	ARI	31	12	3	1	32%
4	J.McKissic	DET	29	9	4	0	31%
5	N.Hines	IND	41	13	4	0	29%
6	D.Singletary	BUF	29	4	8	0	29%
7	K.Juszczyk	SF	14	6	1	4	28%
8	A.Ekeler	LAC	80	9	20	1	26%
9	J.Samuels	PIT	42	14	1	1	26%
10	K.Hunt	CLE	33	8	3	0	25%

Min. 25 passes

Top 10 Teams, Pct Passes Dropped

Rk	Team	Passes	Drops	Pct
1	ARI	509	17	3.3%
2	ATL	631	22	3.5%
3	TEN	415	16	3.9%
4	BAL	414	16	3.9%
5	NO	539	21	3.9%
6	TB	588	23	3.9%
7	LAC	558	23	4.1%
8	LAR	583	26	4.5%
9	HOU	503	23	4.6%
10	JAX	545	25	4.6%

Adjusted for passes tipped/thrown away.

Bottom 10 Teams, Pct Passes Dropped

Rk	Team	Passes	Drops	Pct
23	NE	577	33	5.7%
24	CLE	497	29	5.8%
25	DEN	456	27	5.9%
26	GB	533	33	6.2%
27	WAS	452	28	6.2%
28	IND	472	31	6.6%
29	MIA	575	39	6.8%
30	PIT	465	32	6.9%
31	BUF	466	33	7.1%
32	DAL	570	41	7.2%

Adjusted for passes tipped/thrown away.

Top 20 Players, Passes Dropped

Rk	Player	Team	Total
1	J.Edelman	NE	11
2	R.Cobb	DAL	10
2	M.Gallup	DAL	10
4	O.Beckham	CLE	9
5	D.Adams	GB	8
5	D.Samuel	SF	8
7	G.Allison	GB	7
7	T.Cohen	CHI	7
7	D.Cook	MIN	7
7	J.Crowder	NYJ	7
7	Z.Ertz	PHI	7
7	M.Evans	TB	7
7	D.Knox	BUF	7
7	P.Lindsay	DEN	7
7	C.McCaffrey	CAR	7
7	D.Metcalf	SEA	7
7	J.Ross	CIN	7
7	C.Samuel	CAR	7
19	15 tied with		6

Top 20 Players, Pct. Passes Dropped

Rk	Player	Team	Drops	Passes	Pct
1	C.Edmonds	ARI	5	21	23.8%
2	S.Michel	NE	4	20	20.0%
3	M.Goodwin	SF	4	21	19.0%
3	D.Inman	2TM	4	21	19.0%
5	K.Ballage	MIA	4	24	16.7%
6	D.Harris	CLE	4	27	14.8%
7	P.Lindsay	DEN	7	48	14.6%
8	C.Rogers	IND	4	28	14.3%
8	D.Knox	BUF	7	50	14.0%
10	P.Laird	MIA	4	30	13.3%
11	G.Allison	GB	7	55	12.7%
12	J.Ross	CIN	7	56	12.5%
12	J.Sprinkle	WAS	5	40	12.5%
14	D.Singletary	BUF	5	41	12.2%
15	M.Johnson	IND	4	33	12.1%
16	R.Cobb	DAL	10	83	12.0%
17	D.Cook	MIN	7	63	11.1%
18	D.Thomas	NYJ	6	58	10.3%
18	J.Wright	CAR	6	58	10.3%
20	T.Gurley	LAR	5	49	10.2%

Min. four drops

Top 20 Yards Lost to Drops by Quarterbacks

Rk	Player	Team	Drops	Yds
1	A.Rodgers	GB	33	364
2	D.Prescott	DAL	41	346
3	C.Wentz	PHI	29	320
4	R.Wilson	SEA	24	289
5	D.Watson	HOU	23	268
6	J.Brissett	IND	26	262
7	A.Dalton	CIN	27	251
8	J.Allen	BUF	26	247
9	J.Garoppolo	SF	25	243
10	P.Rivers	LAC	22	242
11	S.Darnold	NYJ	21	232
11	J.Goff	LAR	26	232
13	B.Mayfield	CLE	29	226
14	J.Winston	TB	23	223
15	D.Carr	OAK	27	217
16	D.Haskins	WAS	21	213
17	D.Jones	NYG	24	203
18	M.Rudolph	PIT	19	193
19	M.Trubisky	CHI	23	185
20	K.Allen	CAR	25	184

Based on yardage in the air, no possible YAC included.

Top 20 Intended Receivers on Interceptions

Rk	Player	Team	Total
1	K.Allen	LAC	8
1	M.Evans	TB	8
1	J.Landry	CLE	8
1	M.Williams	LAC	8
5	O.Beckham	CLE	7
5	E.Sanders	2TM	7
7	T.Boyd	CIN	6
7	R.Woods	LAR	6
9	J.Crowder	NYJ	5
9	S.Diggs	MIN	5
9	C.Godwin	TB	5
9	K.Golladay	DET	5
9	J.Jones	ATL	5
9	M.Jones	DET	5
9	D.Moore	CAR	5
9	J.Washington	PIT	5
9	J.Wright	CAR	5
18	8 tied with		4

Top 10 Completion Percentage Over Expected

Rk	Player	Team	CPOE
1	D.Brees	NO	8.5%
2	R.Tannehill	TEN	7.7%
3	K.Cousins	MIN	6.2%
4	D.Carr	OAK	6.1%
5	R.Wilson	SEA	4.9%
6	M.Ryan	ATL	3.2%
7	P.Rivers	LAC	2.9%
8	P.Mahomes	KC	2.7%
9	D.Watson	HOU	2.6%
10	L.Jackson	BAL	2.4%

Min. 200 passes; CPOE adjusted for passes tipped/thrown away.

Bottom 10 Completion Percentage Over Expected

Rk	Player	Team	CPOE
1	D.Haskins	WAS	-6.7%
2	G.Minshew	JAX	-4.0%
3	T.Brady	NE	-3.8%
4	M.Trubisky	CHI	-3.7%
5	A.Dalton	CIN	-3.7%
6	B.Mayfield	CLE	-2.8%
7	J.Brissett	IND	-2.6%
8	D.Jones	NYG	-2.4%
9	J.Allen	BUF	-2.4%
10	C.Keenum	WAS	-1.5%

Min. 200 passes; CPOE adjusted for passes tipped/thrown away.

Top 10 Plus/Minus for Running Backs

Rk	Player	Team	Pass	+/-
1	A.Ekeler	LAC	108	+8.7
2	D.Freeman	ATL	70	+6.9
3	A.Kamara	NO	97	+6.2
4	C.McCaffrey	CAR	142	+5.5
5	L.Bell	NYJ	78	+4.7
6	D.Washington	OAK	41	+4.2
7	J.Richard	OAK	43	+4.0
8	M.Ingram	BAL	29	+3.6
9	K.Hunt	CLE	44	+3.4
10	R.Freeman	DEN	50	+3.3

Min. 25 passes; plus/minus adjusted for passes tipped/thrown away.

Bottom 10 Plus/Minus for Running Backs

Rk	Player	Team	Pass	+/-
1	T.Gurley	LAR	49	-6.5
2	D.Johnson	HOU	62	-4.5
3	G.Bernard	CIN	43	-4.3
4	P.Lindsay	DEN	48	-4.3
5	K.Drake	2TM	68	-3.5
6	L.Fournette	JAX	101	-3.2
7	T.Coleman	SF	30	-3.1
8	N.Chubb	CLE	49	-2.7
9	T.Cohen	CHI	104	-2.7
10	R.Burkhead	NE	38	-2.6

Min. 25 passes; plus/minus adjusted for passes tipped/thrown away.

Top 10 Plus/Minus for Wide Receivers

Rk	Player	Team	Pass	+/-
1	M.Thomas	NO	185	+24.9
2	T.Lockett	SEA	110	+13.6
3	C.Godwin	TB	121	+11.6
4	S.Diggs	MIN	95	+9.0
5	K.Allen	LAC	149	+8.5
6	C.Ridley	ATL	93	+8.3
7	W.Fuller	HOU	71	+7.8
8	D.Hopkins	HOU	150	+7.5
9	A.Cooper	DAL	119	+6.2
10	M.Jones	DET	91	+6.0

Min. 50 passes; plus/minus adjusted for passes tipped/thrown away.

Bottom 10 Plus/Minus for Wide Receivers

Rk	Player	Team	Pass	+/-
1	J.Wright	CAR	58	-8.4
2	A.Tate	CIN	80	-8.3
3	A.Erickson	CIN	78	-6.9
4	C.Samuel	CAR	105	-6.0
5	O.Beckham	CLE	133	-5.5
6	G.Tate	NYG	86	-5.1
7	S.Watkins	KC	90	-4.8
8	J.Ross	CIN	56	-4.6
9	D.Hamilton	DEN	52	-4.6
10	C.Conley	JAX	90	-4.4

Min. 50 passes; plus/minus adjusted for passes tipped/thrown away.

Top 10 Plus/Minus for Tight Ends

Rk	Player	Team	Pass	+/-
1	T.Kelce	KC	136	+11.5
2	D.Waller	OAK	117	+9.5
3	G.Kittle	SF	107	+9.0
4	A.Hooper	ATL	97	+8.9
5	K.Rudolph	MIN	48	+7.3
6	T.Higbee	LAR	89	+7.0
7	W.Dissly	SEA	27	+5.5
8	H.Henry	LAC	76	+4.9
9	R.Griffin	NYJ	41	+4.5
10	J.Witten	DAL	83	+3.7

Min. 25 passes; plus/minus adjusted for passes tipped/thrown away.

Bottom 10 Plus/Minus for Tight Ends

Rk	Player	Team	Pass	+/-
1	T.Hockenson	DET	59	-8.7
2	D.Knox	BUF	50	-4.9
3	I.Thomas	CAR	30	-4.6
4	J.Doyle	IND	72	-4.4
5	E.Engram	NYG	68	-4.0
6	D.Harris	CLE	27	-3.9
7	J.Sprinkle	WAS	40	-3.0
8	J.James	DET	27	-2.7
9	L.Thomas	DET	28	-2.5
10	V.McDonald	PIT	55	-2.5

Min. 25 passes; plus/minus adjusted for passes tipped/thrown away.

Top 10 Quarterbacks, Yards Gained on Defensive Pass Interference

Rk	Player	Team	Pen	Yds
1	T.Brady	NE	14	234
2	P.Rivers	LAC	16	228
3	J.Brissett	IND	10	217
3	J.Winston	TB	12	217
5	A.Rodgers	GB	12	206
6	M.Rudolph	PIT	7	182
7	K.Murray	ARI	9	177
8	M.Ryan	ATL	8	176
9	B.Mayfield	CLE	14	155
10	A.Dalton	CIN	11	152

Top 10 Receivers, Yards Gained on Defensive Pass Interference

Rk	Player	Team	Pen	Yds
1	C.Sutton	DEN	8	150
2	M.Evans	TB	8	139
3	D.Cain	2TM	4	136
4	J.Washington	PIT	6	119
5	C.Kirk	ARI	5	111
6	C.Samuel	CAR	3	94
7	O.Beckham	CLE	8	85
8	D.Adams	GB	5	84
9	C.Ridley	ATL	3	83
10	R.Anderson	NYJ	4	82

Top 10 Defenders, Yards Allowed on Defensive Pass Interference

Rk	Player	Team	Pen	Yds
1	X.Rhodes	MIN	4	99
2	I.Oliver	ATL	4	95
3	D.Baker	NYG	5	91
4	R.Sherman	SF	4	88
5	L.Johnson	HOU	4	86
6	L.Ryan	TEN	4	84
6	C.Ward	KC	2	84
8	N.Hewitt	NYJ	2	82
9	D.Ward	CLE	3	79
10	E.Apple	NO	5	76
10	T.Flowers	SEA	5	76

Top 20 First Downs/Touchdowns Allowed, Coverage

Rk	Player	Team	Yards	Rk	Player	Team	Yards
1	B.Murphy	ARI	44	11	R.Melvin	DET	32
2	V.Hargreaves	2TM	43	11	L.Wallace	BUF	32
3	T.Flowers	SEA	41	13	J.Alexander	GB	31
4	A.Bouye	JAX	39	13	C.Awuzie	DAL	31
5	J.Coleman	DET	37	13	D.Baker	NYG	31
6	I.Oliver	ATL	36	16	M.Peters	2TM	30
6	X.Rhodes	MIN	36	17	Sl.Griffin	SEA	29
8	C.Davis	TB	35	17	T.Herndon	JAX	29
8	K.Fuller	CHI	35	17	L.Ryan	TEN	29
10	D.Slay	DET	33	17	T.White	BUF	29

Includes Defensive Pass Interference.

Top 20 Passing Yards Allowed, Coverage

Rk	Player	Team	Yards	Rk	Player	Team	Yards
1	A.Bouye	JAX	713	11	R.Melvin	DET	586
2	V.Hargreaves	2TM	694	11	D.Worley	OAK	586
3	I.Oliver	ATL	678	13	C.Awuzie	DAL	576
4	B.Webb	CIN	668	13	R.Darby	PHI	567
5	T.Flowers	SEA	630	15	D.Slay	DET	564
6	K.King	GB	623	16	C.Harris	DEN	555
7	K.Fuller	CHI	622	17	G.Conley	2TM	550
8	J.Coleman	DET	621	18	T.Herndon	JAX	543
9	J.Alexander	GB	614	18	X.Rhodes	MIN	543
10	D.Baker	NYG	603	20	B.Murphy	ARI	538

Includes Defensive Pass Interference.

Fewest Yards After Catch Allowed, Coverage by Cornerbacks

Rk	Player	Team	YAC
1	B.Murphy	ARI	1.6
2	C.Hayward	LAC	1.7
3	R.Sherman	SF	1.7
4	J.Bradberry	CAR	1.9
5	D.Slay	DET	2.1
6	S.Nelson	PIT	2.1
7	J.Ramsey	2TM	2.1
8	J.Jenkins	NO	2.1
9	C.Davis	TB	2.2
10	D.Hayden	JAX	2.2
11	T.Waynes	MIN	2.2
12	M.Davis	LAC	2.5
13	T.White	BUF	2.5
14	J.Haden	PIT	2.6
15	B.Skrine	CHI	2.7
16	R.Melvin	DET	2.7
16	X.Rhodes	MIN	2.7
18	B.Jones	DAL	2.7
19	D.Roberts	NYJ	2.8
20	M.Butler	TEN	2.8

Min. 50 passes or 8 games started.

Most Yards After Catch Allowed, Coverage by Cornerbacks

Rk	Player	Team	YAC
1	B.Webb	CIN	7.3
2	D.Trufant	ATL	6.2
3	D.King	LAC	5.5
4	A.Bouye	JAX	5.5
5	T.Mullen	OAK	5.4
6	D.Worley	OAK	5.3
7	K.Sheffield	ATL	5.3
8	G.Conley	2TM	5.2
9	I.Oliver	ATL	5.2
10	K.Williams	SF	5.0
11	D.Ward	CLE	5.0
12	K.King	GB	4.9
13	M.Hilton	PIT	4.9
14	T.Flowers	SEA	4.8
15	A.Witherspoon	SF	4.7
16	G.Williams	CLE	4.6
17	R.Darby	PHI	4.6
17	A.Maddox	PHI	4.6
17	M.Peters	2TM	4.6
17	C.Ward	KC	4.6

Min. 50 passes or 8 games started.

Top 20 Defenders, Run Tackles for Loss

Rk	Player	Team	TFL
1	B.Baker	ARI	11
1	M.Crosby	OAK	11
1	B.Dupree	PIT	11
1	B.Graham	PHI	11
1	G.Jarrett	ATL	11
1	S.Lawson	BUF	11
7	A.Donald	LAR	10
7	T.Edmunds	BUF	10
7	R.Evans	TEN	10
7	M.Golden	NYG	10
7	J.Hankins	OAK	10
7	J.Hicks	ARI	10
7	D.Lawrence	DAL	10
7	T.Watt	PIT	10
15	J.Bosa	LAC	9
15	C.Dunlap	CIN	9
15	K.Phillips	NYJ	9
15	M.Purcell	DEN	9
19	11 tied with		8

Includes both tackles and assists.

Fewest Avg Yards on Run Tackle, Defensive Line or Edge Rusher

Rk	Player	Team	Tkl	Avg
1	M.Crosby	OAK	32	0.3
2	K.Phillips	NYJ	30	0.4
3	B.Graham	PHI	33	0.4
4	F.Fatukasi	NYJ	25	0.6
5	A.Donald	LAR	32	0.7
6	S.Barrett	TB	25	1.1
7	M.Purcell	DEN	47	1.3
8	D.Tomlinson	NYG	43	1.3
9	T.Watt	PIT	34	1.4
10	Y.Ngakoue	JAX	27	1.4
11	D.Lawrence	DAL	33	1.4
12	P.Ford	SEA	28	1.4
13	S.McLendon	NYJ	29	1.4
14	G.McCoy	CAR	31	1.5
15	W.Gholston	TB	36	1.5
16	F.Clark	KC	25	1.6
17	B.Hill	NYG	33	1.6
18	C.Campbell	JAX	47	1.6
18	J.Hankins	OAK	47	1.6
20	L.Ogunjobi	CLE	40	1.7

Min. 25 run tackles

Fewest Avg Yards on Run Tackle, LB

Rk	Player	Team	Tkl	Avg
1	J.Burgess	NYJ	36	1.6
2	V.Williams	PIT	36	2.2
2	J.Bynes	BAL	36	2.3
4	N.Gerry	PHI	37	2.4
5	J.Bentley	NE	26	2.6
6	R.Evans	TEN	67	2.6
7	Z.Cunningham	HOU	96	2.7
8	T.Edmunds	BUF	73	2.8
9	L.David	TB	61	3.0
10	J.Collins	NE	47	3.1
11	D.Perryman	LAC	47	3.1
12	D.Mayo	NYG	58	3.2
13	A.Walker	IND	65	3.2
14	A.Ogletree	NYG	36	3.2
15	D.Trevathan	CHI	46	3.2
16	M.Milano	BUF	55	3.3
17	J.Walker	ARI	39	3.3
17	N.Bradham	PHI	27	3.3
19	L.Vander Esch	DAL	39	3.4
20	L.Kuechly	CAR	89	3.4

Min. 25 run tackles

Fewest Avg Yards on Run Tackle, DB

Rk	Player	Team	Tkl	Avg
1	K.Moore	IND	25	2.8
2	J.Love	NYG	21	2.9
3	M.Hilton	PIT	24	3.0
4	K.Ishmael	ATL	24	3.4
5	L.Ryan	TEN	39	3.7
6	K.Williams	SF	20	3.8
7	K.Jackson	DEN	34	3.8
8	J.Whitehead	TB	37	3.9
9	M.Burnett	CLE	23	4.0
10	D.Thompson	DAL	26	4.1
11	T.Wilson	DET	47	4.3
12	L.Collins	WAS	73	4.3
13	D.James	LAC	21	4.3
13	K.Joseph	OAK	26	4.5
15	T.Carrie	CLE	21	4.5
16	P.Chung	NE	25	4.6
17	C.Clark	BAL	39	4.6
17	J.Adams	NYJ	38	4.8
19	V.Bell	NO	37	4.9
20	J.Heath	DAL	24	4.9

Min. 20 run tackles

Top 20 Offensive Tackles, Blown Blocks

Rk	Player	Pos	Team	Sacks	All Pass	All Run	Total
1	K.McGary	RT	ATL	13.5	37	9	46
2	J.Davis	RT	MIA	6.0	35	10	45
3	B.Smith	RT	IND	7.3	34	9	44
4	N.Solder	LT	NYG	12.0	40	2	42
5	M.Cannon	RT	NE	6.5	28	9	37
5	J.Webb	LT	MIA	4.5	30	5	37
7	T.Scott	LT	LAC	7.0	28	8	36
8	M.Schwartz	RT	KC	1.5	31	4	35
9	C.Erving	LT	KC	4.5	30	4	34
10	T.Decker	LT	DET	5.3	24	8	32
10	C.Robinson	LT	JAX	8.5	24	8	32
12	C.Hubbard	RT	CLE	5.5	21	10	31
12	K.Miller	LT	OAK	7.0	22	9	31
14	J.Taylor	RT	JAX	9.5	19	11	30
15	D.Humphries	LT	ARI	3.0	23	5	29
15	D.Penn	LT	WAS	6.5	21	8	29
15	R.Wagner	RT	DET	3.5	17	11	29
18	G.Ifedi	RT	SEA	3.5	18	8	28
19	D.Daley	LT/RG	CAR	9.0	21	5	26
19	C.Leno	LT	CHI	5.0	20	5	26
19	S.Tevi	RT	LAC	7.0	19	7	26

Top 20 Offensive Tackles in Snaps per Blown Block

Rk	Player	Pos	Team	Sacks	All Pass	All Run	Total	Snaps	Snaps per BB
1	R.Stanley	LT	BAL	0.0	7	2	9	955	106.1
2	A.Whitworth	LT	LAR	0.5	7	5	12	1121	93.4
3	O.Brown	RT	BAL	2.5	7	7	14	1125	80.4
4	L.Collins	RT	DAL	1.5	12	3	15	1007	67.1
5	D.Bakhtiari	LT	GB	2.8	12	5	17	1100	64.7
6	L.Johnson	RT	PHI	1.5	8	4	12	774	64.5
6	C.Lucas	RT	CHI	1.5	6	2	8	516	64.5
8	B.O'Neill	RT	MIN	1.0	9	6	16	983	61.4
9	T.Lewan	LT	TEN	1.5	8	4	12	730	60.8
10	R.Ramczyk	RT	NO	2.5	13	5	18	1077	59.8
11	T.Brown	RT	OAK	0.3	3	7	10	595	59.5
12	D.Smith	LT	TB	3.0	17	2	19	1075	56.6
13	M.Feiler	RT	PIT	6.5	15	3	18	1016	56.4
13	A.Villanueva	LT	PIT	2.0	18	0	18	1016	56.4
15	T.Smith	LT	DAL	2.0	12	4	16	889	55.6
16	L.Tunsil	LT	HOU	1.0	13	4	17	942	55.4
17	M.McGlinchey	RT	SF	5.5	13	2	15	795	53.0
18	A.Castonzo	LT	IND	3.5	15	6	21	1092	52.0
19	D.Dawkins	LT	BUF	3.0	16	4	20	1039	52.0
20	J.Matthews	LT	ATL	5.0	21	2	23	1189	51.7

Minimum: 400 snaps

Top 20 Interior Linemen, Blown Blocks

Rk	Player	Pos	Team	Sacks	All Pass	All Run	Total
1	M.Deiter	LG	MIA	4.8	29	6	35
1	M.Glowinski	RG	IND	2.3	28	7	35
3	B.Turner	RG	GB	6.0	21	12	34
4	A.Blythe	RG/C	LAR	1.0	16	15	31
5	N.Davis	RG	TEN	5.0	15	14	29
5	I.Seumalo	LG	PHI	4.7	18	11	29
7	J.Daniels	C/LG	CHI	2.0	14	13	28
7	Z.Fulton	RG	HOU	1.5	12	14	28
7	T.Hopkins	C	CIN	5.5	18	10	28
10	L.Warford	RG	NO	2.0	13	13	26
11	P.Elflein	LG	MIN	5.5	16	9	25
12	G.Bradbury	C	MIN	4.0	14	10	24
12	D.Fluker	RG	SEA	3.3	17	6	24
12	B.Price	LG	CIN	2.3	15	9	24
12	A.Shipley	C	ARI	3.5	11	13	24
16	D.Feeney	LG	LAC	3.5	14	9	23
16	J.Sweezy	RG	ARI	1.0	16	7	23
16	D.Williams	LG/LT	CAR	9.0	17	6	23
19	T.Frederick	C	DAL	2.0	12	10	22
19	G.Jackson	RG	OAK	4.8	11	10	22
19	T.Karras	C	NE	1.0	13	8	22
19	J.Pugh	LG	ARI	5.0	18	3	22

Top 20 Interior Linemen in Snaps per Blown Block

Rk	Player	Pos	Team	Sacks	All Pass	All Run	Total	Snaps	Snaps per BB
1	Z.Martin	RG	DAL	0.5	3	5	8	1122	140.3
2	M.Yanda	RG	BAL	0.0	4	4	8	987	123.4
3	B.Linder	C	JAX	0.0	5	4	9	1104	122.7
4	B.Brooks	RG	PHI	1.5	6	3	9	1065	118.3
5	J.Thuney	LG	NE	1.0	7	3	10	1147	114.7
6	R.Incognito	LG	OAK	0.0	4	3	7	778	111.1
7	C.Whitehair	C/LG	CHI	1.5	5	5	10	1091	109.1
8	W.Richburg	C	SF	0.0	2	6	8	858	107.3
9	J.Tretter	C	CLE	2.0	4	7	11	1066	96.9
10	J.Bitonio	LG	CLE	2.5	6	5	11	1066	96.9
11	M.Pouncey	C	PIT	0.0	5	4	9	790	87.8
12	A.Reiter	C	KC	1.0	6	6	12	1053	87.8
13	C.Roullier	C	WAS	2.5	5	5	10	851	85.1
14	K.Zeitler	RG	NYG	1.5	6	6	12	1004	83.7
15	A.Marpet	LG	TB	1.0	9	5	14	1159	82.8
16	M.Skura	C	BAL	1.0	4	5	9	734	81.6
17	B.Bozeman	LG	BAL	3.0	9	5	14	1125	80.4
18	C.McGovern	C	DEN	1.5	5	7	13	1024	78.8
19	A.Mack	C	ATL	2.5	11	5	16	1182	73.9
20	C.Williams	LG	DAL	0.0	8	2	10	733	73.3

Minimum: 400 snaps

Top 20 Tight Ends, Blown Blocks

Rk	Player	Team	Sacks	All Pass	All Run	Total		Rk	Player	Team	Sacks	All Pass	All Run	Total
1	D.Fells	HOU	1.0	6	15	21		6	T.Hockenson	DET	0.5	3	4	8
2	O.Howard	TB	0.5	3	12	15		6	C.Uzomah	CIN	2.0	3	5	8
3	J.Witten	DAL	0.5	4	9	13		13	H.Henry	LAC	0.0	0	7	7
4	L.Stocker	ATL	0.5	4	6	10		13	J.James	DET	1.5	5	2	7
5	M.Williams	ARI	0.5	3	6	9		13	G.Olsen	CAR	1.5	2	5	7
6	J.Akins	HOU	0.5	4	4	8		13	D.Smythe	MIA	1.0	1	6	7
6	N.Fant	DEN	2.0	4	4	8		13	L.Thomas	DET	0.0	2	5	7
6	R.Griffin	NYJ	0.5	5	3	8		13	D.Waller	OAK	1.0	4	3	7
6	T.Higbee	LAR	1.0	2	6	8		19	12 tied with					6
6	J.Hill	NO	2.0	4	4	8								

Most Penalties, Offense

Rk	Player	Team	Pen	Yds
1	L.Tunsil	HOU	18	80
2	G.Bolles	DEN	17	95
3	D.Humphries	ARI	14	87
3	J.Taylor	JAX	14	115
3	A.Whitworth	LAR	14	125
6	G.Ifedi	SEA	13	80
6	C.Leno	CHI	13	99
8	D.Bakhtiari	GB	12	94
8	B.Linder	JAX	12	89
8	G.Robinson	CLE	12	95
11	D.Dawkins	BUF	11	54
11	M.Moses	WAS	11	65
11	D.Penn	WAS	11	66
11	C.Robinson	JAX	11	67
15	T.Decker	DET	10	64
15	D.Dotson	TB	10	71
15	T.Lewan	TEN	10	74
15	A.Villanueva	PIT	10	55
19	11 tied with		9	

Includes declined and offsetting, but not penalties on special teams, turnover returns, or kneeldowns.

Most Penalties, Defense

Rk	Player	Team	Pen	Yds
1	B.Breeland	KC	12	102
1	C.Davis	TB	12	111
1	M.Humphrey	BAL	12	79
4	S.Barrett	TB	11	54
5	T.Mullen	OAK	10	85
5	N.Needham	MIA	10	44
5	J.Phillips	BUF	10	54
5	X.Rhodes	MIN	10	139
9	E.Apple	NO	9	91
9	D.Baker	NYG	9	116
9	R.Douglas	PHI	9	58
9	T.Herndon	JAX	9	56
9	L.Johnson	HOU	9	98
9	L.Joyner	OAK	9	46
9	B.Murphy	ARI	9	79
9	L.Ryan	TEN	9	94
9	R.Sherman	SF	9	100
9	T.Watt	PIT	9	60
9	R.Ya-Sin	IND	9	91
20	8 tied with		8	

Includes declined and offsetting, but not penalties on special teams, turnover returns, or kneeldowns.

Top 10 Kickers, Gross Kickoff Value over Average

Rk	Player	Team	Kick Pts+	Net Pts+	Kicks
1	J.Elliott	PHI	+3.5	-3.6	77
2	J.Sanders	MIA	+3.0	+0.4	65
3	B.Pinion	TB	+2.9	+4.7	97
4	D.Hopkins	WAS	+2.5	+2.5	65
5	J.Tucker	BAL	+2.5	+0.5	100
6	R.Bullock	CIN	+2.4	+5.1	66
7	S.Ficken	NYJ	+2.2	+7.2	57
8	A.Rosas	NYG	+1.9	+5.8	70
9	J.Myers	SEA	+1.9	-0.9	82
10	J.Slye	CAR	+1.7	+2.0	69

Min. 20 kickoffs; squibs and onside not included

Bottom 10 Kickers, Gross Kickoff Value over Average

Rk	Player	Team	Kick Pts+	Net Pts+	Kicks
1	S.Martin	DET	-5.7	-4.9	59
2	Z.Gonzalez	ARI	-4.1	+0.6	83
3	B.McManus	DEN	-2.9	-4.0	72
4	B.Maher	DAL	-2.9	-3.4	64
5	K.Fairbairn	HOU	-2.4	+3.8	79
6	M.Wishnowsky	SF	-2.0	+0.5	96
7	J.Lambo	JAX	-1.5	+1.0	34
8	K.Forbath	DAL	-1.1	-1.5	22
9	C.Santos	TEN	-1.1	-0.5	21
10	E.Pineiro	CHI	-0.9	-0.4	50

Min. 20 kickoffs; squibs and onside not included

Top 10 Punters, Gross Punt Value over Average

Rk	Player	Team	Punt Pts+	Net Pts+	Punts
1	T.Way	WAS	+13.7	+4.8	79
2	B.Kern	TEN	+11.7	+5.1	78
3	B.Anger	HOU	+6.0	+10.9	45
4	J.Bailey	NE	+5.4	+10.5	81
5	L.Cooke	JAX	+5.2	+12.2	75
6	B.Colquitt	MIN	+4.3	+6.9	62
7	T.Morstead	NO	+4.3	+4.9	60
8	L.Edwards	NYJ	+4.2	+10.1	87
9	J.Hekker	LAR	+2.8	+2.2	67
10	K.Huber	CIN	+2.8	+4.2	75

Min. 20 punts

Bottom 10 Punters, Gross Punt Value over Average

Rk	Player	Team	Punt Pts+	Net Pts+	Punts
1	C.Bojorquez	BUF	-10.7	-9.4	80
2	C.Jones	DAL	-9.7	-7.6	51
3	B.Pinion	TB	-6.9	-3.6	57
4	D.Colquitt	KC	-6.6	-0.6	49
5	C.Wadman	DEN	-5.8	-11.9	78
6	T.Long	LAC	-3.4	-7.6	48
7	S.Koch	BAL	-2.8	-6.4	41
8	M.Dickson	SEA	-2.7	-1.2	74
9	M.Wishnowsky	SF	-2.3	+6.4	52
10	R.Allen	ATL	-2.3	-1.9	28

Min. 20 punts

Top 10 Kick Returners, Value over Average

Rk	Player	Team	Pts+	Returns
1	B.Wilson	CIN	+10.1	19
2	C.Patterson	CHI	+7.7	28
3	S.Sims	WAS	+7.3	32
4	J.Agnew	DET	+5.5	17
5	J.Grant	MIA	+5.4	22
6	M.Hardman	KC	+4.9	26
6	A.Roberts	BUF	+4.4	25
8	D.Harris	NO	+4.3	24
8	D.Spencer	DEN	+3.5	14
10	V.Smith	NYJ	+2.4	9

Min. eight returns

Bottom 10 Kick Returners, Value over Average

Rk	Player	Team	Pts+	Returns
1	T.Pollard	DAL	-5.1	14
2	M.Walker	JAX	-3.5	17
3	D.Ogunbowale	TB	-2.9	12
4	T.Thomas	CLE	-2.7	10
5	K.Whyte	PIT	-2.4	14
6	D.Shepherd	GB	-1.8	8
7	J.Natson	LAR	-1.7	12
8	T.Montgomery	NYJ	-1.7	17
9	D.King	LAC	-1.6	15
10	R.Switzer	PIT	-1.5	9

Min. eight returns

Top 10 Punt Returners, Value over Average

Rk	Player	Team	Pts+	Returns
1	N.Hines	IND	+16.9	9
2	D.Johnson	PIT	+8.5	20
3	D.Harris	NO	+8.2	36
4	M.Hardman	KC	+4.9	18
5	B.Berrios	NYJ	+4.7	21
6	J.Agnew	DET	+4.3	19
7	T.Cohen	CHI	+3.3	33
8	P.Williams	MIA	+3.0	10
9	R.James	SF	+2.4	33
10	J.Natson	LAR	+2.2	19

Min. eight returns

Bottom 10 Punt Returners, Value over Average

Rk	Player	Team	Pts+	Returns
1	B.Wilson	TB	-5.3	15
2	D.Westbrook	JAX	-2.9	23
3	R.McCloud	CAR	-2.8	10
4	R.Switzer	PIT	-2.8	8
5	A.Erickson	CIN	-2.4	25
6	T.Austin	DAL	-2.4	17
7	M.Hughes	MIN	-2.4	14
7	M.Sherels	2TM	-2.3	12
9	D.Hilliard	CLE	-1.8	15
10	D.Thomas	2TM	-1.8	26

Min. eight returns

Top 20 Special Teams Plays

Rk	Player	Team	Plays	Rk	Player	Team	Plays
1	J.Gray	NO	16	8	L.Fort	2TM	11
1	T.Matakevich	PIT	16	8	R.Mostert	SF	11
1	D.Watt	LAC	16	8	D.Tranquill	LAC	11
4	M.Killebrew	DET	14	14	U.Amadi	SEA	10
5	K.Hodge	CLE	12	14	D.Hilliard	CLE	10
5	A.Moore	HOU	12	14	T.Moore	SF	10
5	J.Reeves-Maybin	DET	12	14	M.Slater	NE	10
8	T.Apke	WAS	11	14	R.Spillane	PIT	10
8	J.Bethel	2TM	11	14	D.Virgin	DET	10
8	J.Dangerfield	PIT	11	20	9 tied with		9

Plays = tackles + assists; does not include onside or end-half squib kicks.

Top 10 Offenses, 3-and-out per drive

Rk	Team	Pct
1	BAL	12.7%
2	KC	13.5%
3	TB	14.4%
4	ATL	14.5%
5	LAC	14.6%
6	HOU	14.6%
7	DAL	15.3%
8	SF	16.8%
9	IND	17.6%
10	MIN	17.9%

Top 10 Defenses, 3-and-out per drive

Rk	Team	Pct
1	PHI	27.6%
2	BUF	27.1%
3	SF	26.3%
4	NE	25.8%
5	NO	24.9%
6	CHI	24.6%
7	LAR	23.7%
8	PIT	23.1%
9	NYJ	22.6%
10	CAR	22.2%
10	NYG	22.2%

Bottom 10 Offenses, 3-and-out per drive

Rk	Team	Pct
23	SEA	23.3%
24	PIT	23.6%
25	GB	24.1%
26	JAX	24.7%
27	BUF	24.7%
28	CIN	24.9%
29	DEN	28.9%
30	CHI	29.2%
31	WAS	29.7%
32	NYJ	30.6%

Bottom 10 Defenses, 3-and-out per drive

Rk	Team	Pct
23	CLE	18.8%
24	MIN	18.7%
25	ATL	18.6%
26	ARI	17.2%
26	WAS	17.2%
28	IND	17.0%
29	LAC	16.2%
30	JAX	16.1%
31	KC	16.0%
32	HOU	13.0%

Top 10 Offenses, Yards per drive

Rk	Team	Yds/Dr
1	BAL	41.77
2	DAL	39.99
3	KC	39.07
4	LAC	37.47
5	ATL	36.83
6	OAK	35.55
7	HOU	34.63
8	NO	34.50
9	IND	34.36
10	SF	33.58

Top 10 Defenses, Yards per drive

Rk	Team	Yds/Dr
1	NE	23.40
2	SF	25.47
3	PIT	26.45
4	BUF	27.46
5	NYJ	28.39
6	CHI	28.63
7	PHI	28.90
8	TB	29.90
9	LAR	30.03
10	BAL	30.37

Bottom 10 Offenses, Yards per drive

Rk	Team	Yds/Dr
23	NYG	29.96
24	BUF	29.53
25	CIN	29.51
26	CAR	29.26
27	MIA	29.23
28	DEN	29.02
29	CHI	27.82
30	PIT	25.96
31	WAS	24.81
32	NYJ	23.89

Bottom 10 Defenses, Yards per drive

Rk	Team	Yds/Dr
23	JAX	34.45
24	ATL	34.72
25	KC	34.84
26	WAS	35.73
27	MIA	35.78
28	CIN	35.89
29	DET	36.46
30	OAK	37.19
31	HOU	37.64
32	ARI	38.03

Top 10 Offenses, avg LOS to start drive

Rk	Team	LOS
1	NE	32.6
2	SF	31.9
3	NO	31.2
4	SEA	29.6
5	MIN	29.6
6	BAL	29.3
7	ATL	29.2
8	CAR	29.0
9	BUF	28.8
10	KC	28.8

Top 10 Defenses, avg LOS to start drive

Rk	Team	LOS
1	NE	25.2
2	OAK	25.8
3	HOU	25.9
4	DET	25.9
5	NO	26.5
6	SEA	26.6
7	CIN	26.8
8	KC	26.9
9	ARI	27.3
10	BAL	27.4

Bottom 10 Offenses, avg LOS to start drive

Rk	Team	LOS
23	CIN	27.9
24	MIA	27.8
25	TEN	27.5
26	DEN	27.2
27	NYG	26.9
28	OAK	26.9
29	NYJ	26.6
30	DAL	26.2
31	LAC	26.2
32	JAX	25.8

Bottom 10 Defenses, avg LOS to start drive

Rk	Team	LOS
23	LAR	29.3
24	JAX	29.6
25	CHI	29.8
26	NYG	29.9
27	PIT	29.9
28	DAL	30.0
29	MIA	30.4
30	CAR	30.5
31	NYJ	31.3
32	TB	31.7

Top 10 Offenses, Points per drive

Rk	Team	Pts/Dr
1	BAL	3.08
2	KC	2.70
3	NO	2.57
4	DAL	2.51
5	SF	2.47
6	MIN	2.33
7	HOU	2.23
8	GB	2.21
9	ATL	2.18
10	TB	2.14

Top 10 Defenses, Points per drive

Rk	Team	Pts/Dr
1	NE	1.02
2	BUF	1.34
3	PIT	1.55
4	SF	1.65
5	BAL	1.67
6	CHI	1.69
7	DEN	1.75
8	MIN	1.76
9	TEN	1.80
10	GB	1.81

Bottom 10 Offenses, Points per drive

Rk	Team	Pts/Dr
23	CAR	1.73
24	BUF	1.71
25	DEN	1.66
26	JAX	1.64
27	MIA	1.63
28	CHI	1.54
29	CIN	1.53
30	WAS	1.51
31	PIT	1.47
32	NYJ	1.29

Bottom 10 Defenses, Points per drive

Rk	Team	Pts/Dr
23	CIN	2.25
24	DET	2.30
25	NYG	2.30
26	ATL	2.31
27	HOU	2.32
28	CAR	2.34
29	ARI	2.41
30	WAS	2.46
31	OAK	2.51
32	MIA	2.65

Top 10 Offenses, Better DVOA with Shotgun

Rk	Team	% Plays Shotgun	DVOA Shot	DVOA Not	Yd/Play Shot	Yd/Play Not	DVOA Dif
1	MIA	69%	0.3%	-41.0%	5.6	3.7	41.4%
2	NYG	73%	4.5%	-33.1%	6.0	4.1	37.6%
3	DAL	64%	35.1%	7.2%	7.0	5.7	27.9%
4	ARI	88%	7.2%	-18.5%	5.9	4.1	25.7%
5	LAC	71%	12.3%	-12.8%	6.5	4.9	25.1%
6	KC	78%	28.2%	4.9%	6.7	5.4	23.3%
7	BAL	95%	29.3%	8.7%	6.4	4.3	20.6%
8	SF	45%	18.9%	-0.6%	6.5	5.9	19.5%
9	HOU	81%	4.0%	-14.1%	5.8	5.7	18.2%
10	CHI	77%	-5.6%	-23.4%	4.8	4.4	17.8%

Bottom 10 Offenses, Better DVOA with Shotgun

Rk	Team	% Plays Shotgun	DVOA Shot	DVOA Not	Yd/Play Shot	Yd/Play Not	DVOA Dif
23	JAX	68%	-9.0%	-10.4%	5.6	5.3	1.4%
24	NYJ	67%	-24.8%	-24.8%	4.9	4.4	0.0%
25	NE	52%	3.7%	4.4%	5.5	5.3	-0.7%
26	CLE	67%	-5.8%	-2.2%	5.9	5.3	-3.6%
27	PHI	72%	1.4%	5.5%	5.5	4.9	-4.2%
28	DEN	55%	-14.3%	-7.3%	5.2	5.3	-7.0%
29	BUF	62%	-10.6%	-2.9%	5.4	5.3	-7.6%
30	CAR	72%	-18.6%	-5.0%	5.1	5.6	-13.6%
31	TEN	51%	4.2%	19.2%	5.8	6.9	-15.0%
32	WAS	62%	-29.2%	-8.9%	4.6	5.8	-20.3%

Top 10 Offenses, Better DVOA with Play-Action

Rk	Team	% PA	DVOA PA	DVOA No PA	Yd/Play PA	Yd/Play No PA	DVOA Dif
1	TB	18%	58.9%	-6.2%	10.4	6.6	65.1%
2	JAX	14%	55.7%	-7.5%	8.8	5.7	63.1%
3	TEN	31%	67.2%	14.0%	11.2	5.6	53.3%
4	BUF	24%	38.3%	-8.2%	7.4	5.6	46.4%
5	CAR	31%	10.8%	-33.3%	6.7	4.8	44.2%
6	SF	32%	49.2%	10.2%	9.6	6.3	39.0%
7	IND	30%	24.8%	-13.1%	7.7	5.4	37.8%
8	OAK	22%	52.7%	15.4%	7.7	7.0	37.3%
9	CLE	28%	28.7%	-5.9%	8.2	5.5	34.7%
10	WAS	22%	6.6%	-21.3%	7.1	4.9	28.0%

Bottom 10 Offenses, Better DVOA with Play-Action

Rk	Team	% PA	DVOA PA	DVOA No PA	Yd/Play PA	Yd/Play No PA	DVOA Dif
23	LAR	32%	14.5%	15.5%	7.5	6.4	-1.0%
24	PHI	31%	12.9%	14.3%	6.2	5.9	-1.4%
25	ARI	28%	-2.8%	5.3%	6.8	5.7	-8.1%
26	DAL	25%	34.5%	43.1%	8.3	7.5	-8.6%
27	GB	27%	12.0%	23.5%	6.8	6.2	-11.5%
28	HOU	24%	9.6%	21.3%	7.6	6.2	-11.7%
29	KC	32%	37.6%	51.5%	7.6	7.6	-13.8%
30	BAL	33%	43.7%	58.7%	7.0	7.4	-15.0%
31	MIA	18%	-19.0%	7.2%	5.8	5.9	-26.2%
32	PIT	14%	-39.5%	-11.4%	3.8	6.1	-28.1%

Top 10 Defenses, Better DVOA vs. Shotgun

Rk	Team	% Plays Shotgun	DVOA Shot	DVOA Not	Yd/Play Shot	Yd/Play Not	DVOA Dif
1	NE	76%	-29.3%	-15.3%	4.8	4.8	-14.0%
2	LAR	74%	-9.6%	1.7%	5.1	5.6	-11.3%
3	SF	63%	-24.2%	-13.2%	4.8	4.7	-11.0%
4	JAX	59%	6.5%	16.4%	6.0	6.5	-9.9%
5	BAL	72%	-15.7%	-5.9%	5.2	5.3	-9.8%
6	DET	65%	7.8%	15.4%	6.2	5.9	-7.5%
7	DEN	65%	-5.8%	-0.3%	5.6	5.3	-5.5%
8	BUF	68%	-13.4%	-8.2%	5.0	4.7	-5.2%
9	PHI	61%	-6.3%	-1.2%	5.7	5.4	-5.1%
10	IND	65%	0.4%	5.4%	5.9	5.7	-5.0%

Bottom 10 Defenses, Better DVOA vs. Shotgun

Rk	Team	% Plays Shotgun	DVOA Shot	DVOA Not	Yd/Play Shot	Yd/Play Not	DVOA Dif
23	PIT	69%	-13.0%	-28.7%	5.1	4.2	15.7%
24	LAC	61%	12.6%	-4.9%	6.1	4.8	17.6%
25	WAS	59%	15.8%	-2.2%	6.2	5.2	18.0%
26	CIN	60%	21.5%	2.6%	6.9	5.4	18.9%
27	NO	66%	3.6%	-16.8%	5.6	5.2	20.3%
28	MIN	62%	-1.5%	-21.9%	5.6	4.9	20.4%
29	ARI	61%	17.0%	-6.2%	6.6	5.3	23.2%
30	GB	65%	8.0%	-16.0%	6.0	5.3	24.0%
31	NYJ	70%	4.2%	-25.5%	5.8	4.0	29.7%
32	HOU	67%	22.1%	-14.0%	6.8	5.4	36.1%

Top 10 Defenses, Better DVOA vs. Play-Action

Rk	Team	% PA	DVOA PA	DVOA No PA	Yd/Play PA	Yd/Play No PA	DVOA Dif
1	WAS	31%	-11.4%	31.4%	5.7	7.0	-42.8%
2	NYJ	19%	-1.3%	14.0%	7.1	6.2	-15.3%
3	BAL	22%	-22.8%	-11.9%	6.7	5.5	-10.9%
4	MIN	28%	-12.5%	-3.9%	6.9	5.6	-8.6%
5	PIT	22%	-16.1%	-13.6%	6.8	5.3	-2.5%
6	CLE	26%	9.0%	10.4%	8.2	6.0	-1.4%
7	IND	23%	10.6%	11.3%	7.5	6.5	-0.7%
8	NYG	33%	32.1%	31.6%	8.2	6.8	0.5%
9	NO	22%	7.4%	2.0%	7.6	5.7	5.4%
10	HOU	22%	25.4%	19.4%	7.5	7.2	6.0%

Bottom 10 Defenses, Better DVOA vs. Play-Action

Rk	Team	% PA	DVOA PA	DVOA No PA	Yd/Play PA	Yd/Play No PA	DVOA Dif
23	TB	24%	18.8%	-6.2%	7.9	5.7	25.1%
24	PHI	23%	28.0%	-1.1%	8.2	5.8	29.1%
25	MIA	29%	62.6%	33.4%	8.7	7.0	29.2%
26	LAR	24%	20.4%	-10.7%	7.4	5.4	31.1%
27	OAK	29%	53.9%	22.2%	9.6	6.7	31.7%
28	JAX	28%	37.1%	3.5%	9.3	5.9	33.7%
29	BUF	24%	14.3%	-21.7%	6.7	4.8	36.0%
30	SF	32%	4.5%	-39.8%	5.8	4.6	44.3%
31	ATL	28%	51.4%	1.7%	9.2	6.1	49.7%
32	NE	20%	9.6%	-43.1%	6.9	4.7	52.7%

2019 Defenses with and without Pass Pressure

Rank	Team	Plays	Pct Pressure	DVOA with Pressure	Yds with Pressure	DVOA w/o Pressure	Yds w/o Pressure	DVOA Dif	Rank
1	NE	612	37.1%	-79.9%	3.1	-3.5%	6.4	-76.3%	4
2	NO	688	36.2%	-54.2%	3.5	36.8%	7.6	-90.9%	11
3	BAL	605	35.0%	-84.3%	2.8	22.1%	7.4	-106.4%	22
4	GB	610	34.8%	-65.2%	3.5	29.3%	7.9	-94.5%	13
5	PIT	604	34.4%	-83.8%	2.8	19.9%	7.2	-103.7%	18
6	DAL	644	33.9%	-43.1%	3.8	41.7%	7.2	-84.8%	7
7	TB	745	32.9%	-85.1%	2.7	40.5%	8.0	-125.6%	31
8	LAR	633	32.7%	-59.2%	3.9	25.5%	7.0	-84.8%	6
9	CLE	584	32.2%	-65.1%	3.2	45.4%	8.2	-110.6%	24
10	JAX	594	31.8%	-72.2%	3.0	53.1%	8.7	-125.3%	30
11	CIN	563	31.4%	-52.0%	3.1	63.7%	9.5	-115.8%	27
12	BUF	621	31.1%	-79.5%	1.9	16.3%	6.8	-95.9%	14
13	SF	607	30.8%	-105.1%	2.1	12.1%	6.3	-117.2%	28
14	PHI	641	30.6%	-52.7%	3.8	33.2%	7.5	-85.8%	8
14	ARI	676	30.5%	-71.1%	3.5	63.3%	8.7	-134.4%	32
14	MIN	664	30.4%	-86.4%	2.8	28.1%	7.4	-114.6%	26
17	NYJ	655	30.4%	-41.9%	5.1	33.3%	7.1	-75.2%	3
18	IND	628	30.1%	-64.2%	3.9	41.7%	8.0	-106.0%	21
19	KC	659	30.0%	-77.3%	3.1	25.9%	7.3	-103.2%	17
20	CHI	624	29.6%	-82.3%	2.7	30.2%	7.4	-112.5%	25
21	OAK	602	29.6%	-45.8%	4.1	64.2%	9.0	-110.0%	23
22	CAR	625	28.6%	-61.8%	3.8	26.9%	7.5	-88.7%	10
23	NYG	630	28.6%	-20.8%	4.6	53.4%	8.4	-74.2%	2
24	DEN	601	28.3%	-57.5%	3.7	30.0%	7.5	-87.5%	9
25	HOU	647	28.3%	-56.1%	4.4	49.9%	8.3	-105.9%	20
26	LAC	532	28.2%	-36.8%	4.3	31.3%	7.5	-68.1%	1
27	ATL	593	27.0%	-73.6%	3.3	51.1%	8.3	-124.7%	29
28	DET	667	26.8%	-48.6%	3.8	54.4%	8.5	-102.9%	16
29	WAS	613	26.1%	-43.8%	4.0	39.9%	7.6	-83.6%	5
30	TEN	682	25.1%	-66.0%	2.9	38.0%	7.9	-104.0%	19
31	MIA	585	24.1%	-26.6%	4.9	64.5%	8.4	-91.0%	12
32	SEA	657	24.0%	-66.8%	4.6	30.2%	7.7	-97.0%	15
NFL AVERAGE		**628**	**30.3%**	**-63.5%**	**3.5**	**37.6%**	**7.8**	**-101.1%**	

Includes scrambles and Defensive Pass Interference. Does not include aborted snaps.

Author Bios

Editor-in-Chief and NFL Statistician

Aaron Schatz is the creator of FootballOutsiders.com and the proprietary NFL statistics within *Football Outsiders Almanac*, including DVOA, DYAR, and adjusted line yards. He is also responsible each year for producing the Football Outsiders NFL team projections. He writes regularly for ESPN+ and has done custom research for a number of NFL teams. *The New York Times Magazine* referred to him as "the Bill James of football." Readers should feel free to blame everything in this book on the fact that he went to high school six miles from Gillette Stadium before detouring through Brown University and eventually landing in Auburn, Massachusetts. He promises that someday Bill Belichick will retire, the Patriots will be awful, and he will write very mean and nasty things about them.

Layout and Design

Vincent Verhei has been a writer and editor for Football Outsiders since 2007. In addition to writing for *Football Outsiders Almanac 2020*, he did all layout and design on the book. During the season, he writes the "Quick Reads" column covering the best and worst players of each week according to Football Outsiders metrics. His writings have also appeared in *ESPN The Magazine* and in Maple Street Press publications, and he has done layout on a number of other books for Football Outsiders and Prospectus Entertainment Ventures. His other night job is as a writer and podcast host for pro wrestling/MMA website Figurefouronline.com. He is a graduate of Western Washington University.

Fantasy Football Statistician

Scott Spratt is responsible for the KUBIAK fantasy football projections in this book as well as the weekly fantasy projections available on FootballOutsiders.com. He got into analytics through his baseball work for Sports Info Solutions and writing for ESPN and FanGraphs, but he loves football analytics because of the intricacies of the sport. He is a Sloan Analytics Research Paper Competition and Fantasy Sports Writers Association award winner and was a 2018 finalist for FSWA Football Writer of the Year for his writing for Pro Football Focus. He is an elusive native Charlottean and has the Jimmy Clausen-given scars to prove it.

College Football Statisticians

Bill Connelly is a college football writer for ESPN. He lives in Missouri with his wife, daughter, and pets. You can find old work of his at SB Nation, at his former SB Nation blog Football Study Hall, and in his books, *Study Hall: College Football, Its Stats and Its Stories* and *The 50 Best* College Football Teams of All Time*.

Brian Fremeau has been analyzing college football drive stats for Football Outsiders since 2006. A lifelong Fighting Irish fan, Brian can be found every home football Saturday in Notre Dame Stadium. He can be found there every day, in fact, due to his campus facility operations responsibilities. He lives in South Bend, Indiana with his wife and two daughters.

Contributors

Thomas Bassinger has been covering the NFL since 2014 and writing for the *Football Outsiders Almanac* since 2019. He was the leader of the #FixTheBucsUnis campaign until February, when the Buccaneers announced they were finally ditching their alarm clock jersey numbers and bringing back their Super Bowl era ensemble. One month later, Tom Brady signed. Bassinger is a graduate of Penn State University and lives with his family in St. Petersburg, Florida.

Ian Boyd covers Texas and Big 12 football on InsideTexas.com and is the author of *Flyover Football: How the Big 12 Became the Frontier for Modern Offense*.

Parker Fleming is an independent college football analyst from Fort Worth, Texas. He hosts a podcast and writes a newsletter covering TCU, the Big 12, and college football entitled "Purple Theory."

Derrik Klassen is from the Central Valley of California, though he grew up near Tampa Bay, Florida. Covering the NFL draft gave him his start but studying the NFL itself has taken precedent. He has been published at SB Nation and Bleacher Report, and has worked for Optimum Scouting, doing charting and scouting reports for their NFL Draft Guide.

Bryan Knowles has been covering the NFL since 2010, with his work appearing on ESPN, Bleacher Report and Fansided. A graduate of UC Davis and San Jose State University, he's heard rumors that his teams could eventually win a football game but has yet to see the empirical evidence. He currently co-writes Scramble for the Ball with Andrew Potter.

Rivers McCown has written for ESPN.com, Bleacher Report, *USA Today*, and Deadspin, among other places. He's edited for Football Outsiders, *Rookie Scouting Portfolio*, and *Pre-Snap Reads Quarterback Catalogue*. He lives in Houston, Texas with his wife, under the control of two cats and two birds. He wants more jobs, and if you don't give them to him, he'll be forced to keep speedrunning video games and helping design randomizer hacks for them.

Dan Pizzuta has previously written for Bleacher Report, numberFire, and Big Blue View. He got into football analytics after hearing Aaron Schatz on a podcast once and now he's here. He's currently a writer and editor for Sharp Football Analysis.

Anglo-Scot (so, Briton) **Andrew Potter** blames Mega Drive classics John Madden Football and Joe Montana Sports Talk Football for his Transatlantic love of the gridiron game. He joined Football Outsiders in 2013 to help with the infamous Twitter Audibles experiment, and still compiles Audibles at the Line to this day. He also authors the weekly Injury Aftermath report and co-authors Scramble for the Ball with Bryan Knowles. Though outwardly a fan of the New Orleans Saints, inwardly the Angus resident still yearns for his first gridiron love: NFL Europe's Scottish Claymores.

Mike Tanier has been writing *Football Outsiders Almanac* chapters for so long that he feels like Ringo making yet another special guest appearance during a Paul McCartney show. Mike recently wrapped up a six-year run as the NFL Lead Columnist for Bleacher Report; his popular Monday Morning Digest feature will presumably be replaced by TikTok videos, cartoon GIFs of Lamar Jackson, and long apologies. A father of two with almost 20 years of experience as an NFL writer, Mike is proof positive that we all get by with a little help from our friends.

Robert Weintraub is the author of the newly released *The Divine Miss Marble* as well as *The Victory Season, The House That Ruth Built,* and the *New York Times* bestseller *No Better Friend: One Man, One Dog, and their Extraordinary Story of Courage and Survival in WWII.* He has also been a regular contributor to Sports on Earth, Slate, Grantland, *Columbia Journalism Review*, and *The New York Times.*

Carl Yedor was born and raised in Seattle, Washington, and his first vivid football memory was "We want the ball, and we're going to score." In spite of that, he has remained a Seahawks fan to this day, which certainly paid off right around the time he began interning with Football Outsiders in February of 2014. As an undergrad at Georgetown University, he worked with the varsity football team (yes, Georgetown does have a football team) to implement football research into their strategy and game planning, drawing on his coursework in statistics and his high school experience as an undersized offensive guard and inside linebacker to make recommendations. He lives in Arlington, Virginia and started his career as an analytics consultant before transitioning to an internal-facing data science role with a credit union.

Acknowledgements

We want to thank all the Football Outsiders readers, all the people in the media who have helped to spread the word about our website and books, and all the people in the NFL who have shown interest in our work. This is our 16th annual book as part of the *Pro Football Prospectus* or *Football Outsiders Almanac* series. We couldn't do this if we were just one guy, or without the help and/or support from all these people:

- The entire staff at EdjSports, especially Tamela Triplett, Bob Ford, Casey Ramage, and our website technical lead Aram Bojadžjan.
- Erik Orr for cover design.
- Cale Clinton, responsible for compiling both The Week in Quotes on our website and The Year in Quotes in this book.
- Mike Harris for help with the season simulation.
- Excel macro master John Argentiero.
- Jim Armstrong, who compiles our drive and pace stats.
- Our offensive line guru Ben Muth and injury guru Zach Binney.
- Nathan Forster, creator of SackSEER and BackCAST, who is also responsible for improvements on Playmaker Score (originally created by Vincent Verhei).
- Jason McKinley, creator of Offensive Line Continuity Score.
- Jeremy Snyder, our incredibly prolific transcriber of old play-by-play gamebooks.
- Roland Beech, formerly of TwoMinuteWarning. com, who came up with the original ideas behind our individual defensive stats.
- Our editors at ESPN.com, in particular Tim Kavanagh.
- Our friends at Sports Info Solutions who have really expanded what we can do with game charting, particularly Dan Foehrenbach and Matt Manocherian.
- All the friends we've made on coaching staffs and in front offices across the National Football League, who generally don't want to be mentioned by name. You know who you are.
- Our comrades in the revolution: Bill Barnwell (our long lost brother), Brian Burke and the guys from ESPN

Stats & Information, Ben Baldwin, Neil Paine, Robert Mays, Danny Kelly, Kevin Clark, and K.C. Joyner, plus everyone at Pro Football Reference, the football guys from footballguys.com, and all of the young analysts doing awesome work with NFLscrapR all over Twitter.
- Also, our scouting buddies, including Andy Benoit, Chris Brown, Greg Cosell, Doug Farrar, Russ Lande, and Matt Waldman.
- Josh Hernandez and the other folks at EA Sports who make FO a part of Madden Ultimate Team.

As always, thanks to our family and friends for putting up with this nonsense.

Aaron Schatz

Follow Football Outsiders on Facebook

https://www.facebook.com/footballoutsiders

Follow Football Outsiders on Instagram

https://www.instagram.com/fboutsiders/

Listen to Football Outsiders

Look for Football Outsiders, Aaron Schatz, or Scott Spratt wherever you get your podcasts, or go to:

https://www.footballoutsiders.com/podcasts

Follow Football Outsiders on Twitter

Follow the official account announcing new Football Outsiders articles at **@fboutsiders.**

You can follow other FO and *FOA 2020* writers at these Twitter handles:

Thomas Bassinger: **@tometrics**

Dave Bernreuther: **@bernreuther**

Zachary Binney: **@zbinney_NFLinj**

Ian Boyd: **@Ian_A_Boyd**

Bill Connelly: **@ESPN_BillC**

Parker Fleming: **@statsowar**

Brian Fremeau: **@bcfremeau**

Tom Gower: **@ThomasGower**

Derrik Klassen: **@QBKlass**

Bryan Knowles: **@BryKno**

Rivers McCown: **@RiversMcCown**

Ben Muth: **@FO_WordofMuth**

Dan Pizzuta: **@DanPizzuta**

Andrew Potter: **@bighairyandy**

Aaron Schatz: **@FO_ASchatz**

Scott Spratt: **@Scott_Spratt**

Mike Tanier: **@MikeTanier**

Vince Verhei: **@FO_VVerhei**

Robert Weintraub: **@robwein**

Carl Yedor: **@CarlYedor61**

MORE FROM

Like what you read? There are plenty of ways to get more of our content.

BLOG:
SPORTSINFOSOLUTIONSBLOG.COM

OFF THE CHARTS PODCAST
APPLE PODCASTS, SPOTIFY, ANCHOR, AND MORE

TWITTER:
@SPORTSINFO_SIS

SISDATAHUB.COM
ADVANCED NFL STATS AND LEADERBOARDS

NEWSLETTER:
SPORTSINFOSOLUTIONS.COM

Printed in Great Britain
by Amazon